APR 2 8 1996

BARRON

D0076010

LIBRARY
UNIVERSITY OF WISCONSIN
BARRON COUNTY
RICE LAKE, WIS. 54868

THE HISTORY OF THE
UNIVERSITY OF OXFORD
VOLUME VI

THE HISTORY
OF THE
UNIVERSITY OF OXFORD

VOLUME VI

Nineteenth-Century Oxford, Part 1

EDITED BY

M. G. BROCK AND M. C. CURTHOYS

LIBRARY
UNIVERSITY OF WISCONSIN
BARRON COUNTY
RICE LAKE, WIS. 54868

CLARENDON PRESS · OXFORD
1997

Oxford University Press, Great Clarendon Street, Oxford OX2 6DP
Oxford New York
Athens Auckland Bangkok Bogota Bombay
Buenos Aires Calcutta Cape Town Dar es Salaam
Delhi Florence Hong Kong Istanbul Karachi
Kuala Lumpur Madras Madrid Melbourne
Mexico City Nairobi Paris Singapore
Taipei Tokyo Toronto Warsaw
and associated companies in
Berlin Ibadan

Oxford is a trade mark of Oxford University Press

Published in the United States
by Oxford University Press Inc., New York

© Oxford University Press 1997

All rights reserved. No part of this publication may be reproduced,
stored in a retrieval system, or transmitted, in any form or by any means,
without the prior permission in writing of Oxford University Press.
Within the UK, exceptions are allowed in respect of any fair dealing for the
purpose of research or private study, or criticism or review, as permitted
under the Copyright, Designs and Patents Act, 1988, or in the case of
reprographic reproduction in accordance with the terms of the licences
issued by the Copyright Licensing Agency. Enquiries concerning
reproduction outside these terms and in other countries should be
sent to the Rights Department, Oxford University Press,
at the address above

British Library Cataloguing in Publication Data
Data available

Library of Congress Cataloging in Publication Data
Data applied for

ISBN 0–19–951016–4

1 3 5 9 10 8 6 4 2

Typeset by Pure Tech India Limited, Pondicherry
Printed in Great Britain
on acid-free paper by
Bookcraft Ltd, Midsomer Norton
Nr. Bath, Somerset

Preface

The two volumes of *Nineteenth-Century Oxford* begin and end at well-recognized turning-points. The examination statute of 1800 turned the University towards an upward path: the outbreak of the First World War set changes in train for every British institution. The division within this well-defined period is more difficult. The main narrative for Part 1 is given in Chapters 1, 7, 10, and 23, and ends with the passing of the University Tests Act in 1871. A similar treatment for all of the thematic chapters would have entailed much subdivision and some infelicities. It would have seemed eccentric, for instance, in describing Oxford's finances to 1871, to have excluded the Cleveland Commission (1872–4), to which we owe most of our knowledge of them. While, therefore, each part stands by itself, and each has its own scholarly apparatus and index, neither is confined everywhere to one side of a mid-point. In Part 1 Chapters 11 to 14, and 18 to 21, take the story to 1914: in Part 2 Chapters 26 and 30, on the University Press and Oxford architecture, start at 1800.[1] These arrangements have helped to eliminate the need for recapitulation in Part 2; but they would not have sufficed in themselves to keep the volumes within limits of length. A process of exclusion and selection has also been necessary. There could be no question of telling the story of each college; but an analysis of the differences between collegiate Oxford, with its emerging tutorial system, and the continental universities seemed essential. Similarly, while Oxford's nineteenth-century graduates influenced British public life in more ways than could possibly be recorded here, it seemed right to chart their main areas of activity, and these are analysed in Chapter 14.

The footnotes and Index have been arranged in the hope of helping readers to obtain any further information which they may need. The number of people named in the volume is too large for more than a few of them to have been provided with biographical footnotes. An alternative method of identification has therefore been adopted, namely, the provision in the Index of dates of birth and death for most of those mentioned in the text. References in footnotes cannot take the place of a bibliography, if only because they may not mention the secondary work which led the contributor to the primary source cited. The massive *Bibliography of Printed Works relating to the University of Oxford* (3 vols 1968), by E. H. Cordeaux and D. H. Merry, is invaluable for tracing the voluminous writings about Victorian Oxford. It has been supplemented, for publications from 1977 to 1981, by

---

[1] A List of Contents for Part 2 (vol. vii) is given at the end of this volume, pp. 731–2.

the booklets entitled *History of European Universities: Work in Progress*, and thereafter by the 'Continuing Bibliographies' in the journal *History of Universities* from volume vii (1988) onwards. *The Wellesley Index to Victorian Periodicals, 1824–1900* (5 vols 1966–89) has added notably to the stock of bibliographical material.

The full title of a work is cited for the first mention in a chapter: where place of publication is omitted it is London, Oxford or Cambridge. Tables and figures are put at the relevant place within a chapter if essential to the understanding of the argument: otherwise they will be found at the end of it. Many Victorian writers supplemented and altered their works substantially in later editions. As the List of Abbreviations shows, a later edition is sometimes cited where this has happened. In quotations spelling and punctuation have been changed only if this seemed to be needed for clarity. Except in Chapter 12 the University has a capital letter where Oxford University is indicated, but not where the word is used as a generic term.[2]

I was appointed editor for the two nineteenth-century volumes of the *History* in 1977. Mark Curthoys was assigned to them as research assistant in 1982 (at first on a part-time basis) and worked on them in the Clarendon Building until 1991. In 1989 he became their co-editor at my suggestion. As the expressions of thanks scattered throughout the volume show, contributors and editors have met with invariable co-operation and goodwill throughout the University and indeed beyond it. They tender their most grateful thanks for all that help. This volume, like its predecessors in the series, was made possible by generous funding from the University, the colleges, the University's higher studies and Hulme surplus funds and the Nuffield Foundation. Its editors owe much to Lord Bullock, and to his successors as chairmen of the controlling committee, Sir Anthony Kenny and Sir Keith Thomas. They received wise advice from Trevor Aston, general editor of the series until his tragically early death in 1985, and admirable administrative support from Ralph Evans until the project office closed. They thank Professor Brian Harrison for generating the library in that office and for help in many other ways. They record with gratitude the importance of the material produced by Mary Heimann during several months of research. Both of them owe particular thanks to institutions in which one or other was employed during some part of their time as editors—to Christ Church, to the *New Dictionary of National Biography*, to Nuffield College and to the College of St George, Windsor.

The editors also record their gratitude to those people who, in administering facilities and resources, went beyond the call of duty in making them available—to the library staffs in the Bodleian, the Centre for Oxfordshire

[2] For the usage in Chapter 12, on University finance, see Ch. 12 n. 6.

Studies, Christ Church, Nuffield College, the Oxford Union Society, Pusey House and Sion College; and, in libraries and archives where it is not invidious to name a particular individual, to Stella Brecknell (University Museum), Christine Butler (Corpus Christi), Janie Cottis (Magdalen), Caroline Dalton (New College), Robin Darwall-Smith (University), Margaret Kirwan (Oriel), Peter Foden (Oxford University Press), Clare Hopkins (Trinity), and Tony Simcock (Museum of the History of Science); to Ruth Vyse, Margaret MacDonald and Simon Bailey, successively University Archivists; to Philip Moss, who gave every facility in the University Offices; and to Clive Payne and Martin Range of the Social Studies Faculty Computing Centre, whose computing expertise was exceeded only by their patience with the inexpert. Richard Sharp of the Ashmolean Museum generously made available to the editors his knowledge of Oxford prints, and alerted them to the extensive holdings of the Hope Collection. Finally, they express their thanks to all those who worked with great efficiency on the production of this volume, and especially to Cathy Brocklehurst, Judy Godley, Pam Hopes, Margaret Hunt, Beverly Potts, and Marion Rogers; to Laurien Berkeley, the best and most patient of copy-editors; and to Ivon Asquith, Anne Gelling and Anthony Morris of Oxford University Press. It is impossible to be sure that the acknowledgements here and throughout the volume are complete: to anyone omitted an apology is tendered. *Nineteenth-Century Oxford, Part 1*, owes much to many helpers: its faults lie with the editors.

The thanks must end on a personal note. My debt of gratitude to Mark Curthoys cannot be exaggerated. I hope that the committee's decision to appoint him as co-editor proclaims what the volume owes to him more effectively than my own words could. The many contributors who completed their work early are to be thanked for their exemplary patience. Where a contribution did not arrive until recently this happened because I had failed to foresee what would be needed, and so had not sought it until a late stage. Both editors owe much to their wives' forbearance; and both feel an especial gratitude to Eleanor Brock for compiling the volume's Index. Only those who have edited a volume such as this know what a boon it is to have a sharp-eyed indexer on hand during the final stage.

An Oxford which has started to conduct final examinations for classified honours begins to look modern; but this volume concerns a world of thought different from our own. The internal university struggles depicted in it represented two aspects of a momentous question. Was unfettered enquiry compatible with the maintenance of a Christian faith? Was Oxford University a preserve of the Church of England, or an institution serving the whole nation and therefore subject to parliamentary decision? Unless an effort had been made to understand those who held the 'anti-liberal' view on that issue in all its ramifications, this volume would have served to subject them to 'the enormous condescension of posterity';[3] but, when that effort has been made, what has been written necessarily reflects today's dominant view. It is hard to believe now that a university which had continued to inhibit the free play of the enquiring mind would have been furthering either higher education or Christian faith and works.

Michael Brock

Oxford, May 1996

[3] When the late E. P. Thompson used this phrase (*The Making of the English Working Class* (1963), 12) he was concerned with 'the poor stockinger, the Luddite cropper [and] the "obsolete" hand-loom weaver'. It has, however, a wider application.

Contents

Plates: List and Commentary

1   'Interior of St Mary's Church'. Engraving by Henry Le Keux after a drawing by Frederick Mackenzie for the Oxford Almanack, 1834, depicting the arrival of the Vice-Chancellor for the University Sermon. Preceded by the bedels of the faculties, the Vice-Chancellor processes to his throne, while the preacher of the day is conducted to the pulpit by the bedel of divinity (H. L. Thompson, *The Church of St Mary the Virgin, Oxford* (1903), 1–2). Undergraduate noblemen, in full-dress gowns, are shown in an honoured position among the pews nearest the preacher. The single-sheet Oxford Almanacks enjoyed a wide sale, especially among non-resident members of Convocation, for whom the images provided a record of new developments in the University. This drawing was commissioned by the Delegates of the Press to mark the restoration and rearrangement of the University Church by Edward Hawkins, vicar of St Mary's until 1828. Hawkins repositioned the pulpit, extended the seating and included galleries for undergraduates to the north and west: this created an auditorium for upwards of 1,000 attenders at the University Sermon. By the time the Almanack was actually published, the University pulpit had acquired a recent and unexpected significance: from it Henry Bulteel had made a sensational denunciation of the heads (6 February 1831); John Keble had delivered his Assize Sermon on 'National Apostasy' (14 July 1833); and Newman had become a leading Oxford figure as vicar of St Mary's.

2   Cyril Jackson, Dean of Christ Church. A posthumous statue (1824) by Sir Francis Chantrey erected by a subscription among members of the House. The organizing committee of Christ Church men, undergraduates under Jackson, included four prime ministers (Liverpool, Grenville, Canning and Peel). Placed in the north transept of the cathedral in 1825, the statue struck the *Ecclesiologist* (February 1847) as a 'monument of prostituted genius... The sitting figure with its back to the altar, [and] the academical instead of the priestly garb are indeed symbolical of a place where learning has triumphed over religion, and the Bishop is overshadowed by the scholars.' It was removed from the cathedral to the library (where it is pictured) in 1873, and thence in 1957 to its present location in the ante-hall. Chantrey's 'dislike to ornament in sculpture' was remembered as 'extreme' (George Jones, *Chantrey* (1849), 85). He was said to have worked from the portrait (1810) by William Owen in Christ Church Hall; but he 'got his suggestion' for the statue, as Pusey recalled many years later, from a caricature (Liddon, *Pusey* iv. 329).

3 John Parsons, Master of Balliol, from an etching by Robert Dighton, published in February 1808. Dighton produced a series of caricatures of Oxford notables after visiting the city in 1807. Parsons, a high Tory, was one of the instigators, with Jackson, of the examination statute of 1800. His satisfaction at his elevation to the see of Peterborough in 1813 was detected in an address of congratulation to the Regent, which he drafted on behalf of the Hebdomadal Board in the following year, the effusive terms of which, Lord Grenville complained, seemed to confuse 'the goodness of the Creator and the merits of the Prince of Wales' (cited in Ward, *Victorian Oxford*, 38).

4 M. J. Routh, President of Magdalen, 1791–1854, in his stall in the college chapel. A mezzotint by David Lucas, published in 1843, after a portrait by T. C. Thompson (1842). G. V. Cox described Routh's remarkable gestures during chapel services, 'his hands being much in motion, and often crossed upon his breast' (cited in R. D. Middleton, *Dr Routh* (1938), 220). The appearance of few Oxford figures of this period has been described as vividly as that of Routh; yet those who knew him considered that no pictorial representation achieved a true likeness. F. A. Faber, Vice-President of Magdalen, reported that the publication of Thompson's portrait had 'caused great mortification to the members of the College, as well as the public at large'. The print reproduced here is from the collection of engraved portraits donated to the University by the Revd F. W. Hope, and now in the Ashmolean Museum.

5 Edward Tatham, Rector of Lincoln, 1792–1834, by an unknown artist. Tatham was said to have paid £300 for the portrait, which 'still broods', in Dr Vivian Green's words, 'in slightly sinister fashion over the college hall' (*Oxford Common Room* (1957), 61). A contemporary dubbed the likeness 'expressive, though not flattering'. In later life Tatham was too devoted to pig-breeding to wear the clothes depicted at all often. His criticisms of the 1807 examination statute were rudely expressed but pertinent. G. V. Cox, who heard his two-and-a-half-hour sermon on the disputed verse of St John's First Epistle, recorded that 'few, if any, left the church till the conclusion, so strangely attractive was the mixture of learning and coarseness…One old head of a college…was said never to have recovered from the effects of the long sitting' (*Recollections*, 233 n.).

6 Edward Copleston, tutor and later Provost of Oriel, by John Downman. Watercolour over pencil. The portrait was made in 1810, the year of Copleston's celebrated *Reply to the Calumnies of the Edinburgh Review*. Painter and subject were both Devon men. Copleston was judged by Tom Mozley 'the most richly-coloured character' in the University of the time: William Tuckwell called him 'monarch in his day alike of Oriel and Oxford'. Less austere than his younger fellows, he rebuked one of them memorably for careless carving of a haunch of venison: 'Mr Newman', he called down the table, 'you are unconscious of the mischief you have done' (Earl of Malmesbury, *Memoirs of an Ex-Minister* (2 vols 1884) i. 18). His liberalism was thought to have delayed a mitre; but in 1828 he became Bishop of Llandaff and Dean of St Paul's.

7 'Commemoration of the Installation of His Grace the Duke of Wellington as
Chancellor of the University of Oxford in the Theatre on the 10th, 11th, and 13th
June 1834'. Lithograph by Thomas Dighton. Wellington's installation was the
occasion of a great Conservative demonstration in reaction both to the Whig
administration and to mounting Nonconformist pressure to remove subscription
to the Articles as a condition of matriculation and graduation. This engraving was
made to replace the print celebrating an earlier occasion of corporate defiance by
the University, the installation of the seventh earl of Westmorland in July 1759,
the plate for which had become worn after frequent reprintings (see Richard
Sharp, 'The Oxford Installation of 1759', *Oxoniensia* lvi (1991), 153). Accommodation in the Sheldonian Theatre is shown carefully segregated by degree:
doctors and noblemen occupied the semicircle; masters of arts the main floor
area; women were seated in the lower gallery; bachelors of arts and undergraduates filled the upper gallery. J. W. Croker, who was present at the installation,
described 'the burst of applause from all the benches as the Duke entered the
theatre, the shouts of the men, and even the voices of the women were heard, and
the waving of handkerchiefs—and all lasted for ten minutes' (*The Croker Papers*,
ed. L. Jennings (3 vols 1884) ii. 226).

8 'Examination of Candidates for the Degree of Bachelor of Arts, Oxford, April
1842'. Aquatint by R. W. Buss reproduced in Huber, *English Universities* ii. pt 2,
524. James Heywood, the wealthy academic reformer, financed the English
edition of Huber's work, commissioning Buss, whose subjects were more often
theatrical or humorous, to produce the plates. Although his figures bear more
than a suggestion of caricature, Buss's scenes are, in the main, accurate depictions.
The room shown here, on the ground floor of the Schools Quadrangle, was
known as 'the Cockpit' on account of the raised seating provided for spectators
to view the confrontation between examiners and candidates. Undergraduates,
fulfilling the statutory obligation to attend the Schools before themselves entering for the examination, look on as a candidate is examined viva voce while other
candidates, at separate desks, are set written exercises. The presence of only three
examiners indicates that an examination for pass degrees was in progress; by
statute four examiners were required to judge the merits of those seeking honours. The vacant throne-like chairs overlooking the examiners' table were for the
use of the Vice-Chancellor and proctors, who might on occasion scrutinize the
proceedings.

9 'Bird's Eye View of the University and City of Oxford', drawn and engraved by
Nathaniel Whittock. Whittock's view, c.1845, catches Oxford at the point when
the great period of classical building was about to give way to the flood of neo-
Gothic whose herald, the Martyrs' Memorial, already stands defiantly north of St
Mary Magdalen. The new Press building (1830) marked the furthest extent of the
University's recent development. The most outlying college, Worcester, remained
isolated between, as contemporary guidebooks invidiously remarked, the city
gaol in Gloucester Green and the workhouse in Rats and Mice Hill (later Wellington Square). In 1853, when the Parks, to the north of Wadham, were earmarked as the site for the University Museum, figures were cited indicating that

85 per cent of undergraduates were resident within seven-and-a-half minutes' walking distance of the new facility (flysheet dated 1 Mar. 1853 in Bodl. G. A. Oxon. b. 27).

10 'St Mary Magdalen, from St Giles's, c.1812', after a water-colour by William Turner of Oxford (published as the Oxford Almanack for 1896). Turner's view of a still semi-rural St Giles's includes the Robin Hood inn, soon to be demolished and subsequently the site of the Martyrs' Memorial.

11 'North View of the Martyrs' Memorial and Aisle'. Engraving by W. Radclyffe after a drawing by F. Mackenzie, published as the Oxford Almanack for 1850. The public subscription launched in 1838 to establish a memorial to the Protestant martyrs Cranmer, Ridley and Latimer raised a sum insufficient to realize the original object of erecting a new church. Instead an 'Eleanor Cross' was erected, built to the design of George Gilbert Scott in 1841–3, and the surplus was used to add the Martyrs' Aisle to St Mary Magdalen Church (see A. Palmer, *Mary Mag's* (1994), 13). In December 1850 a loyal address from Convocation opposing the establishment of a Roman Catholic hierarchy in England was presented to the Queen (*Herald* 14 Dec. 1850).

12 J. H. Newman, portrait in chalk by George Richmond (1844). One of many likenesses, Richmond's drawing was executed for Henry Wilberforce. He had cautioned Richmond, to the latter's amusement, against 'making a fine gentleman' out of his sitter, and the portrait delighted him. 'I cannot well say', he told Newman, 'how much I like and value it. I almost expect to hear your voice at times' (M. Trevor, *Newman: The Pillar of the Cloud* (1962), 324). Richmond's aim in portraiture was 'the truth lovingly told'. The effect, in this case as in others, was flattering. When Maria Giberne made a copy she gave Newman a more soulful look, but even she included the spectacles without which he was almost blind. The miniature painting by Sir William Ross, and the engraving of it by R. Woodman, which are both from the same period as the Richmond portrait, show a more anxious and less comely man; but Richmond provides an antidote to the *Punch* cartoons depicting a drooping and cadaverous Newman endowed with an immense nose.

13 E. B. Pusey. Drawn by his niece Clara Pusey (summer 1853). Pusey declined throughout his life to sit for artists. In 1878, warned that the governing body of Christ Church were about to beseech him to allow a portrait, he explained that he had long ago been influenced by 'a religious book, which instanced having a likeness taken of oneself as implying that one thought well of one's self': he had been 'surprised' when Newman and Keble allowed likenesses to be made, and 'it became to me a part of my religion not to have it done [though] at times it pained me to decline' (Liddon, *Pusey* iv. 327, 329). Richmond, who had known Pusey well, executed a bust and a portrait posthumously; another bust was made from photographs; but the sketch by Pusey's niece seems to be unique in depicting him as he was in the early 1850s. It may be a little flattering. William Tuckwell, who came to know Pusey in those years, was struck by his always ruffled hair and

'exceeding slovenliness of person'. His 'pale, ascetic, furrowed face' had been, as Tuckwell recalled, 'dusky always, as with suggestions of a blunt or half-used razor' (*Reminiscences*, 136, 138).

14 Richard Whately. Soft-ground etching by F. C. Lewis after William Behnes, published in 1836. Oriel's leading Noetic, Principal of St Alban Hall, and Drummond Professor of Political Economy, Whately left Oxford in 1831 to become Archbishop of Dublin. His manners were less polished than those of his mentor Copleston. He was known in Oxford as 'the white bear', and would scramble through ditches wearing a white hat and rough white coat, accompanied by a great white dog. A colleague's wife, Tuckwell recalled, 'had filled her drawing room with...spider-legged chairs...On one of these sat Whately, swinging, plunging, and shifting on his seat while he talked. An ominous crack was heard; a leg of the chair had given way; he tossed it onto the sofa without comment, and impounded another chair' (*Reminiscences*, 17). He looked to his contemporaries like a Yorkshire ostler, and was, in aspect, the least episcopal archbishop of the century.

15 Ashurst Turner Gilbert, Principal of Brasenose. Mezzotint by S. Cousins after T. Phillips, published in 1836. Gilbert's vice-chancellorship (1836–40) coincided with the first proposals to bring the railway to Oxford, and he was called upon to present the University's objections. He came, however, to apprehend a greater threat to the University from within. Initially sympathetic to the Tractarians as learned defenders of the Church, and critical of both Evangelicals and latitudinarians, Gilbert grew increasingly alarmed at the Romish tendency of the movement.

16 'A sketch from Corpus, c.1843'. Anonymous etching of R. G. Macmullen, fellow of Corpus Christi College. By 1842 the Tractarian movement was involved in controversy at every step. When R. G. Macmullen applied to be examined for the BD he started 'a party quarrel', which, as the Provost of Oriel reported, might 'easily involve all Oxford in the flame' (M. O'Connell, *The Oxford Conspirators* (1969), 383). The struggle, described in Chapter 7, lasted for two years, at the end of which Macmullen obtained the degree despite the obstacles put in his way by Professor R. D. Hampden. He became a curate at St Saviour's, Leeds, and in 1847, like others in that Tractarian outstation, went over to Rome. Taking Roman orders in the following year, he gave his new masters as much trouble as the old. His admiration for Newman made him regret Manning's triumphant career as a Roman Catholic. He contended that Mrs Manning's death, which had made this possible, had been a calamity for the Church. When rebuked by Manning for that remark, he did not withdraw it, but replied: 'I pity the man who repeated it to your Grace' (F. Meyrick, *Memories of Life at Oxford and Elsewhere* (1905), 9).

17 R. D. Hampden. Portrait in oils by H. W. Pickersgill, given to Christ Church by the sitter himself. Hampden, whose doings and misfortunes as a canon and Regius Professor of Divinity are detailed in Chapter 7, was short and swarthy, though someone recalled charitably that he had nicely shaped feet. Notoriously

reserved, he amazed a lady who sat next to him at an Oxford dinner party by saying not a word to her, and during his eighteen years in the Lords as a bishop he never made a speech. According to one Tractarian account, 'he stood before you like a milestone, and brayed at you like a jackass' (Mozley, *Reminiscences* i. 380); but Tractarian comments on Hampden should be treated with reserve.

18   Philip Wynter. Lithograph by J. H. Lynch after B. Delacour, *c*.1840. Vice-Chancellor from 1840 to 1844 and President for over forty years of the old High-Church stronghold of St John's, Wynter was a timid man who found himself trying to keep the peace in the University during the most intense periods of religious controversy. He was lampooned for his reply to an address signed among others by Sir J. T. Coleridge and Gladstone, in which he styled himself 'the Resident Governor of the University' (see J. S. G. Simmons, 'The Duke of Wellington and the Vice-Chancellorship in 1844', *Bodleian Library Record* v (1954–6), 37–52). Subsequently the leader of the Conservative party in the University, he suffered the chagrin of repeatedly being overlooked for ecclesiastical preferment promised to him by Lord Derby, despite the pressing circumstance of having to provide for ten sons.

19   'From the Moral Philosophy Lecture Room, 1841'. Etching signed G. C. William Sewell is shown lecturing as Professor of Moral Philosophy during the year in which his *Christian Politics* was published. His face was characterized, as a friend said, by 'benignity and a pug nose' (W. K. Stride, *Exeter College* (1900), 156). His lectures were admired, though discursive: he might convert an Aristotle lecture into a discourse on Gothic architecture. He was one of Oxford's first and most successful lecturers on Plato, having, as a hearer wrote, 'the power of making [you] recognize the intensity and glowing ardour of Plato's spirit'. On 27 February 1849 in the hall of Exeter College he asked whether any of his hearers possessed J. A. Froude's newly published *Nemesis of Faith*. One of those who did confessed and produced a copy, which Sewell promptly impounded and threw on the fire. Froude resigned his Exeter fellowship on the same day.

20   'Front of Brazen Nose College'. Engraved by Joseph Skelton after a drawing by F. Mackenzie for the Oxford Almanack, 1821. Brasenose, the subject of the first of the twenty-four drawings produced by Mackenzie for the Almanacks (see H. M. Petter, *The Oxford Almanacks* (1974), 88), had built a dozen sets of rooms in 1810 to cope with the pressure of admissions attracted to the college by its high reputation under the successive headships of William Cleaver (1785–1809) and Frodsham Hodson (1809–22).

21   'New College cloisters'. Engraving by John Le Keux after a drawing by F. Mackenzie, published in J. Ingram, *Memorials of Oxford* (3 vols 1837), which originally appeared in parts, 1832–6. One of the most extreme examples of a 'closed' college, its fellowships and scholarships being limited to Winchester College, and having only recently (1834) relinquished its privilege of presenting men for degrees without examination, New College represented to James Ingram, the antiquary and President of Trinity, a laudable example of collegiate

independence. 'From an attentive survey of this college', Ingram added, 'the gratifying reflection arises, that most of the buildings of the founder, after a lapse of more than four centuries, remain substantially entire today.' An early reviewer noted approvingly that the publication of views of Oxford's 'halls of learning imposes a check upon future innovators' (*GM* (1833) i. 348). Ingram was a prominent member of the Oxford Society for Promoting the Study of Gothic Architecture, founded in 1839.

22 'St Alban Hall'. Engraving by W. Radclyffe from a drawing by F. Mackenzie. That Edward Cardwell, Principal of the Hall, was an active Delegate of the University Press probably explains its selection as the subject of the Oxford Almanack for 1851. The Hall was in other respects a slightly curious choice of advertisement for the University during the sittings of the Royal Commission: according to the Commissioners' report, it had just seven undergraduate members in 1851. The future of Oxford's five surviving independent halls was to be determined by successive university commissions.

23 'New Hall of Pembroke College', drawn and engraved by J. H. Le Keux for the Oxford Almanack of 1858, the first year of Dr Jeune's vice-chancellorship. The new staircases in the chapel quad (built 1844–6), pictured with smoking chimneys, and the hall (1848), which could seat 180 undergraduates, making it second only to Christ Church in capacity, were monuments to Jeune's dynamic, reforming mastership and his project to turn Pembroke, hitherto a stagnant backwater, into a leading college (J. H. C. Leach, *Sparks of Reform: the career of Francis Jeune, 1806–1868* (1994), 17–18).

24 'The Bodleian Library, Arts End, in 1842'. Aquatint after a water-colour by R. W. Buss. Arts End takes its name from the folio volumes on arts subjects in the medieval classification which occupy the shelves below gallery level. In this picture the viewer, looking south, sees the Librarian's high-backed chair and desk on the left, and the bust of Sir Thomas Bodley, the Gough map of England, and the library catalogues on the right. The artist omitted the entrance on the far left, to which the Prince Regent had ascended in 1814 groaning audibly. The portraits of former Librarians (now in the Curators' Room) look down from the gallery. From his desk, made in 1832 from the old roof beams of what is now the Upper Reading Room, the Librarian commands the entrance and a view along the central part of the Old Reading Room, now known as Duke Humfrey's Library.

25 'The Union Debating and News Room, Oxford University' (*Illustrated Times* 27 June 1863, 442). The Oxford Union Society's debating-hall (later its library) was designed by Benjamin Woodward, who was also the architect of the University Museum. Early in the long vacation of 1857 his friend Dante Gabriel Rossetti, having turned down a suggestion for a panorama in the Museum, arranged for a band of artists to paint the ten panels above the gallery in the debating-hall, then just completed. They were to give their time, their expenses being defrayed by the Union. (The quantity of soda-water in the expenses account amazed the

Society's treasurer.) Rossetti's helpers included two 23-year-old graduates of Exeter College, William Morris and Edward Burne-Jones. They were influenced by Ruskin's doctrine that the thinker and designer should also be a maker, and by Tennyson's poems: the themes for the panels were taken from the Arthurian legends. The work came to an end in March 1858, when seven panels had been painted in a Pre-Raphaelite style, four of them incompletely. The remaining three were painted a little later for a fee by William Riviere. Like Ruskin's Hinksey road-builders of the 1870s, Rossetti's youthful enthusiasts did not prove very successful as workmen. The paintings could not be viewed to full advantage because the effect of the high windows on the lighting had been neglected. They soon deteriorated, partly because the wall plaster had been damp, and partly from dust and the heat and smoke generated by the gas chandeliers. By 1871 the Society had decided that they could not be reinstated. In 1976, however, colour photographs were taken; and ten years later the paintings were restored to a remarkable degree, as part of the repair of the hall supported by English Heritage and the Landmark Trust. Since then the lighting has been further improved. Of Rossetti's scheme only the external feature has survived in entirety—a stone relief of 'King Arthur and his Knights' carved by Alexander Munro as the tympanum over the original hall entrance. Morris redecorated the roof beams and ceiling during the 1870s: this time he confined himself to patterns of flowers and foliage.

26 The lower (ground-floor) room at the Ashmolean Museum, Broad Street, displaying the Museum's mammal collection. Reproduced as frontispiece to the 1836 catalogue of the collection.

27 The lower (ground-floor) room at the Ashmolean Museum, Broad Street, displaying archaeological and ethnographic items together with paintings from the foundation collection. Photograph (c.1864).

28 The Taylorian Building and University Galleries, elevation and ground-plans. An illustration published in a supplement to the *Oxford University, City, and County Herald* 4 June 1842, while the building was under construction. (Some modifications were made to the ground-plan as actually executed.) In 1894 the Ashmolean collections were moved to an extension built to the rear of the Galleries, and in 1908 the two latter institutions combined to form the Ashmolean Museum of Art and Archaeology.

29 Interior of University Picture Galleries. Water-colour by J. Fisher (c. 1860).

30 Bulkeley Bandinel, Bodley's Librarian, 1813–60. Undated daguerrotype. Bandinel owed his appointment to the Library's staff to his godfather. By the early 1840s he had an annual salary of £550, supplemented by a New College fellowship, a Durham rectory and a fee income of £120 a year. According to a young assistant, 'all the staff trembled at Jupiter's nod': the Librarian 'sometimes lacked the general courtesy which should be exhibited to all duly qualified readers alike' (W. D. Macray, *Annals of the Bodleian Library* (2nd edn 1890), 371 n.). His

disciplinary style was that of *HMS Victory*, on which he had served as a naval chaplain. The courtesy which he showed when Francis Douce visited the Library is, however, commemorated in the Douce collection. The Library's contents doubled during his librarianship.

31 Philip Bliss, University Registrar. Engraving by F. Holl. Bliss was 'the embodiment of the traditions and history of his alma mater' (*DNB*) and a familiar figure to generations of undergraduates at matriculation and degree ceremonies: Edward Bradley included a sketch of him in *The Adventures of Mr Verdant Green*. He retired from the University registrarship in April 1853, shortly after the introduction of the Oxford University Bill. In his *Reliquiae Hearnianae* (1857, 2nd edn 1869), Bliss inveighed against the overthrow of the Laudian constitution: 'I have seen a Prime Minister (himself ignorant of a university education) dictated to by an individual of the House of Commons, and at his bidding, for the sake of parliamentary support, granting a one-sided commission embracing the fiercest of the reformers themselves' (iii. 189–90).

32 'The Geological Lecture Room, Oxford'. Lithograph by Nathaniel Whittock, probably issued to commemorate a special lecture given by Buckland at the Ashmolean Museum on 15 February 1823. Those present have been identified as: (standing and seated behind Buckland) C. G. B. Daubeny and Martin Wall; (front row, seated, left to right) T. V. Short, W. D. Conybeare, J. J. Conybeare, T. E. Bridges, Henry Foulkes, Edward Copleston, P. N. Shuttleworth, E. Legge, possibly William James or Lewis Sneyd; (middle row, standing, left to right) John Kidd, Joseph Dornford, possibly Thomas Arnold, J. E. Tyler, Richard Whately, Peter Elmsley, P. B. Duncan, J. S. Duncan, G. L. Cooke; (back row, standing, left to right) S. P. Rigaud, John Bull, possibly Frederick Barnes, C. T. Longley, Charles Lloyd, J. D. Macbride, remaining three individuals unidentified (see J. M. Edmonds and J. A. Douglas, 'William Buckland, FRS (1784–1856) and an Oxford Geological Lecture, 1823', *Notes and Records of the Royal Society of London* xxx (1976), 141–167).

33 Charles Daubeny. Lithograph by an unknown artist, undated but probably made after Daubeny's tour in 1819 of the Auvergne volcanic region, the subject of his first scientific paper. Professor of Chemistry from 1822 to 1854, and Professor of Botany from 1834, Daubeny belonged to the generation which founded the Ashmolean Society (1828) and which first promoted the idea of a University Museum for the natural sciences (see R. Hutchins, 'Charles Daubeny (1795–1867): the bicentenary of Magdalen's first modern scientist', *Magdalen College Record* (1995), 81–92).

34 The University Museum from a photograph taken in 1861, when the external fabric was practically complete. The keeper's house is to the far right; the small building between it and the main structure was the observatory used by John Phillips, the first Keeper. The chemical laboratories, nearest the camera, whose design was based on the Abbot's kitchen at Glastonbury, exemplified for Ruskin the adaptability of Gothic architecture to new purposes: 'No fixed arrangements

of frieze and pillar, nor accepted proportions of wall and roof, nor practised refinements of classical decoration, could have otherwise than absurdly and fantastically yielded its bed to the crucible, and its blast to the furnace' (H. W. Acland and John Ruskin, *The Oxford Museum* (1859), 66).

35 'Oxford University Museum: View in the Court' (*Builder* 23 June 1860, 399). The original wrought-iron girders proved inadequate to take the weight of the glass roof and parts had to be replaced with cast iron. The contractor, F. A. Skidmore of Coventry, executed metalwork in Oxford colleges and in many cathedrals and churches.

36 'Oxford University Museum: Carved Capitals and Corbel, from Lower Arcade' (*Builder* 18 June 1859, 408). The columns were not, John Phillips, the Keeper and Professor of Geology, pointed out, 'a haphazard collection of pretty stones crowned by pretty flowers' but a scientific arrangement of marbles and granites, to which were added capitals depicting plants and animal species naturally associated with each geological type, the whole being intended to help the memory of the student (Acland and Ruskin, *The Oxford Museum* (1859), 93–101).

37 John Kidd, from an undated drawing by an unknown artist (sometimes attributed to E. U. Eddis). Kidd was the first physician in Oxford to discard the large-brimmed hat and wig together with the gold-headed cane sported by his recent predecessors. The preface to his lecture course in comparative anatomy (1824) predicted a new dawn for Oxford science, while as Regius Professor of Medicine he reformed the examinations for medical degrees in 1833. By 1851, however, he gave an extremely pessimistic account of Oxford's potential as a school of medicine.

38 Henry Acland, drawn by John Everett Millais in July 1853. The drawing was done when Acland stayed with the Ruskins at Brig o' Turk, in the Trossachs, Perthshire, for a week from 25 July 1853. Millais, who was also there, had met Acland in Oxford and was impatient to meet him again. He had found Acland's head 'very noble' and wanted to make a study of it (M. Lutyens, *Millais and the Ruskins* (1968), 75). Ruskin favoured this: he had disliked Richmond's crayon drawing of Acland made seven years earlier. He had another reason for welcoming this friend from his undergraduate days, then on holiday in Edinburgh, to Brig o' Turk. He thought that Millais, who was in a nervous state, needed a doctor's eye. In fact, Millais was tense, not from ill health, but from having fallen passionately in love with Mrs Ruskin. Acland was a man of incessant activity and many parts. A courageous and exceptionally well-connected innovator, he was already known in Oxford both for his work in the Christ Church anatomy school and for his 'extension lectures' in the Town Hall. His report on Oxford's experience in the 1854 cholera epidemic was soon to make him a national figure. His wide interests, exemplified on the scientific side in the layout of the University Museum, help to explain his determination to prevent what his biographer termed the 'flooding of the University with mere

medical students, specializing from the date of their matriculation' (Atlay, *Acland*, 397).

39 A group of Oxford scientists photographed by Charles Lutwidge Dodgson (*c.* 1860). Redistribution of endowments created new scientific posts: George Rolleston (seated left, examining skull) was appointed the first Linacre Professor of Anatomy and Physiology in 1860; the stipend of his demonstrator, Charles Robertson (standing left), a Cambridge graduate, was made up from the proceeds of the Aldrichian and Tomlins trusts; A. G. Vernon Harcourt (seated right), was the first Lee's Reader in Chemistry at Christ Church, endowed under the 1858 Christ Church ordinance from Dr Lee's trust; Heywood Smith (standing right) was a medical student. The specimen under scrutiny is the skeleton of a stonefish, one of the most poisonous of fishes. It belonged to the osteological collection in the Christ Church anatomy museum, which was transferred to the University Museum in 1860, under the charge of the Linacre Professor, and is preserved there, OUM no. 17212 (information supplied by Jane Pickering, Zoological Collections, Oxford University Museum).

40 The Clarendon Laboratory, from an undated photograph. Planned under the supervision of R. B. Clifton, Professor of Experimental Philosophy, the Clarendon began to be operational in 1870. Since much of the apparatus was too delicate to be moved, separate rooms were assigned to each branch of physics. Laboratory space was provided for forty students, with two private laboratories for professorial use (see *Builder* 8 May 1869, 366–7, 369).

41 A. P. Stanley. Mezzotint by G. Zobel after E. U. Eddis, published in 1853. The volume which Stanley holds in this portrait seems to be the report of the Royal Commission on the University, the 'Great Blue Book' of 1852. Well known by 1850 for his reforming views and religious liberalism, he had been both an instigator of the Commission and its secretary. Gladstone was reported to have predicted that commissioners guided by Stanley would 'avoid giving any handle for attack'. He had apparently based this on Stanley's 'ingenuity' or 'ingenuousness': which word he had used was not clear. In the event the report was unanimous, dissent being restricted to an anonymous disclaimer on a single point. Although Stanley, as secretary, was given much of the credit for this, he was not wholly satisfied with the Commission's achievement; but, as he wrote to Jowett on the eve of the Blue Book's publication, 'the great work was to finish it at all' (R. E. Prothero, *A. P. Stanley* (2 vols 1893) i. 431–2).

42 H. L. Mansel. Undated photograph. A tutor of St John's, a Tory and High-Churchman, Mansel was the scourge of 'Germanizers', whether importers of the professorial system or propagators of German theology. His reputation as a common-room wit was confirmed by his satirical skit (1850) upon the appointment of the Royal Commission, which included the much-quoted 'Chorus of Cloudy Professors'. He was a prominent member of the Tutors' Association, convened in November 1852, and was elected a representative of the MAs on the first Hebdomadal Council in October 1854.

43 Thomas Gaisford. Mezzotint by T. L. Atkinson after H. W. Pickersgill, published in 1848. Dean of Christ Church, and Regius Professor of Greek, Gaisford was a blunt critic of reform of the University. Alone of the heads of houses, he declined even to acknowledge the communications addressed to him by the Oxford Commission. In the opinion of his successor as Dean he was 'a man unreasonable in all things except philology, and bookselling, and the management of libraries'. Gaisford's greatest services to the University were as a Curator of the Bodleian and a Delegate of the Press (see H. Lloyd-Jones, *Blood for the Ghosts* (1982), ch. 6).

44 John Conington. Undated photograph (possibly *c.*1856). As a junior fellow of University College, Conington was regarded, along with Goldwin Smith and Henry Halford Vaughan, as a dangerous radical and extreme University reformer. Elected as the first holder of the Corpus chair of Latin in June 1854, Conington underwent an evangelical conversion in the following long vacation, moved by 'the terrors of hell'. He became estranged from his former allies through his unwillingness to support their campaign for tests repeal. A jaundiced account of Conington's tenure of the Latin chair appeared in Mark Pattison's *Memoirs* (1885).

45 Edward Cardwell. Stipple engraving by W. Holl after G. Richmond. This fashionable and decidedly unclerical portrait suggests why Tractarian writers such as R. W. Church viewed Cardwell, one of the most powerful figures on the old Hebdomadal Board, so unfavourably as a wordly political operator. More sympathetic contemporaries recognized him as a learned divine who, during the late 1830s, as Camden Professor of Ancient History, had found it 'impracticable to awaken the calm attention of theological students to the early history of the Christian Church in a time of violent excitement and controversy' (*GM* (1861) ii. 209). Instead he directed his scholarly energies to more recent ecclesiastical history, compiling for publication collections of documents illustrating the government and doctrine of the Church of England since the Reformation, with the express purpose of upholding 'that general sobriety of mind and principle, which, however occasionally deranged by factious men, and at convulsive periods, is among the many blessings conferred upon the nation by the reformed church of England' (*Synodalia* ed. E. Cardwell (1842), xxx).

46 Travers Twiss. Undated photograph (*c.*1860). Pictured in his DCL robe, Twiss, an advocate in Doctors' Commons and an international lawyer of some repute, had been appointed to the Regius chair of Civil Law in July 1855. He sought to 'resuscitate' the higher faculties, but differed from radical reformers in wishing to do so for the more limited purpose of reviving the study of civil law (see his *Letter to the Vice Chancellor on the Law Studies of the University* (1856)). Contemporaries proposed that Oxford should educate more future lawyers as a means of moralizing the legal profession; in 1872 Twiss himself was obliged to give up his public offices, and was effectively ruined, following damaging personal allegations about his wife circulated for the purpose of extortion by an unscrupulous and impecunious London solicitor.

47 Richard Greswell. Etching by Thomas Woollen Smith (1852), an undergraduate
at Worcester between 1851 and 1854. Greswell, 'The Faithful Steward' among
J. W. Burgon's *Lives of Twelve Good Men* (2 vols 1889), was a man of 'child-like
piety' and extreme diffidence, though the most senior in age and academic
standing of the tutors sympathetic to the Tractarians. One of the first married
tutors, he continued to teach Worcester men from his house in Beaumont Street
after vacating his fellowship in 1836. He chaired the committee which secured
Gladstone's election to the University seat in August 1847, and represented the
collegiate ideal enshrined in the 1854 Act.

48 Goldwin Smith, from the series of caricatures 'Great Guns of Oxford', published
by T. Shrimpton (*c.*1874). As the trousers in the caricature show, Smith had
migrated to America in 1868, becoming the first Professor of English and Constitutional History at Cornell University. Oxford thus lost one of its best-known
liberal reformers. Goldwin Smith was not particularly popular in the University
even among those who shared his views. In 1856, when his services to the Executive
Commission following the 1854 Act were at their height, Jowett dismissed him as a
man 'with a crack in his skull' (to A. P. Stanley, 27 Feb. [1856], cited in Ward,
Victorian Oxford, 235). Yet the influence of Smith's writings on Oxford could not
be denied. 'He is', a member of the 'Church party' wrote in 1871, 'in his way, and
with all his bitterness, still something of a prophet' (J. B. Mozley, *Letters*, 320).

49 'Black Matins, or the effects of late drinking upon early risers'. Drawn and
engraved by Robert Cruikshank (1824) and later reproduced in C. M. Westmacott, *The English Spy* (1825). Criticism of the empty and irreverent formality
of college chapels was not confined to pamphleteers. Edward Stanley (later the
fourteenth Earl of Derby and University Chancellor) told the House of Commons in 1834 that compulsory morning and evening chapel attendance by undergraduates, sometimes under the influence of drink, 'was most injurious to the
morals of the youth of the country, and was calculated more to deaden all feelings
for religion, than if all the Dissenters of England were admitted to the honours of
the University' (*Parl. Deb.* 25 Mar. 1834, 3S xxii. 636).

50 Mr Slowcoach's lecture, from *The Adventures of Mr Verdant Green* (1853), 79.
Perhaps the only contemporary image of a catechetical lecture, Edward Bradley's
drawing reflected a weight of testimony to the ineffectiveness of college teaching,
which brought together in the tutor's room classes containing widely differing
abilities and levels of previous education. As the sketch shows, undergraduates,
unlike schoolboys, remained seated (or lolling) while they individually construed
classical texts. Although he departed from the earlier visual convention of gouty
and peevish dons (see A. H. Gibbs, *Rowlandson's Oxford* (1911), ch. 15), Bradley
invoked a new stereotype of dull pedants, which was not an entirely faithful
picture of the predominantly youthful and, as the heads had cause to complain,
sometimes volatile tutorial body.

51 Prescribed academic dress for the different orders of undergraduates, depicted in
N. Whittock, *The Microcosm of Oxford* (1828), opp. pp. 43, 44. From left to

right: a nobleman in undress gown (black silk with full sleeves) and dress gown (purple damask silk, richly ornamented with gold lace), in both cases worn with a square black velvet cap with gold tassel (hence a 'tuft'); gentleman commoner in dress gown (richly ornamented with black silk trimming); commoner (sleeveless gown of black 'prince's stuff'); gentleman commoner in undress gown (black silk); and a scholar (plain gown of black 'prince's stuff' with full sleeves), all worn with a square black cap with silk tassel.

52 'An Oxford Proctor requesting a student to put on his gown, instead of carrying it on his arm, which is now a common custom in Oxford, 1843'. Lithograph by Walker after a drawing by R. W. Buss, reproduced in Huber, *English Universities* ii pt 2, 460. The undergraduates formally 'cap' the proctor, in his capacity as a senior university official, who with equal ceremony challenges them outside the porch of St Mary's. The proctor is accompanied by two university policemen ('bulldogs'). In 1861 the outgoing senior proctor, Robert Gandell, wished that 'the absurd custom of carrying the gown on the arm was not so common' (*Herald* 17 April 1861).

53 'Boat Race on the River Isis'. Aquatint by John Whessell after a painting by the marine artist, J. T. Serres, published in March 1822. This early depiction of a 'bumping-race' between two eight-oared college boats anticipated the celebrated disputed 'bump' between the Jesus and Brasenose eights in June 1822. Eight-oared races between college crews, starting at Iffley lock, dated from after 1815 and became regular occurrences, with agreed rules, during the 1820s (see Richard Sharp, 'A Jesus College Rowing Print', *Jesus College Record* (1992), 24–9).

54 'Oxford Transports, or Albanians doing penance for past offences'. Drawn and engraved by Robert Cruikshank, published in 1824. The author of *The English Spy* (1825; new edn 2 vols 1907) claimed that the scene was 'faithfully delineated' from the recollection of a rowdy wine party at St Alban Hall during the last years of Dr Winstanley's principalship (Winstanley died in 1823), at which he and Cruikshank were guests (i. 235 n. 23). Members of the hall, known as the 'Botany Bay' of the University since men expelled from their colleges for disciplinary transgressions were received there, were not unduly inconvenienced by its relaxed regime. Such extreme representations were denounced as untypical by local observers: 'The discipline of the University prohibits late hours and the evenings devoted to enjoyment are not often disgraced by excess' (*Remarks on the Novel of Reginald Dalton* (1824), 20).

55 'The Hunting Breakfast'. Lithograph published in about 1850 by J. Ryman, after a drawing by G. R. Winter. A slightly implausible, and possibly comic, representation of the hunting set: tea is dispensed, and a scout makes a solemn entrance bearing refreshment, while texts are laid out for study upon a prominently displayed book stand.

56 'Oxford University Amusements'. Engraving by R. W. Buss, 1843. Two undergraduates relax with a pipe and a horn in the sanctuary of college rooms. Each

occupant was responsible for his own furnishings. The Royal Commission heard that 'the growing taste for furniture and decorations' was sometimes the cause of ruinous undergraduate debt (*RCO* (1850), report, 24).

57 *a,b* A. W. Pugin's designs for rebuilding Balliol College in 1843, which included an undergraduate's chamber and bedroom depicted here, aroused nineteenth-century Oxford's sharpest architectural controversy. Pugin, who was a Roman Catholic convert, had denounced the reformers commemorated in the Martyrs' Memorial (lately erected by Balliol's back gate) as 'vile, blasphemous impostors'. By a brilliant, single-handed performance he produced his drawings in two weeks, believing that they would make the fellows 'half-mad for true Christian rooms'. His plans came under the Master's veto and the south front of Balliol was not reconstructed until the 1860s, when the Quaker Alfred Waterhouse used many of Pugin's ideas in designing the building seen today. It may be doubted whether any of the medieval *pauperes Christi*, of whom the Tractarians made much, had inhabited a 'two-room set' which included a canopied bed and a handsome prie-dieu (Sir Howard Colvin, *Unbuilt Oxford* (1983), 108–12).

58 Old Mortality, photographed in Trinity 1860. Standing (left to right) J. F. Payne (Magdalen), J. W. Hoole (Queen's), T. H. Green (Balliol), James Bryce (Trinity), A. J. Mackay (University); sitting (left to right) G. R. Luke (Balliol), A. C. Swinburne (Balliol), John Nichol (Balliol), A. V. Dicey (Balliol), T. E. Holland (Magdalen). Members of Old Mortality, founded in 1856, met weekly to hear and discuss papers on modern literature and philosophy. Of its early members, seven became professors and two heads of house; one was raised to the judicial bench and one served in the Cabinet (see Gerald C. Monsman, 'Old Mortality at Oxford', *Studies in Philology* 67 (1970), 359–89).

59 Christ Church men, photographed shortly after the foundation of the Oxford University Rifle Corps (May 1859), from the album of Cecil Mills. Mills's friends at the House were not generally drawn from among the 'reading men'. Only four of the thirty-three contemporaries identified in the album obtained honours in a final school; Mills was himself obliged to migrate to New Inn Hall before taking a pass degree. Shortly afterwards he was presented by his father to the family living, Barford rectory, Warwickshire. About half of those recorded were members of aristocratic or gentry families, and had no professional occupation after going down from the University; seven others became clergymen and three were elected Members of Parliament.

60 'The Rev. the Vice Chancellor of Oxford, Nov. 1852, and two former Vice Chancellors'. Engraving after a drawing by Thomas Woollen Smith. Dr Cotton, Provost of Worcester and Vice-Chancellor, followed by Dr Plumptre, Master of University College, and Dr Symons, Warden of Wadham, processing to the afternoon sermon at St Mary's. Cotton's small stature was attributed to the effects of starvation as a schoolboy at Charterhouse (see E. P. Wilson, 'An Engraving of Provost Cotton, 1852, by Thomas Woollen Smith', *Worcester College Record* (1994), 33–41).

ACKNOWLEDGEMENTS

Acknowledgement is gratefully made to the following, who have given permission to reproduce illustrations.

Ashmolean Museum:

  Department of Western Art: 6, 20, 22, 23.

  Hope Collection of Engraved Portraits: 4, 14, 15, 18, 19, 31, 33, 41, 42, 43, 45, 47.

Balliol College: 57*a*, 57*b* (by kind permission of the Master and fellows; photographs: The Conway Library, Courtauld Institute of Art).

Bodleian Library: 3 (G. A. Oxon. a. 80, p. 20), 7 (G. A. Oxon. a. 86, p. 53), 8 (43. 1406, opp. p. 524), 9 (G. A. Oxon. a. 42, p. 77), 24 (G. A. Oxon. a. 72, fo 48), 29 (MS Top. Oxon. b. 89, fo 11), 30 (Janitor's list of library objects, no. 409), 49 (G. A. Oxon. a. 72, p. 71), 50 (Manning 8° 146, p. 79), 51 (G. A. Oxon. 4° 92, opp. p. 43), 52 (43. 1406, opp. p. 460), 53 (G. A. Oxon. a. 86, p. 57), 54 (G. A. Oxon. a. 72, p. 70), 55 (G. A. Oxon. a. 72, p. 81), 56 (G. A. Oxon. a. 72, p. 78), 58 (MS Top. Oxon. b. 255, fo 6), 60 (G. A. Oxon. a. 72, p. 78).

Centre for Oxfordshire Studies, Oxfordshire Photographic Archive, DLA, OCC: 16, 35.

Christ Church: 2, 17, 21, 36, 37, 59, Fig. 1.1 (by kind permission of the governing body; photographs 21, 36, 59: M. R. Dudley).

Clarendon Laboratory: 40 (photograph: C. W. Band).

The Keeper of the University Archives: Fig. 7.1.

Lincoln College: 5 (by kind permission of the Rector and fellows).

National Portrait Gallery: 12.

Oxford Union Society: 25 (photograph: C. W. Band).

Oxford University Museum: 34, 39.

Oxford University Press: 1, 10, 11 (photographs: Thomas-Photos).

Pusey House: 13 (photograph: M. R. Dudley).

Ruskin Galleries, Bembridge School: 38 (photograph: Frank Taylor).

University College: 44, 46 (by kind permission of the Master and fellows; photographs: M. R. Dudley).

Figures

Tables

Abbreviations

AA	Ashmolean Library archives
Abbott and Campbell, *Jowett*	E. Abbott and L. Campbell, *Life and Letters of Benjamin Jowett* (2 vols 1897)
Atlay, *Acland*	James Beresford Atlay, *Sir Henry Acland, Bart. K.C.B., F.R.S., Regius Professor of Medicine in the University of Oxford: a memoir* (1903)
Alumni	J. Foster, *Alumni oxonienses, 1715–1886* (4 vols 1888)
BA	bachelor of arts
BCA	Balliol College archives
BCL	bachelor of civil law
BD	bachelor of divinity
BL Add. MS	British Library, additional manuscript
BLitt	bachelor of letters
Bloxam, *Reg. Magdalen*	J. R. Bloxam, *A Register of the Presidents, Fellows, Demies, Instructors in Grammar and in Music, Chaplains, Clerks, Choristers, and Other Members of St Mary Magdalen College in the University of Oxford, from the Foundation of the College to the Present Time* (7 vols 1853–81)
BM	bachelor of medicine
BMJ	*British Medical Journal*
BMus	bachelor of music
Boase, *Reg. Exeter*	C. W. Boase, *Register of the Rectors, Fellows, and Other Members on the Foundation of Exeter College, Oxford (Registrum Collegii Exoniensis)* (OHS xxvii 1894)
Bodl.	Bodleian Library, Oxford
Brasenose Monographs	*Brasenose College Quatercentenary Monographs* (2 vols in 3 OHS lii–liv 1909)
BSc	bachelor of science
CA	Christ Church archives
Calendar	*Oxford University Calendar*, 1810– (published annually by the University)
Clinton, *Literary Remains*	Henry Fynes Clinton, *Literary Remains*, ed. C. J. Fynes Clinton (1854). Includes autobiography and literary journal

The Collegiate University	James McConica (ed.), *History of the University of Oxford* iii: *The Collegiate University* (1986)
Copleston, *Reply*	[E. Copleston], *A Reply to the Calumnies of the Edinburgh Review against Oxford* (1810). Copleston's two later replies (1810, 1811) are of less importance
Cordeaux and Merry	E. H. Cordeaux and D. H. Merry, *Bibliography of Printed Works relating to the University of Oxford* (3 vols 1968)
Corr. on Improvement (1854)	*Correspondence respecting the Proposed Measures of Improvement in the Universities and Colleges of Oxford and Cambridge, Part I* (Oxford) (PP 1854 (90) l. 201–308)
Cox	G. V. Cox, *Recollections of Oxford* (corr. edn 1870). For an appraisal of the value of these *Recollections* see O. Chadwick, *The Spirit of the Oxford Movement* (1990), 137
CUF	Common University Fund
DCL	doctor of civil law
DD	doctor of divinity
Derby Papers	Papers of the 14th Earl of Derby (1799–1869), Liverpool Record Office, 920 DER(14). The letters to Lord Derby have not been foliated. Citations from letters by him are taken from copies in letter-books
Devonshire Commn	[Duke of Devonshire, chairman], *Royal Commission on Scientific Instruction and the Advancement of Science*; appointed 18 May 1870; eighth (and last) report signed 18 June 1875 (PP 1872 xxv c. 536: first and second reports; 1873 xxviii c. 868, 637: third report; 1874 xxii c. 958–95: evidence)
DM	doctor of medicine
DMus	doctor of music
DNB	*Dictionary of National Biography* (66 vols 1885–1901, reissued in 22 vols 1908–9). This series, bringing the record to the death of Queen Victoria, 22 Jan. 1901, has been extended to 1990 by further volumes, and by a *Missing Persons* volume (1993)
Ed. Rev.	*Edinburgh Review*
EHR	*English Historical Review*
The Eighteenth Century	L. S. Sutherland and L. G. Mitchell (eds), *History of the University of Oxford* v: *The Eighteenth Century* (1986)
Enactments in Parliament	*Enactments in Parliament specially concerning the Universities of Oxford and Cambridge and the Halls*

	and Colleges Therein and the Colleges of Winchester, Eton and Westminster, ed. L. L. Shadwell (4 vols OHS lviii–lxi 1912)
Fowler, *Corpus*	T. Fowler, *History of Corpus Christi College, Oxford* (OHS xxv 1893)
FRCP	Fellow of the Royal College of Physicians
Froude, *Remains*	Richard Hurrell Froude, *Remains*, [ed. J. H. Newman and John Keble] (4 vols 1838–9)
FRS	Fellow of the Royal Society
Gazette	*Oxford University Gazette* (28 Jan. 1870–)
Gibbon, *Memoirs*	Edward Gibbon, *Memoirs of my Life*, ed. Georges A. Bonnard (1966)
Gladstone, *Diaries*	*The Gladstone Diaries* (14 vols 1968–94) i–ii (1825–39) ed. M. R. D. Foot; iii–iv (1840–54) ed. M. R. D. Foot and H. C. G. Matthew; v–xiv (1855–96, index) ed. H. C. G. Matthew
GM	*Gentleman's Magazine*
HBM	Hebdomadal Board minutes, OUA. The Board was succeeded by the Hebdomadal Council during Michaelmas term 1854
HCP	Hebdomadal Council papers (printed series Mar. 1882–)
Herald	*Oxford University Herald*
Historical Register, 1220–1900	*The Historical Register of the University of Oxford to Trinity Term 1900* (1900)
Huber, *English Universities*	V. A. Huber, *The English Universities*, ed. and trans. F. W. Newman (2 vols 2nd in 2 1843)
KCA	Keble College archives
LBV	Liddon Bound Volumes; papers collected or transcribed when Liddon was writing the *Life of Pusey*. These constitute the greater part of the Liddon Papers in Pusey House library
LCA	Lincoln College archives
LDN	J. H. Newman, *Letters and Diaries* (planned for 31 vols) i–vii (1801–Dec. 1840), ed. I. T. Ker, T. Gornall and G. Tracey (1978–95); xi–xxxi (Oct. 1845–90), ed. C. S. Dessain and T. Gornall (1961–77)
Liddon, *Pusey*	H. P. Liddon, *Life of E. B. Pusey*, ed. J. O. Johnston, R. J. Wilson and for vol. iv W. C. E. Newbolt (4 vols 1893–7). Liddon arranged material for all 4 vols and left a first draft to 1856

LPL	Lambeth Palace library
LSE	London School of Economics and Political Science
Macleane, *Pembroke*	D. Macleane, *History of Pembroke College, Oxford* (OHS xxxiii 1897)
Mallet	C. E. Mallet, *History of the University of Oxford* (3 vols 1924–7, repr. 1968)
MCA	Magdalen College archives
Memories	C. H. O. Daniel (ed.), *Our Memories* (1893)
Mozley, *Letters*	*Letters of the Revd. J. B. Mozley, DD*, ed. Anne Mozley (1885)
Mozley, *Reminiscences*	T. Mozley, *Reminiscences, Chiefly of Oriel College and the Oxford Movement* (2 vols, 2nd edn 1882). See Chadwick, 139–43
NCA	New College archives
nd	no date given
Newman, *Apologia*	J. H. Newman, *Apologia pro vita sua* (1864), ed. M. J. Svaglic (1967)
Newman, *AW*	J. H. Newman, *Autobiographical Writings*, ed. H. Tristram (1956)
Newman, *Fifteen Sermons*	J. H. Newman, *Fifteen Sermons Preached before the University of Oxford* (1843, 3rd edn 1872)
Newman, *Idea*	J. H. Newman, *The Idea of a University*, ed. I. T. Ker (1976). The nine discourses given in this edition are based on the 1873 text, with the changes made by 1891 incorporated
Newman, *P and P Sermons*	J. H. Newman, *Parochial and Plain Sermons* (8 vols 1868–9). For a list of Newman's Anglican sermons, with dates of first delivery, see J. H. Newman, *Sermons, 1824–1843*, i, ed. Placid Murray (1991), 353–72
np	no place of publication given
OCA	Oriel College archives
OCL	Oriel College MS letters and other papers acquired before 1932, Oriel College library
OHS	Oxford Historical Society
OM	*Oxford Magazine*
ONFRS	*Obituary Notices of Fellows of the Royal Society*
OUA	Oxford University archives
OUS	Oxford Union Society

Palmer, *Narrative*   W. Palmer, *Narrative of Events Connected with the Publication of Tracts for the Times* (1883)

Parl. Deb.   *Parliamentary Debates.* The series is briefly denoted, the sign for 'Third Series' being '3S'

Pattison, *Memoirs*   Mark Pattison, *Memoirs*, ed. V. H. H. Green (1885, 1988)

PCA   Pembroke College, Oxford, archives

PHL   Pusey House library

PP   Parliamentary Papers

Pt 2   M. G. Brock and M. C. Curthoys (eds), *History of the University of Oxford* vii: *Nineteenth-Century Oxford, Part 2*

QJE   *Quarterly Journal of Education*

Quarterly   *Quarterly Review*

QCA   The Queen's College archives

RCO (1850)   *Royal Commission Appointed to Inquire into the State, Discipline, Studies and Revenues of the University and Colleges of Oxford*; appointed 31 Aug. 1850; report signed 27 Apr. 1852; chairman Samuel Hinds, Bishop of Norwich (PP 1852 (1482) xxii), report and evidence

RCOC (1872)   *Royal Commission Appointed to Inquire into the Property and Income of the Universities of Oxford and Cambridge, and of the Colleges and Halls therein*; appointed 5 Jan. 1872; report signed 31 July 1874; chairman Duke of Cleveland (PP 1873 xxxvii C. 856 pts 1–3), report and evidence

RCOC (1919)   *Royal Commission on Oxford and Cambridge Universities*; appointed 14 Nov. 1919; report signed 1 Mar. 1922; chairman, with specific responsibility for Oxford, H. H. Asquith (PP 1922 x Cmd. 1588)

Report and Evidence (1853)   *Report and Evidence upon the Recommendations of Her Majesty's Commissioners for Inquiring into the State of the University of Oxford, presented to the Board of Heads of Houses and Proctors, 1 December 1853* (1853). Unless otherwise stated citations are to the Evidence which is paginated separately to the Report

SCOC (1867)   *Select Committee on the Oxford and Cambridge Universities Education Bill*; appointed 26 June 1867; reported 31 July 1867; chairman William Ewart (PP 1867 (497) xiii. 183–560), report (185) and evidence

Stanley, *Arnold*	A. P. Stanley, *Life and Correspondence of Thomas Arnold D.D.* (1844, 16th edn expanded 2 vols 1898)
Statutes	*Oxford University Statutes Translated* i: *The Caroline Code*, ed. G. R. M. Ward (1845), ii: *1767–1850*, ed. G. R. M. Ward and J. Heywood (1851). For G. R. M. Ward's activities see Ward, *Victorian Oxford*, 124–6
SUL	Southampton University library
TCA	Trinity College, Oxford, archives
Tuckwell (1900)	W. Tuckwell, *Reminiscences of Oxford* (1900). See Chadwick, 137. William Tuckwell (1829–1919) grew up in Oxford and matriculated at New College, October 1848. Also wrote *Pre-Tractarian Oxford: a Reminiscence of the Oriel 'Noetics'* (1909)
The Twentieth Century	B. H. Harrison (ed.), *History of the University of Oxford* viii: *The Twentieth Century* (1994)
UCL	University College London
UOC (1877)	*University of Oxford Commission*; appointed 10 Aug. 1877; chairman (–1880) Earl of Selborne, (1880–) Mountague Bernard (PP 1881 lvi C. 2868), evidence, circulars, etc. Commissioners named in section 4 of the 1877 Act, which received the royal assent on 10 Aug
V. & A.	Victoria and Albert Museum
VCH Cambs. iii	J. P. C. Roach (ed.), *A History of the County of Cambridge and the Isle of Ely* iii (1959)
VCH Oxon. iii	H. E. Salter and M. D. Lobel (eds.), *A History of the County of Oxford* iii (1954)
VCH Oxon. iv	A. Crossley (ed.), *A History of the County of Oxford* iv (1979)
Ward, *Victorian Oxford*	W. R. Ward, *Victorian Oxford* (1965)

List of Contributors

GILES BARBER was Librarian of the Taylor Institution, 1970–96.

RICHARD BRENT was lately a Research Fellow, St John's College, Cambridge. He is the author of *Liberal Anglican Politics: Whiggery, Religion and Reform, 1830–1841* (1987).

ASA BRIGGS (Lord Briggs) was Provost of Worcester College, Oxford, 1976–91.

M. G. BROCK was Warden of Nuffield College, Oxford, 1978–88.

L. W. B. BROCKLISS is Fellow and Tutor in Modern History, Magdalen College, Oxford.

M. C. CURTHOYS is a research editor, *New Dictionary of National Biography*.

C. J. DAY is University Lecturer in Local History and Fellow of Kellogg College, Oxford. He was assistant editor, *Victoria History of Oxfordshire*, 1975–96.

J. P. D. DUNBABIN is Fellow and Tutor in Politics and Modern History, St Edmund Hall, Oxford.

ROBERT FOX is Professor of the History of Science, University of Oxford.

H. C. HARLEY was for many years a medical practitioner in Oxford. He is the author of *Sir Henry Acland and his Circle* (1965).

CHRISTOPHER HARVIE is Professor of British and Irish Studies at the Eberhard-Karls University, Tübingen, and Honorary Professor of Politics at the University of Wales, Aberystwyth.

RICHARD JENKYNS is Fellow and Tutor in Classics, Lady Margaret Hall, Oxford.

JOHN H. JONES is Dean and Archivist, Balliol College, Oxford.

A. G. MACGREGOR is Senior Assistant Keeper, Department of Antiquities, Ashmolean Museum.

OSWYN MURRAY is Fellow and Tutor in Ancient History, Balliol College, Oxford.

P. B. NOCKLES is Assistant Librarian, the John Rylands University Library of Manchester.

I. G. PHILIP died in 1985. He became Secretary of the Bodleian Library, 1945, Keeper of Printed Books, 1966, and Deputy Librarian, 1974. He retired in 1978.

A. H. T. ROBB-SMITH is Emeritus Nuffield Reader in Pathology, University of Oxford.

SHELDON ROTHBLATT is Professor of History and Director, Center for Studies in Higher Education, University of California, Berkeley.

N. A. RUPKE is Professor and Head, Institute for the History of Science, Georg-August University, Göttingen.

K. C. TURPIN was Provost of Oriel College, Oxford, 1957–80, and Vice-Chancellor of the University of Oxford, 1966–9.

W. R. WARD was Professor of Modern History, University of Durham, 1965–86.

J. J. L. WHITELEY is Senior Assistant Keeper, Department of Western Art, Ashmolean Museum.

ROLAND WILCOCK was Principal, West Oxfordshire College, 1960–77.

List of Chancellors and Vice-Chancellors

CHANCELLORS

1792–1809 William Henry Cavendish Bentinck, Duke of Portland
1809–34 William Wyndham Grenville, Lord Grenville
1834–52 Arthur Wellesley, Duke of Wellington
1852–69 Edward George Geoffrey Smith Stanley, Earl of Derby
1869–1903 Robert Arthur Talbot Gascoyne-Cecil, Marquis of Salisbury

VICE-CHANCELLORS

1798–1802 Michael Marlow, President of St John's
1802–6 Whittington Landon, Provost of Worcester
1806–7 Henry Richards, Rector of Exeter
1807–10 John Parsons, Master of Balliol
1810–14 John Cole, Rector of Exeter
1814–18 Thomas Lee, President of Trinity
1818–20 Frodsham Hodson, Principal of Brasenose
1820–4 George William Hall, Master of Pembroke
1824–8 Richard Jenkyns, Master of Balliol
1828–32 John Collier Jones, Rector of Exeter
1832–6 George Rowley, Master of University
1836–40 Ashurst Turner Gilbert, Principal of Brasenose
1840–4 Philip Wynter, President of St John's
1844–8 Benjamin Parsons Symons, Warden of Wadham
1848–52 Frederick Charles Plumptre, Master of University
1852–6 Richard Lynch Cotton, Provost of Worcester
1856–8 David Williams, Warden of New College
1858–62 Francis Jeune, Master of Pembroke
1862–6 John Prideaux Lightfoot, Rector of Exeter
1866–70 Francis Knyvett Leighton, Warden of All Souls
1870–4 Henry George Liddell, Dean of Christ Church

Introduction

M. G. BROCK

In 1800 Oxford University was still an Anglican institution in an Anglican state, one of its foremost duties being to uphold Christian doctrines as they were taught by the Church of England. The momentous changes in examining for degrees which were initiated in that year were intended not to alter, but to confirm, its Anglican efficiency. The tenets of the Church were seen by the British government and the Tory politicians as an essential support for the existing order. Oxford was one of the main props in that system of support: the doubts about its loyalty which had troubled governments sixty or seventy years earlier were no more than a memory. Between 1800 and 1830 the Tories were, almost uninterruptedly, the governing party, and the University, where there was a large Tory majority, could be sure of official favour. The members of Oxford's Convocation upheld St Paul's statement (in The Epistle to the Romans 13. 1) that 'the powers that be are ordained of God'. When congratulating the Prince Regent on the peace after Waterloo they undertook to 'impress upon the youth committed to our care...those Christian principles, which are the only sure foundation of public and private virtue, [and] in a more especial manner...to inculcate ...obedience to civil authority, not merely as a social, but as a religious obligation'.[1]

Until 1854 an intending Oxford undergraduate, unlike his counterpart in Cambridge or the Scottish universities, was required to start by declaring his loyalty to the 'national Church': he could not matriculate without first 'subscribing' to the Thirty-nine Articles. In 1814 the future Lord Westbury entered Wadham College when in his fifteenth year. Though debarred by his youth from taking the oath to observe the University's statutes, he was required to 'subscribe' to the Articles.[2] Oxford and Cambridge were national institutions only in the sense that they upheld the national Church. As late as 1834 the Bishop of Exeter could call them, however provocatively, 'the two great seminaries for instruction in the national religion'.[3]

---

[1] 13 Feb. 1816: register of Convocation, 1815–1820, OUA NEP/*Subtus*.

[2] *Statutes* i. 10, ii. 3; *Parl. Deb.* 3 July 1863, 3S clxxii. 163. For the controversy over subscription in 1772–3 see *The Eighteenth Century*, 166–77. A Cambridge graduand had to declare himself '*bona fide* a member of the Church of England'. See also Ch. 1, n. 21.

[3] *Parl. Deb.* 1 Aug. 1834, 3S xxv. 879 (Phillpotts). Lewis Bagot had used the same term in 1774: *The Eighteenth Century*, 173–4; as had Gladstone privately in Mar. 1829: H. G. C. Matthew, *Gladstone, 1809–1874* (1986), 27.

After 1820, as the memory of the long war against the French revolutionaries and Napoleon began to fade, fears of unorthodoxy became less obtrusive in Oxford. The confident young college fellows who had taken honours in the new examinations began to question long-accepted assumptions. The story of the next phase is not, however, one of a steady and gradual progression to free inquiry. The political upheavals from 1829 to 1833 which ended the Tories' supremacy sparked off an anti-liberal reaction in Oxford. The Tractarian group tried to change a system of ecclesiastical conformity into one in which a particular version of the Christian faith would determine the University's operations. The stir made by this doomed Tractarian effort brought the government into action. In 1850 the Prime Minister, Lord John Russell, intervened with a Royal Commission, and this began the process of establishing the national responsibilities of Oxford and Cambridge.

The changes of this second phase were even more rapid than those of the first. In 1863 John Stuart Mill was advising a friend on the choice of a university.

I think I should recommend [he wrote] to send your sons to one or other of the two old universities. Twenty years ago these were about the last places which I should have recommended in any parallel case; but they are now very much changed, and free enquiry and speculation on the deepest and highest questions, instead of being crushed or deadened, are now more rife there than almost anywhere else in England.[4]

In 1865 Benjamin Jowett, looking back at the Oxford which he had first known nearly thirty years earlier, wrote: 'When I was an undergraduate ... almost all teaching leant to the support of doctrines of authority.' He was sure that any return to these doctrines had become 'impossible'.[5] The defenders of the old order had withdrawn to new positions. In the early 1830s John Henry Newman, fellow of Oriel and vicar of St Mary's Church, was, as he later wrote, defending 'the old orthodoxy of Oxford' during 'the commencement of the assault of liberalism'.[6] Less than twenty years later, about seven years after he had become a Roman Catholic, he gave a series of lectures in Dublin in which he stressed a different aspect of a university's function. In these seminal discourses he pronounced the 'object' of a university to be 'intellectual, not moral'.[7] 'Liberal education', he said, 'makes not the Christian, not the Catholic, but the gentleman.'[8]

---

    [4] J. S. Mill to Mrs Henry Huth, 7 Jan. 1863, in *Collected Works of J. S. Mill* xv, ed. F. E. Mineka and D. M. Lindley (1972), 819.
    [5] Benjamin Jowett to Florence Nightingale, in *'Dear Miss Nightingale'*, ed. V. Quinn and J. Prest (1987), 70.
    [6] Newman, *Apologia*, 62.
    [7] Newman, *Idea*, 5. From the second sentence of the preface, 21 Nov. 1852. Cf the definition by a Tractarian of Oxford's function, 1835, p. 222.
    [8] Newman, *Idea*, 110, Fifth Discourse, delivered 7 June 1852. In the 'Ninth Discourse' (first pub. Feb. 1853), Newman, while insisting on control of university institutions by the Church, repudiated the notion that they were 'seminaries': Newman, *Idea*, 184–5, 197.

In 1853 E. B. Pusey argued against the creation of an honours school of theology, which had been advocated a year earlier in the report of the Royal Commission on Oxford. Religious teaching, he insisted, should not be treated as a particular brand of university instruction: it was not one potential subject of study, but the basis of all subjects. Pusey found the Commissioners' reference to 'the history of doctrine' objectionable. There was, in his view, 'no such real history... the faith having been, once for all, made known to the inspired Apostles, and by them inserted in Holy Scripture, and committed to the Church'. It was therefore wrong to adopt a phrase which 'as commonly used' presupposed 'the human origin of great part of the faith'. 'A young man of twenty-one', Pusey wrote, 'ought to learn only the elements of theology.'[9] Yet a mere fifteen years later, before Parliament had abolished the religious tests, he announced a change of mind and sponsored the creation of the Oxford theology school; and he confirmed in debate that it was to include the study of 'the history of doctrines'.[10]

The Oxford of the 1860s did not resemble a modern university: it was all-male; it had only just begun to provide a range of undergraduate courses, and in research it lagged behind the best German universities; it hardly catered at all for graduate or professional studies—in medical education, for instance, it was still far behind Edinburgh. But the most fundamental changes of all were being made. Oxford's teaching for honours men was efficient; its honours were recognized in the rising professional class, and even among some of the nobility and gentry, as a valid measure of merit. The University was now seen as an institution not of the national Church, but of the nation. Those who wanted to maintain its Anglican basis were still fighting hard and achieving tactical successes; but they were in retreat and were preparing to abandon the ramparts which sixty years earlier had seemed unassailable.[11] Oxford had changed almost as fast as British society. With the passage of the University Tests Act in 1871 the transformation to an undenominational, 'free-thinking' institution was almost complete.

---

[9] E. B. Pusey, *Report and Evidence* (1853), 102–6. Pusey's disapproval of the 'history of doctrine' did not extend to 'ecclesiastical history'.

[10] *The Times* 4 June 1868, 6c. See Pt 2, Ch. 3, and H. P. Liddon's reference, Cuddesdon Sermon, 10 June 1873, to 'a secularized university': *Clerical Life and Work* (1894), 84.

[11] See Ward, *Victorian Oxford*, 253–4; Gladstone's remarks quoted in Liddon's diary, 4 Sept. 1866.

A REFORMING ERA

I

The Oxford of Peel and Gladstone, 1800–1833

M. G. BROCK

The reforms adopted by Oxford University and its colleges between 1790 and 1810 have been described in *The Eighteenth Century*, and further detail is added in the chapters which follow.[1] Most of the reforms came in a piecemeal way, as one college after another improved its practices. Oriel and Balliol, which were relatively free from 'locality' and other restrictions in their fellowships, led the way in making academic promise a decisive consideration in fellowship elections. Oriel's fellowship examinations soon became something of a model. Corpus held rigorous scholarship examinations from the turn of the century and in 1816 Trinity followed suit. Increasing care was taken, by some heads at least, in the appointment of tutors; and the number of undergraduates left in complete idleness was reduced. The system of college tests and progress reports, named 'collections', long in force at Christ Church, was adopted elsewhere. Oriel introduced written work into its collections in 1828.[2] College statutes could sometimes be invoked to impede crucial changes; but, where there was a will to effect reforms, a way could usually be found. Provost Eveleigh and the fellows of Oriel made the decisive first move in 1795 in dealing with one of the college's relatively few restricted fellowships. No candidate from the favoured county, Wiltshire, met the required standard, so that the college was freed to look elsewhere and did so with great effect. Many years later Richard Whately explained how unusual this course then was:

It is felt to be such a hardship to reject a candidate as absolutely unqualified, and the feelings are so much more engaged on the side of an individual than of the public, that a native of the specified county is generally elected as a matter of course, even when utterly deficient in the personal qualities required by the Founder. And thus the

---

I should like to thank Sir Isaiah Berlin, E. G. W. Bill, Vernon Bogdanor, Colin Matthew, J. S. G. Simmons, Reba Soffer and C. A. Stray for help with this chapter.

[1] *The Eighteenth Century*, 235, 623–37. See Chs. 4, 5, 6, and 11, and N. Phillipson (ed.), *Universities, Society, and the Future* (1983), 23–4 (L. Stone).

[2] *LDN* ii. 75. Trinity and Corpus seem to have started collections before 1800. They were introduced in St John's in 1802, and are first mentioned in Balliol in that year.

provisions designed for encouraging learning in a certain district or school have often had a directly opposite effect. At Oriel…however, it was the practice to adhere strictly to the Founder's designs.

Edward Copleston, a scholar of Corpus from Devon, already known for his outstanding ability, was approached by Oriel in 1795 and accepted the fellowship.[3]

Reform in the colleges was stimulated and reinforced by the university statutes of 1800 and 1807, establishing the effective examination system for both honours and pass degrees which forms the subject of Chapter 11. As Chapter 22 of *The Eighteenth Century* shows, the struggle against revolutionary France gave the calls for reform of Oxford's arrangements a new strength; and the examination statute of 1800 was interpreted, and welcomed, as a response to them. Similar calls evoked a response in many different settings. Within a few weeks of the adoption of the statute in 1800 the Marquess Wellesley recommended the establishment of a college at Calcutta. He told the East India Company's Council that:

During the convulsions with which the doctrines of the French Revolution had agitated Europe, erroneous principles…had reached the minds of some individuals in the civil and military service of the Company in India…The progress of the mischief would…be aided by the defective or irregular education of the writers or cadets; an institution tending to fix and establish sound and correct principles of religion and government in their minds at an early period of life would be the best security…for the stability of British power in India.[4]

In his *Elements of General Knowledge*, published in 1802, Henry Kett of Trinity mentioned the great need for sound education 'in the peculiar circumstances of the present times'.[5] As Britain's long-established constitutional principles were based on the Christian message propounded by the Church of England, the country's future leaders needed to learn how principles and message should be propagated and defended. The second edition of William Barrow's *Essay on Education*, published in 1804, included this passage in a new chapter on the universities.

What I would earnestly deprecate in this case and every other is *radical reform*; hasty and general innovation, upon any supposed principles of abstract right and general truth; upon any such fanciful and visionary doctrines as *rights of men* or *the wrongs of women*, whether the design be to regulate a state or a college, the management of our children, or the principles of morals. The plan of prudence and caution the members of the Convocation at Oxford have lately applied to…the discipline and the studies of the University; and in this plan every wise and good man will wish them to persevere.[6]

[3] *Remains of the Late Edward Copleston*, ed. R. Whately (1854), 4–5.
[4] *Asiatic Annual Register, 1802* (1803), p. xix.
[5] H. Kett, *Elements of General Knowledge* (2 vols 1802) ii. 356.
[6] W. Barrow, *Essays on Education* (2 vols 1804) ii. 329–30.

Barrow's emphasis was on improved religious instruction to combat what the *British Magazine* called a 'moral pestilence...a conspiracy directed, not only against the human race in all its dearest interests, but against Heaven itself'.[7] In June 1799 Thomas Rennell, the Master of the Temple, had thundered from the pulpit of St Paul's Cathedral against 'the most lamentable and notorious defectiveness of Christian education in many of our public schools and other great seminaries'.[8] The reform actually introduced by Oxford University in the light of such pleas was an examination system based largely on classical studies. At first sight this may seem a curiously oblique response to urgent calls for instruction in Christian morals, and it did not pass without protest at the time. Why, asked Edward Tatham, the Rector of Lincoln, were 'the youth of a Christian university...to learn their moral philosophy from Aristotle, that uncircumsized and unbaptized Philistine of the Schools?'[9] This protest from the notoriously eccentric Rector proved ineffective, although it was addressed to people who, like him, were ministers of the Gospel.

In 1800 Oxford University was controlled by clergymen to a degree which was very rare elsewhere. In 1805, when the Edinburgh presbytery and synod tried to block the election of John Leslie to the University's chair of mathematics, they failed to secure the General Assembly's support and Leslie held the chair despite an echo of David Hume's views in one of his works.[10] In the Oxford colleges, by contrast, clerical influence was unchallenged. Most of the fellows were in holy orders under the requirements of college statutes; and even in Merton and All Souls, where this requirement was not wholly applicable, some two-fifths took orders, this being the way to preferment.[11] In 1830 about half of the undergraduates aimed to become parsons, almost a third of them being parsons' sons. Of those who actually graduated nearly two-thirds used the BA as a passport to orders in the Church of England. This represented a balance different from that of the German universities where, during the early years of the nineteenth century, law enrolments increased and those for theology declined.[12] Convocation, the University's governing assembly, which enacted the examination statute in 1800, was

---

[7] *British Magazine* i (1800) 425, article dated 29 Apr. See *The Eighteenth Century*, 623.

[8] T. Rennell, *A Sermon Preached in the Cathedral Church of St Paul, 6 June 1799* (1799), 7. See also Rennell's 'Notes' to the sermon, 9.

[9] *The Eighteenth Century*, 630. Similar points were made in an anonymous letter in *GM* ii (1800), 1046.

[10] J. B. Morrell, 'The Leslie affair: careers, Kirk and politics in Edinburgh in 1805', *Scottish Historical Review* liv (1975), 63–82. For a later statement about the 'just influence' of the Church of Scotland in the Scottish universities see *Parl. Deb.* 28 June 1836, 3S xxxiv. 996 (Haddington).

[11] See p. 22 below. A by-law obliged some Merton fellows to take orders: *RCO* (1850), report, 193. For the custom whereby the twelve 'law fellows' of St John's were excused from taking orders see ibid. 238.

[12] C. E. McClelland, *State, Society and University in Germany, 1700–1914* (1980), 117. See pp. 116–22 below.

dominated by parsons: it was their habit to qualify for membership of it by taking their MAs and keeping their names on their college's books.[13] Parsons formed a prominent part of the scene in popular descriptions of Oxford. When J. G. Lockhart was setting the scene for *Reginald Dalton: a Story of English University Life* (1823), he wrote: 'If you have ever happened to travel [the Oxford] road about the end of October...you have probably observed abundance of rosy-cheeked old...parsons...seeing their sons into the Oxford-bound coach, just below the rectory ha-ha.'[14] Why did these clergymen adopt syllabuses in which the place assigned to Christian doctrine was comparatively small, and that assigned to the pre-Christian world very large?

The first answer is that the importance accorded to divinity was not reflected in the size of its share of the syllabuses. Once the examinations had been reformed, no one could qualify for an Oxford BA without showing a knowledge of the Gospels in Greek, the Thirty-nine Articles, and Joseph Butler's *Analogy of Religion* (1736). Excellence in the rest of the examination could not compensate for a failure to meet this basic requirement.[15] For the honours man the divinity component was a small part of the syllabus; but for everyone it held a certain primacy. Secondly, more extended theological studies were regarded as part of an intending clergyman's professional training, and thus as unsuitable in a first degree course. Cyril Jackson, the Dean of Christ Church and chief architect of the examination statute, was a divine of an unusual kind who had started life as a courtier. He could hardly have devised a degree examination suited only to intending parsons. Some three-quarters of those Oxford undergraduates who were peers or peers' sons were at Christ Church;[16] and few of these scions of the nobility were intended for holy orders. Moreover, this was a reform introduced during a time of repression, when a speculative temper among undergraduates was discouraged, theological speculations naturally being regarded as particularly dangerous. The Christian faith, as the Established Church expounded it, was seen as a fixed system. 'There is a timid and absurd apprehension', Sydney Smith wrote in the *Edinburgh Review* of October 1809, 'on the part of ecclesiastical tutors, of letting out the minds of youth upon difficult and important subjects. They fancy that mental exertion must end in religious scepticism.'[17] That appeared in a recently established Whig journal. Sydney

[13] *RCO* (1850), report, 10.

[14] [J. G. Lockhart], *Reginald Dalton* (3 vols 1823) i. 214. For recruitment to the clergy in this period see W. J. Reader, *Professional Men* (1966), 13.

[15] See pp. 347–8 below; J. McVickar, *The Early Life and Professional Years of Bishop Hobart* (1838), 492; W. R. W. Stephens, *W. F. Hook* (2 vols 1878) i. 37; E. J. Whately, *Richard Whately* (2 vols 1866) i. 228.

[16] J. Cannon, *Aristocratic Century* (1984), 52. The figures for 1800–19 are for peers of the United Kingdom; they exclude illegitimate sons and those whose fathers were enrolled after they had come into residence.

[17] *Ed. Rev.* xv (1809), 50.

Smith was a clever Whig parson who, being an Oxford man, knew where to place his barbs. Edward Copleston wrote in reply to the article:

There is one province of education indeed in which we are slow in believing that any discoveries can be made. The scheme of revelation we think is closed, and we expect no new light on earth to break in upon us...We hold it our especial duty...to keep strict watch round that sacred citadel, to deliver out in due measure and season the stores it contains, to make our countrymen look to it as a tower of strength, and to defend it against open and secret enemies.[18]

The Select Preachers' statute was reformed in 1803[19] and Copleston emphasized that ethics, being 'more included within the province of religion than that of philosophy', could not be a subject for undergraduate discussion. 'It is...from the pulpit', he wrote, 'that we are to look for the fullest performance of this branch of education.'[20] No deviation from Anglican teaching was allowed. Subscription did not exclude Wesleyans nor members of the Church of Scotland,[21] but while at Oxford they were obliged to conform. By the statute of 1803 the conformity rules were modernized and tightened, the penalties for mingling 'in any way with a congregation of persons dissenting from the doctrine or discipline of the Church of England' being brought up to date: a third conviction for this offence was to entail expulsion from the University 'for ever'. In religious questions Oxford stood not for discussion and free thought, but for unquestioning acceptance of the Church of England's doctrines. Ironically France, though seen as the source of 'moral pestilence', soon had a university system where the control of thought was more stringent than anything known in Oxford. In 1808 Napoleon ordered the first *grand maître* of the Université impériale, the Marquis de Fontanes, to ensure that appointments were confined to those who would serve as a 'guarantee against pernicious and subversive theories of the social order...and as defenders of morality'. The contrast, however, between Oxford and Edinburgh, and, after a few years, between Oxford and the German universities, was as sharp as the exchange between Sydney Smith and Copleston suggested. Until the Disruption of the 1840s the statutory Presbyterian test was in abeyance in the Scottish universities. Glasgow's Professor of Greek from 1821 (D. K. Sandford) was an Episcopalian,

---

[18] Copleston, *Reply*, 151–2.
[19] *Statutes* ii. 43–56; Cox, 54. The number of sermons was reduced; but those commemorating the failure of the Gunpowder Plot, the martyrdom of Charles I, and the Restoration did not lapse until 1859.
[20] Copleston, *Reply*, 178.
[21] *RCO* (1850), report, 55. The Prince of Orange, being a 'Presbyterian', was unable to matriculate in 1809. He 'pursued his studies' in Oxford 'assisted by academic private tutors': Cox, 63, 75. Undergraduates from the Established Church of Scotland were, however, able to subscribe. They had become an accepted feature of Oxford life by 1800: see W. Innes Addison, *The Snell Exhibitions from the University of Glasgow to Balliol College* (Glasgow 1901). See also n. 359 below.

and Philip Kelland, appointed to Edinburgh's mathematics chair in 1838, an Anglican clergyman. In Oxford doubt and denominational diversity were forbidden. In 1832 Vaughan Thomas of Oriel and Corpus accused his antagonist in the *Edinburgh Review* of being 'fresh from the classroom of a Dr. Britchschneider [*sic*] or a Dr. Wagscheider [*sic*], or some other Teutonic Gamaliel with a name as unutterable as his blasphemies'.[22] This pedagogic stance was not confined to Oxford. Charles Simeon, the leading Cambridge Evangelical, warned undergraduates against neglecting their studies in order to read the Bible. 'I speak not of the daily reading which is necessary for our daily strength,' he said, 'but of reading the Scriptures as a study. Remember secular study, as appointed by the authorities, is here your duty to God. Mathematics are important; they will enable us to think clearly.'[23] Finally, the institution in which Oxford's fellows held their orders was a 'layman's Church'. It was not thought in the least improper for clergymen to concentrate their studies on subjects other than divinity. Parsons imbued with the exalted sense of vocation expected later would not have been acceptable to those who ruled England in 1800: lay people in the governing classes did not want the Church 'to get on stilts'.[24]

The controversies to which Oxford's classical syllabus gave rise are examined in Chapter 3. 'To exercise the mind of the student', Copleston told a friend, 'is the business of education.'[25] In the view of Oxford's spokesmen the classics were unrivalled for sharpening the mind. The Dissenters and radicals with whom the establishment's friends had to contend included, as Whately wrote in his *Elements of Logic*, men of 'cultivated argumentative powers'.[26] A study of Aristotle, who was termed in the statute of 1807 'the master of logic',[27] was therefore desirable. Such views were not entirely out of line with those found elsewhere. The classics were given a high place in the Scottish universities, for instance, and in the Yale University report of 1828.[28] The peculiarity of Oxford's position lay in the contention that the

[22] [V. Thomas], *The Legality of the Present Academic System of the University Re-asserted* (1832), 22–3. Karl Gottlieb Bretschneider (1776–1848) had proposed for discussion a view of St John's Gospel held to be heretical: see Liddon, *Pusey* i. 149; for Wegscheider, ibid. i. 87 n. 1. For Gamaliel see Acts 22. 3. For France see pp. 95–8 below and W. D. Halls, *Education, Culture and Politics in Modern France* (1946), 4–5. For Scottish universities see n. 143 below.

[23] A. W. Brown, *Recollections of ... Charles Simeon* (1863), 193–4.

[24] J. A. Froude, *Short Studies on Great Subjects* (4 vols 1867–83) iv. 168–9, 176–7.

[25] To the Revd J. Penrose (*c.*1810), W. J. Copleston, *Memoir of Edward Copleston D.D., Bishop of Llandaff* (1851), 38.

[26] R. Whately, *Elements of Logic* (2nd edn rev. 1827), pp. xxviii–ix.

[27] *Statutes* ii. 63 (where date is wrongly given as 1803).

[28] J. C. Lane, 'The Yale Report of 1828 and liberal education: a neorepublican manifesto', *History of Education Quarterly* (Bloomington Ind.) xxvii (1987), 331–5; Jurgen Herbst, 'American higher education in the age of the college', *History of Universities* viii (1988), 43–4. The two-part faculty report was accompanied by that of a trustee committee. For a protest in July 1836 that a bill then being debated might injure classical teaching in the Scottish universities see L. J. Saunders, *Scottish Democracy, 1815–1840* (1950), 327.

classics constituted the only effective mind-sharpener, there being no study which could combine, to any considerable extent, mind-sharpening with the acquisition of useful knowledge. This was where the critics dissented. Even Macaulay, when defending classical education for public servants, was inclined to charge the English universities with 'too much attention...to the dead languages'.[29] Tatham's plea for examinations which had modern studies, and especially natural science, within their scope was to be echoed many times. An Oxford prize-man, J. S. Boone, described his ideal university in the fifth dialogue of *The Oxford Spy*, published in 1819:[30]

> There what may modern Europe most concern
> The embryo statesman shall not fail to learn;
> There Britain's annals reap their just applause,
> Our country's heroes, and our country's laws....
> Ethics shall flourish such as Moderns know
> Not as they beamed two thousand years ago.[31]

Sydney Smith pointed out in the *Edinburgh Review* that modern languages were as exacting to study as classical, and far more useful: why did they not find a place in the examination syllabus?[32]

The basic reason for Oxford's concentration on the classics was that the cautious founders of the system were obliged to take over what was to hand. They wanted the rest of Oxford to adopt the teaching arrangements of the leading colleges. Practice at Christ Church formed the principal model for their scheme; and Dr E. G. W. Bill writes that from the middle of the eighteenth century liberal education in Christ Church 'tended to become synonymous with classical education'.[33] Oxford's higher faculties of theology, law, and medicine had decayed to nothing. The system had to be based on classical subjects, since those were the ones in which every college could provide tuition. Oxford undergraduates were older on arrival than those of the Scottish universities, and could be assumed to have been taught Greek as well as Latin before they arrived. During this period about 35 per cent of them came from the nine 'Clarendon schools'.[34] Variable as the standard of Greek teaching was, even among these nine, Oxford was able, without

[29] *Parl. Deb.* 10 July 1833, 3S xix. 526.
[30] Student of Christ Church, 1816. Declined to take honours: Mozley, *Reminiscences*, ii. 201. Won Craven Scholarship and Latin Verse and Newdigate prizes, 1817. This seems to have been the first occasion on which the Craven, formerly available only to founder's kin, was opened (no founder's kin claiming) to a 'regular examination': *Memories*, 41 (H. G. Liddell). *The Oxford Spy* was published anonymously.
[31] Fifth Dialogue, 44–5.
[32] *Ed. Rev.* xv (Oct. 1809), 47–8. See also xliii (Feb. 1826), 333–4 (T. B. Macaulay).
[33] E. G. W. Bill, *Education at Christ Church, Oxford, 1660–1800* (1988), 6.
[34] T. Chalmers, *Use and Abuse of Literary and Ecclesiastical Endowments* (1827) in *Works* (25 vols Glasgow, 1836–42) xvii. 95–6. The nine schools were Winchester, Eton, St Paul's, Shrewsbury, Westminster, Merchant Taylors', Rugby, Harrow, Charterhouse: Public Schools Act, 1864 (27 & 28 Vic., c. xcii), Schedule.

departing from tradition, to establish the classics as the essential basis for the honours examination to an extent which was unique in the English-speaking world.[35] Starting an examination system was a perilous business: in 1785 it had led to serious student riots at Yale.[36] Cyril Jackson, who was no mean political strategist,[37] meant to align Oxford publicly against revolutionary ideas without enraging either the college fellows or the parents of sons who might become undergraduates. By concentrating on the classics, apart from a nugget of divinity, he and Eveleigh were playing for safety; for them modern studies meant involvement in political controversy and an encouragement to undergraduate speculations.[38] Thomas Jefferson could include political economy and natural science in the recommendations when drafting the syllabus for his new University of Virginia in 1818.[39] Jackson and Eveleigh had no such freedom. Like their earlier counterparts at Cambridge they were obliged, while meeting the requirements of the political class, to follow their university's traditions. In Cambridge the High-Church tradition had been weak, natural theology being in favour; and, when the tripos was reformed in the 1750s, Newtonian mathematics, honoured as a support for the 'argument from design', became the basis of the reformed system.[40] In Oxford, where more attention had been paid to the traditional disputations and the knowledge of logic which they entailed, the Greek and Latin classics were seen as central, and mathematics and physics as secondary. In the mid-century Cambridge had adopted mathematics as the study untainted by Jacobite leanings: in 1800 Oxford established the classics as a bulwark against the Jacobins.

An emphasis on the classics, with mathematics in second place, accorded with the inclinations of Oxford's clerical fellows in 1800. These subjects were the staples of gentry education and this was largely in the clergy's hands.[41] 'The nobility and gentry of England', the *British Critic* remarked in 1826, 'when they want a tutor for their sons, a man who is to superintend their morals and improve their minds, do not look out for liberal philosophers, but for a well-bred and regularly educated clergyman of the Church

[35] For defects in the teaching of Greek in the 1820s see R. M. Ogilvie, *Latin and Greek: a History of the Influence of the Classics on English Life, from 1600 to 1918* (1964), 83–5. In the 1860s Taine thought English schoolboys worse than French at Latin, but better at Greek: *Taine's Notes on England*, trans. E. Hyams (1957), 112.

[36] Phillipson (ed.), *Universities, Society, and the Future*, 24 (L. Stone).

[37] See J. Nicholls, *Recollections of the Reign of George III* (2 vols 2nd edn 1822) i. 393.

[38] See J. H. Newman to Charles Anderson, 24 Jan. 1836, in *LDN* v. 212. John Parsons, Master of Balliol 1798–1819, worked with Jackson and Eveleigh in launching the examinations.

[39] H. Hale Bellot, *University College, London* (1929), 10.

[40] J. Gascoigne, 'Mathematics and meritocracy: the emergence of the Cambridge mathematical tripos', *Social Studies of Science* xiv (1984), 547–84.

[41] Under 19 Geo. III, c. 44 (1779) a Dissenting teacher was required to make a declaration of his Protestant Christian faith before a magistrate. The requirement was modified in 1812: 52 Geo. III, c. 155, s. 5.

of England.'[42] For the clergy classics and mathematics sometimes provided more than employment: they were important routes to promotion. Pitt's Cambridge tutor had become Bishop of Lincoln and Dean of St Paul's in 1787 when only 36; and Lord Liverpool, impressed in Disraeli's words 'with the necessity of reconstructing the episcopal bench on principles of personal distinction and ability', took as 'his test of priestly celebrity...the decent editorship of a Greek play'.[43] The 'Greek play bishops' were prominent in the early Victorian scene.[44] Looking back in his *Monographs*, published in 1873, Lord Houghton mentioned an earlier bishop's injunction to ordination candidates 'to improve their Greek and not waste their time visiting the poor'.[45] In the Oxford diocese parochial work sometimes came second to classical pursuits. As late as December 1836 all twenty-two of its deacons had been ordained on 'college titles', and not to curacies. 'The study of Greek literature', Thomas Gaisford is said to have remarked in a sermon when Dean of Christ Church, 'not only elevates above the vulgar herd, but leads not infrequently to positions of considerable emolument.'[46]

The leaning of Oxford's clerical fellows towards Greek was to be of great importance in the evolution of 'Greats'. By the early 1830s it had become so pronounced that Latin studies might have withered had not the Hertford scholarships been founded in 1834.[47] The clergy had a professional concern with the Greek New Testament; and the Greeks, unlike the Romans, were free from the stigma of having persecuted the early Christians.[48] Apart from this, Oxford fellows were caught up in the philhellenism which was so pronounced a feature of the early Romantic age. The Roman models of the eighteenth century had fallen into disfavour.[49] Oxford men of the new age revered the truthful directness of Homer. Peel, whose time at Christ Church had come towards the end of Cyril Jackson's reign, received soon after his

[42] *British Critic* ii (July 1826), 349. This is the second volume in the quarterly series published by Mawman. For the *British Critic* as the organ of the High-Church 'Hackney Phalanx' see *Victorian Periodicals Review* xxiv (1991), 111–18.

[43] Benjamin Disraeli, *Tancred* (1847), bk. II, ch. 4 (Bradenham edn 1927), 72–3.

[44] F. Arnold, *Our Bishops and Deans* (2 vols 1875) i. 176; *Proceedings of the Classical Association* ix (1912), 77 (A. C. Headlam); George Eliot, *Felix Holt*, ch. 2 ('Our bishop...all Greek and greediness'); Anthony Trollope, *Barchester Towers*, ch. 43 (Dr Gwynne on Bishop Proudie); *Clergymen of the Church of England* (1866), 21; Tuckwell (1900), 19.

[45] Lord Houghton, *Monographs, Personal and Social* (1873), 272–3.

[46] Diocesan figure compiled by Dr R. K. Pugh from Bodl. Oxford Diocesan papers d. 21-5. The editors wish to thank Dr Pugh for supplying this information. In Tuckwell (1900), 129, it is implied that Gaisford made his remark in a Christmas Day sermon.

[47] A. H. Clough to J. P. Gell, 8 Apr. 1838, in *Correspondence of A. H. Clough*, ed. F. L. Mulhauser (2 vols 1957) i. 68. The terms 'Greats' and 'Great-Go' were used among under-graduates by 1850 to denote the final examination for classical honours: see *The Adventures of Mr. Verdant Green, by Cuthbert Bede* (1853–7, 1982), 235.

[48] F. M. Turner, 'Why the Greeks and not the Romans in Victorian Britain?' in G. W. Clarke (ed.), *Rediscovering Hellenism: the Hellenic inheritance and the English imagination* (Cambridge 1989), 78–80.

[49] Stanley, *Arnold* i. 181.

graduation Jackson's advice to 'let no day pass' without having his Homer in his hands. Homer, Jackson explained, 'alone of mortal men thoroughly understood the human mind'.[50] In lifelong Homeric studies Gladstone remained convinced that Homer's lines always rang true, while Virgil's, for all their brilliance, were marred by the falsities of an emperor's courtier.[51] It was not only statesmen, such as Derby and Gladstone, who were fascinated by the *Iliad*. When J. H. Newman and Hurrell Froude were in Rome early in 1833 they needed a 'motto' for their *Lyra Apostolica*, the verses on sacred subjects which they planned to send to the *British Magazine*. Their choice fell neither on the Bible nor on the works of the Church Fathers. 'We chose the words', Newman recorded, 'in which Achilles, on returning to the battle says, "You shall know the difference, now that I am back again."'[52] In Oxford free rein could be given to these inclinations. The students, having undergone a longer period of secondary education than those in the Scottish universities, had spent most of their working-time on the classics; and the pace among those who sought honours had been set by Shrewsbury and one or two other schools where Greek was well taught.

Like many other successful reformers the sponsor of the examination statute did not appreciate the extent, or the exact nature, of the change which he had initiated. Jackson can hardly have foreseen that the lists of classical books on which candidates were to be examined would soon determine the shape of Oxford's studies. Those lists bore a very loose relation to his concerns and his literary judgements. His scientific interests have been mentioned in Chapter 24 of *The Eighteenth Century*. He attended meetings of the Lunar Society of Birmingham and had numbered Joseph Black and Thomas Beddoes among his friends. When Peel faced the classical examiners in 1808 his list of works offered did not include either of the Homeric epics which Jackson was soon to press on his attention.[53] Once the reformed system was in place a preponderantly classical syllabus found defenders. John Davison, who was a fellow of Oriel, favoured the exclusion of the 'physical sciences' (and indeed of mathematics) from a university curriculum: he argued that no exercise 'of the judgement' was needed in those studies.[54] But when Copleston replied to the *Edinburgh Review* he did

---

[50] C. S. Parker, *Peel* (3 vols 1891–9) i. 28.
[51] W. E. Gladstone, *Studies in Homer and the Homeric Age* (3 vols 1858) iii. 2, 500 ff.
[52] Newman, *Apologia*, 42. The line (*Iliad* 18. 125) was printed above each month's verses; e.g. in *British Magazine* iii (June 1833), 656. Newman gives the sense of the passage rather than a translation of the line itself. He was concerned at the fascination which classical images had for him: Newman, *Verses on Various Occasions* (1868), 109 (Messina, 9 Feb. 1833). A translation of the *Iliad* by his brother, Francis, was published in 1856.
[53] N. Gash, *Mr. Secretary Peel* (1961), 55.
[54] *Quarterly* vi (Oct. 1811), 180. When reproducing this passage in his Dublin lectures Newman omitted the mention of math. and science: *Idea*, 152, lines 22, 23. For the view that ancient math. was more educative than modern see [R. I. Wilberforce], *Considerations Respecting the Most Effectual Means of Encouraging Mathematics* (1830), 9–11.

not take Davison's extreme line on either the Oxford syllabus or the methods of study which went with it. He conceded that the 'best method' would be one which had not been achieved in 'any modern university', namely a combination of professorial instruction in the Scottish style with the tutorial classes which prevailed in Oxford. He insisted, however, that the balance of advantage lay with Oxford's methods, and denied that these were based on a narrow range of studies: the classical syllabus comprehended historical as well as literary works, and the options in the mathematics-and-physics examination included astronomy. Copleston stressed that an undergraduate's work need not be confined to the examination syllabus: the professors gave lectures or took classes in modern history, political economy, chemistry, mineralogy, botany and anatomy, and 'the best works in...the elements of law and politics are in the hands of many students with the full approbation of those who regulate their studies...Any student also may obtain assistance from the Professors of Saxon and Oriental learning.' The *Edinburgh Review* rejoined effectively by asking how many of Oxford's professors were actually offering lectures, and how many of those who did were managing to attract an audience.[55]

Despite the rejoinder there was something in Copleston's claim. William Conybeare, who was in Peel's year at Christ Church, took a first in classics and then became a distinguished geologist. Looking back, he saw advantages in the early honours examination which had been lost soon afterwards. He and his contemporaries, he told the 1850 Commission, had not been required 'to devote all their powers exclusively to one narrow line of academical study'.[56] The effort towards improvement and reform was not confined to classics and mathematics: it comprehended many subjects during these early years. 'Natural philosophy' (theoretical physics, in modern terms) was included among the subjects for the Oriel fellowship examinations.[57] The Aldrichian professorship of Chemistry was filled for the first time in 1803, the Hebdomadal Board improving the professor's accommodation in 1811 and obtaining salary increases for him, and for the Professor of Experimental Philosophy, two years later.[58] The Prince Regent endowed a readership of mineralogy in 1813, and one in geology five years later;[59] and in 1825 the first

---

[55] Copleston, *Reply*, 146, 154–5. See also the syllabus for John Kidd's chemistry lectures in his *Answer to a Charge against the English Universities Contained in a Supplement to the Edinburgh Encyclopaedia* (1818); *Statutes* ii. 63–4; *Ed. Rev.* xvi (Apr. 1810), 186; *Edinburgh Annual Register for 1809* (Edinburgh 1811), 413. The extent to which Scottish professors were in personal contact with students is discussed in G. E. Davie, *The Democratic Intellect* (1961), 25. Hamilton later called for a 'combination' of the two systems: *Ed. Rev.* liii (1831), 426. For an echo of this see J. H. Newman to S. Rickards, 7 Feb. 1840, in *LDN* vii. 232.

[56] *RCO* (1850), evidence, 221.

[57] *Memories*, 121–2 (no. 18, G. A. Denison).

[58] Ward, *Victorian Oxford*, 51. Aldrich's will was proved in 1798.

[59] HBM 1803–23, 504. Although these posts are called professorships in *Historical Register, 1220–1900*, 69, the Calendars for the years concerned show them to have been readerships. For

holder of those readerships, William Buckland, was rewarded for supporting the biblical account of the Flood with a Christ Church canonry. Grenville, the University's Chancellor, had found little difficulty in pressing that preferment on the Prime Minister, Lord Liverpool, who was reported by the Regius Professor of Divinity to be 'bitten with the mania for modern sciences'.[60]

Oxford's leading figures were as ready as the politicians and the court to encourage scientific work, and indeed modern studies in general, though the resources they were able to obtain for these subjects were small. The opposition to undergraduate work in science and technology did not start until 1830 (see Chapter 16). In 1828, on the Vice-Chancellor's advice, steam-engines were the subject set for the Chancellor's Latin Verse Prize, a model engine being put for demonstration in the Clarendon Building.[61] Four years later, when the British Association met in Oxford, Faraday 'elicited a spark from a magnet', using 'the large natural magnet in the Ashmolean Museum'.[62] Gaisford, when advising Van Mildert on the syllabus for the new University of Durham, included natural philosophy among the 'essentials'.[63] As Dean of Christ Church he obliged the undergraduates there to attend 'a course of Physics, to write an abstract thereof, and be examined therein'.[64] Outside influences even did something to overcome the Oxford parsons' dislike for novel or controversial 'speculations', and for subjects which smacked of commerce, or were thought to be recommended only for their supposed utility.[65] Henry Beeke, the Regius Professor of Modern History appointed in 1801, and Edward Nares, his successor thirteen years later, undertook, as a condition of their appointments, to lecture on political economy. Nares received advice on sources from Lord Liverpool, and obeyed the customary instruction to pay for two modern language teachers.[66] In 1825 Henry Drummond, whose family were bankers, offered an endowment for a political economy chair. This was accepted, the Chan-

the difficulty of attaching titles to such appointments see *The Eighteenth Century*, 667–8. For further details, see p. 546 below.

[60] Lloyd to Peel, 4 Jan. 1825, BL Add. MS 40342, fo 187.

[61] Jenkyns to Grenville, 31 May 1827, BL Add. MS 59415, fo 158; R. T. Gunther, *Early Science in Oxford* (3 vols 1923–5) i pt. 3, 205, iii. 335; Tuckwell (1900), 41.

[62] John Tyndall, *Faraday as a Discoverer* (1868), 32 n.

[63] Gaisford to Van Mildert, 24 Aug. 1831, *Durham University Journal* xxv/6 (June 1928), 420. I am grateful to Dr C. D. Watkinson, Durham University Library, for this reference.

[64] Henry Acland's words: PP 1872 xxv. 173 n.; *QJE* viii (1834), 67; *Letters of William Stubbs*, ed. W. H. Hutton (1904), 19. There was a similar requirement at Balliol: Ward, *Victorian Oxford*, 108.

[65] On 'materialism' see p. 49 below (W. Palmer). On continuing suspicions of 'commercial taint' see S. Rothblatt, *Revolution of the Dons* (2nd edn 1981), 257.

[66] Ward, *Victorian Oxford*, 50; *A Versatile Professor: Reminiscences of Edward Nares*, ed. G. C. White (1903), 28–43; J. Black, 'A Regency Regius', *Oxoniensia* lii (1987), 174–7; P. R. H. Slee, *Learning and a Liberal Education* (Manchester 1986), 49; Nares to Vice-Chancellor, 19 Jan. 1829, Bodl. MS Top. Oxon. b. 23, fos 43–4; Cox, 152. For the origin of the instruction about the two teachers of modern languages, see *The Eighteenth Century*, 115, 474.

cellor insisting that the professor should be required both to lecture and to publish.[67]

The dominance of the honours lists came slowly. Peel and Gladstone were exceptional in their undergraduate achievements, as in much else. No first classes had been awarded in mathematics until Peel gained one in Michaelmas 1808: he was thus the first candidate to achieve a 'double first'. When Gladstone gained the same distinction in 1831, fewer than 70 per cent of undergraduates took degrees, and only some 20 per cent achieved honours.[68] Moreover, Gladstone belonged, like Peel, to a minority of a minority: fewer than one-fifth of those who gained honours by 1834 had done so in mathematics as well as in classics. Edward Stanley, later Earl of Derby and Prime Minister, was as scholarly as any honours man.[69] He won the Chancellor's Latin Verse Prize in 1819 and later found time, despite his three premierships, to translate the *Iliad* into blank verse. Yet he left Christ Church without taking a degree.

During the Regency years, however, as the honours system became fully established, it became increasingly difficult to persuade undergraduates to study any subjects outside the examination syllabus. When Nares gave his history lectures for a second year in 1817 his audience dropped to seven. He fared better with political economy, but the audience even for these lectures included very few undergraduates.[70] In the same year Copleston told the Chancellor: 'The lectures on astronomy, chemistry, and experimental philosophy are badly attended. Sometimes there are not enough to form a class, and this notwithstanding the ability of the professors and their earnest endeavours to procure attendance.'[71] Some of the university prizes did a little to keep knowledge of the modern world alive. When G. A. Denison won the Chancellor's English Essay Prize in 1829, his entry on 'the power and stability of federative governments' ranged from 'the Lycian confederacy', via the Hanseatic League, to the American tariff of 1824.[72] But efforts to require attendance at a modern history course as a qualification for the MA failed.[73] Among the science professors Buckland stood out as a brilliant lecturer. Some of his hearers no doubt regarded his criticisms of coal fires in bedrooms as one of his eccentricities: others may have been brought

[67] Ward, *Victorian Oxford*, 53; R. Brent, 'God's providence: liberal political economy as natural theology at Oxford, 1825–1862' in M. Bentley (ed.), *Public and Private Doctrine* (1993), 85–107. For Sydney Smith's prediction that political economy lectures 'would be discouraged in Oxford, probably despised, probably not permitted', see *Ed. Rev.* xv (1809), 51 and p. 135 below.

[68] See Fig. 11.1.

[69] Christ Church collections-book, 1810–38, CA li. b. 4, 163.

[70] *A Versatile Professor*, 241.

[71] Copleston to Grenville, 2 June 1817, BL Add. MS 59416, fo 80.

[72] *Oxford English Prize Essays* iv (1830), 290–2. On the importance attached to university and college prizes see T. Chalmers, *Endowments* (1827), 85 n.

[73] J. H. Newman to R. H. Froude, 9 Jan. 1830, in *LDN* ii. 186.

to realize what exhaustion of the coal seams could mean.[74] He attracted large audiences year after year; but he and John Kidd, who became the Regius Professor of Medicine in 1822, were the exceptions: no other professorial lecturers were equally successful.[75] Baden Powell, who became Professor of Geometry in 1827, was advised by Copleston not to spend too much time and energy on lecturing. 'The credit of the University', Copleston added, 'will be chiefly consulted by such philosophical essays and scientific researches as form your principal employment.'[76] The mineralogy lectures, which had an attendance of fifty-seven in 1817, were down to nine in 1834: over the thirty-six years 1814–49, although twenty-five people attended on average, fewer than two-fifths were undergraduates.[77] By 1832 the decline in the size of science classes had become a matter of public discussion.[78]

When it was realized that the class list might soon dominate all else there was some dismay. 'This university', Charles Lloyd told Peel in 1825, 'has already lost so much of its academical character and has become nothing but a large school, that I should not willingly see that character still farther diminished.'[79] Gaisford, when Dean, discouraged Christ Church men from entering for honours.[80] The President of St John's inveighed from the pulpit against the 'unchristian spirit of emulation' which the honours system had encouraged.[81] The system's great defender Copleston wrote to his successor at Oriel about 'the quackery' of the examination schools. 'Every election to a fellowship', he told Edward Hawkins in 1843, 'which tends to discourage the narrow and almost technical *routine* of public examinations, I consider as an important triumph.'[82] Such triumphs had been a recurrent feature of the Oriel fellowship elections. Richard Whately, J. H. Newman, Hurrell Froude, and Thomas Mozley had no first classes. The college's fellowship examining was somewhat informal. R. W. Church recalled:

We were told we might have as long as we liked for our papers till it got too dark to see, but we should not have candles.... It used to be said that when James Mozley was in ... he kept on till the last, and when it got dark lay down by the fire and wrote

---

[74] 'Diary of James Ramsay, later first Marquess of Dalhousie, while at Christ Church, 1829–1833', 1 Feb. 1831, CA typescript copy.

[75] *Memories*, 91–2 (R. W. Browne), 146 (G. A. Denison); Pattison, *Memoirs*, 67–8.

[76] 5 Mar. 1827: Copleston, *Copleston*, 114–15.

[77] G. L'E. Turner, 'Experimental science in early nineteenth-century Oxford', *History of Universities* viii (1989), 126–7. For further details see Ch. 16.

[78] [R. Walker], *A Few Words in Favour of Professor Powell and the Sciences* (1832), 4. See also J. E. Stock, *Memoirs of Thomas Beddoes* (1811), 24.

[79] 26 Jan. 1825, BL Add. MS 40342, fo 200.

[80] E. G. W. Bill and J. F. A. Mason, *Christ Church and Reform* (1970), 26.

[81] [G. Cox], *Black Gowns and Red Coats* (1834), pt 3, 8 n.

[82] 2 May 1843, Copleston, *Copleston*, 188. See p. 21, 27–8 below and Newman, *Idea*, 138. For the Balliol fellowship examination see Pattison, *Memoirs*, 97.

by the firelight...an English essay of about ten lines...such as no other man [in Oxford] could have written.[83]

E. B. Pusey, racked by a headache, tore up his answers: these were then pieced together by one of the fellows. He followed this by leaving the hall after an hour, but was persuaded to return for the final days, completed the exam, and was elected.[84] 'It may have been necessary', F. D. Maurice wrote in 1835, to establish the honours regulations. 'The "pressure from without" is said to have been strong at the time they were adopted, and the motives for yielding to it, and introducing a worldly leaven into University legislation and morality may have been very cogent.' For Maurice this did not dictate policy a generation later: academic honours 'are certainly not part of our ancient University system, nor, I confess, do I see any means of reconciling them with the principle of it'.[85]

These rearguard actions and protests had little effect. The University was not ruled by Copleston and Gaisford. The Vice-Chancellor of collegiate Oxford bore no resemblance to a powerful American university president. He had no power to reverse policy, as Timothy Dwight had done at Yale in the 1790s, or Ashbel Green at Princeton after 1812.[86] Gaisford's policy, accompanied as it was by the decline just then of Westminster School, served merely to injure Christ Church. From 1831 to 1835 the House produced twenty-eight firsts: from 1841 to 1845 only six.[87] On one occasion when Oriel defied the class lists, D. K. Sandford, the first-class man who had been rejected for a fellowship, retaliated in the *Edinburgh Review*.[88] The personal nature of his attack deprived it of any considerable effect; but such publicity did the college little good. The pressures of war which provided the original impulse for the honours system had been replaced by something more enduring. Assessment of competence was becoming Treasury policy.[89] It would be many years before Britain became anything approaching a full-blown meritocracy; but the day of the successful examinee had already arrived. The President of the Board of Control presented an Indian writer-

[83] Liddon, *Pusey* i. 67. For a reconstruction of the 'ten lines' see Mozley, *Letters*, 56 n. Despite them, Oriel did not elect J. B. Mozley. The fact that his brother Tom was a fellow there probably told against him.

[84] Liddon, *Pusey* i. 57. Newman was persuaded by his tutor not to withdraw from the Oriel examination: A. D. Culler, *The Imperial Intellect* (1955), 32.

[85] [F. D. Maurice], *Subscription no Bondage* (1835), 73–4, by 'Rusticus', whose identity was soon known.

[86] J. McLachlan, 'American student societies in the early nineteenth century' in L. Stone (ed.), *The University in Society* (2 vols Princeton 1975) ii. 468–9.

[87] H. Lloyd-Jones, *Blood for the Ghosts* (1982), 84.

[88] [D. K. Sandford], *Ed. Rev.* xxxv (July 1821), 310–12. This was followed by [A. W. Hare], *Letter to D. K. Sandford* (1822); D. K. Sandford, *Letter to Peter Elmsley* (1822); *Blackwood's Edinburgh Magazine* xi (June 1822) 678–80; D. K. Sandford to E. Copleston, 22 Dec. 1823, in Copleston, *Copleston*, 92.

[89] E. W. Cohen, *Growth of the British Civil Service, 1780–1939* (1941), 66–7.

ship to the University in 1828; and Thomas Pycroft of Trinity, who topped the list in the examination for this, became the first in a distinguished line of 'competition wallahs'.[90]

The Commissioners reported in 1852 that, in fifty years, the system had become not merely more rigorous, but narrower in scope. In their view Conybeare's successors had lacked his freedom both outside the honours syllabus and within it. Increased numbers had necessitated a radical alteration in examining techniques. In Peel's time the Lit. Hum. honours examination was oral: by Gladstone's year it consisted largely of written work, though he was tested in his viva voce in eight classical works (apart from the Greek Testament).[91] The unintended effect of this change was to narrow the circle of works studied and to increase the importance of Latin and Greek composition; and this was reinforced by the effect of the scholarships 'for the promotion of classical learning and taste' founded by Dean Ireland in 1825.[92] The Commissioners commented: 'Complete acquaintance with a few books is hardly sufficient to compensate for the loss of the more free and comprehensive reading of the earlier period.'[93]

The change which the Commissioners noted was matched by others, however, which made for breadth. The tutors of this era were not dedicated academics looking towards a university career. They were migrants whose future lay in the Church. Each hoped to be senior enough after ten or fifteen years to be offered a college living. When that came his way he would resign his fellowship and leave for his parish, free at last to marry. The psychology of the migrant affected the whole University. Copleston, its most efficient defender in these years, aimed at, and in due course obtained, a mitre. After twelve years in the Regius chair of Modern History, Henry Beeke left for the deanery of Bristol. Only a minority of the tutors were deeply interested in the minutiae of classical scholarship, whereas all of the best ones were concerned with the subject-matter. This confirmed their bias towards Greek texts, and led them to emphasize historical works as well as poetry and drama; and it inclined them to seek modern parallels when reading ancient authors. In 1816 a second-year scholar of Corpus told a friend in Trinity College, Dublin: 'Our tutors are most excellent, one of them most exquisite; it is the highest treat to hear him construe the tragedians and quote parallel passages from Shakespeare, Milton, and the whole circle of British poets, from memory.'[94] Gladstone's 'epitome' of Aristotle's *Rhetoric* included examples of the speeches of Canning, Peel and Palmerston to illustrate the

[90] G. O. Trevelyan, *The Competition Wallah* (1864).
[91] Gladstone, *Diaries* i. 392. See the extract from Gladstone's moral philosophy essay in Mallet iii. 228. For extracts from early question papers see *QJE* iv (Oct. 1832), 202–3, 206.
[92] Huber, *English Universities* ii pt 2, 524–5 (ed.'s note).
[93] *RCO* (1850), report, 62. The Commissioners' comments are discussed in Ch. 15.1.
[94] William Whitmarsh Phelps (1797–1867) to R. T. P. Pope, 14 Nov. 1816, in C. Hole, *W. W. Phelps* (2 vols 1871) i. 109–10.

Aristotelian categories.[95] Defending 'subscription' in 1835 F. D. Maurice pointed out that logic could hardly be branded as useless scholasticism when it had been taken up with such enthusiasm by the Benthamites and Utilitarians.[96] In the previous year the *Oxford University Magazine* had explained that honours finals were not 'confined (as many persons imagine) to Greek and Latin. Those who bring most general information to bear upon the exam have generally been most sure of success. Modern history, modern poetry, and modern philosophy have been introduced indirectly to a great extent.'[97] When the revised examination statute was issued in 1830 Literae Humaniores were defined as comprehending 'not only the Greek and Latin tongues, but also the histories of Greece and Rome'; and permission was given for answers on the ancient world to be 'illustrated occasionally by the writings of the moderns'.[98] By then the University was moving towards Greats, which was to become one of its most celebrated educational achievements.[99] The weaker candidates were the sufferers under the classical syllabus. After 1830, when they had been segregated into a separate pass school, it was starkly clear that they had derived little or no benefit from the few classical texts with which they had struggled, always reluctantly and often too late. J. A. Froude, who was an undergraduate during the later 1830s, wrote: 'The idle or dull man had no education at all. His three or four years were spent in forgetting what he had learned at school. The degree examination was got over by a *memoria technica*, and three months' cram with a private tutor.'[100]

By contrast, the classical courses followed by Peel and Gladstone lacked nothing in thoroughness, though they differed in at least one respect from the Greats course as it stood sixty years later. Peel seems to have read no Plato and Gladstone only the *Phaedo*.[101] Aristotle had been supreme at Oxford for too long for Plato to be allowed an easy entry. At Cambridge, where the classical course was new, the Platonism of the Romantic Age made quicker headway. Richard Chenevix Trench, who was at Trinity, Cambridge, from 1825 to 1829, described his fellow members in the Apostles' Club as 'that gallant band of Platonico–Wordsworthian–Coleridgean–anti-Utilitarians'. In Oxford there was no Plato question in the logic paper until

---

[95] H. C. G. Matthew, *Gladstone, 1809–1874* (1986), 20.
[96] Maurice, *Subscription no Bondage*, 60.
[97] *Oxford University Magazine* i (1834), 99.
[98] *Statutes* ii. 166; cf ii. 135 (1826). See *Reflections Occasioned by the Flirtations of Alma Mater and the Stagyrite* (1820), 9: 'we demand the enfranchisement of modern philosophy'.
[99] M. L. Clarke, *Classical Education in Britain* (1959), 101. For earlier hints of Greats see *The Eighteenth Century*, 481.
[100] Froude, *Short Studies* iv. 179–80.
[101] Gash, *Peel*, 55; Matthew, *Gladstone*, 20. For F. D. Maurice's complaint about the disregard of Plato at Oxford see *Athenaeum* 3 Dec. 1828, 912. Gladstone read the *Republic* soon after he had gone down: Gladstone, *Diaries* i. 568–9 (23 Aug. 1832).

1847.[102] In stressing the historical element in the classical course Copleston made particular mention of Thucydides, in whose pages undergraduates could study, 'unmixed with the prejudiced and perverse clamours of party, the fatal consequences of misrule and anarchy, of wild democracy, of unlimited or unjust power'.[103] Copleston may have exaggerated the historical features of the course as it was in 1810; but their importance after the changes of 1830 cannot be doubted. Gladstone was examined in Herodotus and Thucydides; and he had prepared himself for examination in Polybius and Livy. He read Thucydides from time to time in later life;[104] but the greatest of Greek historians does not seem to have made a deep impression on him. In 1831, as always, no one could predict which books would sink most deeply into the honours men's minds, or indeed what would be imprinted where the impression was strongest. Copleston gave a fair summary of the lessons imparted by Thucydides in the eight books of the *History* seen as a whole; but some undergraduates may have been particularly impressed by the fourth book. That would not have led them to Copleston's conclusions. The demagogic Cleon kept his promise to take Pylos in forty days, a feat which hardly exemplifies 'the fatal consequences of wild democracy'. During this period, as in any other, 'safe' texts were almost as hard to find in the ancient world as in the modern. Shelley's *Necessity of Atheism*, which appeared in 1811, a year after Copleston wrote the words quoted above, illustrates this difficulty: in 1811 the classics could include perils for a young man even graver than democratic inclinations or an undue interest in the 'loves of gods and goddesses',[105] for the pantheistic views which exposed Shelley to the charge of atheism were derived from the elder Pliny.[106]

Gladstone never doubted the efficacy of the classical curriculum to which he had been subjected; nor does he seem to have realized that the restriction of an honours man's studies to classics and mathematics had been to some extent unintended.[107] He was well taught for his classical subjects. Robert Biscoe, a Christ Church tutor who had taken a first in classics less than ten years earlier, earned universal praise for his 'college lectures'. His Aristotle

---

[102] *Letters and Memorials of Archbishop Trench*, ed. [Maria Trench] (2 vols 1888) i. 10; G. R. G. Mure, *Philosophy* xii (1937), 296. For the neglect of Plato at Oxford earlier see *The Eighteenth Century*, 498, 528–9. For Jowett's part in promoting the study of Plato see Abbott and Campbell, *Jowett* i. 132, 261. The view that Aristotelian studies helped to promote Tractarianism is discussed on pp. 210–11 below.

[103] Copleston, *Reply*, 159.

[104] There are at least fifteen Thucydides entries in the *Diaries* during Gladstone's undergraduate years, and five thereafter. He also read the 'summary' prefixed to Hobbes's translation of the *History* (1629): *Diaries* i. 213 (24 Nov. 1828). For Arnold's influence in bringing Thucydides into the leading schools see Stanley, *Arnold* i. 15; T. Arnold, *Miscellaneous Works* (1845), 396–7.

[105] Byron, *Don Juan*, Canto I (1819), stanza 41.

[106] Pliny, *Natural History*, 2. 5 (De Deo); T. Medwin, *Shelley*, ed. H. B. Foreman (1913), 37, 50.

[107] See W. E. Gladstone, *Gleanings of Past Years* (7 vols 1879) vii. 23–4, inaugural address, 1860, Glasgow University.

class, which Gladstone attended, was famous enough to attract men from other colleges.[108] Moreover, the restrictions which work for a double first imposed were not serious for an undergraduate of Gladstone's exceptional energy. His modern reading included Rousseau's *Social Contract* and a good deal of Burke.[109] He founded a literary society in Christ Church.[110] He quieted his mind when his mathematics finals were starting by reading some Wordsworth each day; and his list of subjects for those finals included mechanics, hydrostatics, optics and astronomy.[111] Even Gladstone could not do everything, however. Unlike his friend Martin Tupper, whose stutter precluded an attempt at high honours, he did not attend Buckland's lectures and 'geological rambles';[112] and in one case at least, that of political economy, his mentors' suspicions about undergraduate 'speculations' did him no good. Copleston was himself an expert on currency and poor law questions; but, although he had included political economy in the lectures available at Oxford, he had defended excluding it as an undergraduate subject. 'Many points', he wrote, made him 'think it a fitter employment for the mind in an advanced period of life.' 'Theoretical views of society', he added, were of little use to that large majority of undergraduates whose problem would be 'adapting themselves promptly to the limited relations of life in which they were placed.'[113] Such doubts did not disappear with the establishment of the Drummond chair. Professor H. C. G. Matthew has pointed out that Gladstone would have benefited from reading one work which figured prominently in the Edinburgh curriculum. For a future prime minister a little of Adam Smith on the British economy would have outweighed many pages of Aristotle on a pre-Christian, slave-based society.[114]

The most damaging effect of Oxford's largely classical examination syllabus has not yet received enough attention. Defending the mind-sharpening properties of a classical syllabus of little utility could easily entail decrying the educational value of more useful studies. The Oxford which Peel and Gladstone knew was not free from this snobbish or blinkered view.[115] It was mitigated by recurrent pleas to undergraduates not to be outdone by their social inferiors in modern and technical knowledge; but these ran counter to

---

[108] M. F. Tupper, *Autobiography* (1886), 56–7.

[109] Gladstone, *Diaries* i. 374; 360, 362, 365.

[110] Ibid. i. 264–5. J. Morley, *Gladstone* (3 vols 1903) i. 59–60. John Taylor Coleridge had founded one in Corpus in 1809: *Pelican Record* xviii (1927), 60.

[111] Gladstone, *Diaries* i. 396–7. See also *Letters of Frederic, Lord Blachford*, ed. G. E. Marindin (1896), 11–12.

[112] Tupper, *Autobiography*, 59; D. Hudson, *M. Tupper* (1949), 12. If Gladstone had been better informed scientifically, the Ayrton–Hooker troubles, 1872, might have been avoided: Gunther, *Early Science in Oxford* iii. 212.

[113] Copleston, *Reply*, 173–4.

[114] Matthew, *Gladstone*, 21.

[115] See Davison's *Quarterly* article, vi (Oct. 1811), 166–91.

the examination requirements;[116] and once the honours examinations became dominant such pleas were apt to be disregarded. 'Practical applications', whether in research or teaching, tended to be viewed with suspicion. It was easily assumed that an interest in them betrayed not a thirst for knowledge, but a commercial materialism unworthy of a university.[117] In 1823 Buckland consulted anxiously about an invitation to lecture at the Royal Institution, and ended by refusing it. He feared compromising 'the dignity of the University' by acceptance. For all his unconventionality this immensely gifted geologist shrank from lecturing to people who were concerned with mining problems.[118] It became accepted doctrine in Oxford that professional studies in law and medicine, and those in chemistry, mineralogy, or geology which had an industrial application, could be pursued only in a large city. This view was not unfounded in the conditions of Victorian Britain; but it became an excuse too easily used when change and adaptation had been proposed.[119] Such inhibitions and excuses were to prove harmful, not merely within the University, but far beyond it.

Whatever the shortcomings of post-war Oxford, there was widespread agreement about the improvement achieved since the reforms had been launched. In 1827 'a septuagenarian' who had been an undergraduate in the 1770s recorded in the *Gentleman's Magazine*: 'Oxford ... has acquired altogether a new character from the moment that the present exercises for degrees were established.'[120] J. W. Ward, later Earl of Dudley, who had graduated in 1802, told Copleston as early as 1815: 'The whole character of the University has been changed since I left it.' Four years later he was writing: 'Drunkenness has disappeared, and laziness is comparatively rare.'[121] There can be no doubt of the change, much as Ward exaggerated its completeness. By 1819 academic ambitions had spread beyond baronets' sons such as Peel, for in that year the heir to an earldom, Viscount Sandon, took a double first.[122] Another earl's heir, Viscount Ashley, arrived at Christ Church as Sandon left, to be

---

[116] For Buckland's plea see p. 64 below.

[117] See Baden Powell's protest against this view in *The Present State and Future Prospects of Mathematical and Physical Studies* (1832), 21–7.

[118] Buckland later changed his stance on such issues (see p. 560 below).

[119] See the objection made by [J. B. Mozley] (*Quarterly* xciii (June 1853), 168) to the Royal Commission's proposals.

[120] *GM* xcvii (1827), pt 2, 202–3. See also *Report and Evidence* (1853), 173 (Pusey); *Quarterly* xxxix (1829), 124; *Memoir and Letters of the Rt. Hon. Sir Thomas Dyke Acland*, ed. A. H. D. Acland (1902), 8.

[121] 18 Mar. 1815, 29 Dec. 1819, in *Letters of the Earl of Dudley to the Bishop of Llandaff*, ed. E. Copleston (1840), 91, 237. For evidence of a similar improvement in Cambridge see *Diaries and Correspondence of James Losh*, ed. E. Hughes (Surtees Society clxxi 1962) i. 154. In some Oxford colleges there seems to have been a reduction in drunkenness even before 1800: A. Heber, *R. Heber* (2 vols 1830) i. 27; G. Battiscombe, *Keble* (1963), 13. See, however, *LDN* i. 36, and n. 248 below.

[122] Sandon, later 2nd Earl of Harrowby, was the first heir to a peerage to do so: *Christ Church Annual Report* (1956), 19.

asked by his tutor: 'Do you intend to take a degree?' Ashley replied that he 'would try', and took a first in classics.[123] In 1831 a future Governor-General of India, also an earl's son, noted: 'A first nowadays is something quite useful.'[124] By then high Oxford honours were famous enough as a distinction to be satirized north of the border. In 1822 'Christopher North' wrote in *Blackwood's Edinburgh Magazine* about a friend 'going into Covent Garden a few years ago simultaneously with the Prince Regent. The audience, of course, rose out of respect to His Royal Highness...on which the delighted tyro... exclaimed... "these good people, who mean well I dare say, have been informed that I am in the first class, and about to stand for Oriel".'[125] On the second page of *The Eighteenth Century* Edward Ferrars is quoted from Jane Austen's *Sense and Sensibility* as saying that, having been 'entered at Oxford', he had 'been properly idle ever since'. When *Sense and Sensibility* was begun in 1797 that was a fair representation: by 1811, when the novel was published, it had become a little dated. The new century's image of Oxford appeared in another fictional Ferrars. 'William Pitt Ferrars', Disraeli wrote in *Endymion*, 'went up to Oxford about the time that the examinations were reformed and rendered really efficient... The name of Ferrars figured among the earliest double-firsts. Those were the days when a crack university reputation often opened the doors of the House of Commons...An old colleague of the elder Mr Ferrars, a worthy peer with many boroughs, placed a seat at the disposal of the youthful hero.'[126]

The writers in the *Edinburgh Review* seasoned their criticisms of Oxford (described in Chapter 3) with acknowledgements of the improvement achieved. The issue of April 1810 carried a tardy recognition of the 1807 examination statute ('the new plan for Oxford education'): 'The improvement upon the old plan', the reviewer conceded, 'is certainly very great.'[127] From that time Oxford's undergraduate numbers started to rise (Fig. 14.2).[128] In July 1821 D. K. Sandford, the first-class man rejected by Oriel, wrote in the *Edinburgh*:

A young man who has carried off the highest honours...at Oxford...will be found with quite enough of critical scholarship for the most learned avocations, with his mind in a proper state of ferment and anxiety for further knowledge, and with an

---

[123] E. Hodder, *Shaftesbury* (3 vols 1886) i. 52.

[124] Ramsay, Diary, 20 May 1831. Ramsay lost his eldest brother in 1832. This upset his honours work; but his performance in the pass examination was so good that he was awarded an honorary fourth class.

[125] *Blackwood's Edinburgh Magazine* xii (1822) 111. The *nom de plume* was that of John Wilson, Professor of Moral Philosophy, Edinburgh University, 1820–51. He had won the Newdigate Prize in 1806 while a gentleman commoner at Magdalen.

[126] *Endymion* (3 vols 1880) i. 18–19.

[127] *Ed. Rev.* xvi (Apr. 1810), 187.

[128] There were similar increases at Cambridge and Trinity College, Dublin: L. Stone, 'Size and composition of the Oxford student body', in Stone (ed.), *University in Society* i. 6, 59–60, 91–2; R. B. McDowell and D. A. Webb, *Trinity College, Dublin, 1592–1952* (1982), 85–7.

expansion of intellect and a maturity of taste, which, less than twenty years ago, we might have looked for in vain as the fruits of university instruction.[129]

Even Sir William Hamilton ended his powerful criticism of the University in June 1831: 'So great an improvement has been effected...that in some essential points Oxford may, not unworthily, be proposed as a pattern to most other universities.'[130] The Cambridge tripos contained nothing comparable to the compulsory divinity in the Oxford examination.[131] Oxford was gaining the favour of leading Evangelicals such as Wilberforce and Hannah More, as will be recounted in Chapter 7; but it also stood well with a famous man who was unsympathetic to evangelicalism. Sir Walter Scott told Lord Montagu in 1824:

I rather prefer Oxford to Cambridge, chiefly because the last great university was infected long ago with liberalism in politics and at present shows some symptoms of a very different heresy which is sometimes yet blended with the first: I mean enthusiasm in religion. I mean not that sincere zeal for religion in which mortals cannot be too fervid, but the far more doubtful enthusiasm which makes religion a motive and pretext for particular lines of thinking in politics and temporal affairs.[132]

Scott had advised Montagu a few weeks earlier against Edinburgh University.

I am more and more convinced of the excellence of the English monastic institutions of Cambridge and Oxford. They cannot do all that may be expected, but there is at least the exclusion of many temptations to dissipation of mind. Whereas with us, supposing a young man to have any pretensions to keep good society...he is almost pulled to pieces by speculating mammas and flirting misses. If a man is poor, plain, and indifferently connected, he may have excellent opportunities of study at Edinburgh. Otherwise he should beware of it.[133]

Scott's words signalled a striking reversal. During the eighteenth century the fame of some Scottish professors had drawn English students north of the border. A number of these became prominent: an analysis of the 'university men' born between 1685 and 1785 who are noticed in the *Dictionary of National Biography* (some 2,500) shows 343 receiving their university education in Edinburgh, of whom 152 were Englishmen.[134] In science, Jefferson told Dugald Stewart in 1789, 'no place in the world can pretend to a competition with Edinburgh', and this remark did not represent an

---

[129] *Ed. Rev.* xxxv (July 1821), 304. For this review see also n. 88 above.

[130] *Ed. Rev.* liii (June 1831), 426.

[131] See J. H. Monk, *Letter to the Bishop of Bristol* (1822), 12–13. 'Moral philosophy' was a compulsory subject at Cambridge.

[132] *Letters of Sir Walter Scott*, ed. H. J. C. Grierson and others (12 vols 1932–7) viii. 300.

[133] Ibid. viii. 256. 'A metropolis', Newman wrote, 'is not the place for a number of resident youths': *LDN* xxvii. 36. For the requirement of residence in college, see pp. 147–8 below. For 'entrapment' in Oxford see [Thomas Little], *Confessions of an Oxonian* (3 vols 1826) i. 211.

[134] N. Hans, *New Trends in Education in the Eighteenth Century* (1951), 18, 24, 31.

absurd exaggeration.[135] At the end of the century the rich were inclined to supplement the experience of Oxford with some study north of the border. Before coming up to Corpus in 1799 J. W. Ward went to Edinburgh, studying under Dugald Stewart and lodging with him.[136] In 1807 Jackson wrote in sharp annoyance about an outbreak of 'the Scottish disease' in Christ Church;[137] and in the following year a group of Christ Church men, who had just completed their residence and were later to form the nucleus of Grillions Club, travelled to Edinburgh to sit at the feet of Stewart, John Playfair, and Thomas Hope. In 1809 the Duke of Bedford chose three years with Playfair for Lord John Russell in preference to either English university; and it was in Edinburgh University's Speculative Society that Lord John trained himself for a political career.[138]

Edinburgh's numbers rose above 2,000 by 1825; but thereafter they fell sharply.[139] For medicine English students continued to cross the border; but, that apart, once Oxford's reforms took hold, the drawbacks of a Scottish university for any English parent who could afford an Oxford college began to loom large.[140] Louis Simond, who visited Edinburgh in 1810, reported: 'The students do not appear to me subject to much, if any, collegiate discipline.'[141] Sir Walter Scott's warning was well grounded in the light of the lax Scottish marriage laws.[142] The fact that Edinburgh University was undemanding about church attendance, and omitted to observe denominational restrictions when appointing professors, did not strike a conscientious Anglican parent as an advantage;[143] and even Whiggish families might be doubtful of a university where, in Sir James Mackintosh's words about Edinburgh, 'every mind was in a state of fermentation'.[144] As the fate of the Dissenting academies shows, few fathers wanted their sons to be exposed

[135] Papers of Thomas Jefferson, ed. J. P. Boyd (1950–) xv, 204.

[136] Ward (Viscount Dudley, 1823; Earl of Dudley, 1827) corresponded with Mrs Stewart all his life: Letters to Ivy, ed. S. H. Romilly (1905).

[137] To H. C. Jones, 25 Oct. [1807], Correspondence of Hugh Chambres Jones, 1800–52, fo 40, copy in CA.

[138] Acland, ed. Acland, 11–12; Spencer Walpole, Lord John Russell (2 vols 1889) i. 46 ff., D. B. Horn, Short History of Edinburgh University, 1556–1889 (Edinburgh 1967), 92–3.

[139] R. D. Anderson, 'Scottish university professors, 1800–1939', Scottish Economic and Social History vii (1987), 35.

[140] For difference in costs of study, Edinburgh and Oxford, [J. G. Lockhart], Peter's Letters to his Kinsfolk (3 vols Edinburgh 1819) i. 189–90. Brougham stressed a similar disparity when launching his London college: Parl. Deb. 3 June 1825, NS xiii. 1034–5.

[141] L. Simond, Journal of a Tour...in Great Britain (2 vols 1815) i. 498.

[142] Under Scots law an interchange of consent before witnesses validated a marriage.

[143] Report of the Royal Commission on Scottish Universities, 33, 84–5 (PP 1831 (310) xii. 143, 194–5); Simond, Journal of a Tour i. 501; Horn, Edinburgh University, 150–2; R. D. Anderson, Education and Opportunity in Victorian Scotland (1983), 53.

[144] Memoirs of Sir James Mackintosh, ed. R. J. Mackintosh (2 vols 1835) i. 29–30. For William Lamb's view of Glasgow University (c. 1800) see Lord David Cecil, The Young Melbourne (1939), 68.

to bold speculations, and so tempted into free thought.[145] By 1800 the great Whig luminary Samuel Parr was praising the English universities for removing students 'from the contagious example of crowded and dissipated cities', and so enabling them 'to escape the contamination of...metaphysical novelties'.[146] The Edinburgh professor's income depended largely on how many he could attract to his lectures. He was thus thought to be tempted to dazzle and seduce the young with novel theological and political theories. These dangers were a recurrent theme among the *Quarterly* reviewers. In 1820 the *Quarterly* condemned the German universities for outdoing Edinburgh and producing students 'who are all speculative to a degree surpassing even the highest flights of those in our northern capital; and are all puffed up...with their perfect fitness to introduce a new order of things and to become the regenerators of Europe'. 'A tutorial system of education', according to the *Quarterly* of January 1838, 'has always been connected with monarchical principles and institutions—a professorial...almost always with a democracy or a leaning to the doctrines of democracy.' The author of the article was an Exeter College tutor, William Sewell.[147] By the 1820s the Scottish universities were subject to troubles which were investigated by a Royal Commission. The Commissioners recommended an honours examination system similar to Oxford's;[148] and when J. D. Forbes became Edinburgh's Professor of Natural Philosophy in 1833, he borrowed the new technique of written examination papers from Oxford and Cambridge.[149]

This chorus of approval did not include the most prominent of Oxford's radical critics; it would have needed more than the new honours system to win them round. In September 1817 William Cobbett fired a broadside against classical education; he pointed out that Virgil, apart from being 'a gross flatterer of a tyrant', had given agricultural advice shown by Jethro Tull to be wholly misleading.[150] James Mill, writing in the supplement to the *Encyclopedia Britannica*, published in 1818, argued that nothing could be worse than a university 'united with an ecclesiastical establishment'.[151] 'Upon beholding the masses of buildings at Oxford', Cobbett reported in November 1821, 'devoted to what they call "learning", I could not help

[145] L. Wainewright, *The Literary and Scientific Pursuits which are Encouraged and Enforced in the University of Cambridge* (1815), 17–18 n. A surviving 'academy', Manchester College, was to come to Oxford in 1889: Pt 2, Ch. 3.

[146] Preached 15 Apr. 1800. S. Parr, *A Spital Sermon* (1801), notes, 112.

[147] *Quarterly* xxiii (July 1820), 447; lxi (Jan. 1838), 215.

[148] *Report of the Royal Commission on Scottish Universities*, 146–7; report signed 28 Oct. 1830. Thomas Chalmers had included something similar in his reform proposals: *College Endowments*, 88.

[149] Horn, *Edinburgh University*, 161.

[150] *Weekly Political Pamphlet*, xxxii (Sept. 1817), 1072. See also Tom Paine, *Age of Reason* (2nd edn 1795), pt i, 37.

[151] F. A. Cavanagh (ed.), *James and John Stuart Mill on Education* (1931), 67–8; *Works of J. S. Mill* i, ed. J. M. Robson and J. Stillinger (1981), 109.

reflecting on the drones they contain and the wasps they send forth.'[152] Jeremy Bentham wrote to Simon Bolivar in 1825 that Oxford and Cambridge were 'two great public nuisances...storehouses and nurseries of political corruption in its most baleful forms';[153] and in 1837 Thomas Attwood told his wife: 'Oxford and Cambridge are the ruin of England. It takes every man twenty years to *unlearn* all the nonsense which he learns there; and most persons die under the trial, like Liverpool, Canning, and Castlereagh.'[154]

Radical condemnation was one side of the coin, princely approval the other. By the end of the war Oxford was high in the favour of the court. A visit by the Tsar's sister in May 1814 was followed a month later by that of the Tsar himself and the King of Prussia.[155] The Duke of Clarence came in 1816, the Grand Duke Nicholas of Russia in 1817, and another Russian grand duke and the Archduke Maximilian of Austria in 1818.[156] The arrangements for the allied sovereigns in 1814 were imperfect. The arrival of Lords Yarmouth and Cathcart was mistaken for that of the Tsar, while the undergraduates alleviated the excessive heat in the Sheldonian galleries by breaking every window within reach, and Blücher, fighting his way out at the end of the ceremony, declared this 'the hottest struggle he had ever been in'.[157] None of that had a deterrent effect.[158] Oxford was a place where the Prince Regent was sure of an enthusiastic reception. He had been obliged to cancel his visit to the Tsar's London hotel because he had been 'threatened with annoyance in the street'. When he entered the Sheldonian an immense cheer went up. Six years later the gownsmen sided with him in 'the Queen's affair' against Caroline's supporters in the town.[159] By then Edward Gibbon's sneering prediction in the *Autobiography*, that England's universities would neither reform themselves nor submit to be reformed by Parliament, belonged to an earlier age.[160] The effectiveness of Oxford's reforms was acknowledged widely. As for parliamentary intervention, by the time that the *Autobiography* was published in 1796 the French Revolution had made tampering with settled institutions look very dangerous. Reviewing it, Mackintosh showed the Whigs' new tone: 'Ought a philosopher to lament

[152] *Political Register* xl (Nov. 1821), 1385.
[153] 13 Aug. 1825, UCL microfilm. I am grateful to Mr N. B. Harte for help with this quotation.
[154] C. M. Wakefield, *Thomas Attwood* (1885), 317.
[155] Cox, 78, 79–82; *New Monthly Magazine* i (June 1814), 461, (July 1814), 554. The Tsar's sister, the Grand Duchess Catherine, widow of Prince George of Oldenburg, was known in Britain as the Duchess of Oldenburg.
[156] Cox, 88, 89; Ward, *Victorian Oxford*, 40.
[157] G. Hamilton-Edwards, 'An undergraduate in Regency Oxford', *Oxford* xx/1 (May 1965), 69 (reminiscences of William Cotton).
[158] Many British ceremonies were ill performed until the later 19th century: [Lord R. Cecil], *Saturday Review* 9 Feb. 1861, 140–1.
[159] H. Nicolson, *Congress of Vienna* (1946), 112–15; Hamilton-Edwards, 'An undergraduate in Regency Oxford', 69; *Memories*, 107 (W. S. Cole).
[160] Gibbon, *Memoirs*, 49. Gibbon's alarm at the progress of the French Revolution turned him against political reforms during his last years.

that the rights and privileges of great societies are not, even for the specious object of reformation, subjected to the discretion of the legislature?...The principles of orders and bodies of men are the mounds and barriers which protect the rights of individuals.'[161] The Acts of 1818 and 1819 establishing the Charity Commissioners specifically exempted Oxford and Cambridge from their investigations.[162] When Henry Brougham, who had inspired those Acts, was declaiming four years later against 'the influence of the Crown', he referred sarcastically to Oxford's ability to curry favour with the government of the day.[163]

Effective as the reforms were, many imperfections remained in the Oxford which Gladstone knew. The methods of tuition used during this period are described in Chapter 4. A few of the catechetical classes, or 'college lectures', were excellent.[164] There is no reason to doubt John Coleridge's account of the admirable teaching at Corpus which is cited at the end of the chapter on 'Reformers and Reform' (Chapter 22) in *The Eighteenth Century*: indeed it is confirmed by the remark of another Corpus man quoted earlier;[165] but Corpus was a very small college consisting largely of scholars selected by examination, and therefore untypical.[166] The variation in effectiveness from one college lecture to another was immense; and most of the comments made on them during the early years of the new system were much less rosy than Coleridge's.[167] Good college tutors were hard to come by,[168] and Robert Biscoe was the exception even in Christ Church. 'Went to Hussey at 12,' James Ramsay noted in 1830; 'it is quite a farce; we only construe a section every here and there, but he hardly ever asked us a single question.'[169]

Dissatisfaction was not entirely due to the tutors' deficiencies. Reginald Heber, who had entered Brasenose in 1800, thought that the opening years of the century had brought a great improvement where they were concerned. Revisiting Oxford in 1818 he reported to a friend:

[161] *Monthly Review*, NS xx (May 1796), 79–80.
[162] 58 Geo. III, c. xci, s. 12; 59 Geo. III, c. lxxxi, s. 7.
[163] *Parl. Deb.* 24 June 1822, NS vii. 1292–4.
[164] See e.g. Frederic Rogers (later Lord Blachford) on R. H. Froude: R. W. Church, *The Oxford Movement* (1891), 51–2. 'College lecture' was sometimes used to denote any class where there was discussion or questioning. Thus Frederick Oakeley described Charles Lloyd as 'the very prince of college lecturers' when writing of the classes which he conducted as Regius Professor of Divinity for 'all the élite of graduate Oxford': *Reminiscences of Oxford by Oxford Men*, ed. L. M. Quiller Couch (Oxford Historical Society xxii 1892), 324–5.
[165] p. 22 above. Arnold was not, however, quite as enthusiastic as Coleridge made out; Arnold to Longley, 28 Jan. 1835, Stanley, *Arnold* i. 347.
[166] *RCO* (1850), report, 230.
[167] J. Veitch, *Sir W. Hamilton* (1869), 30; T. J. Hogg, *Shelley* (2 vols 1858) i. 258–9; A. Milman, *Dean Milman* (1900), 22; C. Wordsworth, *Annals of my Early Life* (1891), 39; *RCO* (1850), evidence, 12 (R. Lowe); Pattison, *Memoirs*, 40, 58, 62–3, 69.
[168] W. Sewell, *Second Letter to a Dissenter* (1834), 28.
[169] Ramsay, Diary, 20 Jan. 1830.

The tutors...are so different a race from the former stock as to occasion a very ludicrous comparison. The old boys never stirred from home; these pass their whole vacations on the continent, are geologists, system-mongers, and I know not what. It is possible that, when we were lads, we rather underrated the generality of those set over us; but I cannot help thinking that this race of beings is, on the whole, considerably amended.[170]

Even the best tutors were sometimes presented with unmanageable tasks. There were wide differences in attainment within a single class, especially where the Greek texts were concerned.[171] Progress was made at the pace of the slowest, and those who had been taught the classics well before arriving in Oxford were apt to become hopelessly bored.[172] According to Fynes Clinton's testimony, the standard of Greek teaching improved in the University during this period;[173] but an incident from 1831 illustrates how great the difficulties were. In that year a Shrewsbury boy, who had matriculated but not yet come up, won the Ireland scholarship against a strong field which included Gladstone.[174] A college lecture in a class which put a Salopian scholar with some almost Greekless commoners must have been an impossible proposition for any tutor.

The solution for these difficulties was clearly an effective university entrance examination. Copleston seems to have been the first to advocate this.[175] The case was taken up in the 1820s by Richard Whately and by Arnold as headmaster of Rugby;[176] but the University did not impose a uniform entrance requirement until 1926. The stages by which the goal was approached are outlined in Chapter 11. During nearly a hundred years of postponement the basic problem never changed. The supply of young men whose parents were willing and able to defray the costs associated with the Oxford BA course was, or was feared to be, limited. An entry hurdle of any difficulty thus threatened the less popular colleges and halls with financial losses. Moreover, the schools told Whately that an Oxford entrance examination would entail

requiring of masters what it was out of their power to perform...We could never hope that they could instruct properly more than a very small proportion...at the largest [school] of all (Eton), if any boy turned out a sound scholar (except the few who have private tutors), it must be in spite of the system pursued there, and not in consequence of it...The master's bread depends on his reputation...but...[that]

---

[170] To E. D. Davenport, 27 Nov. 1818, Heber, *Heber*, i. 499.
[171] Pattison, *Memoirs*, 44–5. For a comparison between private tuition in classics and that provided in the best schools see R. L. Edgeworth, *Essays on Professional Education* (1809), 75–6.
[172] M. Pattison, *Essays*, ed. H. Nettleship (2 vols 1889) i. 480.
[173] H. Fynes Clinton, *Literary Remains* (1854), 230. See also pp. 514–6 below.
[174] S. Butler, *Samuel Butler* (2 vols 1896) i. 252.
[175] W. Tuckwell, *Pre-Tractarian Oxford* (1909), 38.
[176] *Appendix to Report of the Committee Appointed 23 March 1829*, Bodl. G. A. Oxon. b. 21; Stanley, *Arnold* i. 347.

depends...too much on a small number of first-classes and prizes gained by boys he has brought up...As for the smaller schools, they bait their hooks for fond mothers with roast beef and plum pudding, salubrious air, clean sheets, etc.[177]

Newman, writing in the 1850s, described how the proposal for an entrance examination had been received in Oxford:

Some of [the halls]...supported themselves by taking as members those who either would not be received, or had actually been sent away, by the colleges. The existence then of these societies mainly depended on the sufferance within the University of incompetent, idle, or riotous young men. As they had no endowments, they asked high terms of admission, which, of course, they could not fail in obtaining from those who needed to be in some society or other, with a view to academical advantages, and who could not secure a place in any other body...Nothing would have been more fatal to such establishments than any successful effort to purify the University of unworthy members...The independence and interests of both endowed and unendowed Houses were at once touched by [the proposal for an entrance examination]; and a vigorous opposition was set on foot, in particular by the head of one society, which abounded in gownsmen of...unsatisfactory character...The private interest prevailed over the public; had the question fairly come before colleges generally, it might perhaps have been carried in the affirmative; but it had to be decided first in the Board of Heads of Houses; and they...naturally were unwilling to handle a question which concerned so nearly some of themselves.[178]

By the time that this was written Newman would believe nothing good about the Board of Heads; but his account rings true.

The college lecture system was subject to another defect which Charles Lyell, who had taken a second in classics in 1819, pinpointed eight years later in a *Quarterly* article: each college tutor was expected to tackle too wide a range of work.[179] Daniel Wilson, later Bishop of Calcutta, told a friend in 1807 of his difficulties as a young tutor at St Edmund Hall. He wrote from the village where he was curate:

Next term I have to lecture on Aristotle and the tragedies of Aeschylus...the New Testament has to be critically and copiously dealt with, and Aldrich's *Ars Logica* to be entered on. I will do what I can. If I cannot do for my pupils all that my wishes and the duties of my office require, yet nothing shall be wanting that goodwill, kindness, and careful study can accomplish...My main object must be so to instruct

[177] Whately, *Whately* i. 79–80.
[178] J. H. Newman, *Historical Sketches, Third Series* (1873), 237–8. In the 1872 edition, the first under this title, this volume in the three-volume series was designated as the *First Series*. In 1873 new title-pages were issued and it was redesignated as the *Third Series*. The first part of *Historical Sketches* iii (pp. 1–251, entitled 'Rise and progress of universities'), first appeared anonymously in the *Catholic University Gazette* of Dublin, 1854. The collected sketches were published in 1856, under the author's name, entitled 'Office and work of universities'. The collection has been republished more than once since Newman's death under the title 'University sketches': see M. Tierney's edition, 1953.
[179] *Quarterly* xxxvi (June 1827), 249.

them in the saving knowledge of God, and so imbue their minds with true piety, that, however little they may profit by me in secular matters, they may nevertheless learn to love God, to believe in Christ, to despise and reject the vain traditions and fancies of men, to estimate aright the value of the soul, and to know and be ready to proclaim the excellent glory of the Cross. If they know and understand these things savingly and experientially, they know all.[180]

This approach was not confined to the Evangelicals of St Edmund Hall. When Keble became an Oriel tutor in 1818 he thought that unless a tutorship was considered 'as an aspect of pastoral care...it might seem questionable whether a clergyman ought to leave a cure of souls for it'.[181] When Newman entered on his tutorial duties at the same college eight years later he prayed: 'May I engage in them in the strength of Christ, remembering I am a minister of God, and have a commission to preach the Gospel...and that I shall have to answer for the opportunities given me of benefiting those who are under my care.'[182] Tutors who looked on the academic side of their appointments as secondary to the pastoral did not necessarily think the burden of many different lecture topics insupportable. At this early stage there was no prospect of obtaining relief from a poorly paid and partly non-resident professoriate. The *Edinburgh Review*'s sneers about Oxford's professorial lecturing did not apply only to non-residents who could hardly afford to come to Oxford. Gaisford is said never to have lectured during his long tenure as Regius Professor of Greek.[183]

Faced with college tutors who were coping with too many subjects, and members of the class who slowed it to a snail's pace, many honours men resorted to sessions with a private tutor. To gain a double first without any such aid, as R. D. Hampden did in 1813, was regarded as a remarkable feat;[184] but aids of this kind were of variable value. They did not always provide much alleviation. 'Read some more *Choephoroe*', James Ramsay noted after one of his bouts with Aeschylus; 'it is hard in all parts and in innumerable places almost unconstruable. Saunders makes little of it, and I have but thrown away £50 on him this year.'[185] The private tutors were, however, normally under some degree of college control and a number of them went on to become college tutors.[186] Charles Lloyd, who was Peel's private tutor, became his friend for life.[187] The practice of seeing under-

[180] J. Bateman, *Daniel Wilson* (2 vols 1860) i. 113.
[181] J. T. Coleridge, *Memoir of John Keble* (2nd edn 2 vols 1869) i. 73.
[182] Newman, *AW* 209.
[183] *Quarterly* lxi (Jan. 1838), 213; Lloyd-Jones, *Blood for the Ghosts*, 102.
[184] *Some Memorials of R. D. Hampden*, ed. H. Hampden (1871), 6.
[185] 21 May 1833: Ramsay, Diary. Ramsay realized that the text was corrupt. Saunders rose to be Dean of Peterborough.
[186] Cox, 174. Bill, *Education at Christ Church*, 237–8.
[187] W. J. Baker, *Beyond Port and Prejudice: Charles Lloyd* (Orono M. 1981), 31–5. See also *LDN* ii. 209 n. 1.

graduates singly for what later came to be known as private hours or tutorials was largely confined during this period to these private 'coaches'.[188] Copleston wrote of college tutors: 'My beau-ideal was that a tutor should see all his own pupil's exercises, and remark upon them; that he should talk to him about the lectures he was attending, whether in his own classes or not; be ready to assist his difficulties, observe his conduct, and see more especially that his religious instruction went on.'[189] Henry Kett, for many years a Trinity College tutor, was said in an obituary to have 'united the character of friend with that of tutor'; but there may not have been many college tutors who approached Copleston's ideal.[190] The tutorial system as it is now known emerged only when the efforts of the coaches began to be replaced by those of college tutors. One rule of crucial importance for future tutorial relationships was, however, already a statutory requirement. Under the terms of the 1807 statute no examiner was 'allowed to examine a candidate of the same house with himself'.[191] This principle has affected the University's examination procedures ever since. Oxford undergraduates have been able to regard their tutor as their friend because they have known that he would not, in any university examination, be their judge.[192]

Many of the comments on the improvements at Oxford came from people who thought of the University chiefly as a teaching institution. Its place in the world of learning during these years is hard to define. A defender of Cambridge wrote in 1815 that the English universities had been founded, not 'to be foremost in...discoveries and improvements', but 'for preserving and communicating sound learning and...qualifying the young for discharging some of the most important functions in civil society'.[193] There was a price to be paid in works of scholarship when the most active fellows were appointed to tutorships and other college offices.[194] No work produced during this period by an Oxford tutor outmatched that of one young honours man who did not adopt a scholar's life: George Cornewall Lewis's translation of Boeckh entitled *The Public Economy of Athens* was published in 1828, the year in which the translator, aged 22, took a first in classics and a second in mathematics. Lewis was later to be Chancellor of the Exchequer. The ablest of the Oriel fellows were primarily concerned, as Chapter 7

[188] Lloyd and his successors in the Regius professorship of Divinity gave 'private instruction' to intending ordinands: F. Oakeley, *Historical Notes on the Tractarian Movement* (1865), 12.

[189] D. W. Rannie, *Oriel College* (1900), 201–2.

[190] *GM* xcv (1825), pt 2, 184.

[191] *Statutes* ii. 63.

[192] An examiner in Oxford finals is absent from the viva voce, and silent during the Board's discussions, when the class of a candidate whom he or she has tutored is decided. The significance of the Oxford rule was not always appreciated outside the University: see Isaac Lowthian Bell's answer to Question 1802, 7 Mar. 1862: *Royal Commission, Durham University* (PP 1863 xlvi. 364).

[193] Wainewright, *Literary and Scientific Pursuits*, 87 n.

[194] Bill, *Education at Christ Church*, 233. See also T. Chalmers, *Use and Abuse of Literary and Ecclesiastical Endowments*, in *Works* xvii. 92, 108.

shows, not with scholarship in the modern sense of the term, but with demonstrating the reasonableness of Christianity. In the publications of the University Press the classics came second to theology.[195] Charles Lloyd has already been quoted as telling Peel that Oxford had lost much of its 'academical character' and had 'become nothing but a large school'.[196] This was to be echoed by later generations. Looking back after more than sixty years, Wilamowitz saw the deaths of Elmsley and Dobree in 1825 as marking the end of the great era of English classical scholarship which Bentley had inaugurated in 1691, and this judgement was given an inaccurate English endorsement by Housman in 1903.[197] It may have been unfair to Gaisford, who, for all his limitations, enjoyed a European reputation;[198] but, even apart from this, in a comparison between English and German methods, the advantages did not all lie in one side, as Chapter 2 shows. In a recent study of the transformation of German classical scholarship after 1780 Dr Grafton concludes: 'German scholars ceased to be able to communicate with ordinary educated men. Indeed, the nature of the methods they taught ensured that Germany did not have—as England, with its cheerfully amateur classicists, did have—a public of "ordinary educated readers" interested in debating the meaning of catharsis in Aristotle's *Poetics*, or the viability of the Athenian economy.'[199]

The contribution of Copleston and Whately to political economy was significant. 'By reassuring Oxford', Professor Waterman writes, 'that Cambridge theology and Cambridge political economy were not utterly subversive of religion and good order—and by well-advertised corrections to their more obnoxious features—Copleston and Whately enabled Christian political economy to...enter the mainstream of respectable opinion'.[200] In Regency England, however, universities scarcely held first place for research and scholarship. Much of the pioneering English work in science, virtually all in technology, and some even in classical fields, was done elsewhere.[201] The *Quarterly Review* for October 1830 included an article by David Brewster entitled 'Decline of science in England'. Brewster listed fourteen eminent British scientists and inventors. While three of them had begun as Cambridge mathematicians, there were no names from Oxford.[202] George

---

[195] *Critical Review* vii (1806), 118–19; W. Vincent, *Defence of Public Education* (1801), 14; Clarke, *Classical Education in Britain*, 96.

[196] 26 Jan. 1825, BL Add. MS 40342, fo 200.

[197] C. O. Brink, *English Classical Scholarship* (1986), 115, 148–9. Elmsley was Camden Professor of Ancient History, Oxford; Dobree, Professor of Greek, Cambridge. Blomfield, *pace* Housman, had become Bishop of Chester in 1824.

[198] Tuckwell (1900), 131. Gaisford's scholarship is assessed in Lloyd-Jones, *Blood for the Ghosts*, 81–102.

[199] A. Grafton, 'Polyhistor into philolog: notes on the transformation of German classical scholarship, 1780–1850', *History of Universities* iii (1983), 184.

[200] A. M. C. Waterman, *Revolution, Economics and Religion* (1991), 216.

[201] P. Mathias (ed.), *Science and Society, 1600–1900* (1972), 78–80; A. E. Musson and E. Robinson, *Science and Technology in the Industrial Revolution* (Manchester 1969), 161–5.

[202] *Quarterly* xliii (Oct. 1830), 320. See also a slightly different list, 327.

Grote, the historian of Greece, and William Leake, the classical topographer and numismatist, were not products of any university. Newman was to maintain as late as 1852 that the learned societies in London and other large cities were 'far more suited... as instruments' of research than Oxford and Cambridge.[203] Before Peel came up to Oxford in 1805 he attended science lectures at the Royal Institution.[204] Oxford was still an insular university. Cornewall Lewis's translation of Boeckh broke new ground. It was said that until Pusey went to Germany in 1825 only two or three of its senior members knew German.[205] Although some 5 per cent of the undergraduates of the period had been born overseas, very few of these were foreign nationals, almost all being sons of some planter, military officer, or clergyman who had accepted an overseas posting. The Ashmolean Society, founded in December 1828 to advance Oxford's scientific studies, subscribed to only one foreign journal.[206]

'Have... public endowments', Adam Smith asked in *The Wealth of Nations*, 'contributed to encourage the diligence, and to improve the abilities, of the teachers?'[207] If he had held his Snell exhibition at Balliol during the Regency and not in the 1740s, he might have returned a less emphatic negative to his question: but, however effective Thomas Chalmers might be in arguing that universities needed endowments, it could hardly be denied that some of Oxford's were wasted. Even where there was a will to curb idleness and abuses, the difficulty of altering college statutes could impede remedial action.[208] William of Wykeham had inserted a rubric in New College's statutes in 1379 to ensure that the college would maintain academic standards. This was used until 1834 to exempt New College men from the need to take the university examination in order to graduate.[209] Mark Pattison, who was an unsuccessful candidate for a Balliol fellowship in

---

[203] Newman, *Idea*, 7.

[204] Parker, *Peel* i. 16.

[205] Liddon, *Pusey* i. 72. Pusey told Liddon: 'only two persons... were said to know German'. Liddon identified them in a footnote as Edward Cardwell and 'Mr. Mill of Magdalen' (? William Mills). In fact Pusey's predecessor in the chair of Hebrew, Alexander Nicoll (1793–1828), not only knew German but corresponded with leading German theologians: J. L. Speller, 'Alexander Nicoll', *Journal of Ecclesiastical History* xxx (1979), 451–9. Some German commentaries on the New Testament were written in Latin. The translations of J. D. Michaelis's works on the New Testament, which were published from 1793, were by Herbert Marsh (1757–1839), a Cambridge scholar. Niebuhr's *History of Rome*, vol. i, appeared, translated, in 1828 by two young Cambridge scholars, Connop Thirlwall and J. C. Hare.

[206] P. Corsi, *Science and Religion: Baden Powell and the Anglican Debate, 1800–1860* (1988), 130 n.

[207] *The Wealth of Nations* v. i. 3, art. 2.

[208] Chalmers, *Use and Abuse of Literary and Ecclesiastical Endowments*, 148; *Ed. Rev.* xlii (Aug. 1825), 350–1 (Brougham). For college statutes see Ch. 4, and *The Eighteenth Century*, 235 (Brasenose).

[209] A. W. Hare, *Letter to George Martin* (1813), 33; J. Buxton and P. Williams (eds.), *New College, 1379–1979* (1979), 66–7; Tuckwell (1900), 179; Cox, 258; *Eighteenth Century*, 469 n. 2.

1838, thought the examination there 'vastly inferior to the system pursued at Oriel': he could 'hardly think that the election was influenced' by it.[210] J. B. Mozley's principal rival for a Magdalen fellowship in 1840 commanded a 'great interest'. 'Very few went by the examination itself,' Mozley reported. He was elected thanks largely to the lucky chance that two or three of those enrolled in the 'great interest' could not attend for the vote.[211]

Mozley's account, being contemporary, may be fairly reliable. Later tales of such abuses have to be treated with reserve, since the Victorians liked to contrast their own purity with the squalor of an earlier time. The researches of G. D. Squibb QC established, however, that some who gained privileges as founder's kin had little or no right to them. 'The pedigrees that satisfied college authorities', G. D. Squibb wrote, 'were of varying degrees of accuracy, ranging downwards from the imperfect to the erroneous.' Nineteen scholars were elected to Winchester College on the basis of the same erroneous pedigree, the last of them becoming a fellow of New College in 1837.[212] The founder's kin elected as Craven scholars until their privilege was abolished in 1858 were not prominent in the honours lists by comparison with those who won the scholarship when there was no effective kinship claim. While sixteen of these latter had taken honours, only four of the founder's kin had done so.[213] John Bull, a canon of Christ Church from 1830 until his death in 1858, also held during all those years a Prebendal Stall in York, a canonry of Exeter, and the valuable living of Staverton.[214] Inevitably there were a few fellows who either did not want a college living or were too eccentric to be presented to one. John Frowd, who held a Corpus fellowship for more than forty years, came into the latter category.[215] He and Moses Griffith of Merton were the source of many anecdotes. Griffith died in 1859 in possession of the fellowship to which he had been elected sixty-four years earlier. He customarily spent the term in Bath to avoid the undergraduates. Once in the vacation, when he was dining in hall, alone as he thought, he spied a scholar also at dinner and ordered the manciple to put a screen between him and this young diner.[216] The idle and the eccentric naturally provided the best stories, and it was easy for a later generation to overlook that Canon Bull had been a good scholar and tutor with a double first. Similarly, nepotism in the appointments to Christ Church studentships can

---

[210] Pattison, *Memoirs*, 97.
[211] Mozley, *Letters*, 108.
[212] G. D. Squibb, *Founder's Kin* (1972), 93.
[213] Ibid. 51. See n. 30 above.
[214] Tuckwell (1900), 18–20; H. L. Thompson, *Christ Church* (1900), 186, 190, 196; F. Boase, *Modern English Biographies* (6 vols 1892–1921) i. 468. Bull endowed an Oxford vicarage but amassed a 'small fortune': will proved, 31 May 1858, effects 'under £80,000'.
[215] Tuckwell (1900), 24–7. The mantrap story in G. Smith, *Reminiscences* (1910), 279, belongs to Frowd's later period.
[216] 'Nestor' [William Tuckwell], 'Oxford Memories', *Speaker* 29 Oct. 1898.

hardly have been as common as was later suggested. Gladstone, for instance, cannot be thought to have owed his studentship to it, and the declining fortunes of the House after his day resulted less from defects among the 'canoneer' Students than from the difficulties of Westminster School.[217]

The damaging criticisms were the ones made at the time by those who knew the University well. A pamphlet by Pusey published in 1833 included the statement that Oxford did not require its many intending ordinands to undergo adequate professional training. He wrote: 'One fortnight comprises the beginning and end of all the public instruction which any candidate for holy orders is required to attend previously to entering upon his profession.'[218] It was also notorious that college testimonials for ordination were not always restricted to men of good character.[219] 'It always appeared to me', Copleston wrote privately in 1834, 'that Oxford stood much more in need of reform, as to the use and distribution of its revenues, than the Church of England.'[220]

The patterns of student life which were developing during this early reformed period are described in Chapter 8; but three particular features need to be mentioned here. The first is the extent of the differences between the various 'sets' within a college and between one college and another. One type of undergraduate was distinguished from another by his academic dress, by his place in hall, and, in Brasenose at least, by the quality of the food which he ate there:[221] noblemen and gentlemen commoners came at the top of the scale, servitors at the bottom. To some extent these distinctions were a matter of college policy. It was dangerous for a freshman to join a set too expensive for him. In the 1870s Gladstone deplored the disappearance of this rank-ordering. 'The distinctions of the outer world', he said, 'should have their echo in Oxford...that...protected poor men from the temptations to high expenditure.'[222] Fashionable colleges such as Christ Church, Oriel and Brasenose maintained waiting-lists: others, which had failed to attract the sons of the rich and the great, might be barely full. Charles Lloyd

[217] *Reminiscences of Oxford*, ed. Quiller Couch, 312–13 (Frederick Oakeley); Bill and Mason, *Christ Church and Reform*, 30. For stories of nepotism and allied evils see Tuckwell (1900), 29, 134.

[218] E. B. Pusey, *Remarks on the Prospective and Past Benefits of Cathedral Institutions* (1833), 16; W. S. Cole, 'On the importance of...the pastoral office', in *Two Sermons Preached before the University of Oxford* (1831), 9; Cox, 130–1. For the same defect at Cambridge see R. N. Adams, *Commencement Sermon*, 4 July (1830), 14–16. F. R. Hall, *A Letter to R. M. Beverley* (1834), 32. See also *Ed. Rev.* lx (Oct. 1834), 212.

[219] H. B. Bulteel, *Sermon on 1 Corinthians ii verse 12 Preached before the University of Oxford at St Mary's, on Sunday February 6 1831* (1831), 46–8; E. Burton, *Remarks upon a Sermon Preached at St Mary's on 6 February 1831* (1831), 6; Cox, 140–1; Gladstone, *Diaries* i. 343–4. For Bulteel see also n. 261 below.

[220] To Berens, 10 Feb. 1834, Copleston, *Copleston*, 158.

[221] Heber, *Heber* i. 26–7.

[222] G. W. Kitchin, *Ruskin in Oxford and Other Studies* (1904), 1–3. The dinner-party in the Christ Church deanery at which Gladstone said this was held, in Kitchin's account, 'about twenty-five years ago'.

told Peel in 1825 that this variety among the colleges might be 'of advantage to the community'. 'A clergyman', he wrote, 'who can only allow his son £100 a year, will hardly be persuaded to send him to a college where he might mix with noblemen and men of wealth, or, if he refuses to mix with them, must be exposed to a certain degree of humiliation and annoyance.'[223]

The less formal distinctions were almost equally important. The experiences of the undergraduate who had been through the 'socializing' process of a boarding-school differed from those of his neighbour who might have been educated entirely at home.[224] Within each college the minority who aimed at good honours had to work hard in both term and vacation,[225] while someone who was not greatly concerned at the possibility of being 'ploughed', or did not even aim at a degree, was free to be idle and to expend his energy in high-spirited pranks. During one of her 1814 visits the Tsar's sister was said to have questioned a noble undergraduate:

'May I ask what your Lordship's studies are?'
'General, madam.'
'But what particular books do you read?'
'None, madam.'[226]

In Magdalen during the early 1820s most of the gentlemen commoners wore 'red coats' and two of the others in that small community were driven to adopt defensive measures. 'As both of us had a considerable flow of conversation, and knew more than most of our companions,' one of the two recorded, 'we were, when together, generally successful in suppressing hunting talk.'[227] Christ Church included both the diligent and the idle in abundance. The diary of J. J. Buxton for 1809, the year after Peel went down, survives in the archives of the House: it never mentions work at all.[228] In February 1816 W. W. Phelps, giving a view from Corpus, advised a friend not to try for Christ Church. 'I believe', he wrote, 'its only society is that of bucks and bloods, who, of course, are not naturally eager for learning.'[229] The class lists for this period, even apart from extant letters and diaries, show this to have been a grossly unfair assessment;[230] but the 'bucks and bloods'

---

[223] 26 Jan. 1825, BL Add. MS 40342, fos 198–9. See Ch. 8 below.
[224] The experiences of Frederick Oakeley, who entered Christ Church in 1820, illustrate the difficulties encountered by one undergraduate who had not been toughened by school: *Reminiscences of Oxford*, ed. Quiller Couch, 303–4, 317–18.
[225] For vacation work see Gladstone, *Diaries* i. 249–63 (12 July–15 Oct. 1829); *Memories*, 95 (R. W. Browne).
[226] Milman, *Milman*, 27–8.
[227] J. H. Gray, *Autobiography*, ed. by his widow (privately printed 1868), 241.
[228] W. G. Hiscock, *A Christ Church Miscellany* (1946), 90–2. Sir James Graham (Christ Church, 1810–12) was almost equally idle: C. S. Parker, *Graham* (2 vols 1907) i. 12.
[229] To R. T. P. Pope, 24 Feb. 1816, Hole, *Phelps* i. 87.
[230] See Viscount Sandon to his eldest sister, Susan, 26 Oct. 1816, in *Christ Church Annual Report* (1956), 19–20.

seem to have been fairly prominent next door to Corpus. In 1823 there was prolonged rioting in the House, Lord Castlereagh being expelled.[231] The tightening of discipline which followed occasioned riotous bonfires, much red paint on the Dean's and canons' doors, and the transplanting of the Dean's cabbages to a quad.[232] When the Duke of Wellington's second son was to be rusticated for helping to break down a gate in one of these disturbances, the Duke withdrew both of his sons and sent them to Cambridge.[233] Some of Gladstone's Christ Church contemporaries lacked his high-mindedness. Lord Conyers Osborne died 'in a wine-party frolic' in the House, as Martin Tupper recorded, 'having been back-broken over an armchair by the good-natured but only too athletic Earl of Hillsborough'.[234]

Secondly, all parts of the undergraduate scene reflected the uneven effect of the reforms on an earlier Oxford. Mark Pattison's *Memoirs* convey a vivid sense of this patchwork process of change. Before he came up he was given a disparaging view of Oriel and Balliol, the two colleges where reform had gone farthest. 'We call those', the ill-fated Lord Conyers Osborne had told him, 'the two prison-houses.' Soon after Pattison arrived he discovered that Lord Conyers's aristocratic views were not shared everywhere, and that

if you wanted to get honours you must first get a scholar's gown, and preferably at Balliol. In 1808 ... in my father's time, the 'scholars' were not regarded as gentlemen. They did not associate with the commoners, but lived among themselves, or with the bible clerks. They were nicknamed 'charity boys'. In twenty-five years this had quite changed. The scholar's gown, from being the badge of an inferior order, had become a coveted distinction.[235]

Despite this change, and although a first had become 'something quite useful', a professional man and his son could not afford to forget that in their world patronage remained an operating principle: 'making good connections' at college was thought to be important.[236] If the wealthier undergraduates were setting the tone of the college, a freshman might be tempted,

---

[231] *The Times*, 30 May 1823, 3d, 2 June, 3b; Ward, *Victorian Oxford*, 39.

[232] J. Pycroft, *Oxford Memories* (2 vols 1886) i. 41–2; R. Cruickshank, 'A scene in Tom Quad' in C. M. Westmacott, *The English Spy* (1st edn 'by Bernard Blackmantle' 1825–6; 1907 2 vols) i, between 130 and 131; F. T. Whitington, *Augustus Short* (1887), 8. For riots a few years later, Ramsay, Diary, 23 Feb. 1830, 13 May 1833. Pycroft, writing some sixty years after the events, was confused about the dates.

[233] *Journal of Mrs Arbuthnot*, ed. F. Bamford and Duke of Wellington (2 vols 1950) i. 387; T. De Quincey, *Collected Writings*, ed. D. Masson (16 vols 1889–90) ii. 45–6.

[234] Cox, 259; Gladstone, *Diaries* i. 344–5; Ramsay, Diary, 18 Feb. 1831. For violence in Edwardian Oxford see Pt 2, Ch. 31.

[235] Pattison, *Memoirs*, 26–7, 72. For the prestige of Trinity's scholarships, see Newman, *AW* 36–7, R. Palmer, *Memorials, Family and Personal, 1766–1865* (2 vols 1896) i. 114–15.

[236] E. Bulwer (Bulwer-Lytton, 1843; Lord Lytton, 1866), *England and the English*, ed. S. Meacham (1833, 1970), 150–3; Thomas Hughes, *Tom Brown at Oxford* (3 vols 1861) i. 39; S. Rothblatt, *Tradition and Change in English Liberal Education* (1976), ch. 9: 'A liberal education in practice: George Robert Chinnery'.

despite the gradations in rank, into a set which was too expensive for him and so into debt.[237] R. H. Barham, author of the *Ingoldsby Legends*, matriculated at Brasenose, then an 'expensive college', in 1807. He remembered a contemporary there who, having gone deeply into debt, had written to his father confessing all. The father replied at once, expressing his forgiveness and undertaking to pay; but the letter was delayed by the mail-guard and the son had blown his brains out before it arrived.[238] Other tragedies were of a different and much newer kind: more than one undergraduate suicide seems to have resulted from fear of failure in the final examinations.[239]

During the Napoleonic Wars and their immediate aftermath, undergraduate 'discussion groups' were discouraged. The fear in the 1790s of any association which might disseminate revolutionary ideas, and the consequent discountenancing of the Society for Scientific and Literary Disquisition, has been described in *The Eighteenth Century*.[240] In 1811 the President of Queens', Cambridge, refused to allow undergraduate participation in founding a Cambridge branch of the Bible Society, saying that if he appeared 'as a leader in any plan which originated with undergraduates', he might be 'thought to encourage insubordination'.[241] To John Henry Newman, and his fellow editor of the *Undergraduate*, the University authorities seemed in 1819 to 'require reverence of arbitrary rule'.[242] Yet even in these early years the regime was not one of total and uniform repression. In 1829 Charles Lloyd, by then Bishop of Oxford, told the Lords that twenty years earlier he had 'belonged to a debating club in Oxford...and that club had continued to exist because...it had been found impossible to put it down. When the members...were hunted out of one room they met immediately in another.'[243] Shelley's friend Thomas Hogg described University College, a little prematurely, as 'Liberty Hall';[244] and rebellious voices could be heard in the Sheldonian Theatre itself. During the preparations for Grenville's installation as Chancellor in 1810 Richard Brinsley Sheridan had been

[237] R. S. Hawker to W. W. Martyn, 7 Feb. 1852, P. Brendon, *Hawker of Morwenstow* (1975), 49.

[238] R. H. D. Barham, *R. H. Barham* (3rd edn 1880), 21–2.

[239] Ramsay, Diary, 25 May 1833. Overwork for the exams was said to have led in some cases to nervous breakdown, or even to permanent mental collapse: *Oxford: academical abuses disclosed by some of the initiated* (1832), 12. Peel and Gladstone felt the strain: Parker, *Peel* i. 21; J. Morley, *Gladstone* (3 vols 1903) i. 76.

[240] *The Eighteenth Century*, 342–3.

[241] S. Rothblatt, 'The student sub-culture and the examination system in early nineteenth-century Oxbridge' in Stone (ed.), *The University in Society* i. 267. The Bible Society included Dissenters and was therefore controversial. The President of Queens', Isaac Milner, being an Evangelical, was involved, 1811–13, in a controversy with Herbert Marsh (1757–1839) about its possible activities in Cambridge. See D. A. Winstanley, *Early Victorian Cambridge* (1940), 18–25.

[242] S. Rothblatt, 'Student sub-culture', 265; Cox, 97. See also p. 299 below. Newman was soon revealed to be an editor: Newman, *AW* 41. For an instance of 'arbitrary rule' see the account in the *DNB* entry for John Parsons (1761–1819) of his suppression of the Balliol Junior Common Room.

[243] *Parl. Deb.* 24 Mar. 1829, NS xx. 1417.

[244] *Shelley* i. 290.

proposed for an honorary doctorate; but under a threat of opposition his name was withdrawn. When he entered the Theatre, however, he had to be seated among the doctors in response to shouted demands for him to be accorded that privilege. On this occasion one undergraduate panegyrist strayed from the 'Church-and-king' line. He congratulated Grenville on presiding over the university which had educated John Hampden.[245] The Master and fellows of University College seem to have resolved on expelling Shelley only when Copleston forced their hand.[246] T. L. Beddoes paraded his democratic views, but was allowed by Pembroke to take his MA.[247] Hartley Coleridge's opinions on politics and church endowments may have been a factor in Oriel's withdrawal of his fellowship at the end of the probationary year in 1820; but by his own statement his intemperance had become a problem.[248] Augustus Hare took his degree from New College, and became a tutor there a few years later, although he had published a pamphlet in 1813 attacking the college's degree privileges. The fact that his Attic Society was heavily discouraged during the decade which ended with the Six Acts of 1819 is not surprising.[249]

Early in the 1820s the political climate changed. The fears aroused by the French Revolution and by Bonaparte receded, and the freezing conditions imposed by the long war gave way to more genial weather. In 1821 and 1822 Van Mildert and Howley, two bishops much respected in Oxford, pronounced the country to be, in Howley's phrase, out of 'immediate danger'.[250] The new atmosphere was liberal, that term being used as yet in a general, rather than a party, sense. In these more confident years university and college authorities were less disquieted about the discussions which undergraduate societies might hold; and this made Gladstone's Oxford very different from Peel's. When the thaw came a group of undergraduates secured permission for a United Debating Society; and this first met for debate in April 1823. The subjects for discussion were to be 'the historical previous to the present century and the philosophical exclusive of religion'.[251] The Society was dominated by Christ Church men and met in the House. While its application to acquire its own rooms was before the Vice-Chancellor it suffered the misfortune of being denounced in *John Bull*. The editor of that none-too-respectable paper, Theodore Hook, had a nephew in

---

[245] Cox, 69–70; W. A. Pantin, *Oxford Life in Oxford Archives* (1972), 89; *GM* lxxx (1810), pt 2, 71–2 (installation, 5 July; honorary degrees, 6 July).

[246] N. I. White, *Shelley* (2 vols 1947) i. 113.

[247] *Poems by the Late T. L. Beddoes with a Memoir*, ed. T. F. Kelsall (1851), pp. cxxix, cxxxiii.

[248] H. Hartman, *Hartley Coleridge* (1931), 73, 75–6.

[249] A. J. C. Hare, *Memorials of a Quiet Life* (3 vols 1872–6) i. 168–85.

[250] W. Howley, *Charge to the Clergy of the Diocese of London* (1822), 10; J. C. D. Clark, *English Society, 1688–1832* (1985), 269–70 (Van Mildert's charge to Llandaff clergy, 1821).

[251] D. Walter, *The Oxford Union* (1984), 21. For the rule in the Cambridge Union see J. Burrow, *A Liberal Descent* (1981), 15–16.

Christ Church, and was engaged in defending the House against the recrim-
inations of one of its members. In the course of these proceedings the Hooks
directed attention on to Oriel with an allegation about William Wilberforce's
sons Robert and Samuel. These two were reported to have maintained
during the Society's proceedings that Charles I had been rightly deposed;
and one of them was alleged to have gone farther 'by making a direct attack
on the established church'.[252]

Oxford's senior members were susceptible to aristocratic grandeur; and
adroit use of this fact saved the Society. Its Oriel members included the Hon.
Harry Vane, who was to succeed many years later as Duke of Cleveland. At
a hurriedly summoned special meeting he vouched for the impeccable
sentiments of the two Wilberforces and secured a vote *nem. con.* of 'regret
and indignation' at the conduct of *John Bull*. He then stated that these two
blameless members of his college had been misreported, and secured a
further vote to the effect that *John Bull*'s attitude was 'of such a nature as
to prejudice the society in the eyes of the authorities of this University'.[253]
The Society survived to be reconstituted at the end of 1825 as the Oxford
Union Society. It acquired its own rooms in 1829 and invited members of the
Cambridge Union over in that year for a debate on the respective merits of
Byron and Shelley.[254]

Religious themes were excluded from debate in the Union until the
Second World War.[255] The other restrictions disappeared almost at once.
The subjects of debate in 1826 included mechanics' institutes (approved by a
majority of one), the East India Company's monopoly, the abolition of
slavery, the unpaid magistracy, primogeniture, unanimity in juries, the
power of the legislature over church property, and the corn laws.[256] The
Union which Gladstone dominated was not debarred from debating current
political issues. On 11 November 1830 he recorded, as secretary, that the
motion condemning Wellington's government as 'undeserving of the confidence of the country' had been carried by one (57 to 56). The mover's exuber-
ance overcoming secretarial propriety, he added: 'Tremendous cheering from
the majority of one'. The last five words were deleted by another hand.[257] A
debate of far greater importance for him was held on three evenings in May
1831. The Union, having condemned the Duke, was engaged in condemning

[252] *Laws and Transactions of the United Debating Society, Oxford, Established March 1823*
(1872), 43; *John Bull* 6 June 1824, 189a, b; A. R. Ashwell and R. G. Wilberforce, *S. Wilberforce* (3
vols 1880–2) i. 28–31; Mozley, *Reminiscences* i. 118, 120–1.
[253] Histories of the Society, H. Morrah (1923), C. Hollis (1965).
[254] Gladstone, *Diaries* i. 270. For the Union as 'a school for public speaking', *c.*1830, see
Palmer, *Memorials, Family and Personal* i. 140. For later suspicions that debating was diverting
undergraduates from their studies, see A. H. Clough to J. P. Gell, 18. Nov. [1838], *Correspondence of A. H. Clough* i. 85.
[255] For a religious debate during the Second World War see *The Twentieth Century*, 180.
[256] *Proceedings of the Oxford Union Society* (1841), 31–8.
[257] Morrah, 47.

his opponents for introducing their Parliamentary Reform Bill. Gladstone carried an amendment by 94 to 38 to the effect that the Bill threatened 'to break up the very foundations of social order'. His speech greatly impressed his Christ Church friend the Earl of Lincoln. It was glowingly reported to the latter's father, the Duke of Newcastle; and in the following year the Duke offered Gladstone a parliamentary seat at Newark.[258] That was a far cry from the Oxford of Peel's undergraduate years. He too had left Christ Church for the House of Commons, but he had been given no chance to achieve debating triumphs as an undergraduate. He was elected for a seat in a corrupt Irish borough obtained with his own father's money.[259]

The rules and practices for religious worship are discussed in Chapter 7. Even here the 1820s brought some increase in freedom. While there was little or no relaxation in compulsory chapel attendance, or even in compulsory communion,[260] the enforcement of orthodoxy seems to have become less strict. An attempt was made in 1828 to prevent undergraduates from attending St Ebbe's Church, where the preacher was a fiery Evangelical, Henry Bulteel: it failed, though backed by the Vice-Chancellor's authority.[261] 'Dr Chalmers has been passing through Oxford', Gladstone told his father on 27 October 1830, 'and I went to hear him preach on Sunday evening, though it was at the baptist chapel...his sermon was admirable.'[262] One Sunday in May 1833 Hugh Jones of Jesus recorded in his diary: 'Received the sacrament in the college chapel and heard a sermon from Mr Clough, with which I was exceedingly pleased. Went to St. Mary's at 2. To St. Peter's at 3, heard a very good sermon, and got into college by dinner time. Went to the Baptist chapel at 7, heard a most excellent sermon from...the resident minister...This has been a blessed day to my soul...I felt particular comfort at the Baptist chapel.'[263]

Whatever may have been the case earlier, it seems clear that by 1830 no attempt was made to enforce the rule forbidding attendance at Non-

[258] W. E. Gladstone i: *Autobiographica* (Royal Commission on Historical Manuscripts 1971) 40. For Disraeli's unwise reference to this amendment see *Parl. Deb*. 27 Apr. 1866, 3S clxxxiii. 94–5, 129–30.

[259] Gash, *Peel*, 60.

[260] E. Hawkins, *A Letter to the Author of 'An Appeal to the Heads of the University of Oxford' upon Compulsory Attendance at the Communion* (1822); it had become known that the author of this anonymous 'Appeal' was an Oriel gentleman commoner (J. C. Colquhoun). For Newman's efforts see Newman, *AW* 89, the names of those concerned being given in Newman to Lord Blachford, 22 Oct. 1884, in *LDN* xxx. 419. See also Newman, *Fifteen Sermons*, 153 n. 4. For drunkenness at communion see Newman, *AW* 37–9.

[261] Ward, *Victorian Oxford*, 76.

[262] Morley, *Gladstone* i. 59; Gladstone, *Diaries* i. 326. See also *Diaries* i. 347 and n. 268 below. Chalmers was a family friend of the Gladstones: Matthew, *Gladstone*, 15.

[263] H. Jones, diary, 26 May. Hugh Jones's father (d. 1820) had been a Methodist minister. The son was a fellow of Jesus, 1837–46; Residentiary Canon, St Asaph, 1860; Chancellor, 1890; Archdeacon, 1892. I am grateful to Prof. E. M. Hugh-Jones for telling me about this diary and providing a typescript of it.

conformist chapels. Colleges varied greatly in the quality of the services provided; and the judgement made by an undergraduate might bear little relation to his denominational allegiance. In March 1830 James Ramsay, who was soon to become an active member of the General Assembly of the Church of Scotland, made a comparison unflattering to Christ Church. He recorded: 'To New College chapel. Truly it is magnificent. The chapel itself is beyond my praise—the organ has the most lovely tones I ever heard; the singing is proverbial and full cathedral service is performed. It is the most *devotional* place I ever was in and forms such a contrast to the mockery of prayer which is performed in our chapel.'[264] Later statements about constraints on undergraduates are apt to obscure how much movement there had been by 1830. Looking back after nearly fifty years Gladstone said of his time at Christ Church: 'The temper which too much prevailed in academical circles was that liberty was regarded with jealousy and fear, something which could not wholly be dispensed with, but which was to be continually watched for fear of excesses.'[265]

Real though the restrictions were, undergraduate Oxford had an air of freedom and spontaneity by the end of the 1820s. In March 1833 James Ramsay recorded that he had read Aristotle's *Ethics* 'very hard all morning. They certainly are very fine discipline for the mind,' he added; 'it signifies little, I should think, whether you remember them or not...It is the exertion, the labour necessary for understanding and following out his arguments, which constitutes their value to a young man.'[266] Team games were in their infancy in the universities, walking being the undergraduates' most popular form of exercise;[267] and, as the ablest of them strode along, they debated the unanswerable questions. Gladstone remembered walking the six miles to Marsh Baldon with F. D. Maurice to hear an Evangelical sermon, and discussing it during the long walk home.[268] His inclinations as an undergraduate were not quite those of that other future Chancellor of the Exchequer who had translated Boeckh's great work, but the same ardour of spirit characterized both. The Oxford which nurtured Cornewall Lewis and Gladstone had recovered, among the honours men, not merely the rigour but the sense of intellectual excitement which would be regarded today as one hallmark of an effective university.

* * *

[264] Ramsay, Diary, 21 Mar. 1830. See also E. S. Purcell, *Manning* (2 vols 1896) i. 67; J. W. Burgon, *Lives of Twelve Good Men* (2 vols 1888) i. 410.
[265] Speech given at the Palmerston Club, Oxford, 30 Jan. 1878, in Morley, *Gladstone* i. 60.
[266] Ramsay, Diary, 13 Mar. 1833.
[267] Tuckwell (1900), 125–6.
[268] F. Maurice, *F. D. Maurice* (2 vols 1884) i. 109; Gladstone, *Autobiographica* 141; Gladstone, *Diaries* i. 308, where the preacher is identified incorrectly as a Methodist (John Porter). He was George Porter, fellow of Queen's and vicar of Toot Baldon. I am grateful to the Revd Marcus Braybrooke for his help in making this identification.

The people who produce great educational reforms are apt to differ from those whom the reforms produce.[269] The honours system had revealed powers and released energies without, as yet, cramping individuality, and during the 1820s its products began to make their mark. Thomas Arnold and John Williams, two of the firsts in classics of 1814, became the pioneers in a transformation of Britain's secondary schools.[270] In post-war Oxford the younger fellows who had taken honours bore little resemblance to their staid seniors. The youngsters had the intellectual adventurousness of men whose ability had been publicly certified. Their centre lay in the Oriel Common Room, and their central figures became known as the Oriel Noetics. This Greek term is perhaps best translated simply as 'the intellectuals'.[271] The Noetics' views are given in the Note which follows this chapter. They were not, in origin at least, a party, for the two intellectual currents to which they responded were diametrically opposed to each other.

The more dominant of these currents in the perception of contemporaries, the liberalism of the 1820s, has already been mentioned. It was personified at first by Copleston, but during most of the 1820s by Richard Whately. In his memoirs Blanco White refers to Whately as 'a distinguished leader of whatever liberal spirit existed at Oxford'.[272] The watchwords which alarmed and exasperated Oxford's Tories held no terrors for these two. They were at one with 'the spirit of the age': they marched with 'the march of intellect'.[273] They had no quarrel with an England in which the production and distribution of newspapers were always being accelerated. Copleston was thrilled by the advent of the railways.[274] Whately had little time for the shibboleths of yesterday. He was said to regard High and Low Church as 'equal bigotries'; and a powerful plea for disestablishment published in 1826 was attributed to him.[275] His theology was liberal in that he aimed to substitute rational thought for what he regarded as prejudice and superstition. By 1827 the first signs had been received that geological research did not tally on all points with the Old Testament;[276] and in the following year Whately used

[269] For a stronger version see Macaulay, *Critical and Historical Essays*, ed. F. C. Montague (3 vols 1903) ii. 248 (Sir William Temple).
[270] Arnold was headmaster of Rugby School, 1828–42; Williams, the first Rector of Edinburgh Academy, 1824–7, 1829–47.
[271] Noesis is the fourth and final stage in Plato's chart for the growth of intelligence: *Republic* VII. 510–11. David Newsome's suggestion in *The Parting of Friends* (1966), 66—'the free thinkers'—is more suitable perhaps for the Noetics' later stages than for their activities before 1829.
[272] *Autobiography of Blanco White*, ed. J. H. Thom (3 vols 1845) iii. 129.
[273] William Hazlitt's *The Spirit of the Age* first appeared in book form in 1825. T. L. Peacock entitled ch. 2 of *Crotchet Castle* (1831) 'The march of mind'. For the two phrases in use in an Oxford controversy see Ward, *Victorian Oxford*, 59, and [J. A. Giles], *Reply to an Expostulatory Letter* (Feb. 1829), 4.
[274] Tuckwell, *Pre-Tractarian Oxford*, 47.
[275] Mozley, *Reminiscences* i. 23; Newman, *Apologia*, 24–5. See also n. 296 below.
[276] John Fleming, 'On the geological deluge as interpreted by Baron Cuvier and Professor Buckland', *Edinburgh Philosophical Journal*, xix (Apr. 1826), 205–39. See also p. 555 below.

the thin anonymity of an *Edinburgh Review* article to pronounce that the Bible had been designed to teach religion, not science: it was 'not intended to preclude enquiry, or to supersede the exercise of our natural faculties... on subjects within their reach'.[277]

The other current was less political, and, for some years, less easily discerned. In every European country the early Romantic age was characterized by a reaction against the views associated with the Enlightenment.[278] In 1841 Newman described how this had affected Oxford. He wrote: 'There is... a great progress in the religious mind of our Church to something deeper and truer than satisfied the last century. I have always contended... that it is not satisfactorily accounted for by any particular movement of individuals... The poets and philosophers of the age... Sir Walter Scott, Mr Wordsworth, Mr Coleridge... all bear witness to it.' Newman added that he had wanted the Church of England to lead this movement by giving 'free scope to the feelings of awe, mystery, tenderness, reverence, devotedness'.[279] In his circle the dislike of enthusiasm characteristic of the Church of England during the eighteenth century had evaporated.[280] So had the contempt for the ages of superstition prevalent in the Enlightenment. The age of reason had ended in violence; and it was easier to look kindly on the Middle Ages once the institutional relics of medievalism had been swept away. The young Oxford clergyman who personified the emotional intensity of the Romantic age revered the early or the medieval Church: Hurrell Froude, as Newman recalled, had been a student of medieval Christianity, 'smitten with the love of the Theocratic Church'.[281] Newman and his friends were inclined to regard their own day as materialistic, godless, and too easily tempted into 'speculating wantonly on sacred subjects'.[282] They saw a danger to religious belief in some of the social and educational advances which gave the liberals such confidence. William Palmer came to Oxford from Trinity, Dublin in 1828. Looking back to that time he wrote: 'England was filled to overflowing with glory and power. Wealth flowed into her coffers from innumerable sources. The commerce of the whole world centred in her... A new generation arose which knew not God in his great works. They deemed that all those favours and blessings had come from man himself.'[283] Intellectual

---

[277] *Ed. Rev.* xlviii (Sept. 1828), 172.

[278] C. F. Harrold, 'The Oxford Movement: a reconsideration' in J. E. Baker (ed.), *The Reconsideration of Victorian Literature* (Princeton 1950), 37–8.

[279] J. H. Newman, *A Letter... to the Revd. R. W. Jelf* (1841), 27–8. For Newman's view of Coleridge's influence see *Essays Critical and Historical* (2 vols 1872) i. 268.

[280] [A. P. Stanley], 'The Oxford School', *Ed. Rev.* cliii (Apr. 1881), 310–11.

[281] Newman, *Apologia*, 34–6. These attitudes may be contrasted with those of Gaisford (or of Lord Melbourne). Gaisford, though he edited the Early Fathers from the late 1830s, is said to have dismissed their works once as 'sad rubbish': P. Sutcliffe, *Oxford University Press* (1978), 10.

[282] Newman, *P and P Sermons* viii. 69 (no. 304, 26 June 1831).

[283] Palmer (1803–85), *Narrative*, 19. For the era of 'speculative liberalism' see also J. B. Mozley, *Essays Historical and Theological* (2 vols 1878) ii. 27–8. Mozley was writing in 1844.

pride was the particular abhorrence of Palmer and his like. An anonymous publication announced in 1827: 'The virtue of paganism was strength: the virtue of Christianity is obedience.' Its senior author was Augustus Hare, who had by now taken holy orders and turned his back on his rebellious youth.[284] John Keble's *Christian Year*, which appeared in the same year and had an immense success, showed that the effects of the Romantic age and its sensibilities on Christian belief were by no means confined to Oxford. 'The Oxford [Movement's] leaders believed', wrote J. A. Froude looking back, 'that they were fighting against the spirit of the age. They were themselves most completely the creatures of their age.'[285]

Most of the intellectual leaders among the Oriel fellows responded to both of these currents of thought, and in each person the combination operated differently. Wide divergences of view resulted. Baden Powell and John Davison were both regarded as Noetics. In the year before he returned to Oriel as Professor of Geometry Baden Powell said in a sermon: 'That knowledge must always be a good thing appears to me almost self-evident.'[286] A year earlier Davison, preaching on the National Schools, had expressed a different view of education:

What is knowledge? Evil spirits have it, and in great perfection. Bad men may have it...Consider some of the objections which are entertained against the wide and general diffusion of education. Persons...neither weak in judgement, nor disinclined to benevolence...doubt its utility on this extended scale...They suspect that it tends rather to unsettle men in their proper business and duties...But the education, of which alone I profess to be the advocate, is exempted from the force of these alleged objections...To read and understand the scriptures, and to be initiated in the essential doctrines therein taught, is the basis of that learning which our National Schools inculcate. Unity in the Church of God; duty to parents; obedience to magistrates; fidelity to masters; these are precepts of Christianity, and our National Schools enforce them.[287]

Newman later wrote of Whately: 'He...opened my mind, and taught me ...to use my reason...I became very intimate with him in 1825.' Yet, even at this time, there were divergences of tone between the two.[288] In his sermons during 1825 Newman warned his hearers against their exceptional exposure to temptation from living in 'an age and country in which, more than in any other, men have the opportunity of what is called rising in life'.[289] He

[284] [A. and J. Hare], *Guesses at Truth, by two brothers* (2 vols 1827) i. 1.

[285] Froude, *Short Studies* iv (1883), 166.

[286] Baden Powell, *The Advance of Knowledge* (1826), 3: sermon preached 27 Apr. 1826.

[287] John Davison, *Remains and Occasional Publications* (1840), 236, 239. Sermon preached 11 Sept. 1825.

[288] Newman, *Apologia*, 23; Newman, *AW* 66; Newman to Whately, 14 Nov. 1826, with Newman's note, 10 Nov. 1860; to William Mansell, 10 Oct. 1852, in *LDN* i. 307, xv. 175–9.

[289] Newman, *P and P Sermons* vii. 58 (no. 53, 23 Jan. 1825).

condemned 'an irreligious veneration of the mere intellectual powers'.[290] In the following year he used his first University Sermon to warn against the dangers of scientific research: 'As the principles of science are...more fully developed, and become more independent of the religious system, there is much danger lest the philosophical school should be found to separate from the Christian Church, and at length disown the parent to whom it has been so greatly indebted. And this evil has in a measure befallen us.'[291] In his *Apologia* Newman recalled his article on poetry in the *London Review* of January 1829, and 'how dissatisfied' Whately had been with it.[292] One passage ran: 'With Christians a poetical view of things is a duty; we are bid to colour all things with hues of faith, to see a Divine meaning in every event...The virtues peculiarly Christian are especially poetical—meekness, gentleness, compassion, contentment, modesty, not to mention the devotional virtues.'[293]

These examples are taken from a period of four years starting in January 1825. During these years such divergences were not disruptive. Oxford's young intellectuals took care not to inflame too many sensitivities. In October 1828, when Pusey was seeking the Hebrew chair and assuring Lloyd of his orthodoxy, he wrote that he would not preach on issues where his High-Church views clashed with the position of the Evangelicals.[294] Some of Whately's writings startled old-fashioned readers;[295] but there was no doctrinal laxity in his plea for disestablishment. It was indeed presented as reinforcing orthodoxy. Once it could be said that no one had been subjected 'to Christian ecclesiastical discipline...except by his own choice', a well-known principle would apply: 'Those who *choose* to become, or to continue, members of any...club or institution should make up their minds either to conform to the regulations to which they have thus freely subjected themselves, or else to withdraw.'[296] Dispersed though the younger intellectuals were across the liberal-to-anti-liberal spectrum, they all had one attitude in common: none of them greatly respected the views of their seniors. The older fellows regarded the preservation of the Church establishment, and of the social system which it supported, as falling outside the area of discussion. They were resolved to overlook its manifest imperfections. J. H. Newman's youngest brother, Francis, recorded in old age a conversation which had taken place soon after his election to a Balliol fellowship. The eminent mathematician John Brinkley had been made Bishop of Cloyne.

[290] Ibid. i. 52 (no. 83, 12 June 1825).
[291] Newman, *Fifteen Sermons*, 14 (no. 151, 2 July 1826).
[292] Newman, *Apologia*, 23.
[293] Newman, *Essays Critical and Historical* i. 23.
[294] To Lloyd, 6 Oct. 1828, PHL LBV 108/10. For the relationship between the Noetics and those who later became Tractarians see Mark Pattison's review of Mozley, *Reminiscences*, *Academy* 1 July 1882, 1c.
[295] J. H. Overton, *The Church in England* (2 vols 1897) ii. 311.
[296] R. Whately, *Letters on the Church by an Episcopalian* (1826), 71.

Francis Newman remarked to Balliol's senior resident fellow that Brinkley's mathematical skill hardly seemed proof of the 'spiritual qualities' needed in a bishop. His senior responded:

When you are older you will know how very undesirable it would be for ministers of state to fancy they could sit in judgement on clergymen, and, as from above, could pronounce that one surpassed another in spirituality or in any quality properly ecclesiastical. No! They may judge rightly of men's intellect; but happily they stop there.[297]

This was not a position which the young high-flyers could accept. Although Keble feared 'liberalistic tyranny' he was almost as doubtful about the benefits of establishment as Whately.[298] Arnold was moving towards the notion of broadening the establishment to include all Christian sects.[299]

E. B. Pusey also broke free from the recent past, though in a particularly indirect and confusing way. Gladstone used to say later that during his undergraduate years Pusey had been 'eyed with suspicion...as leaning to rationalism'.[300] The suspicions were mistaken. Although a strong liberal in politics, and 'a desperate radical' to Harriett Newman, Pusey was opposed to religious rationalism. It is significant, however, that he attributed its spread among the Lutheran theologians of Germany, not to any new liberal notions, but to what he called 'dead orthodoxy': yesterday's men had prepared the ground for the evil.[301] Newman was equally unwilling to accept his seniors' views. By the later 1820s proposals for Catholic Emancipation, that is, for permitting Roman Catholics to sit in Parliament, had become a recurrent feature of the parliamentary scene. They were always opposed by Oxford's Tory majority, who were solidly anti-Catholic. Indeed support for Catholic Emancipation was a touchstone of liberalism. When the annual petition opposing it came before Convocation 'in 1828 or 1827' Newman voted in the minority against petitioning. He wrote in the *Apologia* that he had done so, partly because he had been impressed by Whately's views on the separation of Church and state, and partly from dislike of 'the bigoted "two-bottle orthodox"'. Newman was no liberal; but, like the other

---

[297] *Memories*, 67. F. W. Newman resigned his fellowship in 1830, as he was no longer willing to subscribe to the Articles and thus could not take his MA. He became a prominent Unitarian.

[298] Keble to A. P. Perceval, 25 June 1827, 25 Mar. 1829, PHL LBV 11/28.

[299] Arnold to F. C. Blackstone, 14 Mar. 1828, Stanley, *Arnold* i. 77.

[300] Morley, *Gladstone* i. 57. Newman, in Gladstone's account, had been suspected 'as a low churchman'.

[301] LDN ii. 62; E. B. Pusey, *An Historical Enquiry into the Probable Causes of the Rationalist Character lately Predominant in the Theology of Germany* (pt 1, May 1828); Liddon, *Pusey* i. 164-5, 171, 176-7; E. B. Pusey, *Collegiate and Professorial Discipline* (1854), 53-4. In 1848 Pusey withdrew the 1828 study, and the sequel published in 1830, from sale and 'assiduously acquired the remaining copies': L. Frappell, '"Science" in the service of orthodoxy' in P. Butler (ed.), *Pusey Rediscovered* (1983), 1. In his will (1875) Pusey expressed a wish that neither study should be republished: Liddon, *Pusey* i. 176.

young fellows who were helping to make the pace, he questioned his seniors' traditional assumptions and disliked their self-indulgent habits. He had no wish to defend the existing order and the privileged classes: he did not intend, as he wrote a few years later, 'to make...life easy to the rich and indolent'.[302] The young men were far from being of one mind; but each of them was closer in outlook to the others than to the majority of the heads and older fellows.

By 1828 it was generally thought that Oxford's future lay with the liberals. Whately was a more dominating figure than any of those who expressed doubts about the liberal tenets. Keble left Oxford in 1823, while Hurrell Froude did not become a fellow of Oriel until 1826. It was not known that Newman, after his illness in November 1827 and the death of his sister Mary a few weeks later, had began to turn against liberalism.[303] In January 1828 he and Pusey overrode Froude's pleas to them to banish 'the pride of talent' and 'an ignoble secular ambition' from Oriel by bringing Keble back as Provost.[304] They judged that Edward Hawkins, one of the Noetics, would be more effective in dealing with the college's fashionable set; and their votes, which Pusey later regretted bitterly, helped to elect Hawkins to the provostship.[305] During these years the most substantial statements of the anti-liberal position came not from Oxford, but from Hugh James Rose, who became Christian Advocate of Cambridge University in 1829.[306] Newman still conveyed a fairly orthodox impression, as this passage from his Easter sermon to the Oriel undergraduates in 1827 shows:

So much do institutions such as ours...unavoidably bear the appearance of mere seats of learning and science that those who do not know us well may think our spiritual office lost in our literary occupations...I entreat you to account otherwise ...Believe that we consider our offices in this place, not as of this world, but as important stations in the church of Christ to which we have been called by Christ himself. Account of us as thinking much and deeply of your eternal interests, as watching over your souls as those who must give account.[307]

Those present may not all have appreciated the intensity of conviction and imaginative power which underlay these orthodox statements. 'I have

[302] Newman, Apologia, 26. J. H. Newman, Tract 1 (Sept. 1833), ed. A. Stephenson (Didcot 1985), 16.

[303] Apologia, 26.

[304] Newman's account of Froude's view: Newman, AW 91.

[305] Newman to Pusey, 29 June 1882, to Lord Blachford, 4 Nov. 1884, in LDN xxx. 107, 432; I. Williams, Autobiography (1892), 48–9; Pusey, Sermon at the Opening of Keble College Chapel (1876), 24. For Newman's approval of Hawkins's early reforms see Newman to Rickards, 6 Feb. 1829, in LDN ii. 117–18.

[306] See H. J. Rose, Cambridge Commencement Sermon, 2 July 1826, 'The tendency of prevalent opinions about knowledge considered', Eight Sermons... (1831), 183–206; Rose, The State of the Protestant Religion in Germany (1825). Pusey's Historical Enquiry (n. 301), was a reply to Rose.

[307] Newman, Sermons, 1824–1843 i (1991), ed. P. Murray, 340–1 (no. 160, 15 Apr. 1827).

Froude's authority', Newman told Blanco White in March 1828, 'for lowering the intellectual powers into handmaids of our moral nature.'[308] Even
this remark did not go beyond the orthodoxy of the time. Howley, when
Bishop of London, stressed that Christian faith required 'the prostration of
the human understanding before the revelation of God'.[309]

The liberal advance, though slow, was uninterrupted. Oxford's liberals
'met for a time', as Newman later wrote, 'with no effectual hindrance...
except (what indeed at the moment was most effectual, but not of an
intellectual character) the thorough-going toryism and traditionary Church-
of-Englandism of the great body of the colleges and Convocation'.[310] In
February 1826 one of the University's parliamentary seats went to a candidate acceptable to the liberals, T. G. Bucknall-Estcourt.[311] In 1827 the first
Drummond Professor, Nassau Senior, gave his opening political economy
lectures. In accepting the Drummond chair the University had agreed to the
donor's stipulation that political economy would be 'retained in its proper
place...as the servant, but not as the supplanter, of revelation'.[312] Nassau
Senior seems to have interpreted this requirement with some freedom. His
doctrines entailed a liberal interpretation of the Gospels. 'The pursuit of
wealth', he said, 'is, to the mass of mankind, the great source of moral improvement.'[313] When the repeal of the Test and Corporation Acts was proposed in
February 1828 Pusey was delighted. He thought those Acts 'both in their
means and end a disgrace and deterrent to religion. They, more than anything else, keep alive the bitterness of party spirit among Christians, agreeing
in the same essentials of faith, in England.'[314] Russell challenged the University to defend the Acts by petitioning against this concession of equal
civil rights to Nonconformists; but no petition was forthcoming;[315] and in
March the opponents of Catholic Emancipation failed to show their old
strength. Their annual anti-Emancipation petition to the House of Commons was adopted by a majority of less than two to one, four heads, all of
them under 50, voting in the minority.[316] Outside Oxford the liberal tide
was flowing still more strongly. A survey conducted in the mid-1820s by a
Unitarian minister suggested that Oxford and Cambridge were the only

---

[308] 1 Mar. 1828, in *LDN* ii. 60.
[309] See Pusey, *Collegiate and Professorial Discipline*, 73.
[310] Newman, *Apologia*, Note A, 256. This note first appeared in the 1865 edition.
[311] Ward, *Victorian Oxford*, 68; Liddon, *Pusey* i. 91.
[312] H. Drummond to Grenville, 8 June 1825, in OUA Convocation Register, 1820–1828, 347.
[313] N. W. Senior, *Introductory Lecture on Political Economy* (1827), 12–13. For Newman's
rejection of this view, Newman, *Idea*, 85–9.
[314] To Maria Barker, 21 Feb., Liddon, *Pusey* i. 133; D. Forrester, *Young Dr. Pusey* (1989),
14–15.
[315] *Parl. Deb.* 26 Feb. 1828 (Russell), 25 Apr. (Lyndhurst), NS xviii. 688, xix. 118; Ward,
Victorian Oxford, 69–70.
[316] Ward, 70–1; Lloyd to Peel, 13 Mar. 1828, Peel, *Memoirs*, ed. Lord Mahon and E. Cardwell
(2 vols 1856–7) i. 311.

universities in the world to impose religious tests generally: it seemed indeed that, except in the University of Pisa, no such tests were imposed even on those enrolled for divinity degrees.[317] Brougham made an able defence in February 1828 of the decision to have no theological instruction in his new 'London university';[318] and in June it was announced that King's College, London, the answer by the Church to that 'godless academy in Gower Street', would impose no religious tests on its students.[319] By September Lord Eldon had concluded gloomily that Oxford was no longer a reliable ally in the anti-Catholic cause.[320] In November, when a disappointed Tory applicant complained at the appointment of 'a relation of that great radical, Lord Radnor' to Oxford's Hebrew chair, Wellington replied: 'I appointed Mr Pusey because I have reason to believe that he is the best scholar.'[321] By now the world of the Regency had been left far behind. In 1812 the liberals under Copleston had been too few to demand a scrutiny on the anti-Catholic petition; and a year earlier Peter Elmsley had been passed over for the Regius chair of Greek because he was a Whig who had written for the *Edinburgh Review*.[322]

Despite all of this, Oxford's liberals were still in a minority and no sudden crisis was expected. Newman's 'effectual hindrance' to liberalism had not been removed. The champions of 'traditionary Church-of-Englandism' distrusted anyone who did not regard defence of the Establishment as his primary duty. The view which they abominated was the one proclaimed by Brougham in April 1825 during his inaugural address as Lord Rector of Glasgow University:

Real knowledge never prompted either turbulence or unbelief; but its progress is the forerunner of liberality and enlightened toleration...for men will no longer suffer themselves to be led blindfold in ignorance, so will they no more yield to the vile principle of judging and treating their fellow creatures, not according to the intrinsic merit of their actions, but according to the accidental and involuntary coincidence of their opinions. The great truth has finally gone forth...that man shall no more render account to man for his belief, over which he has himself no control. Henceforward, nothing shall prevail upon us to praise or to blame anyone for that which he can no more change than he can the hue of his skin, or the height of his stature.[323]

---

[317] J. Yates, *Thoughts on the Advancement of Academical Education* (2nd edn. 1827) viii. 24–7, 42, 44–6. See also *Ed. Rev.* lx (1834–5), 220, 432. For absence of tests in Trinity College, Dublin see Whately, *Whately* ii. 37–8; and in Scotland see *Parl. Deb.* 24 Mar. 1834, 3S xxii. 583 (Spring-Rice). For 1733–89 see pp. 78, 89 below.

[318] *The Times* 28 Feb. 1828, suppl. 1e.

[319] Ibid. 23 June 1828, suppl. 1c. F. J. C. Hearnshaw, *King's, London, 1828–1928* (1929), 51. The decision was commended in the *Athenaeum* 26 Nov. 1828, 905.

[320] To Lord Stowell (nd), H. Twiss, *Eldon* (3 vols 1844) iii. 56.

[321] Liddon, *Pusey* i. 188. The appointment was attacked in the ultra-Tory Sunday paper *The Age*: *LDN* ii. 115.

[322] Ward, *Victorian Oxford*, 38; Lloyd-Jones, *Blood for the Ghosts*, 80. Elmsley had given up contributing to the *Edinburgh* because of its 'irreligious and Jacobinical tone': Butler, *Butler*, i. 88.

[323] 6 Apr. 1825, H. Brougham, *Speeches* (4 vols 1838) iii. 96–7. For Gladstone's objection to this statement (1828) see Morley, *Gladstone* i. 81.

To a traditionalist the University's liberals looked like Brougham's covert allies. They were also accused of intellectual snobbery. Oriel's high-flyers naturally enjoyed little popularity with the more earth-bound members of other colleges; and a note praising them in the *Edinburgh Review* did not improve their standing in Oxford. Their common-room talk was reported with distaste to 'stink of logic'.[324] To a section of Oxford opinion 'liberal' was a term of abuse.[325] The 'bigoted "two-bottle orthodox"' seemed safe for a good few years.

In politics, as a prime minister of a later time remarked, 'the expected does not happen.'[326] In June 1828 Daniel O'Connell, the insurgent Irish leader, seized the chance of a by-election in Clare and achieved a political masterstroke. He stood, as a Roman Catholic, for the vacancy and was elected triumphantly. The law which prevented him from taking his seat did not prevent his election for it. Hitherto Wellington, the Prime Minister, had opposed Catholic Emancipation. He now saw that, if he was to retain any control over Ireland, he would have to induce his supporters to retreat. Catholic Emancipation had to be forced through Parliament at once. He could not achieve that without the help of Peel, who led the Commons and sat for Oxford University. The Duke persuaded Peel to stay in office and help in making this reversal; and he kept his plan secret until the last moment, so that Peel's letter to the Vice-Chancellor resigning his university seat did not arrive until the first day of the parliamentary session (5 February 1829). It was read to Convocation immediately after the adoption of the usual anti-Emancipation petition, and as Peel was revealing the plan to the Commons in the Address debate.[327] The shock among Oxford's MAs was immense. Peel had been elected by the University twelve years earlier as its anti-Catholic champion, and as a reliable counterweight to its pro-Catholic Chancellor.[328] 'I cannot doubt', he wrote in his resignation letter to the Vice-Chancellor, 'that the resistance which I have hitherto offered to the claims of the Roman Catholics has been one of the main grounds upon which I have been entitled to the confidence and support of a very large body of my constituents.'[329] The country parsons and some of the older fellows were enraged at Oxford's Protestant champion turning round and, as they thought, betraying them. The position of Newman and the others who had declined to support anti-Catholic petitions differed a little from this. When it became known that Peel was to be nominated for re-election, they

[324] *Ed. Rev.* xxxvi (Oct. 1821), 254 n.; Newman, *AW* 73; Newman, *Apologia*, 156; Palmer, *Narrative of Events*, 20; Tuckwell, *Pre-Tractarian Oxford*, 59, 61.
[325] See [Giles], *Reply to an Expostulatory Letter*, 9.
[326] H. H. Asquith, *Letters to Venetia Stanley*, ed. M. and E. Brock (1982), 61.
[327] Gash, *Peel*, 561.
[328] Ibid. 212–18.
[329] 4 Feb. 1829, Bodl. MS Top. b. 23, fo 46.

GRAND CONCERT,

UNDER THE PATRONAGE OF THE

REV. THOMAS GROWLER,

For the Benefit of Mr. PEELigrini,

ON WEDNESDAY, FEBRUARY 25, 1829.

ACT I.

OVERTURE	"Military Symphony."	HAYDN.
TRIO	"When Arthur first in Court began."	
	Signor PEELIGRINI, PHILLPOTTI, and ISCARIOTTI.	
SONG	"There's no *place* like *Home*."	BISHOP.
	Signor PEELIGRINI.	
SONG	"I care for nobody—no not I,	
	"And nobody cares for me."	D—R of C—— C——.
BALLAD	"How happy could I be with either."	BEGGAR'S OPERA.
	PHILLPOTTI.	
GRAND CONCERTO (*Jews' Harp obligato*)		Mr. JUDAS PEELIGRINI.
CHORUS	"The juice of the Orange is gone,	
	"Then let's make the best of the Peel."	
	By the Common Room of C—— C——.	

ACT II.

OVERTURE		JUDAS (not) MACCABÆUS.
COMIC SONG	"Cautious ever, Cautious ever."	
	B——P of O——D.	
ARIA	"Largo al *Factotum*."	
	Duke of W——N.	
SONG	"Turn again."	THE LATE POPE.
	Signor BLANCK WHITO.	
FANTASIA	"*Bass*-Viol."	SIGNOR DAWSONI.
SONG	"Ce m'est égal."	PHILPOTTI.
SONG	"The Soldier tir'd of *wars alarms*."	
	Duke of W——N.	
SONG	"Let justice the traitor to punishment bring"	
	CONNELLI.	
BALLAD	"No Churchman am I for to rail and to write."	
	B——P of O——D.	

FINALE—FULL CHORUS—"Uprouse ye then, my merry merry men."

SIGNORE PROTESTANTE.

FIGURE 1.1 The by-election, February 1829: 'Grand concert'. Cast, as depicted, in order of appearance: *Thomas Vowler Short*, Senior Censor, Christ Church, most fervent supporter of *Peel*, who retains the home secretaryship by turning 'green' and betraying Ireland's Orangemen; *Henry Phillpotts*, Dean of Chester, hitherto a ferocious anti-Catholic; unprincipled and in search of a mitre (appointed Bishop of Exeter by Wellington, Nov. 1830); *Samuel Smith*, Dean of Christ Church, lukewarm supporter of Peel, presiding over a *Common Room* divided between upholders of Protestantism and Judases; *Charles Lloyd*, Bishop of Oxford, once Peel's private tutor; no defender of the Church of England; *Wellington*, a military commander miscast as Prime Minister, who has ordered his followers to turn about; *Blanco White*, a convert from Roman Catholicism, now apparently returning to it; *George Dawson*, a Secretary to the Treasury, Peel's brother-in-law and lately his Under-secretary at the Home Office; shown by his 'ratting' to be base and vile; *Daniel O'Connell*, agitator and leader of the Irish Catholics. Peel's name in this lampoon echoes that of Niccolò Paganini, the violinist (1784–1840), who was then famous throughout Europe. Source: Christ Church Library MSS

objected to a procedure under which Oxford's MAs were required to change their minds at the behest of the government. 'To men with the least independence of spirit', in Tom Mozley's phrase, this was an intolerable demand.[330] 'It is not pro dignitate nostra', Newman wrote to a friend on 6 February, 'to have a rat our Member.'[331]

A less scrupulous statesman might have delayed his resignation until the end of the session. In Croker's view resigning was 'a democratical and unconstitutional proceeding'.[332] If Peel had been exceptionally perceptive, he would have realized that the view of Oxford's MAs obtainable from the London clubs and the fashionable colleges might be an incomplete one.[333] If he had been less proud, instead of merely giving Oxford a chance to re-elect him, he would have pressed his friends to forestall opposition by taking the necessary steps with the utmost speed. As it was, those friends hesitated for a few days and this was fatal. Peel's opponents found a personable Christ Church candidate in Sir Robert Inglis, and he polled 755 votes (including seventy-nine from Christ Church) against Peel's 609. There were unedifying scenes in which the half-stifled throng of country parsons shouted down Peel's proposer and seconder, and broke the windows of the Convocation House for air.[334] The backwoodsmen of Oxford and of many rectories had revolted against the public figures and the liberal intellectuals. Peel's supporters included two-thirds of the first-class men who had voted, fourteen professors out of twenty, all but four of the prize-men, thirty-eight out of forty MPs, and every single nobleman in the lists.[335] Newman, Keble, and Froude voted in the majority and the first two were prominent campaigners for the Evangelical Inglis. Keble was particularly well placed to influence the country clergymen, being one of them himself. The election was bitterly fought amid the mutual accusations of malpractice inseparable from such contests. Each side accused the other of abetting indiscipline by enlisting undergraduate support; and Peel's friends were said to have used their influence in nominating to benefices to put pressure on parsons.[336] Those who thought the liberal path the only safe one for Oxford were aghast. 'The clergy generally, and of Oxford especially, have cut their own throats,' Thomas Arnold concluded, 'in the judgement of all enlightened public men.'[337] Those who had always disliked, or who had turned against, a liberal

---

[330] Mozley, *Reminiscences* i. 141.

[331] To Rickards, in *LDN* ii. 118.

[332] *Correspondence and Diaries of J. W. Croker*, ed. L. J. Jennings (3 vols 1884) ii. 7. See Peel, *Memoirs* i. 338.

[333] Newman, *Historical Sketches, Third Series*, 231–2. See n. 178.

[334] N. Gash, 'Peel and the Oxford University election of 1829', *Oxoniensia* iv (1939), 162–73.

[335] Gash, *Peel*, 563. The analyses of the poll differ a little from each other. See also *The Times* 11 Mar. 1829, 3a, b, 12 Mar., 3a. From Lincoln College 41, including all the fellows, voted for Inglis: 4 for Peel: V. H. H. Green, *The Commonwealth of Lincoln College, 1427–1977* (1979), 422.

[336] *Parl. Deb.* 24 Mar. 1829, NS xx. 1415 (Lansdowne); *LDN* ii. 133–4.

[337] To J. Lowe, 16 Mar. 1829, in Stanley, *Arnold* i. 221–2.

stance were correspondingly delighted. Peel's defeat, Newman wrote, would be a great vindication for the University as 'a religious, straightforward, unpolitical body'.[338] This characterization delineated not what Oxford was in 1829, but the University which Newman wanted.[339]

The University had maintained close links with the government of the day for many years. These now began to be loosened, for what some Oxford clergymen later thought insufficient reasons.[340] Admitting a few Roman Catholics to Parliament could not endanger the Church of England; and it was romantic to suppose that ousting Peel would prevent their admission. Yet those who refused to turn about with him were not wholly mistaken in thinking themselves betrayed. Wellington and Peel had shown that, in a crisis, they did not give the interests of the Church first place. Keble was right when he implied in his election pamphlet that these two had not been compelled to act by the need to keep Ireland at peace.[341] Their reason for defying the majority of Churchmen by a sudden reversal of policy was political. To break O'Connell's power, and safeguard the electoral system which sustained them, they needed to curtail voting rights in the Irish counties. The House of Commons would not accept the curtailment unless it was accompanied by Catholic Emancipation.[342] Unwittingly the outraged Oxford parsons, by defeating Peel, were helping to expose the electoral system to new dangers; for his retreat to a close borough, by favour of a particularly notorious borough owner, advertised the system's seamy side and so made it vulnerable to attack.[343]

In that Peel's defeat marks the start of the Oxford Movement, the story of what followed it belongs largely to Chapter 7. No more than a bare outline of its more immediate consequences can be given here. It released Newman from any remaining inhibitions about liberalism, and he proclaimed his opposition to it with a promptitude which startled at least one of his friends. 'His sudden union with the most violent bigots was inexplicable to me,' Blanco White wrote later. 'Rouse all the bigotry of Kent,' Newman adjured a friend at the start of the campaign.[344] Nine days after it ended he showed in a sermon how little use he had for political economy and all that went with it. Christians, he said, should treat with 'especial caution' those pursuits which 'tend to the well-being of men in this life: the sciences, for instance, of good government, of acquiring wealth, of preventing and relieving want, and

[338] To Harriett Newman, 17 Feb. 1829, in *LDN* ii. 122.
[339] By 1854 Newman had concluded: 'Never has learned institution been more directly political...than Oxford': *Historical Sketches, Third Series*, 222.
[340] C. Wordsworth, *Scottish Ecclesiastical Journal*, i/21 (16 Sept. 1851), 195; P. B. Nockles, *The Oxford Movement in Context* (1994), 86.
[341] Keble, *Queries Addressed to Members of Convocation* (16 Feb. 1829), third query; Peel's memorandum, 12 Jan. 1829, in Peel, *Memoirs* i. 293.
[342] M. Brock, *The Great Reform Act* (1973), 53–4.
[343] Ibid. 56–7.
[344] *Autobiography of Blanco White* iii. 131; Newman to S. Rickards, 15 Feb. 1829, in *LDN* ii. 121.

the like, are... especially dangerous,... fixing, as they do, our exertions on this world as an end'.[345]

Newman had come to see Whately's views as being 'based on the pride of reason and tending towards infidelity'.[346] On 13 March 1829 he told his mother about his attitude to 'free enquiry':

Without meaning, of course, that Christianity is in itself opposed to free enquiry, still I think it *in fact* at the present time opposed to the particular form which that liberty of thought has now assumed. Christianity is of faith, modesty, lowliness, subordination; but the spirit at work against it is one of latitudinarianism, indifferentism, republicanism, and schism.... The talent of the day is against the Church. The Church party... is poor in mental endowments... On what then does it depend? On prejudice and bigotry... Moral truth is gained by patient study, by calm reflection, silently as the dew falls, unless miraculously given, and, when gained, it is transmitted by faith and by 'prejudice'...[347]

After the election, party lines were redrawn in Oxford and made much tighter. The next few years belied Matthew Arnold's notion of Oxford as 'unravaged by the fierce intellectual life of our century'. Whately resented any criticism of his views by Hawkins.[348] Newman he gave up as lost, and he took a 'humorous revenge' on this renegade who had opposed Peel, as the *Apologia* records:

Whately was considerably annoyed at me... As head of a house, he had duties of hospitality to men of all parties; he asked a set of the least intellectual men in Oxford to dinner, and men most fond of port; he made me one of this party; placed me between Provost This and Principal That, and then asked me if I was proud of my friends.... He saw, more clearly than I could do, that I was separating from his own friends for good and all.... [He] attributed my leaving his *clientela* to a wish on my part to be the head of a party myself. I do not think that this charge was deserved.[349]

The event which freed Newman to take up a leader's role was one which he certainly did not plan. Hawkins dismissed him, and his friends Hurrell Froude and Robert Wilberforce, from their Oriel tutorships. The details of this episode, and its effects on Oriel, are described in Chapter 6. The three were devoted college tutors who were later said to have bestowed 'on their pupils as much time and trouble as is usually only expected from very good private tutors'.[350] It would hardly be an exaggeration to see in their efforts

[345] Newman, *P and P Sermons* vii. 30 (no. 189, 8 Mar. 1829).

[346] See his exchange of letters with Whately, Oct. 1834, in Whately, *Whately* i. 234–40.

[347] *LDN* ii. 129–31. Newman later wrote more strongly against 'free enquiry': *Tract 85* (1838), 72–3. For his reaction to Baden Powell's Easter sermon, 1829, see Corsi, *Science and Religion*, 97. For a retrospective view see J. A. Froude, *Nemesis of Faith* (1849), 153.

[348] M. Arnold, *Essays in Criticism*, First Series (1865, 1965), preface; Whately to Hawkins, 11 Oct. 1831, OCL MS Hawkins ii. 182.

[349] Newman, *Apologia*, 26–7. Whately was Principal of St Alban Hall.

[350] Mozley, *Reminiscences* i. 229, 313–14; *Letters of Lord Blachford*, 7. Newman was less successful with idle gentlemen commoners: Newman, *AW* 89; Culler, *The Imperial Intellect*, 52–6; *LDN* xviii. 459, xxx. 409–36 (8 Oct.–14 Nov. 1884).

the germ of the modern tutorial system; but, as the quotations already given suggest, their guiding aim was not that of a modern Oxford tutor. According to his *Autobiographical Memoir*, Newman had 'held almost fiercely that secular education could be so conducted as to become a pastoral cure. He recollected that Origen had so treated it, and had by means of the classics effected the conversion of Gregory, the Apostle of Pontus, and of Athenodorus, his brother.'[351] In the post-election atmosphere tutors with such views who had campaigned for Inglis were doomed to clash with a Provost who had been one of Peel's most prominent supporters. Although Hawkins showed excessive rigidity, his difficulties were real. He had inherited a policy of attracting undergraduates from the country's leading families.[352] He did not want influential parents to suspect that their sons were being exposed to religious influences which they might regard as excessive or unsuitable. The dismissals were, however, an error which did Oriel serious damage. They also had an effect far beyond it.

Freed from tutorial work, Newman became the chief spokesman of the opponents of liberalism in Oxford. His doubts about the propriety of scientific studies had hardened into outright opposition to them. In October 1830 he said in a sermon: 'Sciences conversant with experiments on the material creation tend to make men forget the existence of spirit and of the Lord of spirits.'[353] By this date he was critical not only of some university studies, but of all attempts to link Christian belief with attempts at social amelioration. On 6 March 1831 he told the University:

In the more advanced periods of society a greater innocence and probity of conduct and courtesy of manners will prevail; but these, though they have sometimes been accounted illustrations of the peculiar Christian character, have in fact no necessary connection with it. For why should they not be referred to that mere advancement of civilization and education of the intellect which is surely competent to produce them?...Christianity professes to prepare us for the next life. It is nothing strange then, if principles, which avowedly direct the science of morals to present beneficial results in the community, should show to the greater advantage in their own selected field of action. Exalted virtue cannot be fully appreciated...on the public field of life, because it addresses itself to an unseen tribunal.

Newman made clear in this sermon that he now regarded liberalism as a far greater threat than either 'traditionary Church-of-Englandism' or the emotional self-indulgence of some Evangelicals. He took it as an assumption that 'the freedom of thought, enlightened equitableness, and amiableness, which

---

[351] Newman, *AW* 91. See also Newman to C. P. Golightly, 3 Jan. 1831, in *LDN* ii. 307.

[352] Ward, *Victorian Oxford*, 20. For Pattison's view of the results of this clash, see *Memoirs*, 56–7.

[353] Newman, *P and P Sermons* i. 225 (no. 264, 24 Oct. 1830). I am grateful to Prof. Valerie Pitt, for help over this sermon. For Newman's view later see 'Catholicus', 'The Tamworth Reading Room', letter 7, *The Times* 27 Feb. 1841, 5e. For Keble's view see Mozley, *Reminiscences* i. 179.

are the offspring of civilization, differ far more even than the piety of form or of emotion from the Christian spirit, as being "not pleasant to God, forasmuch as they spring not of faith in Jesus Christ, yea, rather, doubtless, [as] having the nature of sin"'.[354] Gladstone heard this sermon and noted it as containing 'much singular, not to say objectionable, matter'.[355]

An effective refutation of 'the liberalism of the day...could not be done', as Newman wrote later, 'by negatives. It was necessary...to have a positive Church theory.'[356] Now that the Church did not have the firm support of the state in the University and elsewhere, on what authority could it rely? Newman's answer is given in one of his letters of August 1830: '*Moral* truth is not acceptable to man's heart; it must be enforced by authority of some kind...A system of Church government was *actually established* by the Apostles, and is thus the *legitimate* enforcement of Christian truth. The liberals know this—and are in every possible manner trying to break it up.'[357] According to this account of the apostolical Church those who did not recognize the bishops' authority, as it had been conferred through the apostolical succession, were beyond the pale. Preaching some months earlier, Newman had announced: 'We are the English Catholics...There is not a Dissenter living but, inasmuch and so far as he dissents, is in a sin.'[358] A number of the bishops did not take a high apostolical view of their position, as Newman well knew, so that he was involved paradoxically in exalting the episcopal office without any assurance of support in this from the episcopacy. His doctrines were also liable to create difficulties in both the University itself and the country rectories. Oxford could maintain subscription to the Articles only by insisting that this did not entail membership of the Church of England;[359] and a view of holy orders which allowed the Church to 'get on stilts', while it might be popular at a time of confusion and disillusionment, was unlikely to remain acceptable in the longer run.[360] The sudden hardening of the opposition to liberalism made it difficult to remember that many Oxford clergymen did not belong naturally in the camp of the anti-liberals: such people were likely to take the University gradually towards what came to be known later as a 'Broad-Church' position. The 'Apostolicals' were a divisive force in the University and the

[354] Newman, *Fifteen Sermons*, 40, 42 (no. 288). Quotation from the Thirty-nine Articles, Article 13, 'Of works before justification'.

[355] Gladstone, *Diaries* i. 347. Gladstone also heard Newman preach on 25 Sept. 1831 (ibid. 384); he thought this 'a good sermon'. Newman had preached it first in 1824 (no. 24).

[356] Newman, *Apologia*, 100. See also Froude, *Remains* iii. 192 (passage written in 1833).

[357] To Simeon Lloyd Pope, 15 Aug. 1830, in *LDN* ii. 265. Newman's *Tract I* (Sept. 1833; repr. ed. A. Stephenson 1985) is based on this theme. For Arnold's prediction, 18 Nov. 1836, that 'the priestcraft heresy' would end in 'pure popery' see Stanley, *Arnold* ii. 53.

[358] Newman, *P and P Sermons* iii. 191, 202 (no. 218, 29 Nov. 1829). See also H. Froude's letter, 28 Aug. 1830, *Remains* i. 244.

[359] Pusey to Gladstone, 25 Apr. 1834, Liddon, *Pusey* i. 293. See also n. 21 above.

[360] See n. 24 above.

Church. Although they hardly acknowledged this even to themselves, theirs was a partisan stance; and they had no solid ground for believing that they could establish themselves as the majority party.

Moreover, the anti-liberals were not always careful to stress the English character of their catholicism. In a sermon of 1831 Hurrell Froude called the Anglican clergy 'ministers of the Catholic church'.[361] Most of the 'bigots' whose votes had ousted Peel did not see the parson's role in that light. Some of them may even have believed in the linkage to which Edward Irving referred when he spoke of 'papal apostasy and its even more abandoned sister, Protestant liberality'.[362] The doctrines which Newman and Froude had adopted were bound to be as unacceptable to liberals from the Oxford stable as they could be to any bigot. Arnold's first volume of sermons, published in 1829, included a comparison between 'careless and unspiritual churchmen' and 'zealous and holy dissenters' much to the latter's advantage. To Arnold the bond of union between one member of the Church of England and another was, in itself, 'earthly and unimportant': it was the 'union of goodness and holiness' which mattered. Whately explored various manifestations of prejudice and superstition in his *Errors of Romanism*, which appeared in the following year.[363] These were, however, no more than hints of future trouble. 'Objectionable matter' such as Gladstone noted was of no great account while the tide ran strongly against liberalism.

Once Peel had been ejected, Oxford's liberals knew what they had to face; but they had no thought of giving up the fight. As members of the Hebdomadal Board Whately and Hawkins were nearer to the levers of power than were the newly emerging anti-liberal leaders. Both of them sat on a committee, appointed on 23 March 1829, to revise the examination statute.[364] Whately wanted to modernize the curriculum on grounds of both prudence and principle. Preaching in October 1830 for the National School in the little town where he was rector he said:

There are but two ways of preserving the established order of things; one is to keep the lower orders in a state of ignorance and degradation; the other that the higher orders should avail themselves of their own ample opportunities to cultivate their own minds and acquire a superiority of knowledge and intelligence. Which of these two is the more honourable procedure is a question which need not be discussed, because...the choice is not allowed us. It *is* in the power of the higher orders to improve their own education: to keep the mass of the people in a state of blind and brutish ignorance is not...I wonder not much...that some should think the education of the poor an evil: I do wonder at their not perceiving it to be *inevitable*...The

[361] Froude, *Remains* ii. 237 (Sermon XVIII).

[362] 'Last sermon in the Caledonian Church', 29 Apr. 1827, in *Collected Writings of Edward Irving*, ed. G. Carlyle (5 vols 1864–5) iii. 507.

[363] Arnold, *Sermons* (3 vols 1829–34) i. 93–4; R. Whately, *The Errors of Romanism Traced to their Origin in Human Nature* (1830).

[364] Ward, *Victorian Oxford*, 58.

main question is *how* they shall be educated and *by whom*. That many of the most zealous anti-Christians are strenuous promoters of the education of the people is undeniable. They think that, as men become enlightened, Christianity will die away *because it is not true*. Those who are of the opposite opinion ought to show it in their conduct. For our opponents are surely right in regarding education as favourable to the detection of error and establishment of truth.[365]

Whately succeeded Nassau Senior in the political economy chair in 1829. With this subject, as he told a friend, 'religious truth...appears to me to be intimately connected, at this time especially...For it seems to me that before long political economists, of some sort or other, must govern the world... Now anti-Christians are striving very hard to have this science to themselves, and to interweave it with their own notions.'[366] In his *Introductory Lectures on Political Economy* Whately expressed a view of the subject very different from Newman's:

That political economy should have been complained of as hostile to religion will probably be regarded a century hence...with the same wonder, almost approaching to incredulity, with which we of the present day hear of men sincerely opposing, on religious grounds, the Copernican system.

Whately looked towards British universities

Sending forth into the world, to assume the office of legislators and directors of public affairs...men qualified for the high profession they are to follow by a preparation analogous to what is required even of the humblest artisan.[367]

These were persuasive pleas, because the conviction that the upper classes would not hold their own in the new Britain without understanding something of its workings was growing in Oxford. In March 1830 William Mills, the first holder of the revived moral philosophy chair, told his hearers 'very impressively that unless they applied themselves to useful knowledge the lower classes would get over their heads; in short, that the scouts would become gentlemen commoners, and the bed-makers countesses, unless they could keep that start by education which they had obtained by rank and affluence'.[368] In February 1831 Buckland, as James Ramsay noted, 'earnestly recommended us to study mineralogy and such things lest, in the present march of intellect, we should...find ourselves more ignorant than our shoeblack'.[369]

---

[365] R. Whately, *The Duty of those who Disapprove the Education of the Poor...* (1830); sermon preached at Halesworth, 7 Oct. 1830. For an instance of aristocratic opposition to popular education, see A. Aspinall, *Politics and the Press* (1949), 12.

[366] Whately, *Whately* i. 66–7.

[367] R. Whately, *Introductory Lectures on Political Economy* (1831), 29–30, 236–7.

[368] James Robert Hope to his sister, in R. Ornsby, *J. R. Hope-Scott* (2 vols 1884) i. 27.

[369] Ramsay, Diary, 1 Feb. 1831. Lord Derby echoed this in Oxford, June 1855: *Acland*, ed. Acland, 173. See also *QJE* iv (Oct. 1832), 197–8; Baden Powell, *The Present State and Future Prospects of Mathematical and Physical Studies* (1832), 38–9.

Whately dominated the committee on the examination statute and there the liberals achieved some success. A suggestion that examiners should be allowed to take a candidate's moral character into account was defeated, and the recommendation for written papers accepted.[370] The broadening of the classical papers so that they included ancient history and allowed reference to modern authors has already been mentioned. This did not bring the syllabus very close to political economy, however; and the diehards prevented any further inclusion of natural science in it.[371] Whately and his friends might have been a little more successful if they could have resisted the temptation to ridicule their opponents' arguments. Their lampoons on Inglis's supporters and on the examination diehards were hilarious, but wounding.[372] No tactics could have produced a decisive success for Oxford's liberals, however: the tide in the University was flowing too strongly against them. Whately, Arnold and Hawkins had become national figures, receiving in May 1830 the liberal accolade of being libelled in *John Bull*;[373] but, while the revolution of July 1830 in France strengthened liberals elsewhere, in Oxford it merely deepened the rift between them and their opponents.[374] In that year Milman's *History of the Jews* appeared, only to be attacked by the High Church and withdrawn from sale;[375] and Pusey began his retreat from liberalism. When the second part of his study of the German rationalists was published in May he gained the approval of the *Edinburgh Review* for maintaining that Episcopal churches were as vulnerable as Presbyterian to the ravages of rationalism; but by November he had concluded that the German theologians were in a worse case than he had supposed.[376] At Eton Gladstone had written a revolutionary poem in praise of the Cato Street conspirators:

> I hymn the gallant and the good
> From Tyler down to Thistlewood.[377]

He was now a rising Tory star in the Oxford Union. In November 1830 Wellington was defeated and the Whigs succeeded to office. This completed the change of attitude in Oxford which the Peel by-election had begun. The

---

[370] *Memorial Annexed to Report of the Committee Appointed 23 March 1829*, Bodl. G. A. Oxon. b. 21. See also Ch. 11.

[371] Corsi, *Science and Religion*, 112–19.

[372] *Circular Letter of Advice and Justification from the Committee for Ensuring the Election of Sir Robert Inglis* (1829); *Address to the Lower Division of the House of Convocation* (1830).

[373] *John Bull* 2 May 1830, 141a, b; 9 May, 148c, 149a. Arnold was dissuaded from bringing a libel action: Stanley, *Arnold* i. 233–4.

[374] Cf Arnold to G. Cornish, 24 Aug. 1830 (Stanley, *Arnold* i. 235) with Froude to Newman, 1 Aug. (*LDN* ii. 260).

[375] Overton, *Church in England* ii. 313.

[376] Pusey, *An Historical Enquiry*, pt 2, 15; *Ed. Rev.* liv (Aug.–Dec. 1831), 252; Pusey to Tholuck, 8 Nov. 1830, PHL LBV 127/7.

[377] John Chandos, *Boys Together: English public schools, 1800–1864* (1985), 218.

University's Tories no longer saw salvation in any government. Gladstone's stance in the Union, where he condemned first Wellington's cabinet and then their opponents and successors, was characteristic both of his fellow undergraduates and of their mentors. The Tractarians-to-be were confirmed in their suspicions that the Establishment tied the Church either to trimmers or to its outright foes, when what was needed was a firm stand on principle. On 28 November 1830 Hurrell Froude wrote to his father:

I cannot but believe that the Church will surprise people a little when its latent spirit has been aroused, and when the reasons for caution have been removed by disconnecting it with the state. And, though I am not blind to the evils which must accompany such a convulsion, so that I would not for the world have a hand in bringing it about, I own it is not with unmixed apprehension that I anticipate its approach.[378]

In December William Wilberforce wrote to a friend:

It is curious to observe the effects of the Oxford system in producing on the minds of young men a strong propensity to...tory principles. From myself and the general tenor of our family and social circle, it might have been supposed that my children, though averse to party, would be inclined to adopt liberal...principles, but all three of my Oxonians are strong friends to high Church and King doctrines.[379]

He did not exaggerate. On 2 January 1831 Samuel Wilberforce, whose supposedly Cromwellian principles had given the United Debating Society such trouble a few years earlier, wrote to a friend in terms tinged with the intransigence of Charles I. He expressed his forebodings at 'Britain's demi-radical government with the true march-of-mind spirit, and the whole of Europe shaken to its base by the volcanic throes of revolution'.[380]

When the agrarian disturbances began late in 1830 the university authorities swore in special constables; but the introduction of the Parliamentary Reform Bill on 1 March 1831 caused little alarm in Oxford. 'What great interest has [the Church]', Newman asked a friend on 13 March, 'that things should remain as they are?'[381] The petition of April 1831, which was opposed in Convocation by a sizeable minority, ventured on criticism of the Bill, only, in Hawkins's phrase, with 'great mildness';[382] but Parliament

---

[378] To Archdeacon Froude, in P. Brendon, *H. Froude* (1974), 105.

[379] To William Gray, 31 Dec. 1830, in *Private Papers of William Wilberforce*, ed. A. M. Wilberforce (1897), 157.

[380] To P. Boyle, in Ashwell, *Wilberforce* i. 59–60. See also Newsome, *The Parting of Friends*, 7, 212. According to Ashwell (i. 45) Samuel Wilberforce's 'very high toryism' originated in the events of 1829.

[381] Cox, 134–5; the absence of a petition against the Bill from Oxford was mentioned in the Commons, 30 Mar. 1831: *Parl. Deb.* 3S iii. 1192 (Denman); Newman to J. W. Bowden, in *LDN* ii. 317.

[382] Hawkins to Inglis, 22 Apr. 1831, OCL 1152. Not presented because of dissolution: Bodl. MS Top. b. 23, fos 372–3. The petition of Mar. 1832 was stronger: HBM 1823–33, 142–3, 173–4.

was dissolved on the day on which Hawkins wrote, and the government's sweeping electoral victory soon dispersed this complacency. In 1829 most of Oxford's fellows had thought Wellington's government indifferent to the interests of the University and the Church of England: by May 1831 they faced from the government's supporters not indifference, but unconcealed hostility. The Whigs were blamed for unleashing a radical agitation against the country's established institutions. During the election Gladstone was reported by his private tutor, Charles Wordsworth, to be 'quite furious' in the anti-reform cause.[383] A weighty criticism of Oxford in the June number of the *Edinburgh Review* (the first of Hamilton's articles)[384] was followed in July by a gloating anticipation of a University Reform Commission from the *Westminster*.[385] By that date Oxford's fellows and undergraduates were united in hostility to the government's Bill. The undergraduate petition against it, drafted by Gladstone and massively supported, was reproduced in *The Times*; and it attracted a short debate when presented in the Commons on 1 July.[386]

The undergraduates' indignation at the government's proceedings did not flag even after Gladstone had gone out of residence. When it became known on 10 May 1832 that the cabinet had demanded a creation of peers, and that William IV had refused, 914 undergraduates and 'bachelor residents' out of 1,193 signed an address of thanks to the King during a single day.[387] That was a frightening week for their seniors, as it was rumoured that, if the Birmingham Political Union's militants marched on London, the Oxford colleges were to be sacked *en route*.[388] Such alarms were soon over. The King and the Tory peers withdrew from their exposed positions; the Bill received the royal assent; and Oxford's leading figures had to decide how to cope with the possibility that the Reform Act had handed the future to the radicals. Many observers, both in Oxford and elsewhere, feared that the 'popular party' might gain an ascendancy in the reformed House of Commons.

The Church was under a more immediate threat than the University. The Lords had rejected the Bill on its first appearance in their House in October 1831; and the bishops' contribution to the majority against reform then had

---

[383] Wordsworth, *Annals*, 84 n. 1; Perry Butler, *Gladstone: Church, State and Tractarianism* (1982), 33.

[384] *Ed. Rev.* liii (June 1831), 384–427. For an analysis see pp. 141–3 below.

[385] *Westminster Review* xv (July 1831), 56–69. See also *Parl. Deb.* 8 July 1831, 3S iv. 982–8, Hume questioning civil list grant for Oxford readerships (on the origin of this see p. 17 above). The University's stamp duty payments were said to amount to 'more than six times the grant': *Parl. Deb.* 13 Apr. 1832, xii. 477 (Inglis).

[386] *Parl. Deb.* 1 July 1831, 3S iv. 580–2 (Mahon and Morpeth); *Commons Journal* lxxxvi (1830–1), 600; Wordsworth, *Annals*, 84. Text in *Votes and Proceedings*, 1831, ii appx 51.

[387] Ramsay, Diary, 18 May 1832.

[388] W. Palmer, 'The Oxford Movement of 1833', *Contemporary Review* xliii (May 1883), 638. See also G. W. E. Russell, *Collections and Recollections* (1904), 108. For cholera in Oxford, July 1832, see Cox, 250–1.

aroused a storm of indignation which had not subsided.[389] Twenty years later Newman summarized the reactions of Oxford's heads and older fellows to the prospect of an anti-clerical House of Commons, sympathetic to the Nonconformists: 'Calm, perhaps selfish, calculators at Oxford said: "Nothing can touch us; the establishment will go, but not the colleges."'[390] No doubt such things were said; but the sharp reactions in the University to the threat posed by the reformed House were very various and exposed deep differences of principle. The leading liberals had learned that reform movements are apt to run out of control and their reaction was gloomy. On 26 October 1831 Thomas Arnold wrote to a friend: 'All in the moral and physical world appears...exactly to announce the coming of the "great day of the Lord", i.e. a period of fearful visitation to terminate the existing state of things, whether to terminate the whole existence of the human race neither man nor angel knows.' Whately and Arnold assumed that the Church would be the reformers' first target. 'I fear its days are numbered,' Whately wrote during the crisis of May 1832.[391] 'The Church, as it now stands,' Arnold told a friend a few weeks later, 'no human power can save.'[392] Whately had become Archbishop of Dublin in October 1831, so that neither leader was in Oxford, where their liberal views were at a great discount.

The Oxford heads met the new era with a gesture which, while showing the University to be conciliatory and forward-looking, would discourage any undue emphasis on its links with the Church. When the British Association visited Oxford in June 1832 for the first of its regular annual meetings, four scientists, who included a Quaker and a Sandemanian (John Dalton and Michael Faraday), received Honorary DCLs without fee.[393] The visit went well, though one of Oxford's less forward-looking dignitaries, preoccupied with the recent alarms, caused a moment of suppressed hilarity while Faraday was eliciting the spark from the Ashmolean magnet. He warned the gathering that the experimenter was 'putting new arms into the hands of the incendiary'.[394] Scant attention was paid during the visit to the sensitivities of the anti-liberals. Buckland, as Tom Mozley recalled, 'always coarse, was emboldened to unwanted profaneness. A very distinguished Cambridge professor, having to deliver a lecture to the ladies in the Radcliffe Library,

[389] A. P. Perceval, *A Collection of Papers Connected with the Theological Movement of 1833* (1842), 25; *The Times* 9 Oct. 1832, 2b, 8 Nov., 2c, d.

[390] Newman, *Historical Sketches*, Third Series, 233. The Act (2 Wm. IV, c. 45) did not affect elections for Oxford and Cambridge universities (s. 78). For the effect of this in 1853 see p. 325 below.

[391] Stanley, *Arnold* i. 267; Whately, *Whately* i. 159.

[392] Stanley, *Arnold* i. 278.

[393] HBM 1823–33, 176–7 (11 June 1832). None of the four were members of the Church of England, according to *Ed. Rev.* lx (Jan. 1835), 375. See also p. 559 below.

[394] Tyndall, *Faraday as a Discoverer*, 32 n.

congratulated them on the thirst for knowledge they had inherited from their great-grandmother, Eve.'[395] It fell to a Unitarian minister (Lant Carpenter) to express the Association's thanks to their hosts. He said privately that 'Oxford [had] prolonged her existence for a hundred years by the kind reception he and his fellows had received.'

The anti-liberals disapproved entirely of the heads' gesture. To them the University was completely identified with the Church. Keble thought that, in honouring a 'hodge-podge of philosophers', the University had 'truckled sadly to the spirit of the times'.[396] Newman condemned the decision whereby the scientists were brought to Oxford and 'dissenters of all hues ...allowed to gaze upon its buildings'.[397] He was concerned to show in his University Sermons that Oxford had a duty to guide and purify the Church, and that all its activities should be subordinated to this. He had none of the cautious conformism of his seniors. Where his convictions pointed he followed: it was not in him to modify his message from prudence or alarm. He stands in the Oxford tradition of Wyclif and Wesley—inspired, disruptive and a stranger to moderation. His was by now the dominant voice among the younger fellows; and, as Jowett said later, in Oxford 'it was an age of young men'.[398] On 11 December 1831 Newman traced 'the usurpations of the reason...[to] the Reformation. Then, together with the tyranny, the legitimate authority of the ecclesiastical power was more or less overthrown.' A warning followed against 'societies in which literature or science has been the essential bond of union, to the exclusion of religious profession': they were a 'dangerous artifice of the usurping reason'.[399] Should a man 'be led by a speculative turn of mind, or a natural philanthropy', he contended on 27 May 1832, 'then his opinions become ultimately impressed with the character of...definite unbelief.'[400] Three months later he inveighed against identifying the 'vision of Christ's kingdom with the elegance and refinement of mere human civilization', and uttered his 'firm conviction that it would be a gain to this country were it vastly more superstitious, more bigoted, more gloomy, more fierce in its religion, than at present it shows itself to be'.[401] Newman wrote later: 'I earnestly denounced and abjured [the proposition that] virtue is the child of knowledge, and vice of

[395] Mozley, *Reminiscences* i. 179.
[396] Liddon, *Pusey* i. 219. Keble had become Professor of Poetry in 1831.
[397] *British Critic* xxiv (July 1838), 144. See also Newman to Mrs Bowden, 15 Sept. 1847, in *LDN* xii. 115; Newman, *Stray Essays on Controversial Points* (privately printed 1890), 82; *History of Universities* x (1991), 161–4 (P. Nockles).
[398] W. Ward, *W. G. Ward and the Oxford Movement* (1890), 149. Jowett spoke of the later 1830s, but his remark applies to the whole decade.
[399] Newman, *Fifteen Sermons*, 69, 72 (no. 321).
[400] Ibid. 128 (no. 338).
[401] Newman, *P and P Sermons* i. 315, 320 (no. 341, 26 Aug. 1832). For Whately on 'the noxious admixture of superstition' see *Errors of Romanism*, 75.

ignorance, [and the corollary that] education, periodical literature, railroad
travelling, ventilation, drainage, and the arts of life, when fully carried out,
serve to make a population moral and happy.'[402] He had become thorough-
going in condemning institutions of social and educational amelioration, and
included temperance societies in his attack.[403] His assault on the liberalism
of the time reached a climax in his sermon of 4 November 1832 when he
expressed doubts about the benefits of educational progress:

Nothing...is more common than to hear men speak of the growing intelligence of
the present age, and to insist on the Church's supplying its wants; the previous
question being entirely left out of view, whether those wants are healthy and
legitimate, or unreasonable—whether real or imaginary—whether they ought to be
gratified or repressed: and it is urged upon us that, unless we take the lead in the
advance of mind ourselves, we must be content to fall behind. But surely our first
duty is not to resolve on satisfying a demand at any price, but to determine whether it
be innocent. If so, well; but if not, let what will happen. Even though the march of
society be conducted on a superhuman law, yet, while it moves against scripture
truth, it is not God's ordinance. It is but the creature of Satan.[404]

Newman and his friends were not willing to maintain the system which had
brought them to prominence. They had no time for an Oxford which
required conformity while it inched towards pluralism. The assumption on
which such a university rested had been stated by a reviewer for the *British
Critic* in 1827: 'The pursuits by which man will...render himself a fitter
recipient for an immortality of happiness are the very means by which, in
general cases, he will most effectually promote the secular welfare of himself
and his fellow creatures.'[405] Convenient optimism of that kind was no longer
acceptable to Newman.[406] He and his associates were thus disposed to take a
new course; but they distrusted the Conservative opposition almost as much
as the Whigs. They were waiting to see whether the latter were able, and
willing, to control their radical allies. 'We can hardly be too passive,' Keble
wrote in October 1832.[407] 'I shall do all I can', Newman had written a few
days earlier, 'to support the Whigs, so far forth as they are conservatives.'[408]
   The cabinet were in no position to meet Newman's requirement. They
needed an Irish Coercion Act; and they could not obtain one unless they
adapted the Church of Ireland in the light of its limited role in a largely
Roman Catholic country. The result was the Irish Church Temporalities
Bill, under which ten Irish bishoprics were to be suppressed. This was

[402] Newman, *Apologia*, 260–2, Note A, Proposition 18.
[403] Ibid. 49.
[404] Newman, *Fifteen Sermons*, 151–2 (no. 344).
[405] *British Critic*, i (Jan. 1827), 207. For the *British Critic* at this date see n. 42.
[406] See J. H. Newman, *Loss and Gain* (1848), 328 (Reding's remarks).
[407] To A. P. Perceval, [postmark 13] Oct. 1832, PHL LBV 11/28.
[408] To Hurrell Froude, 4 Oct. 1832, in *LDN* iii. 100.

denounced by Keble as a sign of impending 'national apostasy' in the Assize Sermon at St Mary's, Oxford, on Sunday 14 July 1833.[409] Five days later two archbishops and nine bishops voted for the Bill on its second reading in the Lords. They included Whately and Copleston.[410]

Keble might have been more careful had he known more about politics. 'He had set off', as Newman said of him many years later, 'in the company or at the head of many others, on a road which he had not explored.'[411] The Bill which he denounced had originally included a hint about lay use of Church revenues; but it had been shorn of that clause weeks before he spoke.[412] It was hardly a foretaste of worse things: the wiser radicals already knew that there were more votes to be lost than gained in any further 'attack' on the Church of Ireland: such moves looked too like a helping hand for Roman Catholics.[413] In a broader sense, however, his sermon was a response to fears and expectations which were widespread even among well-informed politicians. In 1833 almost everyone who cared about the Church of England expected it to be attacked and wanted to see it stoutly defended. Those fears were not to fade until the radicals had met their Waterloo in the general election of 1837; and until they faded appeals such as Keble had made would enjoy widely based support. That story is told in Chapter 7.

Newman reached home from a visit to Sicily, where he had been seriously ill, five days before Keble spoke. As had happened some years earlier, his illness had helped to impel him towards a new initiative.[414] He always considered the Assize Sermon as marking 'the start of the religious movement of 1833'.[415] Although nowadays the movement is seen as starting in 1829, his view is understandable. Great landslips had awaited the displacement of a pebble. In the Assize Sermon it was displaced; and the first phase of reform in Oxford came to an end.

---

[409] For Keble's decision to publish the sermon see Battiscombe, *Keble*, 152. Pusey's copy was uncut when he died: Liddon, *Pusey* i. 276. The note of extreme alarm was sounded no less clearly by A. P. Perceval at the Chapel Royal, St James's, on 21 July: Perceval, *Papers Connected with the Theological Movement*, 28.

[410] *Parl. Deb.* 19 July 1833, 3S xix. 1017–18.

[411] Newman to Liddon, 19 June 1878, in Battiscombe, *Keble*, 233. Newman referred to Keble's retrospective view. The remark may apply more to his own view, or to the facts themselves.

[412] *Parl. Deb.* 21 June 1833, xviii. 1073–5 (Stanley).

[413] As Barnes of *The Times* had warned Lord Durham: J. C. Hobhouse, Lord Broughton, *Recollections of a Long Life*, ed. Lady Dorchester (6 vols 1909–11) iv. 261–2. See also Froude, *Short Studies*, iv. 172–3.

[414] See also the reference in Newman, *Apologia*, 42–3, to Southey's *Thalaba*: Valerie Pitt, 'Demythologising Newman' in D. Nicholls and F. Kerr (eds), *John Henry Newman: reason, rhetoric and romanticism* (Bristol 1991), 17.

[415] Newman, *Apologia*, 43.

NOTE

The Oriel Noetics

RICHARD BRENT

The Noetics[1] were primarily responsible for Oriel's intellectual dominance of Oxford University during the 1820s. Although historians have recalled them chiefly as the proponents of the theological liberalism that provoked the Tractarian defence of the Church, they were, in their own right, leading agents in the process of Anglican renewal, which had commenced as a reaction to the religiously sceptical French Revolution. In the 1830s, as a consequence of receiving important preferment in the Church and University, the Noetics assumed the additional role of ecclesiastical statesmen. The religious and political significance of this group of Anglican dons and divines has largely escaped the notice of historians, partly, it may be suggested, because it was submerged in the High-Church reaction which followed the liberal reforms of the late 1820s and 1830s, and partly because liberal chroniclers of nineteenth-century thought have been more interested in tracing the origins of nineteenth-century agnosticism than in exploring such accommodations of liberalism with religious orthodoxy as the Noetics represented. Thus any reader will search the *Dictionary of National Biography* in vain for an acknowledgement of the existence of the Noetics; it is revealing that the only member of the Oriel Common Room whose life Leslie Stephen himself noted was Joseph Blanco White, whose religious trajectory led from Catholicism to Unitarianism.

It is important to realize that the Noetics never constituted an organized party in opposition to the Tractarian cohorts. Accidents of time and place were one cause of this. When, for example, the greatest Noetic crisis occurred in 1836, as a consequence of the appointment of Hampden to the Regius chair of Divinity at Oxford, five leading Noetics had left the city and one had died two years previously. Only three remained as resident members of the University and capable of taking immediate action. Even more importantly, a diversity of intellectual interests, political affiliations and theological conclusions (though not approach) prevented the formation of a united party front. If Hampden may be said to be the theologian of the group, then Thomas Arnold was its historian and Baden Powell its scientist. Copleston was a liberal Tory of the Grenvillite school, whereas Blanco White was a Holland House Whig. Whately, for a time at least, was prepared to contemplate Church disestablishment and certainly advocated the spiritual independence of the Church from the state; Arnold, conversely, envisioned a utopia in which Church and state were one.

But the prime reason why the Noetics failed to act in a thoroughly partisan spirit was because their ultimate aim of Church comprehension prevented them from

---

[1] For the meaning of the term see p. 48. above. The leading Noetics are listed in Table 1.1. According to the *OED*, the first published mentions of the term, in relation to Oriel, occur in Mozley's *Reminiscences* (1882) and Pattison's *Memoirs* (1885), although in both instances the authors allude to an existing oral usage. An unpublished letter from S. Wilberforce to H. Froude, 9 Oct. 1827, refers to Froude's recent abandonment of 'the Noetick School': P. Brendon, *H. Froude* (1974), 77. I would like to thank Professor Colin Matthew for the advice which he has given on previous drafts of this note. I also wish to acknowledge the help of the late Dr Angus Macintyre.

doing so. They saw their task not so much as fighting an internal battle for the soul of Anglicanism, as reviving and defending a national Christianity, capable of opposing secularizing liberalism. The Anglican Church was to become Christianity's national corral and not its bullring. In this task they saw themselves, until the 1830s at least, as co-operating with all Churchmen, and certainly, before the decade of reform, High-Churchmen of the Hackney Phalanx were supporters of the Noetic defence of Christian doctrine. Thus in the *British Critic*'s review of Hinds's *Rise and Early Progress of Christianity* (1828), this High-Church organ noted the Noetics' 'entire freedom from *any* sort of contemporary latitudinarianism'.[2] When the Church party warfare began in the 1830s, it was the Tractarians who initiated it.

The singularity of the Noetic defence of revealed religion consisted in a demonstration of its reasonableness. The inspiration for the argument was found in the work of the eighteenth-century Bishop of Durham Joseph Butler. In the latter's *The Analogy of Religion*, first published in 1736, the argument had been that there were two dispensations of providence, the natural and the biblical; that the problems encountered in comprehending both were analogous; consequently, since it was known that God was the first cause of nature, it was probable that he was also responsible for scriptural revelation. On the Butlerian assumption that the publication of Christian truth in the Bible was akin to that in nature, the Noetics proceeded to argue that the same method should be used in understanding the Bible as was used in scientific inquiry, namely induction. Hampden wrote in the introduction to the second edition of his Bampton Lectures that 'the same rule of proceeding applies to Theology and Science . . . we must study the Sacred Records, as we study Nature. The method of Induction is to be used here as there.'[3] Much early Noetic writing consisted either in proving the reasonableness of the scriptures (for example, Davison's work on prophecy), or in indicating the requisite conditions for a correct interpretation of the Bible (Whately's Bampton Lectures of 1822).

The initial targets of Noetic wrath were the Unitarians and Evangelicals, who threatened to undermine orthodox Anglicanism. By means of their inductive theology, the Noetics were able to argue not so much that Evangelicals and Unitarians were doctrinally unsound in relation to the Thirty-nine Articles as that they were careless and false interpreters of scripture. Such animadversions were well received by their fellow Anglicans. Thus Baden Powell's *Rational Religion Examined* (1826), which was primarily a refutation of Unitarianism, was in accordance with the editorial policy of the *British Critic* of the 1810s and 1820s; indeed, Van Mildert, the theological leader of the Hackney Phalanx, used his influence to secure the Savilian chair of Geometry for Powell. Copleston, likewise, in his *Enquiry into the Doctrines of Necessity and Predestination* (1821), mounted an attack on Calvinism, in the course of which he described the doctrine of election as 'contrary to the whole tenor and complexion of the Christian doctrines as revealed by our Lord'; Calvin's fault was to overlay the facts or truths of scriptural revelation with an imperfect 'garb of human metaphysics' or 'dross of earthly disputation'.[4] Copleston's pupil Whately

---

[2] *The British Critic, Quarterly Theological Review and Ecclesiastical Record*, v (1829), 136.
[3] R. D. Hampden, 'The scholastic philosophy considered in its relation to Christian theology', *The Bampton Lectures for 1832* (2nd edn 1837), pp. xlviii–ix. See also pp. 223–4 below.
[4] E. Copleston, *Enquiry into the Doctrines of Necessity and Predestination* (1821), 160, 172.

continued the controversy in his *Essays on Some of the Difficulties in the Writings of St Paul*, a work, according to the *British Critic*, 'on the whole worthy of most decided commendation'.[5]

During the 1830s, in an atmosphere of political and religious liberalism wrought by the repeal of the Test and Corporation Acts and Catholic Emancipation, the Noetics increasingly turned their attention to a consideration of the standing of Anglican dogmas. In his Bampton Lectures in 1832 Hampden discussed the origins of the main creeds and formularies of the Christian Church. On the assumption that the truths of Christianity were facts and not axioms akin to the first premisses of mathematics, he suggested that deductions from these facts (creeds and formularies) were not so much apodictic conclusions as humanly construed definitions. Church dogma or theological opinion was simply the 'various result of the necessary action of our minds on the truths made known to us by the Divine word'.[6] Given this, the younger Noetics, especially Hampden and Arnold, argued for greater toleration of Dissenting sects: such disagreements as existed were grounded primarily on questions of opinion rather than on essential truths of Christianity. Hampden, in particular, in his pamphlet *Observations on Religious Dissent* (1834), argued for the admission of Dissenters to the University of Oxford; Arnold, in his work on the *Principles of Church Reform* (1833), went so far as to suggest the need for a revision of the creeds and formularies of the Church of England, in order that the national Church might be more truly representative of the people. By the mid-1830s the Noetics had established themselves as the theological advocates of liberal ecclesiastical reforms.

Not surprisingly, such advocacies appealed to the Whig–liberal governments of the 1830s, with the consequence that they bestowed high office on the Noetics. In 1831 Whately became Archbishop of Dublin; Hampden was appointed to the Regius chair of Divinity at Oxford in 1836; Arnold returned to the University in 1841 as Regius Professor of Modern History. The Noetics also became government advisers. Copleston's opinions were sought on ecclesiastical appointments; Arnold acted as one of the first fellows of the Whig-founded University of London; Hampden advised on the question of university reform and the preparation of the Deans and Chapters Act of 1840; Whately played a leading role in the drafting of various Irish tithes measures, the institution of the Irish National Board of Education and—scarcely surprisingly for the friend of the economist Nassau Senior—the development of Irish poor law legislation. The associations which grew up between the Noetics and the Whigs were as much personal as political. Copleston was a frequent visitor at the Spencers' country house, Althorp, and Baden Powell visited the home of the Whig Chancellor of the Exchequer in the 1830s, Thomas Spring-Rice. Viscount Morpeth, later 7th Earl of Carlisle, was a fervent admirer of Arnold and a strong supporter of Hampden. Lord John Russell declared himself to be a follower of Arnold, preferring the simple words of Christ to dogmatic interpretations of them. The consequence of these friendships and appointments was that a movement which had commenced as part of a general process of Anglican renewal began to be identified with one particular party or sect, namely the liberals. High-Churchmen and Evangelicals increasingly saw the Noetics as the religious branch of a political movement, bent on the

---

[5] *British Critic* v (1829), 389.
[6] R. D. Hampden, *Observations on Religious Dissent* (2nd edn 1834), 22.

destruction of the Church, and the Noetics were thus to suffer unduly from the calumnies of their fellow Anglicans.

In retrospect, the Noetics have been seen primarily as the precursors of the Broad-Church movement of the 1850s and 1860s, a claim not without foundation. Baden Powell was one of the contributors to the notorious *Essays and Reviews* (1860), while Hinds chaired the Oxford Reform Commission of 1850; Dean Stanley was both the pupil and biographer of Arnold. But the discontinuities were equally important. The later Broad-Church generation were German-inspired, post-Kantian theologians who believed that assent to Christianity was ultimately a matter of faith not reason, an argument of which the Noetics were largely ignorant. The consequence was that some of the leading Oriel liberals such as Hampden and Whately used their charges to their clergy to attack the essayists of 1860. The truth was that the Noetics were the last representatives of an eighteenth-century defence of Anglicanism which stressed the reasonableness of assenting to Christian doctrines. They continued to adhere to a Butlerian apologetic, which such later liberals as Stanley and Pattison rejected as inadequate in the face of advancing scientific knowledge. The inability of the Noetics to cope with new geological and biological theories rendered their theology increasingly redundant, while the only scientist of note among them, Baden Powell, progressed—to the dismay of his erstwhile colleagues—from Noeticism to Broad-Churchmanship.

TABLE 1.1

ORIEL NOETICS

name	birth	Oriel fellowship	residence in Oxford after graduation	Appointment	Date appointed
Copleston, E.	1776	1795	1795–Jan. 1828	provost of Oriel	1814
				bishop of Llandaff	1828
Davison, J.	1777	1800	1800–17	tutor, Oriel	1810
Whately, R.	1787	1811	1811–22	principal of St Alban Hall	1825
			1825–31	Drummond professor of political economy	1829
				archbishop of Dublin	1831
Hawkins, E.	1789	1813	1813–82	provost of Oriel	1828
Hampden, R. D.	1793	1814	1814–16	principal of St Mary Hall	1833
			1829–47	Regius professor of divinity	1836
				bishop of Hereford	1847
Arnold, T.	1795	1815	1815–19	headmaster of Rugby	1828
				Regius professor of modern history	1841
Powell, B.[a]	1796	—	1827–60	Savilian professor of geometry	1827

TABLE 1.1 (*contd.*)

name	birth	Oriel fellowship	residence in Oxford after graduation	Appointment	Date appointed
White, J. B.	1775	(SCR member 1826–32)	—	—	—
Hinds, S.[b]	1793	—	1827–31	vice-principal of St Alban Hall	1827
				bishop of Norwich	1849

[a] Powell was an undergraduate at Oriel 1814–17.
[b] Whately had been private tutor to Hinds, then an undergraduate at Queen's College, Oxford.

2

The European University in the Age of Revolution, 1789–1850

L. W. B. BROCKLISS

OXFORD AND CAMBRIDGE IN THE LATE EIGHTEENTH CENTURY: A UNIQUE PROVISION

Understanding the peculiar position of Oxford and Cambridge among European universities from 1800 onwards entails a glance at the eighteenth century. In 1789 Europe contained about one hundred and fifty universities. Fifty were located in just two countries—France and Spain—while the rest were fairly evenly distributed among the other states of the Continent in proportion to their size and population. Small states, such as the German principalities, usually had only one university, while the other great powers, often themselves a congeries of distinctive regions, normally possessed one or two per province. The kingdoms of Great Britain and Ireland, which contained seven universities (two in England, four in Scotland, and Trinity College, Dublin), followed the common European pattern. In fact, with a combined population of only 13–14 million, the British Isles was better provided with universities than the more populous Austrian Empire.

The universities of the late Middle Ages and early-modern period were typical *ancien régime* institutions with a common European identity forged in the first centuries of their existence. Whatever their date of foundation, continental universities in the eighteenth century were privileged,

Unless otherwise stated this chapter is based on the following secondary authorities: L. Liard, *L'Enseignement supérieur en France, 1789–1889* (2 vols Paris 1888–94); A. Aulard, *Napoléon 1er et le monopole universitaire* (Paris 1911); J. Verger (ed.), *Histoire des universités en France* (Toulouse 1986), chs 7 and 8; F. Paulsen, *Die deutschen Universitäten und das Universitäts-Studium* (1902, 2nd edn Hildesheim 1966; Eng. trans. by F. Thilly and W. W. Elwang, *The German Universities and University Study*, London 1906); C. McClelland, *State, Society and University in Germany, 1700–1914* (1980); M. and J.-L. Peset, *La universidad española, siglos XVIII y XIX: despotismo ilustrado y revolución liberal* (Madrid 1974); H. Engelbrecht, *Geschichte des österreichischen Bildungswesen* (3 vols Vienna 1982–4) iii, chs 12–13; *The Collegiate University* and *The Eighteenth Century*; J. B. Mullinger, *The University of Cambridge* (3 vols 1873–1911); A. Grant, *Story of the University of Edinburgh* (2 vols Edinburgh 1884); J. Coutts, *A History of the University of Glasgow* (Glasgow 1909); J. M. Bulloch, *A History of the University of Aberdeen, 1495–1895* (1895); R. G. Cant, *The University of Saint-Andrews: a short history* (Edinburgh 1970); R. B. McDowell and D. A. Webb, *Trinity College, Dublin, 1592–1952: an academic history* (1982).

self-governing corporations, entirely male preserves, usually confessionally
closed, and only accessible to those who had been sufficiently trained in the
language of learned instruction, Latin. University privileges were legion.
They might be fiscal and judicial as well as academic, but their most important right in law was the power to bestow the degrees of bachelor,
licentiate and doctor on faculty students. The faculties were the fundamental
units of university organization. Their number and nomenclature was determined by the medieval division of human knowledge into four parts:
grammar and philosophy (called the arts), theology, civil and canon law,
and medicine.[1]

The faculties' primary function was to teach and examine in their particular subject area. The historical responsibility to examine had become
peculiarly significant by the end of the eighteenth century. Traditionally,
universities held a monopoly in the teaching of the sciences, but from the
time of the Renaissance an increasing number of rival educational institutions had been founded offering a similar curriculum. The English Dissenting academies are a case in point.[2] However, the educational primacy of the
universities was never effectively challenged because they alone were empowered by state and Church to offer degrees. This ensured the universities
a central role in the acculturation of an important section of Europe's
administrative and professional élite. In most parts of eighteenth-century
Europe it was impossible to enter certain kinds of state employment, such as
the judiciary, hold a major cure of souls, plead at the Bar, or practise
medicine without a university qualification. As a result, most university
students on the eve of the French Revolution were seeking a professional
meal-ticket. The development of the university as a degree factory was not a
late nineteenth- and twentieth-century occurrence, as some historians have
maintained.[3] On the contrary, in the Church at least, attendance at university was a prerequisite of career advancement from the late Middle Ages.[4]

---

[1] Not all universities had four faculties. In Italy the faculties of arts and medicine were
frequently combined, while in Spain there were often separate faculties of civil and canon law.
The French universities of Orléans, Rennes, and Dijon only had faculties of law. Universities
sometimes allowed religious Dissenters to study but seldom to take degrees except in medicine.
Only the new University of Göttingen (founded in 1733) deliberately set out to woo students from
different religious backgrounds, although even there the faculty of theology was strictly Lutheran.
[2] For these see H. McLachlan, *English Education under the Test Acts: the history of Nonconformist academies, 1662–1820* (Manchester 1931).
[3] This argument is advanced especially in K. H. Jarausch (ed.), *The Transformation of Higher
Learning, 1860–1930: expansion, diversification, social opening, and professionalization in England, Germany, Russia and the United States* (Chicago 1983); also in the specifically English
context in H. Perkin, *The Rise of Professional Society: England since 1880* (1989).
[4] All recent studies of the medieval university stress this rapid professionalization: e.g. R.
Southern, 'The changing role of universities in medieval Europe', *Historical Research* lx/142
(June 1987). Actually assessing the relative career prospects of university and non-university
educated clerics is still in its infancy: see R. N. Swanson, 'Learnings and livings: university study
and clerical careers in later medieval England', *History of Universities* vi (1986–7), 81–103.

Oxford and Cambridge, as two of the earliest university foundations, had helped to shape this common institutional identity. However, in the course of the early-modern period the development of the two English universities had been idiosyncratic. By the turn of the eighteenth century, if they remained recognizable members of the educational genus, they were no longer a representative species but a distinctly distant relative (see Fig. 2.1). Their peculiarity was most obvious in their administrative organization. The majority of universities were ultimately run by a committee or council headed by an elected rector or principal. Furthermore, the appointment of a university's officers and administrators was usually in the charge of one or all of the faculties, so that the real locus of power in the average university lay with the separate and independent faculty boards. This was definitely not the case at eighteenth-century Oxford and Cambridge. The English universities had a faculty organization but the faculties had virtually ceased to exist except for the conferment of higher degrees. At Oxford, the head of the University, the Vice-Chancellor, was not an elected figure at all, but the appointee of the absentee Chancellor. The latter was not an academic but an influential nobleman who was elected to his office for life by a poll of the University's MAs, both resident and non-resident. The Vice-Chancellor, however, had limited powers, for his actions were determined by the Hebdomadal Board, an oligarchic body comprised of the heads of the halls and colleges and the two proctors. At Oxford (and Cambridge), therefore, it was the colleges, not the faculties, which really controlled the University. Admittedly, other universities (especially the older foundations) had colleges too. Nevertheless, nowhere else did the colleges gain such power at the expense of the faculties. By 1500 the University of Paris possessed as many as forty colleges (some, like the Sorbonne, extremely prestigious), but Oxford's Alma Mater never showed any sign of developing into a collegiate institution. Until 1789 the rector was elected from among the members of the faculty of arts while the rectorial council was comprised of the three deans of the faculties of theology, law and medicine, and the procurators of the four 'nations', which were regional societies of resident MAs.[5]

The power of the colleges at eighteenth-century Oxford and Cambridge can be attributed chiefly to a peculiar curricular bias. In many continental universities by this date the faculty of arts no longer existed as a serious teaching faculty. In the late Middle Ages, grammar and philosophy had not been studied simply for their own sake but as the source of conceptual and analytical tools essential for the study of the other sciences. Hence the faculties of theology, law and medicine became known as the 'higher' faculties. In the Renaissance era the propaedeutic value of arts instruction

---

[5] See M. Targe, *Professeurs et régents de collège dans l'ancienne université de Paris aux XVIIe et XVIIIe siècles* (Paris 1902), ch. 1.

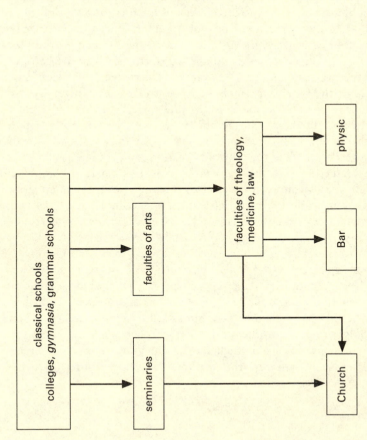

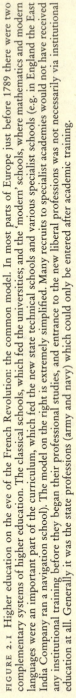

FIGURE 2.1 Higher education on the eve of the French Revolution: the common model. In most parts of Europe just before 1789 there were two complementary systems of higher education. The classical schools, which fed the universities; and the 'modern' schools, where mathematics and modern languages were an important part of the curriculum, which fed the new state technical schools and various specialist schools (e.g. in England the East India Company ran a navigation school). The model on the right is extremely simplified. Many recruits to specialist academies would not have received any institutional training before they began their professional studies, and entrance to the new liberal professions was not necessarily via institutional education at all. Generally it was the state professions (army and navy) which could only be entered after academic training.

was given even greater prominence, as humanists in the name of progress succeeded in turning the study of grammar or linguistic logic into the study of the language and literature of ancient Rome and Greece, and in emptying the philosophy course of extraneous but often stimulating *quaestiones*. In consequence, study in the arts became the exclusive province of boys and teenagers, and in an age which began to appreciate the distinctiveness of childhood, its teaching was frequently transferred from the university to a new institution, the municipal gymnasium or college. Thereby, the faculties of arts were often reduced to finishing-schools. At best, they were attended by students seeking to brush up their philosophy before proceeding to a 'higher' faculty; at worst they became simple examining boards in universities where graduands in theology and medicine had first to take an MA.[6]

At Oxford and Cambridge, in contrast, the study of arts was never eroded. Indeed, in the post-Reformation era its study paradoxically became their dominant concern. Whereas other universities in the seventeenth and eighteenth centuries became predominantly schools of law and theology,[7] churning out graduates to feed an insatiable confessional leviathan, the English *studia* were overwhelmingly filled with students in the humanities (which included, at Cambridge, mathematics) and philosophy. The paucity of students in the higher faculties reflected the anomalous structure of the English early-modern state. A small, largely amateur judicial system founded on common, not Roman law made the study of civil law at Oxford and Cambridge of only academic interest. The real training-ground for judges and JPs was the Inns of Court.[8] At the same time the Church of England was uniquely uninterested in theological training for its ministers. Elsewhere ordinands for the priesthood were accepted only after a period of study in a theological seminary or faculty, but in England a simple degree in arts was sufficient qualification. The buoyant attendance of arts students at the two universities, on the other hand, reflected an educational revolution *manqué*. In this country, the Renaissance had also left an indelible mark on a course in arts and encouraged the foundation of a host of municipal grammar schools. The English grammar schools, however (with the exception of a few élite institutions such as Eton and Westminster) had never threatened

---

[6] The emasculation of the role of the faculties of arts was particularly acute in France. For the development of the college there see R. Chartier, M.-M. Compère and D. Julia, *L'Éducation en France du XVIe au XVIIe siècle* (Paris 1976), chs 5–6. The college provision in 1789 is cartographically depicted in D. Julia (ed.), *Atlas de la Révolution française, ii: L'Enseignement, 1760–1815* (Paris 1987), 30. In Catholic countries the colleges were predominantly controlled by the regular orders, especially the Jesuits: cf the map in R. Mandrou, *From Humanism to Science, 1480–1700*, Eng. trans. (Hassocks 1979), 312–13.

[7] In the 18th century, medical students were nearly always an insignificant proportion of the students in the three higher faculties: see the later section 'The continental university and the student body'.

[8] The Inns of Court were really England's third university: see W. R. Prest, *The Inns of Court under Elizabeth 1 and the Early Stuarts, 1590–1640* (1972).

the monopoly of the arts faculties, since they restricted their activities to the study of the elements of Latin and Greek. For a full course in the humanities and philosophy, it remained necessary to attend the universities.[9]

The emergence of Oxford and Cambridge as arts universities was crucial to the development of college power. Originally intended for poor students, the colleges opened their doors to paying guests relatively early in their history. Being dedicated, at least in theory, to promoting discipline as well as good learning, they were the ideal institutions to act *in loco parentis* to teenage arts students living away from home. In the course of the second half of the sixteenth and early seventeenth centuries, this they duly became, their position cemented by the development of another idiosyncratic feature of the English universities, the tutorial system. In other universities teaching in all faculties was via the traditional hour-long *lectio*, in part dictated, in part extempore. The new municipal schools invented more dynamic ways of inculcating knowledge of the Latin and Greek humanities, which involved classroom exercises and homework. Even there, though, students were taught *en masse* with little attention to individual need or ability. The idea of personal or small-group tuition based around guided private reading was very much a creation of Oxford and Cambridge. Begun as a supplement to lectures, the tutorial system eventually became the linchpin of arts teaching at the two universities. The tutorial system undoubtedly had defects; in particular, tutors in the eighteenth century paid little attention to natural philosophy. None the less, its great potential advantage over the formal lecture was the close rapport that could be built up between tutor and student. Whatever the value of the tutorial system as a pedagogical method, its development had an important consequence: at Oxford and Cambridge the colleges became the University.[10]

The invention of the tutorial system can in large part be explained by reference to a further peculiar feature of the English universities: their gentry clientele. The Renaissance humanists had believed that the new course in the humanities and philosophy had an intrinsic moral and civilizing value. It was not to be taught simply to future members of the liberal professions, but to all members of the élite, especially the military and landowning nobility who had traditionally been uninterested in formal learning. There is little evidence, however, that in general the early-modern faculties of arts and their institutional rivals the municipal colleges succeeded in attracting a new clientele. The large majority of students in the humanities and philosophy

---

[9] The history of the foundation of the English grammar schools is given in F. Watson, *The English Grammar Schools to 1660: their curriculum and practice* (1908); also W. A. L. Vincent, *The Grammar Schools: their continuing tradition, 1660–1714* (1969). Between 1480 and 1660 benefactors in ten counties founded and endowed 436 schools.

[10] The best study of the 18th-century Oxford collegiate curriculum is E. G. W. Bill, *Education at Christ Church, Oxford, 1660–1800* (1988), chs 4 and 5.

remained bound for a career in the Church, law or medicine, and if nobles attended these institutions, then they did so as younger sons bound for the liberal professions. Indeed, after 1600 members of the European nobility (generally the wealthy and titled) who did accept the broader, moral value of an arts education preferred to entrust their elder sons to a personal tutor or to send them to specialist academies, where they could mix with their own kind and study the cultural inheritance of the classical world in less depth or in partial translation.[11] It was only in England that the gentry internalized the humanist ethic and sent their elder sons to the universities in large numbers. In consequence, the Oxford and Cambridge colleges from the mid-sixteenth century were faced for the first time by an invasion of teenage 'amateur' students with no incentive for formal study. The tutorial system was an admirable device for ensuring that their study was both reasonably profitable and well policed. It quickly established a deep and permanent hold on the imagination of the English landed élite. Even in the eighteenth century Oxford and Cambridge continued to educate the aristocracy and country gentry in considerable numbers, despite the existence of a plethora of alternative institutions.[12] In consequence, both Oxford and Cambridge, although primarily schools for the clergy, were not simply degree factories. In that the English universities educated the squire and the parson, the lords temporal as well as the lords spiritual, they trained the élite as a whole and not just a professional rump.

For various reasons, therefore, Oxford and Cambridge on the eve of the French Revolution were very different from continental universities. They also bore little resemblance to their Scottish sisters. Like the English grammar schools the Scottish burgh schools chiefly provided instruction in Latin grammar. The arts faculties of the Scottish universities in consequence continued to flourish in the eighteenth century. Scotland, on the other hand, was a country whose ministers, lawyers and increasingly physicians sought a training in the higher sciences, so that the universities always provided tuition on a broad front. In the Scottish universities, moreover, the faculties always remained the dominant administrative force. This was scarcely surprising, for residential colleges were to be found only at St Andrews. Teaching in the arts faculty thus remained lecture-based and largely impersonal.[13]

---

[11] For this development in Germany, see N. Conrad, *Ritterakademien der frühen Neuzeit. Bildung als Standesprivileg im 16. und 17. Jahrhundert* (Göttingen 1981). General comments in J. Hexter, 'The education of the aristocracy in the Renaissance' in *Reappraisals in History* (1961), ch. 4.

[12] For an idea of the educational choice on the eve of the French Revolution, see N. Hans, *New Trends in Education in the Eighteenth Century* (1951).

[13] Aberdeen comprised two colleges: King's and Marischal's. These, however, were legally separate universities providing tuition in at least two of the three higher sciences besides lectures in arts. They were not residential colleges within a university. Trinity College, Dublin was a similarly confusing designation.

In the course of the next fifty to sixty years the distinctiveness of Oxford and Cambridge became still more marked. In the period 1789–1850 Oxford at least underwent many (usually positive) changes, as Chapter 1 and those that follow show. Nevertheless, before the reforms of the 1850s the University remained essentially unaltered, collegiately organized, confessionally closed and primarily filled with both 'amateur' and 'professional' students in arts taught through the tutorial system. The most important developments occurred in the ways students in arts were examined: through the introduction of more rigorous procedures, an extended curriculum, a system of classification and an additional and separate school (in mathematics and physics) for the intellectually gifted. In contrast, the universities on the Continent experienced a sixty-year period of unprecedented and traumatic upheaval. By the mid-nineteenth century virtually no continental foundation survived in its eighteenth-century form and many did not survive at all.

The root cause of the upheaval lay in two movements which touched Britain more lightly than elsewhere: the radical Enlightenment and the French Revolution. In the course of the eighteenth century the intellectual avant-garde became bitterly hostile to the extant university system, and their critique was acted on all over Europe by supporters of the events of 1789. Given Britain's relative isolation from the revolutionary maelstrom, it might be thought that the history of Oxford in the age of Copleston and Pusey could be written without reference to the continental experience. Such a view would be mistaken. In the first place, the changes that took place at Oxford need to be placed in their European context to appreciate correctly their limited and evolutionary character. Secondly, and more importantly, the European university world was not turned upside-down in the course of the French Revolutionary and Napoleonic Wars without engendering a positive response. Out of the revolutionary ferment appeared a new concept of the university as an institution for objective research rather than professional acculturation. Transferred eventually to England after 1850 this 'modern' concept of the university was to find in Oxford and Cambridge (and their American imitators) a particularly good soil in which to breed. The history of Oxford *after* 1850, therefore, cannot be understood without an introduction to the history of the European university in the age of the liberal revolution.

THE UNIVERSITY AND THE ENLIGHTENMENT

From the emergence of the institution in the twelfth century the university's curriculum had been organized around the analysis and exploration of a series of textual authorities judged to contain the quintessence of knowledge in a particular science. In the Renaissance humanists had objected to the ahistorical and speculative approach to textual exegesis favoured by the late medieval scholastics, and called for the replacement of many Arab authors in the light of the rediscovery of forgotten gems of Graeco-Roman antiquity. Nevertheless, the challenge had gone no further and the universities had found no difficulty in adapting the curriculum to the humanist critique.[14] Thereafter for at least a century the universities were largely immune from serious criticism.[15] This immunity was based primarily on consumer satisfaction. As long as the liberal professions accepted the propaedeutic and moral value of a training in the humanities and philosophy and felt that the education received in the higher faculties was professionally valuable, the universities' role remained unquestioned. In the course of the eighteenth century, however, a section of that élite, known to historians as the *philosophes*, rejected these core assumptions.

The *philosophes* were a mixture of ecumenical Christians and unbelievers who suspected theological dogmatism and believed in the possibility of the moral and material amelioration of mankind if man's natural capacity for empathy and self-improvement were only released.[16] Much of the writing by the *philosophes* was directed towards the reform of contemporary social and economic institutions which through their corporate character were deemed to encourage social disharmony and individual decadence. But the movement was also passionately interested in education as a vehicle in particular for producing 'enlightened' men like themselves. The *philosophes* viewed the organization of eighteenth-century higher education as grossly inadequate. On the one hand, they believed that cultivation and moral enlightenment arose from the study of contemporary literature, ethical rationalism and post-Cartesian natural science; it was not the product of the lengthy study of classical languages and a jejune acquaintance with Aristotelian logic and metaphysics still in many countries the dominant part of the philosophy course. On the other hand, they believed that training for the liberal professions should be practical and relevant and no longer based on the study of outmoded textual authorities. Consequently, by the mid-eighteenth century the universities were the subject of a flood of criticism unparalleled in their history. The *philosophes* did not want to abolish

---

[14] In fact the traditional curriculum was invigorated. Cf C. Schmitt, 'Towards a reassessment of Renaissance Aristotelianism', *History of Science* xi (1973), 159–93. The most detailed recent study of the assimilation of the humanist critique is N. Siraisi, *Avicenna in Renaissance Italy: the canon and medical teaching in Italian universities after 1500* (Princeton 1987), esp. pt 2.

[15] There were plenty of complaints about abuses in the way the statutes were maintained, but in general nobody seriously challenged the viability of the curriculum itself. On academic indiscipline in France, especially in faculties of law, see L. W. B. Brockliss, *French Higher Education in the Seventeenth and Eighteenth Centuries: a cultural history* (1987), 75–82. The only country where there was a sustained attack on the university curriculum was England in the era of the Civil War and Commonwealth: see C. Webster, *The Great Instauration: science, medicine and reform, 1626–1660* (1975), ch. 3 and appxs I and II.

[16] The clearest account of the movement is P. Gay, *The Enlightenment: an interpretation* (2 vols 1973). Gay, however, exaggerates its anti-Christian and liberal dimension. His exposition needs to be refined in the light of the essays presented in R. Porter and M. Teich (eds), *The Enlightenment in National Context* (1981).

these institutions, but they wanted to reform them in accordance with their own highly original conception of professional acculturation.[17]

A trenchant example of the movement's disdain for the contemporary university is contained in the reform programme written by the French *philosophe* Denis Diderot in 1775–6 for the Empress Catherine II of Russia.[18] In Diderot's opinion, the traditional course in the humanities and philosophy was a waste of time. Students spent six to seven years studying 'two dead languages which are only of use to a handful of citizens', and which, moreover, they never successfully assimilated.[19] They then proceeded to the philosophy class where the emphasis even in the scant study of the natural sciences was on useless metaphysical themes: 'under the heading of physics students wear themselves out in listening to arguments about the elemental structure of matter and the nature of the universe; there is not a word about natural history, not a word of solid chemistry, very little on the movement and fall of bodies; there are few experiments, even less anatomy, nothing on geography'.[20]

According to Diderot, the curriculum in the higher faculties was just as inadequate. Future lawyers were trained in Roman, not French, law and procedure, so a graduate left university no better placed 'if someone debauches his daughter, kidnaps his wife or contests the ownership of his land, than the most inconsequential citizen'.[21] The theology faculty, on the other hand, by concentrating on confessional polemic, produced fanatics, not pious pastors. Its alumni 'are the most useless, intractable and dangerous

[17] Critiques were produced in virtually all parts of continental Europe, even Spain and Portugal, where the Enlightenment took root only slowly. See the essays in J. A. Leith (ed.), *Facets of Education in the Eighteenth Century* (Studies on Voltaire and the Eighteenth Century clxvii 1977), 13–27. There are two particularly good studies on the movement in France: G. Snyders, *La Pédagogie en France aux XVIIe et XVIIIe siècles* (Paris 1965), 345–435; and H. Chisick, *The Limits of Reform in the Enlightenment: attitudes towards the education of the lower classes in eighteenth-century France* (Princeton 1981), which addresses the problem of the élitism of the *philosophes*. The most famous educational treatise of the age is Rousseau's *Émile* (1762).

[18] D. Diderot, 'Plan d'une université pour le gouvernement de Russie', in *Œuvres complètes*, ed. J. Assézat (20 vols Paris 1875–7) iii. 409–534. This work was not edited in Diderot's lifetime. The most influential mid-18th-century French critique of the university is contained in L. R. C. de La Chatolais, *Essai d'éducation nationale ou plan d'études pour la jeunesse* (Paris 1763).

[19] Diderot, 'Plan', 435. This and other translations from the original given below are my own, except the ones cited in nn. 56 and 59 below.

[20] Ibid. 436. Diderot's comment on the humanities and philosophy courses follows closely D'Alembert's critique of the college curriculum in the *Encyclopédie*: see D. Diderot (ed.), *Encyclopédie, ou dictionnaire raisonnée des sciences, des arts et des métiers* (17 vols Paris 1751–65) ii. 526–8.

[21] Diderot, 'Plan', 437. The accusation was grossly unjust. In fact, French faculties of law had taught a compulsory course in French law since 1679, if it was admittedly only a minor part of the course: see the comments in Brockliss, *French Higher Education*, 277–82. The most recent study of this innovation is C. Chêne, *L'Enseignement du droit français en pays de droit écrit, 1679–1793* (Geneva 1982).

subjects of the state'.[22] Only the Paris faculty of medicine provided an acceptable education. But even there much was still amiss since the emphasis was on theoretical learning and no attention was paid to clinical experience. 'In consequence, a young physician wins his medical spurs at our expense, and only becomes skilful by dint of murder.'[23]

After such an acerbic analysis, Diderot's own description of the ideal university curriculum contains few surprises. Study in the humanities and philosophy colleges should henceforth be dominated by mathematics and the natural sciences. Much greater time should be given to the study of ethics, civics and history. Tuition in classical languages should only be given right at the end of the course for a single year. In the higher faculties the watchword was utility. Professors were to produce not *savants* but social workers who would be dedicated to the pursuit of a kinder, juster and healthier world. Significantly, Diderot accorded the highest status among the three 'professional' faculties to medicine, not theology as was traditionally the case. 'We must remember that public health is perhaps the most important of all the objects' for which a university exists.[24]

In the second half of the eighteenth century the critique of the universities by the *philosophes* did not go unheeded. The absolute monarchs who ruled over the greater part of Europe in this period were dedicated state-builders. Primarily interested in strengthening their military power, they lent a sympathetic ear to any programme of reform that promised a more prosperous, populous and contented commonwealth, especially one that ostensibly promoted socio-cultural change but not political revolution. Indeed, through its emphasis on the destruction of corporatism, the programme of the *philosophes* seemed to augment, not weaken, the ruler's authority by removing the innumerable protective cocoons that stood between ruler and subject. In consequence the *philosophes* gave birth to a new and much more vigorous stage in the history of absolute monarchy, aptly dubbed by historians 'enlightened despotism'.[25]

In the four decades before the French Revolution no institution of the *ancien régime* escaped the scrutiny of Europe's reforming monarchs. The universities were no exception, and in virtually every continental country commissions were established to investigate means of bringing the training

---

[22] Diderot, 'Plan', 438. The most detailed analysis of the inadequacies of French theology faculties at this date is to be found in Abbé T. J. Pichon, *Des études théologiques ou recherches sur les abus qui s'opposent au progrès de la théologie dans les écoles publiques et sur les moyens possibles de les réformer en France* (Paris 1767), esp. 60–156.

[23] Diderot, 'Plan', 438–9. Diderot exaggerates the French case, but not greatly: see Brockliss, *French Higher Education*, 395–6. Only Strasbourg among the faculties of medicine offered any clinical training: see E. Wickersheimer, 'La Clinique de l'hôpital de Strasbourg au XVIIIe siècle', *Archives internationales d'histoire des sciences* xvi (1963), 253–76.

[24] Diderot, 'Plan', 497.

[25] The best short introduction to the relationship between the Enlightenment and state-building is T. C. W. Blanning, *Joseph II and Enlightened Despotism* (1970).

of the liberal professional élite 'up to date'. Never before had the universities been subject to such continuous and purposeful harassment. In the past as long as the curriculum had been politically and religiously orthodox rulers had been happy to leave the power of deciding what constituted 'useful' knowledge to the universities themselves. Princes had always intervened in university life from time to time, but mainly to exercise their power of patronage, not to control the curriculum or restructure the institution.[26]

Ultimately, however, the enlightened despots failed to effect a radical shake-up of the university system. As in the case of other institutional reforms that they launched or mooted, their initiatives were always firmly opposed by the powerfully entrenched forces of conservatism, especially the Church. Rulers, therefore, had to move cautiously. In general, the princes and their advisers limited their ambitions to expanding rather than redefining the faculty curriculum, so that more 'relevant' subjects might be taught alongside the traditional syllabus. Thus by 1790 law students in most countries were expected to follow courses in natural, national and public law and, in German universities in particular, a course in the novel ethical science of cameralism or state management (usually established in the faculties of arts). Nevertheless, the lawyers' staple diet still consisted of civil law, regardless of its courtroom value.[27] In a similar fashion, the new emphasis that came to be placed on formal instruction in practical medical subjects, such as botany, chemistry, obstetrics, and less commonly clinical medicine, never displaced the prominence traditionally given to theoretical studies.[28]

Additionally, rulers paid some attention to standardizing the curriculum of the different universities under their control in an attempt to end the wide divergences that often pertained between faculty courses. This was done by

[26] The English crown also used Oxford as an instrument of patronage. James II's famous expulsion of the fellows of Magdalen in 1687 began as an attempt to foist an unwanted president on the College: see L. Brockliss, G. Harriss and A. Macintyre, *Magdalen College and the Crown: essays for the tercentenary of the restoration of the college, 1688* (1988).

[27] Only the case of the German universities has been studied in detail: see N. Hammerstein, *Ius und Historie. Ein Beitrag zur Geschichte des historischen Denkens an deutschen Universitäten im späten 17. und im 18. Jahrhundert* (Göttingen 1972), esp. chs 3, 6 and 7; and Hammerstein, *Aufklärung und katholisches Reich. Untersuchungen zur Universitätsreform und Politik katholischer Territorien des Heiligen Römischen Reich deutscher Nation im 18. Jahrhundert* (Berlin 1977). Also of interest is E. Hellmuth, *Naturrechtsphilosophie und bürokratischer Werthorizont. Studien zur preussischen Geistes- und Sozialgeschichte des 18. Jahrhunderts* (Göttingen 1985). Some sort of natural-law teaching, although often in the faculty of arts, was available in many Protestant universities from the mid-17th century: see H. Coing, 'Die juristische Fakultät und ihr Lehrprogramm', in Coing (ed.), *Handbuch der Quellen und Literatur der neueren europäischen Privatrechtsgeschichte* (Frankfurt 1973–88) ii pt 1, 46–7. The first cameralist chairs were founded at the Prussian universities of Frankfurt-on-Oder and Halle in 1727. For the development of this new science, see A. Nielsen, *Die Enstehung der deutschen Kameralwissenschaft im 17. Jahrhundert* (Jena 1911), and J. Brückner, *Staatswissenschaft, Kameralismus und Naturrecht* (Berlin 1977).

[28] Cf e.g. the reform of the Viennese medical faculty: see F. J. Brechka, *Gerard Van Swieten and his World, 1700–1772* (The Hague 1970), 134–70.

ordering all university professors in a given discipline to build their courses around specified textbooks. But this was usually the limit of the state's interference with academic freedom. Universities retained their individuality and independence, based on their corporate identity, their privileges and their endowments. No real step could be taken towards creating an integrated national university system, when, as in Spain, each institution was the subject of a separate inquiry.[29] Only in the Austrian Empire were universities reduced to departments of state with the imposition from the mideighteenth century of government officials, called directors, as heads of the faculty boards. It was only in Catholic Austria, too, that a more thoroughgoing structural reform was carried through. Under the doctrinaire Emperor, Joseph II, the number of universities was rationalized to one per province, the official language of instruction became German and the faculties were forced to open their doors to Protestants and Jews.[30]

THE UNIVERSITY AND THE FRENCH REVOLUTION

The French Revolution of 1789 occurred in the one important European absolutism where there had been no government-sponsored university reform.[31] Given this fact and given the revolutionaries' commitment to 'enlightened' reform (which would now be implemented in a novel, liberal political context), the university question inevitably loomed large in the proceedings of the National Assembly and its successors. In the period 1789 to 1795 a great variety of plans for reforming French higher education were presented to or drawn up by the politicians in Paris. These can be basically divided into two different approaches to the problem: the one characterized by the ideas of the later foreign minister of Napoleon, Talleyrand, then Bishop of Autun; the other by the ideas of a leading *philosophe*, Condorcet, secretary to the Académie des sciences. Both men were agreed on the need for extensive reform of the education of the liberal professional élite. Both wanted the classical education of the colleges replaced by a curriculum which emphasized mathematics and the natural sciences. Both,

[29] As a result, the pace and degree of reform was different from place to place: for two instances see G. M. Addy, *The Enlightenment in the University of Salamanca* (Durham NC 1966), 93–191, and S. Albiñea, *Universidad e Ilustración: Valencia en la época de Carlos III* (Valencia 1988), ch. 3.

[30] From his youth Joseph had been anxious to turn the university system upside-down. In 1766 he suggested the closure of the University of Vienna because students were drawn from their studies by the enticements of the capital: see A. Arneth, *Maria-Theresia und Joseph. Ihre Correspondenz* (Vienna 1868), pt 3, 348–9. On the absence of religious tests in the continental universities by the 1820s see Ch. 1 n. 317.

[31] There was an interest in university reform in government circles but little enthusiasm was shown by the crown and its ministers: see D. Julia, 'Une réforme impossible: le changement du cursus dans la France du 18e siècle', *Actes de la recherche en sciences sociales* xlvii–viii (1983), 53–6; C. Bailey, 'French secondary education, 1763–1790: the secularization of ex-Jesuit colleges', *Transactions of the American Philosophical Society* lxviii/6 (1978), *passim*; Brockliss, *French Higher Education*, ch. 3 and 189–90.

too, demanded not just the reform but the abolition of the extant universities (all twenty-four). However, on what should replace these there was no agreement between the two.[32]

Talleyrand, whose plan was discussed in the National Assembly in September 1791, wanted to abolish the very concept of a university. In his opinion a generalist secondary education in the reformed colleges of the *ancien régime* should form the prelude to specialist studies at a one-subject professional school. There were to be four types of professional school, for Talleyrand believed that, in addition to members of the three traditional liberal professions, future entrants to the army and navy officer corps also needed institutional training. The number and locale of these schools would depend on the country's needs. There would be ten law schools but only four for medicine, while the military schools would be situated on the frontier. Talleyrand's plan envisaged a complete modernization of the professional curriculum. In the law schools, for instance, the study of Roman law would be reduced to the inculcation of a set of principles of equity. He also introduced complete state control. The professional schools would have no endowment and the professors would be civil servants.[33]

Condorcet's reform programme was formulated a little later and eventually debated in the Convention of the First French Republic in December 1792. In its restructuring of the college curriculum it was extremely innovative. The colleges were to be replaced by *instituts* which would not only provide much more mathematics and natural science but allow the pupils total freedom of choice from among the subjects on offer. Condorcet did not believe that there was a set body of knowledge that the student had to absorb before he began his professional studies. While agreeing that the purpose of secondary education was to develop the mind, he insisted, contrary to the traditional wisdom, that 'the study of every science quickens [its faculties] and contributes to their development and perfection'.[34]

Condorcet's conception of the replacement for the universities was equally iconoclastic. All specialist education for the liberal professional élite was still to take place on the one site, but the new institution would be called a *lycée*, not a university. This institution (of which nine were proposed) would be both a professional school and a vehicle of Enlightenment values, offering the chance to both young and old, men and women, to imbibe the liberating nectar of higher knowledge. How the *lycées* would be organized

[32] The best recent account of the revolutionaries' plans for the reform of higher education is contained in R. R. Palmer, *The Improvement of Humanity: education and the French Revolution* (Princeton 1985). This covers the decade 1789–99.

[33] Talleyrand, *Rapport sur l'instruction publique, fait au nom du comité de la constitution de l'Assemblée nationale* (Paris 1791); repr. in C. Hippeau (ed.), *L'instruction publique en France pendant la Révolution* (Paris 1881), 33–184.

[34] Condorcet, 'Rapport et projet de decret sur l'organisation générale de l'instruction publique', in Hippeau, 212.

was not made clear, but it is evident from Condorcet's theory of knowledge that he considered the four-faculty system redundant. This theory of knowledge was outlined in his plans for the final tier of his educational programme, the National Society of Arts and Sciences. This was to be a learned academy filled with the best brains of the country whose task was to increase the sum of human wisdom and supervise the state educational system. Its members were to be divided into four classes: mathematics and the physical sciences; the political and moral sciences (including law); the applied sciences (including medicine, mechanics and military science); and literature and the *beaux-arts*. The division represented a completely novel conception of the categories of knowledge. Condorcet himself recognized that including medicine and mechanics in the same section might seem strange. But he justified the classification on the grounds that the applied sciences were all closely connected. 'A physician, for instance, who is involved in hospital work and has to consider the manner of placing or moving patients who must undergo a serious operation or be given a complex dressing, would find it advantageous to rub shoulders with machine-builders and engineers.'[35]

Both the Talleyrand and the Condorcet plan are highly significant documents. In their different ways, and much more clearly than earlier reform programmes such as Diderot's, they illustrate why the European university in the late eighteenth century was in a period of crisis from which it could never be fully extricated by the compromise reforms of the enlightened despots. Put simply, the universities no longer had a monopoly in the propagation of knowledge. It was not just that the four university sciences could often be studied in other institutions (as was earlier pointed out). Rather, the four university sciences no longer contained the sum of human wisdom, now that knowledge had been greatly extended by the Scientific Revolution. The seventeenth century saw the development of a novel mathematical and experimental method of establishing the relations between natural phenomena, which had a profound effect on the way one particular branch of philosophy, physics, was conceived.[36] At the same time the New Science encouraged and sometimes even gave birth to the rapid growth of a variety of applied mathematical and observational disciplines which by the eighteenth century had firmly established an independent cognitive status: ballistics, architecture, engineering and surgery, to name but the most important. These new sciences could be fitted only with difficulty into a university curriculum where knowledge, even a knowledge of physics, was transmitted chiefly through textual analysis. Yet in the age of the

[35] Ibid. 230–1.
[36] Studies of the Scientific Revolution are legion. One of the most sensitive accounts of the new epistemology of natural philosophy is contained in I. B. Cohen, *The Newtonian Revolution* (1980).

Enlightenment the new mathematical and observational science could not be ignored. Their military and civil 'utility' was all too obvious, and where the state itself did not take the initiative in institutionalizing their teaching, it eventually capitulated to pressure from below. The traditional liberal professions retained their position of pre-eminence in the non-noble status hierarchy in the period 1300–1700 because their members alone required a training in a scientific discipline to earn their bread. The creation of new scientific disciplines clearly applicable in a variety of occupations for which theoretical knowledge had formerly been unnecessary presented an obvious opportunity for the social advancement of new professional groups. Once entry to these careers was also based on theoretical learning, then they too would become liberal professions rather than mechanical or military arts.

In the course of the eighteenth century institutionalized instruction in these new mathematical and observational disciplines was slowly established. Inevitably, institutionalization occurred outside the university's walls (see Fig. 2.1). By 1789 nearly every country in Europe was endowed with a series of military, engineering and surgical academies, particularly servicing the needs of the ruler's war-machine.[37] Only in northern Italy was there an attempt (albeit half-hearted) to provide training for the new liberal professions within the university, through the establishment in the faculty of arts of chairs in architecture, engineering and agriculture, and the development within the faculty of medicine of courses for human and animal surgeons.[38] The implications for the traditional university of the emergence of these new institutional centres of learning were tremendous. The very name became a misnomer; the university was no longer a *studium generale*. In a revolutionary era, when every institution of the *ancien régime* was being carefully scrutinized, the university could no longer exist in its old form. There were only two possibilities. Either the university must be abolished and its faculties changed into specialist, separate institutes, or, as in Condorcet's plan, the university must be reconstituted so that it once again had a monopoly over the dissemination of wisdom.

[37] The situation in France can be studied through the essays in R. Taton (ed.), *L'Enseignement et diffusion des sciences au xviiie siècle* (Paris 1964). Significantly in Russia institutionalized military training was established *before* university education: see J. L. Black, *Citizens for the Fatherland: education, educators and pedagogical ideals in eighteenth-century Russia* (New York 1979), chs 2–3. Two important recent studies of the development of independent surgical education are T. Gelfand, *Professionalizing Modern Medicine: Paris surgeons and medical science and institutions in the eighteenth century* (Westport Conn. 1980), chs 5–7; and M. C. Burke, *The Royal College of San Carlos: surgery and Spanish medical reform in the late eighteenth century* (Durham NC 1977), chs 4–7.

[38] P. Vaccari, *Storia della Università di Pavia* (Pavia 1957), 156; M. Roggero, *Il sapere e la virtù: stato, università e professioni nel Piemonte tra settecento ed ottocento* (Turin 1987), 132–46; M. Ghetti, 'Struttura e organizzazione dell'università di Padova dalla metà del 1700 al 1797', *Quaderni per la storia dell'Università di Padova* xvi (1983), 77–8, 89.

With the coming of war with Europe in February 1792, the subsequent overthrow of the 'constitutional monarchy' and the eventual collapse into the Terror, the revolutionaries were too preoccupied to concern themselves more than occasionally with restructuring the system of French higher education. Before the fall of Robespierre in July 1794 only one definite decision was taken: in September 1793 the universities and colleges of the *ancien régime* were formally abolished, their endowments having already been nationalized the previous March. In the more peaceful Thermidorian era, however, with the Republic much safer from external and internal enemies, the revolutionaries took up educational reform in earnest. By this time Talleyrand was in exile and Condorcet dead, the victim of his Girondin sympathies. Nevertheless, it was their programmes which continued to dominate the ensuing debate. Of the two, it was to be the Talleyrand alternative that was finally embraced and enshrined in a series of laws passed in the final months of 1794. The Thermidorians voted for the establishment of a generalist secondary education in the arts and sciences which would be located in departmental schools called *écoles centrales*. From these the future professional élite would feed into specialist schools which were to be divided by function and discipline. Schools offering training for the state professions would be known as *écoles de service publique*; those for private occupations, as *écoles spéciales*. There were to be schools for virtually every conceivable branch of knowledge: astronomy, geometry, mechanics, natural history, medicine, veterinary science, rural economy, antiquities, political science, painting, architecture and music. At the same time, the majority of the schools would be professionally orientated, not narrowly professional, so Condorcet had not been defeated completely. Moreover, again as he had envisaged and in keeping with the secularist outlook of the Republic, there would be no state schools for theological studies. But the underlying ideology was clear: the university had no more place in the new age than monasteries, serfdom or slavery. As Daunou made clear in his speech to the Convention introducing the law for setting up the *écoles spéciales*, only in single-subject schools could professional training be effectively imparted.

The system of special schools, too little known or at least too seldom established until now, will focus mental effort more immediately and actively on definite goals. The system will continually incite competition, through the eternally useful sight of a purpose which is always close at hand. It will remove the temptation to be lazy by always keeping before the student's eyes the image of success, reputation, and wealth. The system will concentrate the student's strength, which has too often been allowed to be dissipated. It will diminish the number of mediocre men in every profession and increase to the glory of the nation and for the public good the number of extraordinary men in a single [profession].

It will be easy to root this type of teaching in a people who wish to shake off every prejudice.... In the special schools, the sciences will be more reasonably and less fanatically revered. There will be no more altars erected to them, but their benefits will be appreciated.[39]

There were several reasons why the Talleyrand model was the one accepted. The Republic was financially pressed: it was much cheaper to establish and staff separate professional schools which could be founded piecemeal than encyclopaedic *lycées*. Moreover, the Thermidorians had already begun to found specialist professional schools before the Daunou law was promulgated. In the course of the Revolution not only the universities but virtually all the new professional schools, such as the surgical and military academies, had been abolished. This might have been of little immediate consequence but for the high attrition rate of trained personnel in the people's war. By the summer of 1794 the army was starved of engineers, physicians and surgeons and the Thermidorians responded to the shortage by founding in the autumn the École polytechnique and three *écoles de médecine* (at Paris, Montpellier and Strasbourg), where for the first time in France top-class medical and surgical instruction was given in the same institution.[40] The exigencies of the moment, however, were not the sole factor militating in favour of the Talleyrand option. In the light of the development of the sciences in the seventeenth and eighteenth centuries it was the more logical solution. Before 1600 not only had the university taught the gamut of the sciences, but each of the four traditional sciences and their subsidiary branches were united through their dependence on the same analytical tools: humanist exegetical techniques and Aristotelian verbal logic. Knowledge was truly one. The emergence of a science of natural philosophy and a variety of new, applied sciences dependent upon empiricism and mathematical logic destroyed this unity. The late eighteenth-century university taught neither every science nor, with the advent of an experimental, mathematical physics, a series of integrated sciences. Condorcet might reconstruct the university as the single guardian and propagator of man's accumulated wisdom but the *lycée* was at best an umbrella institution.

The creation of a new higher-education system in France took time. The departmental *écoles centrales* were established as planned fairly quickly, but they had a brief history. Compared with the colleges, they were few in number (there were only some ninety departments but there had been some 400 colleges in 1789), and parents disliked the 'modern' curriculum, with its heavy emphasis on mathematics and natural science. Educated during the final years of the *ancien régime*, the majority of the traditional liberal

---

[39] Daunou, 'Rapport' (27 vendémiaire, an IV), in Hippeau, 481. Daunou claimed that the Thermidorian committee had drawn freely on all previous educational plans (see p. 483).

[40] The École polytechnique was initially called the École centrale des travaux publiques. For the most recent discussion of its foundation, see B. Belhoste, 'Les Origines de l'École polytechnique: des anciennes écoles d'ingénieurs à l'école centrale des travaux publiques', *Histoire d'éducation* xlii (1989), 13–54.

professional élite in the 1790s still hankered after the classical curriculum of the former colleges and took advantage of their right under the Constitution of 1794 to send their sons to private institutions.[41] Recognizing this Napoleon in 1802 abolished the *écoles centrales* and replaced them by a network of municipal colleges and *lycées* (not to be confused with Condorcet's encyclopaedic institutions of higher learning). The municipal colleges were essentially feeder schools teaching the lower levels of secondary education, whereas the *lycées* were restricted to the large town. From the beginning the *lycée* curriculum paid as much regard to the study of the classics as of the natural sciences. However, it was the end of the Napoleonic era before the *lycées* became popular. The fact that the *lycées* were intended to be boarding-schools with a military ethos (students wore uniforms) alienated parents, as did their confessional pluralism. The French liberal professional élite by and large wanted its children brought up as Catholic humanists and still preferred to send its sons to other schools. Ultimately, Napoleon only conquered this reluctance by elevating the classics to a position of supremacy once more and restricting the scope of the curriculum offered by the private sector. After 1815 the *lycées* (temporarily rechristened royal colleges) became the dominant institution involved in teaching the final years of the secondary-school curriculum. In the period 1815–48 their number increased from thirty-seven to forty-six and they eventually educated one-fifth of all secondary-school pupils.[42]

The professional schools fell as Daunou had intended into two groups (see Fig. 2.2). One was comprised of a network of specialist military and engineering schools, dependent in part upon the École polytechnique and opening the door to prestigious careers in state service. The École polytechnique was essentially a feeder school. Its students (admitted by a competitive examination) received a sophisticated training in higher mathematics before going on to more strictly professional studies at appropriately named *écoles d'application*. The second group, founded from 1802, consisted of a series of private professional schools. Napoleon was an enthusiast for the concept of the specialist academy and on one occasion suggested the foundation of twenty-nine different types (including one for historical studies).[43] In the end under the reorganization effected by the Minister of the Interior,

[41] The curriculum was extremely progressive and would have been applauded by Diderot. For a good study of its *raison d'être* see S. Moravia, *Il tramonto dell'illuminismo: filosofia e politica nella società francese, 1771–1810* (Bari 1968), 347–69. Detailed research on the sociology of attendance at the *écoles centrales* is in its infancy: see Julia, *Atlas*, 40–5 (statistical maps and analysis).

[42] R. D. Anderson, *Education in France, 1848–1870* (1975), 20. There are virtually no modern studies of the development of individual *lycées*. An exception is O. De Vaux, 'Les Lycées impériaux...des casernes: mythe ou réalité: l'exemple du lycée de Toulouse', *Revue historique* cclxxiii (1985), 159–65.

[43] For Napoleon's deeper thoughts on the structure of a school of history see *Letters of Napoleon*, ed. and trans. J. M. Thompson (1934), 178–87.

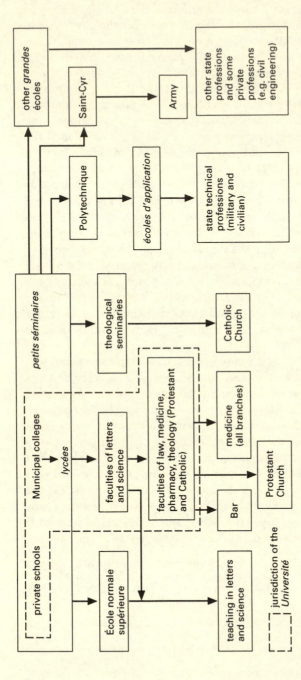

FIGURE 2.2 Higher education in the nineteenth century: the French model. The French model became more complex in 1875 with the creation of 'free' (i.e. non-state) faculties, which accommodated the aspirations of the Catholic Church. The Université was dismantled in 1896 with the establishment of sixteen self-governing universities, although the rest of the system remained intact. The École normale supérieure became part of the University of Paris in 1903.

A variety of institutions prepared students for the faculties and the *grandes écoles*. The *lycées* had the edge because they offered special high-level mathematics teaching for those taking the entrance examination to the *écoles*. These included some private foundations, e.g. the École centrale des arts et manufactures, founded 1829.

Entrance to the École normale supérieure, to the École polytechnique and to Saint-Cyr was by competitive examination only. In the mid-19th century c.600 sat the entrance examination to the Polytechnique; only 25% succeeded. Entrance to the faculties of letters and science was only with a bachelor's degree in letters and, in the case of medical students, a bachelor's degree in science (either, 1852–8). Prospective teachers in municipal colleges, private schools, *lycées* and the faculties of letters and science had to hold a baccalaureate, licence or doctorate in their broad subject area; the level of degree depended on the level at which they wished to teach. Teachers in church schools were exempt. Pharmacy was given faculty status only in 1840. The state faculties of theology did not function since they were boycotted by the French Catholic Church.

Fourcroy, schools within the 1789 boundaries of France were only created in the traditional university disciplines: three in medicine (which included the study of surgery, for physicians and surgeons were henceforth united in one profession), three in pharmacy, nine in law and two in Protestant theology. Both the *écoles publiques* and the private professional schools were carefully monitored by the government. The curriculum in each case was prescribed, appointments were scrutinized closely, and the state kept control of the purse-strings. Nevertheless, the private professional schools looked very much like the old faculties with a streamlined and professionally relevant curriculum. Whereas the *écoles publiques* offered diplomas, the private professional schools awarded degrees, as before a *sine qua non* for professional practice. Graduands, moreover, still had to pass oral examinations, and prepare and defend theses, which were often in Latin, although the language of the classroom was now French.[44]

The system of private professional schools was refined in 1808. Their number remained unchanged, except for the addition of five in Catholic theology.[45] But the schools were now given the old-fashioned name of faculties and students had to gain a degree in arts, the bachelor of letters, before they matriculated. To accommodate this requirement Napoleon created a new institution: the faculty of letters. Twenty-seven were envisaged for the territory occupied by France in 1789, but only six were functioning when the system was reviewed in 1816 and there were still only eleven in 1848. The faculties of letters also licensed humanities and philosophy teachers in the *lycées*, municipal colleges and secular private schools. Would-be secondary-school teachers in mathematics and the natural sciences, in contrast, had to appear before a different examining tribunal: the faculties of science, another creation of 1808, of which only five were extant in 1816 and ten on the fall of Louis Philippe.[46] Both the faculty of letters and the faculty of science ostensibly had a teaching role in that they were intended to provide instruction at a higher level than that supplied by the *lycées*. Before 1870, however, the majority performed their teaching duties perfunctorily. The number of chairs was small, professors often doubled as masters in the local *lycée*, and there was seldom a large audience as degrees in both faculties could be obtained without attending faculty lectures. Most faculties of letters only gave instruction in philosophy, history and French and Latin

[44] Cf the regulations laid down for a doctorate in medicine: *Recueil de lois et règlemens concernant l'instruction publique depuis l'édit de Henri IV en 1598 jusqu'à ce jour* (8 vols Paris 1814–28) ii. 334–78.

[45] The medical map was complicated by the creation from 1806 of a growing number of independent *écoles secondaires de médicine*. These could not give degrees but students who attended the *écoles* could count their time there towards qualifying for a faculty degree. There were 22 by 1841.

[46] More work was found for these faculties from 1836, when medical students had also to become bachelors of science by the end of their second year.

literature. Only at Paris were there a large number of chairs and the possibility of hearing lectures on subjects outside the relatively narrow *lycée*
curriculum. In the capital, however, an important group of potential students was eventually siphoned off into a rival institution, the École normale
supérieure. Also founded in 1808, the École normale was a training college
for professors in the *lycées* and the faculties of letters and science. It contained some 300 students, and entrance, as in the case of the École polytechnique, was by a competitive examination. The pupils at the École
normale initially attended the Paris faculties but by 1830 were receiving
virtually all their instruction within the school.

The 1808 reform also revived the use of the term *université* but gave it a
novel meaning. Bringing to fruition an initiative begun in 1806, Napoleon
brought all the private professional schools and the *lycées* under one administrative umbrella. The country was divided into provinces and each province endowed with an institution called an *académie* whose chief official,
the rector (again an old term), was in charge of the faculties and *lycées* within
his region. The rectors were responsible to a central administrative council,
headed by the *grand maître* (a masonic touch?), who reported annually to
the Emperor through the Minister of the Interior. The whole edifice was
given the label the Université impériale. It was not a university at all in the
traditional sense of the word, but a state department of education that
controlled a series of separate professional schools and their feeder institutions: these had no corporate identity, no fiscal independence and little
curricular freedom. The Université impériale even controlled private secondary schools. Masters in the private sector had also to be graduates in
letters or science, and private institutions were subjected by the local *académie* to a *per capita* tax.

For some reason or another the Université impériale included only the
private professional schools. The École polytechnique and the other military
and engineering schools remained outside the *grand maître*'s sway. Nor were
they ever organized beneath another bureaucratic hierarchy. They and later
specialist technical schools, such as the short-lived École nationale d'administration founded in 1848, were directly under the control of either the War
or the Interior Minister. The Université impériale, therefore, did not marry
the visions of Talleyrand and Condorcet. It made little logical sense as an
institution and was subject to continual revision. Any pretence that the
Université was a self-governing institution was gradually eroded. In 1824
the *grand maître* became the Minister of Education and Religion (from 1829
the Minister of Instruction) and in 1850 the Second Republic abolished the
académies. Had that régime survived, the faculties and *lycées* would have
been thereafter directly under the aegis of a minister of state.

The creation of this new system of higher education in revolutionary and
Napoleonic France had great repercussions for the rest of the Continent. As

its development took place in a period which saw France take control directly or indirectly of the area of Europe that forms the greater part of the present European Community, the new institutional model of liberal professional training, like the other new institutions of revolutionary France, was exported in the knapsacks of the nation's soldiers. Wherever the French went, university and college endowments were seized, the college curriculum was restructured, universities in unfavourable geographical locations were closed and the others turned into one or more professional schools. The process resulted in the loss of several of Europe's most prestigious universities: Louvain in 1797, Luther's Wittenberg a few years later (permanently closed), and even the Prussian educational flagship Halle (only founded in 1694).

In the parts of Europe integrated with France university reform was swift and thorough. In 1801–2, when Piedmont-Savoy was occupied by Jourdan, the University of Turin was instantly remodelled. The faculties of arts and theology were permanently closed and the university turned into five separate écoles spéciales in law, medicine, the mathematical and physical sciences, design and veterinary medicine. On orders from Paris, however, this experiment was abandoned, and Turin eventually became the site of just two professional schools: law and medicine. In 1808 these, together with the resurrected faculty of theology, became faculties of the Université impériale administered through the Turin académie. The experience was never a happy one. Under the kings of Sardinia Turin had been a well-endowed, pampered university. The French in contrast starved the professional écoles of funds. The endowment was sold off and the proceeds invested in government bonds. Far from the académie receiving the interest as was intended, a large proportion of the return disappeared into Napoleon's war chest.[47]

In Napoleon's satellite kingdoms, where rulers were permitted a degree of latitude in the introduction of French institutions, reform, though no less thorough, was more sensitively handled. In the kingdom of Italy Napoleon's stepson Eugène Beauharnais inherited three universities of antiquity and distinction: Bologna, Padua and Pavia, the last only recently 'reformed' by its Austrian overlord. All three lost their corporate independence and were placed under the control of a civil servant responsible to the kingdom's Minister of Education. All three, too, saw a shake-up of the traditional faculty system that brought the end of the study of theology. Nevertheless, they retained an existence as separate institutions and the restructuring of the faculties strengthened the eighteenth-century tendency (unique to the

[47] F. Boyer, 'Les Institutions universitaires en Piémont de 1800 à 1802', *Revue d'histoire moderne et contemporaine* xvii (1970), 913–18; D. Outram, 'Education and politics in Piedmont, 1796–1814', *Historical Journal* xix (1976), 611–33; Outram, 'Military empire, political collaboration, and cultural consensus: the Université impériale reappraised: the case of the University of Turin', *History of Universities* vii (1988), 287–303.

north of Italy) of incorporating within the curriculum the new mathematical sciences. This was particularly true of Padua, where the trend was confirmed by the creation of a separate faculty in physics and mathematics devoted to the production of surveyors, architects and engineers. On the other hand, such moves should not be seen as an attempt to reconstruct higher education on the lines advocated by Condorcet. Even in the kingdom of Italy Talleyrand's ideas, thanks to the whole-hearted support they received from Napoleon, were dominant. As in France specialist military academies and technical schools proliferated, equally fed by the gymnasiums-turned-*lycées*. Moreover, the universities did not have a monopoly in preparing students for the private professions. Milan, for instance, was the site of an independent veterinary college, and from 1809 was host to a school of practical eloquence for trainee barristers. Here the would-be Cicero fresh from law school would learn to 'speak in public with brevity, efficacy, and dignity'.[48]

France's iconoclastic influence, however, was not felt only in the parts of Europe that fell under her sway. From the moment that the revolutionaries abolished the French universities and opted for a system of higher education based on independent professional schools, similar demands were to be heard from educational pundits all over Europe. It was as if revolutionary France had finally effected what every enlightened critic had subconsciously desired but before 1789 had never dared to enunciate. The attack was particularly brutal in German-speaking countries, where calls for the immolation of the institution could be heard as early as 1792.[49] In one German state, moreover, Prussia, the abolitionists found solid support within the government. The year 1797 saw the advent to power of Julius von Massow, a convinced believer in the redundancy of the university as an institution of instruction. In the following years, and especially after 1801, he worked towards the gradual phasing-out of Prussia's four universities (including Halle) and their replacement by a series of professional schools in the capital, Berlin. It was possibly only his removal as a Francophile after Prussia's defeat by Napoleon in 1806 which prevented the fulfilment of his plans.[50]

Indeed, as the nineteenth century dawned, the university looked a doomed species. Its only governmental defenders were to be found in

[48] Vaccari, *Storia della Università di Pavia*, ch. 9; E. Brambilla, 'L'istruzione pubblica della republicca cisalpina al regno italico', *Quaderni storici* xxiii (1973), 491–526; M. C. Ghetti, 'Struttura e organizzazione dell'Università di Padova dal 1798 al 1817', *Quaderni per la storia dell'Università di Padova* xvii (1984), 135–65 (esp. 159).

[49] e.g. J. H. Campe, *Allgemeine Revision des gesamten Schul- und Erziehungswesens* (Vienna 1792). References to this and other abolitionist diatribes from the 1790s can be found in R. S. Turner, 'University reformers and professorial scholarship in Germany, 1760–1806', in L. Stone (ed.), *The University in Society* (2 vols Princeton 1974) ii. 501–3. Turner treats the abolitionist movement in Germany as an independent tradition reaching back to 1760.

[50] U. Muhlack, 'Die Universitäten im Zeichen von Neuhumanismus und Idealismus', in P. Baumgart and N. Hammerstein, *Beiträge zu Problemen deutscher Universitätsgründungen der frühen Neuzeit* (Nendeln 1978), 301–3.

Russia, where in 1803 Tsar Alexander I established six universities along traditional faculty and corporate lines at the apex of a national system of education. The new universities were quintessential representations of the eighteenth-century Enlightenment compromise, 'modern' only in their confessional pluralism, absence of instruction in theology, and the division of the arts curriculum between two separate faculties of philosophy and natural science. Intended to exist beside a number of extant military academies and engineering schools, they were clearly not an attempt to create a new institution which would be a genuine contemporary *studium generale*. Their novelty lay primarily in the additional administrative brief of the university councils. Under the edict of foundation, the country was divided into six educational provinces and each university was supposed to control and supervise the gymnasia and the county and village schools within its region.[51] In the context of the educational spirit of the age, Russia's enthusiasm for the university was the exception that proved the rule. Arguably, the foundation reflected the fact that prior to 1803 the country had only one university, Moscow, established in 1755 and never host to more than a handful of students. The university was a new institution in Russia; it could hardly be seen as a medieval fossil, frustrating the build-up of state power. Arguably, too, the foundation reflected the fact that in the 1790s, in response to the French Revolution, Russia had once more retreated behind its cultural curtain. Alexander's advisers, who included the conservative Minister of Education Zavadovski, probably had no idea that most European governments now viewed the university as a terminological anomaly.

Ultimately, of course, the university did survive. Only in nineteenth-century France was the creation of an alternative higher-educational system permanent (until the reforms of 1892). Elsewhere the collapse of the Napoleonic empire and the restoration of many of the old rulers led in turn to the restoration of the traditional university. Admittedly, the university system of continental Europe in the period 1815–48 was very different from that of the pre-revolutionary era. In the first place, it was leaner, as many small, out-of-the-way universities were abolished and never restored. Sixteen universities were lost in the territory of the old Holy Roman Empire; in the Spanish kingdom of Castile the number fell from seventeen to seven. Secondly, the French creation of a state-run higher-educational system left its mark. The restored universities were generally no longer corporate, independent bodies loosely attached to the state apparatus, but state-funded and state-run institutions subject to a common national curriculum and constant governmental supervision and harassment. This was particularly so in the Austrian Empire, where the Theresan and Josephist reforms had anticipated the state

---

[51] J. T. Flynn, *The University Reform of Tsar Alexander I, 1802–1835* (Washington 1988), 14–25, 177–80, 243–4. Instruction was in Russian except at Dorpat, where German was used.

university of the Restoration era. According to the 1837 regulations for Pavia, the faculty director of studies had progressed from being a government intermediary to a government spy. Henceforth, the director was to ensure enforcement of the prescribed curriculum 'by the means of repeated impromptu visits during the lectures'.[52] Thirdly, the restored rulers felt no allegiance to the traditional four-faculty model. A new emphasis on secularization resulted in many universities being permanently shorn of their faculties of theology. At the same time, there was a growing acceptance that the restored faculty of arts taught a mishmash of incompatible disciplines and that entrants to the higher faculties had no need to have studied both the philosophical and natural sciences in detail. In recognition of this fact, Russian universities quickly ceased to be the only ones where the arts curriculum was institutionally divided. As early as 1815 the universities in the new kingdom of Belgium-Holland were endowed with separate faculties of science.[53] Nevertheless, despite these provisos, the universities of the Restoration era were definitely more than professional schools. Through their traditions, ceremonies and administrative organs (however emasculated) they retained a firm link with their medieval roots.

Given the widespread absorption of the French critique of the institution at the turn of the nineteenth century, the survival and resurrection of the universities after 1815 needs explanation. At first glance, the restored university would seem as much a terminological absurdity as its eighteenth-century predecessor. Only a limited attempt was made to adjust the curriculum to the needs of the new liberal professions, even when the faculty of arts was split into two. The northern Italian universities with their commitment to training engineers and surveyors remained, as always, exceptional.[54] Institutional tuition in the applied empirico-mathematical sciences still remained largely outside the university in a complex of military and engineering academies. Indeed, the number of such professional schools continued to expand as rulers and their advisers sought to imitate the formidable network established in revolutionary France. The creation of the highly successful Vienna Polytechnic in 1815 is just one example. A system of higher education based on a number of separate professional schools, therefore, would seem to have been the logical development.

That this was not to be the case can be easily explained in the short term. Continental Europe's universities were restored as part of

[52] Vaccari, *Storia della Università di Pavia*, 253–5.

[53] V. Cousin, *De l'instruction publique en Hollande* (Paris 1837), 345–8; Cousin contains a French translation of the royal decree of Aug. 1815 establishing a new law of higher education. Science faculties had already been established in the Napoleonic kingdom of Holland as part of the Université impériale. Separate faculties of science were established only slowly elsewhere before the mid-19th century; in Germany none had been founded.

[54] e.g. the 1815 reform of Padua: see Ghetti, 'Struttura della Università di Padova dal 1798 al 1817', 170.

a wider conservative reaction. Whatever Europe's governmental élites thought of the French Revolution in its pre-imperialist stage, the experience of occupation or military humiliation led a growing proportion to denounce all that it stood for. The disaster that had befallen the European states system and the social order at the hands of Napoleon was seen as the inevitable culmination of a half-century of enlightened reform which had weakened traditional institutions, especially the Church and the local noble-dominated estates. As supporters of this viewpoint tended to be well represented in the councils of Europe's absolutist rulers after 1815, the universities inevitably enjoyed a new lease of life. Their rejuvenation was apt in a court universe dominated by disciples of Metternich. Even if many monarchs and their bureaucrats saw themselves as heirs to the tradition of enlightened despotism, the increasing need to rely on the privileged orders in the face of the nascent liberal and nationalist movements ensured there could be no radical educational initiatives. Even more than in the pre-revolutionary decades state-building in the Restoration had to be conducted *sotto voce*. The universities, it was hoped, could be used to inculcate establishment values. Significantly, in the Habsburg dominions religious instruction became a compulsory part of the propaedeutic course in the faculty of arts.

In the long term, however, this explanation is insufficient. Between 1830 and 1860 the absolute rulers of Europe were either pushed aside or forced to reach an accommodation with the forces of nationalism and liberalism. Had the universities been sustained in the mid-nineteenth century only by a wave of traditionalist nostalgia, they would never have survived this second era of revolution. In Spain, for instance, the final arrival of the liberals in power in the 1830s led to a further round in the reform of the country's universities, but no call for their abolition. The state's grip was tightened but the institution received the liberals' blessing. Indeed, if the historic but geographically isolated University of Alcalá was unceremoniously closed, a new university was founded in the capital to mark the dawn of the liberal era. The ease with which the universities survived this age of transition, therefore, must be attributed to a deeper cause.

The answer to the conundrum lies in an ideological shift in the conception of a university. The reaction to the attempt of Napoleon and his clients to redraw the educational map of Europe not merely bred nostalgia for the institution he and his henchmen denigrated. In Protestant northern Germany this reaction coincided with and encouraged the crystallization of a new vision of the university's *raison d'être*. In the first decade of the nineteenth century, as the Prussian establishment worked for the institution's destruction, a small band of intellectuals on the fringe of public life fitted it up with a new legitimacy. The institution ultimately survived on the Continent because the Germans invented the research university.

GERMAN IDEALISM AND THE RESEARCH UNIVERSITY

In the late Middle Ages the universities had been centres of both teaching and research. Professors were always chiefly occupied in communicating an inherited wisdom, but at the same time many (e.g. the Oxford Mertonians of the fourteenth century) saw their role as being one of refining and adding to the sum of knowledge. While all the sciences were dependent for their development on the same tools of logical analysis, there was no problem in the maintenance of this dual activity. Indeed, the idea that teaching and research might be separated was completely foreign to the medieval mind. In the course of the sixteenth and seventeenth centuries, however, the position dramatically changed. As universities became increasingly professional schools dedicated to maintaining theological and political orthodoxies, so they generally ceased to be centres of active inquiry in the metaphysical and moral sciences. At the same time the promotion of a new mathematical and empiricist analytical approach to natural philosophy guaranteed that the universities would play only a minor part in the Scientific Revolution. In general they lacked the facilities and funds required to carry on original work. Research in the natural sciences had an entirely different institutional locus: the academy. First founded in the second half of the seventeenth century, there were few important countries a century later that did not have one.[55] By the eighteenth century, then, it was universally accepted that the university was a teaching institution *tout court*. Virtually all the exciting and often anti-establishment developments in philosophy, theology and natural science occurred outside its walls. A few professors might be engaged in original research (Newton had held the Lucasian chair in Mathematics at Cambridge), but this was a personal choice. If the average professor put pen to paper, he wrote a textbook, not a learned paper. There can be no doubt that the state approved of this restricted role. The Prussian government declared in 1770: 'the ultimate purpose of the universities is the instruction of youth. A professor of a university has fulfilled his office satisfactorily if he thoroughly teaches the youth what is known and discovered in his subject.'[56]

[55] The secondary literature is immense: *inter alia*, H. Brown, *Scientific Organizations in Seventeenth-Century France, 1620–1680* (Baltimore 1934); J. E. McClellan III, *Science Reorganized: scientific societies in the eighteenth century* (New York 1985); F. Hartmann and R. Vierhaus (eds), *Der Akademiegeschichte im 17. und 18. Jahrhundert* (Bremen 1977); L. Boehm and E. Raimondi, *Università, accademie e società scientifice in Italia e Germania del cinquecento al settecento* (Bologna 1981); R. Hahn, *The Anatomy of a Scientific Institution: the Paris Academy of Sciences, 1666–1803* (Berkeley 1971); K. T. Hoppen, *The Common Scientist in the Seventeenth Century: a study of the Dublin Philosophical Society, 1683–1708* (1970); W. S. Knowles-Middleton, *The Experimenters: a study of the Accademia del Cimento* (Baltimore 1971); M. Purver, *The Royal Society: concept and creation* (1967). No academy was founded in the Habsburg lands.
[56] Cited in Turner, 'University reformers', 527; German attitudes to the duties of the mid-18th-century professor are discussed, pp. 515–29. The universities did play a considerable part in

The idea that the university might once more be an institution dedicated to the expansion of knowledge first surfaced in Germany in the 1790s. Its first significant supporter was Kant, the author in 1798 of a seminal pamphlet entitled *Streit der Fakultäten*. Kant was a professor at the isolated Prussian university of Königsberg who had defied the prevalent ethic and dedicated his life to both teaching and original thought. The new 'critical' philosophy which he perfected and published in the 1780s does not seem to have been taught to his students. It was perhaps for this reason that Kant was left alone by the Prussian authorities until 1794, after he published a book on natural religion which the King judged detrimental to Christianity. The pamphlet was his response to royal harassment. In Kant's opinion the university was a vital public institution, but one in which the three 'higher' faculties and the faculty of philosophy had distinctive functions. The former prepared public servants to minister to the spiritual, moral and physical well-being of the people. The faculty of philosophy, on the other hand, was dedicated to the pursuit of truth in what Kant called the historical (meaning empirical) and rational (meaning deductive) sciences. Whereas the government had the right to police the content of the curriculum of the higher faculties, for they were the guardians of the status quo, it had no right to interfere with philosophy. Professors of philosophy should be free even to criticize the foundations of the higher sciences.

It is absolutely essential that within the university there is a faculty involved in public scientific instruction which, being independent of the orders of the government, has the liberty, if not to give orders, at least to give a judgement on everything of scientific interest, that is to say on truth. In this faculty reason must have the authority to speak openly, for without this liberty, truth cannot be made manifest (and this will be prejudicial even to the government). Reason, moreover, is free by its very nature and can welcome no order directing something to be received as the truth (no *crede*, simply a free *credo*).[57]

In the following years Kant's vision was enthusiastically embraced by his philosophical disciples, such as Fichte, Schelling and Wilhelm von Humboldt. But just as these disciples subtly changed his philosophy and created German Idealism, so they developed his view of the research university in a new direction. In so doing they found a new justification for the university as an institution. Kant had wanted to release professors of philosophy from the stranglehold of theological and political orthodoxy. He provided no real reason why teaching and research should be combined in the one function,

medical research in the early-modern period and university posts provided a livelihood for a number of experimental philosophers. Nevertheless, there was no necessary connection between the university and research: see the suitably balanced assessment of R. Porter, 'What part did the universities play in the Scientific Revolution?' in H. de Ridder-Simoens (ed.), *A History of the University in Europe* (4 vols 1991–   ) ii (1996).

[57] I. Kant, *Streit der Facultäten* (1798), ed. K. Reich (Hamburg 1959), 12.

nor why philosophy and the three other traditional sciences should be housed under the one roof. The Idealists provided the answer.

In the first place, they believed unreservedly in the unity of knowledge. Each science was a part of a greater whole and was of interest only in so far as it provided a deeper understanding of ultimate truth. There was a need, therefore, for a new type of university, one truly meriting the name, where adepts of the different sciences would unite together to pursue the meaning of the universe. Total knowledge, however, was beyond man's grasp: it was something towards which the race continually strove. The university, then, would not be in the business of providing definitive answers. As Humboldt emphasized, the pursuit of knowledge was a perpetual activity: 'It is a peculiarity of higher scientific institutions that they deal with science in the form of an as yet unresolved problem and are hence for ever involved in research.'[58]

In the second place, the Idealists believed that a commitment to and engagement in the search for ultimate truth was the sole path to the fulfilment of an individual's humanity. It was only through the search for the whole that one could gain self-understanding. The university, then, could not be reduced to an academy of learned scholars, a sort of Baconian Solomon's House. It had to be an institution for individual *Bildung* where the professional servants of truth would initiate the nation's youth in the great human adventure. Professors had to be both researchers and teachers. It was envisaged that the two roles (as in the medieval university) would be carried on in conjunction. The students would not form a passive audience, listening politely as the teachers expounded their wisdom. Rather, totally committed to their studies as the particular representation of ultimate truth, the students would be encouraged to seek existential confirmation of the benefits of *Bildung* through continually challenging their professors' ideas. The pursuit of truth would thereby become a combined activity, pupil and teacher advancing *ad astra* hand in hand. The Idealists saw the university as a missionary institution. Henceforth it was to be the breeding-ground of the perfect man. The university would replace the Church as the guardian of mankind's spiritual health. The university, claimed Fichte in 1811, was the ideal vehicle for the spiritual evolution and liberation of mankind:

The uninterrupted and steady progress of the intellectual education of our race is ...the sole condition under which the supernatural...can continually appear in mankind in new and fresh transfiguration, and can be exhibited by man in the

---

[58] Quoted in O. Vossler, 'Humboldt's Idee der Universität', *Historisches Zeitung* clxxviii (1954), 263. Humboldt's most notable description of the new university was in his 1809 pamphlet *Ueber die innere und äussere Organisation der höheren wissenschaftlichen Anstalten in Berlin*. Besides Vossler, other accounts of Humboldt's educational ideas can be found in C. Menze, *Die Bildungsreform Wilhelm von Humboldts* (Hanover 1975); E. Spranger, *Wilhelm von Humboldt und die Reform des Bildungswesens* (Tübingen 1960).

external world. The continual employment of the understanding is the sole means by which the human race fulfils its destiny and whereby each generation wins its place in the series of generations. The University, however, is the institution expressly devised to secure the non-interruption and steadiness of this progress; because it is the place where each generation hands on, consciously and according to principle, its highest intellectual education to the succeeding generation, in order that the latter may extend it and hand it on thus extended to its successor, and so on to the end of time.... Now if the University is this, it is clear that it is the most important institution and the most holy thing which the human race possesses.... [The] University is the visible representation of the immortality of our race because it lets nothing perish that truly exists.[59]

Theoretically the university was to be open to all. *Bildung* was equally necessary for members of every class. On the other hand, genuine participation in the activities of the research university would require of its students initial training in a variety of linguistic and logical skills. For this reason entrance to the university would be dependent even more than before on completion of a course at the gymnasium. Collegiate education, however, would need to be reformed if the gymnasium was to fulfil its propaedeutic role. Like the *philosophes*, the Idealists wanted to reduce the dominance of Latin. But, in contrast, they remained enamoured of classical studies, insisting that pride of place should now be given to Greek, hitherto the poor relation. In Humboldt's opinion the ideal curriculum would consist of classics, mathematics and history. The purpose of the course was not just to teach ancillary skills, but to introduce the pupil to human potential through studying man's highest moral and intellectual achievements. In other words, the gymnasium would inculcate both the tools and the values of *Bildung*. Language, it was felt, was the most perfect expression of the human spirit, and of all languages the most perfect was classical Greek. Indeed, some writers thought that the gymnasium should teach the Greek language and culture to the exclusion of virtually everything else.[60] It was for this reason that the Idealists as educational thinkers have been called neo-humanists. Renaissance humanists had also stressed man's potential for development and had insisted that a training in classical language and literature had a predominantly moral value.[61]

[59] J. G. Fichte, 'Concerning the only possible disturbance of academic freedom' (1811), ed. and trans. G. H. Turnbull, in *The Educational Theory of J. G. Fichte* (1926), 263–4. Fichte's most developed scheme for university reform was his 1807 work 'Deduced scheme for an academy to be established in Berlin', ibid. 170–258.

[60] For an extreme statement see F. Passow, *Die griechische Sprache nach ihrer Bedeutung in der Bildung deutscher Jugend* (1812). The best account of the new concept of the gymnasium is to be found in K. E. Jeismann, *Die preussische Gymnasium in Staat und Gesellschaft* (Stuttgart 1974).

[61] A good introduction to German neo-humanism is E. M. Butler, *The Tyranny of Greece over Germany* (Boston 1958).

Given the Idealists' exalted conception of the university, the traditional institution was inevitably faced with radical restructuring. In a university devoted to total knowledge the age-old division into four faculties was declared redundant. The philologist Wolf, for instance, envisaged their substitution by eight subject sections: philosophy, mathematics, philology, history, theology, jurisprudence, natural science and medicine.[62] Redundant, too, was the concept of professional studies. Students should choose to study a particular discipline simply because they found it of compelling interest. As a result, it was expected that philosophical subjects would be most in demand, for these were the sciences most easily devoted to the cultivation of the ethic of *Bildung*. This insistence on freedom of student choice had immediate repercussions on the relationship between the university and the state. Princes should no longer demand that their servants were trained in a particular discipline, but employ anyone who had finished a university course. In Humboldt's eyes the state would only benefit. *Bildung*, not professional education, was the key to an efficient administration. On the other hand, the Idealists had no wish to strengthen the university's corporate independence. Their watchwords were freedom of thought and freedom of study, not freedom of organization. Indeed, appalled by the petty jealousies and wranglings inherent in contemporary university life, the Idealists demanded an end to self-government and complete state control of appointments. According to Humboldt, 'it is no more advisable for teachers to govern themselves than it is for a troupe of actors to direct their own affairs'.[63]

Above all, the new university called for a new pedagogical technique. The traditional hourly lecture was unsuited to a concept of learning based upon the interaction of professor and student. In its place was championed the seminar or laboratory practical class in which students could be gently guided by the professor in a voyage of personal exploration and eventually contribute something to the development of the subject themselves. Admittedly small-group teaching had not been completely excluded from the early-modern university. Apart from the obvious case of the Oxford and Cambridge tutorial system, it was a commonplace for professors in many universities to offer extra-curricular lessons to a handful of private pupils. From the sixteenth century medical professors, for instance, were in the habit of offering clinical instruction to the chosen few in the local hospital.[64] However, the idea of using small-group teaching as a way of expanding the

[62] Muhlack, 'Die Universitäten im Zeichen von Neuhumanismus und Idealismus', 307–8. F. A. Wolf (1759–1824) is primarily remembered for his pioneering *Prolegomena ad Homerum* (1795) (ed. A. Grafton, Princeton 1986).

[63] Quoted in Muhlack, 313.

[64] On the development of this practice see J. J. Bylebyl, 'The School of Padua: humanistic medicine in the sixteenth century' in C. Webster (ed.), *Health, Medicine and Mortality: the sixteenth century* (1979), 339–50; and Ch. 17 (Robb-Smith).

sum of knowledge was definitely an Idealist invention. A philology seminar had been founded at the Hanoverian university of Göttingen in the late eighteenth century in order to give advanced instruction in the classics to theological students bound for a teaching career in the gymnasia. With the blessing of the Prussian government, Wolf established a similar institution at Halle in the 1800s, but quickly turned it into a vehicle for training classical scholars rather than teachers. As Wolf was closely identified with the Idealist cause, one of the great promoters of the peculiar value of ancient Greece, his seminar inevitably became the movement's pedagogical model.[65]

At the turn of the nineteenth century the Idealists were very much on the fringe of the establishment. Prussia's defeat at Jena, however, was followed by a period (albeit short) of royal disillusionment with enlightened despotism which allowed reformers of a different stamp to gain a hearing. As far as the Idealists were concerned, their great opportunity arrived in February 1809 with the appointment of Humboldt as head of the religious and education section of the Ministry of the Interior. As was pointed out above, there had been plans earlier in the decade to centralize higher education in Berlin. After 1806 the need to restructure the country's liberal professional education was plain for all to see, for defeat brought the loss of Prussia's western territories, which included the chief university at Halle. For Humboldt the crisis was heaven-sent. He manipulated governmental anxiety about the education of the state's servants to gain permission to found an Idealist university in the capital. The new university duly opened in the autumn of 1810. In many respects it was a traditional university of the Josephist Enlightenment, and there was no certainty that the Idealists would prosper in it. The state controlled appointments, the four-faculty structure was retained, and Humboldt failed in his attempt to give the new institution an endowment. Moreover, he was removed from office in November and his replacement, Von Schuckmann, was a Prussian of the old era. The King and his *Kabinett* clearly saw the university as a professional school.

Nevertheless, the University of Berlin quickly became established as an Idealist show-piece.[66] Humboldt had not only endowed the philosophy faculty with a wide range of chairs in history and languages, the major fields of contemporary Idealist research. He had also been quick to fill the chairs with Idealist friends and sympathizers, such as the Roman historian Niebuhr, and had written into the statutes a guarantee of freedom of

---

[65] W. Erben, 'Enstehung der Universitätsseminare', *Internationale Monatsschrift für Wissenschaft, Kunst und Technik* (1913), 1247–64, 1335–47. This still remains the essential source. For Wolf's ideas, see F. A. Wolf, *Ein Leben in Briefen*, ed. S. Reiter (3 vols Stuttgart 1935) i. 52–63.

[66] The standard account of the foundation of the new University is M. Lenz, *Geschichte der königlichen Friedrich-Wilhelms Universität zu Berlin* (4 vols in 5 Halle 1910–18) i and iv. Lenz exaggerates Humboldt's contribution to its erection: cf. Muhlack, 310–26.

publication. More importantly, the Von Schuckmann era was short. In 1817 he was replaced in turn as minister by Von Altenstein, who held the post for more than twenty years. Von Altenstein was an Idealist enthusiast who filled the university with people like Hegel. By the 1820s a new type of university had been created within a traditional shell. Ostensibly the institution performed the same function as its eighteenth-century predecessor. Numerically, the University was dominated by the three higher faculties, packed with students seeking a professional qualification (see Table 2.1). The faculty of philosophy, on the other hand, if short of students, was staffed with professors who regarded the absorption of knowledge as its own reward and sought to educate their students in the delights of their discipline through the institution of the seminar. For the first time a faculty was filled with professors who were publishing scholars and whose fame was independent of their lecturing abilities. The historian Ranke, for instance, who was barely audible in the lecture-hall, founded in the 1820s the Berlin seminar which was the cradle of German historiography.[67]

In the 1830s and 1840s the new conception of the university became widely promulgated throughout Protestant Germany. In Prussia success was guaranteed with Von Altenstein in control of the system. In other Protestant states governmental enthusiasm was less in evidence, but the new idea of the research imperative was quickly taken on board by individual professors. As a result, it was only in the Prussian universities that permanent government-funded seminars, laboratories and institutes were established in any number before 1850. Thus in the natural sciences the Prussian government founded general seminars at Bonn in 1825, Königsberg in 1834 and Halle in 1839,

TABLE 2.1

ATTENDANCE AT THE UNIVERSITY OF BERLIN, BY FACULTY,
1811–1860

faculty	1811[a]	1820	1830	1840	1850	1860
philosophy	21	169	241	360	335	436
law	43	247	633	447	571	353
medicine	65	333	302	404	223	319
theology	69	161	611	396	183	314
total	198	910	1,787	1,607	1,312	1,422

Notes: Only matriculated students included.
  [a] Figures for the summer semester throughout.
Source: R. Kopke, *Die Gründung der königlichen Friedrich-Wilhelms-Universität zu Berlin* (Berlin 1860), 297–9.

---

[67] Supporters of the Humboldtian ideal *did* exist in the higher faculties: e.g. the legal theorist Savigny and the theologian Schleiermacher.

while Königsberg also had a specialist seminar for mathematics and physics from 1834. No other Protestant German state, however, established a natural-science seminar before 1850, when the Göttingen mathematico-physical seminar was opened. Outside Prussia there were many private initiatives—at Göttingen Wilhelm Weber had started a physics laboratory as early as 1833–4—but little government sponsorship.[68] As the new university ethic was diffused through Protestant Germany, it was subtly altered. Its Idealist creators had stressed that research in any discipline should ultimately be directed at an understanding of the totality of being. But this aim, even in Prussia, was quickly lost from view. Hegel and his disciples in chairs of logic, ethics, and metaphysics obviously continued to subscribe to the Idealist programme. Professors in other disciplines within the faculty of philosophy, in contrast, increasingly emphasized the value of research in their own particular subject for its own sake. Hegelians never controlled many faculty posts.[69] At the same time the ethic was widened, although not without difficulty, to include formerly marginal disciplines like chemistry, which had been traditionally seen as a craft, not a science. When Liebig opened the first chemistry laboratory seminar at Giessen in 1826, the Prussian university establishment looked askance at the innovation.[70]

This distortion of the original ideal was of marginal importance in the development of a new ideological underpinning for the university. If the Romantic idea of the university as the institution for the search of ultimate truth was jettisoned, the conception of the university as the institutional locus for the pursuit of knowledge *per se* was enthusiastically embraced. In Protestant Germany by 1850 the university had an unambiguous *raison d'être*. Even if in reality it continued to train people for the traditional liberal professions, it did not in theory exist as a series of discrete professional schools. The fact, moreover, that it continued to ignore most of the applied

[68] R. S. Turner, 'The growth of professorial research in Prussia, 1818 to 1848', *Historical Studies in the Physical Sciences* iii (1971), 143–50; A. Grafton, 'Polyhistor into Philolog: notes on the transformation of German classical scholarship, 1780–1850', *History of Universities* iii (1983), 159–92; C. Jungnickel, 'Teaching and research in the physical sciences and mathematics in Saxony, 1820–1850', *Historical Studies in the Physical Sciences* x (1979), 3–47; D. Cahan, 'The intersection revolution in German physics, 1865–1914', *Historical Studies in the Physical Sciences* xv (1985), 3–13; relevant essays in K. M. Olesko (ed.), *Science in Germany: the institution of institutional and intellectual issues* (Osiris 2nd ser. 5 1989); relevant essays in G. Schubring (ed.), *'Eisamkeit und Freiheit' neu besichtigt. Universitätsreformen und Disziplinenbildung in Preussen als Modell für Wissenschaftspolitik im Europa des 19. Jahrhunderts* (Stuttgart 1991).

[69] Cf comments in J. E. Craig, *Scholarship and Nation Building: the universities of Strasbourg and Alsatian society, 1870–1939* (Chicago 1984), 12–16.

[70] R. S. Turner, 'Justus Liebig versus Prussian chemistry: reflections on early institute-building in Germany', *Historical Studies in the Physical Sciences* xiii (1982), 128–62. It has been argued that Liebig was interested in the professionalization of science research, not the promotion of Humboldtian *Bildung*: see J. Ben-David, *The Scientist's Role in Society* (Englewood Cliffs NJ 1971), ch. 7. For the development of chemistry as a scientific discipline see C. Meinel, '*Artibus academicis inserenda*: chemistry's place in eighteenth and early nineteenth century universities', *History of Universities* vii (1988), 106–9.

sciences no longer made the institution look terminologically absurd. Its province was the universality of theoretical knowledge, not of knowledge *tout court*. The teaching of the applied, mathematically based sciences could be happily entrusted to institutions outside its walls (see Fig. 2.3). The foundation of a number of flourishing polytechnics in Protestant Germany in the first half of the nineteenth century, therefore, was now in no way an indication of the university's inadequacy, its failure to fulfil its intended role. Rather, the establishment of nine multi-purpose technical colleges by 1870 was the inevitable concomitant of the new university ethic.

Outside Protestant Germany the new ideal gained little support before mid-century. Occasionally individual professors in the philosophical and natural sciences did try to establish research schools. But their seminars lacked the support of their colleagues and adequate financial backing.[71] In general, neither the state nor the professoriate could as yet conceive of the university as more than a professional school.[72] Before 1850 it was only in the medical faculty that a significant proportion of the professoriate even engaged in personal research, let alone founded a seminar. And medicine had been the one faculty where professors, especially of anatomy, had continually shown an interest in expanding the horizons of their discipline since the Renaissance.[73] The lack of commitment to the new university ethic was particularly strong in France, where the Enlightenment conception of higher education had been most firmly established. There were supporters of the new idea of the teacher-researcher among the professors of the faculties of arts and sciences. Indeed, in 1836-7 the two Paris faculties (collectively called the Sorbonne) positively endorsed the concept in communications with the Ministry of Public Instruction. But the state authorities, while making sympathetic noises, did nothing in response, and by 1848 even promising ventures such as the research undertaken in the Montpellier faculty of science had collapsed.[74] It was only in the three medical faculties that there was a sustained interest in research, the Paris school in particular being considered before 1830 Europe's leading centre in physiology and

[71] e.g. Thomas Thomson's attempt to found a chemistry research school and laboratory at Glasgow in the years 1819 to 1835: see J. Morrell, 'Chemist breeders: the research schools of Liebig and Thomas Thomson', *Ambix* xix (1972), 1–46; and Morrell, 'Thomas Thomson: Professor of Chemistry and university reformer', *British Journal for the History of Science* iv/15 (1969), 245–65 (esp. 263 on the failure of other British professors of chemistry in the 1820s even to attempt to set up a research laboratory).

[72] One new university established on Humboldtian lines was at Athens in 1837: see K. Zormbala, 'Die Gründung der Universität Athen 1837 durch die Bayern—nach welchem "deutschen" Modell?' in Schubring (ed.), *'Eisamkeit und Freiheit'*, 268–73.

[73] Cf what was said, n. 56, above. Of the great early-modern anatomists only Harvey did not hold a university post.

[74] T. Shinn, 'The French science faculty system, 1808–1914: institutional change and research potential in mathematics and the physical sciences', *Historical Studies in the Physical Sciences* x (1979), 271–302.

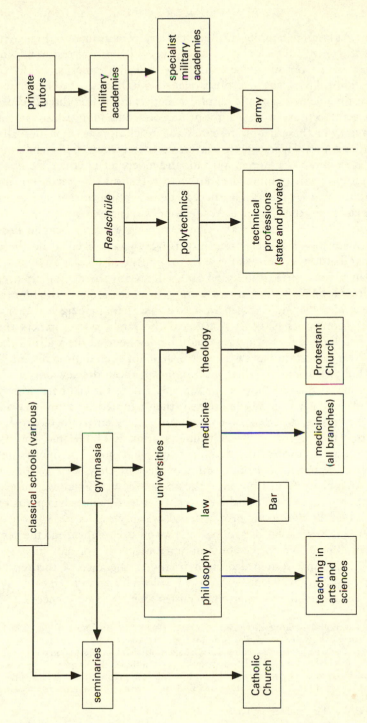

FIGURE 2.3 Higher education in the nineteenth century: the Prussian model. The Prussian model broadly holds true for the whole of Germany, except that some states demanded a compulsory period in the philosophy faculty before beginning professional studies. Tübingen after 1815 had a separate faculty of cameralism.

Entrance to universities was via the gymnasia and only with the abitur certificate. Medicine and the Bar were state professions in Prussia; entrants had to take a series of state examinations after university in order to qualify.

pathology.[75] At no time, moreover, was there any commitment in France to the idea of the university as the peculiar locus of theoretical research. Not only did few professors subscribe to the new research ethic, but many of those who did held posts in the professional schools outside the Université. France's great mathematicians and natural scientists in the first three decades of the nineteenth century were mainly professors and administrators in the *grandes écoles*. For these people research and teaching were not mutually supporting activities. Their professorial posts merely kept body and soul together.[76] Research was a more important and independent concern carried on under the protective umbrella of either the Institut, the revolutionary successor to the various Parisian learned academies of the *ancien régime*, or its later replacement, the revivified Académie des sciences.

The failure of the new university ethic to penetrate widely beyond Protestant Germany before 1850 is not surprising. In fact, even in northern Germany the battle was not totally won, as illustrated by the attempt by professors in Saxony in 1846 to found an academy for the natural sciences along traditional lines. By then there were many professors at the universities of Jena and Leipzig engaged in active research (Leipzig had had a mathematics seminar as early as 1826). All the same, as researchers the professors still looked for an institutional identity beyond the walls of the university, clear indication that the new ethic had not been thoroughly internalized within their faculty.[77] What was important about the new university ethic on the eve of the revolutions of 1848 was not that it had been widely disseminated, but that it had been created, then adopted by a professorial hard core. As a result, the ethic had enough supporters across the Continent to ensure that the advent of the new liberal regimes of the mid-century would not mean a return to the dark days of the 1790s. The universities would survive the transition from absolutism because they were no longer necessarily an archetypal institution of the *ancien régime*. There was now a radically different conception of the university, which many champions of liberalism, especially within the professoriate, warmly espoused.

Moreover, this was the age of nationalism as well as liberalism and the new university ethic pandered to the contemporary penchant for national glorification. A university system dedicated to the furtherance of theoretical knowledge could be an agent of national cultural aggrandizement. The formidable success of the German universities after 1830 only encouraged

---

[75] See E. Ackerknecht, *Medicine at the Paris Hospital, 1794–1848* (Baltimore 1967); J. Lesch, *Science and Medicine in France, 1790–1855* (Cambridge Mass. 1984).

[76] Many of France's mathematicians and scientists held more than one position in the *grandes écoles* under the system known as *cumul*. Significantly, posts in these schools were not necessarily held by research scientists, or gained only after a scientific apprenticeship: see D. Outram, 'Politics and vocation in French science, 1793–1830', *British Journal for the History of Science* xiii (1980), 27–43.

[77] Jungnickel, 'Teaching and research in Saxony', 26–47.

this belief. In the first three decades of the nineteenth century the country that played the most important role in the development of mathematics and natural science was France, where research and teaching were most clearly two separate activities. Thereafter the torch of invention was passed to the north German states and burned not in the Institut and the Académie des sciences but in the universities. Protestant Germany, however, was not just the creative centre of natural science in the mid-nineteenth century. It also excelled through its universities in the philosophical disciplines. Thereby, the concept of German nationhood was undoubtedly strengthened and given respectability in the eyes of established nations, which was exactly what Humboldt had intended.

Given Germany's success, no country in the culturally competitive age of nationalism could afford not to have a research-orientated university system. In the twenty years after 1850 the new ethic was rapidly internalized. In the Austrian Empire Humboldtian reforms began with the fall of Metternich and proceeded apace, even in the reactionary years of the 1850s, thanks to the support of the Education Minister Thun-Hohenstein.[78] By the 1860s even in France there were signs that teaching and research were no longer regarded as antipathetic activities. Above all, at the École normale supérieure Louis Pasteur helped to produce a new breed of research-orientated science professors. When Victor Duruy became Education Minister in 1863, the critics of the French university system gained an ally in the administration. Five years later Duruy attempted to give research an official place in the Université by creating the École pratique des hautes études in the capital. This was a research institute with no institutional locus, staffed by *directeurs des études* drawn from the professoriate of the different Parisian *écoles* and *facultés*. Any professor could be a member, provided he was willing to supervise research. The École pratique introduced a research component into French higher education without dismantling the existing bipartite system (see Fig. 2.2).[79]

The spectacular international power-play of Bismarck's Prussia only hastened the acceptance of the new Humboldtian ideal. Prussia's military and diplomatic triumphs may have had little to do with the cultural achievements of its universities. As institutions dedicated to pure knowledge, their direct contribution to Prussian state-building was slight. German economic growth

[78] See D. A. Halbwidl, 'Conservative politics and higher educational reform in Austria: the career of Leopold Leo Thun-Hohenstein, Minister of Education and Culture, 1849–1855', paper presented to the History of Universities Conference at Glasgow, 30 June 1990.

[79] For recent accounts of Duruy and the reform movement see Anderson, *Education in France*, 225–39; R. Fox, 'Science, the university and the state' in G. L. Geison (ed.), *Professions and the French State, 1700–1900* (Philadelphia 1984), 93–103; C. Zwerling, 'The emergence of the École normale supérieure as a centre of scientific education in the nineteenth century' in R. Fox and G. Weisz (eds), *The Organization of Science and Technology in France, 1808–1914* (Paris, 1980), 31–60.

in the second half of the nineteenth century was promoted through the research of the polytechnics and specialist institutes. Nevertheless, to envious outsiders cultural and international hegemony were inextricably connected.[80]

THE CONTINENTAL UNIVERSITY AND THE STUDENT BODY

The dramatic changes which swept through the European university system in the period 1790–1860 scarcely affected the student population. Whatever the *raison d'être* of an institution of higher learning, the presence of the majority of students was determined, as it always had been, by a need for a professional qualification. In consequence, the 'higher' faculties continued to enjoy the lion's share of attendance (see Tables 2.1–4). There was, how-ever, a significant change in the relative popularity of two of the faculties: medicine and law. Until the end of the eighteenth century few laymen were attracted to medical studies, and the law faculty in most universities always contained a much larger number of students.[81] In the first half of the nine-teenth century the position changed. Law faculties normally continued to contain the larger number of students, but the balance was significantly

TABLE 2.2

ATTENDANCE AT FRENCH UNIVERSITIES, BY FACULTY, 1789–1914

faculty	1789	1836/7	1846/7	1865/6	1876	1914
letters	a	?	?	?	238	6,586
science	a	?	?	?	293	7,330
law	2,700	4,900	?	?	5,239	16,465
medicine	500	2,334	1,052	1,766	2,629	8,533
pharmacy	a	?	?	?	846	1,337
theology	?	?	?	?	108	?
preparatory schools of medicine	a	?	823	1,002	1,851	1,786
grandes écoles	?	?	1,000[b]	?	?	?

[a] Faculty did not exist at this date.

[b] 1850; this is a minimum figure: there were 449 admissions to the chief *grandes écoles* in 1850.

Sources: J. Verger (ed.), *Histoire des universités en France* (Toulouse 1986), 303; R. D. Anderson, *Education in France, 1848–1870* (1975), 59; R. Fox and G. Weisz (eds), *The Organization of Science and Technology in France, 1808–1914* (Paris 1980), 12, 70; R. Chartier, M.-M. Compère and D. Julia, *L'Éducation en France du XVIe au XVIIIe siècle* (Paris 1976), 274.

[80] Despite the fear of German domination, progress in establishing research facilities in the late 19th century could be very slow: see G. Weisz, 'Reform and conflict in French medical education, 1870–1914' in Fox and Weisz, 61–94.

[81] For the situation in France in 1789 see Chartier *et al.*, *L'Éducation en France*, 274 (table). Montpellier with 200+ students was the only medical faculty of any size.

TABLE 2.3

ATTENDANCE AT PRUSSIAN UNIVERSITIES, BY FACULTY, 1805–1913

faculty	1805[a]	1826–30[b]	1835	1845	1855	1870[c]	1913[c]
philosophy							
no.	?	?	1,387	1,699	1,558	2,645	13,187
%			(21.4)	(28.1)	(25.9)	(38.4)	(47.8)
law							
no.	?	?	1,624	1,526	1,794	1,238	5,184
%			(25.1)	(25.2)	(29.8)	(18.0)	(18.8)
medicine							
no.	?	?	1,152	1,026	908	1,526	6,088
%			(17.8)	(16.9)	(15.2)	(22.1)	(22.1)
theology							
no.	?	?	2,313	1,803	1,752	1,481	3,105
%			(35.7)	(29.8)	(29.1)	(21.5)	(11.3)
total (no.)	1,840	5,853	6,476	6,054	6,012	6,890	27,564
technical institutes	?	?	114	185	580	1,212	4,906

Notes: Figures for all of the German universities would produce a higher proportion of law students. The faculty's share is depressed by the importance of theological studies in Protestant northern Germany.

[a] Estimate.

[b] Annual average.

[c] Prussia had six universities in 1815–66 and nine thereafter, when the state's boundaries were expanded. Before 1806 Prussia had five universities.

Source: R. Fox and G. Weisz (eds), The Organization of Science and Technology in France, 1808–1914 (Paris 1980), 315; H. V. Wehler, Deutsche Gesellschaftsgeschichte, 1700–1848 (2 vols Munich 1987) i (1700–1815), 180; R. A. Müller, Geschichte der Universität von der Mittelalterlichen Universitas zur deutschen Hochschule (Munich 1990), table 2, p. 81.

redressed. Indeed, in the Belgian universities medical students in some years outnumbered the lawyers. There were several reasons for this development. In part, it reflected the greater status attributed to practising medicine; in part, it reflected the fusion of the professions of surgery and physic (and sometimes even of pharmacy). In France, for instance, before 1789 only physicians had been university-trained and the surgeons had received formal education in separate écoles de chirurgie.[82]

The students who did attend the faculties of arts or the new separate faculties of philosophy and science mainly did so under compulsion. In

[82] On the development of the French medical profession in the 18th century see M. Ramsey, Professional and Popular Medicine in France, 1770–1830: the social world of medical practice (1988), pt 1. There were seventeen écoles de chirurgie in 1789: see Brockliss, Higher Education, 482 (map).

A REFORMING ERA

TABLE 2.4

ATTENDANCE AT BELGIAN UNIVERSITIES, BY FACULTY,
1817–1912

faculty	1817–19[c]	1831–4	1846–9	1861–4	1909–12
philosophy and letters					
no.	239	458	1,472	723	2,480
%	(16)	(15)	(29)	(10)	(12)
science					
no.	139	328	774	844	5,349
%	(10)	(11)	(15)	(12)	(23)
law					
no.	597	1,108	1,348	1,836	4,355
%	(42)	(36)	(27)	(25)	(18)
medicine					
no.	448	1,222	849	1,906	3,741
%	(31)	(38)	(17)	(26)	(16)
theology[a]					
no.	—	—	175	330	303
%	—	—	(3)	(5)	(1)
écoles spécialisés[b]					
no.	—	—	402	1,635	6,409
%	—	—	(8)	(22)	(27)
total (no.)	1,423	3,116	5,020	7,274	22,637

[a] From the closure of the University of Louvain in 1797 until the foundation of the Catholic University of Louvain in 1835 there was no theological faculty in Belgium.

[b] During the 19th century a number of specialist schools were founded in Belgium, some attached to the universities, others not; only those attached to a university are included here.

[c] Triennial *totals* throughout.

Source: Jan Art, 'Les rapports trienniaux sur l'état de l'enseignement supérieur: un arrière-fond pour des recherches ultérieures sur l'histoire des élites belges entre 1814 et 1914', *RTNG-RBHC* xvii (1986), 208 (table).

some countries, such as Bavaria, it was impossible to move directly from a classical school to a professional faculty without a period of propaedeutic study in a university arts faculty. Where no such regulation pertained, as in France, then the faculty of arts and its successors continued to function as examining boards. Admittedly, in Prussia, where immediate entry to the higher faculties was possible, philosophy studies attracted a growing proportion of students, and by 1860 at the University of Berlin the philosophy faculty was the largest of the four. Nevertheless, it would be dangerous to conclude that the Prussian faculties were peculiarly filled with devotees of Humboldtian *Bildung*. Many of the students would have been lawyers taking courses in cameralism (*Staatswissenschaft*), while the bulk of the faculty would have been prospective gymnasium professors. Arguably, the arts faculties became more populous in Prussia and several other European states in the first half of the nineteenth century because they too had become professional schools. An important educational development of this period was the professionalization of secondary-school teaching. Formerly, the college and gymnasium professors were 'generalists' drawn from the unbeneficed clergy. After 1815 it was increasingly expected that secondary-school teachers would be 'specialists' who had studied their speciality (be it classical languages, mathematics or natural science) in greater detail at university. Attempts were even made to provide complementary training in pedagogy. Witness, for instance, the lectureships set up in the faculties of philosophy and science in Belgium–Holland in 1827.[83]

Not surprisingly, given the cost of university education and the fact that continental Europe was still a pre-industrial society, the majority of students in the period 1790–1860 were drawn from a small proportion of the population. On average, three-quarters of the students came from landed, professional, or business backgrounds. In Germany at least, 40–50 per cent of the students had fathers who had attended university before them; in other words, they belonged to the *Bildungsbürgertum*, an élite group of bureaucrats and members of the liberal professions who consisted of a mere 2 per cent of the population. The lower orders, however, were represented to a certain extent, in contrast to the position at Oxford and Cambridge. In German universities a fifth to a quarter of all students were the sons of artisans, peasant proprietors, and petty officials. At the Paris École normale the fraction, at least in the years 1808–29, was even higher—as much as two-fifths. Even in Russian universities 13 per cent of the intake in 1865 came from peasant stock.[84]

The continental universities, therefore, continued to attract, as they had always done, a hard core of social climbers who understandably sought to raise their status by entering the liberal professions (usually the Church or

[83] Cousin, *De l'instruction publique en Hollande*, 196, 394–5 (French trans. of edict). St Petersburg University actually began life as a pedagogical institute under Catherine the Great and continued to fulfil this role for many years: see Flynn, *The University Reform of Tsar Alexander I*, 66–70.

[84] K. H. Jarausch, 'Der neuhumanistische Universität und die bürgerliche Gesellschaft, 1800–1870', *Darstellungen und Quellen zur Geschichte der deutschen Einheitsbewegung im neunzehnten und zwanzigsten Jahrhundert* xi (1981), 32–40; D. R. Brouer, 'Social stratification in Russian higher education' in Jarausch (ed.), *The Transformation of Higher Learning, 1860–1930*, 247–8; Zwerling, 'The Emergence of the École normale supérieure', 51–4. Among the British universities, Glasgow was also notable for the size of its lower-class intake: see W. M. Mathew, 'The origins and occupations of Glasgow students, 1740–1839', *Past and Present* xxxiii (1966), 78, 85.

school teaching). How many managed to do so is impossible to say. In that the majority of students never graduated, it can be assumed that many fell by the wayside. Moreover, individual states did little to encourage social mobility through education. In Prussia until the mid-1860s, for instance, entrants to the legal profession had not only to gain a degree, but also to undergo a period of unpaid 'practical' training in the courts as part of a series of separate state qualifying examinations.[85] Admittedly, in most countries poor students had the chance to subsidize their secondary and higher education by seeking support from state or municipal bursaries, which either supplemented or replaced previous individual endowments. These, however, were always few in number and not sufficiently remunerative. In Germany university study cost 250–350 thalers per annum, but bursaries were worth in general only 10–50 thalers.[86] It is likely, too, that the bursaries were given in preference to the orphaned children of state servants, so that few actually came into the hands of the lower orders. Certainly, this was what happened in France with the bursaries created by Napoleon for *lycéens*. In 1806, 4,000 *boursiers* attended the *lycées*, but only 884 owed their good fortune to success in a competitive examination rather than their father's position.[87]

At least the poor had some access to university study in this period. For women, on the other hand, the opportunity still did not exist. Some educational reformers at the end of the eighteenth century had argued in favour of opening up higher education to women. Condorcet for one had believed that women could benefit from gaining a deeper knowledge of the arts and sciences, although accepting that they should not be allowed entry to the liberal professions.[88] But his radical initiative was dismissed along with the rest of his programme. French universities did not open their doors to women until the 1860s and then with reluctance. In 1862 the first woman was permitted to take the baccalaureate, but only forty-nine had done so twenty years later. In 1868–9 there were four women in the Paris medical faculty, but three were foreigners, and by 1882 only five French women had graduated as medical doctors. The German university system was even more unwelcoming. Dorothea von Schlözer, daughter of the historian A. L. von Schlözer, was awarded an honorary doctorate in philosophy at Göttingen as

[85] Even once qualified they could find themselves unable to practise at the Bar, for until 1878 Prussian courts operated a *numerus clausus*. Tenured posts in the legal bureaucracy were equally hard to come by. In the 1820s only twenty salaried appointments were made each year: see M. John, 'Between estate and profession: lawyers and the development of the legal profession in nineteenth-century Germany' in D. Blackbourn and R. J. Evans (eds), *The German Bourgeoisie* (1991), 165–7, 176–8.

[86] H. V. Wehler, *Deutsche Gesellschaftsgeschichte, 1700–1848* (2 vols Munich 1987) ii (1815–48), 515.

[87] Initially Napoleon had intended that one-third of the proposed 6,400 bursaries would be reserved for the sons of soldiers and civil servants. By 1865 there were only 1,588 bursaries and there were eight applicants for every scholarship: see Anderson, *Education in France*, 13.

[88] Condorcet, 'Rapport', 279–88.

early as 1787. But her elevation set no precedents. Women were not allowed to study in German universities until the very end of the nineteenth century, although by 1909–10 their numbers had quickly risen to 1856.[89]

Given the socially and sexually restrictive access, it is no surprise to find that the first half of the nineteenth century did not witness any rapid advance in the proportion of the adolescent population receiving university education. In Germany in 1815 it is estimated that 0.71 per cent of 18-year-olds were in university. By 1871 this figure had risen, but only marginally, to 0.96 per cent. Neither figure was inspiring when it is remembered that in late sixteenth-century Castile some 3.2 per cent of males aged 16 to 24 attended university.[90] However, even if the increase merely kept abreast of population growth, the total number of students in universities on the Continent did rise, and rise substantially (see Table 2.5). The figures for France, Belgium, Prussia–Germany and Russia (four very different nineteenth-century states) suggest that between the French Revolution and the 1860s student numbers at least doubled and in some cases trebled. In the German and French cases there seems to have been a rapid rise in the first thirty years of the century (perhaps chiefly post-1815) followed by a slow decline, then recovery over the next forty. This European-wide expansion is highly significant, for it is the received wisdom (although one difficult to chart, given the absence of statistical data) that attendance at Europe's universities stagnated or declined in the period 1650–1800.[91]

Furthermore, the size of individual universities grew out of all proportion to the overall increase. Before 1550 there had been several large universities in Europe. Paris, for one, may have had 10,000 students.[92] The collapse of attendance in the faculty of arts, however, and the proliferation of 'national' foundations ensured that by the eighteenth century the largest institutions only had 2,000 students, while most had no more than 3–400. In the first half of the nineteenth century, however, the abolition of so many smaller

[89] Anderson, *Education in France*, 189–92; R. A. Müller, *Geschichte der Universität von der Mittelalterlichen Universitas zur deutschen Hochschule* (Munich 1990), 88. The most recent account of the growing presence of women in the German universities is J. Albisetti, *Schooling German Girls and Women: secondary and higher education in the nineteenth century* (Princeton, 1988).

[90] Jarausch, 'Der neuhumanistische Universität', 21 (table 1); R. Kagan, *Students and Society in Early-Modern Spain* (Baltimore 1974), 199–200. Other, only slightly less impressive, percentages were recorded in other early-modern states: see W. Frijhoff, 'Surplus ou déficit? Hypothèse sur le nombre réel des étudiants en Allemagne à l'époque moderne, 1576–1815', *Francia* vii (1979), 210–11.

[91] See the essays in D. Julia, J. Revel and R. Chartier (eds), *Histoire sociale des populations étudiantes* (2 vols Paris 1986–9) i; Kagan, 200 (map); Frijhoff, 205–6 (tables). The history of student attendance for France cannot be reconstructed because matriculation registers do not usually exist except for faculties of law; in this faculty numbers seem to have risen: see R. Kagan, 'Law students and legal careers in eighteenth-century France', *Past and Present* lxviii (1975), 63–4 (graphs).

[92] L. W. B. Brockliss, 'Patterns of attendance at the University of Paris, 1400–1800', *Historical Journal* xxi/3 (1978), 512–15 (tables).

TABLE 2.5

ATTENDANCE AT GERMAN AND RUSSIAN UNIVERSITIES, 1800–1914

A. Germany		B. Russia[a]	
year	no.	year	no.
1800	5,500–5,600[b]	1800	50
1819	8,277	1812	1,500
1825	12,480	1824	2,667
1826–30	15,158[c]	1836	2,000
1846–51	11,701[c]	1848	4,500[d]
1866–71	13,128[c]	1859	5,000
1914	75,000	1911	37,906

[a] Russia's six universities had increased to nine by 1900.

[b] A crude estimate; there were 2,764 *new* students in Germany in 1806–15 (annual average).

[c] Annual average.

[d] In 1850 the state limited university numbers to 3,000 (the limit lasted until the late 1850s).

Sources: H. V. Wehler, *Deutsche Gesellschaftsgeschichte, 1700–1848* (2 vols Munich 1987) ii (1815–48), 513; R. A. Müller, *Geschichte der Universität von der Mittelalterlichen Universitas zur deutschen Hochschule* (Munich 1990), 80, 81, 85; W. Frijhoff, 'Surplus ou déficit? Hypothèse sur le nombre réel des étudiants en Allemagne à l'époque moderne, 1576–1815', *Francia* vii (1979), 205; J. T. Flynn, *The University Reform of Tsar Alexander I, 1802–1835* (Washington 1988), 30, and 'Russia's "University Question", 1802–1863', *History of Universities* vii (1988), 8–10; K. H. Jarausch (ed.), *The Transformation of Higher Learning, 1860–1930* (Chicago 1983), 89–96; *British Magazine* i (1830), 56.

institutions in a period of growth led to the appearance once again of large student populations, especially in the capital cities (where universities were often being formed for the first time). In Vienna in 1835–6 there were 5,420 students at the University and a further 705 at the Polytechnic. In Paris at the same date there were some 6,200 students in the faculties of law and medicine alone, and perhaps another 1,000 in the *grandes écoles*. The University of Berlin in the 1830s was considerably smaller but never less than 2,000 students when the non-matriculands are counted.[93]

The reappearance of large numbers of students in the capital cities of Europe was an administrative headache. Most students were 'foreigners' from other towns who found accommodation where they could and lived a life outside the classroom completely unsupervised. There were no residential colleges of the Oxford and Cambridge kind where they could be

[93] R. Köpke, *Die Gründung der königlichen Friedrich-Wilhelms-Universität zu Berlin* (Berlin 1860), 297–9 (tables).

protected from the temptations of city life. The early-modern student had hardly been a paragon of virtue. Law students in particular had been notorious for drinking, brawling and whoring.[94] His nineteenth-century successor, however, lived in a much more liberated environment where Romantic culture emphasized the right of the individual to 'experience' life to the full and youth was encouraged to be self-conscious. Students began to claim that they had a special *déclassé* identity, ironically at the very time that the traditional corporate personality of the university was being dissolved. This new identity could often be a passport to vice. In Germany it encouraged the creation of organized student fraternities with idiosyncratic rituals whose members were bound by a tight discipline enforced through a court of honour. To the horror of the authorities, many student societies became the forum for ritual slaughter as the duel became the hallmark of student as well as aristocratic society.

As the period progressed, however, student rowdyism was the least of the government's worries. In some respects it was contained by the very reforms that had brought such large numbers of students to the capital cities. One of the traditional reasons for student misbehaviour at least in France lay in the irrelevance of large parts of the curriculum to professional needs (in this respect the *philosophes* were correct) and the ease with which some (certainly not all) universities granted degrees.[95] Both problems were successfully addressed by reformers at the turn of the nineteenth century, who made the law and medical curriculum more practical and introduced a more rigorous standardized examination system. Nineteenth-century students, especially medical students, had to work.[96] Student vice, therefore, was likely to be a recurrent but not a permanent state of affairs.

What really worried the authorities after 1815 was the growth of student political radicalism. In Germany especially students played an important role in the burgeoning movement for national liberation and liberal reform. The original student political societies which sprang up in the euphoria following the defeat of Napoleon were successfully crushed, but by the mid-1840s a much more formidable association had developed, nationally organized and with its own newspaper. All over Europe in 1848 students mounted the barricades and helped overthrow (albeit temporarily in most cases) the incumbent regimes.[97] Student radicalism was very much a con-

[94] Cf the picture of student life in the 17th and 18th centuries presented in Brockliss, *French Higher Education*, 95–104.

[95] Ibid. 71–82, 276–82.

[96] Cf the picture of the relative workload of lawyers and medical students in early 19th-century Paris in F. L. Poumiès de la Siboutie, *Souvenirs d'un médecin de Paris*, ed. A. Branche and L. Dagoury (Paris 1910), 88–9.

[97] Specific studies of student political activism include E. H. Attbach, 'Vanguard of revolution: students and politics in Central Europe, 1815–1948' in S. M. Lipset (ed.), *Students and Revolution* (New York 1968); and P. Robertson, 'Students on the barricades: Germany and Austria in 1848', *Political Science Quarterly* lxxxiv (1969), 367–79.

tinental problem. Oxford and Cambridge students were scarcely renowned for their anti-establishment views (Shelley's rustication for atheism was exceptional). The development of the phenomenon had several causes. Primarily it was a reflection of the political instability of most European states after 1815. Student agitation was just a part of a much larger movement of opposition which was directed, significantly, by members of the very liberal professions to which the universities gave access. There was no generational gap: even many university professors were liberals and nationalists, like the radical historian of the Paris faculty of letters Jules Michelet. Many students, in addition, may have been attracted to radical politics as a protest against declining job opportunities. It has been argued that the great upsurge in university attendance in the first part of the period led to an over-production of graduates, who found difficulty making a living from or sometimes even following their chosen profession. In Prussia, for instance, in 1835 there were supposedly 262 candidates for every 100 livings, 265 for every 100 judicial posts (and most law graduates wanted to enter the bureaucracy), and 194 candidates for every 100 state medical appointments. Radical reform that would bring expanded opportunities through the creation of a German national state must have seemed very appealing.[98]

The rapidity with which the graduate market became saturated in early nineteenth-century Europe is a reminder that the structure and content of higher education might be a subject of debate, but its social and professional role remained unchanged. The growth of the universities in the period 1800–60 was necessarily limited, not just by the restrictions on access but also by the relatively modest requirements of the most advanced pre-industrial societies for educated men. The *Bildungsbürgertum* in Prussia in 1840 (including students and graduates awaiting posts) comprised a mere 32,000 people, 0.4 per cent of the male population.[99] Inevitably, once the demand for graduates had been met, university attendance declined quite markedly in some countries in the 1830s and 1840s. Families with an idea of the state of the market did not waste money educating sons unnecessarily. This point emphasizes that the rise in student numbers over the period should not be exaggerated.[100] However vibrant recruitment might have been compared

[98] K. H. Jarausch, 'The sources of German student unrest, 1815–1848' in Stone (ed.), *The University in Society* ii. 533–69; L. O. Boyle, 'The problem of an excess of educated men in Western Europe, 1800–1850', *Journal of Modern History* xlii (1970), 471–95; R. S. Turner, 'Social mobility and the traditional professions in Prussia, 1700–1848', *Journal of Central European History* (1980); Ramsey, *Professional Medicine in France*, 105–22.

[99] R. S. Turner, 'The *Bildungsbürgertum* and the learned professions in Prussia, 1770–1830: the origins of a class', *Histoire sociale/Social History* xxv/13 (1986), 106–7.

[100] In fact, it should be noted that structural changes could result in individual universities not experiencing any growth over the period; e.g. the Spanish university of Valladolid, where the five faculties were effectively reduced to two (law and medicine) in the mid-19th century: see *Historia de la Universidad de Valladolid* (2 vols Valladolid 1989) ii. 424–5 (tables).

with the previous century and a half, the expansion pales into insignificance beside the birth of the mass university in the four decades before the First World War. Berlin would have 8,000 students by 1914; Paris 4,000 studying medicine alone. It was only after 1870 that the continental university would be socially transformed, becoming much more meritocratic, plebeian and impersonal. The concept of the 'modern' university developed in a period when the university was socially still an institution of the *ancien régime*, primarily a vehicle with state connivance for the perpetuation of the existing liberal professional élite.

OXFORD AND THE WIDER UNIVERSITY WORLD

On the eve of 1848 there were some sixty universities in Europe (counting the French Université as a single institution). In contrast to the position in 1789 the university system no longer presented a homogeneous face. By the mid-nineteenth century there were four separate models. In the first place, there still existed a number of traditional, corporate universities, generally located on the periphery of Europe. The four Scottish universities are a case in point. So, too, are the six Russian foundations, though their coats of arms should perhaps have borne a bastard-bar. A second group was formed by the state universities of the Restoration era, traditionally organized in many respects but whose conservative clothing hid a Frankenstein's monster. Some had had their arts faculties divided in two, many had had their theological faculties lopped like useless limbs, and all had lost their institutional life-blood, their freedom from government interference and direction. This group included the universities of Austria, Spain, Belgium and Holland. A third model was represented, uniquely, by the French Université. In France the traditional university system had been completely dismantled and replaced by a network of discrete faculties and their feeder schools formed into a single administrative unit under government control. Each of these three models had one common characteristic: their *raison d'être* was functional; each system was there to train and examine entrants to the liberal professions, to impart knowledge, not create it. Each was thus distinguished from the final model, the Humboldtian university. To the casual observer the German universities would have looked little different from their statist neighbours. They, too, were government-controlled, four-faculty institutions, turning out graduates for the liberal professions. What was different was the novel conception of the university which an increasing number of German professors shared. The university was not primarily to be a professional school but an institution of creativity and liberalism which would perfect the moral development of individuals and increase the sum of human knowledge. Thanks to Prussian military might and economic success, it was this fourth model in the form of the research university which would become predominant in the second half of the century.

In 1789 Oxford and Cambridge had stood out as institutional anomalies. The corporate, collegiate, arts university was a distinctive, unrepresentative species of the educational genus. Sixty years later it was just as difficult to assimilate the two English universities with their sister institutions in other parts of Europe. Although there were now four separate models of the university, none bore any resemblance to Oxford and Cambridge. By 1850 Oxford had half a century's experience of reforms and stood on the threshold of far-reaching changes. Reform, however, had done nothing to change the basic structure of the University. Oxford was a fatter, better-groomed, and more serious educational animal by 1850, but the leopard of learning had not changed its characteristic spots. On the other hand, an end to the homogeneous university of the eighteenth century had paid dividends as far as the European renown of the old English universities was concerned. Largely ignored in the century of the Enlightenment, by the mid-nineteenth century they had become a source of interest (albeit still limited) to foreign visitors and educationalists, who saw them now not as an anomaly but as yet another alternative model. Oxford was particularly attractive to traditionalist Catholics, all too prone to imaginative reconstructions of the past. Thus the French Abbé Du Clos, visiting Oxford in 1847, was charmed by a university 'which…gave him an idea of what the old French convents must have been'.[101]

The survival of the collegiate, corporate, arts university in the British Isles during the period is at first sight surprising. Even in the eighteenth century Oxford in particular had been a prime candidate for state-led reform. The European university, if it was nothing else, was a defender of the political and religious establishment, whereas Oxford before 1760 was a Tory and High-Anglican enclave in defiant opposition to the Whig and latitudinarian mainstream.[102] Thereafter, if the accession of George III brought a growing reconciliation between the University and the regime, this was no guarantee that Oxford, or Cambridge for that matter, would remain immune from criticism. The Channel was no barrier to Enlightenment educational thought or the educational ideas of the French revolutionaries and the German Idealists. Throughout the period 1770 to 1850 there were constant demands from Whigs and radicals that the universities be reformed on utilitarian principles. The attacks launched in the *Edinburgh Review* in 1808–9 and the 1830s were typical: Oxford's undergraduate curriculum had no use in the real world; the colleges had stifled the professional education of the higher faculties; the Anglican monopoly was keeping out Dissenting talent.[103] By

---

[101] Cited in A. Pollen, *John Hungerford Pollen, 1820–1902* (1912), 117. A more significant visitor was the future Austrian education minister Thun-Hohenstein.

[102] Cambridge was traditionally Whig and latitudinarian although the situation was more complex than once thought: see J. Gascoigne, *Cambridge in the Age of the Enlightenment: science, religion, and politics from the Restoration to the French Revolution* (1989).

[103] For a detailed analysis of this critique see Ch. 3 below.

the mid-nineteenth century there were even the first demands from within the University (notably from Jowett) that Oxford should contribute to research by increasing the status and number of specialist teachers.

Moreover, utilitarian critics did not have to look far afield for an alternative university model which could form the basis for reform of Oxford and Cambridge. Although the Scottish universities underwent no significant structural modification in the century 1750 to 1850, they did prove uncommonly adaptive to contemporary intellectual developments. The existence from the beginning of the eighteenth century of strong faculties of arts staffed by specialist lecturers proved particularly advantageous in the age of the Enlightenment. At Edinburgh especially the arts curriculum was continually expanded by the foundation of new chairs in emerging disciplines. By 1800 Edinburgh had chairs in chemistry, natural history, astronomy, and agriculture, plus a professorship in rhetoric, established in 1760, whose holder was supposed to teach English literature. Many of these chairs were filled by men of powerful and innovative intellect, such as Joseph Black, Adam Smith and Dugald Stewart, who used their position to popularize and expound their novel ideas. Scotland was the one European country on the eve of the French Revolution where the jibes of the *philosophes* were decidedly misplaced: north of the border the university was the institutional locus of the Enlightenment.[104] The utilitarian bent of the Scottish universities was illustrated above all by the international reputation of the Edinburgh medical faculty at the turn of the nineteenth century. Founded only in 1726, the Edinburgh faculty had played a pioneering role in the introduction of clinical medicine and the development of vitalist physiology. In the early nineteenth century its numbers expanded quickly. By the 1820s, if its curriculum was beginning to look rather jaded compared with the instruction available at Paris, the faculty was attracting 700 students annually, half of whom came from outside Scotland.[105]

The intellectual vibrancy, international *élan* and numerical strength of the Scottish universities in the first decades of the nineteenth century were an ideal stick with which to beat their effete English counterparts.[106] However, despite parliamentary support during the 1830s, the attack was never suc-

[104] R. L. Emerson, 'Scottish universities in the eighteenth century' in J. E. Leith, *Facets of Education in the Eighteenth Century* (Studies on Voltaire and the Eighteenth Century clvii 1977), 453–74; J. B. Morrell, '"Science"; "patronage"; the University of Edinburgh in the late eighteenth century: its scientific eminence and academic structure', *Isis* lxii (1970), 158–71; A. Chitnis, *The Scottish Enlightenment and Early Victorian English Society* (1986), chs 1 and 2.

[105] R. G. W. Anderson and A. Simpson (eds), *The Early Years of the Edinburgh Medical School* (Edinburgh 1976); C. Lawrence, 'The Edinburgh medical school and the end of the "old thing", 1790–1830', *History of Universities* vii (1988), 259–86. The Glasgow medical school also expanded rapidly in the same period: see D. Dow and M. Moss, 'The medical curriculum at Glasgow in the early nineteenth century', *History of Universities* vii (1988), 227–57 (esp. 243).

[106] See Ch. 3 below. There were some 4,400 students in Scottish universities in 1824; over 50% attended Edinburgh.

cessfully carried home. Until the establishment of the Royal Commission of 1850, Oxford and Cambridge kept their detractors at arm's length. Ironically, the professionally orientated Scottish universities were to be the subject of a Royal Commission as early as 1826 (admittedly on Edinburgh's request),[107] but the two English universities kept the state at bay for many years.

The reasons for this successful rearguard action were several. In the first place and most importantly, the British Isles never experienced revolution or defeat. It was, after all, the French Revolution and the revolutionary wars that gave birth to the new system of higher education on the Continent. The enlightened despots on their own had not succeeded in radically altering the role of the universities. Arguably, only a revolution in Britain could have drastically altered the educational status quo. Moreover, the retreat from the Enlightenment and all things French that the revolutionary era encouraged on this side of the Channel won for the English universities in particular new and much needed support. At the thought of the dangers to property that might flow from irreligion within the élite, the gentry began to send its elder sons in even larger numbers to Oxford and Cambridge that they might be brought up in godliness and good learning, a strategy that began to be aped by the wealthy middle class. Whatever the radicals might think, two institutions devoted to teaching religious and political orthodoxy through a study of the classics suddenly seemed very useful indeed. Of course, the story told in Chapter 1 might have ended very differently if the war with France had been lost. Fortunately for Oxford, it was a tremendous national victory and victory naturally bred complacency with the status quo in all its forms. It is worth pointing out that the only other country in Europe still wedded to the idea of the corporate university was the equally complacent and victorious Russia.[108] Understandably, then, until the reform era inaugurated by Catholic Emancipation in 1829, engendered this time by a home-bred panic, calls for the reformation of the University fell on deaf ears. And even in the 1830s Oxford had plenty of friends in the two Houses, such as the young Gladstone, who declared in 1835 that the status quo 'should not be vexed by the interposition of Parliament'.[109]

Secondly, the utilitarian critique in England was weakened by its lack of support from the legal and medical professions. In other countries much of the impetus for a more specialized and practical system of higher education had come from the liberal professions anxious to raise the quality of candi-

---

[107] *Evidence, Oral and Documentary, Taken and Received by the Commissioners Appointed by His Majesty George IV, July 23rd 1826; and reappointed by his Majesty William IV, October 12th, 1830; for visiting the universities of Scotland* (PP 1837 xxv–viii). The problem in Scotland was the misuse of the appointment powers of the university councils and their municipal allies. Professorships remained in the hands of the same families for many generations.

[108] It is perhaps then fitting that Tsars Alexander I and Nicholas I received honorary degrees from Oxford.

[109] Cited in Mallet, iii. 298–9.

dates for membership. The state, furthermore, very often believed that its civil servants should undergo specific institutionalized training, usually in national law. In England, however, even by 1850 there was still no clearly laid-down educational path for entrants to the liberal professions. Hence the continued relative inconsequentiality of the higher faculties at Oxford and Cambridge. The situation scarcely changed in the first half of the nineteenth century. The Church, despite pressure from the Tractarians, steadfastly held out against introducing compulsory theological training, and there was no Anglican theological college catering specifically for graduates before the 1830s (Cuddesdon outside Oxford was not founded until 1845). Similarly, the legal profession was recruited as it had always been, largely through apprenticeship, with only barristers requiring formal training at the Inns of Court. Even the growing number of medical practitioners during the period had little impact on the pattern of university recruitment, in contrast to other countries. In England, idiosyncratically, there had never been a legal requirement for physicians to hold medical doctorates. At the turn of the nineteenth century the manner of licensing medical practitioners radically changed, but not their manner of training. Graduate physicians remained a minority, even if a growing number of medical men were taking courses in the famous London and provincial hospitals.[110] Nor did the government show much sign of demanding a specific training for prospective civil servants. Indeed, the civil service reformers of the 1850s, though they favoured university entrants, deliberately turned their back on specialist training.

This view in itself was in part the result of a third factor that helped the cause of the educational status quo: the contribution of Oxford's conservatives to the Europe-wide debate on university reform. Oxford did not sit back and ignore the radical critique of its role. On the contrary, it attempted to turn the critical tide by developing its own highly articulate defence of an education in the humanities. A crucial figure in this campaign was Copleston of Oriel. His riposte, published in 1810, to the attack in the *Edinburgh Review* is discussed in Chapters 1 and 3. In it he stressed the value of the mental training received from the study of the classics and mathematics. His defence proved a highly successful and adaptive ideology. Many of his views were to be echoed in Newman's classic mid-century lectures. It was a defence, moreover, which promoted reform from within. Thus, when critics in the 1830s and 1840s continued to assert that the curriculum was still too narrow and allowed no room for choice, the University moved to forestall the impending Royal Commission by establishing two further schools in natural sciences and history with law.[111]

Fourthly, Oxford and Cambridge retained their traditional character in this period because, to a great extent, the broad constituency whose backing

---

[110] I. Loudun, *Medical Care and the General Practitioner, 1750–1850* (1986), esp. chs 2, 7 and 8.
[111] See pp. 313–15 below.

was required for radical reform was successfully bought off. The British Isles in the period 1660 to 1832 was definitely, as has been recently emphasized, a confessional society.[112] Nevertheless, it was a peculiar example of the phenomenon, for it was relatively tolerant of heterodox opinion and the three kingdoms which came together to form the British state in 1800 supported two different Protestant establishments. As a result, it was always possible for Protestant Dissenters to find an educational alternative to the university system in their home country. They were at liberty to found their own schools or travel to another part of the king's dominions where the religious subscription demanded of university students was more to their taste. Catholics, too, had no difficulty in sending their sons abroad to colleges specifically founded for their needs. A large proportion of the clergy of the Irish Catholic Church in the eighteenth century was educated at the University of Paris.[113] Disenchanted Whigs and radicals could deploy similar tactics. If they wanted to give their sons an 'enlightened' education within the British Isles, they could always send them to a Scottish university; and many did.[114]

From the 1790s, moreover, significant steps were taken to accommodate the educationally disaffected further. In 1793–4 it became easier for Irishmen who did not belong to the Established Church to gain degrees at Trinity College, Dublin, and from 1795 Irish Catholics had their own national seminary at Maynooth. Fifty years later a further attempt was made to appease Dissenting opinion in Ireland with the creation of non-denominational colleges at Belfast, Galway and Cork.[115] The demands for a shake-up of the English university system were also eventually met. In 1828 the utilitarians led by Henry Brougham were able to open their own professorial, non-denominational and non-residential college in London, while by the late eighteen thirties, Anglican Churchmen who bewailed the expense of an Oxford education were able to take comfort in the foundation of rival confessional institutions at King's, London, St David's, Lampeter, and Durham. From 1836 students from these and many other non-denominational and non-Anglican establishments could even gain a degree with the incorporation of the new University of London. This was a state-financed

---

[112] J. C. D. Clark, *English Society, 1688–1832: ideology, social structure and political practice during the ancien régime* (1985).

[113] McLachlan, *English Education under the Test Acts*; A. C. F. Beales, *Education under Penalty: English Catholic education from the Reformation to the fall of James II, 1547–1689* (1963); L. W. B. Brockliss, 'The University of Paris and the maintenance of Catholicism in the British Isles, 1426–1789: a study in clerical recruitment' in D. Julia and J. Revel (eds), *Histoire sociale des populations étudiantes* (2 vols Paris 1986–9) ii. 577–616.

[114] For further details about the popularity of a Scottish education in the early 19th century, see pp. 28–30 above.

[115] Despite attempts at accommodation Trinity College, Dublin remained a sectarian institution throughout the period. Even in 1850 less than 10% of the students did not belong to the Church of Ireland.

institution whose sole function was to examine students from affiliated bodies all over the British Isles and, after 1850, from the Empire. By 1853 sixty-eight medical and thirty-two non-medical institutions enjoyed affiliated status.[116] The sting of the critics of university corporatism and confessionalism was thereby successfully drawn. In the course of the period 1790–1850 the traditional universities of the three constitutive parts of the United Kingdom lost their degree-giving monopoly, but they thereby shielded themselves from radical reform.

Finally, reference should be made to the significance of the great wealth of the colleges. Although a natural target of reforming criticism, the college endowment of Oxford and Cambridge was never appropriated, unlike the property of colleges attached to continental universities. Oxford and Cambridge could provide a traditional and expanding arts education from their own funds. They had no need to go cap in hand to the government and risk unwanted state interference as a quid pro quo.

As a result of these various factors Oxford and Cambridge were able to swim against the European tide in the first half of the nineteenth century. Indeed, so successfully had the Coplestonian ethic been propagated that when the sword of Damocles finally fell in the shape of the 1850 Royal Commission, its cutting edge proved remarkably blunt. The universities lost their confessional character (and then not entirely until 1871), but otherwise they remained substantially unchanged. In the second half of the nineteenth century, Oxford was still a corporate, collegiate institution dispensing a largely non-professional education in the arts and sciences. The critics, then, continued to fulminate, especially in the light of the nearly unanimous acceptance on the Continent of the Humboldtian research ethic. In the long term, however, the survival of this neo-medieval institution was a blessing in disguise.

By the end of the nineteenth century Oxford, too, would have to accept that research had a part to play in the university's life. As an arts university, not a professional school dominated by a utilitarian faculty of law, the transition would be relatively painless. Apart from medicine, the research emphasis in the Western world in the late nineteenth century focused on just those areas—philology, mathematics, history and natural science—to which the University after 1850 devoted its teaching resources. But the new ethic would be introduced into an institution largely independent of state control

[116] On the background to these foundations see N. Harte, *The University of London, 1836–1986* (1986), 61–112, and C. E. Whiting, *The University of Durham 1832–1932* (1932), chs 1–2. Durham rapidly became a separate university with a right to award its own degrees. By the 1840s University College, King's College, and the University of Durham were all giving courses in engineering; so too was Trinity College, Dublin (see McDowell and Webb, *Trinity College, Dublin*, 180–5). That entry to the liberal professions in England was not dependent upon a university qualification is emphasized by the small numbers initially taking a University of London degree. Even in 1850 only 70 were examined for a BA and 18 for a BM: Harte, 106.

and the continued beneficiary of private endowments. Such an institution was unknown on the Continent. It formed a truly alternative model for the modern university, one which continental academics, mainly quasi-civil servants paid and appointed by the government, would look on with envy. More importantly, it offered a model which would prove in the long run influential all over the English-speaking world. Although the new civic universities founded in England, the Empire and the United States were initially utilitarian establishments intended to purvey a practical and professional education, over time they absorbed in their turn this conception of the university as an independent, corporate seat of learning.[117] This, of course, was a medieval ideal. It had been largely lost in England, as elsewhere, in the early-modern period and when resurrected after 1800, it took the distorted statist form of the Humboldtian Idealists. Had Oxford and Cambridge not withstood the educational whirlwind of the era of the liberal revolution, this noble concept of a self-governing, unbeholden community of scholars might have been lost for ever.

Moreover, this alternative model of the modern university was, paradoxically, the closest to the Humboldtian ideal. The concept of the creative university where professors and students made a mutual contribution to the advancement of knowledge could not be easily rooted in German institutions (even the new University of Berlin) when these were primarily devoted to professional training. Ultimately, it was institutionalized by perverting the original conception in such a manner that only the brightest students benefited from the new way of learning. The creative university became embodied in the laboratory and the seminar, exclusive institutions for the dedicated postgraduate, while the majority of students continued to be taught as before by the magisterial lecture. The development of the mass university after 1870 guaranteed that the boundary between teaching and research (never intended by Humboldt) would harden further. *Brotstudenten* became, and have remained, in continental universities statistics on a university register. In the Anglo-American world, in contrast, it has been the tradition in the twentieth century (if one not always steadfastly maintained) that undergraduates are also individuals, at university not to be spoon-fed but nurtured through a process of personal exploration. This Humboldtian viewpoint became a central part of the Anglo-American university thanks to the Oxford and Cambridge tutorial system. The collegiate, arts-dominated English universities of the first half of the nineteenth century were already committed to *Bildung* (albeit of a specific kind, the creation of English

---

[117] On the influence of Oxford and Cambridge on the universities of the English-speaking world, see ch. 22 by A. H. Halsey in *The Twentieth Century*. Underpinning this influence was the pervasive belief in the value of a liberal arts education. In the first half of the 19th century this was solidly embedded, even in the frontier culture of the nascent United States: see J. Herbst, 'American higher education in the age of the college', *History of Universities* vii (1988), 37–59.

gentlemen). The transplantation of the Humboldtian university to Oxford and Cambridge, therefore, took place in a peculiarly favourable environment. It was not a question of just tacking on research seminars to professional schools, but of developing in a more rigorous and scholarly way the existing pattern of undergraduate education. The development of Oxford as a world-famous research university was not at the expense of the majority of students, whose intellectual and moral development continued to be a crucial concern. This belief that the undergraduate 'mattered' spread throughout the Anglo-American world, even where lack of resources prevented the wholesale replication of the tutorial system. A profound debt of gratitude is owed by university-educated people in English-speaking countries to Dean Jackson and his successors for keeping this attitude alive. They struggled to make the education provided by early nineteenth-century Oxford respectable and respected: for this they should be revered.

3

Oxford and its Critics, 1800–1835

ASA BRIGGS

The last two chapters have been devoted to what can now be discerned about Oxford during the first three decades of examination reform, when it is compared with the other European universities of that day. This chapter, by contrast, concerns what was perceived and written at the time by Oxford's critics and defenders. Some of the comments mentioned below were related more closely to the political views of the writer than to the observed facts. A period which began during a long war and ended with political upheaval was seldom favourable to dispassionate observation.

That Samuel Parr, the great Whig, had joined the Tories by 1800 in defending the existing order has been mentioned in Chapter 1. 'After the recent downfall... of similar institutions in foreign countries,' he said in his Spital Sermon, 'our universities are the main pillars, not only of the learning, and perhaps the science, but of the virtue and piety... which yet remain among us.'[1] This provoked a much younger Whig, the Reverend Sydney Smith, to ask in the first number of the *Edinburgh Review*, as a graduate of Oxford,

Is it... true that very many of its professors enjoy ample salaries without reading any lectures at all?... Oxford so far differs from Dr. Parr, in the commendation he has bestowed upon its state of *public* education, that [its governors] have, since the publication of his book, we believe, and forty years after Mr Gibbon's residence, completely abolished their very ludicrous and disgraceful exercises for degrees, and have substituted in their place a system of exertion, and a scale of academical honours, calculated (we are willing to hope) to produce the happiest effects.[2]

This comment heralded the beginning not merely of a notable controversy, but of a new and more important phase in the history of the periodical press.[3]

The criticisms of Oxford which the *Edinburgh* mounted between 1808 and 1810 have been mentioned in *The Eighteenth Century*.[4] Francis Jeffrey

---

[1] S. Parr, *A Spital Sermon* (1801), 112 n. See also p. 30 above.

[2] *Ed. Rev.* i (Oct. 1802), 23–4. That article, like all the others in the quarterlies then, was anonymous when first published.

[3] The *Quarterly Review* was founded, 1809, 'not as a corollary, but in contradiction to' the *Edinburgh*: W. Hazlitt, *The Spirit of the Age* (1825), in *Complete Works* xi, ed. P. P. How (1932), 126.

[4] *The Eighteenth Century*, 632–4.

started these with some prudence: in January 1808 he quoted a comment from 'a Cambridge fellow' who was alleged to have called his university 'bad enough, Heaven knows, but not so bad as Oxford'. The fellow apparently alluded to the examination reform recently initiated at Oxford as an attempt 'to imitate' the Cambridge system.[5] Jeffrey's prudent approach was not adopted by his colleagues, who clearly regarded Oxford as an easy target. Playfair wrote in the same number that at Oxford the mathematical 'dictates of Aristotle' were 'still listened to as infallible decrees'. This would have been incorrect if published before 1800: by January 1808 it was a preposterous statement which showed Playfair to be ignorant about recent examination changes.[6] Payne Knight meanwhile termed the new edition of Strabo from the Oxford University Press 'this ponderous monument of operose ignorance and vain expense'.[7] In October 1809 Sydney Smith asserted that 'a set of lectures upon political economy would be discouraged in Oxford, probably despised, probably not permitted'.[8]

Copleston fell on the errors in these articles with devastating effect. He pointed out (*pace* Playfair) that Oxford undergraduates had not studied Aristotle's *Physics* for many years, and (*pace* Smith) that the political economy lectures of Oxford's Regius Professor of Modern History were well known.[9] The *Strabo* was edited by a Bath physician, Thomas Falconer. In his preface he had used some faulty Latin, much of it hallowed by long academic usage. In drawing attention to this Payne Knight had exposed his own deficiencies as a classic.[10] Copleston gave him the severest drubbing of all.[11] Oxford's friends naturally pronounced England's triumph to be complete.[12] More interestingly, a young Scot at Balliol, William Hamilton, said the same.[13] The *Edinburgh*'s team had mishandled a strong case, and their efforts to repair the damage had little effect.[14]

In the long run their criticisms of a system under which a classical course was compulsory were bound to prevail. Copleston maintained that mental

---

[5] *Ed. Rev.* xi (Jan. 1808), 378. Quotation from [R. Southey], *Letters from England by Don Manuel Alvarez Espriella, translated from the Spanish* (3 vols 1807) ii. 297.

[6] Ibid. 283.

[7] *Ed. Rev.* xiv (July 1809), 441. Payne Knight was equally erroneous on Thomas Tyrwhitt's edition of the *Poetics*, and on the Grenville *Homer* (ibid. 431): see Copleston, *Reply*, 34–8.

[8] *Ed. Rev.* xv (Oct. 1809), 51.

[9] Copleston, *Reply*, 16–18, 154. Sydney Smith's mistake was long remembered: *British Critic* ii (July 1826), 344.

[10] M. L. Clarke, *Classical Education in Britain, 1500–1900* (1959), 96.

[11] Copleston, *Reply*, 31–103.

[12] *British Critic* xxxvii (Mar. 1811), 356; W. C. Townsend, *The Paean of Oxford* (1826), 25; *London Magazine* iv (Feb. 1826), 232.

[13] J. Veitch, *Sir William Hamilton, Bt* (1869), 35–6, quoting two of Hamilton's letters, Aug. 1810. Hamilton made a successful claim to a Nova Scotia baronetcy in 1816. *Janus, The Edinburgh Literary Almanack* (Edinburgh, 1826), 23–4, was equally severe on the reviewers.

[14] See the excuse made for Playfair's disregard of the examination reforms (*Ed. Rev.* xvi (Apr. 1810), 165–6) and Copleston's exposure of it (*Second Reply*, 1810, 44–5).

training was all-important and that classical studies constituted by far the best method of achieving this.[15] The double contention was plausible only if modern studies in general, and modern languages in particular, were regarded as dangerous or tainted by commercial connections. In 1810 they were so regarded by many parents in the governing class. To keep undergraduates away from modern controversies and modern speculations was regarded as a paramount need.[16] Nothing could have been better calculated to prolong that attitude than an incompetent attack on the university methods which rested on it. In the later stages of this long controversy few of the statements made were either wholly false or fair and accurate. According to the *Encyclopaedia Britannica* of 1817 Oxford had 'expelled Locke' and still neglected scientific studies. The historical charge, which came from Dugald Stewart, attracted the attention of Grenville. Oxford's Chancellor pointed out that Locke's expulsion had been the work not of the University authorities, but of Christ Church. He laid hold, in Dugald Stewart's words, 'of Dr Fell as a scapegoat'.[17] The second accusation was answered when John Kidd, the Aldrichian Professor of Chemistry, published details of his lecture course;[18] but there was no denying by 1817 that Oxford undergraduates were reluctant to engage in studies lying outside the examination syllabus.

Some of the comments during this era on the German universities included or implied criticisms of Oxford as damaging as those in the *Edinburgh*. Henry Crabb Robinson, who was at the University of Jena in 1802, recorded of his fellow students: 'I thought I had never seen young men combining so many excellences of head and heart.'[19] In 1819, when the Carlsbad Decrees followed the assassination of Kotzebue, the German universities were defended in a London pamphlet, and praised for their 'irresistible spirit of freedom'.[20] Thomas Hodgskin's account of his travels in Germany was published in the following year. He had gone there 'untarnished' by any university, though armed with a questionnaire devised by Bentham. His report was far from uncritical, but he judged the princely rulers of Germany, 'checked and informed' as they were by public opinion, to be running more effective universities than those of England. He thought the revenues of Göttingen, the best-endowed German university, well used:

[15] Copleston, *Reply*, 104–35, 159–65.
[16] See pp. 10–12, 24 above.
[17] Dugald Stewart to S. Parr, 30 Sept. 1817, in S. Parr, *Works*, ed. J. Johnstone (8 vols 1828) vii. 550. The *Encyclopaedia* and Supplements had been 'Edinburgh productions' since the start in 1768. The *Quarterly* corrected Dugald Stewart on the expulsion of Locke: xvii (Apr. 1817), 70–1.
[18] J. Kidd, *An Answer to the Charges against the English Universities* (1818); syllabus of course on pp. 23–42. W. T. Brande (1788–1866) was the author of the article containing 'the charges'.
[19] T. Sadler (ed.), *The Diary, Reminiscences and Correspondence of Henry Crabb Robinson* (3 vols 1869) i. 145.
[20] *A Memoir of Charles Louis Sand: including a narrative of the circumstances attending the death of Augustus von Kotzebue: also a defence of the German universities* (1819), p. xxxiii.

in total they only just exceeded the combined incomes of four heads of houses in Oxford or Cambridge. He drew the contrast:

Göttingen has no good things to bribe its younger members to a continued adherence to taught opinions. There is no warm and well-lined stall of orthodoxy, and no means are taken to influence the students' conscience through their stomachs.... There is probably no country of Europe in which larger funds are appropriated to [the universities] than ... England, and, owing to our rigid adherence to Gothic regulations, there is no one in which so little good is effected by them.[21]

The *London Magazine* reported in 1822 that even a German critic who favoured the political stance of the English universities thought little of their intellectual standing.[22] These criticisms of Oxford came predominantly from Whigs and radicals. They were scarcely echoed among the Tory majority in the aristocracy and the professional class. Even if Kotzebue had received no more than his deserts, the fact that his assassin was a student could be taken as a sign of an anarchic university system.[23] 'From the University of Berlin', an American visitor had reported in July 1816, 'a free spirit has gone forth that has wrought like a fever through all Germany.'[24] Few Tories approved of a university which was having that feverish effect.

The German universities were depicted in the more conservative journals as hotbeds of indiscipline and sedition. The students were reported to move at will from one set of lectures to another; they even migrated from university to university; and the professor's only way of holding his hearers, and so securing their attendance fees, was said to lie in offering them attractive but unsafe speculations; he was subject to none of the restraints which a connection with the aristocracy would have provided: they were separated from normal society by the absence of vacations.[25] The speculations of the German theology faculties, which were mentioned in Chapter 1 as troubling H. J. Rose and E. B. Pusey, came to be viewed as particularly dangerous.[26] 'The Professors', the *Quarterly Review* reported in July 1820, 'are in a state of most degrading dependence on the goodwill of the students.'[27] Five years later the *Quarterly* was again denouncing the German universities, which were 'still kept together by the fame of public lectures, [where] the constant object of the professor' was 'to aim at some striking novelty'.[28] In 1826 the

[21] T. Hodgskin, *Travels in North Germany* (2 vols Edinburgh, 1820) ii. 265–9. Cf. W. Howitt, *The Student-Life of Germany* (1841).

[22] *London Magazine* vi (Aug. 1822), 166–72. The remarks of 'Dr Niemeyer', who had visited Oxford and Cambridge, were quoted.

[23] *Quarterly* xxiii (July 1820), 446–8 (see the quotation, n. 27 below). Among the works reviewed in this article were those named in nn. 20, 21 above.

[24] George to Elisha Tickner, 6 July 1816, in *Life, Letters, and Journals of George Tickner*, ed. G. S. Hillard (2 vols 1876) i. 103.

[25] *Janus; or, The Edinburgh Literary Almanack* (Edinburgh 1826), 19.

[26] Pp. 52–3 above.

[27] *Quarterly* xxiii (July 1820), 447.

[28] Ibid. xxxiii (Dec. 1825), 266.

Edinburgh Literary Almanack judged the German student to need, 'after quitting his college, another education of a very different sort ere he is in any degree fitted for mingling in the ordinary intercourse and duties of society'.[29] In his defence of 'subscription' in 1834 William Sewell wrote: 'We...know the nature of the German universities, and we have no wish to be like them.'[30]

There was a later echo of all this when *Tom Brown at Oxford* appeared in 1861. A girl, who is visiting for Commem week, is warned about 'the most dangerous man in Oxford—a Germanizer and a rationalist'. She asks which is the worse—a Germanizer or a Tractarian? Tom replies: 'The Germanizer, of course...because one knows the worst of where the Tractarians are going. They may go to Rome, and there's an end of it. But the Germanizers are going into the abysses, or no one knows where.'[31]

During the 1820s comments such as these were not the only ones made. As the war, and the post-war turbulence, receded a more balanced view of the German scene began gradually to make its appearance. In 1825 F. D. Maurice reminded the readers of the *Metropolitan Quarterly Magazine* of the time when 'no one dared to translate a German play lest he should have a foul bill of health assigned him as coming from a region in which Kotzebue was supposed to be scattering the seeds of death...In vain it was argued...that German critics had denounced Kotzebue in severer terms than even English ones.'[32] In the same year Fynes Clinton wrote: 'When this is the state of classical education at Oxford, can we expect in the cultivated classes of England the lofty speculations, or the depth and extent of research, for which the Germans are distinguished?'[33] Charles Lyell explained two years later in the *Quarterly Review* that German rationalism and heresy could hardly be attributed to the professorial system of the German universities, since education for the sacred ministry had 'for ages been conducted under such a system in the Scotch universities without any approach to the same inconvenient results'.[34]

The salient facts were now becoming better known. In 1830 the *British Magazine* pointed to the smallness of university provision in England by comparison with continental countries:

The six universities of the Netherlands are increasing...fast...Germany contains at least thirty universities, and as an example of their flourishing condition, the numbers of the seven in the Prussian dominions rose from 3,382 in 1820 to 5,954 in 1827. In

[29] *Janus* (1826), 19–20.
[30] W. Sewell, *Letter to Earl Grey* (1834), 15.
[31] [T. Hughes], *Tom Brown at Oxford* (3 vols 1861) ii. 186.
[32] F. Maurice, *F. D. Maurice* (2 vols 1884) i. 63.
[33] H. Fynes Clinton, *Literary Remains* (1854), 229–30.
[34] *Quarterly* xxxvi (June 1827), 252. Cf lxxiii (Dec. 1843), 103–5, on the drinking and duelling prevalent among German students.

Russia, of whose barbarism people are in the habit of talking so much, and so ignorantly, within the present century four new universities have been established...If Great Britain has loitered in the rear...let her energies be called forth.[35]

'If we are "the worst-educated nation in Europe", Thomas Carlyle wrote in 1830, the Germans 'are much more unquestionably the best.'[36] In 1833 the *Quarterly Journal of Education* complained: 'While Germany, with far less means, is daily making rapid advances in literature, and sending forth productions of great ability, the University of Oxford is obliged to the labours of German writers for the mere class-books which she prints for the use of her "Alumni".'[37] In 1834 Thomas Acland described the atmosphere of Berlin University, which he was visiting, to F. D. Maurice. The theology professors 'all seem', he wrote, 'to think *Wissenschaft* more important than soundness of creed'.[38]

The less one-sided account of university life from the periodicals in George IV's reign did not apply only to the universities of Germany. The proposal for a London university and the appointment of a Royal Commission on the Scottish universities had a sobering effect. The London scheme owed a great deal to Edinburgh (which supplied six members of the original Education Committee), and something to Germany (as Thomas Campbell, its originator, had first discussed it while studying at Bonn). It enshrined an undenominational, and indeed secular, approach to university organization to which Oxford was entirely opposed; and it was heralded by an anonymous 'puff' from Brougham in the *Edinburgh Review* which included a covert attack on Oxford and Cambridge: 'The plan of sending young men of eighteen or nineteen to live together for the three most critical years of their lives, at a distance from their parents or guardians, subject to no effectual or useful control, and suffered to drink, dice, and wench as they please...is one of the most extravagant follies that ever entered into the minds of men.'[39]

Despite these provocations Copleston's comments in the *Quarterly* were adept and conciliatory. He argued that, while there might well be a need 'sooner or later' for new universities, the first requirement was to discover whether Oxford and Cambridge could not enlarge 'their present capacity

---

[35] *British Magazine* i (Jan. 1830), 56.

[36] Thomas Carlyle to Macvey Napier, 27 Jan. 1830: *Collected Letters of Thomas and Jane Welsh Carlyle* (Durham NC 1970–) v. 64.

[37] *Quarterly Journal of Education* (Jan.–Apr. 1833), 330–1. This had been founded in 1829 by the Society for the Diffusion of Useful Knowledge: C. W. New, *Life of Henry Brougham to 1830* (1961), 356. For German editions of classical works published in this period by the Oxford University Press see Clarke, *Classical Education in Britain*, 96–7.

[38] Quoted in F. D. Maurice to the Revd J. A. Stephenson, in *Maurice* i. 167–8. Detailed information on the German universities became available during the 1840s: see W. C. Perry, *German University Education* (1845).

[39] *Ed. Rev.* xlii (Aug. 1825), 352–3.

... by some interior regulation adapted to the change of times'. He wished to see not a parliamentary investigation of Oxford and Cambridge, but 'a feeling' among the fellows of each college 'that they were bound in honour and in conscience to execute the will of their founder *substantially*'.

Copleston ended with a plea for changes in university and college statutes which is notable both in its boldness and in the admissions made or implied:

Our hopes of a ... remedy ... must be founded in the progress of liberal opinion, in the more enlarged view which men daily take of their social interests and their social duties, and still more perhaps in that enlightened religion of the heart, which forbids them to seek, in a pretended veneration for statutes, a real screen for their own indulgence. This, indeed, is the last excuse with which we are disposed to come to any compromise, pleaded as it sometimes is by those who well know that a hundred rules are in fact daily dispensed with, and wisely too, because the observance of them would be burdensome to the present individuals, as well as useless to the public, and yet scruple to sacrifice others of the same kind to the public good, because their own ease or comfort is promoted by their continuance ... The same munificence which change of manners has ... rendered abortive, would instantly be transferred, if the hand of the benefactor were again warm with life, to the encouragement of studies in that mode which is alone adapted to the present age. It is by such a continual adaptation only, that the dignity of these institutions, and the hold they have upon public opinion, can be maintained.[40]

By the mid-1820s no one suggested that the eminence of Oxford's sons put its performance beyond criticism;[41] and its almost exclusive concentration on classical studies was deplored on all sides. This was indeed one of the few subjects on which the *Quarterly* and the *Westminster Review* agreed.[42] Macaulay wrote in the *Edinburgh* of February 1826 that curricula as unbalanced as those of Oxford and Cambridge could have been maintained only in universities which held a monopoly position.[43] In June 1827 Charles Lyell surveyed the overworked tutors and underemployed professors of Oxford in the *Quarterly Review* and concluded:

Our universities are called upon to make no daring inroads upon their ancient constitution. ... The only preliminary objects necessary ... in order to bring about a gradual and salutary change, seem simply these:—to secure to the students the opportunity of being examined before competent boards, not only in the departments of science now encouraged, but in all those ... under the faculties of theology, law and medicine; to award honours fairly to industry and talent on whatever branches of knowledge, whether ancient or modern, moral or physical, they may be displayed ... Certain acquirements may ... with propriety be exacted in common from all, before a degree of bachelor of arts is granted, as is the practice in the

---

[40] *Quarterly* xxxiii (Dec. 1825), 272–5.
[41] *Ed. Rev.* xliii (Feb. 1826), 338; *GM* i (1827), 506; W. Friend, *Samuel Parr* (2 vols 1828) ii. 363–4.
[42] *Westminster Review* iv (July 1825), 152; *Quarterly* xxxvi (June 1827), 260–1.
[43] *Ed. Rev.* xliii (Feb. 1826), 326–7, 331, 333–4.

universities of France, Germany, and Italy...If a large portion of our youth are so lamentably ignorant upon quitting school, that it would be too much to require such qualifications of them upon their matriculation...we...see no reason why they may not be demanded of them at their first examination, when they have completed half their residence at Oxford or Cambridge.[44]

Lyell's comments were not the only ones in 1827 which had a modern ring. In July of that year a writer in the *Gentleman's Magazine* was concerned to refute the view that the methods of Oxford and Cambridge might 'be well enough calculated for the gifted *few*, yet ill-suited to the *many*'; and in 1830 the *Quarterly* noted that the academic appointments intended 'to provide the best possible system of instruction for the young' might not be the best for promoting research.[45] The *Athenaeum* drew the moral from the appearance of Brougham's 'godless college'. Had Oxford and Cambridge 'changed their systems, made them more adapted to be useful and popular...before the projection of the London University, it is more than probable it would never have been thought of'.[46]

This era of comparatively good feelings was brief. After the general election of 1831 drastic reform was deemed the order of the day, and universities which had resisted the Reform Bill, and returned its opponents, were at a discount. In 1827 the *Westminster* had welcomed the Drummond chair for Oxford and had hoped that the professors would present 'the abstruse study' of political economy 'in an attractive shape to a large number of intelligent young men'. In his *Westminster* article four years later Thomas Hogg announced that Oxford University had 'long ceased to exist except for the purpose of electioneering'. Far more important was what Newman called 'the storm...from the North', which now broke again on Oxford with redoubled force.[47] Sir William Hamilton's *Edinburgh Review* article of June 1831—the first in a series of five—opened a whole new area of controversy.[48] The main thesis of these articles was stated on the first page: 'Comparing what it actually is with what it possibly could be, Oxford is, of all academical institutions at once the most imperfect and the most perfectible.'

Hamilton was a quarrelsome man whose Whig politics had kept him out of Edinburgh's moral philosophy chair in 1820. Ten years earlier he had

---

[44] *Quarterly* xxxvi (June 1827), 264. For this exceptionally perceptive article see also pp. 34, 143, 556.

[45] *GM* xcvii. pt 2 (1827), 7; *Quarterly* xliii (Oct. 1830), 328.

[46] *Athenaeum* 9 July 1828, 575c.

[47] *Westminster Review* viii (July 1827), 189; xv (July 1831), 61. Newman, *Idea*, 138. *Oxford: academical abuses disclosed by some of the initiated* (1832) was an attack similar to Hogg's, but better informed.

[48] *Ed. Rev.* liii (June 1831), 384–427; liv (Dec. 1831), 478–504; lix (Apr. 1834), 196–227; lx (Oct. 1834), 202–30, lx (Jan. 1835), 422–45; repr. in W. Hamilton, *Discussions on Philosophy and Literature, Education and University Reform* (1852). In the second edition's preface (1853) Hamilton commented on the Royal Commission's report.

gained an extremely impressive first in Lit. Hum.; but he felt no gratitude to Balliol or to Oxford. His tutor had been inefficient: he had hated wasting his time in 'college lectures'; and he may have resented not having been considered for a Balliol fellowship.[49] By 1831 he had acquired a remarkable knowledge of Europe's universities and their history. He deployed this to argue that the existing organization of Oxford was illegal, as the colleges had gradually usurped the University's statutory functions: that this had been done surreptitiously by successive Boards of Heads without Convocation's sanction was a subordinate point, since Convocation would, in any event, have had no authority to endorse the changes.[50] As a result of that process high university officers promised regularly on oath to see that the statutes were obeyed when they had no intention whatever of seeing to this: nine of the 'ten degrees still granted in Oxford' were 'in law and reason utterly worthless'.[51] Hamilton made full use of the local and other restrictions which affected fellowship elections. As for the tutorial system, it was staffed by clerical celibates as they waited their turn to marry and leave Oxford.

That there is much of good, much worthy of imitation by other universities in... Oxford, we are happy to acknowledge...But this good...is only favoured in so far as it is compatible with the interest of those private corporations, who administer the University exclusively for their own benefit. As *at present organized*, it is a doubtful problem whether the tutorial system ought not to be abated as a nuisance. For if some tutors may afford assistance to some pupils, to other pupils other tutors prove equally an impediment. We are no enemies of collegial residence, no enemies of a tutorial discipline...A tutorial system in subordination to a professorial (which Oxford formerly enjoyed) we regard as affording the condition of an absolutely perfect university. But the tutorial system, as now dominant in Oxford, is vicious in its *application*—as usurping the place of the professorial, whose function, under any circumstances, it is inadequate to discharge; and in its *constitution*—the tutors as now fortuitously appointed being, as a body, incompetent even to the duties of subsidiary instruction.[52]

In its more lurid features Hamilton's indictment was exaggerated and even absurd; but when the accusation of conspiracy by generations of college heads had been put aside, there was substance in his criticisms. With the decline in the number of halls during the sixteenth century, and the increased teaching responsibilities falling then on both colleges and halls, Oxford had become a 'collegiate university'; and in the eighteenth century the system of higher degrees devised in medieval times had fallen into decay.[53] The result was a university constitution ill-adapted to the 1830s. Hamilton made

---

[49] Veitch, *Hamilton*, 30, 41–2, 57–61, 96–103.
[50] *Ed. Rev.* liv (Dec. 1831), 483 n.
[51] Ibid. 484.
[52] *Ed. Rev.* liii (June 1831), 398.
[53] *The Collegiate University*, 51–5; *The Eighteenth Century*, 481–91.

Copleston's phrase about 'rules ... daily dispensed with' look discreditably facile. He underlined the impropriety of Oxford's leading figures taking oaths to uphold practices which had patently fallen into disuse: in the light of the legal opinion of 2 June 1759 he brushed aside any excuse that the University's statutes could not be amended.[54]

The views underlying Hamilton's articles were neither notably perceptive nor constructive. He did not realize that 'college lectures' were often ineffective, not because the tutor was incompetent, but because the absence of a university entrance examination made the range of competence within the class impossibly wide. His call for a change whereby the colleges would be held down, while the halls proliferated as they had once done, was profoundly mistaken: in the residential University of the 1830s it was the weaker halls which stood to lose most from a reform such as the institution of a university entrance examination. Hamilton helped to launch the misconception that unendowed halls would be able to compete effectively with endowed colleges.[55] In 1831, however, his misconceptions counted for little: his first article caught the reform tide at its height. He made the colleges look like a collection of close boroughs; and his attack, though pompously and pedantically expressed, proved very formidable.

Hamilton's call for 'a Royal or Parliamentary Visitation' of Oxford and Cambridge had a force which transcended party boundaries. Four years earlier Lyell had pointed out in the Tory *Quarterly*: 'Every step in the progress of the human mind—every political change—every variation in the religious opinions of the mass of the community, or even in the manners and fashions of the age, may materially influence the practical operation of academical laws. Statutes of high antiquity may not only become inoperative, through the lapse of time, but become productive of evil consequences.'[56]

Hamilton's articles owed their first impact to the fevered conditions of 1831; but they remained effective even when the march to radicalism was seen to have been slowed. The last of them appeared in January 1835. By then Wellington had become Oxford's Chancellor. He had no wish to be seen as the enemy of all reforms, and he lost no time in recommending the Board of Heads to 'take into consideration the circumstances in which they were placed, and to adopt such ameliorations as might be considered safe and necessary'; and in May 1837 he gave the House of Lords a reassuring prediction of statutory reform at Oxford: 'The head of each college had considerable influence within his own sphere, and, in their united capacity as

---

[54] *Ed. Rev.* liv (Dec. 1831), 501–2. Hamilton did not make his view about amending university statutes clear in his first article.

[55] See pp. 310–11 below.

[56] *Quarterly* xxxvi (June 1827), 217.

a board, he believed they would be disposed to make such improvement in the statutes as would give satisfaction to the public.'[57]

This was an empty assurance. The Board of Heads might propose a reform; but that would do no good if it proved unacceptable to those 'whose ignorant votes in Convocation', as the *Quarterly Journal of Education* phrased it, could 'stop the progress of improvement'.[58] Moreover, the right of Convocation to change the University's statutes, asserted successfully in 1759, had been challenged in 1836. When it looked as if a statute depriving the Regius Professor of Divinity of some of his powers would be passed, he had obtained an opinion that, if the University did this, it would exceed its authority. This reversal of the 1759 opinion is discussed in Chapter 7. It came from John Campbell, the Whigs' Attorney-General, and Stephen Lushington, who was a radical, and it might not have been upheld in court. Lushington wrote to Brougham: 'J. Campbell and myself have given an opinion that the proposed statute is illegal. What a clatter when the opinion is published in the University. I presume they will forthwith obtain a counter-opinion from Wetherell.'[59] None the less, Campbell and Lushington had made constitutional reform from within look impossibly difficult: even if Oxford's Convocation had the will to enact changes, had it the authority? The Earl of Radnor told the Lords in December 1837 that the 'steps adopted... against Dr. Hampden' had been 'perfectly illegal'.[60] Wellington's statements to the peers became less and less convincing. 'With respect to the colleges', he said in July 1838, 'I have received accounts from several of them that they are reviewing their statutes.'[61] Brougham replied that, as long as qualified people were available to take up closed fellowships, 'even the Court of Chancery had not the power to throw them open'.[62] Legal impediments apart, while the Tractarian controversies lasted, modernizing college statutes remained impossibly difficult, as Chapter 7 shows.[63]

By 1837 the reform tide had ebbed, but Oxford's many friends in Parliament could not be expected to defend its unreformed features for ever. The

---

[57] *Parl. Deb.* 23 May 1837, 3S xxxviii. 979–80. See also Copleston's statement on 8 May (ibid. 670) that Oxford's statutory position was 'unsatisfactory and embarrassing'. The reply to Hamilton stated that only the Visitor could 'interfere with a college's statutes': [J. Ingram], *Apologia academica* (1831), 34. For the limitation on a Visitor's powers see p. 172 below.

[58] *QJE* iv (Oct. 1832), 193.

[59] Lushington to Brougham, 3 May 1836, in S. M. Waddams, *Law, Politics and the Church of England: the career of Stephen Lushington, 1782–1873* (1992), 304. Sir Charles Wetherell was a Tory and the University's standing counsel. For the 1759 opinion see *The Eighteenth Century*, Ch. 7. By advice of the Royal Commission the legality of the statutory changes was confirmed in the Charter of 10 July 1856: *RCO* (1850), report, 6; *Laudian Code*, ed. J. Griffiths (1888), pp. xxvi–vii (C. L. Shadwell's introduction).

[60] *Parl. Deb.* 21 Dec. 1837, 3S xxxix. 1388.

[61] *Parl. Deb.* 9 July 1838, 3S xliv. 7.

[62] Ibid. 9. The problem of college statutes is discussed at the end of Ch. 4.

[63] See p. 232.

statement with which Hamilton had ended his article in June 1831 was echoed six years later by the Prime Minister in the Lords: 'universities never reform themselves: everyone knows that.'[64] A 'Royal or Parliamentary Visitation' had begun to look like the only way of 'giving satisfaction to the public'.

[64] *Ed. Rev.* liii (June 1831), 427; *Parl. Deb.* 11 Apr. 1837, 3S xxxvii. 1020 (Melbourne). Given in direct speech in *Mirror of Parliament*, Wm IV 3rd session ii (1837). 932.

4

The 'Unreformed' Colleges

M. C. CURTHOYS

At the beginning of May 1848 the venerable Dr Routh, President of Magdalen, who was then in his ninety-third year, planted a cedar of Lebanon in the college grounds to mark the four-hundredth anniversary of the first charter given to his college. This scene during the year of revolutions, one observer remarked, presented a curious contrast with the planting of liberty trees 'by our neighbours across the channel'.[1] Charles Daubeny, a fellow of Magdalen, later commented that the avoidance of revolutionary 'political convulsions' in England had ensured the survival of her two ancient universities with their wealth and constitutions intact.[2] Like all the Oxford colleges, Magdalen had experienced no decisive breach with the past for two centuries; and the successful resistance to James II's assault on the college's independence was carefully commemorated. Dr Plumptre, the Master of University College, reminded the Archaeological Institute meeting in June 1850 that Oxford's buildings were 'memorials' to a long history of independence from external interference. A visit to Oxford by the United States' minister had prompted the Master's reflection that his college, which had celebrated its six-hundredth anniversary in the previous year, had been a place of education several centuries before the discovery of America.[3] As Plumptre spoke, however, plans to establish a Royal Commission to investigate the University and colleges were being laid by Lord John Russell's Whig administration; and the colleges faced the most far-reaching intervention since the Interregnum.

During the early nineteenth century the colleges experienced a resurgence in popularity 'if the number of new members be considered a criterion', Philip Bliss, later to become Registrar of the University, reported to the Chancellor, Lord Grenville, in 1817.[4] In some colleges undergraduate admissions doubled between 1800 and 1830. Overall, 2,156 undergraduates matri-

[1] *Herald* 13 May 1848; R. D. Middleton, *Dr Routh* (1938), 188. The tree failed to flourish and was removed later in the century.
[2] *Report of the Twenty-Sixth Meeting of the British Association for the Advancement of Science, Cheltenham 1856* (1857), p. lxx.
[3] *Herald* 22 June 1850; George Bancroft had received an hon DCL in 1849.
[4] Bliss to Grenville, 17 Oct. 1817, BL Add. MS 59417, fo 206.

culated at colleges in the first decade of the nineteenth century; this increased to 3,647 in the decade 1820–9.[5] Those seeking admission as commoners to one of the colleges in high repute during the early 1820s—Balliol, Christ Church or Oriel—had to join waiting-lists three or four years in advance of their intended residence. In 1823 Copleston's waiting-list for commoner places at Oriel, which he could fill 'two or three times over' up to 1827, was closed.[6] Even very well-connected parents had trouble securing rooms. Sir Walter Scott eventually obtained a place for his son at Brasenose in 1823, through a connection with one of the University's MPs, Richard Heber, who was a Brasenose graduate, but not without much waiting and uncertainty. It took the intervention of Peel, at the request of the Duke of York, to obtain a place at a 'respectable college' for the son of Charles Young, the actor.[7]

Many colleges moved to meet the demand for places by embarking on building projects; nearly half of them added to their rooms between 1800 and 1850.[8] But there were disturbing signs that some of the largest and most handsomely endowed foundations were unwilling to pull their weight. 'It is not the *interest* of any college, as a body, to increase the number of their undergraduate members,' Copleston confided to the Chancellor, 'and it is but too evident that public spirit alone without the concurrence of interest, or without some impulse given from a powerful quarter, is insufficient to induce men to make this sacrifice and to burden themselves with the trouble and anxiety attending upon increased numbers of young men.'[9] Merton, which was free of any statutory limitation on non-foundationers and, unlike Oriel, of constraints on its site, was cited as an example of a college unwilling to expand.[10] All Souls, which was held to be 'not so much a place of elementary education as of cultivated society', confined its educational activity to the instruction of four Bible clerks.[11] Magdalen considered itself bound by statute to admit no non-foundationers other than gentlemen commoners. No non-foundationers were admitted to New College until Philip Shuttleworth, elected Warden in 1822, relaxed the policy by taking in gentlemen commoners; Lord Eldon's grandson became a member of the college with the status of Nobleman. But the numbers involved were inevitably small.

Cambridge responded to the surge of new entrants after 1815 by extending the permission to live in lodgings. Oxford, having recently tightened up

[5] L. Stone, 'The Oxford student body' in L. Stone (ed.), *The University in Society* (2 vols 1975) i. 59.
[6] Copleston to Grenville, 1 Sept. 1823, BL Add. MS 59416, fo 92.
[7] Peel to C. Lloyd, 24 June 1824, C. Lloyd to Peel, 27 June 1824, BL Add. MS 40342, fos 165, 169. J. C. Young matriculated at Worcester.
[8] The Hebdomadal Board estimated that 170 rooms had been added: *RCO* (1850), appx E, 56.
[9] Copleston to Grenville, 11 May 1825, BL Add. MS 59416, fo 100.
[10] R. Whately to Grenville, 13 Mar. 1825, BL Add. MS 59418, fo 114.
[11] J. Ingram, *Memorials of Oxford* (3 vols 1837) i. 15.

its residence requirements, did not follow this path, but looked instead to its surviving independent halls to accommodate the surge of admissions. Unendowed and therefore largely dependent on undergraduate fees, most of the halls had an incentive for growth and were not hampered by founders' restrictive statutes. Magdalen Hall, whose revival under the principalship of John Macbride was noticed in 1820,[12] moved in 1822 to the Catte Street site of Hertford College, where the nucleus of a chapel and hall were already in place. At a relatively modest cost of £16,000 the hall was able to provide some fifty undergraduate rooms.[13] Elsewhere Grenville, concerned that the shortage of college places strengthened the case for the establishment of a university in London, used his patronage as Chancellor to install active and energetic principals into the halls. Peter Elmsley was appointed to St Alban Hall in 1823; and he was followed on his death in 1825 by Richard Whately, who brought with him as Vice-Principal Samuel Hinds, later chairman of the 1850 Royal Commission. Accommodation in that hall was extended from twelve sets of rooms in 1823 to nineteen by 1827, and its members began regularly to appear in the class lists. James Blackstone, under whose principalship New Inn Hall had been emptied of undergraduates and used instead 'as an Inn for his family when they attend any public amusements in the town', gave in to pressure from the Chancellor and stood down in 1831.[14] Blackstone's successor, J. A. Cramer, expended a considerable sum on buildings to restore the hall to a state of efficiency. Among Grenville's last acts as Chancellor was to appoint R. D. Hampden, one of the Oriel Noetics, to the headship of St Mary Hall, where academic standards and discipline were habitually low; the hall soon claimed a member in the first class. The fifth of Oxford's halls, St Edmund Hall, whose principal was elected by Queen's College, enjoyed an era of growth and established itself as the centre of evangelicalism in Oxford.[15] During this period the proportion of undergraduates educated at the halls rose from between 9 per cent of matriculations (1800–9) to 11 per cent (1820–9), a share which they maintained up to 1850, Magdalen Hall growing to become the fourth largest society in Oxford.

Both the colleges and halls enjoyed a virtual monopoly, to the exclusion of the university professoriate, of official undergraduate teaching. The tutorial system, as the term was understood in the first half of the century, was based upon what were termed college lectures; in practice they resembled what later generations would have recognized as a type of class teaching. Part of the inner life of the colleges (and hence sometimes described as 'private', as opposed to the 'public' instruction offered by the university's professors),

[12] *GM* (1820) ii. 112.
[13] Copleston to Grenville, 11 May 1825, BL Add. MS 59416, fo 102.
[14] Whately to Grenville, 17 Nov. 1827, BL Add. MS 59418, fo 141; Copleston to Grenville, 17 May 1825, BL Add. MS 54916, fo 107.
[15] J. N. D. Kelly, *St Edmund Hall: almost seven hundred years* (1989), 68–9.

college lectures were unseen by outsiders and rarely documented. One version of their working was given by Richard Whately, in an account published in 1831:

Let the stranger to Oxford imagine a long table, spread with books, maps, or mathematical diagrams, as the occasion may require, and thronged with students, generally from the age of sixteen to twenty-one; and at the head of this class, (usually from five to fifteen in number,) a master of arts presiding, and conducting the business; and he will have before him a picture of the most essential and the every-day business of a college or hall—a college lecture. Every head of a house appoints a certain number of tutors for lecturing its own members. They are not, however, lecturers, in the ordinary signification of the word... If the subject of the lecture be a classical author, the several members of the class are called on in turn, to translate a portion; questions are put by the tutor, as occasion offers, and remarks are made by him, on points of grammar, philology, and criticism, as well as on the subject-matter of the book, whether it be history, philosophy, or poetry. At the same time, directions are given, as often as may be needful, respecting the mode of preparing for these lectures, the books to be consulted, method of analysing and illustrating, and the like... By far the most usual, and also the most approved practice, is for each student to attend two, three, or even four tutors,—each lecturing in a different branch of literature or science; by which means one great advantage of the division of labour is obtained.[16]

This depiction of an earnest gathering of learners around a table was the statement of an ideal perhaps rarely attained. As a description of essentials, however, Whately's description held true: the system rested on text-centred class teaching, usually in a tutor's own room. College lectures worked effectively in colleges such as Corpus and Oriel, where both students and tutors were picked men. Elsewhere, as the examples given in Chapter 1 show, the underlying problems of a vast range of ability among the learners, and the lack of opportunity for tutors to specialize, widely discredited this type of teaching. Anonymous pamphleteers in the early 1830s, who claimed recent personal experience, complained of spending twelve or sixteen hours a week with fifteen other hapless learners, listening to 'the dogmas of some sapient blockhead, called a "tutor"'.[17] At most colleges, another critic alleged, so ill-qualified were the tutors that undergraduates were 'doomed to listen day after day to the same childish observation, or to hear a tedious passage of some Greek or Latin author translated into English, without the tutor making any observations whatever, either through carelessness or inability'.[18] These allegations were supported by a well-informed critic, writing in 1833 in the same journal which had carried Whately's earlier favourable account: pupils received no individual help to speak of, and

---

[16] *QJE* ii (1831), 16–17.
[17] *Oxford: academical abuses disclosed by some of the initiated* (1832), 10.
[18] *Thoughts on reform at Oxford. By a graduate* (1833), 15–16.

although the procedure at college lectures was described as 'conversational', it was understood to be 'contrary to form' for undergraduates themselves to venture queries of the lecturer.[19]

Attendance at lectures, generally conducted in the mornings, six days a week (though, in some colleges, not on saints' days and other religious holidays), was compulsory. Their frequency, intended as much for disciplinary as for educational reasons, served to magnify their inutility. In the 1840s lectures at a strict college, Wadham, might amount to seventeen a week, and a freshman at Balliol in 1839 was surprised to find that the number of lectures a week (fourteen) exceeded the level of attendance which had been required of him at Eton.[20] It was not merely the undergraduates for whom college lectures were irksome. D. K. Sandford, who took up the Greek chair at Glasgow University after graduating at Christ Church in 1820, reckoned that Oxford tutors were occupied for seven or eight hours a day.[21] This may have been an extreme estimate and probably included private teaching undertaken by college tutors in addition to their official lectures. When he succeeded W. G. Ward as mathematics lecturer at Balliol in January 1843, Frederick Temple recorded his college lectures as totalling fifteen per week, which seems to have been the usual teaching-load.

This surfeit of teaching was subsidized by college endowments; tuition fees, which commonly ranged from about £16 to £25 a year, were said in 1853 to be lower than those charged at King's College, London, or at the recently founded theological colleges at Wells and Chichester. Colleges could afford comparatively generous teacher–pupil ratios, which were, taking the colleges as a whole, in the region of one tutor to fifteen undergraduates actually in residence.[22] Yet one of the most marked developments of this period was for undergraduates to resort to private tutors to provide the teaching they needed. The 1834 Oxford declaration against repeal of undergraduate subscription to the Thirty-nine Articles contained the signatures of eighty-seven individuals 'immediately concerned with the instruction and discipline of the place'—college tutors, deans, and lecturers—while an additional forty-one appeared under the category of 'resident members of the University of Oxford, engaged, as private Tutors, in furthering the established system of education'.[23] Exactly how extensively the services of these latter were used, or how essential they were to get through the prescribed course, is unclear. A commentator generally hostile to the colleges, the geologist Charles Lyell, cited the information given to him by an Oxford

[19] QJE v (1833), 329.
[20] S. Childers, The Life and Correspondence of the Right Hon. Hugh C. E. Childers, 1827–1896 (2 vols 1901) i. 13; E. H. Coleridge, Life and Correspondence of John Duke Lord Coleridge (2 vols 1904) i. 64.
[21] Ed. Rev. xxxv (1821), 308.
[22] Report and Evidence (1853), evidence, 181–2, 477.
[23] Bodl. G. A. Oxon. c. 50 (124). See also p. 213 below.

tutor that in 1840 and 1841 some 250 undergraduates used private tutors, paying £40 or £50 a year (more than twice the cost of college tuition fees). But these, as Lyell acknowledged, represented only about a fifth of resident undergraduates; and even allowing for the fact that they were probably concentrated among undergraduates in their final year, among whom the proportion using the services of a private tutor was probably greater than a fifth, it is by no means clear that they constituted a majority.[24] George Rawlinson, a tutor at Exeter, gave an entirely different picture: only five of his thirty-five pupils who completed their residence between 1842 and 1846 had at no time sought the assistance of a private tutor.[25] Other authorities doubted the need to pay for private tuition at all. Rowland Muckleston of Worcester, where the teaching was said to be good, believed 'numbers of those who read with private Tutors do so more from a sort of fashion, and from a want of self-reliance, than from the necessity of the case'.[26] This may have been true in the case of men who had neglected their college work, and who sought to be 'crammed' prior to taking a pass degree. But for 'reading' men private tutors offered two facilities which could not be generally obtained from their college tutors: specialized tuition and individual attention.

A notice circulated within the University in May 1829, contemporary with the inquiries of the Hebdomadal Board's Committee on Examinations, and possibly carrying the sanction of that Committee, 'respectfully suggested' to private tutors that instead of trying to cover a wide range of books and subjects, they should 'confine themselves respectively to some one branch of study, of which they might make both themselves and their Pupils thoroughly masters'.[27] Whately's suggestion in 1831, quoted above, that such a division of labour was the 'most approved practice' was a significant observation, coming in the aftermath of the celebrated Oriel tutorial row from one who was privy to the proceedings in the college. Apart from his religious objections to the demand of the Oriel tutors to have exclusive responsibility for their individual students, Provost Hawkins's side of the argument was that students would thereby be deprived of more specialized instruction. Where teaching was subdivided, 'the students have the benefit of the instruction of all the Tutors indiscriminately'.[28] Most colleges, however, had only two or three tutors, so it was hardly possible for a division of expertise to be made a reality; only Christ Church, which had separate readers in divinity, rhetoric, logic, and Greek philology, was believed to be able to achieve this.[29]

---

[24] C. Lyell, *Travels in North America* (2 vols 1845) i. 287.
[25] *RCO* (1850), evidence, 216.
[26] *Report and Evidence* (1853), evidence, 253.
[27] Bodl. G. A. Oxon. c. 45 (52); another copy in Bodl. G. A. Oxon. b. 21.
[28] Hawkins to H. Jenkyns, 10 June 1830, BCA MS Jenkyns VB; cf Ward, *Victorian Oxford*, 75.
[29] *Report and Evidence* (1853), evidence, 78–9.

Osborne Gordon, tutor and Censor of Christ Church, believed that it was the desire for 'direct personal assistance' that especially caused undergraduates to pay for private tuition.[30] This was something that college tutors clearly might provide, and there is evidence that a growing number after 1830 did so. Whately's account had indicated that some tutors on occasions met their pupils individually, and this is corroborated by the testimony of R. W. Browne, who had been a tutor at St John's between 1831 and 1835. He included individual consultations with undergraduates in his estimate of the time which college tutors devoted to their official duties, though he suggested that these meetings were 'occasional' and tended to be at the onset of examinations.[31] By 1850 many undergraduates were receiving closer and more regular individual attention from their college tutors: Richard Congreve at Wadham and Henry Mansel at St John's were two of the most prominent among a generation of tutors who gathered able students around them.[32] Mansel demonstrated the absorption of the methods of private tutors within the official system; after graduating he became one of the foremost private tutors of his generation and continued to take private pupils after his appointment to a tutorship of St John's in 1850. Mark Pattison, a conscientious tutor at Lincoln, recorded in his diary early in 1851 his discovery that his peers at other colleges took large numbers of individual pupils and that some, notably Jowett of Balliol, were taking college pupils in the evenings.[33] Pattison's evidence to the Royal Commission, probably written during the winter of 1850–1 (and certainly before his embitterment at the outcome of the Lincoln College rectorship election in November 1851), is the most significant statement of the new attitude. It has been described as 'a sustained argument to prove the necessity in higher education of a personal relationship between the teacher and the taught'.[34] Pattison contended that a regenerated college tutorial system incorporating the best features of private tuition represented the most effective means of educating 'a cultivated clerisy'. Private tuition had shown the importance of 'the act of communication' between the tutor's mind and his pupil's, the personal influence upon the pupil of close contact with 'a superior mind' and 'the gentle pressure and aid' of a tutor who had mastered the same material as his pupil.[35] Its weakness was the demand on the part of private pupils to be given ready-made knowledge, and the lack of authority on the part of the teachers. The principle underlying the catechetical method, that the student should be required 'to master for himself' some of the standard books in his

[30] *Report and Evidence* (1853), evidence, 210.
[31] *RCO* (1850), evidence, 344.
[32] C. S. L. Davies and J. Garnett (eds), *Wadham College* (1994), 45; J. W. Burgon, *Lives of Twelve Good Men* (2 vols 1889) ii. 173.
[33] Bodl. MS Pattison 129, fo 35ᵛ.
[34] J. Sparrow, *Mark Pattison and the Idea of a University* (1967), 92.
[35] *RCO* (1850), evidence, 48.

subject, remained sound.[36] Its requirement that the pupil play an active part in the learning-process 'is the nearest approach we make to the Socratic principle of education'.[37] The weakness of catechetical lecturing lay not in the method, but in the daily practice: if college tutors were better-qualified and ill-prepared students excluded, an ideal combination of lecturing with individual supervision might be achieved. Pattison himself seems to have faithfully carried out his own prescriptions, pupils coming away from his college lectures 'with the feeling of roused inquiry' rather than with pre-pared examination answers.[38] In some colleges, however, official teaching continued to supply neither: at Brasenose in the 1850s, where teaching arrangements were 'chaotic', one undergraduate 'was excused all college teaching' when he was found to be working seriously for honours.[39]

Colleges had to try to control the young men in their charge as well as to teach them. College discipline, like college lectures, had to apply both to a wider range of undergraduate ages than was later usual—generally from 16 to 23—and to extremes of future expectations. Having fulfilled the basic ob-ligations as to gate hours and attendance at chapel and lectures, undergrad-uates were left very much to their own devices. As Edmund Goodenough, a Christ Church tutor, wrote in 1815, the undergraduate, on entering a college, was 'placed in an intermediate state between the close confinement of a School and the entire liberty of action which he is afterwards to enjoy in the world'.[40] Taxed in 1838 as to why undergraduates were not subjected to more frequent roll-calls, A. T. Gilbert, the Principal of Brasenose, explained that it would represent 'a mode of discipline unsuited to the age and station and the manly character of the young men themselves; we cannot institute military discipline in the university; it must be one combining restraint and freedom'.[41] Undergraduates felt, and were consciously allowed, considerable independence in their own rooms; one of the factors which the authorities admitted prevented them from suppressing gambling was the understanding that college officers never entered undergraduates' rooms. An incident at Oriel in 1840, when there was some undergraduate resentment against a young tutor taking rooms on a staircase usually occupied by gentlemen commoners, suggested the sensitivities touched by any hint of encroachment by the authorities.[42] W. G. Meredith, an undergraduate at Brasenose be-tween 1821 and 1824, described to his friend Benjamin Disraeli the state of the college at night: 'It is quite amusing to hear the noise in our quad,

---

[36] Ibid. 44.
[37] Ibid. 48.
[38] A. J. Church, cited in V. H. H. Green, *The Commonwealth of Lincoln College, 1427–1977* (1979), 436.
[39] F. L. Latham, 'B.N.C. in the Fifties', *Brazen Nose* i (1911), 159.
[40] E. Goodenough to unnamed correspondent, 30 Oct. 1815, Bodl. MS Top. Oxon. d. 156.
[41] PP 1837–8 HL (227) xx. 767.
[42] T. Hughes, *James Fraser, Second Bishop of Manchester. A memoir, 1818–1885* (1887), 27–8.

which usually takes place at about eleven or twelve o'clock. After liberally imbibing the liquors which are of every description from Champagne to gin and water, they institute what is called a Vauxhall, and promenade up and down the grass plot smoking, and drinking malt, till a very late hour.'[43] There was no suggestion of any intervention by the resident fellows.

At least one Oxford college experienced the disciplinary problems faced by other institutions charged with educating and accommodating young men of means in the 1820s. Recurrent disturbances and nightly carousing among the students at Manchester College, York, a Unitarian academy, had brought the tutors to the point of despair in 1828.[44] A riot in 1822 at the East India Company's college at Haileybury, the sixth since 1808, led to proposals for tighter surveillance of the students, including inspections of their rooms.[45] At Christ Church the authorities appeared temporarily to be in danger of losing control; in Michaelmas 1824 Dean Smith considered that there were more undergraduates in residence than the authorities could manage, and during the summer of 1825 Charles Lloyd was 'in expectation of what the University has not often seen, a positive rebellion'. Disagreements surfaced among the Chapter and censors over how to deal with rowdy late-night supper-parties, the source of much trouble. Smith adhered to the traditional line that 'young men are to be taught the use of their liberty and must abide by the consequences'; Lloyd believed this view outmoded, and that the parties should be stopped as incompatible with 'academical pursuits'.[46] Some timely removals of troublesome individuals, a sanction not so readily available to professors at Haileybury,[47] brought calm to Christ Church by the end of the year. This college apart, however, there was no appearance in this period of open revolt: in 1843 the detonation of two barrels of explosives by undergraduates in Exeter College was a Guy Fawkes night prank rather than a deliberate defiance of authority.[48]

Infractions of college discipline in minor cases, such as missing chapel, might be punished by written impositions.[49] Repeated offences were met by confinement within the college ('gating') or deprival of rights to use the buttery ('discommoning'). Further levels of sanction involved rustication for a period, or removal from the college, usually to one of the halls, and finally expulsion. Discipline was administered impersonally and often with considerable formality; persistent offenders might find themselves arraigned

---

[43] W. G. Meredith to B. Disraeli, 13 May 1822, Bodl. Dep. Hughenden 12/1, fo. 6.

[44] J. Seed, 'Manchester College, York: an early nineteenth century Dissenting academy', *Journal of Educational Administration and History* xiv (1982), 14.

[45] P. James, *Population Malthus* (1979), 328.

[46] Lloyd to Peel, 26 Jan. 1825, 27 Nov. 1825, 23 Mar. 1825, BL Add. MS 40342, fos 199, 285, 230.

[47] F. C. Danvers, *Memorials of Old Haileybury College* (1894), 86.

[48] Boase, *Reg. Exeter*, p. clxv.

[49] An apparently genuine example was cited in B. Blackmantle, *The English Spy* (2 vols 1825, new edn 1907) i. 156.

before an assembly of the head and fellows and admonished as to their future conduct. On occasion, ceremonial acts of submission to authority were demanded. During the troubles at Christ Church, eighteen undergraduate Students, parties to what appears to have been a demonstration against the authorities of the House at the founder's dinner in June 1825, were brought before the Dean and Chapter and were admonished; one of them was 'required to prepare a Latin Epistle to the Dean and Canons acknowledging the offence and asking pardon for it', which he was to read out in the Chapter House in the presence both of the Dean and canons and of the other reprimanded Students.[50] A similar sanction was applied at Trinity in 1831. A petition signed by fifty-three undergraduates was presented to the President in protest at the length of the impositions set by the Dean, whose severity had already provoked the breaking of his windows. The President and resident fellows viewed the petition as 'in itself an act of disobedience to Authority', one of the signatories being reminded by the plain-spoken Trinity tutor Thomas Short that 'you are not here as a free citizen of England, but *in statu pupillari*'. Those scholars who had signed, including Roundell Palmer, were reprimanded by the President. The remainder were required publicly to acknowledge the impropriety of their proceedings in the presence of the resident fellows.[51] At Corpus, in the following year, all the undergraduates were assembled in the college hall to witness the admonition of an undergraduate exhibitioner for surreptitiously entering the college after 9 p.m.; his public act of contrition caused the college authorities to withdraw a more severe penalty threatened.[52]

Occasional ritual sanctions did little to reassure parents who expected college discipline to protect their sons against falling into debt. Little urgency, however, was attached by the colleges to curtailing the costs of Oxford residence as they basked in influential patronage after 1815. In 1825 Copleston rather blithely considered annual college charges of no more than £100 for 'rooms, diet, and instruction' to be modest, and additional personal expenditure to be 'just what a gentleman must spend wherever he is, provided he wishes to live as other gentlemen do'.[53] Extravagance in the latter case the colleges claimed to be powerless to prevent; parents who complained about debts run up by their sons beyond their normal college battels were reminded by a later writer that the colleges were not boarding-schools, nor were tutors 'school ushers'.[54] Many of the colleges' own practices were held by critics to prevent economical living. Poor housekeeping, it was alleged, kept charges in some colleges artificially high; average battels in

[50] Chapter Act of 14 June 1825, CA D&C i. b. 9, fos 56–7.
[51] TCA A1 Liber Decani, Michaelmas 1831; J. Pycroft, *Oxford Memories* (2 vols 1886) i. 39.
[52] Fowler, *Corpus*, 316.
[53] W. J. Copleston, *Memoir of Edward Copleston, D.D., Bishop of Llandaff* (1851), 9.
[54] *Herald* 19 Feb. 1848.

some were 50 per cent higher than those in the better-run colleges.[55] The continued practice of admitting gentlemen commoners was widely criticized, though this period saw their gradual disappearance as a distinct class. Trinity admitted its last gentleman commoner in 1808, and University College ceased the practice in the 1830s, followed by Corpus in 1849. By 1850 most colleges had ceased to admit them. Where they remained, gentlemen commoners were no longer exempt from ordinary college discipline, and the rights which their payment of double fees brought them had been whittled down to 'some few privileges of their table' in hall and the permission to enjoy expensive amenities, such as additional servants and the ownership of a horse.[56]

There was no relaxation, however, in the idea that a college education was to produce 'gentlemen'; indeed, there was a significant growth in the provision on staircases and in undergraduates' rooms of personal service considered appropriate to young men of that standing. Like many collegiate developments in this period, the rise of the scouts was unstatutory, unofficial and to a large extent unsupervised.[57] In the late eighteenth century staircase scouts, or bedmakers as they continued to be officially known, were already undertaking duties which had formerly been performed by servitors or, in the case of wealthier students, by private servants employed by the undergraduates themselves. In 1776 the word 'scout' first appears in Pembroke's governing body minutes; by that date menial functions had already been transferred from servitors to scouts at Christ Church; at Magdalen, for a trial period in 1802, college servants replaced the choristers in waiting at table in hall, and the arrangement was made permanent in the following year.[58] By 1850 the domestic system of the colleges depended upon a large complement of servants and, according to the testimony of the Bursar of Balliol, service charges (over £12 a year at his college) were the second-largest single charge on undergraduates after tuition fees.[59] Although nominally paid by the colleges from fixed charges levied on battels, the scouts, like other college employees, swelled their incomes both by additional charges levied for services, profits made on provisions supplied to undergraduates' rooms, commissions received from tradesmen to whom they introduced their undergraduate masters and, most notoriously, the various perquisites which had grown to enjoy the sanction of custom. By mid-century there were attempts to bring the system more closely under college control. Servants at Magdalen were placed on a fixed stipend by a college order of March 1855;

---

[55] *Prose Remains of A. H. Clough* (1888), 71; *Thoughts on Reform at Oxford*, 21.

[56] *RCO* (1850), evidence, 355.

[57] C. Platt, *The Most Obliging Man in Europe* (1986), 15.

[58] Macleane, *Pembroke*, 498; E. G. W. Bill, 'A catalogue of treasury books' (typescript 1955, CA), 81; Bloxam, *Reg. Magdalen* i, p. xiii.

[59] *RCO* (1850), evidence, 144.

in the same year one of H. G. Liddell's first acts on his appointment as Dean of Christ Church was to bring the entire charge for scouts within battels.[60]

The colleges supplied the trappings of gentility; but they offered, it was alleged, no guarantee of morality; Henry Bulteel had pointed this out with sensational effect in his sermon on the indiscriminate giving of testimonials of good conduct to intending ordinands.[61] The Tractarians promoted the idea of reforming college discipline on the principles of poverty and obedience, the monastic ideal finding expression in Pugin's plans for the rebuilding of Balliol.[62] Schemes proposed after 1840, often under Tractarian inspiration, to create affiliated halls for poor scholars intending to enter the Church were concerned as much with imposing a more closely regulated regime as with reducing costs. 'Industry and economy' were the principles upon which, in March 1851, a committee of Magdalen fellows proposed to establish a hall for poor scholars in the college grounds: a regime of compulsory frugality was to be imposed on the scholars, who were to be completely segregated from the rest of the college; all meals were to be had in common; and each undergraduate was to have only one room, furnished by the college 'plainly and uniformly'.[63] Such an austere regime, for which there were parallels among the training colleges for elementary teachers founded by the Anglican National Society in the previous decade, would have represented a fundamental break with existing traditions of collegiate education in Oxford.[64] Its promoters, however, pointed to earlier precedents in the rules of life prescribed by early college statutes, of which translations had recently been published (Magdalen in 1840, Corpus in 1843, Merton in 1847).

Those statutes reminded a younger generation how much of the original communal ideal of college life had been lost. 'Our existing system of College habits so far separates the Undergraduate from the Fellow', Mark Pattison told the 1850 Royal Commission,[65] 'that his merely being lodged under the same roof makes him no real member of the family, brings him into no contact with his seniors. The relation between the student and the College official is, in general, as distant and technical as that between the officer and the private in our army.' During the Hebdomadal Board's exercise in statute revision, in 1837, the re-enactment of the section in the Laudian Code which required each undergraduate to be assigned a tutor called attention to the priority which had in earlier centuries been attached to tutors' responsibil-

[60] Order of the Dean, Dec. 1855, CA xlii. a. 1; MCA CP/1/14, p. 14. I owe this Magdalen reference to Dr Janie Cottis.

[61] H. B. Bulteel, *A Sermon on I Corinthians ii. 12 Preached before the University of Oxford, at St. Mary's, on Sunday, Feb. 6, 1831* (1831), 46.

[62] H. Colvin, *Unbuilt Oxford* (1983), 109–11.

[63] *Corr. on Improvement* (1854), 285–6.

[64] R. W. Rich, *The Training of Teachers in England and Wales during the Nineteenth Century* (Bath 1933), 87.

[65] *RCO* (1850), evidence, 43.

ities for moral and religious supervision.[66] How far this role should be taken
had given conscientious tutors cause for reflection in the early decades of the
century. In the twenty years following Provost Hawkins's dismissal of the
Oriel tutors, a growing number of college teachers did regard their office as a
pastoral one. In 1840 William Sewell of Exeter argued that teaching-loads
should be reduced to enable tutors to carry out the 'cure of souls' which he
considered their office to represent.[67] Under two Tractarian tutors, Isaac
Williams and W. J. Copeland, the scholars at Trinity formed a high-minded
set at whose gatherings, one of them recalled, 'never once did I hear a word
uttered, or a subject discussed, which might not have been spoken or
discussed in a lady's drawing-room'.[68] Of the liberals, A. P. Stanley, who
taught at University College from 1842, regarded college tutoring as a serious
vocation and declined offers of ecclesiastical preferment. He gave time to his
pupils individually, taking them on walks, and inviting them to breakfasts,
while attempting to raise the level of his college lectures to a standard which
would make them more useful to his pupils in the examinations.[69]

These developments of the late 1840s, important though they were later to
prove, had yet to make much of an impact on the popular perception of the
colleges. Declining aggregate admissions to the colleges after 1830—a fall
which was more pronounced at Oxford than at Cambridge—were brought
to public attention by the statistical inquiries of Baden Powell, the Savilian
Professor of Geometry, and James Heywood, the Mancunian promoter of
university reform.[70] Their findings were linked to the early attempts to
estimate the wealth of the colleges; Harry Longueville Jones, who had
proposed in 1836 the establishment of a university college in Manchester,
presented data to the British Association two years later suggesting that
Oxford college revenues exceeded £150,000 a year.[71] The way was open for
invidious international and local comparisons. Jones related endowment
incomes to the numbers of members on the books of each college, producing
a monetary 'stimulating force per head' in a table which did not display
All Souls and New College to their advantage.[72] Numbers on the books,
obtainable from the *Calendar*, were a purely formal indicator of membership. The interest in establishing exactly how many undergraduates were in
residence caused Heywood to collect what seems to have been a unique set
of figures showing the actual populations of the colleges and halls in May

---

[66] *Statutes* ii. 233.
[67] *Quarterly* lxvi (1840), 181.
[68] W. R. W. Stephens, *The Life and Letters of Edward A. Freeman* (2 vols 1895) i. 46.
[69] R. E. Prothero, *The Life and Correspondence of Arthur Penrhyn Stanley D.D.* (2 vols 1893)
i. 183–92.
[70] *Quarterly Journal of the Statistical Society of London* v (Oct. 1842), 235; ix (Oct. 1846), 194.
[71] R. D. Thomson, *British Annual and Epitome of the Progress of Science for 1839* (1838), 102.
Corrected figures appeared in Huber, *The English Universities* ii pt 2, p. 576.
[72] Huber, 578.

TABLE 4.1

UNDERGRADUATES IN RESIDENCE, MAY 1842

college	fellows	scholars	exhibitioners	Bible clerks and servitors	noblemen	gentlemen commoners	commoners	total
All Souls				4				4
Balliol		10					63	73
Brasenose		20					79	99
Christ Church	17[a]			11	4	23	99	154
Corpus		9	4			4		17
Exeter	2	5					104	111
Jesus		5		5			26	36
Lincoln		13		1			27	41
Magdalen		5		4		4		13
Merton		10		2			23	35
New	18			2		2		22
Oriel		3		4	1	6	45	59
Pembroke		13		1			24	38
Queen's		10	4				54	68
St John's	9			2		3	44	58
Trinity		10					55	65
University		8	1				40	49
Wadham		8		2		1	57	68
Worcester		8		1		5	56	70
Magdalen Hall						18	64	82
New Inn Hall						2	5	7
St Alban Hall							6	6
St Edmund Hall				1			24	25
St Mary Hall				1		2	19	22
total	46	137	9	41	5	70	914	1,222

Source: J. Heywood, 'Statistics of the universities of Oxford and Cambridge', *Quarterly Journal of the Statistical Society of London* v (1842), 243. [a] Students.

1842. His 'academical census', part of which is summarized in Table 4.1, demonstrated that some of those colleges known to be the wealthiest were educating the fewest undergraduates. Merton, with one of the largest endowments, was shown to be among the smallest colleges.[73] Magdalen edu-

[73] E. F. Percival, *The Foundation Statutes of Merton College, Oxford* (1847), 129.

cated just thirteen undergraduates, and was subjected to unflattering comparison with Trinity College, Cambridge, which was said to enjoy a similar endowment and yet to have nearly 300 men in residence.[74] These radical observations were no more than a head of house had been privately reporting to the university Chancellor some twenty years earlier.

In a further elaborate arithmetical exercise, published in 1853, Sir William Hamilton used the examination class lists between 1838 and 1847 to generate a table which claimed to show 'the comparative efficiency of the Oxford Houses as seminaries of education'.[75] Assigning points to the honours obtained by each college, and relating them to student numbers, Hamilton arrived at a collegiate ranking. His purpose was not primarily to compare one college with another (though it afforded him 'great satisfaction' that his old college, Balliol, emerged at the top) but rather to expose the extent of differences between the best and worst. Balliol was found to perform more than four times better than the weaker colleges, such as Jesus and Pembroke, and by some measures the differences were even greater. Linked to a survey of the qualifications of the tutors in each college, Hamilton's results were intended to demonstrate that Oxford's tutorial monopoly was not only illegal but often incompetent as well.

Utilitarian calculations were foreign to the purposes of the *Memorials of Oxford* (1837), a combination of architectural and constitutional history complied by James Ingram, President of Trinity. Royal commissions were denounced as threats to the chartered liberties of the colleges, whose past benefactors Ingram recorded in detail, and whose present affluence was celebrated in the accompanying engravings of Oxford's buildings. Ingram's book inspired William Sewell to draw a contrast between cities of Mammon, London and Birmingham, 'in which wealth is created for man', and Oxford 'in which it has been lavished, and still is expended, for God'.[76] Francis Wayland, President of Brown University, who made a comparative study of university systems during a visit to Europe in 1840–1, was less impressed. He described the Oxford colleges as 'palaces', the surroundings as 'princely' and the inhabitants 'gentlemanly'. None the less, he considered the 'luxurious ease', social exclusiveness and religious narrowness to amount to 'a monstrous perversion' of the objects for which the colleges had been given their wealth.[77] External benefactors showed little enthusiasm for the residential collegiate ideal in this period: existing colleges attracted few new endowments and those which were received came mainly from internal

[74] *RCO* (1850), report, 152.
[75] W. Hamilton, *Discussions on Philosophy and Literature, Education and University Reform* (2nd edn 1853), 746–7.
[76] *Quarterly* lxi (1838), 205.
[77] F. Wayland and H. L. Wayland, *A Memoir of the Life and Labors of Francis Wayland, D.D. LL D* (2 vols New York 1867) ii. 41.

donors.[78] No new college had been successfully founded since Worcester in 1714. The hopes vested in the halls a generation earlier had proved largely illusory. While they retained an important function in providing a route into the University for older or married men, they tended, with the exception of St Edmund Hall, to revert to their earlier character as places of refuge for those obliged to remove themselves from their colleges. The most damning verdict on them came from William Hayward Cox, Vice-Principal of St Mary Hall for twelve years: none of the five independent halls, he asserted in 1850, 'either on the score of economy or intellectual advantage, can compete with the collegiate system, even in its present faulty state'.[79]

Presiding over what appeared to be an increasingly vulnerable system of domestic education were the heads of houses. The nineteen college head-ships were, with the exception of Merton, tenable only by clergymen, as a result of either college statutes or the connection of headships with church livings. Twelve of the heads holding office between 1800 and 1850 were to receive ecclesiastical promotions. Warden Shuttleworth of New College, whose ambitions were immortalized in rhyme, finally secured a bishopric in 1840.[80] Most were elected in their mid-forties and, taking advantage of the freedom to marry which they alone among members of college foundations enjoyed, remained in Oxford for good; fifty-seven of the sixty-nine heads of colleges and halls who held office between 1800 and 1850 died in post.

Described by the 1850 Royal Commission as 'posts of honour and influence', college headships had become 'lucrative offices' carrying emoluments varying from £600 to £3,000 a year.[81] Francis Jeune's income as Master of Pembroke in 1850 has been reckoned by his biographer to have amounted to about £1,400, a remarkable sum when set against his college's total income for the year of about £4,750.[82] Jeune's contemporaries were wealthy men: of thirteen for whom information is available, twelve left estates valued at more than £10,000.[83] 'I must state the very solemn idea suggested to Oxford natives of that day by the title, much more by the sight and presence' of the heads, bedel Cox recalled.[84] Memoirists conventionally held up for notice their individual qualities of 'dignity of deportment', 'urbanity' and 'suavity' of manners and their avoidance of 'enthusiasm' in religion.[85] For the less reverent pen they offered an appealing subject. J. G. Lockhart's 1823

[78] D. Owen, *English Philanthropy, 1660–1960* (Cambridge Mass. 1965), 346.

[79] *RCO* (1850), evidence, 94.

[80] Tuckwell (1900), 169.

[81] *RCO* (1850), report, 182.

[82] J. H. C. Leach, *Sparks of Reform: the career of Francis Jeune, 1806–1868* (1994), 35.

[83] The thirteenth left over £8,000. Values obtained from the *Calendar of the Grants of Probate* (1858–   ).

[84] Cox, 160.

[85] *GM* (1824) ii. 84 (Thomas Lee, Trinity); (1828) i. 370–1 (Michael Marlow, St John's); (1833) ii. 276 (William Tournay, Wadham); (1836) ii. 545 (George Rowley, University); (1838) ii. 560 (John Collier Jones, Exeter); (1843) ii. 551 (Thomas Bridges, Corpus).

novel *Reginald Dalton* was unusual among early novels of Oxford life as a production of a graduate of the university; its depiction of a college head—a 'rubicund old gentleman in grand canonicals and a grizzle-wig', resting his gouty leg on a footstool, beside a table of reading-matter including 'the *Courier*, a number of the *Quarterly*, and a novel of Miss Edgeworth'[86]— conveyed a widely held impression of worldliness. Although Lockhart was criticized for his 'false and gaudy colouring of this picture of Oxford life and manners',[87] his fiction was an understatement set beside the actual deathbed scene, in 1826, of Peter Vaughan, Warden of Merton. Vaughan breathed his last under the shadow of episcopal censure for his greedy pluralism, and amidst the noisy lamentations of the mistress whom he had notoriously harboured for many years in his lodgings.[88]

Few heads were conspicuous for scholarship, though they enjoyed more leisure for its pursuit, and for the dissemination of its results, than most residents of the time. Dean Gaisford and Dr Routh were the two heads with the most substantial scholarly reputations, though others, such as Philip Wynter of St John's, who laboured upon an edition of the works of Joseph Hall, the Stuart divine, and James Ingram of Trinity, whose historical in-quiries drew him away from college business, were recognized as industri-ous. 'With the exception of four or five of the body, no Head of a College has written a work which would repay the trouble of a perusal,' a critic alleged in 1850; and even a loyal defender of the heads could find only six 'Authors or Editors' among them, including the principals of the halls, who were noticeably the more distinguished body of men.[89] Their involvement in education was even more slight. They were responsible for admissions and their polished manners doubtless came into play in dealings with parents. Other than this, their work amounted to presiding over college collections at the end of term and overseeing college discipline; the Principal of Jesus, it was reported in 1851, 'takes no part in the instruction'. The Evangelicals, Symons of Wadham and Jeune of Pembroke, delivered regular Sunday lectures on the Articles in their college chapels.[90] Acknowledging the effi-ciency of Symons's theological lecturing, James Garbett, a fellow of Wad-ham, considered it 'a mistake of the first order, that heads of houses should hold aloof from all the duties of instruction, and only touch the under-graduate sphere at the disciplinary point'.[91]

[86] J. G. Lockhart, *Reginald Dalton* (Edinburgh 1823), 300–13.

[87] *Remarks on the Novel of Reginald Dalton, with extracts from that work illustrative of life in Oxford* (1824), 3.

[88] J. R. L. Highfield, 'Two accounts of the death of Dr Peter Vaughan, Warden of Merton College, Oxford', *Oxoniensia* xxxix (1974), 93–4.

[89] *Letter to the Rt Hon Lord John Russell M.P. on the Constitutional Defects of the University and Colleges of Oxford* (1850), 48; *Report and Evidence* (1853), evidence, 464.

[90] *RCO* (1850), evidence, 317, 344, 363, 376.

[91] J. Garbett, *University Reform: a letter to the Warden of Wadham College, Oxford* (1853), 17.

By the ritual of mutual bowing, the heads marked the distance in ordinary relations between themselves and the undergraduates.[92] The position of the heads in relation to other Oxford residents was scarcely less formal. With their freedom to marry had come a physical detachment from the other members of their colleges, as they established themselves in extensive and sometimes secluded lodgings. They and their families formed a distinct and exclusive social circle in early Victorian Oxford; heads dined in their college halls only on the occasions of gaudies or feast-days.[93] Roundell Palmer of Magdalen was one who believed that the family lives of the heads had tended to distance them from the bachelor fellows, creating a lack of sympathy on either side which contributed to the constitutional conflicts of the 1830s and 1840s.[94] Matters were not eased by the prerogatives which heads claimed in college business. Some used their authority to abridge the rights of college governing bodies. Benjamin Symons, in conflict with the young, radical Wadham fellows in the late 1840s, claimed 'the power of determining what subjects shall be discussed at College meetings'.[95] As one of the few heads to sympathize with the Tractarians, Dr Routh was held in personal affection in Magdalen. After an entertainment in his drawing-room in 1849, the 'easy familiarity between the Fellows and their Head' was noted by James Mozley; but even there the fellows were exasperated in 1851 when their reform scheme was quashed 'summarily' by the President exercising his power of veto.[96]

While radicals made the obvious charge of sinecurism,[97] the heads were also held to have grown forgetful of their paternal responsibilities by a younger generation which likened colleges to families or parishes. This was the contemporary thrust of the story that Provost Hawkins of Oriel delayed to put on his cap and gown before emerging from his lodgings to inspect the body of an undergraduate mortally wounded by a fall from an upper window.[98] J. T. Round, a former tutor of Balliol, professed to admire the existing university constitution on the ground that it was founded upon the filial principle of obedience to fathers, and J. R. Bloxam of Magdalen lamented Routh's passing as the loss of 'a father and a friend';[99] the reality of the office of head in the unreformed university more often strained the loyalty and imagination of even their most determined supporters.

[92] *Memoirs of a Highland Lady: The autobiography of Elizabeth Grant of Rothiemurchus*, ed. Lady Strachey (1928), 133.

[93] *The Oxford University and City Guide* (1824), 190.

[94] *Parl. Deb.* 18 July 1850, 3S cxii. 1469.

[95] *RCO* (1850), report, 245; B. H. Jackson (ed.), *Recollections of Thomas Graham Jackson* (1950), 24, 104; J. S. Reynolds, *The Evangelicals at Oxford, 1735–1871* (1975), pt 2, p. 2.

[96] Mozley, *Letters*, 208.

[97] See T. J. Hogg's invective in *Westminster Review* xv (July 1831), 62.

[98] D. W. Rannie, *Oriel College* (1900), 188.

[99] *Report and Evidence* (1853), evidence, 465 n.; Bloxam, *Reg. Magdalen* ii, p. ccx.

Next on the foundations were the 'brother' fellows, who were about 550 in number (including the Students of Christ Church). The majority were clergymen, all were unmarried, and most were young. Although fellowships or studentships were not yet clearly distinguished from scholarships at Christ Church, Exeter, New College and St John's, where there were in total about fifty undergraduates in the former category in 1842, the overwhelming majority were graduates. Most college statutes required fellows to enter holy orders within a certain period after their election. It was calculated that 90 per cent of Oxford fellowships could be held permanently only by clergymen, though at any one time there might be a number waiting—or delaying—to take orders. In 1840, in round figures, 330 (60 per cent) out of some 500 graduate fellows were actually in orders. Some of the remainder took advantage of those fellowships which could be held permanently by laymen. Oriel permitted three lay fellows to study common law or medicine. There was a concentration of lay fellows at Merton, where there was no statutory requirement to enter orders, and at All Souls, where exemptions from the obligation to enter orders were granted by the college as a matter of course.

All fellowships were held subject to the condition of celibacy; and marriage was the most common cause for them to be relinquished. Forty-eight of the eighty-three men elected to fellowships at Exeter College between 1800 and 1840 vacated them for this reason. College founders had regarded fellowships as supports for needy scholars and had attached to them property disqualifications. What 'poor' or 'needy' meant in the nineteenth-century context was never clear; but usually a fellowship was vacated when the holder obtained ecclesiastical preferment over a certain value. A general disqualification applied to the ownership of real property. At University College the limit was set at an annual income of £80, obliging A. P. Stanley to surrender his fellowship upon coming into an inheritance; at Jesus £100 a year in land was 'understood to vacate a Fellowship'.[100]

Subject to these conditions, almost all fellowships could be held for life. The principal exceptions were the fellowships at Wadham and the Michel foundation at Queen's, in both of which tenure was limited. In practice, the tenure of a fellowship was likely to be temporary. A brisk turnover was maintained by the purchase of livings following the repeal in 1805 of the limitations on college patronage imposed by the 1736 Mortmain Act. Taking the colleges as a whole, it was reckoned that fellowships were held on average for ten years. Thorold Rogers found that, during the decade 1840–9, about three-quarters (395 out of 550) of the fellowships became vacant.[101] Such a rapid succession had a striking effect on the composition of college

---

[100] RCO (1850), evidence, 361.
[101] J. E. T. Rogers, Education in Oxford (1861), 212–13.

governing bodies, which were, by later standards, remarkably youthful. Within five years of being admitted to the University as an 18-year-old, a man might participate in college government; more than two-thirds of fellows in 1840 were aged under 35.

James Heywood's 1842 survey found that a minority (196 out of the 550) of college fellows were actually resident in Oxford. So long as teaching was concentrated in two or three hands in each college, there was little occupation for the remainder. Only fifty-four fellows (about 10 per cent of the whole) held college tutorships in 1845; and the other college offices, such as deans, bursars, and librarians, would barely have doubled this figure. Opportunities for higher study no longer existed to keep others in Oxford, a fact which St John's recognized in 1829, when BA fellows were given general permission to go out of residence.[102] Accordingly it was felt that those without college posts were better employed in parochial work or school-teaching outside the university; and in the case of lay fellows engaged at the Bar, or very occasionally in the practice of medicine, residence outside Oxford was essential.

Widespread non-residence was a symptom of a larger malaise. When, in 1825, legislation was drawn up to increase colleges' borrowing-powers for new accommodation, Grenville objected to the draft preamble, which stated solely that the purpose of the colleges was 'education'. This omitted the original intention of college founders to collect together pious and learned men 'to prosecute conjointly the studies not merely of youth, but of mature and even advanced age'.[103] The preamble was amended, but the reality in most colleges was unchanged. One exception was Magdalen, where the memory of Gibbon's aspersions upon the idleness of its fellows still rankled.[104] Influenced by the Oxford Movement, whose leaders favoured enforcing the condition of residence, there was an identifiable group of fellows who shared common interests in the history of the Church and its liturgy.[105] Perhaps the most influential was J. R. Bloxam, who resided in the college from 1836 to 1863, holding a variety of college offices, but not a tutorship. Although his claim to have restored in 1844 a more 'orderly and reverential' celebration of the May Morning ceremony may have been overstated,[106] the influence of his antiquarian researches upon the revival of church ritual was widely acknowledged. His patient biographical compi-

---

[102] W. C. Costin, *The History of St John's College, Oxford, 1598–1860* (1958), 246.

[103] Lloyd to Peel, 26 Jan. 1825, BL Add. MS 40342, fo 200; Grenville to Peel, 27 May 1825, BL Add. MS 54918, fo 121; PP 1825 i. 209.

[104] Samuel Wilberforce was involved in an exchange at the quatercentenary gaudy in 1858 when he suggested, speaking in reply to the founder's oration, that Gibbon may have had some grounds for his criticisms: W. D. Macray, *A Register of the Members of St Mary Magdalen College, Oxford* (8 vols 1894–1911) v. 140.

[105] They are described in R. D. Middleton, *Magdalen Studies* (1936).

[106] R. Judge, 'May Morning and Magdalen College', *Folklore* xcvii (1986), 19–25.

lations of members of Magdalen's foundation sought to show, in the academic context, how the medieval collegiate model might still represent the basis for a learned community of celibates. The moving testamentary acknowledgement by Charles Daubeny, the chemist and botanist, of his sense of debt to Magdalen College where, remaining unmarried, he had spent most of his adult life as a lay fellow, eloquently illustrated the point. Bloxam added a gloss, which would perhaps have been unwelcome to Daubeny himself, since the latter had been a critic of Oxford's clericalism. Daubeny's works, in Bloxam's words, were 'the fruits of a life chiefly spent in tranquil intellectual occupation, under the fostering wing of one of those great semi-monastic establishments which are peculiar to this country'.[107]

Much of Oxford scholarship in this period was produced by individuals unsupported by college endowments. William Palmer of Worcester, the liturgical scholar, Manuel Johnson, the Radcliffe Observer, and Henry Octavius Coxe, Bodley's Librarian, all had college attachments; but none benefited from a fellowship. The divorce of the colleges from the promotion of learning was most obvious in the case of the professoriate. A minority (nine out of twenty-five in 1840) of university professors and readers held positions on college foundations. Christ Church, whose canonries could be held by married men, alone managed to incorporate professors within its governing body, though not without raising contentious constitutional issues. As a cathedral foundation, Christ Church's position was unique. Its concentration of professors, including William Buckland, who had been obliged to relinquish his Corpus fellowship on his marriage in 1825, and E. B. Pusey, whose installation to a canonry followed shortly after his marriage, only served to confirm the observation of political economists that in England the endowments of the Established Church, rather than those of the universities, offered the most substantial supports for learning.[108]

Rarely the centre of intellectual advances, the colleges were identified as storehouses of 'leisurely thought, of multifarious but undigested erudition'.[109] An account of the life of resident dons during this period finds them, at Lincoln, maintaining a well-stocked library and sharing a common culture with the educated gentry and clergy.[110] Whatever their other failings, the fellows of Queen's have been credited with the wise expenditure of a considerable benefaction to the library, given by an old member of the college in 1841.[111] The diary of a fellow of New College, John Egerton,

---

[107] Bloxam, *Reg. Magdalen* vii. 197.
[108] T. Chalmers, *On the Use and Abuse of Literary and Ecclesiastical Endowments* (Glasgow 1827), 53.
[109] *British Critic* xxiv (1838), 134.
[110] V. H. H. Green, *Oxford Common Room: a study of Lincoln College and Mark Pattison* (1957), 21–2.
[111] R. Drummond-Hay, 'The library of the Queen's College', *Queen's College Record* iv (1970), 26.

who was intermittently in residence between 1825 and 1827, records an existence whose chief intellectual element was attendance at sermons delivered by the leading figures in the University. Days were otherwise occupied in college business, pro-proctorial duties during the year in which New College supplied a proctor, dinners, walks and a wide range of outdoor recreations, including cricket and watching the eights. A shooting expedition procured a woodpecker for dissection in the Christ Church anatomy school by Dr Kidd, who wished to examine the mechanism of its tongue.[112] Evenings frequently ended in the common room, where whist, backgammon or billiards would continue until the early hours.

For those fellows who resided in Oxford the common room was the focus of college life. 'Instead of a monastery', Richard Cobden reported after a visit in December 1853, 'the University is rather a great nest of clubs, where everybody knows everybody, and all are anxious to have a stranger of any note to break the monotony of their lives. I might have lived at free quarters for weeks amongst them. The best of fare, plenty of old port and sherry, and huge fires, seem the chief characteristics of the colleges.'[113] At the turn of the century both the fare and the furnishing of common rooms was sometimes rudimentary. At Pembroke the Senior Common Room in the early nineteenth century had no curtains, the chairs were uncushioned, and the floor bare until the acquisition of a rug in 1839.[114] The fellows of Jesus were remembered sitting outside the bursary with their pipes and ale.[115] In the following decades there was a general increase in comforts. The London daily papers were available in the common room, providing subjects for wagers and, perhaps most important of all, news of the prospects for preferment. Members of Christ Church Common Room kept a 'dodge book', recording payments levied on members whenever livings, offices or degrees came their way. On his appointment to the Regius professorship of Divinity, a combination of chair, canonry and living at Ewelme, Charles Lloyd incurred a total 'dodge' of 5 guineas.[116]

The life of a resident was agreeable enough for three or four years, Maria Edgeworth was told by a Magdalen fellow in 1821. Thereafter the daily round was likely to become tedious and worse: 'men shut up in colleges are apt to grow stiff in all their opinions and this *uncontradicted* life is dangerous'.[117] Those who remained in Oxford without teaching or other duties were often a cause of contention within their colleges, as boredom gave scope for squabbles over place, preferment and personality. Narrow preoccupations

---

[112] Egerton diary, 7 Apr. 1827, Cheshire Record Office, copy in NCA. I am indebted to Caroline Dalton for drawing my attention to this source.

[113] J. Morley, *Life of Richard Cobden* (1906), 611.

[114] Macleane, *Pembroke*, 483 n.

[115] *Memories*, no. 5 (June 1889), 18.

[116] CA MS CR 28, fos 27, 31.

[117] C. Colvin (ed.), *Maria Edgeworth: letters from England, 1813–1844* (1971), 248.

of a material sort predominated in the fellows' betting-book of Queen's for the early years of the century, as a later college historian noted.[118] Chafing against the college customs in force at All Souls, to which he had been elected a fellow in 1840, Henry Acland was reminded that 'these little etiquettes are a main element for holding together the good feeling which pervades the very various elements of the society'.[119] Common rooms have been identified as playing an important part in maintaining the social cohesion of the colleges during a period when their members were often sharply divided in matters of public controversy. One of the most extreme and controversial Romanizers among the Tractarians, J. B. Morris, a fellow of Exeter, was nevertheless nominated University Preacher by his college just before his secession to Rome 'to show that his brother fellows did not mistrust his loyalty to the Church'.[120] Friendships and civilities in the Balliol Common Room survived the extremes of theological strife during the 1840s.[121]

Eligibility to college fellowships and undergraduate scholarships was traditionally hedged about with a mass of conditions, attached over the course of six centuries by successive generations of benefactors. Taking all the limitations into account, it was reckoned in 1850 that only twenty-two fellowships at Oxford were genuinely open. These comprised twelve at Oriel, which had opened its fellowships to competition in the 1790s, and ten at Balliol, where all but two fellowships had been thrown open in 1806. The most common restrictions, affecting a majority of the colleges, enjoined a preference (in some cases absolute, in others *ceteris paribus*) for natives of certain localities. It was estimated that 116 fellowships were limited to the counties and dioceses of southern England and South Wales, eighty-one to the North, and three to the Channel Islands.[122]

The field of eligible fellowship candidates was narrowed further where election was limited to undergraduate members of the college foundation, comprising scholars and their equivalents. In some cases this amounted to an automatic right of succession. The colleges most affected were Corpus, Trinity, Wadham, Jesus, Pembroke and Worcester (all colleges founded after 1500), and those foundations linked to schools, New College and St John's in particular. At Magdalen the demies and at Queen's the taberdars by custom proceeded to fellowships, though Magdalen could fill some of its fellowships from outside. The older foundations were generally free to recruit from other colleges: University, Balliol, Merton, Exeter, Oriel, Lincoln, Brase-

[118] R. H. Hodgkin, *Six Centuries of an Oxford College* (1949), 165–6.
[119] Atlay, *Acland*, 77.
[120] Boase, *Reg. Exeter*, p. cli.
[121] P. Hinchliff, 'Jowett and the Church of England' in J. Prest (ed.), *Balliol Studies* (1982), 131–2.
[122] J. Heywood, *The Recommendations of the Oxford University Commissioners* (1853), p. xvii.

nose, All Souls and Magdalen all did so. All Souls, having no undergraduates
other than its few Bible clerks to draw upon, necessarily had to look outside
its walls for recruits. In 1843 Trinity broke from its former practice and
elected an outsider to a fellowship.[123] Rates of internal recruitment, however, remained generally high; nearly 80 per cent of all fellows in 1840 had
been undergraduates at the colleges where they held their fellowships.

Much depended upon the actual methods of electing fellows: elections to
closed fellowships might attach great weight to considerations of merit
among those competing; while fellowships which were technically open
were not necessarily awarded on a competitive basis. At Merton and All
Souls elections were largely determined by patronage, and applications
needed to be 'supported by personal interest or high connexions'.[124] In
1833 Viscount Sidmouth, whose nephew was a fellow of Merton, was approached by James Hope's father to support his son's candidacy. Sidmouth
was not optimistic: his nephew was apparently 'overloaded for the next
Election. In addition to applications from other quarters he has two from
me, at the earnest request of relatives who, like yourself, are old and highly
valued friends.'[125] Elections by nomination were condemned by Jowett
without qualification as 'the disgrace and abuse' of Oxford.[126] While the
exercise by the Dean and canons of Christ Church of their personal patronage to appoint to Studentships certainly laid them open to well-founded
charges of nepotism, indiscriminate condemnation overlooked Dean Gaisford's promotion of a string of promising classical scholars.[127] Whatever the
particular merits of the case, the retention of appointments by patronage in
Oxford, when they had much earlier been replaced at the Cambridge colleges
by examinations, proved indefensible. Attempts were made to minimize, so
far as founders' statutes allowed, the effects of local restrictions, of which
there were said to be three times as many at Oxford as at Cambridge.'[128]
During the mastership of Dr Plumptre University College advertised in the
Calendar that the restrictions attached to its fellowships were not absolute.
Brasenose, which as early as 1815 had unsuccessfully sought the permission
of its Visitor to permit performance in the honour schools to be taken into
account in its elections to fellowships, was able during the 1840s to extend
eligibility to its endowments to natives of an area of Lancashire and Cheshire
'computed to contain a population of nearly four million inhabitants'.[129]

[123] H. E. D. Blakiston, *Trinity College* (1898), 217–18.
[124] *RCO* (1850), report, 168.
[125] R. Ornsby, *Memoirs of James Robert Hope-Scott* (2 vols 1884) i. 49.
[126] *RCO* (1850), evidence, 36.
[127] For the Chapter's defence of their practices see E. G. W. Bill and J. F. A. Mason, *Christ Church and Reform, 1850–1867* (1970), 12–14. Osborne Gordon, William Linwood, Frederick Blaydes and H. G. Liddell were among those nominated to canoneer studentships after 1830.
[128] *Parl. Deb.* 4 May 1837, 3S xxxviii. 511.
[129] *Corr. on Improvement* (1854), 246.

At Queen's, on the other hand, the issue of whether the founder's preference for natives of Cumberland and Westmorland was an absolute one had been contested for 500 years and continued to divide the fellows.[130] The results of these variations were clear enough. At the three colleges which had most enthusiastically adopted election by examination from a wide field, Balliol, Oriel and Trinity, over 40 per cent of graduate fellows in 1840 had taken firsts. In six other colleges, Merton, Queen's, Lincoln, All Souls, St John's and Pembroke, a majority of fellows had obtained no honours at all; the pool of competence from which colleges in that position could appoint tutors was severely limited.

Elections to undergraduate scholarships also began to involve a competitive element. Corpus, where all the scholarships had a county or diocesan limitation, was the first to use a rigorous examination in its elections. The reputation of the competition attracted the picked men of a region. The announcement in the Salisbury newspaper of an election to a Wiltshire scholarship at Corpus in 1815 brought forward William Phelps and a small field of candidates, who were put through an examination lasting five days.[131] In 1816 Trinity, whose scholarships, worth £70 a year, were among the most valuable in the University and were practically free from local restriction, introduced an open competition in place of the old system by which scholars were nominated by the president and college officers from among the resident commoners.[132] Such was the success of these new methods by the 1830s that those colleges which lacked endowments for undergraduates began to be placed at a disadvantage in recruiting or retaining talent. University College, Oriel and Exeter had cause for complaint on this account and applied some of their corporate revenues to founding open scholarships.[133] Colleges linked to particular schools through closed endowments were at the mercy of changing standards over which they might have little control. St John's was said to benefit from its connection with Merchant Taylors', but the candidates from the closed Reading school foundation were less satisfactory, and unqualified candidates had to be rejected; Pembroke was injured by its dependence upon Abingdon School.[134]

Contemporaries designated colleges 'open' or 'close', by analogy with parliamentary boroughs, in a range that encompassed Balliol and Oriel at one end and, to take three examples, New College, Queen's and Jesus at the other. By any wider measure all would have appeared 'close'. Connections

---

[130] J. R. Magrath, *The Queen's College* (2 vols 1921) ii. 155, 168; E. M. Thomson, *The Life and Letters of William Thomson, Archbishop of York* (1919), 26.

[131] C. Hole, *The Life of the Reverend and Venerable William Whitmarsh Phelps, MA* (2 vols 1871) i. 65.

[132] Blakiston, *Trinity College*, 216.

[133] *Report and Evidence* (1853), evidence, 356; Boase, *Reg. Exeter*, 203; *Corr. on Improvement* (1854), 215, 218.

[134] Leach, *Sparks of Reform*, 41.

with Cambridge were few enough; Frederick Metcalfe, a Cambridge graduate elected to a fellowship at Lincoln in 1844, was an extremely rare example. Links further afield were fewer still. William Palmer, the member of Worcester Common Room already mentioned, was one of a trickle of incorporations, amounting to two or three a year, from Trinity College, Dublin. Religious tests would have been an obstacle to foreigners, had they seen a purpose in entering one of the colleges or halls. Colleges did not expect to admit them. Warden Tournay of Wadham was suspicious of those born outside Great Britain. He levied additional caution money from a native of Belfast in 1812, and, as legend had it, he declined to admit a Channel Islander, Bonamy Price, on the ground that he was a Frenchman.[135]

Within the British Isles the colleges could still claim a wide-ranging constituency. A petition in 1838 against a proposal by the Provost and fellows of Queen's to open the endowments of the college was signed 'by virtually every literate person' in Cumberland and Westmorland.[136] The memorialists affirmed 'a deep interest in your Ancient and distinguished College' and spoke of the connection as 'a Privilege which we value so highly, and which we feel it our bounden duty to protect, to the utmost of our power'; the college, which needed little encouragement to do so, backed down.[137] Local preferences like those at Queen's linked individual colleges to distant regions: C. A. Heurtley recalled that the journey from Louth in Lincolnshire to Corpus in 1823, to sit for a scholarship, took twenty-seven hours. For one of his competitors, from Berwick-upon-Tweed, reaching Oxford was an even more considerable undertaking.[138] The Snell foundation, which sent a regular supply of exhibitioners from Glasgow University to Balliol, exposed Oxford to Scottish influences and critics.[139] Jesus preserved the Welsh connection, while in 1841, 34 Irish students from throughout the University celebrated 'a grand Irish dinner' on St Patrick's Day.[140]

Nor was active membership of the colleges confined to those currently receiving instruction or otherwise in residence. Incumbents of college livings, of whom there were over 400 in 1850, represented outposts of their foundations, forming part of the larger body of non-resident graduates (1,873 in 1820, and 3,236 by 1850) who had retained their names on the books of their colleges. A German observer, Professor V. A. Huber of Marburg, was impressed by the attachment which graduates showed towards their old colleges, regarding the sentiment as a peculiar characteristic

---

[135] Wells, *Wadham*, 159. There were more substantial grounds for Tournay's doubts in this case than tradition allowed, *Memories*, no. 6 (May 1890), 28.

[136] C. Hibbert (ed.), *The Encyclopaedia of Oxford* (1988), 348.

[137] QCA 2. V. 135. Mr J. M. Kaye kindly supplied details of this document.

[138] *Memories*, no. 2 (Mar. 1889), 5.

[139] W. I. Addison, *The Snell Exhibitions from the University of Glasgow to Balliol College, Oxford* (Glasgow 1901).

[140] *Memories*, 2nd ser. no. 2 (Apr. 1895), 20.

of the English system.[141] Such connections had an obvious political utility; and non-resident MAs were rallied from afar to vote in parliamentary elections, or to support college members in elections to university offices, or else to determine matters of university legislation in Convocation. As protection for the colleges in the face of external attack, the strength of feeling which old members retained for their colleges was frequently cited in the 1820s as a potent force. An example of their former influence was given topical restatement in 1848 by T. B. Macaulay's historical account of how 'a powerful, active, and intelligent class, scattered over every county from Northumberland to Cornwall' had been roused to activity in the face of James II's depredations upon Magdalen.[142]

No such forces could be rallied to the aid of the colleges in 1850, much as some heads attempted to liken their policy of non-co-operation with the Royal Commission to that earlier struggle against arbitrary authority. The colleges' independence was ultimately undermined by a constitutional failure of self-government. Unlike the University, which had acquired and used the power to alter the Laudian Code of statutes, most of the colleges were statutorily prevented, even if they had been willing, to effect substantial reform from within. In the face of threats of government intervention, much was made of the existing regulatory authority of college Visitors. But it became clear that in most cases this power was restricted to interpreting statutes; the Visitor could not innovate.[143] For actual alteration an Act of Parliament was necessary, which governing bodies showed no desire to obtain. Six colleges were said to be embarked on statute revision in June 1838, though there was little subsequent public evidence of progress.[144] In the unusual case of Merton, where the governing body was found to possess large powers of statutory innovation, this power was invoked by a Tractarian element among the fellows in an attempt to impose clerical restrictions where none had previously existed. Merton's stewardship of the trust founded by Thomas Linacre for the provision of medical lectureships, whose admittedly small revenues had been diverted to other purposes, together with its earlier reluctance to expand, did not suggest an energetic commitment to academic renovation.[145] Considerable scope for innovation existed at Christ Church, where the dean and Chapter were largely unham-

[141] Huber, *English Universities* ii pt 1, p. 324.

[142] T. B. Macaulay, *The History of England*, ed. C. H. Firth (6 vols 1914) ii. 926.

[143] For a discussion of the authorities on this disputed point see 'Power of Visitors in eleemosynary corporations', *Law Magazine* xix (1838), 16–18; 'On the legislative power of the colleges', ibid. xix (1838), 257–9; R. Phillimore (ed.), *The Ecclesiastical Law by Richard Burn* (9th edn 4 vols 1842) i. 439c; *Parl. Deb.* 11 Apr. 1837, 35 xxxvii. 1032; *RCO* (1850), legal statement by Mr Dampier, 2; *RCO* (1850), evidence, 370–1.

[144] *Parl. Deb.* 9 July 1838, 3 S xliv. 3; 21 July 1843, 3 S lxx. 1298; Ward, *Victorian Oxford*, 357 n. 29.

[145] M. Pelling, 'The refoundation of the Linacre lectureships in the nineteenth century' in F. Maddison, M. Pelling and C. Webster (eds), *Linacre Studies* (1977), 271, 275.

pered by statutory restrictions; but activity there was paralysed by a constitution which excluded the tutors from an active part in college government.[146]

The failure of internal statute revision, despite Wellington's exhortations, practically sealed the fate of the unreformed colleges, as their defence of chartered rights increasingly bore the appearance of perpetuating an ossified system. At Magdalen, which considered itself bound by statute not to open its foundation, the president and fellows were found to have fewer scruples about ignoring their founder's injunctions in matters touching their own material rewards. The procedure by which college decisions at another wealthy, closed foundation, New College, were vested in the warden and thirteen senior fellows was thought to exist on very doubtful statutory authority.[147] One of the last acts of the unreformed Lincoln College governing body was the notorious headship election of November 1851, which took place in time to be mentioned in the Royal Commission's report. Whatever the merits of the case, reformers regarded that election as evidence of the incapacity of governing bodies, as then constituted, to have regard to considerations other than narrow self-interest.[148]

The subsequent activity of the Executive Commissioners in redrawing college statutes, opening most fellowships to competition, reducing the number restricted to clergymen and making the first steps towards a redistribution of college endowments to support the professoriate is described in Chapter 23. Perhaps the most significant result of their work was the creation of reconstituted governing bodies, which set about addressing the problems of teaching, discipline and expense. The college system was to be transformed in the process.

---

[146] Bill and Mason, *Christ Church*, 7.
[147] Paper by Revd W. B. Heathcote on the theory of college meetings, Mar. 1847, NCA MS 862.
[148] *RCO* (1850), report, 182, evidence, 387; Green, *Oxford Common Room*, 170.

5

Balliol: From Obscurity to Pre-eminence

JOHN H. JONES

Balliol came near to total collapse in the closing years of the eighteenth century. Numbers had fallen much more sharply in mid-century than in the University as a whole and lost ground had not been regained. The buildings were in extreme disrepair and the college was in debt. A fellowship had been sequestered (in modern jargon, a post had been frozen) since 1775, and the dividend which would have been paid to its holder had been used for corporate—'Domus'—purposes; but this had sufficed for little more than essential repairs and interest on outstanding loans. In 1800 there was still a net debt (Fig. 5.1) and there were only four admissions in that year. The stage was nevertheless set for improvement. The first outsiders—'extranei'—had been elected to fellowships in the 1780s, largely as a result of the influence of Richard Prosser (fellow, 1773–93). One of these, elected in 1785, was John Parsons, who had been an undergraduate at Wadham. Holding the office of bursar during John Davey's mastership (1785–98), he had re-established administrative efficiency: from this period, minutes of college meetings were recorded in detail and in English, business-like accounts were kept and the college started to use the services of banks regularly.

Parsons was elected Master in 1798. One of the prime movers behind the examination statute of 1800, he also tightened up the academic arrangements in his own college—introducing, for example, collections on the Christ Church model. He was not a liberal reformer, however: he was a Tory disciplinarian primarily interested in bolstering the Protestant establishment. A substantial faction in the college resented his attempts to impose a regimented system of lectures and examination which they thought 'an insult upon sense and learning'. But the Master acquired a fervent adherent in Richard Jenkyns, who was elected to a fellowship in 1803, and soon

Citations (with in many cases extensive quotations) of almost all the printed and MS material used in this chapter can be traced through the author's *Balliol College: a history, 1263–1939* (1988, 2nd edn 1997), ch. 14, and in his chapter 'Sound religion and useful learning: the rise of Balliol under John Parsons and Richard Jenkyns, 1798–1854' in J. M. Prest (ed.), *Balliol Studies* (1982). Reference is given here only to sources which cannot be located in this way.

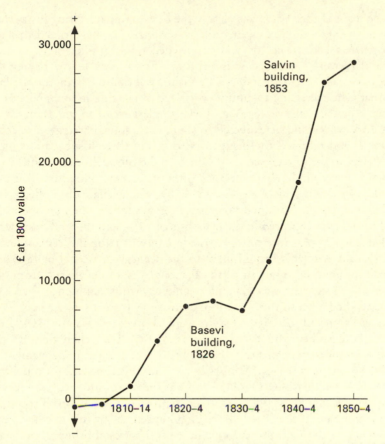

FIGURE 5.1 The financial position of Balliol, 1800–1854. Five-year averages of the balance of debts, cash in hand and credit with the bank at the end of the financial year.

became the principal college tutor. Jenkyns had been a scholar of the college, and as such had enjoyed a relatively smooth progression to a fellowship. The 1507 statutes, which were still in force, left the fellowships on the ancient foundation free of regional or other restrictions, but gave existing scholars a *ceteris paribus* advantage. The extent to which this advantage could be stretched was still a fiercely disputed issue, despite recent precedents for the election of outsiders. The election of William Vaux of Christ Church in 1806 provoked two appeals to the Visitor, which focused the arguments. The appeals were lodged by three scholars who had been passed over, and two dissident fellows. The principal basis of both appeals was that three eligible scholars with adequate qualifications had offered themselves and that according to the statutes one of them ought to have been preferred to an *extraneus*. Parsons, advised by Prosser behind the scenes, made a vigorous

reply: he insisted that Vaux was clearly the best candidate, citing his performance in the new public examination as evidence. He also argued that the
ceteris paribus preference for scholars needed to be applied with caution
because they were appointed without competition, each fellow having the
private patronage of a scholarship. The Visitor was Shute Barrington, Bishop
of Durham. In exercising its unique privilege of electing its own Visitor in
his favour in 1805, the college had given the last word in its affairs to an
ardent Tory who could be expected to support Parsons. Barrington rejected
the appeals and rebuked the instigators so firmly that all subsequent elections (except to the two closed fellowships on the Blundell foundation) were
conducted on a completely open basis without further contention. Barrington held office until his death in 1826, by which time the college was
completely controlled by men who had been elected in open competition.
Balliol names first appeared in the class lists of 1808, and the first firsts were
obtained in 1810. An intermittent trickle continued for the remainder of
Parsons's rule. After his appointment to the deanery of Bristol in 1810 and
bishopric of Peterborough in 1813, Parsons was often absent from the
college. His vicegerent was generally Jenkyns, whose influence therefore
grew, extending even to the control of admissions from 1816.

Noel Ellison and Charles Ogilvie were elected fellows in 1816. Like
Charles Girdlestone, who followed in 1818, they had taken firsts in the
schools. Tradition gives this trio the credit for the marked improvement in
the fortunes of the college which began at about this time and soon led to a
waiting-list for admissions. Ogilvie, who was the most influential and served
longest, was a vigorous and outspoken figure among Oxford Protestant
High-Churchmen in the 1820s, describing himself as 'an attached and zealous member of the Church of England as by Law established'. For many
years a correspondent of Hannah More, the Evangelical writer, who was
'much pleased' with Ogilvie's report 'of the good discipline and studious of
character' of Balliol,[1] Ogilvie exemplified the extent of religious seriousness
in the University in the pre-Tractarian period.

The first twenty years of the nineteenth century also saw a return to
solvency (Fig. 5.1).[2] Without this recovery the college would have been
held back later by inability to build new accommodation for increased
admissions. Rising revenue from ancient estates in Northumberland, beneath which coal-mining developments were taking place, was responsible.
The principal beneficiaries were the Master and fellows. The income remaining after various fixed allocations of funds and expenses was divided into
fifteen equal shares, one for each fellow, two for the Master and only one for
Domus. But Domus was absorbing the dividend of the unfilled fellowship as

---

[1] Hannah More to C. A. Ogilvie, 21 Apr. [1816], Bodl. MS Eng. lett. d. 124, fo 105.
[2] Based on the bursars' accounts and banking records, BCA.

well as its own share, and in 1802 the Master and fellows resolved[3] to increase the Domus share of all Northumberland profits in excess of £700 from the normal one-fifteenth to one-third. This sacrifice of immediate dividends by the Master and fellows enabled the college to clear its debts by 1816. As a result, the next Master, Jenkyns, who succeeded Parsons in 1819, came to preside over a college whose realizable wealth was growing at a healthy rate, and one which was in a position for the first time in decades to fund the full complement of fellows.

Jenkyns was a small and sometimes ridiculously pompous man—the 'Little Master'; and accounts are dominated by affectionately told but ludicrous anecdotes. He was no great scholar but made no pretensions in that direction, writing nothing for publication except obituary notices for the *Gentleman's Magazine*. He was primarily a shrewd organizer and good judge of men who had an inflexible view of what was right, and usually got his way. One of the earliest problems of his reign came from the will of Thomas How, a former fellow, who made a bequest for the foundation of two closed exhibitions for the sons of Somerset and Devonshire clergymen. The bequest was refused. The region which would have been favoured by this arrangement was the home ground of the closed Blundell foundation, which had proved a parasitic burden during the previous 200 years. The foundation supported two scholars from Blundell's School in Tiverton, Devon: they had a right of succession to Blundell fellowships, which carried all the privileges of the Domus fellowships. Any Domus fellowship falling vacant could be claimed by a Blundell scholar if no Blundell fellowships were free, and held until one was. This had at times created an overwhelming inbred Devonshire party in the college. Jenkyns regarded the Blundell foundation with almost obsessive suspicion, declaring it to be 'the very bane of our Society'. They were to have 'their *pound* of flesh—but not an ounce more'.

Although the college was powerless to reform the Blundell foundation, it had complete freedom of action in elections to the Domus scholarships, which were not restricted by geographical or other limitations. The only obstacle to completely open elections was the individual right of fellows to nominate scholars, which they agreed to surrender in May 1827. In future the scholarships (which were also doubled in value) were to be filled by 'a general competition of candidates, whether members of the College or not'. The examination was to be similar to that for fellowships, but set at an appropriately lower level; there was to be only one a year and the Master was to give it 'greater importance and notoriety' by advertisement. From the very first open examination (November 1827) under the new regulations, large numbers of strong candidates were attracted. The cream of them were

[3] English register, 12 June 1802, BCA.

no doubt drawn by one of the few available opportunities to demonstrate their prowess: the rest simply hoped to do well enough to earn the offer of a commoner place. Commoner places were at the sole disposal of the Master, who chose to fill many of them with competent runners-up in the scholarship examination, which thus became in effect a competitive general admissions examination. A new residential block had been built in 1826 'in consequence of the deficiency of Rooms to satisfy the very numerous and pressing applications for admission', but the college was soon oversubscribed again. By the mid-1830s Balliol was generally recognized as the leading college: its open scholarships and fellowships were the greatest distinctions a young man could aspire to in the University, and it was dominant in the honour schools, having risen as Oriel and Christ Church declined (Fig. 5.2).

In 1834 the scholarship scheme, 'having been found productive of the best results', was, 'with a view of enforcing its perpetual observance', formally embodied in the statutes after confirmation by the Visitor. It was the unanimous view of those who saw its effects at first hand that this reform was the making of Victorian Balliol. To whom is the credit due? H. W. C. Davis tells us that Jenkyns merely concurred 'not because he expected any good from the change, but because the tutors were unanimous on the other side',[4] and local tradition singles out Ogilvie as the key figure. Ogilvie certainly played a large part in the affair, but he was very much the Master's man, and it seems

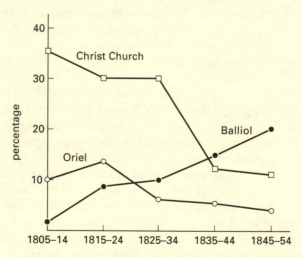

FIGURE 5.2 Number of firsts obtained as percentages of the total number awarded, 1805–1854. Ten-year averages.

[4] H. W. C. Davis, *Balliol College* (1899), 205.

hardly plausible to suggest that Jenkyns, who was ruling all departments of the college with an iron hand, acquiesced weakly in a radical change to which he was opposed. There is no hint of this in the immediate documents. In any case it is quite clear that the Master's influence on the execution of the new scheme was considerable. He was effectively tutor for admissions and handled all the correspondence. He also had two votes in the elections. On one occasion he got his way when in a minority of two against three: the doubling of his vote made it three-all and the tie was broken by the statutory obligation of the most junior fellow (who was of the original majority) to change sides.

The practice of awarding prizes from Domus funds for firsts in the honour schools was introduced early in the 1820s. In his will, made in 1827, George Powell, the senior fellow, endowed a prize for an English essay competition. Richard Prosser's will of 1828 provided for six exhibitions, which were to be awarded annually to the six undergraduates who, in the opinion of the Master, senior dean, senior tutor, and mathematical lecturer, were the most distinguished. Nor was the competitive spirit confined to the academic side of student life, for it was in the same period that Balliol rowing was institutionalized. In 1823 there was a 'boat match between the rowers of Balliol and Christ Church which was won by the former, after a well contested race',[5] and two Balliol men rowed for Oxford in the first university boat race of 1829, in a boat lent by Balliol for the occasion.

The leading tutors in the late 1820s were Ogilvie, J. T. Round and George Moberly, assisted by J. M. Chapman and Frederick Oakeley. The role of the college tutor was the delivery of college lectures to classes. Although those who wanted more individual assistance usually made their own arrangements with a 'private tutor' or 'coach', in 1836 and 1837 'a Senior Fellow of the name of Carr occasionally looked over the weekly essay, dividing the work with the Master'. Nor, it seems, was there much informal social contact between tutors and undergraduates.

The rapid turnover of fellows brought a new generation of tutors in the 1830s. Round retired from Oxford in 1831; and Ogilvie, who had at one time been 'generally designated in public opinion as the future Master of Balliol', dropped out of the teaching in 1830, resigning in 1834, despite Keble's lament that Oxford 'would become a very sink of whiggery' without him. Moberly vacated his fellowship by marriage, also in 1834, but remained as the first married tutor of the college for nearly a year before leaving to be headmaster of Winchester. Tutorial appointments were the Master's prerogative and Jenkyns invited A. C. Tait to fill Moberly's place. Tait was the leading tutor for the next seven years, together with, for most of the time, Robert Scott; W. G. Ward was mathematical lecturer; J. G. Lonsdale and

[5] *Oxford University and City Herald*, 14 June 1823.

E. C. Woollcombe came in the early 1840s. In 1838 it was agreed, probably under Scott's prompting, that 'the use of the books in the Library should, under certain conditions & the vigilant attention of the tutors, be allowed to the undergraduates of the college', a privilege previously reserved for fellows. Frederick Temple succeeded Ward as mathematical lecturer in 1843, and when Tait resigned to become headmaster of Rugby in 1842, Benjamin Jowett and W. C. Lake were appointed to the tutorial strength.

The academic development of the college between 1830 and 1845 took place against a background of political and religious controversies. The Balliol common room was often riven by these. The grip of the High-Church Tories on the college had begun to weaken in the late 1820s with the election of men like Oakeley. He surprised Jenkyns by voting for Robert Peel (and by implication for Catholic Emancipation) in 1829, and relations between them became uneasy. Jenkyns found himself with fellows who were either edging towards Roman Catholicism with the Tractarians or moving in the opposite direction with Thomas Arnold. The Tractarian movement, in which Oakeley and Ward were prominent, was profoundly disturbing to Jenkyns, and in 1841 (at the instigation of Tait, Woollcombe and Scott) he put pressure on Ward to resign his mathematical lecturership, on the ground that his pupils were being contaminated with deviant doctrine. The split in the common room also intruded into fellowship elections. In the summer of 1838 A. P. Stanley, scholar of the college and a rising liberal star, was discouraged from entering the forthcoming fellowship election, and therefore offered himself to University College, where he was elected. Tait struggled hard to avoid the loss of a good man, but the party within the college who, like Scott, were suspicious of both 'Taitians and Wardians' had their way. Scott's conservatism was disturbed not only by the prospect of open elections introducing into the college fellows with dangerous views, but also by the established practice of electing fellows who had no intention of proceeding to holy orders, and who planned to resign before the statutes obliged them to do so. In 1837 he petitioned the Visitor for clarification, asking whether all fellowship candidates should be required to enter into an undertaking to take orders. Jenkyns professed his 'own entire freedom from doubt' on the matter, and successfully defended the current practice as being not only statutable but in the interests of the college. Other intense disagreements occurred. Pugin's Catholic-inspired plans for rebuilding the college were hotly contested, and eventually defeated, in 1843.[6] W. G. Ward's increasingly extreme theological views, which led to his degradation by the University in 1845, were a further cause of contention. But the college held together, avoiding the divisions which proved so damaging in Oriel. The Master and fellows remained on warm personal terms, and continued

---

[6] See pt 2, Ch. 30.

to co-operate effectively in matters concerning the welfare of the under-graduates.

Jenkyns received the deanery of Wells in 1845, which he held in conjunc-tion with the mastership, in what was generally regarded as a recognition of his work in raising Balliol to pre-eminence and steering it through recent difficulties. After 1845 religious controversy died down, and the impression given by the college register is of a return to the traditional material concerns of administering college estates and making appointments to college livings. The university reform movement, however, represented a new source of anxiety to Dr Jenkyns. Replying to the Royal Commissioners' first approach to Balliol in 1850, Jenkyns held himself responsible only to the Visitor, a position which he had adopted in 1837, in the face of an earlier attempt to subject the colleges to parliamentary scrutiny. It was not that he feared what a commission might say. What worried him was the erosion of the college's independence as a corporation which had been 'founded and endowed solely by the munificence of private individuals'. The college had been subject only to its own statutes and the authority of its Visitor for nearly 600 years. Under the 'salutary influence of such Visitatorial power', the college had faithfully and, it was hoped, 'successfully laboured to promote the cause of sound religion & useful learning'. It did not shrink from the 'strictest examination' of its 'own lawful Visitor', but deprecated any 'extraneous interference which would supersede the provision wisely made by the Founders themselves for regulating the objects of their bounty'. He stuck to this line—as did most other heads of houses—and Balliol made no official answers to the Commission's questions. By this time, however, Jenkyns's dominance over his governing body was diminishing. He was now nearly 70 and absent at Wells much of the time, whereas the fellows into whose hands the actual running of the College fell—Woollcombe, Jowett, Lake and Henry Wall—were young, already very experienced in academic politics and full of self-confidence. Jowett, Lake and Wall felt able to tell the Commission that, although they could not assist in their capacities as college officers, they would as individuals be glad to help and make available the college books and information which they happened to have in their possession. When the Commission reported in 1852, it had little to say that was critical of the college, and indeed used it as an example to support the case it made for the general abolition of closed scholarships and fellowships.

The principal internal business of the college during Jenkyns's last years was a rebuilding programme. The hall was enlarged, new kitchens were built and a row of dilapidated buildings near the back gate was demolished to make way for a plain and functional new building. Jowett was much in-volved in the execution of the work, and his hand is clear, for example, in the inclusion of a basement chemical laboratory in the plans.

Jenkyns died in the Master's lodgings on 6 March 1854, a few months after completion of the new buildings. 'He found Balliol', *The Times* pronounced, 'a close college among the least distinguished collegiate bodies at Oxford: he left it almost entirely open, and confessedly the foremost of all.'[7]

[7] *The Times* 7 Mar. 1854.

6

The Ascendancy of Oriel

K. C. TURPIN

Towards the end of the eighteenth century an alumnus of Oriel and a high steward of the University, Edward, Lord Leigh of Stoneleigh in the county of Warwickshire, left the college the whole of his library; this necessitated the erection of a new building to house it. In this neo-classical building on the north side of the middle quadrangle of the college the library was accommodated on the first floor but, mindful of their other needs, the Provost and fellows provided two common rooms on the ground floor, in the larger of which it became the custom to place the portraits of provosts. Among these portraits are those of John Eveleigh, Edward Copleston and Edward Hawkins, the three provosts who cover the period with which this chapter is concerned. Eveleigh, Provost from 1781 to 1814, sowed the seeds of Oriel's distinction in the earlier part of the nineteenth century, Copleston, Provost from 1814 to 1828, reaped the harvest, and Hawkins, Provost from 1828 to 1882, partly owing to changing circumstances, partly because of his own personal idiosyncrasies, saw the college gradually lose the pre-eminence it had achieved under his two predecessors.

Eveleigh was painted by Hoppner, who depicted an elderly cleric of mild appearance wearing a wig, holding a folio and tranquilly regarding the spectator. The portrait of Copleston by Thomas Phillips gives rather a different impression. Unlike Eveleigh and Hawkins he looks not at the spectator, but into the middle distance. In his hand he holds the diploma of doctor of divinity conferred on him by the University and he clearly expects to be active outside his college. The third provost, Hawkins, and the one who held office longest, was painted in the twenty-fifth year of his reign by Sir Francis Grant in the high-Victorian style. His features are clear-cut and handsome, displaying dignity and benevolence, but with a touch of chilliness. In his hand he grasps a packet of papers, probably relating to college business, which, in life, he grasped no less firmly.

With Eveleigh began the sequence of events which led to Oriel's years of great distinction. Oriel was fortunate in that, of its eighteen fellowships, twelve were entirely open, that is to say, they were not restricted either to candidates who had been members of the college or to those who were from particular schools or localities. Six were restricted to particular localities; but even here the college managed, in the absence of suitably qualified candidates from the localities concerned, to elect a candidate without the territorial qualification. Copleston himself, for example, was elected in 1795 to a fellowship restricted to candidates born in Wiltshire whereas he was a Devonian.[1] There was no examination, since his reputation, supported by a scholarship at Corpus, and the winning of the Latin Verse Prize in 1793, was sufficient.

Subsequently elections were by examination, in a procedure described by Dean Church.[2] A candidate had to call on the provost and seek his leave to stand. The provost would enquire about the candidate's plans and his means, since independent means were held to exclude a man. If the provost granted leave, he told the candidate to write a Latin letter to each of the fellows stating the grounds on which he desired election and on which he thought he might be entitled to it. These letters were a serious exercise and were meant to test a candidate's power of putting his own personal case, wishes and intentions into Latin. He then had to call on the dean and was invited to dine, when he was 'trotted out and observed upon'.

The examination began on Monday in Easter week and lasted four days. On the first day there was a translation of a longish passage of English into Latin together with an English essay. In Church's case the essay subject was a passage of Bacon, in Newman's case a statement of Cicero regarding the saying 'Know thyself'. All the papers for the day were handed out at 10 a.m. and the examination continued without a break until dusk; but refreshments, no doubt much needed by the candidates, were served during the course of it. The second day brought a Latin essay and a passage of English for translation into Greek, the third day a passage of Greek for translation into English and a paper of 'so-called' philosophical questions. In Newman's time this paper included mathematical questions. On the fourth day, Thursday, there was Latin translation into English. Composition and translation therefore were the main parts of the examination: otherwise the general questions were designed to find out how a candidate could treat topics which interested cultivated men. During the examination each candidate had a viva voce examination before the provost and the assembled fellows consisting of Latin and Greek translation. The successful candidate was summoned by the provost's butler to the Tower Room of the college the day after the examination, where he was congratulated by the provost and fellows. He was later admitted in chapel as a probationer fellow, a status he held for one year until his admission to a full fellowship.

The method of the examination was old-fashioned, and contrasted rather pointedly with the newer methods of setting questions, which implied a

[1] *Report and Evidence* (1853), evidence, 354–5.
[2] R. W. Church to H. P. Liddon, 31 Jan. 1883, in Liddon, *Pusey* i. 66.

good deal 'of modern or of somewhat pretentious reading, in history, philology and modern books of philosophy and political science'. What Oriel wanted was not necessarily in the first place wide reading, so much as a high standard of Latin, Greek and English allied with good sense. The most important papers were Latin prose composition and the English essay; and men who were first in these papers usually maintained their lead in the rest of the examination, whilst those who failed there seldom recovered themselves. Next in importance were the Latin essay and the unseens; the general paper was more of a makeweight, useful in helping to decide a difficult choice.

The papers were read and considered by the whole body of fellows together and in the case of a translation paper into Latin or Greek, or the English and Latin essays, each sentence was read aloud and went round the fellows in turn for discussion and criticism. It was, as Church said, a very tedious process, but thorough in the case of both examinee and examiner.

Provost Eveleigh died suddenly in December 1814, and Copleston, at the age of 38, was his obvious successor, receiving a unanimous invitation from the fellows to undertake the office of provost. As senior treasurer of the college from 1805 to 1810 he had shown some financial ability to the college's benefit, beginning a process of increasing the rents rather than taking fines, which involved some internal borrowing on college funds so as not to prejudice the interests of the fellows who depended on a share of the fines for their dividends. By establishing this practice during his period of office as treasurer, which was prolonged considerably beyond the customary period, Copleston calculated that he had been able to treble the income of the college, liquidate all its debts and get the estates better tenanted.[3]

Copleston's reputation as a tutor was considerable, both within Oxford and outside, and it was based not only on the excellence of his tuition, but also on the personal interest he took in his pupils together with his ability to make them conscious of this.[4] When he became Provost his contact with the young was not so close but he did have the sole responsibility of appointing the tutors from among the fellows, of assigning their pupils to them and of presiding at the terminal examinations.

The admission of undergraduates was an important responsibility of the provost since the opinion of the public about the standing of a college was determined not only by the intellectual calibre of the head and fellows and the efficiency of the tuition, but also by the social rank and behaviour of the students. Oriel under Copleston was 'eminently a gentlemanly college'[5] and during the first thirty years of the nineteenth century the college possessed all three elements required for distinction in that it had all that there was of

[3] W. J. Copleston, *Memoir of Edward Copleston, D.D., Bishop of Llandaff* (1851), 19.
[4] J. Hughes to W. A. Copleston, 28 Mar. 1851, in Copleston, *Copleston*, 27.
[5] Pattison, *Memoirs*, 46–7.

original intellect at that time in the University, its tutors were energetic and well qualified and an entrance examination sifted the commoners. The college register for the years 1800–11[6] shows that of the 194 undergraduates admitted, four were the sons of noblemen and six of baronets. The parents of 120 were described as 'armigerous', and of fifteen as 'gentlemen', whilst thirty-five were in holy orders and fourteen were doctors. Of the 134 undergraduates whose later careers are known, seventy-five took holy orders, sixteen became barristers, twenty-one were landed gentry, three went into the army, eight became fellows of colleges and six became doctors. Four went into politics, and three of these are included in the category of landed gentry.

A glimpse of an undergraduate's life at Oriel at that time is provided in the diary of William Hale, who came into residence in April 1814 having been admitted as a commoner from Charterhouse in the previous year.[7] The rooms allocated to him had belonged to a gentleman commoner who had found the college too strict and had departed after residing for only one term; the books the latter had left behind were a curious medley 'of profane and sacred learning', the former being mainly concerned with horse-racing. Davison became Hale's tutor and took a personal interest in him, asking him to stay up on at least one occasion so that he might be able to give him extra tutorial attention. Hale's health at one time gave cause for concern, which was attributed to overwork, and Keble, who was not then a tutor, wrote him playful letters and advised him not to be anxious about reading.[8] Though a possible first, Hale took a second in mathematics and Literae Humaniores. Oriel, he thought, was 'the most comfortable [college] in the University'. He knew almost all the resident members of it, 'and it is a great thing to say there is scarcely an objectionable man in it'.[9] He went to professorial lectures on comparative anatomy and described in May 1815 a geological expedition to Shotover under the guidance of Buckland, the party consisting mainly of fellows of colleges, a number of bachelors of arts–and himself. He was probably the only undergraduate and was amused 'to behold the great dons putting off their wonted stiffness and indulging in mirth and jokes'.[10] In college Hale managed to have a wide circle of acquaintances and he was for a time steward of the undergraduate book club; a correspondence with one of his friends, John Strutt, later Lord Rayleigh, dealt with the serious problem of finding a suitable successor to himself in that post.[11]

Copleston advised his successor, Hawkins, on the admissions problems, which caused such perpetual anxiety. He stated as a leading principle: 'I

---

[6] C. L. Shadwell, *Registrum Orielense* (2 vols 1893, 1902).
[7] William Hale's diary, 1814–1816, OCL 137.
[8] Keble to Hale, 25 Oct. 1816, OCL 127, 16 Jan. 1818, OCL 130.
[9] Hale diary, 17 May 1814.
[10] Ibid. 22 May 1815.
[11] J. Strutt to W. Hale, 20 Oct. 1816, OCL 126.

always disallowed the claim of preference founded on priority of application. If a college is to be filled upon any other principle than a stage coach
this claim cannot be allowed.'[12] The popularity of the college made the
handling of applications for admission a delicate matter since offence had
to be avoided and the claims of the sons of old members given due weight.
The same was true of the applications from influential persons hitherto
unconnected with the college: to oblige them might well be to the college's
ultimate advantage. Accommodation at Oriel was limited because of the
cramped site, which allowed no room for extensions.[13] Just over fifty undergraduates could be provided for and even then some men had to be squeezed
into unsatisfactory rooms. Fellows, unless they held college offices requiring
residence within the college, were not allocated rooms and had to lodge in
the town. The most satisfactory solution would have been to acquire St
Mary Hall, which lay between the college and the High Street; but the
Principal, Dr Dean, declined Copleston's offer of the 'best lodgings in
High Street' and refused to budge.[14]

   The nature of the Noetic group which held sway in the Oriel Common
Room during the first thirty years of the nineteenth century has been
described in the Note which follows Chapter 1. It is possible to exaggerate
the unity of the group. Davison, for example, though a great admirer of
Copleston and Whately, was not a disciple of either.[15] And unity was further
threatened when Copleston resigned as Provost, at the end of January 1828,
on his elevation to the see of Llandaff: this plunged the fellows into the
excitement and contention of a headship election. As a fellow, Copleston
had sometimes felt impatient with his predecessor, Provost Eveleigh, and
Copleston's own regime did not escape criticism.[16] On the occasion of the
fifth centenary of the college Copleston had reflected somewhat complacently on the flourishing state of the college, the excellent discipline and the
harmony of the fellows.[17] There were those who thought otherwise, mainly
because of Copleston's liking for men of good birth, his worldliness and the
lax discipline. James Tyler, the Dean, was accused of 'tuft and silk court-
ing';[18] and holy communion was not thought by some of the fellows to be
taken sufficiently seriously.[19] There was no doubt some substance in these
criticisms, and young men of good birth were often a nuisance; but the
fellows were before long to discover that there was much to be said for a

---

[12] Copleston to Hawkins, 27 Oct. 1829, OCL 1332.
[13] Mozley, *Reminiscences* i. 88–9.
[14] Pattison, *Memoirs*, 108.
[15] W. Tuckwell, *Pre-Tractarian Oxford: a reminiscence of the Oriel 'Noetics'* (1909), 18.
[16] *Letters of the Earl of Dudley to the Bishop of Llandaff* (1841), 84, 292.
[17] Copleston, *Copleston*, 109.
[18] J. H. Newman to S. Rickards, 19 Mar. 1827, in *LDN* ii. 8.
[19] *LDN* i. 286 n. See also Ch. 1 n. 260.

provost who had interests outside the college and the University and therefore sat loose to the details of college administration.

On Copleston's resignation, there was no one outstanding fellow upon
whom all could agree. The possibilities were John Keble and Hawkins.
Hawkins started with considerable advantages, having been resident in the
college since his election as a fellow in 1815. He liked the details of business
and had wisely kept on good terms with all the factions in the college.[20] He
was stricter with the young men than Copleston or Tyler, reassuring those,
such as Newman, who were uneasy about the laxity prevailing towards the
end of Copleston's time. Of the fellows resident in the college Dornford was
a leading supporter of Hawkins, winning over Newman and Pusey to his
side.[21] Keble had gone out of residence in 1823 to assist his father in parochial
work. Though he had been a good tutor and was academically distinguished,
he was thought by some fellows to be too shy and unpractical for the rough
and tumble of running a college.[22] The choice between Hawkins and Keble
was settled by Keble standing down for personal and family reasons, though
if there had been a clear call for him he would have been willing to undertake
the office.[23] Hawkins, therefore, was elected without a contest.

The first sign of trouble ahead appeared over the by-election in February
1829 which was described in Chapter 1. Peel's committee was supported in
Oxford by seven heads of houses, including Hawkins and Richard Whately
(who was by then Principal of St Alban Hall). The Oriel Common Room
was divided between those who supported Peel—Hawkins, Thomas Davies,
Henry Jenkyns, John Awdry and E. B. Pusey—and those who supported
Inglis—Joseph Dornford, Keble, Newman, Robert Wilberforce and Hurrell
Froude. From the election Newman dated the end of familiar relations
between Hawkins and many of the fellows, and it was the background to
the dispute between the Provost and the tutors over the organization of
tutorial work.

There were four tutors at that time: Dornford, who was tutor from 1823
to 1832 and dean from 1828 to 1832; Newman and Froude, appointed in
1826; and Robert Wilberforce, appointed in 1828. Their ages were respectively 34, 27, 25 and 26. Hawkins was 39. Newman, Froude and Wilberforce
were intent on keeping up a high intellectual standard and were not afraid of
innovations in college practice to secure it. Their first step, with the cordial
approval of Hawkins, was to send down men who were unsatisfactory and
beyond reform; the number of gentlemen commoners was also reduced from
twenty to eight or nine. Unprepared candidates for admission were rejected
and chance vacancies were given to well-recommended and picked men.

[20] Mozley, *Reminiscences* i. 38.
[21] Newman to Lord Blachford, 4 Nov. 1884, in *LDN* ii. 44 n.
[22] Ibid. 45 n.
[23] J. T. Coleridge, *A Memoir of the Rev. John Keble* (2nd edn 2 vols 1869) i 177–8.

Paper work was introduced into the collections examination.[24] One novel but sensible suggestion by Wilberforce, made to Newman in September 1828 but not pursued, was that freshmen should come up at one period in the year.[25] The change which eventually occupied the centre of the stage and brought about the clash with the Provost concerned the organization of the college lecture system. The existing system was for the tutors to meet at the beginning of term to arrange the lecture classes and determine which each student should attend. On entry to the college each student had been assigned by the provost to a tutor, but when students were assigned to classes, no account was taken of who their tutors might be, and the decision which tutor should take any particular class was determined by the choice of each tutor in turn, according to seniority.[26] What the tutors did was to introduce a 'most important and far reaching improvement', whereby the bad men were thrown into large classes and time saved for the better sort, who were put into very small lectures, principally with their own tutors. Judging from the fact that Newman did not want these changes talked about, it is clear that the tutors realized that they might be skating on thin ice.[27]

Hawkins discovered that there had been some changes when in the spring of 1829, during an examination for an exhibition, he found that the tutors did not know all of each other's pupils. He then told the tutors, apparently rather abruptly, that this situation could not be allowed to continue. Newman, who was the tutor mainly concerned in the negotiations with the Provost, argued that as the University Statutes required each student to be placed under a tutor by his college, the office was a university one: the head of the college made the appointment to it, but once this had been made, the tutor, Newman contended, was responsible to the University for the due performance of his duties.[28] Moreover, he asserted that under the old system it was impossible for the tutors to find enough time to give that personal and pastoral attention to their pupils which in his view, and also Keble's, made the office a suitable one to be held by a cleric.[29] The Provost, on the other hand, maintained that the old system did not preclude a tutor from giving adequate personal attention to his pupils:[30] this point was supported by Copleston, whom he consulted in the course of the disagreement.[31] He also questioned Newman's interpretation of the university statutes as giving a tutor independence of the college and its head in his tutorial work[32] and

[24] Newman to Samuel Rickards, 6 Feb. 1829, in *LDN* ii. 117.
[25] R. I. Wilberforce to Newman, 3 Sept. 1828, in *LDN* ii. 98.
[26] Hawkins to Newman, 15 May 1830, in *LDN* ii. 228.
[27] Newman to Rickards, 6 Feb. 1829, in *LDN* ii. 118.
[28] Memorandum on the Oriel tuition, 9 July 1830, in *LDN* ii. 246–50.
[29] Newman to Hawkins, 8 June 1830, in *LDN* ii. 233.
[30] Hawkins to Newman, 9 June 1830, in *LDN* ii. 239.
[31] Copleston to Hawkins, 3 May 1830, in *LDN* ii. 213.
[32] Hawkins to Newman, 15 May 1830, in *LDN* ii. 232.

suggested that Newman, under a deep sense of his own responsibility, 'had a little forgotten that of the Provost'.[33]

The dispute continued from the spring of 1829 to the summer of 1830, exacerbated, it appears, by a growing difference in religious views.[34] The impasse was terminated by the Provost not assigning any more pupils to the three tutors. In this way he lost the services of three most able tutors, and in the longer term sowed the seeds of protracted opposition to himself by the fellows which was to have a debilitating effect on the college. The system which the tutors wished to follow was apparently not a novel one; it was, as Hawkins admitted, in operation in other colleges[35] and it should have been possible to reach some compromise. Failure to do so can fairly be laid at the door of the Provost, who was not prepared in this, as in many other matters during his period of office, to contemplate any change at all. But the mention in Chapter 1 of Newman's insistence on a tutorship as a cure of souls should not be forgotten. The three tutors were pressing for a scheme which would increase their influence on the religious views of the ablest students. Hawkins's reluctance to sanction that is understandable.[36]

Under the old tutorial system Oriel had its successes in the Schools— eighteen first classes in the eight years before 1828, of which eleven were in classics and seven in mathematics; but Newman maintained that these successes had been achieved by private and personal tuition on the part of Whately, Keble, Davison and Tyler, which represented an additional expense for undergraduates. In the four years from Michaelmas 1825 to Easter 1829 under the old system only two firsts were gained. But in the four years from Michaelmas 1829 to Easter 1833, during part of which period Newman and his colleagues were tutors, there were eleven firsts. Subsequently, in the four years from Michaelmas 1833 to Easter 1837, under the restored old system only five firsts were gained.[37] As Newman pointed out, under his system pupils received free what they had to pay for under the old, and, since under the old system the extra tuition was optional and not free, idle men who really needed it tended not to seek it. The conclusion must be that the tutors had the better of the argument on educational grounds, even though the development of greater specialization in university studies would have required considerable modification in their scheme.

To assist him in the emergency caused by the virtual dismissal of the three tutors the Provost turned to Hampden, a former fellow of the college

[33] Hawkins to Newman, 9 June 1830, in *LDN* ii. 240. On the personal clash see also Newman, *AW* 125–6, and M. Trevor, *The Pillar of the Cloud* (1962), 86.

[34] Copleston to Hawkins, 3 May 1830, in *LDN* ii. 214.

[35] Hawkins to Newman, 15 May 1830, in *LDN* ii. 230.

[36] For the 'preposterous intellectual and emotional demands' later made by a Tractarian tutor (W. G. Ward, Balliol) on his 'favourite pupil', see *Oxford Diaries of A. H. Clough*, ed. A. J. P. Kenny (1990) xix.

[37] *LDN* ii. 243 n. For the college's decline, see E. J. Whately, *Richard Whately* (2 vols 1866) i. 417.

resident in Oxford, who, although well qualified to be a tutor, was neither a fellow nor resident in the college, a great break with tradition. George Denison was also appointed a tutor in 1830 and Clement Greswell in 1832.[38] However, whereas the Provost had in his own hands the appointment of tutors, the college elected to the offices of dean, treasurer, junior treasurer and librarian; and at the elections in October 1833 the rebel fellows put up an alternative list to the names which the Provost would have preferred, and carried it.[39] Newman held the office of dean in the years 1833–4 and 1834–5.

In another issue arising indirectly from the tutorial differences the fellows were not so successful in getting their way. This concerned the position of gentlemen commoners in the college, who in Newman's opinion were the ruination of the place.[40] They had certain privileges, one of which was to dine with the fellows at high table;[41] the admission of gentlemen commoners was one of the 'laudabiles consuetudines' of the college, a 'praiseworthy custom', but not one specifically covered by the statutes. The fellows wished to get rid of them; the Provost did not; and the matter was discussed in college meetings in 1832. Hawkins took the view that a simple majority in the governing body in favour of a change was not sufficient to bring it about; the senior fellows must have greater weight and the Provost could in the last resort refuse to allow a change if he was very much against it.[42] The foundation statutes of the college were ambiguous, but did assign a special position to the senior members of the governing body in the making of changes; and Hawkins chose to exercise what he took to be his power to refuse to put to a college meeting any question involving an alteration to the *laudabiles consuetudines* of the college.

The lack of any cordial co-operation between the Provost and fellows during Hawkins's long reign was a fatal weakness in the college. During the years of the Tractarian controversy Hawkins came to feel himself 'like the Captain of a crew on the verge of mutiny',[43] and was driven to controlling his rebellious governing body by various expedients. These included occupying college meetings with details of 'all the posts, barndoor fowls, and chimney pots' on the college estates, to the exclusion of more contentious business.[44] Dissension arose on the most trivial issues. Newman and Keble resisted the presentation to the college of a bust of Richard Whately; and the college subsequently refused to accept a portrait of Copleston, which the sitter had intended for the Oriel hall. The portrait went, instead, to

[38] W. J. Copleston, a nephew of the former Provost, seems to have been the least efficient of the tutors under the new dispensation: Pattison, *Memoirs*, 45.
[39] Mozley, *Reminiscences* i. 236.
[40] *LDN* i. 305 n.
[41] Mozley, *Reminiscences* ii. 157.
[42] Provost's note on his powers, 20 Apr. 1832, OCL 5.
[43] D. P. Chase to W. A. Greenhill, 6 Jan. 1880, OCL 1262.
[44] Newman to Froude, 14 June 1834, in *LDN* iv. 272.

Copleston's old college, Corpus. R. W. Church resigned his tutorship in 1842 following a disagreement with the Provost over Tract 90; and further conflict with the fellows arose when Hawkins attempted to withhold testimonials from Oriel ordinands whom he suspected of adherence to Newmanite principles.

Under the Ordinance drawn up by the Executive Commissioners in 1857, democratic rule was substituted 'for a (rather unlimited) monarchy'.[45] The arrangements for the instruction and discipline of junior members were put under the control of the Provost and fellows, rather than the Provost alone. There were to be two stated general meetings a year, where questions were to be settled by majority vote. Voting became more frequent in college meetings. At the Easter audit in 1864 the old question of gentleman commoners came up; Hawkins was in the minority (11 to 3), and it was agreed to admit no more of them. In 1865 Hawkins and J. W. Burgon were alone in opposing the decision that persons not members of the Church of England should be allowed to enter their names for admission.[46] On the educational side of the college, where the Provost had exercised unquestioned authority since the days of Newman's tutorship, the fellows set up by ordinance an educational staff to organize teaching for the honour schools. The Provost's comments on the new arrangements, to which he was evidently opposed, show how difficult his opposition and passion for detailed objection must have made college meetings.[47] In 1874 Hawkins retired from the management of the college, withdrawing to the canonry of Rochester annexed to the headship since 1714, where he died in 1882, at the age of 93, having lost his last battle with the fellows of Oriel to prevent the severance of the provostship of the college from the canonry of Rochester. This change enabled the fellows to elect David Binning Monro, a distinguished Presbyterian layman and Vice-Provost of the college, as his successor.[48]

---

[45] Chase to Greenhill, 6 Jan. 1890, OCL 1262. See PP 1857 xxxii. Sess. 2, 201–15.

[46] Hawkins's view was contrary to the spirit, though not to the letter, of the 1854 Act, section 43, under which no one matriculating could be required to subscribe to the Articles.

[47] Provost Hawkins's notes, 6, OCA; memorandum by Provost Hawkins, 10 Feb. 1868, OCA.

[48] The Provost's lodgings had been occupied since 1874, partly by Monro and partly by the college dean, Arthur Butler, together with Butler's wife and small children: C. Colvin, 'A don's wife a century ago', *Oxoniensia* l (1985), 267–78.

'AN AGE OF YOUNG MEN'

7

'Lost Causes and ... Impossible Loyalties': The Oxford Movement and the University*

P. B. NOCKLES

> The truth is that this moment, which swept the leader of the Tractarians, with most of his followers, out of the place, was an epoch in the history of the University. It was a deliverance from the nightmare which had oppressed Oxford for fifteen years. For so long we had been given over to discussions unprofitable in themselves, and which had entirely diverted our thoughts from the true business of the place ... By the secessions of 1845 this was extinguished in a moment ... In 1845 the darkness was dissipated, and the light was let in in an instant.
>
> (Pattison, *Memoirs*, 123–4)

Mark Pattison's famous retrospect on the Oxford Movement's impact on the University contained something of the rancour and bias of a disillusioned, lapsed convert, who came to regret once having fallen under the spell of its leader, John Henry Newman.

What was this Oxford Movement which could rouse such passionate retrospective antipathy in a former adherent? What had this Movement to do with the University? In essence, it represented a rallying together in the early 1830s of a body of young Oxford MAs and tutors led by Newman, John Keble, Hurrell Froude and later E. B. Pusey in defence of the High-Church or 'catholic' tradition of the Church of England in response to a liberal and Erastian challenge to the Church's apparent rights and independence. In particular, the Movement's genesis is traditionally regarded as the protest inspired by these young Oxford High-Churchmen in 1833 in response to the suppression of ten Anglican bishoprics in Ireland. The most famous and immediate product of the Movement, a series of publications

*When Matthew Arnold referred to Oxford in 1865 as a 'home of lost causes' (*Essays in Criticism*, First Series, preface) he seems to have had the Oxford Movement particularly in mind. See his passage on Newman in 'Lectures on the study of Celtic literature' (1867), *Complete Prose Works*, ed. R. H. Super (11 vols Ann Arbor, Mich. 1960–77) iii. 305.

known as the 'Tracts for the Times' from which its followers acquired the
title 'Tractarians',[1] may have been addressed to Churchmen at large, but
soon became notorious as being the 'Oxford Tracts'. As the Movement
developed, 'Puseyites' and 'Protestant papists' were some of the kinder
terms of description invoked by their detractors.

Pattison's verdict conveyed a vivid sense of a unique and distinctive epoch
in the annals of Oxford University. The classic accounts of the Movement,
from Newman's own *Apologia pro vita sua* to R. W. Church's famous
history, all convey, from their various standpoints, the same impression.
Thus, if for Pattison 1845 represented 'deliverance', for Church it represented 'that catastrophe'.[2] Neither was in any doubt as to the significance of
the events of that year as the end of an era in the University. G. V. Cox's
comment—'Instead of High Church, Low Church or Broad Church, Oxford talked of high embankments, the broad gauge and low dividends:
Brunel and Stephenson were in men's mouths instead of Dr Pusey or Mr
Golightly; and speculative theology gave way to speculation in railway
shares'[3]—might seem flippant, but it accurately conveys something of the
suddenness with which the preoccupations of the previous fifteen years
appeared to be extinguished.

To attribute to the Oxford Movement absolute consistency and a high
degree of coherence and unity in purpose and direction would be misleading: in reality it often lacked these qualities. It developed and underwent
modifications in response to the flux of ideas and changing circumstances.
The evolution of theological principles meant that the party of 1845 was
manifestly not the party of 1833. The Movement increasingly diverged,
more especially after 1841, from the classic High-Anglican tradition which
the University of Oxford had broadly upheld since the seventeenth century.[4]
On questions as fundamental as the rule of faith, the merits of the Reformation and the relationship of Church and state, the Tractarians came to differ
markedly from the strong body of old High-Churchmen within the University, who had often supported the Movement at first and who came to
express, albeit sometimes reluctantly, their unease and, ultimately, dissent.
This divergence was to be critical.

From its origin the Movement had a clear and definite vision and ideal of
the University and its relation to Church and nation, though justice has not
always been done to the Movement's positive educational ideals. The Trac-

---

[1] The first use of the epithet 'Tractarian' appears to have been in 1839 by the Master of the
Temple Christopher Benson: *Discourses upon Tradition and Episcopacy* (1839), 101. Many years
later Newman confirmed this: J. H. Newman to J. T. Coleridge, 7 Feb. 1869, in *LDN* xxxi. 87.
O. Chadwick, *The Spirit of the Oxford Movement* (1990), 135–6.
[2] R. W. Church, *The Oxford Movement: twelve years, 1833–1845* (1891), ch. 19.
[3] Cox, 355.
[4] P. B. Nockles, *The Oxford Movement in Context: Anglican High Churchmanship, 1760–
1857* (1994), esp. 282–306.

tarian conception of the University gave priority to the achievement of religious and moral excellence and the preservation of doctrinal truth rather than the pursuit of intellectual attainments. To the Tractarians the University was an ecclesiastical institution, likened by Pusey to a cathedral foundation. As such, in Dean Church's words, it became 'the fulcrum from which the Tractarians hoped to move the church'.[5] The battles of the period were fought in defence of a preconceived vision and ideal of the University. It was not so much a case of blind reaction on the old Tory, pre-1829 model, as a veritable counter-attack and counter-revolution, whose appeal yet lay beyond the bounds of a 'Tractarian' party, but rather carried a great bulk of the junior university along with it, conservative Evangelicals and old High-Churchmen as well as 'Tractarians'.

The Tractarian movement infused university life at Oxford with a moral purpose, religious zeal and earnestness not witnessed since the age of Laud.[6] The religious state of Oxford in the period immediately preceding the Movement has almost inevitably been seen to present a sharp contrast. Oxford's clerical heads and fellows were depicted in liberal journals, and more grossly in the radical pamphlets, prints and cartoons of the day, as combining the worst traits of bigotry and worldliness. They were charged with clinging to 'the loaves and fishes' of establishment privileges, and maintaining a religion of forms without the spirit. The various undergraduate 'sets' of the day were classified in an anonymous pamphlet of 1832 as 'the drinking and hunting', 'the gentlemanly', 'the book-worms', and 'the saintly hypocritical, canting, psalm-singing, Methodistical set'.[7] Even as caricature these accounts[8] convey little idea of the true state of religion at Oxford when Gladstone came into residence. Far more serious and challenging was the religious and moral, rather than political, critique inspired by Evangelicalism.

Pre-Tractarian Oxford's religion came out badly from the Evangelical standpoint. Itself a vigorous reaction to the supposed torpor and indifference of eighteenth-century religion, Evangelicalism had appeared to concentrate within itself much of the rising religious and moral earnestness of the early nineteenth century, especially among the middle classes. Yet, although early Methodism through the Wesleys and the 'Holy Club' had taken root in Oxford in the 1730s, the University had subsequently turned its back on the broader Evangelical revival. Indeed, in Evangelical eyes, the University of Oxford had brought upon itself disgrace and infamy, by the expulsion of six

---

[5] Church, 407.

[6] See Principal Shairp's testimony in R. T. Davidson and W. Benham, *Life of Archibald Campbell Tait* (2 vols 1891) i. 106.

[7] *Oxford: academical abuses disclosed by some of the initiated* (1832), 11–12. A similar critique and satire of the state of the University was contained in G. Cox, *Black Gowns and Red Coats; or, Oxford in 1834* (6 pts 1834) and J. S. Boone, *The Oxford Spy; a dialogue in verse* (1818). William Tuckwell considered neither to be a faithful portrait: Tuckwell (1900), 115–16.

[8] [T. J. Hogg], 'The universities of Oxford and Cambridge', *Westminster Review* xv (1831), 62.

students from St Edmund Hall for reputedly being Methodists.[9] Although there was nothing at Oxford comparable with the Evangelical movement fostered at Cambridge by the preaching of Charles Simeon, Evangelicalism nevertheless retained adherents among a minority of the University.[10] But Oxford retained the eighteenth-century bias against what was called 'enthusiasm', and Evangelicals were frequently assailed on this account from the pulpit. For their part, Evangelicals at Oxford, as elsewhere, would accuse the so-called 'orthodox' clergy of not 'preaching the gospel'; and the severe judgements against the religion of the majority of the University should be seen in the context of this rather narrow Evangelical attitude.[11] Likewise, the inherited evangelicalism of the young Gladstone played its part in forming his view that the period of his residence at Oxford, from 1828 to 1831, was one in which the University was still sunk in spiritual lethargy or 'frozen indifference'. As an undergraduate Gladstone was quite repelled by the 'steady, clear but dry Anglican orthodoxy' that then held sway. Though he heard Newman preach, as was recounted in Chapter 1, he could not then perceive the slightest indication of the incipient Oxford Movement. 'There was nothing at that time', he later recalled, 'in the theology, or in the religious life, of the University to indicate what was to come.'[12]

In comparison to her religious pretensions, the University's devotional life undoubtedly left something to be desired. Attendance at college chapel could be a boring duty, and conduct was sometimes unseemly. Bedel Cox recalled the university sermons as 'dry, cold discourses', little attuned to stimulate piety. Good sermons were rare and the congregations 'thin and listless'. A comment from the *Athenaeum* in November 1828, then in the sympathetic hands of F. D. Maurice, is revealing. A father is represented as warning his Oxford-bound son: 'I am not quite sure that your devotional feelings will be much improved by frequenting the theological lectures at St. Mary's; for you will occasionally find some difficulty in following the very learned professor, on account of the crumpling of newspapers, the exchange of novels, and the earnest questions from your neighbours about the odds against the favourite at the Derby.'[13] Similar strictures were advanced

---

[9] Described in *The Eighteenth Century*, 165–6.

[10] J. S. Reynolds, *The Evangelicals at Oxford, 1735–1871* (1953), ch. 5; cf. A. C. Dormer, *A Century of Evangelical Religion in Oxford* (1938), 5, 11–12; Ward, *Victorian Oxford*, 75.

[11] J. C. Philpot, *A Letter to the Provost of Worcester College, Oxford, on Resigning his Fellowship, and Seceding from the Church of England* (1835); H. B. Bulteel, *A Sermon on 1 Corinthians ii verse 12 Preached before the University of Oxford at St Mary's, on Sunday February 6, 1831* (1831), 46–7.

[12] W. E. Gladstone, *A Chapter of Autobiography* (1868), 52–3; D. C. Lathbury, *Correspondence on Church and Religion of W. E. Gladstone* (2 vols 1910) i. 2–6.

[13] Cox, 236–43; *Memories of Dean Hole* (1893), 291; *Athenaeum* 19 Nov. 1828, 888. For the unreliability of attendance at sermons in St Mary's as a test of religious vitality see *A Letter to the Vice-Chancellor of the University of Oxford on the Subject of University Sermons, by a tutor* (1853), 4–5.

against the deficiencies in the University's theological instruction. John Randolph, who was Regius Professor of Divinity from 1783 to 1807 (and, from 1799, simultaneously Bishop of Oxford), was content to give infrequent lectures by candle-light to small groups of drowsy undergraduates.[14] Sir James Graham recalled, when he had high political office, the scanty attention paid to religion during his residence in Oxford, between 1810 and 1812.[15]

Yet the religious state of pre-Tractarian Oxford was not as defective as critics made out. 'The popular reputation of all national institutions of a moral and religious intention is borrowed from a past time,' J. H. Newman's brother, Francis, commented; 'both veneration and disgust, under ordinary circumstances, outlasting their causes at least half a century.'[16] By the 1820s many of the criticisms of the religious state of the University were manifestly out of date. Thomas Hogg's demand in 1831 that 'the chairs of theology (be) filled, not by drones and sluggards, but by professors whose talents would adorn the science they taught'[17] would have been less than fair during Randolph's tenure of the Regius chair. To make the charge in the age of Charles Lloyd (Regius Professor of Divinity, 1822–9) and Edward Burton (1829–36) was absurd. The 1800 examination statute had stimulated more rigorous religious instruction in the colleges. In 1820 Henry Handley Norris, a High-Churchman, reported to the American bishop, John Henry Hobart, that 'our universities, Oxford especially, have been repairing the decay of discipline...a competent knowledge of the evidences and principles of Christianity is made indispensable to everyone'.[18] There is considerable evidence in favour of an improvement in religious tone and principles starting perhaps twenty years before the official dawn of the Movement. To some Evangelicals 'orthodox', 'decorous' Oxford was proving more attractive than Simeon's Cambridge. It was to Oxford rather than Cambridge that William Wilberforce chose to send his three younger sons; and to Oriel rather than St Edmund Hall.[19] Another moderate Evangelical, Hannah More, commented in 1818 that she was 'much changed' in her estimate of the

---

[14] Cox, 139–40.

[15] C. S. Parker, *Life and Letters of Sir James Graham* (2 vols 1907) i. 12. Graham did not take a degree. For criticisms of compulsory attendance in college chapels see *Parl. Deb.* 25 Mar. 1834, 3s. xxii. 636 (Stanley); Wordsworth, *Prelude* (1850) iii. 418–19 in the Cornell 'reading text', *The Fourteen Book 'Prelude'*, ed. W. V. B. Owen (Ithaca, NY 1985), 72.

[16] Huber, *English Universities* ii pt 2, p. 512; cf F. Oakeley, *A Letter to the Duke of Wellington* (1835), 4.

[17] [Hogg], 'The universities of Oxford and Cambridge', 56. Hogg had matriculated in 1810.

[18] J. McVickar, *The Early Life and Professional Years of Bishop Hobart* (1838), 492. Bishop Jebb of Limerick also testified to a High-Church religious revival in Oxford by 1820: see J. Jebb to C. A. Ogilvie, 11 Aug. 1819, Bodl. MS Eng. lett. d. 123, fo 34. Cf *A Letter to the Author of an Enquiry into the Studies and Discipline Adopted in the Two English Universities, as Preparatory to Holy Orders in the Established Church, by a graduate of the University of Oxford* (1824), 15–16.

[19] D. Newsome, *The Parting of Friends* (1966), 60–1.

religious merits of the two universities: 'I used greatly to prefer Cambridge, but this summer I have had so much intercourse with men of talents and piety from Oxford that I believe not only that the general discipline is much stricter but in two or three colleges religion is in more esteem.'[20] This improvement was not universal. Isaac Williams, a young High-Churchman who was to be prominent in the Oxford Movement, complained in 1832 that Oxford was 'very dead', and that he was often the only person present at university and saint's-day sermons in St Mary's.[21] None the less, during these years pre-Tractarian Oxford underwent a religious and moral revival that was specifically based on High-Church and Tory principles. The regeneration of Oxford which Bishop Jebb dated some years prior to the Movement had 'been wrought out from within, and in no small degree in hostility to the Evangelical party of the Church'; the series of learned theological works that issued from Oxford during the period 1817–22, hailed by Jebb as evidence of the University's revival, was of a distinctly High-Church character.[22]

The High-Churchmanship of the seventeenth century associated with Archbishop Laud, himself responsible as Chancellor for the famous statutes of 1636, continued to maintain its hold. This was more than a mere political religion made up of Jacobite sympathies and a horror of whiggery. Eighteenth-century High-Churchmanship, not least in Oxford, is sometimes said to have lost its earlier spiritual vitality in the reaction against the emotionalism and 'enthusiasm' of Methodism and evangelicalism. There was no shortage of representatives of the 'high-and-dry' strain, of which Godfrey Faussett, Lady Margaret Professor of Divinity from 1827 to 1853, was a later survival. Faussett shared with his eighteenth-century predecessors an antagonism to some of the more spiritual manifestations of High-Churchmanship. However, there were many others for whom High-Church allegiance involved not only high theological doctrines of the Church, sacraments and apostolical tradition, as well as the politics of 'Church and king', but also elevated religious ideals of asceticism, spirituality and devotion.[23] These ideals were exemplified by the Oxford 'Hutchinsonians', followers of the somewhat esoteric anti-Newtonian scientific theories of the Hebraist John Hutchinson, who formed a kind of eighteenth-century Oxford movement.[24] In their mysticism, emphasis on typology, anti-rationalism, high sacramentalism, asceticism, interest in patristic learning, devotional fervency and imaginativeness, the Hutchinsonians anticipated many of the religious traits

[20] E. M. Forster, *Marianne Thornton, 1797–1887: a domestic biography* (1956), 78.
[21] *The Autobiography of Isaac Williams B.D.*, ed. G. Prevost (1892), 52–3.
[22] J. Jebb to C. A. Ogilvie, 18 Mar. 1818, 8 May 1819, Bodl. MS Eng. lett. d. 123, fos 22, 30.
[23] For a sympathetic portrait of one of pre-Tractarian Oxford's orthodox tutors see C. E. H. Edwards, *An Oxford Tutor: the life of the Rev. Thomas Short, B.D. of Trinity College Oxford* (1909), 43–50.
[24] R. Spearman, *Life of J. Hutchinson*, prefixed to *A Supplement to the Works of John Hutchinson Esq.* (1765), pp. i–xiv.

later associated with the Tractarians. Through their real leader, George Horne, President of Magdalen College from 1768 to 1791, they exerted a considerable influence by the practical inculcation of a fervent and deep High-Church spirituality among the younger men.[25]

The vigour of High-Church religion in pre-Tractarian Oxford owed much to the revival of patristic studies and patristic learning. Five important 'torch-bearers' in this respect were William Cleaver, Principal of Brasenose College from 1785 to 1809, Thomas Townson, a fellow of Magdalen from 1737 to 1752, and, above all, Martin Joseph Routh, Horne's successor at Magdalen, whose tenure of the presidency lasted from 1791 to 1854, and the Regius professors Charles Lloyd and Edward Burton. Of all these, Routh, remote and cloistered as his life was, was probably the most influential. His *Reliquiae sacrae*, published between 1814 and 1818, with its massive display of patristic learning, harked back to the Caroline divinity of seventeenth-century Oxford.[26]

Charles Lloyd's divinity lectures provided the most direct personal influence over the future leaders of the Tractarian Movement, transmitting a sense of the Church of England's catholic liturgical and patristic heritage.[27] It was a legacy that those leaders would build upon, but the differences between the future Tractarianism and the old High-Churchmanship of Lloyd and Burton should not be underestimated. Lloyd's early death removed a steadying influence, which might have caused the Tractarian Movement to take a less radical course.[28] Before 1829, however, there was a striking theological and political consensus within the University. Common ground and a unity of purpose existed among many of the so-called Noetics and the more moderate High-Churchmen, in a broad-based Anglican renewal against the opposing claims of Unitarianism and rational Dissent on the one hand and Roman Catholicism on the other.[29] Equally notable, in view of the denunciations against Bible societies and Evangelical preachers as 'engines of Jacobinism' and 'enthusiasm' earlier in the century, was the harmony in Oxford between Protestant High-Churchmen and many Evan-

[25] H. Best, *Four Years in France* (1826), 25–35.

[26] J. W. Burgon, *Lives of Twelve Good Men* (2 vols 1889) i. 1–115. For Newman's veneration of Routh see J. H. Newman to F. Rogers, 7 Jan. 1837, in *LDN* vi. 7–9. A fifth volume of *Reliquiae sacrae* was published in 1848.

[27] F. Oakeley, *Personal Reminiscences of the 'Oxford Movement': a lecture addressed to the Islington Catholic Popular Club* (1855), 4–5; F. Oakeley, *Historical Notes on the Tractarian Movement* (1865), 12–14. On Lloyd's relation to the Tractarians see J. H. Philpot, *The Seceders, 1829–1869* (1930), 15; A. Maguire, *The Oxford Movement: strictures on the 'Personal Reminiscences' and revelations of Dr Newman, Mr Oakeley, and others* (1855), 328–9; W. J. Baker, *Beyond Port and Prejudice: Charles Lloyd of Oxford* (Orono M. 1981), 214–15.

[28] E. Churton, *Memoir of Joshua Watson* (2 vols 1861) i. 294; Cox, 31–2; Gladstone, *Chapter of Autobiography*, 52–3.

[29] R. Brent, *Liberal Anglican Politics: Whiggery, Religion, and Reform* (1987), 148–9; P. Corsi, *Science and Religion: Baden Powell and the Anglican debate, 1800–1860* (1988), 73–83; cf P. Hinchliff, *Benjamin Jowett and the Christian Religion* (1987), 9–10.

gelicals on the eve of Catholic Emancipation. The Evangelical Hannah More welcomed John Miller's 'High-Church' Bampton Lectures of 1817, which were to provide a philosophical inspiration for Tractarianism.[30] Such co-operation was aided by the somewhat undoctrinal emphasis and preoccupation of Oxford High-Churchmanship at this time. Theological works of a High-Church character such as Lloyd's *Formularies of Faith* (1825) and Burton's *Testimonies of the Ante-Nicene Fathers* (1826) were certainly produced in the University, but they tended to be uncontentious. A common devotion to the old constitutional principles on which Church and state and the University rested united all parties. Anti-Catholicism could lead both wings of the Church within Oxford to overlook fine theological distinctions, as when that refugee from Spanish Catholicism Blanco White, even though well on his way to eventual Unitarianism, was taken up by the University and granted, in 1826, the unusual distinction of an MA by diploma 'on account of those able and well-timed publications by which he has powerfully exposed the errors and corruptions of the Church of Rome'.[31] In 1829, when a Parliamentary candidate capable of ousting Peel was needed, Protestant High-Church resident members turned to Sir Robert Inglis, a staunch Churchman but reputedly an Evangelical; consistency on constitutional principles and in defence of the establishment could more than offset any doctrinal differences.[32] Philip Bliss, the Protestant High-Church Registrar of the University, feared that Inglis 'would not "go down" with a large majority of our members of Convocation, on account of his principles in religion being supposed to be Evangelical'; but, in the event, Inglis numbered among his supporters Charles Ogilvie, and even Keble and Newman. What mattered, insisted the editor of the High-Church *Standard*, was Inglis's basic 'attachment to the Church of England', and the fact that he was 'more high-church than most of the bishops ... in the matter of the Test and Corporation Acts'.[33]

The rejection of Peel in 1829 marks more accurately the origin of the Movement than Keble's 1833 Assize Sermon condemning the suppression of the Irish bishoprics; and those involved in it may be termed Tractarians from the earlier date, though the Tracts had not yet been devised even when the Sermon was delivered. Since the 1770s Oxford had been a pillar of the establishment in the broadest sense. The defeat of the Home Secretary and

[30] See H. More to C. A. Ogilvie, 2 Apr. 1816, 21 Mar. 1818, Bodl. MS Eng. lett. d. 124, fos 103–4, 129.

[31] OUA WP/γ/24(4), HB 24 Apr. 1826, fo 53; J. B. Mozley, 'Blanco White', *Essays Historical and Theological* (2 vols 1878) ii. 96.

[32] See *A Letter of Congratulation to Sir R. H. Inglis Bart, by a member of the University of Oxford* (1829), 8.

[33] P. Bliss to unnamed correspondent, 19 Feb. 1829, BL Add. MS 34750, fo 148. Bishop Jebb took a similar view of Inglis: J. Jebb to C. A. Ogilvie, 12 Feb. 1829, Bodl. MS Eng. lett. d. 123, fo 65; J. Jebb to M. Routh, 14 Feb. 1829, MCA 407, fo 21.

Leader of the Commons represented a reversion to the University's eighteenth-century traditions of independence and opposition, in which a strong party within the University insisted upon Oxford's detachment from the political nation.[34] Like Oxford Jacobitism in the earlier period, the Tractarian Movement depended for its life-blood on the non-residents, represented in Convocation. Mainly comprising country clergymen and gentry, this 'external university' was organized through an intricate network of connections and country associations. The uproarious scenes in February 1829, described in Chapter 1,[35] signalled the first phase of a broadly based, anti-liberal alliance within the University. In its early years the Movement made particular headway among the 'Vinegar Tops', as William Palmer of Worcester described the country clergy,[36] and it was towards these clerical non-residents that the early Tracts were primarily directed.

When it enjoyed Convocation's favour, between 1829 and 1837, the Tractarian Movement flourished. As that favour was gradually withdrawn, the Movement in Oxford went into retreat and became increasingly isolated, numerous though its younger devotees always remained. The climax occurred in February 1845 when the '1,300 wild country parsons', as the young Benjamin Jowett described them, assembled in the Sheldonian Theatre to give their final condemnation. Among Oxford residents the constituency of the Movement was very much the university of young MAs (generally fellows and tutors), designated 'juniors' in contradistinction to the 'senior' university of the heads of houses. MAs were entitled to vote in Convocation, and thus had an important voice in the University, but the power to execute statutes or to initiate legislation lay with the formal governing body, the Vice-Chancellor and his Hebdomadal Board made up of the heads, who, from their age, station and freedom to marry, formed a quite distinct society from the rest of the University. MAs had a minority representation on the Board through the two annually elected proctors, who could also exercise a veto on legislation in Convocation. The Movement came increasingly to feed off the tension between these two elements in unreformed Oxford's oligarchic constitution, as the gulf between seniors and juniors lent force to the theological contests.

The Peel contest propelled Newman, among others of the future Tractarians, on a new path radically divergent from that of his erstwhile Oriel Noetic friends.[37] Contemporaries hoped that the election would prove merely a temporary disturbance to the quiet routine of official university life. Robert Marsham, Warden of Merton, and one of the leading figures on

---

[34] Ward, *Victorian Oxford* xiii., 80.
[35] See pp. 56–9 above.
[36] C. Wordsworth, *Annals of my Early Life* (1891), 154.
[37] See Ch. 1 n. 349; and H. Tristram, 'Catholic Emancipation, Mr Peel, and the University of Oxford', *Cornhill Magazine* lxvi (Apr. 1929), 410.

the Oxford committee for the re-election of Peel, had looked forward to the speedy termination of what he expected to be a good-humoured, 'amiable contest'.[38] When Blanco White looked back, however, he saw the election as marking 'the first manifestation of the mental revolution' that was to lead to the 'Protestant Popery' of the Tractarian Movement.[39] In his retrospective account, he stressed that before the election ideological differences within the University had been submerged by the strength of personal bonds. Oxford Noeticism was always more a frame of mind and a theological temper rather than a rigidly liberal creed (see Note following Chapter 1). It encompassed a wide shade of opinion, some of it very 'High-Church',[40] and drew in many for whom the least contact with 'liberalism' would, in later years, be anathema. Blanco White felt truly at home in this climate, and even referred to his 'union of heart' with avowed Protestant High-Church-men like Ogilvie.[41] The Catholic Question had been simmering for years and it hardly seemed possible that its settlement could produce any lasting personal division within the University. Partly owing to the liberal influence of the Noetics, some observers held that Oxford had become 'very much liberalised on this subject within the last few years'.[42] Newman's period under Richard Whately's influence, and his opposition in 1827 to the petition against the Catholic claims, have been mentioned in Chapter 1. The Noetics seemed to have all before them. Their intellectual supremacy in the University was still unquestioned. Their position consolidated by elevation to positions of authority—Copleston to the see of Llandaff in 1828 and replaced as Provost of Oriel by Edward Hawkins with the support of Newman and Froude, and Whately to the principalship of St Alban Hall in 1825—the Noetics enjoyed close London political ties with some of the younger liberals and whigs.[43] The University's rejection of Peel proved to be a body-blow from which the Noetics never recovered. Dismayed by the popular passions roused by the election, they increasingly turned to their London parliamentary friends in the way that would characterize the Oxford liberals of the 1830s. This only served to isolate them and heighten their unpopularity in the University. Whately, like other Noetics, conspicuously failed to grasp the depth of feeling and principle that was setting his erstwhile allies on their new course.

[38] R. Marsham to R. Peel, 14 Feb. 1829, BL Add. MS 40398, fo 261.
[39] J. H. Thom, *The Life of Joseph Blanco White* (3 vols 1845) ii. 198–9, iii. 131.
[40] Significantly even Edward Copleston, the most prominent of the Oriel Noetics, regarded himself in 1814 as 'more a high churchman' than most of his Oxford contemporaries: W. J. Copleston, *Memoir of Edward Copleston D.D., Bishop of Llandaff* (1851), 47. He regarded Arnold's views as 'rash and dangerous': W. Tuckwell, *Pre-Tractarian Oxford: a reminiscence of the Oriel 'Noetics'* (1909), 45.
[41] Thom ii. 129.
[42] P. Shuttleworth to Lord Holland, [Feb. 1828], BL Add. MS 51597, fo 125.
[43] See p. 74 above.

For Newman and many future Tractarian opponents of Peel in 1829, Keble perhaps excepted, Catholic Emancipation was a subordinate issue in the election. Newman continued to believe that Emancipation would not represent a particular injury to the Church of England.[44] Instead, the triumphant vindication of the independence of the University was the all-important outcome. 'We have achieved a glorious victory,' Newman wrote. 'We have proved the independence of the Church and of Oxford. So rarely is either of the two in opposition to Government, that not once in fifty years can independent principle be shown.'[45] By challenging and discrediting the Noetics, and defending the rights of both University and Church against what they saw as the 'insolence' of the self-styled 'talent' of the University, Newman and his friends took the important step that was soon to establish their moral and religious leadership at Oxford. In doing so, they brought about a new alignment of forces within university politics, forging a coalition of Tractarians, Protestant High-Churchmen, and conservative Evangelicals in the face of what they saw as a threat from liberalism. Among the bulk of MAs, the great concern was whether the University was to be 'infected by the liberality of the age, and is willing to sacrifice experience to experiment'.[46]

In 1829 Oxford University and the Church of England had been affronted, and a renewed sense of their inseparability was born. As the old constitutional safeguards broke down, there developed a more urgent sense of the University's duty to act as the voice of the Church, indeed as its 'appointed Guardians and Guides', and not to be subservient or truckling to any ministry or London parliamentary 'friends'. The appeal in 1829 to the country clergy, often of lowly and humble status, fitted the Tractarian rhetoric of exalting examples of popular piety and zeal against false teaching in high places. They gloried in Whately's charge of fomenting 'popular tumult'.[47]

The experience of 1829 had taught the Tractarians never again to put the trust of the University in the hands of politicians.[48] Wellington's election as Chancellor in 1834 in succession to Lord Grenville was regretted by many of them,[49] though they contented themselves with the reflection that he was at least preferable to Peel, whose candidature had been promoted by the liberal Tories.[50] The Archbishop of Canterbury would have been their preferred candidate, as symbolic of the ecclesiastical nature of the University.

[44] J. H. Newman to H. Newman, 16 Mar. 1829, in *LDN* ii. 132.

[45] J. H. Newman to Mrs Newman, 1 Mar. 1829, ibid. 125; cf Newman, *Apologia*, 72–3.

[46] [Edward Burton], *The Substance of Two Speeches Delivered in Convocation on Thursday, February 26th, 1829* (1829), 5; Bodl. MS Bliss B421, item 56.

[47] R. Whately to R. Peel, 1 Mar. 1829, BL Add. MS 40399, fos 11–12.

[48] J. Keble to J. H. Newman, 28 Mar. 1829, in *LDN* ii. 135.

[49] For an account of the Wellington chancellorship election see N. Gash, 'Oxford politics in the Chancellor's election of 1834', *OM* lvi (1938), 543–4, 574–5.

[50] *LDN* iv. 178; cf J. Christie to W. Palmer sen., 15 Feb. 1834, LPL MS 2837, fo 11; Ward, *Victorian Oxford*, 84–6.

The University was, in Keble's view, 'so very wrong in going to the Duke when they might have the Archbishop, and I think it moreover so very doubtful how his Grace will be advised on the great ecclesiastical points.'[51] This set-back would ultimately jeopardize Tractarian hopes of complete ascendancy in the University.

To many in 1833–4 it seemed that the 'Tory reaction' in the University, based on the triple alliance of Tractarians, High-Churchmen and Evangelicals, would hold up. Oxford Evangelicals such as Benjamin Symons and John Hill felt the almost apocalyptic sense of danger to the Church, and appreciated that it was the University that must stand foremost in the breach.[52] The more conservative among the old Noetic grouping, Edward Hawkins and John Davison, began to dissociate themselves from their more liberal colleagues. Davison approved of Keble's Assize Sermon, and even endorsed the original plan of the Tracts.[53] Newman claimed Davison to be 'more or less connected with us'.[54] Hawkins did not go this far, but he expressed strong private disapproval of Arnold's *Principles of Church Reform* (1833) and Lord Henley's Church reform proposals of 1832.[55] His public attempts to distance himself from Whately's opinions, and to prevent the latter from being seen as the 'leader of the Oriel school', had begun several years earlier.[56] In 1833 Keble, when commending Hawkins's book on the Old Testament, expressed relief that he did not belong to 'Whately's school'.[57]

In the early stages of the Movement, many accepted the leadership of the Tractarians, who would later recoil from them once the full theological implications of the Movement became apparent. 'At first rise', Vice-Chancellor Gilbert recalled in 1839, 'and for some succeeding years, they were looked upon not unfavourably by many of all ranks in the Church.'[58] The Movement originally had a wide appeal among all those who were conservatively disposed in religion and politics in the face of infidelity, secularism, and the inroads of dissent. One wing of the original Movement comprised the Association in Defence of the Church, founded in Oxford in 1833,[59] and

---

[51] J. Keble to C. A. Ogilvie, 18 Jan. 1834, Bodl. MS Eng. lett. d. 124, fo 68.

[52] An avowed Evangelical such as Anne Tyndale could even express approval of some of the Tracts: A. Tyndale to E. B. Pusey, 11 Nov. 1833, PHL Pusey Papers, PUS 104/1.

[53] J. Davison to J. Keble, 16 Aug. 1833, KCA MS 50.

[54] J. H. Newman to J. W. Bowden, 23 Sept. 1833, in *LDN* iv. 54; *British Critic* xxxi (Apr. 1842), 391. Liberals continued, however, to claim Davison as an ally: see T. Arnold to an old pupil, 17 Aug. 1840, in Stanley, *Arnold* ii. 187–8.

[55] Hawkins regarded Arnold's pamphlet as a 'burlesque upon reform': E. Hawkins to R. Whately, 4 Feb. 1833, OCL MS Hampden Controversy 412.

[56] Whately to Hawkins, 11 Oct. 1831, OCL MS Hawkins ii. 182. See p. 60 above.

[57] J. Keble to E. Hawkins, 7 Mar. 1833, OCL MS Hawkins viii. 751.

[58] J. Garbett, *Dr Pusey and the University of Oxford. A Letter to the Vice-Chancellor of the University of Oxford* (1843), 8; A. T. Gilbert to Wellington, 26 Dec. 1839: SUL 2/250/64.

[59] J. H. Newman to R. H. Froude, 9 Sept. 1833, in *LDN* iv. 47–9; cf J. Keble to J. Davison, 13 Aug. 1833, KCA MS; J. Mozley to A. Mozley, 20 Sept. 1833, in Mozley, *Letters*, 36–7; Palmer, *Narrative*, 48–53, 91–118.

representing such learned figures as William Palmer of Worcester College, Charles Ogilvie of Balliol and Vaughan Thomas of Corpus. In Hurrell Froude's idiosyncratic parlance, such men as Palmer, for all their rigid High-Church principles and detestation of liberalism in all its forms, were 'Zs'— conservative, Protestant High-Churchmen as distinct from the Tractarians themselves, for whom he claimed the title 'Apostolicals' and code-name 'Ys', both of whom were distinguished from the Evangelicals or 'Xs'.[60] A follower and later annalist of the Movement, William Copeland, was entirely justified in insisting on the importance of keeping 'the Movement, which was from within, as clear as possible from the external circumstances, with which it came into contact'.[61] Palmer was always nervous about the publication of the Tracts and repeatedly advised caution and a committee of revision to avoid 'unguarded expressions'.[62] Such caution was regarded with increasing impatience by Froude, who counselled Newman to 'throw the "Zs" overboard'.[63]

The Tractarians were happy to avail themselves of support from the 'Zs' in the early years, for this lent the Movement influence in the important constituency of country parishes.[64] None the less, the Tractarians remained determined to shape the Movement in their own way and on their own terms. The church coalition of resistance to state power in 1833 was essentially different from the unity of church parties in the 1820s, whose position rested on the support of the state and the maintenance of the status quo. For a time the uneasy coalition of 'Zs' and 'Ys' held, their inner differences remaining concealed so long as the common threat of a radicalized Whig government appeared potent. Once the threat of radicalism receded, the coalition began to fall apart.

The differences were as much psychological as initially overtly theological, consisting in what Newman in his *Apologia* summed up as 'the principle of personality'. For Newman, men like Palmer and other Oxford 'Zs' lacked 'any insight into the force of personal influence and congeniality of thought in carrying out a religious theory, a condition which Froude and I considered essential to any true success in the stand which had to be made against liberalism'. Palmer had too many establishment connections, among 'high church dignitaries, archdeacons, London rectors, and the like'.[65]

This mentality gave the Tractarians a real sense of detachment from the University of the seniors, notably that close-knit and aloof oligarchy the

---

[60] Froude, *Remains* i. 429.

[61] W. J. Copeland to the Warden of Keble College, 22 Sept. 1879, KCA MS E 82.

[62] W. Palmer to A. P. Perceval, 23 Aug. 1833, PHL LBV 14/6 (transcript); cf W. Palmer to A. P. Perceval, 6 Jan. 1841, LBV 14/16.

[63] R. H. Froude to J. H. Newman, 17 Nov. 1833, in *LDN* iv. 112–13; cf J. H. Newman to J. W. Bowden, 13 Nov. 1833, ibid. 98–9.

[64] J. H. Newman to R. I. Wilberforce, 29 Oct. 1833, OCL 1013.

[65] Newman, *Apologia*, 47; W. Ward, *William George Ward and the Oxford Movement* (1889), 53.

heads of houses. They were always wary of bowing to committees of supposedly 'sound, safe men', always ready to appeal to 'grass-roots' feeling among the 'juniors' over 'men of rank and station'. Of the utmost significance in this context was Newman's later avowal in the *Apologia*: 'Living movements do not come of committees, nor are great ideas worked out through the post, even though it had been the penny post.'[66] In his eyes, official bodies such as the Hebdomadal Board stood for inertia and a debilitating conservatism.

In the *Apologia*, Newman described how the traditional pedagogic relationship of tutor and pupil was personalized by himself and his immediate followers in a way that fostered the spread of Tractarian ideas and principles.[67] Largely unencumbered by official responsibilities in the University, the Tractarian leaders, as young men, were well placed to influence those younger still, giving an immediacy and depth to their personal religious impact on undergraduates and junior resident graduates. The Movement captivated the junior university largely because of the peculiar, personal nature of Newman's advocacy and the discipleship which, albeit unconsciously, he fostered. Followers hung on his words, and even imitated his gait and gestures. 'Credo in Newmannum' was to become the watchword for a generation of undergraduates and younger MAs. If the country clergy initially saw in the Movement a conservative force, the junior university tended rather to be moved by the appeal of Tractarianism as a genuinely counter-revolutionary movement, in its widest spiritual, doctrinal, and intellectual aspects.

By 1836 Philip Shuttleworth, the anti-Tractarian Warden of New College, noted that 'our undergraduates I fear are much bitten by the self-mortifying spirit of Newman and Pusey'.[68] Three years later the Vice-Chancellor, A. T. Gilbert, complained of the influence which Newman was exerting from the pulpit of St Mary's, which, Gilbert alleged, Newman was using as 'more of an organ for propagating his views among those who are educating for the Church, than the plain instruction of an ordinary congregation'.[69] This influence was often moral and ethical rather than doctrinal: many who came under Newman's spell were to remain aloof from the characteristic doctrinal shibboleths of the Movement. Some of the testimonies to the power of Newman's preaching came from those who were never in any sense 'Tractarian'. 'After hearing these sermons you might come away still not believing the tenets peculiar to the High Church system,' J. C. Shairp

---

[66] Newman, *Apologia*, 46.
[67] Ibid. 132–4.
[68] Bodl. MS Eng. hist. c. 1033, fo 230.
[69] A. T. Gilbert to Wellington, 26 Dec. 1839, SUL 2/250/65. According to an undergraduate contemporary, however, Newman's University Sermons attracted doctors of divinity and masters of arts more than undergraduates. P. Le Page Renouf to his father, 7 May 1841, PCA 69/9/1/25.

recalled, 'but you would be harder than most men if you did not feel more than ever ashamed of coarseness, worldliness, if you did not feel the truth of things of faith brought closer to the soul.'[70] The influence even touched future liberals of the Arnoldian school. In the case of Frederick Temple, there were 'legacies of the [Oxford] school which he never lost—an awe and reverence about his religion and worship which all could see, and the sense of a supernatural presence which inspired them'.[71]

The Tractarian ethos owed much to its Oxford setting. The absence of a parallel movement at Cambridge is striking, since the strength of the 'orthodox' party there in the period 1790–1830 is well attested;[72] the 'Hackney Phalanx' had closer ties with Cambridge than Oxford. Moreover, Hugh James Rose, who, of all the so-called 'Zs', was probably closest in spirit and sympathy to the Oxford Tractarians, had been Christian Advocate at Cambridge in the 1820s and one of the first to sound the alarm in defence of the Church. In fact, while it is true that largely through the ministry and preaching of Charles Simeon, Cambridge Evangelicals were a far more powerful and influential party than their Oxford counterparts,[73] the old High-Church party remained dominant in both places. But Cambridge was to experience no equivalent manifestation of religious revival. Joseph Romilly's diaries during the 1830s contain several unflattering references to occasional 'Puseyite' sermons in the university pulpit, usually from visiting preachers, but no indication of an equivalent groundswell of junior support for the Movement as at Oxford. Romilly could express relief that what he called 'the Newmania sect at Oxford' had made so small an inroad on the sister university, save for individual supporters such as W. H. Mill and J. J. Blunt, Lady Margaret Professor of Divinity, and younger followers such as Pusey's correspondents W. J. Irons and John Fuller Russell.[74]

Part of the explanation may lie in Cambridge's very different ethos and, to some extent, physical character. The sheer size of Cambridge's biggest colleges, Trinity and St John's—Trinity had twice as many undergraduates as Oxford's largest college, Christ Church—may have made it more difficult to establish there that very personal, 'pastoral' relationship of tutor to pupil that Newman and his allies so effectively used to inculcate moral and religious influence at Oxford. It was possible at Cambridge for individual religious leaders to emerge and sway men, yet the tutors never came under

[70] J. C. Shairp, *John Keble* (1866), 17. See also Mountstuart E. Grant Duff, *Notes from a Diary, 1873–1881* (1898) ii. 121.

[71] *Memoir of Archbishop Temple*, ed. E. G. Sandford (2 vols 1906) ii. 486–7.

[72] A. M. C. Waterman, 'The Cambridge "via media" in late-Georgian Anglicanism', *Journal of Ecclesiastical History* xlii (July 1991), 419–36.

[73] D. A. Winstanley, *Early Victorian Cambridge* (1940), 18–28; V. H. H. Green, *Religion at Oxford and Cambridge* (1964), 222–54.

[74] *Romilly's Cambridge Diary, 1832–1842*, ed. J. P. T. Bury (1967), 158. See also W. J. S. Simpson, *The Contribution of Cambridge to the Anglo-Catholic Revival* (1933), esp. 15–33.

Simeon's influence to the extent they came under Newman's at Oxford. 'At Oxford the tutors endeavour to bias the mind by authority—at Cambridge by evidence,' observed an anti-Tractarian polemicist.[75] The different intellectual traditions and curricular emphasis of Cambridge were undoubtedly significant. The bias of Cambridge theology was towards the evidential divinity of the school of Paley and Tomline, rather than to the patristic studies favoured at Oxford.[76] The High-Church intellectual heritage at Oxford had never fully embraced the Paleian emphasis on utility and natural reason, preferring instead to accord a high place to the study of Aldrich's logic textbook and Bishop Butler's *Analogy of Religion*. Butler's moral philosophy, rooted in Aristotelianism, tended to permeate Oxford's system of education, leaving an indelible mark on Gladstone as well as Keble, Froude and Newman. Aristotle was especially praised for grasping that classic Tractarian insight that mere 'head-knowledge' was not enough, that 'heart-knowledge' was essential. The Balliol tutor Frederick Oakeley later pointed out the tendency of Oxford's Aristotelian bias to make men's minds more receptive than at Cambridge to Tractarianism:

The Aristotelian ethics, with the Christian philosophy of Bishop Butler as their commentary and supplement, entered into the academical education of all the more cultivated minds of Oxford, and contributed, in a pre-eminent degree, to form their character and regulate their tone...None can read Mr. Froude's 'Remains', for instance, without seeing that, with him, and with those with whom he corresponded, the ethical system of Oxford had exercised no small influence in the formation of mental habits...constantly he used to appeal to this great moral teacher of antiquity ('Old Stole', as he used playfully to call him), against the shallow principles of the day.[77]

In 1836 F. D. Maurice drew a comparison between the Platonism of Cambridge and the Aristotelianism of Oxford, symbolized by Coleridge, on the one hand, who was to influence certain prominent Cambridge figures, and Newman, whom he described as 'an eminent Aristotelian divine', on the other.[78] Sometimes the poetic and Romantic sensitivity of Tractarian theo-

---

[75] *The Life and Defence of the Conduct of the Venerable and Calumniated Edward Bonner, Bishop of London: by a Tractarian British Critic* (1842), p. v; L. Stephen, *Sketches from Cambridge* (1865), 13.

[76] M. M. Garland, *Cambridge before Darwin: the ideal of a liberal education, 1800–1860* (1980), 52–9; D. L. Lemahiu, *The Mind of William Paley* (Lincoln, Nebr. 1976), 152–83; A. M. C. Waterman, *Revolution, Economics and Religion: Christian Political Economy, 1798–1833* (1991), 182–3.

[77] Oakeley, *Historical Notes on the Tractarian Movement*, 180; F. Oakeley, *Remarks on the Study of Aristotelian and Platonic Ethics, as a Branch of the Oxford System of Education* (1837), 26–9. Peter Maurice, chaplain of Jesus, considered Tractarianism 'the natural result' of Oxford's Aristotelian studies: *The Ritualism of Oxford Popery: a letter to Dr MacBride* (1867), 111.

[78] F. D. Maurice, *Moral and Metaphysical Philosophy* (1882) i. 182; F. D. Maurice, *Has the Church, or the State, the Power to Educate the Nation? A course of lectures* (1839), 68. In that Newman had been concerned more with the Neoplatonists than with Plato, Maurice was hardly exaggerating. For the contrast between Oxford and Cambridge in Platonic studies see p. 23–4.

logy gave it a Platonic flavour, largely through the influence of the Alexandrian Platonists, whom Newman studied so attentively. The epistemology of Tractarian thought was, however, primarily Aristotelian. As Newsome has observed, Newman and other Tractarian leaders might have been 'born' Platonists, but became Aristotelians through their Oxford education.[79]

By assigning pre-eminence to mathematical attainments, Cambridge, in the eyes of Oxford Tractarians, shared the Noetic fault of exalting the intellect at the expense of moral example and religious truth: Cambridge, moreover, had fatally compromised with the forces of latitudinarianism by allowing Dissenters to matriculate as members of the University. George Moberly, fellow and tutor of Balliol, compared the state of religious instruction in the two universities: 'how different is their religious system from ours. In our colleges a Roman Catholic, or Socinian, would feel their doctrines denied more or less directly every day of their lives. In the regular course of our religious reading, every form of dissent would in turn be exposed and refuted. We have instituted, and we wish to perfect, a higher system of religious instruction than is there possible.'[80] Cambridge was in no position to take a vanguard position in the real counter-revolution to the forces of liberalism and secularity: that lead, as the Tractarians believed, belonged to Oxford alone. As Newman put it, 'Let Cambridge wish us well, and cheer us to our work. We have at present the post of danger and honour; it may be hers another day!'[81] The zeal and earnestness which the Tractarians diverted to their own use in Oxford ran at Cambridge into the channel of Arnoldian liberalism, and so to the Broad-Church school of F. D. Maurice, Connop Thirlwall, Julius Hare and Adam Sedgwick. Though this school did have some temperamental affinities with Tractarianism, drawing inspiration from seventeenth-century Cambridge Platonism and Coleridgean influences, the 'Cambridge Movement' proved uncongenial to fastidious Oxford Tractarian tastes. And for Tractarians like Froude it was not long before the term 'to Cambridgize' entered their vocabulary, carrying the same force of opprobrium as 'to protestantize' or 'to Miltonize'.[82]

[79] D. Newsome, *Two Classes of Men: Platonism and English Romantic thought* (1974), 62–72. According to Jeune (*Studies of Oxford Vindicated* (1845) 15) some attributed Tractarian errors to Plato's seductive imagination. As the same people thought Bishop Butler equally blameworthy their testimony against Plato should be treated with reserve. Hurrell Froude admired some, but by no means all, of Plato: *LDN* ii. 349.

[80] G. Moberly, *A Few Thoughts on the Proposed Admission of Dissenters into the University of Oxford* (1834), 14; cf W. Sewell, *The Attack upon the University of Oxford in a Letter to Earl Grey* (2nd edn 1834), 36.

[81] J. H. Newman to H. J. Rose, 17 Mar. 1834, in *LDN* iv. 209. Newman contrasted 'the exemplary sobriety and decorum' of the Oxford Union with the supposed licence and rampant liberalism of its Cambridge counterpart: ibid. 210.

[82] J. H. Newman to R. H. Froude, 14 June 1834, in *LDN* iv. 278. See also Newman's comment: 'These [Cambridge] fellows take up everything as a matter of literature—and their opinions come and go like Spring fashions': J. H. Newman to C. Cornish, 28 Dec. 1838, in *LDN* vi. 363.

The challenge to Anglican hegemony in the universities provided the immediate rallying-point for the Tractarian Movement. Newman almost welcomed the liberal assault on the status quo: 'I have all along been triumphing at our enemies being blunderers enough to attack the *Universities*, which are the best organised, the most popularly constituted of our ecclesiastical institutions, and most intelligible to the nation.'[83] The earliest challenge to the Anglican religious and legal monopoly of university education at Oxford and Cambridge, albeit indirectly, had come in 1825 with the foundation of a non-denominational University of London, inspired by the Whig politician and Benthamite Henry Brougham.[84] Oxford put up a bitter rearguard resistance to the demands of this new institution in Gower Street for corporate university status conferred by royal charter.[85] This campaign was conducted as vigorously by the conservative 'Church and state' old guard in the University as by the embryonic Tractarian party. Unlike subsequent anti-liberal campaigns, it was led from above. As early as 1828 Wellington had presided over what was, in effect, a great protest meeting, and in 1834 his call to the University for resistance to London's charter delighted the Tractarians.[86] The overwhelming conservative majority in Oxford insisted that a 'University' of London could not be chartered unless it taught the religion of the Thirty-nine Articles. Without teaching theology such an institution could not pretend to teach universal knowledge and could not call itself a university. As counsel for the University before a hearing of the Privy Council, the former Attorney-General, Sir Charles Wetherell, used precisely the arguments that would soon find expression in Tractarian claims on behalf of the University's rights and definitions of her status. Like the Tractarians, the Protestant constitutionalist Wetherell maintained that Oxford degrees were no mere badges of intellectual attainment or proof of knowledge, but the mark of a Christian, and specifically Church of England, education.[87]

A new challenge was represented by the introduction of a bill in the House of Commons by the Unitarian MP for the southern division of Lancashire, G. W. Wood, to allow the admission of Dissenters into the universities and to abrogate religious tests. A revised bill proposed to abolish subscription at matriculation and on taking any degree, but left intact the right of each college to exclude undergraduates who would not attend chapel. Wood's bill passed its third reading in the Commons by a large majority on 28 July 1834. Presented to the Lords by the radical Earl of Radnor, it was strenuously opposed by Wellington and the Duke of Glou-

---

[83] J. H. Newman to R. H. Froude, 14 June 1834, in *LDN* iv. 278.
[84] C. New, *The Life of Henry Brougham to 1830* (1961), 366.
[85] OUA WP/γ/24(5), fo 10, HBM 17 Feb. 1834. *The Times* 23 June 1828, supple. 1c;
[86] J. H. Newman to J. W. Bowden, 14 Mar. 1834, in *LDN* iv. 205.
[87] OUA MR/8/2/2.

cester, Chancellor of Cambridge, and ultimately defeated by a majority of 102.

Oxford Churchmen had been alerted to the threat to religious tests even before the introduction of Wood's bill. A petition to Parliament had been signed by sixty-three resident members of Cambridge University, including two heads, nine professors and eleven tutors, calling for the admission of Dissenters there to degrees in arts, law and medicine. In fact Oxford fears about Cambridge liberalism proved exaggerated, for although the petitioners included such distinguished names as Professor Adam Sedgwick, they were very much a minority at Cambridge. It was only because they had despaired of any success in their university senate that the petitioners had appealed over its head to Parliament.[88] In response to the Cambridge campaign and Wood's bill, it was the Regius Professor of Divinity, a moderate High-Churchman, Edward Burton, who was at the apparent forefront of organiz-ing meetings of protest at Oxford. A committee was set up consisting of Burton, the Lady Margaret Professor, Godfrey Faussett, and William Sewell, as well as Pusey and Newman. A declaration of 'Members of the University immediately connected with the instruction and discipline of the place' was drawn up against any alteration of subscription or admission of Dissenters, and signed by most Oxford tutors. A declaration of approval and concur-rence was then signed by twenty-five heads and forty-one private tutors, more than 1,900 of the 2,519 members of Convocation, over 2,000 parents and guardians of undergraduates then in residence, by 1,050 to 1,200 of the undergraduates themselves and, finally, by many thousands of parishioners in the nation at large.[89] The declaration was taken to embody the Universi-ty's official view; and Oxford's cause was popularized to a remarkable degree through the medium of newspapers, magazines and the extensive parochial network. The young Gladstone was deputized to rally the Christ Church MPs in its support. 'I never remember any occasion on which so strong or unanimous a feeling has been shown in Oxford,' Burton told the Chancellor, Wellington.[90] Six out of ninety tutors did not sign the original declaration, and there were rumours of a counter-declaration drawn up by Arnold and circulated by Bonamy Price from Rugby,[91] while Baden Powell, by now an advanced liberal, published a leaflet of *Reasons for not Joining in the Declaration*. In the end 'all the recusants came in' except two, while even such notorious liberals as Philip Shuttleworth, Warden of New College, and

---

[88] Winstanley, *Early Victorian Cambridge*, 88–90.
[89] G. Rowley to Wellington, 4 May 1834, in J. Brooke and J. Gandy (eds), *Prime Ministers' Papers: Wellington's political correspondence* (1975) i. 525. During this phase the term 'declara-tion' was used confusingly to denote (1) statements in favour of subscription, and (2) a proposed Declaration of allegiance to the Church of England which should supersede subscription. It is given a capital letter only when used in sense (2).
[90] E. Burton to Wellington, 24 Apr. 1834, in *Wellington's Correspondence* i. 513.
[91] J. H. Newman to R. H. Froude, 14 June 1834, in *LDN* iv. 278.

R. D. Hampden himself signed the declaration. They were encouraged by the wording of the declaration, which some Tractarians regretted had not put the case more strongly.[92]

The great Tory demonstration at the formal installation of Wellington as Chancellor in June 1834 seemed to be the fitting climax to a remarkable year in which the 'Tracts for the Times' could be viewed as only one manifestation of a much wider revival of 'church spirit' at Oxford.[93] Misgivings about the suitability of Wellington were for the time being forgotten. If Lord Holland had occasion to lament Wellington's assumption of 'a much more decided tone of high church politicks', Newman took comfort from signs of improvement in the Chancellor: 'He now sees with his eyes, what the narrow circle of town life could not inform him, the keenness and energy, and the diffusive and expansive force, and the actual wide reception of principles which are in London dead, and to a London inhabitant visionary...The Duke will gain good (I trust) from being among us.'[94] Oxford was to be the symbol of a counter-revolution from within the Church against her liberal enemies.

Tractarian tactics now lay in keeping up the momentum of the subscription controversy. 'Having established a raw, our game is to keep it from healing,' Newman confided.[95] The great bulk of the pamphlet literature which stirred the controversy emanated from the Tractarian camp. For the first of many occasions over the next few years, the university authorities lost control of events to the 'juniors', now effectively under Tractarian direction, as the leadership of the Hebdomadal Board was thrown off. The heads of houses were not consulted and, like Wellington, had reservations about the direction in which the coalition of 'juniors' were pushing matters. Nevertheless, the Board had lamely to yield to the clamour it was powerless to control. The heads were only brought to committing themselves to a petition against Wood's bill by a wish to give 'as great an appearance of unanimity as possible'.[96] It took a great deal of swallowing of pride for them to thank Sewell and Vaughan Thomas for their exertions. Wellington complained that his own defensive strategy for the debates in the Lords had been seriously compromised by the abrasive impetuosity of the Oxford agitators.

The publication of Hampden's controversial *Observations on Religious Dissent*, with its bold advocacy of the admission of Dissenters and the

[92] J. F. Christie to W. Palmer jun. (Magdalen), 15 May 1834, LPL MS 2837, fo 13.

[93] *The Correspondence and Diaries of the Late Rt. Hon. John Wilson Croker*, ed. L. T. Jennings (2 vols 1884) ii. 225–9; cf H. Twiss, *The Public and Private Life of Lord Chancellor Eldon, with selections from his correspondence* (3 vols 1844) iii. 227–32.

[94] *The Holland House Diaries, 1831–1840: the diary of Henry Richard Vassall Fox, third Lord Holland*, A. D. Kriegel, ed. (1977), 321; J. H. Newman to R. H. Froude, 14 June 1834, in *LDN* iv. 268. Cf R. Jenkyns to G. W. Hall, 18 Jan. 1834, PCA 60/11/36.

[95] J. H. Newman to R. H. Froude, 14 June 1834, in *LDN* iv. 270.

[96] G. Rowley to Wellington, 4 May 1834, in *Wellington's Correspondence* i. 525.

abolition of all doctrinal tests on religious and not merely tactical grounds, marked the first breach in Oxford's hitherto united front against her external liberal assailants.[97] The Tractarians dreaded giving Hampden publicity, but once his pamphlet went into a second edition, they felt bound to assail it. Newman wrote a sharp letter to Hampden, protesting at his pamphlet marking the 'beginning of hostilities in the University', and lamenting 'that by its appearance the first step has been taken towards interrupting that peace and mutual good understanding which has prevailed so long in this place, and which if once seriously disturbed will be succeeded by dissensions the more intractable because justified in the minds of those who resist innovation by a feeling of imperative duty'.[98]

The Hebdomadal Board was coming under increasing pressure from another quarter to do something about undergraduate subscription. Wellington was finding it hard to justify in the House of Lords Oxford's practice of making youths as young as 16 subscribe to articles of religion far beyond their understanding, and in April 1834 he urged the necessity for some form of strategic retreat.[99] In his view the likelihood of continued 'inquisitorial jealousy of the institutions of the country' by Parliament made such action pressing. In November 1833 Philip Shuttleworth had suggested some substitute for the existing form, but his plan had been rejected by the Board by 14 votes to 7.[100] Now, a year later, the heads disregarded their Chancellor's advice and voted by 10 to 7 against change. Edward Cardwell, Wellington's principal correspondent on the Board after the Vice-Chancellor, expressed regret,[101] but the Chancellor was furious and proceeded to lecture the heads on not knowing 'what was passing in the world'. Continued pressure had the desired effect and the heads caved in. The form of Declaration in lieu of subscription was brought forward, and just carried at the Board by 11 to 10, though four of the five absentees at the crucial meeting on 10 November, according to Cardwell, would have opposed the motion.[102] The worst fears and suspicions of the Tractarians were confirmed, and their indignation at the supineness and vacillations of 'these trumpery heads' boiled over.[103]

Just as in the wider national sphere, the Tractarians were beginning to despair of further reliance on establishment and the Church–state connection, and to preach a falling-back upon unfettered 'Apostolical principles'

---

[97] J. H. Newman to H. J. Rose, 20 Aug. 1834, in *LDN* iv. 323.

[98] J. H. Newman to R. D. Hampden, 28 Nov. 1834, in *LDN* iv. 371.

[99] Wellington to E. Cardwell, 22 Apr. 1834, Wellington to G. Rowley, 27 Aug. 1834, in *Wellington's Correspondence* i. 512, 646–8; Wellington to E. Cardwell, 3 Mar. 1835, SUL MS Wellington 2/246/22; Wellington to G. Rowley, 18 June 1835, SUL MS Wellington 2/246/74.

[100] OUA WP/γ/24(5), fo 2, HBM 11 Nov. 1833.

[101] E. Cardwell to Wellington, 3 Nov. 1834, in *Wellington's Correspondence* i. 714–15.

[102] E. Cardwell to Wellington, 10 Nov. 1834, in *Wellington's Correspondence* i. 726; J. H. Newman to R. H. Froude, 14 Nov. 1834, in *LDN* iv. 360.

[103] F. Christie to W. Palmer jun., 25 Nov. 1834, LPL MS 2837, fo 17.

alone, so the sudden turn of events within the University at the end of 1834 began to engender in them for the first time a sense of 'separateness', of being increasingly a party within rather than the actual representatives of the 'official' University. In this spirit, Newman confided to Keble,

I am sure no harm (please God) can happen to Apostolical principles. If the University is liberalized, those who hold them will only be so much more thrown into relief, detached from all those secular connections and influences with which it is their duty now to keep united—Nothing would tend more to the spreading of the Truth among those who could 'receive it', than for it to be thrown out and embodied in a party.[104]

The 'apostolical' message of the early Tracts seemed more relevant than ever and needed to be acted upon in the present crisis: 'The innovators urge that "our friends in both Houses of Parliament say they wish to defend us but find our present position so difficult!" Does not this illustrate our Tract No. 19? Thus, in order that our defenders may pass well in the eyes of men of the world, the Truth is to be given up.'[105] The Tractarians continued for a while to rest their hopes for Oxford on the efforts of their Chancellor in his battles in the Lords,[106] but under his influence the Board pressed ahead in March 1835 with its proposal to substitute a simple test of conformity to the Church of England at matriculation in lieu of subscription to the Articles.[107] This coincided ominously with the reintroduction of Radnor's bill in March 1835, and the virtual certainty that the Whigs would be back in power within a few weeks. Still in alliance with conservative Evangelicals like John Hill and Protestant High-Churchmen like Vaughan Thomas and Sewell, the Tractarians more openly set the pace and tone of opposition than they had in the previous year. A committee began meeting in Pusey's rooms in Christ Church, and a new declaration was drawn up and signed by eighty members of Convocation before the end of March.

Oxford's 'parliamentary friends', especially Wellington, were again embarrassed by the passions roused. Non-residents were called up from the country, and, amidst rowdy scenes, the measure was thrown out in Convocation on 20 May by 459 to 57.[108] The heads were utterly humiliated. Completely out of touch with the mood of the 'juniors', Wellington still remained confident that his view of the expediency of substituting a Declaration for subscription was in accord with the wishes of the majority of Convocation. It took repeated delicate hints from Rowley and Cardwell to convince him that this impression was erroneous.[109] Reformers on the Board had succeeded

[104] J. H. Newman to S. Wilberforce, 10 Nov. 1834, in *LDN* iv. 355.
[105] J. H. Newman to J. Keble, 10 Nov. 1834, in *LDN* iv. 353.
[106] J. H. Newman to J. W. Bowden, 1 Dec. 1834, in *LDN* iv. 372–3.
[107] E. Cardwell to Wellington, 23 Mar. 1835, SUL MS Wellington 2/246/38.
[108] G. Rowley to Wellington, 20 May 1835, SUL MS Wellington 2/246/56.
[109] G. Rowley to Wellington, 15 June 1835, SUL MS Wellington 2/246/73.

in blocking a proposal to petition against Lord Radnor's bill, but the Tractarians, determined to press home their advantage, rallied the MAs. A memorial called on the Vice-Chancellor to bring the Board to a reconsideration of its earlier decision. Again the Board completely capitulated.[110] The final triumph was achieved with the throwing-out of Radnor's bill in the Lords in July 1835. The *de jure* governors of the University, the Chancellor and the heads, had been ignominiously brushed aside, and forced to follow lamely in the wake of the Tractarians, who, as the mouthpiece of junior feeling, could be said by the summer of 1835 to be almost its *de facto* rulers. Their achievement fell little short of a democratic revolution in Oxford.

The violence of the reaction to such an apparently modest measure exposed the Tractarians to charges of malevolent party spirit and deliberate subversion of the university constitution. It was made repeatedly clear that the great bulk of those who favoured the proposal did not approve of the admission of Dissenters.[111] The Board insisted that the Declaration was to be 'neither more nor less exclusive than the present test' of subscription.[112] In the face of Pusey's protest that 'the character of our church' was at stake,[113] Hawkins insisted that there was to be no alteration or relaxation of principles at all; only a change of form, so as 'to clear our system from objections'.[114] Benjamin Symons, Warden of Wadham and a prominent Evangelical, defended the alteration on conservative grounds, arguing that the Declaration represented a tightening rather than a relaxation of doctrinal safeguards.[115] A large group of essentially moderate High-Churchmen such as C. T. Longley and Edward Denison were prepared to abandon subscription to the Articles at matriculation and graduation so long as existing usages concerning religious discipline and instruction remained untouched.[116] Significantly there were several, including those on the Board, who did not vote in favour because the proposal did not go far enough.[117]

---

[110] E. Bayly to Lord Holland, 16 June 1835, BL Add. MS 51597, fo 194; Lord Holland to Lord Radnor, 17 June 1835, PHL Rad. 1/2/24; E. Cardwell to Wellington, 20 June 1835, SUL MS Wellington 2/246/85; OUA WP/γ/24(5), fo 56, HBM 20 June 1835.

[111] E. Cardwell to Wellington, 19 Apr. 1834, in *Wellington's Correspondence* i. 508.

[112] OUA WP/γ/24(5), fo 50, HBM 16, 23 Mar. 1835.

[113] [E. B. Pusey], *Questions Respectfully Addressed to Members of Convocation on the Subjoined Declaration which is Proposed as a Substitute for the Subscription to the Thirty-Nine Articles at Matriculation* (1835).

[114] [E. Hawkins], *Oxford Matriculation Statutes: answers to the 'Questions Addressed to Members of Convocation' by a bachelor of divinity, with brief notes upon church authority* (1835), 16–17.

[115] [B. Symons], *A Letter to a Non-resident Friend upon Subscription to the Thirty-Nine Articles at Matriculation* (1835), 1–2, 7. F. D. Maurice's view that the proposed declaration would prove more offensive to Dissenters than the existing subscription (*Subscription no Bondage* (1835), p. ii) was shared by Peel: *Parl. Deb.* 20 June 1834, 3S xxiv. 705–6.

[116] C. T. Longley to Lord Radnor, 30 Dec. 1834, PHL Rad. 1/2/8; E. Denison, *A Review of the State of the Question Respecting the Admission of Dissenters to the University* (1835), 49–50.

[117] E. Bayly to Lord Holland, 16 June 1835, BL Add. MS 51597, fo 194.

Much of the vehemence which the Tractarians showed stemmed from fears that there existed a conspiracy to liberalize the University. These had more foundation than has sometimes been allowed. Three members of the Board, Shuttleworth, Hampden and the liberal Proctor Edmund Bayly, were in clandestine correspondence with that arch-apostle of philosophical whiggery Lord Holland. Hampden's correspondence with the Earl of Radnor also reveals the extent of the collusion of Oxford liberals with leading Whigs. All three broke the secrecy of the Board's deliberations, keeping Holland informed of all the latest developments and expressions of feeling of individual heads and others, and even seeking advice concerning the course of action the government wished them to take.[118]

Of the three correspondents, Shuttleworth was certainly the most moderate and anxious to advise the greatest caution and ministerial sensitivity to university feeling. He warned Holland that he 'knew only of two persons in the whole University who are willing to see Lord Radnor's bill carried to the full extent of its provisions'.[119] Shuttleworth contended that 'extreme propositions' for change would only unite Oxford opinion 'in support of a system which will not admit of vindication in some important particulars'.[120] Bayly was less cautious, undertaking to exercise his proctorial veto at the behest of the Whig government against any petition put to Convocation opposing the Radnor bill.[121] Of the three, Hampden was the most ready to subordinate the cause of the University to that of the Whig ministry. Unwilling to forgive Convocation for throwing out the Declaration, Hampden became convinced that, since the University would never act voluntarily, external pressure should be brought to bear. He told Radnor on the day after the Convocation vote:

I have been anxious that the University should make a change in the matter of the Tests by its own act. But there is a great reason to fear from what has passed on this occasion, that any such thing is quite hopeless, and that we must therefore be eventually indebted for the benefit . . . to other hands. There is a very active party here bent on resisting any alteration of our practice with the most determined enthusiasm and a clamour is raised against those who express an opinion in favour of it.[122]

Radnor passed on this first-hand diagnosis to Lord Holland, who hoped that the University and Convocation would keep up its show of implacable opposition; the public and Parliament would be provoked and the way opened to external interference.[123] In similar vein, Arnold actually looked

[118] The irregularity of these disclosures was admitted by both Bayly and Shuttleworth: BL Add. MS 51597, fos 146–7, 196.

[119] P. Shuttleworth to Lord Holland, 19 June 1835, BL Add. MS 51597, fos 146–7.

[120] Shuttleworth to Lord Holland, 21 June 1835, BL Add. MS 51597, fos 148–9.

[121] E. Bayly to Lord Holland, 18 June 1835, BL Add. MS 51597, fo 196.

[122] R. D. Hampden to Lord Radnor, 21 May 1835, PHL Rad. 1/2/18.

[123] Lord Holland to Lord Radnor, 23 June 1835, PHL Rad. 1/2/28.

forward to the defeat of the Declaration proposal in Convocation in May 1835, precisely because he was 'convinced that Oxford now is like Oxford in the 16th century, and will never be reformed effectually, except from without. I often think of the instructive fact, that the Reformation was carried by a Reforming Government supported by a small minority of the clergy, against the majority of the clergy, the country gentlemen and the populace.'[124]

Although the Tractarians were only one element in the coalition fighting the liberal model of university reform, their intellectual contribution was the most crucial and lasting. Most defenders of the University, including moderate liberals and advocates of limited reform such as Hawkins, took it as axiomatic that the universities were corporations which had 'a right to expect that their charters shall not be interfered with, unless they can be shown to have been transgressed'.[125] All other divisions could be set aside in the defence of self-government. 'I think there is no one point on which all are agreed', Vice-Chancellor Rowley informed Wellington, 'except in deprecating the interference of the legislature in a matter of internal regulation.'[126] Noetics such as Hawkins argued strongly against parliamentary interference on principle,[127] and until Hampden's change of heart in 1835, Arnold alone was radical on this point. It was the Tractarians, however, who made the most extravagant assertions of the independence of the University. If Parliament made tests illegal, Newman contended, the Vice-Chancellor as the executor of the University's own statutes was bound to continue to impose them until specifically rescinded by Convocation. And even if the University were to be empowered by new statutes to admit Dissenters, the power and right of the colleges to exclude them would remain.[128]

The supporters of Wood's and Radnor's bills, on the other hand, constantly argued that the universities were national bodies, and acted on the principle of 'free admission to the national universities for all members of the nation'.[129] The only sense in which the great bulk of Oxford Churchmen would admit that the universities were national institutions was 'in so far as they were connected with the National church', but 'in no other point of view were they to be regarded as national institutions, for it could not be

---

[124] T. Arnold to R. D. Hampden [nd], in *Some Memorials of R. D. Hampden*, ed. H. Hampden (1871), 38.

[125] Denison, *Review*, 6; *The Speech of Henry, Lord Bishop of Exeter on Occasion of a Petition from Certain Members of the Senate of Cambridge University, presented to the House of Commons on April 21, 1834* (1834), 11.

[126] G. Rowley to Wellington, 21 June 1835, SUL 2/246/87.

[127] [E. Hawkins], *A Letter to the Earl of Radnor upon the Oaths, Dispensations and Subscriptions to the Thirty-Nine Articles at the University of Oxford* (1835), 26.

[128] *Parl. Deb.* 28 July 1834, 3S xxv. 635.

[129] *Eclectic Review* xiii (1835), 266; F. C. Parry, *The Dissenters and the Universities; or, the civil rights of the Dissenters most effectually secured by the erection of a new university* (1835), 6.

pretended even that they were supported by the nation'.[130] The universities were only national in the sense that the Church of England claimed to be; Dissenters could no more be admitted to Oxford *per se* as Dissenters without conformity to some test or doctrinal standard than they could be admitted to the Church of England.[131] An argument that rested on the endowed character of the University and colleges was not unassailable, however. Not all founders had belonged to the Church of England, and there was no liberal taunt more sorely felt or keenly rebutted than the suggestion that consistency demanded the return into Roman Catholic hands of those colleges founded before the Reformation.[132]

Even Oxford's moderate liberals were agreed that 'national' meant 'Anglican'. Hawkins, Longley and Denison, who supported abrogating the matriculation test, could join with Newman and Pusey on this point. They did not dispute what Copleston described as 'the fair right' of 'the colleges and perhaps the University... to require all their members to be conformists to the Church of England'.[133] Most of those who favoured Radnor's bill agreed that Dissenters could only be admitted 'with the full understanding that no abandonment of the present statutes or usages with regard to religious discipline, instruction or examination was to be required or expected'.[134] The more radical Arnoldian liberals such as Bonamy Price, who held to an ideal of religious comprehension within the University as in the Church as a whole, tended to employ essentially prudential arguments. They had little sympathy for the Dissenters as such, and took it for granted that Dissenters would be morally 'improved' by their contact with Churchmen.[135] It was never doubted that Church of England principles, however liberally defined, would continue to hold sway. Altering tests, Hampden admitted, might raise a danger of heterodoxy, but 'the danger is more than counterbalanced by the probability of conformity to ourselves from the ranks of Dissent'.[136]

Thus far, there was no vast gulf of opinion within the University. The Tractarians widened the debate to include not only the meaning and propri-

---

[130] *Parl. Deb.* 1 Aug. 1834, 3S xxv. 881; cf *The Universities and the Dissenters... A letter to Sir R. H. Inglis* (1834), 6; memorandum of the Bishop of Exeter, Aug. 1834, in *Wellington's Correspondence* i. 653–6.

[131] *Quarterly* li (Mar. 1834), 519.

[132] Huber, *English Universities* ii pt 2, pp. 551–2; for a rebuttal of this charge see R. H. Inglis to P. Bliss, 2 July 1833, BL Add. MS 34571, fo 247; cf *The Universities and the Dissenters: substance of a speech delivered in the House of Commons on Wednesday, 26 March, 1834 by Sir Robert Inglis Bart in reference to a petition from certain members of the Senate of the University of Cambridge* (1834), 12.

[133] E. Copleston to E. Hawkins, 24 June 1835, OCL 403.

[134] C. T. Longley to Lord Radnor, 30 Dec. 1834, PHL Rad. 1/2/8.

[135] B. Price to W. E. Gladstone, 30 Apr. 1834, BL Add. MS 44353, fo 130.

[136] R. D. Hampden, *Observations on Dissent* (1834), 38; cf R. D. Hampden to Lord Radnor, 2 June 1835, PHL Rad. 1/2/21.

ety of subscription, but the whole relationship between religion and education. They and their conservative allies had vehemently opposed the ideal of
comprehension expounded in Hampden's *Observations on Dissent* on the
ground that it was tantamount to sanctioning 'indifferentism'. 'How does
Dr Hampden support the proposed change?', Henry Wilberforce asked.

Not on grounds of national, political, or academic expediency; nor yet of abstract
justice; but by arguments purely theological. He would remove the subscription,
because he objects to all tests and creeds as conditions to communion, and sees no
valid reason for any separation between ourselves, and those who 'unhappily' reject
the doctrines of Our Lord's divinity and atonement.[137]

Newman wanted the spectre of doctrinal heterodoxy brought to the forefront of the debate, enabling the Tractarians to stand as defenders of the
Thirty-nine Articles, linking those who supported the relaxation of subscription with the earlier movements of 1772 and 1773 and, by implication,
with the Socinianism and Arianism of the earlier period.[138] By appearing to
be in the vanguard of the defence of doctrinal fundamentals and the 'scriptural truths' enshrined in the Articles, the Tractarians attracted the support
of Evangelicals such as Hill and Symons, and Protestant High-Churchmen
such as Vaughan Thomas and Godfrey Faussett. The cause might be anti-
liberal, but few could doubt that it was also Protestant.

The Tractarian championship of the Articles in 1835 needs some explanation, for Newman was already uneasy with the Articles on theological
grounds, complaining that they 'countenance a vile Protestantism'.[139] The
contradiction was not so great as it first seems. It was not their doctrinal
content, nor even their suitability as barriers of Protestant exclusion, that
mattered. Most Protestant High-Church defenders of existing practice such
as Faussett and Bishop Phillpotts followed the line of the official apology
put forth by Archdeacon Powell in 1757 that the first subscription simply
meant that undergraduates acknowledged a general assent to the Articles
'grounded on the authority of others. And nothing farther I suppose, does
any man conceive to be meant by their subscriptions.'[140] To the Tractarians,
subscription meant much more than this. In a letter to Arthur Perceval,
Newman explained

The advantage of subscription (to my mind) is its witnessing to the principle that
religion is to be approached with a submission of the understanding. Nothing is so
common, as you must know, as for young men to approach serious subjects as
judges—to study them as mere sciences. The study of the Evidences now popular

[137] [H. W. Wilberforce], *The Foundations of the Faith Assailed in Oxford* (1835), 14.
[138] [B. Harrison], *1835 and 1772: the present attack on subscription compared with the last in
a letter to 'a resident member of Convocation'* (1835).
[139] J. H. Newman to R. H. Froude, 13 May 1835, in *LDN* v. 70.
[140] *Speech of Henry, Lord Bishop of Exeter*, 5.

(such as Paley's) encourages this evil frame of mind—the learner is supposed external to the system . . . In an age then, when this great principle is scouted, subscription to the Articles is a memento and protest—and again actually does, I believe, impress upon the minds of the young men the teachable and subdued temper expected of them. They are not to reason, but to obey;—and this quite independently of the degree of accuracy, the wisdom etc. of the Articles themselves. I am no great friends of them—and should rejoice to be able to substitute the Creeds for them.[141]

Thus the Tractarians rested their defence of subscription on the ground that religion was to be approached with a submission of the understanding. While Protestant High-Churchmen regarded the tests as little more than fences of the establishment, the Tractarians bestowed a quasi-sacramental efficacy upon the act of subscription.[142] It was the solemn duty of all members of the University 'to regard her as the sacred ark wherein the truth has been preserved . . . not as sceptical disputants, who would investigate for themselves a new road to the shrine of truth; but as humble and teachable disciples, labouring to ascertain what has been the church's faith and practice'.[143] To tamper with this system of subscription was to strike at the very keystone of the 'catholic' character of university education. But the 'catholic principle' which the Tractarians glorified remained an embarrassment to the University's 'parliamentary friends' like Wellington,[144] and a matter to be explained away even by staunch defenders of the status quo like Bishop Phillpotts.

In the wake of the attempts of Radnor and the liberals to impose the admission of Dissenters and an alteration in the system of undergraduate subscription, the Melbourne government's appointment of the now notorious Hampden as Regius Professor of Divinity, in February 1836, seemed like a deliberate blow against the University. Convinced by Whately and Copleston of Hampden's orthodoxy, Melbourne disregarded Archbishop Howley's own list of candidates, which included Newman and Keble and was headed by Pusey's name. And although it was sometimes alleged that Melbourne acted without knowledge of the state of feeling in Oxford, it is clear from Melbourne's correspondence with both Oxford liberals and Vice-Chancellor Gilbert, whose private protest was curtly rebuffed, that the Prime Minister knew what he was doing.[145] This was a partisan appoint-

[141] J. H. Newman to A. P. Perceval, 11 Jan. 1836, in *LDN* v. 197.
[142] [C. P. Eden], *Self-Protection: the case of the Articles* (1835), 23–4.
[143] [Wilberforce], *Foundations of the Faith Assailed*, 6; cf Oakeley, *Letter to Wellington*, 15–16.
[144] Wellington to E. Cardwell, 22 Apr. 1834, in *Wellington's Correspondence* i. 512.
[145] *Lord Melbourne's Papers*, ed. L. G. Sandars (1890), 497; R. Whately, *Remains of the Late Edward Copleston D.D.* (1854), 55; W. Palmer sen. to W. Palmer jun., 27 Feb. 1836, LPL MS 2834, fo 81; cf J. H. Newman to H. J. Rose, 11 Feb. 1836, in *LDN* v. 231; B. H. Kennedy to G. W. Hall, 30 Mar. 1836, PCA 60/11/36, p. 36; H. A. Woodgate, *Letter to Viscount Melbourne on the Recent Appointment to the Office of Regius Professor of Divinity in Oxford* (1836), 6; B. Harrison to W. E. Gladstone, 8 Mar. 1836, BL Add. MS 44204, fo 83; Melbourne to A. T. Gilbert, 17 Feb. 1836, SUL 2/248/154; R. Whately to E. Hawkins, 15 Mar. 1837, OCL ii. 221.

ment. Hampden, despite his niece and biographer's later assertion that he had no 'party' connections, had strong links with London parliamentary Whigs, and his promotion was viewed in liberal circles as a measure of retaliation at Oxford's Tory High-Church defiance in 1834-5.[146]

Within days of the appointment, a public meeting of members of Convocation had assembled in the common room of Corpus Christi College, and drawn up memorials to the King and the Archbishop of Canterbury, complaining both that Hampden's appointment would have 'disastrous consequences to the soundness of the faith' and that he lacked the essential confidence of the University.[147] The memorial to the Archbishop, which attracted the most signatures, formally charged Hampden with maintaining 'orally and in printed publications doctrines and principles fundamentally opposed to the Church of England'.[148] The feelings of the 'juniors' were reflected in the pressure now brought to bear by MAs on the Hebdomadal Board.[149]

Liberal supporters of Hampden believed that the outcry was fomented at the instigation of the Tractarians.[150] Shuttleworth thought that they had seized on the appointment as giving 'an opportunity of rallying'.[151] The ostensible objection to the appointment was the supposed rationalism of Hampden's Bampton Lectures of 1832. Baden Powell thought that there was little in this objection, and that no substantial argument 'to show the impropriety of the appointment' had been made 'but what is wholly mixed up with the peculiar theology' of the Tract writers.[152] Certainly, the long time-lag between the delivery of the Lectures and the objections raised against them at the moment of the appointment seemed suspicious and gave apparent substance to the liberal charge.[153] The Lectures had not

[146] C. Fox to P. N. Shuttleworth, 25 Feb. 1836, Bodl. MS Eng. hist. c. 1033, fo 12.

[147] Diary of John Hill, 13 Feb. 1836, Bodl. MS St Edmund Hall 67/10, fo 54; cf E. Cardwell to Wellington, 11 Feb. 1836, SUL 2/247/13.

[148] E. Cardwell to Wellington, 15 Feb. 1836, SUL 2/247/22. There was a confident expectation at this stage that Hampden would have to withdraw, and that Denison would be appointed Regius Professor in his stead. See J. F. Christie to W. Palmer jun., 15 Feb. 1836, LPL MS 2837, fo 21; E. Cardwell to Wellington, 11 Feb. 1836, SUL 2/247/13; E. Bayly to Lord Holland, 12 Feb. 1836, BL Add. MS 51597, fos 194-5.

[149] J. H. Newman to E. B. Pusey, 24 Jan. 1836, in *LDN* v. 213-15. Newman's exasperation with the heads was increased by the Board's vote of 20 to 4 against giving Convocation the opportunity to condemn the Bampton Lectures: J. H. Newman to H. J. Rose, 29 Feb. 1836, in *LDN* v. 245; E. Cardwell to Wellington, 29 Feb. 1836, SUL 2/247/35.

[150] *Correspondence between the Rev. Dr Hampden Regius Professor of Divinity in the University of Oxford and the Most Rev. Lord Archbishop of Canterbury* (1838), 11.

[151] P. Shuttleworth to Lord Holland, 1 Mar. 1836, BL Add. MS 51597, fo 136.

[152] Baden Powell, *Remarks on a Letter from the Rev. H. A. Woodgate to Viscount Melbourne, Relative to the Appointment of Dr Hampden* (1836), 4; cf. *Specimens of the Theological Teaching of Certain Members of the Corpus Committee at Oxford* (1836), 3-4, 36-8.

[153] *A Letter to His Grace the Archbishop of Canterbury, Explanatory of the Proceedings at Oxford, on the Appointment of the Present Regius Professor of Divinity, by a member of the University of Oxford* (1836), 4; E. J. Whately, *Life and Correspondence of Richard Whately*

hitherto stood in the way of Hampden's advancement in 1834 to the princi-palship of St Mary Hall, which entitled him to a position on the actual Hebdomadal Board itself, or in 1834 to the chair of moral philosophy.[154] One anti-Hampdenite, Hugh James Rose, regretted that more critical notice had not been taken of the Lectures at the time of delivery.[155] The Tractarian answer was that they had not then wished to give publicity to a work intended for limited readership,[156] and that Hampden's opinions were now rendered dangerous in a way they had not been before, for 'the Bampton Lectures, however unread as they were, and unreadable as they might be...had now the authority of a Regius Professor of Divinity'.[157]

The 'Corpus Parliament', which now co-ordinated the agitation, was the organic descendant of the ad-hoc committee of Protestant High-Church-men, conservative Evangelicals and Tractarians which had met in Pusey's house to direct the anti-liberal campaign over subscription. Among non-Tractarians, it included the Calvinist Evangelical Vice-Principal of St Ed-mund Hall, John Hill; R. L. Cotton, an Evangelical soon to become Provost of Worcester; C. P. Golightly, later to be an inveterate enemy of Tractarian-ism and the Protestant High-Churchman Vaughan Thomas. Moreover, 'se-nior' opinion was better represented in the anti-liberal camp than in 1834-5, with A. T. Gilbert, Principal of Brasenose, and Edward Cardwell, Principal of St Alban Hall, both favouring strong measures. Although Newman was responsible for the Corpus committee's main piece of controversy against Hampden with his *Elucidations*, and Pusey's writings on the subject at-tracted prominence, the Tractarians at most only directed and exploited a protest movement that would have existed without them. An anonymous pamphlet commented on the breadth of the coalition against Hampden: 'what party? Look at the "Record" and "British Magazine". Are they likely to agree on any one point if they can possibly help it? Look through the list of names affixed to the various documents. You will find there specimens of what are termed High churchmen, and the lowest of those who are desig-nated the Low church.'[158] While it held together, this proved to be an irresistible combination.

D.D., Late Archbishop of Dublin (2 vols 1866) i. 390–1; E. Bayly to Lord Holland, 9 Mar. 1836, BL Add. MS 51597, fo 216; *An Elucidation of Mr Woodgate's Pamphlet, in a letter to a friend* (1836), 8; [T. Arnold], 'The Oxford malignants and Mr Hampden', *Ed. Rev.* lxiii (Apr. 1836), 225–7; *The Holland House Diaries*, 344.

[154] *Hampden*, 20–34, 105; *A Letter to His Grace the Archbishop of Canterbury*, 4; Lord Grenville to R. D. Hampden, 20 Apr. 1833, Hampden Controversy 1a; Whately, *Remains of Copleston*, 56–7.

[155] H. J. Rose to W. Hale, 10 Feb. 1836, OCL 134; J. Miller, *Conspectus of the Hampden Case at Oxford* (1836), 14.

[156] [J. H. Newman], *Elucidations of Dr Hampden's Theological Statements* (1836), 3.

[157] Mozley, *Reminiscences* i. 362.

[158] *A Non-Resident M.A.'s Self-Vindication for Attending to Support the Vote of Censure on Dr. Hampden's Writings* (1836), 12.

The Board was now under pressure to petition against Hampden's appointment, and would have carried a resolution to this effect but for Hampden's sudden personal appearance at the meeting, where he voted for himself.[159] Such 'low and vulgar and weak tactics of defence...lowered him in estimation', in the view of one Board member.[160] Attempts to quash further discussion of the matter were defeated,[161] and the Board went ahead with another proposition, namely, the submission to Convocation of a statute depriving the Regius Professor of Divinity of certain powers. Among these were the appointment of select preachers and the right to a seat among the six doctors empowered by statute to judge heresy cases.[162] Hampden refused to compromise. Although his inaugural lecture earned some grudging commendation from a few opponents of his appointment, there was no formal retraction.[163] Some of Hampden's friends on the Board, notably Hawkins, attempted to prove that a friendly interpreter could find Hampden orthodox, but few were convinced. When, on 22 March, Convocation voted on implementation of the statute proposed by the heads, Hampden's supporters could muster no more than thirty votes. E. G. Bayly was then proctor, and exercised his veto to halt the statute,[164] but new proctors came into office in the Easter term and the way was opened for a formal condemnation. In late April 1836 Cardwell presented the same statute as that of 22 March, with minor verbal alterations. The heads voted by 14 to 11 to have the statute promulgated in Convocation on 2 May, despite Hampden's protests.[165] On 5 May, amidst tumultuous scenes, Convocation formally passed the statute by 484 to 94, with no proctorial veto ensuing. The anti-Hampden campaign apparently had run its course and triumphed.

[159] P. Shuttleworth to Lord Holland, 1 Mar. 1836, BL Add. MS 51597, fo 134; R. Hampden to R. Whately, 2 Mar. 1836; *Hampden*, 58; J. H. Newman to F. Christie, 14 Feb. 1836, in *LDN* v. 234.

[160] R. Jenkyns to H. Jenkyns, 14 Mar. 1836, BCA MS Jenkyns VI/A.

[161] E. Bayly to Lord Holland, 4 Mar. 1836, BL Add. MS 51597, fos 206–7; E. Hawkins to C. T. Longley, 9 Mar. 1836, LPL Longley MS i. 109–10.

[162] OUA WP/γ/24(5), fo 75, HBM 7 Mar. 1836; E. Bayly to Lord Holland, 7 Mar. 1836, 11 Mar. 1836, BL Add. MS 51597, fos 212, 217–18.

[163] Hawkins felt that the inaugural lecture had 'pretty well silenced the cry against his personal faith': E. Hawkins to R. Whately, 31 Mar. 1836, OCL MS Hawkins 416. For Evangelical praise of the lecture see J. W. Cunningham to R. D. Hampden, 19 May 1836, OCL MS Hampden Controversy 65. Even Pusey had to admit that the inaugural lecture was 'in direct contradiction with what he before stated': *Mr. Hampden's Past and Present Statements Compared* (1836), 3; R. Jenkyns to H. Jenkyns, 17 Mar. 1836, BCA MS Jenkyns VI/A/1a. Others insisted that the lecture changed nothing: *Does Dr. Hampden's Inaugural Lecture Imply any Change in his Theological Principles?* (1836), 3–5; B. Harrison to W. E. Gladstone, 29 Mar. 1836, BL Add. MS 44204, fo 90.

[164] E. Bayly to Lord Holland, 21 Mar. 1836, BL Add. MS 51597, fos 229–30; E. Cardwell to Wellington, 22 Mar. 1836, SUL 2/247/47; *Hampden*, 68; E. Hawkins to R. Whately, 31 Mar. 1836, OCL 416.

[165] E. Bayly to Lord Holland, Mar. 1836, BL Add. MS 51597, fos 231–2; Lord Holland to P. Shuttleworth, 5 May 1836, Bodl. MS Eng. hist. c. 1033, fo 49; E. Cardwell to Wellington, 5 May 1836, SUL 2/249/66.

Hampden's supporters raised the charge that the proceedings of 5 May had been 'unstatutable'. Lord Holland's secret correspondent on the Board, Edmund Bayly, took the lead in suggesting courses of action to thwart the anti-Hampden campaigners. It was Bayly who argued that the Select Preachers' statute passed by Convocation represented an interference by the University 'with the prerogative of the Crown in depriving it of those rights which have been heretofore annexed to the office of Regius Professor of Divinity'.[166] Hampden sought legal opinion to test the legality of the statute. The Attorney-General, J. Campbell, and Dr Stephen Lushington came down in favour of Hampden on the ground that the passing of the statute violated 'the restrictions imposed by the Laudian Code, and [was] passed by the assumption and exercise of a power which has not been conceded to the University'.[167] The statutes of the University could only be made or altered with the consent of the Crown. This caused Philip Bliss, the University Registrar, to produce the 1759 legal opinion of R. Wilbraham and J. Morton, which upheld the University's freedom to pass or alter statutes without regard to royal authority.[168] Significantly, Melbourne was reluctant to press Hampden's legal case in Parliament, urging Hampden to rest content with standing his ground at Oxford.[169] The University, with the Tractarians in the vanguard, had again repelled a liberal challenge. Yet how much of a triumph really was it, and for whom?

The Hampden controversy represented the zenith of Tractarian political influence within Oxford; and liberals such as Edmund Bayly complained that the Board, in allowing itself to be the subject of Corpus dictation, had 'nullified its own existence as the Initiative of this University' and given way to a democratic agitation.[170] The victory over Hampden proved to be less decisive than the Tractarians had hoped, however. J. A. Cramer, Principal of New Inn Hall, was only one of several on the Board who understood it as a merely temporary and provisional measure, to be rescinded when Hampden had exonerated himself.[171] The great weakness of the censure was its vagueness—nearly all on the Board would go out of their way to insist that no formal charge of heterodoxy was implied. Hawkins challenged the heads to accuse Hampden of heresy, and to institute a full and fair trial.[172] If the

[166] E. Bayly to Lord Holland, 9 Mar. 1836, BL Add. MS 51597, fos 215–16.

[167] 'Considerations on the power of the University to make, alter, or repeal statutes, without any royal licence', Bodl. MS Top. Oxon. c. 209; [V. Thomas], *Oratiunculae cum oratiuncula non habitae cum habito concertatio* (1836), 33–4; SUL 2/247/68; 'Legal opinions on the statute, May 5, 1836, depriving the Regius Professor of Divinity of the right of sitting at a board of inquiry into heretical doctrine, and at the board for nomination of preachers', PHL MS Hayward-Cox 5252, Pa. 268.

[168] SUL 2/247/68; L. S. Sutherland, 'Laudian statutes in the eighteenth century' in *The Eighteenth Century*, 202–3.

[169] Lord Melbourne to R. D. Hampden, 9 June 1836, OCL MS Hampden Controversy 34.

[170] E. Bayly to Lord Holland, 7 Mar. 1836, BL Add. MS 51597, fo 211.

[171] J. A. Cramer to R. D. Hampden, 22 Dec. 1847, OCL MS Hampden Controversy 175.

[172] E. Hawkins to R. Whately, 18 Feb. 1836, OCL 413.

object really was to vindicate the orthodoxy of the Church and University, then, as Whately argued, the censurers of Hampden should have appealed to episcopal authority rather than a self-constituted tribunal.[173] The closest that proceedings against Hampden came to meeting the Tractarian demand for a formal theological indictment came with an appeal to the bishops to withdraw their sanction to certificates of attendance at the Regius Professor's lectures, which were ordinarily required of intending ordinands. As early as February 1836 the Board considered a request that the bishops be urged to refuse to recognize such certificates 'so long as the Chair of the Regius Professor of Divinity continues to be filled by one on the soundness of whose doctrinal opinions the University can place no reliance'.[174] Each bishop would judge for himself whether Hampden was a fit instructor, though ideally the Tractarians would prefer a consistent anti-Hampden stand by the whole bench. The proposal did attract support on the Board, but in the end the latter voted to do nothing.[175] Bishop Phillpotts wrote to Exeter College to declare that he would dispense with certificates of attendance at lectures given by the Regius Professor, but his example was not generally followed. When, in November 1836, the Vice-Chancellor, A. T. Gilbert, in his private capacity as Principal of Brasenose, announced his intention not to sign testimonials for ordinands who had attended Hampden's lectures,[176] his action was criticized even by anti-Hampdenites.[177] The Chancellor, ever fearful of the prospect of internal schism, urged Gilbert to back down.[178] When a case arose in which an individual bishop refused to examine a member of Brasenose who could not produce the necessary certificates, a legal battle looked in prospect to decide who was the final arbiter of theological orthodoxy in such a case. Gilbert withdrew his prohibition, and Hampden continued to attract larger attendances to his lectures than any of his predecessors.[179]

Other internal measures against Hampden were equally ineffectual. In December 1836 the Chancellor, who had disapproved of Hampden's appointment, questioned his principalship of St Mary Hall, not, however, on theological grounds, but because of Hampden's alleged breach of university statutes by his non-residence at the hall.[180] Hampden mistook this as an

[173] R. Whately to J. E. Tyler, Sept. 1836, LPL MS 2164, fo 124; R. Whately to E. Copleston, 21 Nov. 1836, OCL MS Hampden Controversy 20. R. Whately, *Statements and Reflections on the Church and the Universities* (1848), 8; *An Elucidation of Mr Woodgate's Pamphlet*, 26.

[174] E. Cardwell to Wellington, 26 Feb. 1836, SUL 2/247/32.

[175] C. P. Golightly to P. S. Dodd, 12 Mar. 1836, LPL MS 1805, fo 137; I. Williams to Jeffreys, Mar. 1836, LPL Keble dep. 9/10.

[176] A. T. Gilbert to Wellington, 16 Nov. 1836, SUL 2/247/88.

[177] P. N. Shuttleworth to Lord Holland, 1 Mar. 1836, BL Add. MS 51597, fo 136.

[178] Wellington to A. T. Gilbert, 25 Jan. 1837, SUL 2/247/125.

[179] A. T. Gilbert to Wellington, 25 May 1837, SUL 2/248/90; J. H. Newman to H. Wilberforce, 31 May 1837, in *LDN* vi. 74.

[180] Wellington to R. D. Hampden, 14 and 23 Dec. 1836, OCL MS Hampden Controversy 303, 307.

indication that Wellington was acting in league with the Regius Professor's theological enemies.[181] Wellington was not a man for theological niceties, which he thought best left to the bishops: his indignation had been aroused because 'Dr. Hampden did not conduct himself as he ought towards the Chancellor of the University nor even towards a Gentleman.'[182] Indeed, anxious at all times to secure peace in the University, the Chancellor had initially done no more than suggest that the elevation of Hampden to a bishopric might enable Oxford to be rid of him.[183] Not surprisingly, Tractarian dissatisfaction with the man they labelled with irony their 'Military Chancellor' and 'parliamentary friend' intensified during 1836. In March Pusey had not wanted to entrust the Corpus declaration to the Duke's hands: 'We have (against our will) been too much mixed up with politics already, so that unless he acted as Chancellor... one should most like to see it in the hands of a religious churchman.'[184]

Hampden's clerical opponents from the moment of his appointment had sought to make it an anti-Erastian cause, asserting the independence of Church and University against the pretensions of a reforming ministry. The Church and not the ministry should choose the religious leaders of the nation. Traditional High-Churchmen had regarded the royal supremacy as the best safeguard of church interests, but a Whig ministry, by foisting unacceptable appointments on Church and University, was deemed to be subverting the Crown's as well as the Church's independence.[185] Following the decline in the influence of the Crown after the constitutional revolution of 1829–33 and the King's false move in November 1834, royal prerogative now meant Whig ministerial prerogative. Whig ministers and liberal Churchmen could now exploit the benefits of church patronage which, in previous decades, had operated in the interests of Tory High-Churchmen. An appeal was made to William IV, asking the King 'to take his ecclesiastical appointments into his own hands'.[186] Lord Holland was sensitive to the constitutional implications of the resistance to the appointment, complaining to his Oxford ally Shuttleworth, 'there never was so impudent an attempt as that to transfer the appointment from the prerogative guided by responsible advisers, to the impression of "the many" which those who conveyed it did not dare to acknowledge as their own'.[187] Hampden likewise saw it as an attempt to introduce 'a democratic force' in the making of appointments, swayed 'by the prevailing opinions, feelings, and humours of the clergy'.[188]

---

[181] R. D. Hampden to Wellington, 21 Dec. 1836, SUL 2/247/100; OUA WP/α/57/5/7.
[182] Wellington to A. T. Gilbert, 7 Mar. 1837, SUL 2/248/8.
[183] Wellington to E. Cardwell, 2 Mar. 1836, SUL 2/247/34.
[184] E. B. Pusey to W. E. Gladstone, Mar. 1836, PHL LBV 85/18 (transcript).
[185] *LDN* v. 232.
[186] E. B. Pusey to W. E. Gladstone, Mar. 1836, PHL Pusey MS.
[187] Lord Holland to P. N. Shuttleworth, 29 Feb. 1836, Bodl. MS Eng. hist. c. 1033, fo 47.
[188] *Hampden*, 107–8.

For the Tractarians the theological aspect of the case was paramount, and this owed much to the 'mental revolution' of 1829. H. W. Wilberforce wrote many years later that 'Dr Hampden was singularly unlucky in the moment at which his lectures were preached. Only five or six years earlier he might have said all he actually did say without any great danger of awakening the University from its sleep.'[189] However, if there was a new polarization in the 1830s, this was not entirely the fault of the Tractarians. On the contrary, the terms of the theological debate were moved no less in new directions by the liberals, as they were in other directions by the Tractarians. During the 1820s Noeticism was not tantamount to doctrinal liberalism; no one could reasonably have disputed the orthodoxy of Copleston, Hawkins and Davison. After 1829, however, Noeticism moved in the direction of a more self-conscious liberalism. A marked shift can be detected in Hampden's position from writings of the 1820s as editor of the High-Church *Christian Remembrancer* to his authorship in 1834 of *Observations on Dissent*.[190] Baden Powell was another who crossed the boundary from an apparent moderate High-Churchmanship to doctrinal ultra-liberalism in the same period. Even Arnold was a more hardened liberal in 1836 at the time of his violent 'Oxford Malignants' article than when in genuinely eirenic spirit he supported Catholic Emancipation in 1829.

The Tractarian theological charges against Hampden were not unfounded. Although there was a vagueness about the terms of the formal censure against the Regius Professor, doubts about Hampden's orthodoxy were not confined to a fanatical minority: here again his niece's protestations cannot be accepted. The familiar liberal charge was that the Tractarians distorted Hampden's meaning by the use of selective quotation, especially in Newman's *Elucidations*.[191] His opponents seemed to be trying to institute little short of an *auto-da-fé* on the model of the sixteenth- or seventeenth-century Inquisition.[192] This impression was mistaken. Even Hampden's

---

[189] [H. W. Wilberforce], 'Dr Hampden and Anglicanism', *Dublin Review* xvii (July 1871), 76.

[190] Ibid. 72. Corsi distinguishes an 'early Noetic school', identifiable with Copleston and Davison, from 'the late Noetic school, or more accurately…Whately's school': *Science and Religion*, 74. Edward Churton considered that 'the Oriel school' had collapsed by 1836, and that Hampden was but 'the trail of the school': E. Churton to W. Copeland, July 1837, Sutton Coldfield MS Churton.

[191] *The Propositions Attributed to Dr Hampden by Professor Pusey Compared with the Test of the Bampton Lectures, in a series of parallels* (1836), pp. ii–iv; W. W. Hull, *Remarks Intended to Show how far Mr Hampden may have been Misunderstood and Misrepresented* (1836); F. W. Newman, *Contributions Chiefly to the Early History of Cardinal Newman* (1891), 89–92.

[192] *State of Parties in Oxford* (1836), 41–2; *The Oxford Persecution of 1836, extracts from the public journals, in defence of the present Regius Professor of Divinity, and his appointment to that chair, and in condemnation of the proceedings at Oxford subsequent to that appointment* (1836); Blanco White to E. Hawkins, 11 Apr. 1836, OCL 108; Thom, *Life of Blanco White* ii. 222. For the Noetic Nassau Senior's account of the *auto-da-fé* at Oxford, see *Hampden*, 66–8. These proceedings were less severe in effect than those by which F. D. Maurice was deprived of his chair at King's College, London, in 1853. In the *Apologia* (53) Newman playfully rebutted

more moderate or conservative supporters among the liberals had private theological qualms about the Bampton Lectures. They did not have the theological imprimatur of the old Oriel school, despite an attempt by Hampden to suggest that John Davison had approved of them.[193] Davison's widow disputed this.[194] Hawkins also had decided reservations.[195] Shuttleworth privately acknowledged to Lord Holland that

unfortunately in his writings [Hampden] has been ambitious of taking a new view of things, and he has alarmed many very moderate and liberal men in this place, not so much for himself as for the possible mischief he may do to the younger part of the University by his teaching. I take for granted however, that he has learned a severe lesson by what has taken place, and will be more on his guard for the future.[196]

A sense of the paramount importance of revealed dogma to which the claims of reason must owe subservience was the great unifying theological principle which united the triple alliance of the anti-Hampden phalanx. Hampden's apparent attempt to separate 'fact' from 'doctrine' was thought rationalistic in its consequences. At this stage, it was enough to unite all anti-liberals simply to assert that Hampden's 'rationalism' was subversive of 'scriptural truth'. Many of the early theological statements of objection to Hampden by the Corpus committee tended to be couched in terms designed to win the assent of conservative Evangelicals. In his *Brief Observations upon Dr. Hampden's Inaugural Lecture*, Pusey concentrated on Hampden's supposed denial of 'preventing and co-operating grace', misuse of scripture, failure to assert that Jesus was of one substance (homo-ousian) with the Father, and for a defective interpretation of the Atonement as reconciling man to God rather than the reverse.[197] Evangelicals were especially impressed by the way Pusey made Hampden appear to speak slightingly or irreverently of each of the Articles. John Hill and Golightly, two robust Protestants, relished the task of compilation and citation. Certainly, there was quite as good an 'Evangelical' case to be made out against Hampden as there was a 'High-Church' one. Evangelicals were offended by Hampden's apparently anti-dogmatic use of scripture—he did not, like them, appear to deduce dogma from self-evident scriptural truth, and, above all, rejected scripture-consequences.

Tractarian objections to Hampden emphasized his irreverence for the Fathers of the Nicene and later periods and apostolical tradition in general.

---

any Inquisitorial leanings: 'Not even when I was fiercest could I have cut off a Puritan's ears, and I think the sight of a Spanish *auto-da-fé* would have been the death of me.'

[193] *Correspondence between Hampden and the Archbishop of Canterbury*, 11.
[194] *British Critic* xxiv (Oct. 1838), 490; *LDN* vi. 317.
[195] E. Hawkins to R. Whately, 18 Feb. 1836, OCL 413.
[196] P. N. Shuttleworth to Lord Holland, 1 Mar. 1836, BL Add. MS 51597, fo 136. See also Shuttleworth 'on incautious sentiments...in some of your writings': to Hampden 17 Mar. 1836, OCL MS Hampden Controversy 73.
[197] [E. B. Pusey], *Brief Observations upon Dr. Hampden's Inaugural Lecture* (1836), 4–6.

When Tractarians accused him of setting aside the 'received principles of interpreting scripture', they evidently meant apostolical tradition and the Vincentian canon.[198] Significantly, in the second edition of his *Dr. Hampden's Past and Present Statements Compared*, Pusey added sections on tradition and the Church that bolstered the 'Tractarian' emphasis. The scriptures themselves, he claimed, were to be interpreted 'as expanded by the consent of catholic antiquity, or the agreement of the universal church'.[199] Hampden, he argued, was attacking the Anglican position and not the Roman.

Hampden's opinions were, moreover, judged objectionable on moral grounds. Instead of asserting the obligation of reverence and 'teachableness' of a young mind in obedience to the authority of the Church, Hampden sanctioned a 'self-willed' reliance on private judgement and freedom of speculation. Clearly, the Tractarians would have preferred to shun intellectual debate of Hampden's actual propositions altogether. As Pusey explained to his German friend Professor Tholuck, in words which in themselves present a classic statement of the Tractarian mentality,

We had not to dispute a point, or show whence the mischief came, but we had to give the alarm and to cry 'Fire'; if people took the warning and ran to extinguish the fire, the end was secured. In our present state, it was enough to show that Dr. Hampden's system, as a system, went counter to that of the Articles, to show the leprous spot, and warn people to flee the infection.[200]

For in the last resort, Newman, Pusey and the Tractarians thought they discerned in Hampden's theological liberalism an incipient unbelief; against it, they insisted on the insufficiency of empiricism as a foundation of faith. Since Oxford represented the historic bulwark of that faith, the Tractarians believed that the University's independence and integrity should be protected and preserved.

In March 1837 Lord Radnor gave notice in the House of Lords to revive the possibility of a parliamentary inquiry into the internal state of the University. The attack was now concentrated on the colleges, which were accused of having departed from their statutes and the intentions of their founders. The renewed external threat cemented the anti-liberal alliance of 1834–6 as the heads joined with the great body of 'juniors', under Tractarian leadership, to petition against the bill, which was defeated in the Lords in April 1837.[201] Undaunted, Radnor used a discussion of the

---

[198] On the centrality of a defence of the Catholic principle of dogma in the Tractarian case against Hampden see E. R. Fairweather, '"Apostolical tradition" and the defence of dogma: an episode in the Anglo-Catholic revival', *Canadian Journal of Theology* xi (1965), 277–89; S. Thomas, *Newman and Heresy: the Anglican years* (1991), 76.

[199] E. B. Pusey, *Dr. Hampden's Past and Present Statements Compared* (2nd edn 1836), 23–4.

[200] E. B. Pusey to A. Tholuck, 6 Mar. 1837, PHL LBV 127/10 (transcript).

[201] A. T. Gilbert to Wellington, 25 Mar. 1837, SUL 2/248/38.

Hampden case as a cue for making a major university reform speech but, well briefed by Gilbert and Philip Bliss, the Chancellor again successfully fended off the challenge.[202] In private, however, tensions were already developing between the line of defence favoured by Wellington and the one to which the majority were inclined in Oxford. Wellington feared the adoption of extreme tactics of opposition, advising the Vice-Chancellor:

We must not forget the great object of our Institution. The University cannot be a party in opposition to the Government. The Government may ill treat the University, but we ought to avoid to take any course which can be attributed to feelings of party; and which might afford a pretext for adopting measures which would be attended by the most fatal consequences to the Church.[203]

He urged some accommodation of external criticisms, calling on the colleges to put their houses in order, repealing from their statutes 'all that is anomalous and obsolete' and substituting new provisions 'more suitable to the circumstances of the University and of the times'.[204] Progress was slow, and Wellington's position became more difficult as the publication of college statutes exposed the extent of abuses and of non-observance. And there was little prospect of reforms of the sort Wellington hoped for so long as Tractarian strength in the colleges grew. By 1837 some colleges could already be identified as Tractarian strongholds. 'At Exeter', Newman exulted, 'right opinions are strong. At Magdalen, Trinity, University and Oriel, nucleuses are forming... Christ Church alone is immobile.'[205] A Cambridge visitor who dined with the fellows of Queen's in 1837 heard the view confidently expressed 'that nothing could withstand the influence' of the Tractarians, and that 'every man of talent who during the last 6 years has come to Oxford, has joined Newman'.[206]

Attempts to speed up the process of revision of the University's statutes came up against the opposition of a Tractarian-dominated Convocation. One broadsheet saw no safety in the pragmatic adjustment advised by the Chancellor:

It is possible that political friends who understand neither our principles nor our practice, and who may think that they are supporting us while in reality we are supporting them, may be urging us on to this measure; but if the safety of the

[202] Wellington to A. T. Gilbert, 9 May 1836, SUL 2/248/85; *Speeches of Wellington in Parliament* ed. J. Gurwood (2 vols 1854) ii. 104–8, 138–41.
[203] Wellington to A. T. Gilbert, 12 Apr. 1837, SUL 2/248/48; Wellington to E. Cardwell, June 1837, SUL 2/248/105.
[204] SUL 2/249/52–62; R. Palmer, *Memorials, Family and Personal* (2 vols 1896) ii. 230–2.
[205] J. H. Newman to H. W. Wilberforce, 14 Mar. 1837, in *LDN* vi. 42. Oriel, Trinity and Exeter were the leading strongholds of Tractarianism.
[206] John Fuller Russell to Pelham Maitland, 18 Nov. 1837, PHL Russell Papers.

University of Oxford is to rest on a political party, not on truth, reason, and religion, we had better at once abandon it to its fate.[207]

Convocation sanctioned the abolition of the oath of supremacy at matriculation, but the likelihood of opposition caused the Board to draw back from a proposal to reopen the question of subscription at matriculation. Cardwell reported to Wellington that several members of the Board, 'who on a former occasion were friendly to the measure, gave their votes against it on the present occasion, solely from the fear of making the Convocation suspicious and adverse to any other propositions which might issue from the Board'.[208] The prospect of more thoroughgoing statute revision prompted a deluge of largely Tractarian-inspired papers and pamphlets advocating the constitutional rights of Convocation in relation to the Board. The Board, it was contended, had no right to embark on a revision of this scale 'without first proposing the general question to Convocation'.[209]

At this point, when the Tractarians were at the height of their power within the University, there were the first signs of misgivings about their Movement. The political situation was no longer that of 1833. After the general election of July 1837 the fear that the parliamentary radicals might mount a successful attack on the Church was a thing of the past. The Tractarians had ceased to look like a conservative band whose leadership the old High-Churchmen could accept; by now they resembled a disruptive and possibly revolutionary party in Oxford. Wellington increasingly saw them as a recalcitrant and factious party, hindering his attempts launched in a spirit of Peelite conservatism to make the University less vulnerable to external criticism. The Hebdomadal Board moved in 1839 and 1840 to restore the position of the professoriate and to introduce a limited recognition of modern studies into the undergraduate curriculum. Convocation was in no mood to facilitate the Board's work, and the proposals were finally thrown out in June 1840.[210]

The first element in the triple alliance of the mid-1830s to react against Tractarian leadership after 1837 were the Evangelicals. Though in many respects the Movement's natural enemies, the Evangelicals had been won over by skilful Tractarian appeals in the anti-Hampden campaign. There was

---

[207] 'Some remarks by a member of Convocation for objecting to the proposed revision of the university statutes, and to the revised portion of them which has just been published', SUL 2/248/140.

[208] E. Cardwell to Wellington, 21 Nov. 1837, SUL 2/248/133.

[209] A. T. Gilbert to Wellington, 23 Nov. 1837, SUL 2/248/141. For an exposition of the constitutional case against the Board see E. Greswell, *A Letter to his Grace the Duke of Wellington, Chancellor of the University of Oxford, on the Proceedings in the House of Convocation on Thursday the 23rd inst.* (1837); *An Address to Members of Convocation* (1837).

[210] Ward, *Victorian Oxford*, 108–9. On Tractarian educational ideas see P. B. Nockles, 'An academic counter-revolution: Newman and Tractarian Oxford's idea of a university', *History of Universities* x (1991), 137–97.

a surprising amount in the earlier numbers of the Tracts calculated to appeal to Oxford Evangelicals. In one early Tract, 'The gospel a law of liberty', and in his famous letters to the *Record* newspaper in 1833, Newman had successfully disarmed potential Evangelical opposition. Yet scope for a fuller theological understanding was stifled by Newman's own self-confessed determination 'to frighten our peculiar brethren'; by 1837 he was hoping that the Hampden case would open the eyes of Evangelicals to the inadequacies and dangers inherent in their own religious position.[211] Fundamental theological differences on the questions of baptism and justification became more explicit with time. Pusey's lengthy and scholarly treatises on baptism in Tracts 67 and 69, which appeared in 1835 and 1836, went beyond traditional High-Churchmen's insistence on the doctrine of baptismal regeneration, for long a point of dispute with Evangelicals. Hostile reaction to these views came largely from outside Oxford. John Hill, the influential Vice-Principal of St Edmund Hall, though aware of what he called 'the evil doctrines' of the Movement, strove hard to reassure the Islington conference of Evangelical clergy that those doctrines were not representative of 'the true character and state of Oxford'.[212]

The first sign of an Evangelical backlash against the Tractarians within the University itself came in 1837 with a fierce pamphlet by the Low-Church chaplain of New College, Peter Maurice. Maurice detailed various 'popish' ritual and ceremonial innovations apparently being practised by individual Tractarians in Oxford, accusing Newman himself of being guilty of such acts in the University church.[213] Pusey was soon complaining that 'the walls of Oxford have been placarded...with "Popery of Oxford" and its citizens have been edified with the exhibition of Newman's and my name as Papists'.[214] Maurice was an eccentric figure, and the impression made by his charges did the Tractarians little immediate harm.

More damaging was the publication in March 1838 of the first two volumes of Hurrell Froude's *Remains*, edited by Keble and Newman. The revelation of Froude's expressions of antipathy towards the English Reformers and Reformation, objects of veneration for traditional High-Churchmen as well as Evangelicals, was almost calculated to alienate friends as well as to provoke avowed foes. The cry of 'popery' among Evangelicals and Low-Churchmen was entirely predictable; it was more serious that old High-Churchmen, such as Edward Churton, thought publication highly

[211] J. H. Newman to Lord Lifford, 13 Sept. 1837, J. H. Newman to Miss M. R. Giberne, 24 July 1837, in *LDN* vi. 42, 104.

[212] Diary of John Hill, 4 Jan. 1837, Bodl. MS St Edmund Hall 67.

[213] P. Maurice, *The Popery of Oxford Confronted, Disavowed and Repudiated* (1837).

[214] E. B. Pusey to B. Harrison, 26 Mar. 1837, in Liddon, *Pusey* ii. 12–13. Pembroke College was also deemed a hotbed of ritualistic practices. See P. Le Page Renouf to Mrs M. J. Renouf, 10 Nov. 1840, PCA 63/9/1/7.

imprudent.[215] For impressionable undergraduates and younger MAs ready to 'lionize' and craving the inspiration of an heroic exemplar, Froude's mixture of personal 'catholic' holiness and asceticism, uniting a romantic visionariness with youthful zest and sense of fun, exerted a strong appeal. The *Remains* were in perfect tune with the romantic medievalism which the Movement consciously fostered and identified with historic Oxford.[216] Yet, in deciding to publish the *Remains*, the Tractarians were appealing to one, albeit important and youthful, section of the University at the risk of alienating the rest.[217] From 1834 to 1837 the Tractarian orchestration of the subscription and anti-Hampden campaigns had enabled them to assume the right to speak for the great conservative body of the University as a whole. The publication of the *Remains* amounted to a forfeiture of that right, and set the Movement within the University on to the path of sectarianism.

The evidence that the old conservative alliance had been broken became evident in May 1838 with the first assault on the Movement by a staunchly Protestant High-Church figure, the Lady Margaret Professor of Divinity, Godfrey Faussett. Now that Hampden as Regius Professor was effectively muzzled, Faussett became practically the mouthpiece of Oxford orthodoxy; in a sermon from the pulpit of St Mary's, Faussett lashed the Tractarians on essentially old-fashioned Tory High-Church grounds for inspiring a spirit of 'ecclesiastical insubordination' and 'enthusiasm'.[218] The Tractarians may never have cared for Faussett as an individual, nor had much regard for him as a divine,[219] but it was on his favour or at least neutrality that their earlier tactical ascendancy had depended. To have made an enemy of Faussett as well as Hampden was to prove a serious misjudgement.

The developing realignment of parties in Oxford found early expression in a plan to erect a memorial to commemorate the Protestant Oxford Martyrs of 1555–6, Cranmer, Latimer and Ridley. In November 1838 a committee of thirty-four was set up in Oxford to raise subscriptions. By June 1842 over £7,000 had been collected, the foundation-stone of the new Memorial having been laid a year earlier, in May 1841.[220] It was widely believed that the

---

[215] E. Churton to A. P. Perceval, 23 Feb. 1839, PHL LBV 2/30 (transcript). See Samuel Wilberforce's castigation of the 'mischievous delirium of publishing Froude's unguarded thoughts to a morbidly sensitive and unsympathizing age. I feel assured that that work has put back church principles for fifty years': S. Wilberforce to W. F. Hook, 11 Jan. 1839, Bodl. MS Wilberforce d. 38, fo 144. For the use made in the Commons of quotations from the *Remains* see *Parl. Deb.* 30 July 1838, 3S xliv. 818 (Morpeth).

[216] W. J. Baker, 'Hurrell Froude and the reformers', *Journal of Ecclesiastical History* xxi (1970), 243–59.

[217] P. Brendon, 'Newman, Keble and Froude's *Remains*', *EHR* lxxxvii (1972), 699–716.

[218] G. Faussett, *The Revival of Popery: a sermon preached before the University of Oxford at St Mary's on May 20, 1838* (1838), 12–14.

[219] [T. Mozley], 'The Oxford Margaret Professor', *British Critic* xx (July 1841), 214–43.

[220] Diary of John Hill, 13 May 1841, Bodl. MS St Edmund Hall 67/13, fo 68.

project derived its impetus from the strong reaction against the 'Romish character of the Movement' in general and Froude's *Remains* in particular.[221] Although prominent Evangelicals such as John Hill, and J. D. Macbride, Principal of Magdalen Hall, along with the Whig and liberal Evangelical Philip Shuttleworth, were moving forces on the committee, the Memorial was not an exclusively party affair. The committee also included several leading Protestant High-Churchmen such as Vaughan Thomas, Charles Ogilvie, Edward Greswell, C. P. Golightly and even William Sewell, who had been active on the Corpus committee against Hampden.[222] It even enjoyed the blessing of the High-Church bishop, Dr Bagot. Such High-Churchmen differed from the Evangelicals in their interpretation of the doctrines and essential message of the reformers, but would never have regarded the latter in any light but that of martyrs to be venerated. To the strictest of the old High-Churchmen subscription to the Memorial was no less a blow for Protestant orthodoxy than the campaign against Peel in 1829, the defence of subscription in 1835, and the opposition to Hampden's appointment in 1836. The project had precedents in the traditional anti-Romanism and anti-liberalism of pre-Tractarian Oxford Churchmanship; one scheme for the publication of a commemorative print had been floated in 1826 as a specifically Tory Oxford expression of resistance to the Catholic claims. The idea of a Martyrs' Memorial seems to have been even older; Philip Shuttleworth described it in 1839 as 'a hobby-horsical scheme of myself and others 20 years ago'.[223] Shuttleworth contended that the present scheme had been intended to be as uncontentious as possible, avoiding any expression on the inscription 'which Mr. Newman or his friends could say was, by any amplification, directed against themselves'.[224]

It was symptomatic, however, of the increased recklessness of the Tractarians after 1838 that having originally agreed to countenance the Memorial, they withdrew co-operation.[225] Once this attitude of opposition became clear, the project fell increasingly into the hands of more extreme Protestant elements in the University. The Memorial committee dropped its former caution, concluding 'that many sincere Protestants would be offended by the very sparing manner in which we had alluded to the points of difference between our church and that of Rome'. Words 'against the errors of the Church of Rome' were agreed to be added to the inscription.[226] The implication was by now undisguisedly anti-Tractarian, and Bishop Bagot threatened to withdraw his sanction, but in the face of support for the new

[221] W. K. Hamilton to W. E. Gladstone, 20 Feb. 1839, BL Add. MS 44183, fo 190.
[222] Diary of John Hill, 3 Nov. 1838, Bodl. MS St Edmund Hall 67/12, fos 74–5.
[223] P. Shuttleworth to Lord Holland, 6 Jan. 1839, BL Add. MS 51597, fo 153.
[224] P. Shuttleworth to H. Martyn, 5 Jan. 1839, Bodl. MS Eng. hist. c. 1033, fo 102.
[225] E. B. Pusey to B. Harrison, 5 Nov. 1838, PHL LBV 90/77 (transcript). Keble was from the start opposed to the scheme: J. Keble to E. B. Pusey, 18 Jan. 1839, PHL LBV 50/14.
[226] Diary of John Hill, 13 Nov. 1838, Bodl. MS St Edmund Hall 67/12, fo 77.

wording from such staunch High-Church anti-Hampdenites as Vaughan Thomas, Bagot's objections were overcome.[227]

Conservative Oxford Churchmen were now thoroughly disillusioned with the apparent direction of the Movement. In 1839 the Vice-Chancellor, A. T. Gilbert, who had supported the Tractarians so firmly against Hampden as 'learned and able advocates' of the Church and University against liberals and Whigs, became alarmed. He confided his fears to Wellington: 'They [the Tractarians] are accused of designing the reintroduction of Popery, a design which I am quite certain their leaders do not entertain...I feel, however, persuaded that however unconsciously they are, in effect, pioneers of that superstition.'[228] Having upheld the orthodoxy of the University against Hampden, Gilbert was no less anxious to discountenance what he considered to be Tractarian errors in the opposite theological direction. Such concern was understandable in the light of allegations that fear of Tractarian doctrines at Oxford was driving parents to send their sons to Cambridge.[229] Attempts were made to prevent the election of potentially troublesome Tractarians to college fellowships. Newman was convinced as early as November 1837 that this was the reason for James Mozley's failure to win a fellowship at Lincoln College.[230] In 1838 another such unsuccessful candidate was explicit on this point, asserting that 'it would, I have no doubt, seriously injure any one's chance at any college now being connected so openly with Newman and Pusey'.[231]

Meanwhile the first substantive doctrinal issue to divide the University as a direct consequence of Tractarianism centred on the relative role and importance assigned to apostolical tradition in the schema of Christian doctrine. Article VI laid down that holy scripture 'contained all things necessary unto salvation', a principle stressed by Low-Churchmen and Evangelicals. The High-Church tradition which the Tractarians inherited, while accepting that scripture was 'sufficient' as the basis or rule of faith, also maintained that it required the interpretation or at least corroboration of otherwise doubtful points, which an appeal to apostolical tradition provided. The continuity of this High-Church teaching on tradition within the University in the half-century preceding the Movement had been upheld by the annual Bampton

[227] Ibid. 31 Jan. 1839, fo 91.
[228] A. T. Gilbert to Wellington, 29 Dec. 1839, SUL 2/250/64.
[229] *A Letter of Remonstrance, Addressed to an Undergraduate of the University of Oxford, Concerning the Tenets of Dr Pusey and Mr Newman* (1840), 20; [E. Fry], *The Listener in Oxford* (1839), 22. For a private comment see S. Wilberforce to R. I. Wilberforce, 29 Nov. 1838, in A. R. Ashwell and R. G. Wilberforce, *S. Wilberforce* (3 vols 1880–2) i. 129. For Hawkins's fears that undergraduates were not concentrating on their classical studies, see A. H. Clough to J. P. Gell, 18 Nov. [1838], in *Correspondence of A. H. Clough*, ed. F. L. Mulhauser (2 vols 1957) i. 85.
[230] *LDN* vi. 172; cf F. Nolan, 'A study of Mark Pattison's religious experience, 1813–1850' (Oxford DPhil thesis 1977), 113.
[231] Mozley, *Letters*, 78; see also 107.

Lectures.[232] Why then did the Tractarian revival or reassertion of the claims of apostolical tradition provoke such an outcry? Part of the reason was that more than mere reassertion was at stake. As the liberal divine Baden Powell pointed out, in Tractarian hands the old High-Church theory of tradition 'received a more full and striking development' than ever before.[233] On this issue as on others, the Tractarians acted not as passive legatees of the High-Anglican inheritance: on the contrary, Newman saw it as their task 'to catalogue, sort, distribute, select, harmonise and complete' the catholic tradition in Anglicanism.[234] For old High-Churchmen apostolical tradition was essentially conservative and corroborative of scriptural truths, whereas for the Tractarians, as for the nonjurors of the previous century, apostolical tradition could be reformative and dynamic in its implications.[235]

The radical nature of the Tractarian view of tradition, asserted at this sensitive period in the Movement's history, helped further fracture the conservative anti-Hampden alliance. That alliance had been cemented by Hampden's apparent denigration of dogmatic authority in the name of religious liberty. For Evangelicals and many Protestant High-Churchmen the main threat posed by Hampden had been to the authority of the Bible. For the Tractarians, it was apostolical tradition that had also been assailed, and Hampden and his friends saw in Tractarian teaching on tradition the 'Achilles heel' of the Movement. If the Hampdenites could expose the Tractarian view of tradition as essentially unscriptural, they could emerge as the sounder Protestants and retrieve a grudging respect from many of their former opponents. Here was a chance to turn the tables on the Tractarians.[236]

H. A. Woodgate's ultra-High-Church Bampton Lectures in 1838,[237] described by Shuttleworth as 'the most direct attack made against Protestantism in this place',[238] presented the pro-Hampden party with their opportunity. Shuttleworth's counter-blast, *Not Tradition but Revelation*, which he described as 'a kind of protest against those opinions which are making such formidable progress in our University',[239] was in itself slight and its arguments readily disposed of. But he did speak for Evangelical and conservative Protestant orthodoxy. He now urged Hampden to make himself

[232] T. C. Snow, 'The early Bampton Lectures, 1780–1831', *Proceedings of the Society of Historical Theology* (1912), 37–43.

[233] Baden Powell, *Tradition Unveiled; or, an exposition of the pretensions and tendency of authoritative teaching in the church* (1839), 5, 8–9.

[234] J. H. Newman, *Lectures on the Prophetical Office of the Church, Viewed Relatively to Romanism and Popular Protestantism* (1837), 30.

[235] O. Chadwick, *The Mind of the Oxford Movement* (1960), 39.

[236] R. Whately, *Statements and Reflections on the Church and Universities* (1848), 33.

[237] Woodgate insisted that the Church held knowledge of doctrine to be antecedent to the perusal of holy scripture: H. A. Woodgate, *The Authoritative Teaching of the Church Shown to be in Conformity with Scripture, Analogy, and the Moral Constitution of Man* (1839), p. xiv.

[238] P. N. Shuttleworth to H. Martyn, 24 Aug. 1838, Bodl. MS Eng. hist. c. 1033, fo 100.

[239] P. N. Shuttleworth, *Not Tradition but Revelation* (1838), 39.

acceptable to this strand of anti-Tractarian feeling in Oxford. In a lecture entitled *On Tradition*, delivered in November 1838, Hampden responded with an 'ultra-Protestant' assault on 'sacerdotal authority' which delighted Evangelicals. In place of apostolical tradition, he gave as the main aid to the interpretation of scripture not 'unaided reason' as might have been expected, but the Holy Spirit. The arguments of Woodgate and the Tractarians were presented as the greatest threats to scriptural orthodoxy.[240] How far Hampden had moved away from his earlier latitudinarianism became apparent when his work was set alongside the contribution of the Oxford liberal Baden Powell. Baden Powell's *Tradition Unveiled* was much more in the rationalizing spirit of Hampden's earlier writings. It criticized 'ultra-Protestant' biblical literalism as playing into Tractarian hands. It even commended the Tractarians as exhibiting 'more rational views of the grounds of religious belief, and of the general nature of Christian doctrine' and for purifying the Church 'from the repulsive tenets of a vulgar fanaticism' which he identified with Evangelicalism.[241] Tradition was a false idol certainly, but the letter of the Bible alone was equally false—the only alternative to both was reason and the unlimited exercise of private judgement. Shuttleworth was quick to apprehend in Baden Powell's pamphlet the revival of the very anti-dogmatic spirit in reaction to which Tractarians and Evangelicals had united between 1834 and 1836.[242] In short, Baden Powell's brand of extreme theological liberalism was but the reverse side of the Tractarian coin—both were subversive of the canons of Evangelical Protestant orthodoxy which Shuttleworth upheld and with which increasingly, Hampden, whether sincerely or not, was identifying himself.

It was left to Edward Hawkins to assert a moderate, middle position more acceptable to the mainstream of conservative Protestant feeling in the University in his Bampton Lectures on the subject in 1840. Hawkins sought to reassert the old balance between scripture and apostolical tradition, against what he perceived as Tractarian excesses, while by implication the ultra-latitudinarian and the 'sola scriptura' positions were both also challenged. While authoritative tradition was rejected, and the influence of the 'Noetic' dependence on reason rather than authority was evident, it was also made clear that the Word of God as contained in the scriptures was addressed to Christians already instructed by the Church. Hampden had been mistaken in implying that tradition meant the opinions of individual men: it meant far more than that.[243] The heads, who had the power of appointing Bampton lecturers,

---

[240] R. D. Hampden, *Lecture on Tradition, Read before the University in the Divinity School, Oxford, on Thursday, March 7th, 1839, with additions* (1839), 7–8, 13.

[241] Baden Powell, *Tradition Unveiled*, 16–17.

[242] P. N. Shuttleworth to H. Martyn, 22 Feb. 1839, Bodl. MS Eng. hist. c. 1033, fo 104.

[243] E. Hawkins, *An Enquiry into the Connected Uses of the Principal Means of Attaining Christian Truth* (1840), 38 ff., 55 ff. Hawkins emphasized that his Bamptons were a conscious repudiation of the Tractarian theory of tradition: E. Hawkins to R. Whately, 28 Sept. 1840, OCL 422.

had pressed Hawkins to accept the office. His performance delighted the Protestant High-Church old guard. 'He has amply fulfilled our expectations,' Gilbert reported.[244] The heads were hopeful that peace might return and divisions heal. Tract 90, which was published on 27 February 1841, dashed these hopes.

As is well known, in Tract 90 Newman set out to demonstrate that, though drafted 'in an uncatholic age', the Articles were 'patient' of a 'catholic' rather than Protestant sense.[245] As he was to write in the *Apologia*, it had become to him 'a matter of life and death' to demonstrate this. The reaction elicited in Oxford was one of immediate hostility. 'Poor Golly is almost distracted with excitement,' Mark Pattison reported of C. P. Golightly.[246] Among the heads, Edward Cardwell's response was typical: 'The object of the Tract appears to be to introduce such an interpretation of the 39 Articles as would make them consistent with the real system of the Church of Rome, and exclusive only of its local and grosser corruptions.'[247] Philip Wynter, President of St John's and Vice-Chancellor from 1840 to 1844, pointed out another danger: the Tract 'suggested a mode of interpreting those passages [in the Articles] which if adopted would render subscription to the Articles themselves a mere mockery'.[248] Prompted by the famous Letter of the Four Tutors, A. C. Tait of Balliol, H. B. Wilson of St John's, T. T. Churton of Brasenose and J. Griffiths of Wadham,[249] the Hebdomadal Board was moved to denounce Tract 90, with only two dissentients, Routh of Magdalen and Richards of Exeter. See Fig. 7.1.[250]

Newman was later to be portrayed as having been the subject of a cruel campaign of obloquy and persecution by the heads. Church described the Board's action as 'an ungenerous and stupid blunder' and maintained that the heads 'had not so much condemned as insulted him'.[251] There was now a distinctly constitutional as well as theological basis to Tractarian resentment, for they questioned the very title of the heads to act as theological arbitrators or censors in the University. In contrast to 1836, when the censure of Hampden was vociferously demanded from the heads, James Mozley considered in 1841 that they had overstepped their powers: 'It is generally thought that the Heads of Houses have gone quite out of their sphere in deciding on the theology of a work; they are merely a committee for

[244] A. T. Gilbert to Wellington, 24 May 1840, SUL 2/250/129.
[245] [J. H. Newman], *Remarks on Certain Passages in the Thirty-Nine Articles* (Tracts for the Times, no. 90, 1841), 4, 82–3.
[246] M. Pattison to E. Pattison [1841], Lincoln College archives LCA MS Pat./II/A.
[247] E. Cardwell to Wellington, 10 Mar. 1841, SUL 2/251/21.
[248] P. Wynter to Wellington, 15 Mar. 1841, SUL 2/251/27.
[249] *The Protest against Tract for the Times, No. 90, Resolution of the Hebdomadal Board, and Mr Newman's Letter to the Vice-Chancellor* (1841), 3–5.
[250] OUA WP/γ/8/24(5), fo 237, HBM 12 Mar. 1841.
[251] Church, *The Oxford Movement*, 292; Newman, *Apologia*, 242.

AT a Meeting of the Vice-Chancellor, Heads of Houses, and Proctors, in the Delegates' Room, March 15, 1841.

CONSIDERING that it is enjoined in the STATUTES of this University, (TIT. III. SECT. 2. TIT. IX. SECT. II. §. 3. SECT. V. §. 3.) that every Student shall be instructed and examined in the Thirty-nine Articles, and shall subscribe to them; considering also that a Tract has recently appeared, dated from Oxford, and entitled " Remarks on certain passages in the Thirty-nine Articles," being Nº 90 of the Tracts for the Times, a series of Anonymous Publications purporting to be written by Members of the University, but which are in no way sanctioned by the University itself;

RESOLVED, That modes of interpretation such as are suggested in the said Tract, evading rather than explaining the sense of the Thirty-nine Articles and reconciling subscription to them with the adoption of errors, which they were designed to counteract, defeat the object, and are inconsistent with the due observance of the above-mentioned STATUTES.

P. WYNTER,

Vice-Chancellor.

FIGURE 7.1 The Hebdomadal Board condemns Tract 90. *Source*: OUA WPγ/24(5), no. 78

practical business; besides that, some of them are laymen.'[252] Keble denied
that the heads' censure had any theological validity, regarding it as 'not an
act of the University... merely the opinion of the majority of individual
members of the Board'.[253] The Tractarian spirit of submission to established
authority was proving to be selective; Convocation was the only authority
which Keble was now able to acknowledge. Ironically, the varied opponents
of Tract 90 proved the more faithful in upholding the traditional religious
powers vested in the governing authorities of the University.

In a striking reversal of roles, liberals now appeared as conservative
defenders of the Articles, while the Tractarians, who had defended the
Articles to the hilt in 1836, 'now tell us that they are a bondage which, as
they cannot be got rid of, must be evaded to the utmost of our power'.[254]
Hampden seized his moment and preached a conservative defence of the
Articles against Tractarian casuistry, insisting, in sharp contrast to the ambivalent language of his earlier works, on the Articles' literal and dogmatic
nature.[255]

The wide reaction to Tract 90 outside the University convinced the heads
of the necessity for some unequivocal sign that Tractarianism did not represent the official teaching of the University. The mood of resident opinion
was more favourable to the heads' action than Tractarians assumed: 'the
general feeling is that some interference was absolutely required and that the
Heads of Houses have done perfectly right in putting forth their protest'.[256]
There were some complaints, moreover, that this official action had been too
long delayed, and that the declaration against Tract 90 should have been
applied to the whole series of the 'Tracts for the Times'.[257]

Unease did arise in some quarters that the heads were in danger of
appearing to usurp spiritual powers properly belonging to the bishops.
Conservative High-Churchmen such as Palmer of Worcester and Sewell
took issue with their intervention against Tract 90 on this strictly constitu-

[252] J. Mozley to T. Mozley, 5 Apr. 1841, Mozley, *Letters*, 116.

[253] J. Keble, *The Case of Catholic Subscription to the Thirty-Nine Articles Considered with Especial Reference to the Duties and Difficulties of English Catholics in the Present Crisis; in a letter to the Hon. Mr Justice Coleridge* (privately printed 1841), 8.

[254] P. N. Shuttleworth to unnamed correspondent, 31 May 1841, Bodl. MS. Eng. hist. c. 1033, fo 226.

[255] R. D. Hampden, *The Thirty-Nine Articles of the Church of England: the eleventh of the public course of lectures, in Trinity term, read before the University, in the divinity school, Oxford, June 1, 1842* (2nd edn 1842), 40–1.

[256] J. R. Hall to C. T. Longley, 23 Mar. 1841, LPL MS Longley, vol. i, fo 205. Newman himself conceded that his teaching was 'not calculated to defend that system of religion which has been received for 300 years, and of which the Heads of Houses are the legitimate maintainers in this place': Newman to Keble, 26 Oct. 1840, *LDN* vii. 417.

[257] [C. P. Golightly], *Correspondence Illustrative of the Actual State of Oxford with reference to Tractarianism, and of the Attempts of Mr Newman and his Party to Unprotestantise the National Church* (1842), 32–5; [R. Whately], *The Controversy between Tract XC and the Oxford Tutors* (1841), 3.

tional ground.[258] Palmer, Churton and Archdeacon Thorp, while repudiating Tract 90, drew up a declaration and protest to the heads, taking issue with their manner of proceeding as a violation of the academic constitution as enshrined in the rights of Convocation.[259] On this strictly constitutional ground, several younger Protestant High-Churchmen would retain their old alliance with the Tractarians and remain out of sympathy with the Board, bringing an unexpected new source of strength to bolster the faltering fortunes of the Movement.

It was doubtful whether the Board had in practice exceeded its powers. In March 1841 they had merely warned the University against evasive modes of interpretation of the Articles, as part of their statutory duty to banish false teaching from the University and protect the faith of its members. The word of counsel from the Board on such a matter did not need to be submitted to Convocation.[260] The Vice-Chancellor, Philip Wynter, took particular care to meet and rebut arguments to the effect that the Board had no such function. In a fragment from his manuscript 'Memoir', dated 1845, Wynter commented

One of the charges against the Board was that it had interfered in a matter purely ecclesiastical—that the proceedings taken were of that character—proceedings as it was alleged, entirely beyond their province. So much was said upon this point by some individuals who called upon me, that I authorised one of them (Mr. Sewell) to state on my authority that the censure was academical, that care had been taken by the Hebdomadal Board not to deal with the Tract ecclesiastically, but merely to warn the junior members of the University upon a point which directly involved an honest and faithful observance of the statutes.[261]

The heads themselves in their official capacity astutely avoided discussion of the theological basis for their action, and this avoidance attracted the criticism of Low-Churchmen, who complained at the lack of theological substance in the censure.

The university authorities never claimed, as Tractarians maintained, that the University was the interpreter of the meaning of subscription to the Articles. Its role was to administer subscription and to repudiate evasions or quibbles likely to unsettle, as Wynter put it, 'the minds of our younger members'.[262] Keble was to be strongly criticized for appearing to deny the heads this judicial power.[263] One of the many traditionally minded

[258] W. Palmer [Worcester] to W. Gresley, 16 Mar. 1841, PHL Gres. 3/40/1; R. Palmer to W. Palmer [Magdalen], 24 Mar. 1841, LPL MS 1861, fo 217.
[259] See 'Protest of Edward Churton MA against the proceedings concerning Tract XC', Bodl. MS Wynter dep. d. 3, fo 5.
[260] P. Wynter to Wellington, 15 Mar. 1841, SUL 2/251/27–8.
[261] 'Memoir of Dr Wynter' [1845], PHL LBV 135/79 (transcript). Provost Hawkins emphasized to Richard Church that 'the resolution was drawn up so as to avoid the appearance of a theological censure': R. W. Church to J. Keble, 25 Mar. [1841], KCA MS E 80.
[262] 'Memoir of Dr Wynter' [1845], PHL LBV 135/79 (transcript).
[263] J. Jordan, *A Second Appeal to the Rt. Rev. The Lord Bishop of Oxford on the Divinity of the Tract Writers, more particularly with reference to their views of subscription to the Thirty-*

Protestant High-Churchmen in Oxford to whom Tract 90 seemed to strike at the very root of the ecclesiastical conception of the University, Robert Scott, fellow of Balliol, assured his Balliol colleague Tait of his support for the Letter of the Four Tutors. The grounds of his approval are significant:

There was undoubtedly a cause why the University, which exists on the condition of teaching—i.e. affixing a sense to—these Articles, should protest against their having a no-sense-at-all peremptorily fixed upon them . . . this publication struck a blow at the very mission of the University; and therefore the interference could never at another time have been so well timed.

Scott actually accepted the Tractarian point that the Board had confounded itself with the University, and even agreed with Keble that such a decree as that issued by the Board against Tract 90 should have come from Convocation, 'or at any rate from the statutable committee of Heresies', but thought that the heads were wise in practice to take this course, since an endless split would otherwise have resulted.[264] If it was the duty of tutors to instruct undergraduates in the Articles—and this all the pamphlets in defence of Oxford's system of subscription at matriculation in 1834–5 had taken for granted—then it could not be a matter of indifference to the Board in what sense those Articles were subscribed and their meaning conveyed.

Isolated as a theological force within the University after 1841, the Tractarians increasingly relied on the recurrent constitutional grievance among all 'juniors'. Jealous of the prerogatives of the heads, they were determined to sustain their power as a political as well as spiritual force in the University. The Movement undoubtedly became narrower in scope and focus and more sectarian and party-spirited in character; but two internal university controversies during 1841–2, surrounding the Poetry professorship election and revival of the Hampden question, were to reveal that the Movement's power to divide the University was greater than ever, and that its ability to win to its side a large body of moderate opinion was still considerable.

During the contest in 1841 for the chair of poetry between Isaac Williams, fellow of Trinity College, and James Garbett, fellow of Brasenose, the candidates came to be judged not as poets but as representatives of rival theological parties. Williams, the Tractarian candidate, had done much to foment opposition from Evangelicals in Oxford. His supporters insisted that his writings had been designed to heal divisions,[265] but his Tracts 80 and 87, 'On reserve', had struck at the root of the Evangelical tenet of individual conversion and understanding of the doctrine of Atonement. Lord Ashley, the leading lay representative of the Low-Church party, declared his opposi-

---

nine Articles, as maintained by Mr Keble in his 'Case of the Catholic Subscription Considered' (1841), 18.

[264] R. Scott to A. C. Tait, Apr. 1841, LPL MS Tait, vol. lxxvii, fo 34.
[265] Correspondence Relative to the Professorship of Poetry in the University of Oxford (1841), 3.

tion to Williams as a 'public teacher' in the University on the grounds that his published doctrine on reserve would tend to 'obscure the perspicuity of the Gospel by the philosophy of Paganism'.[266] Unhappy that the heads had not adopted a firmer policy of proscription against the Tractarians, many Evangelicals hoped that the defeat of Williams would open the way for the final expulsion of the Movement's supporters from Oxford.

At the outset of the campaign, college loyalties were a stronger determinant of allegiance than religious opinion. Though many anti-Tractarians supported Garbett on account of his Low-Church opinions, Garbett's election committee included Protestant High-Churchmen who desired peace and opposed any exclusion of the Tractarians. A. T. Gilbert, the late Vice-Chancellor, chaired the committee in his capacity as head of Garbett's college and was careful to dissociate himself from attempts to turn the contest into a religious struggle.[267] Even with such influential backing for Williams's opponents, there was a real chance that the Tractarian candidate might have triumphed. His prospects were dramatically changed, however, by what even a sympathizer described as an 'outrageously injudicious circular' in his support produced by Pusey in November 1841. Newman believed that Pusey had blundered badly by 'hoisting the flag of party'. Reaction was immediate. Wadham, an evangelically inclined college, began to take up Garbett's cause entirely on 'religious grounds'.[268]

Both sides believed that poetry and theology were inseparable. Non-liberal enemies of the Movement felt just as strongly as the Tractarians that religion ought to colour every aspect of academic life and teaching. The issue was, what form of religion? Opposition to Williams was raised, not because the Tractarians seemed bent on using the professorship as a medium for inculcating religion, but because that religion would be Tractarian. Pusey's circular had said as much. Keble had asserted the inherent affinity between catholic principle and true poetic feeling; only a sound 'catholic' could be a true poet.[269] Moreover, some Tractarians claimed that the influence which the poetry chair would give them would render nugatory the heads' censure of Tract 90.

At the same time the Tractarians feared that a humiliating defeat for Williams would bring grave consequences, encouraging their enemies to take strong measures against them. For the first time Newman began to harbour 'a great dread of Convocation', whose rights the Tractarians had formerly championed against the 'arbitrary' heads. Significantly it was

[266] Lord Ashley to R. Palmer, Dec. 1841: E. Hodder, *The Life and Work of the Seventh Earl of Shaftesbury, K.G.* (3 vols 1886) i. 389–90.
[267] *Correspondence Relative to the Professorship of Poetry*, 4–5.
[268] W. B. Jones to A. C. Tait, 17 Dec. 1841, LPL MS Tait, vol. lxxvii, fo 121; diary of John Hill, 16 Dec. 1841, Bodl. MS St Edmund Hall 67/13, fo 98.
[269] Keble, *The Case of Catholic Subscription: letter to Mr. Justice Coleridge*, 17.

among the influential non-residents, who had been called up with great success in 1829 and 1834–6, that the Tractarians were now losing ground. As the election campaign progressed, a powerful body of moderate High-Churchmen, led by Gladstone, alarmed at the rising theological strife within the University, attempted to effect a compromise. Proposing that both sides withdraw in the interests of the Church, the mediating party feared that polarization and proscription might threaten not merely 'extreme' opinions, but the kind of traditional, orthodox High-Church values with which the University had been long associated. In particular, Gladstone feared the opportunity that would be given to unauthorized theological censors, and sought a pronouncement from the bishops to avert the risk of laymen and lawyers becoming 'public witnesses to the soundness of the theological opinions' of the clergy.[270] Gladstone and his like-minded friends were almost as unwilling as were the Tractarians to admit the authority of the heads to adjudicate on a matter of national religious controversy; they rejected the conservative anti-Tractarians' insistence upon the University's jurisdiction over religious matters where unsound teaching appeared to be jeopardizing the traditional faith of her members. It was not that they absolutely denied the right of theological superintendence in theory; they objected rather to the apparently one-sided way it was exercised. Sir Francis Palgrave repeated a familiar Tractarian charge when he told Gladstone that the University had already 'abdicated her high functions as censor of heresy and error by permitting members of her body to promulgate such opinions as those of Milman, Arnold, Buckland etc. etc. etc. unchecked'.[271]

Having been so active in promoting the idea that all issues should be treated as issues of conscience to be decided on theological grounds, the Tractarians were in no position to lower the theological temperature of the contest. This ensured the failure of Gladstone's mediation. In the event, no election took place, but an assessment of pledged votes showed 921 for Garbett and 623 for Williams—not as decisive a majority against the Tractarians as their opponents might have wished.[272] Far from paving the way for an easy vanquishing of the Movement, the contest showed the extent of support which the Tractarians could still command, an impression which was confirmed by the revival of the Hampden controversy in May and June 1842.

There had been a growing feeling, not least in the Evangelical camp, that since 1836 Hampden had 'worked his theological passage' by his orthodox Protestant anti-Tractarian writings and lectures. Hampden's stand in defence of the Articles hastened the process of reinstatement. Edward Cardwell

---

[270] W. E. Gladstone to Viscount Sandon, 14 Dec. 1841, BL Add. MS 44358, fo 287.
[271] F. Palgrave to W. E. Gladstone, 13 Dec. 1841, BL Add. MS 44358, fo 282.
[272] T. Mozley to A. Mozley, 23 Jan. 1842, in Mozley, *Letters*, 126; diary of John Hill, 20 Jan. 1842, Bodl. MS St Edmund Hall 67/13, fo 108.

expressed the widespread conviction that 'the unobjectionable nature of the doctrines maintained by Dr Hampden in his recent lectures and sermons, has induced many of us to think that the vote of no confidence may now be fairly withdrawn'.[273] The Tractarians interpreted the moves by the heads to rehabilitate Hampden as a tactical ploy,[274] and their suspicions were kept alive by the distinctly anti-Tractarian animus of the heads' 1842 Theology statute. Pushed through Convocation with unseemly haste, the statute effectively restored Hampden's power as Regius Professor by placing him at the head of the five members of the new Theology Board.[275] Criticized by one writer as 'a pretence for reviving the Hampden question',[276] the measure was privately admitted to be a prelude to the heads' attempt, in June 1842, to repeal the punitive statute of 1836. Wellington explicitly linked the two proposals.[277] Hampden remained as theologically suspect in the eyes of the Tractarians and their allies in 1842 as he had been in 1836. The new development was that his Tractarian opponents had to contend with both the narrow rump of his original liberal supporters and a substantial body in the University who were now ready to abandon their earlier theological objections to him. The Tractarians were particularly scornful of the changed allegiance of the Evangelicals, their erstwhile allies in 1836, following Hampden's metamorphosis into the 'champion of the Reformation'. The rallying of Evangelicals behind Hampden was attacked as a logical outcome of certain inherent 'rationalistic' tendencies in the Evangelical system, to which Newman had drawn attention in Tract 73.[278] The somewhat eccentric fellow of Magdalen William Palmer was the most candid and unguarded of Hampden's Tractarian critics. He argued that the principles of the Bampton Lectures were perfectly consistent with traditional 'Protestant' principles. The 'orthodox' Protestant opponents of Hampden in 1836, Vaughan Thomas, Sewell and Ogilvie, had been inconsistent, Palmer contended, because Hampden's 'rationalism' and 'Protestantism' were synonymous.[279] This sort of language served only to drive Hampden and the Evangelicals closer together. It appeared to give credence to the old liberal charge that the spirit of the original campaign against Hampden had been essentially un-Protestant and 'popish' in nature, Evangelicals and other Protestants having been made innocent dupes of Tractarian fanaticism. 'It was by his Protestantism

[273] E. Cardwell to Wellington, 23 May 1842, SUL 2/252/113.
[274] *British Magazine* xxii (1842), 93; *Christian Remembrancer* xv (June 1848), 465.
[275] T. Gaisford to W. Howley, 23 Nov. 1841, Bodl. MS Wynter dep. d. 4, fo 136; R. Peel to Wellington, Dec. 1841, BL Add. MS 40459, fo 96.
[276] *British Critic* xxxii (1842), 161–4.
[277] Wellington to E. Cardwell, 8 June 1842, SUL 2/252/124; E. Cardwell to Wellington, 23 May 1842, SUL 2/252/113.
[278] *British Critic* xxxii (1842), 182.
[279] W. Palmer [Magdalen], *A Letter to the Rev. Dr. Hampden, Regius Professor of Divinity in the University of Oxford* (1842), 5–7.

and not by any heresy', one writer commented, 'that Dr Hampden made himself obnoxious to the semi-papists.'[280]

The arguments of both Palmer and ultra-liberal opponents disguised the extent of continued conservative Protestant misgiving about Hampden even in 1842. Many Oxford Evangelicals remained hesitant about withdrawing the censure. John Hill was not untypical in wrestling with his conscience, reluctantly voting for repeal 'as being most charitable and the least of two evils'.[281] If the Tractarians had not given the impression that there was an inseparable link between their campaign to oppose repeal and their self-confessed endeavour to 'un-Protestantize' the Church of England, many other Protestants and Evangelicals would have been inclined to vote against repeal. To the Tractarians, it was all along a matter of upholding the dogmatic principle against specific heresy and the spirit of rationalism. They believed the intention of the 1836 statute to have been both permanent and specific, despite the evidence to the contrary. Criticizing the heads for trying to act as theological censors in the case of Tract 90, the Tractarians now chided them for failing to act up to this character in the case of Hampden. According to Roundell Palmer,

those who opposed Dr. Hampden (and we were the majority) do so in the undoubting conviction that he has taught, not only heresy, but the very principle of heresy in opposition to the principle of a definite dogmatic theology. The Heads of Houses have shown themselves publicly to be at issue with the governing body of the University upon one or other of these questions—(1) what is heresy? or (2) whether heresy ought to disqualify a Regius Professor from the exercise of theological functions at Oxford?[282]

In calmer moments individual Tractarians were more realistic. James Mozley admitted that the statute of 1836 was, in truth, a 'miserable thing', vulnerable to removal as circumstances changed.[283]

Even in 1842 it was still possible for Tractarians to gain victories, for the proposal to withdraw the censure was lost by 334 to 219 when it came to Convocation.[284] The majority was much smaller than in 1836, but in the circumstances this was hardly surprising.[285] Given that the affair, like the poetry chair contest, had become a party battle of Tractarians against the rest, even that margin of success was no mean achievement.

Party spirit coloured a new controversy which broke out in 1843. The sermon which Pusey preached at Christ Church on 14 May 1843, *The Holy Eucharist, a comfort for the penitent*, might at almost any other time in the

---

[280] *North British Review* viii (Feb. 1848), 546.
[281] Diary of John Hill, 7 June 1842, Bodl. MS St Edmund Hall 67/13, fo 127.
[282] R. Palmer to J. R. Godley, June 1842, LPL MS 2498, fo 25.
[283] J. B. Mozley to A. Mozley, 31 May 1842, in Mozley, *Letters*, 131–2.
[284] E. Cardwell to Wellington, 7 June 1842, SUL 2/252/123.
[285] *British Critic* xxxii (July 1842), 182.

University's history have attracted little attention, let alone controversy. It was intended by Pusey to be something of a balance or corrective to the harsh implications of his earlier writings on the heinous nature of post-baptismal sin, which even many sympathetic to the Movement had criticized as severe and one-sided. Pusey thought he had disclaimed Transubstantiation,[286] and was quite unprepared for the storm which was raised against him. In the context of the perceived Tractarian excesses of the recent past, the Movement's enemies were not inclined to give Pusey the benefit of the doubt.

Godfrey Faussett played the leading part in the subsequent action. By virtue of his office, Faussett was the primary judge of sermons, and delated Pusey's sermon to the Vice-Chancellor. Following the strict letter of the statutes, a court of Six Doctors was convened to examine the sermon, and it was found 'to contain opinions at variance with the doctrines of the Church of England'.[287] Offered the opportunity to recant, Pusey refused, and the Vice-Chancellor, Wynter, had no alternative but to suspend Pusey from preaching for two years. The craving for martyrdom which many of the leaders of the Movement seem to have felt was fulfilled.

The heads were again unlucky in their choice of issue to challenge the Tractarians. They succeeded in rekindling sympathy for the Movement in those old High-Church quarters at Oxford where it was almost extinct, drawing from Thomas Mozley the comment that 'all persons who are not quite with the Heads of Houses' clique are disgusted'.[288] Even an avowed enemy of the Movement, Edward Cardwell, admitted confidentially to the Chancellor that it was difficult to find sentences in Pusey's sermon 'in direct opposition to the declared doctrines of the Church of England'.[289] Two of the Six Doctors, Edward Hawkins and R. W. Jelf, stated respectively 'that the preacher did not design to oppose the doctrine of the Church of England' and that no part of the sermon 'could be reasonably complained of, if properly examined'.[290] Given such apparent admissions, there might seem to be some basis for the Tractarian complaint that the heads were again assailing religious teaching whose theological nature they either did not understand or else deliberately misconstrued.

The Tractarians further castigated the heads for political partisanship stemming from a craven desire to court the government of the day. As in the mid-1830s, the Oxford authorities were suspected of keeping too much of a 'weather eye' on Westminster, censuring Pusey in order to ingratiate themselves with the Peel administration. Mark Pattison certainly believed

[286] E. B. Pusey to P. Wynter, 22 May 1843, Bodl. MS Wynter dep. d. 3, fos 27–8.
[287] E. Cardwell to Wellington, 25 May 1843, SUL 2/253/24.
[288] T. Mozley to A. Mozley, 4 June 1843, in Mozley, *Letters*, 141.
[289] E. Cardwell to Wellington, 25 May 1843, SUL 2/253/24.
[290] [E. Hawkins], 26 May 1843, Bodl. MS Wynter dep. d. 3, fo 65.

that the government had been urging the university authorities 'to put down the Tractarian party' on 'the first plausible pretext',[291] while Pusey's friend Thomas Henderson reported the 'widely spread feeling that jealousy for the purity of the faith was not alone the ground on which your condemnation was sought'.[292] However, it would be a mistake to conclude that there were no valid theological objections raised against the sermon. On the contrary, the verdicts of the Six Doctors did have specific theological substance. Hawkins's private statement of what he considered to be Pusey's doctrinal errors filled many closely written pages. The two key theological tenets in Pusey's sermon singled out for condemnation in the submissions of the Six Doctors were that of 'a substantial bodily presence' in the Eucharist as contrary to Article 28, and that of 'a continual sacrifice in the eucharist for remission of sins'.[293] Though Pusey sheltered behind lengthy quotations from the ancient Fathers sometimes shorn of context, many traditional High-Churchmen denied his claim to be simply restating classic Caroline Anglican teaching.[294] Of the Six Doctors themselves, only Benjamin Symons could be classed as out of sympathy with the traditional Protestant High-Church tradition of the University. One of the doctors, Richard Jelf, 'a member of the same chapter with Dr. Pusey', in Cardwell's words, 'and ... for many years ... his most intimate friend', was thought to be, if anything, predisposed to favour the accused.[295] It was well known that other doctors such as Thomas Gaisford, Dean of Christ Church, or Cardwell himself might have been selected. They would have had still less sympathy with Pusey's teaching than those who sat in judgement on the sermon.

It was only the continuing constitutional grievances of the 'juniors' against the power exercised by the heads which won for Pusey an otherwise surprising degree of support at this time and smothered the strictly theological issue. Pusey's main line of protest against the sentence had rested on the claim that the Vice-Chancellor's action was 'unstatutable as well as unjust'.[296] Determined to appeal to the broader and more popular ground of the academic rights of Convocation, the Tractarians now worked in unison with older and widely respected advisers outside the University, such as Sir John Coleridge, Gladstone, Lord Dungannon and Edward Badeley. This gave weight and respectability to Pusey's cause. A formal address of protest, signed by 300 non-resident members of Convocation, was presented to the

[291] M. Pattison to E. Pattison, 5 June 1843, LCA MS Pat./II/B.
[292] T. Henderson to E. B. Pusey, 17 June 1843, PHL Pusey Papers, Pus. 19/19.
[293] E. Cardwell to Wellington, 1 July 1843, SUL 2/253/43.
[294] J. S. Edison, *The Doctrine of Dr Pusey's Sermon* (1843), 72–3; J. Garbett, *A Review of Dr Pusey's Sermon and the Doctrine of the Eucharist According to the Church of England* (1843), pp. viii, xxvi.
[295] E. Cardwell to Wellington, 25 May 1843, SUL 2/253/24.
[296] For Pusey's protest see SUL 2/253/28.

Vice-Chancellor deprecating 'the construction of the statute, under which Dr. Pusey has been condemned'.[297] To Wynter, this seemed like a direct challenge to his authority. He refused to receive the protest, censuring its signatories and promoters in memorable terms for 'an unbecoming and unstatutable attempt to overawe the Resident Governor of the University in the execution of his office'.[298] Wynter's self-description was unfortunate, and seemed to be tantamount to usurpation and a considerable affront to the rights of non-resident MAs. Wynter's reproof was considered more appropriate for an unruly 'set of schoolboys' than for grave and learned gentlemen of the legal and political world.

Pusey determined to have the issue settled in the courts. An opinion was obtained from the Tractarian sympathizer Roundell Palmer, who advised that the Vice-Chancellor's action had been unlawful and suggested an application to the Court of Queen's Bench to prevent him from carrying out his 'pretended sentence'. Even the Queen's Advocate, Sir John Dodson, and the Attorney-General, Sir Frederick Pollock, pronounced the sentence as having 'nullity of law',[299] but the question of how far the civil courts could have cognizance over a matter of university discipline was a contentious one and remained unresolved. Pusey also took counsel with Badeley and James Hope. Like Palmer, they judged that the sentence was 'no ecclesiastical censure; as quite independent of the Church; as a mere arbitrary and unconstitutional exercise of magisterial authority in the University'.[300] However, even Hope, Badeley and Palmer had misgivings as to whether Pusey could carry his point either in a suit in the vice-chancellor's court, or in a civil suit under the Church Discipline Act.

According to the strict letter of the statutes, the Vice-Chancellor had not exceeded his powers, and his actions were supported by historical precedents. The only firm ground of complaint, apart from that of supposed natural justice, was that the statute was obsolete and had been applied in a one-sided way.[301] Few conservative High-Churchmen were impressed by this argument. It was surprising that so many of the followers of the Movement should have sought to assail proceedings which were 'conceived in rather a Middle-Age spirit'. Moreover, the force of the complaint that the Lady Margaret Professor had acted as both accuser and judge was diminished by the consideration that it was the inevitable consequence of the anti-Hampden statute of 1836 which the Tractarians had engineered.[302] The

[297] SUL 2/253/55.
[298] P. Wynter to E. Badeley [nd] (copy), SUL 2/253/56; cf P. Wynter to Wellington, 4 Aug. 1843, SUL 2/253/54.
[299] Liddon, *Pusey* ii. 354.
[300] Ibid. ii. 353.
[301] *British Critic* xxxiii. (July 1843), 241, 254–6, 258; *The Plea of the Six Doctors Examined* (1843), 5, 7, 9–10.
[302] Liddon, *Pusey* ii. 310.

Tractarians could hardly have expected a better hearing from Hampden than the one they were given by Faussett. Furthermore, the statute did not allow, let alone require, Wynter to grant a public hearing to the accused.[303] As James Garbett put it, 'any summons into the presence of the Vice-Chancellor is not for the purpose of a disputation and a wrangling defence but . . . as a preliminary to that compulsory retraction which the law confers the full power to extort'.[304] A young man, as in the case of J. B. Morris after two controversial sermons preached in St Mary's in 1839, might be simply warned or asked to retract.[305] A doctor of divinity could not expect such leniency, 'for he surely had had time to digest his sentiments, and power to express them accurately'.[306] Little would have been gained by further attempts at explanation in Pusey's case; the Vice-Chancellor's correspondence with him only served to strengthen Wynter's initial conviction that the sermon was heterodox in tendency.

In his biography of Pusey, Liddon did less than justice to the difficulties which faced Wynter as Vice-Chancellor. Wynter's correspondence reveals, at the worst, a somewhat diffident man, rather too much in the shadow of the great Provost Hawkins of Oriel, dogged by an almost over-scrupulous and painful sense of devotion to duty, which Pusey himself was willing to acknowledge.[307] In fact such was Wynter's reputation as a staunch anti-liberal Churchman that Shuttleworth had been surprised by his stand against Tract 90: 'I had my fears that his bias would be in the other direction.'[308] Wynter was as much opposed to whiggery and to what he castigated as 'low church principles' as he was to Tractarianism.[309] For more than a year prior to Pusey's sermon, Wynter had resisted relentless pressure from Golightly to take action against Tractarian preachers, and was exposed to private criticisms from Evangelicals for not doing enough to clear the name of the University from the Tractarian 'heresy'.[310] Wynter had grounds for his indignation at the aspersion cast by Sir John Coleridge that he had meekly capitulated to outside pressures. In so far as this applied to pressure from Wellington, Coleridge's charge was wide of the mark—the Chancellor was,

[303] P. Wynter to E. B. Pusey, 3 June 1843, Bodl. MS Wynter dep. d. 3, fo 65; Bodl. MS St Edmund Hall 67/14, fo 17.
[304] Garbett, *Pusey and the University of Oxford*, 16.
[305] J. H. Newman to J. R. Bloxam, 25 Oct. 1839, MCA MS 307, no. 27.
[306] *British Magazine* xxiv (1843), 87.
[307] E. B. Pusey to J. B. Mozley, 20 Dec. 1844, in Mozley, *Letters*, 158–9.
[308] P. Shuttleworth to A. C. Tait, 10 Mar. 1841, LPL MS Tait, vol i, fo 9.
[309] P. Wynter to Wellington, 13 Apr. 1842, SUL 2/252/76. For a Tractarian admission that Wynter was 'a sort of high churchman' see *Christian Remembrancer* viii (Oct. 1844), 537. Disraeli later described Wynter as a representative of the 'orthodox church and state party': W. Costin, *The History of St John's College Oxford, 1598–1860* (1958), 250.
[310] See e.g. W. Goode to C. P. Golightly, 29 May 1843, LPL MS 1806, fo 103; C. Bickersteth to C. P. Golightly, 5 June 1843, LPL MS 1804, fo 34; P. Wynter to C. P. Golightly, 6 Dec. 1842, LPL MS 1811, fo 250.

on this occasion, all for doing nothing, for fear of 'reviving the Pusey controversy'.[311]

The Tractarian challenge to the authority of Wynter and the heads seemed to represent further evidence that they had abandoned their earlier attempt to identify and assimilate the University *qua* ecclesiastical institution with what they interpreted as an authoritative voice of the Church catholic in England. Their appeals were now to 'liberty of conscience', and their tirades were directed against the heads for being 'Inquisitors'.[312] Bedel Cox recollected with approval 'a remark made at the time, "that Dr. Pusey was now made to wear the cap which in 1836 he had fitted on Dr. Hampden's head"'.[313] As they showed by delating a sermon on the Eucharist by James Garbett in 1844, the Tractarians themselves had no insuperable objection to such an application of that statute.[314] They were driven, instead, to rely on special pleading and even sarcasm to make good their complaint of persecution at the hands of the university authorities.

W. F. Hook reminded Pusey that their difficulty now in convincing anyone of the theological nullity of the Vice-Chancellor's action was exacerbated by the fact that 'we have told our people to regard as heresy what the Church pronounces to be such, and the Church and University are so identified in the minds of men—University men'.[315] It was impossible to escape the conclusion that, ultimately, ecclesiastical authority, whether wielded by university authorities or bishops, was a wholesome revival of sacred discipline when applied against the Movement's opponents, but suddenly became an illiberal and tyrannical exercise of arbitrary power when applied against the Movement itself. Moreover, the Tractarian attempt to appeal beyond the jurisdiction of the University to the lawcourts squared uneasily with the logic of the whole Tractarian campaign since 1829 on behalf of the independence of the University. In the heat of ecclesiastical partisanship, the Tractarians in 1843 were prepared to separate the cause of 'the Church' from that of the 'official University' in a way which overturned the principles of 1829. Henry Woodgate went so far as to state 'that the university is only a lay corporation, and therefore has no authority, properly so called, in ecclesiastical matters'.[316] Pusey felt no compunction about flouting the authority of the heads, while Keble, finding that Bishop Phillpotts disapproved of the censure, resorted to the novel argument that the Vice-Chancellor's sentence need not be obeyed unless it was ratified by one

[311] Wellington to E. Cardwell, 31 May 1843, SUL 2/253/26.
[312] *A Letter to the Rev. the Vice-Chancellor of the University of Oxford and the Learned Doctors who Assisted him on a Late Occasion. From Torquemada the Younger* (1843), 12.
[313] Cox, 328.
[314] *Christian Remembrancer* viii (July 1844), 1–8; Bodl. MS Wynter dep. d. 5, fos 141–8.
[315] W. F. Hook to E. B. Pusey, 4 June 1843, in Liddon, *Pusey* ii. 349.
[316] H. A. Woodgate, *Considerations on the Present Duty of the University of Oxford with Reference to the Late Proceeding against the Regius Professor of Hebrew* (1843), 20.

or more bishops.[317] This was an argument hastily shelved when the bishops in turn assailed the Movement.

At length Sir William Follett, who was slower to reply than Dodson and Pollock, gave advice rather different from theirs. He upheld that much-vaunted ecclesiastical independence of the University which the Tractarians had so strongly insisted upon ever since 1829. It was surprising that it should take Follett's opinion finally to convince Pusey and his friends that if, as was only right, the statute under which the Six Doctors had condemned Pusey was 'taken merely as one of the regulations of the University for those who voluntarily choose to become members of it, and agree to its rules, then the rules of the ordinary courts of law were not applicable'.[318] By pursuing the case, the Tractarians had called into question the University's powers of internal regulation and placed a fatal weapon in the hands of those liberals bent on secularizing the University and removing its clerical character. For the moment, jealousy of the 'seniors' meant that the majority of even non-Tractarian 'juniors' were prepared to overlook the inconsistency and anomaly of a Movement so committed in theory to authority, but in practice always chafing under it and attempting to throw it off.

Another opportunity soon presented itself for the Tractarians to exploit the constitutional sensitivities of the MAs and to embarrass the Vice-Chancellor. It was proposed to grant an honorary DCL to Edward Everett, the United States minister to Britain, in June 1843. Everett was a Unitarian, 'afflicted with the leprosy of Socinianism', as one Tractarian commentator put it, 'and until he be washed of that disease he is an alien from the church, and therefore unfit to receive the honours which she has to bestow'.[319] In the wake of the heads' recent punitive measures against the Movement, the Tractarians might have reason for complaint at this connivance at heresy.[320] In fact, the cases of Pusey and Everett were scarcely comparable. It was a perfectly legitimate exercise of the high religious office of the university authorities to reprove the public purveyor of false teaching within the University's precincts. Honorary distinctions, in contrast, conferred no right of teaching within the University and 'had never been conferred or withheld with any reference to the religious tenets of the individual'.[321] Foreign dignitaries were regular recipients of honorary degrees and many were non-Anglicans: Romanists and even Muslims had been included.

On the day of the ceremony, amid rowdy scenes directed against an unpopular proctor, the cries of 'non placet' went conveniently unheard by

[317] J. Keble to E. B. Pusey, 25 Oct. 1844, PHL LBV 50/71; *British Critic* xxxiv (1843), 498.
[318] Liddon, *Pusey* ii. 354.
[319] *English Churchman* i (1843), 424.
[320] Liddon, *Pusey* ii. 351; R. W. Church to F. Rogers, 28 June 1843, *Life and Letters of Dean Church*, ed. M. C. Church (1895), 40–4.
[321] P. Wynter to Wellington, 30 June 1843, Bodl. MS Wynter dep. d. 4, fo 314. See p. 68 above.

the Vice-Chancellor, and Everett's degree slipped through. Many among the large body of non-Tractarian, traditional High-Churchmen were irritated at the Vice-Chancellor's violation of the rights and liberties of MAs in Convocation, in effect granting the degree purely on his own authority and refusing a scrutiny demanded by persons opposing the grant.[322] The Tractarian Charles Marriott was certainly expressing a view widely held among MAs when he informed Wynter sternly, 'that any concession that a degree so conferred can possibly be accounted valid would be a surrender of those rights which we are bound to maintain'.[323] These apparent rights were further infringed in the so-called Macmullen affair, which dragged on from 1842 to 1844.

R. G. Macmullen, Dean of Corpus Christi College, was an impetuous and controversial Tractarian. Required by his college statutes to proceed to the degree of bachelor of divinity, he made the necessary application to the Regius Professor of Divinity, the uncongenial Hampden. Traditionally the exercises for the degree took the form of Latin disputations, but these had become something of a sham. Edward Burton, Hampden's predecessor, had introduced a new procedure requiring two English essays on subjects assigned by the professor.[324] Asserting the authority of his office, Hampden sent Macmullen two distinctly Protestant tenets to 'prove'—on the Eucharistic presence and sacrifice, and on the subject of apostolic tradition. Knowing that Macmullen espoused a high Tractarian position, and that the two theses set required a repudiation of both doctrines, Hampden was laying a trap.[325] Macmullen refused to accept the subjects and brought an action against Hampden in the vice-chancellor's court, claiming that the professor had exceeded his powers. The dispute raised the question to what extent should the divinity exercises be made a test of sound doctrine, as defined by the Regius Professor, rather than 'merely a trial of learning and talents'?[326]

Wynter's support for Hampden's claim to control the exercises for the degree[327] enjoyed Wellington's approval. But it was seen to represent a further *de facto* enlargement of the powers of the University's ruling body at the expense of Convocation. The Board went further, seeking to make these incursions upon Convocation's presumed privileges permanent in a new Theology statute, introduced in February 1844. The new statute proposed to give the Regius Professor the power which Macmullen had contested, placing all divinity degrees under the control of a board chaired by the Vice-Chancellor. The University's constitution, which it was becoming

[322] W. Sewell to P. Wynter, 29 June 1843, Bodl. MS Wynter dep. d. 4, fo 321.
[323] C. Marriott to P. Wynter, 1 July 1843, Bodl. MS Wynter dep. d. 4, fo 327.
[324] E. Burton to G. Rowley, 24 Jan. 1830, OUA NW/21/1.
[325] R. G. Macmullen to E. B. Pusey, 17 June 1842, PHL, Pusey Papers, Pus. 18/11.
[326] *Dublin Review* NS 17 (July 1871), 92–3.
[327] R. G. Macmullen, *Copies of the Correspondence in the Case of the Regius Professor of Divinity and Macmullen* (1844), 12.

familiar among opponents of the Board to describe as 'a popular one', seemed to be subverted by 'taking the conferring of the most important class of Degrees out of the hands of Congregation, and lodging it in the hands of two individual functionaries'.[328] It was claimed that Congregation and the whole body of the University were the ultimate judges of a candidate's fitness for his degree—not the Regius Professor. The Tractarians could still count upon wide support for resistance to the pretensions of the heads, and the new statute was defeated in Convocation by 341 to 21.[329]

High-minded pleas in favour of university democracy were not, however, Macmullen's sole motivating force. Tractarian partisanship and antipathy to Hampden played their part. Hampden, it is true, did not emerge from the affair with any more credit than when he was the object of censure in 1836 and 1842. His stubborn exercise of the keenly disputed rights of his office seemed to square ill with his earlier demands for liberty of conscience, according to Dean Church turning 'what had been a mere formal exercise into a sharp and sweeping test of doctrine, which would place all future divinity degrees in the University at his mercy'.[330] Yet any reform which had as its object a sharper definition and specification of the religious-teaching office of the University, and a setting-aside of lax custom developed during a period of relative torpor and indifference, might have been expected to enjoy Tractarian favour. Had it not represented a bolstering-up of Hampden's position, the reform might have been welcomed by the Tractarians as a positive enhancement of the religious character of the University.

Hampden's use of his powers found support from Faussett and the majority of Tory old High-Churchmen, who endorsed what they felt to be a legitimate attempt in notoriously disturbed times to resist a straining of the limits of Church of England orthodoxy by the Tractarians. The two propositions which Hampden sought to impose on Macmullen were fully in accordance with traditional Protestant High-Church doctrine. Fifteen years earlier, men of that party, like Charles Ogilvie, would not have hesitated to subscribe to them unreservedly. The Board's endeavour to make Macmullen conform to certain defined theological limits appeared to be vindicated by the fact that within three years he had abjured the Church of England and joined the Church of Rome.

The deep-seated sense of alienation from and antipathy towards the Hebdomadal Board felt by the Tractarians and their allies by the late summer of 1844 drove them into committing their most extreme act of defiance. When Philip Wynter's four-year term of office came to a close in September, they determined on taking the unprecedented step of opposing the nomination of his successor, Benjamin Symons, the Evangelical Warden

[328] *The New Examination for Divinity Degrees* (1844), 13.
[329] OUA WP/γ/24(6), fo 67, HBM 13 May 1844.
[330] R. W. Church, *Oxford Movement* (1891), 322.

of Wadham. By custom, if not statute, the office of Vice-Chancellor went in rotation among the heads, and the power of nomination was held to reside with the Chancellor. The opposition raised against Symons thus represented an implied challenge to the Chancellor's authority. The Tractarian plot, organized during the summer of 1844,[331] badly backfired when the great bulk of MAs rallied to Symons's defence.[332] In the end, Convocation supported Symons by 882 votes to 183.[333] Coming so soon after the decisive rejection of the Theology statute in May, the challenge to Symons was a major tactical blunder. As even Liddon admitted, this was 'an act out of exasperation rather than of wisdom' on the part of Tractarians.[334]

Wellington, outraged when he heard reports of the intended opposition, which he treated as a mark of personal disrespect and want of confidence, threatened resignation if the vote against Symons succeeded.[335] Sir Charles Wetherell's legal advice subsequently confirmed Wellington's view that the Chancellor alone possessed the right of nomination,[336] to the embarrassment of Wynter, who had allowed an election to be held.[337] In challenging Wellington's constitutional prerogatives, the Tractarians had touched a sensitive nerve. Tractarianism might or might not be heresy, but that it was subversive the Chancellor was now in no doubt.

The Tractarians justified their stand against Symons partly on personal and theological grounds—Symons was reported to have said that the party ought to have been 'put down long ago'[338]—and partly as an act of constitutional self-defence, a protest against the supposed 'aggressions upon the constitution of the University' by the late Vice-Chancellor. 'If the Vice-Chancellors were to be dictators', Roundell Palmer wrote, 'their election by rotation could not be submitted to by those who had the power to resist it.'[339] The claim that, in the past, the Vice-Chancellor had been 'little more than a functionary', but that in recent years holders of the office had assumed extended powers,[340] was borne out neither by the statutes nor by precedent. The challenge to Symons divided the Tractarians from some of their erstwhile allies among High-Churchmen such as Sewell, Churton and Hook. To

---

[331] *Pages from the Diary of an Oxford Lady, 1843–1862*, ed. M. J. Gifford (1932), 6.

[332] C. P. Golightly to W. Bricknell, Sept. 1844, PHL Bricknell Papers.

[333] P. Wynter to Wellington [1844], Bodl. MS Wynter dep. d. 4, fo 436; diary of John Hill, 8 Oct. 1844, Bodl. MS St Edmund Hall 67/15, fo 3. See J. S. G. Simmons, 'The Duke of Wellington and the vice-chancellorship in 1844', *Bodleian Library Record* v (1945).

[334] Liddon, *Pusey* ii. 413.

[335] Wellington to P. Wynter, 29 Sept. 1844, Bodl. MS Wynter dep. d. 4, fos 424–5.

[336] Wellington to P. Wynter, 2 Oct. 1844, Bodl. MS Wynter dep. d. 4, fo 432.

[337] P. Wynter to Wellington, 30 Sept. 1844, Bodl. MS Wynter dep. d. 4, fo 427.

[338] *Letters with a Few Remarks Concerning Rumours which have Lately been in Circulation Calculated to Prejudice the Appointment of the Warden of Wadham College to the Vice-Chancellorship* (1844), 7–8.

[339] R. Palmer to J. R. Godley, 24 Nov. 1844, LPL MS 2498, fo 49.

[340] *The Times* 9 Oct. 1844; *English Churchman* ii (1844), 616–18.

Churton the Tractarians seemed bent on precipitating a crisis.[341] A. T. Gilbert feared that 'these reckless men will bring a visitation upon the university, if they are not stopped';[342] if the University failed to restrain the offenders, 'the Civil Power' would intervene. With prophetic insight, Gilbert predicted that the Tractarians would come to 'rue' the external interference that they seemed to be inciting. In opposing Symons, the Tractarians had raised the alarming prospect that an unpopular system of oligarchic government would be replaced by something far worse. These apprehensions gave the edge to the fury of conservative Protestants within the University, whether old High-Church or Evangelical, who were united in opposition to the incipient rising liberalism of some younger elements.[343]

In the forefront of those bent upon bringing the constitutional crisis to a head was a distinctly 'Romanizing' party among the younger tutors and MAs who by 1843–4 had gained prominence within the University. Represented by such figures as W. G. Ward and Frederick Oakeley, both fellows of Balliol, J. B. Morris and J. D. Dalgairns of Exeter and T. W. Allies of Wadham, this party became a source of acute embarrassment not only to old High-Churchmen sympathetic to the Movement, but to moderate Tractarians and even Pusey. The Romanizing party projected its views through the periodical the *British Critic*, which had effectively fallen into its hands after 1841, and which it used to direct a ceaseless attack upon the Oxford authorities.[344] Within college common rooms, this extreme party carried the process of division and distraction over the merits and claims of Tractarianism to new lengths. Sometimes these disputes took bizarre and petty forms, as in the case of the Balliol 'Civil War of 1843', when proposals for the architectural restoration of the college buildings by Pugin became a matter of theological controversy.[345]

The spirit of self-denial and asceticism among the Romanizers commanded undoubted respect, even among the most Protestant-minded of the resident body. In particular, independent, moderate resident MAs such as Hussey of Christ Church, C. P. Eden of Oriel, Sewell of Exeter, Francis Faber of Magdalen, W. A. Greenhill of Trinity, Henry Wall of Balliol and Hobhouse of Merton, who had helped swell the Tractarian majorities in the disputes between the heads and the Tractarians in the early 1840s but had deplored the Movement's tactics in the vice-chancellorship contest,[346] re-

[341] E. Churton to E. B. Pusey, 28 Dec. [1844], PHL LBV 41/15.
[342] A. T. Gilbert to C. P. Golightly, 20 Sept. 1844, LPL MS 1806, fo 9.
[343] T. T. Churton to C. P. Golightly, 18 Sept. 1843, LPL MS 1805, fo 19.
[344] Ward, *Ward and the Oxford Movement*, ch. 10.
[345] J. Jones, 'The civil war of 1843', *Balliol College Record* (1978), 60–7.
[346] E. Churton to J. Watson, 6 Feb. 1843, PHL Chur. 2/3/6; R. Scott to R. Davidson, 30 July 1886, PHL Sco. 1/8/4. For the view of an aged High-Churchman, see *Reflections Discriminative and Pacificatory, on Recent and Still Passing Events in our Church and our Elder University, by a graduate of the last century* (1845).

cognized the moral elevation and sincerity of purpose of the extreme party. Any revival of the influence of the Movement depended on heeding the counsel of the independents and not fostering new points of controversy. These counsellors now considered that the work of the Movement in relation to the University had already been done,[347] and that the Movement's followers should direct their energies to carrying out 'church principles' in the parishes, as Hook was doing in Leeds.

The emergence of the Romanizing school marked the loss of control by the Tractarian leaders over their followers. Newman later admitted as much: 'Years after, a friend, writing to me in remonstrance at the excesses, as he thought them, of my disciples, applied to me my very own verse about St. Gregory Nazianzen, "Thou couldst a people raise, but couldst not rule" ...At no time could I exercise over others that authority which under the circumstances was imperatively required.'[348] Some younger conservative High-Churchmen in the University such as Palmer of Worcester were still prepared to exonerate the leaders from blame for secessions to Rome by men like Sibthorp of Magdalen, Seager of Worcester and a Cambridge graduate, Francis Wackerbarth;[349] and Palmer went on to produce a history of the Movement in an attempt to 'draw some line between sound church principles and Ultra & Romanising views' but 'without censuring the Tracts'.[350] Events soon proved it to be a fruitless task, and enemies of the Movement derided him for the attempt.[351] As if to disprove such a distinction and to embarrass the old High-Churchmen, in direct response to Palmer's *Narrative of Events Connected with the Oxford Movement*, W. G. Ward produced a provocative, unashamedly Romanizing treatise, *The Ideal of a Christian Church*. Ward's book provoked a final crisis. The heads, with the Evangelical Symons now at the helm, decided on strong measures.

A committee of the Hebdomadal Board found little difficulty in picking out objectionable passages in Ward's book, and the Board pressed ahead with a condemnation of the book and its author, submitting three propositions to Convocation in December 1844. The first condemned Ward's book, and the second proposed to deprive him of his degree. Finally, the Board sought to impose a new condition to subscription to the Articles, adding a declaration that they were assented to in the sense in which 'they were both first published and were now imposed by the University'.[352] Had the heads rested content with the first two propositions only, they would have carried

---

[347] E. Churton to E. B. Pusey, 3 Jan. 1845, PHL LBV 41/16.
[348] Newman, *Apologia*, 63.
[349] W. Palmer to W. Gresley, 20 Nov. 1841, PHL Gres. 3/40/3; W. Palmer to W. E. Gladstone, 3 Aug. 1843, BL Add. MS 44360, fo 302.
[350] W. Palmer to W. Gresley, 15 Sept. 1843, PHL Gres. 3/40/6.
[351] W. S. Bricknell to C. P. Golightly, 9 Nov. 1843, LPL MS 1805, fos 87–8.
[352] Church, *Oxford Movement*, 377; for a defence of the necessity for these measures, see B. Symons to Wellington, 16 Dec. 1844, SUL 2/254/106.

the bulk of the University—High- and Low-Church—with them. However, by attempting to enforce what appeared to be, for some, a 'new test', the heads blundered against the same independent instincts of non-Tractarian juniors which they had antagonized before. Such was the pressure of opinion against this apparent innovation that the heads were compelled to withdraw the proposition in January 1845—substituting for it a proposal that Convocation should formally condemn Tract 90.[353]

Convocation considered the resolutions on 13 February 1845, a momentous day in the annals of the Movement. The first proposition was passed comfortably, the second with a smaller majority, but the third, owing to the dramatic intervention of the two Tractarian proctors with the cry of 'non placet', failed.[354] In short, the heads had overplayed their hand. Dean Church's description, in his history, of the February meeting as the 'rout' of the Movement was an over-simplification. A term as strong as that is applicable only if the meeting is seen is conjunction with Ward's announcement just afterwards of his impending marriage. By that announcement the defeated Movement was exposed to ridicule. The laughter arose, as Wilfrid Ward wrote in his Life of his father, from 'the broad fact that the English clergyman who advocated clerical celibacy was himself about to marry'. Many years later Stanley commented:

The contest had reached a white heat—lawsuits, prosecutions of every kind were talked of—the weapons of both sides were drawn and sharpened—when suddenly the Oxford Movement collapsed at its centre. This is not the place or time to describe the entirely personal reason of a defeat so singular and so total; suffice it to say that it was a defeat in which the sense of the ludicrous aspect prevailed over every other feeling.

Taken in isolation, the heads' victory on 13 February was of the pyrrhic kind. 'Such another victory and we are ruined,' one of their supporters observed.[355] For Tract 90 escaped condemnation in Convocation, the body which the Tractarians had always argued was the final court of appeal in the University.

Although the Tractarians escaped more lightly than might have been expected, the Hebdomadal Board did not avoid being showered with obloquy for the last of what were regarded as a series of acts of tyranny and persecution. If the Oxford Movement is viewed in isolation strictly in terms of the history of religious ideas and spirituality, Gladstone's charge that the measures of the heads were conducted in 'a cold, effete and repressive temper' might be sustained.[356] Even an avowed opponent of Tract 90,

[353] E. Cardwell to Wellington, 4 Feb. 1845, SUL 2/254/112.

[354] E. Cardwell to Wellington, 17 Feb. 1845, SUL 2/254/117.

[355] Ward, Ward and the Oxford Movement, 350; Ed. Rev. cliii (Apr. 1881), 323–4; W. Dalby to P. Bliss, 19 Mar. 1845, BL Add. MS 34575, fo 535. Ward's letter announcing that he was to marry appeared in The Times, 3 Mar. 1845, 5d. In Church's view (Oxford Movement, 336), those who looked below the surface realized that the Movement had not been completely routed.

[356] W. E. Gladstone to S. Wilberforce, 29 Dec. 1844, BL Add. MS 44393, fos 53–4.

A. C. Tait, reprimanded the heads for their 'distance' and lack of under-standing of the feelings of the junior body of the University during this final controversy.[357] Tait affirmed that he had not met anyone in Oxford 'who has not positively declared his intention of opposing the Test'.[358] Had the opposition to the third proposition been confined to Tractarians and the younger liberals, the heads could still have got their way. It was the opposi-tion to it among the orthodox, moderate majority of residents that proved fatal to the measure.[359] As in 1841 the heads undoubtedly failed to take sufficient account of the objection that they were enforcing a strict inter-pretation of subscription against those who sought latitude in a 'catholic' direction, while observing an apparent laxity towards those whose latitudi-narianism lay in a liberal-Protestant direction.[360]

Dean Church suggested that the heads were motivated by an ignorant, old-fashioned belief that the appeal of Romanism for Oxford graduates and MAs lay in 'a silly hankering after the pomp or the frippery of Roman Catholic worship, and at best a craving after the romantic and sentimen-tal'.[361] Yet it can be argued that the heads took the steps which they did in the Ward affair precisely because they recognized the reality and depth of the appeal of Romanism in the junior university, and acted according to their duty as guardians of the faith of the young. For where 'Romanizing' dan-gerously impinged upon the University, and where it absolutely demanded the attention and response of the authorities, was not in any love of cere-monial, private ascetic practices, or even private opinion in favour of this or that Romish doctrine. Rather, the heads saw it as tampering with and subverting the University's traditional test and bulwark of the orthodox faith of the young under its care, subscription to the Thirty-nine Articles. It was to preserve the meaning and intention of that test that the heads in 1844–5, as in 1841, took their stand.

In the mid-1830s, the campaign which the Tractarians had spearheaded in defence of the existing subscription had presupposed some consensus on the sense or meaning of the Articles as imposed by the University. Tract 90 had destroyed this common ground, though some Tractarians belatedly and not altogether convincingly argued that no such consensus had existed since the controversies of 1772.[362] Tract 90 was revolutionary in justifying for the first time an interpretation of the Articles in a 'catholic' or non-'traditionary' sense. The doubts thereby thrown on the meaning of subscription to the

[357] A. C. Tait, *A Letter to the Rev. the Vice-Chancellor of the University of Oxford, on the Measures Intended to be Proposed to Convocation on the 13th of February, in connexion with the case of the Rev. W. G. Ward M.A.* (1845), 12, 5–7.
[358] A. C. Tait to R. Jenkyns, 30 Dec. 1844, BCA MS Jenkyns VI. B.
[359] See e.g. E. Churton to W. Gresley, 17 Dec. 1844, PHL Gres. 3/7/49.
[360] W. E. Gladstone to S. Wilberforce, 16 Jan. 1845, BL Add. MS 44393, fo 71.
[361] Church, *Oxford Movement*, 338.
[362] G. D. Ryder, *Subscription to the Articles* (1845), 21.

Articles induced some of the heads, including Hawkins at Oriel, to require as an additional condition of election to college fellowships a repudiation of the interpretation of the Articles advocated in that Tract. R. W. Church's refusal to disavow Tract 90 prompted Hawkins to remove him from his tutorship, and the granting of a testimonial to C. P. Eden was delayed on similar grounds.[363] At Balliol, where W. G. Ward was removed from his tutorship, even the liberal A. C. Tait supported the policy of the Master.[364]

Many of the younger High-Churchmen in the University, acknowledging the right of individual colleges to carry out such a policy, considered that this was sufficient protection, and believed that the Board's proposed 'new test' went too far in granting 'enormous' unprecedented powers to the Vice-Chancellor.[365] Had the scope of the measure been more limited, 'the opposition to its reception', Wickham told Jenkyns, 'would have been confined to the advocates of No. 90, and to mere latitudinarians fretting at all tests and restraints, and longing for an unlimited field for their speculations'.[366] In the event, the opposition encompassed moderate High-Churchmen who, though they disapproved of Tract 90, suspected that the heads were showing undue subservience to ministerial and 'ultra-Protestant' lay pressure, compromising the University's independence.[367] The reverse was the case, for Wellington had favoured caution and moderation, arguing first that no special notice should be taken of the *Ideal* because 'it has not been delivered as a sermon, above all not preached in the presence of the university, but was simply a pamphlet', and then urging the Board to delay until Ward had been heard, 'in order to be certain that the measures which the Convocation should make to prevent evasion or mistake in future, might to a certainty be effectual'.[368] The heads' concern for the preservation of the University's Protestant orthodox doctrinal purity caused these cancellarial urgings to be overruled.

The heads felt obliged to introduce a new declaration in December 1844 precisely because the censure against Tract 90 in March 1841 had not proved sufficient to stem the spread of 'false' and 'evasive' modes of interpreting the Articles. Ward's book was apparent proof of this. The declaration was required, Henry Hallam explained, as 'a guarantee to the world that the University of Oxford will give a protestant education to the youth she

---

[363] R. W. Church to G. Moberly, 26 June 1842, in *Life of Church*, 36–7; E. Hawkins to C. P. Eden, 30 Oct. 1843, OCL 83.

[364] R. E. Prothero, *Life and Correspondence of A. P. Stanley* (2 vols 1893) i. 297–8.

[365] W. Gresley, *Suggestions on the New Statute to be Proposed in the University of Oxford* (1845), 7.

[366] E. D. Wickham to R. Jenkyns, 29 Jan. 1845, BCA MS Jenkyns VI. B.

[367] F. D. Maurice, *On the Right and Wrong Method of Supporting Protestantism: a letter to Lord Ashley, respecting a certain proposed measure for stifling the expression of opinion in the University of Oxford* (1843), 22–3.

[368] Wellington to B. Symons, 28 Nov., 17 Dec. 1844, SUL 2/254/100, 2/254/108.

instructs'.[369] Further, the proposed declaration was not an innovation, as the detractors alleged, but was claimed by its proponents as simply intended to 'reinvest the existing statute with the force of which it had been deprived'.[370] The object was not to create some novel authority, but 'to preserve a power, already possessed'.[371] There was even some criticism of the proposition against Tract 90 for not being specific enough.[372]

The logic of the heads' case was strong. Their assumption that the sense of the Articles imposed by the University was the same as that imposed by the Church had never before been questioned. If it was true, as the Tractarians had always insisted, that the University and the Church of England were interchangeable, and that the former really did have a religious-teaching or 'prophetical' office, then it was hard to fault the Board's actions. For this reason, Palmer of Worcester without irony congratulated the heads for proving more attached to the Articles, and more concerned to preserve 'the securities for the reception of the Church's doctrines in the University' in 1845 than in 1835.[373]

The older generation of 'Zs' were still more emphatic in their support of the principle behind the action of the heads. As Joshua Watson, leader of the 'Hackney Phalanx' maintained,

The cards were dealt to them, and if they had refused to play, they had surely failed in their duty to the University as 'custodes juventutis academicae'. Nothing could release the body from their obligation to protect those entrusted to their charge from looking upon the bonds of subscription as merely ropes of sand...I wish for justice, and I think it has as little been dealt to the Hebdomadals as to the six doctors heretofore.[374]

The older generation of Oxford liberals were no less inconsistent than the Tractarians. Whately and Hampden, who had been all for latitude of interpretation in 1835–6, joined Copleston in pressing the heads to close off any such leniency in 1844–5.[375] The younger liberals, such as Jowett and Stanley, delighted in exposing the double standards of both sides.[376] Detesting all tests of belief, they at least could claim some consistency. As Maurice put it, 'If the Heads of Houses may sit in judgment on Ward's book today, they may try Buckland for his geology tomorrow, and Bunsen

---

[369] H. Hallam to W. E. Gladstone, 10 Feb. 1845, BL Add. MS 44361, fo 80.

[370] *The Case as it is, with reference to a proposed declaration considered in a letter to a friend* [nd np Dec. 1844–Jan. 1845], 1–2; B. Symons to A. C. Tait, 15 Jan. 1845, LPL MS Tait, vol lxxvii, fo 285.

[371] C. A. Ogilvie to unnamed correspondent, 6 Jan. 1845, BCA MS Jenkyns VI. B.

[372] E. Cardwell to Wellington, Feb. 1845, SUL 2/254/112.

[373] *English Churchman* iii (1845), 42.

[374] Churton, *Watson* ii. 152.

[375] E. Copleston to E. Hawkins, 6 Nov. 1844, OCL 54; *Hampden*, 117–18; J. Keble to H. A. Woodgate, 28 Jan. 1845, PHL Woodgate Papers, Wood/1/11/6.

[376] Abbott and Campbell, *Jowett* i. 117–18.

(who is a DCL) for his book on Egypt the next day.'[377] The Tractarians now relied on such liberal support in escaping the fetters which the heads wanted to force on them. Dean Church later played this down in his history of the Movement,[378] and Newman was loath to acknowledge it in the *Apologia*,[379] while the Protestant High-Church party were as keen to highlight the link, complaining that the Tractarians were 'in communication with avowed infidels'.[380] Certainly Newman's view that he was driven from the University by liberals cannot be sustained without qualification.[381]

There were notable similarities between the advanced Tractarian and liberal theories of university subscription. Charles Ogilvie and Hawkins stressed the similarity of the Ward case with the Arian subscription controversy of the previous century.[382] Both Tractarians and liberals appeared to deny the equation of the University with the Church as imponents of the Articles; by the new test the University was narrowing 'the theological terms upon which it admits members further than the church in England has already narrowed them'. Pusey likewise objected to the new test on the grounds that he would have to receive it 'not from the Church, but from the University, in the sense in which it is proposed to be by them'.[383] It was a distinction which Protestant High-Churchmen and early Tractarian defenders of the Articles would have alike considered untenable. In other ways, the Tractarians came more than ever to part from their earlier idealistic view of the University as handmaid and minister to the Church. They doubted the power of the Vice-Chancellor to summon persons deemed suspect of unorthodox teaching.[384] Above all, they ceased to regard the Vice-Chancellor in the light of his office alone, seeing him only in terms of his supposed personal theological beliefs.[385] Thus, they described the Board as 'a board of Puritan divines' designed to 'render Calvinism our Oxford creed'.[386] The collapse of the old Protestant High-Church consensus ensured that the offices of university authority had become tainted by considerations of theological partisanship and personal animus.

[377] F. D. Maurice to J. Hare, 15 Jan. 1845, in F. Maurice, *F. D. Maurice* (2 vols 1884) i. 400.
[378] Church, *Oxford Movement*, 393.
[379] A. P. Stanley, 'Subscription', *Macmillan's Magazine* liii (Jan. 1881), 209–10.
[380] *The Standard* 28 Dec. 1844.
[381] Newman, *Apologia*, 184; for a further discussion of this see P. B. Nockles, 'Oxford, Tract 90 and the Bishops' in D. Nicholls and F. Kerr (eds), *John Henry Newman: reason, rhetoric and romanticism* (Bristol 1991), 28–87; Nockles, *Oxford Movement in Context*, 294–300.
[382] C. A. Ogilvie, *Considerations on Subscription to the Thirty-Nine Articles Submitted to the Serious Attention of Candidates for Holy Orders* (1845), 11–12.
[383] Liddon, *Pusey* ii. 419.
[384] *English Churchman* iii (1845), 46.
[385] E. Churton to W. Gresley, 27 Jan. 1845, PHL Gres. 3/7/50; G. Moberly, *The Proposed Degradation and Declaration* (1845), 18–23.
[386] J. Williams to W. F. Hook, 24 Dec. 1844, papers of Mrs Barnaby Green, Lamberhurst, Kent.

By repudiating the right of Convocation to settle matters of doctrine, the Tractarians downgraded the status of the University as an ecclesiastical entity.[387] In 1841 they complained that the Vice-Chancellor's censure had not been ratified by Convocation. There could be no such objection in 1845. Instead of accepting the verdict of Convocation, the Tractarians argued that only an episcopal judge could take cognizance of the matter,[388] and Roundell Palmer offered to take legal proceedings on behalf of Ward on the ground 'that the Convocation of the University had exceeded its jurisdiction by assuming cognisance of an (alleged) ecclesiastical offence by a clergyman of the Church of England'.[389] Even the University's hitherto undisputed power to degrade was questioned, and legal confirmation of its right to do so had to be sought.[390] Again, the Tractarians found themselves hand in hand with liberals, who denied the right of 'MAs to say whether statements, x, y, z, agree or not with the Articles'.[391] By setting aside the theological function of both the Vice-Chancellor and Convocation, in the face of by no means total defeat, the Tractarians were abandoning the University, allowing the 'catholic' cause to be separated from it in a way which went against the animating principles of its origins and early history. In the long term, the only beneficiaries of this in the University were bound to be the forces of liberalism and even secularization. The eventual triumph of those forces came about not as a result of the Movement being turned out of the University, but rather because the Movement chose, of its own accord, to turn its back on the University. What the partisans of the Tractarians achieved through the controversies of the early 1840s was, as Sheridan Gilley has put it, 'nothing less than the destruction from within of the old Protestant high church ideology of unreformed Oxford'.[392]

Should the year 1845 be taken as the date of the demise of the Oxford Movement? At one level, as such diverse contemporary observers as G. V. Cox, Mark Pattison and Dean Church all agreed, the events of 13 February 1845 really did mark the end of a chapter or phase in the history of the University of Oxford. The suddenness of the breach was exacerbated by the profound and almost permanent sense of alienation from the 'official' University felt by Tractarians in the wake of the proceedings against Ward, though the number of outright seceders was, as Keble predicted, 'small

[387] *Some Answer to a Question, How did you Vote on the 13th? In a letter to a friend, by a junior MA, one of the 386* (1845), 12.

[388] R. C. Sewell, *A Letter to Members of Convocation in the University of Oxford* (1845), 11.

[389] Ward, *Ward and the Oxford Movement*, 344.

[390] For the legal case in favour of the University's power to degrade see OUA NW/21/8; E. Cardwell to Wellington, 7 Feb. 1845, SUL 2/254/115–16. For the case against see *Case as to the Proposed Degradation in the Statute of February 13, submitted to Sir J. Dodson and R. Bethell* (1845).

[391] A. H. Clough to T. Burbage, 31 Dec. 1844, in *Correspondence of Arthur Hugh Clough*, ed. F. L. Mulhauser (2 vols 1957) i. 143.

[392] S. Gilley, *Newman and his Age* (1990), 12.

indeed'; there were fifty-seven Oxford seceders to Rome between 1841 and 1847.[393] Keble signified his own alienation by declining to wear the MA hood for a period after Ward's degradation. After 1845 a faithful historian of the Movement should turn his focus to the world beyond Oxford. The University of Oxford falls into the background as the Movement concentrated its energies on the parochial world outside. By the 1850s it is patently impossible to write about the University almost solely by reference to the Movement's history, as was the case in the 1830s and early 1840s.

Church's famous reference to the events of 1845 as 'catastrophe' might have been applicable to the Movement as a university movement: it was certainly inappropriate if the Movement is viewed in the wider, national context. Yet, even in the former instance, it was a verdict perhaps too much influenced by Church's tendency to portray the Movement through the figure of Newman. Newman's departure for Rome in October 1845 was a great blow, though he had already been in effective retirement in Littlemore. Tractarianism in Oxford was far from dead, although as a political force in the University it was now rapidly on the wane. Benjamin Symons reported to Wellington in December 1845 that 'the party, which has for some years past been seeking occasion for disturbing our quiet, have of late been much less aggressive. They have been content to attract less notice, and to leave our discipline and institutions unassailed.'[394] Within the University, as in the parishes, Tractarianism remained a potent force in its private, spiritual and devotional aspect. Indeed, the peak of Tractarian-inspired moral, religious and ethical earnestness coupled with ascetic religiosity was probably reached in Oxford in the years after 1845. In 1851 Edward Churton could cheerfully note that 'all seems going on well at Oxford; there is a good spirit in the place, and no decline of zeal or earnestness'.[395] What had changed was that the centre of the Tractarian orbit had been transferred from Oriel and St Mary's to Christ Church and the Cathedral. For, with Newman gone, the party had regrouped under Pusey's leadership, with Charles Marriott in assistance. Tractarianism proved to be entrenched in particular colleges. This deterred the heads, despite a public call for action from Golightly, from moving against Pusey over his 1846 sermon on absolution, which in content was as controversial as that on the Eucharist three years earlier.[396] As late as 1847 the Movement's most bitter opponents were lamenting that it could still 'number five hundred partisans among the members of Convocation'.[397]

[393] J. T. Coleridge to E. Coleridge, 10 June 1845, BL Add. MS 44137, fos 243–4; *Oxford Protestant Magazine* i (1847), 245–8.
[394] SUL 2/254/158.
[395] E. Churton to W. Gresley, 5 Mar. 1851, PHL Gres. 3/7/93.
[396] Liddon, *Pusey* iii. 53–67.
[397] *Oxford Protestant Magazine* i (1847), 14.

It was the power and influence not of the Tractarians but of the conservative heads which most spectacularly collapsed in the wake of Ward's degradation. The University election of 1847 when Gladstone, the favourite of the Tractarians, triumphed over Round, the candidate most favoured by the heads, was acclaimed as 'a victory of the Masters over the Hebdomadal Board'.[398] An opportunity for the heads to reassert their authority had been lost. Instead, the election represented a settling of scores for February 1845, and in that sense almost something of a belated Tractarian triumph. It was a triumph on which the remnant of the Movement, under wise guidance, might have built. However, in the next few crucial years prior to the fateful Oxford University Act of 1854, the Tractarian remnant sought to take political revenge on the heads and Protestant High-Church old guard. They thus divided the broadly conservative forces in the University, and helped pave the way for the liberal triumph of the 1850s. Tractarianism would continue to flourish, but within the University, as within the Church of England at large, it was to be on the basis of a toleration by the state of all theological opinions and not on the *ancien régime* principle of Anglican confessionalism and hegemony. For the Oxford Movement had failed in its attempt to effect a restoration of ecclesiastical authority either in the University or more broadly in Church and state. The Tractarian counter-revolution, begun with such high hopes in the early 1830s, had been fatally maimed by the internecine theological strife of the following decade. It survived 1845 but in 1854, with the enactment of University reform, it was given its last rites.

[398] J. B. Mozley to R. W. Church, 6 Aug. 1847, in Mozley, *Letters*, 184. For this election see p. 312.

8

The Oxford of Mr Verdant Green

M. C. CURTHOYS AND C. J. DAY

The mid-century debate on Oxford reform generated a profuse and influential literature. The Great Blue Book 'sold like hot cakes' (see Chapter 10), and provoked official counter-statements by the University and a lively controversy among pamphleteers. One contemporary contribution to this debate, Newman's Dublin lectures, continues to be studied as a classic statement of the case for a liberal education (see Chapter 9). None of these statements, however, reached a wider audience than *The Adventures of Mr. Verdant Green* by Edward Bradley ('Cuthbert Bede'), first published in 1853 and achieving a sale of over 100,000 copies within twenty years.[1] And none, perhaps, was as powerful as the genre of the university novel, which *Verdant Green* significantly developed, in fixing in the public mind the notion that Oxford and Cambridge represented the ideal type of English university education.[2] Although Bradley himself was a graduate of the new university of Durham, and *Verdant Green* was originally conceived as a depiction of Durham student life, the published novel was very precisely located in mid-century Oxford. Bradley had little difficulty in drawing a humorous contrast between the conventional case for a collegiate education, as expressed by the University's numerous early nineteenth-century apologists, and the reality of Oxford life.[3] But the narrative has a positive outcome: Mr Verdant Green comes through unscathed, obtains his degree and is safely 'married and done for'.

Such a satisfactory outcome to an Oxford career was rarely found in the work of an earlier generation of writers and illustrators who had made the University their subject. The picture of Oxford life among the vignettes of places of fashionable resort described by the journalist Charles Molloy Westmacott in *The English Spy* (1825), illustrated with cartoons by Robert Cruikshank,[4] was one of unrelieved depravity, sharpened (probably for the

[1] C. A. Wilson, '*Verdant Green* or "A book written in spite of itself"', *American Oxonian* xx (1933), 27–31.
[2] See M. R. Proctor, *The English University Novel* (Berkeley 1957).
[3] Bradley presented a pastiche of the traditional arguments in the Revd Larkyns's urgings that the young Verdant Green be sent to the University: *The Adventures of Mr. Verdant Green, by Cuthbert Bede* (1853–7, 1982), 11–13.
[4] G. Everitt, *English Caricaturists and Graphic Humourists* (1886), 116.

purpose of blackmail) by reference both to specific incidents and to notable local characters of the day. The arrival of the freshman on the Oxford coach—a favourite episode in university fiction—sets the tone, for the driver is said to be a former undergraduate, the son of a head of house, fallen on hard times as a result of habits of dissipation acquired at the University. Scenes of drunkenness and licentiousness follow, sustained by a network of corrupt retainers, until a sentence of rustication finally brings an end to the revels. Adopting the characteristic tone of much of the Oxford fiction of the 1820s, *The English Spy* observed student life as an extension of the sprees and rambles of the sporting men and fashionable rakes of Regency London.[5]

By contrast, the fictional Mr Verdant Green arrived in Oxford from a quiet Warwickshire manor, clad in an outfit made by his village tailor. He belonged neither to Christ Church nor to one of the independent halls whose aristocratic excesses and lax discipline, respectively, had supplied much of the material for the grosser accounts of student life in unreformed Oxford. Brasenose, Verdant Green's thinly disguised college, was regarded as a respectable society, suffering comparatively little from the statutory restrictions which isolated the closed foundations, or from the poverty or obscurity of the less distinguished colleges. By electing a succession of socially well-connected heads, Brasenose confirmed its historic connections with gentry families and established a tone associated with a 'marked but not exclusive predilection for the exercises and amusements of out-door life'.[6] Two Brasenose men, both clergymen, produced popular and more favourable depictions of university life in the 1840s than had been usual a generation earlier. Prints by G. R. Winter, who captained the Oxford University Boat Club in 1848, published by James Ryman, the Oxford stationer, reminded many a mid-Victorian graduate of episodes from his undergraduate days. In decorous contrast to Cruikshank's racy caricatures, Winter's illustrations of the hunting-breakfast, where the beverage most prominently displayed is dispensed from a teapot, or the cricketing-scene on Bullingdon Common, where the sometimes extremely lively proceedings in the marquee are concealed from view, could suitably decorate the study of a country parsonage. Most influential of all was a humorous handbook to Oxford, which went through several editions after its publication in 1843. Written by S. R. Hole, a sporting man who entered Brasenose in 1840, *Hints to Freshmen* warned its intended readers of their 'lamb-like innocence', introducing the theme which Bradley was so successfully to exploit of the freshman duped: the newcomer might be encouraged by his seniors to wear a gaudy

---

[5] For example, T. Little, *Confessions of an Oxonian* (1826); S. Beazley, *The Oxonians* (1830). See also the Oxonian character Bob Logic in P. Egan, *Life in London* (1822), 73–4.

[6] F. Madan, 'Brasenose' in A. Clark (ed.), *The Colleges of Oxford: their history and traditions* (1891), 265.

waistcoat on his first visit to his tutor, or else hasten to the Clarendon Building to see Daniel O'Connell present the Ireland scholarship.[7]

Hole drew on a tradition of prescriptive literature about student life produced before the majority of undergraduates had come to share the experience, standardized later in the century, of a public school education. Entry to Oxford was more of a leap in the dark for undergraduates in this earlier period, especially for the significant number of them, including the fictional Verdant Green, who had been educated at home or by private tutors. Unwritten codes of university and college discipline were a traditional snare. More difficult to negotiate was the social life of undergraduates, which did not encourage the integration of outsiders. 'It is a queer place, quite unlike anything we have been accustomed to—I mean the colleges, their forms, etiquettes, etc.', J. C. Shairp reported to a Scottish friend after his first term at Balliol in 1840; 'Ours is a very crack college, but one is scarcely prepared for the hauteur that many of the men, who consider themselves of the best style, assume.'[8] One rule which freshmen were advised to observe was not to speak to another undergraduate without first being introduced; another was to beware of candour under the influence of drink offered by senior men. Initial impressions were crucial—and might be fatal. The first term was occupied in elaborate rituals of leaving and returning cards, and attending parties given by senior men. On the basis of these performances sets were formed as individuals were taken up or dropped, the latter accomplished by the notorious Oxford 'cut'.[9] Being a freshman was a disagreeable experience; for those with no previous school experience it was particularly so. Mark Pattison, having been schooled at home in an isolated country rectory, never forgot the maladroitness of his early months at Oriel, describing with a bitter poignancy the social disaster of the first wine party at which he was host.[10]

It was regarded as crucial for the freshman to find his appropriate level within the highly stratified student world. This might no longer be automatically dictated by his background. Distinctions of social status were still marked by the prescribed academic dress; Shairp sent his sister an Oxford view which depicted a nobleman in his elaborate gown and gold-tasselled cap. But these marks of rank were already in decline, as colleges gradually dropped the status of gentleman commoner and as aristocratic patronage of the University receded from the high point of the 1820s. There were only five noblemen in residence in the whole University when Shairp came up, however, so a 'tuft' would have been a rare sighting indeed. In place of the

---

[7] S. R. Hole, *Hints to Freshmen in the University of Oxford* (1843), 7.

[8] W. Knight, *Principal Shairp and his Friends* (1888), 43.

[9] [John Campbell], *Hints for Oxford* (1823), ch. 2; *Hints on Etiquette for the University of Oxford* (1838), 18.

[10] Pattison, *Memoirs*, 37, 81.

traditional divisions of rank, contemporaries noted the prevalence of informal 'sets' within an undergraduate body which comprised an enormous
range of financial means and future prospects, and an even greater range of
academic abilities. Arriving at Christ Church in 1844 as one of the diminishing number of servitors, the future historian William Stubbs attempted an
analysis of his contemporaries. Within the three main groupings of 'fast'
men, 'slow' men, and 'reading' men, there were further subdivisions of
'gentlemen' and 'cads', among whom Stubbs observed still further minute
segmentation.[11] While college institutions implied communality, daily practice often reinforced division. At Worcester, the arrangement of the tables in
hall reflected the character of the three distinct groups of undergraduates
within the college, identified as the 'sinners', 'smilers', and 'saints'.[12] The
growing practice of small groups messing together in hall, ordering elaborate
dinners from an extensive bill of fare, marked a departure from the traditional idea of a common table.[13] Taken together with the local peculiarities
of each of the colleges and halls, these arrangements reflected a remarkably
heterogeneous internal scene. Later in the century a more self-consciously
united undergraduate body came into being, whose common interests were
catered for by a burgeoning undergraduate press. No comparable constituency existed at mid-century; and in its absence publications such as Newman's early production *The Undergraduate* (1819) and its various successors
were doomed to be short-lived.

  The making of acquaintances at college involved an exchange of hospitality which was, especially for wealthy students, relentless. Edward Knatch-
bull-Hugessen, a gentleman commoner at Magdalen, recorded that he
entertained in Michaelmas term 1848 eighty men at dinner and twenty-seven
at lunch, and was himself entertained by twenty-one at dinner and by ten at
lunch.[14] Large breakfast parties took place after morning chapel, although
reading men might well avoid them. It was said, moreover, that these were
often drowsy gatherings as a result of the earliness of the hour; civilities were
likely to be curtailed as individuals left to attend their college lectures.
Luncheon was not yet firmly established as a formal meal since, despite a
gradual postponement over the course of the first half of the nineteenth
century, the dinner-hour was still fixed in the late afternoon. At Lincoln the
move from three to four o'clock had taken place in 1804; from four to five in
1821, where it stood until 1854. Christ Church dinner was fixed at five from
1825 to 1858.[15] The early-evening period naturally lent itself to formal
socializing. While the fellows retired to their common rooms, undergraduates

[11] *Letters of William Stubbs*, ed. W. H. Hutton (1904), 20–1.
[12] C. H. O. Daniel and W. R. Barker, *Worcester College* (1900), 220.
[13] Macleane, *Pembroke*, 484; W. H. Rooper, *Reminiscences of my Life* (Bournemouth 1893), 25.
[14] L. M. Quiller Couch (ed.), *Reminiscences of Oxford* (OHS xxii 1892), 399.
[15] V. H. H. Green, *The Commonwealth of Lincoln College, 1427–1974* (1979), 397.

made up parties and repaired to their rooms for dessert, wine and cigars. J. G. Lockhart evoked a characteristic scene at a wine party, where inhibitions gave way to conviviality and song.[16] In reality, wine parties were so central to the pattern of socializing that their character reflected the range of under-graduate sets, as Bradley recognized in his drawings of a 'fast' and 'slow' wine. They might be high-minded affairs; at a wine party given by A. H. Clough, who attended twenty-three such parties in Michaelmas 1840 alone, conversation turned upon the merits of Coleridge's *Aids to Reflection*.[17] Parties of reading men would break up at seven to return to their books or more sober conversation in smaller groups. For others, the wine might be a prelude, interrupted only by evening chapel, for a night of carousing.

Those venturing outside their college gates after dusk were required to wear academic dress, a deterrent to misdemeanour and a practical aid to the proctors in detecting wrongdoers. One of the freshman's first acts was to acquire a gown, 'a garb of orderly submission and obedience', as an Oriel tutor put it.[18] To appear in the streets before one o'clock in the afternoon without a cap and gown was to commit a breach of the university statutes, a copy of which was presented to everyone matriculating. Academic dress functioned to mark what one mid-century proctor defined as 'the working time' of the day.[19]

For undergraduates and senior members alike afternoons were given over to leisure. Heads and tutors might be seen among those individuals or small groups taking constitutional walks on the way to Joe Pullen's tree on Head-ington Hill, or beyond Summertown to Five Mile Drive (whose construc-tion was paid for by members of the University in about 1820); or further afield to Bagley Wood, Shotover, or Hinksey. Others might take a 'pull' in a skiff on the river down to Sandford or Nuneham. Those who could afford it took a ride on horseback.[20] Such were the approved ways of using recrea-tional time in a period when the prescriptive literature spoke of 'relaxation' or 'exercise' as the proper activity for the interval between a morning of study and dinner, refreshing the mind and body for an evening of reading before bed.[21]

New forms of amusement were viewed with suspicion. Vice-Chancellor Jenkyns of Balliol took alarm in 1825 at a proposal to establish a gymnasium open to undergraduates. He had no objection to fencing, or 'the manly amusement of tennis', but feared from his experience of students' enthu-siasm for boxing that this new development would encourage 'low and

[16] J. G. Lockhart, *Reginald Dalton* (Edinburgh 1823), 339.
[17] *The Oxford Diaries of A. H. Clough*, ed. A. Kenny (1990), p. xxxvi.
[18] [C. Daman], *Ten Letters Introductory to College Residence* (1848), 8.
[19] H. Pritchard, 'Procuratorial experiences and observations in the year 1852–1853', OUA WP/γ/8(21).
[20] R. W. Hiley, *Memories of Half a Century* (1903), 140.
[21] *Remarks on the Novel of Reginald Dalton* (1824), 4.

abandoned company and gambling practices'.[22] Pugilism enjoyed phases of popularity in the mid-1830s and again in the mid-1850s.[23] Billiards also defied official discouragement and the censure of moralists.[24] Commenting on its continued attraction to undergraduates in 1861, Thorold Rogers noted that 'as usual, the constant *habitués* of this amusement are among the most disreputable persons to be found'.[25] A prohibition of play before one o'clock in the afternoon and after nine at night was the most that the proctors were able to do to curb the sport. On occasion the authorities were obliged to prohibit even less improving pastimes: in November 1846 the Hebdomadal Board, acting at the instigation of the senior proctor, forbade undergraduates from 'Shooting at animals provided for the purpose in traps or cages'.[26]

Fox-hunting offered one of the greatest challenges to the official view of the exercise proper for the University to countenance among its junior members. Highly visible in their red coats, followers of the chase set out in the morning for their day's sport well before the time normally prescribed for leisure. One huntsman regarded this as a benefit to scholarship: 'a good fixture of the Duke [of Beaufort], or Sir Thomas Mostyn, carried off the surplus idle population, who would otherwise be constantly tormenting and interrupting the hard-reading men'.[27] Opportunities to join the hunt had considerably increased during the early nineteenth century; almost all the county of Oxfordshire was hunted, boundaries having been agreed between the principal hunts in 1834.[28] Although their youthful inexperience on occasion earned the displeasure of the masters of some Oxfordshire hunts, undergraduates were welcome at the Heythrop in the 1820s under the mastership of the Duke of Beaufort, a tradition which was maintained under Beaufort's successor, Lord Redesdale.[29] Sheer expense—the hire of a horse suitable for the purpose cost at least two guineas a day—put the sport beyond the pockets of the majority of undergraduates, but its influence was widely felt. Hunting spawned other equestrian events: point-to-point steeplechases (or 'grinds' as they came to be called) took place in the 1840s; at Exeter the college grind was said to have inspired the holding of the first college athletics sports.[30] Sporting men, skilled in managing animals, kept

[22] R. Jenkyns to Grenville, 17 Feb. 1825, BL Add. MS 59415, fo 102.
[23] F. Gale, *The Life of the Hon. Robert Grimston* (1885), 36; *Sir William Gregory: an autobiography*, ed. Lady Gregory (1894), 47; Lord Redesdale, *Memories* (2 vols 1915) i. 103; T. Hughes, *James Fraser, Second Bishop of Manchester* (1887), 25.
[24] [Campbell], *Hints for Oxford*, 55–6.
[25] J. E. T. Rogers, *Education in Oxford* (1861), 127–8.
[26] OUA WP/γ/24(6), notice no. 45(a); cf *Adventures of Mr. Verdant Green*, 351.
[27] *Sporting Magazine* (Dec. 1827), 70. We are indebted to Dr J. D. Pickles for drawing our attention to this article.
[28] *VCH Oxon*. ii. 351, 356.
[29] R. Carr, *English Fox Hunting* (1976), 80; *VCH Oxon*. ii. 356; G. T. Hutchinson, *The Heythrop Hunt* (1935), 105.
[30] Boase, *Reg. Exeter*, clxi.

dogs in defiance of rarely enforced regulations. C. L. Dodgson, who entered Christ Church in 1850, recalled that there were seventy dogs on the premises 'day and night'.[31]

Although the first match against Cambridge took place as early as 1827, cricket remained a minority undergraduate pursuit in this period.[32] Strongly associated with certain public schools—Eton, Harrow and Winchester—undergraduate teams were constituted as private clubs such as the Bullingdon or the Old Wykehamists, and their opponents were commonly club sides from outside the University. Intercollegiate matches were not yet established on a regular basis, only a minority of colleges having teams in the 1840s. The general character which cricket held in unreformed Oxford may be inferred from a fixture which took place in 1843 between New Inn Hall and St Mary Hall: none of the players taking part obtained academic honours, and all of those fielded by New Inn Hall had been obliged to migrate from the colleges at which they had originally matriculated.[33] Walter Fellows's drive in practice at the Christ Church ground in 1856 entered the annals of the game as the biggest hit on record; in the summer of his feat, however, the Dean and Chapter of Christ Church deprived him of his Studentship on account of his failure to pass the BA examinations in the required time.[34] Cricket was considered an expensive pastime, whose followers set out from the colleges in carriages laden with provisions to be consumed in the marquees erected at the boundary. An early tactician of the game, James Pycroft of Trinity, took this heavy eating and drinking into account in his advice to captains; while the excessive consumption militated against running between the wickets, Pycroft believed that the bowling rather than the batting side was the more disadvantaged during the innings after the meal was taken. This, he casually observed, might serve as a hint 'in giving and taking the odds'.[35] In 1850 a proctor gave a grim assessment of the type of sociability promoted by the Bullingdon Cricket Club, denouncing the presumably Rabelaisian choruses sung at its dinners as 'a curse and disgrace to a place of Christian education'.[36]

Undergraduate cricket sides frequently included one or two professional bowlers; and it was particularly alleged as a criticism of equestrianism and pugilism that undergraduates were exposed to the 'low' company of grooms, hunt servants, prize fighters (who acted as trainers and sparring partners) and other members of the sporting fraternity. Rowing, by contrast, was from the outset rooted in the colleges, and professionals were soon afterwards

[31] *Letters of Lewis Carroll*, ed. Morton Cohen (2 vols 1979) i. 226.
[32] On the development of organized sport, see Pt 2, Ch. 22.
[33] *Bell's Life* 2 July 1843.
[34] Chapter Act, 25 June 1856, CA D&C i. b. 10, fo 168; *Wisden Cricketers' Almanack, 1994* (1994), 259.
[35] [J. Pycroft], *The Principles of Scientific Batting* (1835), 34.
[36] *RCO* (1850), evidence, 182.

excluded from participation.[37] Although the actual innovation of eight-oared rowing seems to have come from Eton, the association of college rowing with developments in the public schools was less marked than in the case of cricket. Two of the colleges whose undergraduates established eights before 1830, Jesus and Queen's, did not have close links with those schools, while the Brasenose crew of 1827 numbered only one former pupil of a Clarendon school. This comparatively weak dependence on previous schooling—any undergraduate could become proficient at rowing without prior experience—may explain why the sport swiftly attracted a large number of student participants. In 1849 twenty eights took part in the summer races, some colleges mustering more than one crew. Only three colleges—Corpus, Magdalen and New College—which were then among the smallest in the University, failed to enter.

Despite the early popularity of rowing, it would not have appeared inevitable to an observer of the University in 1850 that team games would come to supplant individualistic forms of physical recreation. Verdant Green was depicted trying his hand at many of those on offer, and specifically the gymnasium and fencing-school conducted by Archibald MacLaren, a pioneer teacher of physical education. MacLaren's school enjoyed a considerable vogue in the 1850s, Edward Burne-Jones and William Morris being among the undergraduates who received instruction there, and his methods received wide publicity when he opened a purpose-built gymnasium in 1859.[38] Contemporary with the University Museum for the natural sciences, the new gymnasium was inspired by a similar scientific purpose, to study physical exercise on systematic lines.[39] Gymnastics, MacLaren contended, were more valuable than games for the bodily development of undergraduates, which was his prime object. The ultimate failure of this view to gain a hold in Oxford owed much to the tendency, already visible at mid-century in the case of rowing, to invest team games with morally beneficial results. One of the earliest college oarsmen, Augustus Short, a future bishop, considered that the 'strict habit of life' engendered by training with his college eight saved him from the temptations which Oxford conviviality presented. Hole, too, applauded oarsmen as 'Fine, manly, open-hearted fellows' with firm handshakes.[40]

If rowing was coming to enjoy a special position among Oxford sports, all of them shared a characteristic noted by a German observer of the English educational scene: unlike their continental counterparts with their secret fraternities and rituals, students at Oxford (and Cambridge) enthusiastically

---

[37] W. E. Sherwood, *Oxford Rowing* (1900), 11; C. Dodd, *Oxford and Cambridge Boat Race* (1983), 34.

[38] See the introduction by John Christian to A. MacLaren, *The Fairy Family* (1985), p. xi.

[39] P. E. McIntosh, *Physical Education in England since 1800* (1968), 92.

[40] F. T. Whitington, *Augustus Short* (1888), 8; Hole, *Hints to Freshmen*, 31.

shared the common pursuits of the country at large.[41] Few activities were more effectively to reunite the ancient universities with the nation than their patronage of sport. The potential interest in the boat race with Cambridge was illustrated by the celebrated seven-oared race rowed at Henley in July 1843. Oxford won, despite rowing one man short, 'amidst the most deafening shouts of applause' generated by a large crowd, many of whom had bet heavily on the outcome.[42] And whatever academic reservations might have existed about fox-hunting, there was no question that those undergraduates who joined the field were signifying an attachment to an established county institution.

None of the facilities for this burgeoning undergraduate sporting-scene were laid on by the University or the colleges; and in leisure, as to some extent in teaching, private enterprise was an important provider. MacLaren's gymnasium was an obvious case in point. Oxford tradesmen feature prominently in evocations of student life in this period. Expensive confections prepared by pastry-cooks in the town were smuggled through college gates in defiance of sumptuary regulations: Jubber's desserts were an Oxford institution. Stable-keepers serviced the thriving market for horses. The most celebrated was Charley Symonds, whose stables in Holywell Street provided at their peak accommodation for 100 horses, as well as an unspecified number kept at livery for members of the University.[43] Sporting men favoured the St Aldate's stables of Samuel Quartermaine, who owned a Grand National winner, and those of his successor, Joseph Tollitt. Isaac Sadler kept 'a large stud' of noted hunters, and could also boast Derby and Oaks winners.[44] Intrepid sportsmen ventured to the public houses of Fisher Row to haggle with dog-dealers for a likely looking terrier; Cuthbert Bede's character Filthy Lucre was probably Mr Luker, keeper of the Packet Inn in George Street.[45] Undergraduate clubs found venues in rooms let by Oxford shopkeepers: the sporting club founded in 1863 which originally met in the High Street premises of Joseph Vincent, printer and bookseller, famously adopted his name. Robert Morier of Balliol was one of the last undergraduates to enrol in Angelo's fencing-school,[46] which was succeeded by Mac-Laren's venture. The keepers of the tennis-courts in Oriel and Merton streets, notably the Tompkins dynasty and James Russell ('Duck-legged Jem'), offered tuition and put on exhibition matches.[47] Private enterprise

[41] L. Wiese, *German Letters on English Education*, trans. W. D. Arnold (1854), 24, 131.
[42] *Herald* 6 July 1843.
[43] C. Bede, 'Charley Symonds', *Fores's Sporting Notes* (1888) v. 26–34. Jubber's daughter achieved brief fame in 1834 when J. H. Newman refused to conduct her wedding because she had not been baptized: *LDN* iv. 278.
[44] *Oxford Chronicle* 26 Apr. 1890.
[45] M. Prior, *Fisher Row* (1982), 259 ff.
[46] See Bodl. MS Top. Oxon. b. 269.
[47] J. Potter, *Tennis and Oxford* (1994), 65.

also found a place in the intellectual scene. Before the establishment of the Taylor Institution, foreign-language teachers met such demand as there was for coaching in the modern European languages. Those whose neglect of study or college discipline incurred written impositions could, it was said, purchase the necessary paperwork from enterprising local scribes.

There was no place, however, for promoters of public amusements. The university authorities succeeded in restricting these to occasional musical performances; plays were never permitted during term. Undergraduate theatricals, which had been banished from the University since the seventeenth century, revived, though they took place outside Oxford itself. Early performances by the Oxford Dramatic Amateurs were staged in 1847 at the Henley Regatta, Maidenhead, and London. Their popularity during the 1860s brought a renewed prohibition in 1869, which was not lifted until Jowett's vice-chancellorship in the 1880s.

Vehicles, which offered a chance to escape from this enforced dullness, always attracted proctorial vigilance. Fast tandems were said to be irresistible to a class of undergraduates 'whose stay at the University profits neither themselves or others'.[48] The coming of the railway threatened to bring the metropolis and its temptations within the range of undergraduate day trippers. Giving evidence to a House of Lords committee on the Great Western Railway Bill in 1838, A. T. Gilbert, the Vice-Chancellor and Principal of Brasenose, pointed to the hazards presented to undergraduates by London's gambling-dens and the lure of the capital's women, while Robert Hussey, Censor of Christ Church and university proctor, feared that the Ascot Races would be brought within easy reach.[49] As a result the University succeeded in winning for its officers significant rights of search and enquiry in stations and on trains when the railway finally opened in 1844.[50]

In the last years of the unreformed University the more traditional hazard of debt came into prominence. There was always a special problem that clergymen's sons and those destined for the Church might be dazzled by Oxford's facilities for expensive consumption. A country parson from a family 'who have been constantly clergymen for 200 years' wrote in 1815 to Lord Grenville, the university Chancellor, enclosing a bill totalling £114 7s 3d run up with a wine-merchant by his son while in residence at Wadham. His college tutor had been warned when the first signs of overspending had become apparent; yet the student had not been prevented from obtaining further credit.[51] The year of 1848 began with spectacular revelations from the London Insolvent Debtors' Court concerning the case of Edward Napleton Jennings, a commoner of Worcester, who had been arrested for

[48] RCO (1850), evidence, 183. In a tandem the horses were harnessed one behind the other.
[49] PP 1837–8 HL (227) xx. 234, 258.
[50] Oxford Railway Act, 6 & 7 Vic., c. 10; J. Williams, The Law of the Universities (1910), 58.
[51] W. Royse to Grenville, 21 Jan. 1815, BL Add. MS 59417, fo 136.

accumulating debts of over £2,337 with only a silver pencil-case valued at three shillings to his credit.[52] Disclosure that Jennings, the son of a Yorkshire clergyman who had eight children to educate, had been enabled to run up credit on such a scale brought an avalanche of correspondence from worried parents to *The Times*, which devoted leading articles to the subject.[53] Hard on the heels of the Jennings scandal came that of Charles Throsby, who came before the same court after being detained by creditors owing some £750 from his career as an undergraduate at Exeter College.[54] The system of extended credit, by which tradesmen allowed undergraduates to run up such large debts, had been satirized half a century earlier;[55] and the annual spectacle of large numbers of tradesmen soliciting the freshman's custom with the assurance that they wanted his orders not his money was universally deplored. Although some establishments attempted to hold themselves aloof, few could afford the lofty tone of Elliston and Cavell's 1836 billheading 'No Credit Given'.[56] Asked why he had permitted Jennings to run up a debt of £70 without discovering the undergraduate's address and warning his father, Thomas Randall, a hatter, pointed out that any Oxford trader so doing might as well shut up shop, for he would be boycotted. The system then prevailing was to present a bill after two years, when interest of 5 per cent was charged.[57] An Oxford Tradesman's Association was founded in the wake of the Jennings case, and attempted to prevent solicitation and enforce the prompt settlement of bills, but the initiative was short-lived.

If much censure was passed upon Oxford businessmen the university authorities fared little better. Commenting on another case, in 1852, an Insolvency Commissioner remarked: 'It seemed to him that young men went to Oxford to get initiated into debt: that seemed to be the education they got at Oxford.'[58] The Jennings and Throsby cases were extreme: the former was an accomplished confidence trickster and neither of them was a 'mere boy', much as their counsel sought to present them in that vulnerable light to the court. Most bills submitted by tradesmen for payment within the University's jurisdiction were relatively small. But cases which actually came before the courts represented only a fraction of the extent of debt; and the intense interest which they generated arose because of the common

[52] *The Times* 1 Jan. 1848, 6. On the case see Ward, *Victorian Oxford*, 139; *Oxford Tradesmen versus the Insolvent Jennings: a verbatim copy of the schedule of Edward Napleton Jennings... discharged under the Insolvent Act, December 31st 1847* (1848).
[53] *The Times* 3 Jan. 1848, 4; 12 Jan. 1848, 4.
[54] *The Times* 7 Aug. 1849, 4.
[55] *Directions for the Conduct of a Young Gentleman at Oxford* (1795).
[56] M. L. Turner and D. G. Vaisey, *Oxford Shops and Shopping* (1972), 48–9.
[57] *Herald* 17 Mar. 1848; *Oxford Chronicle* 8 Jan., 12 Feb. 1848; *Oxford Protestant Magazine* i (Feb. 1848), 632–40.
[58] OUA WP/α/58(7).

knowledge that the adult lives of many university men, who treated liabilities incurred at Oxford as debts of honour, were blighted by the visits of duns.

In the opinion of one tutor, 'idleness' was 'the parent of extravagance at Oxford'.[59] A majority of undergraduates sued for debt by tradesmen in 1847 belonged to just four societies, where reading men were distinctly thin on the ground: Worcester, Christ Church, New Inn Hall and St Mary Hall. The patterns of consumption involved in debt cases tell the same story. Wine merchants headed the list of tradesmen entering actions against undergraduates in the Chancellor's Court during 1847; and although the high place held by boot-makers seems less reprehensible, the bills incurred by students with them were too large to be consistent with necessity.[60]

The prominence of liquor bills among undergraduate debts pointed to the issue of intemperance. That heavy drinking continued to be accepted among both junior and senior members of the University alike was one of the most striking respects in which mid-century Oxford lagged behind changes in public opinion in the outside world.[61] In 1836 a traveller on the night coach to Cheltenham 'was much shocked and disgusted' when five university men entered the coach at Oxford 'intoxicated, and lewd in their conversation'. Temperance advocates complained that they were able to make little headway in the University, one remarking in 1862 on the beneficial influence which a Temperance Hall might exert on senior and junior members alike: 'Such a Temperance Hall would act as a silent monitor to many a poor undergraduate, and even to many a poor Fellow who is on the downward path to ruin here, and hell hereafter, through drink.'[62] Tobacco was a milder vice associated with student life; the cigar shop of Henry Gattie, a retired actor, was said to be a favourite resort of 'collegians'.[63] The spread of the habit in respectable society at large has been attributed to its acceptance after 1840 among undergraduates at both Oxford and Cambridge, who were not to be dissuaded by moral reformers.[64] An alliance between undergraduates and town youths disrupted a lecture given by the Secretary of the British

<hr />

[59] *The Times* 6 Jan. 1848, 3.

[60] The 147 separate actions brought by tradesmen in 1847 comprised: wine merchants (21); boot- and shoemakers (20); booksellers (15); chemists, grocers, and ironmongers (9); tobacconists (8); upholsterers (7); tailors (6); watch- and clockmakers (5); stable-keepers (4); china-dealers, confectioners, gilders and carvers, hoteliers and innkeepers (3); auctioneers, coffee-house keepers, gunsmiths, mercers, saddlers (2); accountants, billiard-table keepers, breeches-makers, clerks, clothes-cleaners, dog-dealers, haberdashers, jewellers, masons, music-sellers, stationers, trunk-makers (1). Figures extracted from Chancellor's Court Register, 1840–57, OUA Hyp/A/71.

[61] B. H. Harrison, *Drink and the Victorians* (1971), 98.

[62] *British and Foreign Temperance Intelligencer* 31 Dec. 1836, 56; *Proceedings of the International Temperance and Prohibition Convention, held in London, September 2nd, 3rd, and 4th, 1862* (1862), 136. We are indebted to Professor Harrison for these references.

[63] *GM* (1844) ii. 654.

[64] N. Gash, *Robert Surtees and Early Victorian Society* (1993), 317.

Anti-Tobacco Society in 1855 by the tactic of laying down a screen of smoke.[65]

Apart from the ravages of drink and smoking, an undergraduate's health might be 'destroyed by another cause too delicate for us to mention', Alfred Bate Richards of Exeter alleged soon after his graduation in 1841.[66] Undergraduates were surrounded by the temptations and dangers presented by prostitutes in both the city of Oxford and surrounding villages. A Snell exhibitioner writing in 1823 warned freshmen of 'the intoxicating dews of guilty pleasure'.[67] Though rarely mentioned in later accounts of student life, the pervasiveness of this concern can hardly be overstated. In the late 1820s the correspondence received by the Vice-Chancellor included information about women soliciting on the road through Bagley Wood, and a complaint from a Jericho householder that his wife had been accosted by undergraduates who were evidently accustomed to propositioning female residents of the neighbourhood.[68] A writer in 1847 estimated that there were up to 100 women on the street each night, reckoning their total population to be between 300 and 500.[69] Although the opportunities for vice were not in doubt, there was a conflict of testimony among the proctors as to extent of 'gross immorality' among undergraduates. Henry Pritchard of Corpus, proctor in 1852–3, recorded instances of discovering undergraduates in brothels, but considered them 'extremely rare' and drew some satisfaction from the belief that the worst instances occurred in places outside Oxford and were committed by 'gross delinquents' who were likely to 'baffle' any proctorial attempts to interfere with their pleasures. Others viewed the situation with less equanimity; and prostitution in Oxford became a symbol for some Tractarians of the rottenness of the old regime. J. H. Pollen, Pritchard's predecessor as proctor, and later a secessionist to Rome, was an active supporter of the Oxford Female Penitentiary, and during his proctorship was particularly vigorous in intercepting undergraduate expeditions to Abingdon and other outlying places.[70]

The prevalence of prostitution coloured mid-century discussion of student lodgings. Permission to live outside college was limited to those who had completed three years of residence and those few who for special reasons received the Vice-Chancellor's dispensation to lodge out. At one of the earliest meetings of the new Hebdomadal Council, Pusey unsuccess-

---

[65] *Herald* 3, 10 Nov. 1855.

[66] A. B. Richards, *Oxford Unmasked* (1842), 38.

[67] [Campbell], *Hints for Oxford*, 19.

[68] Bodl. MS Top. Oxon. b. 23, fos 358, 502.

[69] *Oxford Protestant Magazine* i (May 1847), 111. See also A. J. Engel, '"Immoral intentions": the University of Oxford and the problem of prostitution, 1827–1914', *Victorian Studies* xxiii (1979), 79–107.

[70] A. Pollen, *John Hungerford Pollen, 1820–1902* (1912), 220–1.

fully proposed a complete prohibition of even these few exemptions.[71]
Pusey seems to have thought that, provided undergraduates were required
to sleep within college walls, vice was effectively curbed. This confidence
was not shared by all, but contemporaries were probably right to observe
that, given the concentration of young men, Oxford was, outwardly at least,
a remarkably orderly university city. A tightening in 1816 of the statute
requiring the wearing of academic dress in public helped to achieve the 'great
order and decorum' in Oxford's streets described by guidebooks.[72] This was
not the immediate conclusion which would be drawn from university novels, where the town–gown row was an essential incident and a favourite
subject for illustrators; depictions of brawls outside Oxford's historic buildings provided an entertaining contrast to the contemporary genre of topographical prints peopled by grave academic figures, heading perhaps for
divine service or some other elevated purpose. In reality, disturbances were
uncommon events. They intensified at times of political excitement, such as
the Queen Caroline affair in 1820, the general election of May 1831, and
during the Reform agitation of 1867. But annual disorder on the fifth of
November was not invariable. C. T. Longley found 'not the least symptom
of disturbance' in 1827 or 1828, and this seems to have been the case during
the following decade; for later proctors the night was less tranquil, but by
patrolling the streets they could keep the violence within bounds. The easiest
option would have been to close all college gates on the night, but as one
proctor pointed out, 'the blood of youth' required some outlet, 'and will
only be raised to fever heat if it be denied'. This implied containment: events
were sufficiently predictable for future proctors to be advised that the worst
would be over by ten o'clock.[73]

If the fifth of November had something of the character of ritualized
blood-letting, the Encaenia ceremony at the end of Trinity term was a
recognized occasion for licensed disorder. As one of the rare occasions in
the university year when undergraduates gathered *en masse*, the ceremony
offered an opportunity for them to vent their feelings towards unpopular
proctors and other university officials. In general the proctorial system
enjoyed the consent of the students whose lives it regulated, not least
because they had a degree of self-interest in its maintenance. While they
were liable to be fined for minor transgressions, such as not wearing academic dress, students enjoyed protection from ordinary criminal jurisdiction. In their daily duties, proctors were treated with civility; students rarely
offered resistance or ran away when challenged. One of John Ruskin's
contemporaries paid a sovereign fine in halfpennies, dropping them at the

[71] W. A. Pantin, *Oxford Life in Oxford Archives* (1972), 10–11.
[72] *Statutes* ii. 113; *The Oxford University and City Guide* (1824), 191.
[73] OUA WP/γ/8(21), fo 25.

feet of the proctor, but this was as far as defiance went.[74] Reaction to perceived injustices, however, was likely to take a much more boisterous form in the Sheldonian, when the commotion created by the undergraduates seated in the upper gallery sometimes reduced the official proceedings to farce. No consideration was given to visiting dignitaries caught up in the row. Receiving an honorary degree in 1857 before setting out to suppress the Indian mutiny, Lieutenant-General Sir Colin Campbell was observed to tremble 'with indignation at the example of insubordination and license' shown by the students during the formalities.[75]

The most serious disruption occurred in 1843 as a protest against the proctorship of W. E. Jelf, a Christ Church tutor who displayed an Evangelical zeal in attempting to enforce a moral reformation of student life: his agenda included a general ban on dining-clubs, hunting, racing, and tandem-driving, and a crusade against 'the abodes or agents of vice'.[76] Jelf's appearance at the Sheldonian met with what seems to have been an organized attempt to disrupt the proceedings; the uproar prevented Matthew Arnold from reading his Newdigate Prize poem 'Cromwell', and drowned the 'non-placets' raised by Tractarian MAs against the honorary degree conferred upon the American Unitarian Edward Everett. Summary and unusually severe sentences of rustication were imposed on the ringleaders, one of whom protested 'that he considered he was only doing that which had been previously allowed'.[77] Later disturbances went unpunished, however, and the occasion was acknowledged by one tutor in 1852 as 'a wholesome check upon authority, in its nature and by necessity somewhat despotic'.[78]

The rowdy arena of the Encaenia ceremony also provided a rare opportunity for expressions of undergraduate opinion on political questions as the names of notable figures of the day were called out and cheered or booed according to the state of opinion. These reactions, carefully recorded by visiting newspaper reporters as an indication of the opinions of the coming generation, suggested that while undergraduates in mid-Victorian Oxford were a cause of anxiety to their parental 'governors' through falling into debt or bad company, they remained true to the influences of their homes in political matters. Melbourne, Russell, 'Brougham and London University', Daniel O'Connell, Feargus O'Connor and 'the Chartists' were cries guaranteed to raise a howl. Peel, whose name had been cheered vigorously in 1839, joined the demonology after 1846. The heads might have consoled themselves that they had allies among the junior members, who jeered at the

---

[74] J. Ruskin, *Letters Addressed to a College Friend during the Years 1840–1845* (1894), 14.

[75] R. Michell, *Orationes Creweianae* (1884), 61 n.

[76] *RCO* (1850), evidence, 182; for Jelf's unpopularity at Christ Church see J. Powell (ed.), *Liberal by Principle* (1996), 55–6.

[77] OUA WP/γ/8(9). Cambridge ceremonies also witnessed undergraduate disorder: *Romilly's Cambridge Diaries, 1842–1847*, ed. M. E. Bury and J. D. Pickles (1994), 41 (21 Jan. 1843).

[78] *Herald* 26 June 1852.

prospect of a Royal Commission in 1850. Visiting honorands were exposed to this applause or censure more directly. Having compromised his High-Church credentials by supporting a parliamentary bill for the removal of Jewish civil disabilities, Gladstone, elected MP for the University in 1847, knew that he was in for a noisy reception when he attended the Encaenia in the following year to receive an honorary DCL.[79] If the gallery was unsure what to make of Gladstone, and remained divided over his merits in the following decades, the Encaenia of 1848 was memorable for the unity of its enthusiastic patriotism in the face of revolution abroad and the Chartist movement at home.[80] The undergraduates forced the organist to strike up the National Anthem, foreshadowing the loyal enthusiasm which greeted the Prince of Wales when he came into residence in 1859, and the revival of the volunteer movement in the face of the Anglo-French war scare. John Morley was one name among the earliest recruits to the Oxford University volunteers, whose numbers peaked at 517 in 1863—about a third of all undergraduates in residence.[81]

Enthusiasm for the volunteers waned. More permanent and even more impressive in the extent of its membership was the Oxford Union Society, which included over two-fifths of undergraduates in the late 1840s, rising to about a half in 1860.[82] Some 1,000 undergraduates belonged when the Union celebrated its half-centenary in 1873. An earlier generation had secured the principle of freedom of discussion in matters other than theology (see Chapter 1), and the celebrity of the Union as a debating society grew after the decision to permit newspaper reports of the speeches made in February 1850 on the motion 'That the state of the nation imperatively requires a return to Protection'.[83] In the context of undergraduate life as a whole, however, the importance of the Union lay in its remarkable growth as a literary society, with an impressive library (from which books could be borrowed) covering modern subjects outside the university curriculum and not represented in college libraries. Subscriptions to a wide range of contemporary periodicals and newspapers testified to a greater determination among the undergraduates running the Union to keep abreast of trends in the contemporary world than was shown by many of their seniors.[84] By 1850 blackballing had practically ceased and subsequent rule changes made applications for membership a formality.[85] So strong was the sentiment in

[79] Gladstone, *Diaries* iv. 47.

[80] *Herald* 8 July 1848.

[81] R. L. Abbott, *The Muster Roll of the 1st (Oxford University) V.B. The Oxfordshire Light Infantry from 1859 to 1887* (1887).

[82] Register of members elected, 1844–1873, OUS Archives.

[83] H. A. Morrah, *The Oxford Union, 1823–1923* (1923), 132.

[84] See E. B. Nicholson's descriptions of the library in *Oxford University Magazine and Review* (Dec. 1869), 177; *London Society* (Nov. 1873), 450.

[85] A ballot was only to be held if requested: *Rules and Regulations of the Oxford Union Society, corrected to August 1867* (1867), 2.

favour of openness that there were attempts to remove even the modest restriction which required all candidates for membership to have resided in the University for one term.[86] With its property securely vested in trustees, the Union was able to purchase permanent premises in 1853, the new debating-hall being opened in 1857 and the library in 1863. Use of these facilities—and free stationery and postage—could be had for the comparatively small sum of £1 entrance fee and a terminal subscription of £1 2s.

Other undergraduate societies tended to have transient existences. Programmes of debates at St Edmund Hall in the late 1830s have survived; and a debating and book club founded at St John's in 1849 has left a printed rule-book.[87] Queen's College was unusual in 1850 in having a musical society.[88] More firmly established were the social clubs, most of which had come into being in the previous half-century. The Phoenix Common Room at Brasenose could claim to be the oldest. Its twelve members gathered for weekly dinners in uniforms prescribed by a regulation made in 1823, dining on Sundays until 1842 when, in response to the 'violent opposition' of the Brasenose dons to this violation of the Sabbath, the day was moved to Tuesday.[89] Other dining clubs were the Archery Club at St John's, dating from 1830, and its offshoot, the King Charles Club, founded in 1845. A secret club for the purpose of taking hot luncheons was in existence in Pembroke at about the same time.[90] Henry Chaplin's elderly guardian expressed some surprise on hearing that his charge had been elected a member of the Christ Church Society in 1859; 'At the time I was at Oxford [1805], there were no clubs for undergraduates that I ever heard of.'[91] Loder's, as the Christ Church Society came to be known, dated from 1814, and managed to unite some of the intellectual as well as the social élite of the college at its weekly wine parties. Members had included at various times George Cornewall Lewis, John Ruskin, and the future third Marquess of Salisbury.[92] Another Christ Church club, the Mitre, founded in 1820 with premises in the hotel of that name, was little more than a wine club for hunting-men and fell heavily into debt.[93]

Serious-minded undergraduates in this period enjoyed both the freedom of intellectual speculation which their predecessors in the 1820s had first come to enjoy (see Chapter 1) and a greater liberty in other areas of

---

[86] OUS minute-book vii (1848–52), 194, 378, OUS archives.

[87] J. N. D. Kelly, *St Edmund Hall* (1989), 76–7; *Rules of the Saint John's Debating and Book Club* (1854).

[88] R. H. Hodgkin, *Six Centuries of an Oxford College* (1949), 196.

[89] F. Madan, 'The Phoenix Common Room, 1782–1900' in *Brasenose Monographs* ii pt 2 (OHS liv 1910), 97, 110.

[90] *The Bystander* xxiii (1909), 230, 356; Macleane, *Pembroke*, 486.

[91] Marchioness of Londonderry, *Henry Chaplin: a memoir* (1926), 19–20.

[92] *Rules of the Christ Church Society* (1878), 14.

[93] Mitre Club minutes, 1820–43 (copy), CA MS 648; C. K. Firman, 'The Mitre Club, 1820–1843', *American Oxonian* liii (1966), 12.

university life.[94] Admittedly the talent of this generation could not look forward with the same certainty to the rewards which the old Church–state connection had offered in the period when Peel and Gladstone were undergraduates. But the rupture of that link removed many constraints. Oxford was less aristocratic in 1845 than it had been in 1825; and the forms associated with the dominance of the old 'high and dry' religion had been relaxed. Regency Oxford demanded a stiff regime of elaborate dressing for dinner in breeches, shoes and stockings, and even the wearing of white ties. Twenty years later, youthful experiments in matters of dress or manner of life were less likely to be seen as defiance of constituted authority; nor were such expressions of individualism yet subjected to the sort of peer-group pressure sometimes exerted in the later decades of the century. Coming to Balliol in 1842, Matthew Arnold was able to throw aside the restraints of his father's school; no less experimental were those influenced by the Tractarians, such as Edward King at Oriel, who adopted strict ascetic regimes in daily life and religious observance.[95]

Although the formal university curriculum was narrow and religious tests remained in force, this generation of reading men arguably enjoyed more freedom to follow their own intellectual interests than their successors, who were tied to the pursuit of honours and the demands of fellowship examinations or the civil service competition. 'We tried to think widely on life and learning,' George Kitchin, who came up in 1846, recalled; 'independence was curbed by the Thirty-Nine Articles; it ranged all the more freely elsewhere.'[96] The academic self-help which had created the Union library nurtured vacation reading parties, where intercollegiate groups gathered to read with the leading young tutors of the day. The Lake District and Highlands were favoured destinations, but some ventured further afield. Walsham How of Wadham read with Clough in Ireland during the long vacation of 1842 and with Richard Congreve in Dresden in 1843.[97] Particularly formative for the personnel of mid-Victorian academic liberalism, reading parties were no less significant experiences for High-Church undergraduates. H. P. Liddon joined a group at St David's, led by William Stubbs, which kept a common diary representing the reading party as a monastic community with Stubbs as Lord Abbott and Liddon as 'Coquinarius'.[98] Some of the atmosphere of these parties was preserved in Oxford by essay and discussion groups: the Decade, whose membership had included Jowett, A. P. Stanley and Matthew Arnold; its successor, the Essay Society and, among

[94] C. Harvie, *The Lights of Liberalism* (1976), 34.
[95] G. W. E. Russell, *Edward King, Sixtieth Bishop of Lincoln* (1912), 6.
[96] G. W. Kitchin, *Ruskin in Oxford, and other studies* (1903), 33.
[97] H. Birks, *The Life and Correspondence of Thomas Valpy French* (2 vols 1895) i. 12; F. D. How, *Bishop Walsham How: a memoir* (1898), 20, 23.
[98] J. O. Johnston, *Life and Letters of Henry Parry Liddon* (1904), 11.

lesser-known societies, the Hermes, which heard Henry Smith, later the
Savilian Professor of Geometry, lead a discussion on communism, and the
Cosmopolite, 'formed chiefly with a view to cultivate more tolerant and
enlarged sympathies than Oxford men generally had'.[99]

Discussion and argument about literary, political, and theological questions continued on afternoon constitutional walks, the favoured recreation
of reading men.[100] Excursions into the Oxfordshire countryside developed
interests in botany and geology or ecclesiastical architecture. It has perhaps
been too readily assumed that opportunities to pursue these activities were
curtailed by the more regulated leisure patterns later associated with the rise
of organized sport;[101] but there is no doubt that the idea of independent and
individual recreation was particularly strong in this generation. So also was
the idea of Oxford as a rural university. Celebrated in Matthew Arnold's *The
Scholar-Gipsy* and *Thyrsis*, which were inspired by rambles with Clough in
Easter term 1843 to North Hinksey,[102] these images of a university untainted by industrialism were later to exert a strong appeal to the university
extension movement.

The Arnoldian experience of Oxford was hardly shared by the likes of Sir
John Astley, who regarded his twelve months at Christ Church in 1846–7 as
'the most wasted' of his life.[103] A contemporary, who entered Trinity College in 1847, recalled the pervading idleness and the failure of the dons to
occupy undergraduates' time.[104] To many—perhaps the majority—of students in the 1840s, the liberty which the old system allowed, as much by its
decay as by any intended purpose, did not represent the opportunity for
broadening the mind which a rather smaller body of reading men so effectively exploited. For Mr Verdant Green, if he is taken as a cipher for the
representative commoner of his day, the intellectual and moral influences
exercised by Oxford's official system of education were minimal. *The Adventures of Mr. Verdant Green* appeared at the very moment when Oxford
was changing; the first sign of this being the move to broaden an antiquated
curriculum, which, it was freely acknowledged, did the majority of learners
little or no benefit.[105]

---

[99] *The Recollections of the Very Revd. G. D. Boyle, Dean of Salisbury* (1895), 125; J. E. Butler,
Recollections of George Butler (Bristol 1893), 33.

[100] E. A. Towle, *Alexander Heriot Mackonochie: a memoir* (1890), 16–17.

[101] See D. Newsome, *Godliness and Good Learning* (1961), 206.

[102] *Oxford Diaries of Clough*, p. li; see below p. 716.

[103] J. D. Astley, *Fifty Years of my Life* (1894), 28.

[104] A. Y. Marshall, *The Oxford Undergraduate of Twenty Years Ago* (1874), 32.

[105] [B. Jowett and A. P. Stanley], *Suggestions for an Improvement of the Examination Statute*
(1848), 10.

9

An Oxonian 'Idea' of a University:
J. H. Newman and 'Well-Being'

SHELDON ROTHBLATT

John Henry Newman's *The Idea of a University* is unquestionably the single most important treatise in the English language on the nature and meaning of higher education. The only twentieth-century name in similar circulation to Newman's is Alfred North Whitehead's. But neither in scope nor importance do Whitehead's essays rival Newman's discourses and lectures. The very thought of speaking about universities as if they incorporate a central principle or purpose is Newman's. He was inspired, it is certain, by Samuel Taylor Coleridge, who was the first nineteenth-century thinker in England to discuss institutions as if they were much more than mere adaptations to changing circumstances, or more than utilitarian solutions to historical challenges. Institutions (and Coleridge extended the argument to cover character or personality) have an underlying historical identity that persists despite apparent outward transformations. They have an ultimate 'aim'.[1] Before Coleridge it was Edmund Burke who taught the English the importance of history and tradition, and, what is more, in opposition to radical polemicists of the age of the French Revolution, developed the paradox that tradition could actually be used in the service of change.

Newman's 'quasi-germanique'[2] title is often appropriated. Thus we have twentieth-century books entitled *The Concept of a University* or (as befits our more plural world) *Conceptions de l'université*, wherein Newman is joined by Karl Jaspers, Whitehead and even Napoleon Bonaparte.[3] Newman is the starting-point, although hardly the end-point, of the most widely known statement on the nature of the modern (that is, contemporary) public university, Clark Kerr's Godkin Lectures at Harvard of 1963. Kerr's first chapter is entitled 'The Idea of a Multiversity'. Lapidary phrases taken from Newman adorn college bulletins and recruiting brochures in the United

---

[1] R. O. Preyer, 'The Romantic tide reaches Trinity: notes on the transmission and diffusion of new approaches to traditional studies at Cambridge, 1820–1840', *Annals of the New York Academy of Sciences* ccclx (20 Apr. 1981), 54.

[2] J. Drèze and J. Debelle, *Conceptions de l'université* (Paris 1968), 14.

[3] Ibid.; and K. R. Minogue, *The Concept of a University* (1973).

States,[4] and he is often examined in connection with discussions of Roman Catholic education by continental scholars and clerics.[5] There is in general a Newman 'industry' of formidable proportions. Surely he has travelled well.

An 'idea', if it is to be functional, if it is to form the basis upon which a new institution is to arise, should possess two qualities: simplicity and clarity. But Newman as a person was anything but simple, and the large volume of Newman hermeneutics demonstrates that he was anything but clear as a thinker, that is, straightforward, apparent. Anyone who has worked through the *Idea*, or the autobiographical *Apologia pro vita sua*, realizes that an attempt to reduce Newman to quotation threatens the rhetorical integrity of his argument. No sooner is a statement made than he proceeds to render it more intricate. Polarities of argument, upon which the reader relies, are synthesized or transformed as ideas are dissolved into example and qualification and extended through discourse.

We turn, for instance, to the famous opening definition of the *Idea*. 'The view taken of a University in these Discourses', Newman begins, 'is the following:—that it is a place of *teaching* universal *knowledge*. This implies that its object is, on the one hand, intellectual, not moral; and, on the other, that it is the diffusion and extension of knowledge rather than the advancement.'[6]

The definition appears certain, a restatement of the contemporary public controversy shaped by German scientific conceptions of research. Teaching, according to Newman, takes place in a university, but discovery—the advancement of knowledge—is institutionalized elsewhere, as in an academy or other learned society. Teaching and the advancement of learning differ profoundly in this as well, in that the teacher leads a public life, spending his days in 'dispensing his existing knowledge to all comers', but the researcher seeks seclusion and quiet. 'The greatest thinkers have been too intent on their subject to admit of interruption; they have been men of absent minds and idiosyncratic habits, and have, more or less, shunned the lecture room and the public school.'[7]

The argument is joined. There are two rival conceptions of a university. However, the student of Newman would do well to hesitate over the rhetorical placement of the word 'implies' in the famous definition and thus cautioned will proceed slowly along the axis of further discussion. A

---

[4] To take only one example nearly at random, Augustana College in Sioux Falls, South Dakota, affiliated with the American Lutheran Church.

[5] See J. H. Walgrave, 'J. H. Newman et le problème de l'université catholique', in N. A. Luyten (ed.), *Recherche et culture* (Fribourg 1965). Apparently, however, Newman did not attract much attention in Victorian Scotland (possibly because the Scots had their own ancient idea of a university). See R. D. Anderson, *Education and Opportunity in Victorian Scotland* (1983), 83 n.

[6] Newman, *Idea* (1976), 5.

[7] Ibid. 8, 6–7.

qualification is about to issue, as Newman introduces a distinction between a university in its *essence* and a university in *practice*, between, to be specific, a university without a church connection and one with: he suggests thereby a different and more symbiotic relationship between the intellectual and moral forms of education, presented earlier in the celebrated opening as opposing conceptions. The 'idea' of a university, he is saying, may presuppose *intellectual* education, but in practice more is needed.

Another example of how seemingly direct statements of a university's mission are developed or transposed within a highly complex reasoning structure is Newman's discussion of what today is called 'academic freedom', *Lehrfreiheit*. Since this is a crucial issue in twentieth-century conceptions of knowledge and university autonomy, and since purist sentiments respecting the importance of the pursuit of truth without constraint—historically, the 'Platonic-Pythagorean' notion of the cultivation of knowledge for its own sake—do appear in the *Idea*,[8] it is important to give Newman's own words an even closer contextual reading. For phrases and ideas strikingly familiar to us today as axioms and clichés are less familiar when connected as he prefers.

I say [Newman wrote] that it is a matter of primary importance in the cultivation of those sciences, in which truth is discoverable by the human intellect, that the investigator should be free, independent, unshackled in his movements; that he should be allowed and enabled, without impediment, to fix his mind intently, nay exclusively, on his special object, without the risk of being distracted every other minute in the process and progress of his inquiry, by charges of temerariousness, or by warnings against extravagance or scandal.[9]

This seems clear enough, but the wary reader should pause for a minute over the words 'those sciences' and the clause 'in which truth is discoverable by the human intellect' and should be a little uneasy about the rather mitigated word 'distracted'. Even warned, the reader may be puzzled by the next paragraph where, while talking about 'what are called the *dogmas* of faith', Newman announced that 'none of us should say that it is any shackle at all upon the intellect to maintain these inviolate'.[10] Further on Newman expressly rejected the position that a scientist should be allowed, within the university, to use his science to contradict dogma. Next he wrote that 'when I advocate the independence of philosophical thought, I am not speaking of any *formal teaching* at all, but of investigations, speculations, and

[8] Ibid. 52, 135. My understanding of the purist strain in Western liberal learning has been enhanced by discussions with William Bouwsma and Bruce Kimball. See also P. A. Dale, 'Newman's *The Idea of a University*: The Dangers of a University Education', *Victorian Studies* xvi (1972), 5–36, who convincingly argues against the common tendency to make Newman an exponent of the idea of the pursuit of truth for its own sake.
[9] Newman, *Idea*, 379.
[10] Ibid. 379–80.

discussions'.[11] And the trump card, when finally played, is Newman's warning that 'there must be great care taken to avoid scandal, or shocking the popular mind, or unsettling the weak'.[12] No unambiguous 'idea' of a university is anywhere in sight.

Difficulties in pinning down Newman's idea of a university are compounded by an additional problem. It is a commonplace of Newman studies to remark that his idea of a university is not, let us say, just a Coleridgean extrapolation of essence from changing historical circumstances, but that it is also in some important way Oxford's idea of a university as derived by Newman from his long sojourn within its walls and gardens. Since he came to Oxford as a boy of 16 and remained there for nearly thirty years, it is only natural that *The Idea of a University* should reflect the singularities of that special educational environment. Yet Newman was uncomfortable with the suggestion—it was more in the vein of an accusation—that the sentiments and ideas he expounded in his famous book of the 1850s corresponded closely to the Oxford, or as it came to be known, to the 'English' idea of a university. In Dublin, where he presided over the series of conferences that led to the *Idea*, his assignment was to create an institution that would serve as a centre for English-speaking Roman Catholics. The English idea was unacceptable to members of the Roman Catholic hierarchy in Ireland, for Oxford and Oxford's education was believed to be class-specific, that is, developed especially for a particular clientele. Oxford (and Cambridge) were patronized by the wealthier sections of society and therefore produced (in Newman's ironic words) 'that antiquated variety of human nature and remnant of feudalism...called a "gentleman"'.[13] By contrast, potential Roman Catholic students were of humble background and modest incomes. Furthermore, the Irish bishops initially wanted to found a seminary rather than a university, and their objectives were accordingly more limited. Differences between Newman and the Irish bishops are always present in the many discussions and deliberations comprising his *Idea*.

Whether Newman was uncomfortable with the suggestion or not, the case can certainly be made that in conception, purpose, structure and tone, Newman's idea of a university is both English and 'Oxford'; but since in Newman's lifetime there were several competing 'Oxford' ideas or, better,

[11] Newman, *Idea*, 379.
[12] Ibid. 381. See also 199: the duty of the Church was 'not to prohibit truth of any kind, but to see that no doctrine pass under the name of Truth but those which claim it rightfully'. One of the main points of contention in the famous quarrel with Charles Kingsley that led to the writing of *Apologia pro vita sua* was the matter of truth for its own sake. See Newman, *Apologia*, p. li. It is worth repeating the observation that if Newman's definition of truth disappointed English liberals, it was more flexible than views held at the time by members of the Roman Catholic hierarchy. In fact, according to Culler, some of Newman's theories of teaching, especially his emphasis on the *internal* transformation of personality, remained more Protestant than Catholic. See A. D. Culler, *The Imperial Intellect* (New Haven 1965), 14, 22, 226.
[13] *Idea*, 5–6.

variations on a common theme, it is more accurate to say that Newman's 'Oxford' idea of a university derives from memories of the college life he led in the 1820s. It is that experience, the particular expression of a union of certain Oxford traditions with certain changes in the wider English culture, that animates the *Idea of a University* and provides it with intellectual force and emotional appeal. An 'Oxford' idea of a university is indeed Newman's idea, and the Irish episcopacy was correct in so perceiving it. Newman's rejoinder was to explain, in a memorable *summa*, why the 'Oxford' idea was appropriate for a Roman Catholic university.

Because Newman's 'idea' is neither simple nor direct, it has been suggested that the subtitle, which uses the word 'discourses', is a more accurate representation of his method.[14] This is a reasonable emendation; but 'idea', even if it is confusing, places Newman within the tradition of Burke and Coleridge and gives his work a special impact or effect. An 'idea' inhabits or haunts the mind in ways that a discourse cannot.

This does not dispose of the criticism that Newmanesque discoursing is profoundly contradictory or inconsistent. Such conclusions are plausible. Newman's life was filled with tension, disappointment and crises. Family difficulties, career frustrations, controversy, misunderstandings inevitably enter the inner psychic and mental circuitry of an emotional and sensitive man. This is not the place to engage in debates about whether Newman 'deconstructs' his own text or whether he has successfully merged Christianity and humanism or resolved in some plausible fashion mid-nineteenth-century debates between religion and science.[15] The point to be made is that Newman, in stipulating the essence of a university, is indeed, as he says, also concerned about its actual design and functioning. Hence it is not so much the problem of knowledge *qua* knowledge that leads to such equivocation or confusion as one may notice in Newman, but the immensely practical and bedrock consideration of educating the young. Newman, like all his contemporaries—like all his predecessors—had to deal with the historical fact that universities were composed of undergraduates who came to be taught, and the question of authority must inevitably arise wherever the education of young people not yet mature in mind and person is in question. The Catholic University in Dublin over which Newman presided as Rector for seven years admitted students who were only 16 years of age. This was typical of most 'post-secondary' institutions at the time. It was true of non-medical students at the University of London and of students in Scottish

---

[14] F. McGrath, *Newman's University: Idea and Reality* (1951), 281. *The Discourses on the Scope and Nature of University Education* were first published in volume form 2 Feb. 1853. In 1873 the *Discourses* were combined with *Lectures and Essays on University Subjects* under the title *The Idea of a University*.

[15] For which see Ker's extensive introduction to *Idea* and Dale, 'Newman's *The Idea of a University*', 34 (who contends that Newman is *not* a 'Christian humanist').

universities as well as in American colonial foundations like Yale or Harvard.[16] Oxford undergraduates, however, tended to be nearer the age of 18, although John Keble was not quite 15 when he went up to Corpus Christi College in 1807 and Newman was less than two years older. He was, however, the only one of his age among the nineteen undergraduates entering Trinity College in 1817.[17]

The problem of authority was compounded by the absence or blurring of distinctions between the university and the upper secondary school in the first half of the nineteenth century. Teachers at the university held much the same view of the pedagogical role as their counterparts in schools. They expected to exercise moral superintendence over young persons placed under their care. While they may have disagreed over the nature of the proper 'discipline' to be exercised, and often enough in the two senior universities of England were rather relaxed in the exercise of their responsibilities, there was no question in their minds but that a university, whatever else it might be, was also a place in which young persons were subject to discipline—moral, intellectual or, in past ages, corporal. It was therefore in keeping with the usual idea of a university that knowledge be disseminated only when young minds were carefully prepared to receive it. It was also in keeping with the idea of a university that there was false learning as well as right learning, error as well as truth. Views similar to Newman's had always been expressed in Oxford. A decade before his arrival there the Rector of Lincoln College, Edward Tatham, called a university a 'seat of *Universal Learning* increasing and to be increased, from the nature of men and things, with the lapse of time: it is also the place of *Universal Teaching*, which is its first and most important duty'. Although placing rather more stress than would Newman on the importance of advancing learning and adjusting university teaching accordingly—'otherwise it may occupy young men in studies that are obsolete and in errors that are exploded'—Tatham's apparent advocacy of truth was not unlimited. He too appreciated the fact that immature minds could be damaged by unsifted opinions. No matter how progressive the studies of a university might be, they should also, he emphasized, 'be in the *Right or Initiative Method*; otherwise it will lead [the students] *from*, instead of *to*, the Truth, into Sophistry instead of Science, in all parts of learning, and involve them in darkness and confusion'.[18]

The question of knowledge cannot be separated from the question of teaching. Newman's idea, but also the English and the Oxford idea of it,

[16] Which is not to say that there were no mature university students. For example, in America between 1821 and 1830 students 25 years old or above made up 16.9% of the graduating population. At places like Brown they made up over one-third. I. C. Mohsenin, 'Note on age structure of college students', *History of Education Quarterly* xxiii (Winter 1983), 493.

[17] McGrath, *Newman's University*, 299.

[18] E. Tatham, *An Address to the Members of Convocation at Large on the Proposed New Statute Respecting Public Examinations in the University of Oxford* (2nd edn 1807), 1.

presupposes yet another institutional connection, that between a university and a college or (for consistency) the idea of a college. Newman's clearest statement of the relationship between college and university appeared originally in 1854 and is usually reprinted under the title *Rise and Progress of Universities*. In this book-length discussion Newman makes a distinction between university and college. The teaching-method of the first is professorial, of the second tutorial. The university exists for the pursuit of knowledge, but the function of the college is the development of character. In Newman's day these were conventional summaries of the division of labour between the two educational institutions in the English universities. Yet Newman makes a more interesting separation of the two. The 'essence' of a university, he says (by essence he means the historical idea rather than any scholastic reference to inherent qualities) is knowledge, but the essence of a college is 'integrity'. The dissemination of knowledge ultimately produces progress, and therefore in time universities embody the principle of progress. But colleges represent stability. If universities are centres of movement, colleges are places of order. If universities are sail, colleges are ballast.[19] Here is an unmistakable borrowing of Coleridge's two desiderata that institutions should incorporate at one and the same time: the principle of progress and the principle of permanence.[20]

Newman goes on to say that the 'strict idea' of a university is sufficient for its being, but it is the college that stretches 'being' into 'well-being'.[21] The distinction, he says, is based on Aristotle's discussion of happiness where the philosophical conception of 'integrity' appears. Integrity—in this case 'well-being'—is a gift or addition, external to the thing itself. The thing—'being'— may stand alone and function regularly, but it remains flawed, not quite fulfilled. Such is the relation between a university and a college. Such is the integrity provided for the first by the second.

Rarely and only obliquely does the *Idea of a University* make reference to the idea of a college. 'Integrity' there is identified with the Roman Catholic Church. It is the Church that 'steadies' the university in the performance of its 'office of intellectual education'.[22] Newman was participating in the establishment of a new university in Ireland which would function as an intellectual centre for English-speaking Catholics, and some 'ballast', or reassurance, was required to counteract professorial speculations possibly inimical to dogma or Church teaching.

But if we ask what does Newman *feel* (an appropriate question for a Georgian romantic), apart from what he may *say*, there can be no doubt that for him the proper institution for granting integrity to the university is the

---

[19] J. H. Newman, *Historical Sketches* iii (1873). See Ch. 1, n. 178. *Rise and Progress of Universities*, Chs. 2, 15, and 17–20 are especially relevant.
[20] S. T. Coleridge, *On the Constitution of Church and State*, ed. J. Colmer (Princeton 1976), 44.
[21] Newman, *Historical Sketches*, iii. 182.
[22] Newman, *Idea*, 5.

college, even though, given its special purpose, the college acts on behalf of the Church, or is its surrogate.[23] It was and had always been the college that held his loyalty and affection. True, in the 1850s he castigated Oxford for emphasizing the college over the university, the antiquated idea of a gentleman over the acquisition of knowledge; but if knowledge was his being, the old college system was the source of his well-being. He yearned for it even if he could not reproduce it in the very different environment of Victorian Ireland.

The topic warrants special elaboration. Newman's discussion of the idea of a university proceeds in two cognitive modes, two planes of knowing or perceiving. The first may be called intellectual. He discusses knowledge, the proper ends of knowledge, the relationship of the several fields of knowledge, and moral qualities engendered or inhibited by learning. He discusses the meaning of liberal education and its antithesis, servile education, and the spheres of influence of secular and religious learning. This form of discussion predominates in the substance of the *Idea*. The second mode is emotional and is conveyed through Newman's famous multifaceted prose. The Edwardian critic Sir Arthur Quiller-Couch said of the *Idea* that it is 'sinuous, sinewy, Platonic'. Some critics speak of his Ciceronian, Gibbonian, Attic and Hebraic styles, or of his regal, elegiac or academic styles. Others of his 'simple, curled and cumulative styles'.[24] But what is more to the point is Newman's recognition and use, especially in the *Apologia*, of what he himself understood as 'states of mind', predispositions to likes and dislikes, tastes, hopes and fears, or 'indefinite, vague, and withal subtle feelings which quite pierce the soul and make it sick'.[25] States of mind move an argument along as effectively as fact and reason, and it may be said that what often moves *The Idea of a University*, or what makes it so rhetorically appealing, are not the facts and reasoning—these, as we have seen, are not always easy to grasp in the form Newman gives them—but the states of mind behind the arguments, always suggesting a deeper, richer, more important strain of knowing and understanding. Walter Houghton underscores these distinctions by noting the startling difference in biographical method between John Stuart Mill's *Autobiography* and Newman's *Apologia*. One is the record of a mind, the other of a person.[26] One is partial and the other whole. Although the difference can be overstated, there is some broad truth to it.

The idea of a university is cerebral. The idea of a college is a state of mind. A university 'is a place of *teaching* universal *knowledge*', runs the famous

[23] Newman, *Historical Sketches* iii. 182. But not 'feeling' in the modern popular form of a rejection of self-control in favour of *élan vital*. This qualification is essential for understanding Newman's holism, represented institutionally by the union of university and college. See John Barrie, 'Bantock on Newman: A Nineteenth-Century Perspective on Contemporary Educational Theory', *British Journal of Educational Studies* 34 (Feb. 1986), 76.

[24] W. E. Houghton, *The Art of Newman's 'Apologia'* (New Haven 1945), 46.

[25] JHN to Jemima Newman, 10 May 1828; *LDN* ii. 69.

[26] Houghton, op. cit., 51–3.

definition, but if we were to tamper with this line, rewrite it to emphasize that a college 'is a *place* of teaching', we would come closer to where Newman's own sentiments reside. Some French commentators have understood this by rendering 'place' as *milieu*.[27] A college is a milieu, not an institution, an environment that acts immediately upon the mind of young persons, engendering moods and dispositions, loyalties and affections. 'It is the shrine of our best affections, the bosom of our fondest recollections, a spell upon our afterlife, a stay for world-weary mind and soul, wherever we are cast, till the end comes.'[28]

These extraordinary, almost desperate images of security and sanctuary have a force often missing from the intellectual discussions comprising the bulk of the *Idea*. Expressed again and again in Newman's letters, diaries, essays and occasional writings, they are not his exclusive possession. They belong to his generation, the young undergraduates who read Sir Walter Scott and listened to or played Beethoven (as he did), and wished (as he did) that 'the Arabian Tales were true: my imagination ran on unknown influences, on magical powers, and talismans'.[29] Newman's generation began arriving in Oxford midway through the period of the wars against France. Romantics experiencing the profound cultural changes of the last years of the eighteenth century and the opening decades of the nineteenth, they wanted a college to be a milieu. They spoke of it or of buildings and gardens as having a separate spirit or existence, implying that places and people interact and interconnect. As an undergraduate wandering about the colleges at night, Newman wanted to be encircled by Oxford, to be drawn into its life for ever. He would walk about the colleges, peering 'into the deep, gas-lit, dark-shadowed quadrangles', wondering how he could make his attachment permanent, wondering, to be precise, whether he would ever be a 'Fellow of this or that College'.[30] How is it, Newman asks, at a critical moment in Discourse VI of the *Idea*, that England has been 'able to subdue the earth, able to domineer over Catholics.... how is this to be explained?'[31] And he answers, with reference to English public schools and Oxbridge colleges, that they possess 'a self-perpetuating tradition, or a *genius loci*... which haunts the home where it has been born, and which imbues and forms more or less, and one by one, every individual who is successfully brought under its shadow. Thus it is that, independent of direct instruction on the part of Superiors, there is a sort of self-education in the academic institutions of Protestant England.'[32] The genius of the place influences the teachers as well, 'for they themselves have been educated in it, and at all

---

[27] Drèze and Debelle, *Conceptions de l'université*, 46.
[28] Newman, *Historical Sketches* iii. 215.
[29] Newman, *Apologia*, 15–16.
[30] Newman, *AW* 50.
[31] Newman, *Idea*, 130.
[32] Ibid. 130–1.

times are exposed to the influence of its ethical atmosphere'.[33] 'Real teaching', says Newman, can only occur where space encourages 'intercommunion'.

Upon first seeing Cambridge in 1832, he wrote 'there is a *genius loci* here, as in my own dear home—and the nearer I came to it the more I felt its power'.[34] The 'genius of the place': the recurrence of the phrase in Newman deserves an historical comment. The habit of attributing special qualities to a place, *a fortiori* of attributing gender, moods and other human qualities to buildings, streets and gardens, begins perhaps with Vitruvius, is carried into the Italian Renaissance and reappears in the writings of French Enlightenment and Scottish School of Common Sense theorists. But although the habit of imbuing a place with a unique genius or inspiration in order to create a milieu was present in the eighteenth century, aestheticians were also attracted to neo-classical formalism, to rules and Platonic forms. A building or a painting is an emblem. A portrait represents attributes and qualities such as courage, self-sacrifice, chastity, devotion or virtue, but these can only be apprehended through examination and reflection, what may be called intellection. In the Scottish School of Common Sense, particularly in the writings of the highly influential associationist Archibald Alison, direct communication replaces the prior emphasis in aesthetics on intellectualizing experience. In the theory of associations the mind instantly receives impressions and perceptions of a building, situation or painting. No longer is the object viewed a representation or a form that stimulates learned but 'objective' responses. It is instead a personal composition. Furthermore, subjective meaning can be enhanced or directed by associations suggested to the beholder by his imagination, his experience and expectations, or by history and historical allusion. As in all associational psychology, early experience makes for lasting impressions. The associations formed in childhood and youth are particularly strong.[35] In the *Apologia* Newman referred to 'the pleasures of memory', the attractions of 'historical sites and beautiful scenes', and, as if to mark the sharp break with eighteenth-century sensibility, he contrasted these pleasures with Grand Tourism, with visits merely for the purpose of studying 'men and manners'.[36]

Newman arrived at Oxford when the new mode of perception and understanding had established itself. Undergraduates were talking about their university and college experiences with an affection conspicuously absent

[33] Newman, *Idea*, 131.

[34] J. H. Newman, *A Packet of Letters*, ed. J. Sugg (1983), 12–13. And he goes on: 'I do really think the place finer than Oxford, though I suppose it isn't, for every one says so. I like the narrow streets—they have character.'

[35] For 'the genius of the place' see G. L. Hersey, *High Victorian Gothic: a study in associationism* (Baltimore 1972), pp. xviii, xix, 1–24; also G. H. Hartman, *Beyond Formalism* (New Haven 1970), 311–36.

[36] Newman, *Apologia*, 41.

in the eighteenth century.[37] Students then had not customarily thought of colleges as sanctuaries from the world, as special places where past associations could be directly translated into contemporary styles of feeling and youthful aspirations find encouragement. Now in the early decades of the nineteenth century a revolution in expectations and associations was taking place. A youth subculture had established itself in the ancient quadrangles, drawing young people even more closely together. One result was self-conscious separation from the world of senior dons. Newman remembered this world of separate spheres when later he wrote of 'a state of things, in which teachers were cut off from the taught as by an insurmountable barrier; when neither party entered into the thoughts of the other. I have known places where a stiff manner, a pompous voice, coldness and condescension were the teacher's attributes, and where he neither knew, nor wished to know...the private irregularities of the youths committed to his charge.'[38]

Debating societies, sporting and drinking clubs, constant rounds of expensive entertaining, a serious interest in literature and politics—these were for the most part new, that is, new in the sense that the college was seen to be the natural home for such activities. In the eighteenth century the 'world' (usually London) and the 'way of the world' were more important for undergraduates than the college or university. And in the nineteenth century the colleges and universities had responded to youthful energy and ambition, or, travelling in parallel lines, had encouraged zeal and industry by intensifying academic discipline, by introducing new examinations and honours, and by establishing prize competitions. The religious revivals of the early nineteenth century contributed immeasurably to the new mood. Factions, sets, friendship circles, affinity groups, Evangelical or 'high-and-dry' societies are a more pronounced feature of the student landscape, and within the university itself, sometimes college-based but not always, undergraduates engaged private tutors for intensive sessions of study in ways hardly typical of earlier generations.

One of the least understood dimensions of this enlarged, enhanced, turn-of-the-century undergraduate world is its special quality of youthfulness. Historically young people have usually been expected to model themselves upon adults, to anticipate socialization into career or polite society by adopting manners, bearing, styles of dress and attitudes common to their elders. Our current emphasis on independence (of thinking, at least), on personal autonomy, on self-reliance and initiative and on the emotional states that sustain such behaviour was not culturally typical of the periods before Newman, nor—it would be a mistake to imply a complete change had

---

[37] For a lengthier discussion of these changes see S. Rothblatt, 'The student sub-culture and the examination system in early nineteenth-century Oxbridge' in L. Stone (ed.), *The University in Society* (2 vols Princeton 1975) i. 247–303.

[38] Newman, *Historical Sketches* iii. 75.

occurred—was it characteristic of the period in which Newman came of age. Yet we have reason to believe that from the 1790s onward developments were occurring within landed and professional families (at least those feeding the universities) which would, within several decades, produce a more questioning and demanding student, a more earnest undergraduate likely to be attracted to teachers who, perhaps unwittingly, appealed to youthful idealism or stirred youthful aspirations. More attention was being paid in the home to upbringing as a dynamic process. Parents could not as yet avail themselves of what today would be called developmental psychology. It was not customary to divide the life cycle into discrete stages of biological, sexual and emotional growth, yet there is evidence of considerable thought being given to schooling as it affected personal development. It is not, as it is sometimes represented to be, merely a case of parents selecting schools according to the best career opportunities for sons, although that factor is never absent. There was also a desire to place them in educational environments conducive to moral growth. The great aristocracy was still willing to release its progeny into the world at an early age, there to acquire a knowledge of men and manners thought necessary for a governing stratum, but in other social groupings there were genuine fears that irreparable damage would be done to inexperienced children if care was not exercised in the proper choice of friends and teachers. The fears were strongest among the clergy, lesser gentry and professional families which were the principal patrons of Oxford.[39] In these families youth or adolescence ('adolescence' not yet having an age-specific or sexual meaning) was considered to be the 'dangerous age', and young people had to be sheltered or protected from adverse influences.[40] Parents seemed to be particularly anxious about the fate of their sons in boarding-schools and residential colleges and kept up a personal correspondence with headmasters, college heads and college tutors in an effort to assuage anxieties that proper supervision was not being exercised. Private tutors, consequently, played a special role by acting *in loco parentis*, being engaged by families to follow sons to college, or, recommended to parents by heads of houses, used as watchdogs, as pedagogues in the original Greek sense.

Gradually, over a number of decades, the whole way in which residence at university was looked at by parents and sons was transformed. College tutors overlapped in function with private tutors. Both stood in the place of a parent, and the undergraduate began to see the college as in effect his home towards which it was legitimate to express affection and from which, in return, he had a right to expect a certain amount of solicitude. This would not be true of all students, but it was true of the special ones, the Newmans,

---

[39] See Pt 2, Ch. 1.
[40] P. Spacks, 'The dangerous age', *Eighteenth-Century Studies* xi (1978), 417–38.

for example, or the Macaulays at Cambridge, and of youthful poets and rebels like Percy Bysshe Shelley, who never dreamed that his flamboyant espousal of atheism would result in expulsion in 1811. G. M. Young once wrote that Shelley was the first undergraduate 'recognizable as such'.[41] Young always enjoyed leaving readers with the burden of filling in the blanks, of recognizing an undergraduate upon sight. Possibly he meant that the mixture of idealism, the special prominence accorded to being young, a sense of estrangement from an incomprehensible adult world and a desire to challenge authority were first joined together in the early nineteenth century to create a type of student response altogether new.

Newman felt all these influences, the influences derived from a new mode of aesthetic perception, the influences originating in a family life in which relationships were emotional if not always satisfactory, and in which a family crisis, such as his father's business failure, was likely to have a traumatic impact. He felt the strong passions released by the religious revivals (for a time he fell under the dominance of a strong-willed, Evangelical master at Ealing School), the influences of a newly established student subculture where the undergraduate was both insider and outsider.[42] It is not always remembered that Newman was the editor of England's first authentic student publication, called *The Undergraduate*, which he and a friend, John William Bowden, founded early in 1819. The magazine enjoyed a brief popularity, and then disappeared, as was typical of student publications where the problem of continuity of editorial leadership had not yet been worked out. The tone of *The Undergraduate* was believed to be threatening to authority, which may be another reason why its youthful authors decided to stop publication. But the episode was an example of his early commitment to ideas and to issues, a foreshadowing of the controversialist he was to become, an example of an exploration of the idea of a university forming itself in a very young mind. Newman loved Oxford as William Wordsworth, in the early 1790s, could not love Cambridge. Wordsworth looked back to a Cambridge where Isaac Newton's statue stood in the antechapel at Trinity College,

> his prism and silent face,
> The marble index of a mind for ever
> Voyaging through strange seas of Thought, alone.[43]

---

[41] 'Hogg and Shelley... seem to me the first undergraduates, recognizable as such, on record': G. M. Young, *Victorian England: portrait of an age* (1957), 92 n.

[42] Expressed sociologically, this combines a profound attachment to an institution's prevailing or inherent values, or an idealization of those values, with some of the feelings associated with marginal status. See R. Merton, 'Insiders and outsiders: a chapter in the sociology of knowledge', *American Journal of Sociology* lxxviii (1972), 9–47.

[43] W. Wordsworth, *The Prelude*, book III, lines 61–3. As Ben Ross Schneider has so well explained, Wordsworth's undergraduate experience at Cambridge was mixed. Intellectually he

Images of perdurable rock, stillness, distance, separation, scientific and rational detachment usurp space meant for prayer and communication and empty it of life and human association. How different Newman!

The idea of a college incorporates a sense of the genius of the place. It is a milieu, and within that milieu a special form of communion takes place between teacher and taught. But that special form of communion did not exist as a regular collegiate experience when Newman was an undergraduate at Trinity College, Oxford. It came later, in 1826 to be precise, when Newman, then a fellow of Oriel College, was appointed one of four tutors in the college.

To appreciate Newman's conception of a college one must mention the famous controversy, discussed in Chapters 1 and 6 of this volume, with Provost Edward Hawkins over the Oriel tutorial system. Newman, along with his close friends Hurrell Froude and Robert Wilberforce, also tutors, was dissatisfied with the conventional responsibilities attached to an Oriel tutorship. They introduced a new system in which a single tutor monopolized the moral and educational superintendence of students assigned to him, taking over some of the functions of the private tutor and altogether increasing his influence. Serious students received far more attention than indifferent (usually wealthy) students in what clearly was an effort to influence their religious views, or so it has been plausibly suggested, and Newman virtually said as much himself. Hawkins appears to have first expressed disapproval only in 1829 when the issue of Catholic Emancipation led to a sharp break with Newman.[44]

It was not exactly a novelty in Oxford for a college tutor to wish to establish some kind of influence over a student shortly after he came into residence. Oxford teachers had often argued that liberal education was more effective when commenced early. The great Edward Copleston had argued this point when answering the criticism of the Edinburgh reviewers earlier in the century.[45] It was a corollary of the assumption that associations were best and most lastingly formed when the mind was most impressionable.[46] Hawkins objected that the innovations promoted favouritism. Newman answered that he and his associates had transformed the tutorial office from an administrative and pedagogical one into a high clerical undertaking. 'I have ever considered the Tutorship a religious office, not unlike the

<hr />

owed the rational studies of the place more than one might suppose given the personal indignities he suffered as a sizar (that is, a poor scholar) and as a north-countryman whose accent invited ridicule. See *Wordsworth's Cambridge Education* (Cambridge 1957), 40, 51 and ch. 9.

[44] W. Robbins, *The Newman Brothers* (Cambridge Mass. 1966), 18, 20, 35; Newman, *Apologia*, 62–3; D. Newsome, *The Parting of Friends* (1966), 92–5.

[45] Newman, *Idea*, 445.

[46] Newman, *Historical Sketches* iii. 235.

Pastoral', he wrote in 1831.[47] There was always danger, he said in a letter of 1826, that a college tutor would regard his office as merely an opportunity to advance himself in a career. Newman thought of it more in Weberian terms as a calling. But he also believed that success in Oxford's examinations virtually required specifically tutorial instruction, a belief which in the long run proved to be entirely correct.[48]

Why was this revolutionary or disturbing? Oxford was in so many respects a religious or at least an ecclesiastical institution. Surely moral, even religiously moral, superintendence was very much part of the tradition of college teaching. But for Newman these were formulae. Oxford teaching had become 'intellectual' he said in the *Apologia*, not 'moral', that is, not religiously moral, not 'real teaching'. Intellectual culture had nothing to do with conscience, for which it merely substituted a moral sense. Sin against human nature replaced sin against God. 'Taste' was more important than duty. Oxford's famous academic reawakening, as exemplified by the new examination statutes and such paragons as the Oriel Noetics, was, as he would later say, liberal, utilitarian, rational, Protestant and 'anti-dogmatic'. Religious authority had given way to private judgement.[49] Undergraduates were perfunctorily cautioned against committing sins, but no intense personal effort was made to cure their souls, to prevent perdition, to rescue, develop and cultivate their inner sense of being, their special human but also spiritual quality.

There is a striking passage in *The Idea of a University* which states exactly what happens to a university when it lacks the ballast of a college, when it makes its object only the cultivation of intellect without the integrity of moral instruction. A university becomes 'a set of examiners with no opinions which they dare profess, and with no common principles, who are teaching or questioning a set of youths who do not know them, and do not know each other on a large number of subjects, different in kind, and connected by no wide philosophy, three times a week, or three times a year, or once in three years, in chill lecture-rooms or on a pompous anniversary'.[50]

The passage is a Burkean echo of a world turning upside-down. From three times a week to once in three years—the inversion, followed by

---

[47] *LDN* ii. 307. The dispute with Hawkins has always attracted attention. See M. R. O'Connell, *The Oxford Conspirators: a history of the Oxford Movement, 1833–1845* (1969), 114–16; M. Ward, *Young Mr Newman* (1948), 179–81.

[48] Newman, *A Packet of Letters*, 9; *LDN* ii. 211–12. In his tutorial activities, as well as generally, Newman had many sides. His moods switched abruptly from chatty informality to shy aloofness, from light-hearted common-room talk to stern disapproval. Ward suggests he had some of the emotional problems of a near-stutterer (Ward, 76–7, 179, 247, 317).

[49] Newman, *Idea*, 165; Newman, *Apologia*, 54–7. See also Culler, *The Imperial Intellect*, 22. For the relevant passage in Newman's Easter sermon in Oriel, 1827, see p. 53 above.

[50] Newman, *Idea*, 131.

disconnection, is devastating, and the place, the milieu, has turned cold and formal. Its integrity is gone. Its well-being has become only being. Newman once wrote that 'an academical system without the personal influence of teachers upon pupils is an arctic winter; it will create an ice-bound, petrified, cast-iron university, and nothing else'.[51] Here, finally, is the Oxford counterpart to Wordsworth's marble statue of Isaac Newton. And a pompous anniversary replaces the genius of the place. This is not Newman's preferred way of remembering Oxford. This is not the Oxford of youthful companions, of quadrangles by moonlight, of snapdragons growing on the walls opposite the rooms he kept as a freshman—the Oxford that is part of natural creation, that is alive and human.[52] Nor does it suggest the unforgettable approach to the city and the University via the Henley Road, across Magdalen Bridge and past Magdalen Tower and the great Magdalen elms, and finally around the famous curve in the High.[53]

Despite its fame, Newman's *Idea* is not the most prevalent conception of a university today, not even, it may be suggested, in the form of its natural offspring the American liberal arts college, church-related as well as independent. Within modern, technological, bureaucratic, democratic societies other conceptions of a university are in the ascendancy: the idea of a university as a place of original inquiry and as a home for specialist learning; or, more broadly, the university as a service centre for all the varied cultural, vocational, professional, technological demands that can be placed on it. It is also a sanctuary for the avant-garde and a place from which theories of social reconstruction issue. The most common idea of a university, argued Clark Kerr, is that it can no longer be described as having one.

The Catholic university established in Ireland which owes much to Newman's inspiration before and during his brief tenure as its rector modelled its constitution on the Belgian Catholic University of Louvain of 1831, but its teaching-structure was Oxbridge, in so far as its limited resources allowed. Newman established a professoriate, but also, to begin with, he created three collegiate houses of fifteen to twenty students in each where a certain degree of tutorial instruction and communication took place. Tutors, he noted, were half companions, half advisers.[54] Formal discipline he left to deans. Newman also established a medical school, and he specified professorial chairs in both engineering and agriculture. In some form, depending upon how one defines them, his creations lasted until 1908. Newman's university incorporated collegiate, professorial and professional functions. But the special quality

[51] Newman, *Historical Sketches* iii. 75.
[52] Newman, *Apologia*, 213.
[53] Of which Culler makes effective use in the opening to *The Imperial Intellect*, but the description is originally William Tuckwell's: Tuckwell (1900), 3.
[54] McGrath, *Newman's University*, 340; from Newman's 'Memorandum to the Bishops', composed in Apr.–May 1854.

of a university, that which made undergraduate teaching essential to its survival, was the idea of a college. 'The principal making of men must be by the tutorial system,' he declared in 1851;[55] and the making of men was the real ideal of a university. Deny it as he might, or attempt as he would to calm the ruffled feathers of the Irish Catholic hierarchy by typically brilliant arguments, the fact remained that Newman's idea of a university was finally the English idea of one.

Was it also Oxford's? Did Oxford have an 'idea' and was that 'idea' similar to the one being expounded in Dublin by the famous controversialist who left Oxford in 1846 and did not see the University again for many years, 'excepting its spires as they are seen from the railway'?[56]

However much Oxford had rejected Newman—Hawkins had forced him out of the tutorship in 1831 and Tract 90 of the Oxford Movement had been condemned by the Hebdomadal Board—it is astonishing to realize that Newman's idea of a university was indeed Oxford's. New and younger dons professing an ethic of teaching similar to his continued to gravitate towards positions of authority within the colleges. Some of them were not to Newman's taste. They were the 'liberal' disciples of the Oriel Noetic Thomas Arnold. But whether or not he approved of them, their objectives were similar to his: the restoration of the collegiate spirit, the revival (or extension) of the tutorial system in order to restore to the teaching relationship the personal influence of the tutor. Furthermore, the Royal Commissioners who reviewed the financial structure and curriculum of Oxford from 1850 to 1852 were sympathetic to Newman's idea, at least to this extent, that in their eyes a university was a place for the dissemination of knowledge; although for them, with respect to this object, it did not matter whether its structure was professorial or collegial. After the 1850s and 1860s the movement for university reform recommenced on a new basis, and in those decades a different idea formed to challenge the older one. That idea was the advancement of knowledge, known then as the movement for the 'endowment of research'. 'Integrity', the idea of a college as ballast, was no longer essential even to the 'idea' of a university. Newman, in short, propounded his *Idea* at precisely the last moment when circumstances allowed for its realization.

In one respect the Oxford about to be born, the 'Young Oxford' as new generations of mid-Victorian dons would call it, did not meet Newman's conception of what a university ought to be. In his extraordinary portrait of that 'remnant of feudalism', the English gentleman, Newman had provided the lineaments of the nineteenth-century courtier in a fashion never to be replicated again. But Newman's own feelings towards this special social product of the English university were ambivalent. He was attracted to

---

[55] McGrath, *Newman's University*, 121; from the postscript of the report to the Catholic University Committee, submitted Oct. 1851.
[56] Newman, *Apologia*, 213.

him even as finally he had to reject him. For the gentleman, unquestionably moral, was not conspicuously Christian. He was secular, even pagan. 'At this day the "gentleman" is the creation, not of Christianity, but of civilization,'[57] that is, of intellectual culture. And the difference was precisely this, that civilization, or, as he also called it, 'the world', was 'content with setting right the surface of things', but the Church aimed 'at regenerating the very depths of the heart'.[58] In 'The Tamworth Reading Room' Newman had phrased the same sentiment this way: 'glory, science, knowledge, and whatever other fine names we use, never healed a wounded heart, nor changed a sinful one'.[59] In so far as a university was a place of disseminating knowledge, it had to be supplemented by a college, for knowledge could only adjust the surface of things, but a college transformed human nature through its 'regenerative quality',[60] which rested finally on a pastoral conception of teaching.

The Oxford University that Newman entered when he came into residence in 1817 was in many respects unsatisfactory. Newman was distressed by the sinful conduct of youthful aristocrats and other wealthy men who set a poor example for earnest but vulnerable sons from country parsonages and respectable landed families. The Oxford of some forty years later was on the edge of a major internal transformation. The foundations of the modern or present tutorial system were being laid. The golden age of Oxford teaching was about to commence. Young dons incorporated a sense of calling into their ministrations to the young. And the young as a generation were noticeably more responsible. They were becoming better disciplined and more civilized. But in other important dimensions Oxford was not conforming to Newman's idea of a university. The dons who came after him wanted a career as 'professional' academics. Newman had feared this would make them less sensitive to the religious basis of their collegiate duties. Young men were better-behaved, but they were not particularly pious. Compulsory chapel every day was gradually disappearing, religious subscription was about to become obsolete. Celibacy, which Queen Elizabeth had once personally insisted upon, was becoming less universal as a requirement for holding collegiate office, although hanging on through the remainder of the century and making a comeback from time to time. Very shortly Oxford students and dons would succumb to all the temptations of the 'anti-dogmatic' principle associated with Victorian liberalism against which Newman had fought.

---

[57] Newman, *Idea*, 174.
[58] Ibid.
[59] Newman, 'The Tamworth Reading Room' in E. Jay (ed.), *The Evangelical and Oxford Movements* (1983). Newman's seven letters on the Reading Room had originally appeared, under the anonymity of 'Catholicus', in *The Times* Jan.–Feb. 1841.
[60] Newman, *Historical Sketches* iii. 235.

Discontented as he was with the official but dispassionate avowal of Christian belief he had experienced as an undergraduate, Newman could still maintain that, with all its faults, the Oxford of 1817 was in some sense Christian. The Oxford of the 1850s was becoming less so. A statement such as this conceals many important qualifications. However, while admitting that some exaggeration is inevitably required of generalizations, it may still be asserted that whatever the English or Oxford idea of a university would be in the future, it would be secular, and in every imaginable way.[61]

[61] Newman's discoursing on the idea of a university was doubtless begun in reaction to the establishment of what became University College London, and continued in reaction to the examining London University chartered by Order in Council in 1836. Newman's idea of a university is a refutation of the utilitarian ethos of the godless institution in Gower Street and the equation of a university education with preparation for examinations. But Newman was an exceedingly practical man, and Kieran Flanagan ('The Godless and the Burlesque: Newman and the other Irish universities', in James D. Bastable (ed.), *Newman and Gladstone: Centennial Essays* (Dublin 1978), 270) takes pleasure in establishing that Newman rapidly incorporated several of the central features of the examining university model into his own foundation. It also appears that he would even have agreed to an affiliation or 'connection' with the new Queen's University of Ireland, adapted from the 1836 University of London, if support could be found in the Roman Catholic community. See *LDN* xviii. 77–9, 77 n. However, none of this is altogether inconsistent with Newman's position that colleges give 'integrity' to a university. Precisely because universities cannot avoid being utilitarian, collegiate foundations are all the more necessary.

10

From the Tractarians to the Executive Commission, 1845–1854

W. R. WARD

By 1845, when pressure for reform began to revive, events had demonstrated that the constitution of the University, designed (so far as it had been designed at all) to stop changes being made, was indeed incapable of satisfying the new demand. It followed that those whose concern was with university extension or the reform of studies could not fail to be constitutional reformers, and were always likely to be linked with those outside the University like James Heywood, MP for North Lancashire from 1847 to 1857, who wanted to repeal the tests[1] or apply German models of university organization.[2] These three themes, constitution, studies, and outside intervention, were to preoccupy Oxford for a decade.

From the moment the Russell government won its parliamentary majority in 1847, Oxford liberals scented the possibility of state intervention, and drew fresh hope from the prospect of catching the government's ear. For a decade from the mid-1840s the Oxford liberals appeared to be the coming men, and although as a party they never quite came, their perception of themselves was shared by their opponents. Reinforced by former High-Churchmen like H. H. Vaughan, Mark Pattison and J. A. Froude, a central connection, based on Rugby and Balliol, picked up unexpected reinforcement from the Evangelical wing of Churchmen. The central figure of the group had been Thomas Arnold. Arnold had died in 1842, and proved irreplaceable as a party figure-head; but his favourite pupil, A. P. Stanley, who had matriculated at Balliol in 1833, perpetuated the memory and message of the prophet in his tremendously successful *Life of Arnold*

This chapter is based on very extensive sources and some of the footnotes necessarily refer to more than one step in the narrative. Readers seeking further information on a particular episode may wish to consult the references given in Ward, *Victorian Oxford*, 365–85.

[1] In 1843 W. D. Christie, MP for Weymouth 1841–7, began to make annual attempts to abolish the university tests, and brought the Protestant Dissenting deputies into the campaign in 1844: B. L. Manning, *The Protestant Dissenting Deputies* (1952), 372.

[2] See e.g. Walter C. Perry, *German University Education* (1845); Huber, *English Universities* i, p. vi; ii pt 2, pp. 597 ff.

(1844), and was now, as fellow and tutor of University College, an important figure in his own right. So were the other Rugby and Balliol men W. C. Lake (now a fellow of Balliol) and Arthur Hugh Clough (fellow and tutor of Oriel). Another Arnoldite, Richard Congreve, had gone up to Wadham, where he was now a fellow and tutor. He was in Paris when the revolution of 1848 broke out, and came back a positivist. Rugby continued to be the focus of the whole group. A. C. Tait, the Balliol tutor who had led the attack on Tract 90, succeeded Arnold as headmaster. Frederick Temple, another Balliol liberal, was offered the succession to Tait in 1849, and actually became headmaster in 1857. At the school itself Bonamy Price, former scholar of Worcester and in 1868 Drummond Professor of Political Economy, flowed 'with a continuous stream of German Divinity and Bible-Philology',[3] not to mention proposals for the reform of Oxford.

The Rugby group made it a matter of pride to be a 'set', but not an exclusive one, and they brought in, or acted with, men of quite different origins. Of these the most important was Stanley's friend Benjamin Jowett, fellow of Balliol. Where doctrine was concerned Jowett's instincts were negative. As an undergraduate he turned against his Evangelical upbringing, and he could not stand the modish catholicism of the 1830s. At the time of Tract 90 he had hoped to obtain a simplified version of the Thirty-nine Articles. When this proved unobtainable, he became an implacable foe of subscription, while advising prospective ordinands to subscribe if they were in general sympathy with the church establishment; for Jowett, as a tutor and purveyor of culture, was irked by Dissenters as well as by subscription.[4] Early in 1841 he was writing a paper 'On Strauss's theory of Christianity', and after visiting Germany with Stanley in 1844 and 1845, he returned an ardent Hegelian, and open to the influence of the Tübingen school. New studies of this type would end the reign of authority in the Oxford schools. A strong rationalist, Jowett never had much patience for Gladstone, and was indeed as tetchy with colleagues and elders as he was patient with pupils. One particular bugbear was H. G. Liddell, of Christ Church, already celebrated as joint author of the famous Lexicon. Jowett thought him less orthodox than himself, and found Liddell's knack of succeeding without making enemies, and his representing himself as the rising leader of liberal Oxford,[5] difficult to tolerate. Among like-minded colleagues Jowett's aversions included Baden Powell, Savilian Professor of Geometry 1827–60. As a professor with an interest in the development of the professoriate, as a scientist and as a liberal theologian who was prepared to support Jowett in the Essays and Reviews, Baden Powell was a committed reformer.

[3] A. H. Clough to J. P. Gell, 18 Apr. [1839], in Correspondence of Arthur Hugh Clough, ed. F. L. Mulhauser (2 vols 1957) i. 90.

[4] Benjamin Jowett to R. R. W. Lingen, 18 Aug., 22 Sept. 1846: BCA MS Jowett, I.F. 7/4, 7; Abbott and Campbell, Jowett i. 124.

[5] G. Smith, Reminiscences, ed. A. Haultain (New York 1910), 103.

Another contributor to the *Essays and Reviews* was H. B. Wilson, a fellow and former tutor of St John's who had joined Tait in the protest of the Four Tutors in 1841. He had become Rawlinsonian Professor of Anglo-Saxon in 1839.[6] Like Jowett, Wilson had Evangelical origins, and there were generally a few professing Evangelicals who acted with the liberal group. Much the most important of these was Francis Jeune, who became Master of Pembroke in 1843. In the early 1830s Jeune had had a reputation as a radical tutor,[7] but in 1834 had gone off to be a reforming headmaster at King Edward's school in Birmingham. Promoted by Russell in 1838 to be Dean of his native Jersey, he worked for the establishment of Victoria College, St Helier. Jeune had left behind in Pembroke a handful of liberal fellows who did what they could to rescue the college from its confusion of close foundations, and at the next opportunity, after a contested, tied and finally disputed election, they brought him back as Master.[8] Jeune was pledged to the idea that the way to fill a college was to keep down the cost of battels, and in five years he raised the Pembroke intake from almost nothing to the third largest in the University. He brooked no resistance from the conservative element in the college, and, though the Regius chair of Divinity eluded him in 1847,[9] he was clearly basing a successful career upon a formula of evangelicalism and reforming drive. He was already the man depicted by Dr Cardwell in 1858 as a 'thorough reformer, with great talent and all sorts of information: energetic and impetuous, but clear-headed and good-tempered: low-church politically rather than doctrinally: vehement as a preacher, but not impressive: his pervading faults are ambition and restlessness'.[10]

Not all Rugby men evolved towards a steadily thinner faith. John Conington came up from Rugby in 1843 and in the following term carried off both the Hertford and the Ireland scholarships. In due course he obtained a fellowship at University College after a rival had taken him to court. Not surprisingly he too became regarded as a dangerous radical in academic affairs,[11] and being unwilling either to take orders or to pursue legal studies, seemed to have barred his own way to a career. The year 1854 proved a great turning-point for him, when he was appointed to the new chair of Latin, and underwent a profound spiritual crisis. He emerged from this crisis confirmed in the evangelicalism in which he had been reared, and something of a saint, a spiritual odyssey which some liberals found hard to forgive.[12]

[6] B. Jowett to A. P. Stanley, 9 Sept. [1850], BCA MS Jowett, III. S. 52. For the Letter of the Four Tutors, see p. 240 above.

[7] Correspondence of J. Keble with T. Keble [1831, 1833], KCA MSS.

[8] OCL 425; Bodl. MS Wynter dep. d. 5, fos 97–100; *Pages from the Diary of an Oxford Lady, 1843–1862*, ed. M. J. Gifford (1932), 5: Macleane, *Pembroke*, 463–4.

[9] *The Times* 18 Nov. 1847, 3.

[10] Edward Cardwell to Earl of Derby, 15 Mar. 1858, Derby Papers, 123.

[11] *Liberty! Equality! Fraternity!* [1848], Bodl. G. A. Oxon. b. 26.

[12] Bodl. MS Pattison 50, fo 404; *The Recollections of the Very Revd. G. D. Boyle, Dean of Salisbury* (1895), 145 ff.; Pattison, *Memoirs*, 128–9; *Memorials of W. C. Lake*, ed. K. Lake (1901),

Of all the liberals none became more censorious towards those who believed, or, still worse, 'subscribed' willingly, than Goldwin Smith. The son of a Reading physician and railway company director, he felt oppressed by the ordinary Anglican conventions of his upbringing, and was converted to the cause of university reform by a double failure in fellowship elections after a brilliant classical career. Fetching up as Stowell Civil Law fellow at University College, he rapidly gained repute as a tutor, journalist and prophet.[13]

A galaxy of liberal talent did not, however, produce a programme, nor clarify the ambiguities of their relations with Dissenters. The liberals loathed Dissenters, but could not do without their parliamentary assistance; the Dissenters wanted to be rid of the university tests, but had no great enthusiasm for sending their sons to Oxford. But moves were afoot. Jowett tried and failed to get Roundell Palmer, a lay supporter of the Tractarian remnant second in importance only to Gladstone himself, to lead a campaign based on opening fellowships and suppressing many of them to endow professorships and demyships for the sons of the middle class. Outside the University, during the winter of 1847–8, James Heywood got up a petition for a university commission. This Unitarian initiative killed the scheme in Oxford, where only thirty-nine signatures could be obtained, but it revealed some significant straws in the wind. In November 1847 Russell had proposed a commission to inquire into schools and colleges of royal foundation, only to be dissuaded from proceeding by Prince Albert; but when Heywood's deputation presented him with their memorial complaining of the clericalism and intellectual backwardness in the universities and the college system, Russell promised his serious consideration. The following August, when there were the usual radical challenges to Treasury grants for professorial stipends, Russell went out of his way to recommend changes in the standing of professors and concessions for Dissenters, while Gladstone almost promised that something would be done about university extension.[14] The Duke of Wellington, the university Chancellor, characteristically urged the Vice-Chancellor to broaden the basis of university studies, reform the statutes and reduce undergraduate expenses.[15] Meanwhile *The Times* became much less friendly to the universities.[16]

74. See also the memoir by H. J. S. Smith prefixed to *Miscellaneous Writings of John Conington*, ed. J. A. Symonds (1872) and T. H. Ward, 'The late Professor Conington', *Macmillan's Magazine* xxi (Dec. 1869), 146.

[13] Mozley, *Letters*, 320; Pattison, *Memoirs*, 56; J. R. Magrath, *The Queen's College* (2 vols 1921) ii. 168–9; BL Add. MS 44218, fos 79–82.

[14] *Guardian* (1848), 333, 354, 550; *Royal Commission of Inquiry for the Universities of Oxford and Cambridge: memorial presented, 10 July 1848* (np, nd), Bodl. G. A. Oxon. c. 64 (163). For the Treasury grants see pp. 17 and 67.

[15] B. P. Symons to Duke of Wellington, 1 July 1848, Wellington to B. P. Symons, 19 July 1848, SUL MS Wellington 61 2/155/124–6.

[16] *The Times* 24 Aug. 1848, 4.

These signs of movement in the political world were accompanied by changes in opinion in Oxford which threatened to make the University once again ungovernable. The first question, that of university extension, was one on which the post-Tractarian party was still able to speak for many of the tutors, and on which the Hebdomadal Board set itself against a great deal of university opinion. Both Evangelicals and High-Churchmen were interested in enlarging Oxford's usefulness by providing cheaper accommodation. The Evangelicals, with powerful lay support, had put up a memorial to the Hebdomadal Board in 1845, and High-Churchmen, led by Charles Marriott, fellow of Oriel and former Principal of Chichester Theological College, sought to develop the proposal in their own way. The Tractarians had roseate views of both the colleges and the poor scholars they claimed colleges had originally been intended to serve. Colleges were the Anglican answer to Roman Catholic monasteries; they were anti-professorial, and provided tutors with a pastoral vocation. A new college might inculcate the catholic virtues of poverty and obedience, and offer an alternative to the liberal faith in free trade in talent. In Pusey's imagination the poor scholars came increasingly to figure as the *pauperes Christi*, 'the very wealth of the university, of the state and of the church'.[17] On this basis Gladstone, Sir John Taylor Coleridge and others became interested in the idea in the summer of 1845. The long-drawn-out history of the schemes for a High-Church college or hall falls outside the scope of this chapter. Suffice it to say that Marriott felt bound to work for a college, notwithstanding that a college required a much greater endowment, since he saw no chance that the Vice-Chancellor would appoint him as the head of a hall; but when his ill-health finally killed the scheme in 1856, nothing had been accomplished. In 1870 his party opened Keble College on a different basis.[18] After the University Act of 1854 the Evangelicals obtained their hall under E. A. Litton, an Irishman, a double first, former fellow of Oriel and a theologian; but plans for it came to an end when he obtained preferment in Gloucestershire in 1860.

University extension through colleges or halls for poorer men proved unobtainable, but the call for it exacerbated relations between the heads and the tutors in the University at an awkward moment, for the heads' reply to the Evangelicals' memorial was a cold douche of realism. They held it folly to establish new foundations when there was a surplus of accommodation in the old, when matriculations had stagnated for twenty years and when 200 new sets of rooms (the annual intake of the University being about

---

[17] *Guardian* (1851), 449. See also W. Sewell, *Journal of a Residence at the College of St Columba in Ireland* (1847), pp. xv–xvii; BL Add. MS 44251, pt 1, fos 1–2; OCL 1072; Liddon, *Pusey* iii. 83. The later use of 'university extension' to denote provision for those who would not be full-time resident students did not become general until the last quarter of the century.

[18] Correspondence of C. Marriott with E. B. Pusey, 1846, *passim*, PHL; BL Add. MS 44281, fo 38. For Keble College see Pt 2, Ch. 6. For Litton's hall, see Ward, *Victorian Oxford*, 203.

400) had recently been built.[19] They considered it undesirable to create a new class of servitors in affiliated halls, and unlikely that poorly endowed new foundations would be cheaper than the old. Jeune indeed reckoned that, by requiring undergraduates at Pembroke to purchase from the college kitchen at a fixed tariff, he enabled his men to live almost as cheaply as undergraduates at Bishop Hatfield's Hall in Durham, the cynosure of the Oxford advocates of apostolic poverty. The heads took the view that spare funds were best devoted to creating bursaries for the poor, and, spurred on by parental and cancellarial pressure and cases in the courts, they maintained that the worst feature of the present situation was the ease with which undergraduates could accumulate debt.[20] That on all these points the heads were right did not alter the fact that they were counselling inaction at a moment when the political world was beginning to demand action, and that their inertia could be ascribed to prejudice by the two most vigorous theological parties.

How menacing theological prejudice could become was made apparent in the parliamentary election of 1847.[21] It had been known for some time that one of the University's sitting MPs, Thomas Grimston Bucknall-Estcourt, would not stand again, and when he made his intention public in May 1847 the Hebdomadal Board was ready with another good candidate, the Peelite Edward Cardwell, former Secretary to the Treasury, sometime scholar and fellow of Balliol, a double first and nephew to his namesake, the Principal of St Alban Hall, who was private secretary to the Chancellor. The choice of Cardwell showed the conservative court politics of the Board at their most business-like, and on this ground he carried the support of some liberals, including Jeune, G. H. S. Johnson and Hayward Cox. However, a group of High-Churchmen in London and Oxford put up Gladstone, who was at that moment out of Parliament, and who prized the Oxford seat above all others as conferring independence from patrons and electors, and as constituting its incumbent in effect Member for the Church of England. Not a single head appeared on his committee, which was led by Richard Greswell, tutor of Worcester, who had married money and devoted himself to good works on behalf of his college, the University and the Church. The committee was composed chiefly of resident fellows and tutors, of whom only Frederick Temple had liberal inclinations at the time. Gladstone himself, claiming never to have read the Tracts, was bitterly attacked as a Tractarian by the liberal *Oxford Protestant Magazine* for having voted for W. G. Ward in 1845.

[19] E. Cardwell to Duke of Wellington, 16 Mar. 1846, SUL MS Wellington 61 2/254/163; HBM 1841–54, no. 43 (repr. in *RCO* (1850), appx 55–7); BL Add. MSS 44362, fos 109–10; 44363, fo 5; *Oxford Protestant Magazine* i. (May 1847) 121–2; *Return of Matriculations, 1845–1849* (PP 1850 (7) xlii. 450); J. W. Mackail, *Life of William Morris* (2 vols 1907) i. 32.
[20] BL Add. MS 44363, fos 230–1. For undergraduate debts see Ch. 4 above.
[21] For a fuller account of this election conflict see Ward, *Victorian Oxford*, 141–5.

Party was falling into confusion in Oxford as at Westminster. Both Cardwell and Gladstone advocated free trade, which was expected to reduce tithes by a quarter; each had favoured the Maynooth grant, and, in the famous phrase of *The Times*, the anti-popery fire-engine played on both candidates with absolute impartiality. However ill-manned that engine might be among the residents, a platform of Protestantism and protection was sure of powerful backing among the clergy in Convocation. After some confusion the Protestant and protectionist party put forward a candidate of their own, Charles Gray Round, member for North Essex, and long ago a first-class man at Balliol. He speedily gathered half a dozen heads, many Protestant High-Churchmen, Evangelicals like John Hill, and the Tractarian fellow traveller William Sewell. Confusion was now trebly confounded. Tories and Protestant High-Churchmen were found in all three camps; liberal support was divided between Cardwell and Gladstone, Cardwell taking the lion's share. Most of the Evangelicals backed Round, but the more intelligent favoured Cardwell or Gladstone. The Tractarians generally supported Gladstone, although Sewell had gone to Round. Even the college was not the electioneering unit of old. Dr Routh could not vote for Gladstone because his election would give both seats to Christ Church; on the other hand, both Cardwell and Round were Balliol men. Further movement began when, after a bitter campaign, Cardwell's committee withdrew him on 21 June. Cardwell had appeared as a candidate much like Gladstone, but inferior, and a creature of the Hebdomadal Board to boot. The issue now became simpler, for most of the liberals came over to Gladstone; only the heads were stranded, and five ultimately abstained.

Polling-day was a stampede, but the issue was never in doubt. All parties agreed to support Inglis, who had represented Oxford since 1829, while Gladstone held second place throughout, defeating Round by 997 votes to 824. The juniors had given the heads the biggest trouncing they had had since the Hampden affair in 1836. Only four heads voted with the majority, sixteen for Round. Talent, as measured by first classes, prize-men and foundationers, was with Gladstone; the isolation of the heads could hardly be more publicly demonstrated. Moreover, they had taken their drubbing at the hands of an improbable coalition of liberals and Tractarians; and the future history of the University and the Church was marked by the fact. Gladstone was the only candidate the juniors had a hope of carrying, and they must stick together and compromise their differences in policy. In the end Gladstone was able to take a section of his High-Church supporters with him into liberalism, and helped them to transform the rigid orthodoxy and the high Tory politics of their recent past into the liberal catholicism of Gore and the Lux Mundi group.[22]

---

[22] On this see W. R. Ward, 'Oxford and the origins of liberal catholicism in the Church of England', *Studies in Church History* i (1962), 233–52.

This alliance of the juniors was always precarious. It was strained in one direction when Russell (supported by the majority of Oxford heads) raised Dr Hampden to the see of Hereford, and Prince Lee to Manchester; and strained in another when Gladstone voted for the removal of Jewish disabilities. But it was powerfully reinforced when the body of working tutors began to move for reform, and to discover that they had much in common. The ball had been set rolling in the spring of 1846 by the professors; they submitted a memorandum to the Board, urging that the examination system be modified to include the modern sciences and literature which they taught, or, at the very least, that undergraduates be required mandatorily to attend their classes. The nostrums now began to pour from the press. The Hebdomadal Board appointed a committee;[23] and Dr Jeune pressed on it a scheme which underlay most of the later discussion. He proposed to exact more work from undergraduates by increasing the number of their examinations from two to three, and ensuring that Responsions were taken early enough to fulfil some of the functions of a matriculation examination. The High-Church *Guardian* now urged the tutors to take the matter into their own hands, which, emboldened by their success in carrying Gladstone's election, they did, foreshadowing the more formal organization of the Tutors' Association five years later. Osborne Gordon, Censor of Christ Church, proposed that Jeune's scheme be developed to require undergraduates to take a second, new school, after Greats;[24] and this idea reappeared in a memorial presented to the Hebdomadal Board in March 1848 by fifty-nine of the sixty-three tutors, urging that the third examination should comprise theology, moral philosophy, history (ancient or modern) or mathematical and physical science.[25] In that revolutionary year even the heads responded to their constituents: they appointed a committee, accepted the principle of the third examination and negotiated freely with the tutors.[26]

Among those now to enter the fray anonymously were Jowett and Stanley.[27] They disclaimed any desire for a Scottish or a German university, but wanted to find something for professors, and to keep passmen employed. Moreover, they wanted a theology school. This proposal instantly aroused the wrath of High-Churchmen, who maintained both that sacred studies would be demeaned by being made 'the vehicle of academic honours', and that theology as conceived by the liberals was a misnomer, for it consisted

[23] HBM 1841–54, fos 103, 106; *Statutes* ii. 364–8.
[24] O. Gordon, *Considerations on the Improvement of the Present Examination Statute...* (1847).
[25] *Guardian* (1848), 182.
[26] HBM 1841–54, fo 137. By early 1849 the tutors were dissatisfied with the participation they had enjoyed, and discussed the formation of a 'Tutorial Society' to keep up the pressure on the Board: Mozley, *Letters*, 198.
[27] [B. Jowett and A. P. Stanley], *Suggestions for an Improvement of the Examination Statute* (1848); Abbott and Campbell, *Jowett* i. 193.

solely of biblical criticism and omitted dogmatic works like Pearson on the Creed.[28] When early in 1849 the heads were ready to legislate, no theology school was proposed. The main outlines of the heads' scheme remained unchanged. There were to be three examinations, and all candidates were to graduate in Greats, and in one of three other schools, mathematics, natural sciences or history, and attend two professorial courses. Points of detail apart, criticism fastened on two chief issues, the fourth school and the appointment of examiners. To many High-Churchmen the proposed history school was no more than a soft option to be prepared for by 'historical novels or novel-like histories as Macaulay's'; to the devotees of standard texts it was arbitrary: 'if...the examiner and the candidates have studied *different* historians, as they well may, the acquirements of the candidate may be most praiseworthy, and yet be wholly inappreciable by the examiner'. Even the liberal Clough asked for 'the stronger aliment of political economy'.[29] The arguments over the appointment of examiners who called the tune to which the whole University danced were labyrinthine, but the issue was simple enough. The heads proposed to transfer the nomination of examiners to professorial boards; the college interest was determined to keep them in the hands of the Vice-Chancellor and proctors.

The proceedings of Convocation on 20 March 1849 upon this statute turned out to be a prelude to events to come. The colleges discouraged non-residents from coming up to overturn the labours of the residents, and few appeared, apart from the headmasters of the great public schools. Here was plainly foreshadowed the Congregation of the reformed University. The Hebdomadal Board divided the statute into twenty-eight parts, and, in the course of a five-hour session, divisions were taken on each, so that the loss of some parts need not involve the loss of the whole.[30] By the end of the proceedings the outlines of the statute survived, but most of the details, and especially those dearest to the liberals, were lost.[31] The principle of three examinations, the establishment of a natural sciences school and compulsory attendance at professorial lectures were carried without difficulty; but the appointment of examiners by boards was decisively defeated, and the modern history school was lost by six votes. In short the Hebdomadal Board had been able to make progress where, and only where, they could carry the support of the general body of tutors and professors. The case for making the body initiating legislation more representative of the opinion of the residents had been underlined. This was indeed the moral of

[28] R. Hussey, *Remarks on Some Proposed Changes in the Public Examinations* (1848), 19; *Guardian* (1848), 228, 241–2.

[29] *Guardian* (1849), 125, 142, 157–8; A. H. Clough to E. Hawkins, 3 Mar. [1849], OCL 292 *Correspondence of Clough* i. 248; *The Fourth School*, Bodl. G. A. Oxon. c. 65 (179).

[30] The voting was recorded in *The Times* 21 Mar. 1849, 8.

[31] The *Guardian* (1849), 173–4, had declared against the statute, much disturbing Jowett: B. Jowett to R. R. W. Lingen [16 Mar. 1849], BCA MS Jowett, I.F. 7/31.

the Convocations of December 1849 and March 1850, to which the revised statute was presented. As tempers rose, it proved impossible to confine the discussions to residents. History was saved by a whisker in December, but a syllabus (finally drafted by Jeune)[32] could not be obtained till concessions had been made to the views of H. H. Vaughan and to 'the stronger aliment of political economy'. Moreover, no amount of Hebdomadal campaigning could save the appointment of examiners, even of the new schools, from the hands of the Vice-Chancellor and proctors. Four years of effort and a major concession to the college interest had secured an examination statute very much on the lines originally proposed by Jeune.

Nor was the next step any more convincing. Some provision would now have to be made for the teaching of the natural sciences school. Richard Greswell and others launched a scheme (described in detail in Chapter 22) for a science museum to house laboratories and lecture-rooms, the collections of the Ashmolean Society, Hope's entomological bequest, and Greswell's own scientific library. The rich men of the University, however, would not subscribe, and the Hebdomadal Board created another furore by proposing to make a substantial grant from the profits of the Press. The *Guardian* ridiculed extravagance 'in building a receptacle for dried insects', and the post-Tractarians would not allow that profits from prayer-books should be expended in sciences, which attracted no students, rather than on the sons of poor clergy and university extension. The scheme failed in Convocation by 88 votes to 47.[33] Convocation had willed the end of scientific education, but not the means, and would not do so until university reform had been carried.

This was the direction in which the liberals now turned their energies. Stanley and Jowett began to work on a history of the University and a plan for its reform, collecting material and ideas which would eventually go into the Blue Book of 1852, and assembling collaborators like Goldwin Smith, Temple and Johnson, who were to take a leading part in the enforcement of reform from the outside.[34] James Heywood's annual motions in the House of Commons gave the subject an airing without creating any menace. Both liberals and conservatives suspected, however, that Russell might yield to private pressure; Stanley applied it; and Jeune stated a case for a commission, which Russell used. On 23 April 1850, three weeks before the new

[32] HBM 1841–54, fo 180.

[33] R. Greswell to Lord Derby, 3 May 1853: Derby Papers, 8/2; Cox, 366, 380–1; R. Greswell to M. J. Routh, 30 July 1849, MCA MS D. 5. 16; *Guardian* (1851), 449, 453, 467. For the Convocation vote, see p. 649 below, and H. M. and K. D. Vernon, *A History of the Oxford Museum* (1909), 48–50.

[34] B. Jowett to A. P. Stanley [1848–9], BCA MS Jowett, III. s; Jowett to R. R. W. Lingen [13 Mar. 1849], ibid. I. F. 7/30; Abbott and Campbell, *Jowett* i. 172–7. Goldwin Smith gave up his tutorship at University College in 1854. Thereafter he was almost as much an 'outsider' as the two others mentioned.

examination statute was finally adopted, Russell announced that he could not agree to the terms of Heywood's motion: he would, however, advise the Crown to issue a royal commission of inquiry.[35] The announcement was the beginning of a great deal of public and private politics. Prince Albert pressed Russell to leave the inquiry to the universities; Jowett, Stanley, Lake and Goldwin Smith pressed him to stand firm.[36] William Thomson of Queen's obtained an interview, and Goldwin Smith enforced the liberal doctrine in a series of letters to *The Times* over the signature 'Oxoniensis'.[37] There were also frantic efforts to appeal to, and to brief, the university MPs.[38] The Hebdomadal Board, in the absence of Dr Jeune, published a manifesto asserting that all was well with the University, and were advised by Wellington to hold their peace.[39] When the debate came on in Parliament on 18 July, Roundell Palmer challenged the legality of the Commission, while Gladstone insisted that, impolitic as the Commission was, its inquiries must redound to Oxford's credit. Russell would not yield, and obtained a majority of 22.[40]

Russell could secure no co-operation from the Hebdomadal Board in the nomination of his Commission, but produced a powerful liberal team on his own.[41] At the head was Samuel Hinds, Bishop of Norwich, Whately's old henchman. A. C. Tait had led the liberal assault upon Tractarianism. Dr Jeune had been in the thick of the fray since 1846. J. L. Dampier was appointed to 'keep the commission right in its law', and Baden Powell to look after the science interest. H. G. Liddell added Westminster to Rugby among the great schools represented in the Commission. G. H. S. Johnson had held chairs of both astronomy and moral philosophy. The Secretary and Assistant Secretary, Stanley and Goldwin Smith, were straight from Jowett's reform factory. The party complexion of this body was bound to add to the animosity it encountered. To those who held that any such commission was illegal under the Bill of Rights, or was simply impolitic, were added those who loathed Russell and his Erastianism, and those who believed that a

[35] Bodl. MS Top. Oxon. e. 80, fo 6; R. E. Prothero, *Life and Correspondence of A. P. Stanley* (2 vols 1893) i. 419–20; *Diary of an Oxford Lady*, 16; *Parl. Deb.* 23 Apr. 1850, 3S cx. 747–55 (Russell).

[36] D. A. Winstanley, *Early Victorian Cambridge* (1940), 226; *Fraser's Magazine* xlii (July 1850), 86; Abbott and Campbell, *Jowett* i. 178; *Lake*, 78.

[37] E. H. Thomson, *Life and Letters of William Thomson, Archbishop of York* (1919), 26–9; *The Times* 20 May 1850, 4; 3 June, 5; 12 June, 5; 22 June, 8.

[38] BL Add. MS 44230, fos 229–34. Cf E. A. Litton, *University Reform* (1850); BL Add. MSS 34578, fo 99; 44251, pt 1, fos 18–22; 44369 *passim*.

[39] *Fraser's Magazine* xlii (July 1850), 87; Hebdomadal Board to Wellington, 16 May 1850, SUL Wellington MS 61 2/256/33–6; Lord John Russell to Wellington, 8 May 1850, BL Add. MSS 44566, fo 153; 34578, fo 75.

[40] *Parl. Deb.* 18 July 1850, 3S cxii. 1455–1525.

[41] F. C. Plumptre to Wellington, 16 Aug. [1850]; Lord John Russell to Wellington, 7 Aug. 1850, SUL MS Wellington 61 2/256/60, 2/256/54–5; BL Add. MS 34578, fos 123–5; Bodl. MS Top. Oxon. e. 80, fos 15–19.

partisan inquiry would be offered and would receive only liberal evidence. The Hebdomadal Board agreed that 'all matters relative to the commission of inquiry should be referred to a committee to consist of all members of the Board with the exception of the Master of Pembroke', and were suddenly able to command a majority in Convocation of 144 against the Commission.[42] But the only hope of escape was that the Russell government would founder and be replaced by one in which Gladstone would be able to stop the Commission. In the event Russell survived another year, and Derby, who succeeded him, was surprised by the Bishop of Norwich into allowing the Commission to continue to work in Downing Street as before.[43] The inquisition would have to be faced.

Conservatives now attempted to discredit the report in advance as entirely predictable liberal propaganda, but were given the lie both by the report and by the proceedings which led up to it. Boycotted by the Board and by most of the colleges, the Commission received good Tory testimony from Robert Scott and H. L. Mansel, and discovered that not all liberal nostrums were mutually compatible; indeed all Tait and Stanley's diplomacy was needed to get the Commission itself to make a unanimous report.[44] Nevertheless, after the turmoil of the last six years there was much agreement among the witnesses on four matters: the Hebdomadal Board did not constitute an acceptable governing body; professorial teaching should be revived and somehow fitted in with the tutorial system; all foundations should be opened; and there was a general belief that the student population could be increased by the opening of cheap halls which consorted oddly with the equally general conviction that costs in the present colleges were hardly capable of reduction. All these views left their mark on the report.

The Commission insisted, first, that the University must have undisputed power to alter the Laudian Code.[45] They took it for granted that government by the Hebdomadal Board could not continue, and made proposals which were heavily influenced by H. H. Vaughan. The central recommendation was to revive Congregation, the ancient house of teachers of the University. It should be composed of the Board, together with professors and public lecturers, and the senior tutor of each college. They should discuss, in English, measures which they or the Hebdomadal Board had prepared. The Board should retain its administrative functions and Convocation its veto. In addition, the professors should form a standing delegacy for the

[42] E. Cardwell to Duke of Wellington, 22, 26, 29 Oct. 1850, SUL MS Wellington 61, 2/256/69–72; HBM 1841–54, fos 195–6; Mozley, *Letters*, 205–6; *Guardian* (1851), 385.

[43] Mozley, *Letters*, 207; R. T. Davidson and W. Benham, *Life of Archibald Campbell Tait* (2 vols 1891) i. 163.

[44] Davidson and Benham, *Tait* i. 165; Prothero, *Stanley* i. 431–2. As it was, Jeune entered an anonymous disclaimer (*RCO* (1850), report, 167) to the majority's opposition to terminable fellowships: BL Add. MS 44295, fo 9.

[45] *RCO* (1850), report, 6–7. See Ch. 3 n. 59.

supervision of studies, examinations and libraries, thus constituting a body
very like the Senate recently created at Owens College, Manchester, itself the
prototype of a series of new university constitutions.[46] Like everyone else,
the Commissioners thought that Oxford did not educate a large enough
student body to justify its endowments, and, like everyone else, they had no
very convincing remedy to prescribe. They gave their blessing to halls,
admitting that they did not know how their capital cost was to be met,
and were driven back on Vaughan's prescription of lodgings for both members of colleges and a new race of non-collegiate students. The Commissioners were not empowered to discuss the university tests, but they noted in
passing that subscription was a barrier to university extension, and neither
excluded all who were not members of the Church nor included all who
were.[47]

More than half the report on the University was devoted to examinations.
The Commissioners wished to introduce a matriculation examination, even
at the risk of temporarily diminishing the entry. The examination statute of
1850 should be developed by ending the privilege of Greats as the compulsory school. Classical studies and the rudiments of religion should be wound
up at an intermediate examination, and the final school be chosen among
four options, theology, moral philosophy and philology, jurisprudence and
history, and mathematical and physical science. This provision would reverse the progressive narrowing of the present system, but it would also
break the back of the tutorial system, which already creaked audibly under
the breadth of the studies it was required to cover. To the Commissioners,
this defect afforded a golden opportunity to build up professorial teaching;
certain hours in the day should be sacred to the professors, who should be
organized in boards corresponding to the four final schools. There was not
the least prospect that the Commission would obtain the professorial oracles
for which they were looking, without better methods of appointment (for
which they looked mostly to the Crown), and without much higher pay.
This embarrassing question took the Commissioners to the colleges, and to
the ideas of Jowett, Stanley and Goldwin Smith.[48]

The Commissioners dispatched the original purposes of the colleges in
cavalier style. Colleges were no longer eleemosynary, and sustained neither a
common life nor the spiritual purposes envisaged by the statutes. Fellows
did not reside for study in the sense intended by the founders. Indeed
founders' wills had so little contemporary relevance that colleges must be
empowered to renew their statutes on modern principles. The Commissioners were sufficiently possessed of the liberal dogma of free trade in talent

[46] *RCO* (1850), report, 14–16.
[47] Ibid. 35–6; H. L. Thompson, *Henry George Liddell... a memoir* (1899), 127; Davidson and
Benham, *Tait* i. 168. On 'subscription' see Ch. 1 nn. 21 and 359.
[48] *RCO* (1850), report, 104–9.

as to require unhesitatingly the opening of all the fellowships, only twenty-two out of 542 being truly open at the moment. The Commission did not face the fact that 'closeness' unaccompanied by other vices did not seem ruinous, and that as things stood practically all the first-class men and many of the seconds were provided for. But there was no doubt that a general opening of foundations would simplify the whole system and put paid to real abuses. The Commission did not wish to compel fellows to reside, and so allowed fellowships to cushion the early years of a professional career away from Oxford; and, in the interests of college residence, they resisted the pressure to abolish the qualification of celibacy. But they absolutely condemned the obligation of fellows to take holy orders, and resisted the efforts of Jeune to speed up the turnover of fellowships by putting a time limit upon them, the majority being unwilling to impose any new restrictions upon fellowships until it was absolutely necessary.[49] The most revolutionary proposal sprang from the conviction that there were too many fellowships. An average of thirty-five fellowships fell vacant annually, but there were only thirteen first-class men a year. The application of such an enormous capital to sinecures could not be justified; nor could the demonstrable reluctance of colleges to endow new studies. Some fellowships should therefore be appropriated to the new schools; others should be suppressed to endow university teachers or be united with chairs. Others should go to endow scholarships; and yet others to support the tutorial system itself, for the Commissioners could see increasing difficulty in filling tutorships at present rates of pay while appointments worth £500 per annum multiplied in the Church, the professions and the public schools. The colleges (for whom they prescribed in detail) were, in short, to be cannibalized for their own development as well as that of the University.[50]

The Blue Book sold like hot cakes, and was so well received as to mark a clear point of no return. Journals as different as *The Times* and the *Guardian* were agreed that the report must be taken seriously.[51] It had not in fact sacrificed chartered independence to state action, nor even to the centralized management of property in the style of the Ecclesiastical Commissioners. The bureaucratic regulation of perceived abuses, called by historians the 'revolution in government', was not in evidence here. Indeed the prospects for reform of a relatively conservative kind were enhanced by the evidence in the press of common ground, and the futility of the flanking attacks on either side. On the left, the Dissenters were at odds among themselves, the Unitarian *Prospective Review* being deeply impressed with the affection Oxford inspired among her sons, while the *British Quarterly*, in the voluntaryist style, wanted to build up the private tutors and condemned the

[49] Ibid. 149–69.
[50] Ibid. 172–80.
[51] *The Times* 22 May 1852, 6; 28 Aug., 8; *Guardian* (1852), 45, 345, 681.

matriculation examination as tying the schools to Latin and Greek.[52] On the right, the *Quarterly Review* held that the Commissioners had no real constitutional plan apart from 'a general wish to stuff in professors', the untried portion of the university community; they did not understand what 'poor scholars' or even 'close' foundations really were; their belief that unattached students would regenerate the University was ludicrous.[53] But it was a sign of the times that the *Guardian* was soon defending the report against both the radicals and the conservatives, and looking for a parliamentary combination of liberal conservatives and liberals 'to free the universities from their shackles, increase their usefulness, but not destroy their principles': an enabling Act would do the trick.[54]

It was a question whether this was so, or whether, at a time when it was impossible to predict from month to month what the complexion of the government might be, legislation might be obtainable. But in Oxford, at least, there was a general stir. Within a few days of the publication of the Blue Book, fifty-six residents approached the Hebdomadal Board with the request that a delegacy of Convocation be appointed to consider the professoriate, university extension and other reforms, only to be rebuffed on the grounds that the Board already had the matter in hand.[55] In the colleges, too, reform met mixed fortunes. In Magdalen there were strenuous efforts to discipline the gentlemen commoners and the demies, to open fellowships and endow new chairs, but they encountered the wooden opposition of the aged President Routh; and when he died in December 1854, the election of his successor, Frederic Bulley, was 'determined ... by dislike of reform'.[56] At Corpus the Latin lecturership of the college was re-established as a university chair, but there was no confidence between the President (who wanted an enabling Act permitting changes to be made under the sanction of the Visitor) and the liberal party among the fellows, led by J. M. Wilson, Professor of Moral Philosophy, who wanted a parliamentary commission and the enlargement of the lay element in the governing body of the college.[57] Queen's was still in public ill-odour for turning down Goldwin Smith for a fellowship some years before; now the factions of the college began to air their differences in public. The minority took the view that the foundation which had in practice been confined to Cumberland and West-

[52] *Prospective Review* viii (July 1852), 347–92 (W. Bagehot); *British Quarterly Review* xvi (Nov. 1852), 289–357 (F. B. Zincke and Robert Vaughan).

[53] *Quarterly* xciii (June 1853), 152–238 (J. B. Mozley).

[54] *Guardian* (1852), 384, 401, 424–5, 441, 489, 521, 569, 696; (1853), 645, 660–1, 693. The Tractarian *Christian Remembrancer* came round to much the same point: xxv (Jan. 1853), 192–212.

[55] *The Times* 26 June 1852, 8; BL Add. MSS 44372, fo 149; 44251, pt 1, fo 46.

[56] F. Jeune to W. E. Gladstone, 25 Jan. 1855, BL Add. MS 44221, fo 218.

[57] James Norris to Vice-Chancellor, 28 Dec. 1853, in *Correspondence on Improvement of Oxford* (1854), 15; BL Add. MSS 44318, fos 15–18; 44378, fos 46–7, 94–5, 100; T. Fowler, *Corpus Christi College* (1898), 324.

morland was by statute open, with certain preferences *ceteris paribus*. This was absolutely denied by the majority, who had nevertheless agreed to a gradual raising of the examination achievements of fellowship candidates. It was now urged on Gladstone that a candidate's prospects ought not to depend on the shifting balance of college parties, and that a settlement imposed from the outside would enormously reduce the effort expended on college intrigue.[58] In Pembroke the problem was the resistance put up by the schools which would suffer by the opening of college scholarships. Jeune could stand being abused in public; he could not bear that the college got, 'at the best...a class of men not bad enough to keep from a fellowship, not good enough to become teachers'.[59] The college resolved to apply for a special Act, and an interesting correspondence among Russell, Lord Derby and the college Visitor followed. Derby professed willingness to help so far as he could without overturning founders' wills; Russell thought it too late in the session for a bill; and Gladstone observed that even in a special Act the general implications of the proper tenure of fellowships could not be avoided.

As so often in the past, Jeune had set the ball rolling, and on 12 December 1853 Palmerston, as Home Secretary, applied to Lord Derby to know what progress the colleges had made, 'and what they may desire from Parliament in the form either of prohibitions, of enabling powers, or of new enact-ments'.[60] The replies of the heads to the inquiry made on Lord Derby's behalf by the Vice-Chancellor reveal the whole spectrum of college attitudes under the threat of state intervention.[61] Dean Gaisford of Christ Church was truculent: 'As this college has no statutes it has no need of prohibitions, of enabling powers, or new enactments.' Jenkyns of Balliol would have nothing to do with the reforming schemes of his college colleagues, which could certainly not proceed without legislation. Dr Wynter of St John's, the most stubborn opponent of reform, evasively replied that a college committee had been through the statutes, and would recommend changes which would require an enabling Act. University College, Oriel and Worcester regarded the changes made in the past generation as enough to meet the need. All Souls could not even propose changes without an Act, and prayed to be

---

[58] *RCO* (1850), report, 203–5; BL Add. MS 44376, fos 227–8; J. Barrow, *The Case of Queen's College, Oxford* (1854); J. Fox to Vice-Chancellor, 6 Jan. 1854: in *Correspondence on Improve-ment*, 12–13; W. Thomson, *An Open College Best for All* (1854); *Ed. Rev.* xcix (Jan. 1854), 182–3 (A. C. Tait).

[59] F. Jeune to Lord Derby, 15 June 1853, Derby Papers, 8/1, fo 7. See also Lord Derby to E. Cardwell, 3 May 1853, to F. Jeune, 5 and 9 May, to Headmaster, Pate's Grammar School, Cheltenham, 9 May, ibid. 182/1, fos 87–96; E. Cardwell to Lord Derby, 4 May 1853, ibid. 157/10. Macleane, *Pembroke*, 448–50; BL Add. MS 44221, fo 11; *Correspondence on Improvement*, 18, 34.

[60] *Correspondence between Viscount Palmerston, the Chancellor of the University, and the Board of Heads of Houses and Proctors* (Delegates Room 25 Feb. 1854), 4.

[61] Most of the replies of the heads, including that of Gaisford, which follows, are in *Correspondence on Improvement*.

spared the wholesale butchery of their fellowships proposed by the Commissioners. New College and Trinity were in the hands of their Visitors; President Wilson of Trinity feared that even legislation could not annul the moral force of the college oath. The liberal heads, Jeune, Cradock of Brasenose and Richards of Exeter, where there were elaborate plans for opening and reforming their foundations, were all in favour of legislation. Thus by the end of 1853 the threat of outside intervention had driven the colleges to examine their statutes, and in many cases to admit the need for legislation. It had also shown how deeply entrenched were the forces of conservatism; in many colleges diehard heads and fellows would obstruct any progress under an amending Act.

Three unpleasant events which had taken place in Oxford within a few months of the publication of the Blue Book had shown the tenacity of conservatism. In 1847 Gladstone's candidacy for the university seat had been opposed on a protectionist and Protestant basis; and if protectionism was now a lost cause, the furore over the Ecclesiastical Titles Bill had given a great fillip to Protestant fervour, and exposed a lack of mutual comprehension between Gladstone and some of his warmest friends. Even in the mid-1840s Gladstone had shuddered at the injury to the Church caused by the patronage and policies of Peel, the politician he revered above all others. What the Church needed was liberty, liberty to profit fully from its real resources of inner vitality. And the Church could not sustain a claim to liberty without acknowledging the just claims to liberty of Jews, Roman Catholics, Dissenters and others. To friends like J. B. Mozley and Sir William Heathcote, Gladstone seemed to be abandoning the Church establishment without a fight;[62] liberals suspected that he would thwart any effective measure of university reform; conservatives were angry that he did not rescue the Derby government. One reason why Gladstone had fought hard in 1847 was that it was a firm eighteenth-century tradition that sitting members not be opposed as long as they were willing to serve. In May 1852 when a general election was expected within weeks, it suddenly became clear that the heads, Protestants and protectionists who had fought him in 1847, would, tradition notwithstanding, renew the contest. Their candidate, Robert Bullock-Marsham, Warden of Merton, was of small merit, but was almost alone among the heads in not being disqualified from the Commons by holy orders. On this occasion Gladstone had the advantage over his opponent of an election machine in good heart, and Lord Derby was still sufficiently hopeful of Gladstone's support to refuse his open backing to the conservative candidate.[63] In the event Gladstone triumphed easily by 350 votes; the sinister features of the poll were that the heads had

---

[62] BL Add. MSS 44372, fo 174 (cf fos 47–53); 44208, fo 23.
[63] P. Wynter to Lord Derby, 26 June 1852, Derby Papers, 156/3; Lord Derby to P. Wynter, 29 June, ibid. 180/1, fo 188; Lord Derby to W. E. Gladstone, ibid. 179/2, fo 131.

voted 12 to 5 against him (5 abstaining) and so had many of the liberals most clearly associated with the Blue Book.[64] His right-hand man in Oxford, A. W. Haddan, pointed the moral. 'Those who did not elect you', he told Gladstone, 'although undoubtedly as a body anxious for reform from *within*, are... speaking generally, of the party opposed to compulsory Government or parliament interference as utterly ruinous.' The question of state intervention still separated Gladstone's juniors from the liberals, but if the Hebdomadal Board, which could not be reformed from within, continued to behave as at present, the gap would certainly narrow.

This was the significance of two events later in 1852. After the election, Marsham's committee published a statement signed by Wynter, as chairman, rejoicing that they had enabled 750 electors to protest against further attempts to sever the union of Church and state. Earlier in the election campaign Gladstone had rebutted a much milder statement that he was out for disestablishment, and he was furious at this impeachment of his good faith. Wynter replied that it was no part of his duty to read election documents and that 'in every official position which I have occupied, I have uniformly made it a point to avoid as much as possible reading any documents which have appeared in newspapers or other periodical publications, on the subject of acts or proceedings with which my name has been connected';[65] and he successfully obstructed all Gladstone's attempts to force the publication of their correspondence. This contempt for the organs of public opinion was almost an invitation to the juniors to exploit them to the full. And almost at once the power of the heads was displayed again, and more publicly. On 13 September 1852 the Duke of Wellington retired to bed with 'the Oxford Blue Book, with a pencil in it; and he said to Lord Charles Wellesley, who was with him, "I shall never get through it Charles, but I must work on." '[66] The Duke, who had been an obstinate university reformer, died that night, and his death enabled the university politicians again to show their true colours. There had been persistent rumours in Oxford that a London committee was grooming a candidate for the chancellorship, and it was assumed that this meant that a body such as the National Club was going to promote Lord Shaftesbury. The various High-Church factions in the University were therefore under pressure to act quickly. A group of post-Tractarians met at Oriel to put forward Gladstone's friend, the Duke of Newcastle; the ruling knot of heads were all out for Lord Derby

[64] BL Add. MS 44183, fos 36–51. A fuller account of this election is given in Ward, *Victorian Oxford*, 170–4. The election papers are collected in *A. W. Haddan's Election Papers, 1852*, Bodl. G. A. Oxon. a. 129.

[65] Wynter to Gladstone, 24 Aug. 1852, Bodl. MS Wynter dep. d. 5, fos 216–17. See also BL Add. MSS 44372, fos 298–332; 44373, fos 7–11. Cf Edward Hawkins, Provost of Oriel, who 'except in stirring times of peculiar interest... only read a weekly newspaper': Hawkins to Gladstone, 24 Dec. 1852, BL Add. MS 44206, fo 57.

[66] Cox, 386 n. Cf *The Times* 24 Sept. 1852, 4 f, 5a.

(notwithstanding his youthful assaults on the Irish Church and the university tests). Derby agreed to stand if an uncontested election could be arranged. As an accomplished classical scholar, head of the protectionist Tories, Prime Minister with church preferment in his gift, a man 'decidedly hostile to the Puseyite tendency, and ready to watch over the Protestant character of the Church', he was an ideal candidate.[67] Samuel Wilberforce, Bishop of Oxford, was laid on to outmanœuvre Newcastle's party with the argument that Derby must win, and that to oppose him unsuccessfully would look like a Low-Church victory. Derby thus had his uncontested triumph. He owed it to the way in which the strongest political group among the juniors had for once been outmanœuvred, but the contest was renewed in a different part of the field before the end of the year.

In December the government of Derby was defeated on its budget proposals after a powerful attack by Gladstone. With the defeat of both Whig and Tory governments in a year, tempers ran high, and a group of drunken Tories at the Carlton Club threatened to throw Gladstone out of the window into the Reform. Instead Prince Albert's attempt to solve the constitutional crisis gave them an opportunity to throw him out of Oxford, since one of its consequences was a by-election in the University. The new Aberdeen coalition consisted of six Whigs, including Russell and Palmerston; six Peelites, including Gladstone; and the radical Molesworth, abhorred by the orthodox as the editor of Hobbes. It was predictably denounced from one wing by Archdeacon Denison as latitudinarian politics, the precursor to latitudinarianism in religion, and from the other by Hugh Stowell, the Protestant firebrand, as 'a cabinet more deeply tainted with the leprosy of Tractarianism than any which has yet existed'.[68] Gladstone incensed his enemies and upset his friends by letting Russell into office, and then joining him in the cabinet as Chancellor of the Exchequer. As the law then stood, accepting office entailed re-election to Parliament. Dr Lempriere, fellow of St John's College, conservative agent, London organizer for Marsham at the last election and one of the revellers who attacked Gladstone at the Carlton, scoured the country for a candidate, and well-authenticated notices appeared in the press as to who this would be. The name presented on nomination day was, however, a complete surprise, Dudley Perceval, the son of Spencer Perceval, who had not even kept his name on the books of the University. He was, however, a member of the committee of the rabid National Club, and was proposed by the High-Church Denison and the Evangelical Macbride. An election at least gave Gladstone the opportunity, normally denied him by the traditions of the

---

[67] Prince Albert, Memorandum, 27 Feb. 1852, in *Letters of Queen Victoria*, First Series, ed. A. C. Benson and Viscount Esher (3 vols 1907) ii. 456.

[68] G. A. Denison, *The Coalition of 1852* (1853); H. Stowell, *An Address to the Electors of the University of Oxford* (1853); *Nonconformist* 5 Jan. 1853, 2.

University, of explaining his new venture to his constituents, but in the early stages of the poll he trailed behind his opponents. When he established a lead, however, his opponents would not let him off the hook; discovering that the University was excluded from the provisions of the Reform Act for shortening the period of polling, they kept open the poll for fifteen days, and dragged out the pamphleteering much longer.

Triumphant at last in a contest he considered utterly discreditable, Gladstone was bound to reconsider his position. It was clear that, whatever the traditions of the University, the party opposed to him would never give him any respite. Nor was there any question who they were: seven heads had voted or paired for him, thirteen against. There can be no doubt that this last bitter experience helped to move Gladstone quite sharply towards the view that the University needed overhauling by outside authority. By the same token this brought him nearer to the liberals. Whereas in 1852 most of the liberals had kept off,[69] fifty now came to his side, and it was widely noted that he was liberalizing his Tractarian friends. The decisive liberal–catholic coalition was getting nearer.[70]

With the heads fighting so strenuously to regain the initiative, and becoming the natural channels for the government's enquiries as to progress in Oxford, it was natural that the working residents should make their own views known. On 8 November 1852 the committee of the Tutors' Association which had met during the long gestation of the new examination statute revived the Association at a large meeting in Oriel, and arranged for meetings twice a week.[71] The revival of the Association very greatly furthered the crystallization of Oxford opinion; the strong conservatives were dominant in the Hebdomadal Board, which provided a constitutional focus for their views; the liberals had a programme in the Blue Book, and a leader in Dr Jeune; now the bulk of the working residents, who liked neither the authoritarianism of the one nor the commitment to professors and state compulsion of the others, could work out their own policies. Professional parity provided a bridge among men whose political views covered a range from H. L. Mansel on the conservative right, to Lake on the liberal left, and included Gladstone's constituency organizers Woollcombe and Haddan. Moreover, before the tutors' first report was published, Gladstone was in office and the Association then had the advantage of access to the man in power which during Russell's ministry had been enjoyed by the liberals, and, during Derby's Indian summer in 1852, by the Hebdomadal Board.

[69] OCL 164; BL Add. MS 44372, fos 178–9.
[70] The papers of this election are collected in *A. W. Haddan's Election Papers, 1853*, Bodl. G. A. Oxon. 4 to 57. See also BL Add. MSS 44208, fos 21–4, 31–2, 39; 44183, fo 31; 44206, fo 64; 44258, fo 79–80; Bodl. MS Acland d. 69, fo 28. For 15-day poll see p. 68 above.
[71] *Guardian* (1852), 728; BL Add. MS 44183, fo 55; *Reports of the Oxford Tutors' Association*, no. 1 (1853), 4.

The tutors' first report on university extension was hastily compiled by a committee by the second week in December, and accepted by the Association in the last week of January 1853. The tutors would not countenance the Commissioners' suggestions of lodgings, but were clear that the college monopoly must be broken by cheaper alternatives. Affiliated and independent halls were accepted readily; the worry was occasioned by private halls, which were expected to give rise to theological strife. The committee's draft, however, was submitted to Gladstone, and his approval helped to save the halls when the Association met to accept the report.[72] Later in the term another committee, appointed to discuss the university constitution, reported, and had its draft accepted in April. The tutors had no sympathy for either the Hebdomadal Board, an isolated, irresponsible and ill-qualified body, or the Congregation overweighted by professors, which the Royal Commission had proposed. The harmonizing principle of the constitution should be that of representation, a principle to which the tutors as a body were pledged. The contentious question was the representation to be allotted to professors; Gladstone's allies Woollcombe and Haddan wished to concede none at all, but in the end professors were diluted with public examiners and moderators, and allotted one of three electoral constituencies. Nine members of a new Hebdomadal Board should be elected by the heads, nine by tutors and resident MAs and nine by professors and examiners. Again, the tutors' hand was strengthened by the knowledge that Gladstone had seen their draft and much preferred their proposals to those of the Blue Book.[73]

While these discussions were proceeding, J. B. Mozley persuaded the Association to seek expert evidence, instead of waiting for it to come in as both the Commissioners and the Hebdomadal Board had done. In May 1853, therefore, questionnaires went out on, amongst other things, the possibility of reviving professional education in Oxford. The replies eventually formed an interesting series of appendices to the Association's reports. But the main work of the Trinity term was to clarify the vexed relations of the professorial and tutorial systems. George Rawlinson made it clear to Gladstone that although the tutors had no objection to the development of the professoriate, they wanted professorial teaching to remain subordinate to the tutorial system. The tutors were prepared to require undergraduates to attend professorial lectures, but their circumlocutions about the moral and indirect influence of the professoriate left the impression that they wished to kill professorial influence altogether. Gladstone was privately informed that, having reluctantly accepted a much reduced professoriate, the tutors were bitterly opposed to financing it by compulsorily suppressing

---

[72] Reports of the Oxford Tutors' Association, no. 1, passim; BL Add. MS 44282, fos 209–12; Guardian (1852), 836; (1853), 58.

[73] Reports of the Oxford Tutors' Association, no. 2 (1853); BL Add. MSS 44282, fos 217–22; 44230, fos 250–3; 44258, fos 107, 121.

fellowships, and wished to leave the matter to college discretion.[74] The tutors' final report on the college system was not accepted till March 1854, and was of smaller importance since decisions had already been taken elsewhere which would settle the future of the colleges. It was a very conservative document. Colleges should remain the centre of the University and nothing should be done to destroy their moral and religious influence. No uniform system should be imposed on them, only a proportion of the fellowships should be completely open and the obligation upon fellows to take holy orders should in general remain. Fellows would find plenty of employment in the new halls, but fellowships existed to promote study, not employment. Some machinery would be needed for overhauling college statutes for the future; at present, Parliament should break college oaths, and simply provide enabling powers, looking to compulsion later. If Parliament were to lay down detailed regulations for colleges, a parliamentary committee would be needed to discuss them with the colleges. This recommendation showed how far the tutors had been driven against their inclinations, and the fact was bound to influence Gladstone's legislation.[75]

While the score of tutors who managed the Association had been preparing recommendations in consultation with Gladstone, the heads had been influencing him in another way. By the beginning of November 1852 the committee of the Hebdomadal Board had reported, and the Vice-Chancellor wrote to Lord Derby requesting a royal licence to repeal three statutes of the Caroline Code, the first prescribing the nomination of collectors in Lent, now a meaningless form, the second establishing the proctorial cycle, which was now out of date, and the third constituting the Hebdomadal Board. This was all the assistance the University would need on the side of legislation, but they would also like a licence to increase their holdings of lands in mortmain. To neither of these requests was Derby sympathetic. He could not move the Crown without being informed of the proposed changes. It was clear that the heads had no programme, that the colleges were not ready to be included in a comprehensive enabling measure and that an extension of mortmain was completely contrary to public policy. It was also clear, as Derby intimated in private correspondence and at his public installation in June 1853, that they must acquire a programme quickly.[76] For Russell, briefed by Gladstone, made a statement in the Commons (4 April 1853) that the government would allow the University the grace of the present

[74] Mozley, *Letters*, 217–19; *Reports of the Oxford Tutors' Association*, no. 3 (1853); BL Add. MSS 44282, fos 223–4; 44529, fo 15; 44230, fos 262–7 (repr. in *Lake*, 180–90).

[75] *Reports of the Oxford Tutors' Association*, no. 4 (1854); BL Add. MSS 44282, fo 225; 44230, fos 268–77.

[76] R. L. Cotton to Lord Derby, 16 Nov., 6 Dec. 1852, J. W. Henley to Lord Derby, 10 Dec. 1852, Derby Papers, 157/12; E. Cardwell to W. P. Talbot, 2 Nov. 1852, ibid. 157/10; Lord Derby to E. Cardwell, 22 Apr. 1853, ibid. 182/1, fos 79–84; HBM 1841–54, fos 251–3, 255, 257, 259–62; *Guardian* (1853), 397.

session to settle their affairs, but would accept no plan of reform which did not meet five requirements: the opening of fellowships so that they became the rewards of merit and work; constitutional reform to secure the representation of the main elements of the University in the governing body; measures to increase the numbers of students and limit the disadvantages of poor students; and the application of college resources towards the revival of the professoriate. Finally, it might be prudent to limit the term of fellowships.[77]

The major development of the summer was that Pusey and Marriott came round to defending the status quo, and Pusey not only presented a substantial treatise as evidence, but canvassed his friends to give the heads' report a respectable appearance by doing the same.[78] When the report was produced in December 1853, however, it was a mouse, incapable of being disguised, by any embellishment, as a lion. The heads felt, with some reason, that the new examination system should be allowed to prove itself before further changes should be made, and could not conceive a matriculation examination of a standard low enough not to exclude some candidates who were now properly admitted. They doubted the demand for university extension, and were against unattached students and private halls. They burked the professorial question, simply supporting the combination of professorial and tutorial teaching which had been envisaged in the new examination statutes, and hoped to endow new chairs without taking college funds. They were well satisfied with the university constitution, but were prepared to appoint non-members of the Board to their delegacies more often, and to enlarge the Board by adding eight elected members of Convocation. They were against the wholesale opening of fellowships, and would countenance only marginal relaxations of the obligation to enter holy orders.[79] Pusey's evidence was at least based on a great general idea, and was acclaimed by the *Guardian* as showing that the issue between the Commission and its critics was 'a question between religion and irreligion—between moral restraint and licence'.[80] At bottom, Pusey felt that the literary heritage of the Catholic past was the sole defence of faith and morals against the destructive modernisms of the day. Magnifying the personal instruction of professors was in principle idolatry. Professors would do only for science, which amounted to the purveying of facts, but not for liberal education. Likewise teaching must be kept in clerical hands, and government in the Hebdomadal Board. What the Board needed was access to the views of residents. Pusey proposed the creation of a second board equal in numbers to the first, each to have the

---

[77] BL Add. MSS 44206, fos 83–8; 44528, fos 93, 95–7, 121, 123–5; *Ed. Rev.* xcix (Jan. 1854), 174; *Correspondence between Viscount Palmerston... and the Board.*

[78] Two undated letters of E. B. Pusey to J. Keble [May and June 1853] and another of the same period to Charles Marriott, KCA MSS; BL Add. MS 44251, pt 1, fos 74–6.

[79] *Report and Evidence* (1853), report (111 pp.).

[80] *Guardian* (1854), 9.

initiative in recommending measures to the other, the measures agreed by both to go to Convocation. This proposal, clearly designed to stop changes being made, went against the intentions of almost everyone other than Pusey and the Board.[81] The heads' report was published in December 1853 just as Palmerston required his progress report. The Senior Proctor, D. P. Chase, moved that a delegacy be appointed to prepare constitutional changes, and was defeated.[82] When the heads' proposals appeared they revealed themselves to be hiding behind their old enemy Dr Pusey, and to be asking for precisely his scheme of two boards.[83]

The constitutional issue now dwarfed every other, and there were three options available, that of Pusey championed by the heads, the representative option of the tutors, and the Hebdomadal Board, 'stuffed with professors', of the Royal Commission. H. H. Vaughan now made a last attempt to save the day for the third of these,[84] but was already left behind by the tide of events. For forty-one of the liberals who had hitherto adopted the Blue Book platform, led by J. M. Wilson, sent up a petition to Lord John Russell urging a tripartite Hebdomadal Council (after the manner of the Tutors' Association) elected by a Congregation consisting of all university and college officers. The powers of Convocation should remain unchanged.[85] There were three reasons for this major concession to the position of the tutors. In the first place the liberals saw that the tutors were now willing to accept a broadly based Congregation, and made their own contribution to the reconciliation with the High-Churchmen which had been gradually effected. Then, secondly, the liberals believed that the government had given up a full university and professorial system, and, knowing that there was no future for the heads' plan, feared the boasts of the Tutors' Association spokesmen that they 'would have it all their own way with Mr Gladstone'.[86] And, thirdly, the power of Gladstone's connections was displayed again in January 1854 in the election of Sir William Heathcote as a university burgess. This by-election was brought on by the resignation of Sir Robert Inglis, now old and ill. The Oxford post-Tractarians wanted to put forward Roundell Palmer, but Gladstone's London committee absolutely refused to surrender the claims of their chairman, Sir William Heathcote. As pupil and patron of Keble, a lay sympathizer of the Tractarian party and a cultivated gentleman

---

[81] *Report and Evidence* (1853), 1–173. The evidence is summarized in Liddon, *Pusey* iii. 381–6.
[82] HBM 1841–54, fos 291, 298.
[83] The scheme was worked out by Hawkins in consultation with Pusey: BL Add. MS 44206, fo 114; cf 44251, pt 1, fo 82.
[84] H. H. Vaughan, *Oxford Reform and Oxford Professors* (1854).
[85] BL Add. MSS 44376, fo 246; 44377, fos 193, 199; 44230, fos 278, 283–4, 288; *Guardian* (1854), 136. There is a copy of the petition in *University Reform Papers, 1854*, Bodl. G. A. Oxon. c. 70.
[86] H. G. Liddell to Gladstone, 18 Feb. 1854, BL Add. MSS 44236, fo 267, cf fos 262–3; 44377, fos 253–5. Gladstone gave a broad hint to Liddell that the government favoured the tutors' line: BL Add. MS 44529, fo 49.

of the old school on easier terms with the Derbyites, Heathcote was in any case a strong candidate. The heads, who for years had been sending frail candidates to defeat, could not now find a candidate of any kind, and lost all to the Gladstonians.[87] The liberals accordingly flocked to make their peace.

Oxford opinion was now substantially polarized between the heads' scheme and that of the tutors who had Gladstone's ear. The heads' last throw was to send Pusey privately to persuade Gladstone to postpone the government's announcement until Convocation had voted upon the Hebdomadal scheme. Disastrous confusion was the consequence. The government had no intention of accepting the heads' constitutional proposals, and informed Lord Derby accordingly. Derby assumed (an assumption the Oxford tutors and liberals knew to be in error) that the government intended to introduce a full professorial system, and encouraged the heads to resist. The heads therefore canvassed the outvoters while the juniors did not, and carried their motion by 212 votes to 161, the minority being composed almost entirely of resident fellows. The heads were never less credible than in this victory, and the University generally looked to the bill being drawn for the government by Gladstone.[88] Gladstone's personal evolution was now a crucial element in the political equation. In January 1852, before the publication of the Blue Book, he had still wanted to 'avert Parliamentary interposition altogether'.[89] Even after the Blue Book, he regarded anything more than enabling legislation as an absolute last resort.[90] By the end of September 1852, much wounded by the Hebdomadal Board in the parliamentary and cancellarial elections, he held that, unless there were substantial changes (which he did not believe would be forthcoming from the heads), there must be parliamentary intervention radical enough to prevent repeated interference in future.[91] After the bitter by-election of January 1853, at a public luncheon in Oxford, Gladstone made it as clear as his public circumlocutions ever made anything clear that there would be parliamentary intervention with his support. In cabinet Russell found him 'very radical', and was content to leave the management of the affair to him.[92] When Hawkins produced the

[87] For a fuller account with references see Ward, *Victorian Oxford*, 187–8.

[88] This compressed narrative is based on BL Add. MSS 44271, fos 49–53; 44281, fos 103–42; 44282, fo 246; 44377, fos 201–2, 205, 218; E. B. Pusey to Sir William Heathcote, 13 Feb. [1854], PHL Pusey 138/4; Pusey to J. Keble [16 Feb. 1854], KCA MSS (parts repr. in Liddon, *Pusey* iii. 392–3); R. L. Cotton to Lord Derby, 10 to 25 Feb. 1854, Derby Papers, 157/12; Lord Palmerston to Lord Derby, 16 Feb. 1854, ibid. 8/2 (this letter was drafted by Gladstone, who would give no ground: BL Add. MS 44743, fos 143–9); Lord Derby to R. L. Cotton, 16 Feb. 1854, Derby Papers, 182/2, fos 220–2; E. B. Pusey to Lord Derby, 23, 27 Feb. 1854, ibid. 8/2; C[harles] M[arriott], *How are we to Vote on the Proposed Constitution for the University?* (20 Feb. 1854); *Guardian* (1854), 151–2, 165, 173, 182–3.

[89] Gladstone to Hawkins, 5 Jan. 1852, OCL Gl. 10.

[90] BL Add. MS 44236, fo 261; cf MS 44318, fo 10.

[91] BL Add. MS 44183, fos 52, 57.

[92] *Diary of an Oxford Lady*, 20; F. Temple to A. H. Clough, 3 Feb. 1853, in *Correspondence of Clough* ii. 373.

heads' report in December 1853, Gladstone told him it was too late to preserve the independence of the University; all that could be saved was the fundamental principles of the place—the connection with the Church, religious discipline and 'the predominance of the higher studies'.[93]

On these principles Gladstone began to construct his bill, assisted by a draft bill submitted by Jowett at the end of 1853. Jowett wanted a general settlement rather than a chaos of college schemes promoted under enabling powers, and he wanted the whole settlement enforced in the Act. He anticipated the liberals' compromise with the Tutors' Association by adopting the tripartite Hebdomadal Council: it was to be elected by a constituency of tutors. Jowett looked to a general opening of foundations, and to a redeployment of college wealth; but having provided that colleges might appropriate one-sixth of their fellowships to scholarships, and the same proportion to new studies, dared not plunder more for the endowment of chairs. In January 1854 Gladstone circulated this draft among the ministers and the Education Committee, together with one of his own incorporating a commission, and in mid-February gave both drafts extensive private circulation in Oxford to sound out the views of residents.[94] The principal differences between the two were that Gladstone thought that a commission would secure a result gentler and better in detail, whereas Jowett thought it would be ruinous to general principles; that Gladstone had some respect for college oaths, whereas Jowett had none; and that Gladstone had the High-Church faith in private halls, whereas Jowett looked for expansion to multiplying scholarships.[95] An immense and confused correspondence followed the circulation of the drafts, to which Gladstone replied with infinite patience. The two chief points of comment were the election of the proposed Hebdomadal Council and the tenure of fellowships. On the first point Gladstone admitted that the government was moving against sectional and in favour of congregational election, influenced partly by the evils inherent in small electorates, and partly by the willingness of the liberals, the great advocates of professors, to accept the scheme. The fellowship question was very difficult. Gladstone thought fellowships would never be safe as long as they were formally sinecures; many of his Oxford supporters were against change, and though he got them to accept that a quarter of fellowships, for the sake of the new studies, should be held by laymen, the liberals protested vigorously that this was far too favourable to the clergy.[96]

[93] BL Add. MS 44206, fos 103–4.
[94] BL Add. MSS 44376, fos 210–15, 218–19, 246–51; 44529, fo 16; 44743, fos 2–12, 119–20; 44377, fo 215; 44580, fos 45–7; 44183, fos 72–5.
[95] BL Add. MSS 44743, fos 119–20, 130–1; 44377, fos 10–14, 19, 113–15.
[96] BL Add. MSS 44183, fos 66–70, 77–8, 85, 93–4, 99–100, 108–9; 44236, fos 264, 272–8; 44377, fos 206–8, 273–4; 44230, fos 275, 313–16, 318–20; 44251, pt 1, fos 103, 130, 144, 149, 170–1; 44374, fos 9–10, 33–4; 44378, fo 46.

The bill, introduced by Russell on 17 March 1854, was in the main a compromise between the schemes of Gladstone and Jowett (who both warmly supported it),[97] and bore the marks of the strenuous discussion in Oxford. Gladstone secured his commissioners, and Jowett his tripartite Hebdomadal Council. This was to be elected by a Congregation composed of university officers, the senior tutor of each college, and such other residents as could produce a certificate that they were habitually engaged in study. Congregation was to discuss proposals of the Hebdomadal Council in English, and though it gained no power of amendment, its members might forward amendments in writing to Council. Gladstone obtained his point about oaths, which were to be restricted, but not prohibited; and also the opening of private halls under licence from the Vice-Chancellor. Half the fellowships were to be opened, certain preferences to schools on lines suggested by Jowett being retained. Colleges were to allot up to a quarter of their fellowships to laymen, and restrictions were placed on non-residence. Fellows must not only reside, but must either be tutors, office-holders or incumbents of parishes within three miles of Carfax, or hold a certificate of study. Colleges might produce new statutes for the approval of the Commissioners, devoting up to one-fifth of their income to the support of chairs, and suppressing fellowships to raise the income of fellows up to £250 per annum, to erect new buildings or to establish affiliated halls. Here Jowett's suggestions had been developed in the direction of the Blue Book. The new statutes were to be approved by the Commissioners before the beginning of Michaelmas term 1855; failing this the Commissioners were to make the statutes themselves, which, subject to the approval of the Queen in Council and to no address being moved against them in either House of Parliament, should become binding.[98]

Once published, the bill went down to Oxford again for comment. The wilder conservatives were furious; the Vice-Chancellor, Pusey and Keble querulous, and not at all mollified by Gladstone's proper stress on the bill's conservative character, and its resolute refusal to increase the influence of the Crown;[99] and the complex arrangements about fellowships and special connections of colleges with schools enabled the Hebdomadal Board to fight its last stand. The Board moved Convocation to petition against the bill lock, stock and barrel, secure in the assurance of support from threatened schools and the confidence that Lord Derby would accept the cue to throw the bill out of the Lords. The tutors and the *Guardian* came out immediately in support of the bill, and, in the end, the heads were humiliated by a victory by

[97] BL Add. MS 44378, fos 26, 33–4, 78–82.
[98] A copy of the bill in its original shape was printed in the *Guardian* (1854), 248–9.
[99] BL Add. MSS 44378, fos 44, 70; 44281, fos 143–4, 149; J. T. Coleridge, *Memoir of John Keble* (2nd edn 2 vols 1869) ii. 380–90.

two votes only, a result which guaranteed a second reading for the bill in the Commons.[100] The serious feature of the voting was the abstention of the more extreme liberals who had connections in the Commons. Prominent among them was H. G. Liddell, who was reputed to be personally piqued at not being appointed to the Executive Commission, and who proceeded to give Gladstone the roughest time he ever had with a bill.[101] It was unfortunate that Gladstone had to introduce his bill at a most peevish and disorderly time of a peevish and disorderly Parliament, a Parliament which knew that the Oxford consensus on which the bill was based was weakened by the secession of Pusey and Marriott on the one flank and the stronger liberals on the other.

The upshot was that Derby was briefed by an Oxford delegation led by the Vice-Chancellor to play havoc with the details of the bill in committee, while a phalanx of radicals led by Blackett and Heywood also attacked it clause by clause. The two together substituted sectional for Congregational election of Council, the radicals in the name of independence for professors, the Tories to rescue the heads from an electoral caucus of Tractarians. (Congregational elections had been suggested by various Blue Book witnesses.) The privileges of schools were also a thorny topic, and Sir William Heathcote himself carried a clause protecting the claims of Winchester on New College.[102] Not only was the balance of the bill upset by these tactics, but the delays threatened the whole enterprise. By the beginning of June, twenty-seven clauses relating to the University had been passed, but thirty-one relating to colleges remained, to which seventy-five amendments had been tabled. Gladstone was low in spirits, but determined to fight. He abandoned the whole of the college provisions of the bill, and made college reform a simple matter of arrangement between governing bodies and the Commissioners, the college being empowered to reject any scheme of the Commissioners by a two-thirds majority. Even then Roundell Palmer carried an amendment extending this arrangement to schools whose privileges were threatened.[103] The opening of foundations was now clearly threatened. Gladstone was mortified, and Jeune, foreseeing his college being held to

[100] BL Add. MSS 44221, fos 23–4, 29–30, 37, 43–4, 49–54; 44282, fos 268–74; 44183, fos 106–9; *Guardian* (1854), 257, 262, 264–5, 285.

[101] BL Add. MS 44208, fo 97. Liddell's biographer asserts (H. L. Thompson, *Liddell* (1899), 146) that he refused to serve on the Commission, though pressed to do so, but no trace of this has been found in Gladstone's correspondence: Bodl. MS Acland d. 68, fos 8–11. The liberals objected with some reason that Gladstone was preserving an artificial ascendancy of the clergy in Oxford, and Liddell, who ascribed all the feuds there to Gladstone's 'culpable weakness' (Bodl. MS Acland d. 69, fos 30–3), received no further offers of preferment until the death of Stanley in 1881, when he felt too old to succeed to the deanery of Westminster.

[102] *Guardian* (1854), 348, 357; BL Add. MS 44208, fos 76, 82–91.

[103] BL Add. MS 44221, fos 109, 114; *Guardian* (1854), 451; R. Palmer, *Memorials, Family and Personal, 1766–1865* (2 vols 1896) ii. 200–1.

ransom by the corporation of Abingdon, desperate.[104] Worse, however, was to come. After all Gladstone's promises to maintain the Anglican character of the University, James Heywood moved the abolition of the tests on 22 June, and in a good house obtained a majority of 91.[105]

This unforeseen result aroused consternation in Gladstone's camp, and clearly illuminated flaws in the Aberdeen coalition. For some time past the Dissenters had been renewing their educational and other claims, and the publication of the religious census of 1851 during the winter of 1853–4 added new grist to their mill. Yet they seemed able to make little progress. In the early months of 1854 half the divisions in the Commons were on ecclesiastical questions, and under government leadership they went consistently against the Dissenting interest; indeed in the very week Heywood moved against the test, the cabinet defeated Clay's Church Rate Abolition Bill. Nonconformist tempers were inflamed to a pitch reminiscent of the worst days of the schools question, and their agitating organizations were set to work. The question of the tests was an ideal question on which Nonconformists could sink their differences, and, more importantly, draw on outside support normally denied them. A Dissenting petition to Russell was signed by radicals like Cobden and Hume, and Catholics like O'Connell. Russell, too, seems to have been not quite candid, leaving the petitioners with the impression that 'although the cabinet could not themselves propose such a measure...they would not oppose it if proposed on the part of dissenters by independent members of the House'.[106] This invitation to pressure would be accepted by Cambridge members, who saw no reason for the greater strictness of the Oxford matriculation test, and still more by Derby, who twenty years previously had supported the admission of Dissenters and saw no reason to avoid embarrassing Gladstone now. In the Commons Lord Stanley deprecated government claims that Heywood's clause would not get through the House of Lords, and fifty Tories trooped into the Nonconformist lobby.[107]

Heywood's success was a surprise, but no fluke; and, particularly when he determined to claim no more for Dissenters than admission to the BA degree, Gladstone felt that the verdict of Parliament could not be reversed. As was well as known, Provost Hawkins had been campaigning for twenty years for Oxford to modify the religious test for the BA course, while retaining teaching and government in the hands of the Church. A step

---

[104] BL Add. MS 44221, fos 146–7, 150; F. Jeune to Lord Derby, 6 July 1854, Derby Papers, 8/1; *Diary of an Oxford Lady*, 49. There was also much distress in Jesus, where the college had determined to open its foundations to natives of the principality subject to a *ceteris paribus* preference: BL Add. MS 44381, fos 169–70.

[105] *Parl. Deb.* 22 Jan. 1854, 3S cxxxiv. 511–95.

[106] *Christian Reformer* (Apr. 1854), 247; *Inquirer* 25 Mar. 1854, 178.

[107] *Parl. Deb.* 22 Jan. 1854, 3S cxxxiv. 556; *Nonconformist* 28 June 1854, 525.

beyond that had now been taken by the Unitarian Heywood. The Tractarians were full of woebegone talk about withdrawing from Oxford, and the
Hebdomadal Board was seized with such confusion that all motions at its
meeting fell to the ground.[108] There were more surprises to come in the
House of Lords. The High-Church press left the peers in no doubt about
their duty on the tests, and could fairly argue that private halls were a very
different proposition if there were to be no tests. But Derby admitted to
Hawkins that his opinions on the admission of Dissenters had not changed,
and he was widely believed to be impatient to get off to the races.[109] At all
events, no Tory whip was put on, and when the government peers found
themselves unexpectedly in a majority, Goldwin Smith persuaded Gladstone
to get them to reverse some of the changes made in the Commons. Congregational election of the Hebdomadal Council was restored, and some of
the sting was taken out of Roundell Palmer's clause protecting the privileged
schools. The bill went back to the Commons much as the government
wanted it.[110]

Through an extraordinary chain of events, Oxford was now to be governed on principles somewhat different from any of those championed
during the previous four years. At the top, as the tutors had suggested,
was an elected council consisting of the Vice-Chancellor and proctors with
six heads, six professors and six members of Convocation. The electing
body, however, was to be Congregation, an institution which the tutors
had not originally wanted at all, and not the Congregation which the Oxford
liberals had wanted as late as the launching of the bill, for the official element
in it was now swamped by the inclusion of all residents. No one could
foretell how far foundations would be opened, or what would be the outcome of the Commissioners' negotiations with the colleges. The great gai-
ners from the Act were Gladstone's friends among the tutors, but they were
irked by the removal of the tests as far as the bachelor's degree, which
entailed changes in the examination of religious knowledge, and put a
different complexion upon private halls. It was no wonder that Keble was
chagrined about Gladstone, or that die-hard Tories should see betrayal
everywhere.[111] And their disorientation might well be reflected among

[108] Coleridge, *Keble* ii. 404; Liddon, *Pusey* iii. 399; J. Keble, *A Few very Plain Thoughts on
the Admission of Dissenters to the University of Oxford* (1854); BL Add. MSS 44183, fos 133–4;
44251, pt 1, fos 230, 233–6; 44221, fos 164–9; HBM 1841–54, fos 337–9; correspondence of E. B.
Pusey with J. Keble, various undated letters of June and July 1854, KCA MSS; R. L. Cotton to
Lord Derby, 1 July 1854, Derby Papers, 157/12; cf MCA MS D. 7. 4.
[109] *Guardian* (1854), 523, 530–1, 546; T. Gaisford to Lord Derby, 21 June, 30 June 1854;
E. Hawkins to Lord Derby, 5 July 1854; B. P. Symons to Lord Derby, 6 July 1854; Lord De La
Warr to Lord Derby, 12, 13, 17 July 1854; Derby Papers, 8/2; Lord Derby to Provost of Oriel, 6
July 1854, ibid.; ibid. 182/2, fos 319–24; R. Palmer, *Memorials, Family and Personal* ii. 201–2.
[110] Smith, *Reminiscences*, 106–7.
[111] *Letters of Frederic, Lord Blachford*, ed. G. E. Marindin (1896), 158; P. Bliss, *Reliquiae
Hearnianae* (2nd edn 3 vols 1869) iii. 189–91.

latter-day historians, for this reform followed none of the patterns said to be comprised under the 'revolution in government'; to Gladstone's chagrin it did not quite follow the other great nineteenth-century pattern of taking institutions out of politics. Utilitarianism had almost nothing to do with it; the constitutional ineptness of nineteenth-century Britain concerned it very nearly.

FOUR SURVEYS,
1800–1914

11

The Examination System

M. C. CURTHOYS

The undergraduate honours course, occupying three or four years' study of a single subject, culminating in a series of three-hour written examinations and a published class list, became an established institution in many English universities during the twentieth century. For most of the nineteenth century these features were peculiar to Oxford and Cambridge: the Oxford system originated in 1800;[1] the Cambridge Senate House examination and tripos lists had rather earlier, eighteenth-century, origins.[2] Brought into being at a time when the influences most strongly felt in the universities were clerical and aristocratic, the examinations came to assume functions unforeseen by their creators. Later notions of credentialism did not form a significant element in the original arrangements. The award of a written certificate or diploma was never an element in the Oxford degree ceremony;[3] under the new system the much sought-after *testamurs*, on which the examiners certified that a candidate's performance had been satisfactory, were printed on scraps of blue paper inferior to contemporary tradesmen's bills.[4] Those who gained 'honorary' distinction appeared in a class list originally published on paper of the grade used for packaging tea.[5]

By 1870 examinations had come to dominate undergraduate education at Oxford. The *Oxford University Gazette*, established in January 1870 to publish the university notices formerly posted in college butteries, assigned much of its space to lists of examinees and the details of changes in examination regulations. Those regulations were the subject of a major overhaul in 1872, with the immediate result that the information which a student needed to know about the examinations, formerly contained within a few

---

This chapter was to have been written by the late T. H. Aston. I wish to acknowledge the benefit of conversations with him on the evolution of examinations. I am also grateful to Brian Harrison and Janet Howarth for many helpful comments and suggestions on early drafts.

[1] A short history of the Oxford examinations is given in *Report of the Committee on the Structure of the First and Second Public Examinations*, suppl. 3 to *Gazette* (Mar. 1965), 15–24.
[2] J. Gascoigne, *Cambridge in the Age of the Enlightenment* (1989), 7–8.
[3] J. Wells, *The Oxford Degree Ceremony* (1906), 61.
[4] There are collections of *testamurs* in Bodl. MS Top. Oxon. d. 83 and OUA 3/1/39.
[5] [J. Campbell], *Hints for Oxford* (1823), 42.

pages of the *University Calendar*, came to fill an entire volume, *The Examination Statutes and Decrees*. These, in turn, were of such complexity that a
simplified account, *The Student's Handbook to the University and Colleges
of Oxford* (later *The Oxford University Handbook*), appeared in 1873 as a
semi-official successor to the existing guides to the examinations, of which
the most famous was Montagu Burrows's, *Pass and Class* (1860). For the
benefit of intending candidates, the Oxford publisher James Parker had since
1863 advertised for sale past papers 'printed directly from the Examiners'
copies', a venture undertaken by the Clarendon Press after 1874.[6] Elections
to college fellowships and scholarships by competitive examination had
meanwhile become the general rule. Oxford entered the field of external
examining in 1857 with the foundation of the Local Examinations Delegacy,
as the railway and later the parcel post linked candidates (mainly schoolchildren) throughout the country with distant examiners.

In their lavish scale and elaborate decoration the palatial new Examination
Schools, opened in May 1882, symbolized the triumph of the examination
idea in Victorian Oxford. John Ruskin, who, on his return to the University
in 1870, had found the influence of examinations all-pervasive as compared
with his undergraduate days, thought it 'expressive of the tendencies of this
age' that Oxford had spent a vast sum on a highly ornamented building 'for
the torture and shame of her scholars'.[7] The Schools, which were the most
expensive capital project undertaken in nineteenth-century Oxford, were
planned on a scale sufficient to process over 4,500 candidates a year.[8] Such a
weight of numbers prompted 'bureaucratic' measures in a university otherwise deficient in central administration. In 1890 the laborious task of collecting the names of the candidates was transferred from the proctors to a
permanent officer, the Secretary to the Board of Faculties. A series of
registers recording each undergraduate's progress through the system was
created in 1893, when the cumbersome business of issuing *testamurs* was
abolished.[9]

Examinations and their modification became a major preoccupation of
college tutors and a significant factor in the development of academic
professionalism. As early as 1822, when changes to the examinations were
under discussion, the defect of Oxford's unreformed constitution in denying
them powers to initiate legislation had become evident.[10] Once tutors had

---

[6] *Calendar* (1874), 22; between 1870 and 1873 past papers were published as supplements to
the *Gazette*.

[7] *The Works of John Ruskin*, ed. E. T. Cook and A. Wedderburn (39 vols 1903–12), xxxi. 29;
xxxiii. 363.

[8] R. Wilcock, *The Building of the Oxford University Examination Schools, 1876–1882*
(1983); Report of the Committee on Invigilation, 25 Nov. 1882, HCP 3 (1882).

[9] *Journal of Education* NS xii (July 1890), 375; NS xv (Apr. 1893), 225. The undergraduate
registers are in OUA UR 2/1/1–92.

[10] T. V. Short, *A Letter Addressed to the Very Revd the Dean of Christ Church, on the State of
the Public Examinations in the University of Oxford* (1822), 5.

acquired a partial voice on the Hebdomadal Council, in 1854, and a powerful influence in Congregation, they lost no time in bringing examination questions to the fore in university legislation. In 1859 thirty-two speakers took part in a debate lasting two days on a new examination statute.[11] 'It is amusing, but at last it grows wearisome', E. A. Freeman commented in 1888, 'to see the gravest men with the gravest countenances pottering away at some peddling change in Group A1, Preliminary that, Additional subject the other... never thinking that an University exists for the promotion of learning, and not simply for the purpose of putting Group A1 into a new shape every term.'[12] Stipends paid by the University to examiners in 1877 amounted to £3,731, a sum roughly equivalent to the salaries of six professors.[13]

These elaborate arrangements originated in the examination statute of Trinity term 1800, whose essentially conservative objectives have been described in Chapter 1. Lord Eldon's description of his farcical BA examination in 1770 appeared to stand in the sharpest contrast to the rigour of the new procedures, and was commonly quoted in the nineteenth century as evidence of the decadence of Oxford's old regime.[14] But the exercises which Eldon described had long been ceremonial, and their purely symbolic character was understood as such by the participants in a period when responsibility for organizing the curriculum devolved upon the colleges. Much inevitably depended upon the energy with which each college chose to undertake its educational work.[15] In some—Christ Church, in particular—the level of efficiency seems to have been high. There is a strong case for seeing the 1800 statute as an attempt by the heads of the leading colleges to enforce their standards upon the rest.[16] Edward Tatham, the Rector of Lincoln, attacked the development as one of Cyril Jackson's schemes to secure the hegemony of Christ Church in the University, and the early success of Christ Church men in the examinations appeared to bear him out. But another head of house, Edward Copleston of Oriel, was more willing to acknowledge the general benefit which had been conferred. By the system of which Jackson was principal architect, 'a new spirit was breathed into the University, and the *comparative* importance of his own College was proportionably reduced, a consequence to which he could not be blind, but which did not restrain him from promoting zealously what he felt to be an act of duty'.[17] Christ Church was unable in the long term to maintain its earlier pre-eminence once other colleges had been stimulated

[11] *Guardian* 23 Mar. 1859.
[12] A. Herbert (ed.), *The Sacrifice of Education to Examinations* (1889), 167.
[13] *UOC* (1877), circulars, 10–11.
[14] *RCO* (1850), report, 59.
[15] *The Eighteenth Century*, 369, 476.
[16] E. G. W. Bill, *University Reform in Nineteenth-Century Oxford* (1973), 15.
[17] *Letters of the Earl of Dudley to the Bishop of Llandaff* (1840), 192 n.

into activity. One such, New College, came under pressure to surrender its privilege of bringing forward its men for graduation without submitting to university exercises. Described in 1826 as 'in many respects an independent university',[18] New College gave up the custom in 1834, but only after lengthy debate. Arguing for the change, Augustus Hare, an undergraduate and later tutor of the college, had pointed out the difficulties inherent in a college acting as a degree-validating institution. Severity and impartiality were well-nigh impossible to uphold in internal college examinations:

Our senior fellows must not only be devoid of self-interest, but must rise superior to frailty. They must be wholly careless of popularity, deaf to the importunities of friendship, and ever and entirely bent on the performance of a harsh and ungrateful duty. You must believe that they will instantaneously change with change of place, that from kind friends they will become rigid examiners, that their smiles in the court will prove severity in the hall, that they will shake an undergraduate by the hand one instant, and pluck him if he deserve it the next.[19]

Hare's point was underlined by the subsequent history of college collections. Instituted during the late eighteenth century amidst signs of renewed collegiate vigour, collections proved difficult to enforce with anything like consistency. Thomas Gaisford, Dean of Christ Church from 1831, certainly made them a terrifying ordeal in an attempt to restore their importance, and therefore Christ Church's independence, in relation to the university examinations. On four days prior to his death in June 1855 he was said to have been presiding over college exercises.[20] In other colleges, however, the importance of collections was much diminished. 'To-day are Collections or college examinations; almost a farce. If a man is idle he copies his neighbour, or perhaps two join to work together,' wrote an undergraduate at Pembroke in 1855, whose testimony is the more powerful since the college was then under the reforming regime of Dr Jeune.[21]

There was no such laxity about the University's procedures after 1800. Once examiners began to reject unqualified candidates, what had been an empty form in which failure was almost unknown became a real test of attainment with a very real threat of rejection. During the first decade little more than 5 per cent of those who entered failed to receive *testamurs*.[22] After 1810, however, the failure rate rose to nearer 20 per cent, and by 1850 it was about 25 per cent. Although these figures include candidates who

[18] *Janus; or, The Edinburgh Literary Almanack* (Edinburgh 1826), 5 n. For evidence of Christ Church's independence in the 18th century see E. G. W. Bill, *Education at Christ Church Oxford, 1660–1800* (1988), 142.

[19] [A. W. Hare], *A Letter to George Martin, Esq.* (nd [1814]), 21.

[20] *GM* (1855) ii. 99.

[21] *Letters of George Birkbeck Hill*, ed. L. Crump (1906), 53.

[22] Senior Proctor's list of candidates, OUA SP/59; register of public examinations, 1801–14, OUA UR/3/1/13/1.

withdrew before the trial began, such loss of nerve, which involved the forfeiture of fees paid, indicated that the proceedings were no formality. One sign of the new rigour was the complaint of hard-pressed parents of intending ordinands that a 'pluck' brought with it the expense of additional residence.[23] Those undergraduates of high social rank who wished to graduate could no longer shirk the exercise, since the customary privilege which allowed noblemen and gentlemen commoners to take honorary MA degrees at the conclusion of their residence was quietly withdrawn.[24] Two such awards after 1810 were both for intellectual merit: the fourth duke of Dorset, a nobleman at Christ Church and a diligent classical scholar, was presented for an honorary degree in 1813, his hopes of entering for honours having been dashed by the loss of his sight in one eye after an accident while playing tennis; in 1829 the Hebdomadal Board conferred a degree on Thomas Pycroft in recognition of his successful performance in the competition for an East India Company writership, which had cut short his university studies.[25] The exception to this general pattern was the ordinary qualification for the MA degree itself. An examination for this degree briefly existed between 1800 and 1807. Thereafter it was dropped, the only requirement imposed being a further period of a minimum of three weeks' residence. This, too, ceased to be required after 1859.[26]

All undergraduates who wished to graduate BA, and therefore proceed to their MA, had now, regardless of their social rank, to risk the silence with which the examiners passed over those who had failed to satisfy them. It was, enthused a pamphleteer writing in 1826, 'a silence which must move the heart of the most dead to feeling, a degradation which must harass the mind of all not totally depraved, as severely as bankruptcy'.[27] In the post-Waterloo years, Thomas Vowler Short, tutor and Censor of Christ Church, recorded instances where his pupils shied away from the trial: 'he was alarmed at Brabazon's fate & could not be got to face the enemy,' Short wrote of one nobleman who drew back from an encounter with the examiners.[28] Undergraduate slang, it has been noted, was quick to respond to this new fact of student life, 'pluck', 'gulf' and 'plough' being among the more common usages for failure.[29]

[23] *GM* (1820) i. 32.
[24] The principle that honorary MAs could be conferred on gentlemen commoners was reaffirmed in 1803: HBM 2 Mar. 1803. Sir Oswald Mosley, who matriculated at Brasenose in 1802 and was created honorary MA in 1806, seems to have been one of the last gentlemen commoners to receive this privilege.
[25] *GM* (1816) ii. 196–7; HBM 16 Apr. 1829.
[26] *Herald* 27 June 1807; *RCO* (1850), evidence, 25; Cox, 60–1; Hebdomadal Orders, 1859, no. 268, OUA HC/1/7/1.
[27] W. C. Townsend, *The Paean of Oxford* (1826), 44–5.
[28] 'History of my pupils', CA Cen. i. a. 4, p. 144.
[29] S. Rothblatt, 'Failure in early nineteenth-century Oxford and Cambridge', *History of Education* xi (1982), 9; M. Marples, *University Slang* (1950).

Although the introduction of honours proved the most influential legacy of the 1800 statute, the original 'extraordinary examination', which adopted the Cambridge practice of ranking the most able candidates in order of merit, in a class limited to twelve names, was soon abandoned. Only fourteen individuals appeared in the honours lists between 1801 and 1806 and the attempt to copy Cambridge was not repeated. Instead, in 1807 the Hebdomadal Board reverted to the plan outlined in 1773 by John Napleton, a Brasenose tutor;[30] under the new statute candidates considered worthy of honorary distinction were placed in two alphabetically arranged classes. Large numbers of undergraduates were immediately attracted to come forward by the new scheme, whose popularity brought its own problems. Having no grading within it, the second class, which in 1808 comprised nearly 80 per cent of those who obtained honours, was thought to be too large. One disgruntled graduate complained of the unequal range of merit 'promiscuously huddled together into that broad-bottom class'.[31] More precise grading was allowed in 1809 when a line was drawn through the second class, the lower division (described as 'below the line') being formally designated the third class in 1825. This expedient proved counter-productive in another way. Marginal candidates, fearing the 'degradation' of appearing in the third class, preferred the anonymity of an ordinary pass degree.[32]

There was also a demand for a more precise classification at the top end of the scale. The examiners in mathematics, whose moving force was Baden Powell, Professor of Geometry, sought the restoration of an order of merit to generate in Oxford the competition for which the Cambridge tripos was famed. In their efforts to encourage the most able to strive to their utmost, the mathematics examiners had awarded a book to F. W. Newman in recognition of his performance in Easter 1826. Their action was 'much abused as presumptuous, unwise and unconstitutional', and strong resistance developed to any further subdivision of the first class.[33]

Such points of detail preoccupied a committee of the Hebdomadal Board appointed in March 1829, when the influence of the Noetics in the University was at its height. Their professed object was to create a self-activating mechanism to stimulate both teaching and study throughout the University.[34] In doing so, they reaffirmed that 'the standard for each class be absolute and

---

[30] J. Napleton, *Considerations on the Public Exercises for the First and Second Degrees in the University of Oxford* (1773), 32; see *The Eighteenth Century*, 615.

[31] *Herald* 4 June 1808.

[32] A. P. Saunders, *Observations on the Different Opinions Held as to the Changes Proposed in the Examination Statute* (1830), 24 n.; memorial sent to the Vice-Chancellor by the mathematics examiners, 6 Dec. 1828, Bodl. MS Baden Powell 31.

[33] C. Lloyd to Peel, 2 July 1826, BL Add. MS 40342, fo 360.

[34] Ward, *Victorian Oxford* 58; OUA WP/γ/24/4, fos 101, 113; 'Report of the Committee appointed by a resolution dated March 23, 1829, to discuss the construction of a new Examination Statute', Bodl. G. A. Oxon. b. 21; the evidence collected by the Committee is in Bodl. MS Top. Oxon. d. 15.

positive'.[35] Theoretically, all the candidates could be in the first class, and individual classes could be (and sometimes were) empty.[36] Honour schools never became strictly competitive between individuals, and this may be one reason why private coaching never became as necessary for success in Oxford as it seems to have been in Cambridge. The committee's practical objection to an order of merit lay in its likely deterrent effect; they considered alphabetical classes to be the best device for achieving the desired end of encouraging more students to try for honours.[37] At the committee's suggestion the fourth class was added in 1830, both to raise the status of the third and to deepen the scope of honours by bringing in passmen who had 'really satisfied' the examiners, as distinct from those who had merely avoided being 'plucked'.[38] This was the origin of the curious experiment of the 'honorary fourth', awarded between 1831 and 1865 to candidates for pass degrees who had shown more than ordinary diligence or ability. Here the university authorities revealed the gulf between their own and undergraduate perceptions of the class list. From its inception, the honorary fourth was widely resented by its recipients, embarrassed rather than complimented by seeing their names published among those at the foot of the class list. One of the first candidates to receive the award, in 1831, feared that it would look as if he had gone in for honours and failed to do well.[39]

Appearances were of critical importance since the early examinations took place in the presence of an audience. Great emphasis was placed upon securing publicity for the proceedings (hence the title, 'public examinations'), the attendance of undergraduates as spectators being secured by the requirement that they had to produce a certificate of having sat in the gallery of the rooms where the examinations were held on two previous occasions before they could themselves appear for examination.[40] So much store was set by this regulation that dispensations were very rarely granted. One of the first generation of students to be exposed to the new rigour gave his mother a dramatic account of his public ordeal:

There is a room in the schools fitted up for the purpose, with seats for the Vice-Chancellor and Proctors at one end of it, and all round benches for the other members of the University, so that you make a public exhibition. Six sour Masters of Arts sit at a large table in the middle of the chamber, and ask questions concerning

[35] Report of the Committee (1829), 7.
[36] Such a system of classification encouraged the α–γ scale of grading, which seems to have been generally used in Oxford examinations. See G. E. Thorley's Lit. Hum. mark-book for 1874–5, which appears to be the earliest extant: Bodl. MS Top. Oxon. d. 131. On Oxford marking see F. Y. Edgeworth, 'The statistics of examinations', Statistical Society Journal li (1888), 605 n.
[37] QJE ii (July 1831), 8.
[38] Whately to Hawkins, 29 Nov. 1829, OCL 6/563; Copleston to Hawkins, 17 June 1830, OCL 6/746.
[39] C. N. Gray, Life of Robert Gray (2 vols 1876) i. 13.
[40] Lists of those given certificates of attendance are in OUA SP/23.

religion, mathematicks, logic, algebra, languages, and heaven knows what, to which the trembling undergraduate answers from the other side of the table. You may imagine my agony... for the whole time previous to the dreadful day I could neither eat nor sleep, nor speak, nor scarcely move.[41]

George Moberly fainted in the street before his examination in 1825; Francis Jeune completely broke down in his viva in 1827.[42] It was a scarcely less daunting experience for the examiners, who were obliged to act in the full glare of public scrutiny. J. H. Newman collapsed under the strain of examining in November 1827, having spent the previous long vacation engaged, like many of the candidates, in 'getting up' the necessary preparatory reading.[43] By contrast, Mark Pattison redeemed his own disappointing class by a highly effective performance as a public examiner in 1848, which he regarded as a turning-point in his academic career.[44]

Public displays of attainment had been firmly established by the prize competitions founded from the late eighteenth century onwards, whose winners recited their compositions before the large and illustrious audience gathered at the annual Encaenia ceremony. While theatrical performances remained under an official ban, large crowds of undergraduates were attracted to the Schools[45] in anticipation of academic drama. Sir William Hamilton's oral examination in 1810, for which he had offered a list of books unequalled among his contemporaries, lasted for twelve hours over the course of two days, in front of a large audience, and concluded with the thanks of his questioners.[46] The public examinations were also occasions for the show of aristocratic virtue, much importance being attached to the willingness of young noblemen and gentlemen commoners to come forward to try for honours.[47]

After 1820 the method of oral examining was overwhelmed by the sheer number of candidates. In 1810, 188 came forward; in the peak year of 1827 the figure reached 404. Limited by statute to dealing with six candidates per day, the examiners were occupied in the task for almost half the academic year. The outcome was a decisive shift towards written work as the method of assessment. Written work had been set in the BA examinations since 1807, but initially it seems to have played a subordinate part in the proceedings.[48] A candidate who was due to be examined on the same day as Peel was set to

---

[41] *Letters from and to Charles Kirkpatrick Sharpe, Esq.*, ed. A. Allardyce (2 vols Edinburgh 1888) i. 111. The first batch of candidates under the new statute was examined on 4 Dec. 1801; Sharpe was among the second, on 15 Dec. 1801, OUA UR/3/1/13/1.

[42] C. A. E. Moberly, *Dulce domum: George Moberly, his family and friends* (1911), 23 n.

[43] A. J. C. Hare, *Memorials of a Quiet Life* (2 vols 1872) i. 211–12; *LDN* ii. 37.

[44] Pattison, *Memoirs*, 120–2.

[45] i.e. the rooms in the Schools Quadrangle where the examinations were held before 1882.

[46] *Testimonials in Favour of Sir William Hamilton, Baronet* (np nd), 11 n.

[47] *Report and Evidence* (1853), report, 20.

[48] *Statutes* ii. 63; Short, *Letter*, 17.

answer questions in writing while waiting his turn.[49] Within twenty years exercises on paper had become a much larger part of the examination. In 1827 William Jacobson worked on written answers for three days, before being examined viva voce.[50] This represented a further burden on the examiners, who still had to set individual exercises for each candidate.[51]

The situation was revolutionized in 1830, when the examiners were permitted 'to try several persons at the same time, at answering the same questions'; this opened the way for printed papers to be set.[52] In 1828 the mathematics examiners had introduced printed papers following the example of their Cambridge counterparts. The first printed papers in Literae Humaniores were used in Easter 1831, covering logic, rhetoric, criticism and history, and Greek, Latin and English passages for translation. Their value as evidence of the state of Oxford education was immediately recognized by an anonymous writer who, in 1833, reviewed the recent papers, comparing them unfavourably with those set by the London University examiners.[53] This judgement may, however, have been based on inadequate information since these printed questions were not the whole story. The examination also included a long essay, or thesis as it was sometimes described, on moral philosophy, which was intended to occupy the whole day; and the subject of this was dictated to the candidates.[54] The Hebdomadal Board's inquiry was told by an examiner that the viva was 'best adapted to ascertain the acquaintance with the contents of the book and its details', whereas written work allowed 'the display of original thought and the talent of the examinee in combining and applying what he has read'.[55] In the long term, the introduction of printed papers increased the importance of essay work in Lit. Hum., although contemporaries observed the more immediate effects to have been a tendency towards narrowness and an emphasis on technical detail.[56]

Although paper work, lasting five days for those seeking honours,[57] was rapidly established after 1830 as the decisive element of the BA examination, a peculiarity of the Oxford system, compared to Cambridge and London, was the survival of the viva. One explanation for this lies in the importance attached by the Oxford examinations to religious knowledge. No one, it was laid down in 1800, was deemed worthy of a *testamur* 'who has been found to have neglected the elements of religion', and it was reaffirmed in 1807 that,

---

[49] B. C. Roberts, *Letters and Miscellaneous Papers* (privately printed, 1814), 73.
[50] J. W. Burgon, *Lives of Twelve Good Men* (2 vols 1889) ii. 242.
[51] Bodl. MS Top. Oxon. d. 15, fos 14–15; Report of the Committee (1829), 2.
[52] *Statutes* ii. 169.
[53] See p. 530.
[54] *Life and Letters of Frederic Lord Blachford*, ed. G. E. Marindin (1896), 9.
[55] Bodl. MS Top. Oxon. d. 15, fo 27.
[56] W. J. Copleston, *Memoir of Edward Copleston D. D., Bishop of Llandaff* (1851), 188; cf D. S. L. Cardwell, *The Organisation of Science in England* (1972), 145.
[57] *Oxford University Magazine* i (1834), 99.

in preference to all other subjects, 'the elements of religion are to claim first place'.[58] In 1830 it was specified that the examination in the rudiments of faith and religion should always be oral. 'The Divinity is conducted viva voce only,' Henry Vaughan wrote to his father in 1833. 'The candidate is expected to know the Articles of our Church, to be able to support them by quotation from Scripture. He is also examined upon the history of the Bible.'[59] Far from fearing that a public examination in religion would encourage danger-ous controversy,[60] the authorities saw the viva, which took a catechetical form (that is, the candidate answered, and was given no opportunity to dispute), as a means of enforcing public submission by the undergraduate to a test of his knowledge of the Articles of the Church. Failure in divinity was irredeemable by excellence in the other subjects, as Nassau Senior had found when he was plucked in 1811.[61] Much was made of such occasions when candidates, perhaps over-confident of their intellectual abilities, were found to have neglected their religious studies and suffered the disgrace of rejection. 'It has long been the glory of Oxford', J. T. Round, who had examined in the 1820s, observed, 'that when her ablest and most accom-plished Students stand up to be examined for the degree of BA, which is the turning point of life, *the first* book which is placed in their hands is the *Greek Testament*.'[62] To emphasize its importance both the examiner and the undergraduate rose from their seats for this part of the examination.[63]

Previous attendance at the examinations as a spectator ceased to be re-quired of candidates after 1849. Instead, during the brief period when a substantial revival of the authority of the professoriate appeared possible, all undergraduates were required to produce certificates showing that they had attended professorial lectures before they could enter the examinations. This requirement was dropped in 1859. Meanwhile, although now voluntary, audiences continued to attend the examinations, though in rather smaller numbers than formerly. The examination in 1880 of D. S. Margoliouth, subsequently Laudian Professor of Arabic, was one of the last occasions where a performance was met by the applause of an audience.[64] Accommod-ation for 'listeners' was provided for in the new Examination Schools, but

---

[58] *Statutes* ii. 40, 62.

[59] Bill, *University Reform in Nineteenth-Century Oxford*, 21.

[60] Cf S. Rothblatt, 'Student sub-culture and the examination system' in L. Stone (ed.), *The University in Society* (2 vols Princeton 1975) i. 293. There was anxiety about the method of disputations, revived for higher degrees in theology by Edward Burton, Regius Professor of Divinity in 1830, but even in this case there was agreement that an audience should be present to prevent the exercises 'soon becoming formal': MS Top. Oxon. c. 81, fo 225; *LDN* ii. 218; *QJE* ii (1831), 14.

[61] Bloxam, *Reg. Magdalen* vii. 169–70, 174.

[62] *Report and Evidence* (1853), evidence, 489.

[63] *Memoirs of Archbishop Temple*, ed. E. G. Sandford (2 vols 1906) ii. 430; *Statistical Society Journal* ix (1846), 201–2.

[64] *Guardian* 15 Dec. 1880, 1741.

the rearrangement in 1883 of the times of examinations so that vivas in finals were held in the long vacation reduced the likelihood of an audience being present.[65] Ceasing to be primarily a public occasion, the importance of the viva rapidly declined. Pressures of space to accommodate growing numbers of students simultaneously working on printed papers had been the chief reason for building the new Schools, though the architect, Thomas Jackson, contrived to conceal the purpose of the vast writing schools that lay within by erecting on one side of the entrance a sculptured panel showing a viva voce examination in progress.[66] Jackson's panel almost became a memorial at the moment of its erection, for the examiners then in office apparently attempted to use the opening of the new Schools building as an opportunity to do away with the labour of compulsory viva voce examining altogether. They were only prevented from doing so by the intervention of the Vice-Chancellor (Jowett) and proctors. The incident was said to have produced 'a decided reaction in favour of this time-honoured institution' and although, by the early twentieth century, the majority of vivas were reported to be mere formalities, renewed attempts at abolition were defeated.[67] Gradually dispensed with in preliminary examinations,[68] the viva remained a require-ment in every final honour school except mathematics, even at the cost of summoning candidates back to Oxford during the vacation. Such was the concern to uphold this principle that when, in 1906, a candidate was pre-vented by illness from returning to Oxford from his home in Birmingham to be orally examined, the Vice-Chancellor, by some accounts, authorized the examiners to conduct the viva by the use of a ten-minute trunk call on the new telephone link—an incident which reassured the *Isis* that the Oxford authorities were not the 'antiquated old fossils' popularly depicted.[69] In a longer perspective, their openness to change was more strikingly represented by the speed with which they had abandoned traditional methods of oral examining, still widely used in universities elsewhere in Europe.

A European observer would have been as forcefully struck by the com-paratively small part played by Oxford's professors in the assessment of candidates for degrees. Examining was largely in the hands of college tutors, nominated in rotation by the Vice-Chancellor and proctors, who showed some preference towards members of their own colleges. In the early years

---

[65] *Gazette* vi (30 May 1876), 407.

[66] On the other side he depicted the conferring of an MA degree, for which there had been no examination for three-quarters of a century: Wilcock, *Building of the Examination Schools*, 29–32.

[67] J. Wells, 'Literae Humaniores' in A. H. M. Stedman (ed.), *Oxford: its life and schools* (1887), 261; *Journal of Education* (July 1883), 247; in 1908, 55% of Lit. Hum. vivas were formal: OUA FA/4/7/2/1, 46, 61.

[68] The viva was dropped from classical Moderations in 1884 and Responsions in 1890, but retained in pass and divinity Moderations.

[69] *Isis* 20 Oct. 1906, 13; R. A. J. Earl, *The Development of the Telephone in Oxford, 1877– 1977* (1983), 24.

the nominators also conspicuously overlooked certain colleges, which may well have been a reflection on the reputed competence of their tutors. By contrast Balliol, Brasenose, Christ Church and Oriel, all of whose standing was high, supplied five or more public examiners between 1810 and 1830. When St Edmund Hall considered that one of its men had been ill used by the examiners, in 1807, the Hall's Vice-Principal warned that 'if the members of small colleges are to be overlooked in the Examining schools and subjected to neglect, or caprice, or injustice, the consequences to the reputation of the University may be easily imagined'.[70] His anxieties seem to have been allayed by the requirement that there were never to be two examiners from the same college or hall, although it was probably true, as Newman found at Trinity, that undergraduates from colleges whose tutors had not held the office were at a disadvantage in not being so well prepared for the type of questions likely to be put.[71] But no direct influence could be gained by candidates so favoured, because from 1807 examiners were not permitted to examine members of their own colleges, a prohibition which was extended in 1858 to those who had acted as private tutors.[72] Each examiner was bound by oath to give no 'testimonial to any undeserving party, or refuse one to the worthy', and the proctors regularly inspected the proceedings.[73]

Statutes to transfer the nomination of examiners to professorial boards were rejected by Convocation in 1849 and 1850,[74] and the Royal Commission's support for professorial control was successfully contested by both the Tutors' Association and the Hebdomadal Board. To the argument of J. M. Wilson, Professor of Moral Philosophy, that examinations conducted by non-specialists paid insufficient attention to scholarly advances in particular subjects and led to concentration on the routine of instruction,[75] Pusey, himself a professor, replied that tutors were best placed to carry out the task: 'In any question of education, there can be no comparison between the practical wisdom of persons habitually employed in the training of young men and the daily formation of their minds, and that which is likely, for the most part, to be possessed by persons engaged in abstract sciences.'[76] After the creation in 1872 of boards of studies to determine the composition of the various courses of study, examiners remained influential in establishing and passing on what was described as the 'vital tradition' of the Oxford honour schools, a body of lore whose continuity was ensured by including on each

[70] *The Rev. D. Wilson, Vice-Principal of St Edmund Hall, Feels himself called upon to State in the most Explicit Manner the Circumstances of the Examination of his Pupil* (np 1807), 11.

[71] Newman, *AW*, 40.

[72] *Herald* 20 Feb. 1858; *Calendar* (1860), 143.

[73] *Statutes* ii. 30; OUA WP/γ/8/19, fo 10.

[74] *The Times* 21 Mar. 1849, 8; 24 Apr. 1850, 5; Ward, *Victorian Oxford*, 149; Bill, *University Reform*, 124–8.

[75] *RCO* (1850), evidence, 262.

[76] *Report and Evidence* (1853), evidence, 92.

board of examiners at least one examiner who had held the office on a previous occasion.[77] Younger tutors sought to be initiated into the traditions of the Schools, to form an impression of the level of attainment generally shown by undergraduates and to discover what might reasonably be expected. Even when representatives of the newly created faculties were added to nominating boards in 1882, tutorial control was unshaken in the largest honour schools, Lit. Hum. and modern history.[78]

A new development in the second half of the century was the co-option of scholars from outside Oxford to join the boards of examiners. Non-resident members of Convocation had always been eligible to hold the office, but few did so before 1850. When examination subjects began to extend beyond the range of expertise available in Oxford, outsiders inevitably had to be recruited. In the early years of the law and history school, before the colleges had established staffs of specialist tutors, eminent Oxford graduates were invited to help conduct the examinations. In 1853 Henry Hallam, who had graduated from Christ Church in 1799, questioned candidates on their reading of his *View of the State of Europe during the Middle Ages*, an event which not surprisingly attracted large numbers of interested spectators.[79] Two years later there was another astute appointment to an examinership, that of the fifth Earl Stanhope, the historian of the eighteenth century, who had graduated in 1827. Stanhope, like Hallam, helped the fledgling honour school to maintain its place in the public eye. After 1872 the office of examiner ceased to be restricted to Oxford MAs. The freedom to appoint external examiners was immediately used to bring Michael Foster, the Cambridge physiologist, to take part in the natural science school during 1873–5; Arthur Gamgee and Edward Schafer, Professors of Physiology at Owens College and University College London respectively, examined in the 1880s and 1890s. In recondite areas of knowledge, such as oriental languages, the heavy reliance on the specialist knowledge of outside examiners was much criticized. A lack of specialist teachers in Oxford to fill the position of examiners offered one ground for objection in 1903 to the proposal for a modern languages honour school.[80] The latter objectors took no account of the existence of established scholars in the women's societies; no woman was appointed an examiner until 1922.

The emergence of new, specialized academic disciplines was reflected in changes to the structure of the BA course and the examination system which regulated it. Between 1800 and 1914 the common basis of the curriculum was progressively eroded, though much of the traditional course survived.

[77] C. Cannan (ed.), *The Student's Handbook to the University and Colleges of Oxford* (9th edn 1888), 159.

[78] *OM* 8 Nov. 1908, 61. For the faculties (1882), see Pt 2, Ch. 2.

[79] J. E. Butler, *Recollections of George Butler* (Bristol 1893), 88.

[80] *Oxford Times* 16 May 1903; *OM* 29 Apr. 1903, 290.

Before 1850 every undergraduate had to pass two examinations to qualify for the BA degree. The first, Responsions ('Little-Go'), introduced in 1808, was an elementary examination in Greek, Latin and logic or Euclid, generally taken at the end of the first or during the second year of residence. The second was the public examination ('Great-Go') in the rudiments of religion and those subjects described in 1807 as Lit. Hum. taken in the third or fourth year of study. A common course of study was prescribed for all, though honours men went far beyond the minimum required.

Mathematics, which was originally one of the subjects prescribed for the BA in 1800, was the first to break away from the common core. In 1807 a voluntary mathematical examination was established, with its own class list, although it took place at the same time, and was conducted by the same board of examiners (who included at least one mathematician),[81] as the main examination in Lit. Hum. When a separate board of mathematics examiners was created in 1825, they lost no time in urging upon the Hebdomadal Board that the mathematical examination should be allowed greater independence.[82] All that they gained was the concession in 1826 of an interval of three weeks after the Lit. Hum. examination to allow candidates in mathematics more time to prepare. By 1830 the climate within the University was unfavourable to further separation, and Hurrell Froude went so far as to propose reuniting the two class lists, making mathematics a constituent part of a single examination as it had been before 1807.[83] Joint honours were evidence of the continuing viability of a general course of study: between 10 and 15 per cent of those who took honours in Lit. Hum. before 1850 also did so in mathematics. Robert Peel, who pioneered the double first in the original meaning of that distinction, was one of seven future Chancellors of the Exchequer educated at Oxford before 1850 who had obtained honours in the voluntary mathematical examination.[84]

Compulsory Lit. Hum. preserved the common arts course for all undergraduates until 1864. The first recognition of other subjects as a qualification for a BA degree came rather half-heartedly in 1850, when examinations were instituted in natural science and law and modern history, each with its own board of examiners. All those who sought a degree had to obtain at least a pass in one of these, or in mathematics, in addition to Lit. Hum. In practice this change lengthened the degree course by as much as a year without providing more than a token recognition of the new disciplines, whose

[81] G. L. Cooke, Professor of Natural Philosophy, was on the board for six years between 1808 and 1815.

[82] P. Corsi, *Science and Religion: Baden Powell and the Anglican debate, 1800–1860* (1988), 110.

[83] A. P. Saunders, *Observations on the Different Opinions Held as to the Changes Proposed in the Examination Statute* (1830), 9; *Considerations Respecting the Most Effectual Means of Encouraging Mathematics at Oxford* (1830); repr. in Froude, *Remains*, pt 1, vol ii, p. 333.

[84] The others were Francis Thornhill Baring, Charles Wood, George Cornewall Lewis, W. E. Gladstone, Robert Lowe and Stafford Northcote.

students were delayed by compulsory Lit. Hum. from embarking on their preferred studies. Others found the requirement to take a second school a burden to be got through in the shortest possible time, cramming their reading for the additional subject into six months after they had taken Lit. Hum. (the examinations being held twice a year, in May and November).

Single-subject specialization was eventually permitted in 1864, when those who had obtained a minimum of third-class honours in any one honour school were permitted to proceed to their degrees. This exemption was extended in 1870 to those who gained fourth classes. Once compulsory Lit. Hum. had been cast aside, the claims for the recognition of further alternative areas of study made themselves felt. A theology honour school was created in 1869, and jurisprudence and modern history came into being as separate entities in 1872. New honour schools were created in the arts: oriental languages, divided into Indian languages and Semitic languages, in 1886; English language and literature in 1893, and modern languages in 1903. From 1886 the particular branch of the natural science school in which candidates had specialized—chemistry, physics, physiology, zoology, botany or geology—was specified, astronomy being added to the list in 1895, and engineering science in 1909.

A parallel trend was the gradual separation of the examinations of those seeking honours and those who were content to try for a pass degree. Originally all candidates, regardless of their ambitions, were examined together by the same examiners, who recorded at the foot of the class list the number, but not the names, of those who had achieved the minimum standard to qualify for a degree. After 1830, on the basis of lists submitted in advance by candidates of the classical books in which they were prepared to be examined, the examiners sifted out those who were seeking honours, and dealt with them separately. The same principle operated for the new degree-qualifying subjects created in 1850. For each subject the reading required from those seeking honours was specified; a lesser amount, designated as the 'minimum', was prescribed for those aiming only at a pass.[85] Thereafter the two forms of BA course began to part company. In 1865 a separate board of examiners was instituted to assess those seeking only a pass in Lit. Hum. A more fundamental difference was created in 1872 when the pass school was reconstituted, on the lines of the London pass BA and the Cambridge poll degree, as a combination of subjects (or 'Groups').[86] Passmen were henceforth required to take three subjects, one of which had to be a language, to obtain their degree. These could be taken at intervals, enabling Cecil Rhodes, for example, to spread his final BA examinations over four years, between 1877 and 1881. Most opted to do Group A1, which required a

---

[85] *Calendar* (1855), 136–7.
[86] SCOC (1867), Qs 1276, 2455; D. A. Winstanley, *Later Victorian Cambridge* (1947), 151.

Greek philosophical work and a portion of a Greek or Latin historian; as a result the school was often described as 'pass Greats'.[87]

The reformed pass school potentially represented a significant curricular innovation. It gave the earliest recognition in the Oxford course to English and modern languages, and offered undergraduates the chance to combine ancient and modern, literary and scientific subjects. This potential was never fully exploited. Few took modern languages; candidates were warned that a working knowledge of French would not satisfy examiners whose concerns were largely grammatical.[88] The science options were rarely taken, nor were they encouraged by the Museum professoriate. Other modern subjects proved to be makeweights; B3 (political economy, 'pol. econ.') acquired instant and enduring popularity as an easy option. The pass course nevertheless had its defenders, who felt that it had a useful role in combining humane studies with subjects more closely connected to the student's future occupation. Groups B4 (a branch of legal study, 'contracts'), D (elements of religious knowledge) added in 1886, and E (military studies) created in 1904, were taken by intending lawyers, clergymen and army officers respectively. In 1907 the recently created certificate and diploma courses were allowed to count towards a pass degree, enabling a student intended for business to combine his classical books with reading for the diploma in economics; or the prospective agriculturalist to combine them with the rural economy diploma.[89] This also offered a route to graduation for those taking diplomas in the new disciplines of geography and anthropology.

The mixed pass school offered one approach to the contested issue of specialization. After 1864 the security for common, preliminary studies rested on the requirement that all candidates should pass Moderations. This exercise was established in 1850 as an intermediate stage in the BA course, usually taken at the end of the second year. Moderations ('the first public examination', as it was confusingly termed, being in fact the second examination taken after matriculation) comprised a pass and an honours examination in classical subjects and a voluntary examination in pure mathematics. For those not seeking honours, pass Moderations in Latin, Greek and a choice of mathematics or logic was intended to provide a stimulus for exertion in mid-course, ending 'the ample leisure for all mischievous and idle pursuits' which the gap between Responsions and the final examinations had often produced.[90]

Moderations offered a ledge to which defenders of the classical curriculum could retreat once the compulsory Lit. Hum. barrier had been breached.

---

[87] In the 1890s nearly 90% of passmen took A1; in the 1900s nearly 80% did so. The remainder offered either classical oriental languages, or modern European languages.

[88] Stedman (ed.), *Oxford*, 211.

[89] J. L. Myres, *Diplomas and Degree Examinations* (1906).

[90] [B. Jowett and A. P. Stanley], *Suggestions for an Improvement of the Examination Statute* (1848), 19.

This second line of defence held from 1864 to 1887. All undergraduates, no matter which final honour school they intended to read, had to spend at the very minimum the first year working for a predominantly classical examination. For Oxford scientists this represented a particular grievance, and some looked to faculty bifurcation, creating a distinct science degree with its own preliminary requirements shorn of Greek, as a solution. London University had been awarding undergraduate BSc degrees since 1860 and the practice had been adopted elsewhere in Europe; the London LL B offered a similar precedent in the case of law.[91] But Oxford's proposed BNS (bachelor of natural science) degree, allowing scientists to offer German or French as an alternative to one of the two classical languages, foundered in 1880 upon divisions among the scientists and legal doubts about the status and privileges attached to the new credential.[92]

With the defeat of separate science degrees there was little alternative to a fissure in the arts course itself. The creation in 1882 of faculties with control of the various honour schools which fell within their subject area encouraged a concerted attack on Moderations by non-classicists. In November 1886 the scientists freed themselves from Moderations, when the natural science preliminary, set up in 1871 as part of the final examination, was recognized as a qualifying part of the first public examination. Mathematical honour Moderations was accorded equal status. Lawyers also obtained their own jurisprudence preliminary. The historians, divided among themselves over E. A. Freeman's ambitious scheme for an ancient and modern history honour Moderations, which was defeated in 1886, ended up with nothing. For nearly thirty years modern historians had to take the jurisprudence preliminary if they wished to avoid having to take classical Moderations. Only the Theology Board declined the chance to establish its own intermediate examination, doubting whether the interests of theology would be advanced 'by such a premature specialization'.[93]

The lurch after 1882 into what was described as 'that kind of specialization which is most foreign to the spirit and traditions of Oxford'[94] brought a reaction in the following decade. No special preliminary examination was devised for the new oriental languages school; orientalists usually took classical Moderations. Candidates for the new honour school in English language and literature were required to submit to the discipline of classical Moderations, and modest proposals by the historians to introduce historical papers into pass Moderations were defeated in 1897.[95] Modern linguists did

[91] PP 1872 xxv, Q. 3359.
[92] *Gazette* vii (8 May 1877), 375; ix (20 May 1879), 366; *The Times* 23 May 1879, 10; *Gazette* x (3 Feb. 1880), 233; x (27 Apr. 1880), 346; *The Times* 28 Apr. 1880, 7.
[93] Minutes of the Theology Board, 30 May 1883, OUA FA/4/19/1/1, p. 9.
[94] *Oxford and the Nation: by some Oxford tutors* (1907), 28.
[95] A. L. F. Beeston, 'Arabic teaching at Oxford', *OM* ns lxxii (1991), 19; *Gazette* xxvii (16 Mar. 1897), 383; *The Times* 18 Mar. 1897, 7.

obtain a preliminary in 1908 and the historians finally secured their Previous examination in 1914. Candidates for ordinary degrees, meanwhile, continued to be denied remission from the classical grind of pass or honour Moderations.

These changes left Responsions in the last line of defence for the traditional curriculum. The only significant change in its content between 1808 and 1914 was that after 1850 elementary mathematics was required from all candidates in place of logic. The examination became a byword for pedagogic conservatism; non-Euclidean proofs were eventually permitted in the geometry examination in 1902,[96] and unseen translations were allowed in 1900 in place of set books in the classical papers, but staples like the Greek grammar paper were defended to the last by an alliance of traditionalists and private crammers.[97]

Responsions became essentially an examination of work done at school, taken at progressively earlier points in the undergraduate course. After 1849 the examination could be taken in the first year and the limits of standing were abolished altogether in 1864: the stronger colleges began to require their undergraduates to take Responsions in their first term of residence. As the line between school and university work became more sharply drawn, college tutors were less willing to prepare students for this elementary exercise, and the institution of school examinations, which from 1874 were recognized as exempting candidates from Responsions, hastened the process of shifting the task of preparation on to the schoolmasters.[98] By a piecemeal addition of new exemptions, nearly fifty alternative qualifications were recognized before 1914, ranging from the certificate of the Joint Matriculation Board to the French baccalaureate, provided that those qualifications included Greek, Latin and mathematics.[99] Intending undergraduates who were unable to enter school examinations, or who were not up to the standard (which was higher than Responsions), were enabled from 1881 to take a special examination 'in lieu of Responsions' held in Oxford during September before term began. This soon became the most popular route through the first stage of the examination system.

No university entrance examination existed at Oxford before 1914. As late as the 1890s nearly 20 per cent of undergraduates took Responsions after they had come into residence. Admissions were in the hands of the colleges, and the University was required to matriculate any man whom a college chose to admit. Sooner or later an undergraduate wanting a degree would

---

[96] G. Howson, *A History of Mathematics Education in England* (1982), 262 n. 44.

[97] *OM* 20 Feb. 1895, 240–1; *Gazette* xxxi (4 Dec. 1900), 192; *OM* 21 Nov. 1907, 98; *OM* 28 Nov. 1907, 107; *Athenaeum* 10 Dec. 1904, 806; 16 Dec. 1911, 769–70.

[98] Minute-book of the Tutors' Committee, 20 Nov. 1867, QCA. Certificates of the Oxford and Cambridge Joint Board were recognized in 1874, the Oxford Locals in 1877, and the certificate of the Scottish Education Department in 1889.

[99] *Examination Statutes* (1914), 11–16.

have to surmount the Responsions hurdle, and by 1900 the majority of colleges required intending students to have passed Responsions or some equivalent before coming into residence. In some, however, this remained only a recommendation, for weaker colleges were in no position to place obstacles in the way of commoners on whose fees they depended. The history of proposals for matriculation examinations, dating from Richard Whately's initiative in 1828, was one of resolute collegiate obstruction.[100] Lord Curzon's renewed call in 1909 to the University to 'grapple with the problem on broad and courageous lines' only stirred F. J. Lys, the Bursar of Worcester, to conjure up dire visions of falling numbers and lost revenues; a vociferous campaign achieved the defeat of a proposed university matriculation examination in 1914, one of the last acts of Congregation before the outbreak of war.[101] By then, however, the biggest obstacle to implementing a university matriculation requirement was the absence of any general school-leaving qualification correlated with university preliminary examinations. Any such reform depended on the existence of a consensus about what subjects should constitute the common basis of education for 18-year-olds. As the celebrated battles in Edwardian Oxford and Cambridge over compulsory Greek showed, no such agreement existed. Greek remained compulsory in both universities until after the First World War.[102] It was not until 1926, nearly a century after Whately's original proposal, that Responsions finally became a university entrance examination.

One ancient feature in degree examining, the centre-piece of the 1800 reform, outlived compulsory Greek for entrance by a decade. Compulsory divinity was not finally abolished until 1931, though non-Anglicans were permitted, after 1855, to offer a miscellaneous selection of 'substituted matter'. By the late nineteenth century, however, the divinity examination had become a shadow of the awesome proceeding undergone by earlier generations of nervous examinees. Its demise dated from Jowett's attempted nomination in 1883 of R. F. Horton, a Congregational minister and fellow of New College, to a vacant examinership in the rudiments of faith and religion.[103] During the ensuing controversy, a compromise was reached by which Group D was added to the pass school with the same Anglican denominational safeguards as those attached to the theology honour school. At the same time the compulsory divinity examination, from which the Thirty-nine Articles were excluded, was downgraded to a second-year

---

[100] RCO (1850), report, 68; Guardian 4 May 1859, 392; See above p. 33.

[101] Lord Curzon of Kedleston, Principles and Methods of University Reform (1909), 114; OM 11 June 1914, 389–92.

[102] C. E. Mallet, A History of the University of Oxford (3 vols 1927) iii. 471, implies that in 1911 Oxford mathematicians and scientists were released from Greek. The statute proposing this was, in fact, defeated by a vote of Convocation (595 to 360): Gazette xlii (29 Nov. 1911), 213.

[103] Horton's nomination was defeated by a large vote (155 to 576) in Convocation: Gazette xiv (11 Dec. 1883), 179, (24 Dec. 1883), 197.

exercise, 'holy scripture', comprising a written paper followed by a viva. 'Divvers', as the new exercise became widely known, was placed in the hands of the pass moderators, who might be of any religion, or none. They were rapidly overwhelmed by the system of oral examining, much as their predecessors had been in the 1820s. Earlier safeguards limiting the number of vivas in Moderations to sixteen per day were swept away. The result was soon apparent, as one candidate recorded: 'March 13 [1893]. Golf with Austin and W. E. C[leaver]. Divinity Schools at 2 p.m. Viva at 5.15. George asked four questions, to which I answered "Don't know". Verdict— "Don't know much about Samuel, but perhaps enough, and Gospels good." Testamur at 5.30. Record time?'[104] In 1911 the pass moderators reckoned that they were conducting holy scripture vivas at a rate of eighty a day, in what was freely acknowledged to be a 'blasphemous farce'.[105]

An aspect of the system which remained roughly constant between 1800 and 1914 was the comparatively high proportion, by historical rather than modern standards, of undergraduates who qualified for their degrees. Fiction and colourful anecdotage might suggest otherwise, particularly that informed by the experiences of the high-born, who might have little incentive to work for degrees, or those well-documented literary figures—such as Shelley, Swinburne and Max Beerbohm—who left the University without graduating. Yet the majority of undergraduates throughout this period stayed the course: taking the undergraduate population as a whole, the proportion graduating rose from just under 60 per cent in the second decade of the century to over 70 per cent by the 1850s. There was a slight fall during the 1870s, which was attributable to the liberal admissions requirements adopted by the censors of the Unattached students.[106] These were tightened in the following decade, when over 75 per cent of Oxford students graduated. After 1890 the picture is distorted by increasing numbers of students who matriculated to obtain the BMus degree and the small contingent coming up to read for the research degrees of BSc and BLitt (instituted in 1895). The University Registrar attempted a calculation of BA graduation rates between 1882 and 1901 excluding these students, and arrived at a figure of 76.7 per cent.[107]

Global figures mask the crucial division among undergraduates in the late nineteenth century: the gulf between 'passmen' and 'classmen', which widened after 1872. An experienced college tutor who had taught many passmen, P. A. Wright-Henderson of Wadham, deplored the division as an entirely artificial one, institutionalized by the examination system, and

---

[104] *Memorials of Lionel Helbert* (1926), 38; Revd H. B. George was a moderator in Hilary 1893: *Gazette* xxiii (28 Mar. 1893), 370–1.
[105] HCP 88 (1911), 245–6; 95 (1913), 7; *Oxford and the Nation*, 97.
[106] About a third of the students unattached to a college or hall admitted from 1868 to 1883 graduated (excluding those who migrated to colleges).
[107] *Gazette* xxxix (2 Mar. 1909), 465.

founded on the questionable assumption that the passman was an entirely different creature from his counterpart reading for honours.[108] One pass coach complained that under the new regime the passman was to be goaded through examinations 'by penalty and through fear', a charge not denied by Edwin Palmer, Corpus Professor of Latin, who in 1877 admitted to regarding pass education as 'a sort of police supervision'.[109] Pass examinations embodied the less-eligibility principle: whereas honours men were permitted some choice in the questions to be answered, the passman was expected to attempt all the questions set and was exposed to interrogation on minor points of detail of set texts and grammar. Subjecting passmen to an increasing number of examinations helped to bring potential idlers more frequently to account. But the strategy had the unforeseen practical result of limiting the consequences of failure, which was already ceasing to involve exposure to public shame. Being ploughed was less catastrophic than in the first half of the century—a comparatively small amount of work had to be repeated—and by becoming a commonplace event, it could even be regarded with levity. By its character and the methods of teaching which it called into being, the pass school was in danger of becoming a joke; L. R. Farnell left a vivid picture of the 'galley-slaves' drilled for the examination by a successful pass coach.[110] Of the two undergraduates depicted by William Warde Fowler, a Lincoln tutor, in 1904, the passman conformed comfortably to the prevailing stereotype: a muscular Brasenose commoner who cheerfully occupied the interval between his failure in 'pol. econ.' in Trinity term and retaking the paper in Michaelmas with a cricketing tour of the West Indies.[111]

With such images in their minds, some examiners attempted to use their office to force up standards. In 1874 the increasing rigour of Responsions was alleged to be driving intending ordinands to theological colleges, while a sudden increase in the number of 'plucks' in 1877, brought to light by C. L. Dodgson, led to a warning by G. R. Scott of Merton that country squires were also in danger of being forced out of the University.[112] In the early twentieth century a desire to expel the passmen was alleged to lie behind a new wave of purges in Responsions. A similar determination was shown in 1907 by the examiners in final pass Group A1, who, without notice, altered the practice of a quarter of a century and reversed the order of the philosophy and the history papers. One candidate fainted when he discovered the change, and an abnormally high number withdrew.[113]

---

[108] P. A. Wright-Henderson, *Glasgow and Balliol and Other Essays* (1926), 121.
[109] James Rumsey, *Pass Examinations in Oxford* (1876), 4; *UOC* (1877), evidence, Q. 1627.
[110] L. R. Farnell, *An Oxonian Looks Back* (1934), 72–3.
[111] W. Warde Fowler, *An Oxford Correspondence of 1903* (1904), 15, 89.
[112] *Guardian* 11 Nov. 1874, 1457; C. L. Dodgson, *Responsions: Hilary 1877* (np nd); *OUC* (1877), appx, 127.
[113] *Guardian* 14 Nov. 1906; *Times Educational Supplement* 6 Feb. 1912, 15; 2 Apr. 1912, 40; *Varsity* 7 Feb. 1907, 209.

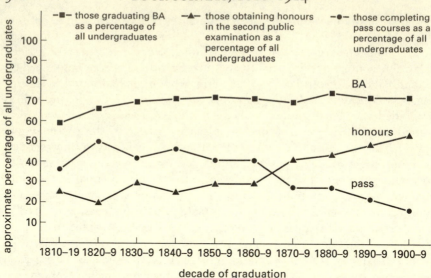

FIGURE 11.1 Proportion of Oxford men qualifying for pass and honours degrees, by decade of taking the second public examination, 1810–1909

The results of this pressure bearing down on the passmen are shown in Fig. 11.1. At mid-century passmen accounted for the great majority of undergraduates; nearly a half of undergraduates took only an ordinary degree, in addition to those who took no degree at all. The balance suddenly and emphatically turned in the generation matriculating in the mid-1860s. During the following decade over 40 per cent of all undergraduates (60 per cent of those who graduated BA) had taken honours, while passmen dropped to under 30 per cent. The downward trend continued to the end of this period; of those matriculating in the academic year 1909/10 only 16 per cent took pass degrees.

The numbers of undergraduates obtaining honours in each honour school after 1865 are shown in Fig. 11.2. Despite losing its compulsory status after 1864, Lit. Hum. experienced an almost continuous increase in numbers, peaking in the early twentieth century. Growth during the 1860s and 1870s was admittedly modest, and the school's association during those decades with free-thinking scepticism may well have narrowed its appeal. The new theology school and the modern history school looked safer to Churchmen than the Greats school from which the religious element had gradually been excluded. Lit. Hum. recovered sharply in the 1880s; the resurgence of Greats was perhaps the most remarkable curricular development of late nineteenth-century Oxford. It was not until the turn of the century that it was decisively overtaken by modern history. Jurisprudence enjoyed rapid growth and was swelled after 1905 by the Rhodes scholars, for whom it was the most popular

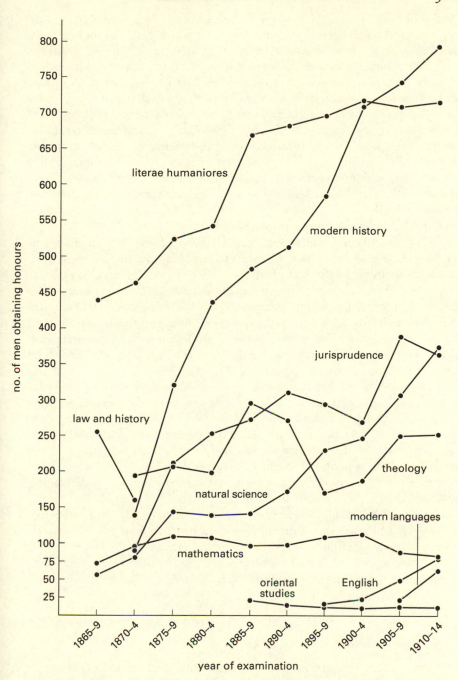

no. of men obtaining honours

literae humaniores

modern history

jurisprudence

law and history

natural science

theology

mathematics

modern languages

oriental studies

English

year of examination

FIGURE 11.2 Subjects taken by successful candidates in final honour schools (men), 1865–1914

choice of honour school. Theology declined in the 1890s, probably because of the counter-attraction of the new pass Group D, which was more closely tailored to the needs of clerical education. Oriental languages, always a minority subject, came near to being discontinued in the early 1890s, when there were more examiners than candidates. The English and modern languages schools had made only a limited impact on the studies of Oxford men by 1914. Numbers taking mathematics were inflated before 1865 by 'honorary fourths' and classical double firsts (see Table 11.A1); thereafter it was confined to specialists and attracted on average twenty successful candidates a year. More controversial was the performance of the natural science school, whose slow growth is discussed elsewhere in these volumes.[114] By the eve of the First World War, however, natural science was the third-largest honour school.

Within this broad picture three refinements can be added. There were considerable collegiate variations, such as the predominance of Balliol in Greats and Keble in theology (Table 11.A2); these differences were even more pronounced in the case of the pass school (see Table 11.A3).[115] Between each honour school there were, in addition, well-understood differences in prestige. Lit. Hum. continued to be described in the *University Handbook*, in 1913, as 'the premier school in dignity and importance', despite ceasing to be the largest school.[116] When modern history overtook it for the first time, in 1898, the *Isis* declared the development 'only to be expected'. Modern history, it pointed out, was thought to be one of the easiest schools to get through, less demanding in some respects than the pass school, and more pleasurable.[117] These differences partly reflected the distribution of college scholarships and exhibitions. As late as 1910 over a half were awarded in classics, ensuring that a disproportionate share of the most able recruits were likely to read Greats. The dearth of commoners taking the natural science school left competitively recruited scholars and exhibitioners—few as they were—as a dominant element among those reading for the school. As a result, the majority of those classed in Lit. Hum., mathematics and natural science were firsts or seconds. By contrast, about 60 per cent of those in jurisprudence, modern history and theology between 1875 and 1914 were thirds or fourths. Sudden increases in the failure-rate in these latter schools, which were overwhelmingly populated by commoners, suggest that the examiners periodically felt the need to reassert standards.[118]

[114] See Ch. 22 and Pt 2, Ch. 20.

[115] For comparable Cambridge figures see A. I. Tillyard, *A History of University Reform* (1913), 301.

[116] *Oxford University Handbook* (1913), 135.

[117] *Isis* 11 June 1898, 326.

[118] In the 1890s the proportion of candidates in Lit. Hum., math. and natural science who were not, for whatever reason, classed was about 5%; in jurisprudence, modern history and theology the average was over 10%, and in some years over 15%.

In the early twentieth century nearly a half of Oxford students completing their courses had done so in either Greats or pass Greats (Table 11.A4). Classics remained entrenched during the earlier stages of the examination system, which inevitably reflected the prevailing balance of the public school curriculum: even after 1887, when alternatives were allowed, over 60 per cent of undergraduates had taken pass or honour classical Moderations (Table 11.A5). Those alternatives were not all interchangeable, and the late Victorian undergraduate embarked, almost from his first year, on a clearly marked progression of examinations (the route to each final honour school being illustrated by diagrams in the *Student's Handbook*). Differences in these routes affected the overall duration of the BA course: a majority of those reading natural science took four years, as did almost all Greats men, whereas by the end of the period, history, jurisprudence and theology were more commonly completed in three years (Table 11.A6).

The first women students to sit as candidates for final honour schools, in Trinity term 1884, did not do so as matriculated members of the University and, not being permitted to graduate, they were not subjected to the same rigid course structures as male undergraduates.[119] The statute admitting them to certain of the public examinations 'contained no reference to residence or to membership of any institution, nor did it prescribe Responsions or any intermediate examination'.[120] Although all Oxford's undergraduate examinations were opened to women during the ten years up to 1894, and women candidates sat the same papers at the same times as the men, the publication of the results contrived to ensure that the two groups were kept distinct. Separate class lists were published in the *Gazette*, the men in customary Latinized form, the women in English: Emily Penrose, to whom the Lit. Hum. examiners chaired by W. A. Spooner awarded a first in 1892, had achieved the same distinction as that conferred at the same time by 'Gulielmus A. Spooner' and others upon, for example, 'Myres Joannes L. e Coll. Nov'.[121]

Women candidates entering the schools were also not required to conform to what a French observer in 1895 called 'the sacred tradition of the white tie and the gown'.[122] The proctors' memorandum to undergraduates on matriculation, first produced in 1904 presumably in response to the arrival of Rhodes scholars, stipulated that coloured shirts or collars were no more admissible than coloured waistcoats.[123] Subfusc reinforced what had become one of the collective experiences of late Victorian student life. For undergraduates in the early nineteenth century, who were examined singly over a

---

[119] The position of women in the University is discussed in Pt 2, Ch. 10.
[120] A. M. A. H. Rogers, *Degrees by Degrees* (1938), 16.
[121] *Gazette* xxii (4 Aug. 1892), 607, 612.
[122] J. Bardoux, *Memories of Oxford* (1899), 75.
[123] Bodl. G. A. Oxon. c. 107.

period of several weeks, the experience was very much an individual trial; solitary candidates sheltered under the Schools Tower 'amidst the compassionate exhortations of their friends to "keep the pecker up"'.[124] After 1883, when the final honour schools were held only once a year, and the academic year assumed its modern pattern, all those following the same course of study went in together: Edwardian student periodicals described the scene on the first day, as the crowds made their way down to the Examination Schools and waited for the electric bells to summon them to the designated examination hall. These later generations entering the Schools were also older, in general, than their predecessors. Nearly half of those who matriculated in 1818/19 had taken the public examination by the age of 21; in the late 1890s only a quarter did so. By then, nearly two-thirds taking their final schools were aged between 22 and 24, and nearly a tenth were 25 or older.

Undergraduates responded to the demands made on them with remarkable compliance. Consent was encouraged by the general willingness of examiners to adhere to the injunction of the 1800 statute against undue harshness.[125] Describing the examination to his mother in 1821, W. F. Hook commented that the examiners behaved 'very good-naturedly to me'. His impression was shared by others.[126] The same indulgence may not always have been extended towards the obviously rakish characters who presented themselves at the examiners' green-baize table. Yet few examiners incurred the public odium to which H. A. Woodgate of St John's was exposed after his tenure of office in 1827–8, when he was said to have shown relish 'in seeing men floored'.[127] Examiners very rarely came in for abuse from hecklers in the undergraduate gallery at the Encaenia ceremony. Indeed, in 1850 the masters of the schools were 'much applauded' from that quarter, perhaps confirming the allegation of Robert Lowe, who had examined Responsions in the 1830s, that the standards which they exacted were minimal.[128] The worst that Travers Twiss, a former public examiner, had to endure when introducing the honorands (in Latin) as Regius Professor of Civil Law were such well-worn interruptions as 'That will do, Sir; now construe' and 'We won't detain you any longer.'[129] By the end of the century undergraduate journals and college debates permitted more considered expressions of opinion; but, though college and university discipline were much commen-

[124] F. A. W. Buckley, *The Natural History of Tuft-Hunters and Toadies* (1853), 39 n.
[125] *Statutes* ii. 33.
[126] W. R. W. Stephens, *The Life and Letters of Walter Farquhar Hook* (2 vols 1878) i. 37; *An Eton Boy: being the letters of James Milnes Gaskell*, ed. C. M. Gaskell (1939), 181; *Letters of Hartley Coleridge*, ed. C. E. Griggs and E. L. Griggs (1936), 19.
[127] Philodicaeus, *A Brief Appeal to the Good Sense of the University of Oxford on Classification of Merit* (1829), 16.
[128] *Herald* 15 June 1850; A. P. Martin, *Life and Letters of the Rt Hon Robert Lowe, Viscount Sherbrooke* (2 vols 1893) i. 29.
[129] *Oxford Undergraduate's Journal* 13 June 1866, 74.

ted on, little was said about examinations, which were treated as inevitable, fixed occurrences. The motion that 'the present or any system of Examinations is as injurious as it is painful' was lost without a division in the Union in 1876; and in 1880 the same body rejected the suggestion that all honours examinations should be abolished (31 to 59).[130] One perceived act of defiance did, however, receive a stern response. A. E. Housman, who had obtained a first in classical Moderations in 1879, but who had no taste for the philosophy and ancient history required in Lit. Hum., handed in papers regarded by the examiners as 'so ludicrously bad' as to amount to treating the proceedings with contempt. He was, unusually, failed outright, without being credited with passes in the equivalent pass school groups which the honours examiners were permitted to award candidates who were not classed.[131]

Extensive cheating might have been as dangerous to the system as defiance. When the major shift to written work was under discussion in 1830, Richard Jenkyns, Master of Balliol, exhibited his habitual dread of undergraduate misconduct by proposing that at least two examiners should be on duty 'to keep watch over the Pens and Pockets of the writers'.[132] Collusion and cribbing in the pass school seems, however, to have become a significant problem by 1870;[133] one tutor noted in 1869 that in the examination room candidates seeking help from their neighbours were prepared to ignore the normally rigid undergraduate etiquette forbidding conversation between men who had not been previously introduced.[134] In 1882 it was considered to be necessary to have one invigilator for every fifty candidates to ensure the 'stricter superintendence' of candidates in the new Schools building, the design of which enabled the examiner to 'command' every part of the room.[135] Such precautions led university reformers to draw an unfavourable contrast between the ethics of Oxford passmen and the 'honor codes' established by student classes in North American universities.[136] The proctors' manuals for the end of the century do not, however, suggest that the incidence of cheating was significant. An instance of flagrant misconduct by an examiner was brought to light by a candidate in the pass school who, though placed at an advantage by the irregularity, felt honour-bound to report the matter to his tutor.[137]

---

[130] *Proceedings of the Oxford Union Society, 1871–1878* (1878), 164; ibid. *1878–1884* (1891), 59.

[131] P. G. Naiditch, *A. E. Housman at University College London: the election of 1892* (Leiden 1988), 202–3. He was obliged to return to Oxford to take Groups A1, A2 and B3 in Michaelmas 1881 and Trinity 1882 in order to qualify for his degree.

[132] R. Jenkyns to Vice-Chancellor, 31 May 1830, Bodl. MS Top. Oxon. d. 15, fo 61.

[133] *Cornhill Magazine* 11 (1865), 230; *Oxford Undergraduate's Journal* 23 Feb. 1871, 957.

[134] R. F. Clarke, *The Influence of Pass Examinations* (1869), 11.

[135] See the architect's comments in *Gazette* vi (30 May 1876), 407; HCP 3 (1882), reports of 3 and 10 Nov. 1882.

[136] *Oxford and the Nation*, 23.

[137] The case of Philip Aldred, 1881, OUA WP/β/1/2, fo 44. The proctors' manual, 1911–12, records a case of expulsion for cribbing in schools: OUA WP/γ/7/6, fo 127.

If there was a sustained questioning of the value of examinations as a form of educational practice, it came not from the undergraduate victims but from the University's senior members. In his Creweian oration, delivered at the Encaenia ceremony in July 1800, William Crowe spoke of the consensus within the University which had marked the passage of the examination statute.[138] By the end of the 1820s this unity of purpose was lost amidst a reaction against the examination system in general and the award of honours in particular.[139] The class list was always open to the religious objection that it aroused feelings of pride and envy. William Wilberforce warned his sons of the dangers of 'emulation', though the historian of Oxford evangelicalism has noted that its adherents enjoyed significant success in the Schools.[140] None the less, the potential force of this criticism was acknowledged in 1829 by the Hebdomadal Board committee, which cited 'strong objections on moral grounds' to the idea of a competitive order of merit.[141] A more fundamental question, which anticipated some Tractarian misgivings about the examinations, divided the committee: did the examiners' oath to admit no 'unworthy' candidate oblige them to consider the moral merits of the candidates? As things stood, the University's highest distinctions might be conferred on a student of notorious character. Baden Powell lampooned the impracticability of applying moral criteria in a sketch of examiners confronting candidates with porters' lists of those who had missed chapel or who had kept irregular gate hours. Four members of the committee, Richard Whately, Edward Hawkins, Philip Wynter and R. A. Thorp of Corpus, claimed that they were expressing the view of a majority of college tutors that the public examinations should be purely a 'test of *literary* merit'.[142] Doubts persisted among the generation influenced by Tractarianism as to whether the types of knowledge rewarded in the Schools served religious purposes; Edward King, later Regius Professor of Pastoral Theology, who read only for a pass degree, has been identified as an exemplar of 'the Tractarian emphasis on the priority of moral attitude over intellectual virtuosity'.[143]

Those who resented the narrow reading demanded by the schools offered another element of opposition to the class list after 1830. This view enjoyed particular currency at Christ Church, where it drew upon traditional ideals of gentlemanly scholarship. Sir Henry Acland, later Regius Professor of Medicine, who took only a pass degree in 1840, but who published in the year of his graduation a treatise based on wide classical reading entitled *The*

[138] W. Crowe, *Oratio Creweiana* (1800), 18.

[139] See p. 20.

[140] A. R. Ashwell, *Life of the Right Reverend Samuel Wilberforce* (3 vols 1880) i. 13–14; J. S. Reynolds, *The Evangelicals at Oxford, 1735–1871* (Abingdon 1975), 92–3.

[141] Report of the Committee (1829), 7; cf *Herald* 26 Dec. 1829.

[142] Bodl. MS Baden Powell 31 (13); Memorial annexed to the Report of the Committee (1829), 4.

[143] G. Rowell, *The Vision Glorious* (1983), 141–2.

Plains of Troy, was an embodiment of the ideal. The strength of this sentiment lent purpose to the otherwise anachronistic distinction of the 'honorary fourth', enabling examiners to raise up patently well-read candidates,
including J. R. Bloxam, John Ruskin and Robert Cecil (a future Chancellor
of the University), who had chosen only to read for pass degrees, from
among the otherwise anonymous ranks of passmen. For these men, as for
the Tractarians, the pursuit of high honours had no appeal: the proportion
gaining firsts in Lit. Hum. during 1840–9 was the lowest of any decade
between 1810 and 1899.

A second wave of criticism arose in the 1870s. This was expressed most
vehemently by Mark Pattison and A. H. Sayce, a fellow of Queen's and later
Professor of Assyriology, and was identified with the movement for the
endowment of research.[144] 'Originality, bold speculation, unremunerative
study, are antithetic to all the qualities fostered by an examination,' Sayce
contended.[145] A younger generation of scholars who had studied at German
universities returned impressed by the disinterested pursuit of scholarship
which the German system seemed to encourage. English universities, which
founded their education upon punishments and rewards, compared unfavourably; 'the system here', R. W. Macan, a tutor at Christ Church, told the
Selborne Commission in 1877, 'seems to be based upon the supposition that
the undergraduate does not wish to learn'.[146] The rhetoric directed against
examinations in the 1870s was more muted in the following decade, as some
critics became reconciled to a system which presented opportunities for
disciplinary specialization. The scheme devised by the philologists in 1887
for a modern languages school illustrated the extent to which the research
party of the previous decade now saw specialized honour schools, controlled
by professors, as the most effective means of furthering their interests in
Oxford. R. W. Macan and Henry Nettleship, both 'Germanizers' in the
1870s, became keen proponents of new honour schools. 'The ideal University', Macan wrote in 1891, 'should be prepared to examine its *alumni* in any
sufficiently large and prominent subject which is capable of scientific treatment.'[147] The researchers followed the path of an earlier generation: Henry
Acland helped to draw up the natural science school, and Ruskin himself
suggested in 1874 the establishment of an honour school of fine art.

Oxford's rigid format of written examinations placed a heavy premium
upon knowledge that was 'testable', and this constraint also attracted critics.
Little headway was made by those who advocated that theses should count

[144] M. Pattison, *Suggestions on Academical Organisation with Especial Reference to Oxford*
(Edinburgh 1868), 242–70; M. Pattison, 'Review of the situation' and A. H. Sayce, 'Results of
the examination system at Oxford' in *Essays on the Endowment of Research* (1876), 17–22, 124–
48; *UOC* (1877), evidence, Q. 4115; *Academy* 11 Dec. 1875, 603.
[145] Sayce, 'Results of the examination system', 144.
[146] *UOC* (1877), evidence, Q. 4609.
[147] R. W. Macan, 'Oxford prospects', *Educational Review* i (Nov. 1891), 5.

towards classes, though a voluntary option was introduced in the modern history school in 1907.[148] The limitations imposed by conventional examining seem to have dissuaded the anthropologists from seeking honour school status in 1914; in the anthropology diploma course the final assessment attached great importance to evidence of individual research, including 'printed matter, essays, collections of notes' undertaken by students during their course-work.[149] The natural science honour school alone achieved some success in breaking away from the restrictions of paper work. The first regulations for that school, produced in 1852, pre-dated the opening of the University Museum; and, in the absence of suitable accommodation, made no provision for practicals. But in 1858 the natural science examiners memorialized the Hebdomadal Council to provide laboratory accommodation and materials for practical examinations. Acland introduced practicals into the BM examination in the same year,[150] and by 1862, when the Museum was in full operation, part of the honours examination in all three constituent parts of the natural science school—chemistry, mechanical philosophy and physiology—was practical. In the early twentieth century Oxford chemists and physicists underwent a practical examination at the University Museum occupying two or three days.[151]

Despite the appeal of its arguments, the movement to reduce the importance of examinations at Oxford in this period has to be accounted comparatively weak, and ultimately unsuccessful. Auberon Herbert's national manifesto of 1888, *The Sacrifice of Education to Examination*, produced surprisingly little resonance in Oxford.[152] One explanation was that Herbert's main targets were the divorce of teaching from examining, competitive examinations for government offices and excessive pressure on schoolchildren.[153] To the undergraduate honour schools, which were not founded upon external examining and were not strictly competitive between individuals, these complaints were barely applicable. Moreover, the college system offered important safeguards. In a residential institution, as J. B. Mozley, the Regius Professor of Divinity pointed out in a sermon entitled 'The Principle of Emulation', published in 1876, moral and social influences could be brought to bear to restrain the excesses of competition.[154] Though he

[148] P. Slee, *Learning and a Liberal Education* (1986), 148.

[149] *Student's Handbook* (1909), 314; minutes of the Committee for Anthropology, 31 Jan. 1913, 24 Feb. 1913, 6 Mar. 1914, OUA UDC/M/14/1.

[150] Hebdomadal Council minutes, 29 Nov. 1858, OUA HC/1/2/1, p. 252; Statute to be Promulgated, 28 Feb. 1859, Bodl. G. A. Oxon. b. 29; *Lancet* 19 June 1858, 609; *Calendar* (1862), 140 n.; see the surviving physiology and anatomy practical papers, set in 1859, and chemistry papers for 1864, in the collection of unpublished natural science papers, Bodl. MS 2626 d. 35.

[151] *Gazette* iii (14 May 1872), 200–1; *Student's Handbook* (1906), 167, 169.

[152] *Journal of Education* (Feb. 1889), 98.

[153] J. Roach, *Public Examinations in England, 1850–1900* (Cambridge 1971), 280–1.

[154] J. B. Mozley, *Sermons Preached before the University of Oxford and on Various Occasions* (1876), 266–8. The sermon was originally delivered at Lancing College, but its implications

regarded the class lists as pernicious, Pattison directed his attack more particularly against what he described as the 'gold fever' generated by examinations for lucrative college scholarships and fellowships.[155] Among other radicals there was little demand for the complete abolition of the practice of awarding honours. Thomas Fowler, who followed Pattison's line in university politics, defended the final schools in 1876, suggesting only that their competitive potential might be reduced by having just two grades.[156] Even the relentless Tractarian moralist William Heygate of St John's, who reviewed the temptations and potential evils of the class lists in his novel *Godfrey Davenant at College* (1849), finally concluded that they served a valuable purpose in suggesting to young men's minds the great scrutiny to come.

If academic opinion was often ambivalent towards the public examinations, the outside world was more whole-hearted in its approval. Prizes or honourable distinctions were a feature of many systems of higher education; in few, as James Bryce pointed out in comparing Oxford (and Cambridge) with America, did they attract so much notice beyond the walls of the University.[157] Former graduates were always important in sustaining the pre-eminence of the class list. One product of the schools, Gladstone, never ceased to regard his own experience as beneficial, urging upon Ruskin, in 1878, 'the value of the sudden strain and effort, the vast concentration of mind, the hasty calling into play of all the intellectual powers, as a training for political life'.[158] Of Oxford events, only the boat race and the Varsity matches outdid the class list in regular national newspaper coverage, a fact exploited in 1864 by a hoaxer who placed a forged Greats list in *The Times*, ranking Alfred Robinson, later a leading tutor at New College, in the fourth class, and leaving Courtenay Ilbert, one of Jowett's favoured pupils, as the sole occupant of the first.[159] The seriousness with which university honours were regarded was barely overshadowed by greater events. In August 1914, alongside a column headed 'The sunset of peace', *The Times* announced, 'Oxford "Greats" List. Winchester and New College Successes'.[160]

were discussed in relation to the opening of Oxford examinations to women, *Guardian* 26 Mar. 1884, 470.

[155] *UOC* (1877), evidence, Q. 4115.

[156] T. Fowler, 'On Examinations', *Fortnightly Review* xxv (1876), 424. George Rolleston similarly advocated a reversion to two classes: W. Turner (ed.), *Scientific Papers and Addresses by George Rolleston* (2 vols 1884) i. p. li.

[157] J. Bryce, *The American Commonwealth* (3 vols 1888) iii. 445–6.

[158] J. Ruskin, *Letters to M. G. and H. G.* (privately printed 1903), 14, cited in H. C. G. Matthew, *Gladstone, 1809–1874* (1986), 20.

[159] *The Times* 10 May 1864, 11; 11 May 1864, 9.

[160] *The Times* 6 Aug. 1914, 9.

APPENDIX

TABLE 11.A1.

HONOURS AWARDED BY SUBJECT (MEN); SECOND PUBLIC EXAMINATIONS, 1807–1914

year	Literae Humaniores	mathematics	natural science	law and history	jurisprudence	modern history	theology	oriental studies	English	modern languages
1807–9	134	32	—	—	—	—	—	—	—	—
1810–14	343	63	—	—	—	—	—	—	—	—
1815–19	343	67	—	—	—	—	—	—	—	—
1820–4	395	66	—	—	—	—	—	—	—	—
1825–9	340	77	—	—	—	—	—	—	—	—
1830–4	522	105	—	—	—	—	—	—	—	—
1835–9	540	124	—	—	—	—	—	—	—	—
1840–4	481	124	—	—	—	—	—	—	—	—
1845–9	444	132	—	—	—	—	—	—	—	—
1850–4	472	141	5	68	—	—	—	—	—	—
1855–9	382	104	57	158	—	—	—	—	—	—
1860–4	314	114	53	154	—	—	—	—	—	—
1865–9	438	72	54	253	—	—	—	—	—	—
1870–4	461	93	82	167	84	136	188	—	—	—
1875–9	525	114	137	—	222	323	212	—	—	—
1880–4	545	106	126	—	253	437	199	—	—	—
1885–9	672	94	131	—	273	485	292	16	—	—
1890–4	660	96	172	—	314	512	270	14	—	—
1895–9	697	109	229	—	294	584	171	11	13	—
1900–4	719	113	245	—	270	716	185	9	21	—
1905–9	711	84	304	—	387	748	250	11	49	19
1910–14	718	80	374	—	367	797	250	11	79	62

Source: Calendar.

TABLE 11.A2.

COLLEGES OF SUCCESSFUL CANDIDATES IN FINAL HONOUR SCHOOLS, 1875–1914

college	Literae Humaniores	mathematics	natural science	jurisprudence	modern history	theology	oriental studies	English	modern languages
All Souls	18	1	1	1	11	4	0	0	0
Balliol	634	85	144	149	408	25	13	2	8
Brasenose	226	40	46	122	137	47	1	4	0
Christ Church	305	55	179	104	344	86	2	13	4
Corpus	307	49	28	82	143	12	0	2	2
Exeter	208	39	85	145	191	148	4	4	10
Hertford	205	57	39	49	100	55	2	3	4
Jesus	212	77	96	17	109	97	6	9	1
Keble	175	6	95	48	355	288	2	6	3
Lincoln	179	2	30	80	179	39	0	8	3
Magdalen	210	47	155	118	272	29	2	8	2
Merton	181	43	83	128	204	67	1	8	2
New	560	40	169	295	543	68	1	10	4
Oriel	178	3	30	140	132	60	0	5	1
Pembroke	145	27	25	42	63	39	1	3	5
Queen's	252	85	83	77	152	89	4	13	4
St. John's	232	24	105	110	225	159	9	13	5
Trinity	294	3	108	249	319	47	2	16	3
University	289	36	78	232	310	41	0	10	7
Wadham	210	9	37	60	112	69	9	7	4
Worcester	146	48	17	89	101	73	9	4	6
halls	38	6	11	14	51	84	1	4	1
Non-Collegiates	43	14	72	30	141	203	11	10	2

Source: Calendar.

TABLE 11.A3.

PROPORTION OF UNDERGRADUATES TAKING PASS
DEGREES, AS A PERCENTAGE OF ADMISSIONS TO EACH
COLLEGE IN THE ACADEMIC YEARS 1893/1894, 1898/1899,
1903/1904, 1909/1910

%	college		%	college	
⩾25	St Edmund Hall	46	10–24	Magdalen	20
	Keble	44	(contd)	Merton	20
	Oriel	31		Jesus	19
	Wadham	27		Trinity	18
	Brasenose	25		Lincoln	15
10–24	Christ Church	24		Queen's	14
	Non-Collegiate	24		St John's	14
	Exeter	23		University	11
	Hertford	23	<10	Corpus	8
	Worcester	22		New	6
	Pembroke	21		Balliol	5

Source: OUA Undergraduate Registers.

TABLE 11.A4.

SUBJECTS TAKEN AT THE
SECOND PUBLIC EXAMINATION BY THOSE
WHO GRADUATED BA, 1880–1909
(% OF GRADUATES)

course of study	decade of graduation		
	1880–9	1890–9	1900–9
Literae Humaniores	21.2	23.3	22.9
mathematics	3.5	3.5	3.2
natural science	4.5	6.9	8.8
jurisprudence	9.2	10.5	10.5
modern history	16.1	18.8	23.4
theology	8.6	7.5	7.0
oriental studies	0.3	0.4	0.3
English	n.a.	0.2	1.1
modern languages	n.a.	n.a.	0.3
(joint honours)	(2.7)	(2.7)	(2.8)
pass school	39.3	31.6	25.3
total graduates	100.0	100.0	100.0

n.a. = not applicable.
Source: *Calendar*.

TABLE 11.A5.

NUMBER OF UNDERGRADUATES PASSING THE FIRST PUBLIC EXAMINATION
AS A PERCENTAGE OF UNDERGRADUATES MATRICULATING, 1855–1909

year		classical honour moderations	pass moderations	mathematical moderations[a]	preliminary jurisprudence	preliminary natural science	total
1855–9:	no.	476	1,042	(93)			1,518
	%	25	55	(5)			80
1860–4:	no.	592	1,048	(108)			1,640
	%	29	52	(5)			81
1875–9:	no.	843	1,970	(154)			2,813
	%	24	56	(4)			80
1880–4:	no.	975	2,355	(162)			3,330
	%	26	61	(4)			87
1895–9:	no.	1,012	1,681	176	390	200[b]	3,459[b]
	%	24	40	4	9	5[b]	82
1905–9:	no.	915	1,963	196	429	300[b]	3,803[b]
	%	20	41	4	9	6	80

[a] Before 1887 mathematical moderations was a voluntary examination, which did not qualify candidates to proceed to a final school.
[b] Figures for the natural science preliminary are approximate, based on the average of sample years; the resulting totals are estimates.

Sources: Calendar, Gazette.

TABLE 11.A6

DURATION OF UNDERGRADUATE STUDIES FOR THOSE
MATRICULATING 1893/1894, 1909/1910
(NO. OF STUDENTS)

course of study	1893/4 (no. of years)		1909/10 (no. of years)	
	3	≥4	3	≥4
Literae Humaniores	2	138	14	117
mathematics	6	15	7	7
natural science	12	28	26	35
jurisprudence	26	27	50	14
modern history	41	70	86	63
theology	11	12	26	11
English	—	—	11	4
modern languages	—	—	6	2
pass school	85	104	69	86
total	183	394	295	339

Source: OUA Undergraduate Registers.

12

Finance and Property

J. P. D. DUNBABIN

In 1753 Sir William Blackstone wrote proudly of the All Souls accounts that they made it impossible for the manciple 'to wrong the College even to the Amount of forty shillings, without being immediately detected'; indeed, two minor instances apart, 'I cannot conceive that any Alteration can possibly be made in them for the better...'. But in 1869 his successors had to report 'that up to this time no regular account has been furnished to the College of its gross annual income and expenditure'. Something indeed was audited each year, but the rents actually received were some 19 per cent above those there shown. 'In the absence of any account of the sinking fund, the committee are unable to state what has become of... [this] difference... but they presume that it was regularly paid into the College bankers, and... formed a fund from which sums were from time to time taken as required, to compensate fellows for fines lost by the non-renewal of leases.'[1]

All Souls was an extreme case—with Lincoln, the only college quite unable to tell the Cleveland Commission what its income had been before 1869. But breakdown in the traditional systems of accounting was widespread, though not universal, in the mid-nineteenth century. Its manifestations varied from college to college. In Magdalen the chief problem was over-complication. The traditional system (which was in principle capable of being double-checked) survived in form till 1882, but became vitiated by the proliferation of fictitious balances—the chief sum deemed to be handed over from one bursar to another, £1,636 in 1725 and £7,642 in 1800, had risen to £96,713 in 1881, by which time the accounts balanced on over £160,000, though true annual income was under £40,000. More usually the problem was one of omission. Where rents were increased beyond the traditional figures that featured in the old accounts, the balance might be channelled elsewhere (usually being divided more directly among the college fellows). Thus in 1812 Exeter was taking, in respect of Kidlington rectory, the traditional corn-rent, a long-standing augmentation, an 'improved rent' and a

[1] Sir William Blackstone, *Dissertation on the Accounts of All Souls College Oxford 1753*, ed. W. R. Anson (Roxburghe Club cxxix 1898), 11, 28; *RCOC* (1872), pt 2, 528. The report was made available to the Commission in Jan. 1873.

'further improved rent'. The chief source of income, over and above the traditional rents, was, and long had been, the 'fines' (or premiums) charged lessees for the renewal of their leases. By 1800 this system was working smoothly, and the sums involved were often recorded in separate books for ease of calculation. But, for the historian, trouble comes when colleges started to discontinue it; for fellows who would have been entitled to receive fines had the leases been renewed were often compensated from other sources—and 'fine-books' do not necessarily distinguish between fines actually paid and those simply borrowed from other college funds. In the case of All Souls, as we have seen, the additional rents received when the leases fell in were earmarked to cover this, but no account was kept of the process. Lastly, accounts were geared towards traditional ways and rates of paying fellows. Where the University Commissioners altered these in the mid-1850s, they provided at least an occasion for change. Accordingly New College's splendid series of vellum rolls (*Computus bursariorum*) ends in 1855. And some colleges were more successful than others in finding replacements.

Faced with this confusion the Cleveland Commission on the Property and Income of the Universities of Oxford and Cambridge bullied the colleges into the production of accounts in a more or less common form for 1871, and into the provision of a great mound of partially digested information on their property, income and expenditure. This led, from 1883, to University taxation of the colleges on the basis of a common system of printed accounts[2] that lasted (in essence) until 1967. By 1910, these accounts, too, had come to seem defective, and in 1912 a Board of Finance was charged with clarifying and harmonizing them as part of the drive for university reform.[3] But if the 1883 format left much to be desired, it still represents a great improvement on what went before—and much extends the range of questions a historian can usefully discuss.

By the early nineteenth century Oxford was, in financial terms, running smoothly. The university was overwhelmingly centred on the colleges. These provided scholarships, chapel services, and some teaching. But this was not the chief concern of most college fellows, who looked to their college to provide a kind of club, food and rooms if they were resident, and in any case a modest annual dividend. Most hoped eventually to secure livings; and 1805 saw the removal of all legal restrictions on college purchases of advowsons for their members. All this was underpinned chiefly by landed property, though perhaps never quite as exclusively as one would deduce

---

[2] Whereas traditional college accounts had been mostly of the charge–discharge variety (which survived on some landed estates to the end of the century), these were on the double-entry system that now represented best practice and that (for instance) parishes were required to adopt in 1867: M. J. Jones, 'The accounting system of Magdalen College, Oxford, in 1812', *Accounting, Business and Financial History* i (1991), 141–61.

[3] P. 399 below, and *Twentieth-Century Oxford*, 639, 640–1.

from the accounts; and most of the records of college meetings relate to the management of this property. Some was let directly at commercial (or 'rack-') rents—and rising levels of rent during the Napoleonic Wars encouraged colleges to run out a few leases and shift to rack-rents. But almost, though not quite, all colleges adhered to the system of beneficial leases, where rents remained at traditional (and increasingly unrealistic) levels and the lessee paid periodic 'fines' (usually every seven years) for the renewal of his lease.

This (and the not dissimilar tenure of copyhold) had been normal in the late-medieval and early-modern period. But from the 1630s onwards in south-central England, and the eighteenth century in the west, it was increasingly abandoned, leaving college, cathedral and crown lands as anomalies. Crown lands were particularly under-rented, and Pitt put an end to the system from 1794 as part of his general financial reforms. The Napoleonic Wars saw rapidly rising rents; so both colleges and cathedral chapters raised the level of their fines, but both generally stopped short of major tenurial change. The 1830s, however, saw the advent of externally imposed ecclesiastical reform, one aim of which was to secure the more rational and efficient management of church property. Accordingly beneficial leases of church property were brought to an end in Ireland, and the new Ecclesiastical Commission sought after 1840 to follow suit in England—arousing a major storm by its handling of Norwell (Notts.) in 1845.[4] From the late 1830s to the mid-1850s the terms of the transition were fought out between the lessees, the Commission and its partisans through pressure groups, public inquiries, and Parliament. Colleges were able to stand on the sidelines. But the general climate must have encouraged them to embark on the business of running out their own leases, which (unlike both Crown and Church) they were able to do without any formal financial concessions towards 'the just and reasonable Claims of the present' lessees 'arising from the long continued Practice of Renewal'.[5] Their actions were given official blessing from the late 1850s. Nevertheless, the process was a slow one, little more than half-complete by 1871; and its aftermath was to affect colleges' finances for the rest of the century.

Raising money is one side of the coin, spending it the other. Oxford's critics and reformers sought to transform it into a place primarily devoted to

[4] L. Stone, *The Crisis of the Aristocracy, 1558–1641* (1965), esp. 321; P. Bowden, in J. Thirsk (ed.), *The Agrarian History of England and Wales*, iv: *1500–1640* (1967), 686 ff.; *Reports of the Surveyor General of His Majesty's Land Revenue* PP 1812 xii. 513 ff.; W. H. Grey, *Church Leases* (first pub. 1847; 1851); G. F. A. Best, *Temporal Pillars* (1964), ch. 8, sect. 3.

[5] The insertion of these words into the Episcopal and Capitular Estates Management Act, 1851 stilled the lessees' opposition. The Ecclesiastical Commission had originally offered no concessions; but after the 1851 Act lessees apparently secured, in recognition of their prescriptive claims, an improvement of between 5% and 7% (they had at one stage been seeking between 15% and 25%) in the terms on which their beneficial leases were enfranchised: PP 1856 xi, Qs 740–63. In 1794 the Treasury had allowed most Crown lessees a 5% reduction on market rents, while the 1833 Irish Church Act provided for a 4% discount on the leases' sale price.

teaching or research (they were divided on which). Such a transformation had a multitude of implications. More students meant a need for more buildings to put them in. Fees and charges would generate more money, though the general feeling was that the cost of attending the university should be controlled (through a closer supervision of kitchens and servants) and subsidized by the expansion of scholarships. If fellows came to seek a lifelong tutorial or scholarly career, they would have less need of college livings and more of pensions—and by the end of the nineteenth century colleges had switched from buying to selling advowsons (albeit in a small way) for the benefit of their pension funds. But above all the change raised the question of relations between colleges and the central institutions of the university.[6] For everybody agreed that the University had an important, some felt virtually an exclusive, role to play in the provision of research and teaching as well as of libraries, museums and laboratories. Yet it had little property of its own, and an income not much larger than that of a wealthy college. From the 1850s reforms sought to enable it to harness college incomes; but the way in which these reforms turned out was, and remains, controversial.

Traditionally colleges had at least two basic kinds of external income, *recepta ordinaria* and *extraordinaria* as the Merton accounts term them. The former consisted chiefly of the reserved rents of properties let (or, occasionally and confusingly, once let) on beneficial lease. These were partially indexed to the price of corn, but should not otherwise have varied greatly from year to year. Defenders of the system always claimed, with substantial though not complete justification, that since the reserved rents were well below current market rates, they were paid punctually and cheerfully even in bad years. The effect was to shield colleges, in their corporate capacity, from short-term fluctuations. For, especially where their dependence on internal income—and hence on attracting enough paying undergraduates— was slight, their basic running-costs were covered by their ordinary receipts. Prosperity or adversity came chiefly through shifts in the extraordinary receipts, and was passed on to the individual members of the foundation in the form of a greater or lesser surplus to be divided. And if (say) building or repairs presented any unusual demands, the college could either make a levy (for 'domus') on the extraordinary receipts or suspend a fellowship— vacancies occurred fairly regularly through marriage or preferment[7]— and divert its dividends to fill the gap. The revelation of the outcome of these calculations had come to be the great day of late Victorian All

---

[6] In this chapter the University has a capital letter if the reference is to the central institutions when seen apart from the colleges.

[7] The first Commission took the average tenure of a fellowship to be ten years: *RCO* (1850), report, 172.

Souls, being followed by a singsong, traditional oyster supper and obstacle races.[8]

'Extraordinary' receipts fluctuated wildly. This was due partly to irregular wood sales and the varying energy shown in holding manorial courts and collecting copyhold fines, but chiefly to the fact that in some years the leasehold properties coming up for renewal (and thus producing fines) were more valuable than in others. Admittedly the cycle was predictable. And if an expected fine was not paid, or if, as was increasingly the case in the mid-century, the college decided to refuse renewal of a lease and so forgo the fine, its equivalent could be advanced from 'domus' (or any other fund with money to spare), subject usually to subsequent repayment. But for the individual fellow even this meant a sequence of fat and lean years. One fellow of Exeter has recorded his profits for 1805/13.[9]

1805/6 Probationer Fellow, £14; Sub-Dean, £28; room rent, £8; (total £50)

1806/7 Fellow, £85; Moderator, £11; 'Reading Prayers' (half-year) £6; room rent, £8; (£110)

1807/8 Fellow, £45; not resident; room rent, £8; (£53)

1808/9 Fellow, £94; [left blank]; room rent, £8; (?£102)

1809/10 Fellow, £100; Lecturer, £13; 'Reading Prayers' (20 weeks), £10; room rent, £8; (£131)

1810/11 Fellow, £77; Lecturer, Sub-Dean, Librarian, £39; Prayers, £17; room rent and commons, £21; (£155-rounded)

1811/12 Fellow, £90; Sub-Dean, Librarian, £21; Prayers, £18; room rent and commons, £23; (£153-rounded)

1812/13 Fellow, £141; Sub-Dean, £25; Prayers, £15; room rent and commons, £23; (£203-rounded)

Under the traditional arrangements, then, colleges were not in the long run likely to get into grave financial difficulties, while the perceptions of most of their members probably focused on year-to-year fluctuations that the historian is bound to average out. Nor, as we have seen, are college accounts designed to facilitate generalization. Nevertheless, there are indications of a gradually increasing prosperity. This appears most clearly in the case of colleges with a high dependence on internal income (Table 12.1), like Balliol and Wadham (and, probably, Exeter, though the accounts do not show it).

Another fairly small group of colleges comprises those relatively quick to abandon the system of beneficial leases, and consequently more dependent than most on trends in rack-rent. This would include Jesus, Balliol and Exeter (Table 12.2). Of most colleges, though, it is hard to say more than that their external income at least maintained its position in money terms

[8] Sir Charles Oman, *Memories of Victorian Oxford* (1941), 127 ff.
[9] Exeter College archives MS A. III. 21, 'Notebook of college income and its division'.

TABLE 12.1

INTERNAL REVENUE OF BALLIOL AND WADHAM, 1800–1850 (£)

	1800	1810	1820	1830	1840	1850
Balliol ('final accounts'						
internal revenue (%)	37	52	48	54	51	—
total net income	5,800	8,400	13,200	14,300	15,300	—
constant 1826 £s	*3,800*	*5,500*	*11,500*	*15,100*	*15,000*	—
Wadham (bursars' accounts)						
internal revenue (%)	40	51	66	63	68	64
total net income	6,100	8,300	11,200	11,800	14,000	12,800
constant 1826 £s	*4,000*	*5,400*	*9,700*	*12,500*	*13,700*	*17,400*

Note: Constant 1826 £s calculated from Gayer, Rostow and Schwartz's index of 'Domestic and imported commodities', in B. R. Mitchell with P. Deane, *Abstract of British Historical Statistics* (1962), 470.

TABLE 12.2

EXTERNAL REVENUE OF JESUS, BALLIOL AND EXETER, 1800–1850 (£ p.a.)

	1800	1810	1820	1830	1840	1850
Jesus						
('Domus', 'Sir L. Jenkins',						
'Meyricke' accounts)						
gross external income	3,800	6,500	7,200	9,300	9,900	9,800
fines	2,500	—	200	—	—	—
total	6,300	6,500	7,400	9,300	9,900	9,800
constant 1826 £s	*4,100*	*4,200*	*6,400*	*9,800*	*9,700*	*13,400*
Balliol ('final accounts')						
rents, arrears, and domus						
(net)[a]	3,600	4,100	6,900	6,600	7,500	—
constant 1826 £s	*2,400*	*2,700*	*6,000*	*7,000*	*7,300*	—
Exeter						
computus rectoris, receipts[b]	2,100	1,800	2,200	?3,500[b]	3,100	3,000
fines (decennial average)	800	600	500	200	100	0
additional rents earmarked						
for stipends (decennial						
average)	1,000	1,500	2,000	2,200	2,600	3,200
total	3,900	4,000[c]	4,700	?5,800[c]	5,800	6,200
constant 1826 £s	*2,600*	*2,600*	*4,100*	*?6,200*	*5,600*	*8,400*

[a] Balliol had run out its most valuable leases in the 18th century, and its 19th-century income from fines was negligible. See also p. 175 above.
[b] Inclusive of arrears. The treatment of these is difficult; but this factor is unlikely to be important except perhaps in 1830.
[c] Rounded.

TABLE 12.3

	1800–9	1810–19	1820–9	1830–9	1840–9	1850–9
Merton (*liber rationarius, computus generalis*)						
'ordinary receipts'	2,700	3,200	2,800[a]	3,400	3,600[a]	6,700
fines and manorial profits	1,000	2,200	3,000	2,500	3,400[a]	3,000
total	3,700	5,400	5,800	5,900	6,900[ab]	9,600[b]
constant 1826 £s	2,700	3,800	5,800	6,300	7,900[a]	10,100
Magdalen (*libri computi* and *indenturae magnae*)						
distributed to members of foundation	4,400	6,200	5,900	7,300	8,300	7,500[c]
proportion of fines not forming part of this distribution	3,000	4,700	4,300	3,500	3,400	3,800[c]
total	7,400	10,900	10,200	10,800	11,800[b]	11,300[c]
constant 1826 £s	5,400	7,600	10,100	11,600	13,500	12,800[c]

[a] The 'ordinary receipts' for 1822 and 1823 were not totalled. More seriously the accounts were in considerable disorder in the 1840s and the total of fines could be lower; but the figure given agrees quite well with Merton's statement to the Royal Commission (see below, p. 382).
[b] Rounded.
[c] Figures for 1850–4.

and must therefore have increased in real ones.[10] This is certainly the impression given by the main accounts and the fines of All Souls, Brasenose, Lincoln, New College and Wadham, taken collectively, though the calculation leaves much to be desired.[11] And some confirmation is provided by those of Merton and Magdalen (Table 12.3).

[10] Prices rose steeply during the Napoleonic Wars, then fell sharply; despite considerable subsequent fluctuation they were lower in 1850 than in 1820; thereafter the tendency was upwards, especially in the early 1870s. The later 1870s, and more especially the 1880s and early 1890s, saw a substantial drop. To a rise at the turn of the century there succeeded, first a slight decline, then an increase, which accelerated in the years immediately before 1914.
[11] Total main accounts and fines of All Souls, Brasenose, Lincoln, New College and Wadham, 1800–1850 (£)

	1800	1810	1820	1830	1840	1850
rents, rent-charges, etc.[a]	15,900	16,300	17,200	19,600	21,800	23,200
decennial average of fines	10,500	14,100	13,000	10,900	9,800	7,800
total	26,400	30,400	30,200	30,500	31,600	31,000

[a] All Souls *summa firmarum*; Lincoln, rents and rent-charges; New College, rents and corn rents; Wadham, rents; Brasenose, rents, net arrears and miscellaneous receipts—an uncomfortably catch-all heading; the Brasenose figure in the top column is for 1821 not 1820. This is not a complete account of external income.

After the middle of the century we are on slightly firmer ground. For though the first Royal Commission was largely cold-shouldered, some colleges did provide information on their financial state *circa* 1850; and the Commission also reported hearsay on the value of fellowships at others. Two decades later the Cleveland Commission managed to get nearly all its questions answered, and must provide the fullest picture ever given of the university's external income and assets. In Table 12.4 the findings of these Commissions are juxtaposed with some further evidence added from the more reliable of the college accounts. This picture is clearly mixed. Balliol's external income fell sharply, Jesus's slightly, and New College's very slightly, in real terms. But most of the colleges in the table experienced a gratifying increase in their gross external receipts, even allowing for a 25 per cent rise in prices between 1850 and 1871. These gains will have come partly from rising

TABLE 12.4

COLLEGE INCOMES, 1850–1871 (£)

	1850	1871	Increase (%)
All Souls			
corporate external	9,622	15,486[a]	61
Balliol			
land, houses, tithe and interest	5,059	5,188	3
'Domus'		2,286[c]	
Lincoln			
corporate external (excl. room rents)	3,794	6,545	73
Merton			
corporate rents, fines, interest	7,120	15,911	123
Pembroke			
external (corporate and awards)	3,343	5,352[d]	60
internal	1,427	2,401	68
total	4,770	7,753	63
Corpus Christi	c 7,000–8,500	14,166[e]	39[f]
		11,783[g]	

	1850	1870	
Jesus			
gross external	9,829	11,465	17
Wadham		1871	
external	4,596	8,378	82
internal	8,206	7,467	−9
total	12,802	15,845	24

	1860	1870	
Brasenose			
rents, fines, interest, etc.	7,919	9,364	18
internal and misc.	2,145	4,317	101
total	10,064	13,681	36

	1860	1871	
New College			
fines received	3,352	—	
other external	20,149	22,417	−5
	23,501	22,417	
fines borrowed	1,203	2,369	
total	24,704	24,786	

[a] Excl. fines.
[b] Not stated; £2,612 net in 1840.
[c] Trust.
[d] Corporate and trust.
[e] Gross corporate external.
[f] At least.
[g] Net coporate external.

Sources: All Souls to Corpus Christi, and New College 1871: *RCO* (1850), evidence; *RCOC* (1872), pts 1 and 2 (these give Pembroke's 1850 total as £4,743, but seem to disregard its small estate on beneficial lease); Jesus and Wadham: accounts as in Tables 12.1, 12.2; Brasenose: condensed abstract of accounts (B 2. b. 12); New College 1860: NC8 833, income and expenditure, esp. pp. 52–3.

rents during the so-called 'golden age' of English agriculture (though neither Balliol nor Jesus appears to have derived great advantage therefrom) and partly from the gradual substitution of rack-rents for the traditional system of fines and beneficial leases.

In the century and a half before the end of the Napoleonic Wars fines (for the renewal of leases) had been the most dynamic element in college incomes, growing (for a sample of four colleges) from a third of the size of their traditional rents in the 1690s almost to equality with them in the 1810s.[12] The middle of this decade was admittedly marked, for a number of colleges, by some rather leaner years. Thus in December 1814 Magdalen resolved that 'in consequence of the fall in the price of grain Fifteen per Cent be deducted from the valuation upon which the Fines of this year were set'.[13] But, taken as a whole, the decade probably saw the peak of fine income for most, though not all, colleges (see Table 12.5).

[12] See *The Eighteenth Century*, 276.
[13] This, and all subsequent unattributed references to resolutions by Magdalen, are taken from the order-books: 1786–1810, MCA CMM 1/2; 1811–34, CMM 1/3; 1835–54, CMM 1/4; 1854–70, CMM 1/5; 1870–84, CMM 1/6; 1885–1902, CMM 1/7; 1903–23, CMM 1/8.

TABLE 12.5

AVERAGE RECEIPTS FROM FINES, 1800–1870 (£p.a.)

college	1800–9	1810–19	1820–9	1830–9	1840–9	1850–9	1860–9	1870–9
All Souls	2,242	3,027	3,235	2,633	2,045	1,482[a]		
Brasenose	1,882	3,174	3,114	2,176	c.2,656[b]	3,156[d]	2,132[d]	c
Exeter	763	611	511	182	114			
Lincoln	614	964	c.745	706	580	257[d]		
Magdalen	3,972	6,229[e]	5,690	4,612	4,567	5,125[f]		
Merton[g]	1,934[g]	2,183	2,982	2,496	3,383[h]	2,957	2,320[d]	
New College	5,233	6,616	5,321	4,901	4,138	2,647		
Wadham	553	688	594	468	334	289[i]		
total	17,200	23,500	22,200	18,200	17,800	c.15,900	n.a.	n.a.

Notes: n.a. = not available; Balliol fines always well below their mid-18th-century levels.

[a] To 1856.
[b] Average of five years only.
[c] Average receipts for 1870–3 £2,240 p.a., thereafter slight.
[d] Negligible.
[e] Average of nine years only.
[f] 1861–1 average receipts £3,791 p.a., 1864–9 probably £4,244 + £2,093 p.a. advanced internally.
[g] *Liber Rationarius* listing of fines, perquisites of court, sealings. The fine-book suggests that in 1800–9 only half the fines received were carried to the *Computus generalis*, so the figure given here is adjusted accordingly.
[h] 1840s accounts are confused and one year is missing.
[i] Copyhold enfranchisement began in 1858, the proceeds sometimes being included in the fines in the 1860s; with them, the average 1860s receipt is £271 p.a.

Sources: All Souls: rent rolls; Brasenose: calculation of fines, 1789– (B2d21); Exeter: dividend books; Lincoln: register of the fines; Magdalen: *indenturae magnae*; Merton: *libri rationarii*; New College: 'record . . . of the college properties, their value and fees and fines . . . from *c.* 1770 to 1860' (Steer 9652); Wadham: bursars' accounts.

The level of fines demanded had risen appreciably in the eighteenth century and continued to do so. Thus in 1800 Merton noted that 'A year and a half['s clear value] was this Mich taken for the first time'.[14] In 1811 Christ Church also went to one and a half years, Magdalen to one and three-quarters and Brasenose a fraction higher. By 1825 Merton was calculating on one and three-quarters (a level still in force *circa* 1850). From July 1830 Magdalen demanded two and a quarter years' clear value, less a 5 per cent allowance for repairs and land-tax. Brasenose practice fluctuated in the 1830s and 1840s, but by the 1850s it too was normally taking two and a

[14] Merton fine-book, Merton College archives MS 2.19B. The fine demanded for the renewal of house property did not reach this level till 1819 and in 1823 was again reduced to one and a quarter years (ibid., Annunciation 1819 and 1824).

quarter years with an allowance for land-tax. All Souls, admittedly, still remained at one and a half; and in 1853 Charles Neate (of Oriel) assumed that two years' clear value was general. But the twilight of the system probably saw a further increase for those leases colleges were prepared to renew. Certainly the individual fines taken by Magdalen in the later 1860s often show a sharp jump, while in 1870 Brasenose advanced again to two and a half years' clear value.[15]

If, then, the level of fines demanded continued to rise, but receipts did not, it can only be because colleges were, by the 1820s, refusing to renew an appreciable number of leases. Initially this meant either that those entitled to divide the fines forwent them in the general interest or that they were compensated from some other college fund. Thus Merton told the 1850 Royal Commission that for the past seven years it had had an annual deficit of £1,200, the product 'wholly' of the non-renewal of leases. The deficit had

been supplied, without disturbing the customary administration of the college, out of a previously accumulated fund. That fund is now exhausted, but the leases alluded to being also on the eve of expiration, it is obvious that the increased income to arise from the rack-rent value of those estates, when in possession, will still enable the College to pursue the same beneficial system in future, and probably at an accelerated rate.[16]

But in the course of the 1850s it came to be felt that this process of self-reliance was too slow. There were probably several catalysts—parliamentary intervention to set aside old statutes and promote internal reform must have prompted ideas of seeking the relaxation of the old legal restrictions on estate management. There were practical reasons, too, for doing so, notably the need to be free to grant ninety-nine-year building leases. And a model was to hand in the Church Estates Acts, on which the Universities and Colleges Estates Act of 1858, in particular, was modelled. It also seems reasonable to accept the tradition, reported by C. L. Shadwell (Oriel) in 1898, that the fracas aroused by the Ecclesiastical Commissioners' assault on beneficial leases of church property, and by the counter-mobilization of the lessees, led colleges in the 1850s to seek to resolve the situation in their favour while there was yet time. The upshot was an approach (through university MPs) to Parliament by colleges in both Oxford and Cambridge,

[15] Merton fine-book, Merton College archives, *sub anno*; Magdalen order-books, MCA MS ES 2/10, 11, 27, and fine-book, 1721, MCA MS CP 3/13; 'Calculation of fines, 1789– ', Brasenose College archives; *RCO* (1850), report, 195, 219–20; C. Neate, *Observations on College Leases* (1853), 6; Christ Church fine-book, 1799–1811, CA MS xxiii b. 2. By 1840 Christ Church was referring to 'the old mode of taking $1\frac{1}{2}$ on a *Gross* value' and explaining that it had shifted to $1\frac{1}{4}$ or 2 years on a net one, or, in the case of the tithe (which after commutation now approximated 'more nearly to the certainty of money payments'), $2\frac{1}{2}$—though it claimed that in practice the difference between $1\frac{1}{2}$ on gross and $2\frac{1}{2}$ on net value 'is not so great as might be supposed' (CA MS Estates 25, fo 122; 28, fo 288); $2\frac{1}{2}$ years later came to be assumed as the general level.

[16] *RCO* (1850), report, 195–6.

which in 1858 and 1860 secured them—apparently uncontentiously—greatly increased powers to deal with their estates.[17]

The 1860 Act permitted colleges to raise loans to compensate their present members for fines forgone by running out leases. There was no compulsion—Brasenose found the terms of borrowing too restrictive and continued the old system for another dozen years. But the legislation certainly provided an additional stimulus, especially to colleges with large estates. And, to judge by their replies to the Cleveland Commission, most colleges must have decided either in the later 1850s or in the 1860s to end the system. However, the way in which they did so was to have repercussions for the rest of the century. At one extreme was Merton, which ran out all its beneficial leases without incurring debt. At the other was Christ Church, which by 1886 had borrowed more than £200,000 (or over three times its income on revenue account) to replace fines.[18] In theory rising returns from rack-rents should have made repayment easy. But in practice it was accepted that these returns might be delayed by the need to spend considerable sums on rehabilitating the estates once they came into hand. So repayments might be bunched towards the end of the thirty-year maximum over which they could be spread. Christ Church fell into this trap, and probably also into the related one of over-valuing their estates when calculating the sums to be borrowed as fine loans—their lessees, after all, no longer had occasion to contest such optimism. On top of this came the unexpected fall in agricultural rents after 1879. And the result was that, though the ending of beneficial leases did increase Christ Church's income—up by 18 per cent in 1897 on the land and tithes emancipated in 1874–6 with the aid of fine loans—the burden of debt repayments led in 1886 to a college panic and row over economies[19] and in 1897–8 to successful lobbying for a degree of legislative rescheduling.[20]

Another problem was the condition of the estates themselves. In 1889 Sir William Harcourt asserted roundly in Parliament that 'if there was any property out of order or dilapidated, it was sure to be College property... one could always tell College property as one passed on the road'.

[17] C. L. Shadwell, *The Universities and Colleges Estates Acts, 1858 to 1880, their history and results* (1898), esp. 15–18 (which ascribes much of the credit for the outcome to C. W. Lawrence, Steward of New College and Christ Church). Charles Neate's *Observations on College Leases* warns of the dangers of lessees securing parliamentary recognition that they had rights of ownership.

[18] CA MS Estates 134, fo 45. Of the £203,557 fine loans outstanding in 1886, £139,958 represented external borrowing, though by 1897 all the college's debt had been refinanced by internal reborrowing. See nn. 20 and 141 below.

[19] See CA MS Estates 134, fos 25–46. The row occasioned an able memorandum by C. L. Dodgson (Lewis Carroll, fos 39–42), and was resolved by asking Bartholomew Price (Pembroke) to help compile a report on the college's financial position. The report came down on the optimistic side. But by 1897 it was clear that Christ Church was in for a decade of deficits.

[20] PP 1897 xlv (esp. Qs 781, 787 and tables); CA MS Estates 135, esp. fos 202 ff., 283, 322 ff., 392–7.

This naturally raised a number of hackles; but there was a widespread feeling that, though it was now out of date, it had once been true.[21] There are a priori grounds for expecting buildings on beneficially leased college estates to have been somewhat below average. But such estates (which constituted nearly a sixth of Oxfordshire) did not attract any special attention from the agricultural writers of the late eighteenth and early nineteenth centuries. And as late as 1851 Caird's specific criticisms were rather of the Marlborough estates, though he added a general stricture that Oxfordshire landlords tended to be little interested in agriculture and their agents over-legalistic lawyers. In 1854 Clare Sewell Read repeated this stricture; but he also declared that 'Speaking generally, the property of the university is badly managed', and (after explaining the mechanics of beneficial leases) continued:

When the lessee is the actual occupier of the land, and a man of sufficient capital, then these leases are often beneficial, the lands well tilled, and the holding kept in good order. But should the estate be leased to a middleman, who underlets the farm,[22] and who took the lease simply with a view to making a good per-centage of his money, then the estate presents a most wretched and dilapidated appearance. The lessee is supposed to keep the buildings in repair, and is only allowed by the college such timber as grows on the estate. He cares nothing about the condition of the premises or the land. If he added to the buildings, or drained and improved the soil, he might have to pay an exorbitant fine.[23]

In the next quarter-century conditions were probably much worsened by the running-out of beneficial leases, which left the lessees even less incentive to maintain the property. And the Oxfordshire section of the report on the *Employment of Children...and Women in Agriculture* found room for an ideological broadside: cottages were in a bad way on the estates of 'life-renting' landlords, but far worse on those of 'collegiate...and all corporate bodies, whose members manage and divide the income of the estate...the life-renter has a conscience, but the corporate landowner has none, and the system of beneficial leases, to which some of them still cling, is simply an abomination'.[24] Its remarks do not seem to have been particularly well researched, but they were alarming. Charles Neate thought that the position of colleges as landed proprietors was threatened, and Dean Liddell of Christ

[21] See NCA 11470 for correspondence between Alfred Robinson (the Bursar), Harcourt and others about Harcourt's assertion; also Shadwell, *The Universities and Colleges Estates Acts*, 26–7.
[22] This was probably more usually the case, though Read did not say so. Often, however, the lessee's interest was more traditional and less speculative than Read implies. And college property was frequently intermingled with other holdings; its tillage would not then be remarkable, though its buildings might well be neglected.
[23] James Caird, *English Agriculture in 1850–1851* (first pub. 1852; 1968), 24–8; Clare Sewell Read, 'On the farming of Oxfordshire', *Journal of the Royal Agricultural Society of England* xv (1854), 257–9.
[24] PP 1868–9 xiii. 170; the report also quotes, highly selectively, from Read.

Church was anxious that the Cleveland Commission should go into the allegations about cottages.[25]

Against this background, colleges always assumed that, when beneficial leases ran out, a great deal of spending would be needed to put the estates to rights (and often so to upgrade them as to attract a better class of tenant); this

TABLE 12.6

COLLEGE ESTATE EXPENDITURE TO 1883 (£)

college	information given to Cleveland Commission[a]	estate loans to 1883 (amount originally borrowed)	charges in respect of estate loans (1883)	gross corporate income from estates (1883)
University	1871: 6,000 programme started	c.10,000	200	6,500
Balliol	—	400	—	6,000
Merton	1867–71: 9,200 spent on repairs and improvements	none	0	17,200
Exeter	—	none	0	4,900
Oriel	1867–71: 14,400 spent on repairs and improvements	24–30,000	2,700	11,200
Queen's	1869–70: 7,400 borrowed for improvements	c.21,000	1,200	14,200
New	1860s: 20,000 spent on rack rent estates; much needed for beneficially leased ones	98,200[bc]	800	31,300
Lincoln	—	none	0	5,000
All Souls	40,000 borrowed for estate improvements and college buildings	48,000	2,900	22,300
Magdalen	28,500 borrowed for estate improvements	23,000[c] 34,000[d]	500	36,900
Brasenose	—	—	0	7,700
Corpus Christi	very large repairs needed	50,100[bc]	1,300	18,000
Christ Church	—	1,300	100	49,000
Trinity	1867–71: 2,200 spent on repairs and improvements	3,300[b]	—	7,000

[25] Liddell to Price, May 1872; the Duke of Cleveland preferred to ignore the cottage question, feeling that inquiry would only show that colleges differed as widely in this connection as did private landlords (PCA MS 60/14/59, 60).

college	information given to Cleveland Commission[a]	estate loans to 1883 (amount originally borrowed)	charges in respect of estate loans (1883)	gross corporate income from estates (1883)
St John's	1867–71: 19,300 borrowed, 19,700 spent on repairs and improvements; the newly erected farm buildings were insured for c.21,000	100,300[cbe]	3,600	20,000
Jesus	improvement loan of 3,000 under consideration	6,500	300	11,300
Wadham	—	5,400	400	5,100
Pembroke	—	none	o	3,100
Worcester	—	5,300	300	4,700

[a] Where the Cleveland Commission did not comment on estate improvements, colleges may not have spent very heavily on them. But other colleges may have spent more than is here recorded. Nor of course was all subsequent estate expenditure financed out of loans.
[b] Fine loans.
[c] Estate loans.
[d] Purposes unstated.
[e] St John's estate loans were much bigger than its fine loans—hence the reversal of order.

attitude also led to the improvement of their existing rack-rent property. Sometimes colleges were very proud of their achievements. St John's wanted to take the Cleveland Commission on a conducted tour of the north Berkshire estates it had rehabilitated after their leases fell in. Such estate expenditure could be accounted for under so many headings and financed in such different ways that it is impossible to make any complete inventory. Still, Table 12.6 represents an attempt to sketch the situation up to 1883.

As so often, colleges varied, half being relatively unexposed, and half having—at some stage before 1883—borrowed at least the equivalent of a year's corporate estate income. Clearly estate rehabilitation could often not have been carried out without loans. The Universities and Colleges Estates Act of 1858 had accordingly provided legal facilities for raising these; and would-be lenders were quick to turn it to account. In 1859 the Land Improvement Company circulated material advertising loans at 5 per cent for 'beneficial agricultural improvements' to be paid off by a rent-charge on the improved lands.[26] How far such expenditure was wise, it is now

[26] Jesus College's archives, box 2, list 1, 13, miscellaneous documents.

impossible to say. Some was unavoidable; some, for example the erection of new cottages, socially desirable. Some (notably that associated with building development) greatly increased college income. But there were mistakes, like the grubbing-up of woods to permit arable farming on marginal lands that had to be reafforested a couple of decades later. During the 'golden age' the fashion in agricultural investment was to encourage a cost-intensive 'high farming' that was later to prove vulnerable to falls in price (and especially corn price) levels. All Souls was badly hurt in this way. And in 1881 one writer recalled sourly that

in those palmy days of scientific farming any tenant would pay 6 per cent for works of drainage and other improvement. The College simply pledged its credit and lent the tenant its capital . . . Without dipping their hands into their own pockets, the Colleges were to see their estates put into apple-pie order . . . No wonder College Bursars became amateur Hopes and miniature Mechis, and facile land-agents signed with readiness the documents necessary to procure the consent of the Copyhold Commissioners.[27]

The freedom to manage college estates—which came rather suddenly in the 1850s—did, after all, entail the freedom to make mistakes.

So far we have made little mention of the University as distinct from the colleges. And not unreasonably so, since until the 1850s it seems not to have felt much need of money. Indeed its contributions to extraneous causes were then reported as averaging £1,200 per year.[28] That it could make them was largely due to the largesse that flowed in from the University Press. This was one of Oxford's nineteenth-century success stories.[29] In 1780 nobody had been prepared to bid for the exercise of the University's special privilege to publish Bibles, so the University was forced itself to enter the business (albeit for many decades in partnership with other printers and booksellers). A century later a separate London publishing presence was emerging; in 1896 a New York branch was opened; and by then the Press (with its staff of 540) claimed to be the largest employer in Oxford. Bibles still constituted the foundation of its prosperity. From 1825 the old Clarendon Building had been outgrown, and in the next decade £30,000 was spent on new premises in Walton Street, and £3,000 on the conversion of the Clarendon Building into University offices. In 1836 the Delegates of the Press offered the University £1,050 per annum; in 1841–5 they contributed £33,000 towards the building of the University Galleries; in 1850 £60,000 of surplus profits were handed over to the University, and throughout the 1850s such payments were rarely

[27] G. Faber, *Notes on the History of the All Souls Bursarships and the College Agency* (privately printed), 74–80; 'Oxoniensis' [A. C. Tait], 'The colleges as landlords', *Fraser's Magazine* ns lxxxvii (May 1881), 590–1 (Hope and Mechi were leading agriculturalists of the day).
[28] *RCO* (1850), report, 127–8.
[29] A full account will be found in Pt 2, Ch. 26.

less than £10,000 per annum. They then dwindled after 1863, disappearing altogether in 1871 and 1872. But by the 1880s the Press was more confident, partly, no doubt, as a result of the remarkable demand for the Revised Version New Testament (of which over a million copies were sold on the first day). And Vice-Chancellor Jowett could write in 1883: 'If we can strengthen the institution somewhat I see no reason why in the next ten years the income and business of the Press might not double, as it has done in the last ten or fifteen years, supplying a golden egg to the university and with good effects on science and literature'.[30] Contributions, £3,500 in the years 1879–81, rose to £4,000 in 1882, then in 1883 to £5,000 per annum (a level maintained until 1907, when it was reduced to £2,000 per annum, then discontinued in 1921). And a further £39,500 passed to the University's capital account over the years 1886–97. Without all this, as the Press's Secretary observed in 1892, 'in these times of agricultural depression and increasing Academical demands, the University would have been in great straits'.[31]

The Press, then, was an invaluable resource. But if, in mid-century, this had enabled the University to be complacently generous—reformers took particular exception to its 1850 gift of £2,500 towards colonial bishoprics and the University of Toronto—'increasing Academical demands' subsequently began to constrain it. Criticism of Oxford's financial arrangements had been sharply voiced since at least the 1820s, reforms had been attempted in the 1830s, and in 1841 canonries at Christ Church were assigned to the existing Lady Margaret professorship of divinity and to two new chairs in theology. In 1850 the pace quickened with the Royal Commission on the 'State, Discipline, Studies and Revenues of the University and Colleges', which in 1852 recommended flatly

that the University ought not to spend its revenues on objects not academical. It is, as we have seen, inadequately supplied with Lecture-rooms, Museums and Laboratories. The Examiners for Scholarships are unpaid. Most of the Professorships are so ill-endowed as not to afford a maintenance for the Professors. There are many branches of learning and science which are not at all represented by Professors.[32]

Lord John Russell and Gladstone built on these recommendations in 1854 with a bill that would *inter alia* have pressured colleges so to reform their statutes as to devote up to a fifth of their incomes 'towards the foundation or better endowment of professorships and lectureships for the instruction of

---

[30] To Price, PCA MS 60/14/103.
[31] P. Sutcliffe, *The Oxford University Press: an informal history* (1978), esp. pp. xxv–vi, 4–7, 51, 79–80, 191; PP 1876 lix. 352; *University and College Accounts* (1883–). In 1896 the Press also made over to the Chest its Sandford Mill Estate with a rent of £793 p.a.; but repairs cost so much that 'taking one year with another the University received little or no revenue from this estate' and sold it in 1918: RCOC (1919), appx, 99.
[32] RCO (1850), report, 127–8. For the two new Regius chairs (moral and pastoral theology and ecclesiastical history) see 3 & 4 Vic. (1840), c. 113.

the Members of the University at large'. The sequel is described in Chapter 10. The measure met concerted Tory and radical obstruction at the committee stage, and to ease its passage the degree of compulsion on colleges was relaxed.[33] Some moves were admittedly made in Russell's direction during the subsequent reform of college statutes, but only minor ones. In 1871 colleges were contributing for such purposes £14,200, or between 4 and 5 per cent, of their disposable income. Pressure revived in early 1871, during the passage of the University Tests Act, and Gladstone promised to place Parliament 'in a position to deal effectively with the subject of Fellowships, and make the great and noble endowments of the colleges in their Universities as efficient as possible for the purposes for which they were intended'. His first step was to find out, through a Royal Commission (the Cleveland Commission), what these endowments were.[34]

This Commission, as we have seen, did much to fix on the colleges a common form of accounts, in itself a considerable advance, but one with a most regrettable lacuna. For though the Commission was able to standardize treatment of external college income, it was baffled by the complexities of internal accounting—understandably so, since in 1938 simply to list the charges on undergraduates demanded a sheet of paper nearly two feet square.[35] The result, though, was that the Cleveland Commission could not 'say with certainty in all cases whether profit... accrues to a College from its reception of students or not. In many cases, and notably in some Colleges in Oxford which are poorly endowed, considerable profit accrues... [which] forms a very important part of the whole income of the College, and amply compensates for the insufficiency of the endowment.'[36] This is a dimension of collegiate resources that can easily be overlooked; and it was unfortunate that the accounting system that emerged from the reforms was inappropriate for efficient internal management.

Things might, indeed, have turned out otherwise. For another strand of reform sought to lower the costs of an Oxford education. Traditionally college servants looked for much of their income to fees collected directly from undergraduates and/or to profits from undertaking the college's catering. In 1865 an undergraduate agitation in Christ Church against food prices—bread and butter cost 60 per cent more than in the shops—made a big splash in the London Press (perhaps because it was led by the son of the proprietor of *The Times*), and occasioned major reductions, fixed-price dinners, the installation of a Steward (domestic bursar) and the placing of

---

[33] *Annual Register*, 1854, ch. 5; *Parl. Deb.* 17 Mar. 1854, 3S cxxxi. 909; 1 June, cxxxiii. 1212–14; 15 June, cxxxiv. 213–14; Ward, *Victorian Oxford*, 190 ff.

[34] *Parl. Deb.* 23 Feb. 1871, 3S cciv. 779. For the doings of the Cleveland Commission, see Pt 2, Ch. 2.

[35] *OM* lxiii (1945), 109. Overall charges varied much less (as between colleges) than did their component parts.

[36] *RCOC* (1872), pt 1, 30–1.

the cook and butler on salaries (plus, admittedly, half the profits of their department).[37] Pembroke reached the same goal more discreetly, holding its servants to fixed tariffs after 1845, and in 1868–70 assuming direct responsibility for the provision of food and services and reducing its servants to paid employees.[38] Moves in this direction were probably quite common. But they still left a good deal to be desired—the Cleveland Commission noted that internal college management received less specific attention than in Cambridge, where 'an officer of the College generally superintends and directs all the departments, such as the kitchen and the buttery, and takes charge of the College buildings'.[39] Indeed it was not until 1909 that Oxford Domestic Bursars started meeting regularly to exchange notes.[40] And the pattern of service, whereby meals were ordered individually and carried up to students' rooms, must have been labour-intensive. Certainly an inquiry in connection with the Asquith Commission found it to be so, and also commented adversely on the prices at which colleges bought food—though the colleges claimed that this was an aberration of post-war inflation, soon controlled, and that in the late 1930s charges for meals in Halls were still almost at 1914 levels while other undergraduate charges had lagged well behind inflation.[41]

In the 1870s, however, the emphasis was rather on ascertaining the extent of college property and external income, with a view to tapping it for the support of 'University purposes'. Accordingly the Cleveland Commission was asked to estimate the prospective increase in such income, and duly did so. In fact this was an impossible task. For the most obvious source of increase lay in the running-out of beneficial leases; and, as the Commission recognized, 'it will . . . be found in most cases on the expiration of the leases that the property is in a condition requiring a large outlay to place it in a proper order'. In framing its estimate,[42] the Commission did not allow for this. Nor, more reprehensibly, did it take into consideration the fact that running out leases meant forgoing income from fines. Both improvement and fine loans took about thirty years to pay off; so the full benefit from the ending of beneficial leases might not come through for a generation. Ignoring all this the Commission assessed the prospective increase in college incomes at £98,800 per annum (approximately 38 per cent) for Oxford (excluding St John's) by 1891, plus a further £24,300 per annum from the ending of copyholds for lives that could not be so precisely dated. Fortunately the Commission also erred on the other side, by leaving out of

[37] E. G. W. Bill and J. F. A. Mason, *Christ Church and Reform, 1850–1867* (1970), 132–41; Christ Church scrapbook, Bodl. G. A. Oxon. c. 272, fo 15.
[38] 'Note on domestic administration', by Mr A. Lawes, PCA.
[39] *RCOC* (1872), pt 1, 37; see also n. 103 below.
[40] Bodl. G. A. Oxon. b. 140, unsorted box.
[41] *RCOC* (1919), report, 140–55, and appx 9, 10 (in which Oxford compares unfavourably, in many ways, with Cambridge); *Oxford* v (1939), 51.
[42] *RCOC* (1872), pt 1, 32 (which unfortunately misprints 1895 for 1890).

consideration income from new building developments. There were already indications that this was likely to rise, and it did so strongly, partly offsetting the disappointing performance of agricultural lands and tithes.

The Commission's estimates certainly stimulated the process of reform. In late 1874 Hebdomadal Council asked colleges, in the light of the recent report, what sums they 'would be able and willing to contribute to University purposes'. Most replies were discouraging, seldom extending beyond the provision of some fellowships for the endowment of professors.[43] But Council proceeded to produce a succession of estimates of University needs. Both the Commission's estimates and Council's statements of needs were cited by the government spokesman, the University's Chancellor, Lord Salisbury, as necessitating further reform legislation and Commissioners. He personally laid more stress, however, on the £55,000 per annum that could be saved by discontinuing 'idle Fellowships' 'not filled by any person occupying an educational office'.[44] When these Commissioners were appointed in 1877, they began by asking colleges whether the Cleveland figures needed any correction. Most of the colleges, especially the wealthier ones, then submitted markedly lower estimates, Magdalen anticipating a gain of income by 1891 of £9,984 per annum in place of Cleveland's £19,462, Christ Church that its income would be £3,964 *less* in 1890 than in 1876 (whereas Cleveland expected it then to be £34,040 above its 1875 level).[45]

Provost Magrath of Queen's recalls the Commissioners as 'disposed to make light of the difficulties in running out the beneficial leases', and as being so anxious 'to discover a clear annual surplus for University purposes' by stereotyping payments as to be impervious to his 1878 warnings that a 'College with a large number of fixed payments and a fluctuating income may in periods of agricultural depression become bankrupt'.[46] But in fact the Commissioners seem to have accepted the points put to them. Their chairman, Mountague Bernard, in an open letter explaining their decisions, mentioned, as offsets to the Cleveland estimates of increases in income, charges for the repayment of fine (and college building) loans, 'the extraordinary repairs and improvements necessary at the expiration of the beneficial leases' and 'the recent reduction of agricultural rents ... and the prospect of some depreciation in the future'. He declared himself 'unable to form any estimate of the future total income of the colleges which I should not regard as speculative', and stressed that 'no heavy *immediate* charge can be imposed on the Colleges for University purposes ... And in imposing *prospective*

[43] *Questions submitted to Colleges, and the Answers...*, Bodl. G. A. Oxon. 8vo 1001, 14.

[44] *Parl. Deb.* 24 Feb. 1876, 3S ccxxvii. 795–9.

[45] Christ Church felt the Cleveland Report 'calculated to mislead' since it 'took no account of the large deductions necessary for the payment of interest on the borrowed money, and for the repayment of the capital': *SCO* (1877), circulars, 61. The doings of the Selborne Commission are described in Pt 2, Ch. 2.

[46] J. R. Magrath, *The Queen's College* (2 vols 1921) ii. 199–201.

charges it must be borne in mind that the amount they will realize, and the time within which it will be realized, are matters of much uncertainty.'[47]

In the circumstances the Commissioners were cautious, and provided for a range of outcomes. They certainly stereotyped college payments to their heads (at a variety of levels), fellows (at £200 per annum for future appointments),[48] and not infrequently tutors (in such a way as to give these a *maximum* total income of £800 per annum, or a little more if they were also college officers). But college Visitors were also empowered, in the event of insufficient revenue, to suspend vacant fellowships and awards, and reduce tutorial payments and, pro rata, the charges laid on colleges by statute. These charges were of two kinds: defined support for specific professorships (and other University causes), and a progressive levy on colleges' net external incomes. Since support for professors, etc. could be set off against liability for most Common University Fund (CUF) taxation, the effect was to relate the latter to fluctuations in college incomes (whereas in Cambridge a fixed sum was demanded almost regardless).[49] However, 'If at any time it shall appear to the Visitor that the revenues of the College have become more than sufficient to provide for its expenditure, the Visitor may...make an order directing that any part of the surplus revenue shall be applied to purposes relative to the College [other than the increase of emoluments] or the University'; or the college might propose one itself.[50] In practice such superfluity only become apparent in the case of Magdalen, which in 1904 prepared a scheme earmarking a third of its prospective post-1906 surplus; the University questioned the scheme's adequacy, but did not quite reach the point of invoking the Visitor.[51]

Since Council's statements of University needs in the mid-1870s were not fully costed or quantified, one cannot say definitely how far they were or were not met.[52] They had fallen into three categories: buildings, new

---

[47] M. Bernard, *A Letter to the Right Hon. W. E. Gladstone on the Statutes of the University of Oxford Commission* (1882), 12–13. Bernard had succeeded Lord Selborne as Chairman in 1880.

[48] Vested interests survived. Sir Charles Oman recalls that 'As the old foundation' fellows of All Souls 'died out, or married, the survivors profited so much by the gradual appreciation of the college estates that a non-resident doctor fellow might be getting £800 a year, and a professor-fellow of the old foundation something like £2,000': *Memories of Victorian Oxford* (1941), 127–8.

[49] In Cambridge, though, the system of fluctuating dividends for fellows was allowed to continue (subject to a maximum).

[50] PP 1882 li. 641 (for scheme of CUF taxation) and *passim*. Another reason for this provision, as Bernard's letter makes clear (p. 43), is that the very prospect of a surplus was new; previously all income beyond the college's basic running-costs was simply divided between the head and fellows.

[51] See e.g. Magdalen College, *Report of the Finance Committee*, 1904, Bodl. G. A. Oxon. c. 179, fo 15, and minutes of the Bursarial Committee, esp. Dec. 1912 and Feb. 1913, MCA BCM/1/1.

[52] Had all the proposals put to the Commissioners by the various special interests been adopted, apart from the very expensive School of Practical Medicine, it would have cost over £50,000 p.a.: Bernard, *Letter*, 11.

University teaching-posts and an improvement in professorial pay. The fullest statement of building needs, that of 1875, amounted to £109,000 plus additional lecture-rooms, office and museum space (for which Lord Salisbury added on, rather generously, another £100,000 when introducing his Oxford University Bill in 1876). Next year's report added the important rider 'that the claims upon University funds...are made on behalf of several objects equally indispensable to the progress and well-being of the University, and that it would therefore be obviously undesirable if the amount expended on any single item were to be so great as to cripple the development of the University in other directions'. Unfortunately this process had already started in connection with the new Examination Schools, whose projected cost rose between 1875 and 1876 from £50,000 to £60,000. In 1877 a contract was signed for £71,500. And the final building cost to the University was about £107,000 (plus £38,000 for the site).[53] It would be churlish to begrudge a great building; but, in financial terms, it was over-elaborate. Nevertheless, it did not wholly pre-empt other developments. Plans to move the Bodleian Library foundered, on aesthetic and conservative as much as financial grounds, and the whole was left alarmingly unprotected against fire. But in 1878–84 some £26,500 was spent on restoring and refacing the quadrangle, and in 1883–90 space within it (vacated by the removal of the old schools and the Arundel marbles) was refitted for over £4,000.[54] And, in the University Museum area, 1875–7 saw a new Observatory, 1877–9 additional chemistry laboratories, 1882–5 the Pitt-Rivers Museum, and 1884 the Physiology Laboratory (whose £10,000 cost was opposed chiefly on anti-vivisectionist grounds).[55] All in all, the building needs identified in the mid-1870s may broadly be said to have been met—though partly, as had always been anticipated, by borrowing.[56] (For a more general listing of building costs and a comparison with Cambridge, see Appendix 12.2.)

Turning to new University teaching-posts, Council had recommended, in 1877, the gradual addition of about thirteen professors and twenty readers or demonstrators. The Commissioners envisaged the eventual addition of nine new professorships and two readerships, plus the appointment in 1883–4 of seven readers.[57] Their priorities were not followed to the letter. But the University's teaching staff continued to expand, albeit rather more slowly than at Cambridge (Table 12.7). Of their income it is hard to say much. In

[53] R. Wilcock, *The Building of Oxford University Examination Schools, 1876–1882* (1983), 29. See also the Note following this chapter. The University Museum had also greatly exceeded the original estimate of building costs (£30,000): see pp. 654–6 and Table 12.A3 below.

[54] Sir Edward Craster, *History of the Bodleian Library, 1845–1945* (1952), esp. 142, 227–8.

[55] *VCH Oxon.* iii. 57–8; H. M. and K. D. Vernon, *A History of the University Museum* (1909), 90–5.

[56] £60,000 for the Examination Schools (finally paid off in 1909), £10,000 for Physiology.

[57] Bernard, *Letter*, 13–14, 18. The 1883–4 readers were to come from the CUF, topped up if necessary by a temporary contribution from University funds.

TABLE 12.7

UNIVERSITY TEACHERS AT OXFORD AND CAMBRIDGE,
1851–1913

	1851	1876	1886	1899	1913
Oxford	32	46–7	68	97	123
Cambridge	25	34	68	—	153

Sources: RCO (1850), appx F (professors and readers); PP 1852–3
xliv. 179–81; PP 1876 lix. 330–1 (when one professorship was in
the process of establishment); PP 1886 li. 521 ff.; *Calendar*;
RCOC (1919), appx 1, 120–1. (The Asquith Commission's Oxford figures for 1913 are slight underestimates.)

the early 1850s the median was around £300 per annum, to which level six
professorships had recently been increased. In 1876 the average may have
been about £575 per annum,[58] that is perhaps slightly less than the income of
the average college tutor (as opposed to lecturer). The Commissioners then
fixed most full-time professorships at either £900 or £600 per annum (which
latter figure a number of people would have regarded as on the low side).[59]
In 1913 most professors seem to have received £900 per annum, while the
average income (from both University and college sources) of all University
teaching staff was probably rather over £600 per annum.[60] Where progress
was least was in the matter of pensions. In 1875/6 Council had called for a
system of pensions for retired professors; but nothing happened until 1912,
when it accepted a gift of £10,000 to initiate one. The war then supervened.[61]

A major factor in the increase of the professoriate was, as had always been
intended, rising contributions from the colleges. The 1850s reforms had
imposed on colleges specific liabilities for the support of professors, and in
1876 a committee of Hebdomadal Council had argued that 'Should Colleges
be willing to contribute to University funds, the most convenient form
of doing so would be to take upon themselves the payment…of some
of the Professors' stipends now charged to the University.'[62] The 1877

[58] PP 1876 lix. 330–1. Bernard, 21, remarks on the accidental variations: Christ Church
canons apart, the two most highly paid professors owed their respective £1,000 and £1,500
p.a. to their colleges' 'having forborne…to make a composition with them which would have
secured them £750 at a time when their actual incomes were much less'.
[59] In 1876 Salisbury favoured £1,000 p.a. (£954 in 1881 pounds), in 1922 the Asquith
Commission £1,200 (perhaps £698 in 1881 pounds or £36,900 in late 1995 pounds).
[60] The calculation (necessarily approximate) is based on figures given by the *RCOC* (1919),
appx 1, 116 ff. The average is obviously affected by the relative mix of professors, readers and
lecturers.
[61] *RCOC* (1919), report, 189–90, and appx 1, 131.
[62] Bodl. G. A. Oxon. c. 33, fo 155.

Commissioners followed this course. Bernard expected the 'appropriation to the Professoriate out of College revenues' to rise, eventually, by a little over £17,500 (exclusive of the detachment of a Rochester canonry from the provostship of Oriel to found a new chair); this would account for 'a large proportion' of all University taxation of the colleges, since it could be written off against their liabilities to the CUF.[63] In fact the relevant statute was broadly drawn and covered not only the University payments specifically imposed on colleges by the Commissioners, but also other contributions including the provision of fellowships for the holders of other University posts. In 1898, besides seventeen statutory professors and readers, five others had fellowships at colleges other than All Souls; by 1912 these figures had risen to twenty-two and nineteen. In the twentieth century the effect was to increase the overlap between Oxford's collegiate and University sections: in 1886, 11.9 per cent of these colleges' fellows also held University lectureships or other senior University posts,[64] 12.5 per cent in 1898, 19.9 per cent in 1912; the proportion of fellows actively engaged in inter-collegiate work will have been higher.

In 1871 the colleges had paid professors (and other University post-holders) £14,100. By 1913 their payments for 'University purposes' had risen to at least £45,400 (£39,000 by statute, the remainder voluntary). As Bernard had anticipated, most of this (£30,700) represented payments to professors and other University teachers, and relatively little cash passed directly to the University. Indeed the CUF that had been set up specifically to manage 'college contributions' received only some £9,300. Until 1914, therefore, the CUF was of no more than moderate importance,[65] and this has led some people to play down the significance of University taxation of the colleges. A different perspective would emerge if one compares college expenditure for 'University purposes' with, say, the £42,100 spent by the University itself on academic stipends. Whether college contributions were adequate in the light of their own resources can only be a matter of opinion; they had more than doubled since their introduction in 1883, and in 1913 accounted for 11.7 per cent of college spending other than on external property.[66] The Chancellor, Lord Curzon, however, had noted that most (though not all) colleges were 'far better off than when the Statutes of 1882 were passed', and had

[63] Bernard, *Letter*, 13–14, 17.

[64] University demonstrators holding fellowships have had to be excluded for reasons of comparability between the different dates.

[65] See also Appx 12.1 below. After 1945 the Fund was to prove of great importance, first as the vehicle through which the now comparatively affluent University could aid the colleges and, later, as the channel for capital grants from richer to poorer colleges.

[66] The 1913 figures derive from HCP 99 (1914), 63 ff. (though even here differences of definition produce minor divergencies in the accounts). The colleges put their own spending (independent of the University) on 'education and research' at £58,000 (1913 total excluding Corpus Christi, plus Corpus' 1914 spending), though it is not clear what proportion of fellows' and tutors' pay this covered.

claimed to find 'a general consensus' that their CUF payments 'admit of substantial increase. The University being poor, the Colleges, which are its federal constituents, are the first who should be called on to support it'. On the eve of the First World War things seem to have been moving in this direction. Despite the voluble hostility of President Case of Corpus, the new University Board of Finance (created in 1912) was to exercise surveillance over both college contributions and college finances generally, reporting to Council on 'the economy of administration, and...the interests of the University involved'. The University had also started to take legal advice on college contributions and the related question of the disposition of 'surplus' college revenues; and in 1913 it began the process of telling colleges the results (presumably as a prelude to action).[67] But none of this had any tangible consequences; and after the war the Asquith Commission pronounced itself satisfied that the University received from the colleges 'the full contribution which they can properly be asked to make'.[68]

Be that as it may, the University's own internal revenue was larger than college contributions. It derived chiefly from degree and admission fees, and from standard charges on all university members who kept their names on the books. In so far as people continued to do this after they had gone down, it contained an element of 'alumnus support'. At Cambridge, indeed, the Asquith Commission was told that the Chest's 'increased income is largely due to the increased number of Members of the University (11,430 in 1882 and 15,094 in 1913)', though the number of 'residents' in those years had been only 2,818 and 3,263. Oxford managed to expand its internal revenue fairly steadily, though it did not raise the rates of its capitation tax until 1913.[69] But Cambridge (admittedly a slightly larger place) did distinctly better, and, in the half-century after the Cleveland Commission, emerged as the wealthier University even though its colleges remained collectively poorer than their Oxford counterparts.[70]

Plotting Oxford University's income is difficult: it was dispersed among a multiplicity of departmental and other funds; and for the years to 1914 there are true consolidated accounts only for 1871 and 1913, while the 'general account: revenue', which is all that is really available for the interim, significantly understates the true total (see Table 12.8). This suggests that, in money terms, the University's income was broadly stationary for the decade

[67] Lord Curzon of Kedleston, *Principles and Methods of University Reform* (1909), 150; *Gazette* 6 Mar. 1912, 498–9; Bodl. G. A. Oxon. c. 153 (Case and Vice-Chancellor Heberden's 2 Dec. 1912 letter to colleges), and Bodl. G. A. Oxon. b. 140 (for the more moderate comments of a Committee of College Bursars in 1911); HCP 84 (1909), 49–52; HCP 94 (1913), pp. xii, xiii, xxxvii; HCP 96 (1913), 23.

[68] See also *Twentieth-Century Oxford*, 641–2.

[69] *RCOC* (1919), appx 1, 100, 141. Cambridge raised its University charge on undergraduates from £0.85 p.a. to £2 p.a. in 1894, Oxford from £2 to £2.50 in 1913.

[70] See Appx 12.1 below.

TABLE 12.8

OXFORD UNIVERSITY'S INCOME, AFTER DEDUCTING EXTERNAL
EXPENDITURE, 1856–1913

year	income	
(a) 1856, 1871, 1913		
1856	22,900	(excl. income from trusts)
1871	47,600	(incl. £15,400 from trusts)
1913	118,900	(incl. income from trusts, £6,500 from the endowment fund and £4,300 of government grants to departments, but not £1,800 of income tax repaid)

(b) General account I, revenue and CUF cash receipts from colleges only, 1884–1913

1884	58,100	
1888	60,100	
1893	59,000	
1898	59,700	
1903	74,400	
1913	84,000	

Sources: (*a*) Abstract of the general account of the University: Bodl. G. A. Oxon. c. 72, p. 380; *RCOC* (1872); *HCP* 99 (1914), 65; (*b*) University and college accounts.

1888–98 (which covered the worst onset of late nineteenth-century agricultural depression), but that otherwise it grew steadily. In real terms some allowance must be made for changes in purchasing-power. So in the 1880s and mid-1890s the university was doing distinctly better than the figures suggest, but not quite so well in the immediately pre-war years. Sometimes people must have realized this. A proportion of external receipts had for centuries been indexed to corn prices on the Oxford market (which were, indeed, still collected in 1996 for the information of estates bursars). But late Victorian and Edwardian England was strongly pervaded by 'money illusion'. Nor, in the university context, was it entirely illusion, since so many stipends and payments were fixed. Changes in the value of money affected their recipients as individuals, but applied only to a proportion of University and college finances. However, when all allowances are made, the University's income was clearly on a rising trend. Objectively it was not doing badly. But whether people felt this or not depended on their perception of university needs. By the turn of the century this had again begun to expand,[71] one external stimulus being Cambridge's 1899 appeal for an endowment

---

[71] In the 1898 Creweian Oration the Public Orator 'grimly accepting the genteel poverty of this University drew an amusing picture of the wealth and luxury of the University of California': *Oxford Times* 28 June 1898. G. B. Hill's *Harvard College by an Oxonian* (1894), 16–20, also observes that 'in England rich men found families; in America they found Universities, or they enlarge them', and notes admiringly that gifts and bequests to Harvard were currently running at over £100,000 p.a.

fund, another, Cecil Rhodes's benefaction to trustees of £3,345,000 in 1902. Thereafter, the 1870s assessments of University requirements were paralleled by a round of papers on 'the more pressing Needs of the University'. This time, however, reformers looked to meet them by launching in 1907 a public appeal for £250,000; of this £123,000 had been subscribed by 1912.[72] These results were broadly comparable with those achieved at Cambridge,[73] but were eclipsed by the half-million raised by Joseph Chamberlain to establish the new University of Birmingham.[74]

Even in 1914 the Oxford colleges still (in financial terms) greatly outweighed the University. We have already sketched their progress before 1870, and must now investigate whether, as was believed both by contemporaries and by subsequent tradition, their revenues thereafter dropped 'down the bottomless abyss of agricultural depression'. The short answer is that they did not. A calculation of net college incomes, disregarding both borrowing and the costs of loan charges and 'contributions for University purposes', gives the figures shown in Table 12.9. The most that can be said is that there was a slight dip in 1893 (during the second wave of agricultural depression); but the

TABLE 12.9

NET COLLEGE INCOMES, DISREGARDING BORROWING, LOAN CHARGES AND PAYMENTS FOR 'UNIVERSITY PURPOSES', 1871–1913

year	income (£)	constant 1900 pounds
1871 excl. Hertford	297,400	219,300
1883 excl. Hertford	336,100	267,000
incl. Hertford	342,400	272,000
1888	344,500	340,700
1893	335,600	337,600
1898	352,800	378,500
1903	363,000	374,600
1908	399,900	388,200
1913	417,000	357,900

[72] Of this over £43,300 had been spent (over £20,000—with a further £2,000 promised—on library storage below the Radcliffe Camera) and quite a lot of the remainder promised; so the resultant income only swelled the University's trust funds in 1913 by £2,223: *OM* 16 Oct. 1913, 10–11; University accounts.

[73] In 1899–1907 the Cambridge University Association raised £115,000, and a special appeal for the Library, £18,000; but the same period also saw some £100,000 worth of gifts and bequests, some (though not all) inspired by the appeal: letter from Duke of Devonshire, 15 Feb. 1907, to the *Morning Post*.

[74] In the 1870s Sir Josiah Mason had devoted over £200,000 to establishing the Mason Science College. In upgrading this into Birmingham University, Chamberlain (encouraged to think big by Andrew Carnegie and an inspection of American universities) raised the equivalent of

general picture is of growth, albeit one whose contours were much affected by changing price levels.

Contemporary complaints, though, became more comprehensible if we widen our calculations to include both borrowing and the costs of debt service, plus those of 'contributions for University purposes'; this gives us some idea of what was available for immediate college spending (see Table 12.10).

TABLE 12.10

COLLEGE INCOMES, INCLUDING BORROWING,
LESS LOAN CHARGES AND PAYMENTS FOR
'UNIVERSITY PURPOSES', 1871–1913

year	income (£)	constant 1900 pounds
1871 (excl. Hertford)	285,900	210,800
1883 (incl. Hertford)	283,100	224,900
1888	270,900	268,000
1893	259,400	261,000
1898	274,900	294,900
1903	283,400	292,400
1908	317,600	308,400
1913a	331,000	284,200
1913b	362,400	311,100

Note: 1883 excl. Hertford: £276,800 (constant pounds *219,900*).

Sources: For 1871, Cleveland Commission (net external, trust and special and internal income, less payments for University purposes). For 1883–1913a, College accounts—'General Account I—Revenue'. For 1913b, net external, trust and special and internal income, less contributions for University purposes: *Gazette* xlv (18 May 1914), 179. These figures are more comprehensive than those derived from college revenue accounts only. Christ Church's payments for University purposes in 1871 include those for all canons and professors and for 'Chapel'; for 1883–1913a they are those listed in the accounts plus the entire contribution to the Chapter Fund; both figures are somewhat too high. For 1913b they are those stated in the *Gazette*.

Keble's accounts are not included since they were compiled on a different basis.

£650,000. Much of this went on buildings, the last two laboratories leaving heavy debts. Chamberlain had meant to raise a further £500,000 by way of endowment, but his stroke prevented this. In 1920 the university successfully appealed for £500,000 to clear its debts of £138,000 and resume development: F. W. Burstall and C. G. Burton, *Souvenir History of the Mason Science College and of the University of Birmingham, 1880–1930* (Birmingham 1930), esp. 11, 31, 41; E. W. Vincent and P. Hinton, *The University of Birmingham: its history and significance* (Birmingham 1947), 25–6, 28, 34–5, 38, 162, 183; J. L. Garvin and J. Amery, *The Life of Joseph Chamberlain* (6 vols 1933–69) iv. 217–19.

The growth in money income between 1871 and 1883 had been more than offset by a drop in borrowing,[75] by the increase in the cost of servicing past debt and by higher payments for University purposes. Thereafter the figures in current pounds—those of which contemporaries would have been most aware—do indicate a distinct (though not disastrous) decline in 1893, and otherwise a long period of stagnation from which colleges did not break out until after 1903. In constant pounds, however, there seems to have been a slight improvement between 1871 and 1883, distinct progress in the 1880s, checks in the early 1890s and around the turn of the century, a peak in 1908 and a (perhaps misleadingly steep[76]) decline thereafter. Of course not all college spending was sensitive to price changes. But, taken together, Tables 12.9 and 12.10 suggest a considerable overall improvement in colleges' finance, checked only briefly around 1893.

Naturally all colleges did not follow quite the same pattern. In current money, University College's disposable income (as calculated in Table 12.10) fell from 1871 to 1893 and then rose steadily; Trinity's shot up (with the running-out of large beneficial leases) and then remained close to, or slightly below, the 1883 figure for the rest of our period; Hertford was the only college never to show any relapses. The rank order of college incomes[77] did not change very greatly, and it does not seem that all the gains made in our period were monopolized by a few untypical colleges. One can, however, point to a number of 'losers', or colleges that went through difficult spells; and it is understandable that one should hear more of these than of those colleges that had nothing to complain of. Balliol, broadly speaking, did well, with a rise of over a third in disposable income between 1871 and 1883; but in current (though not in constant) pounds, this had by 1893 declined by a tenth—hence, in part, the appeal after Jowett's death in that year for a memorial fund to remedy this. Exeter and Lincoln were both poorer, in current pounds, in 1913 than in 1871. In Exeter's case this resulted largely from a decline in its undergraduate numbers and hence its internal income; in Lincoln both internal and external income followed a curve of decline and renewal. But if one calculates in constant rather than current pounds, recovery set in after 1883 and soon brought both colleges above their 1871 levels. Pembroke's fortunes broadly resembled those of Lincoln. But in both Wadham and Worcester the fall in external income was so steep that in

[75] Five colleges borrowed in 1871, Magdalen and Christ Church very substantially. Unfortunately the post-1883 accounts do not always distinguish between 'fines' (income) and 'fine loans' (borrowing); where they do not, half the stated total has been allocated to each. Fine loans are, however, appreciable only in 1883.

[76] 'Repairs and improvements on estates', which are deducted to arrive at net external income, rose by £26,400 p.a. between 1903 and 1913 (probably because there was more money, in current pounds, around). Were this increase added back into income, 1913 would, in constant pounds, be only slightly down on 1908.

[77] Changes in comparative college incomes since c.1660 are charted in *Twentieth-Century Oxford*, pp. 657–8.

current money neither regained its 1871 level, while even in constant pounds this was rarely achieved. Both would, no doubt, have welcomed the problems of the far richer Corpus, Christ Church and All Souls. Corpus' disposable income increased until 1888, then fell for a decade before fully recovering in current (but not constant) pounds by 1913. Christ Church's income in 1871 had been boosted by £9,765 worth of loans; and though the college had little to complain of thereafter in terms of gross revenue, the effort of debt repayment caused it (as we have seen) severe problems around the turn of the century. All Souls did well between 1871 and 1883; but its basic income (as measured in Table 12.9 in current pounds) had by 1893 lost almost all these gains, with full recovery not achieved until the twentieth century; and these difficulties were so magnified by deductions for loan service and University taxation that, in current pounds, its disposable income never (and in constant pounds only in 1908) regained the 1883 level.

Further detail is made difficult by variations both in college policies and in the sources of their incomes. Worcester is a classic instance of a college caught by the agricultural depression. The bulk of its external income came from land rather than houses, so though the yield from the latter nearly tripled, this did not make much difference; gross rent for land, £5,882 in 1871, fell to £2,886 in 1893, and only recovered to £3,022 in 1913. Other colleges changed their financial profiles: University's internal income rose steadily, to overtake external (as here calculated) in 1893, but by 1913 its external income was again slightly the greater. Merton did not borrow until the twentieth century, and then only incurred charges of £775 per annum (on loans for internal building). As a result, it generally had more disposable income than All Souls, despite that college's considerably greater unadjusted income. Between 1880 and 1913 All Souls borrowed £130,200 for estate development. But this did lead to results, its stated gross income from 'houses' (more accurately ground-rents) rising from £16 in 1883 to £12,600 in 1913.[78] The pattern of Christ Church's estate borrowing was rather different: fine loans for its existing members of £203,600 (to 1886), estate improvements (1886–1913) £42,300. Its income from 'houses' rose only from £2,800 in 1883 to £5,200 in 1913; and, as we have seen, the burden of loan charges led it into a number of financial panics. Lastly the burden of contributions for University purposes fell very unevenly. In part this reflected deliberate college decisions: Magdalen was embarrassingly well off before the First World War, and its £10,100 payment in 1913 (up from £5,600 in 1903) reflected this. In part it resulted from the estimates by various commissions of college circumstances: All Souls' burden was always very high, but then it had fewer other claims on its resources than the undergraduate colleges. Another factor was the prevailing lack of interest in internal income: University taxation fell

[78] For slightly different figures, see Faber, *All Souls Bursarships*, 92, and p. 430 below.

only on external income, so Balliol's contribution never rose above £316, though that of Jesus (always the poorer, on the criteria used for this chapter, after 1883) rose from £280 in 1871 to £1,003 in 1913.

It will be seen that I tend to play down, some would say underplay,[79] the impact of the agricultural depression. Nevertheless, some colleges clearly were, and others felt themselves to be, squeezed. One obvious response was caution in regard to new commitments. The 1877 Commissioners imposed on All Souls, *inter alia*, a £1,000 per annum payment to the Bodleian. But 'owing to agricultural depression All Souls...found it impossible to reach that figure until 1906, and from 1887 to 1898 Bodley would have received nothing at all from the College had not its Warden, Sir William Anson, paid in £100 a year anonymously out of his private purse'.[80] A longer-running problem was that of Corpus. This had allowed (or encouraged) the Commissioners to prescribe for it the ambitious targets of five professorial and twenty-two or twenty-three other fellows, and of thirty-six scholars. But its gross income peaked in 1888 (at £22,211), then declined to a trough (of £17,349) in 1898, and from 1893 to 1900 the corporate account was continuously in deficit (to the cumulative total of £7,408) producing in the President what a junior colleague later called the 'hallucination' that 'the college was on the verge of bankruptcy'.[81] Contrary to tradition, this did not prevent expenditure on head, fellows, tutors, college officers and professors from being higher in 1898 than in 1888. But by 1904 there was clearly no longer any expectation that the Commissioners' targets would be met: in reciting them for the *University Calendar*, Corpus altered their preamble from 'When' to 'If ever the provisions of the Statutes...can be fully carried out'. However, the University was now pressing Corpus to do more, even establishing in 1909 one of the professorships (Romance Languages) specified in the statutes. Corpus repeatedly dragged its heels; and though in 1910 it took on another of its statutory chairs (Moral Philosophy), in 1914 it finally turned Romance Languages down.[82] The problem seems to have been not simply money, but also a bitter division within the governing body between the professorial and tutorial parties, exacerbated after 1905 by suspicion of the dictatorial tendencies of President Case.[83] Another way of postponing expenditure was to put

[79] See e.g. A. J. Engel, *From Clergyman to Don* (1983), ch. 5.

[80] Craster, *History of the Bodleian Library*, 160. Anson maintained that 'the order which shall be followed' in meeting the various contributions for University purposes 'is left to our discretion', though he was anxious to hasten the college's assumption of the full liabilities imposed on it: H. H. Henson (ed.), *Sir William Anson, 1843–1914* (1920), 70, 80.

[81] G. B. Grundy, *Fifty-Five Years at Oxford* (1946), 102.

[82] Both chairs attracted benefactions in 1909; the £6,654 for Moral Philosophy yielded dividends of £247 p.a., but the £1,000 for Romance Languages disproportionately little at £28 p.a.

[83] Grundy, ch. 6; T. H. Aston, 'The effects of the late nineteenth century agricultural depression on the University and its colleges, 1870–1914', OUA, Keeper's Oration, 1977; college accounts (which make it clear that payments from the Tuition Fund were not, as has been claimed, suspended in the 1890s).

off building. It was not always taken—Corpus was induced by a generous contribution from Case to lay out £5,800 on the library and the President's house in 1905–6.[84] But shortage of money fortunately prevented Wadham from demolishing the King's Arms.[85] And Merton abandoned some rather alarming projects in 1882 in consequence of the state of its agricultural rents,[86] though they were revived (on a smaller scale, but still including a white elephant of a warden's lodgings) in 1905–10. More generally, capital account expenditure on college buildings seems to have fallen from an average of £17,900 per annum in 1883–7 to £15,200 per annum in 1888–92, £3,100 per annum in 1893–7 and £3,600 per annum in 1898–1902; it then leapt to £23,000 per annum in 1903–7 and settled at £19,600 per annum in 1908–12.

More painful economies were to cut stipends or pay them in arrears (as, for example, in Jesus and Wadham in 1882). This was less common than might have been expected. The alternative adopted by Pembroke, one of the hardest-hit colleges, was to keep stipends at their statutory level (£200 for a fellow), indeed to increase tutors' pay in 1882 (from the £300 set in 1879 to £375),[87] but to take every opportunity of reducing the number of fellows. In December 1889 it petitioned its Visitor to permit a fellowship recently released by death to be kept vacant until 'the Corporate Revenue of the College is sufficient to meet the stipend of a new Fellow without rateably diminishing the charges created by the College Statutes'. Charges for the Master, ten fellows and twelve scholars were £3,670, whereas over the last six years estate profits and room rents, less fixed charges, had averaged only £2,940, 'the deficiency having been supplied from the internal revenue which the college derives from Matriculation and Graduation Fees, Annual Dues from members of the College and similar items which are necessarily of an uncertain character and fluctuating amount'. There was no prospect of an increase in revenues, and the college was hampered for lack of funds. However, it 'possesses a number of Fellows amply sufficient to carry on the business, discipline and educational work of the College, having five Fellows resident within the College walls' (2 deans, 2 tutors, 1 bursar) 'and two Lecturers besides one Professor Fellow residing within the university' plus three non-resident fellows. The Visitor (Lord Salisbury) allowed a ten-year suspension of the vacant fellowship. Further petitions followed in 1892 (in respect of the fellowship vacated by Professor Price's elevation to the mastership), 1897 (fellowship vacated by marriage), and 1899 (on the determination of a non-resident's seven-year fellowship). In 1904 a petition for

---

[84] Case contributed a further £7,000, one condition being that he could control the design.
[85] J. Wells, *Wadham College* (1898), 172.
[86] Aston, 'College and university estates'.
[87] Convention book, 1858–83, 13 June 1879 and 5 Dec. 1882, PCA 2/1/4; lecturers' pay also rose. The new rates were held till 1895, when a more complicated division of the Tutorial Fund was resolved on.

the renewal of the seven-year suspension granted in 1897 added, to the usual information, the contention

That any addition to the existing number of Fellows would probably force the Governing Body to increase the charges upon Undergraduate members of the College. At present these are kept as low as possible. And the Master and Fellows would be most reluctant to tax the junior members of the College in order to provide stipends for Fellows from whom, as not being engaged in College work, the Undergraduates would derive no advantage.

Salisbury and his successor, Goschen, were both accommodating. But when, on the next opportunity in 1908, the standard petition was again put in, Lord Curzon, the new Chancellor and Visitor, balked, remarking of the claim 'that the Undergraduates ought not to be taxed to pay for a Prize Fellow not engaged in tutorial work' that the Master and fellows could agree 'with an ordinary, i.e. a non-tutorial Fellow, to take part in the educational work of the College. They might even desire to elect a Fellow on these terms at no distant date'. Curzon did, however, concede a three-year suspension. When this expired, Pembroke initially intended simply to ask for a further seven years, but thought better of it and decided in February 1912 to appoint to a new 'Tutorial Fellowship with special regard to the philosophical work of Literae Humaniores'.[88] Thus fortified, it petitioned in June for the suspension of another fellowship vacant by death: estate profits, etc. had averaged £2,435 per annum in 1903–11, while with seven fellows annual charges would now be £3,100 per annum and the college 'is most reluctant to increase these charges upon its junior members, and would prefer to lower them, when possible, as it has recently done by reducing its' BA and MA fees. Curzon was unimpressed, interviewed the Bursar, established that Pembroke was 'likely to be decidedly better off in the immediate future', and asked 'what the College proposed to do with this surplus'. Eventually he allowed a three-year suspension to permit repair and improvement of college and estate buildings, but added that Pembroke should then

proceed to fill the remaining Fellowship contemplated by the Commission; and I need not remind you ... that even if an additional fellow be not then required for the internal work of the College, it will be open to you to associate a Prize Fellowship with any conditions as regards work or research, inside or outside the University, as may be thought desirable in the interest of the Higher Education.[89]

Pembroke represents an extreme case of the tendency to protect the position of fellows involved in teaching, if need be at the expense of the remainder. This sometimes took the form of the suspension of fellowships:

---

[88] R. G. Collingwood was elected.
[89] Convention book, 1883–93, pp. 72–3, fos 125–6, 131; 1894–1903, fos 86–9, 130 ff.; 1904–15, fos 7 ff., 81 ff., 89–90, 154, 156, 165 ff., 176–7.

in 1898 Lincoln's statutes were altered to permit a seven-year suspension if the fellowship dividend had been 25 per cent below £350 for three consecutive years.[90] Overall fifteen fellowships were returned as suspended in 1886 (eight at Magdalen), and the *University Calendar* suggests that twelve were suspended and two vacant in 1913. But actual suspensions probably mattered less than the general trend in numbers. Precise calculations are subject to irritating minor differences (of definition and as between sources), but Tables 12.11 and 12.12 probably represent a fair approximation.

The number of fellows seems to have remained fairly steady until the onset of reform in mid-century, then to have declined progressively until

TABLE 12.11

NUMBERS OF FELLOWS, TUTORS ETC.
(EXCLUDING ALL SOULS), 1815–1912

year	no. suspended or vacant	remainder	employment	%
1815	18	495	EO	9[a]
1842	21	489	EO	12[b]
1865	21	368	EO	18[c]
1871	29	317	T/LC	30
			CO	9
			UP	3
1886	15[d]	271	EC	45
			UL+	12
1898	20	257	T/LC	49
			CO	4
			UL+	12
1912	14	271	T/LC	56
			CO	4
			UL+	20

Note: EO = engaged in educational work in Oxford; T/LC = tutors/lecturers in their own college; CO = college officers; UP = University professors, of whom one-third were also T/LC; EC = employed in educational work of the college; UL+ = holding university lecturerships or above.
The number of fellows holding university demonstratorships (not shown here) will have increased appreciably by 1912.

   [a] 1814.
   [b] 1845.
   [c] 1858.
   [d] Vacancies not stated.

Sources: *Calendar* (the calculations of percentages 'engaged in educational work in Oxford' are those of Engel, *From Clergyman to Don*, 292; and for 1871 *RCOC* (1872), pt 1, for 1886 PP 1886 li. 571 ff.

[90] V. H. H. Green, *The Commonwealth of Lincoln College, 1427–1977* (1979), 523.

TABLE 12.12

COLLEGE PAYMENTS TO FELLOWS, TUTORS ETC.
(EXCLUDING ALL SOULS), 1871–1912 (£)

(*a*) University to Worcester

	1871	1886
fellows (excl. university professors/readers)	90,200	59,800
college officers, tutorial fund payments to teachers (not necessarily fellows), pension funds	38,700	52,600
total	128,800	112,500
total 1914 pounds	111,400	130,500

(*b*) University to Hertford

	1886	1893	1898	1903	1908	1912
fellows (excl. professors/ readers)	61,300	56,300	53,500	53,500	56,500	58,600
college officers; tutors and lecturers, being fellows	38,200	41,000	40,800	44,700	49,500	49,800
pension funds	5,300	8,000	10,500	10,500	12,700	18,200
tutorial payments to persons not fellows of the college making them	10,500	10,400	10,700	11,000	10,700	12,800
total	115,400	115,800	115,500	119,800	129,400	139,400
total 1914 pounds	133,900	136,500	145,200	144,900	147,200	142,200

the mid-1880s, after which it more or less stabilized. Detailed changes resulted from the decisions and fortunes of individuals. But university reform seems to have exercised a more powerful downward influence on numbers than agricultural depression, though the latter contributed to preventing the realization of the Commissioners' 1881 targets. The tendency of increasing numbers of fellows to devote themselves to educational work in Oxford also started in mid-century, though it gathered pace from the 1870s and had clearly become the norm by the eve of the First World War.

It is harder to be definite about pay, not only because this could fluctuate wildly from year to year—fellows of Queen's on the Old Foundation got £629 each in 1870 as against their usual average of £310[91]—but also because there were wide variations between the earnings of different types of fellow in any given year. The range of earnings (from all college sources) at Lincoln is set out in Table 12.13.

[91] *RCOC* (1872), pt 1, 71. For the provost the figures were £1,984 and £1,046, for fellows of recent appointment £483 and £247.

TABLE 12.13

EARNINGS OF FELLOWS AND TUTORS AT LINCOLN COLLEGE,
1800–1912 (£)

year	highest income £	1914 pounds	tutorial fees	lowest income
1800/1	363	179	138	33[a]
1815/16	306	187	87	56[a]
1816/17	345	209	134	113[b]
1837/8	529	417	326	79[a]
1856/7	637	509	319	262[a]
1871	762	660	462	300
1878/9	717	658	305	377[a]
1886:				
5 tutors	583	655	217	
2 other fellows	366	411	—	
1898:				
5 tutors	496	564	230	
3 other fellows	266	302	—	
1912:				
6 tutors	524	524	195	
2 other non-professorial fellows	329	329	—	

Note: 'Highest income' includes 'tutorial fees'. In 1878/9 there were three tutors, earlier two; in 1871 these earned £462 and £328 respectively, but such disparities were unusual. The highest income in 1871 was at least £762 but could have been up to £25 more.

For 1886, 1898 and 1912 the payments are averages. Further payments (in 1886 £370, 1898 £330, 1912 £375) were made to the college officers and chaplain, who were generally (but not necessarily) fellows; individual fellows may also have earned money by teaching for other colleges.

[a] Non-resident.
[b] Resident.

Sources: RCOC (1872), pt 1; 1914 pounds are derived from the indices in Mitchell (with Deane), *Abstract of British Historical Statistics*, 343–5, 470.

The 1877 Commissioners thought the current payments too large, and future fellows were restricted to a maximum of £200 per annum (apart from their earnings as college officers, chaplains, etc.), or, if tutors, of £300 per annum plus the produce of the tutorial fund. Dr Green tells us that in the late nineteenth century 'A Fellowship was worth £350 a year, but the dividends sometimes fell below this level'; in 1885 they were made up to a floor of £310 by drawing on the building fund. Lincoln's fortunes emphasize the importance both of tutorial earnings and of the numbers of people between whom college income (whether tutorial or corporate) had to be divided. The amount the college paid out to both fellows and tutors was higher, in money terms, in 1912 than in 1886, but so was the number of recipients.[92] Similarly the three St John's tutors of 1880 earned an average of £667 (inclusive of their fellowships), the four of 1905 one of £643.[93]

The experience of Corpus also shows a considerable rise in earnings to 1871, with the greater value of money continuing this in real terms in 1886, but growing numbers then exerting a downwards pressure. In 1814 it told its Visitor that, as a result of past inflation and the improvement of the College revenues, 'The present annual value of a Fellowship, with all its advantages, cannot be estimated at less than £200' (about *100* 1914 pounds). In 1854–5 a senior fellow received £274 (*228*), a junior £258 (*215*); and in 1871 a fellowship was put at £300 (*274*), a tutorship at £330 (*301*). Subsequently, in 1886, eleven non-professorial fellows averaged £288 (*324*), and three who were tutors a further £366 (*411*). In 1898 twelve non-professorial fellows averaged £280 (*318*), and five tutors a further £215 (*244*) plus £90 (*102*) per head contributed to their pension fund. In 1912 eleven non-professorial fellows averaged £243 (*243*), and six tutors a further £344 (*344*), plus £229 (*229*) per head for the pension fund. The predicament of Corpus tutors in the later 1890s stemmed chiefly from the increase in their numbers. But they felt rather hard-pressed, and with some reason if they concentrated on take-home pay and disregarded the pension fund (instituted in 1890). The need for improvements was much stressed in the next decade, and in 1909 special tutorial stipends were introduced as a supplement to the tutorial fund.[94]

Balliol was another college conscious of the deficiencies of its tutors' pay, and its 1904 appeal, *The Needs of Balliol*, put their problems into a comparative context. Only one tutorial fellow had ever received the maximum of £590 per annum envisaged in the statutes; 'Practically no one can now obtain more than £540, and only a few can be granted so much'. One reason for what was clearly seen as an unfavourable situation *vis-à-vis* other colleges was the deficiency of endowments, which meant that undergraduate awards had to be financed from the tutorial fund, leaving less available for division between the tutors. Another was that Balliol fellows did not receive free rooms or allowances, which, it was claimed, meant they were thus £50 to £80 per annum worse off than those of other colleges. The appeal, however, improved the situation, two people being paid an extra £100 in 1906–7 from the fund's income, and five £50.[95]

[92] Green, *Lincoln College*, 390–1, 523, 573–4; *RCOC* (1872), pt 1; college accounts; *Calendar*. For 18th-century trends, see *The Eighteenth Century*, 238–9, 254.

[93] T. Hinchcliffe, *North Oxford* (New Haven 1992), 165. An average St John's lectureship in 1905 was worth £382.

[94] Fowler, 300, 342; *RCOC* (1872), pt 1; college accounts. There were in addition, for example, payments to college officers (c. £550 p.a. in 1886–95, £650–90 in 1898–1910, £740 in 1912–13). These are harder to allocate to individuals, but will in some cases have provided a worthwhile supplement.

[95] Bodl. Firth b. 36, fo 74.

For the university as a whole, Table 12.12 suggests a significant shift of payment away from fellows as such towards tutors and college officers (broadly overlapping categories covering those fellows active in college life).[96] Fellows, whether active or inactive, secured 70 per cent of the total payments recorded here in 1871, but only 42 per cent in 1912, by which time payments to college officers and tutorial fellows, plus provision for their pensions, had risen to 49 per cent. We can also get some idea of the average income of tutorial fellows, though of course factors like seniority will have led to substantial departures from this average, at least in connection with payments from tutorial funds (Table 12.14). These figures somewhat understate tutors' welfare, since they will have received free meals, some will have earned money by teaching for other colleges that will not show in the second part of the table, and a number will have received money from other funds.

TABLE 12.14

AVERAGE PAYMENTS TO TUTORIAL FELLOWS AND COLLEGE
OFFICERS (EXCLUDING ALL SOULS), 1871–1912

	year	no. of recipients	average receipt (£)	1914 pounds
18 colleges (University to Worcester): fellowship + payments to college officers and tutorial fund payments (whether or not made to fellows)	1871	123	597	516
	1886	118	702	814
19 colleges as above + Hertford: fellowship + payments to college officers, tutorial fund payments to fellows and provision for pensions	1886	125	595	690
	1898	145	556	699
	1912	164	666	678
As above, excl. provision for pensions	1886	125	552	641
	1898	145	484	608
	1912	164	552	563

Sources: *RCOC* (1872), pt 1; college accounts (revenue and tuition accounts). See also n. 97.

[96] It is harder to discuss the income of college heads as accounts do not necessarily show that derived from church livings held *ex officio*, while some apparent reductions may (as at Pembroke) be in respect of their tenure of professorial chairs. The stipends of individuals were, on occasion, sharply reduced, through their own generosity and/or for their colleges' necessities. The total returned for the nineteen historic colleges in 1883, £24,800, was well down on the 1871 Cleveland figure of £30,000 (though the Cleveland figure may have been more comprehensive). From 1883 there was little overall change, the 1893 total being £23,100 and the 1913 total £25,900. Most, though not all, heads were paid markedly better than either tutors or professors.

There are also some other problems.[97] But incomes clearly increased after 1871 both in money and still more in real terms. After 1886 they were clearly affected by the growing tendency to set money aside for college pension funds. These must be regarded as remuneration, but tutors derived no immediate benefit from them—and indeed the accounts suggest that until 1914 far more was put into such funds than was paid out in pensions.[98] Another important development was the growing number of fellows who were full-time teachers and who would have received payments from tutorial funds, thus reducing the 'jackpot' that, at least up to the 1870s, had often been divided out between a rather small number of senior tutors. Lastly, we should note the very considerable impact on real incomes of changes in the price level.

Three more imponderable factors also bear on our estimate of the college tutors' position. The first is their prospects in other careers. In the past a majority of fellows had gone on to take up church livings, and in the 1880s and 1890s a third of fellows were still clergymen. So it may be relevant that the average value of the 439 college benefices in 1871 was £427 per annum. With the subsequent decline in wheat prices, and hence in tithes, it will have fallen appreciably. This does not seem, before 1900, appreciably to have inclined fellows towards secular careers outside the university, but it may well have helped to tip the balance away from the Church and towards academe.[99] The second factor is marriage—also, in the past, a common reason for resigning fellowships. Some tutorial fellowships were still restricted as late as the 1930s; but restrictions were lifted piecemeal from 1869 onwards and, by 1886, 25 per cent of fellows were married.[100] This undoubtedly brought major new financial demands. The 1898 Creweian Oration decried Oxford's 'unfounded reputation for wealth and luxury' and depicted its tutors as in danger of having, 'like the Megarians in Aristophanes, to put their too numerous families up to auction'.[101] Lastly, private means. The general rule had been that fellows must resign if their (non-tutorial) income exceeded the value of their fellowship. This was abandoned with the 1850s reforms. There is no knowing what proportion of late nineteenth-century fellows enjoyed (like Alfred Robinson) private means, but it was not insignificant.

[97] Except for 1886 (where they come from PP 1886. il 570 ff.) the numbers of recipients derive from University Calendars. Those for tutors, lecturers and college officers are comparatively straightforward. But one cannot distinguish with complete confidence between ordinary fellows and those holding professorships or other University posts whose college fellowship payments are subsumed in the accounts under 'Payments for University Purposes' and who therefore cannot be counted here.

[98] The Corpus fund, started in 1890, had by 1912 accumulated a balance of £15,097.

[99] Engel, *From Clergyman to Don*, 286 (subject to the correction of a misprint); RCOC (1872), pt 1, 199.

[100] Engel, 107 ff.; PP 1886 li. 571 ff.

[101] *Guardian* 1 July 1896, 1022.

Finally, we turn from the chief purpose to which colleges put their income, the payment of head and fellows, to a brief survey of that income's sources, which were, in order of magnitude, external, internal (including tuition fees), and trust. As we have seen, relatively little stress was placed on internal income; qualms were expressed about placing burdens on junior members, and most discussion was of the proper use, or lamentable shortfall, of endowment income. Nevertheless, internal income—basically fees[102] and charges, since there was little attempt to make a profit on catering[103]—rose from £58,900 (20 per cent of all net income) in 1871 to £147,800 (36 per cent) in 1913. Some colleges built themselves up very largely on this basis. Keble, founded in 1868, was already, in terms of undergraduate numbers, the sixth-largest college by 1871. Its financial system, however, differed sharply from that of traditional colleges. More typical was Hertford. This did in fact have an endowment that, being kept in the hands of trustees, was always excluded from the official accounts. But, if we take only the income shown there, it was by the 1890s broadly on a par with Pembroke and Worcester. In terms of undergraduates in residence, it moved rather higher in the twentieth century, while if measured by numbers (though not prestige) of fellowships, it was one of the larger colleges. Older colleges, too, might depend substantially on internal income, as did Exeter (67 per cent of its disposable total, as calculated in Table 12.10, in 1871), University (55 per cent in 1903) and Wadham (61 per cent in 1908).

But, in financial terms, extra undergraduates could also be rather a nuisance if they necessitated additional college building. From 1868, admittedly, the University allowed them to live in lodgings, and the proportion who did so shot up to over a third of the total by 1883, then broadly kept pace with the growth in student numbers. Some will have lived in lodgings to save money as non-collegiate students, but most were attached to the traditional colleges. And these might well feel some obligation to increase their accommodation. New College's ordinances, looking towards an undergraduate population of the normal type, date from 1857. In 1861 a committee was established to consider accommodation, and Merton was approached in 1866 about the purchase of houses in Holywell. Since these had been leased out, purchase was not easy, but a site was assembled by 1871 and thirty-eight sets of rooms completed in 1873 for some £16,500. By then numbers 'had

---

[102] In 1871 tuition fees were usually £21 p.a. but sometimes £25 or £27: *RCOC* (1872), pt 1, 31. Balliol tried increasing tutorial fees in the 1870s 'with the result that the college lost numbers, and the experiment was given up': *The Needs of Balliol* (1907), Bodl. Firth b. 36, fo. 75[a].

[103] Grundy records with pride the success of his wife when appointed Domestic Supervisor at Oriel, the first woman ever to fill such a position. It led to pressure to reform Corpus along similar lines, and also took her (via wartime catering at an army hospital) to food control and local politics: Grundy, *Fifty-Five Years at Oxford*, 109, 130. After the war the Asquith Commission led to the general introduction of catering accounts, albeit still in an incomplete format.

grown so much that it was seen to be desirable to proceed without much delay to erect another portion', and two more staircases, plus a house for a married tutor, were added in 1875–7 for £11,300.[104] Another staircase and a resident tutor's house were built for £9,849 in the 1880s,[105] and on the death in 1895 of the Bursar, Alfred Robinson, his friends offered money to complete the design as a memorial to him (£14,200 for a gate-tower and two more staircases). The £2,620 they subscribed 'made it feasible to undertake at once what would otherwise have been delayed for some years for financial reasons'. Magdalen began its academic reform and educational expansion rather before buildings were ready—in 1875 a third of its undergraduates were in lodgings. By 1876 building had been recommended in principle, though there was some concern that it be financed otherwise than by the suppression of fellowships. This did not prove possible; but work started in 1880 and cost some £34,000. Many other colleges also constructed new undergraduate accommodation. But building could equally stem from aesthetic or prestige considerations. Even New College spent a good deal more on the restoration of its chapel (1877–88) than on its 1870s Holywell buildings. And though Brasenose nearly doubled in area, this related less to pressure of numbers than to an ambition to expand to the High that had been evident since the early eighteenth century. Plans had been drawn up from time to time, and in 1807–10 a building fund was established.[106] But the prospect of losing shop rents was decisive. By the 1880s, though undergraduate numbers remained steady, such considerations, while still felt, were no longer as influential, and some £24,000 was then expended; the scheme was finally completed (for another £20,000) in 1911, and only around then did undergraduate numbers rise.[107]

According to G. C. Brodrick (Warden of Merton) nearly all the older colleges had extended their buildings by the 1880s, 'mostly by the aid of private munificence'. Such aid might be spontaneous (as in the case of New College's Robinson tower); a lever to secure a particular outcome (W. A. Fearon contributed £2,000 towards New College's controversial hammer-beam chapel roof);[108] or even unwelcome—Walter Morrison was so overcome by a Balliol gaudy speech in 1911 praising the beauties of the Old Chapel, demolished in 1857, that at breakfast next morning he offered £20,000 to build a replica; the college seemed willing, but its old members

---

[104] Contract for building in Holywell, 19 Jan. 1875, NCA 3159. For an architectural appreciation of the Holywell buildings see Pt 2, Ch. 30.

[105] Memorandums on building costs, 1882–6, NCA 3176.

[106] This is said to have been consequent upon a rise in college numbers and of resulting pressure from the University.

[107] J. Buxton and P. Williams (eds), New College, Oxford, 1379–1979 (1979), 247–55; H. George, New College, 1856–1906 (1906), 52 ff.; VCH Oxon. iii. 154, 207; college accounts (the figures for Magdalen and Brasenose are of internal building expenditure on capital account, and could include other projects also); Magdalen order-books, 1854–84.

[108] Buxton and Williams (eds), New College, 263.

protested against the waste, and the money was finally steered towards Egyptology and professorial pensions.[109] Subscriptions were as often deliberately sought after. Jowett 'plumed himself on his dexterity in drawing money out of a man's pocket! Mere circulars he regarded as of little or no use...“you must write yourself”, he insisted, “to every individual person from whom you hope to get anything”'. And he urged the purchase of well-sited but correspondingly expensive land as a cricket ground by saying, 'I will give £3,000, if the Fellows can make up £2,000; and then I will beg £5,000 from my old pupils; and there's your £10,000.'[110]

This takes us to the more general topic of benefactions and trust funds. They were a mixed lot. Table 12.15 shows the variety received by Brasenose. Some of these benefactions were obviously intended to be spent (or drunk), others to form a continuing trust fund, or to swell existing funds, for the purposes specified.

TABLE 12.15

TRUST FUNDS AND BENEFACTIONS RECEIVED
BY BRASENOSE, 1833–1908 (£)

year	purpose	gift
1833	stipend for a preacher	63
1842	three exhibitions	4,313
1875	scholarship[a]	3,300
1885	Divinity Prize	105
1892	organ	1,240
1894–5	cricket ground and pavilion	1,200
1899	library[a]	3,000
1902	chapel panelling	500
1904	fellow's bequest: wine-cellar and money for building	4,000
1908	two exhibitions	5,000

[a] These gifts were made by transferring stocks, not cash, to the college.

Source: Brasenose Monographs iv. 40–1 (OHS lii 1909).

[109] H. Hartley, 'The Successors of Jowett', in R. H. C. Davis and R. Hunt (eds), A History of Balliol College (1963), 233–4.
[110] Abbott and Campbell, Jowett ii. 100; H. Hartley, 'Benjamin Jowett: An Epilogue' (citing A. L. Smith), in A History of Balliol College, 219; J. Jones, Balliol College: a history, 1263–1939 (1988), 217. Jowett had been looking since the early 1850s for somewhere more convenient than the traditional facilities at Cowley Marsh. The present Master's Field was brought into use in 1891 and rounded off as a memorial to him. The acquisition of such sports-grounds was another cost consequent upon the late 19th-century increase in undergraduate numbers and athleticism. New College's sports-ground, in the same area as Balliol's, also seemed impossibly expensive (it was building-land) until the Bursar came up with an anonymous benefaction: George, New College, 101.

Some colleges had many such funds, others few; and in 1871 their net income varied from £8,200 at Christ Church and £3,700 at Magdalen to £51 at Worcester. Some colleges were fortunate in attracting large benefactions—like Oriel's £100,000 legacy from Cecil Rhodes[111]—while others were particularly energetic in pursuing them. We have noted Jowett's fund-raising propensities. Later Balliol, inspired by Thomas Brassey (who himself is said to have owed the idea to the Master's wife), launched an appeal for £50,000 in 1904 and followed it up with others.[112] The college history says that without this 'financial support of the old members' it could not have maintained its position, and increasing number of fellows, in competition with wealthier rivals.[113] But of course many trust funds dated back for centuries. The older ones often held landed property; but, overall, funds were more likely than other college endowments to be invested in government stocks, etc. Their arrangement could be very complicated, with one fund feeding its income to another, usually for sensible reasons, though complexity is now (and presumably was then) in part also a bursarial device to curb extravagant impulses on the part of the fellows. Money could even be lost track of for long periods. Thus when a subscription was raised in 1837–40 for stained glass for the Wadham antechapel, the unspent balance of £200 was invested by the then Deputy Bursar, Griffiths; the college forgot about it, but in 1885, four years after his retirement as Warden, Griffiths handed over the fund, now grown to £1,200, asking that its first use be the reinsertion of plain glass.[114]

We cannot be certain of the full value of trust funds, since (especially at Hertford and Balliol) some were held by external trustees and did not figure in the published accounts. But the total net revenue reported for 1871 was £27,700, that for 1913 apparently only £33,900. Trust funds were less flexible than corporate income. But by and large they could be made to serve the colleges' current wishes, whether directly,[115] or indirectly by releasing corporate money for other purposes, or, in the last resort, by borrowing from them. Perhaps the commonest use for trust funds, though, was the provision of undergraduate awards. These increased steadily in absolute numbers (221 were listed in 1815, 941 in 1910) and even, despite slight dips in 1842 and 1886, as a proportion of the total number of undergraduates on the books.[116] The

---

[111] 22.5% for new building, 10% for repairs, 17.5% for general college income, 50% to supplement the income of (and improve high table for) resident fellows; in 1913 these funds together only produced an income of £2,222.

[112] £26,770 had been promised by mid-1907: Bodl. Firth b. 36, fo 74.

[113] Davis and Hunt, *A History of Balliol College*, 226.

[114] Wells, *Wadham College*, 192.

[115] The University, at least, allowed itself some latitude in interpreting funds' purposes, financing its first physics laboratory from an 18th-century gift to erect a riding-school.

[116] Number (including Rhodes scholarships, etc.) and percentage of total on the books: 221 (20.7%) in 1815; 272 (18.0%) in 1842; 396 (23.5%) in 1865; 670 (21.7%) in 1886; 941 (24.7%) in 1910.

system was occasionally criticized as reflecting neither financial need nor current performance, but only good tuition at public schools; and though such attacks were not common, they led to a survey of the 231 new award-holders (other than Rhodes scholars) coming up in October 1911: their awards (to the total value of £15,334 per annum) averaged £66, but supplementary payments from their colleges (£617), other sources such as city companies (£1,700), awards from their schools (£4,377) and county council scholarships (£1,725) brought total receipts per head to an average of £103.[117]

The last type of college revenue, external income, was that which attracted most attention, from reformers, in the prescribed form of accounts, and probably also at college meetings. The historic colleges were all primarily endowed with landed property (and tithes). And for much of our period its management did not differ much from the eighteenth-century pattern. Reserved rents came in more or less automatically. And all the college had to do was to assess a property's true value every seven years so as to fix the appropriate fine, and visit it occasionally to identify the college's holdings[118] and check that the lessee was neither wasting them nor absorbing them into his other possessions. Most of this could be done by any interested college fellow, or indeed by a friendly local gentleman. But by 1800 colleges had started to use professional land agents as well. The trend continued, and must have been stimulated by the Tithe Commutation Act, 1836. For this required the valuation of all the relevant produce, to establish a tithe rent charge and attach it to particular holdings, a process that meant that over the next decade college interests had to be represented at sometimes difficult meetings wherever tithes were held. Magdalen in 1838 allowed the president and bursar special powers to appoint agents to act for the college,[119] and Christ Church (a particularly large tithe-holder) made considerable use in this connection of Benjamin Badcock, an Oxford land agent. Later in the century much college work came to gravitate towards the firm of Field & Castle in Merton Street. Colleges might, of course, have local agents for specific properties. But convenience and familiarity led to most business being conducted through Oxford ones. Thus in February 1904 Messrs Castle reported to Merton on repairs ('Necessary' £1,290, 'Desirable' £1,550) in County Durham, Yorkshire, Leicestershire and Wiltshire. Their report was

[117] 'Return of entrance scholarships and exhibitions awarded to students beginning residence ...in October, 1911', Bodl. G. A. Oxon. b. 140. One (presumably wealthy) scholar in fact declined his £80 emoluments.

[118] See e.g. an 1872 letter: 'I do not know wheare the Property that belong to Christ Church is situated in Ashendon Parish [Bucks]. I have made inquiries dont think there is a man in the place that can point it out. I have heard from inquiry that the greater part or all of it is in Mr Ridgways Farm...'. This occasioned a detailed valuation by an Oxford land agent, which showed that Christ Church's holdings were indeed much intermixed with others: CA MS Estates 6, fos 135, 137.

[119] Magdalen order-book, 9 June 1838.

accepted. Colleges clearly relied heavily on their advisers; and estates committee minutes are full of assurances that Messrs Castle think such and such
a good price, and of decisions to spend 'in accordance with the report of
Messrs. Castle Field and Castle, May 17 1893' (Merton), or that 'tithe on
Magdalen's land at Wandsworth be redeemed as Mr. J' Anson [a London
architect] thinks best'. It is indeed exceptional to find departures from such
professional advice—as when Merton's smaller Gamlingay (Cambridge-
shire) tenants were in 1885 allowed rent rebates only of *up to* 15 per cent,
not of *at least* 15 per cent, as Castle had suggested, or when in 1903 the
Bursar was asked to get a second report on a possible purchase.[120] But this
does not mean that colleges were wholly dominated by their agents. For one
can occasionally detect distinctive college policies, and agents' advice will
have been framed in the light of college attitudes and of detailed and continuous consultation with their bursars.

The growing specialization of the office of bursar was another nineteenth-
century development. Some fellows had always been more knowledgeable
and interested than others—Blackstone (with whom we began) was one
such—but the office had genuinely rotated, usually on a yearly basis. In
New College, though,

The disappearance of the old simple system of beneficial leases, and the gradual
assumption by the College of a position as an ordinary landowner...made the office
of Bursar a very different thing...It could no longer be held by any Fellow willing to
take the necessary trouble with internal management, and it was obviously undesirable that the office should change hands frequently. In 1862 for the first time a Bursar
was deliberately chosen, and was retained in his post until he quitted Oxford thirteen
years later.

Elsewhere the choice of a new style was less deliberate. But at All Souls
Richard Berens served as Acting Bursar from 1808 to 1849, and came so to
manage all college business as to be loosely called 'the Bursar'. On his death
it seemed natural to replace him as 'Acting Bursar', and the position was
formalized by college regulation in 1858.[121] At Lincoln Washbourne West
held the bursarship for over thirty years from 1851; he once preached on
Judas's 'unbusinesslike conduct in accepting such inadequate remuneration
as thirty pieces of silver'.[122] In Pembroke W. H. Price clearly dominated the
scene in the early 1860s. In November 1862 he was thanked and remuner-
ated 'for his long, zealous, and effective service as Bursar and Deputy
Bursar'. Then disaster struck, and in February 1864 we find Bartholomew
Price undertaking (presumably for reasons of family solidarity) to repay the

---

[120] Merton bursars' reports, Oct. 1885, pp. 50–2, Mar. 1887, p. 125, May 1893, p. 110, Mar.
1903, p. 53, Feb. 1904, p. 79, Merton College Archives 6.37–6.40; Magdalen order-book, Nov.
1882.
[121] George, *New College*, 71; Faber, *All Souls Bursarships*, 24–31.
[122] Green, *Lincoln College*, 433.

£1,258 the 'late Bursar' had been discovered to owe the college; the affair apparently blighted Bartholomew's chances of election as Master for nearly thirty years. But such episodes were rare.[123] The *University Calendars* of the early 1870s reveal that, though in theory most bursars were still annually elected, in practice continuity was very much the rule. Non-fellows could be appointed to the job—the Cleveland Commission noted that two colleges had done so. It also described the cost of managing college estates as 'very low';[124] and though it would not assess the efficiency of such management, it reported that 'the average lettings, the absence of arrears, and the apparently small amount of losses from tenants, testify to the care and vigilance of the Bursars'.[125]

The task of estate management could certainly be strenuous. Most colleges, admittedly, had fewer and more compact estates than Magdalen, but it is worth noting the visits paid by the Bursar of Magdalen in 1889 (alone, or accompanied by his President, other fellows or the land agent):

Jan.   Westcott Barton (Oxon.); Chancery Lane and Southwark; Oddington (Oxon.)
Feb.   Wandsworth
Mar.   Wanborough (Wilts.); Horspath (Oxon.)
Apr.   Harwell (Berks.); Quinton (Glos.)
May   Standlake (Oxon.); Selborne, Petersfield, Sheet, Hillhampton, Otterborne, Bramdean, King's Somborne, Cowfold, Uppately, Basing (the Hampshire 'Progress')
June   Chalgrove and Berrick (Oxon.); Hempton (Oxon.); Standlake (Oxon.); Edgehill (War.)
July   Aynho, Astwick, Whitfield, Syresham, Brackley Hatch, Helmdon, Evenley, Plumer's Furze (Northants), Stamford, Kitton, Frampton, Candlesby, Swaby, Wainfleet, Titchwell, Hickling, Brandeston, Lincoln Hall, Caldecott Hall (Lincoln and Norfolk Progress)
Sept. Alton, Selborne and Lyeway Farm (Hants)
Oct.   Standlake; Hempton; Berrick, Chalgrove, Golder (Oxon.)
Nov.   Stainswick, Chapelwick (Oxon.), Wanborough, Denchworth (Oxon.)
Dec.   Hempton; Northmoor and Standlake; Tubney (Berks.)[126]

Originally the formal sealing of new leases had been perhaps the major external business of college meetings. And for the first half of our period much debate could be generated over the appropriate level at which to set

[123] Convention book, 1858–83, fos 9, 25–7 (Pembroke 2/1/4). The St John's Bursar in the 1890s was 'bonded' to the tune of £1,000, but was found in 1896 to have 'borrowed' nearly £3,000; a bailiff had already embezzled over £3,000 in 1889: Hinchcliffe, *North Oxford*, 76–7.
[124] Ostensibly under 3% of external college income; this usually did not include the bursars' salaries, but the cost still appeared low where some or all of these were added in.
[125] *RCOC* (1872), pt 1, 35–6.
[126] Notes of Bursar's visits to estates, MCA MS CP 1/40.

fines and over the running-out of beneficial leases. Lengthy memorandums were submitted on the former question in 1811 to a Magdalen committee that split three ways before compromising,[127] while committees were appointed in July 1854, May 1864 and May 1870 to make recommendations on the latter.[128] But Hereford George recalls, of New College, that discussion most frequently arose in connection with requests, from parishes where the college had property, for subscriptions or donations. These came with little prior notice; and though the warden or bursar's advice, based on past experience, was usually followed, lobbying by interested fellows sometimes produced haphazard decisions. 'As more attention came to be paid to College finance', committees were established to lay down ground rules and relate gifts to the extent of college property in the parish in question. Then, as property began to come into hand, important questions as to purchase, sale, letting or investment might arise at any time, and it was felt that they were better not first raised in a full college meeting. So, initially as an experiment, 'all property questions, including applications for grants of money' were from 1870 first referred to a standing Estates Committee, whose recommendations were in practice rarely discussed afresh in the full meeting.[129] In smaller and poorer colleges such problems might not arise, and there might even be too few resident fellows to constitute a real committee. But larger ones probably arrived, by the late nineteenth century, at arrangements not unlike New College's. Certainly the Merton 'Bursar's Reports' (in effect estates committee minutes) were almost always later endorsed by the governing body.

George's account of New College stresses the requests for local subscriptions and donations. In the eighteenth century these had been rare. Later several factors multiplied them. One was the ending of beneficial leases. Previously colleges had taken (though not always stuck to) the position that such requests should be addressed to the lessees; now they were exposed to a growing number of minor demands.[130] Secondly, Victorian clergymen were increasingly likely to reside in their parishes instead of leaving them to curates. When they did so, they discovered their vicarage to be impossible,

---

[127] President Routh was one of the doves: MCA MS ES 2/10, 2/11, 2/27.

[128] Magdalen order-book.

[129] George, *New College*, 71–3.

[130] Magdalen's order-books record the following gifts to Chinnor: 1813: £30 for church repairs; 1848: £100 plus a subscription of £5 p.a. to the school; 1852: £5 p.a. for the school; 1854, 55, 57: £5 to the Coal Fund; 1859: £5 for an organ and £115 for school building; 1861–3: £75 for church restoration; 1864–5: further contributions refused; 1870: £3 for the organ; 1874: £5 for the British School; 1878: £20 for fittings, £10 for a library; 1887: £20 for enlarging the school; 1889: up to £25 towards the purchase of a reading-room; 1891: £100 for increased school accommodation, but the annual grant was reduced to £5; 1894: 3 guineas for the school; 1895: 2 guineas for the church tower; 1899: the subscription to the voluntary school increased to 7 guineas; 1901: the 2 guinea subscription to the Coal Club (along with sixteen similar subscriptions in other villages) discontinued.

and demanded assistance in building a huge new one; the church was dilapidated and in need of restoration by Sir George Gilbert Scott; and local provision for education was defective—in 1856 the East Garston (Berks.) schoolmistress was incompetent, but had been given the job sixteen years earlier to keep her off the poor rates when she had failed at keeping the accounts of the local shop.

Most of the estate correspondence in Christ Church's muniment-room is about such matters. Occasionally the college was moved by social concern to take the initiative. In 1859 it circulated to all holders of its livings a questionnaire on: the benefice's income; the state of the parsonage and of the church; the condition, management and sufficiency of local schools; and the size, circumstances, moral condition and denominational feelings of the population. More usually it was concerned to ward off external pressure. Thus it explained in 1831 that while

the Dean and Chapter are very sorry to hear the Parish is so heavily burthened by the Labouring Poor...as Trustees of a Charity, they have little or no discretion allowed them—and they cannot be brought to think, as you appear to think, that they have the power to *compel* their tenants to employ any given number of labourers, of any given Parish—All they could...do, would be to *recommend* Messrs. Fountaine and Lusk to employ as many of the D[reyton] B[eauchamp] labourers as the great distance will allow them to do and place as many of them as they conveniently can on the Cottages already existing upon their farms.[131]

We cannot fully quantify college charity, since a common way of augmenting benefices was to grant the incumbent glebe, tithe or other land at a reduced or notional rent. But the figures recorded for actual expenditure by the historic colleges on corporate account on augmentations, donations, etc. were: £17,800 in 1871; £18,300 (6.5 per cent of gross corporate revenue other than dividends) in 1883; £12,900 (4.9 per cent) in 1893; £11,700 (4 per cent) in 1903; £15,700 (4.4 per cent) in 1913. Such figures exceeded the cost of taxes and insurance on estates until 1883, but were considerably less by 1893. In comparison with current (as opposed to capital[132]) estate repairs and improvements, they also fell steadily, from a ratio of over 4 to 5 in 1871 to one of 1 to 5 by 1903 (even less in 1913).

Like other landlords, colleges sometimes blundered into major trouble. From 1859 onwards Queen's were determined to extinguish common rights over Plumstead Common (in metropolitan Kent) and then enclose it for building purposes. In 1866 the fences they erected were torn down, and this led the college into years of unsuccessful litigation, culminating in 1871 in a legally important decision (*Warrick* v. *Queen's College, Oxford*). To make

---

[131] CA MS Estates 1, fo 108–9; 7, fo 115.

[132] College contributions to charity were generally only on current account (though Magdalen, in particular, did spend significant capital sums on rebuilding the schools with which it was specially connected).

matters worse, one of its fellows won a prize for an essay stating, from 'the popular side', the law of public rights over commons. Ultimately the Metropolitan Board of Works bought Queen's out for a sum that just covered the college's legal costs.[133] From 1871 Jesus was involved for nearly thirty years (on and off) in a dispute over the proper application of the Meyricke bequest that generated both litigation and much agitation in Wales, besides threatening to bring the University Reform Commissioners into head-on collision with the Charity Commissioners. As a result Jesus had to relinquish a capital sum of £20,000 to be spent within Wales, but was able to use the remainder for endowment (and Welsh scholarships), but not building.[134] Then in 1886 came the Welsh tithe war. This time Jesus, whose Bursar, Professor Rhys, had links with advanced Welsh politicians, kept its head down, largely conceding demands for tithe abatements in Anglesey, though not in Gloucestershire. Christ Church, however, felt that abatements in Wales would mean abatements elsewhere. So, though prepared to make individual allowances for bona-fide poverty, it stood otherwise on its legal rights. When prevented by riots from collecting them, it insisted (despite some pressure from the Home Secretary) on police protection and, when necessary, employed London specialists to make distraint sales.[135]

Usually, however, life was more placid: H. A. L. Fisher depicts the typical college as 'a steady-going, careful, impoverished [agricultural] landlord'.[136] As colleges recovered legal and actual control of their lands, they had to face four (sometimes interconnected) questions. How should they handle the tenurial transition from beneficial leases to rack-rent? Should they sell their existing estates and invest elsewhere? How should they respond to agricultural depression? Should they diversify out of agriculture? Responses naturally varied, not only from college to college but also from holding to holding; and space will only permit us a distinctly cursory overview.

Where the beneficial lessees of college property occupied it themselves, there might be difficulty in agreeing on dilapidations, but the transition to a system of rack-renting was relatively simple. Usually the lessees stayed on as rack-renters. Occasionally they sought to buy the freehold, an option colleges might find attractive either where their property was so intermixed with the lessee's own that it could not be worked independently, or where the lessee was a powerful local figure or college patron, like Sir Henry

[133] Queen's had chosen its time badly as agitation over metropolitan open spaces was intense in the mid-1860s: G. Shaw Lefevre, *English Commons and Forests* (1894), 77–84; Magrath, *Queen's College* ii. 185–6.

[134] PP 1889 lix. 327 ff.; J. N. L. Baker, 'Edmund Meyricke and his benefaction', *Jesus College Record* (1966), 24–8.

[135] Estate meetings and letters, Nov., Dec. 1886, Dec. 1887, Dec. 1888, June 1889, May, Nov. 1891, Jesus College archives, shelf 8; J. P. D. Dunbabin, *Rural Discontent in Nineteenth Century Britain* (1974), ch. 10 and p. 289.

[136] 'A college progress', *Macmillan's Magazine* lxxv (1896), 22.

Dashwood of Kirtlington, to whom New College sold 127 acres in 1872.[137] But most lessees were middlemen, leasing land from a college (or other corporation) and subletting it, often along with or even intermixed with other land, to tenants. Magdalen wrote to one such, in 1871, emphasizing its determination not to renew leases and readiness to undertake the building and other costs this policy would entail, thanking him and his ancestors for past services over 'so long a period', but stressing that 'Under the Rack Rent system it would not be advisable for the College to allow their Lessees' to sublet, and suggesting an exchange of lands. Next year the lessee on another Magdalen property suggested that his subtenant (whose family had in fact occupied the land on a year-to-year basis since 1795) should step into his place.[138] Generally ad-hoc arrangements were reached with little disturbance of local life—the average beneficial lease in 1871 was only of about 117 acres[139] (considerably smaller, that is, than the average Oxfordshire farm). But very occasionally colleges took the opportunity for a substantial reconstruction of holdings. In 1871 St John's felt that, at the expiry of their beneficial leases, 'very few' of their holdings would remain the same:

The various estates would have to be reapplotted, and farms would be formed from the lands lying contiguous and convenient to each other...Few of the farmhouses at present existing are fit for tenants of an improved character, and as it is the desire of their College that its tenantry should be second to none, houses and homesteads will have to be rebuilt in many instances, and the land cleared of superfluous hedges, and rendered fit for a high state of cultivation.[140]

Balliol had done much the same with its Snell Trust estate. But the scope for such action was limited not only by cost and the fact that different leases fell in at different times, but also by geography—in only 120 parishes did individual colleges own as much as 500 acres.

In 1800 colleges were permitted to sell houses in Oxford, from 1802 to sell land for the sole purpose of redeeming land-tax on other holdings. This latter provision enabled them to dispose of a number of outlying properties to enhance the value of the remainder. But any other sales required a special Act of Parliament. There were to be sales to public utilities, particularly railways, but usually only on a small scale. General power to sell came with the legislation of 1856 and 1858; but the proceeds still had to be reinvested in

[137] *VCH Oxon.* vi. 226.
[138] Notebook of J. E. Henderson, college Bursar, 1871–8, 19 June 1871, and 15 Oct. 1872 (Garsington), MCA MS CP 8/142.
[139] Calculated from *RCOC* (1872), pt 2. These calculations (which take account also of the University's property) were made by computerizing data extracted from the Cleveland returns—not an entirely error-free procedure since they were not designed for the purpose. I am indebted to the University Computing Service and to Clive Payne for assistance. I have retained (and would be prepared to make available) the printouts, which include material that it was not possible to use for this chapter.
[140] *RCOC* (1872), pt 2, 472.

land, or lodged with the Copyhold Commissioners at 3 per cent interest until such reinvestment was possible. In 1872 colleges held consols with a face value of some £421,000 deriving from land sales, some dating back to the canal age but most of post-1858 vintage.[141] We have no comparable figures from a later date, but can follow both sales and purchases from 1883 onwards through the colleges' capital accounts (Table 12.16).

TABLE 12.16

SALES, PURCHASES AND ESTATE IMPROVEMENTS (CAPITAL ACCOUNT), 1883–1914 (£)

	1883–7	1888–92	1893–7	1898–1902	1903–7	1908–12	1913–14
sales	50,300	53,900	182,700	148,800	81,500	74,600	69,600
enfranchisements of rights (incl. tithes), sales of way-leaves, etc.	7,300	8,300	7,100	14,900	10,800	14,200	5,900
total	57,500	62,200	189,800	163,700	92,300	88,700	75,500
p.a.	11,500	12,400	38,000	32,700	18,500	17,700	37,700[a]
purchases	49,200	51,000	81,000	242,200	76,400	98,300	21,500
enfranchisement expenditure	3,100	2,800	5,500	15,600	1,700	700	1,000
subtotal	52,300	53,800	86,500	257,800	78,100	99,000	22,500
p.a.	10,500	10,800	17,300	51,600	15,600	19,800	11,300[a]
estate improvements	86,200	60,300	71,900	83,400	106,400	57,400	17,600
p.a.	17,200	12,100	14,400	16,700	21,300	11,500	8,800
total	138,500	114,100	158,400	341,300	184,500	156,400	40,100
p.a.	27,700	22,800	31,700	68,300	36,900	31,300	20,100

Note: Part of the table is continued, for a sample of nine rich colleges, to the 1970s: J. P. D. Dunbabin, 'College finances and property in the twentieth century', in Trevor Rowley (ed.), *The Oxford Region* (Oxford University Department for External Studies 1980), table 2.

[a] The 1913–14 figures for this sample are: sales, £32,200 p.a.; purchases, £10,700 p.a.

This would suggest that the rate of sales had slowed by the 1880s, and that they were then almost balanced by purchases. The 1890s saw much more activity, probably reflecting both agricultural depression and increased house-building. Sales greatly exceeded purchases in 1893–7, but purchases then

[141] £376,800 for all colleges except New College, which did not specify the origins of its funds; to this I have added New College's holdings on corporate but not trust account. Land sales clearly constituted the colleges' largest source of consols with the Copyhold Commissioners. In 1880 (at Alfred Robinson's instance) the colleges obtained legislation permitting them to reborrow these; they thus refinanced almost all their external debt (on which they had previously had to pay 4%).

rebounded. Thereafter dealings declined, though not to the level of the 1880s. As with other large landlords, sales rose strongly just before the First World War, though they were not yet on the scale of 1919–20, when six colleges between them sold £331,800 worth of land.[142] If we make allowance also for estate improvements, the colleges only disinvested from their estates in 1893–7 and 1913–14. Sales and purchases of agricultural land were usually meant to produce more compact holdings. Thus in 1872 Brasenose sold land 'at Cold Norton, Broadstone, Enstone, Little Tew, &c.' and in 1875 bought some 580 acres at South Leigh out of the proceeds. Similarly, in 1908 it bought 230 acres at Ivington Court (Herefordshire), where it already had widely scattered property; 'The effect of the purchase is to create a good estate practically in a ring fence'.[143] Such consolidation, however, altered the broader geographical distribution of college property surprisingly little between 1871 and 1918.[144]

Land sales were most readily made, and fetched the best prices, at times of agricultural prosperity (notably in the period on either side of the First World War). But Table 12.16 suggests that, in the 1890s though not the 1880s, they could also be a response to agricultural depression. Another response was to try to spend one's way out of trouble. In the prosperity of the early 1870s St John's had (as we have seen) been determined to upgrade its estates; in 1878 it was arguing that, while the results of this process had been disappointing, 'in the present state of agricultural prospects...it appears that by such expenditure alone, productive or unproductive, can suitable tenants be found for the farms at all'.[145] Certainly tenants might demand improvements as an alternative to rent reductions or even as a condition of continuing to farm. Alternatively, colleges might help them diversify out of arable by laying land down to grass (or even larches). But overall it looks as if colleges spent more freely on improvements when agriculture and rents were doing well.[146] A tenant's simplest approach to agricultural depression was, of course, to seek a rent reduction, and many sent in notices to quit to force one. This could backfire: when the bad (and non-resident) tenant of Ibstone Farm did so in October 1888, Merton let it

[142] Oriel, All Souls, Christ Church, Jesus, University, Worcester: *RCOC* (1919), appx, 358. See also *Twentieth-Century Oxford*, 658–9.

[143] *Brasenose Monographs* vi. 8, 46, 47.

[144] See the maps and tables in *Twentieth-Century Oxford*, 664–70.

[145] *SCO* (1877), circulars, 60.

[146] College estate repairs and improvements (revenue and capital accounts)

	1883	1893	1903	1913
repairs and improvements (revenue account)	26,800	35,200	45,100	71,500
five-yearly average of estate improvements on capital account	17,200	14,400	21,300	8,800[a]
total	44,000	49,600	66,400	80,300

[a] Two-yearly average.

to a neighbouring farmer, lending him £800 capital with which to work it. All Souls also, as it thought, called the bluff of the tenant of 898 acres in Romney Marsh, and for many years refused to reduce the rent from £1,569 per annum. But, when the tenant quit in 1894, he could be replaced only at £1,125 per annum, and by an outsider who did not understand marsh-farming, reduced the land to thistles and had to be got rid of; the college then had to pay about £1,000 to restore it to order, and relet it in a number of lots for about £900 per annum.[147] But such sagas were unusual. Colleges usually felt, with Merton, that 'It is better to let it even at a much reduced rent than to take it in hand',[148] and were disposed to bargain. The outcome could be a permanent rent reduction (the best solution from the tenant's perspective, since it also lowered his rates), or a more temporary allowance—'As agriculture appears to be improving Mr. Franklin recommends an allowance for 1887 and 1888 instead of a permanent reduction'.[149] Or, less formally, the bursar was often simply authorized to grant allowances up to a certain figure at the rent audits if he found it necessary. In 1892 'a most disastrous... [year] for farmers worse even than 1879', Merton was faced with a number of early applications and decided to set aside £1,000 for allowances of up to 15 per cent; but £400 was sufficient to meet demands. However, next year, which was 'even more disastrous', it anticipated that the full £1,000 would be required and the bursar was authorized to offer up to 20 per cent.[150] A variant, employed on an appreciable but not a major scale, was to permit tenants to run up arrears of rent to be paid off in better times.

In December 1893, at the nadir of the agricultural depression, Merton noted that its estate income was constant: 'the diminution in several items being compensated by an increase in House rents amounting to £400, this item has risen steadily since 1883 from £800 to £2,800, and has contributed with Dividends, which have increased from £2,000 to £4,100...to maintain the financial equilibrium'. For some colleges, of course, this was never true. And even for the aggregate of all historic colleges the fall of gross incomes from land, copyholds, tithe and other rent charges over the decade (£26,000) slightly exceeded the increase in that from houses (£21,200). But from then on houses easily compensated for declining agricultural rents, with gains of £34,500 (against a fall of £3,500) by 1903, and £37,500 (as compared with a rise of £20,100) by 1913.[151] 'Dividends' also increased (by £1,900 from 1883

---

[147] Memorandum by J. J. Done, printed in Faber, *All Souls Bursarships*, 82–4. The 1878 rent had been £2,040.

[148] Bursar's reports, 1 July 1890.

[149] Ibid. 3 Nov. 1888: the tenant wished *inter alia* to leave the arable fallow for a season; it did not answer and the Radstone farm came into Merton's hands.

[150] Ibid. 3 Dec. 1892, 2 Dec. 1893. In Dec. 1894 up to 15% was to be allowed, in May 1895 up to 10%. Further relief was provided nationally by the Agricultural Rating Act, 1896, which remitted half the rates on agricultural land.

[151] These figures (calculated from L. L. Price, 'The accounts of the colleges of Oxford, 1883–1903; with special reference to their agricultural revenues', *Journal of the Royal Statistical*

to 1893, a further £3,100 by 1903, then £7,200 by 1913). But houses were by a large margin the main non-agricultural source of external income. For, unlike the Ecclesiastical Commissioners, the colleges never had any substantial mining royalties (though Balliol's 1860s rebuilding was eased by revenue from a Northumberland colliery), while wood sales appear to have declined from their peak during the Napoleonic Wars. (Probably they had been overdone: New College hall was reroofed with college oaks in the 1860s; but these were the last trees of that size in England, and to restore the chapel in traditional style the college would have had to use Baltic timber, which it distrusted.)[152]

Colleges were always aware of the general possibilities of building. Brasenose had seen the Hulme Trust estate in Lancashire so developed from 1770 and its rents rocket.[153] In 1836 it decided to run out certain leases 'as the property is closely adjoining the increasing City of Gloucester'. But the Kingsholme lease was in fact renewed in 1845, which later gave rise to sour comments on the opportunities missed: 'It is a great pity that this land was renewed...as it is Building Land' (1852), and '1860 Building was going on very actively all round'.[154] One factor that made it difficult for colleges to join in was the law preventing them from leasing away houses for more than forty years. It was possible, as Queen's showed in Southampton, to use beneficial leases as a form of building lease, the lessee covenanting to erect certain buildings in lieu of a fine. But most developers wanted more security than forty years. Magdalen had in fact secured legislation in 1776–7 enabling it to grant ninety-nine-year building leases in Southwark, and between 1846 and 1855 five Oxbridge colleges followed suit. Then in 1858 this power was generalized.[155] By 1871 Oxford colleges were controlling[156] ground-rents from ninety-nine-year leases of £10,000 per annum (almost all in Oxfordshire, Surrey, Middlesex and Gloucestershire), and the rateable value of the houses in question was £45,100 per annum. The Cleveland Commission noticed this activity, and also more conventional building for rent, but did not attach any great importance to it. In fact ground-rents proved considerably more lucrative than the agricultural value of the land in question, and (as Table 12.17 shows) they constituted the most dynamic, though certainly not the largest, element in college incomes in the period to 1914. They were, though, highly vulnerable to inflation after the Second World War.

Society lxvii (1904), 610–11, and Dunbabin, 'Oxford and Cambridge college finances, 1871–1913', 638) are for revenue account. They do not include 'fines and fine loans'.

[152] George, *New College*, 58–9, 62. For coal see also p. 176 above.
[153] *The Eighteenth Century*, 287.
[154] Calculations of fines, 1787–, Brasenose College archives B2d21.
[155] All Souls (1846, Middlesex), Christ Church (1851, Middlesex), Magdalen (1852, Surrey), Sidney Sussex (1853, Lincs.), St John's (1855, Oxford): *Enactments in Parliament* ii. 255 ff., iv. 314, 337–9.
[156] Some of the proceeds went for trust purposes outwith the college.

TABLE 12.17

GROSS COLLEGE CORPORATE INCOME FROM LANDS AND HOUSES,
1871–1913 (£)

	1871	1883	1893	1903	1913
land, copyholds, tithes, etc.	187,200	234,600	212,500	203,700	229,400
houses, rack-rent and beneficial lease	16,400	23,400	35,500	51,500	56,900
houses, long lease	6,300	12,300	21,400	39,900	72,000
houses (total)	22,700	35,700	56,900	91,400	128,900

Note: Fines and fine loans, which might come under either, or neither, category have been excluded.

For most colleges the benefits of building probably came through a rather undramatic mixture: some rehabilitation of existing houses (especially at the end of leases) and their reletting at enhanced rents; some new building; occasional prudent purchases of land to provide existing holdings with the road access necessary for development, or profitable sales of land for building; some 'long', ninety-nine-year building leases, possibly after minor drainage or road-works. Obviously bursars and their advisers kept an eye on possible future developments—we have noted Queen's ill-fated attempt to enclose Plumstead Common for building. But they were often only responding to general trends in the area, or even to specific approaches from would-be developers. Thus in 1887 Merton considered the future of fifteen acres at Watford whose beneficial lease would fall in next year. The land agent reported that part could be developed by spending a little over £2,000 on roads, and sold in three to five years' time for a price that (suitably discounted) suggested that the whole property was now worth £12,000; a bid of £10,000 had already been put in for it. Merton accepted his recommendation to sell, and drove the bidder up to £12,500 (plus costs).[157] Similarly, the college must for two decades have watched the growth of North Oxford, which had obvious implications for its Holywell property. In 1878 it was undecided as to what to do about the Holywell houses when their leases fell in. In 1884 and 1885 it was receiving applications for building leases, and decided to commission a plan for the development of the estate. This was submitted in December 1885 and adopted. But by then an application had already been received for land on which to build a new college (Mansfield),[158] and this was soon followed by another college (Manchester), and

---

[157] Bursar's report, 17 June and 7 Oct. 1887, Merton College archives 6.37.
[158] Ibid., 28 June 1884, 21 Nov., 16 Dec. 1885, 22 and 30 Jan. 1886; *Report of the Committee on the Future Income and Expenditure of the College* (29 Nov. 1878), Merton College archives D.1.32.

by Balliol, New College and Merton's own cricket grounds. So more land was sold (as opposed to leased) than had been expected; and, though there was some development, it was much less dense (though presumably not less profitable) than had been anticipated.

But two more positive approaches deserve to be briefly mentioned. First, All Souls. Until the early 1880s it had had no policy for exploiting its suburban land in Middlesex beyond that of selling as soon as it would fetch £800–£1,000 an acre. The college agent's junior partner, J. J. Done, who had had experience in managing building estates in Manchester, proposed that the college should itself lay down sewers and roads; but the Bursar turned this down as too risky. There are signs that this was a controversial issue within the college, and it may have entered into the 1888 election to the estates bursarship (the only one ever to be contested). Certainly the new Bursar (H. O. Wakeman) soon enquired about arrangements 'for letting building land', and in 1889 All Souls accepted Done's own bid for a small building lease at £50 per annum. Done rapidly grew in favour, taking over the full management of the college's Middlesex estates in 1892. And in 1893 Wakeman was writing to him that 'Middlesex has certainly come to the rescue at a critical time and it is satisfactory to see the larger income now deriving from building leases...which in itself goes far to justify the policy which we have followed in our large capital expenditure on roads, etc.' It was a courageous policy, given that All Souls had burnt its fingers badly on borrowing to improve its agricultural estates and that the Warden was at the time having himself to fund some of the prize fellowships. Income from building leases shot up (from £424 in 1889 to £2,492 in 1894, £9,260 in 1904 and £12,875 in 1914), compensating for the sharp fall in agricultural income. But, as we have seen, All Souls was (relatively speaking) more burdened with debt charges than any other college. So its disposable income did not rise appreciably till after 1904; and the really dramatic gains seem to have come with the 1930s suburban building boom.[159]

So much for Middlesex. In Oxford nineteenth-century suburban development inevitably calls St John's to mind. The possibilities were first revealed when the Poor Law Guardians decided not to erect a workhouse on what is now Park Town and in 1854 sold the site for development. The speed with which lots were at first taken up revealed a latent demand for middle-class housing, suppressed by the colleges' inability to offer more than forty-year leases. So St John's Steward, the solicitor F. J. Morrell, persuaded it to develop on the basis of ninety-nine-year leases, and the necessary powers were obtained (over 455 acres) from Parliament in 1855. The first lease was granted in 1856, but building did not become general until the 1860s, after which it rippled northwards and westwards. St John's was, as we have seen

---

[159] Faber, *All Souls Bursarships*, 39, 56–62, 65–6, 68–70, 78–80, 92.

in the agricultural context, ambitious and ready to spend money. It also kept a tight grip on the style of development through its architect (from *c.*1860–1886 W. Wilkinson), who not only drew the plans, assessed the ground-rents and negotiated with the numerous local property developers, but also vetted the design of each house and enforced rules to ensure high standards of workmanship (and in certain areas, social exclusiveness)[160] and to prevent shoddy building. Where faults were found or complaints made, the St John's Bursar never failed to demand a full account which, it is fair to say, Wilkinson was normally able to give.[161] In North Oxford, *Si monumentum requiris, circumspice.*

North Oxford was one way in which the colleges changed the face of the city. A more unexpected one was through Merton's early connections with William Morris. From 1902 he rented the old livery stables at the corner of Holywell and Longwall, converting it into 'The Oxford Garage' (and 'Morris Cycle Works'). In 1910 Merton agreed to build him a small factory (final cost £3,763), on which he would take a twenty-one-year repairing lease at £300 per annum. The building was completed in 1911, and from it in 1912 he launched his first car, the Morris Oxford. The investment was big enough to give Merton some thought, but was not, in principle, unusual—Merton often put up the capital for farm buildings, machinery for corn-mills, etc. to be repaid from enhanced rents. But from Morris's perspective it was important, since he was operating on a shoe-string (his 1912 company's only outside capital was Lord Macclesfield's £4,000 preference shares), essentially assembling bought-in components. Fortunately the car was immediately successful, and Morris was able to take on larger and more suitable premises, a disused school in Cowley.[162] His venture was to change the pattern of employment in Oxford more profoundly than ever the coming of the railways had done.[163]

[160] The class of houses did, however, fall with the contours towards working-class Hayfield Road. Most college development was middle class, but not all. Oxford slum clearance in St Thomas's parish in 1866 produced the Christ Church Model Dwellings, and the college built another tenement block in 1893: *VCH Oxon.* iv. 195–6.

[161] *VCH Oxon.* iv. 197–8; A. Saint, 'Three Oxford architects', *Oxoniensia* xxxv (1970), 84–5; *Oxford Journal* 20 Jan. 1885 (Morrell's obituary). For a fuller and more nuanced account see Hinchcliffe, *North Oxford, passim.*

[162] Merton bursar's reports, esp. 5 Mar., 28 May, 4 June 1910; college accounts; R. J. Overy, *William Morris, Viscount Nuffield* (1976), ch. 1 and pl. on p. 58.

[163] University hostility to railways is sometimes claimed to have prevented Oxford from developing into a manufacturing town. But it appears not to have been the decisive factor in persuading the GWR to prefer Swindon for its workshops: *VCH Oxon.* iv. 215; Hinchcliffe, *North Oxford,* 159–61. See also pp. 459–60 below.

APPENDIX 12.1 UNIVERSITY INCOME IN OXFORD AND CAMBRIDGE

Comparative Income

Table 12.A1 seeks to give a comparative view of the income of Oxford and Cambridge universities.

The 1871 figures for Oxford colleges exclude £27,000 of loans treated as income, and also expenditure from external income or trust funds on augmentation of benefices, interest and repayments of loans, management, reports and rates on estates and trust fund investments and balances. Those for Cambridge University exclude sale of stock; no Cambridge colleges treated loans as income, but external expenditure has been excluded as at Oxford; four Cambridge colleges did not return their takings from tuition fees, and all Sidney Sussex's corporate income has had to be treated as external. Oxford colleges owned more land than did Cambridge, but had been slower to extinguish beneficial leases.

Oxford University's 1920 figures include all its government emergency grant, though a fraction was not in fact brought into account in that financial year. The Cambridge college figures exclude some 'bed-making' charges.

Oxford's 1913 income (for University and colleges combined, excluding £1,808 income tax repaid to the University and avoiding double-counting of college cash payments to the University) was £511,600.

Common University Fund Taxation of Colleges in Oxford and Cambridge

Taxation of colleges for University purposes was arranged differently at the two universities, and too much may have been read into this difference. What follows is a perhaps presumptuous attempt to clarify a highly technical subject with many pitfalls. College payments for University purposes may be stated as in Table 12.A2.

Cambridge colleges paid less in 1871 to support professors, etc. than did their Oxford counterparts (indeed only Downing and Trinity are recorded as having so contributed). In both universities the subsequent reform Commissions imposed further college obligations to support professors. But Oxford colleges were often required to provide all (or most) of a professor's stipend, whereas Cambridge statutes generally envisaged professorial fellowships as ordinary ones, subject that is (save at Trinity) to a maximum dividend of £250 per annum. (Also some Oxford colleges were required to make direct payments to other University institutions.) So it is not surprising that Oxford colleges were authorized to set, against their CUF taxation liability, sums paid 'for any University purpose mentioned in... [their] Statutes, including the emoluments of any Fellowship... attached to Professorships'. In Cambridge, too, colleges were permitted an offset 'for each Professorial Fellowship' of up to a maximum of £200, that is of all or most of its cost. Accordingly, in 1920, which was typical of the years when the scheme was fully operational, though a notional £30,076 CUF taxation was levied, Cambridge University actually received only £23,613 in cash. However, other college contributions to University purposes did not reduce CUF liability; so they were not specially recorded in the accounts and the Asquith Commission was only told that they were 'substantial'.

TABLE 12.A1

OXFORD AND CAMBRIDGE UNIVERSITY INCOMES, c.1851–1920 (£s ROUNDED)

	Oxford 1856	Cambridge 1845–51 (average)	Oxford 1871	Cambridge 1871	Oxford 1920	Cambridge 1920
external (net) and misc.	7,400	2,400	13,000	2,000	16,900	16,300
internal	12,500	6,600	18,500	20,100	82,200[a]	113,800[b]
trust (1871 and 1920, net)	n.a.	9,100	15,000	9,900	41,600	46,300
University Press	2,900	900	—	—	2,000	—
cash receipts from colleges	(small; incl. above)	1,100[c]	—	—	27,600	23,600[d]
government grants			—	—	12,100[d]	23,000[d]
subtotal (University)[e]	22,900[f]	20,200	46,600	32,100	182,500	223,000
government emergency grants			—	—	30,000[g]	30,000
subtotal (University)					212,500	253,000
colleges (net external and trust, internal and tuition fees, less cash paid to the University)[e]	n.a.	n.a.	289,600[h]	285,700[i]	613,800[j]	466,500[k]
total (University and colleges)[e]	—	—	336,200[l]	317,800	826,400	719,600

Notes:

[a] Fees and dues, deducting £4,843 non-recurrent war-time 'emergency fund' receipts. [b] Fees and dues. [c] Cambridge's receipt, to 1851, of £1,130 p.a. from the state was eclipsed by the tax (discontinued shortly thereafter) on matriculations and degrees, which is said to have netted £3,051 p.a. [d] Old grants to University departments. [e] Rounded where necessary. [f] Not including trust income. [g] Including £1,648 not brought to account in 1920. [h] Oxford colleges, excluding Keble; Oxford colleges and halls, excluding Keble, £299,300; both figures are net of £27,194 borrowed and treated as income. [i] Excl. Sidney Sussex's tuition fees. [j] Men's colleges, excluding Keble. [k] Men's colleges, excluding Selwyn; some undergraduate payments for bedmakers are not included. [l] Men's colleges, £345,800 including halls.

Sources: PP1852–3 xliv. 146–50, 237–8; *Abstract of the General Account of the University [of Oxford]*, Bodl. G.A. Oxon. c. 72, 38o; RCOC (1872); RCOC (1919).

TABLE 12.A2

OXFORD AND CAMBRIDGE COLLEGE PAYMENTS FOR UNIVERSITY
PURPOSES, 1871–1913 (£)

	1871	1884	1888	1893	1898	1903	1908	1913
Oxford								
Direct college payments to professors etc.	14,100	18,400	18,600	19,500	21,800	22,700	26,200	30,300
payments by colleges to the CUF or other University institutions	—	4,500	4,000	5,600	4,800	6,800	11,000	15,100
CUF receipts from college contributions under statute (incl. above)	—	2,900	4,000	4,400	3,600	5,400	8,300	9,300
Cambridge								
college payments for university professors and purposes	2,000							
notional CUF receipts *inclusive* of allowances to colleges for fellowship payments to professors	—	5,700	13,200	18,100	22,700	28,100	30,500	30,100

Sources: for 1871, *RCOC* (1872); for other Cambridge figures, *RCOC* (1919), appx 1, p. 142; for Oxford in 1913, HCP 99 (1914); other Oxford figures derive from the *University and College Accounts*, with the addition to the 'Direct College payments to Professors' of £4,500 in respect of the Christ Church canon professors—to judge by a comparison with 1913 they may slightly underestimate total college payments.

In Cambridge the original CUF statute laid down fixed sums to be paid each year, which were then annually reapportioned among the colleges according to their taxable incomes. Agricultural depression, etc. led the Chancellor on a number of occasions to invoke a let-out clause, so the target of £30,000–£30,500 per annum was reached in 1906 rather than 1897 (as originally specified). Thereafter payments remained constant, to the University's discomfort during the wartime inflation. In Oxford net external college revenue plus income from trusts more than 50 years old in 1877 was taxed progressively, up to a maximum rate of 35 per cent. This system (though complex) was obviously better adapted than the Cambridge one to inflation, and the Asquith Commission preferred it.

Total college contributions to 'University purposes' were always higher in Oxford than in Cambridge. But since most took the form of payments to professors, etc., the actual receipts of the Oxford CUF fund were lower—too low, probably, to be of any great importance up to 1914. Still differences between the Universities were perhaps less than they seemed. For the Cambridge CUF fund was used quite largely to relieve the University Chest of the cost of 'Stipends and Salaries'—between 1883 and 1918 Chest expenditure under this heading fell by £6,200 per annum, with CUF expenditure rising by £10,600 per annum. It was, however, permissible in Cambridge (though not Oxford) to apply up to a third of the Fund's income to building or to loan repayment; from 1886 it was held available for these purposes, which helped the University considerably with its building programme, especially perhaps in the 1880s and early 1890s.

Sources for Appendix 12.1: *RCOC* (1919), appx 1, 141 ff., 196 ff.; PP 1881 lxxii (Cambridge college statutes), PP 1882 li. 280, 641 (statutes determining CUF contributions).

APPENDIX 12.2   UNIVERSITY BUILDING IN OXFORD AND CAMBRIDGE

TABLE 12.A3

UNIVERSITY BUILDING, OXFORD, 1830–1884 (£)

year		amount
1830s	conversion of Clarendon Building (vacated by Press)	3,000
1844	Taylorian and University Galleries	69,700
1853–65	purchase and planting of University Parks (which *inter alia* provided science area sites)	38,000
1855–72	Science Museum and laboratories	100,000
1872	Clarendon laboratory	12,000
1875–7	Observatory	5,700
1874, 1878–9	new chemistry blocks	7,600
1877–82	Examination Schools	146,000
1878–84	restoration of Bodleian	26,500
total		408,500

Note: A slight overlap with Table 12.A4 is probably offset by under-recording.

Sources: 1830s, p. 390 above; 1844, OUA TL/M/1/1, 4 Feb. 1847; 1853–65, *Guide to the Trees and Shrubs in the University Parks Oxford* (1977)—a not quite inclusive figure; 1855–72, PP 1872 xxv, Qs. 3280, 3282; 1872, ibid., Q. 3282 (incl. £1,000 for apparatus); 1875–7, *The Builder* xxxvi (1878), 484–90 (excl. the purchase cost of one telescope and donation of another); 1877–82 and 1878–84, p. 396 above.

The figures in this appendix are not exact. But they suggest that the level of University building in Oxford during our period was broadly comparable with that in Cambridge. We should, however, note the Asquith Commission's judgement of Oxford science that 'Many generous benefactions have been received, but nothing

TABLE 12.A4

UNIVERSITY EXPENDITURE ON CAPITAL ACCOUNT, OXFORD,
1883–1918: AVERAGE P.A. (£)

years	amounts
1883–7	7,544
1888–92	5,315
1893–7[a]	7,283[b]
1898–1902	4,939
1903–7	1,030
1908–12	2,869
1913–18[a]	6,698[c]

[a] 1893–7 and 1913–18 also saw some 'investment' expenditure on the acquisition of city centre sites or properties.

[b] Boosted by the restoration costs of St Mary's spire (£14,500 in 1894–8).

[c] Very high in 1914–15 (Dyson Perrins laboratory etc.), very low in 1917–18.

TABLE 12.A5

UNIVERSITY CAPITAL EXPENDITURE, OXFORD, 1883–1918 (£)

	amount
University 'internal' capital expenditure, 1883–1918 (as in Table 12.A4 above)	185,000
plus Indian Institute (1883), by subscription	21,000[a]
Radcliffe Science Library (1901–3) (Drapers' Co.)	15,000[b]
Electrical Laboratory (1908–10) (Drapers' Co.)	23,000[c]
School of Rural Economy, laboratory (1907) (St John's College)	8,200[d]
total	252,000

Sources:

[a] *Statement of Receipts and Expenditure . . . to November 25, 1886*, Bodl. G. A. Oxon. 4° 262(30).

[b] *Gazette* 15 June 1897, 584.

[c] Incl. £1,000 for equipment: *Gazette* 20 Oct. 1908, 89; *Nature* 23 June 1910, 511.

[d] College accounts.

TABLE 12.A6

UNIVERSITY BUILDING, CAMBRIDGE, 1821–1851 (£)

	amount
expenditure from University Chest on sites, buildings (and fittings)	59,300
expenditure from trusts, subscriptions, and Library Subscription Fund	142,700
purchase by University Chest of mineral collection and astronomical instruments	3,200
total	205,200

Source: PP 1852–3 xliv. 230.

TABLE 12.A7

UNIVERSITY BUILDING, CAMBRIDGE, 1862–1918 (£)

	amount
expenditure by University for new buildings for various departments	174,000
plus for sites (1882–1918)[a]	c 70,000
for new buildings met by benefactions or external sources	178,000
subtotal	c 422,000
plus School of Physiology (Drapers' Co.)	
Squire Law Library (Squire trustees)	
Institute of Genetics (private benefaction)	

Notes: funds were short in the 1850s, leading to the suspension of work on the Fitzwilliam 1847–70; so the 1852–61 gap in these figures is unlikely to be serious.

[a] £52,000 plus a rent-charge of £731 p.a.

Source: RCOC (1919), appx, 142.

comparable with the large sums which scientific studies had attracted to many other Universities in recent times' (Report, 104).

The low level of Oxford's capital expenditure 1903–12 is surprising, given the renewed concern over its 'more pressing needs'. Two partial explanations can perhaps be suggested: the increase in the number, and co-ordination of the specialisms, of college scientific laboratories; and the unusually high level of University estate expenditure in 1898–1907 (average £2,297 per annum) stemming from the misfortunes of the Sandford Mill and the 1899 inundation of Elmley (Isle of Sheppey).

NOTE

The University Chest, 1868–1914

ROLAND WILCOCK

Before the establishment of the Curators of the Chest the handling of all University income and expenditure apart from fines collected by the proctors was the personal responsibility of the Vice-Chancellor alone. Handing over to a successor was for some Vice-Chancellors a troublesome and anxious business.[1] By the mid-1860s the manner in which the University's finances were being handled had become a matter of general comment, and limited attempts were made to deal with the question. At length, in June 1868, a statute passed Convocation to transfer to a new body of nine persons—'Curatores cistae academicae'—all the financial duties hitherto discharged by the Vice-Chancellor. In addition the Board was to take over the responsibilities of the

[1] A letter dated 3 July 1863 from Francis Jeune (Vice-Chancellor, 1858–62) to his successor, John Prideaux Lightfoot, is preserved in the office of the present Secretary of the Chest.

Delegates of Estates. The Vice-Chancellor and proctors were members of the Board of Curators *ex officio*, the former usually taking the chair; among the six elected Curators, the Hebdomadal Council, the University Press and, after 1882, the Common University Fund, were always represented.[2]

A clause in the 1868 statute allowed the Curators to appoint a salaried Secretary. Only two held office before 1914—Alfred Stowe (1868–73), a fellow of Wadham, and William Blagdon Gamlen (1873–1919). An MA of Exeter, Gamlen had been called to the Bar in 1870 before his appointment, at the age of 29, as the first professional on the University's full-time non-academic staff.[3] His salary was fixed in 1875 at £400, rising by increments to £600.[4] He was assisted in the Chest office in the Clarendon building by two clerks.

Two episodes concerning University buildings during the early years of the Curators' activities illustrate the flexible conditions in which they initially operated. In the case of the erection of the Examination Schools (1876–82) the freedom of decision and action enjoyed by the Curators make the building almost as much a monument to them as to the architect, Thomas Jackson. Their decision to allow him to use Clipsham stone marks an epoch in Oxford buildings. In the decrees of Convocation of 15 June 1876 at which Jackson's designs were accepted and the Curators authorized to proceed with their execution, the only reference to finance was to authorize them to borrow by mortgage not more than £60,000. The plans were accompanied by a brief and imprecise estimate of cost. No budget for the project was ever drawn up and over the six years of building work the Curators met expenditure as it arose from what funds were available. Neither Council nor Convocation were involved in any decision on how money was being spent. Ultimately the erection of the building cost the University over £107,000—excluding £34,000 in interest on the mortgage—against the 1876 estimate of £64,000. A significant part of the increase was accounted for by the Curators' willingness to allow Jackson to realize his scheme of elaborate decoration in the building.

The Bodleian restorations were entrusted to the Curators almost contemporaneously with the assignment for the Examination Schools with even looser terms of reference. They were authorized to spend 'such sums...as may be necessary' on the repairs to the fabric. From May 1876 until the last of six contracts was completed in 1884 it was the Curators of the Chest who directed the restorations round the Schools Quadrangle that give the Bodleian its present appearance, spending on behalf of the University £28,000 for the purpose. It was at their instigation that Jackson undertook the work, and they allowed him to use Clipsham stone.

[2] The agenda and minute-books of the curators are in OUA. The 2120 Chest meetings on which this note is largely based (10 July 1868–29 Aug. 1914) generated some 25,000 minutes.
[3] See the obituary by L. R. Farnell, *OM* 23 May 1919, 303–4.
[4] *Gazette* v (9 Mar. 1875), 499.

Such lavish provision was possible in the circumstances which prevailed up to the early 1890s; the yearly income in the revenue account kept ahead of expenditure with generally an adequate margin, though at times the Curators faced cash-flow problems. For the ten years after 1882, when fees and dues levied from members of the University were raised, income exceeded expenditure by an average of £2,000. Any concern generally felt about the soundness of the University's financial base was probably moderated by annual contributions from the University Press, and by the beginning of the practice of using dues compositions (i.e. fees from life members) to meet current expenditure instead of investing them as required by statute. From 1893/4, however, the published accounts began to show a yearly adverse balance, amounting, by 1903, to nearly £6,000. In 1910 the Curators of the Chest were able to meet claims on the University's General Fund only by resorting to balances held by them on account of trust funds and the Common University Fund. By 1911/12 the University had absolutely no means of meeting any increase in current expenditure.

The Hebdomadal Council can hardly be said to have been in a position, or to have shown much inclination, to exercise any direction or control of University finance. Its typical financial Act was to propose or, more rarely, to refuse decrees for expenditure, leaving the Curators of the Chest to find the wherewithal. For nearly twenty years after the Curators' establishment Council had no particular procedure or system for dealing with money grants. It was without apparent enthusiasm that in 1885, in response to a memorial from members of Congregation, Council adopted a procedure for the submission and consideration of applications for grants, and by amendment of statute made it possible for Convocation to have a more adequate opportunity to discuss money grants. Similarly, it required a memorial from Convocation in 1894 to lead Council, again by amendment of statute, to make it obligatory that all decrees proposing money grants of more than £100 be considered by Congregation before going to Convocation. In 1898 Council accepted a proposal from the Curators of the Chest that all such decrees should be accompanied by a statement saying where the money was coming from.

The Curators' original statutory functions were very modest: receiving all monies due under various heads to the University; paying all charges upon it; investing any balance not immediately required; and presenting to Convocation an annual historical account of the money involved. After 1882 the Curators were also charged with the responsibility for seeing that colleges complied with the statute requiring them to make contributions for University purposes. In practice, the Curators themselves appear not to have been inhibited by the humble role formally assigned to them. As early as 1870 they passed on to Council, uninvited, an estimate of the current yearly income and expenditure of the University. In 1877 came the first of a series of intermittent but not infrequent requests from Council for financial fore-casts or general financial statements or advice regarding aspects of University finance. From the 1890s Council grew into the habit of asking the Curators' opinion on proposed money grants, and appeared to recognize them as its only source of financial advice and information. Council, how-ever, was not consistent in its attitude, receiving on more than one occasion a protest from the Curators at not being consulted. The latter did not always play a reactive role. At times of approaching or actual crisis—1894–8, 1901–3 and 1910–14—they took or proposed steps intended to ameliorate the situation. One outcome of the 1903 crisis was the adoption by the Curators of the practice of providing Council each spring with an estimate of income and expenditure for the current year.

The University did little, however, to recognize the Chest's contribution to its financial management. Indeed, the Chest appears to have been gen-erally held in low esteem. The office of Secretary did not become mandatory until 1912. Throughout his forty-six years of tenure, Gamlen, who was never elected to a college fellowship, had to deposit with the University 'security for the due discharge of the duties of his office'. For his part, Lord Curzon, the Chancellor of the University, gave a very limited account of the Chest's role in the context of his proposals for university reform set out in 1909[5]; and this was summarized as follows in the case for a new Finance Board which he made on Council's behalf in the following year: 'whether it has been desirable or not, the Chest has come to be regarded as unconcerned with the financial policy of the University...We propose, therefore, to leave the Curators of the Chest as they now are, namely, as an Account Office, an Estates Committee and Office of Works for the University.'[6]

[5] For the proposal about a new Finance Board, see Lord Curzon, *Principles and Methods of University Reform* (1909), 161, 163–71.
[6] *Principles and Methods of University Reform: report of the Hebdomadal Council, with an introduction submitted on behalf of the Council by Lord Curzon of Kedleston* (1910), p. xxvii. See Pt 2, Ch. 32 and *The Twentieth Century*, 639–41.

13

The University and the City

C. J. DAY

Prolonged disputes between town and gown in the sixteenth and seventeenth centuries had left the University assailed but unbroken, firmly entrenched behind its battery of charters and privileges; and for much of the eighteenth century the city was content to derive a comfortable living from a small but lavish academic community.[1] The nineteenth century seemed likely to open with a challenge to the University's hegemony when, on 10 February 1800, the Mayor, Richard Cox, failed to attend St Mary's Church for the St Scholastica's Day ceremony, the city's annual act of expiation for the great riot of 1355. The Corporation, however, refused him its support upon learning that 'Mr. Cox, some years since, in company with some young friends, said if ever he served the office of mayor he would not submit to such a humiliation. His acquaintance reminded him of his promise.' The University is sometimes thought to have been slack in defence of its privileges at this period but the Delegates of Privileges met on 11 February and agreed to demand the fine of 100 marks (£66) to which it was entitled. Cox, a banker, paid out of his own pocket and the money was given to the Radcliffe Infirmary.[2] Next year the Delegates met before the ceremony and requested the Vice-Chancellor to demand the citizens' attendance, which continued unchallenged for a further two decades.[3] A formal approach by the Corporation in 1824 suggesting that 'five centuries of annual humiliation was sufficient atonement' met with a sympathetic response, and in 1825 the University released the city from its obligation.[4]

Attention then inevitably turned to that other manifestation of civic subordination, the oath to uphold the University's privileges sworn each year at St Mary's Church by the new mayor accompanied by sixty-two citizens. The ceremony was even older than that of St Scholastica's Day,

---

[1] This chapter covers the period 1800–1914. It is significant that only the 18th-century volume of this series (vol. v) has no separate section on town–gown relations.
[2] Oxford City archives F. 5. 10, pp. 8–11; OUA WP α 17(8a), 11 Feb., 1 Mar. 1800; OUA NEP/Pyx/A/8; Bodl. MS Top. Oxon. d. 247, fo 94.
[3] OUA WP/α/17(8a), 4 Feb. 1801.
[4] Oxford City archives B. 5. 5, 1 June, 11 Nov. 1824; 7 Feb. 1825; ibid. D. 5. 17, fos 121–2; *Herald* 5, 12 Feb. 1825.

being part of the settlement imposed by the papal legate in 1214 following the riot and subsequent dispersal of the University in 1209;[5] and the University was reluctant to dispense with it, feeling that it went to the heart of constitutional relations between the two bodies. The ceremony had by 1834 become a public scandal, since it was impossible to find enough respectable citizens to take part, the numbers being made up of 'persons in the lowest stations of life, collected from the streets'. The annual hubbub in St Mary's persuaded the University to concede a private ceremony at the Vice-Chancellor's lodgings attended only by the mayor and four citizens.[6] The oath was finally abandoned in 1859, after a succession of radical mayors had flatly refused it. The Delegates of Privileges met the initial challenge, in 1856, with uncertainty, and in 1857 Convocation approved a motion requiring the swearing of the oath by only 36 votes to 11; it was hardly the time to be seen defending to the death a privilege so firmly rooted in the Middle Ages.[7] However, the intransigence of the mayor, Isaac Grubb, a Baptist baker and corn-dealer whose boast was that he had 'no connexion with the University and nothing for which to thank any member thereof',[8] hardened attitudes, and in February 1858 Convocation voted 64 to 9 to institute legal proceedings.[9] A potentially ruinous chase through the lawcourts was prevented by William Gladstone and Edward Cardwell, MPs for the University and city respectively, who successfully proposed a compromise: the oath would be taken once more, in 1859, after which it would lapse, the city paying for the required Act of Parliament.[10]

The abolition of ritualistic displays of the University's authority left untouched its routine exercise directly through the university courts and indirectly through the statutory bodies that administered the city. The Chancellor's court, in which the Vice-Chancellor deputized, had exclusive jurisdiction in all civil causes except those involving freeholds in which one party was a resident member of the University; the Vice-Chancellor in his own right as an *ex officio* magistrate exercised criminal jurisdiction, comprising petty-sessional powers, in cases involving a resident member of the University.[11] The jurisdictions were somewhat wider than might at first

[5] *VCH Oxon.* iv. 54.

[6] Oxford City archives B. 5. 6, pp. 9, 15, 21, 35, 39–40, 50, 80, 96–7; OUA NEP/H8, letters of Jan., Apr. 1834; OUA MR/3/4/2; *Herald* 29 Aug., 5 Sept., 4 Oct. 1834. A reference in *Report of the Commission on Municipal Corporations in England and Wales* (PP 1835 (116) xxiii. 238) to the St Scholastica's Day ceremony is presumably in error for the mayor's oath.

[7] OUA WP/α/17(8b), *passim*; WP/α/56(6); Oxford City archives B. 5. 8, p. 523; C. 5. 1, 6 Nov. 1857; *Oxford Journal* 1, 15 Nov. 1856; 7 Nov., 12 Dec. 1857.

[8] Cox, 401.

[9] *Oxford Journal* 6 Feb. 1858.

[10] OUA NWP/4 (1, no. 8); OUA NEP/H8; Oxford City archives C. 5. 1, 1 Jan., 18 Mar., 13 May 1858; 26 May, 9 Nov. 1859; *Oxford Journal* 30 Jan., 27 Mar., 8, 15 May 1858; 5 Feb., 23 July 1859; *Oxford Chronicle* 23 July 1859; *VCH Oxon.* iv. 246.

[11] *Halsbury's Statutory Instruments* v. 276; OM 12, 19 Nov. 1890.

1. The arrival of the Vice-Chancellor for a University Sermon
    (from the Oxford Almanack, 1834)

2. Cyril Jackson

3. John Parsons

4. M. J. Routh

5. Edward Tatham

6. Edward Copleston

7. The installation of the Duke of Wellington in the Sheldonian Theatre, 1834

8. An examination in progress in the old Schools, 1842

9. The University and the City, c.1845

10. St Mary Magdalen, from St Giles', *c.* 1812

11. The Martyrs' Memorial, 1850

12. J. H. Newman

13. E. B. Pusey

14. Richard Whately

15. Ashurst Turner Gilbert

16. R. G. Macmullen

17. R. D. Hampden

18. Philip Wynter

19. William Sewell

20. The front of Brasenose College, 1821

21. New College cloisters, 1833

22. St Alban Hall, 1851

23. The new hall of Pembroke College, 1858

24. The Bodleian Library, Arts End, 1842

25. The Oxford Union debating hall, 1863

26. Ashmolean Museum, the mammal collection, 1836

27. Ashmolean Museum, the archaeological and ethnographic collections, *c.*1864

PLAN OF THE FIRST FLOOR.

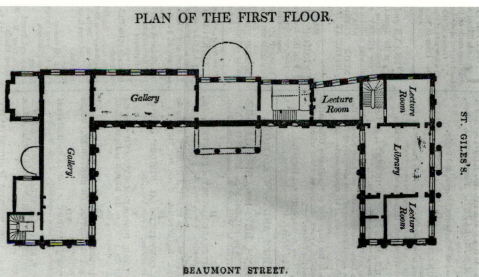

Gallery

Gallery

Lecture Room

Lecture Room

Library

Lecture Room

ST. GILES'S.

BEAUMONT STREET.

THE GROUND PLAN.

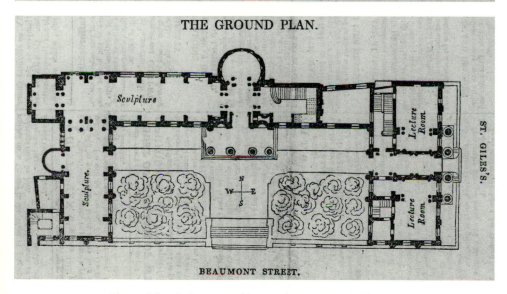

Sculpture

Sculpture

Lecture Room.

Lecture Room.

ST. GILES'S.

BEAUMONT STREET.

28. Plans of the Taylorian Building and University Galleries, 1842

29. The University Galleries, *c.*1860

31. Philip Bliss

30. Bulkeley Bandinel

32. William Buckland lecturing, 1823

33. Charles Daubeny

34. The University Museum, c.1861

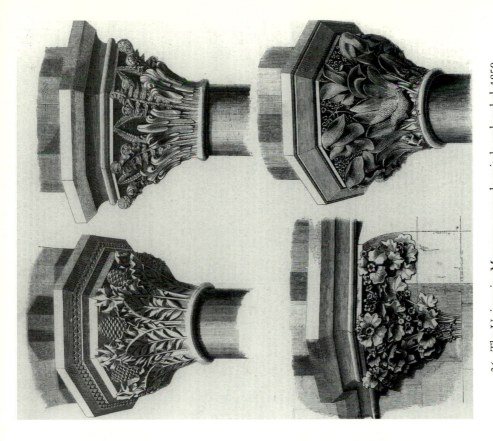

36. The University Museum, carved capitals and corbel, 1859

35. The University Museum, interior view, 1860

38. Henry Acland

37. John Kidd

39. George Rolleston, Charles Robertson, A. G. Vernon Harcourt,
and Heywood Smith, *c.*1860

40. The Clarendon Laboratory

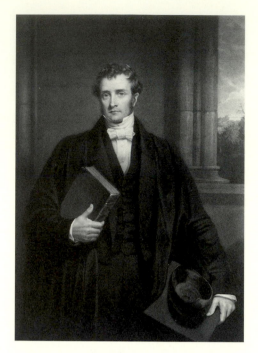

41. A. P. Stanley

42. H. L. Mansel

43. Thomas Gaisford

44. John Conington

45. Edward Cardwell

46. Travers Twiss

47. Richard Greswell

48. Goldwin Smith

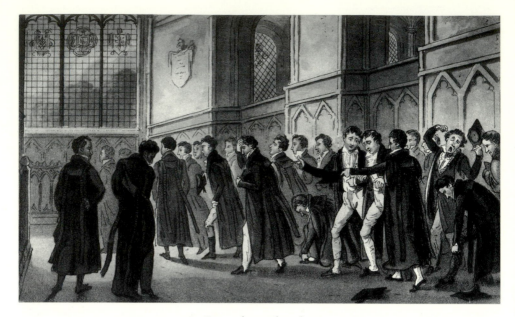

49. Compulsory chapel, *c.*1824

50. A college lecture, *c.*1849

51. Prescribed academic dress, 1828

52. A proctor confronts an undergraduate not wearing his gown, 1842

53. An early intercollegiate bumping race on the Isis, 1822

54. A boisterous wine party in the early 1820s

55. Huntsmen taking breakfast, *c*.1850

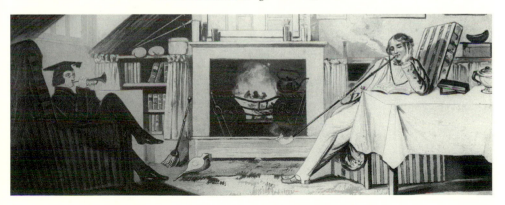

56. Undergraduates relaxing in college rooms, 1843

57a and 57b. Pugin's designs for an undergraduate's chamber and bedroom, 1843

58. Old Mortality, 1860

59. Christ Church men, c. 1860

60. The Vice-Chancellor processing to St Mary's, 1852

appear, for among members of the University were those tradesmen known as 'privileged persons' who had signed the matriculation register and were therefore protected by university privilege from the city's jurisdiction and from the obligations imposed upon freemen.[12] By the nineteenth century the privilege had become restricted to those whose occupations were traditionally of close concern to the University, notably university and college servants, booksellers, bookbinders, printers, stationers, and barbers. Demarcation disputes, which had largely died away in the eighteenth century, occasionally became troublesome again, but by and large the truce held. Freemen did not seek to invade the privileges of matriculated tradesmen, though they were prepared to protect their own position with threats of legal action; the University was rather more relaxed, acting against tradesmen only when its privileges were threatened or when pressed by privileged persons to control competition among their number. William Wise, a matriculated stationer, was discommoned (i.e. forbidden any contact with members of the University) in 1804 at the behest of 'their high mightinesses, the booksellers of Oxford' when he attempted also to sell books; and it was the booksellers Joseph Parker, Joshua Cooke and Robert Bliss who brought the action in the Chancellor's court that led to the discommoning of the unmatriculated bookseller Nathaniel Bliss, mentioned below.[13] There were reckoned in 1829 to be 250–300 matriculated tradesmen; but the number declined later in the century, especially after the Municipal Corporations Act of 1835 swept away trading restrictions: the last tradesman to matriculate seems to have been William Bacon, tobacconist and 'cricket depot proprietor', in 1856.[14]

Townsmen took a pragmatic view of the University's civil jurisdiction. It was quicker and cheaper than the ordinary judicial process, and by most accounts offered fair dealing. While townsmen were happy to use the civil court, there was little liking for the University's criminal jurisdiction. No self-respecting high-Victorian civic body could remain unconcerned when its mayor's court was compelled to halt proceedings and hand over cases to a rival jurisdiction, as happened on a sensational occasion in 1890. On 6 November Catherina Riordan, a London 'woman about town', shot and wounded James Bright, Master of University College. Miss Riordan had been thrown over by John Haines, a fellow of the college, in favour of Bright's daughter—an act of betrayal for which she held the unfortunate Master and his family responsible. The case had just about every element

---

[12] For an account of privileged persons see *VCH Oxon.* iv, *passim*.
[13] OUA WP/α/17(8ᵃ⁻ᵇ); WP/α/43(1); W. Wise, *An Appeal from Custom to Conscience* (1804) (copy), Bodl. 2581 f. 31; notice of Wise's discommoning, Bodl. Don. b. 12(103); *VCH Oxon.* iv. 209.
[14] OUA WP/α/56(3), fo 7. 19th-century matriculants included bakers, barbers, booksellers, college and university servants, grocers, instrument-makers, joiners, musicians, perfumers, pharmacists, stationers, surgeons, and victuallers: OUA matriculation register; Dutton & Allen, *Directory of Oxon.* (1863).

that a riveted public could desire: an eminent public figure seriously though not mortally wounded, an attractive wronged woman of unstable temperament and shadowy background, an innocent and distraught fiancée, a promising career in ruins, and every prospect of further skeletons in the cupboard. In the circumstances it is no surprise that little attention was paid at first to the curtailment of committal proceedings in the mayor's court by the university Bedel-at-Law claiming the case for the Vice-Chancellor. The city's subsequent grievance at having to bear the expense of a case claimed by the University soon widened to encompass the entire issue of university jurisdiction.[15] The Hebdomadal Council came close in June 1891 to conceding the Vice-Chancellor's petty-sessional powers in return for the appointment of a joint Bench, a compromise operating successfully at Cambridge. In May 1893 an agreement was reached with the City Council whereby the University would accept a mixed Bench and cease to exercise petty-sessional jurisdiction over non-members of the University except in street-walking cases, control over which had been confirmed to the University in 1825.[16] The Vice-Chancellor's authority, shared with the mayor, to permit public performances was also to be retained.[17] The Corporation withdrew its consent at the last moment, mistakenly believing, despite warnings from university councillors, that further pressure would bring additional concessions.[18] The matter remained unresolved, and an agreement of 1899 stipulated only that the Vice-Chancellor would warn city magistrates if he intended to claim jurisdiction. That agreement was confirmed in 1914; and the system remained unchanged, though little used, until in 1968 the Vice-Chancellor's powers, like those of other *ex officio* JPs, were removed by the Justices of the Peace Act. The University's civil jurisdiction ceased in 1977.[19]

There was in the exercise of university jurisdiction less of the triumphalism that had so soured relationships with the town in the past. When, in 1814, the bookseller Nathaniel Bliss responded to a notice of discommoning by obtaining an injunction in the Court of King's Bench the University was anxious to avoid the affair being portrayed as a town–gown issue.[20] In truth the town had long ceased to be the chief threat to university jurisdiction: the main protagonist was now the legal profession itself, hostile to franchises, and the struggle increasingly lay between a local and a national jurisdiction.[21]

[15] OUA NEP/Pyx/H6; *Oxford Times* 8, 15, 22 Nov. 1890; 9 May 1891; *Oxford Review* 7–26 Nov. 1890. Riordan received a six-year sentence; Haines resigned and became a private tutor.
[16] Act for the Preservation of the Peace in the Universities, 6 Geo. IV, c. 97.
[17] The right of veto was confirmed by the Oxford Police Acts of 1868 and 1881: 31 & 32 Vic., c. 59; 44 & 45 Vic., c. 39.
[18] OUA NEP/Pyx/H6; *Oxford Times* 3, 10, 17 June 1893.
[19] OUA MR/3 (4, no. 24); Justices of the Peace Act 1968, c. 69; Administration of Justice Act 1977, c. 28, s. 23; *VCH Oxon*. iv. 247.
[20] OUA WP/α/43.
[21] For university jurisdiction generally, see W. A. Pantin, *Oxford Life in Oxford Archives* (1972), ch. 5.

Montagu Burrows, in 1877, cited joint action on the statutory bodies administering Oxford as the greatest single factor in improving relations over the previous hundred years.[22] The Oxford Paving Commission, one of the first such bodies in the country, was set up in 1771 on the initiative of Nathan Wetherell, the Vice-Chancellor, to supervise the paving, cleansing and lighting of the city. It marked a shift in power in Oxford to bodies on which city and University were represented evenly and which were jointly financed. The Commission's capacity for comprehensive planning and administration marked a decisive break with the past, and the experience of co-operation and joint action in the face of common problems was to make inconceivable a return to the implacable hostility, let alone the violence, of former times.[23] In the first years of the Paving Commission university representatives were highly influential.[24] The University, therefore, shared responsibility for the physical transformation of the city which in the later eighteenth century and earlier nineteenth swept away much of its remaining medieval fabric. A further joint body, the Oxford Market Committee, comprising six university and six city members, was charged under the 1771 Act with building a covered market for the sale of perishable goods. The Committee did not have to contend with the politically sensitive issues of the assize of bread and ale and the appointment of clerks of the market, which remained a university prerogative, or with tolls, which the Corporation retained, and it is generally reckoned to have been a useful example of co-operative endeavour.[25]

While the experience of working together on statutory bodies undoubtedly helped break down barriers, it might at times fuel old rivalries. When, in 1848, the University Paving Commissioners, led by Richard Harington, Principal of Brasenose College, proposed taking advantage of the borrowing-powers created by the Health of Towns Act to undertake much-needed sanitary improvements, they were supported by some Conservative Commissioners but successfully opposed by the town's Liberals and radicals, fearful of the expense and of central-government interference.[26] Support for the University's position on extra expenditure was undermined by its own campaign to halve its share of the rates from two-fifths to one-fifth on the ground of Oxford's recent suburban expansion. A compromise of one-third was eventually agreed, with ill grace.[27] It was nevertheless becoming apparent that the Paving Commission's powers were inadequate for a city whose

[22] Oxford Chronicle 6 Jan. 1877.
[23] The Eighteenth Century, 221–5; VCH Oxon. iv. 232–3.
[24] Oxford City archives R. 6. 5.
[25] Market Committee minutes, ibid. FF. 2. 1–5; VCH Oxon. iv. 307–10; M. Graham, 'Building of Oxford covered market', Oxoniensia xliv (1979), 81–91.
[26] Herald 29 July, 28 Oct. 1848; Oxford Protestant Magazine i (1847), 297.
[27] Oxford City archives B. 5. 7, pp. 211–13; Bodl. G. A. Oxon. c. 64(37); Oxford Journal 26 Feb. 1848; Oxford Protestant Magazine ii (1848), pp. 44–8; Oxford Mileways Act, 11 & 12 Vic., c. 37.

population had almost tripled since 1771. An attempt in 1858 to adopt the Local Government Act of that year was broken, ironically, by an alliance of Liberals and the University, which was afraid of losing its influence in local government. The Act was finally adopted in 1864, although four college heads remained in opposition to the end, and a Local Board of Health replaced the Paving Commission. The University was generously represented by the Vice-Chancellor and fifteen elected members on a Board of forty-seven.[28]

There was continuity of personnel from the Paving Commission to the Local Board, and university representatives, led by four college heads, James Sewell of New College, Edward Cradock of Brasenose, John Lightfoot of Exeter and Henry Liddell of Christ Church, were more prominent than had become usual. Also active was Robert Jackson, fellow of New College and Henry Acland's rival for the chair of Clinical Medicine in 1857, elected as parish representative for Holywell.[29] Nevertheless, the Board was at first as reluctant as its predecessor to commit itself to long-term expenditure, although it was accepted in the wake of serious cholera outbreaks in 1832, 1849 and 1854 that new drainage and water-supply systems were essential. Until the Corporation in 1854 purchased the lake at South Hinksey created by gravel extraction for the railway-line, the city waterworks had been at Folly Bridge, downstream of at least five sewage outfalls and the gasworks; not surprisingly, only 340 houses took the supply.[30] Major improvements were forced through after a long struggle notable for the persistence of Liddell, George Rolleston and Henry Acland, who at one time came close to despair, complaining in 1866 that 'the longer I live here, the more unbearable it seems to me. The dean [Liddell] and I have both been pointedly told that whatever he or I proposed at the Local Board would have been equally and violently opposed.'[31]

The Paving Commission and Local Board provided a model for the eventual settlement of the age-old issue of policing the city. Until 1868 policing between 9 p.m. and dawn was provided by the University, a right it had won in the Middle Ages and which it was reluctant to concede so long as prostitution remained a problem.[32] The Delegates of Privileges noted with satisfaction in 1819 that the 'superior authority' of the proctors in the matter of the night watch was respected by the city. Misunderstandings were

[28] *VCH Oxon.* iv. 233, 239. The college heads opposing the change were James Norris of Corpus, Edward Hawkins of Oriel, Philip Wynter of St John's, and John Wilson of Trinity: *Herald* 27 May 1864.

[29] Oxford City archives R. 5. 1; *Herald* 2 Nov. 1867.

[30] *VCH Oxon.* iv. 355.

[31] *Oxford Chronicle* 25 June 1881; Atlay, *Acland*, 364; A. Howe, 'Intellect and civic responsibility' in R. C. Whiting (ed.), *Oxford: studies in the history of a university town since 1800* (Manchester 1993), 23–6.

[32] OUA WP/β/5(23), pp. 5, 9–10.

usually settled tactfully, although co-operation may not have penetrated much below senior level since city constables were known to return after going off duty in order to join in attacks on gownsmen.[33] The university watch, admitted in 1828 to be 'very imperfect', was reformed the following year under the provisions of the 1825 Act for the Preservation of the Peace in the Universities, which allowed for the establishment of a university police force. The new force comprised thirteen constables and two inspectors, whose efficiency led the Municipal Corporations Commission in 1835 to single out Oxford as among the best-policed cities in the kingdom.[34] A new city police force, generally regarded as more or less incompetent, was established in 1836, but the University retained the prerogative of noctivagation.[35] Oxford's growth in the nineteenth century made those policing arrangements increasingly incongruous, but criticism by the Home Office Inspectorate in 1859 had less effect than increasing costs in pushing the University to attempt to unload a serious financial burden on to a now unwilling civic body.[36] It took the Hebdomadal Council's threat unilaterally to discontinue the night watch to bring about the establishment in 1868 of a united police force administered by a joint watch committee, two-fifths of the costs and members of which were the University's. A proviso inserted on University insistence allowed for a review of the arrangements following the census of 1881, as a result of which the University's contributions and representation were reduced to one-third.[37] Anomalies remained: Home Office inspectors, praising the efficiency of the new force,[38] failed to note that the arrest of prostitutes continued to be left to the proctors, apparently because 'it never occurred to the new police that those cases came under their cognizance'.[39] The police were also unsure about their jurisdiction in colleges, even when their assistance was officially requested.[40]

In Oxford the restructuring of local government in 1889 was accomplished on the basis of an agreement that preserved university interests while bringing back into a central role a corporation that had previously little to do beyond 'the management of its property, the payment of its officials, and the more ornamental functions of civic life'.[41] City and University jointly

[33] OUA WP/α/17(8a); WP/γ/8(19), fo 68; WP/γ/24(3), p. 294; 24(4), pp. 26–7, 42; 24(6), p. 174.
[34] OUA WP/γ/24(4), pp. 95, 97, 104, 164; 26(2), fo 61; Act for Preservation of Peace, 6 Geo. IV, c. 97; Report of the Commission on Municipal Corporations, 239; Report of the Commission on Municipal Corporation Boundaries (PP 1837 (238) xxviii. 12).
[35] VCH Oxon. iv. 357.
[36] Report of Inspectors of Constabulary (PP 1859 (17 Sess. 1) xxii. 32–3); Oxford City archives D. 11. 3. 2; ibid. C. 5. 1, 13 June 1864; OUA NWP 4 (2, no. 27a); OUA WP/γ/24(7), pp. 431–2.
[37] OUA WP/γ/24(7), p. 516; Oxford City archives C. 5. 2, fo 15ᵛ; Bodl. G. A. Oxon. 8° 105(13); ibid. c. 229 (2, 5); Oxford Police Act, 31 & 32 Vic., c. 59; Oxford Police Act, 44 & 45 Vic., c. 39.
[38] Report of Inspectors of Constabulary (PP. 1871 (25) xxviii. 34); (1881 (131) li. 63).
[39] Oxford Times 17 June 1893.
[40] Oxford City archives HH. 1. 3, 1 June 1887.
[41] Oxford Chronicle 19 Nov. 1881.

applied for a Provisional Order constituting Oxford a county borough, the powers of the Corporation, the Local Board, the Market Committee, and Police Committee to be vested in one municipal authority, a City Council on which the University and colleges would receive a fifth of the representation. There were to be three university aldermen and nine councillors, six elected by college heads and bursars, three by Convocation.[42] In some ways the new arrangement increased university influence, introducing it into areas from which it had previously been excluded. Civic influence over university affairs remained minimal. There was some hostility to University representation, especially in the East ward where three members of the University stood as Conservative candidates, and there was resentment that senior members would have two votes, one in the wards in which they lived and one in Convocation.[43] All but one University councillor had been members of the Local Board, and they were at once able to play a useful and prominent role on the new Council. Since they rarely acted together as a University 'party', they aroused little resentment. Their role was acknowledged in 1913 when Alderman the Revd W. E. Sherwood became the first University councillor to be elected mayor.[44]

Two important areas, poor relief and education, remained outside the control of the new Corporation, and the University was influential in both. The unification of eleven parishes in 1771 for purposes of poor relief was, unlike the other reforming Act of that year, the Paving Act, a city initiative.[45] College and university buildings were extra-parochial and therefore not rated for poor relief, but the Poor Law Guardians' mounting financial difficulties led to growing demands for contributions.[46] In 1838 they attempted to force the issue by compelling an MA living in New Inn Hall Street to be overseer for St Michael's parish. As a tentative attempt to establish a precedent it was a dismal failure since the Delegates of Privileges responded vigorously and forced the Guardians to back down with a threat of costly litigation.[47] In 1843 the St Michael's overseers distrained on the silver at Exeter and Jesus colleges, but lost the resultant expensive legal battle. Non-contribution by the University and colleges remained a source of resentment until in 1854 the University Rating Act established a new board of thirty-three members, which included the Vice-Chancellor, eight members elected by heads of houses and bursars, and two elected by Con-

[42] Local Government Board's Provisional Orders Confirmation Act, 52 Vic., c. 15 (Local and Personal); *VCH Oxon.* iv. 240. The election of university councillors was modelled on that for the Local Board, for which eleven members were elected by heads and bursars, four by Convocation.

[43] *Oxford Times* 9 Nov. 1889.

[44] Ibid. 15 Nov. 1913; Howe, 'Intellect and civic responsibility', 34–6.

[45] Act for Regulating the Poor in Oxford, 11 Geo. III, c. 14. For education see below.

[46] *VCH Oxon.* iv. 235.

[47] OUA WP/α/17(7).

vocation. The University was to collect its own rates and until 1875 had its own delegacy of appeals. Christ Church, considered still to be extra-parochial, remained unrated for poor relief until in 1862 it offered to contribute in return for the right to appoint two Guardians; Merton, Corpus Christi, St Alban Hall and parts of Oriel lay in St John's parish, and part of St John's College lay in St Giles', both parishes forming part of the Headington Poor Law Union. The University's public buildings remained exempt from poor rates until 1875.[48]

The Oxford Anti-Mendicity Society was founded in 1814 as the Committee for the Relief of Distressed Travellers at the instigation of John Duncan of New College, and re-established in 1827 by Richard Whately of Oriel. It was a subscription society whose purpose was to replace direct alms-giving to vagrants with vouchers redeemable at an Office of Investigation where applicants were examined by the Society's officer, often assisted by undergraduates, and the 'deserving' offered help.[49] Prompted by Col. W. E. Sackville West, Bursar of Keble College and founding member of the London Charity Organization Society (COS), the Anti-Mendicity Society first enlarged its scope to include local poor and then in 1873 merged with the COS under Sackville West's chairmanship.[50] The University dominated the new Society's committee: Samuel Wayte, President of Trinity College, was its President, William Spooner and A. H. D. Acland its Secretaries and several prominent university figures and their wives and daughters served on the committee.[51] The Society's aim of bringing the tenets of economic liberalism to bear upon poor law administration by replacing outdoor relief whenever possible by selective charitable giving backed up by the workhouse test was successfully practised only in Oxford and Cambridge, where it attracted the support of highly influential university liberals and where there were long-established, well-supported appropriate charities.[52] The Society set itself to reduce pauperization by returning to independence those dependent upon public relief, offering advice, financial or medical assistance and help with employment or even emigration. Co-operation with the Board of Guardians was said to have been close in the decade 1876–85[53] when University Guardians, notably W. A. Spooner (New College), L. R. Phelps (Oriel), J. Rigaud

---

[48] *VCH Oxon.* iv. 235–6. The campaign against the University was led by Isaac Grubb, then overseer for St Peter-le-Bailey parish: *Oxford Chronicle* 28 Mar. 1885.

[49] W. A. Spooner, 'The COS, the Board of Guardians, the Pol. Econ. Club', NCA MS 14. 356, fo 2; *Herald* 7 May 1814; *VCH Oxon.* iv. 475.

[50] Spooner, 'The COS', fos 9–13.

[51] Oxford Anti-Mendicity Society and COS, *Reports* etc., esp. *Circular Letter* (1873), Bodl. G. A. Oxon. 4° 165.

[52] Oxford COS, *Report* (1901) (copy), Bodl. G. A. Oxon. 4° 165; C. Harvie, *Lights of Liberalism* (1976), 195; Harvie, 'Intellectuals and poverty: administering the poor law in Oxford and Cambridge, 1860–1906', unpub. paper kindly made available by Prof. Harvie; *VCH Oxon.* iv. 348–9.

[53] Spooner, 'The COS', fos 9–13.

(Magdalen) and J. C. Wilson (Exeter), all active in the COS, came to dominate the Board with the support of some parish representatives.[54] The result was a sharp fall in the number of those given outdoor relief, from 572 in 1870 to 157 in 1883, when, acting upon a recommendation first made by Arnold Toynbee in 1881, the Board agreed to relieve applicants only while their cases were investigated by the COS, employing as investigators the large pool of concerned people, mainly women with university connections, available for such work in Oxford.[55] Undergraduates working for the Society learned, as Sir William Anson remarked in 1887, that 'poverty existed in Oxford as well as in Bethnal Green, Whitechapel, and Seven Dials'. Some of those later going to live and work at the university settlements in London first had their eyes opened by the slums of Oxford.[56] After investigation the Society would offer to assist 'deserving' cases, often generously; others were offered the workhouse.[57] The number of those on out-relief continued to fall, from 157 in 1883 to only 40 in 1899, when the total of those receiving any sort of relief was 437 (1 in 60 of the population) compared to 970 (1 in 23) in 1870.[58] Some of those relieved by the COS would not have qualified for public relief, but even if their number is added to the paupers relieved by the Guardians, the proportion of the population receiving relief fell from 4 per cent in 1872 to between 2 and 3 per cent in the period 1876–1908.[59]

The experiment, as it was later admitted to be,[60] was an administrative and financial success but a political failure, alienating many of those seeking relief and, most disappointingly, unable to command durable support in what was believed to be its natural constituency, the 'respectable' working class. Faltering university and college incomes in the 1870s and 1880s made economy a priority,[61] but lofty talk of 'principles too high to be generally understood'[62] and of a 'harsh and austere but not an ignoble or thoughtless ideal'[63] was an inadequate response to the campaign of opposition led with considerable political skill by Oxford's Conservative MP, A. W. Hall. Scarcely acknowledging the spirit of compassion that had first drawn the

[54] Reports of the Board of Guardians (1826–69), Bodl. c. 127; ibid. (1870–1904), Bodl. Per. G. A. Oxon. 8° 456. Members of the University rarely served as parish representatives, although entitled to if householders: cf Harvie, Lights of Liberalism, 195.

[55] L. R. Phelps, Administration of the Poor Law in Oxford (1900), copy in Bodl. 24724 e. 388 (4); Harvie, 'Intellectuals and poverty'; A. Kadish, Apostle Arnold: the life and death of Arnold Toynbee, 1852–1883 (Durham NC 1986), 156, 166–7.

[56] Spooner, 'The COS', fo 2; Oxford Anti-Mendicity Society and COS, Report (1897–8); Oxford Chronicle 26 Nov. 1887; B. H. Harrison, 'Miss Butler's Oxford survey', in A. H. Halsey (ed.), Traditions of Social Policy: essays in honour of Violet Butler (1976), 49 ff.

[57] Phelps, Administration of the Poor Law in Oxford; Phelps, Statement.

[58] Reports of Board of Guardians.

[59] VCH Oxon. iv. 349.

[60] Oxford Anti-Mendicity Society and COS, Report (1901).

[61] Harvie, 'Intellectuals and poverty'; Harvie, Lights of Liberalism, 195.

[62] Oxford Anti-Mendicity Society and COS, Report (1901).

[63] Spooner, 'The COS', fo 12.

University Guardians into public life, he cleverly caricatured them as a comfortable and unworldly group whose agonizing only made more intolerable the imposition of their rigid principles on a long-suffering population.[64] Hall's claim that the University Guardians cost the Liberal Party the city election in 1885 was an over-simplification, but their unpopularity in key parts of the constituency such as St Ebbe's and St Thomas's played a part in the long-term decline in Liberal fortunes in Oxford.[65]

The criticism levelled at the Guardians seems not to have been extended to the many charitable agencies with which the University was associated. The Christ Church almshouses in St Aldates, absorbed into Pembroke College in 1888, were until the late eighteenth century the only almshouses in the city.[66] The extent to which most charities relied on university support is revealed in their annual reports, and the consequence is apparent in the imposition of the pragmatic moralism characteristic of the COS, whose supporters were to be found on most committees. The Oxford Coal and the Oxford Clothing funds, for instance, were typical in using relief to reward the provident poor: 'Those who have not saved the small amount necessary to spend with a ticket are not properly objects of the charity.'[67] By the later nineteenth century Oxford was so well provided with charitable institutions that it was scarcely possible in the poorer parts of town to be born, to give birth, to subsist or to die without coming to the notice of at least one voluntary agency.[68] In some cases university involvement took the form of increased membership and influence, as with the Medical Dispensary and Lying-In Charity, which attracted little attention when founded in 1807 but which by mid-century was treating 1,000 patients a year.[69] Other agencies and associations were from the start university initiatives, ranging from the Association to Promote the Observation of Laws on the Subject of Morals (1886) to the fund for a cabmen's shelter at the railway station (1894).[70] The Oxford Working Girls' Club, founded in 1887 to provide entertainment and education for factory girls, was based in rooms at New Inn Hall provided by

[64] The debate can be followed in Oxford Anti-Mendicity Society and COS reports and leaflets in Bodl. G. A. Oxon. 4° 165, and in the Oxford newspapers of the period; Howe, 'Intellect and civic responsibility', 29–30.

[65] Harvie, 'Intellectuals and poverty'; Harvie, Lights of Liberalism, 195. The politics of poor relief were not exclusively those of party: J. C. Wilson, lecturer in Jurisprudence at Exeter College, alderman, chairman of the Board of Guardians, and a strong COS supporter, was a leading Conservative: Oxford Times 8 Jan. 1887; VCH Oxon. iv. 252–4.

[66] J. Curthoys, '"To perfect the college": the Christ Church almsmen, 1547–1888', Oxoniensia lx (1995), 379–95.

[67] Coal Fund, Reports (1853–88), Bodl. Per. G. A. Oxon. 4° 264; Clothing Fund, Reports (1849–92), ibid. 4 to 266.

[68] E. H. Cordeaux and D. H. Merry, Bibliography of Printed Works Relating to Oxford City (OHS ns xxv 1976) lists some fifty local non-municipal charities in existence at various times during the 19th and early 20th century.

[69] Reports, Bodl. G. A. Oxon. b. 15, fos 9–11.

[70] Ibid., fos 62–7; b. 156, fos 67–8.

Balliol College and supervised by members of, among others, the Liddell, Müller, Nettleship and Toynbee families.[71] The Oxford House of Refuge for Fallen Women, in Floyd's Row, was begun by John Burgon in 1875 and from 1890 had the proctors automatically on its committee; the mayor only joined the committee in 1897. The refuge fulfilled twin desiderata so far as the University was concerned, expiating sin and removing temptation. In the latter it could claim some success since it was reckoned in 1888 that half the 550 girls who had by then passed through the house might confidently be regarded as reformed.[72]

Charitable and welfare work in Oxford had an effectiveness rarely attained elsewhere. One explanation lay in the participation of a large number of voluntary workers, many of them women from academic families or from recently established 'residential' families on the fringes of the academic world. They were rarely the well-intentioned but ineffectual busybodies of popular myth; possessed of remarkable stamina and determination, usually well organized and supervised, they devoted themselves to their work for long enough to become thoroughly knowledgeable and, as important, respected by those to whom they ministered.[73] Pre-dating the Green–Toynbee circle, on which so much attention has been focused, two earlier role models for women welfare workers, Eleanor Smith and Felicia Skene, represented the academic and non-academic worlds respectively. Felicia Skene came to Oxford in 1845 and, under the imperious influence of Thomas Chamberlain, Student of Christ Church and vicar of St Thomas's, devoted herself to welfare work in that parish. Singled out for praise by Acland for organizing home nursing during the cholera outbreak of 1854, she later became Oxford's first female prison visitor and was closely involved with Chamberlain in founding St Edward's School. Lancelot Phelps generously acknowledged the practical underpinning that she gave to COS theorizing.[74] Eleanor Smith, sister of the Savilian Professor of Geometry, was known in academic circles for her connection with Somerville College and Bedford College, London. To Oxford townspeople she was the sole female School Board member, a pioneer of district nursing and of the Oxford Provident Dispensary, and an indefatigable campaigner on behalf of slum children. Her dedication and energy, combined with a 'somewhat disconcerting outspokenness', gave her what William Spooner recalled as 'a sort of leadership in all matters philan-

[71] Reports (1891–1923), ibid. 8° 795.

[72] Reports (1879–1917), ibid. 8° 657.

[73] Harrison, 'Miss Butler's Oxford survey', 27–72; P. Hollis, Ladies Elect: women in English local government, 1865–1914 (1987), 239, 397, 409–10, 438, 448; E. C. Rickards, Felicia Skene of Oxford: a memoir (1902).

[74] DNB; Rickards, Felicia Skene, 88–9, 103 ff., 188 ff., 292–7; A. B. Simeon, A Short Memoir of the Revd. Thomas Chamberlain (1892); H. W. Acland, Memoir on the Cholera at Oxford in 1854 (1856), 99; W. E. Sherwood, Oxford Yesterday (1927), 69; note of c.1899 in collections re St Edward's School, Bodl. Per. G. A. Oxon. 4° 169.

thropic and charitable ... in a masterful way peculiarly her own'.[75] From the 1870s she began to receive assistance from the families of Liberal academics, notably from Charlotte Green, Bertha Johnson, Alice Kitchin, Georgiana Müller, Charlotte Toynbee and Mary Ward.[76] They were succeeded by protégées such as Lettice Fisher, Mabel Pritchard and Mary Smith,[77] and by non-academics such as Lizzie Hughes and Sophia Merivale, the city's first women councillors.[78] One of their number, Violet Butler, daughter of Arthur Butler of Oriel, produced Oxford's only major contribution to the social surveys of the period, *Social Conditions in Oxford*, published in 1912.

The pervasive influence of that close-knit group did much to reduce the sort of duplication, or even competition, that beset municipal, statutory and voluntary agencies at work in towns elsewhere. At the centre of the network of agencies was the Oxford Sanitary Aid Association, whose Health Committee worked closely with the city's Medical Officer of Health (MOH), the COS, the Invalid Children's Association, the Acland District Nurses, the Diocesan Social Services Committee and other bodies to demonstrable effect: a programme of infant-visiting at the request of the MOH, of instruction and of providing low-cost treated milk helped reduce Oxford's infant mortality by a remarkable 53.5 per cent for the period 1902–19, compared to the 35.7 per cent reduction nationally.[79]

The University had been closely involved with public health in Oxford from the later eighteenth century, quite apart from the Paving Commission and the Local Board of Health. Oxford's principal hospital, the Radcliffe Infirmary, was wholly administered by the University from its opening in 1770 until 1848, when citizens were admitted to its committee of management. Other leading institutions, such as the Warneford Asylum (founded 1826) and the Acland Nursing Home (1882), had close university links; and Oxford's charitable dispensaries relied heavily on practical and financial support from the academic community.[80] The same was true of the ad-hoc committees established during nineteenth-century epidemics. The inaction

[75] *Oxford Chronicle* 30 Apr. 1887; *Oxford Times* 19 Sept. 1896; Hollis, *Ladies Elect*, 148–50; J. E. Courtney, *An Oxford Portrait Gallery* (1931), 215; NCA MS 14, 356, fos 21–2 of loose leaves at end of MS. For her work on the Oxford School Board see below.

[76] The wives of T. H. Green, A. H. Johnson, G. W. Kitchin, Max Müller, Arnold Toynbee and Humphry Ward.

[77] The wives of H. A. L. Fisher, H. A. Pritchard and A. L. Smith. E. Peretz, 'Infant welfare in inter-war Oxford', in Whiting (ed.), *Oxford*, 135–6.

[78] *Oxford Chronicle* 25 Oct., 1 Nov., 8 Nov. 1907, 30 Oct. 1908; Courtney, *Oxford Portrait Gallery*, 215 ff.; Harrison, 'Miss Butler's Oxford survey', 64–7; Hollis, *Ladies Elect*, 24, 397, 409–10; J. Parfit, *The Health of a City: Oxford, 1770–1974* (privately printed 1987), 73. Miss Merivale was, unusually in that circle, a Conservative: *Oxford Chronicle* 8 Nov. 1913.

[79] Oxford Sanitary Aid Association, *Reports* (1907–8, 1910); Oxford Diocesan Social Services Committee, *Reports* (1908–9, 1912); City of Oxford, Medical Officer of Health, *Reports*; Harrison, 'Miss Butler's Oxford survey', 58; Parfit, *Health of a City*, 73–5.

[80] *Oxford Chronicle* 30 Apr. 1887; VCH Oxon. iv. 360–2.

of the Guardians of the Poor, whose responsibility it theoretically was to deal with epidemic disease, led to the setting-up of temporary boards of health on which the University was prominently represented, officially and voluntarily. Vaughan Thomas of Corpus Christi College, chairman of the Warneford trustees, and Henry Acland were the chief motivators and organizers of the boards set up during the cholera epidemics of 1832 and 1854 respectively; the response to that of 1849 was disorganized and acrimonious, only a few doctors and voluntary workers emerging with any credit.[81]

Growing awareness of the need to tackle problems of sanitation and health at source by improving housing conditions focused attention on the role of colleges as landlords of some of the worst dwellings in Oxford. Christ Church, 'awakened to the necessity of removing the scandal of owning such property', took the lead in the 1840s by calling in expired leases and in 1850 initiated a housing improvement committee, comprising citizens as well as academics, to repair and manage its houses 'as a model to others in the city'.[82] In 1866–7 the college replaced some very poor tenements in St Thomas's with two adjoining blocks of model dwellings. It repeated the operation in 1893–4 with its New Buildings, following consultation with Octavia Hill.[83] The Oxford Cottage Improvement Company, which became the most important housing agency in Oxford, was a philanthropic body set up in 1866 as a joint town–gown venture, although the main inspiration, and most of the capital, came from socially concerned members of the University, including undergraduates. Auberon Herbert, fellow of St John's, and G. W. Kitchin of Christ Church seem to have been the originators. C. L. Wingfield of All Souls was the first chairman of the company, five of whose nine directors were academics; another, F. P. Morrell, was the university solicitor. In 1869 forty-eight out of ninety shareholders were members of the University. The company worked closely with the Sanitary Aid Association, whose Rent Committee, with Miss Butler as secretary, managed properties on lines laid down by Octavia Hill. By 1908 the Committee managed fifty-three properties, fourteen privately owned and thirty-nine belonging to the Cottage Improvement Company.[84]

The University, therefore, directly through college ownership and the Delegacy of Lodgings, indirectly through the Cottage Improvement Com-

---

[81] V. Thomas, *Memorials of the Malignant Cholera in Oxford, 1832* (1835); papers re the cholera epidemic of 1832, Bodl. G. A. Oxon. b. 11; W. A. Greenhill and T. Allen, *Reports on the Mortality and Public Health of Oxford in 1849 and 1850* (1854); Acland, *Cholera at Oxford*; Parfit, *Health of a City*, 32–51.

[82] CA MS Estates 78, fos 78–9.

[83] Ibid. fos 127–9, 135, 313–65; *Oxford Journal* 13 Oct. 1866; R. Mole, *Cottage Improvement to Sheltered Housing* (Oxford Citizens' Housing Association 1987), 10–15; M. Sadler, *Michael Ernest Sadler, 1861–1943* (1949), 91.

[84] Oxford Cottage Improvement Co. papers, Bodl. G. A. Oxon. 4° 180; Mole, *Cottage Improvement*, 4–18.

pany and the Sanitary Aid Association, exercised greater control over housing in Oxford than any other body prior to the First World War. Even the suburban expansion of the later nineteenth century was affected by college landownership: St John's in North Oxford and Jericho, and, to a lesser extent, Christ Church in East and West Oxford and Brasenose and University College in South Oxford, were able to influence the pace and nature of development. Their caution and fastidiousness as developers is apparent in the spacious gentility of North Oxford, and their concern, for reasons of morality and sound financial investment, to avoid the creation of slums left its mark in some of the better-quality suburban developments.[85]

The University's impact on education in the city was less pervasive than might be expected. There were schools attached to New College, Magdalen and Christ Church, and the Greycoat Boys' Charity School in Jericho, established by the University in 1708, was maintained by it until its closure in 1865.[86] Financial and academic assistance was given to the city's charitable foundation, the Bluecoat School.[87] The building costs of new suburban schools were often defrayed by contributions from colleges, some of which provided sites on their estates. Brasenose, for example, gave land in Grandpont in 1891, and Christ Church gave a site at Osney in 1904.[88] On an individual level Mary Macbride, wife of the Principal of Magdalen Hall, maintained a girls' school in New Inn Hall Street in the 1830s and 1840s.[89] The Macbrides were among the few from the University to support the Oxford Ragged School at its inception in 1859, although in the 1880s it began to attract generous and widespread assistance.[90]

The political controversy that surrounded the Board of Guardians was matched in the field of education only at the establishment of the Oxford School Board in 1871 and in the running of the High School for Boys. The School Board was applied for by 'radicals', who included Thorold Rogers and Max Müller, but control was won, following a campaign led by Montagu Burrows, by the party favouring retention of religious education in local schools. The Board contained three university representatives: Burrows, Francis Leighton, Warden of All Souls, and G. W. Kitchin, the sole radical.[91] Most unexpected was the election of Eleanor Smith, the only woman candi-

[85] For comprehensive analysis of colleges' impact on suburban development see M. Graham, 'The suburbs of Victorian Oxford: growth in a pre-industrial city' (University of Leicester Ph.D. thesis 1986); Graham, 'Housing development on the urban fringe of Oxford, 1850–1914', *Oxoniensia* lv (1990), 147–66; T. Hinchcliffe, *North Oxford* (Yale 1992); Hinchcliffe, 'Landownership in the city: St John's College, 1800–1968' in Whiting (ed.), *Oxford*, 85–109; *VCH Oxon*. iv. 196–201.

[86] *VCH Oxon*. iv. 445.

[87] Oxford Blue Coat School, *Reports* (copies), Bodl. Per. G. A. Oxon. 8° 368.

[88] *VCH Oxon*. iv. 448, 453.

[89] Bodl. G. A. Oxon. b. 156, newspaper cutting at front of vol.; *VCH Oxon*. iv. 452.

[90] Oxford Ragged School, *Reports* (copies), Bodl. Per. G. A. Oxon. 8° 799.

[91] School Board election papers, Bodl. G. A. Oxon. b. 10; M. Burrows, *Autobiography*, ed. S. M. Burrows (1908), 228 ff.; *VCH Oxon*. iv. 442.

date, who devoted herself thereafter to a prolonged campaign, ultimately fruitless in the face of clerical opposition, for a non-denominational board school and for church schools to be compelled to devote resources to slum children.[92] Church party control of the School Board remained until its responsibilities were transferred in 1903 to the new Local Education Authority.[93] The High School, opened in 1881, owed its foundation largely to the efforts of T. H. Green, supported by Benjamin Jowett, George Rolleston and, from the city, the Liberal alderman James Hughes.[94] University financial support was considerable, both at official and at individual level. The High School aimed to provide a grammar school education which would enable Oxford boys to take advantage of the University's new openness, particularly the relaxation of the rules governing residence.[95] The establishment of what was sometimes called a George Street junior Balliol, with a public school emphasis on the formative value of sport and voluntary work, inevitably attracted criticism, the school's very success in securing scholarships provoking a lively debate in the town on the relative merits of academic or commercial education.[96] The number of scholarships obtained was impressive, the school accounting for a significant increase in the number of local boys admitted to the University. The school was an important rung in Green's 'ladder of learning': in the twenty-five years to 1913, of 109 boys coming to the school with scholarships from elementary schools, eighty passed on to the University.[97] Green was also a supporter of the highly regarded Wesleyan Boys' School, enlisting junior members of the University to take weekly classes and himself helping to prepare senior pupils for training as teachers.[98]

There were in Oxford the usual small private schools, mostly short-lived, for middle-class children, but demand from the growing community of academic families in the later nineteenth century produced an entirely different type of school which either began in North Oxford or was soon transplanted there. Such was the Oxford Preparatory School, later the Dragon School, founded by a group of dons in 1877 primarily for their own children. It was transferred from St Giles' to North Oxford in 1879.[99]

[92] Hollis, *Ladies Elect*, 148–50.

[93] *VCH Oxon.* iv. 442–3.

[94] Hughes was co-founder of Oxford's leading grocery business, the renowned Grimbly, Hughes of Cornmarket Street.

[95] *Oxford Chronicle* 22, 29 Oct. 1887; 7 Oct. 1893; J. L. Marler, 'History of the City of Oxford High School for Boys', typescript 1971 (copy), Centre for Oxfordshire Studies, Central Library, Oxford. Green's role is commemorated on a plaque at the school's entrance. The building now houses the University faculty of Social Studies.

[96] *VCH Oxon.* iv. 458; J. R. Gillis, 'The evolution of juvenile delinquency in England, 1890–1914', *Past and Present* lxvii (1975), 111–12.

[97] 4th Report of the Royal Commission on the Civil Service, minutes of evidence PP 1914 (7338) xvi, Q. 23, 065); G. C. Brodrick, *Memories and Impressions, 1831–1900* (1900), 386.

[98] Kadish, *Apostle Arnold*, 39; *VCH Oxon.* iv. 456.

[99] C. H. Jaques, *A Dragon Century* (1977); obituary of C. C. Lynam, *The Times* 29 Oct. 1938.

Summer Fields, a boarding-school in Summertown, was established in 1864 by Mrs Archibald Maclaren, wife of the gymnasium owner and daughter of an Oxford bookseller, David Talboys.[100] St Edward's School, started by the Revd Thomas Chamberlain in New Inn Hall Street in 1863, was removed to its Woodstock Road site in 1873.[101]

In the field of adult education the most significant development in terms of town–gown relations was the involvement of members of the University in the educational programme of the local Co-operative Society, founded in 1872. The principle of co-operation was warmly supported by university liberals, notably in the 1870s by Rogers and Kitchin. The organization of an educational programme, and university participation in it, were largely the initiative of A. H. D. Acland, Secretary of the University's Delegacy of Local Examinations, who foresaw an opportunity to involve the University in a national scheme of working-class education in association with the Co-operative movement. Acland represented the local society at national congresses held in Manchester (1878) and Edinburgh (1883), and in 1882 he was instrumental in bringing the congress to Oxford, where university buildings were placed at its disposal and where speakers included Sir William Anson, G. C. Brodrick and Arnold Toynbee. Lecture series under the aegis of the Society continued thereafter but the university extension scheme, which would have been the natural means of expanding adult education in Oxford, was concerned in the later nineteenth century to establish its presence nationally, and its gaze, fixed on distant horizons, scarcely fell on its own doorstep.[102]

The city's economic dependence on the University was commonly regarded as near total and assumed to be permanent. Goldwin Smith was typical in claiming the University as source of the city's prosperity and importance 'as certainly as manufactures are the staple of Manchester or shipping of Liverpool'.[103] Sir William Harcourt believed Oxford, on the contrary, to be a poor place and attributed that, too, to the University.[104] The *Oxford Magazine* voiced the accepted wisdom of the day when it remarked dismissively in 1893 that 'apart from the university, the sole industry is beer'.[105] In reality the city's reliance varied considerably from period to period and from group to group; as the population grew, tradesmen could thrive without university business, and there were increasing numbers of

---

[100] R. Usborne (ed.), *A Century of Summer Fields* (1964). For David Talboys see below p. 464.

[101] Papers re St Edward's School, Bodl. Per. G. A. Oxon. 4° 169; Simeon, *Thomas Chamberlain*, 24; R. D. Hill, *History of St. Edward's School* (1963).

[102] *Oxford Co-operative and Industrial Society: an historical sketch, 1872–1909* (1909), 40–7 (copy), Bodl. G. A. Oxon. 16° 110; Oxford Co-operative and Industrial Society, *Reports* (1878 and later edns), Bodl. G. A. Oxon. b. 37; *Oxford Co-operative Record* ii (Apr. 1881) (copy), ibid.

[103] Letter to *Daily News* 1 June 1865.

[104] *Oxford Election Commission: minutes of evidence* (PP 1881 (2856-1) xliv. 1033).

[105] *OM* 7 June 1893, 413.

people, particularly in the poorer outer parishes, who derived little or no economic benefit from the University's presence.[106]

The University's economic importance derived not only from its role as major employer, property owner and consumer of goods and services; it was also a source of capital. Members of the University had been crucial to the financing of the Oxford Canal, opened in 1790. Nathan Wetherell was an important mover in its early stages, members of the University were prominent shareholders, and the Oxford Canal Company enjoyed the unusual distinction of having for much of its existence a chairman in holy orders.[107] The University was joint owner with the city of the wharves at Folly Bridge and therefore profited considerably though briefly when a link was made from the river to the Canal, making Oxford the point of interchange for the shipment of goods between the Midlands and London. Through traffic was removed by the opening of the Grand Junction Canal in 1800.[108]

For a time after the removal of trading restrictions in 1835 trade in Oxford was 'revolutionized for the better' as large numbers of new businesses were established, most hoping for a share of university business.[109] The city's rapidly growing population further stimulated trade; but the University's failure to match the city's growth revealed how dangerously narrow was the economy's base. The University, which in 1801 comprised 10 per cent of Oxford's population, was by 1851 only 6 per cent; and the city slid towards recession. Oxford stood in marked contrast to Banbury, whose success as a marketing and manufacturing centre in the mid-nineteenth century emphasized Oxford's over-dependence on the University. The issue appeared less clear-cut in the later nineteenth century, however, when the University's resurgence shielded Oxford from the protracted decline which the agricultural depression inflicted on its rival in the north of the county.[110] Almost all within the University, and many townspeople, were happy to see Oxford remain a moderate-size market town. Although it is a persistent myth that the University scotched the Great Western Railway's attempts to open a line to Oxford in the 1830s, University and Corporation were at one in wanting to keep Oxford a tight, narrow and conveniently manageable community. A

---

[106] Letter of Richard Greswell in *The Times* 16 June 1865. The city's growing economic autonomy is strongly argued by Howe, 'Intellect and civic responsibility', 20–2.

[107] Of loan capital raised in 1775 and 1786, 26% (£35,000) was raised in the University: J. R. Ward, *Finance of Canal Building in Eighteenth-Century England* (1974), 32–3. *The Eighteenth Century*, 165, 225; H. J. Compton, *Oxford Canal* (Newton Abbot 1976); E. C. R. Hadfield, *Canals of the East Midlands* (Newton Abbot 1970), 18. The cartouche on the Canal House, opened in 1829, depicts the university and city arms, and Britannia, behind whom are a canal boat and the Radcliffe Camera. The Canal House later became the lodgings of the master of St Peter's College.

[108] OUA WP/α/24(3), pp. 208, 209–11; *VCH Oxon.* iv. 208–9.

[109] *Oxford Chronicle* 16 Feb. 1850; *Oxford Protestant Magazine* i (Feb. 1848), 635.

[110] *Oxford Chronicle* 16 Feb. 1850; *VCH Oxon.* iv. 181, 209–10, 215–16; B. Trinder, *Victorian Banbury* (Chichester 1982), chs. 7, 12.

petition in favour of the railway signed by 500 of the 'operative and working classes' was countered by the signatures of 450 inhabitants, including a great many tradesmen afraid that '£50,000 spent at the college will be spent...in London'.[111] The University, though it had petitioned against the proposed line, eventually decided that the development could not be prevented, and that the best concessions obtainable would have to be extracted from the Great Western. It was pleasantly surprised when the scheme foundered on the opposition of local landowners. The Act of Parliament secured by the Great Western in 1843 empowered the University to ban undergraduates from this new and rapid means of escape.[112]

The City Council came to feel that by opposing the railway it had missed a great opportunity, and therefore gave enthusiastic backing to a proposal of 1865 to site the Great Western's workshops at Cripley Meadow. The University, by now somewhat embarrassed at its earlier distrustfulness, was slow to respond until galvanized by Goldwin Smith, who organized opposition in Oxford while encouraging it on the board of the Great Western, of which his father had been a director. When the workshops went to Swindon reaction in Oxford was so furious that a police guard was required for Smith's house. The arguments were revelatory. Smith's flippant and dismissive tone was unfortunate, but he carried university opinion by the familiar argument that Oxford's whole character would be changed, undermining the University's discipline and leaving it subordinate. The dangers were clear: 'everyone knows the character of the students of Paris'. As for the city, more would be lost by the departure of 100 students than could be gained from 500 Great Western workmen. Smith's views were challenged by some within the University, notably by Richard Greswell, at one time a supporter of Smith, and by Thorold Rogers and Charles Neate, who supported townspeople in the belief that the workshops would introduce much-needed skilled employment to the city. Greswell pointed out that the workshops could provide apprenticeships for the large pool of child labour employed by the University Press and 'turned adrift' at the age of 16.[113] Failure to obtain the workshops left a feeling of depression and of resentment against the University: 'Nothing could exceed the admiration of certain resident professors of advanced opinions for the man who earned his bread by the sweat of his brow...But when it was proposed that this superior being should take up his abode in their midst...these professors were the fiercest denouncers of

[111] Oxford City archives B. 5. 6, pp. 341–3; Select Committee on the Oxford and Great Western Union Railway Bill (PP 1837 HL(70) xix. 189; ibid. 1837–8 HL(227) xx. 138–9, 729).
[112] Select Committee (1837–8), 225–6; Oxford Railway Act, 6 & 7 Vic., c. 10 (Local & Personal); VCH Oxon. iv. 294.
[113] OUA WP/α/24(7), pp. 484–5; Oxford City archives C. 5. 1, 2 May 1865; British Transport Historical Records, Rail 253/129–30; Oxford Chronicle 10, 17 June 1865; collection of letters, posters, etc., Bodl. G. A. Oxon. c. 81; G. Smith, Reminiscences, ed. A. Haultain (New York 1910), 280–1; Howe, 'Intellect and civic responsibility', 15–17.

such a proceeding.'[114] The city fathers still liked to hark back to the episode twenty-five years later.[115]

The same arguments were rehearsed in the 1870s when the University campaigned to prevent the siting of a military depot at Oxford, the danger to academic discipline and morals this time being posed by soldiers and camp-followers.[116] Public opinion was outraged by the tactlessness of some of those mobilized to support the University in Parliament. Gathorne Hardy, in a debate in the House in May 1873, juxtaposed 'the moral feeling of the university' with 'the sordid [i.e. pecuniary] feeling of the town'.[117] Lord Randolph Churchill's maiden speech the following year offended Oxford citizens, the army and some on his own side. The roistering and licentiousness that he warned against came perilously close to self-parody: still fresh in Oxford memories was a discreditable undergraduate career which had included assaulting and suborning a policeman after a drunken dinner, and reportedly securing the dismissal of a waiter who had given evidence against him.[118] The government eventually set up a small establishment at Cowley, but the University was satisfied that it had at least saved Oxford from the fate of Aldershot.

The University's rapid growth in the later nineteenth century was possible only because of the availability of lodgings in the town.[119] The census of 1861 returned only twenty lodging-house keepers in Oxford,[120] but the potential supply was large, for 336 houses were licensed in 1868 when the Delegacy for Lodgings was established, and by 1879 there were 579.[121] Those licensed were predominantly college servants or their wives, clerical workers and shopkeepers; but they included prominent citizens.[122] The economic benefits to the town were such that little attention was paid at first to the University's encroachment into new areas. Lodging-houses were concentrated mainly, as might be expected, in the centre of town, but they were also to be found in considerable numbers in Walton Street and along Iffley Road, though not in the socially less desirable Cowley Road.[123] The vigorous defence of the system by University and town when it came under attack

[114] T. F. Plowman, 'Gown and town', *Chambers's Journal* 8 Apr. 1916, 291.

[115] *Oxford Times* 4 Jan. 1890.

[116] Reports, memorials, petitions, etc., 1872–4, Bodl. G. A. fol. A139* (50); ibid. b. 140 (27c, 30); *Report of Oxford Brigade Depot* (PP 1873 (218) xl. 547–9); *Memorial against Proposed Depot* (PP. 1873 (66) xl. 551–3); *Oxford Chronicle* 6 Jan. 1877.

[117] 216 *Parl. Deb.* 23 May 1873, 3S ccxvi. 370–1.

[118] 219 *Parl. Deb.* 22 May 1874, 3S ccxix. 714–15; R. F. Foster, *Lord Randolph Churchill: a political life* (1981), 13–14, 27.

[119] The following para. owes much to T. H. Aston, 'Undergraduate lodgings in Oxford, 1868–1914', OUA, Keeper of the Archives' Oration, 1972.

[120] *Census*, 1861.

[121] OUA LHD/Misc./3(7); Aston, statistical tables.

[122] Aston, 7; Bodl. Per. G. A. Oxon. 4° 245, licensed lodging-house lists.

[123] *Gazette* viii (25 June 1878), map following p. 468.

indicates the extent to which both had come to depend on the provision of lodgings.[124] Not that this made the partnership equal, if only because supply exceeded demand. So much became clear in 1881 when, in a remarkable display of its authority, the University responded to criticism following the death from diphtheria of a student in lodgings in Turl Street by ordering a rapid inspection of about 650 houses and demanding sanitary improvements before the renewal of licences. The Delegacy achieved more in months than the statutory body responsible, the Local Board of Health, had secured in years. The Local Board claimed that the Delegacy had exceeded its powers, and there were many complaints about university tyranny and the return of discommoning, but to no avail as the Delegacy played a strong hand forcefully and obtained from its licensees a grumbling acquiescence.[125] When the demand for lodgings seemed likely to collapse in 1914 the delegates acted with far-sighted generosity, arranging for soldiers, refugees and convalescents to be billeted with their licensees, and urging colleges to help out in any way that they could. In 1918, since 245 houses remained of the 400 that had been on the list in 1914, the University was saved the task of building the system anew.[126]

Although colleges and their members continued to buy predominantly locally, improved communications undoubtedly made it easier to import goods and services. Local tradesmen were highly sensitive to the trend. A. W. Hall knew well the chord he would strike when protesting at a Druids' Dinner speech in 1890 that at one Commemoration Ball the previous year 'every blessed thing down to the very waiters was imported from London (Cries of "Shame!")'.[127] The justification for buying outside Oxford was the high prices charged there; the response was that high prices were bound to result when customers were absent half the year and expected to live the other half on credit. Extended credit remained the norm during most of this period, and some businesses broke under its weight.[128] The city's leading department store, Elliston and Cavell, long refused credit, but by 1892 it, too, was forced to offer customers a discount for the prompt settling of accounts[129]

The University remained the largest single employer of labour in the city until the expansion of the motor industry after the First World War. The

[124] *Oxford Chronicle* 11, 18, 25 Nov.; 2, 16 Dec. 1876; Aston, 12, 15. For the attack by John Burgon in 1876 see below.
[125] OUA LHD/RP1(1); *Report on Sanitary Inspection of Lodging-Houses* (1881–2) (copy), Bodl. G. A. Oxon. 4° 339a (8); *Oxford Chronicle* 19 Mar., 6 Aug., 3 Dec. 1881; Aston, 16–20.
[126] OUA LHD/RP5(1).
[127] *Oxford Times* 4 Jan. 1890.
[128] J. Pycroft, *Oxford Memories* (2 vols 1886) ii. 32, 35–6; M. Graham, *Top. Oxon.* xviii (1972) (copy), Centre for Oxfordshire Studies, Central Library, Oxford.
[129] *Oxford Protestant Magazine* i (1847) 441–8, 636; M. L. Turner and D. G. Vaisey, *Oxford Shops and Shopping* (1972), 48–9.

University Press alone employed 278 people in 1883 and as many as 764 in 1911.[130] For most people, however, university employment was equated with college service, the summit of Oxford's job hierarchy in the later nineteenth century and earlier twentieth: 'When I was a boy, if a man had a job in the gasworks, the printing press, or on the railways he stayed there...Of course there was the college servants; but they wouldn't look at the likes of us.'[131] College service was paternalistic, hierarchical, and strictly regulated; it was also secure, for dismissal, even of persistent miscreants, was relatively rare.[132] Higher servants such as manciples, butlers and head cooks were generally of some standing locally. Since a great deal of college money passed through their hands they might be obliged to provide security in very large sums. Richard Green entered a bond for £1,000, guaranteed by William Green of Magdalen Hall and Alderman William Fletcher, the banker, when appointed head butler of Christ Church in 1803. James Brazier, appointed to the same post in 1848, bound himself in the sum of £3,000, guaranteed by the banker Guy Thomson and the architect H. J. Underwood.[133] It is hardly surprising that praise was lavished on those who dutifully reported tradesmen offering inducements.[134]

The 1851 census recorded 635 college servants, 232 of whom lived in. At Christ Church, where even the head porter had three servants, there were no fewer than forty-seven servants living in, most in the canons' lodgings. More than 27 per cent of Oxford's total employed population, twice the national average, was engaged in domestic service. The proportion would have been high even without the colleges; but college service was responsible for the very high proportion (10 per cent) of employed males in domestic service. Most lived fairly close to their places of work, particularly in St Ebbe's (86 college servants), where recent extensive development had been heavily supported by college servants investing in property. There were also concentrations of college servants in Holywell (62) and St Giles (51).[135]

A profusion of specialized trades and professions was drawn to Oxford by the prospect of university business: cabinet-makers and upholsterers, picture-framers and gilders, booksellers and stationers, printers, bookbinders, and livery stable-keepers all prospered, as did teachers at the numerous private schools that flourished even then on the back of the University's reputation.[136] The itinerant makers of high-quality shoes who came to Oxford, as to Cambridge, in term-time and who moved to London at the

---

[130] H. Hart, *The University Press at Oxford* (1894), 6; C. V. Butler, *Social Conditions in Oxford* (1912), 40 n.

[131] Quoted in J. M. Mogey, *Family and Neighbourhood* (1956), 5.

[132] CA S. xxix. a. 4, fos 6–8.

[133] CA MS Estates 125, fos 8, 11.

[134] CA S. xxix. a. 4, fo 25; ibid. a. 6–8.

[135] PRO HO 107/1737–9; R. J. Morris, 'Friars and paradise', *Oxoniensia* xxxvi (1971).

[136] Based on a study of trade directories and *Census*, 1801–81.

start of the social season were a reminder of the greatest single problem of those reliant upon the University, the seasonality of employment.[137] Local shoemakers claimed in 1890 that they only had six months' work in the year because of the 'peculiarity of Oxford trade',[138] and observers routinely noted the damaging effect of the long vacation in particular on laundries, stables, shops and lodgings.[139] Worse-affected were the crowds of 'hangers-on' to be found 'at or near the college gates ready to offer their services' but who were without even that casual employment for half the year.[140] The case of college servants was alleviated to some extent in 1860 when the Mayor and Vice-Chancellor drew up a joint scheme to find summer employment in holiday resorts, later to become common practice.[141]

Underemployment, which was the curse of the place and which lay behind many of the disputes over the granting of temporary out-relief by the Guardians of the Poor, eased somewhat in the later nineteenth century. The attractions of the university city had always brought in visitors: the owner of the Angel and the Star, Oxford's chief coaching-inns, conducted a census in 1834–5 which revealed that 13,096 travellers stayed in Oxford for at least one night.[142] To tourists were later added university extension students, who came to Oxford for the summer and thus helped alleviate the difficulties of those worst-affected by the long vacation. Professional and professorial families already established in North Oxford were joined after the reforms of 1877 by a trickle of new academic families and by increasing numbers of non-academic families and retired people: 'Oxford is now becoming a residential place,' as the Provost of Queen's remarked in 1890.[143] The scale of university building work was for the first time matched by that in the town, in the house-building boom of the 1820s and 1830s and again in the later nineteenth century. Hyde & Franklin's clothing factory in Shoe Lane, that of W. F. Lucas in George Street, Lucy's ironworks, the breweries and the railway increasingly provided employment independent of the University, as did a growing suburban population that generated its own demand for goods and services.[144] A. W. Hall, looking wistfully at Reading with its biscuit factory and at Swindon with its railway workshops, sighed in 1890 that 'the

---

[137] *Morning Chronicle* 23 Jan. 1851.

[138] Oxfordshire Trades Council pamphlets, Bodl. G. A. Oxon. 4° 551.

[139] e.g. *Herald* 2 Mar. 1844; Acland, *Cholera at Oxford*, 46; *Oxford Poor Parishes Fund: long vacation* (1858), printed notice, Bodl. G. A. Oxon. c. 74 (363); F. M. Gamlen, *My Memoirs* (privately printed 1953), 35.

[140] OUA NWP/4 (4, no. 5); *Oxford Election Commission: minutes of evidence*, 1033.

[141] Cox, 447; Gamlen, *Memoirs*, 32; P. F. Bickerton, *Fred of Oxford* (1953), 5; C. Platt, *The Most Obliging Man in Europe* (1986), 88.

[142] *Select Committee on the Oxford and Great Western Union Railway Bill*, 67.

[143] *Oxford Times* 6 Dec. 1890; 7 June 1893, 413; Oxford Anti-Mendicity Society, *Report* (1896), 5.

[144] *VCH Oxon.* iv. 212–13; letter from 'Oxford citizen', *Oxford Chronicle* 19 Sept. 1896; Howe, 'Intellect and civic responsibility', 20–2.

great need of Oxford is some large industry'. He hoped without expectation for the day when 'some enterprising man could start a factory here'.[145]

It might be supposed that the dependence of tradesmen and college employees laid them open to pressure from the University on political or religious grounds. Although manipulation is occasionally discernible, the evidence is mostly intermittent and anecdotal. In a particularly unfortunate case David Talboys, Oxford's leading classical bookseller and a political radical, was the target in a campaign by Philip Bliss, University Registrar, conducted anonymously through the columns of the *Oxford University Herald*, of which he was part-owner and editor. Talboys, who claimed that voting for the Roman Catholic Thomas Stonor in the general election of 1835 cost him half his business, pleaded with members of the University 'no longer to consult the poll book before venturing to give their orders'. In December 1837 a *Herald* editorial made a thinly veiled suggestion that Talboys be boycotted, and eventually his business and health broke.[146] Talboys's trade was susceptible to pressure. Others were better-placed, or tougher. Isaac Grubb, the Baptist baker and corn-dealer mentioned above, was both, as was the irrepressible temperance campaigner J. J. Faulkner, who, from the vantage-point of his grocery shop opposite Christ Church, delighted in trying to provoke the University at every opportunity. He broke up a meeting of the City Council in 1848 by capping an announcement that he was a Chartist with a declaration that college heads were 'a set of vagabonds, living on the fat of the land'.[147] In the same year he published an address congratulating the French on their 'Great Revolution'; and he countered the Crimean War victory celebrations in 1856 by posting the number of war casualties in his shop window.[148]

It was commonly believed that university and college employees voted to order: 'the [university] police, it is presumed, receive their orders at the Clarendon [Building] what candidates they are to vote for, and at the same place...are made out their voting forms for city councillors'.[149] But such employees were in little need of persuasion. Philip Bliss rejoiced that in the parliamentary election of 1857 Stephen Gaselee, supported by 'ultra revolutionists', was defeated by 'the strength of the college tenants and college servants';[150] Charles Neate, fellow of Oriel College, unseated for bribery at the same election, was said to have received all the votes of his college's

[145] *Oxford Times* 4 Jan. 1890.
[146] OUA SWP/2(3), 1 Dec. 1827; printed addresses by Talboys, Bodl. G. A. Oxon. c. 107 (39–41); *Oxford Protestant Magazine* i (1847), 301–2; S. Gibson and C. J. Hindle, 'Philip Bliss', *Oxford Bibliographical Society* iii (1933), 189, 252–3; *DNB*.
[147] *Herald* 29 Apr. 1848.
[148] Ibid. 11 Mar. 1848; B. H. Harrison, *Drink and the Victorians* (1971), 161, 164.
[149] Printed notice, 1837, Bodl. G. A. Oxon. c. 107 (40). Similar accusations were levelled at the Oxford Local Board and the City Council: *VCH Oxon.* iv. 231.
[150] Commonplace book of P. Bliss, Bodl. MS Top. Oxon. c. 270, p. 47.

employees;[151] only eight out of 161 college servants voted for Stonor in 1835. Yet, as at Cambridge in similar circumstances, there is no reason to suppose that undue pressure was applied or, indeed, was necessary.[152] Those college employees scheduled for corrupt practices by the Oxford Election Commission in 1881 had all been active in the Conservative interest.[153]

Very few employees stood for public office. The last unreformed city council in 1835 included one college servant; two sat in 1868–9, at a time, it has to be said, when there were only six Conservatives in the entire council.[154] Henry Grant, manciple of Christ Church, was unusual in serving as a member of the Local Board and as Conservative councillor for the South ward from 1857 until his death in 1876.[155] Walter Gray, steward of Keble and by far the most prominent college employee in public life, was, significantly, not a local man. Gray helped transform political life in Oxford in the late nineteenth century, displaying initiative and energy far transcending the inventiveness over perquisites that traditionally characterized college service. When he left Keble c.1882 he was well on the way to becoming the most powerful man in the city and, utilizing connections made initially through his college, one of the wealthiest.[156]

The Reform Acts of 1832 and 1867 excluded residents in college from voting in city elections, and the political lives of the two bodies remained largely separate until in the later nineteenth century increasing numbers of academics living in town began to appear on the city's electoral register.[157] The move out of college coincided with a growing interest among University Liberals in local affairs that gathered pace after the defeat of the Liberal government in 1874.[158] Their involvement in the administration of poor law and education in Oxford has been mentioned already. Some turned also to local politics. Thorold Rogers, President of the Oxford branch of the Reform League as early as 1866 and for some years Vice-President of the Oxford Liberal Association, was rumoured in 1867 to be considering standing for the city at the next parliamentary election. Arthur Sidgwick, President of the Association from 1886 to 1911, was consistently its most

---

[151] *Evidence to the Select Committee on the Oxford City Election Petition* (PP 1857 (170 Sess. 2) viii. 43–5).

[152] *Oxford City Pollbook, 1835*; J. R. Vincent, *Pollbooks: how Victorians voted* (1967), 11, 158.

[153] Those found guilty were Thomas Wells, manciple at Brasenose, John Churms, assistant librarian at Magdalen, William Savage, butler at University College, and Henry Turner, rent-collector for Christ Church: *Report of the Commission on Corrupt Practices in Oxford*, pt 1 (PP 1881 xliv c. 2856. 21–3).

[154] Based on a study of newspapers and poll-books in the Bodleian Library and of Council minute-books in Oxford City archives.

[155] Letter of Ann Grant, 25 Oct. 1876, CA; *Oxford Journal* 5 Nov. 1870, 14 Oct. 1876.

[156] For Gray see C. Fenby, *The Other Oxford* (1970); *VCH Oxon*. iv. 231–2.

[157] 2 & 3 Wm. IV, c. 45, s. 78; 30 & 31 Vic., c. 102; speech by L. R. Phelps, *Oxford Chronicle* 28 Oct. 1882.

[158] Harvie, 'Intellectuals and poverty', 6.

generous benefactor; by 1896 the Association's committee included not only several dons, but five college heads, including the Vice-Chancellor, J. R. Magrath.[159] The political issues that excited them, however, were primarily national. Westminster remained at the centre of their consciousness until T. H. Green's pioneering efforts made conceivable, even respectable, the devotion of time and energy to purely local political issues.

Green was among those academic Liberals who campaigned for G. C. Brodrick during the parliamentary elections for Woodstock in 1868 and 1874; but his passionate devotion to the causes of temperance and high-school education drew him increasingly into civic affairs.[160] In 1876 he became the first don to sit on the City Council, representing the North ward until his death in 1882.[161] He was by no means the first university man to play an active role in the city but his open involvement in municipal politics was startling.[162] To stand for election to the City Council while eschewing service on the ostensibly more important statutory bodies such as the Local Board of Health and the Board of Guardians was in itself a highly political act, for the Council at that time was a battleground of party politics. Moreover, Green became involved in local party politics during one of the darker periods of Oxford's notorious political history. Corruption, routine in parliamentary elections, was rumoured also to be rife within the Council and even the Local Board.[163] Green, who was aware of the murky reputation of the Liberal Party apparatus,[164] was wisely not a committee man, serving only on the Council's Schools Committee: the committees were seen as the levers by which the party machine controlled the city.[165] Despite accusations that he was the University's Trojan horse, Green convinced a majority of the electorate of his sincerity in putting himself forward as a fellow citizen, not, as he would have been on the Local Board, a representative of the University. Almost unknown in the city in 1876, he was within a year said to be 'the man most respected and liked by both the colleges and townspeople'.[166] In a touching demonstration of respect, his funeral, which took place on a filthy day in March, was attended by 'the largest combined gathering of citizens and members of the university in memory'.[167]

[159] Oxford Liberal Association, *Reports* (copies), Bodl. Per. G. A. Oxon. 4° 544; Bodl. G. A. Oxon. b. 164, fo. 10; *Oxford Chronicle* 18 May 1867.

[160] *Works of T. H. Green*, ed. R. L. Nettleship (3 vols 1885–8) iii, pp. cxii–xvii; *Oxford Chronicle* 21 Oct. 1876; Harvie, *Lights of Liberalism*, 178–84; *VCH Oxon.* xii. 406; Howe, 'Intellect and civic responsibility', 29–30.

[161] *Oxford Chronicle* 4 Nov. 1876.

[162] M. Richter, *Politics of Conscience: T. H. Green and his age* (1964), 346–7.

[163] *VCH Oxon.* iv. 231, 252–3.

[164] *Oxford Chronicle* 14 Jan. 1882.

[165] *Oxford Times* 12, 19 Nov., 17 Dec. 1881.

[166] Letter of Mrs A. J. Butler, 2 May 1877 (in possession of Mrs C. E. Colvin); *Oxford Chronicle* 21 Oct. 1876.

[167] *Oxford Chronicle* 1 Apr. 1882. Much the same thing was said in 1853 of the funeral of Richard Harington, Principal of Brasenose and chairman of the Paving Commission: *Herald* 24 Dec. 1853.

Although, unlike George Rolleston, Green was spared the *Dictionary of National Biography*'s reproof for wasting his time on university and municipal politics, some were puzzled that he did not play a 'greater part in the wider world'; in that context it is noteworthy that Oxford citizens were among the first to appreciate how central to his political philosophy was the choice that he made.[168] Green's combination of university career and active citizenship was taken as a model by devoted and influential admirers,[169] though only Arnold Toynbee, Green's self-proclaimed political heir, sought to emulate him by standing for election in a city ward. Toynbee's bottom place in the 1882 poll for Green's old seat was blamed on the Conservatism of the North ward's many women voters: by attaching himself, like his predecessor, to the local party apparatus he inevitably suffered from its gathering unpopularity.[170] After the municipal reforms of 1889 Brodrick and others took an easier route on to the Council by representing the University. They thereby avoided friction with those who complained that the University would be overrepresented if its members stood for city wards, but they also let lie their mentor's challenge that Oxford should be but a single community.

University Liberals lent enthusiastic support to the struggle to establish an agricultural trade union in the area. Green and Thorold Rogers shared a platform with Joseph Arch at a meeting held in Oxford in October 1872 to establish the Oxfordshire district of the Agricultural Labourers' Union, an organization that enjoyed the public support also of Kitchin, Rolleston and Henry Smith.[171] An attempt to resurrect trade unionism in Oxfordshire in the early 1890s attracted the energetic involvement of undergraduates and younger dons, with Arthur Sidgwick, though only just turned 50, in the role of elder statesman; he and L. T. Hobhouse were trustees for the Union's finances. For men like Herbert Samuel and Michael Sadler the campaign proved to be formative. The impact on the Union was more ambiguous: it collapsed in 1893 amidst allegations that many labourers had been alienated by the well-intentioned but naïve young Turks from the University. Perhaps the most intriguing aspect of the whole episode was the mentor's role played by the radical college chimney-sweep William Hines.[172]

There were echoes of that campaign in attempts by members of the university Fabian Society to promote closer links with local labour leaders

---

[168] *Oxford Chronicle* 1 Apr. 1882.
[169] Brodrick, *Memories and Impressions*, 385–7; Richter, *Politics of Conscience*, 293, 344–5, 349.
[170] *Oxford Chronicle* 20 Oct., 4 Nov. 1882; Kadish, *Apostle Arnold*, 233. Women were enfranchised for local government elections in 1869: Municipal Franchise Act, 32 & 33 Vic., c. 55.
[171] *Oxford Journal* 26 Oct. 1872.
[172] P. Horn, *Agricultural Trade Unionism in Oxon.* (Oxfordshire Records Society xlviii 1974), 18–20, 39, 94; Horn, 'Farmworkers, dockers, and Oxford University', *Oxoniensia* xxii (1957), 60–70; Horn, 'Agricultural trade unionism in Oxfordshire', in J. P. Dunbabin (ed.), *Rural Discontent in Nineteenth-Century Britain* (1974); H. L. Samuel, *Memoirs* (1945), 15–16; Kadish, *Apostle Arnold*, 200–1; Kadish, *Oxford Economists in the Late Nineteenth Century* (1982), 24.

in the early twentieth century. A. J. Carlyle of University College and John Carter of Pusey House compiled lists of 'fair' employers in Oxford, and Carlyle was instrumental in establishing a Municipal Labour Representation Committee in 1902.[173] The celebrated Oxford tram strike of 1913 allowed 'close students of economic and labour questions' to formulate and test their ideas, an opportunity seized most notably by G. D. H. Cole of Magdalen and G. N. Clark of All Souls, whose pamphlet, *The Tram Strike: a letter to the city and University*, advocated linking wages to need rather than profit and urged a greater role for trade unions.[174] As in the 1890s, the intervention of young academics was more significant for their own political development than for its influence on the strike, which collapsed. Until the city's industrialization the university Left was consistently more radical than that of the town, where labour remained weak, disorganized and stubbornly conservative.[175]

University Conservatives were slower to make an impact on the town's political life. There seem to have been no academics on the committees of the Oxford Constitutional Association, founded in 1868, and the Oxford Conservative Club (1869).[176] The revival of Conservative fortunes that took place in the 1870s owed something to Washbourne West of Lincoln College, Vice-President of the Conservative Registration Association from 1874, and rather more to Montagu Burrows. Burrows helped establish the *Oxford Times*, an increasingly influential Conservative weekly, in 1868. He was a vigorous organizer of election campaigns, involved in everything from securing funds to, in his own words, assembling 'Tory roughs...to shout down the red roughs', thereby stiffening the resolve of timid North Oxford 'villa-Conservatives'.[177] Renewed Conservative confidence was indicated in 1874 when colleges were bedecked in colours for the first time in memory: Sir William Harcourt recalled 'Magdalen tower being from top to bottom blue, which I thought was a great feat of agility as well as electioneering'.[178] In 1880 the Vice-Chancellor and proctors thought it necessary formally to warn undergraduates against involvement in the bitterly fought by-election caused when the Conservatives broke the convention of not opposing the re-election of a newly appointed minister: Harcourt had been made Home Secretary.[179] The

[173] R. C. Whiting, *The View from Cowley* (1983), 18–19.
[174] *Oxford Chronicle, Oxford Times* Apr.–May 1913; pamphlets, etc. re strike, Bodl. G. A. Oxon. b. 162.
[175] *Oxford Chronicle* 30 May 1913; *VCH Oxon.* iv. 221; Whiting, *View from Cowley*, 20–2; Harrison, 'Miss Butler's Oxford survey', 63.
[176] Political papers, leaflets, etc., Bodl. G. A. Oxon. 4° 274; *Oxford Conservative Club Rules and Regulations* (1877), Bodl. G. A. Oxon. 8° 1132 (8).
[177] Burrows, *Autobiography*, 228–35, 252–3; *Report of the Commission on Corrupt Practices in Oxford*, pt 2, 292, 333.
[178] Ibid. 1030, 1036.
[179] Ibid. pt 1, pp. 9–10; P. D. John, 'Oxford and the general election of 1880', *Oxoniensia* lv (1990), 131–46; *VCH Oxon.* iv. 251.

narrow victory of the Conservative brewer A. W. Hall was made possible, alleged the Liberal *Oxford Chronicle*, by the election taking place during term: 'The enormous influence of the Conservative graduates of the university was energetically exerted on [Hall's] behalf and, in spite of the vice-chancellor's mandate...the "senior undergraduate" of Exeter College received valuable aid from the junior members of the university.'[180] It should be noted, however, that the paper's correspondents were less inclined to blame the University, pointing rather to an alliance of parish clergy and publicans and raising the old cry of 'Bible and beer'.[181] The campaign had been lively, Thorold Rogers's Beaumont Street house coming under attack at one point; and it was reckoned corrupt even by Oxford standards, though only the chance discovery of a letter from Montagu Burrows to Thomas Dallin, the university Public Orator, revealing a £3,000 subvention from Conservative Central Office, enabled Hall's election to be challenged. Local Liberals were understandably nervous of an impartial investigation; but, at the insistence of Green and Rolleston, a petition was lodged. During the consequent parliamentary commission of inquiry Burrows and West were interrogated, the latter admitting to 'a very little offence' in providing refreshments while campaigning; neither was personally censured. The constituency was, sensationally, disfranchised until 1885.[182] In that year the section of the 1832 Reform Act prohibiting resident members of the University from voting in city elections was repealed, despite Hebdomadal Council's fears about the likely consequences for public order of undergraduate involvement. The Court of Appeal's decision in November that undergraduate accommodation did not constitute the required twelve months' unbroken residence came just in time for the general election, which in Oxford passed off relatively quietly. Hall was returned triumphant.[183]

An Oxford Socialist League was founded in 1885, largely through the efforts of C. J. Faulkner, senior fellow and Bursar of University College. Its meetings were liable to disruption by rowdy undergraduates, as when in February 1885 a meeting addressed by William Morris and Edward Aveling, son-in-law of Karl Marx, broke up in disorder.[184] More significant was the split in the local Liberal party over Home Rule which, due to university influence, produced more Liberal Unionists in Oxford than anywhere except Birmingham. Brodrick, promoter in 1888 of the Oxford University Unionist League, and his nephew and factotum P. Lyttelton Gell were

[180] *Oxford Chronicle* 15 May 1880. Hall had never graduated, and his college standing was that of the most senior commoner: *Calendar* (1880), 269.

[181] Ibid. 8, 15 May 1880.

[182] *Report of the Commission on Corrupt Practices in Oxford*, pt 2, 294–5, 468, 899–900; John, 'Oxford and the general election' 131–46; C. Fenby, *The Other Oxford* (1970), 42–61.

[183] Registration Act, 48 Vic., c. 15, s. 15; *Oxford Times* 9, 16, 23 May 1885; ibid. Nov.–Dec. 1885; *Oxford Chronicle* Nov.–Dec. 1885.

[184] *Oxford Chronicle* 31 Jan., 7, 21, 28 Feb. 1885.

instrumental in establishing the Oxfordshire Liberal Unionist Association and the Central Conservative and Unionist Club opened in George Street in 1894.[185] Liberal dominance of the city had in any case run its course; but the support of such prominent figures as Jowett, Spooner and Acland made the astutely chosen and popular Unionist candidates for the city almost unbeatable. Sir George Chesney, the weakest Unionist candidate to be fielded until 1914, was said to owe his narrow victory in 1892 to the intervention of Acland, whose considerable local esteem swayed waverers.[186]

The Oxford citizen of nineteenth-century novels and memoirs was conventionally the ingratiating and importunate tradesman, attending hat in hand at the side entrance of the college for the condescension of an order. The stereotype could not, of course, accommodate such dynasties as the Morrells—bankers, brewers, attorneys, MPs, related by marriage to college heads, well-nigh hereditary overseers of the affairs of college, university, county and diocese.[187] Herbert and John Parsons, bankers and mayors, were the brother and cousin respectively of John Parsons, Master of Balliol, where building work in the late eighteenth and early nineteenth century relied heavily on the family bank, Fletcher & Parsons (later the Old Bank).[188] A small élite of such townsmen, themselves likely to be Oxford graduates, moved comfortably in the upper reaches of both worlds. Indeed, a Morrell or a Parsons was as unlikely to socialize with the struggling private tutor as was Goldwin Smith with the Great Western railwayman about whom he pronounced with such confidence. Even late in the nineteenth century it was reckoned to be difficult for outsiders to get a foothold in university society, and despite the growth of suburban North Oxford making next-door neighbours of tradesman and don, their social lives remained largely distinct.[189]

Credit for the first sustained attempt to break down social barriers between the two communities has usually been given to T. H. Green, but they had been under sustained assault from the Aclands from the late 1840s.[190] Oxford people responded warmly to Henry Acland's flamboyant campaigns on social issues, whether in support of child sweeps in the 1840s and 1850s, of improved sanitation in the 1860s and 1870s, or of providing home care for

[185] Papers of Oxford Conservative and Unionist Club, Bodl. G. A. Oxon. 4° 274; Brodrick, *Memories and Impressions*, 398.

[186] W. R. Williams, *Parliamentary History of Oxfordshire* (privately printed Brecknock 1899), 140–1; Atlay, *Acland*, 453; Brodrick, *Memories and Impressions*, 330, 398.

[187] *VCH Oxon.* iv. 184–5; B. Allen, *Morrells* (1994), *passim*.

[188] Bodl. MS Top. Oxon. d. 247, fos 127, 147'; D. Adamson, 'Child's Bank and Oxford University in the eighteenth century', *Three Banks Review* cxxxvi (1982); L. F. Bradburn, *The Old Bank* (privately printed 1977).

[189] E. M. Arnold, 'Social life in Oxford', *Harper's Monthly Magazine* (July 1890), 248; C. E. Colvin, 'A don's wife a century ago', *Oxoniensia* l (1985), 267–78.

[190] *Works of T. H. Green* iii, p. cxix; *Oxford Times* 20, 27 Oct. 1900; Atlay, *Acland*, 179–81, 364–5; T. F. Plowman, *In the Days of Victoria* (1918), 52, 331.

the sick poor in the 1880s.[191] Local pride was tickled by his characteristic assertion to the Royal Commissioners in 1870 that 'one of the best botanists in Oxford is one of the best makers of portmanteaus, and one of our best electricians is a glazier'.[192] Green was no populist, and he died too young to enjoy a sainted old age like Acland's. That Sir Michael Sadler also was able to claim a pioneering role in promoting town–gown relations at the end of the century underlines the old adage that things move slowly in Oxford.[193] G. C. Brodrick, reflecting complacently on his own contribution to the gathering *rapprochement*, yet felt that 'it is hardly to be expected that a complete social amalgamation can be effected between university and city— at least, as long as ladies dominate society, emphasizing a marked difference of habits and culture between the commercial and non-commercial sections of the English middle class'.[194]

Socializing by undergraduates with townspeople was generally discouraged, and invariably so where women and girls were concerned. There was always the worry of entrapment, leading ultimately, perhaps, to the awful fate of one who, sued for breach of promise, 'cost his father a considerable sum and is now doing manual work in Australia'.[195] For many undergraduates, townspeople who were not in trade or in service impinged on their consciousness chiefly as fanciful elements in lurid accounts of town–gown riots, brutish bargees and hod-carriers looming out of the Alsatian fastness of West Oxford only to return vanquished yet again by the scientific and sportsmanlike pugilism of the collegians.[196] The two major riots of the nineteenth century, in 1800 and 1867, were directed chiefly at the price of provisions, but drew in the University. That of 1800 alarmed the University sufficiently for it to encourage the dispatch of troops by the Home Office on the grounds that the civic authorities had capitulated to the rioters: 'The poor...have raised in them a spirit of madness to be laid only by the sword of a dragoon.'[197] There was an ugly moment when John Cooke, President of Corpus and Pro-Vice-Chancellor, a supporter of government action, confronted an angry crowd.[198] But many members of the University seem to

---

[191] Atlay, *Acland*, 181, 362 ff.; *Oxford Chronicle* 30 Apr. 1887; *Oxford Times* 20, 27 Oct. 1900.
[192] Devonshire Commn evidence PP 1872 c.536 xxv. 208.
[193] Sadleir, *Sadler*, 139.
[194] Brodrick, *Memories and Impressions*, 384–7.
[195] *Modern Review* Jan. 1893, 418–20; Aston, 'Undergraduate lodgings in Oxford', 12. *Oxford Chronicle* 11, 18, 25 Nov., 2, 16 Dec. 1876. Burgon claimed that his dislike of the lodgings system derived from the reported experiences of girls entering his House of Refuge; see above.
[196] e.g. *The Adventures of Mr. Verdant Green, by Cuthbert Bede* (3 vols 1853–7, 1982), 161–73; C. M. Westmacott, *The English Spy* (1907), 249–62. Cf W. E. Sherwood, *Oxford Yesterday* (1927), 47.
[197] PRO HO 42/51, nos 59, 154, 319; R. Wells, *Wretched Faces: famine in wartime England, 1763–1803* (1988), 126–7, 238–41; E. P. Thompson, *Customs in Common* (1991), 250–2.
[198] Notice re attack on Cooke, Bodl. G. A. Oxon. b. 111 (90).

have accepted that there were genuine grievances, and the University had long given consumers in Oxford greater protection than was customary elsewhere through Market Committee regulations and generous public sub-scriptions for subsidized prices.[199] In 1867 the Guy Fawkes celebrations, traditional occasion for town–gown disorder, had passed off fairly quietly despite the tension created in Oxford by the news of bread riots in the West Country, but on 9 November a group of undergraduates, ostensibly out to prevent a rumoured disturbance, succeeded in triggering it off. Building workers on strike at Balliol joined in, and it was some days before peace was fully restored. The strict controls imposed by the university authorities, gating those living in college and arranging for those in lodgings to be sworn in as special constables, prevented the sort of provocation that could easily have caused the trouble to spread. The use of the University Volunteers to help clear the streets was thought in retrospect to have been unwise, though preferable to employing the two companies of Grenadier Guards sent from Windsor.[200]

In November 1879 the *Oxford Chronicle* felt able to announce that, despite twenty-one arrests after some apparently half-hearted scuffling, 'town and gown riots have now fortunately become almost a thing of the past'.[201] A resurgence of trouble in the late nineteenth century was due largely to student rowdyism. It commonly took such forms as 'sweeping' the streets arm in arm, or damaging the railway station after sports fixtures. Gas lamps were convenient and routine targets: C. B. Fry, appearing in court in March 1895, was but one of many to whom they proved irresistible.[202] Socialist and Salvationist meetings in particular were considered fair game.[203] Most incidents were explained away as pranks, albeit in the face of the perennial complaint that a young gownsman's high spirits were a town youth's thuggery. But disorder occasionally went beyond excuse. Disruption of Socialist rallies at the Martyrs' Memorial in May and June of 1897 got out of hand when large crowds of undergraduates and local 'roughs' joined forces to assault the speakers. The firing into the air of a revolver by a Wadham man, hardly to be overlooked by even Oxford's tolerant author-ities, resulted in a ban on undergraduate attendance at such rallies. Those disturbances were partly inspired by the excessive enthusiasm generated by the Prince of Wales's visit to open the new Town Hall on 12 May. Student

---

[199] W. Thwaites, 'The marketing of agricultural produce in eighteenth-century Oxfordshire' (Birmingham Ph.D. thesis 1980), 500 ff.; Thwaites, 'The assize of bread in eighteenth-century Oxford', *Oxoniensia* li (1986), 178–9.

[200] Collection re the riots, Bodl. G. A. Oxon. 4° 784; 'Gown and town rows at Oxford', *Dublin University Magazine* lxxi (1868), 363–81; Plowman, *In the Days of Victoria*, 216–21; Sherwood, *Oxford Yesterday*, 9.

[201] 8 Nov. 1879.

[202] C. Ellis, *CB: the life of Charles Burgess Fry* (1984), 18.

[203] See Pt 2, Ch. 31.

uproariousness on that occasion was met with unaccustomed severity by specially drafted detachments of Metropolitan police. There were several arrests, most famously that of F. E. Smith, then a fellow of Merton, charged with disorderly conduct and assaulting the police after intervening to protect a college servant from allegedly over-zealous police attention.[204] A decade later Christ Church's re-emergence as Head of the River was celebrated by setting fire to a marquee being used for the Oxford Historical Pageant. The national newspapermen who again flocked down from London were sold a story of a prank that unfortunately got out of hand, despite evidence of careful planning and of elaborate manœuvres to draw off police and firemen, forewarned and lying in wait.[205] Celebration of the 'Glorious Fifth' of November, which had given the proctors little concern in recent times, returned to the streets in 1907. It was described as the first town–gown disturbance of the century, but the town's role was largely that of onlooker in a battle between undergraduates and police and proctors.[206] For a few years Guy Fawkes' Night disturbances became popular once more. They usually comprised firework-throwing and 'sweeping' the streets, although there was an attack on Ruskin College in 1909.[207] What impressed most was the Vice-Chancellor's decision in 1908 not to claim jurisdiction in the cases of those arrested. A letter to *The Times* from Lord William Cecil regretting the 'modern plan of employing clumsy, lower-class policemen to keep high-spirited gentlemen in order'[208] provoked an overwhelmingly derisive response which demonstrated more clearly than the mutual reassurances of civic and academic leaders how far attitudes had changed.

The reduction of violent outbursts against the University reflected the extent to which the town's own traditional festivities, occasions of drunkenness and licence, had been tamed by the efforts of clergy, teachers, welfare activists, temperance campaigners and youth leaders.[209] St Giles' Fair was a case in point—'the type in brutality and excess of St. Bartholomew's', it was eventually purged of its 'baneful and injurious' influence under threat of permanent closure.[210] It is ironical that in the very period when undergraduates were given to spectacular outbursts of rowdyism they should have become increasingly active in the process of modifying citizens' behaviour

---

[204] The charges were dropped: *Oxford Chronicle* 15, 22, 29 May, 5, 12, 19 June 1897.

[205] *Oxford Review* 30, 31 May 1907; *Oxford Times* 1 June 1907. See also Pt 2, Ch. 31.

[206] OUA WP/7(6), fo 77; *Oxford Review* 7 Nov. 1910.

[207] *Oxford Times* 7 Nov. 1908, 12 Nov. 1909; *Oxford Review* 7 Nov. 1910.

[208] *The Times* 7, 12, 17 Nov. 1908; *Oxford Times* 14, 21 Nov. 1908. Lord William's son Randle was one of those fined for assault. He was sent down later in the month for window-breaking: *Oxford Times* 28 Nov. 1908. Lord William became Bishop of Exeter in 1916.

[209] Gillis, 'Evolution of juvenile delinquency in England', 107.

[210] St John's College archives MS Mun. V B 131; J. R. Green, *Oxford Studies*, ed. Mrs J. R. Green and K. Norgate (1901), 241; S. Alexander, *St. Giles's Fair, 1830–1914* (History Workshop pamphlet no. 2 1970).

through youth clubs, the Boys' Brigade or the Boy Scouts.[211] But too much should not be made of the change in behaviour or of the University's part in it. Unruliness was to some extent simply deflected. Clubs and associations, especially if adopting uniforms, were identified as the new enemy and attacked as such by those, often the poorest, who would not or could not join. At the same time, within the clubs, town–gown warfare was continued by other means as members sought to impose themselves physically and psychologically upon their inexperienced instructors; it was not unknown for police assistance to be required at the Balliol Boys' Club in St Ebbe's.[212] It is fair to note, however, that the experience for both sides was sufficiently rewarding for the schemes to survive and in many cases thrive, and that in time external threats diminished.[213] Meanwhile, student indiscipline continued to provide townspeople with alternative outlets. Besides harassing political meetings they helped hijack trams during the strike of 1913 and were welcomed by students when they joined the noisy displays of defiance towards the university authorities that often accompanied the departure from Oxford of the rusticated malefactor.[214]

Religious life in Oxford was long dominated by the hostility of the city and university authorities towards dissent. The City Council petitioned Parliament against the admission of Dissenters to the University in 1834, and only narrowly passed a contrary petition twenty years later.[215] But growing Nonconformist representation on the Council and on statutory bodies inevitably made relations tense and difficult at times. Criticism of the University abated somewhat after the abolition of confessional tests and was further modified by the strenuous bridge-building efforts of T. H. Green and his followers.[216]

Tractarianism impinged little on the city initially, although daily services were introduced at St Mary the Virgin and St Peter-in-the-East, where J. H. Newman and W. K. Hamilton respectively were vicars in the 1830s.[217] The movement made a greater impact on Oxford parishes with the appearance of vestments, altar furnishings, and Marian devotions in some churches in the 1840s. Most affected was St Thomas's, where Thomas Chamberlain was vicar from 1842 until his death in 1892. He eventually won the grudging

---

[211] Butler, *Social Conditions in Oxford*, 53; J. Jones, *Balliol College: a history, 1263–1939* (1988), 232; C. Bailey, *A Short History of the Balliol Boys' Club* (1950); *Oxford and District Boy Scouts' Chronicle* i, no. 1 (1909).

[212] Bailey, *Balliol Boys' Club*, 9–10; Gillis, 'Evolution of juvenile delinquency in England', 120–1; J. R. Gillis, *Youth and History* (New York 1981), 175.

[213] Bailey, *Balliol Boys' Club*, 11, 18.

[214] *Oxford Chronicle* 19, 26 May 1894, 16 May 1913; *Oxford Review* 26 Feb. 1894, 13 May 1913.

[215] Oxford City archives B. 5. 6, pp. 47–8; *Herald* 22 Apr. 1854.

[216] D. Price Hughes, *Hugh Price Hughes* (1904), 134–6.

[217] Oxfordshire County archives MS Oxf. Dioc. b. 41, fos 175, 177-7ᵛ; H. P. Liddon, *Walter Kerr Hamilton* (1869), 11, 14–15.

respect of his parishioners less for his pronounced ritualism than for his attempts to translate Tractarianism into practical social concern.[218] Chamberlain was an eccentric, isolated individual whose influence died with him. Parish livings, which were mostly in college hands, were increasingly seen as power bases by Tractarians and Evangelicals struggling to attract members of the University, some parish churches becoming in effect alternative college chapels. Thus, St Cross became a Tractarian, St Aldate's an Evangelical, stronghold. N. J. Moody of Oriel took the St Clement's living despite its 'scanty' income for 'the love of souls and the care of the young men of the university'.[219] St Aldate's great advantage was its excellent situation 'from the point-of-view of influencing university men'.[220] The biographer of Canon Alfred Christopher of St Aldate's found it necessary to stress that involvement with the religious life of undergraduates had not led to the neglect of his normal pastoral duties. His curate, Francis Webster of Pembroke College, established the Church Army in Oxford, even for a time uniquely combining 'the functions of secretary of the Union Debating Society and Salvation Army preacher'.[221] In the circumstances the reputed godlessness of much of the population of a place so preoccupied with religion is not surprising.[222] It was claimed in 1917 that the 'religion of the Gown' and the 'religion of the Town' scarcely touched: 'the municipal community hardly, perhaps, reflects the academic movement so conspicuously as do some other mirrors more remote or below the horizon, East London, Central Africa, Calcutta'.[223] Nevertheless, colleges assisted with several of the new churches built in the later nineteenth century for Oxford's growing suburban population, contributing to building funds or even providing sites.[224] And the clergy they supplied were the 'younger shirt-sleeved pastors' such as Montague Noel of St Barnabas's who were prominent in the drive to socialize the young through the clubs, associations and organized activities mentioned above.[225]

In 1914 Oxford was, despite suburban expansion, recognizably the city it had been a hundred years before. There was still open country between the Woodstock and Banbury roads, and villages around the city's periphery were as yet unabsorbed. The city appeared, in J. R. Green's famous account,

---

[218] Simeon, *Thomas Chamberlain*; T. W. Squires, *In West Oxford* (1928), 18–26.

[219] *VCH Oxon.* iv. 256, 375, 377, 379, 389, 402–3, 408; J. S. Reynolds, *Canon Christopher* (Abingdon 1967), 75 ff.

[220] Reynolds, 93.

[221] Oxfordshire County archives MS Oxf. Dioc. d. 350, fo 286; Reynolds, 228–31.

[222] Oxfordshire County archives MSS Oxf. Dioc. d. 575, fos 55–6; d. 178, p. 366b; d. 550, p. 365.

[223] R. W. Macan, *Religious Changes in Oxford during the Last Fifty Years* (1917), 8–9.

[224] e.g. St Philip and St James in north Oxford (1860–1, St John's College), St Frideswide in Osney (1871–2, Christ Church), St Matthew in Grandpont (1891, Brasenose): *VCH Oxon.* iv. 257, 408, 411–12.

[225] Gillis, 'Evolution of juvenile delinquency in England', 110.

'a mere offshoot of the university...a mere assemblage of indifferent streets that have grown out of the needs of the university...as a municipality it seems to exist only by grace or usurpation of university privileges'.[226] But A. W. Hall's 'enterprising man' had by 1914 already begun to manufacture his motor-cars; and the city's rapid and uncontrolled growth from the 1920s would transform the University, in a witty phrase, into 'the Latin Quarter of Cowley', travellers at the railway station being met with the hoarding: 'Welcome to Oxford—home of Pressed Steel'.

[226] Green, *Oxford Studies*, 3–4.

14

The Careers of Oxford Men

M. C. CURTHOYS

The confidence with which early nineteenth-century writers had celebrated an unbroken succession of statesmen, divines and scholars issuing forth from Oxford was not shared by the generation which followed. 'One by one, the university has lost its hold on the great professions,' Thorold Rogers lamented in 1861.[1] A sermon delivered in 1863 by Thomas Espin, formerly a fellow of Lincoln, called the attention of the University to a historic decline in the proportion of recruits to the Church of England ministry educated at Oxford.[2] In the case of the judiciary, Gladstone observed a 'retrogression' in 1867 from the position twenty or thirty years earlier. Fewer than half of the members of the Bench between 1850 and 1875 had been educated at Oxford or Cambridge.[3] Local reputations were not assured of wider recognition: none of the three college fellows A. H. Clough, Mark Pattison and J. A. Froude who were candidates for professorships at the new Queen's colleges in Ireland received appointments when the first were made in 1849.[4] In 1872 an accumulation of evidence supported the contention of the Roman Catholic bishops, when, in opposing the restoration of a Catholic presence in the University, they argued that Oxford's role in educating the leaders of public life was a diminishing one.[5]

Some of these trends were felt in Cambridge, and the movement to restore and to extend the ancient universities' role in English life, the 'silent revolution' described by Lewis Campbell, Jowett's biographer, was common to both.[6] Campbell's assessment of the most influential forces in bringing about this change may not receive universal acceptance, but there is no doubt of the movement's effectiveness, if the educational backgrounds of prominent figures in the world of affairs are taken as a measure. Surveys of office-holders in modern Britain show, from the late nineteenth century until the

---

[1] J. E. T. Rogers, *Education in Oxford* (1861), 197.
[2] T. E. Espin, *Our Want of Clergy. Its causes and suggestions for its cure* (1863), 1–2.
[3] *Parl. Deb.* 5 June 1867, 3S clxxxvii. 1640; D. Duman, *The Judicial Bench in England, 1727–1875* (1982), 42–3.
[4] T. W. Moody and J. C. Beckett, *Queen's Belfast, 1845–1949* (2 vols 1959) i. 63–5.
[5] V. A. McClelland, *English Roman Catholics and Higher Education, 1830–1903* (1973), 274.
[6] L. Campbell, *On the Nationalisation of the Old English Universities* (1901), 5.

middle of the twentieth century, an increasing proportion of leading positions held by men educated at the ancient universities.[7] A century after Gladstone's anxieties about the University's contribution to the judiciary, Oxford men enjoyed a remarkable tenure over the office of Lord Chancellor, including all six of those who held the office between 1940 and 1970.[8] The interval between an individual's education and the eventual attainment of high office ensured that the effects of the educational changes effected by the mid-Victorians continued to be felt in the second half of the twentieth century. Greats, the most influential course of study developed in Victorian Oxford, was well represented among Britain's 'top people' in the 1950s. A prime minister (Harold Macmillan), an archbishop of Canterbury (Geoffrey Fisher), a Lord Chancellor (Gavin Simonds) and a Permanent Secretary of the Treasury (Edward Bridges) had all read that school before 1914, though in Macmillan's case the war had intervened before he could complete the course.

The education of future MPs was one indication of Oxford's standing in the world of politics. Here, also, there was a mid-Victorian perception of decline. Bonamy Price identified a 'progressive diminution of the academical element' among the MPs elected in 1868.[9] Since the early eighteenth century, there had been phases of loosened and then restored attachment between the University and the political nation, as Oxford successively accommodated itself to the Hanoverian regime in the late eighteenth century, liberalism and Nonconformity in the late nineteenth century, and labour in the twentieth century (Fig. 14.1).[10] The link was never stronger than in the last decades of the unreformed Parliament. The proportion of university-educated MPs had grown steadily since 1790, and by 1830 Oxford men accounted for over 30 per cent of the House of Commons. This representation was sustained as the products of the expanding and reforming University of the 1810s and 1820s took their places in Peel's majority elected in 1841. A subsequent decline in the proportion of Oxford-educated MPs illustrated the consequence of Oxford's attempt to uphold religious exclusions in a state where the Estab-

[7] H. Perkin, *The Structured Crowd* (Brighton 1981), 162; W. D. Rubinstein, 'Education and the social origins of British élites, 1880–1970', *Past and Present* cxii (1986), 163–207.

[8] R. F. V. Heuston, *Lives of the Lord Chancellors, 1940–1970* (1987), 15–16.

[9] *Fraser's Magazine* lxxviii (Nov. 1868), 547.

[10] Data on the university education of MPs have been drawn from: R. Sedgwick, *The House of Commons, 1715–1754* (2 vols 1970) i. 139; L. Namier and J. Brooke, *The House of Commons, 1754–1790* (3 vols 1964) i. 111; *The Eighteenth Century*, 358; R. G. Thorne, *The House of Commons, 1790–1820* (5 vols 1986) i. 293; G. P. Judd, *Members of Parliament, 1734–1832* (New Haven 1955), 87; W. O. Aydelotte, 'The House of Commons in the 1840s', *History* xxxix (1954), 254; B. Cracroft, 'Analysis of the House of Commons' in *Essays on Reform* (1867), 179; C. R. Dod, *Parliamentary Companion, 1874* (1874); *Pall Mall Gazette* 26, 28, 29 Dec. 1885; *Cambridge Review* xiv (13 Oct. 1892), 9; H. R. Greaves, 'Personal origins and interrelations of the Houses of Parliament, since 1832', *Economica* ix (1929), 177; J. A. Thomas, *The House of Commons, 1906–1911* (Cardiff 1958), 20; J. F. S. Ross, *Parliamentary Representation* (1948), 57; C. Mellors, *The British MP* (Farnborough 1978), 55; D. Butler and D. Kavanagh, *The British General Election of 1987* (1988), 202.

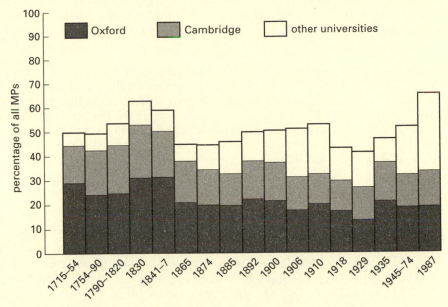

FIGURE 14.1 University education of Members of Parliament, 1715–1987. Includes those who attended more than one university; total university attendance exaggerated by between 1% and 3%
Sources: see n. 10

lished Church was no longer overwhelmingly dominant. When Palmerston won the 1865 election over eighty of the successful candidates were non-Anglicans: for nearly all of this group religious affiliation alone would have ruled out Oxford. Nor was the falling-away of the University's influence on the House of Commons limited to periods of Liberal majority. There was little recovery when the country returned a Conservative administration in 1874: the weakening of aristocratic patronage of the University, which coincided with the Tractarian movement, and the decline in matriculations during the 1850s had reduced the number of potential Oxford-educated MPs on the Conservative side. It took at least twenty years for the effect of the rise in student admissions after 1860 and the repeal of religious tests in 1854 and 1871 to work through. H. H. Asquith came up in 1870 from a Congregationalist background and entered Parliament in 1886; Tom Ellis and Silvester Horne (the latter matriculating as a Non-Collegiate) were other Oxford-educated representatives of late nineteenth-century liberal Nonconformity who helped to halt the downward trend.[11] By 1892 there was a slight recovery, which was sustained in 1900.

[11] On Ellis and Horne see *DNB: Missing Persons*, 207–8, 329.

The University was swift to acknowledge the significance of the return of twenty-nine Labour members in 1906. A committee which reviewed Oxford's relations with the labour movement, chaired by T. B. Strong, the Dean of Christ Church, observed:

Throughout the nineteenth century a considerable portion of those who, as ministers or members of Parliament or public officials, wielded great influence, have received their earliest education in political ideas at the hands of Oxford, and have acknowledged freely that they have learned through it to be more efficient servants of the community. The Trade Union secretary and the 'Labour Member' need an Oxford education as much, and will use it to as good ends, as the civil servant or the barrister. It seems to us that it would involve a grave loss both to Oxford and to English political life were the close association which has existed between the University and the world of affairs to be broken or impaired on the accession of new classes to power.[12]

In 1929, when Labour became the largest single party, the House of Commons had fewer Oxonians, and fewer graduates, than at any other recent time. After 1945, however, the result of Edwardian Oxford's engagement with labour took striking effect. Of the few Labour MPs up to 1935 who had attended University, slightly more had been to Cambridge than Oxford; of those returned between 1945 and 1974 Oxford had educated twice as many as Cambridge.

The educational composition of the House of Lords changed more gradually, and was less subject to fluctuation. In 1799 over a third of the peerage had been educated at Oxford; in 1911 the Oxonian element had fallen to a quarter in a much expanded Upper House.[13] The most notable change there, as in the cabinet, was collegiate: Balliol grew to rival Christ Church in the House of Lords and to supplant it in the cabinet. In the latter, Oxford's presence was remarkably consistent; it educated between a third and a half of those who sat in British cabinets between 1830 and 1940. Nearly a half of the members of the cabinets of the 1820s were Oxford-educated (and Canning's short-lived ministry of 1827 was very much a Christ Church affair); and not much had changed a century later, when slightly over a half of the members of the 1924–9 cabinet were Oxonians. The only period between 1812 and 1940 when Cambridge accounted for a larger share of the cabinet than Oxford arose during the ministries holding office between 1828 and 1841. In those years episcopal appointments also emphasized the damaging implications for Oxford's influence of the collapse of the confessional state. Melbourne promoted Cambridge men to nine out of the thirteen sees

---

[12] *Oxford and Working-Class Education* (1908), 48.
[13] J. Cannon, *Aristocratic Century* (1987), 48, table 9; G. D. Phillips, *The Diehards: aristocratic society and politics in Edwardian England* (Cambridge, Mass. 1979), 86; A. Adonis, *Making Aristocracy Work* (1993), 208, table 7.8.

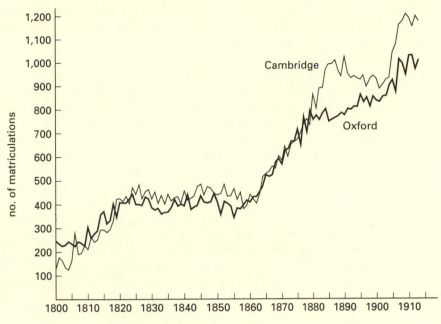

FIGURE 14.2 Oxford and Cambridge matriculations (men), 1800–1913

he had to fill.[14] But this proved a temporary interruption; Oxford men continued to enjoy a majority share of episcopal appointments in the early twentieth century.

Future cabinet members or bishops obviously represented a small fraction of the approximately 63,000 undergraduate men who matriculated at Oxford between 1800 and 1913, the last academic year before the First World War (the equivalent Cambridge figure was about 68,500). The trends in admissions are shown in Fig. 14.2. What follows is based on a survey of the later careers of undergraduates who matriculated in four separate years during the course of the century. The first year illustrates the destinations of those born at the turn of the nineteenth century, who came up in the academic year commencing in Michaelmas 1818, during the period of post-Napoleonic War expansion. The second, for the academic year 1848/9 (the cohort whose university careers were evoked in *The Adventures of Mr. Verdant Green*), examines those who came up on the eve of the first Royal Commission. The third, 1878/9, during the great rise in admissions of the 1860s and 1870s, seeks to establish the effects of the mid-Victorian reforms. The final year

---

[14] R. A. Soloway, *Prelates and People: ecclesiastical social thought in England, 1783–1852* (1962), 17.

surveyed represents those men who graduated at the turn of the century (matriculations during 1897/8), and had become established in careers by the outbreak of the First World War. They were admitted just before the significant influx of overseas students in the early twentieth century.

Vocational categories were never in reality as clear-cut as any tabular statement would at first suggest (see Table 14.A1 and 14.A2). Parsons might be landowners or schoolmasters; barristers might not practise. A period of army service might be no more than a prelude to the management of an estate. Mixed careers became more common later in the century; lawyers might enter business, for example. But a general outline may be established with some confidence, and this suggests a strong similarity between Oxford and Cambridge in the pattern of careers followed by the majority of alumni (Fig. 14.3). At both universities the majority of undergraduates who matriculated before 1850 entered holy orders. Among those who actually graduated, the proportion was nearer three-quarters. Church reform had created a demand for university-educated men, while opportunities for preferment were more widely spread as pluralism was curtailed.[15] The growth in student numbers meant that both universities were supplying the Church with more graduates than at any time since the early seventeenth century; Oxford and

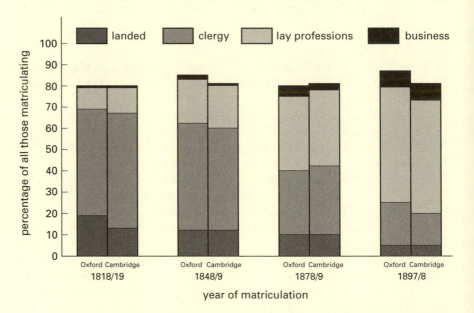

FIGURE 14.3 Principal careers of men matriculating at Oxford and Cambridge, 1818/1819, 1848/1849, 1878/1879, 1897/1898

[15] A. Haig, *The Victorian Clergy* (1984), 21 n. 23.

Cambridge accounted for about three-quarters of all ordinands between 1830 and 1850.

Despite this clerical predominance, undergraduates intended for lay occupations represented a sizeable minority of the total student body in the early nineteenth century. Most of this minority were destined to assume landed responsibilities. Their numbers cannot be precisely established; and the accompanying tables probably understate their representation in the University during the first half of the century. Nearly a third of those admitted between 1815 and 1820 to Brasenose, which has a particularly detailed college register, became country gentlemen.[16] Another perspective is provided by John Bateman's analysis of those territorial magnates in 1873 who owned 3,000 acres and received £3,000 a year in rental. About a quarter of those in Bateman's survey old enough to have attended a university had been at Oxford, and about a sixth at Cambridge. Of the colleges attended by the landowners Christ Church was always pre-eminent (see Table 14.A3). Oriel had educated a significant proportion of landowners among the generation who came to Oxford in the 1820s. After 1830 Balliol and University colleges attracted future landed magnates. Very few great landowners had attended the poor or 'close' foundations: Jesus, Lincoln, New College, Pembroke, Queen's, St John's, Wadham and Worcester.

Before 1850 Oxford played only a small part in educating men for the lay professions and government service. Some graduates acquired government clerkships by patronage; others served in the diplomatic service. In both cases, however, they generally did so rather by virtue of aristocratic birth or connection than their Oxford education. A few purchased army commissions on going down from Oxford. Before 1850 under 10 per cent of Oxford men went on to be called to the Bar, and only about half of these practised. The role of university men in the legal profession was accordingly inconsiderable; it has been estimated that over 40 per cent of the practising Bar in 1835 had not attended a university.[17] In medicine the detachment was even more pronounced. Oxford's medical school existed in little more than name, and the output of medical graduates, already small, declined after 1830. The large majority of practitioners had been educated at the Scottish universities or, increasingly, London.[18]

Professional education had formed an important function of the new London University, whose senate, in contrast to Oxford's overwhelmingly clerical governing bodies, was dominated by medical men and lawyers.[19]

---

[16] A. J. Jenkinson, 'The nineteenth century: the schools, university honours and professions of Brasenose men', *Brasenose Monographs* ii. 67, table 1.

[17] D. Duman, *The English and Colonial Bars in the Nineteenth Century* (1983), 24, table 1.9.

[18] A. H. T. Robb-Smith, 'Medical education at Oxford and Cambridge prior to 1850' in F. N. L. Poynter (ed.), *The Evolution of Medical Education in Great Britain* (1966), 50.

[19] N. Harte, *The University of London, 1836–1986* (1986), 81–3.

Oxford's weakness in these areas was not new; but after 1840 parliamentary inquiries into professional education exposed Oxford's somnolent higher faculties to critical public scrutiny. A parliamentary return in 1846 brought to light the inability of Joseph Phillimore, the Regius Professor of Civil Law, to form a class. Later in the same year, the Select Committee on Legal Education contrasted the 'meagre provision' of law-teaching at Oxford compared with German universities.[20] In 1848 Oxford witnesses appearing before the Select Committee on Medical Registration were obliged to acknowledge that medical education was languishing.[21] The Hebdomadal Board offered little hope for reviving Oxford as a place of professional education. In 1846 Philip Bliss, the University Registrar, foresaw no imminent increase in student numbers, and could find only insurmountable difficulties in the way of introducing professional studies into the Oxford curriculum; such subjects, in his view, were best taken up outside the University.[22] Instead, the Board adopted a narrow policy of protecting the monopoly position enjoyed by Oxford graduates in certain professional areas. Fears that London graduates would encroach upon ecclesiastical and other offices to which Oxford and Cambridge MAs enjoyed an exclusive right had caused the heads to oppose the London University charter in 1834. In the following years the privileges of the handful of holders of Oxford degrees in civil law in the Admiralty and ecclesiastical courts, and those of medical graduates in the Royal College of Physicians, were gradually eroded, although the heads clung to Oxford's vestigial power of medical licensing.[23]

Compulsory attendance at professorial lectures, and the extension of the undergraduate curriculum, represented new, if somewhat half-hearted, initiatives aimed at reviving Oxford's links with the professions. A. C. Tait's pamphlet on the Oxford professoriate, published in November 1839 following a summer spent at the University of Bonn, defined a role for them in offering courses of professional education. Another writer influenced by the German system, Travers Twiss, a tutor at University College and later Regius Professor of Civil Law, saw the need for the Oxford course to incorporate professional studies to overcome the growing tendency 'to regard an Academical education as an uncertain venture of time and money' and of doubtful value in preparing men for the 'scenes of active life'.[24]

[20] *Returns Relative to the Professors of Oxford and Cambridge* (PP 1846 xxxii. 766); *Report of the Select Committee on Legal Education* (PP 1846 x. 3).
[21] See the evidence of Philip Wynter and John Kidd, *Third Report of the Select Committee on Medical Registration* (PP 1847–8 xv. 583–91, 607–14).
[22] *Select Committee on Legal Education*, 309–17.
[23] G. D. Squibb, *Doctors' Commons: a history of the College of Advocates and Doctors of Law* (1977), 104–5; see *Third Report of the Select Committee on Medical Registration*, Q. 3781 (Philip Wynter).
[24] [A. C. Tait], *Hints on the Formation of a Plan for the Safe and Effectual Revival of the Professorial System in Oxford* (1839), 23; [T. Twiss], *Considerations of a Plan for Combining the Professorial System with the System of Public Examinations in Oxford* (1839), 29.

Although the eventual broadening of the undergraduate curriculum in 1850 to include natural science and law owed much to the belief that Oxford could do more to provide preparatory education for the learned professions, the immediate results were not encouraging. Falling matriculations in the 1850s offered little sign of a demand on the part of parents to give their sons whatever advantages could be derived from the University's first timid steps towards introducing pre-professional instruction in the BA course. Indeed, discussion of Oxford's relations with the professions at mid-century was not informed by the sort of overcrowding crisis (the 'excess of educated men') experienced in continental universities;[25] contemporaries saw instead empty college rooms and more fellowships than men qualified to fill them. H. L. Mansel of St John's observed that the continental models of professional education had little relevance in the English context: in Germany, 'Every lawyer, every medical man, every clerk in a Government office is licensed to his post by University certificate.'[26] English university degrees had no such general monopoly, and those privileges which their holders did possess were, as Pusey pointed out in 1853, being abridged.[27]

These pessimistic assumptions were called into question by the growing belief, which the Hebdomadal Board was noticeably slow to recognize, that an Oxford education in general might be a suitable and, indeed, highly desirable preparation for the lay professions. This was particularly urged in the case of the law. Sir John Taylor Coleridge, a judge of the King's Bench, and one of the brilliant group of scholars at Corpus in 1810, argued in 1853 that men might become 'astute, money-making practitioners' without having passed through an academic course, but, for the benefit both of the profession and the public, 'it is most desirable that men should come to the Law with all the training and mental discipline and accomplishment and association which the Academical course alone can give'.[28] His views were supported by a number of other leading High-Churchmen within the legal profession, who responded to a questionnaire on Oxford and professional education circulated by the Tutors' Association in the same year. None believed that Oxford should attempt to provide practical training, but all agreed that a university education was a valuable preparation for the law, and that teaching in the principles of jurisprudence might be attempted, as much for the benefit of students generally as for intending lawyers. Sir John Patteson, Coleridge's brother-in-law and friend of John Keble, and Sir John Awdry both expressed this view.[29] Roundell Palmer and W. H. Tinney,

[25] W. E. S. Thomas, *The Philosophic Radicals* (1979), 450–1.
[26] *RCO* (1850), evidence, 19–20.
[27] *Report and Evidence* (1853), evidence, 128.
[28] Ibid. 502.
[29] J. W. Awdry and J. Patteson, *Suggestions with Regard to Certain Proposed Alterations in the University and Colleges of Oxford, and to the Possibility and Advantages of a Legal Education at the University* (Tutors' Association Papers nos. II and III, 1854), 59–60, 63.

the latter a former fellow of Oriel and Bencher of Lincoln's Inn, took the argument further. Palmer envisaged that, by teaching future practitioners the theoretical elements of their profession, Oxford could help to curb what he regarded as the regrettable tendency of English legal practice to become 'more and more empirical, and unduly dependent upon precedents as distinguished from principles'.[30] Tinney thought the moment favourable for universities to attempt to educate more barristers: trends within the profession away 'from the formal and technical rules and principles' which young graduates found so repellent when they first entered the chambers of a special pleader were tending 'to diminish the importance of the early acquisition of technical skill, and increase that of a superior general education'.[31]

Two solicitors who responded to the Oxford tutors, John Gidley, an attorney at Exeter, and Christopher Childs, who was in practice in Liskeard, laid stress on the need to raise the character of that branch of the profession which, Childs regretted, had acquired 'an unenviable notoriety' for 'cunning' and 'sharp practice'.[32] Gidley, who later sent his son to St John's before entering practice, believed a university education would arouse in solicitors 'an abiding sense of their moral responsibility'.[33] In this they were repeating many of the opinions, some perhaps exaggerated, about the perceived inferiority of the entrants to the profession submitted to the 1846 Select Committee on Legal Education.[34] For other occupations of uncertain status and respectability a preliminary literary education was advocated as a necessary foundation. Music, like medicine, was a profession for which the University in the early nineteenth century certificated candidates whom it had not taught, and the arrangements for the BMus degree were a curious anomaly in that candidates were not required to reside.[35] Generally organists or music-teachers, the recipients of music degrees were often older men, self-taught, and frequently of lower social standing than resident undergraduates. After his appointment as Professor of Music in 1855, Sir Frederick Gore Ouseley endeavoured to raise the standing, socially as much as academically, of Oxford's music degrees, introducing preliminary examinations for music students which required evidence of a classical education.[36]

[30] F. Rogers and others, *Suggestions Respecting the Conditions under which University Education may be Made more Available for Clerks in Government Offices, for Barristers, for Solicitors* (Tutors' Association Papers nos. iv–x, 1854), 90.

[31] Ibid. 96. For these developments see R. Cocks, *The Foundations of the Modern Bar* (1983), 36.

[32] Rogers, *Suggestions*, 106.

[33] Ibid. 109.

[34] W. Holdsworth, *A History of English Law* (17 vols 1903–72) xv. (ed. A. L. Goodhart and H. G. Hanbury), 228–9.

[35] See Pt 2 Ch. 18.

[36] C. Ehrlich, *The Music Profession in Britain since the Eighteenth Century: a social history* (1985), 42–3, 71.

In no area was the displacement of practical men by products of Oxford's literary course of studies accomplished more thoroughly than in the civil service. Here, too, the Oxford Tutors' Association's links with Gladstone, Chancellor of the Exchequer during 1853–5, brought them closer than the Hebdomadal Board to the crucial developments. Early in 1853, before the preparation of the famous Northcote–Trevelyan Report, the Association sought opinions on how far a university education might be an appropriate preparation for administrative posts in government. The fullest response was given by Sir Frederic Rogers, registrar of joint stock companies and a former fellow of Oriel. He was associated with three of the Tutors' Association's respondents from the legal profession, and with Gladstone himself, in the circle of High-Church laymen known as 'the Engagement'.[37] Under the existing system of promotion by seniority, as Rogers showed, university graduates were given no advantage, though he had found that the 'power of intelligent analysis and arrangement' developed by 'getting up' books for Lit. Hum. was an 'admirable training' for civil service work.[38] The ability to cut through paper was also cited by Stafford Northcote, a Balliol contemporary of Jowett and formerly Gladstone's secretary: 'I attribute my own success, such as it has been, entirely to the power of close reasoning which a course of Thucydides, Aristotle, Mathematics &c, engenders or developes, and to the facility of composition which arises from classical studies. There is nothing that can compensate for the want of being able to follow out a train of reasoning, rejecting immaterial and irrelevant issues, and keeping close to the matter in hand.'[39] By 1850 a few university men had risen through the civil service hierarchy, anticipating in many of their characteristics the later development of the Administrative Class. Four such examples were all Oxford men; unlike earlier Oxford-educated public servants such as Charles Greville, who had obtained a position after only a few months' residence in Christ Church, all had obtained academic honours.[40]

The prospect of civil service appointments being opened to competitive examination was an opportunity to carry out the objective of the Royal Commission, announced in the final paragraph of their report, 'to place the University of Oxford at the head of the Education of the country'.[41] Members of the Commission and those who had co-operated with its inquiries were prominent among the educationalists whose views in favour of the Northcote–Trevelyan Report were published in 1855; Francis Jeune, the

---

[37] C. Matthew, 'Gladstone, Evangelicalism and "the Engagement"' in J. Garnett and C. Matthew (eds), *Revival and Religion since 1700: Essays for John Walsh* (1993), 123.

[38] Rogers, *Suggestions*, 77.

[39] Northcote to Rogers, 22 Feb. 1854, ibid. 83.

[40] H. Parris, *Constitutional Bureaucracy* (1969), 143. The examples cited by Professor Parris are T. H. Farrer of the Board of Trade, Edmund Hammond of the Foreign Office, Ralph Lingen of the Education Office, and Frederic Rogers.

[41] *RCO* (1850), report, 260.

only head to serve on the Commission, was the only member of the Hebdomadal Board whose views were cited in the parliamentary paper.[42] The 'Broad-Church' ambition to extend the University's national role was equally apparent, and more immediately effective, in relation to appointments in the Indian civil service, thrown open as a result of the 1853 India Act. The report of the committee, chaired by T. B. Macaulay, commissioned to devise a scheme of examination for Indian appointments, of which Jowett was a member, embodied two principles crucial for linking Oxford to the Indian service. First, it recommended raising the age limit for candidates to 23, opening the competition to those who had completed Oxford's four-year honours course. Second, the principle was asserted that the intending Indian civil servant 'should have received the best, the most liberal, the most finished education that his native country affords'.[43] In the case of Oxford, this meant the classical curriculum, and Macaulay's marking scheme was weighted to place such graduates at an advantage.

Oxford men gained a third of the Indian appointments offered for competition between 1855 and 1859, and during the first fourteen years of the open competition they accounted for the largest number of university recruits. But Lord Salisbury doubted the virtues of the Greats man: successive reductions in the maximum age limits culminating in his decision in 1876 to fix the limit at 19 effectively halted graduate recruitment, although probationers admitted to the service thereafter were permitted to spend two years at Oxford. Nor did the developments of the mid-1850s bring about an immediate influx of Oxford entrants to the home civil service. A channel for Oxford men had been created by the system of limited competition which operated between 1856 and 1870. Between 1834 and 1855, only six recruits to the Treasury had been university-educated; during the period of limited competition nine out of the twenty-two recruits had been at Oxford.[44] In relation to the size of Oxford's graduate output these numbers were small. Even after the implementation of open competition in 1870, Treasury reductions in the number of first-class clerkships effectively reduced the available openings; only 232 such posts were offered for competition between 1870 and 1894.

Before 1890 the dominant influence on career patterns continued to be the Church. During 1853–4, when the Tutors' Association was preparing its reports, the Hebdomadal Board and the theology professors were responding to the more immediate question, posed by the Cathedrals Commission, whether the universities supplied an adequate preparation for those entering

---

[42] *Report and Papers Relating to the Reorganization of the Civil Service* (PP 1854–5 xx. 52–3); J. Roach, *Public Examinations in England, 1850–1900* (1971), 27.

[43] The Macaulay Report was reprinted in *Papers Relating to the Selection and Training of Candidates for the Indian Civil Service* (PP 1876 lv. 300–6).

[44] H. Roseveare, *The Treasury* (1969), 172.

orders, or whether theological colleges, attached to cathedrals, should be established to provide such instruction. The replies from Oxford exposed some significant divisions of opinion, though the majority opinion was firmly in favour of retaining clerical education as a function of the University.[45] A doubling in the number of theology professors in less than a decade, as a result of the creation in 1842 of chairs in pastoral theology and ecclesiastical history, and in 1847 of the Ireland professorship of the Interpretation of Holy Scripture, had made theological teaching more effective: unlike their lay counterparts, the theology professors delivered regular lectures, which were well attended. This promising development threatened to be undermined by a sharp decline in the number of graduates taking orders. About 400 fewer Oxford men were ordained between 1854 and 1863 than in the preceding decade.[46] Compounded by a similar fall at Cambridge, the proportion of ordinands who had not been educated at a university rose to over a quarter (Table 14.A4). None of the parties in Oxford politics wanted clergy education to be lost to the University; liberals because they disliked the sacerdotalism of the theological colleges, High-Churchmen because they feared a further weakening of the link between Oxford and the Church. The less expensive avenues to the University opened up as a result of the reports of the subcommittees of Convocation on university extension in 1866—the Non-Collegiate scheme and Keble College—strengthened by the economical education offered by St Edmund Hall, and the foundation of Hertford College on church principles, proved crucial in reversing the decline in the short term. Keble was soon educating about 250 future ordinands per decade, and the supply from the Non-Collegiates was considerable (nearly a half of the first sixty-two Non-Collegiate MAs were in orders). Between 1882 and 1891 more Oxford men were ordained than in the peak decade before 1850, and they accounted for about 30 per cent of all ordinands between 1872 and 1891 (Table 14.A5). The immediate effect of university extension had been to restore the position of Oxford as an educator of the clergy.

The decisive collapse occurred after 1890. As well as wider social and economic trends, such as the effect of the agricultural depression on clergy incomes, and the general effect of religious doubt, discussion of the causes of this decline pointed also to local causes, particularly the removal by the Selborne Commission of the restrictions which limited the tenure of many college and university offices to clergymen.[47] A committee appointed in 1908 by the Archbishop of Canterbury to report on the supply of ordinands cited the comment of the Dean of Christ Church: 'It is necessary to remember that the University, as the Commission left it, is virtually a secular

[45] See A. Haig, *The Victorian Clergy* (1984), 77.
[46] Espin, *Our Want of Clergy*, 2.
[47] *Official Report of the Church Congress, 1883* (1884), 317.

institution. The Divinity Professorships are still held by Priests, but the University is not concerned as such, either with maintaining, or developing, or arousing a desire for Holy Orders.'[48] Variations in the number of ordinands produced by different colleges in the late nineteenth century suggest how much now depended on the active promotion of the clerical vocation by individual dons.[49] St John's and Exeter, which both retained energetic Church traditions, continued to send over one in five of their undergraduates into the Church before 1914. At Corpus, whose fellows had been among the first to remove clerical restrictions, about one in eight undergraduates entered the Church after 1886. Of the colleges for which figures are available, Balliol showed the most pronounced decline: only one in twenty-five Balliol men at the end of the century took holy orders.[50]

The movement of Oxford graduates into the lay professions, of which the first signs were apparent by 1850, began in earnest after 1870. College registers both date and illustrate the change more precisely (Table 14.A6). Law was the first profession to reflect the new pattern, with results which told upon the composition of the profession itself. By 1885 some 30 per cent of practising barristers had been educated at Oxford, compared to 21 per cent fifty years earlier, while the proportion of non-graduates fell to under 30 per cent.[51] Towards the end of the century the number of both Oxford and Cambridge entrants to the profession levelled off; by then the law absorbed about 11 per cent of the undergraduates at both universities. Behind this stationary figure was concealed a significant change in the distribution of graduates within the profession. In the early nineteenth century it had been very rare for an Oxford or Cambridge graduate to become a solicitor; by 1900 some 40 per cent of Oxford men going into the law did so as solicitors. Although this was significant in so far as it affected Oxford, graduates still made limited inroads on this branch of the profession, which, in contrast to the Bar, remained a largely non-graduate one.[52] To most parents of intending solicitors, the cost and delay represented by a university course, for which the Law Society was less willing than the Inns of Court to make concessions, was a needless addition to the already heavy cost of articles. Moreover, by the end of the century attendance at a public school offered a sufficient social credential, which had not been so widely available, or even acceptable, a generation earlier.[53]

[48] *The Supply and Training of Candidates for Holy Orders: Report of the Committee appointed by the Archbishop of Canterbury* (1908), 16 n.

[49] See the remarks of W. W. Jackson of Exeter in *Official Report of the Church Congress, 1902* (1902), 392.

[50] *VCH Oxon.* iii. 86.

[51] Duman, *English and Colonial Bars*, 24 table 1.9.

[52] H. Kirk, *Portrait of a Profession: a history of the solicitor's profession* (1976), 58.

[53] R. D. Anderson, 'Universities and élites in modern Britain', *History of Universities* x (1991), 244.

It was in medicine that the mid-Victorian project to link Oxford more closely with the professions produced the most controversial results. High hopes were expressed in 1857 by H. G. Liddell, the Dean of Christ Church, when he supported H. W. Acland's candidature for the clinical professorship of medicine; the new honour school of natural science, coupled with hospital instruction in the Radcliffe Infirmary, offered the 'prospect of restoring our ancient alliance with the Faculty of Medicine' in the same manner as the law and history honour school was doing for law.[54] After two decades of Acland's tenure of the Regius and clinical professorships of medicine, disquiet at what seemed the comparatively meagre fruits of university reform produced the celebrated controversy concerning the so-called 'lost medical school' (see Chapter 17). During the same period, Cambridge, which in 1855 had differed little from Oxford in the scale of its medical education, had rapidly expanded its output of medical graduates. In November 1888 it was reported that 120 freshmen admitted at Cambridge during that term were intending to study medicine,[55] a figure that very nearly accounted for the total difference in matriculations to the two universities in that decade. Concern at Oxford's weakness relative both to Cambridge and to the new university colleges, which in the decade after 1870 had systematically joined forces with existing provincial medical schools,[56] was not limited to critics of Acland among Oxford scientists. One petition to the Selborne Commission, regretting the 'slight' contribution which the University made to the science of medicine, included a strong liberal element: James Bryce, G. C. Brodrick, H. F. Pelham and T. H. Green. A Balliol-educated Greats tutor, T. H. Grose, proposed an undergraduate course in medical science in 1889. Jowett himself was the moving force on the Hebdomadal Council, in the face of fierce opposition from Acland, for Oxford to develop a medical school. In November 1878 he secured a committee to investigate ways of 'providing instruction and encouragement for students in Medicine and Engineering'.[57] Evidence which the committee obtained from G. M. Humphry on the arrangements in the Cambridge school influenced Jowett's own preferred scheme for the introduction of human anatomy into the undergraduate natural science honours course, and the use of the Radcliffe Infirmary as a place for clinical training. During his subsequent vice-chancellorship, the medical faculty was established and there was a subsequent increase in the number of Oxford BMs awarded. In 1897 Cambridge, which claimed to be the largest medical school in England, was still

[54] Atlay, *Acland*, 242–3.

[55] *Cambridge Review* x (1 Nov. 1888), 50.

[56] S. V. F. Butler, 'A transformation in training: the formation of university medical faculties in Manchester, Leeds, and Liverpool, 1870–1884', *Medical History* xxx (1986), 115–32.

[57] Hebdomadal Council minutes, 11 Nov. 1878, OUA HC/1/2/2, p. 502; the papers of the committee are in OUA HC/1/5.

producing four times more entrants to the medical profession than Oxford.[58]

Jowett's committee also received evidence from the Cambridge Professor of Mechanism and Applied Mechanics, James Stuart, who described how his Cambridge course attempted to cover what was normally done in the first year of engineering pupillage, with a view to reducing the premium levied upon university graduates entering the profession. This, too, was an area which Oxford had been relatively slow to develop, though before 1880, when very few members of that profession had a university education, this was not a particularly striking deficiency. Early attempts to teach engineering in university courses at Durham and Dublin were said in 1867 to have failed on account of the large pupillage premiums which contractors continued to demand from their graduates; the failure of the former was regarded as the more striking because of its proximity to the engineering centre of Newcastle.[59] Inducements to encourage Oxford men into the profession were unable to overcome these obstacles. Three Whitworth engineering scholarships were awarded to Oxford graduates in 1868: two became lawyers, the other a lecturer in mathematics.[60] But once a body of recognized theoretical basis of engineering knowledge had been established and recognized by the profession, Oxford's slowness to respond was less defensible.[61] When a university department was finally established in 1907, a large part of its clientele was colonial; seven of the twenty-one students attached to the department in 1911 were Rhodes scholars.[62]

Comparatively few Oxford graduates entered those careers like architecture whose method of entry involved lengthy and expensive articles. T. G. Jackson, a rare example in this period of an Oxford-educated architect, paid a 300-guinea premium to Gilbert Scott on entering articles in 1858.[63] Nor did many Oxford graduates act on the suggestion of 'a city man', writing to the *Oxford Magazine* in 1884, that they should consider opportunities in the accounting and actuarial professions.[64] The response to a scheme sponsored by the Surveyors' Institution in 1908 to encourage Oxford men to take the

---

[58] The majority of registered medical students at both universities completed their clinical training elsewhere. See G. L. Geison, *Michael Foster and the Cambridge School of Physiology* (Princeton 1978), 156–7 n.

[59] *SCOC* (1867), Qs 2622, 4061.

[60] D. A. Low, *The Whitworth Book* (1926), 32. I am indebted to Dr Anna Guagnini for this reference.

[61] R. A. Buchanan, 'The rise of scientific engineering in Britain', *British Journal for the History of Science* xviii pt 2 (1985), 227–8.

[62] *Report for the Year 1913–1914 from those Universities and University Colleges in Great Britain which are in Receipt of a Grant from the Board of Education* (PP 1914–16 xix. 440); on the creation of the engineering department, see Pt 2, Ch. 20.

[63] B. H. Jackson (ed.), *Recollections of Thomas Graham Jackson* (1950), 54.

[64] *OM* 12 Nov. 1884, 399.

newly created rural economy diploma course as a preliminary to land-surveying disappointed its promoters.[65]

Journalism, by contrast, was an area in which Oxford graduates had become well-established at the turn of the twentieth century. Newman had regarded with abhorrence the London newspaper writers who descended upon Oxford during the 1829 election; but the Tractarians proved important in establishing Oxford's strong connection with *The Times*. J. T. Delane marked the first in a succession of Oxford-educated editors. Under the management of John Walter III, who had 'a notable loyalty to his University', two of the most prolific leader-writers, Thomas Mozley and G. C. Brodrick, were recruited from Oxford.[66] On the provincial press, C. P. Scott, nephew of the founder of the *Manchester Guardian*, joined that paper after taking schools in 1869, starting a tradition which brought in a succession of Oxford graduates—L. T. Hobhouse, J. A. Hobson and J. L. Hammond; this was maintained when Robert Ensor was recruited in 1901. In the mid-1890s the careers of E. T. Cook at the *Daily News* and J. A. Spender at the *Westminster Gazette* were seen as further evidence that writing for the press was a peculiarly Oxford phenomenon.[67] Impressions were encouraged by the proliferation of undergraduate journalism. At the eighteenth anniversary dinner of the *Isis*, founded in 1892 (its Edwardian competitor, the *Varsity*, started in 1901), one speaker considered 'The chief value of papers like the *Isis* was that they held the place of an honour school of Journalism.'[68] The same could not have been said of the Oxford University Dramatic Society, which has been found to have been strikingly inefficient as a route into the acting profession, though an increasing number of graduates did enter the professional theatre after 1880.[69] Despite the great names, however, the stage, press and authorship, when seen as full-time occupations, absorbed fewer than 2 per cent of undergraduates in the late nineteenth century.

School-teaching, which drew in over one in eight Oxford men after 1890 and probably more if those who were temporarily occupied as schoolmasters are taken into account, was more numerically significant. Regarded for much of the century as an outgrowth of the clerical vocation, the scholastic profession received little distinct notice in the discussions of Oxford's links with the professions at the time of the first Royal Commission. The subsequent

---

[65] F. M. L. Thompson, *Chartered Surveyors: the growth of a profession* (1968), 202; HCP 81 (1908), 189; HCP 98 (1914), 36.

[66] S. Morison, *The History of 'The Times': the tradition established, 1841–1884* (1942), 42; A. J. Lee, *The Origins of the Popular Press in England* (1976), 110.

[67] *OM* 29 Jan. 1896, 143.

[68] *Isis* 30 Apr. 1910, 306.

[69] H. Carpenter, *OUDS: a centenary history of Oxford University Dramatic Society, 1885–1985* (1985), 58; M. Sanderson, *From Irving to Olivier: a social history of the acting profession in England, 1880–1983* (1984), 15.

emergence of a lay teaching profession was as rapid as it was unforeseen. Opportunities grew as new schools were founded or remodelled on public school lines in the two decades after 1860; high salaries in those schools made that a boom period for Oxford graduates entering teaching. Classically educated Oxford graduates held the majority of public school headships between 1890 and 1930; and Oxford and Cambridge between them accounted for the overwhelming majority of assistant-masterships in those schools.[70] One qualification needs to be added. While teaching was a growth area, it never held the same overwhelming importance as a career for Oxford graduates as it did for arts graduates of the newer civic universities. Intending schoolmasters were a minority of those reading Oxford's two largest honour schools in the late Victorian period, Greats and modern history. The nature of both schools reflected the fact that most of their graduates were unlikely to have a future professional interest in the subjects themselves. When headmasters sought to recruit assistant masters to take their classical sixth forms, performance in classical Moderations was a surer guide than the final examination in Literae Humaniores to the type of competence they needed.

While many of those who graduated between 1860 and 1880 enjoyed successful and sometimes lucrative careers in the public schools, those who followed them into teaching, perhaps encouraged by the example of their own schoolmasters, were not always so fortunate. Outside the major schools, the level of salaries was said to have halved in the twenty years after 1870.[71] For those with capital, running a preparatory school could be a profitable undertaking, but for the masters whom they employed conditions were said to be very poor.[72] Teaching had, by 1890, become a buyers' market. The *Oxford Magazine* acknowledged that career prospects in the profession were poor; and the *Isis* pondered how graduates were to obtain a living wage.[73] In 1893 the Vice-Chancellor, Henry Boyd, voiced anxieties, otherwise rarely heard in nineteenth-century England, that university expansion carried with it the risk of creating an academic proletariat.[74] He had, perhaps, mistaken the phenomenon. Traditionally, many graduates had pursued unremunerative vocations in the Church. The plight of preparatory schoolmaster in the 1890s 'without place or honour in the profession, without hope or prospect in his life' was a new manifestation of the older

----

[70] Oxford men held 32 headships out of 50 leading public schools in 1890, and 82 of 148 Headmasters' Conference schools in 1930. Of 1,873 assistant-masterships in HMC schools in 1910, Oxford men held 708 and Cambridge 747.

[71] J. Wells, *Oxford and Oxford Life* (1892), 43; W. H. D. Rouse, 'Salaries in secondary schools', *Contemporary Review* lxxviii (1900), 277.

[72] D. P. Leinster-Mackay, *The Rise of the English Prep School* (1984), 18.

[73] *OM* 28 Feb. 1894, 240; *Isis* 21 Apr. 1894, 226.

[74] *Report of a Conference on Secondary Education in England, convened by the Vice-Chancellor of the University of Oxford and held in the Examination Schools, Oxford, October 10 and 11, 1893* (1893), 24.

problem of the impecunious curate.[75] Lured by the prospects of an immediate starting salary and the opportunity for organized sport, recent graduates entering the teaching profession found that increments might be insufficient to support a family: indeed, headmasters were inclined to think that their subordinates' value declined with age.

A widespread concern that graduates were drifting into schoolmastering, often on unfavourable terms, caused a well-known Trinity tutor, R. W. Raper, to lay the foundations of what became the Oxford University Appointments Committee.[76] The idea of establishing an educational Registry Office in Oxford had first been proposed in 1877 by G. W. Kitchin, Censor of the Unattached Students, many of whom entered teaching.[77] Raper revived the idea in 1885 in response to the growing practice of headmasters to recruit assistant masters through scholastic agencies, who charged graduates a proportion of their first year's salary in return for a placement. He envisaged a non-profit-making agency on the lines of that successfully established at Cambridge by W. J. Lewis, who held a fellowship at Oriel;[78] and in December 1892 the Appointments Committee held its first meeting, with Raper in the chair. In 1907 the Committee received full official recognition from the University.[79]

Careers in the Empire represented about 20 per cent of the Appointments Committee's placements by 1914; and they were of undoubted importance in siphoning off what might otherwise have been an excess of graduates. In 1854 it had been remarked, by way of criticism of the closed scholarship system, that a holder of such an award had resorted to sheep-farming in New Zealand; by the early twentieth century this had ceased to be an unusual sequel to a university career.[80] In the face of agricultural depression at home, many Oxford men chose to pursue landed careers overseas. College registers, like public school lists, show that, by the end of the century, coffee-, tea- or rubber-planting in East Africa, Ceylon or Malaya, fruit-farming in California or Australia, ranching in North and South America, were all likely destinations.[81]

Demand for men who had obtained high classes in the honour schools remained strong in the late nineteenth century; among them, the material

[75] W. T. Sutthery, 'The assistant-master: past, present and future', *Preparatory Schools Review* i (1895), 6.

[76] T. Weston, *From Appointments to Careers: a history of the Oxford University Careers Service, 1892–1992* (1994), ch. 1.

[77] Hebdomadal Council minutes, 15, 29 Oct. 1877, OUA HC/1/2/2, pp. 471, 473.

[78] On the early proposals to recognize the agency see HCP 10 (1885), 19 Jan. 1885; *OM* 4 May 1887, 166.

[79] F. B. Hunt and C. E. Escritt, 'Historical notes on the Oxford University Appointments Committee, 1892–1950', Bodl., repr. from typewriting, 1950.

[80] W. Thomson, *An Open College Best for All* (1854), 15. Cf the account of opportunities for settlers in British East Africa in *Oriel Record* i (Feb. 1909), 31.

[81] W. J. Reader, *Professional Men* (1966), 190.

conditions never really existed for the emergence of a disaffected intellectual class. Like their Cambridge counterparts, those who had headed Oxford's class lists had turned away from the Church to a striking extent in the 1860s; and the Church's inability to obtain its share of first-class men was much discussed in the early 1900s.[82] Headmasters also complained that these men were drawn away from teaching by the lure of more attractive alternatives.[83] Even the Empire seemed to be losing out; in 1911 Lord Selborne criticized the tendency for the ablest men to turn their backs on India and to opt for secure careers at home.[84] The first-class graduate at the turn of the century was likely to be drawn into government service, and was not obliged to go out to the Empire to do so (Table 14.A7). The home civil service, which resumed large-scale recruitment of graduates in the mid-1890s, offered an opportunity to fulfil the public service ideal so strongly promoted in late Victorian Oxford, with the security of an immediate salary and pension rights.[85]

After 1890 a university education became the norm for higher appointments in government service, and Oxford benefited disproportionately. The raising to 23 of the age limit for entry to the Indian civil service in 1892 reopened the service to graduates. In 1895 the home civil and ICS examinations were united into a single annual competition, to which Eastern cadetships were added in 1896. On average about ninety appointments were made a year. Of these Oxford gained over 45 per cent between 1895 and 1914. Although Cambridge obtained rather fewer, the two ancient universities between them accounted for over three-quarters of the total (Table 14.A8). When the diplomatic and foreign services were brought within the combined competition (under certain conditions), the same pattern emerged. Oxford men obtained ten out of sixteen appointments to Foreign Office clerkships, between 1908 and 1913, and fifteen of twenty-one diplomatic attachéships.[86] In the Education Department where, controversially, both administrative and inspectorate posts continued to be recruited by patronage, Oxford and Cambridge more or less scooped the pool.[87] The period of civil service recruitment 1890–1914 marked the true 'zenith of Greats'. Favoured, as the Civil Service Commission intended that it should be, by the allocation of marks in the open competition, Greats now assumed its

---

[82] A. G. L. Haig, 'The Church, the universities and learning in later Victorian Britain', *Historical Journal* xxix (1986), 187–201; P. S. Burrell, 'The growing reluctance of able men to take holy orders', *Hibbert Journal* i (1902–3), 719; *Church Congress Report, 1902*, 392.

[83] *Report of a Conference on the Training of Teachers in Secondary Schools for Boys* (1902), 46; *Oxford Review* 3 Mar. 1913.

[84] *The Times* 28 Oct. 1911, 7.

[85] *Pelican Record* vi (June 1903), 235.

[86] R. A. Jones, *The Nineteenth-Century Foreign Office* (1971), 64; R. A. Jones, *The British Diplomatic Service, 1815–1914* (Gerrards Cross 1983), 142.

[87] *Transactions of the National Association for the Promotion of Social Science, 1875*, 415; G. Sutherland, 'Administrators in education after 1870' in Sutherland (ed.), *Studies in the Growth of Nineteenth-Century Government* (1972), 263–85.

pre-eminent position in the civil service examination.[88] In five years, between 1897 and 1901, 154 of 243 successful Oxford candidates had taken honours in Greats and a further forty-three had taken classical honour Moderations only, having entered for the civil service examination before taking their final schools. Only twenty-nine had read modern history (and some of these took it as a second school).

Others who had achieved high academic attainments in their Oxford careers were drawn into the expanding area of university teaching. The early practitioners in disciplines which had developed outside the existing university curriculum had frequently not attended a university; and when Oxford began to extend its range of teaching some of the new posts went to men who came from outside the university tradition. Once newer disciplines became established in Oxford, graduates of them proceeded to obtain posts at the civic universities or the new universities being founded in the colonies. Here the differences between Oxford and Cambridge's curricular strengths were most apparent. Oxford had educated only half as many fellows of the Royal Society in 1910 (over half of whom held university posts) as Cambridge and fewer than the Scottish universities and London (Table 14.A9). The picture was almost reversed in the British Academy (nearly three-quarters of whose fellows were based in universities) where, of the 100 FBAs in 1910, Oxford had educated nearly a half and Cambridge about a third. There was a well-established tradition of Oxford classicists and philosophers teaching in Scottish universities,[89] and the foundation of the Welsh university colleges drew in others. Few Oxford graduates, however, held positions in the early years of the civic universities when the orientation was towards science and technology. In 1908 J. A. Venn found 170 Cambridge men of professorial rank in English and colonial universities, compared to 105 from Oxford.[90] As late as 1913 only thirty-three of the 180 Oxford graduates employed in London University, the English civic universities, and the Welsh university colleges were teaching mathematics and the natural sciences.

At the beginning of the twentieth century new careers opened up which attached rather less exclusive weight to academic attainment and rather more to what was termed 'character', as exemplified by the qualities of sporting prowess and leadership potential which Cecil Rhodes specified as criteria for his scholars. Jowett's confident assertion, cited in the Northcote–Trevelyan Report of 1853, that 'in more than nineteen cases out of twenty' men who succeeded in examinations 'are also men of character',[91] was qualified fifty

[88] R. Symonds, *Oxford and Empire* (1986), 189–91.

[89] R. D. Anderson, 'Scottish university professors, 1800–1939: profile of an élite', *Scottish Economic and Social History* vii (1987), 43–4.

[90] J. A. Venn, 'The nation: Oxford and Cambridge', *Oxford and Cambridge Review* iv (1908), 41.

[91] *Report and Papers Relating to the Reorganization of the Civil Service*, 470.

years later by the belief of those like Clement Jackson, Bursar of Hertford and tutor to its passmen, that sporting achievements also made Oxford men employable, for participation in athletics 'intensified the lesson of self-reliance and determination'.[92] Appointments in the colonial service, which became increasingly numerous after 1900, were made by nomination rather than competitive examination, and for these 'character', in the sense in which Rhodes understood the term, was at a premium. In assessing the suitability of applicants to the Sudan political service, which was opened to civilians in 1904, the Appointments Committee took note of 'general ability, literary ability, athletic ability, special proficiency in modern languages and character', the object being, as the *Oxford Magazine* noted, to obtain 'all-round men'.[93]

A further area of demand came from the army. An Oxford education had traditionally been an alternative rather than a preliminary to a military career. Army reductions in the post-Napoleonic period probably contributed to the rise in Oxford admissions. Conversely, the increased availability of non-purchase commissions during the Crimean War drew away men who might otherwise have gone to university. Commissions allocated to the universities, limited to sixteen a year, dated from the 1860s, but the candidates whom they attracted proved neither satisfactory to the army nor creditable to the University.[94] Seeing the army as yet another area into which the University might extend its influence, Jowett had little success in his attempts during the 1880s to persuade the War Office to extend the scheme.[95] This position was revolutionized by the Boer War, when large numbers of candidates from Oxford (eighty-seven in 1900 alone) were recommended for commissions by the Vice-Chancellor, in addition to those who entered the service in the ordinary way.[96] Evidence of enthusiastic undergraduate enlistment, and the high calibre of the recruits obtained, encouraged the Akers-Douglas Committee on military education, appointed in 1901, to recommend that the number of university commissions should be increased to 100 a year.[97] Oxford's response was to establish a Delegacy for Military Instruction, adding Group E (military subjects) to the pass school for the benefit of intending officers, while those seeking honours were encouraged to read the modern history school, which introduced a military campaigns special sub-

---

[92] C. N. Jackson, 'Some notes on the Oxford University Athletic Club' in W. B. Thomas (ed.), *Athletics* (1901), 83, 89.

[93] *Royal Commission on the Civil Service*, appx to the third report (PP 1913 xviii, Q. 18,674); *OM* 3 Feb. 1910, 171. See A. H. M. Kirk-Greene, *The Sudan Political Service* (1982); 180 of the 310 members of the Service recruited by 1952 had been at Oxford.

[94] G. Harries-Jenkins, *The Army in Victorian Society* (1977), 98.

[95] Abbott and Campbell, *Jowett* ii. 293–4; OUA HCP 15 (1886), 3 Dec. 1886, HCP 22 (1889) 29 Jan. 1889.

[96] *OM* 29 Oct. 1902, 28.

[97] *Report of the Committee on Military Education* (PP 1902 x. 205–9).

ject. According to the Delegacy, 1910 was a year 'remarkable for an un-precedented development of military spirit in the Undergraduate',[98] and the new university route, whose merits were enthusiastically urged by T. E. Lawrence in the case of one of his brothers, was immediately popular.[99]

Business careers were the third area of growth in the Edwardian period.[100] In 1913, however, H. E. Morgan, an executive with W. H. Smith's, published a series of articles in which he asserted that the public schools and ancient universities 'deliberately and traditionally teach boys and young men of those classes from which we may expect higher intelligence and inherited ability to despise business'.[101] Morgan's complaint has found echoes in a large body of subsequent literature.[102] It was true that the number of fathers of Oxford undergraduates in business greatly exceeded the number of undergraduates who themselves went on to business careers. Although the gap narrowed after 1870 it remained considerable: at the end of the century businessmen who sent sons to the University exceeded undergraduates who went into business by over three to one. Whether these figures demonstrate that the University itself was instrumental in diverting undergraduates away from business is open to question. During most of this period, the University was not seen as an appropriate preparation for a youth intended for business life, any more than it was seen as a useful preliminary to the army. For those intended to take over a family business, or for whom some business opening could be found, a university education would have been both unnecessary and, by delaying entry into employment until after the age of 21, positively damaging. In 1854 E. A. Freeman described the process: 'A father has two sons, one designed to be a clergyman or barrister, the other to be a banker, merchant, surgeon, or solicitor; the first goes to University, he never thinks of sending the second.'[103] A parental decision to send a son to university usually indicated a prior resolution that he was not to enter business.

After 1870 some businessmen did begin to send to Oxford sons who were destined to be their successors, although the resulting delay in enter-ing commercial life continued to be regarded as a disadvantage. In 1878 T. C. Baring, the benefactor of Hertford College, who was backed by a petition of 161 MPs mainly representing 'the commercial classes', supported

[98] *Gazette* xli (8 Feb. 1911), 438.

[99] *The Letters of T. E. Lawrence*, ed. Malcolm Brown (1988), 34.

[100] M. Sanderson, *The Universities and British Industry, 1850–1970* (1972), ch. 2; M. Sander-son, 'Education and economic decline, 1890–1980s', *Oxford Review of Economic Policy* iv (1988), 42. For Cambridge see S. Rothblatt, *The Revolution of the Dons* (1968), 256–7.

[101] *Review of Reviews* xlvii (1913), 21.

[102] M. J. Wiener, *English Culture and the Decline of the Industrial Spirit* (1981), 22–4; C. Barnett, *The Collapse of British Power* (1972), 38.

[103] *Suggestions with Regard to Certain Proposed Alterations in the University and Colleges of Oxford* (Tutors' Association Papers no. xii, 1854), 147.

an unsuccessful attempt by the Law Society to persuade the Selborne Commission to introduce two-year degree courses.[104] Baring's signatories included many with interests in the City of London; and this was a reflection of where Oxford-educated businessmen were most likely to be found.[105] The next development was the recruitment of university men not necessarily having family connections with business into managerial positions. An early and informal instance of this occurred in 1892 when W. F. D. Smith, heir to the W. H. Smith firm, introduced into the business a clergyman's son, C. H. Hornby, who had rowed with Smith in the New College eight in 1888.[106] Executive openings provided a new field of opportunity for the Appointments Committee, whose involvement dated from a successful approach to the North Eastern Railway in 1903 and the establishment of a non-technical traineeship scheme for railway management positions.[107] Placements of this type remained comparatively rare before the First World War; the Appointments Committee arranged twenty-two in 1913. Only about 10 per cent of undergraduates obtained placements through the Appointments Committee, so these figures cannot be taken as a full measure of Oxford's involvement with the business world. Among those undergraduates who came up in 1897, about 8 per cent entered business careers, which exactly matched the proportion at Cambridge. Business became a decidedly fashionable career in Edwardian Oxford, claiming at least two fellows of All Souls. Some much quoted figures have succeeded in concealing this trend. Attempting a rough classification of 2,412 living old members of Balliol listed in an early edition of the college register, its compiler, the college Bursar, enumerated the numbers in the various professions, nineteen bankers being the only entrepreneurial occupation represented. At the same time, he failed to classify over 500 names recorded, and these included a substantial number who were in commercial occupations. A later analysis has found that nearly 10 per cent of Balliol men entered business after 1880.[108] If rather more Oxford men went into business at the end of the nineteenth century than is often supposed, the University continued to play a limited part in educating future business leaders. One survey of 100 company chairmen in 1935 found fewer than a quarter (Oxford eleven, Cambridge twelve) had been educated at Oxford or Cambridge; among 103 managing directors the figure was even smaller (Oxford two, Cambridge four).[109]

---

[104] *UOC* (1877), evidence, Q. 5381; suppl. evidence, 379–80.

[105] Y. Cassis, 'Bankers in British society in the late nineteenth century', *Economic History Review* xxxviii (1985), 213–15.

[106] C. Wilson, *First with the News: the history of W. H. Smith, 1792–1972* (1985), 190.

[107] C. E. Escritt, 'The railway traffic apprenticeship', *Oxford* xxv/1 (1972), 46.

[108] E. Hilliard (ed.), *The Balliol College Register, 1832–1914* (1914) vii, cited in H. Perkin, *The Rise of Professional Society* (1989), 370; Sanderson, *Universities and British Industry*, 51.

[109] D. J. Jeremy, *Capitalists and Christians: business leaders and the Churches in Britain, 1900–1960* (1990), table 1.13. These figures roughly match a survey of chairmen of leading

Where, then, were Oxford men predominant? Their share of cabinet, episcopal and judicial appointments, and seats in the Houses of Commons and Lords, has already been indicated. A broader impression of the impact of Oxford's alumni may be gained from an analysis of those who matriculated at Oxford before 1914 and who were subsequently recorded as attaining a certain level of distinction in *Who Was Who* (those who died from 1897 onwards).[110] These criteria produced a population numbering some 3,600 Oxford-educated men. Among them traditional links with the Church and aristocracy were maintained after 1870 at the same time as new areas of influence opened up (Table 14.A10); but after 1870 the pattern of college attendance of future élite members changed (see Table 14.A11). That Balliol overhauled Christ Church in the cabinet has already been noted. The years after 1870 saw the colleges with traditional gentry connections, such as Brasenose and Merton, overtaken by New College and Magdalen, which both expanded to become among the most prolific educators of future leaders in the world of affairs. Members of Corpus, a small college but one with a strongly competitive examination for classical scholarships, proved particularly successful in the civil service and other careers which favoured academic talent.

There were significant differences, too, between the products of the various honour schools. The contrast between some of the honour schools and the pass school was still more pronounced (Table 14.A12). Oxford's small natural science school, for example, was relatively successful in this respect; its most prominent graduates were concentrated in medicine, higher education and research. The theology school, on the other hand, though it successfully provided a semi-professional education for future parsons, was less likely to prove an avenue to high ecclesiastical office: only 4 per cent of its graduates attained high positions as defined by this survey. Graduates of the newer and, before 1914, small, specialized schools in the arts—oriental studies, English, modern languages—were conspicuously drawn into the world of learning. In the character of its clientele the modern history school most closely resembled the pass school, which it was intended to replace as a course providing a general education for commoners. It became a popular school for the intending clergy, as the first Chichele Professor, Montagu Burrows, had hoped it would be.[111] Those who succeeded to hereditary

companies from 1880; up to 1939 Oxford and Cambridge accounted for between 25% and 30%, the two universities' shares being roughly equal: H. Perkin, 'The economic worth of élites in British society since 1880' (Social Science Research Council Report 1976); Rubinstein, 'Education and élites', 141, table 14.

[110] Since the criteria for inclusion in *Who's Who* changed over time, this survey has attempted to ensure comparability by restricting its range to those who achieved defined positions. All peers, baronets, knights and MPs are included. Criteria for hierarchical occupations include: all bishops and deans; judges and QCs; under-secretary rank in the civil service; generals in the army.

[111] M. Burrows, *Inaugural Lecture Delivered October 30, 1862* (1862), 28.

titles tended to read modern history, if they went in for honours at all, and more MPs educated at Oxford between 1870 and 1914 had read history than any other school. It was the honour school most commonly read for by those whose future importance lay in the business world. But Oxford's traditionally pre-eminent school, Greats, remained the most successful of the large schools in producing high achievers. Before 1914 Greats educated more future high court judges than the jurisprudence school, more bishops than the theology school, and more politicians of cabinet rank than the modern history school.

The period covered by these volumes ended, as it had begun, with the utility of the Oxford course of study as a preparation for 'the active duties of life' in question. 'Practically every member of the ruling class of England passed four of the most important years of his life in Oxford. All the rest of his life he looked at things through Oxford spectacles,' John Perry, Professor of Mechanics at the Royal College of Science and a critic of the influence of Oxford graduates on national science policy, alleged.[112] To the sometimes unflattering comments of businessmen on the products of an Oxford education[113] were added more trenchant criticisms from the labour movement. Ramsay MacDonald's maiden parliamentary speech, in March 1906, criticized the concentration of public offices among Oxford men and attacked the record of Balliol men in the Empire.[114] In 1909 Beveridge, who had no high opinion of his Oxford education, undertook to look outside the universities to find men who were 'in touch with the practical issues of life' to run the new labour exchanges.[115] Two years later, 6,000 teachers and civil servants assembled in the Albert Hall to protest at the hold of the old universities over appointments to the higher civil service.[116] The *Daily Mail* joined in the fray with a series of articles alleging that education at the ancient universities and public schools either turned out 'loafers' or fitted a man 'for nothing but teaching and the civil service'.[117] Anxieties on this score even reached undergraduate periodicals and college debating societies.[118]

The range of occupations to which an Oxford education was a preliminary had greatly expanded since 1800. Yet, as the Edwardian critics illustrated, the precise benefit conferred by a university education, whether at Oxford or anywhere else, remained largely imponderable. Moreover, appointments to government service by a method developed in the 1850s, which assumed that a liberal education was the ideal type, no longer seemed self-evidently to

[112] *Oxford Times* 5 Dec. 1903, 9.
[113] See the remarks of leading businessmen reported in *Strand Magazine* xxxii (1906), 399.
[114] *Parl. Deb.* 5 Mar. 1906, 4S cliii. 122.
[115] J. Harris, *Unemployment and Politics* (1972), 290.
[116] *The Times* 15 May 1911, 3.
[117] Cited in *Wadham College Gazette* (Michaelmas 1912), 96.
[118] *Varsity* 28 Jan. 1913, 3.

serve the needs of a democratic state. Two Royal Commissions appointed in 1912, the Islington Commission, which reviewed recruitment to the Indian civil service, and the MacDonnell Commission, which had a similar remit for the home civil service, obliged the Hebdomadal Council in 1913 to offer a wider justification of Oxford's methods, as Edward Copleston had been called to do, though in rather different terms, a century earlier.[119]

APPENDIX

TABLE 14.A1

PRINCIPAL CAREERS OF OXFORD MEN MATRICULATING IN FOUR ACADEMIC YEARS, 1818/1819, 1848/1849, 1878/1879, 1897/1898

career	year of matriculation							
	1818/19		1848/9		1878/9		1897/8	
	no.	%	no.	%	no.	%	no.	%
landed/no profession	71	18.8	52	11.7	75	10.2	39	4.9
clergy	188	49.7	219	49.3	216	29.2	144	18.1
non-Anglican clergy	0	0.0	3	0.7	4	0.5	11	1.4
law	19	5.0	22	5.0	89	12.0	86	10.8
medicine	3	0.8	6	1.4	16	2.2	21	2.6
higher education	3	0.8	12	2.7	18	2.4	30	3.8
school-teaching	3	0.8	14	3.2	68	9.2	94	11.8
research, libraries	0	0.0	2	0.5	3	0.4	16	2.0
armed forces	2	0.5	25	5.6	15	2.0	62	7.8
government service	7	1.9	7	1.6	33	4.5	93	11.7
miscellaneous professions	0	0.0	0	0.0	3	0.4	8	1.4
arts, literature	2	0.5	2	0.5	11	1.5	14	1.8
commerce, finance	2	0.5	7	1.6	22	3.0	38	4.8
industry, engineering	1	0.3	1	0.2	14	1.9	24	3.0
died young	5	1.3	11	2.5	21	2.8	19	2.4
not known	72	19.0	61	13.7	132	17.8	96	12.1
total	378		444		740		795	

Note: the total for 1897 excludes 30 non-resident students who matriculated for the purpose of qualifying for the BMus degree.

Sources: Matriculation registers, OUA; *Alumni*; professional directories; school and college registers.

[119] For Council's submissions, see *Royal Commission on the Civil Service*, 2nd appx to fourth report, appx 53 (PP 1914 xvi. 933–4); *Royal Commission on Public Services in India*, appx to the report, vol. xi (PP 1914 xxiv. 667–8).

TABLE 14.A2

PRINCIPAL CAREERS OF CAMBRIDGE MEN MATRICULATING IN
FOUR ACADEMIC YEARS, 1818/1819, 1848/1849, 1878/1879,
1897/1898

career	year of matriculation							
	1818/19		1848/9		1878/9		1897/8	
	no.	%	no.	%	no.	%	no.	%
landed/no profession	52	12.5	52	11.7	70	9.6	43	4.6
clergy	222	53.5	216	48.4	232	31.7	137	14.8
non-Anglican clergy	0	0.0	0	0.0	1	0.1	6	0.6
law	28	6.8	37	8.3	98	13.4	106	11.4
medicine	3	0.7	2	0.4	42	5.7	100	10.8
higher education	2	0.5	11	2.5	26	3.6	23	2.5
school-teaching	8	1.9	26	5.8	48	6.6	99	10.7
research, libraries	0	0.0	0	0.0	4	0.5	13	1.4
armed forces	6	1.4	11	2.5	23	3.1	56	6.0
government service	3	0.7	2	0.4	6	0.8	72	7.8
miscellaneous professions	0	0.0	0	0.0	9	1.2	13	1.4
arts, literature	1	0.2	2	0.4	11	1.5	9	1.0
commerce, finance	3	0.7	4	0.8	15	2.1	33	3.6
industry, engineering	0	0.0	1	0.2	3	0.4	40	4.3
died young	12	2.9	16	3.6	9	1.2	23	2.5
not known	75	18.1	65	14.6	135	18.5	155	16.7
total	415		445		732		928	

Sources: Matriculation registers, Cambridge University Archives; J. A. Venn, *Alumni cantabrigienses, 1752–1900* (6 vols 1940–54)

TABLE 14.A3

COLLEGES ATTENDED BY THE GREAT LANDOWNERS
EDUCATED AT OXFORD

no. of landowners	college
> 50	Christ Church (327)
25–49	Balliol (46), Oriel (31), Brasenose (30), University (25)
10–24	Exeter (20), Magdalen (18), Merton (14), Trinity (11), Corpus (10)
< 10	New (6), St John's (6), Pembroke (5), Worcester (5), Magdalen Hall (4), Wadham (3), Queen's (2), Lincoln (1), Non-Collegiate (1), Jesus (0)

Source: J. Bateman, *The Great Landowners of Great Britain and Ireland* (4th edn 1883, repr. 1971)

TABLE 14.A4

ORDINATIONS OF DEACONS IN THE PROVINCES OF CANTERBURY
AND YORK, 1834–1911, BY PLACE OF HIGHER EDUCATION (%)

year of ordination	Oxford	Cambridge	Dublin	Durham	other colleges[a]	literates	total no.
1834–43	38.8	43.1	4.1	3.4	10.6	—	5,350
1844–53	32.9	39.0	8.0	4.4	15.7	—	6,656
1854–63	29.5	36.7	6.4	4.1	23.3	—	6,009
1864–73	30.5	33.3	5.5	3.3	27.3	—	5,990
1872–81	28.7	30.9	4.1	4.3	25.6	6.4	6,560
1882–91	29.6	30.0	3.9	7.0	26.5	2.8	7,644
1892–1901	28.6	31.6	3.7	8.3	25.2	2.5	6,762
1902–11	26.0	25.8	3.2	9.8	30.9	4.1	6,232

[a] Incl. theological colleges and, before 1873, literates.

Sources: Alan Haig, The Victorian Clergy (1984), 32, table 2.2; Report of the Committee of the Lower House of Convocation on Deficiencies in Spiritual Ministration, Chronicle of Convocation vii (1876), 28; annual tables of ordinations, in Official Yearbook of the Church of England from 1883.

TABLE 14.A5

PROPORTION OF OXFORD AND CAMBRIDGE UNDERGRADUATES
ORDAINED, 1834–1911

year of ordination	no. educated at Oxford	percentage of Oxford undergraduates[a]	no. educated at Cambridge	percentage of Cambridge undergraduates[a]
1834–43	2,076	53.5	2,307	53.5
1844–53	2,188	53.5	2,596	58.0
1854–63	1,771	45.0	2,207	50.0
1864–73	1,829	38.5	1,995	41.5
1872–81	1,880	30.0	2,029	32.5
1882–91	2,262	29.5	2,295	26.5
1892–1901	1,932	24.0	2,139	22.5
1902–11	1,624	19.0	1,610	17.0

[a] Ordinands calculated as a proportion of those matriculating five years earlier. Cf Alan Haig, The Victorian Clergy (1984), 30, table 2.1.

Sources: as Table 14.A4.

TABLE 14.A6

PRINCIPAL CAREERS OF MEN ADMITTED TO FOUR OXFORD COLLEGES, 1870–1909

career	Brasenose		Corpus		Keble		St John's	
	1870–99		1886–1909		1870–1904		1875–1909	
	no.	%	no.	%	no.	%	no.	%
landowners UK	64	6.3	4	0.9	24	1.4	13	1.0
landowners overseas	17	1.7	2	0.4	36	2.1	13	1.0
farmers	5	0.5	3	0.7	7	0.4	5	0.4
land agents	14	1.4	2	0.4	14	0.8	2	0.2
clergy	211	20.9	62	13.7	905	51.8	369	28.1
non-Anglican clergy	0		6	1.3	6	0.3	5	0.4
barristers	97	9.6	48	10.6	46	2.6	71	5.4
solicitors	62	6.1	33	7.3	57	3.3	51	3.9
medicine	13	1.3	8	1.8	53	3.0	30	2.3
higher education	17	1.7	18	4.0	28	1.6	51	3.9
school-teaching	74	7.3	58	12.8	266	15.2	102	7.8
other academic	5	0.5	15	3.3	6	0.3	0	
army	53	5.2	14	3.1	30	1.7	19	1.5
government	64	6.3	100	22.1	66	3.8	112	8.5
miscellaneous professions	2	0.2	6	1.3	16	0.9	13	1.0
arts, literature	24	2.4	14	3.1	43	2.5	29	2.2
commerce, finance	65	6.4	17	3.8	27	1.5	23	1.8
industry	25	2.5	7	1.5	24	1.4	11	0.8
died young	35	3.5	6	1.3	41	2.3	13	1.0
not known	164	16.2	30	6.6	53	3.0	380	29.0
total	1,011		453		1,748		1,312	

Sources: Brasenose College Register, 1509–1909 (OHS lv 1909); P. A. Hunt and N. A. Flanagan, *Corpus Christi College, Oxford, Biographical Register, 1880–1974* (1988); B. St. G. Drennan, *The Keble College Centenary Register, 1870–1970* (1970); V. Sillery, *St. John's College Biographical Register, 1875–1919* (1981).

TABLE 14.A7

PRINCIPAL CAREERS OF MEN WHO OBTAINED FIRST CLASSES IN FINAL HONOUR SCHOOLS, OXFORD, 1815–1909

career	years of taking schools									
	1815–19		1835–9		1865–9		1885–9		1905–9	
	no.	%	no.	%	no.	%	no.	%	no.	%
landowners	6	7.8	1	1.4	1	0.6	4	1.4	3	0.9
clergy	36	46.8	41	55.4	35	20.1	50	17.9	26	7.9
non-Anglican clergy	0		2	2.7	0		2	0.7	13	4.0
barristers	17	22.1	14	18.9	45	25.9	30	10.7	23	7.0
solicitors	0		0		3	1.7	5	1.8	3	0.9

career	years of taking schools									
	1815–19		1835–9		1865–9		1885–9		1905–9	
	no.	%	no.	%	no.	%	no.	%	no.	%
medicine	1	1.3	0		9	5.2	13	4.7	20	6.1
higher education	6	7.8	7	9.5	37	21.3	65	23.3	90	27.4
school-teaching	0		2	2.7	15	8.6	39	14.0	35	10.6
other academic[a]	2	2.6	0		0		32	11.5	10	3.0
army	0		0		1	0.6	0		0	
government	4	5.2	2	2.7	9	5.2	24	8.6	73	22.2
miscellaneous professions	0		0		0		0		1	0.3
arts, literature	0		0		4	2.3	1	0.4	6	1.8
commerce, finance	0		0		2	1.2	0		4	1.2
industry	0		0		1	0.6	1	0.4	8	2.4
died young	1	1.3	4	5.4	8	4.6	4	1.4	0	
not known	4	5.2	1	1.4	4	2.3	9	3.2	14	4.3
total	77		74		174		279		329	

[a] Incl. school inspectors and Board of Education examiners.

Sources: *Calendar*; *Alumni*; professional directories; school and college registers.

TABLE 14.A8

UNIVERSITY EDUCATION OF SUCCESSFUL CANDIDATES
IN THE COMBINED OPEN CIVIL SERVICE COMPETITION,
1895–1914

university attended	percentage of successful candidates			
	1895–9	1900–4	1905–9	1910–14
Oxford	51.4	45.1	50.1	48.3
Cambridge	29.6	31.2	31.1	29.1
Trinity College, Dublin	3.8	3.8	3.8	5.7
London	5.9	4.1	2.0	6.1
Scottish	7.2	13.5	9.5	7.8
Royal University of Ireland	2.3	3.6	3.4	2.3
English civic and Welsh	1.1	2.6	1.1	2.1
overseas	4.3	4.7	3.6	4.7
no university	3.6	0.9	1.6	0.9
(attended 2)	(8.7)	(8.8)	(6.8)	(7.9)
total (rounded)	100	100	100	100
no.	470	468	443	559

Source: From 1896, the Annual Reports of the Civil Service Commissioners; for 1895, *OM* xiv (1895–6), 43.

TABLE 14.A9

UNIVERSITY EDUCATION OF FELLOWS OF THE
ROYAL SOCIETY AND FELLOWS OF THE
BRITISH ACADEMY, 1910 (%)

university attended	Royal Society	British Academy
Oxford	12.5	45
Cambridge	28.0	34
London	17.5	6
Scottish	15.0	13
Irish	5.5	5
English civic and Welsh	5.5	1
overseas	12.5	6
(attended 2)	(14.5)	(16)
(attended 3)	(2.5)	—
none	21.5	6
not known	1.5	—
no.	464	100

Sources: *Year-book of the Royal Society of London, 1910*; *Proceedings of the British Academy, 1909–10*.

TABLE 14.A10

OXFORD-EDUCATED ELITE MEMBERS,
BY AREA OF PUBLIC LIFE, COMPARING
MATRICULATIONS BEFORE AND AFTER 1870

category of eminence	matriculation before 1870		matriculation after 1870	
	no.	%	no.	%
peers, baronets, MPs[a]	281	38.3	530	18.1
church	82	11.2	183	6.2
law	74	10.1	354	12.1
government	139	19.0	909	31.0
higher education	89	12.1	488	16.6
arts, literature	14	1.9	63	2.1
medicine	14	1.9	84	2.9
armed forces	13	1.8	59	2.0
other professions	1	0.1	7	0.2
commerce, industry	26	3.5	257	8.8
total	733	100	2,935	100

[a] Excl. those who appear in any of the categories below. This category mainly comprises those who succeeded to titles and MPs who did not hold ministerial office.

TABLE 14.A11

UNDERGRADUATE COLLEGES OF OXFORD ELITE MEMBERS MATRICULATING 1870–1914

élite members	college affiliation
>500	Balliol (511)
250–499	Christ Church (383), New (378)
100–249	Magdalen (216), University (166), Trinity (157), Exeter (115), Brasenose (113), Oriel (104), St John's (103), Corpus (100)
50–99	Keble (99), Merton (80), Non-Collegiate (78), Queen's (70), Wadham (62), Lincoln (61), Hertford (58), Pembroke (51), Worcester (51), Jesus (41), halls (26)

Note: 90 migrants double-counted.

TABLE 14.A12

UNDERGRADUATE STUDIES OF OXFORD ELITE MEMBERS MATRICULATING 1870–1914 (%)

élite category	Undergraduate studies										
	literae humaniores	mathematics	natural science	jurisprudence	modern history	theology	oriental studies	English	modern languages	pass school	did not graduate
peers, baronets, MPs[a]	5.9	4.2	6.2	17.4	22.7	5.0	4.3	13.3	0.0	32.9	34.8
church	7.6	7.0	0.5	1.0	6.4	57.5	0.0	0.0	0.0	10.2	0.0
law	12.1	4.2	4.7	42.5	9.3	1.3	0.0	6.6	14.3	10.2	5.6
ministerial rank	2.1	1.4	0.0	3.5	4.6	0.0	0.0	0.0	0.0	1.6	3.2
home civil service	14.8	15.5	3.8	6.6	7.0	2.5	0.0	0.0	0.0	5.1	2.4
foreign service	1.3	1.4	0.0	1.7	5.7	0.0	8.7	0.0	14.3	2.2	4.1
Indian civil service	17.2	9.9	5.7	4.2	4.9	0.0	21.7	0.0	14.3	6.7	21.4
colonial service	4.5	2.8	1.9	3.8	4.4	2.5	0.0	0.0	0.0	3.8	1.9
higher education, research	26.0	46.5	26.5	4.2	17.8	30.0	65.2	66.6	57.1	6.0	3.0
arts, literature	3.0	0.0	0.9	2.8	2.2	0.0	0.0	13.3	0.0	0.6	2.1
medicine	0.9	1.4	42.7	0.0	0.0	0.0	0.0	0.0	0.0	3.5	0.7
business	3.3	5.6	6.6	9.1	12.6	0.0	0.0	0.0	0.0	10.2	14.2
other	1.2	0.0	0.5	3.1	2.4	1.3	0.0	0.0	0.0	6.7	6.7
total	100.0	100.0	100.0	100.0	100.0	100.0	100.0	100.0	100.0	100.0	100.0
no.	947	71	211	287	546	80	23	15	7	313	535

[a] Excl. those who appear in any of the categories below.

SUBJECTS OF STUDY

15

The Beginnings of Greats, 1800–1872

I
CLASSICAL STUDIES

RICHARD JENKYNS

'It doesn't seem to me that one gains the quintessence of the University unless one reads Greats,' says Michael Fane, the hero of Compton Mackenzie's *Sinister Street* (1913–14); this is the admission of one who, like his creator, has read modern history.[1] Greats is one of the noblest monuments of Victorian education, and in the definitive form which it reached in 1850—language and literature up until the first public examination; history and philosophy thereafter—it seems so lucid and logical in its construction that it might be thought to have sprung fully grown from the head of Zeus. In reality it was the product of an evolutionary process, and that evolution is marked by two characteristics: separation and enlargement. An analysis of this development is one of the keys to understanding the place of classical literature and language in nineteenth-century Oxford.

The bare facts have been given in Chapter 11 and need only the briefest recapitulation here. Seven years after the adoption of the examination statute in 1800 it was seen to comprehend too many subjects. Mathematics and physics were separated from the rest, which were grouped under the name of Literae Humaniores; law and Hebrew were silently dropped. Literae Humaniores at this date included logic and moral philosophy, but no mention was made of metaphysics and history; examination was mostly oral, and so in effect success depended largely on skill in construing the Greek and Latin languages. In 1825 the increase in the numbers of examinees led to the appointment of separate examiners for the two schools of classics and mathematics and the institution of the third-class honours degree. In consequence of the greater number of candidates it became necessary to conduct more and more of the examination on paper, with the result that philosophy and composition grew more important. In 1830 the fourth class was established; Literae Humaniores now included ancient history and political

---

[1] *Sinister Street*, bk iii, ch. 15.

philosophy, as well as rhetoric, poetry and moral philosophy; and permission was given to illustrate ancient by modern authors.[2]

The statute of 1850 created Greats in the form in which it continued, essentially, until 1968 (in broad terms, literary texts in Mods., followed by history and philosophy); this remains one of the forms in which Greats can be studied to this day. The final honour school required composition in Greek and Latin and the study of 'rhetoric' (either Aristotle's *Rhetoric* or some of Cicero's rhetorical works). This apart, the school contained no literary study: the other branches were theology, logic, moral philosophy and political science, and ancient history. It was, in short, a study of history and ideas, based upon the original sources, and backed up by testing of the undergraduate's competence in understanding and manipulating the classical languages.

Before proceeding to the final school, undergraduates had to pass two earlier examinations. During their first year (usually in their second term), they sat Responsions (selections from one Latin and one Greek author, and some simple mathematics); for the fifth term, an entirely new examination was brought in. This, the 'first public examination', also known as Moderations (Mods.), required candidates to be examined in the Gospels (in Greek) and in either logic or mathematics, but the core of it was the study of literary texts, principally the poets and orators. Candidates had to offer a minimum of one Greek and one Latin author; candidates for higher honours were expected to offer four authors in each language, and their attention was particularly directed to Homer, Virgil, Demosthenes and Cicero. Prose composition in both languages was required of all candidates for honours and verse composition encouraged.

As we survey the events of half a century, it becomes clear enough that although some changes came about almost fortuitously, there was a more or less consistent line of development: the object was to enlarge the scope and seriousness of classical studies. The critics from outside the ancient universities were being heeded, it seems. The carelessness with which the Edinburgh reviewers mounted their assault in 1809 has been stressed in Chapter 3. It remains to consider the substance of their criticisms. Sydney Smith, who had been both an undergraduate and a fellow of New College, attacked Oxford's predominantly classical curriculum on a number of grounds.[3] One was that this education consisted too much in the mere accumulation of factual knowledge. Another complaint was against the pursuit of scholarship for its own sake: the danger is that scholars come 'to love the instrument better than the end; not the luxury which the difficulty encloses, but the difficulty; not the filbert, but the shell; not what may be read in Greek, but

---

[2] *RCO* (1850), report, 60–2. For the background to the 1830 statute see pp. 23, 65 above.
[3] *Ed. Rev.* (Oct. 1809) xv. 46.

Greek itself... The glory is to show I am a scholar.'[4] A third objection was that classics was too exclusively a literary study:

The present state of classical education cultivates the imagination a great deal too much, and other habits of mind a great deal too little; and trains up many young men in a style of elegant imbecility... No man likes to add the difficulties of a language to the difficulties of a subject; and to study metaphysics, morals, and politics in Greek, when the Greek alone is study enough without them.... A classical scholar of 23 or 24 years of age is a man principally conversant with works of imagination... All the solid and masculine parts of his understanding are left wholly without cultivation; he hates the pain of thinking.[5]

Underlying all this was the issue discussed in Chapter 1. In 1809 Oxford's clerical fellows were intent on repressing 'speculation' among undergraduates; and Sydney Smith exposed their fears to great effect:

To preserve the principles of their pupils they confine them to the safe and elegant imbecility of classical learning. A genuine Oxford tutor would shudder to hear his young men disputing upon moral and political truth, forming and pulling down theories, and indulging in all the boldness of youthful discussion. He would augur nothing from it but impiety to God, and treason to Kings.[6]

In his famous *Reply to the Calumnies* (1810) Edward Copleston contented himself with asseverating that there was nothing much amiss; but, though he achieved a debating triumph and was rewarded with a doctorate of divinity, his reply was weakly argued. It did not stand the test of calmer and more confident times. The developments of the next forty years provided a recognition of the substance of Sydney Smith's complaints and a positive response to them. The acquisition of competence in Greek and Latin was increasingly seen as a means towards an end; the cultivation of literary taste had to yield its pre-eminence to the 'solid and masculine' study of history and philosophy (it was left to the 1890s, with the foundation of the school of English, to restore to Smith the grievance that the Victorians had earlier removed). The virtue he found lacking in the Oxford of his day, energetic, youthful disputation upon morals, politics and religion, is the very virtue that we find most characteristic of Jowett's Oxford.

This does not mean that the more traditional types of classical attainment were neglected. The Royal Commission of 1850, while approving the reforms of the past half-century in general, feared that they had not been achieved without some loss. Skill in construing, they suspected, might have declined as a result of the shift away from oral and towards written examination, while 'Scholarship, such as Porson or Elmsley represented, is culti-

---

[4] Ibid. 47.
[5] Ibid. 48–9.
[6] Ibid. 50. These passages may be found in *Works of Sydney Smith* (2nd edn 3 vols 1840) i. 189–95.

vated by few in Oxford in our day.'[7] It is hard to know what weight to give to these assessments or what basis the Commission had for making them; was textual criticism in the manner of Elmsley ever the pursuit, on a serious level, of more than a few? It is true that Dean Ireland's scholarship, a prize examination in Latin and Greek, was established in 1825 'for the promotion of classical learning and taste', and that the Hertford scholarships were established in 1834 to check the decline of Latin; but the fact that these prizes became established as the blue ribands of classical ability tells, in part, a different story. The evidence is that the pursuit of composition in Greek and Latin to a very high standard, a practice more favoured in England than elsewhere (as Wilamowitz noted with approval), was not something that the Victorians just tamely inherited from earlier ages. It receives a new prominence in the nineteenth century, and its golden age is from the Victorian period to the middle of the twentieth century.

One further feature of the Royal Commissioners' comments may be noted. After recording their approval of the new school of law and modern history, they remarked: 'We are of opinion that ancient history should be added to this school.'[8] They were too late. The 1850 statute establishing the school had been finally adopted by Convocation on the day on which the Prime Minister announced in the Commons that a Royal Commission was to be appointed.[9] The Commissioners' view was held elsewhere. 'History', Thomas Arnold had pronounced, 'is to be studied as a whole.'[10] 'Why separate modern history from ancient?', the *Guardian* asked in February 1849.[11] The question, echoed in that year by E. A. Freeman, was to be raised twenty-five years later by William Stubbs.[12] All this was in vain: Greats held the field. The reforming party in Oxford had made their move in the nick of time.

Latin verse composition had long been a bone of contention. Sydney Smith had criticized the practice. An Oxford don, defending his university in the *British Critic* for 1826 against attacks from Scotland, felt the need to deny that excessive importance was attached to the exercise, adding that hundreds passed through Oxford without being required to compose a

[7] *RCO* (1850), report, 61–2.

[8] *RCO* (1850), report, 103.

[9] *Times* 24 Apr. 1850, 5d; *Parl. Deb.* 23 Apr. 1850, 3S cx. 748. For the method of appointing examiners, settled three weeks later, see pp. 315–6.

[10] T. Arnold, *Miscellaneous Works* (1845), 399. The passage, dated Jan. 1835, is from vol. iii of Arnold's edition of Thucydides.

[11] *Guardian*, 28 Feb. 1849, 142b.

[12] [E. A. Freeman], *Thoughts on the Study of History* (1849), 121; W. Stubbs to E. A. Freeman, 8 Mar. 1885, *Letters of W. Stubbs*, ed. W. H. Hutton (1904), 264. See also E. A. Freeman, *Comparative Politics* (1873), 296–339 (Rede Lecture, Cambridge, 1872), and 499 n. 34. In 1855 Mark Pattison envisaged the transfer of ancient history to the history school, but thought 'the time…not ripe for that change': *Oxford Essays I* (1855), 295. For Freeman's ancient- and modern-history honour Moderations scheme, 1886, see Ch. 11, p. 355–6.

single verse in Latin, but rather spoiling his case by mocking the *Musae Edinenses* for inaccuracies of prosody.[13] This article is an indication of the way the wind was blowing; the writer, evidently conservative by nature, nevertheless feels obliged to concede a good deal to the reformers: the claim, argued without much enthusiasm, is not that their goals are wrong, but that Oxford is more or less fulfilling them already. Later, when competitive examination was introduced for the civil service, Macaulay was to defend the inclusion of a Latin verse paper, though in somewhat equivocal terms: if the ablest young men had devoted years to the study of the Cherokee language, they should be tested in Cherokee; since in practice they had been writing Latin verses, Latin verses should be examined (he allowed that Scots candidates should be permitted an alternative test).[14] In his *Essays on a Liberal Education* (1867), F. W. Farrar renewed the attack, alleging that 'backward and superstitious Portugal' was the country which had shown 'the greatest outburst of fecundity and facility in the production of Latin Verse'.[15] Yet in a way these attacks are a tribute to the effectiveness with which the art of composition was cultivated. The problem with Latin verses is that the form in which they were most commonly written, the elegiac couplet in the manner of Ovid, requires adherence to a restrictive set of rules, which meant that only a few undergraduates could hope to achieve any sort of naturalness even after long practice. The fact that the attacks concentrated upon Latin verse suggests that this peculiar difficulty was consciously or unconsciously recognized; if prose composition, though compulsory, and even the writing of Greek verse were not so commonly censured, it may be because good standards were attained.

At the same time, attention was paid to the classical authors. It was an avowed purpose of the 1850 reform to promote industry during the second year, and from one point of view giving the poets and orators an examination largely to themselves was to allow a clear importance to this branch of classical study. The establishment of the chair of Latin in 1854 was another earnest of good intentions. But so far we have been considering the enlarging effect of the nineteenth-century reforms; when we turn to the separative effect, the picture is somewhat different, and less satisfactory. The evolution of Greats came from a recognition that the reading of imaginative literature should be part of a wider and more diverse study of antiquity, but its separation from history and philosophy inhibited the development of literary and cultural history and the history of ideas. It was difficult for Oxford scholarship to acquire that comprehensive approach to classical antiquity that the Germans call *Altertumswissenschaft*. It was a further problem that the reading of texts as literature was confined to the first part of the course;

[13] *British Critic* ii (July 1826), 333–56, esp. 337.
[14] G. O. Trevelyan, *Life and Letters of Lord Macaulay* (1876), ch. 13.
[15] F. W. Farrar (ed.), *Essays on a Liberal Education* (1867), ch. 13.

tutors in this subject were turned into 'Mods dons', their work a propaedeutic for the rigours of Greats proper.

Changes of taste also had their effect. In one sense the whole of Greats
was studied in a literary manner, through the reading and analysis of classical
texts that were acknowledged masterpieces. Philosophy was dominated, of
course, by Plato and Aristotle; history was mainly 'source criticism', that is,
wrestling with the works of great minds like Thucydides. Later in the
century, when some historians were trying to introduce epigraphy and
archaeology, which provide types of historical evidence not to be found in
literary texts, they were opposed by Jowett. The idea behind this was that
undergraduates had most to gain from grappling hard with the greatest
intellects and imaginations of antiquity. That was a noble principle, but it
had its disadvantages. The syllabus proposed in 1850 presents classical
literature as a majestic landscape of a few mighty and isolated peaks; missing
the foothills, the student would find it hard to understand the underlying
geology. The Royal Commissioners expressed concern at the steadily narrowing range of authors read. They noted that at the time of writing the
study of fourteen, thirteen or even twelve authors was sufficient for the
highest honours; as late as 1827 a list of twenty authors was not infrequent;
and between 1807 and 1825 undergraduates had been encouraged to study
many works which had since almost entirely disappeared from the university course, such as Homer, Demosthenes, Cicero, Lucretius, Terence, Plutarch, Longinus and Quintilian. The statute of 1850 had addressed this
problem in part by giving a new prominence to the first three of these
authors, while Terence and Lucretius were also commended to candidates
for higher honours; but it cannot be said that the new course ranged widely.

On the Greek side, Homer and the dramatists dominated the study of
verse literature; indeed, no other poet was listed, with the exception of
Pindar, and when the new first public examination was first sat in 1852,
only five of the seventy-one honours candidates, and no ordinary candidate,
brought him up.[16] Lyric (Pindar apart) and didactic, iambic and elegiac verse
were excluded, as was Hellenistic poetry. By contrast, oratory was given its
due: in the examination of 1852, more honours candidates brought up
Demosthenes than any other author except Virgil, and nearly half of them
mentioned the minor orator Aeschines. In Latin Cicero, Virgil, Horace and
Juvenal were most widely studied; Terence was also given prominence in the
syllabus, no doubt because of the purity of his Latin, but it seems that only a
minority chose to read him. Lucretius, second only to Virgil among Latin
poets, was brought up by just two candidates in the 1852 examination.
Indeed, the Latin syllabus was a ragbag. The Greek syllabus could be
said to be focused upon the 'best periods', fifth-century poetry and

---

[16] Register of Moderations, 1852–70, OUA L/15/1, p. 9.

historiography and fourth-century oratory, plus Homer, but the selection of Latin authors had no such coherence. As with the Greeks, 'later' literature was neglected: the only post-Augustan authors included were Juvenal and Tacitus, but neither the age of Cicero nor the Augustan age could be seen steadily and seen whole. The most startling feature of this curriculum is the entire omission of the Latin elegiac tradition: Catullus, Propertius, Tibullus and Ovid were all excluded.

It was not just that the need to find room for history and philosophy was forcing some worthy texts out of the course: what we see here is a shift in taste. Hero-worship has often been identified as one of the characteristics of Victorian culture, and the counterpoise to the veneration offered to the greatest writers and artists was a tendency to undervalue minor art, into which category all but the very best could easily be consigned. Poets were especially at risk. Ruskin declared, 'With poetry second-rate in quality no one ought to be allowed to trouble mankind. There is quite enough of the best.'[17] And Thomas Arnold, who refused to use 'the second-rate Latin poets' such as Tibullus and Propertius at all at Rugby, said in 1842, 'Any examiners incur a serious responsibility who require or encourage the reading of these books for scholarships; of all useless reading, surely the reading of indifferent poets is most useless.'[18] In this we hear an early Victorian reaction to a Regency education. The Royal Commissioners noted the change: 'An intimate acquaintance with the Latin poets, such as accomplished Oxford men at the beginning of the present century possessed, is now rare.'[19] And it was indeed a remarkable change. Latin elegy had been the possession of educated men for centuries, while Ovid's hexameter poem the *Metamorphoses* has been second only to the *Aeneid* among Latin poems in its influence upon European civilization. In cutting undergraduates off from this, the reforms of the earlier nineteenth century were cutting them off from a stream of tradition that went back to the Renaissance, indeed to the Middle Ages. In this respect Mods. as well as Greats was a distinctively Victorian creation.

The new examination did cause some dissatisfaction, the chief complaint being that it repeated at a higher standard the kind of work done in school. That was in a way a tribute to the schools. A Victorian classical education, which survived in a few schools until the end of the 1960s, was at its best an enabling education: the aim was to make the classical languages and their literature part of the furniture of the mind. Pupils would do little if any literary criticism, in our sense of the words, but much could be understood

[17] J. Ruskin, *Modern Painters* (1856) iii pt 4, ch. 12, sect. 6, note, in *Works*, ed. E. T. Cook and A. Wedderburn (39 vols 1903–12) v (1904), 205–6. *Modern Painters* was first pub. in 5 vols (1843–60).

[18] Stanley, *Arnold* i. 130.

[19] *RCO* (1850), report, 62.

that was not written, and a good schoolmaster could hope to convey his own enlightenment. The most able were trained like racehorses; for the less able, the notion was that of Kipling's Mr King: 'It sticks. A little of it sticks among the barbarians.'[20] But whatever the merits of such training, it was not desirable that an undergraduate course should merely continue it; indeed, the more excellent it had been, the more important it was for the University to provide something new. Changes were introduced in 1872 and 1886 to counteract this defect; but these belong to the next volume of the *History*.

II

ANCIENT HISTORY

OSWYN MURRAY

THE OLD LEARNING

The emergence of Oxford as one of the leading universities in the world for the teaching and study of ancient history is a development of the nineteenth century. In the eighteenth century there had indeed been a requirement for candidates for the BA to study 'selected heads out of Greek and Roman Antiquities';[21] and there was some feeling that ancient history offered a way of varying the traditional school curriculum of the ancient poets for older students intending to enter public life. The better colleges included for undergraduate reading many of the major historians of antiquity—in Greek, Herodotus, Thucydides, Xenophon and even Polybius; in Latin, Caesar, Livy and Sallust;[22] but these were read as an exercise in construing, with little concern for their contents. The elucidation of texts *ex historiae monumentis* may be exemplified by the suggestion that Edward Bentham's collection of the three Attic funeral orations could serve as a foundation for the study of Greek history.[23] Oxford had produced no outstanding antiquarians concerned with the ancient world; the two elementary compilations of John Potter (1697) and Basil Kennett (1696) on Greek and Roman antiquities were her main contribution to the maintenance of that tradition, and were so often reprinted that they were clearly in use as standard textbooks throughout the eighteenth century.[24] The Camden chair of history was with few exceptions held by placemen incompetent in and even ignorant

---

[20] Kipling, 'Regulus', written 1908, pub. in *A Diversity of Creatures* (1917).
[21] *The Eighteenth Century*, 472, 477 (Sutherland); 523 (Clarke).
[22] Contrast the practice of Christ Church (ibid. ch. 16, Quarrie) with the more traditional Magdalen (ibid. 524, Clarke).
[23] Ibid. 497 ff. (Quarrie).
[24] Potter's *Archaeologia(e) graeca(e)* (1697–8) went through some seventeen editions until 1837.

of ancient history, who seldom gave their statutory lectures—no great loss, since until the statute of 1839 these were required to take the form of a commentary on Florus.[25] Autodidacts like Gibbon (Magdalen, matric. 1752), William Mitford (Queen's, matric. 1761) or Henry Fynes Clinton (Christ Church, matric. 1799) found in Oxford no incentive to rise 'from dead languages to living science'.[26]

This was the period of which Goldwin Smith said, 'the professoriate was deranged and mute'. The silence of the Camden professors lasted another half century.[27] Thomas Winstanley (1790–1823), editor of Theocritus, was simultaneously Laudian Professor of Arabic. G. V. Cox recorded: 'That he discharged the duties of his two Professorships we may take for granted; the fact that he ever had a class does not come within my "Recollections"; but I do remember that, though himself a remarkably plain, purblind old man, he had a daughter with a lovely face, classic features and a *perfect figure* ("a syllogism in AAA" an eminent logician called her).'[28] His successor, Peter Elmsley (1823–5), was a learned editor of Greek drama, but no historian. On his death after only two years Edward Cardwell was elected, to hold the chair for thirty-five years until 1860. Cardwell was indeed a scholar, although his only productions in ancient history were a small volume of nine *Lectures on the Coinage of the Greeks and Romans*, published in 1832,[29] and an edition of Josephus's *De Bello Judaico* (1837); his main interest was in the history of the English Church. From 1831 he was, like his two predecessors, Principal of St Alban Hall; he was a man of means, and 'one of the best men of business in the university'; prominent in university politics and the management of the Clarendon Press, he established the Wolvercote paper-mill, was private secretary to three successive Chancellors, including the Duke of Wellington and was a personal friend of Peel and Gladstone.

> Hear me, hoary Heads of Houses! ye whose weekly wisdoms meet.
> In reactionary councils and somniferous retreat,—
> Many years have fed your grass plots, many annual lectures shown
> Cardwell's blaze of erudition lighting up the Parian stone.[30]

In 1850 Cardwell was one of the senior figures who gave crucial help in the foundation of the new honour school of modern history and law, but his

[25] Exceptions may be made for Henry Dodwell (1688–91), a Dublin man, and William Scott (1773–85), both of whom won Gibbon's approval: *Miscellaneous Works* (1814) v. 224; *Memoirs*, 65; on them see *Eighteenth Century*, 515–16, Clarke. For the 1839 statute on the chair, see *Statutes* ii. 263–7.

[26] Gibbon, *Memoirs*, 48.

[27] For the history of the Camden chair see H. Stuart Jones, 'The foundation and history of the Camden chair', *Oxoniensia* viii–ix (1943–4), 169–92.

[28] Cox, 191.

[29] These lectures are described in his evidence to the 1850 Commission as 'not sufficiently attended, and...therefore published': *RCO* (1850), evidence, 264.

[30] *A Song of the Encaenia Respectfully Dedicated to the Chancellor* (1853), 8–9.

interest in the promotion of his own chair of ancient history was slight: in his brief and reluctant written reply to the questions of the 1850 Commissioners he recalled that he had fulfilled his duty since the statute of 1839, of delivering two courses of lectures a year 'either on some ancient historians, or on questions connected with Ancient History'; but the numbers attending the lectures had been small—about forty for the popular lectures and about ten for the others. He made no proposals for change, and concluded, 'The study of Ancient History in the University is sufficiently provided for, so far as general regulations are concerned, by the Statute requiring examinations for the first degree.'[31] The Camden Professor found himself under the opposite disadvantage to other professors (whose lectures were ill attended because they were unrelated to undergraduate studies), of lecturing in a central subject already well covered by college teaching arrangements and private tutors.

The publications of the Clarendon Press in the first half of the century confirm the impression of a somnolent backwater in a changing world. Apart from editions of historians (the most important of which was Thomas Arnold's three-volume *Thucydides*, 1830-5, with some important historical appendices) two major historical enterprises were undertaken; both reflect the characteristic Oxford strengths and weaknesses of wide reading in ancient texts and a lack of interest in modern critical techniques.

J. A. Cramer, Principal of New Inn Hall and Regius Professor of History from 1842, published between 1826 and 1832 seven volumes of geographical descriptions of ancient Italy, ancient Greece and Asia Minor.[32] These were learned compilations based on library study, not travel; in the case of Italy, 'the writer who follows so beaten a track must renounce all hope of communicating original information, and content himself with the humbler, though not less useful, task of giving publicity to the researches of others'.[33] For Greece and Asia Minor, Cramer made good use of the systematic travellers from Chandler to Leake, as well as the fanciful *Voyage du jeune Anacharsis* of the Abbé Barthélemy and more recent German scholarship.[34] But the only evidence that Cramer had himself visited any of these parts is a footnote referring to a snowfall in Rome on 12 April 1817.[35] The foundation of the narrative was in fact the systematic collection of relevant passages from ancient writers, 'all of whom I have reperused with attention for the purpose of extracting from them whatsoever was illustrative of local history

---

[31] *RCO* (1850), evidence, 264.

[32] J. A. Cramer, *A Geographical and Historical Description of Ancient Italy* (2 vols 1826); *A Geographical and Historical Description of Ancient Greece* (3 vols 1828); *A Geographical and Historical Description of Asia Minor* (2 vols 1832). He also published classical maps.

[33] Cramer, *Ancient Italy*, preface, p. iii.

[34] Incl. Niebuhr, 'an eminent German scholar': ibid. 346 n.

[35] Ibid. i. 10; it was in Rome on this occasion that he also saw the Aegina marbles, on their way to Munich: *Ancient Greece* iii. 281.

and topography'; the purpose of his work was not to contribute to 'a field of inquiry already exhausted, as it were, by the German antiquaries', but 'to fill up a desideratum in our books of classical instruction', especially for 'students in the Universities'.[36] Such a hope may at least suggest a new level of seriousness in the study of ancient texts at university.

Another Christ Church man cut a larger figure in the literary world. Henry Fynes Clinton had been one of the second set to be examined under the new statute in 1802.[37] The lavishly produced *Fasti hellenici* (1824–7) and *Fasti romani* (1845–50) were famous in their day; they went through several editions and epitomes, and were even pirated in Germany in a Latin translation; so popular were they that the Delegates actually volunteered an honorarium to the author of more than half the expected profit from a new edition.[38] Bulwer-Lytton attested their fame in the middle of the century, when he wrote: 'Here, indeed, was one of those books which embrace an existence; like the Dictionary of Bayle, or the History of Gibbon, or the *Fasti Hellenici* of Clinton, it was a book to which thousands of books had contributed, only to make the originality of the single mind more bold and clear.'[39] It was an extraordinary success for an author of chronological tables, who claimed 'in English expression I want *ease*; I want *fluency*; I want *copiousness*',[40] and who wrote:

It is probable that very few even of those who gain the first honours in the Examination (and these at Oxford are perhaps at this time one in fifteen) carry away with them from the University a taste for ancient learning, or ever cultivate it after they have quitted the University. The demand, then, for the 'Fasti', must be limited to those who are pursuing these studies with a view to the higher Examination; and these would probably be supplied by fifty copies annually.[41]

But as Bulwer-Lytton saw, there is something endearing about the melancholy Clinton, who unexpectedly inherited family money on condition he did not take holy orders, passed twenty years as a silent MP for a rotten borough (1806–26)—'as far as public speaking is concerned, an inefficient Member of Parliament', he wrote[42]—and devoted every moment of his time

---

[36] *Ancient Greece*, preface, p. v.
[37] Fynes Clinton, *Literary Remains* (1854), 12. This volume includes the *Literary Journal* and *Autobiography*. The dates of the entries in these are given in the notes which follow.
[38] Fynes Clinton, *Literary Journal* (1826), ibid. 246. The editions were *Fasti hellenici* ii (1824, 1834, 1841), iii (1834, 1851), i (1834); *Fasti romani* i (1845); ii (1850). It is a fitting tribute to Clinton's obsessions that his brother solemnly records the total number of pages of each of these works—1,724 quarto pages and 1,484 quarto pages respectively, a total of 3,208 quarto pages (364). The works and their *Epitomes* (1851, 1854) were still listed as in print in the University Press catalogue for 1907.
[39] Bulwer-Lytton, *The Caxtons* (3 vols 1849) i. ch. 10, 160.
[40] Fynes Clinton, *Literary Journal* (1821), 169.
[41] Ibid. (1825), 227.
[42] Ibid. (1826), 248.

to the reading of Greek. Perhaps the only man ever to be inspired with a love of Greek history by Mitford,[43] he claims little debt to Oxford:

When I first went thither Greek learning was perhaps at the lowest point of degradation. During the seven years of my residence there (four of them as an Undergraduate) I never received a single syllable of instruction concerning Greek accents, or Greek metres, or the idiom of Greek sentences; in short no information upon *any one point* of Grammar, or Syntax, or Metre. These subjects were never named to me. What I learned was struck out principally in my conversations with my companions Symmons and Gaisford.[44]

What Clinton did acquire was the practice of compulsive reading. During his seven years and eight months at Oxford (April 1799–December 1806) he claims, 'I went through...about 69,322 verses of the Greek poets and about 2,913 pages of prose authors; making together an amount of about 5,223 pages.' He was clearly disappointed with his diligence at Oxford: in the next seven years he achieved 'a sum of 28,887 pages, being almost *six times* the amount of the former quantity'.[45] Subsequently he invented an even more precise way of measuring his activity, which involved listing the whole of Greek literature, and reducing it to a standard page-length of 1,002 letters.[46] In his journal he records his reading with meticulous regularity; Plato's *Republic*, for instance (Plato was, according to him, an author not read at Oxford by anyone),[47] took him five days (403 pages) in May 1819. In that year he recorded that he had read 4,000 pages of Greek a year for the last ten years.[48] He himself claimed, 'A literary object is necessary to me for my mind's health and for my moral safety,'[49] and his brother records, 'when deprived of what was so essential to his intellectual vigour, gloom and despondency assailed him: his mind lost its tone'.[50]

Encouraged by his friend Thomas Gaisford, Clinton organized this massive reading into the compilation of his *Fasti*: these are based, to an even greater extent than the collections of Cramer, on unmediated study of the ancient sources. They tabulate in columns the magistrates, and the civil and the literary chronology of Greece and Rome; their great usefulness is the fact that they present the evidence for each event, citing the actual ancient passages in question and recording their conflicts. But Clinton was a gentleman scholar with firm views on the correct size of a library (750 volumes)

[43] Fynes Clinton, *Autobiography*, 8; and even Clinton could remark, 'defective styles are seldom improved. The practice of forty years, and of ten octavo volumes, has not purified the style of Mr. Mitford': *Literary Journal* (1821), 170.
[44] Ibid. (1825), 230.
[45] Fynes Clinton, *Autobiography*, 23.
[46] Ibid. 47.
[47] See p. 23 above.
[48] Fynes Clinton, *Literary Journal* (1819), 123, 139; cf 157.
[49] Ibid. (1830), 285.
[50] Fynes Clinton, *Literary Remains*, 155.

and a declared intention to limit his book purchases to £10 a year,[51] rather than a student of the antiquarian literature: 'There are *two* methods of study; the one is, the studying an author; the other may be called, studying a subject...Of these two methods of seeking knowledge, the first is much to be preferred.'[52] The truth was to be discovered by the reading of the texts themselves, not in learned controversy; and, of course, inscriptions were beyond Clinton's horizon. He recognized indeed that his 'ignorance of the German language precludes him from profiting by the writers who have illustrated ancient history and literature by works written in that language'; characteristically he claimed that two independent inquiries had more value than learned controversy.[53] Introduced by Gaisford later in life to the young George Cornewall Lewis, he read the latter's translation of Müller's *Dorians*, only to reject its conclusions.[54]

THE NEW LEARNING

Two interrelated factors were important in the transformation of ancient history and its emergence as a separate subject of study. One was internal, and concerned with developments in the tutorial and examination system to meet the educational demands of the age of reform.[55] But these requirements do not in themselves explain why ancient history should have become such an important aspect of classical education at Oxford. This was a consequence of external developments.

This external factor in the establishment of ancient history as an independent discipline was the transformation of historical studies in the universities of Germany. The nineteenth century was the age of scientific history: it was in ancient rather than modern history that the great advances in positivist historiography began; and throughout the century ancient history remained the most advanced area of historical studies. Behind the impetus for change in mid-nineteenth-century Oxford lies the excitement generated by the work of B. G. Niebuhr, August Boeckh and Carl Ottfried Müller.

The superiority of the Germans had been a commonplace of English classical scholarship from the beginning of the century; it is accepted in Copleston's replies to the attacks of the *Edinburgh Review*, and in historical works from Cramer onwards; the 1833 translation of the *Manual of Ancient History* by Professor Heeren of Göttingen (first published in 1799) was well

---

[51] Fynes Clinton, *Literary Journal* (1821), 185 and 183—though he was unable to keep to these limits, and by 1825 his library had grown to 880 volumes: *Literary Remains*, 235.

[52] Fynes Clinton, *Autobiography*, 74.

[53] Preface to *Fasti hellenici* iii (1834), p. iv. He did read vol. i of Boeckh's *Corpus inscriptionum graecarum* on its publication in 1825, and was pleased to find Boeckh agreed with him on many points: *Literary Journal* (1825), 237 and 240; cf the preface to *Fasti hellenici* ii (3rd edn 1841), p. v.

[54] *Literary Journal* (1830), 283; see the use of Müller in the introduction to *Fasti hellenici* i (1834).

[55] See Chs. 11 and 23.

known in Oxford; and a comment by the American translator, George Bancroft, is typical: 'It is to the patient industry of the historians of Germany that we are indebted for the first production of Manuals of history ... and among the various and profound treatises of this class which enrich and adorn their literature, the works of Heeren are distinguished by their extended range of inquiry, as well as by the minute accuracy of their details.'[56] But to the generation of Arnold, Thirlwall and Grote, German scholarship meant more than mere industry.

The story of the reception of the new German historical scholarship in England is a remarkable one. The first version of Niebuhr's *History of Rome* was published in 1811–12; it was translated into English from the 1826 edition by two young fellows of Trinity College, Cambridge, Connop Thirlwall and Julius C. Hare, in 1828–32; almost immediately they had publicly to defend the theories of Niebuhr in the *Quarterly Review*. Subsequently a third volume was translated in 1842 by Leonhard Schmitz and William Smith. Its success was so great that, according to Chevalier Bunsen in his memoir of Niebuhr, 'a much larger number of copies of the English translation ... have been sold than of the German original'.[57]

Leonhard Schmitz[58] had studied under Niebuhr, Welcker and Ritschl in Bonn; a native of Alsace, he married an English woman and came to live in Britain; with the encouragement of Thirlwall and Chevalier Bunsen[59] he went on in 1844 to publish, for the first time and in English, Niebuhr's *Lectures on Roman History* as he had heard them in Bonn (for which service he received a gold medal from the King of Prussia); by 1845 he was Rector of Edinburgh High School. He subsequently published also Niebuhr's *Lectures on Ancient History* (1852), and the *Lectures on Ancient Ethnography and Geography* (1853); he was private tutor to the Prince of Wales and the Duke of Edinburgh. Schmitz was an indefatigable purveyor of the new German learning, writing for the encyclopaedias of his friend William Smith, and starting a new journal in imitation of the *Rheinisches Museum für Philologie, Geschichte und griechische Philosophie*, founded by Boeckh, Niebuhr and C. A. Brandis in 1827. Schmitz's *Classical Museum* ran for seven volumes from 1843 to 1850, and, like its model, emphasized in its explanatory title the new importance of ancient history, describing itself as 'A Journal of Philology,

---

[56] A. H. L. Heeren, *A Manual of Ancient History*, trans. (1829, 2nd edn 1833) iii.
[57] *Niebuhr* ii. 451–2. See n. 70 for full citation.
[58] 1807–90: see *DNB*.
[59] Chevalier, later Baron Bunsen (1791–1860) was the most important single influence on the development of intellectual relations between Germany and Britain during his lifetime. He married an English wife, and lived in Rome for twenty-two years, as Niebuhr's assistant and successor as minister in Rome (1831–8), where in 1836 he founded and was first secretary of the German Archaeological Institute. He was Prussian ambassador in London from 1842 to 1854. He received an honorary degree with Wordsworth from Oxford in 1839. See Frances Baroness Bunsen, *Memoirs of Baron Bunsen* (2 vols 1868, 2nd edn abridged 1869).

and of Ancient History and Literature'. Later Schmitz was also involved in the second wave of German influence on the English-speaking world, writing an introduction to the translation of Mommsen's *History of Rome* (1862).

His collaborator in translating the third volume of Niebuhr's *History*, William Smith, had studied law before learning Greek and Latin at University College London; he became a master at University College School, and in 1842 published his famous *Dictionary of Greek and Roman Antiquities*, 'in which the first scholars of the country took part';[60] between then and 1887 he produced a series of reference works, dictionaries and atlases, together with an edition of Gibbon, which won him a knighthood (1892), the editorship of the *Quarterly Review* (1867–93) and an honorary DCL at Oxford (1870).

In this movement Oxford produced one significant figure: the anonymous translator of August Boeckh's *Public Economy of Athens* (1828, 2nd edn 1842) was the future Chancellor of the Exchequer George Cornewall Lewis; the book was published in the year he obtained his first-class degree in Literae Humaniores. With his Christ Church contemporary the politician Henry Tufnell, he also translated C. O. Müller's *History of the Doric Race* (1830, 2nd edn 1839) and his *History of the Literature of Ancient Greece* (1840–2). But Cornewall Lewis was an exceptional Oxford man, from the last days of the dominance of Christ Church; for in him we see the pull of the London scene with its wider continental scholarship and increasing interest in the political significance of ancient history. He contributed to the first and subsequent numbers of Schmitz's *Classical Museum*; and throughout his later career as a politician and statesman, and his friendships with John Austin, George Grote and John Stuart Mill, he remained fascinated by the detailed scholarship of the Germans.

Most of this revival of classical learning of the mid-century was derivative on German works. When Dr J. W. Donaldson, headmaster of Bury St Edmunds Grammar School, accused the author of the article 'tragoedia' in Smith's *Dictionary* of having copied it wholesale without acknowledgement from his own *Theatre of the Greeks*, it was swiftly shown that both writers had simply 'had recourse to the same German authors'.[61] And the fortunes of the Clarendon Press in the mid-century were founded on two works, Liddell and Scott's *Greek–English Lexicon* (1843) and Wordsworth's *Greek Grammar* (1839–43), the vehicles of the revival of Greek in English education, both of which were explicitly based on German models.

Still, cautiously the protagonists of the new learning set out to emulate their mentors. One of the earliest admirers of Niebuhrian scholarship in England was Thomas Arnold. He had read Niebuhr in the 1820s, and met

---

[60] Abbott and Campbell, *Jowett* i. 228.
[61] *Classical Museum* vii (1850), 495–6.

Niebuhr's friend Bunsen in Rome in 1827; later he visited Niebuhr in Bonn. From 1838 he began publishing a *History of Rome* 'to the revival of the western empire, in the year 800 of the Christian era by the coronation of Charlemagne at Rome', which was explicitly an attempt 'to practise [Niebuhr's] master art of doubting rightly and believing rightly';[62] by his death in 1842 he had reached the Second Punic War in three volumes. Bunsen (to whom the work was dedicated) wrote in 1838: 'Your plan is excellent, your style worthy of the subject, your research and judgment worthy of your great predecessors and standards, Niebuhr and Thucydides.'[63] Another admirer, Connop Thirlwall, wrote his *History of Greece* in eight volumes between 1835 and 1844,[64] again as an attempt to bring Niebuhrian methods to bear on Greek history. Even before Schmitz, he and Hare had founded a Cambridge journal, *The Philological Museum*,[65] which survived from 1831 to 1833. George Cornewall Lewis similarly shows the dominance of Niebuhr in the subject-matter of his two-volume sceptical work *On the Credibility of Early Roman History* (1855).

Thirlwall had the misfortune to publish his *History of Greece* at precisely the same time as his old schoolfellow George Grote was writing;[66] no work has ever been more quickly superseded (although his friend Schmitz translated it into German). With the publication of its first two volumes in 1846, Grote's *History of Greece* was immediately recognized as a masterpiece— 'The best History of Greece extant in any language... Thirlwall is the fit predecessor of Grote, and... none but Grote could have followed Thirlwall.'[67] It combined the new German methodology with a common sense, and with a utilitarian conception of social justice which has remained the basis of all study of Greek history since. The early volumes presented Greek mythology as the expression of the mentality of those later ages which created and retailed it, rather than as the pale reflection of some lost historical past requiring reconstruction by the rational historian: this insight remains the fundamental principle of all modern interpretations. Grote's portrayal of Athenian democracy was in one sense a rebuttal of the obvious prejudices underlying William Mitford's *History of Greece* (5 vols 1784–1818);[68] but it offered a reading of Athenian political life so startlingly modern

[62] T. Arnold, *History of Rome* (1838–43), preface, i. viii–x. Vol. iii was edited posthumously by J. C. Hare.

[63] Frances Baroness Bunsen, *Life and Letters of Baron Bunsen* (2 vols 1868) i. 463.

[64] 2nd edn 1845–52.

[65] Probably named after the earlier *Museum criticum* (1814–26) of J. H. Monk and C. J. Blomfield rather than Niebuhr's *Rheinisches Museum*.

[66] Strangely they did not meet until after both had published: but Grote was three years senior to Thirlwall at Charterhouse, and left school at 16 to enter his father's bank. Grote's *History of Greece* was published at intervals between 1846 and 1856.

[67] W. M. Gunn, *Classical Museum* v (1848), 125–6.

[68] See Grote's critique in the *Westminster Review* for Apr. 1826 (summarized in *Minor Works* (1873), 12–18).

that it immediately placed Greek history at the centre of political debate. In England and elsewhere, Grote ruled supreme for more than two generations.[69]

By about 1850 an image of ancient history had formed on the basis of German scholarship. It was an intellectual discipline, combining close reading of the ancient sources with a critical and imaginative approach; it rested on a massive body of factual knowledge; it approached political and military affairs through the study of agrarian problems and social and economic history. It was far in advance of anything that modern history could offer, and avoided the problems of 'partisanship', or divergent national traditions. The charismatic figure of Niebuhr, one of the architects of Prussian independence from Napoleon, was enshrined in the English version of his biography, published in 1852,[70] and proved that ancient history was not just the most exciting area of history, but also a study especially suitable for the statesman and man of affairs. Grote in turn had made the study of Greek history a central question for the modern political economist.

Yet this image had been formed outside Oxford, largely among schoolteachers and men of affairs. When the *Classical Museum* closed in 1850, the only significant Oxford contributors had been Cornewall Lewis, A. P. Stanley and A. H. Clough: and among 'the slender support which the Journal has met with from the Scholars of this country', Oxford subscribers had been few—though they included H. G. Liddell, John Conington (University), Richard Congreve (Wadham, the future disciple of Comte) and Benjamin Jowett (Balliol), with his friends Stanley and Clough. The Charterhouse that had bred Thirlwall, Hare and Grote as contemporaries before 1810, Trinity College, Cambridge, until the expulsion of Thirlwall (1834), the Rugby of Arnold, utilitarian London and the circle of Chevalier Bunsen were the centres of the new studies; Oxford was late in learning, and much of the best of its scholarship was brought to it from the more advanced public schools. When Stanley arrived at Balliol in 1834 fresh from Dr Arnold's enthusiasms, he found his Livy teacher was still recommending a *History of Rome* by Nathaniel Hooke, Pope's friend, published in 1738: 'I don't know whether he has heard that there is such a book as Niebuhr, but it would seem not; and, if so, it is rather disgraceful, I think. However he is not a good tutor, and so not a good specimen of Oxford.' Stanley was right, for other evidence shows that those who took Livy in this period were expected to know something of Niebuhr.[71] Similarly, Stanley's friend W. C. Lake said

---

[69] It was still a standard work in the 1890s, when my grandfather, reading Greats, acquired prize copies of Grote and Mommsen, and its Athenian section was epitomized in one volume as late as 1907, and used as a textbook for another fifty years.

[70] *The Life and Letters of Barthold George Niebuhr and Selections from his Minor Writings, with Essays on his Character and Influence by the Chevalier Bunsen and Professors Brandis and Loebell*, ed. and trans. Susanna Winkworth (3 vols 1852).

[71] *Letters and Verses of A. P. Stanley*, ed. R. E. Prothero (1895), 26–7. See the evidence of Pycroft, Twiss and Mark Pattison (p. 533 below) for knowledge of Niebuhr.

of the tutor he later replaced, 'Tait's lectures on History were a very inferior matter.'[72] In Oxford there was even a fear that 'the impulse which the genius of Niebuhr had given to historical criticism' would lead to unorthodoxy: 'there were some', in the words of Jowett's biographers, 'who foresaw that the same spirit would not ultimately be warned off from the sacred territory', and Pusey regarded Jowett and Stanley as suspect simply because they had visited Germany.[73]

THE NEW TEACHING

The importance of ancient history slowly increased at Oxford. The freedom in the original examination statutes for candidates to choose their books to be offered resulted, in the event, in relatively standard lists of authors for honours and passmen, for the convenience of candidates and tutors; these always included Herodotus, Thucydides, early Livy and Tacitus. In 1830 the statutes offered a new definition of Literae Humaniores as 'not only the Greek and Latin tongues, but also the histories of Greece and Rome', rhetoric and poetry, and moral and political science 'in so far as they may be drawn from writers of antiquity, still allowing them occasionally as may seem expedient to be illustrated by the writings of the moderns'.[74]

From 1831 written examinations were allowed, to lessen the burden of examining viva voce. The earliest examination papers for Easter term 1831 survive, as do other papers sporadically until a continuous run begins in 1860. Initially answers were written on the question papers in a limited space; from 1852–3 a distinctive blue paper was used, and class and pass papers can be clearly distinguished: classmen read authors, and were examined by a translation paper and two essay papers in Greek and Roman history; passmen read 'texts', blocks of three or four books from the same historical authors, examined by a paper of translation and brief historical questions.

The *Quarterly Journal of Education* for 1833 subjects this innovation to an unfavourable comparison with the examinations of the University of London, and quotes the historical questions asked:[75]

1. Give a sketch of the history of Nineveh, with a comparative estimate of the authorities from which it may be compiled.
2. Influence of Sicily on the politics, arts, and literature of Greece.
3. Trace the principal events of the Macedonian history to the time of Philip.
4. Fix the dates of the following events: Usurpation of Pisistratus, Conquest of Messenia by the Spartans, Siege of Olynthus by Philip, Overthrow of the Thirty at Athens, Battles of Leuctra, Cynoscephalae, and Pharsalus.

---

[72] W. C. Lake, 'Rugby and Oxford: 1830–1850', *Good Words* (1895), 669.
[73] Abbott and Campbell, *Jowett* i. 210.
[74] *Statutes* ii. 166.
[75] 'Oxford examinations', v (1833), 328–43. For the Bodleian's holdings of surviving papers see Cordeaux and Merry, no. 2241.

5. History of Cyrene.
6. Characters of Cleomenes, Cimon, Pausanias, Cleisthenes of Athens.
7. Rise of literature at Rome, at what period, and by what events chiefly pro-moted.
8. Notice any modifications of the office of consul from its rise to the decline of the Roman empire.
9. In what places and at what times were schools of philosophy first established?
10. The occasion of the Jugurthine war.

Most of these questions would now be regarded as suitable only for a dissertation; but the terrifying nature of such a test is mitigated by the realization that a space of at most a few lines was allowed for each answer: on the other hand, all questions were to be attempted. There is in fact little sign that a sceptical or critical spirit was encouraged; all that was required was a narration of the facts as gleaned from ancient authors and modern handbooks. It is only after 1860 that the questions begin to take on a critical nature.

The undergraduate response to this obsession with examinations is well revealed by the immensely popular pamphlet *The Art of Pluck being a Treatise after the Fashion of Aristotle... to which is [sic] Added Fragments from the Examination Papers* by 'Scriblerus Redivivus' (Edward Caswall, later Newman's disciple, Catholic priest and devotional poet), which went through thirteen editions between 1835 and 1893:

Of History useful to Pluck are there four divisions, for the most part; that is to say, Herodotus, Thucydides, Livy and Tacitus; whereof Herodotus produceth Plucks in proportion 40, Thucydides 39, Livy 53, and Tacitus 44; whence it appeareth that Thucydides produceth fewest Plucks, and Livy most. Now the reason of this is, that Thucydides being difficult is most studied, but Livy being easy is studied but a little, being read for the most part (that is to say, the second decade) in an analysis. In the reading of History for Pluck, let each be mindful to consider of chronology as of a separate thing, not to be mixed up with history; for indeed history is of things, but chronology of times. Therefore let him be careful either, first, not to read chronology at all; or secondly, to read it in such a way as for it to have no congruity with history.[76]

The first examination paper was similarly guyed, with questions such as:

1. Give a particular account of the earliest gown and town riots recorded in history. Are there supposed to have been gown and town riots in Athens when it was the University of the world?

7. Niebuhr, from observing that caps have tassels, and that the streets of Oxford are not macadamized, comes to the conclusion that the University was originally in-habited by Pelasgi, which he further confirms by observing that the inhabitants of it depart and return periodically, according to the vacations, in which we see the migratory habits of the Pelasgi exemplified. State the force of the argument.

---

[76] [E. Caswall], *Art of Pluck* (1835), 7.

Historical Essay.

The origin of boat races in the University, with a detailed account of the principal victories gained in them since their commencement, tracing their influence upon the morals and studies of the place, and comparing the Athenian navy at the death of Pericles with the navy of Oxford and Cambridge.

The treatise was finished off with 'a Synchronological table of the principal historical Events at Oxford and Cambridge during the years 1832, 1833, 1834, 1835, and 1836, down to the present era', arranged in parallel columns for the two universities, and consisting of various (mostly true) student escapades, in the manner of Clinton's *Fasti*.

As a young coach James Pycroft published anonymously in 1837 *The Student's Guide to a Course of Reading necessary for obtaining University Honours by a Graduate of Oxford*; it shows the standard expected by a conscientious tutor at that date. The author deprecates the reading of texts 'always armed with Adam's Roman and Potter's Grecian Antiquities... Not to assert that these works are absolutely useless, I speak from observation when I say that, as they are commonly employed, they do more harm than good' (p. 13). Instead of these handbooks he recommends the direct study of the ancient historians: Herodotus should be read with Schweighaueser's *Lexicon* and Heeren's *Commerce and Intercourse of the Nations of Antiquity*. Thucydides should be read in Parker's edition, 'though Arnold may occasionally be borrowed... in three thick volumes... The best translation, is that by Hobbes; and some such aid is undeniably requisite, as a man cannot always have a tutor at his elbow' (pp. 51–2); neither Mitford nor Thirlwall, 'a work of infinitely more research should be as much as looked into till both Herodotus and Thucydides are known thoroughly' (p. 42). With Xenophon's *Hellenica* these works comprise the usual 'portions of Grecian history... given by historians most eligible for the Candidate for Honours' (p. 54). The most useful work on Greek history is in fact 'a History of Greece, published by the Society for the Diffusion of Useful Knowledge, in one volume, of two-columned pages, price five shillings', which is correctly described as 'little else than an epitomized translation' of the chief ancient authors arranged as a consecutive narrative (p. 40).

The recommended reading for Roman history was similar. The most usual texts were the first and third decades of Livy, with Polybius to supplement the missing second decade. Other authors studied were the *Annals* of Tacitus alone, or the *Histories*, *Agricola* and *Germania*. The student needed help only with Livy; again the Society for the Diffusion of Useful Knowledge came to the rescue with a *History of Rome* which had an especially good section entitled 'On the credibility of the history of the early ages of Rome'.[77] The question arises whether it is requisite to read Niebuhr; per-

[77] Arnold's preface, p. xiii, speaks respectfully of this work, and says that it was written by a 'Mr. Maldon'; in fact Henry Malden (1800–76), schoolfellow of Macaulay, undergraduate

haps, but only 'when the contents of Livy are known thoroughly and not till then and when everything has been gleaned from the History by the Society for the Diffusion of Useful Knowledge'. Even then 'Mr Twiss's Epitome of Niebuhr' will suffice (p. 59).[78]

Mark Pattison had a keen memory for the embarrassments of undergraduate life in the 1830s; he records the peril of ignoring this advice:

Then the text of Livy alone did not quite fit one out for answering their questions on the early history of Rome. One was expected at that time to know something of Niebuhr's views; I set out to discover these for myself, not in an epitome, as I ought to have done—there were such things—but by reading for myself the two volumes of Thirlwall's translation. A ploughed field was nothing to this. It was a quagmire, a Serbonic gulf, in which I was swallowed up.[79]

Travers Twiss of University College ('that astute lawyer' whom Pattison never forgave for having cheated him out of a fellowship that was awarded instead to A. P. Stanley, whom he claimed was not eligible) represents the conscientious side of college teaching by fellows. According to the *Dictionary of National Biography* he was 'one of the few Oxford men of his day who possessed a competent knowledge of German, and his "Epitome of Niebuhr's History of Rome" (2 vols, 1836) helped to redeem the university from the reproach of obscurantism'; he published a learned edition of the whole of Livy in four volumes with Niebuhrian notes (1840–1), and was examiner successively in Literae Humaniores and mathematics (1835–40) as well as Bursar, Dean and college tutor, before pursuing a distinguished career in political economy and international law.

It is clear from Pycroft and others that by 1837 'the History of the Greeks and Romans' (p. 86), derived from a reading of selected historical authors, was a central and normal choice in the final examination of Literae Humaniores, since the author talks first and at greater length of ancient history, before going on to deal more briefly with divinity, philosophy, and the Greek and Latin poets; he recommends sixteen books for a candidate aiming at a first class, twelve for a second; the 'Standard Authors' listed are the *Ethics*, Herodotus, Thucydides, Xenophon's *Hellenics* 1 and 2, the first decade of Livy, and two Latin and two Greek poets (p. 87–8). But the limitations of the historical knowledge expected are recognized: although in the viva voce examination questions were asked especially about the content of historical authors, 'Persons uninformed as to the Oxford Education

contemporary of Thirlwall at Trinity, Cambridge (matric. 1818), fellow of Trinity and contributor to the journals of both Thirlwall and Schmitz; second Professor of Greek at University College London (1831–76): see *DNB*.

[78] Pycroft's reading-list and recommendations for study are confirmed in the factual *Hints to Students in Reading for Classical Honours in the University of Oxford* by 'A Classman' (2nd edn 1843).

[79] Pattison, *Memoirs*, 84–5.

suppose that an acquaintance with every point of Ancient History is demanded, if not from the original authorities, at least from modern compilations. Without any attempt at this being expected, a small part of history is required to be derived from the ancient writers, with little else more than sufficient to make that portion connected' (p. 43). And despite the attempt to integrate the Niebuhrian critical method with the study of texts, Pattison could still claim in 1855 about the teaching of ancient history: 'The study of ancient history in Oxford is very greatly in arrear of that of ancient philosophy. The private tutors have not taken up the subject to any great extent, and there are no public lectures corresponding to those of Professors Wall and Wilson.'[80]

THE RISE OF ANCIENT HISTORY, 1850–1872

The examination reforms of 1850 were motivated by a wide range of considerations.[81] There was the desire to pre-empt the unwanted attentions of a Royal Commission. There was the need to establish the position of the professors, and give them an audience. There was the problem of widening the scope of honours in Literae Humaniores and the desire to diminish the importance of the pass degree: the more the attempt was made to raise educational standards and attract the less gifted undergraduates into study for honours, the more obvious it became that some other and better training for the mind than mere mechanical language work was needed. Philosophical and historical texts had always been a major choice in the examinations. The inclusion in the new honours courses of a combined course in modern history and jurisprudence must have suggested that this would eventually threaten the primacy of Literae Humaniores, unless the latter were made less linguistic.

The solution was to remove virtually all language work into a first examination, and to create a final examination centred on ancient history and philosophy. One of the protagonists of the reform was Benjamin Jowett, who was examiner in the first examination of 1851, 'and felt the responsibility of reorganizing the Final Examination in Classics'. The strategy was successful, and Literae Humaniores continued to maintain its numbers through the subsequent creation of separate honour schools from 1864 onwards. The basic structure of 'Greats' was now in place.[82]

One issue that had arisen during the debate over the reforms was the distinction between the study of 'books' and the study of 'subjects', or

---

[80] M. Pattison, 'Oxford studies', in *Oxford Essays* (1855); repr. in *Essays*, ed. H. Nettleship (2 vols 1889) i. 474.

[81] See E. G. W. Bill, *University Reform in Nineteenth-Century Oxford* (1973), chs. 7–10; P. R. H. Slee, *Learning and a Liberal Education* (1986), 12–19.

[82] Abbott and Campbell, *Jowett* i. 215; he had also been examiner in 1849. For the 1850 statute, see *Statutes* ii. 289–326.

periods. In their *Suggestions for an Improvement of the Examination Statute* (1848) Jowett and Stanley had hoped that 'the minute facts respecting Persian Satraps, and Volscian wars, which were apt to engross the Oxford reader of Herodotus and Livy, may give way to the interest of Greek and Roman History as a whole' (p. 27). In the controversy over the proposals by the Royal Commission of 1852 to enlarge the professorial system, it had been pointed out that professors tended to teach subjects, while tutors taught books;[83] this neatly confused the issue, since it was also true that passmen read books while classmen read subjects. But for a long time the various changes in the formal requirements for the study of ancient history in the public examination continued the earlier insistence on the study of authors in their historical context, as the *University Calendar* for 1852 emphasized: 'Candidates for Honours... will have to bring up, as at present, the Greek and Latin Languages, Greek and Roman History, Chronology, Geography, Antiquities; Rhetoric and Poetics; Moral and Political Philosophy. These subjects may be illustrated by Modern Authors. Logic must be tendered by all who seek to obtain a first or second Class, and it is to have great weight in the distribution of Honours.'[84]

At first sight the new syllabus was indeed identical with the old, and was approached in the same way, as can be seen by comparing A. S. Farrar's recommendations in his *Hints to Students* of 1856 with the earlier *Hints to Students* of 1843. However, a comparison of two rather more informative works, *Pass and Class* of Montagu Burrows (1861) and Pycroft's *Student's Guide* of 1837, shows that behind the similarities a far more critical spirit was now encouraged, and this is evident also from the examination questions being asked in the 1860s. For instance, on the first decade of Livy, Burrows expects the student to compare the views of Niebuhr, Arnold and Liddell 'that there is a sufficient basis of historical truth to justify some sort of reconstruction' with that of Cornewall Lewis, 'to consider it all too uncertain to make such labour profitable'. With characteristic conservatism he reveals, however, that 'the former of the two views which have been mentioned is the one which prevails, and is perhaps likely to prevail, at Oxford', and Niebuhr was still sufficient:[85] 'That incomparable historical genius left little for others to do in this department, and since the posthumous publication of the *Lectures*, Arnold, with all his merits, has been comparatively little read, at least for the First Decade, though his eleventh chapter on the Aequi and the Volsci should still be referred to.' Despite his reference to Jowett's hated Volscian Wars, Burrows invokes a larger historical view, describing

what is rightly called the philosophical study of history—the attempt to obtain general views, to analyse the spirit which lies beneath facts, to connect together

---

[83] Bill, *University Reform*, ch. 10.
[84] *Calendar* 1852, 128.
[85] Montagu Burrows, *Pass and Class* (1861), 112–13.

widely separated periods, and to discover the general laws under which the Supreme Governor of mankind, without for a moment resigning His special providence, has yet allowed His creatures to carry on their social existence. But on the other hand, it must not be supposed that any amount of this generalising process can make up for ignorance of facts....It is needless to say that this sort of pseudo-philosophy finds very little favour with Oxford Examiners.[86]

Ancient history has indeed a special relevance for Englishmen, for we owe to the Greeks 'our intellectual education, our philosophy, our history, our oratory and our art', to the Romans 'the practical lessons of administration':

In the present day, few countries can be said to be in a position to make a better use of both teachers than our own. The intellectual is, doubtless, making itself more and more felt in the midst of the practical, but we shall search the records of the gifted Greeks in vain for any parallel to our national history like that supplied by Rome in the slow and gradual development of her political constitution, step by step, along with the elevation of her people in the social scale, and still more the growth of her undying jurisprudence, which, based like our own on custom rather than statutes, commanded popular respect and influenced national character to a degree which has never been witnessed elsewhere.[87]

'In theory the candidate has the option of the authors which he proffers for examination; in practice the authors proffered are generally identical': these are the words of another more pedestrian handbook of the period, that of Thorold Rogers, *Education in Oxford, its Methods, its Aids and its Rewards* (1861). In fact all the handbooks give the same list, which was to some extent dictated by the fixed translation papers in the examination. Finally in 1862 the books recommended for study were formally listed in the *Calendar* for the first time: 'Of *Aristotle*, the Rhetoric, Ethics, Politics. Of *Plato*, the Republic. *Herodotus, Thucydides*. Of *Livy*, ten Books. Of *Tacitus*, the first six Books of the Annals, the Histories. *Bacon's* Novum Organon, *Butler's* Sermons, or Analogy.'[88]

In 1872 the decisive step was taken of specifying periods of ancient history (with a choice of two Greek and two Roman) 'to be studied as far as possible in the original authors'; and the lists of associated set texts were formalized.[89] One sign of the times is that the early decades of Livy were finally dropped, and Polybius entered; doubtless under the influence of Mommsen's *History of Rome*, Roman history now began with the Punic Wars, and the grand speculations of Niebuhr on early Rome were forgotten. The aged Warde Fowler remembered the change in his memoirs:

[86] Montagu Burrows, *Pass and Class* (1861), 109–10.
[87] Ibid. 114–16.
[88] *Calendar* 1862, 140 n.
[89] *New Examination Statutes* (1872), 29–30: 'In Greek History—(1) To the end of the Peloponnesian War. (2) From B.C. 500 to the death of Philip'; 'In Roman History—(1) From the beginning of the First Punic War to the Battle of Actium. (2) From the end of the Third Punic War to the accession of Vespasian'.

On my return to Oxford I found Roman History wanted for both lectures and tuition. There had been a change in the books taken up by statute, and among the new ones was Polybius, to whom I now began to devote myself with ardour, and to write a commentary upon some of his books. The same changes introduced me to Plutarch's *Lives* and the letters of Cicero; I have recently returned to the first decade of Livy with great pleasure and interest, but at that time no doubt it was good to travel over rather wider ground.[90]

Thus the concept of subjects or periods was established, but firmly kept in check by the existence of set books; these same periods and texts remained virtually unchanged for well over a century until the reforms of 1995, with the single addition in 1903 of a third imperial period of Roman history.[91]

After 1850 classical literature was effectively excluded from Greats; indeed ancient history began to invade honour Moderations: 'The subject of Ancient History is much too great a one to be pushed off to the last part of the University course, and this no doubt is the reason why [historical] authors have been inserted in the prescribed list.'[92] There were many protests: of the criticisms of Greats in 1887, 'Even more bitter is the complaint of the Philologists; they say with reason that in a school which calls itself the Final Classical School, the least important place is taken by the knowledge of Latin and Greek.'[93] The official *Student's Handbook* for 1907–8 does indeed still give literature a separate heading with history and philosophy, but then reveals that the main requirement is no more than translation from the texts set under the other two heads. The examination is also stated to include simple language papers (unseens and voluntary proses) set under the rubric 'Scholarship' (pp. 154, 157). Thus the gap between the Cambridge philological study of literary texts and the Oxford attention to historical antiquities, which was noted already in the 1820s, had continued to widen, producing from 1850 a wholly different type of education, in which texts were studied for their content and in context—'still there is some weight in the objection that at Cambridge it may happen…that a man learns two languages of which he never in his life learns the use'.[94] As the *University Calendar* of 1874 put it in a formulation which still survives for ancient history in the *Examination Decrees*: 'Candidates must show such knowledge of Classical Geography and Antiquities and of the General History of Greece and Rome, as well as of the History of Philosophy, or of the History of the period of Philosophy to which the philosophical authors offered by them belong, as shall be necessary for the profitable study of the authors or periods which they take up.'[95]

[90] Warde Fowler, *Reminiscences* (1921), 43.
[91] See Pt 2, Ch. 13.
[92] Burrows, *Pass and Class*, 66.
[93] J. Wells in A. M. M. Stedman, *Oxford: its life and schools* (1887), 263.
[94] [J. Pycroft], *The Collegian's Guide* (1845), 32.
[95] *Calendar* 1874, 83 n. y.

Ancient history in the Oxford of this period slowly began to be dominated by college tutors. It was another generation before the Camden Professor played any serious part in the teaching activities of the University. When Cardwell's long tenure ended with his death in 1861, George Rawlinson was appointed. Rawlinson had been a founding member of the Tutors' Association, which was formed as a result of the Royal Commission of 1850;[96] in 1859 his Bampton Lectures had attempted to demolish the new biblical criticism on historical grounds: he was clearly a safe candidate. He became a prolific author, with the great good fortune of having as his brother the famous Assyriologist, diplomat and soldier Sir Henry Rawlinson, who had transcribed and deciphered the great Behistun Inscription of Darius (1846). George had already published (1858–61, 3rd rev. edn 1875) a briefly annotated translation of Herodotus in four large volumes, whose chief interest is its many supplementary essays on oriental history by his brother and Sir John Gardner Wilkinson, the explorer of Egypt. This was highly regarded in Oxford and recommended by Burrows.

George Rawlinson subsequently wrote four volumes entitled *The Five Great Monarchies of the Ancient Eastern World* (1862–7) and further volumes on Parthia, the Sassanids and Phoenicia. These were successful works of popularization, but they represented the sum of his conception of the duties of the Camden chair. In his evidence to the Commission of 1877,[97] Rawlinson revealed that there had developed a complete rift between himself and the tutors, who tried to prevent pupils from attending his lectures. He even alleged that one tutor had attended his lectures with the specific intent of reproducing them in his college. He also complained that he had been asked to examine only once in sixteen years: 'At present the university provides the instruction, but it does not ask a single undergraduate ever to go near the professors, it makes no provision on the matter at all.'

The truth was somewhat different: Rawlinson had been a canon of Canterbury since 1872; and it is alleged that he would announce subjects unsuitable for undergraduate lectures, descend at the start of the term on Oxford and take a room in the King's Arms, from which he would ascertain that there were indeed no auditors for his first lecture in the Old Clarendon Building—whereupon he would depart for London until the start of the next term. In 1886 the question of the emoluments and duties of Oxford and Cambridge professors was raised in Parliament; Rawlinson gave the following evidence:

In the year 1885 the professor offered three courses of twelve lectures each, but no students sent in their names.

The holder of this office regards himself as required by his office to advance the study of Ancient History generally as much as to teach it in Oxford. He offers his

---

[96] Its members are listed in K. Lake, *Memorials of W. C. Lake, Dean of Durham, 1869–1894* (1901), 76–7.

[97] *UOC* (1877), 250–5, esp. answers 4094–96, 4105, 4111.

teaching but under present arrangements has no hearers. He therefore devotes himself to advancing the subject by books. There is no year since his appointment in which he has not been mainly employed in such work. He has published 19 volumes on Ancient History in the course of the last 25 years. His last work, published in 1885, was entitled *Egypt and Babylon from Sacred and Profane Sources.*[98]

When Rawlinson 'closed his undistinguished tenure of the Camden Professorship of Ancient History' in 1889,[99] 'the last Professor of the old regime'[100] had come to be hated with a venom that can be felt in all the memoirs of the period, and was capable of being recalled in 1945, over fifty years later.[101]

Despite the strictures of Mark Pattison, many of the ancient history tutors of this period were competent scholars, and the notion that Greats in the mid-century 'contained relatively little ancient history' is exaggerated; it derives from Joseph Wells's comparison with the later period of professionalism.[102] G. C. Brodrick came up to Balliol in 1850, when it 'was already, as it has ever since remained, the most eminent place of education in the University'; Oxford was 'becalmed, as it were, between two periods of stormy agitation'. His tutor in ancient history was W. C. Lake, who is briefly mentioned as 'a very clever man, with a knowledge of history then unusual'. That is not surprising, for Lake was from Arnold's Rugby; a boyhood friend of A. P. Stanley, he was an undergraduate at Balliol in 1834 and elected to a fellowship in 1838, the same year as Jowett; he records how with Jowett and Temple 'for several years we worked together in entire harmony, and with perhaps an almost exaggerated feeling that no work could be more important, both intellectually and morally, than that of our tutorships'—a picture somewhat belied by his nicknames of 'Serpent' and 'Puddle'.[103] Brodrick was clearly influenced by Lake, because in 1855 he won the Arnold Essay Prize with an essay entitled 'Roman *coloniae* under the Empire', and the Chancellor's English Essay Prize with an essay entitled 'Representative

[98] *Return of Certain Particulars with regard to the Universities of Oxford and Cambridge,* 23 (PP 1886 (214) li. 541).

[99] The description is that of Francis Haverfield, in *Essays by Henry Francis Pelham* (1911), p. xii.

[100] Jones, 'Camden chair', 189.

[101] G. B. Grundy, *Fifty-Five Years at Oxford* (1945), 103.

[102] Cf C. Schmidt on Hopkins in 1866: in J. Prest (ed.), *Balliol Studies* (1982), 166; see J. Wells in Stedman, *Oxford,* 247.

[103] In 1840 Lake won the university prize in Latin for an essay on the influence of the Roman army on liberty, but there are no scholarly publications. He slept through the death of Arnold (*Lake,* 34), and urged moderation in Tractarian disputes. As Senior Proctor in 1852–3 he was the leading architect of the new school of law and modern history; in 1856, 1858 and 1868 he served on Royal Commissions on Education. He left Oxford in 1858, and later as Dean of Durham was instrumental in saving the University of Durham and founding that of Newcastle: see his reminiscences, 'Rugby and Oxford: 1830–1850', 666–70; 'More Oxford memories', *Good Words* (1895), 828–32. Contrast the unfavourable picture of an arrogant pluralist in Tuckwell (1900), 206 ff.

government in ancient and modern times'. After election as a fellow of Merton, Brodrick left to pursue a career at the Bar.[104]

One of the last products of the old system had been Albert Watson, who took a first class from Wadham in 1851 and was tutor and lecturer at Brasenose from 1854 to 1873.[105] A shy and gentle bachelor in holy orders, he was a convinced liberal and a force in university politics; he represents the new style of permanent college tutor, whose scholarship matched his preoccupation with teaching. Watson's *Select Letters of Cicero* (1870) was a work of careful learning, and a household word for generations of undergraduates from the 1870s, when it replaced the first decade of Livy as a set text;[106] it went through various editions, and finally went out of print in 1915.

The combination of tutorial teaching with scholarship of a rather unadventurous but worthy type began to be typical of Oxford learning: this was of course what Jowett proclaimed and Mark Pattison deplored. The young Warde Fowler was one of the few people able to find pleasure in the company of the cantankerous Rector of Lincoln; but even his sweet nature had few illusions about the standard of lectures in the 1860s: 'It is difficult in these days to realise how utterly inadequate was the ordinary Oxford lecture in classics or ancient history...I remember when my late Headmaster, Bradley, came to Oxford as Master of University College, and was to lecture on Greek history, he asked me whether it would be sufficient to boil down Grote and Curtius!'[107]

There were, however, tutors who combined successfully the two aspects of teaching and scholarship. The most distinguished teacher of ancient history in the 1860s was W. L. Newman (1834–1923). A contemporary of W. W. Merry, Robinson Ellis and D. B. Monro, and a pupil and disciple of Jowett, he was appointed a fellow of Balliol while still an undergraduate in 1854. His lectures on ancient history, law and modern history from 1858 to 1870 were famous throughout the University; his auditors included the philosophers T. H. Green (who described him as 'the best lecturer I have ever heard'), Edward Caird and R. L. Nettleship; the historians J. L. Strachan-Davidson and Evelyn Abbott; and literary figures such as Andrew Lang and J. A. Symonds. He is said to have been equal in importance as a teacher with Jowett and T. H. Green. A weak voice, constant absences through ill health and a rapid delivery did not diminish the effect of his imaginative and wide-ranging command of ancient and modern examples. Lord Bryce wrote: 'His lectures were the first really thorough and philosophical treatment of ancient history Oxford had seen and marked an epoch. They made a great impression. His scholarship was admirable but in ancient

---

[104] G. C. Brodrick, *Memories and Impressions, 1831–1900* (1900), 74–8, 108.
[105] Albert Watson (1828–1904), matric. Wadham 1847, Principal of Brasenose 1886–9.
[106] J. Wells in Stedman, *Oxford*, 246.
[107] Fowler, *Reminiscences*, 29.

history he so overtopped his contemporaries that the linguistic side was less dwelt upon.' J. W. Mackail described him as 'the inspirer and very largely the originator of a new historical school in Oxford. His lectures kindled the interest and helped to shape the studies of Creighton, Dicey, and Pelham as well as those of many others of lesser eminence.'[108]

Newman was regarded as an important representative of the University by the Parliamentary Select Committee of 1867. His extensive evidence was highly critical of the present state of Oxford. In support of Jowett's scheme for broadening access,[109] he claimed that the University should be opened 'to the poor generally; and by the poor, I mean not the poor of one class, but the poor of all; the poor of the upper class, the poor of the upper middle class, and the poor of the lower middle class as well...An increase in the class of poor but able men would help to give a new tone to the place; the present undergraduates, I think, partake to some extent in the general increase of luxury in this country.' But he went further than his mentor: he condemned the new athleticism and the absence of connections with training for the professions; he advocated the abolition of religious tests, the provision of scholarships based on need, opening university prizes to other subjects than Latin and Greek, increasing the number of professors and the age of tutors, and paying for all this by abolishing sinecure fellowships and reducing the emoluments of heads of colleges. He deplored the absence of any teaching in archaeology, ancient art or numismatics. When asked 'why Oxford does so little for classical learning when compared with the universities of Germany', he replied:

I think the reason is, that there is no considerable class of learned men at Oxford who have thorough leisure for study. A great number of the tutors at Oxford are so constantly employed that it is out of their power, except during the vacations, to find much time for study...I could mention two or three books which have made quite a revolution in the education of Oxford, and if a learned class could be constituted at Oxford, such a class as the professoriate would supply, the result might very well be that works of a character which would give an enormous stimulus to Oxford education would appear, and that the University would advance at a tenfold rate, compared with what it does at present.

Asked to cite the books from outside Oxford which had been so influential inside it, Newman named Grote's *History of Greece*, 'Mr. Mill's books' and Mommsen's *History of Rome*.[110] This was a far cry from 1850:

> Not for them, whilst Warrens scribble, Staffords quibble, Walpoles quote
> On a Mill to squander honours, or to robe the fame of Grote.[111]

---

[108] J. W. Mackail, *James Leigh Strachan-Davidson* (1925), 27. For Lord Bryce see L. K. Hindmarsh, 'The benefactors of Balliol', BCA, Hindmarsh papers, M S, 1947.
[109] Abbott and Campbell, *Jowett* i. 367. For the Select Committee's proceedings see p. 727.
[110] SCOC (1867), 77–88.
[111] *A Song of the Encaenia*, 8.

But Newman's radical views were too far ahead of his contemporaries to have any influence on the future of the University;[112] his subsequent career is something of a mystery, and perhaps suggests that he had come to find the demands of education and scholarship too difficult to reconcile in contemporary Oxford. Although he was appointed University Reader in Ancient History in 1868, he retired in ill health to Cheltenham two years later, to live another fifty-three years. It was in retirement that he found time to write one of the few Oxford works of the nineteenth century which can indeed still stand comparison with anything produced by German historical scholarship—his great four-volume commentary on Aristotle's *Politics* (1887–1902).[113] The inspirer of a new school, had he remained in Oxford he might have been its leader; his departure left the way open for Henry Francis Pelham and the triumph of Roman history.

[112] They are, however, echoed by Thorold Rogers, *Education in Oxford* (1861), 67: 'Scholarship, philosophy, and history are borrowed from French and German authors. In scarce any of these has Oxford any native growth. Very little has been added to the general stock of human learning out of the vast endowments of University and collegiate income—endowments equalling the incomes of many States. The most notable among Oxford authors have hated and despised the place of their education, or at least regretted that so vast a power of stimulating causes should have eventuated in such scanty results. But with an active staff of public teachers, and a resolute determination, both within and without the walls of Oxford...'.

[113] W. L. Newman (1834–1923), matric. 1851. He retained his fellowship at Balliol, though refusing his stipend; at his death he had been a member of the college for seventy-two years, and was the last remaining life fellow.

16

Oxford's Scientific Awakening and the Role of Geology

N. A. RUPKE

During the nineteenth century the natural sciences were made a major and integral part of higher education in most European universities.[1] At Oxford, also, the idea of a university was extended to include the natural sciences. A monumental natural history museum and separate laboratory buildings were among the most discussed architectural additions to Victorian Oxford. The teaching of the natural sciences became an independent and respected profession, commonly connected to a well-defined research imperative. Financial support for this from the considerable endowments of the colleges and, much later, from the state, was called for by a growing number of specialized professionals who successfully used the presumed superiority of 'the German system' to argue for the reform of academic science in England. Although most of these developments occurred after 1850, they were the fruits of a natural sciences ideal that took root during the first half of the nineteenth century. In this chapter the growth of this ideal and the influences which shaped it are examined at three levels: first, at the international level of Romantic learning; second, at a national level of Whig reform; and third, at an intramural level of debates about the usefulness of the natural sciences as part of a liberal education.

During the period 1800–50 professors and readers gave classroom lectures on scientific subjects, but these subjects did not enter into the examinations, although candidates could choose to offer experimental philosophy and astronomy. Thus Oxford's formal requirements contained hardly any science, and the little that there was centred on mathematics; i.e. the sort

[1] In this chapter the term 'natural sciences' refers to experimental philosophy (experimental physics), chemistry, botany, anatomy, mineralogy, geology and rural economy (agricultural science); it is distinguished from the 'physical sciences', which included natural philosophy (theoretical physics), geometry and astronomy. At Oxford, the physical sciences had been endowed as early as the second decade of the 17th century (Table 16.1); the progress of these studies to 1800 is described in *The Eighteenth Century*, ch. 24. See further F. S. Taylor, 'The teaching of science at Oxford in the nineteenth century', *Annals of Science* viii (1952), 82–112. For a comparison with Cambridge see H. W. Becher, 'Voluntary science in nineteenth century Cambridge University to the 1850s', *British Journal for the History of Science* xix (1986), 57–87.

of science that could be learned from books rather than from the experimental or observational study of nature. This conformed to a prevailing view of the aims of an Oxford education: that it should be based on textual study, not on practical study of the sort undertaken in the law courts, hospitals or museums of natural history. For professional training in law, medicine or the natural sciences, it was argued that the nation's capital was a much better-suited place. As the *Quarterly Review* commented, in a criticism of the recommendations of the 1850 Royal Commission, the road of the chemist, the mineralogist and the geologist was to the metropolis.[2]

This perception of the natural sciences as intrinsically metropolitan was to a large extent wishful thinking on the part of the traditionalists. For it was during this period of renovation in university studies, heralded by the new examination statutes and the introduction of fellowships by examination at Oriel, that scientific subjects requiring laboratories and museum collections were added to the teaching at Oxford: anatomy, chemistry, experimental philosophy, mineralogy, geology and rural economy, the chair of botany having been founded in the early eighteenth century (Table 16.1). New chairs and readerships in these subjects belonged to the first two decades of the

TABLE 16.1

SCIENCE-RELATED UNIVERSITY POSITIONS AND THEIR
INCUMBENTS, 1800–1850

position	year founded	incumbent	year appointed	degree
Regius Professor of Medicine	1535	Christopher Pegge	1801	DM
		John Kidd	1822	DM
Sedleian Professor of Natural Philosophy	1611	Thomas Hornsby	1782	DD
		George Leigh Cooke	1810	BD
Savilian Professor of Geometry	1619	Abram Robertson	1797	DD
		Stephen Peter Rigaud	1810	MA
		Baden Powell	1827	MA
Savilian Professor of Astronomy	1619	Thomas Hornsby	1762	DD
		Abram Robertson	1810	DD
		Stephen Peter Rigaud	1827	MA
		G. H. S. Johnson	1839	MA
Tomlin's Praelector of Anatomy	1626	Regius Professor of Medicine		
Keeper of the Ashmolean Museum	1683	William Lloyd	1796	BCL
		Thomas Dunbar	1815	MA
		William Thomas Philipps	1822	BD
		John Shute Duncan	1823	DCL
		Philip Bury Duncan	1826	MA

[2] J. B. Mozley, 'The Oxford Commission', *Quarterly* xciii (June 1853), 168.

position	year founded	incumbent	year appointed	degree
Radcliffe's Librarian	1718	Thomas Hornsby	1783	DD
		George Williams	1810	DM
		John Kidd	1834	DM
Radcliffe's Observer	1718	Thomas Hornsby	1772	DD
		Abram Robertson	1819	DD
		Stephen Peter Rigaud	1827	MA
		Manuel John Johnson	1839	MA
Sherardian Professor of Botany	1728	George Williams	1796	DM
		Charles G. B. Daubeny	1834	DM
Lichfield Professor of Clinical Medicine	1772	Martin Wall	1785	DM
		Robert Bourne	1824	DM
		James Adey Ogle	1830	DM
Sibthorpian Professor of Rural Economy	1796	Charles G. B. Daubeny	1840	DM
Aldrichian Professor of the Practice of Medicine	1803	Robert Bourne	1803	DM
		James Adey Ogle	1824	DM
Aldrichian Professor of Anatomy	1803	Christopher Pegge	1803	DM
		John Kidd	1822	DM
Aldrichian Professor of Chemistry	1803	John Kidd	1803	DM
		Charles G. B. Daubeny	1822	DM
Reader in Experimental Philosophy	1810	Stephen Peter Rigaud	1810	MA
		Robert Walker	1839	MA
Reader in Mineralogy	1813	William Buckland	1813	DD
Reader in Geology	1818	William Buckland	1818	DD

Note: Although provisions for the Sibthorpian chair of Rural Economy were made in 1796, no professor was appointed until 1840. In the intervening years, the proceeds of John Sibthorp's estate, in accordance with his will, were used to publish his ten-volume *Flora graeca*.

Sources: *DNB* and *Calendar, 1850. Corrected to December 31, 1849.*

nineteenth century.[3] The institutionalization of the natural sciences during this period took the form of new positions and lecture courses, and some limited extensions to existing buildings, but not yet of formal degree requirements.

In 1806 shortage of space was already said to be hindering the display of apparatus for demonstrations in experimental philosophy.[4] By 1817 encroachments on the space available for the chemistry laboratory and lecture-room in the basement of the Ashmolean gave concern that there was insufficient space for the professor's 'processes and experiments'. Two former readers of chemistry, Martin Wall and Robert Bourne, wrote to the

---

[3] In the case of the readership of experimental philosophy, the small endowment bequeathed by Lord Crewe, which established the post in 1749, was substantially increased in 1810.
[4] HBM 8 Mar. 1806.

Vice-Chancellor making the case for the entire area to be assigned to chemistry. With anything smaller 'Oxford would not support a decent exterior in the eye of the world.'[5] The Hebdomadal Board agreed, and the area was given over. John Kidd's successor, Charles Daubeny, was voted £200 by Convocation in 1823 to make further purchases of apparatus.[6]

Some of the new positions were for the first time paid for or supplemented from public funds, voted by Parliament.[7] The sums involved added up to very little; the total public expenditure for scientific lectures amounted to no more than £400 in 1830 and to a mere £582 even in 1850 (£100 each for mineralogy, geology, experimental philosophy and chemistry, and later a further £182 for botany).[8] Professorial salaries were correspondingly low. In order to make a living, individuals were often obliged to hold positions in combination. Kidd, for example, combined the Regius professorship of Medicine, Tomlin's praelectorship in Anatomy, the Aldrichian professorship of Anatomy, and the mastership of Ewelme Almshouse. This netted him a yearly total of merely £466 18s 10d (after tax).[9] Other professors earned even less. Buckland, on the other hand, was well off; although each of his readerships gave him only £100, he enjoyed a substantial income from 1825 as a canon of Christ Church, and an extra £300 from the living of Stoke Charity in Hampshire. Not many scientists received such ecclesiastical patronage; MDs were more common among them than DDs.

Salaries were supplemented by lecture fees. Buckland charged £2 2s for first attendance at his customary full course of sixteen lectures (or half this sum in the event of a short course of eight lectures), and an additional £1 1s for attendance during a second or a third year. Such sums were fairly substantial, and because the natural sciences were not part of the formal degree requirements, lecture attendances during the first half of the nineteenth century were a good measure of the popularity of the subject and of the lecturer. By far the best-attended courses were Buckland's; he taught a yearly course in mineralogy (1814–49) and another in geology (1819–49), of which a complete attendance register has been preserved (Fig. 16.1). The overall trend shows that the initial popularity of his subjects was considerable; up to and including 1830, numbers averaged some thirty-four for mineralogy and sixty-one for geology, from a total population which averaged slightly over 400 new, matriculated students per year. During the early

[5] HBM 5 June 1817.
[6] R. T. Gunther, *Early Science in Oxford* (14 vols 1923–45) i. 74.
[7] Ch 1 nn. 59, 385.
[8] *Estimates of the Sum Wanted to pay the Salaries or Allowances Granted to Certain Professors in the Universities of Oxford and Cambridge* (PP 1830 xviii. 471; PP 1850 xxxiv. 393).
[9] *RCO* (1850), evidence, 256.

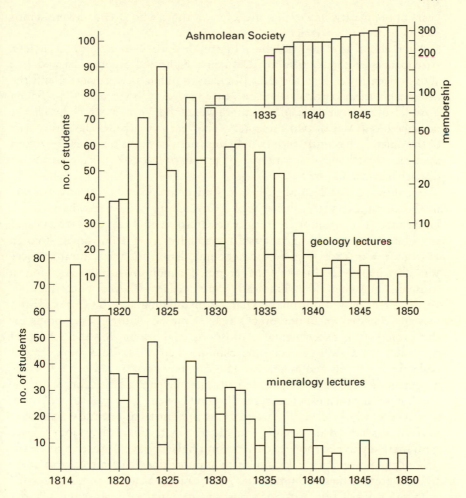

FIGURE 16.1 Ashmolean Society membership and attendance at Oxford's most popular science courses of the early nineteenth century, namely William Buckland's lectures in mineralogy (1814–1849) and geology (1819–1849). When no attendance is indicated, no course was announced owing to foreign travel or indisposition.

As a rule, two courses were offered annually, one in mineralogy and one in geology, starting in Feb. and in Apr. or May respectively. A substantial number of students who attended the lectures in mineralogy also signed up for those in geology. In the autumn of some years extra courses were given, starting in Oct. or Nov. The attendances at these second courses (mineralogy 1825: 28, 1847: 5; geology 1837: 29, 1843: 8, 1844: 7, 1846: 7, 1847: 4) have not been plotted in order to preserve the comparability of the graph's columns. *Source*: List of students attending lectures in geology and mineralogy, 1814–1849, Oxford University Museum, Buckland papers. Also plotted is the annual number of officers and ordinary members belonging to the Ashmolean Society (note the logarithmic scale). Honorary members (climbing from 3 in 1830 to 21 in 1849) have not been included because they were not members of the University. No data are available for the years 1828–9 and 1831–4. *Source*: Lists of members of the Ashmolean Society, Oxford University Museum

years of popularity, however, quite a few of those who attended were senior members of the University.[10]

After about 1830 the numbers began to decline to half or even less. Attendances at the lectures by Daubeny, Kidd and Stephen Rigaud had always been lower than those at Buckland's public performances, and the decline hit them particularly hard. In 1833, 1835, 1837 and 1839 Baden Powell had no students at all, and there were other years in which his classes numbered only one or two students.[11] The year 1830 divides the earlier part of the nineteenth century into two distinct periods in the fortunes of Oxford science: a first honeymoon period of popularity, followed by a period of disenchantment and strife.

In contrast to the declining trend in student attendances, a steady increase in the commitment to science took place among senior members of the University. The Ashmolean Society, established in 1828 for graduates of the University, saw its membership gradually grow, from ninety-two in 1830 to 333 in 1850 (Fig. 16.1). Accommodation for the natural sciences was also improved. In 1832 the cramped conditions of the Ashmolean Museum (now the Old Ashmolean) were partially relieved when the University Press moved out of the Clarendon Building and the empty edifice was appropriated to, among other things, a public lecture-room, rooms for the professor of experimental philosophy and rooms for the reader of mineralogy and geology, including exhibition space for Buckland's famous collection of fossils and minerals. Daubeny, however, stayed behind, in the basement of the Ashmolean, until in 1848 he moved to a laboratory which he had built at his own expense in the Physic Garden.[12]

It is a widely held belief that early in the nineteenth century science at Oxford was a decidedly second-rate affair. Few historians have joined issue with Merz on his assertion that science in England was cultivated outside the pale of the universities.[13] Examples to support this belief are easy to come by; the great names of human and comparative anatomy were associated with the Royal College of Surgeons and its Hunterian Museum (Charles

---

[10] 'List of students attending lectures in geology and mineralogy, 1814–1849', Oxford University Museum, Buckland papers. See also J. M. Edmonds, 'The founding of the Oxford readership in geology, 1818', *Notes and Records of the Royal Society of London* xxxiv (1979), 33–51; J. M. Edmonds and J. A. Douglas, 'William Buckland, F.R.S. (1784–1856) and an Oxford geological lecture, 1823', *Notes and Records of the Royal Society of London* xxx (1976), 141–67. See also Ch. 1 n. 77.

[11] C. G. B. Daubeny, 'To the members of Convocation', 24 Feb. 1839, 11 Mar. 1839, Bodl. G. A. Oxon. c. 55 (31, 42); Daubeny, *Brief Remarks on the Correlation of the Natural Sciences* (1848), 20–2; *RCO* (1850), evidence, 258.

[12] R. T. Gunther, *The History of the Daubeny Laboratory* (1904); A. V. Simcock, *The Ashmolean Museum and Oxford Science, 1683–1983* (1984), 9–10; K. J. Laidler, 'Chemical kinetics and the Oxford college laboratories', *Archive for History of Exact Sciences* xxxviii (1988), 197–283.

[13] J. T. Merz, *A History of European Thought in the Nineteenth Century* (Edinburgh 1896) i ch. 3. See also, from among many more recent examples, C. A. Russell, *Science and Social Change, 1700–1900* (1983), where any discussion of Oxbridge science is omitted.

Bell, Richard Owen); the famous chemists of the period lectured at the Royal Institution (Humphry Davy, Michael Faraday); John Dalton worked in Manchester and William Herschel in Slough. Upon the death of Rigaud, in 1839, Buckland tried to attract John Herschel to Oxford's Savilian chair of Astronomy, but without success.[14]

It is certainly true that among the teachers of what Tuckwell in his *Reminiscences of Oxford* called 'prescientific science' there were several complete nonentities. Nevertheless, five of Oxford's early nineteenth-century scientists rate an entry in the *Dictionary of Scientific Biography*, namely Thomas Hornsby, John Kidd, William Buckland, Charles Giles Bridle Daubeny and Baden Powell. Admittedly, apart from Buckland, their contributions were more to the institutionalization of science than to scientific progress in a cognitive sense. Hornsby's main accomplishment was the foundation of the Radcliffe Observatory. Although Kidd wrote on a variety of scientific subjects, his influence was strongest in the field of science education, and the same has to be said of Daubeny. Powell did some meritorious work on radiant heat and light, but his more lasting contribution was to the debate about the place of science in the University and the relation of science to theology. Although not listed in the *Dictionary of Scientific Biography*, Christopher Pegge, Rigaud and Robert Walker[15] also should be acknowledged for their attempts, by lecture courses, to cultivate a taste for their subjects at Oxford.[16]

In Buckland, however, Oxford had a scientist of the first order. Not only was his skill as a lecturer unrivalled, but his many contributions to the novel subject of geology were second to none. Buckland was a colourful figure whose lecturing antics and idiosyncratic behaviour led to a large number of 'Buckland anecdotes', which have tended to obscure his real scientific significance. Furthermore, he has been too readily dismissed as an obscurantist clergyman-naturalist on account of his well-known advocacy of diluvialism. However, one only has to read further than the title of Buckland's *Reliquiae diluvianae* to discover that his best-known diluvial work was in fact one of the most original treatises of vertebrate palaeontology of the period.[17]

---

[14] William Buckland to J. F. W. Herschel, 20 Mar. 1839, Royal Society library, Herschel letters iv no. 324.

[15] For an assessment of Walker's work see the notice on him by A. V. Simcock in *DNB: Missing Persons*.

[16] D. Oldroyd and D. W. Hutchings, 'The chemical lectures at Oxford (1822–1854) of Charles Daubeny, M.D., F.R.S.', *Notes and Records of the Royal Society of London* xxxiii (1979), 217–59; see also A. P. Willsher, 'Daubeny and the development of the chemistry school in Oxford, 1822–1867' (Oxford BA thesis 1961); N. Miller, 'The development of the Oxford chemistry school, 1800–1850, with particular reference to the works of John Kidd and Charles Daubeny' (Oxford BA thesis 1986). P. Corsi, *Science and Religion: Baden Powell and the Anglican debate, 1800–1860* (1988).

[17] Buckland's geological work is discussed in N. A. Rupke, *The Great Chain of History: William Buckland and the English school of geology, 1814–1849* (1983).

Buckland was one of the founding fathers of historical geology who made original and lasting contributions to the study of fossils. The most sensational of these was his hyena den theory, for which he was awarded the Royal Society's Copley Medal. Caves had been extensively explored since the 1780s and had yielded the remnants of a variety of extinct Pleistocene mammals. In 1821 a hitherto unknown cave was broken open in the Oolitic limestone of Kirkdale in Yorkshire. Inside, a large assemblage of teeth and bones was discovered, and Buckland established that these belonged to a non-symbiotic mixture of carnivorous and herbivorous animals which included extinct species of hyena, elephant, rhinoceros and hippopotamus. Such a mixture, many people believed, indicated that the animals had attempted to seek refuge in Kirkdale Cave from a cataclysmal inundation, or that their drowned carcasses had been swept into the cavern, and that this inundation provided geological evidence for Noah's deluge. Buckland disagreed and argued instead that Kirkdale Cave had been the den of antediluvian hyenas whose dietary habits had produced the seemingly haphazard assemblage of fossil remains. Among the conclusive facts in support of this theory was the observation that most of the fossil bones had been broken and gnawed, and that in some instances tooth-marks were still present. As further proof Buckland fed the shin bone of an ox to a living hyena in order to observe the beast gnaw it, and the broken fragments of this bone proved identical to those from Kirkdale Cave. This did not mean that Buckland rejected the deluge altogether; on the contrary. Up to about 1830 he enthusiastically promoted a form of diluvial geology, in which he attributed to the deluge such phenomena as the extinction of the cave hyenas, the emplacement of what later became known as glacial detritus and the origin of certain valleys.

Among Buckland's other palaeontological contributions was his description of the megalosaurus, the first dinosaur of the geological literature. His interest, however, was not so much in taxonomy, but in ecology, in the question of how prehistoric hyenas or saurians had lived. An ingenious instance of Buckland's ecological predilection was his study of coprolites. These occur in large numbers in Lyme Regis where they were known as bezoar stones, but their precise nature and origin had long eluded naturalists. Buckland managed to prove that the stones were the fossil excrement of ichthyosauri. One of the observations on which he based this coprolitic theory was that the stones were arranged in a spiral whorl and in some instances bore surface impressions of a vascular texture. Buckland managed to reproduce the internal and external features by injecting the intestines of dogfish with cement. Having thus established the origin of the coprolites, he was able to deduce from their composition what ichthyosauri had eaten.

Of the strength of Buckland's ecclesiastical connections and preoccupations there can be no doubt. Buckland descended from a family of Anglican clergymen; he himself was ordained and held a DD; he became a canon of Christ Church (1825) and later Dean of Westminster (1845). His two principal books, *Reliquiae diluvianae* (1823) and his Bridgewater Treatise, *Geology and Mineralogy Considered with Reference to Natural Theology* (1836), both had explicitly religious purposes. They were, none the less, important scientific works. Buckland's use of the biblical deluge provided, throughout the 1820s, a diluvial paradigm which stimulated cave research and the study of what we now call Pleistocene geology. When by the late 1820s and early 1830s it became apparent that the deluge was an inadequate explanation of the 'diluvial' gravel, boulder clay, erratics, etc., Buckland abandoned the diluvial theory and became the first and most fervent advocate in Britain of the idea of glaciation, developed in Switzerland by Louis Agassiz.

Equally, Buckland's Bridgewater Treatise was an authoritative textbook of historical geology. Its use of the design argument lifted the description of fossils beyond common taxonomy to the level of functional anatomy. A famous example was Buckland's interpretation of the megatherium, the extinct giant ground sloth of the South American pampas. The grotesque look of its colossal skeleton had led some naturalists to conclude that it represented a monstrosity, one of nature's failures. The notion of divine design, however, did not allow for ill-designed mistakes, and Buckland skilfully deduced from its feet and teeth the environmental conditions under which the giant sloth had lived.

Buckland's genial temperament was ill-suited to the administrative agitation for educational reform, something he left to Daubeny, Powell and later also to Henry Acland. By contrast, his infectious enthusiasm for geology made him the centre of a circle of geological devotees, at Oxford and in England at large, some of whom eulogized him as the country's answer to France's Cuvier and Germany's Alexander von Humboldt. His colleagues, pupils and protégés included W. J. Broderip, the brothers J. J. and W. D. Conybeare, the brothers J. S. and P. B. Duncan, Charles Lyell, John Ruskin, Hugh Strickland, Roderick Murchison and Adam Sedgwick.

These signs of scientific awakening at Oxford need to be seen as part of a pan-European phenomenon encouraged by the place these sciences occupied in the Romanticism of the period 1780–1830. Its champions rejected the rationalism of the French *savants* and the authority of the *Encyclopédie*. The pendulum now swung away from the religious scepticism of the *philosophes* towards an interest in things metaphysical; there was a resulting emphasis on feeling and intuition, and on the grandeur of nature's primeval forces. This anti-rationalistic *Weltbild* included a keener appreciation of history, whose scope was widened by a more sympathetic investigation of those past ages which the Enlightenment had treated as barbaric. In the new trend towards organicism human civilization was examined in relation to its natural environment, and the successive periods of its history were studied as part of a connected development. Herder, in his influential *Ideen zur Philosophie der Geschichte der Menschheit* (1784–91), traced the development of human life in its close relationship to the natural world, the first volume discussing the earth as a planet, as a theatre of geological upheaval and change, with an atmosphere, oceans and continents fit to support plant and animal life and eventually man.

Geology, the scientific study of rocks and fossils, was the Romantic science *par excellence.*[18] During the heyday of Romanticism geological study went through an exceptionally formative and popular phase. It was intrinsically in tune with the Romantic appreciation of history in that it was primarily concerned with palaeontology and stratigraphy, i.e. with historical geology. Around the turn of the century the notion of extinction became firmly established through Blumenbach's work in Germany, Cuvier's in France and James Parkinson's, for example, in England. Cuvier probably was the greatest scientist of the Romantic period, although Alexander von Humboldt was the greater Romantic. Humboldt's travel accounts fed the Romantic taste for nature's grandeur, for towering mountains, vast coastal stretches, deep mines, catastrophic volcanic eruptions, mysterious caves and gigantic fossils. The cave bear, the mammoth and other extinct mammals became popular images. That several of these species from 'a former world' proved to be much larger than their living relatives fuelled the notion of degenerative change in the course of the earth's history.

This developmental view was portrayed in fairly orthodox biblical colours by several writers who viewed the course of history as an eschatological process having its beginning in a golden age, a paradise, a state of purity, continuing along a line of degenerative change and ending in an apocalyptic conflagration foreshadowed by the deluge. This apocalyptic view of history went hand in hand with an enthusiastic acceptance of the reality of meteorite showers, which had been decried by the *philosophes* as based on popular superstition.[19] Deluc and many others speculated that a comet might have been the cause of the deluge.

Cave palaeontology was a particular craze of the Romantic period. Caves evoked the imagery of portals to the past, so effectively used by Novalis in his *Heinrich von Ofterdingen* (1802). Buckland's cave researches of the 1820s were the culmination of this Europe-wide Romantic preoccupation. Comparative anatomy itself, on which the success of palaeontological reconstructions rested, was first taught as a course of higher education by the Romantics, and its popularity was part of the Romantic fascination with

---

[18] N. A. Rupke, 'The study of fossils in the Romantic philosophy of history and nature', *History of Science* xxi (1983), 389–413. For a dissenting view, see M. Shortland, 'Darkness visible: underground culture in the golden age of geology', *History of Science* xxxii (1994), 1–60.

[19] N. A. Rupke, 'The apocalyptic denominator in English culture of the early nineteenth century' in M. Pollock (ed.), *Common Denominators in Art and Science* (Aberdeen 1983), 30–41.

correspondences. Equally typical of the period was the close connection between Romantic science and the fine arts. Examples are to be found in the work of Goethe and Coleridge, Caspar David Friedrich and John Constable, and in that of a host of others such as Humphry Davy, John Martin and Willem Bilderdijk,[20] whose *Destruction of the First World* (written 1809) was his most celebrated literary work. Together with Byron's *Heaven and Earth* (1823), it demonstrates the substantive part which apocalyptic, 'diluvial drama' played in the Romantic period.[21]

At Oxford the attention which was given to geology was not just the result of the presence of Buckland, of his talent as a lecturer or the quality of his researches. Among Buckland's teachers, Pegge had applied his anatomical skills to the study of fossils. Kidd expanded his chemistry lectures to include mineralogy, and his earliest publications as Aldrichian Professor of Chemistry were the *Outlines of Mineralogy* (1809) and his *Geological Essay on the Imperfect Evidence in Support of a Theory of the Earth* (1815), the latter with a sketch of Wernerian stratigraphy. Daubeny succeeded him in the chair of chemistry. His most original book, also on a geological topic, was the *Description of Active and Extinct Volcanoes* (1826), in which he advocated Humphry Davy's chemical theory of volcanic action (later refuted by K. G. Bischof). Like Kidd, Daubeny was an enthusiastic follower of the diluvial fashion in geology, defending it in *The Diluvial Theory* (1831).[22] Other prominent Oxonians who developed an interest in the study of rocks and fossils included William Daniel Conybeare.[23] On marrying in 1814, he left Oxford but continued to publish on palaeontology, stratigraphy and the diluvial debate. One of Conybeare's lasting scientific contributions was his reconstruction of the plesiosaurus.

Geology found adherents among three successive holders of the modern history chair at Oxford, underlining its interest as a form of history. Henry Beeke (professor from 1801 till 1813), later Dean of Bristol, enthusiastically contributed to the study of Kent's Hole, one of Buckland's hyena dens. He was succeeded by Edward Nares, who occupied the chair for a record twenty-eight years (1813–41). In his Bampton Lectures of 1805 Nares had combined an attack on 'the pretended Age of Reason' with a defence of Deluc; and he again showed his interest in geology with a treatise entitled *Man, as Known to us Theologically and Geologically* (1834). Thomas Arnold, whose tenure as Regius Professor of Modern History was tragically short (1841–2), had been well known for his familiarity with geological matters since his younger days at Oriel, when he, along with several other

[20] A. Cunningham and N. Jardine (eds), *Romanticism and the Sciences* (1990).
[21] N. A. Rupke, 'Romanticism in the Netherlands' in R. S. Porter and M. Teich (eds), *Romanticism in National Context* (1988), 191–216.
[22] Rupke, *Great Chain of History*, ch. 5.
[23] See p. 17 above.

Oriel fellows, had attended Buckland's lectures.[24] Another of the Oriel circle, Richard Whately, second holder of the Drummond professorship of Political Economy established in 1825, emphasized the consanguinity of his subject with geology.[25]

Even poetry reflected geological interests: in this respect also Oxford mirrored the wider world of Romantic culture. John Josias Conybeare, brother of William Daniel and Professor of Poetry (1812–21), was an active participant in the geological travels which Buckland conducted.[26] A later candidate for the professorship of poetry, Isaac Williams, had been awarded the Chancellor's Prize for Latin Verse with his *Ars geologica* (1823) during his student days at Trinity. Buckland's diluvial researches themselves became the subject of versification by Conybeare, Duncan and others, some of it representing jocular imitations of Byron. When in the 1820s Buckland was turned into something of a Byronic hero, a short diluvial play was written in which he and Noah were cast as the two principal characters.[27]

Thus the natural sciences were not developing at Oxford under a utilitarian guise: they were not pursued for economic or financial reasons or even for the purpose of professional training. Quite the contrary; it was the perception of geology as history (albeit history of an antediluvian world), as a branch of humanistic learning, which made it suitable as a fashionable branch of liberal education. Buckland explicitly stated in his inaugural lecture, *Vindiciae geologicae*, when explaining the utility of geology and why it should be given a place at Oxford, that it was 'founded upon other and nobler views than those of mere pecuniary profit and tangible advantage. The human mind has an appetite for truth of every kind, Physical as well as Moral; and the real utility of Science is to afford gratification to this appetite.'

Moreover, Buckland presented the new scientific subjects as complementary to Oxford's system of classical education. He respectfully referred to an 'ingrafting (if I may so call it) of the study of the new and curious sciences of Geology and Mineralogy, on that ancient and venerable stock of classical literature from which the English system has imparted to its followers a refinement of taste peculiarly their own'. In Buckland's opinion, the new sciences were in fact a necessary part of a proper liberal education and should be 'admitted to serve at least a subordinate ministry in the temple of our Academical Institutions'.[28]

[24] 'List of students attending lectures in geology and mineralogy, 1814–1849', Oxford University Museum, Buckland papers.

[25] R. Whately, *Introductory Lectures on Political Economy* (1831), 30–1.

[26] J. J. Conybeare's geological water-colour landscapes were used by Buckland to illustrate his lectures and are preserved in the collection of Buckland's lecture diagrams in the Oxford University Museum.

[27] C. G. B. Daubeny, *Fugitive Poems Connected with Natural History and Physical Science* (1869); Rupke, *Great Chain of History*, ch. 6.

[28] W. Buckland, *Vindiciae geologicae; or, the connexion of geology with religion explained* (1820), 2–5.

Romanticism was anything but homogeneous; as a cultural movement it is far less easy to define than, for example, the Enlightenment, and one might want to list 'pluralism' as one of its characteristic features. There existed a clear difference between the manifestation of Romantic science in Germany, where the predominantly secular metaphysics of *Naturphilosophie* flourished, and England, where Baconian empiricism was the naturalist's epistemological credo helping to keep too much continental free-thinking at bay. Moreover, Romantic science was more explicitly biblical at Oxford than at the continental institutions of higher education, because of Oxford's distinctive role as a nursery of the Anglican clergy. In order to make geology as relevant as possible to the educational purposes of the University, and thus to justify the establishment of the new readerships in mineralogy and geology, Buckland and his colleagues made an effort to link the study of rocks and fossils to the 'deluge' and the 'creation', i.e. to those events of revealed religion on which geological research could shed the light of natural theology.

Within the British scene, it is noteworthy that geology helped to strengthen Oxford's defences against the early attacks of the *Edinburgh Review*. Kidd had added his voice to the debate with his *Answer to a Charge against the English Universities* (1818) in which he upheld the adequacy of the chemistry instruction. The Edinburgh imputation of Oxford's supposed backwardness in scientific matters could readily be dismissed once Buckland's *Reliquiae diluvianae* had made Oxford's geology internationally famous. Copleston was quick to seize the opportunity, and he wrote a glowing review of Buckland's masterpiece for the *Quarterly Review*, in which he contended that Buckland's lecturing success had been 'brilliant beyond example' and had 'infused an appetite for physical knowledge' at Oxford.[29] The debate about the relative merits of Edinburgh and Oxford became intertwined with the controversy over Oxford's diluvial geology. Diluvialism was attacked by John Playfair, Professor of Natural Philosophy at Edinburgh, one of Oxford's *Edinburgh Review* critics. An ageing representative of the Scottish Enlightenment, Playfair passionately defended a deistic system of geology in his *Illustrations of the Huttonian Theory of the Earth* (1802). The *Edinburgh Review* was rather fainter in its praise of Buckland's book than the *Quarterly*, especially with respect to the issue of the deluge, and the *Edinburgh Philosophical Journal* actually attacked 'The Geological Deluge, as interpreted by Baron Cuvier and Professor Buckland'.[30] The novelty and quality of Oxford geology was such, however, that it put

---

[29] [E. Copleston], 'Buckland: *Reliquiae diluvianae*', *Quarterly* xxix (Apr. 1823), 146.

[30] [W. H. Fitton], 'Geology of the deluge', *Edinburgh Review* xxxix (1823), 196–234; J. Fleming, 'The geological deluge, as interpreted by Baron Cuvier and Professor Buckland, inconsistent with the testimony of Moses and the phenomena of nature', *Edinburgh Philosophical Journal* xix (Apr. 1826), 205–39.

Edinburgh (still in the grip of the Hutton–Werner clash) in the shade, an advantage which defenders of the ancient universities did not fail to exploit.

William Conybeare, for example, argued in a somewhat convoluted manner that in the Oxford school of geology 'a striking and satisfactory proof has been afforded in opposition to the misrepresentations of shallow sciolists, that the institutions of academical education are far from unfavourable to the cultivation of the physical sciences, and that an ignorance of the rules of classical composition, and of the languages, and philosophy of polished antiquity, are by no means essential advantages in researches of this nature'.[31] Similarly, young Charles Lyell drew attention, in an essay for the *Quarterly Review* entitled 'The state of the universities', to the popularity of Buckland's lecture courses and those of his counterpart at Cambridge, Adam Sedgwick, who 'have continually attracted as many as the moderate dimensions of their class-rooms could contain'. In view of this, Lyell concluded: 'Our universities are called upon to make no daring inroads upon their ancient constitution—to submit to no sacrifice of existing interests.'[32] William Whewell used stronger language in *The British Critic*; referring to geology, he stated: 'And we do think it strange, that the Universities, which thus unquestionably have been and are the first and most zealous nurses of this youngest of the sciences, should be exposed to the trite and unmeaning charge of cherishing antiquated dogmas and neglecting the advances of modern discovery.'[33]

After 1830, however, Buckland's geology no longer represented such an obvious source of strength to many of Oxford's clerical defenders, and signs of a reaction against the growing influence of the natural sciences could increasingly be seen. Objections had always been raised to Buckland's *Reliquiae diluvianae* by those who adhered to a literal exegesis of Genesis. They immediately recognized that Buckland's diluvialism was only skin deep. Previous generations of scriptural naturalists had attributed the entire stratigraphic record of fossiliferous strata to Noah's deluge. Buckland's hyena den theory, which ascribed only patches of superficial gravel and boulder clay to a deluge, was no more than a shadow of the traditional, full-blooded diluvialism. The accumulation of the fossils was not attributed to any cataclysmal waters, but to the eating habits of many successive generations of hyenas. Furthermore, if the cave fossils had been emplaced before the deluge, even more so had the rock layers in which the caves themselves had been hollowed out, and, by obvious deduction, so too had the massively thick sequences of strata below the caves. The formation of all those rocks would have taken a very long stretch of geological time.

[31] W. D. Conybeare and W. Phillips, *Outlines of the Geology of England and Wales* (1822), p. xlviii.
[32] [C. Lyell], 'State of the universities', *Quarterly* xxxvi (June 1827), 263–4.
[33] [W. Whewell], 'Science of the English universities', *British Critic* ix (1831), 73–4.

Matters were made worse when Buckland failed to discover human fossils in his diluvial deposits, in spite of a protracted international search; even the 'Red Lady of Paviland' seemed to be of a post-diluvian date.[34] From this it followed that the geological deluge was not the same as the biblical deluge in which the antediluvian population had drowned, but had to have occurred before the creation of man. In other words, the historical deluge of Noah had left no geological traces. Even the notion of diluvial action before the creation of man was cast aside when Buckland adopted the glacial theory.

Outside Oxford several Evangelical voices were raised against these heterodox implications. They appeared to undermine the traditional belief not only in the geological importance of the biblical deluge, but also in sacred chronology which limited the age of the earth to some 6,000 years. Authors who commanded a national readership, such as George Penn and George Bugg, attacked Buckland for his heresies. A string of critical pamphlets followed, one of them written by William Cockburn, Dean of York. Not all of the leading divines, it must be emphasized, were on the side of the critics. Shute Barrington, Bishop of Durham, and J. B. Sumner, Bishop of Chester and later Archbishop of Canterbury, were among the supporters of Oxford geology. And although the Evangelical *Christian Observer* published attacks by Henry Cole and George Fairholme on the 'infidel geology', the editor himself, consorting with Conybeare, took up its defence.[35]

The anti-geological attack entered Oxford itself through Frederick Nolan, an Oxford graduate who enjoyed a considerable reputation as a traditionalist theologian. His book on the time of the millennium had just been published when he returned to the University to preach as the Bampton lecturer for 1833. Nolan chose as his title the *Analogy of Revelation and Science*, providing himself with an opportunity to castigate the new geology. Buckland kept a low profile, but both Daubeny and Powell jumped to the defence of science.[36] Daubeny focused on Nolan's lack of scientific expertise, whereas Powell emphasized that the Bible was intended for moral instruction, not for physical truth, which was derived from the study of nature. This distinction was finding broad acceptance among the Oxbridge scientists, and had been made before by Sedgwick in his anniversary address to the Geological Society in 1830. Buckland was not a controversialist and rarely entered the fray of hostile debate. In his Bridgewater Treatise he relegated his retraction of the geological importance of the biblical deluge to a footnote; but in a sermon preached in Christ Church early in 1839, *An Inquiry whether the*

[34] F. J. North, 'Paviland cave, the "Red Lady", the deluge, and William Buckland', *Annals of Science* v (1942), 91–128; Rupke, *Great Chain of History*, ch. 8.
[35] [S. C. Wilks], observation on 'A layman on scriptural geology', *Christian Observer* (1834), 479–96.
[36] C. G. B. Daubeny, 'Apology for British science', *London Literary Gazette* 7 Dec. 1833, 769–71, 789–92; Baden Powell, *Revelation and Science. With some additional remarks occasioned by the Bampton Lectures for 1833* (1833), 30–9.

Sentence of Death Pronounced at the Fall of Man Included the Whole Animal Creation, or was Restricted to the Human Race, he faced up to the heterodox inference which followed from the occurrence of pre-human ichthyosauri and similar extinct monsters, namely that violent death and carnivorous habits had existed before man's Fall, and thus could not have been the consequence of Adam's sin.

It is not surprising that Oxford's diluvialism was regarded by some with suspicion; but the origins of the distrust generated by the scientists' advocacy of natural theology are less clear. Scientific knowledge had often been legitimized among Oxford's clerical majority in the early nineteenth century by appeals to its value as a contribution if not to revealed religion, at least to natural religion. In a variety of inaugural or special lectures, the incumbents of scientific positions went out of their way to demonstrate that their particular subject was a proper branch of natural theology, a rich source of evidence of divine design in nature. Buckland maintained, in his inaugural lecture (1819), that 'Geology contributes proofs of Natural Theology in harmony with those derived from other branches of natural history.'[37] This was no empty rhetoric; as is shown above, Buckland's belief in the argument from design significantly influenced the content of his geological work.

Daubeny, in his *Inaugural Lecture on the Study of Chemistry* (1823), aligned himself with Buckland; and Kidd did the same, in *An Introductory Lecture to a Course in Comparative Anatomy, Illustrative of Paley's Natural Theology* (1824). In yet another inaugural lecture, *On the Study of Botany* (1834), Daubeny once more based the justification for giving his subject a place at Oxford on its contribution to a theological education; it afforded 'to the Divine some of the most beautiful illustrations with which nature can supply him'.[38] The new subject of political economy was promoted in the same way. In his *Introductory Lectures on Political Economy* (1831), Whately maintained that the economic working of human society provided the most striking examples of divine contrivance and was the best introduction to natural theology. In addition to delivering lectures of this kind, Buckland and Kidd each contributed a treatise to the eight Bridgewater Treatises, the voluminous culmination of England's natural-theology tradition.[39]

Although such justifications for the teaching of science continued to be made until well after 1850, they came under strong attack in the course of the 1830s from the Tractarians. In the early 1820s Keble, Newman and Pusey

[37] Buckland, *Vindiciae geologicae*, 18.

[38] C. G. B. Daubeny, *Inaugural Lecture on the Study of Chemistry* (1823), 40; Daubeny, *Inaugural Lecture on the Study of Botany* (1834), 27.

[39] William Buckland, *Geology and Mineralogy Considered with Reference to Natural Theology* (2 vols 1836); J. Kidd, *On the Adaptation of External Nature to the Physical Condition of Man: principally with reference to the supply of his wants and the exercise of his intellectual faculties* (1833).

had all attended Buckland's lectures, and had been warm supporters of the new geology. But a decade later they made a volte-face. By its self-presentation as natural theology, science was now thought to contribute to the Whig attack on Oxford. The only thing to which natural theology could lay claim was proof of the existence of a God and of his various attributes of power, wisdom and goodness (as the general title of the Bridgewater Treatises stated). It had nothing to say on points of doctrine. For this reason the *British Critic*, which had become a Tractarian organ, begged 'most strongly to protest against any more such evidences of religion' as the Bridgewater Treatises provided. Newman emphatically deprecated physical theology in his *Idea of a University*: 'It cannot tell us anything of Christianity at all.'[40]

Natural theology was quintessentially interdenominational in character, and the scientists were suspected of latitudinarian sympathies. This suspicion seemed to be confirmed when in 1832 Buckland invited to Oxford, and presided over, the first full meeting of the British Association for the Advancement of Science. The interdenominational nature of the event was underlined by the conferment of honorary degrees on four Nonconformist scientists, namely David Brewster, Robert Brown, John Dalton and Michael Faraday.[41] The liberal press welcomed this as a step in the direction of opening Oxford to Dissenters; but Newman and his friends were appalled. Many years later Thomas Mozley showed his resentment at Buckland's role in the BAAS event: 'Buckland was at Oxford the representative of science, and the *savants* of the University sheltered themselves under his great name. They certainly considered themselves at war, I will not say with faith, but with a large mass of secondary beliefs, and what is more, with a number of pious traditions, cherished the more fondly because appealing rather to loyalty than to faith.'[42] In the eyes of the Tractarians the scientists had not only compromised the Anglican integrity of Oxford when they hosted the BAAS: they compounded the latitudinarian implications of this when they sided with Renn Dickson Hampden in the controversy over lessening the importance attached to the Church's Thirty-nine Articles.

In the debate about educational reform the Tractarians firmly sided with those traditionalists who regarded science as inferior to classics as a means of cultivating the mind. The anti-scientific sentiment of the 1830s and 1840s was aggravated by the fact that the scientists, too, altered their position. Having earlier disavowed any attempt to associate the teaching of science with 'base' utilitarian applications (Buckland's refusal in 1823 to lecture at

[40] Newman, *Idea*, 365.
[41] J. Morrell and A. Thackray, *Gentlemen of Science: early years of the British Association for the Advancement of Science* (1981), 225–35.
[42] T. Mozley, *Letter to the Revd. Canon Bull* (1882), 20–1.

the Royal Institution has already been mentioned),[43] Oxford scientists in the 1830s became caught up in the enthusiasm for linking scientific education and research with agricultural and industrial progress. Comparisons were made with continental universities, especially the new German universities of Berlin and Bonn, where the professorial system flourished and where the scientists were not treated as second-class citizens. Cambridge forces joined the Edinburgh reform movement when Babbage, a Cambridge man, published a controversial jeremiad, *Reflections on the Decline of the State of Science in England* (1830), echoed the following year by Brewster in his *Edinburgh Journal of Science*, which criticized Oxbridge privilege and aristocratic and Tory dominance of the Royal Society.[44]

Both Buckland and Daubeny increasingly demonstrated an interest in 'public utility'. Buckland was chairman of the Oxford Gas and Coke Company. Daubeny, especially after his appointment to the chair of rural economy, promoted agricultural chemistry. Buckland lectured and wrote about agriculture, artesian wells and water supply, civil engineering, and kindred topics. *Punch* depicted him as 'Professor Buckwheat educing the agricultural mind'. Even his interest in coprolites took an economic turn when he drew attention to their use as fertilizers. Buckland's last contribution to the Ashmolean Society dealt with the potato disease. This utilitarian drift was well illustrated by the case of Hugh Edwin Strickland, the Deputy Reader of Geology during Buckland's terminal illness, who, in a lecture entitled 'On geology, in relation to the studies of the University of Oxford' (1850), not merely reiterated the old justifications for geology which Buckland had used in his inaugural address, but in addition emphasized 'the important relations in which geological science stands to the practical employments of life, which in the present state of our civilisation have become so widely multiplied'.[45]

This change in emphasis coincided with a growing movement to provide not merely a foothold, but a prominent and secure place for the natural sciences at Oxford. In the late 1810s Buckland had modestly referred to the 'subordinate ministry' of the sciences. Kidd, too, had asked for no more than an ancillary role for the physical and experimental sciences: 'These branches of science, in this place at least, may be considered with reference to Divinity, Classics, and Mathematics, in the same light as the supernumerary

[43] William Buckland to Robert Peel, 25 Apr. 1823, BL Add. MS 40355, fos 347–49; see p. 26. Neither Buckland nor Peel thought that the University's 'dignity' would be compromised; but Buckland had to take the views of colleagues into account.

[44] From the fairly extensive literature on 'declinism' see e.g. P. Alter, *Wissenschaft, Staat, Mäzene. Anfänge moderner Wissenschaftspolitik in Grossbritannien, 1850–1920* (Stuttgart 1982), ch. 2; M. Boas Hall, *All Scientists Now: the Royal Society in the nineteenth century* (1984); M. J. Nye, 'Scientific decline', *Isis* lxxv (1984), 697–708.

[45] H. E. Strickland, 'On geology, in relation to the studies of the University of Oxford' in W. Jardine, *Memoirs of Hugh Edwin Strickland* (1858), 217.

war-horses of Homer's chariots; which were destined to assist, but not to regulate, the progress of their nobler fellow-coursers.'[46] When in the 1830s and 1840s it had become difficult to attract a student audience to their lectures, the scientists began to resent the subsidiary place which the University allocated to the study of their subjects. They attributed the decline in scientific interest to inadequacies of the educational system which did not encourage attendance at professorial classroom instruction. In support of a flysheet circulated by Daubeny in 1839 'To the members of Convocation', Buckland ascribed the lecture-room malaise 'to some internal cause in the system of education and public examinations recently pursued, which tends to alienate the attention of our Students from the pursuit of Physical Science'.[47]

However, the decline in scientific interest was not just the result of stiffer competition for honorary distinction in the examinations. Buckland's letter, rather than pinpointing the cause of the disease, drew attention to a possible remedy. The examination system of the 1830s was not very different from that of the 1820s, when geology had attracted as many as ninety students per course. The decline in popularity of the lectures by Buckland and his colleagues reflected the change in how the sciences were perceived at Oxford. Their fashionable novelty had gone, and their Romantic appeal had faded, giving place to an increasingly professional and utilitarian image. At the same time, the generation which had supported Buckland in the 1820s—notably the Oriel Noetics—had dispersed; some who remained loyal to the scientific cause joined the Ashmolean Society and attended its meetings. Others of that generation had turned against the sciences, most prominently Keble and his Tractarian friends.

Whereas Buckland's lecture-room had formerly been crowded, it was now Newman's sermons which were the centre of interest. Whately pessimistically estimated in 1838 that no fewer than 'two-thirds of the steady reading men' were 'Puseyites'.[48] Declining attendances at scientific lectures coincided with the high point of the Tractarian movement. Buckland's fossil discoveries were no longer a match for the ethical power of Newman's pulpit in St Mary's. Buckland grew disenchanted, and in 1845 he was glad to leave for the deanery of Westminster (although he continued to give his lecture courses until 1849).

Buckland excepted, all the scientists reacted to the crisis by pamphleteering in support of reform of the examination statutes. Powell, who was

[46] J. Kidd, *An Answer to a Charge against the English Universities Contained in the Supplement to the Edinburgh Encyclopaedia* (1818), 7–8.

[47] William Buckland to C. G. B. Daubeny, 9 Mar. 1839, MCA Daubeny papers, autograph letters 89; Daubeny, *Brief Remarks*, 22–3.

[48] E. J. Whately, *Life and Correspondence of Richard Whately, D.D., Late Archbishop of Dublin* (2 vols 1866) i. 418.

vehemently opposed to the Tractarians and later served on the 1850 Royal Commission (as did George Johnson), started early. In 1828 a controversy over the students' preparation for the mathematics examinations widened into a demand 'to render *some acquaintance with the first principles of Physical Science a necessary qualification* for the degree of B.A.'.[49] Powell pleaded for the revival of the professorial system of public lectures in his pamphlet *The Present State and Future Prospects of Mathematical and Physical Studies in the University of Oxford* (1832). To these attempts to upgrade the teaching of the physical sciences, Daubeny, Kidd and Ogle added those of the natural sciences. Daubeny became the principal spokesman on behalf of the scientific cause, demanding a more central role for chemistry and other scientific subjects and tirelessly campaigning for an improvement in their academic status. He was particularly active in this respect during the agitations for examination reform in 1839 and 1848. In his *Brief Remarks on the Correlation of the Natural Sciences* (1848) he advocated a solution of compulsory attendance 'on two courses at least of Public Lectures during the third year of residence, leaving it, however, entirely to the option of the Student to select any of those relating either to the Literae Humaniores, as they are termed, or to Mathematics and Physics, according to the School in which he proposes to be examined'.[50] In this he was joined by Acland and Walker, who, together with Duncan, had in 1847 circulated a gravamen intended to improve provisions for lecture-rooms and exhibition space of the natural history collections, at that time still dispersed across Oxford, in the geological museum of the Clarendon Building, in the Ashmolean Museum and in the Anatomical Museum of Christ Church. This concerted effort led to the establishment of a public examination in natural science in 1850; and the case for science was argued in the Oxford Commission's report in 1852, which was the prelude to the building of the University Museum. The discussion of these developments will be found in Chapter 22.

[49] Anon., 'Examination system' (1 Nov. 1833), Bodl. Baden Powell 31 (1).
[50] Daubeny, *Brief Remarks*, 19.

17

Medical Education

A. H. T. ROBB-SMITH

The succession of new endowments which the University received in the late eighteenth century to support medical teaching-posts were the first such benefactions for over a century, and offered the hope that Oxford might re-emerge as a major centre of medical education.[1] As an immediate result, the number of medical graduates increased threefold in the last two decades of the eighteenth century. By the will of Dr Matthew Lee, who died in 1755, Christ Church received a benefaction to establish an anatomy lectureship. The first lecturer was appointed in 1767 and an anatomy school was opened in Christ Church in the following year.[2] In 1770 the Radcliffe Infirmary was opened and, by a bequest of the Chancellor of the University, Lord Lichfield, who died in 1772, a clinical professorship was established. The establishment of facilities for clinical teaching provided the foundation for later developments and represented an early example of the practice of clinical teaching of medical students in hospital wards. And finally, the will of Dr George Aldrich, a graduate of Merton and practitioner in Nottingham, who died in 1797, endowed professorships in anatomy and physiology, the practice of medicine, and chemistry.

In 1801 Sir Christopher Pegge was appointed Regius Professor of Medicine, an office which he held until his death in 1822. A member of a literary family which for several generations had been associated with Cambridge University, Pegge entered Christ Church in 1782 and graduated BA in 1786. He then joined the clinical school newly established at the Radcliffe Infirmary, where medical students had an opportunity to gain practical clinical experience. Convocation elected the first holder of the Lichfield chair of Clinical Medicine in 1780, and the regulations for the professorship were drawn up in the same year (and are described in volume v of this *History*). The Professor was required to attend regularly in the wards, to examine patients and explain their disorders in the presence of students, to see that proper notes were kept of their condition and, lastly, to ensure that these

---

[1] See C. Webster, 'The medical faculty and the Physic Garden' in *The Eighteenth Century*, 710.

[2] E. G. W. Bill, *Education at Christ Church, Oxford, 1660–1800* (1988), 314–15.

notes were available for the students to study.[3] There was much that was novel in these provisions. There had been ward teaching in Italy and Holland as early as the sixteenth and seventeenth centuries, and in Vienna later in the eighteenth century; but this had been limited to a cursory inspection of the patient, a feeling of the pulse and an inspection of a specimen of urine. As medical schools became popular, moreover, anything approaching ward instruction became impossible; weight of numbers dictated an amphitheatre demonstration with a lecture, the patient being present in the theatre. In Edinburgh students were allowed to examine patients in certain wards, but they had no instruction from their professors as to how examinations should be carried out.

The significance of ward teaching grew as techniques of clinical examination became more detailed. There was careful palpation of the abdomen to detect abnormalities, and percussion was used to reveal abnormal fluid or other changes in the chest or abdomen. In the London medical schools this form of instruction could readily be given because of the arrangement of 'firms', in which small groups of about eight to ten students would be attached to each physician and the patients in his wards. Many of those holding teaching positions in the London hospitals at the beginning of the nineteenth century held Oxford medical degrees, and they had had the opportunity to attend the clinical instruction available at the Radcliffe Infirmary during part of the academic year,[4] for the Lichfield professor was required to visit the wards regularly between November and March and on at least two days a week to give lectures on particular cases. Members of the University of at least two years' standing, including undergraduates, who had entered their names as medical students, and had been recommended by their tutors to the Vice-Chancellor for admission to the Infirmary, were entitled to attend the clinical lectures.[5] Those attending these courses, which lasted for two terms, amounting to sixteen weeks, might spend the rest of the year either as a pupil of an able physician or attached to one of the London or Edinburgh schools.

Although it is impossible to say for certain how many Oxford medical students in the early nineteenth century took advantage of these opportunities, the evidence of individuals suggests that many did obtain instruction in Oxford during Michaelmas and Hilary terms, while spending Trinity term and the long vacations in London or Scotland continuing their medical studies. One such was William McMichael, the medical historian and biographer, who graduated BA from Christ Church in 1805 and BM in 1808, and was physician at the Middlesex Hospital between 1822 and 1831, having

[3] Webster, 708.
[4] Ibid. For practices on the Continent see also pp. 87 and 108 above.
[5] See the regulations of 11 Jan. 1786 in Radcliffe Infirmary archives RI/1/4a, p. 192.

been a clinical pupil under Martin Wall at the Radcliffe Infirmary before spending three years at Edinburgh followed by a period at St Bartholomew's. A more distinguished clinician, and a characteristic example of the Radcliffe tradition of careful clinical examination of the patient, was Peter Mere Latham, who matriculated at Brasenose in 1806 and graduated BM in 1814. Following his father's example, Latham went on to the staff of the Middlesex Hospital prior to his appointment at St Bartholomew's in 1824, where he played a major part in the organization of bedside teaching.

In the first decade of the nineteenth century medical teaching at Oxford was in the hands of five individuals, all physicians at the Radcliffe Infirmary. Pegge has already been noticed: to his Regius chair were attached two posts in anatomy—the Tomlins praelectorship, and, after 1803, the Aldrichian professorship in Anatomy and Physiology. Pegge also held the Lee's readership in Anatomy from 1790 until 1816. In 1785 Martin Wall was elected to the clinical professorship, which he held until his death in 1824. Robert Bourne was appointed professor of the practice of medicine in 1803, and gained election to the clinical professorship in 1824, when already in poor health. Like his predecessor, Bourne died in office (in 1829). Botanical lectures were given by George Williams, who was elected Sherardian Professor of Botany in 1796; his reforming activities in the Botanic Garden and the Radcliffe Library are described elsewhere.[6] The first Aldrichian Professor of Chemistry, John Kidd, was appointed in 1803.

The new posts created by the Aldrich benefaction, coupled with the existing Lee's readership, placed the teaching of anatomy and physiology on a firm basis. Pegge's published syllabus of lectures on anatomy and physiology, as Aldrichian Professor, was an admirable conspectus of the functional morphology of the tissues and organs, followed by lectures on respiration, digestion and circulation, taking note of the current views on these subjects by British and continental scientists. At the same time Pegge maintained the earlier tradition of popular anatomy teaching. Dissections were regularly undertaken in the Christ Church anatomy school, where extensive collections of specimens illustrating human and comparative anatomy were accumulated. In his later years ill health curtailed Pegge's activities: in 1808 he had felt it necessary to resign his physicianship at the Radcliffe Infirmary; and in 1816 he left Oxford for Hastings, resigning his Lee's readership; but he returned each term to give his lectures as Regius Professor until 1822, when he died in his High Street lodgings.

John Kidd was appointed Pegge's successor to the anatomy readership and commenced his duties with energy. His claims upon the monies accumulated by the Lee Trust marked Kidd out as 'a great asker' in the view of Samuel Smith, Treasurer of Christ Church. He none the less persuaded the trustees

---

[6] See Webster, 722–3; pp. 692–3, below.

to purchase the first two microscopes in Oxford. Expenditure on the anatomy school, which steadily increased, peaked in 1828 when over £1,000 was
spent on acquiring specimens and books auctioned by Joshua Brookes's
London anatomy school.[7]

Kidd's posthumous reputation has suffered unduly from the damning
verdict of a German visitor who spent one day in Oxford in 1844.[8] And it
was perhaps unfortunate for Kidd's later standing that he lived on into the
age of the mid-Victorian commissions—one of his last acts was to reply to
the questionnaires circulated by the first Royal Commission. During the
1820s, however, he was a popular lecturer, especially in the field of comparative anatomy. He endeavoured to overcome the difficulty in procuring
subjects for human anatomy instruction by acquiring artificial preparations.
J. S. Duncan and Philip Duncan presented to the anatomy school in 1819
'several models in wax beautifully executed at Florence and highly useful for
the purpose of demonstrating several important points in human and comparative anatomy'.[9]

Medical students represented only a minority of Kidd's auditors. The
average attendance at his courses of about twenty-nine a year exceeded the
number of BM degrees awarded at Oxford in the whole decade 1821–30 (see
Table 17.1).[10] Indeed, the output of medical graduates was slightly smaller

TABLE 17.1

OXFORD AND CAMBRIDGE BM DEGREES AWARDED, 1801–1900

year	Oxford	Cambridge
1801–10	25	25
1811–20	24	27
1821–30	20	52
1831–40	28	63
1841–50	13	36
1851–60	21	21
1861–70	28	49
1871–80	45	83
1881–90	88	335
1891–1900	114	581
total	406	1,272

[7] CA MS Estates 140, fo 101; CA lii. b. 1, visitations of Dr Lee's anatomy theatre; CA lv.
c. 20, accounts of Dr Lee's trust; H. M. Sinclair and A. H. T. Robb-Smith, *A Short History of
Anatomical Teaching in Oxford* (1950), 45.

[8] M. Neuburger, 'C. G. Carus on the state of medicine in Britain in 1844' in E. Ashworth
Underwood (ed.), *Science, Medicine and History* (2 vols 1953) ii. 270–1.

[9] CA chapter book, 1819–37, fo 1.

[10] C. Daubeny, *Brief Remarks on the Correlation of the Natural Sciences* (1848), 21.

than forty years earlier, in a period when the numbers of arts graduates nearly doubled; between 1800 and 1870 the average number of Oxford BMs awarded was just over two a year. A similar recession occurred at Cambridge where, in the same period, the output of BMs averaged just three a year. Edward Tatham, Rector of Lincoln College, noticed the trend in Oxford as early as 1810, and regretted that so few were able to take advantage of the excellent provision for clinical teaching: 'And as to the *Clinical Lectures in Medicine*, liberally endowed by a late Chancellor of the University, though the Reader is a Physician of the first practice in Oxford, and of undoubted skill, he has not been able to raise a single class for the last two or three years; though that class should only consist of the number 6.'[11] In the early nineteenth century medical degrees continued to be awarded on the same conditions as in the previous century. Medical graduates passed through the classical arts course before taking their BM, which most did eight years after their matriculation (Table 17.2). Of the colleges, Christ Church was markedly the largest producer of medical graduates, accounting for a fifth of BMs awarded; this probably reflected the interest which the Dean, Cyril Jackson, took in the fortunes of the anatomy school, and the college's connection with Westminster School, which produced a significant number of entrants to the profession. The significant proportion of Oxford medical graduates who had obtained honours in Literae Humaniores suggests the importance which continued to be attached to literary cultivation (Table 17.3).[12] Over two-thirds of those who obtained Oxford medical degrees in the first quarter

TABLE 17.2

DURATION OF STUDIES OF OXFORD BM GRADUATES, BY YEAR OF GRADUATING, 1801–1900 (YEARS)

no. of years between matriculation and BM	1801–25	1826–50	1851–75	1876–1900
5	0	0	0	3
6	1	0	0	6
7	11	12	12	25
8	25	11	21	65
9	3	11	13	58
10	3	4	6	35
11	3	1	3	17
12+	4	3	5	27
incorporated from Cambridge and Dublin	8	10	0	0
total	58	52	60	236

[11] [E. Tatham], *A New Address to the Free and Independent Members of Convocation* (1810), 16.

[12] 'Observations on medical reform. By a member of the University of Oxford', *Pamphleteer* iii (1814), 420.

of the nineteenth century secured election to the fellowship of the Royal College of Physicians (Table 17.4). Oxford medical graduates were often

TABLE 17.3

UNDERGRADUATE COURSES FOLLOWED BY OXFORD BM GRADUATES, BY YEAR OF GRADUATING, 1801–1900 (NO. OF UNDERGRADUATES)

BA subject read	1801–25	1826–50	1851–75	1876–1900
Literae Humaniores	15	15	14	23
mathematics	3	1	5	10
natural science[a]	—	—	32	86
chemistry	—	—	—	14
physiology	—	—	—	67
jurisprudence	—	—	—	2
modern history	—	—	—	3
theology	—	—	—	3
(joint honours)	(2)	(0)	(3)	(7)
pass BA	34	26	12	35
incorporated BA	8	10	0	0
total	58	52	60	236

[a] Before 1886 it was not specified in which branch of the natural science honour school a candidate had specialized.

TABLE 17.4

CAREERS OF OXFORD BM GRADUATES, BY YEAR OF GRADUATING, 1801–1825 AND 1891–1900 (ROUNDED %)

career	1801–25	career	1891–1900
FRCP	69	FRCP	17
		FRCS	10
physicians: London	29	consulting physicians	16
provinces	35	consulting surgeons	9
academic appointments	7	consulting ophthalmologists	4
church	5	consulting obstetricians,	
not known	24	gynaecologists	4
		pathologists	4
		academic appointments	6
		medical officers of health	10
		general practitioners	39
		other	5
		not known	3
total	100		100
no.	58		114

found at the centre of the fashionable London medical world, practising as medical attendants upon the aristocracy and members of the court.[13]

After 1830 changes in the organization of the medical profession as a whole came to have significant repercussions for the Oxford faculty. Until then, being the only universities in England entitled to award medical degrees, Oxford and Cambridge had enjoyed a unique position in relation to the Royal College of Physicians, whose fellowships—with the privilege of practising in London—were restricted to graduates of those universities. As competing medical schools of a high standard had come into being, especially in London and Scotland, the existing position became untenable. J. A. Wilson, physician at St George's Hospital, and himself an Oxford medical graduate, had in 1832 proposed removing the ancient universities' privilege. Change in eligibility to the Royal College's fellowships was brought about in 1837 during the presidency of another Oxford medical graduate, Sir Henry Halford.[14]

A contemporary development was the introduction by John Kidd, appointed Regius Professor at Oxford in 1822, of new regulations for the medical examinations which were agreed in Convocation in December 1833.[15] Seven years were required for the BM and a further three for the DM. The examination, partly oral and partly written, covered the theory and practice of medicine, anatomy, physiology, pathology, materia medica and such parts of botany and chemistry as would illuminate medicine. Some familiarity with the works of two at least of Hippocrates, Aretaeus, Galen and Celsus was expected; and candidates were required to show that they had attended the practice of medicine as well as lectures at some hospital of repute.

Kidd was equally conscientious in his endeavours to broaden the connection between the Oxford medical faculty and the profession at large. He had attended the inaugural meeting of the Provincial Medical and Surgical Association (the forerunner of the British Medical Association) and presided over its third annual meeting, held at Oxford in July 1835, taking the opportunity, in an address to the 300 members gathered in the Radcliffe Library, to make some complimentary remarks on provincial practitioners.[16] In the course of the proceedings the unusual distinction of the degree of DM by diploma was conferred on two of the visitors, John Abercrombie and James Cowles Prichard. The last such honorand had been Edward Jenner in 1813.[17]

[13] I. Loudon, *Medical Care and the General Practitioner, 1750–1850* (1986), 270; cf W. Baillie to Mrs Hamilton, 9 Jan. 1806, cited in L. Rosner, *Medical Education in the Age of Improvement* (Edinburgh 1991), 23.

[14] G. N. Clark, *A History of the Royal College of Physicians* (1966), 682.

[15] *Statutes* ii. 183–9; A. H. T. Robb-Smith, 'Medical education at Oxford and Cambridge prior to 1850' in F. N. L. Poynter (ed.), *The Evolution of Medical Education in Britain* (1966), 45–7.

[16] *London Medical Gazette* xvi (1 Aug. 1835), 635.

[17] *Lancet* (July 1835), 551–2.

Two years later Charles Hastings, founder of the Provincial Medical Association, was one of the names suggested in a memorial submitted to the Hebdomadal Board by Kidd and the other physicians resident in Oxford:

As it appears desirable that the university should keep up its connexion with the medical faculty at least to the usual extent; it is respectfully submitted to the Board of Heads of Houses and Proctors whether this may not be effected in a desirable manner, by an occasional selection from the Medical Profession at large of such individuals as possess a high character among the members of that profession, for the purpose of conferring upon them the Degree of Doctor in Medicine by Diploma.

The Board chose not to act upon the suggestion.[18] Kidd then turned his attention to the growing movement for medical reform and anticipated H. W. Acland in foreseeing that Oxford (and Cambridge) might have more to gain than to lose by relinquishing their licensing powers—'a privilege which is of remarkably confined operation for conjointly they grant a very few licences in each year'—in exchange for acquiring a voice on the proposed national registration body for practitioners.[19]

While Kidd concentrated on matters of medical politics, J. A. Ogle, elected clinical professor in 1830, took steps to revive the instruction given at the Radcliffe Infirmary. He was able to muster a small clinical class in 1834.[20] By the end of the decade, with the support of the governors of the Infirmary, a lecture-room had been fitted out and the range of teaching extended to include materia medica.[21] Between 1836 and 1843 instruction was given at the Christ Church school by George Hitchings, an anatomical surgeon, with the dissection of a body. Two university students were pursuing medical studies in Oxford in 1839. One of them, W. A. Greenhill, a member of Ogle's college, Trinity, attended the clinical lectures at the Infirmary and subsequently continued his medical studies in Paris, before returning to Oxford to practise. Although the BM might be obtained through attending university scientific lectures and clinical instruction at the Radcliffe, Kidd knew of only three students who had done so between 1836 and 1848.[22] Ogle himself admitted that 'the wider range and more ample accommodation of the London Schools' made them preferable as places to pursue professional studies.[23] In spite of able teachers and adequate endowments, the Oxford medical school had suffered an eclipse. The number of BMs graduating in the decade 1841–50 fell to their lowest point since 1770. Stiffening of the examination requirements may have acted as a deter-

[18] HBM 17 Apr., 15 May 1837.
[19] J. Kidd, *Further Observations on Medical Reform* (1842), 15.
[20] *Select Committee on Medical Education* (PP 1834 xiii, Q. 4523).
[21] Minutes of the Radcliffe Infirmary, 27 Feb. 1839, Radcliffe Infirmary archives RI/1/4a/IX, p. 14.
[22] *Select Committee on Medical Registration* (PP 1847–8 xv, Q. 4176).
[23] *RCO* (1850), evidence, 279.

rent, while the exclusion of religious Dissenters continued to isolate Oxford from a large body of the profession; at the same time Oxford medical education suffered from the counter-attractions of the medical schools burgeoning within the new University of London.

To the Royal Commission of 1850 the picture seemed clear: 'Oxford has ceased altogether to be a school of Medicine. Those few persons who take Medical Degrees there with a view to the social consideration which these Degrees give, or the preferments in the University for which they are necessary, study their profession elsewhere.'[24] Supported by Kidd's testimony that Oxford could never be made a more effective school of medicine, since its small population prevented it from ever having an ample field of observation,[25] the Commission saw the University's role as being primarily to provide preliminary teaching in preparation for the examinations of professional bodies.[26] Sir Benjamin Brodie had written to the Commissioners in October 1851 emphasizing the importance of Oxford concentrating on chemistry, botany, the elements of mechanical philosophy and physiology, rather than on the clinical aspects of medical education. Although later to prove controversial, this conclusion enjoyed a wide consensus at the mid-century.

Under the prolific office-holder C. G. B. Daubeny, the posts in chemistry and botany were already developing in new directions. During his tenure of the Aldrichian chemistry professorship, the association of the chemistry post with medical teaching became increasingly tenuous. Although Daubeny had been trained in medicine, and held the position of physician at the Radcliffe Infirmary, he no longer had the concerns of the medical profession in the centre of his interests. In 1826 it was alleged that his activities were concentrated more in the laboratory at the Old Ashmolean than in the Infirmary, and in 1829 he was moved to resign his clinical post.[27] The death of George Williams in 1834 opened the way to Daubeny to add the Sherardian chair of Botany, whose appointment was in the hands of the Royal College of Physicians, to his scientific emoluments. Botany proved to be the earliest of the biological sciences to separate itself functionally from the study of medicine, and during his tenure of the botany chair, which he occupied until his death in 1867, Daubeny worked on the influence of nutrients on plants. Daubeny's successor to the chemistry post in 1855, B. C. Brodie, although the son of the surgeon mentioned above, was not himself a medical graduate; and the Aldrichian chemistry professorship was suppressed in 1866, the endowment being diverted to the support of a demonstrator in the chemistry department of the University Museum.

[24] *RCO* (1850), report, 71.
[25] Ibid., evidence, 256.
[26] Ibid., report, 82.
[27] A. G. Gibson, *The Radcliffe Infirmary* (1926), 116.

There was also a change in the direction of the teaching provided by the Lee's readership in Anatomy at Christ Church after 1830. In Kidd's later years the numbers attending fell away, and the small expenditure on new additions to the collections in the anatomy school suggested a recession from the high point of the 1820s.[28] On Kidd's resignation in March 1845 the Dean and Chapter of Christ Church appointed H. W. Acland. A Christ Church graduate, and fellow of All Souls, Acland returned to Oxford fresh from the influence of Richard Owen at the Royal College of Surgeons, and Allen Thomson, John Goodsir and William Pulteney Alison at Edinburgh. He was soon proposing to Dr Lee's trustees—as his predecessor, Kidd, had done nearly three decades earlier—ambitious schemes of expenditure to keep abreast with developments in biological science:

Within the last twenty-five years, the additions to Physiological and Anatomical knowledge have been so great, and the mode of imparting it has been so altered, that a young Lecturer brought up in the schools of the present day must, if he impart the knowledge we possess, be provided with new, and more extensive apparatus.

In particular the Laws of organic structure have been traced so far, and the Anatomy of each particular animal is found to be so merely a link in the whole chain of organic beings, that it has become *impossible* to treat properly of the Human frame or any other, without an extensive series of drawings and dissections, illustrating the laws of formation and structure in the Animal Series generally.[29]

Over £3,280, in addition to Acland's own stipend, were expended on the anatomy school during his twelve-year tenure of the Lee readership, the first fruits being his published *Synopsis of the Physiological Series at Christ Church Museum* (1853), describing the arrangement of its collections in accordance with Hunterian principles. Courses of practical instruction in embryology and histology were organized,[30] attracting a rare encomium from the *Lancet*, which described the Christ Church school as 'the best *teaching* museum for comparative anatomy and physiology in England'.[31]

Acland's appointment to the Regius professorship in 1857 marked the beginning of a new and later much-contested phase in the history of Oxford medicine. Outstanding as an administrator with vision, and at his best, perhaps, in handling large schemes, such as the institution of the University Museum, modernizing the Radcliffe Infirmary, or pushing through sanitary improvements, Acland exercised a dominating influence over Oxford medical education for half a century. Acland's ideal was that Oxford should educate gentlemen and men of science who would, after undergoing a general literary education coupled with 'fundamental scientific training',[32]

[28] R. T. Gunther, *Early Science in Oxford* (14 vols 1923–45) iii. 195.
[29] H. W. Acland to the Dean and Chapter of Christ Church, 25 Nov. 1845, CA DP ii. c. 2.
[30] Atlay, *Acland*, 147.
[31] *Lancet* 10 Oct. 1857, 368.
[32] *UOC* (1877), evidence, Q. 3107.

go on to medical schools elsewhere to pursue their clinical studies. Visiting the pre-clinical departments of the projected medical school at Johns Hopkins University in Baltimore, in 1879, he was impressed by what seemed to be a vindication of his ideal, in the regulation that students were not allowed to enter upon hospital instruction until they had completed three years of laboratory work in the basic sciences.[33] 'The men who are to advance Medicine in the present day must be disciplined in the modes of Biological research, before serious clinical study,' Acland believed, and this was to be Oxford's contribution to the profession.[34] But such a high ambition inevitably made for a small school, and the numbers of Oxford BMs remained low between 1860 and 1880. Much was made of the high proportion of scientific investigators among them, and the number who went on to hold prestigious teaching appointments. When the Oxford Graduates Medical Club held its inaugural meeting in March 1884 attention was drawn to the number of Oxford medical graduates 'who held important posts at many of the leading metropolitan and provincial hospitals'.[35] In fact this had been a characteristic of medical graduates since the establishment of the Radcliffe clinical school a century earlier (see Table 17.4), and certainly pre-dated Acland's tenure of the Regius chair.

One of Acland's first acts was to remodel the BM examination. His own unhappy experience as a young medical student, when the necessity of studying theoretical and practical aspects of medicine simultaneously had brought him close to a nervous breakdown, no doubt reinforced his view that pre-clinical and clinical studies should be separated.[36] The examinations for the BM were henceforth divided. He also effected changes in the conditions attached to Oxford's most valuable endowments for medical students, the Radcliffe travelling fellowships.[37] An original member of the General Medical Council, Acland was much occupied in national questions. He recalled attending forty-three conferences on medical education, over the course of four years in the 1870s;[38] these wider commitments, however, seem to have caused him to delay initiatives in Oxford to modify the medical curriculum.[39]

With the opening of the University Museum the Regius Professor had, for the first time in the history of the chair, proper accommodation, with a small

[33] H. W. Acland, *Medical Education. A letter addressed to the authorities of the Johns Hopkins Hospital and Johns Hopkins University* (Baltimore 1879), 10.
[34] OUA HC/1/5.
[35] Minutes, 9 Oct. 1884, Bodl. MS Top. Oxon. e. 639, fo 19.
[36] *RCO* (1850), evidence, 236.
[37] PRO HO 73/44, pt 1.
[38] *UOC* (1877), evidence, Q. 3122.
[39] 'Medical Education Committee of Hebdomadal Council: memorandum by the Regius Professor of Medicine, Nov. 4, 1867', Bodl. G. A. Oxon. b. 137; Hebdomadal Council minutes, 29 Jan. 1872, 293, OUA HC/1/2/2; F. K. Leighton (Vice-Chancellor) to Registrar, General Medical Council, 25 May 1868, cited in PP 1882 xxix. 921.

lecture-room and laboratory. This became, much later in the century, the basis for the department of pathology. In April 1864 Acland acquired from Utrecht the Van der Kalk collection of pathological specimens, of which he wrote a synopsis in 1867.[40] Sanitary reform and public health were his other great interests. In the 1873 edition of the Oxford *Student's Handbook* it was announced that 'from time to time the Professor takes members of the University to inspect localities in town or country for instruction in sanitary defects and remedies'.[41]

George Rolleston succeeded Acland to the Lee's readership in Anatomy in 1857, and in 1860, on his appointment to the new Linacre professorship of Anatomy and Physiology,[42] became responsible for the entire range of university teaching in anatomy, physiology and zoology. To these he later added anthropology. Of wide intellectual interests, Rolleston, who had taken a first in Greats in 1850 before graduating BM in 1854, aligned himself closely with Acland's view of Oxford's role in medical education. To Acland he was the embodiment of the ideal associated with the Oxford Museum; Rolleston undertook biological work 'of the widest kind': 'To him Man was the crown of the whole. But Man in his material origin and descent; Man in his evolution, social, moral, and intellectual; Man of every time, character, aspiration; Man in his highest relations to his fellow men, and to God.'[43] Others, as the memoir to him delicately suggested, felt that Rolleston 'lost force' by diversifying into so many areas.[44]

As Lee's Reader Rolleston had continued Acland's work in developing practical courses particularly directed to the needs of those undergraduates reading for the natural science honour school.[45] He maintained this emphasis as Linacre Professor.[46] When chairs and endowments were being rearranged during the 1850s, Ogle had apprehended the danger that consolidation of the existing university endowments for anatomy under the Linacre chair would lead to the neglect of human anatomy.[47] What Ogle feared came to pass, for the old emoluments were used to support a departmental demonstrator, Charles Robertson, who worked on preparing comparative anatomy specimens. The Christ Church Anatomy Reader from 1860 to 1869 was William

[40] The specimens were later transferred to the Sir William Dunn School of Pathology and then to the Nuffield Department of Pathology. A selection of the more important items are kept in the Museum of the History of Science.

[41] *The Student's Handbook to the University and Colleges of Oxford* (1873), 52.

[42] M. Pelling, 'The refoundation of the Linacre lectureships in the nineteenth century' in F. Maddison, M. Pelling and C. Webster (eds), *Linacre Studies: essays on the life and work of Thomas Linacre, c.1460–1524* (1977).

[43] H. W. Acland, *Oxford and Modern Medicine* (1890), 28.

[44] See the memoir by E. B. Tylor in W. Turner (ed.), *Scientific Papers and Addresses by George Rolleston, M.D., F.R.S.* (2 vols 1884) i, p. xliv.

[45] See his report for 1859–60, CA lii. b. 1.

[46] Rolleston to Vice-Chancellor, 7 May 1873, OUA HC/1/5.

[47] Ogle to Goldwin Smith, 25 June 1857, PRO HO 73/44, pt 1.

Church, the last of Acland's own student assistants, who taught both comparative anatomy and physiology. Appointed to a clinical post at St Bartholomew's in 1867, Church was obliged to resign the Lee's readership in 1869 when the Christ Church governing body determined that the reader should be resident.[48] Subsequently, as physician to St Bartholomew's and President of the Royal College of Physicians, Church was twice urged to allow his name to be put forward for the Regius chair, to succeed first, Acland, and then J. S. Burdon-Sanderson. The next holder of the Lee's readership was John Barclay Thompson, a histologist more in theory than in practice, whose lectures included a course offered from time to time over this period entitled 'The osteology and teeth of the ichthyopsida, with some account of their distribution in space and time'.[49] During his fifty-year tenure of the readership Thompson concentrated on providing college tuition for the natural science honour school.

Acland had always regarded human anatomy as an unsuitable activity for undergraduates; it was increasingly excluded from the range of instruction during Rolleston's tenure of the Linacre chair, even though Rolleston's chief research interest was the study of human skeletal remains. Dissections were rare, and intending medical students needing to cover this part of the pre-clinical curriculum were often obliged to do so in London. Nor was the university department keeping abreast of new developments in physiological teaching. It was left to Charles Yule, who came to Magdalen in 1873, having been a Cambridge pupil of Michael Foster, to organize the first course of practical physiology in Britain at the Magdalen chemistry laboratory. Yule, like Rolleston, obtained a Home Office licence under the 1876 Cruelty to Animals Act to undertake vivisection, to the disapproval of Rolleston, who wished to restrict its use to medical students.[50] Meanwhile, it was difficult for intending medical graduates to obtain teaching at Oxford in all the subjects they needed if they were to satisfy the requirements of the London licensing boards.[51]

Clinical teaching at the Radcliffe Infirmary was more or less in abeyance. Between 1837 and 1840 Ogle and his colleagues had organized an excellent course of clinical instruction at the Infirmary, and between 1837 and 1840 there had been some thirty-seven pupils, although only three of these were members of the University. Ogle had combined the Regius and clinical chairs and believed that the two should be permanently attached, so that 'the Institutes of Medicine as set forth theoretically from the school-chair might be illustrated practically at the bedside'.[52] This may well account for

---

[48] SCOC (1867), evidence, Qs 3273, 3275.
[49] Gazette xxi (13 Oct. 1890), 33.
[50] For Yule's syllabus, see UOC (1877), evidence, Qs 3613, 4330–6.
[51] BMJ 26 Jan. 1878, 138.
[52] 'Replies of professors in the University of Oxford to a circular letter addressed to them by the direction of the Oxford University commissioners' (1856), 53–5, PRO HO 73/42, pt I.

Acland's initial determination to stand for election to the clinical chair after his appointment as Regius. Acland's supporters in Convocation carried the day in a contested election, and he commenced with twelve pupils at the Infirmary. These were to be the last whom he introduced to clinical teaching.[53] By 1874 Acland attached so little importance to the chair that he expressed a willingness to surrender it whenever reorganization of the Oxford professoriate took place,[54] convincing the Hebdomadal Council's committee on university requirements, in the following year, of the case for putting its resources to other uses.[55]

When the Selborne Commission, which had been appointed to draw up new statutes for the University and colleges, came to Oxford in November 1877 to hear evidence on the priorities for university spending, the principal testimony which they received on medical education came from Acland and Rolleston. Acland restated the arguments against attempting to create a complete medical school in a small country town. He proposed the suppression of the clinical chair, and the use of its endowments to provide for a chair in comparative pathology.[56] The Commissioners, however, proposed the suspension of the clinical professorship until the University could put forward a positive suggestion as to how clinical instruction should be provided. Acland resigned his office as physician to the Infirmary in October 1879 and the clinical professorship in November 1880. The Hebdomadal Council had agreed in January 1880 that the endowment of the Lichfield chair should be used to support two clinical lectureships attached to the house physician and the house surgeon at the Radcliffe Infirmary.[57] In the meantime the medical staff of the Radcliffe set about providing clinical teaching on their own initiative: courses were announced in Michaelmas 1881 and six students signed on, with a further three joining in Hilary 1882.[58] This arrangement was sanctioned by the Hebdomadal Council in May 1882 when the Lichfield endowment was formally applied to fund lectureships in medicine and surgery at the Radcliffe Infirmary. The first appointments were made in the following year. Each lecturer was required to give a termly course of lectures; tenure was limited to two years, though the holder could be reappointed for a further period.

These developments took place in the wake of a public row which broke out in January 1878 when the *British Medical Journal* carried a letter from 'a member of Convocation' headed 'A lost medical school'; this,

[53] Gibson, *Radcliffe Infirmary*, 267.
[54] Memorandum to the medical committee of the Hebdomadal Council, Nov. 1874, OUA HC/1/5.
[55] *Gazette* v (8 June 1875), 646.
[56] *UOC* (1877), evidence, Qs 3107, 3130.
[57] Recommendations of a committee on medical studies, adopted by the Hebdomadal Council, 26 Jan. 1880, OUA HC/1/5.
[58] See the advertisement in *Gazette* xii (14 Oct. 1881), 28.

reinforced by comments in the *Journal*'s editorial columns, amounted to a personal attack on Acland and Rolleston. Medical education at Oxford, it was alleged, had practically ceased in the previous twenty-five years. There were no lectures in medicine, anatomy or physiology, and under Acland the Regius chair had been turned into a sinecure. Rolleston was held to have diverted the Linacre chair, originally intended for medical education, into abstruse channels. The letter concluded with an attack on the monopoly of clerical and pedagogical interests at the ancient universities.[59]

The tinder for this attack was provided by the Selborne Commission's recommendation that there should be four faculty boards only, medicine being submerged within natural science. As a result of the outcry, the Commission was obliged to hold special sittings in London to hear the views of those who advocated a complete medical school at Oxford. E. R. Lankester, then a fellow at Exeter College, supported by J. F. Payne, a fellow of Magdalen, elaborated a scheme to establish a clinical medical school on a larger scale, as Lankester acknowledged, than that which existed at Edinburgh.[60] Acland's supporters, including many former pupils, rallied to provide contrary testimony.[61]

The controversy was eagerly promoted by Ernest Hart, the unscrupulous editor of the *British Medical Journal*.[62] One cross-current exploited by Hart during the 'lost medical school' row was the body of opinion among general practitioners critical of Acland's role in the General Medical Council. The British Medical Association petitioned the House of Commons in the course of the row, and Sir Charles Cameron, radical MP for Glasgow and a medical graduate of Dublin, raised a parliamentary question as to whether Acland gave any lectures.[63] From the standpoint of those interested in promoting biological research, Lankester kept the matter simmering in his start of session address as Professor of Zoology at University College London in September 1878. He stressed the importance of retaining connections between theory and practice in medical education and denied the validity of the distinction between preliminary and professional studies. His swipes at Oxford clericalism and at the University Museum, Acland's beloved centre for the natural sciences (where Lankester's own early researches were carried out), which he dismissed as 'a sort of Gothic palace', brought the controversy to new heights of acerbity.[64]

[59] *BMJ* 5 Jan. 1878, 34–5; 12 Jan. 1878, 66.
[60] *UOC* (1877), evidence, Q. 5209.
[61] See James Andrew's evidence, *UOC* (1877), evidence, 5405; and the supplementary evidence, 381–91.
[62] For this controversial figure see P. W. J. Bartrip, *Mirror of Medicine: a history of the 'British Medical Journal'* (1990), 63–8.
[63] *Parl. Deb.* 18 July 1878, 3S ccxli. 1843–4; on the professional politics see Pelling, 'The refoundation of the Linacre lectureships', 284.
[64] *BMJ* 5 Oct. 1878, 501, 505.

Acland's response to these critics was to secure the appointment of J. S. Burdon-Sanderson from University College London to the Waynflete chair of Physiology in 1882. The new chair had been created by the Selborne Commission's statutes, which at the same time restricted the Linacre chair to comparative and human anatomy. For the development of the pre-clinical departments it could not have been a better appointment. As professor of physiology, and later as Regius, Burdon-Sanderson was to begin the development of the Oxford school of experimental medicine which was to come to fruition during Osler's tenure of the Regius chair. Almost immediately, however, the plans for laboratory accommodation faced violent opposition from an anti-vivisection clique led by Edward Nicholson and E. A. Freeman. The first challenge came in Convocation in June 1883, when a £10,000 grant for a physiology laboratory was narrowly carried by 88 to 85. A decree authorizing the sale of stock to pay for the laboratory was the occasion of a further division in February 1884; it was carried by 188 to 147. The most famous debate took place on 10 March 1885, when large numbers of non-resident members of Convocation were mobilized in an attempt to prevent an annual grant to the department of £500. It was nevertheless carried, 412 to 244.[65] While these contentions were going on, Burdon-Sanderson, like many an Oxford professor after him, found that he had no department to work in. Magdalen, to which his chair was attached, came to the rescue by allowing him the use of its own laboratory; and Burdon-Sanderson, with his assistant Francis Gotch, found a haven where they continued their research on the electromotive properties of the leaf of Dionaea, undisturbed by the bitterness of Convocation. In the event some £12,000 was spent on the physiology laboratory, which was designed with advice from Michael Foster.[66]

Burdon-Sanderson's other immediate priority was to restore teaching in human anatomy. In 1885 he secured the appointment of Arthur Thomson, from Edinburgh, to a new university lecturership in human anatomy, which in turn necessitated a further subdivision of the Linacre chair. At first the department was located in an inadequate iron-roofed extension to the Museum; but in 1893 a permanent building was opened and Thomson was given the title of professor. By then it had become usual, as Thomson reported, for medical students to remain in Oxford until they had passed their first BM examination, taking advantage of the new facilities. There were forty-three students working in the department in 1890.[67]

The restoration of human anatomy teaching—in the face of Acland's barely concealed disapproval—and the creation of a physiology department

[65] *Gazette* xiii (5 June 1883), 548; xiv (5 Feb. 1884), 272; xv (10 Mar. 1885), 342; R. D. French, *Antivivisection and Medical Science in Victorian Society* (Princeton 1975), 275–6.
[66] Reports and estimates as to prospective outlay on university building, Mar. 1882, HCP 1 (1882), 13–15.
[67] *Gazette* xxi (26 May 1891), 499.

removed the most serious obstacles to the creation of a medical school at Oxford covering the first part of the BM curriculum. It was sometimes suggested in the course of the 'lost medical school' row that G. M. Humphry, the Professor of Anatomy at Cambridge, had been able to establish a complete medical school. An option did exist at Cambridge to obtain a medical degree without first passing through the BA course and there was a small clinical school in Addenbrooke's Hospital just as there was at the Radcliffe.[68] Yet most Cambridge students, like their Oxford counterparts, went to the metropolis to do their clinical training, and graduation through the undergraduate natural science tripos remained the recommended preliminary at Cambridge to further medical study. The real difference between the two universities had been the greater willingness of Cambridge to adapt its teaching to the needs of pre-clinical medical students, enabling them to meet the licensing requirements of the GMC.[69] Acland had always set his face against such accommodation, which he feared would depress the level of Oxford's scientific courses, and he offered only lukewarm support when, in November 1884, Burdon-Sanderson broached with Jowett, the Vice-Chancellor, 'the revival of medical study in the university'.[70] A statute creating a faculty of medicine, distinct from the natural science faculty created in 1882, passed in Convocation in March 1886 and the newly constituted faculty of medicine held its first meeting on 21 May 1886.[71] Medical students pursuing their studies at Oxford were now able to register under the Medical Acts, and the creation of a student Medical Club in 1891 indicated that they were now a growing and distinct group in Oxford.[72] The *British Medical Journal* rejoiced that 'The notice of "The Lost Medical School" will now disappear from our columns.'[73]

Physiology proved to be the fastest-growing area in the biological sciences in late nineteenth-century Oxford. Starting with just six students working in the department in 1883, there were thirty-seven in 1888, and nearly seventy in 1900.[74] The physiological branch of the natural science honour school came to be the most popular undergraduate course preliminary to the BM. Gotch,

[68] G. M. Humphry, 'Medical study and degrees' in *The Student's Handbook to the University of Cambridge* (1866), 235; in Mar. 1879 Humphry advised the Hebdomadal Council that the experience of using Addenbrooke's for clinical training had proved unsatisfactory: OUA HC/1/5.

[69] *BMJ* 19 Jan. 1878, 111; *Student's Guide to the University of Cambridge* (1880), 14; G. L. Geison, *Michael Foster and the Cambridge School of Physiology* (Princeton 1978), 160–1.

[70] Burdon-Sanderson to Vice-Chancellor, 1 Nov. 1884, HCP 9 (1884); see Acland's accompanying warning against an attempt to do too much, 15 Nov. 1884.

[71] *Gazette* xv (9 June 1885), 566; *Gazette* xvi (16 Mar. 1886), 409–12.

[72] R. Macbeth, 'Medical clubs and societies in Oxford' in K. Dewhurst (ed.), *Oxford Medicine* (Sandford-on-Thames 1970), 116–18.

[73] *BMJ* 5 June 1886, 1073.

[74] F. Gotch, 'The department of physiology', in exhibits assembled for the education exhibition at the Imperial Institute, 1900, Bodl. G. A. Oxon. b. 41. See also W. J. O'Connor, *British Physiologists, 1885–1914: a biographical dictionary* (Manchester 1991), ch. 3.

who succeeded Burdon-Sanderson to the physiology chair in 1895, was better remembered as a meticulous teacher, who would spend an hour before each lecture writing a précis of its content on the blackboard, than as an original investigator. But he regarded the researches carried out in the department as its 'crowning prestige'.[75] A summary of its research output was produced from 1894 onwards,[76] much of it the work of Burdon-Sanderson's brilliant young nephew John Scott Haldane, who was disappointed to be passed over in favour of Gotch for the chair, and of Walter Ramsden. Both worked in the field of physiological chemistry, and an extension to the laboratory to accommodate the expanding needs of this subdiscipline was identified by Gotch as one of the most immediate needs of the department in 1902. But Gotch emphatically opposed any moves of the sort which were taking place in continental universities, to separate the new discipline of biochemistry from what he continued to regard as the single science of physiology.[77]

By the last decade of the nineteenth century there was the outline of a good medical school at Oxford covering, as the *Oxford Magazine* announced in its account of the medical statute in 1885, 'the first half of the Medical Curriculum'.[78] The introductory courses in the wards of the Radcliffe proved to be an ideal introduction to the teaching which medical students were going on to receive at the London hospitals in the final part of their clinical studies. A course in materia medica was instituted in 1888.[79] This was still some way short of the complete school which Lankester and others had advocated; and an address in 1893 by the Chancellor, Lord Salisbury, urging the University to do more to exploit the opportunities for clinical teaching at the Infirmary, suggested that the question had not yet been entirely laid to rest.[80]

One of the last controversies in which Acland became involved concerned the tendency of changes in the pattern of studies for Oxford medical degrees to reduce the literary element and to subordinate undergraduate studies more narrowly to the demands of professional examinations. In standing out against this he was supported by many of his former pupils, who apprehended a lowering of the standard of the Oxford medical degrees.[81] The complaint that the Oxford course was too long had often been voiced. In the 1870s it generally took eight years or more to qualify: the regulations

[75] F. Gotch to Vice-Chancellor, 19 Feb. 1898, HCP 49 (1898), 43–5. On the growth of the Oxford department see *Statement of the Needs of the University, being replies to a circular letter addressed by the Vice-Chancellor on February 20, 1902* (1902), 26–8.

[76] *Gazette* xxiv (12 June 1894), 580.

[77] *Statement of Needs*, 26.

[78] *OM* 21 Oct. 1885, 310.

[79] *BMJ* 8 Sept. 1888, 590.

[80] *OM* 8 Mar. 1893, 276.

[81] Acland, *Oxford and Modern Medicine*, 25; H. W. Acland and J. Ruskin, *The Oxford Museum* (1893), pp. xxii–iii; J. S. Burdon-Sanderson, *The School of Medical Science in Oxford* (1892), represented a counter-view.

stipulated that students had to have completed two years of study after their final BA examination before taking the first part of the BM, and another two years before taking the second part.[82] The natural science honour school usually involved a course of four years, one of which was occupied by the classical studies required for Moderations. Acland was adamantly opposed to reducing the duration of study. 'The period of seven years cannot be shortened if our Graduates are to hold an honourable place as men of general culture and professional attainment,' he asserted in 1874.[83] After 1887 science graduates were freed from classical Moderations, effectively cutting one year from the time required to obtain the BM, and moves to align studies for the undergraduate natural science school with the requirements of the first part of the BM brought a six-year qualification period (five years for graduates of affiliated universities) at least theoretically within reach.[84] The BM remained in effect an extended honours course, however, and of those graduating in the 1890s, slightly fewer than a half had managed to do so in under eight years after their matriculation. Those who sought to qualify more quickly did so by taking the examinations of the London conjoint board (MRCS, LRCP). Nearly a quarter of Oxford medical students who had taken the first BM went on to qualify in this way. This in turn was an indication of an increased number of Oxford graduates entering general practice (see Table 17.4), as the influence of the Oxford school spread out into the country much as it had done in the sixteenth and seventeenth centuries.

Acland resigned his chair at the end of 1894, at the age of 75, disappointed at the failure of one of his longest-term projects to mature. In the early 1870s he had set up a small sanitary laboratory in the medical department of the Museum. He envisaged this as the basis of a larger venture, modelled on the work of the Brown Institution in London, to be connected with the establishment of his long-hoped-for chair of comparative pathology. One of his earliest student assistants in the laboratory, Lionel Beale, became a pioneer of diagnostic pathology. Progress had been checked by the early death in 1873 of Acland's assistant, C. C. Pode, and the subsequent 'lost medical school' controversy. In 1891 he revived his earlier plans, only to be rebuffed by the Hebdomadal Council, which gave priority to spending on other biological departments, in particular to the grant to human anatomy.[85] In place of the more ambitious project Acland brought Carl Menge of Munich to Oxford to organize bacteriological classes in the limited accommodation available, and these were continued by James Ritchie, who came to Oxford in 1889 as an assistant to one of the Radcliffe surgeons.

[82] *The Student's Handbook to the University and Colleges of Oxford* (1873), 148–9.
[83] Memorandum to the medical committee of the Hebdomadal Council, Nov. 1874, OUA HC/1/5.
[84] *The Student's Handbook to the University and Colleges of Oxford* (1892), 209.
[85] *Gazette* xxii (29 Mar. 1892), 385.

It was to prove the main work of Burdon-Sanderson, Acland's successor, to establish the teaching of pathology within the medical school.[86] Each year he gave a course of twelve lectures on general pathology and supervised post-mortem examinations at the Radcliffe Infirmary. Lack of accommodation hindered further growth, however, and Burdon-Sanderson became increasingly frustrated by the difficulties in the way of securing the necessary funding for pathology. A repetition of the delays which he had encountered in getting a laboratory in physiology seemed to be in prospect. In November 1896 he addressed an open letter to the President of Magdalen, arguing that the subject could be taught better in Oxford than in London, where medical students were forced to go to learn it as part of their study for the second BM.[87] Committees approved his proposals but there were further delays. The Museum Delegates favoured a large plan for a complete institute of pathology outside the limits of the existing Museum area, but there was no immediate prospect of finding the means. In June 1899 Burdon-Sanderson issued a further memorandum pointing out that Oxford was the only institution in Great Britain where adequate provision for pathology was lacking. Before the year was out Ewan Frazer, who had attended the first of Burdon-Sanderson's courses, offered £5,000 if the University would provide the rest. This was done and the pathology department, largely designed by Arthur Thomson, opened in October 1901, with Ritchie as reader.

In the 1902 statement of needs of university departments the medical faculty commented: 'Fifty years ago the University seemed to have come to the conclusion that it could not conveniently provide courses of instruction specially adapted for students in Medicine.' The endowments originally intended for medicine, it went on, had at that time been 'diverted to the encouragement of studies unconnected with medicine'. Subsequent developments had altered the picture, however, and the faculty considered that there was now in existence 'a prosperous and growing medical school'.[88]

---

[86] *Gazette* xxvi (9 June 1896), 567.
[87] J. S. Burdon-Sanderson, *Medical Education in Oxford. A letter to the President of Magdalen from the Regius Professor of Medicine* (np nd [1896]), 4.
[88] *Statement of Needs*, 23.

CENTRAL INSTITUTIONS, OLD AND NEW

18

The Bodleian Library

I. G. PHILIP

In his novel *Crotchet Castle* (1831) Thomas Love Peacock describes how a party of visitors walked about Oxford on a fine July day 'to see the curiosities of architecture, painted windows, and undisturbed libraries', and how the Reverend Doctor Folliott laid a wager 'that in all their perlustrations they would not find a man reading'. In reality the reverend doctor would not have run any risk in making such a wager on a fine day in the depth of long vacation, at least as far as the Bodleian was concerned, for the Library's archives show that in 1831 no books were ordered by any readers in that library between 29 June and 2 August, and the records of book-orders for the month of May, that is, in full term, do not evidence any great activity.[1] The Bodleian 'entry-books', in which all requests for books were entered day by day, show that in May 1831 books were ordered by readers on only eighteen days in the month, that on these eighteen days the average attendance of readers was between two and three, and that books ordered amounted, in total, to about three or four a day. Even assuming that some of those who ordered books may have returned subsequently to consult a book previously ordered, the average daily attendance is unlikely to have been more than five or six readers and this number rose slowly during the first half of the century. It has been calculated that in May 1845 the average number using the Library was probably about ten a day in the summer term,[2] and only a small minority of these would have been college tutors. A witness to the 1850 Commission described the Bodleian as 'practically to College Tutors useless during Term time, owing to its hours' which were then 9 a.m. to 4 p.m. in summer and 10 a.m. to 3 p.m. in winter.[3] The summer term was in fact the only time the Library could be used with any comfort, for Thomas Bodley's original statute forbidding any 'fire or flame' was scrupulously observed, and there was therefore no artificial light or heat. In a library which was 'either close or cold, and for a great part of the year, both',[4]

---

[1] Library records, entry book. For a detailed and authoritative account of the Bodleian during this period see Sir Edmund Craster, *History of the Bodleian Library, 1845–1945* (1952).
[2] Craster, 25.
[3] *RCO* (1850), evidence, 154.
[4] Cox, 223.

prolonged study required considerable dedication and only scholars of the calibre of Gaisford, Nicoll or Pusey were likely to share the trials of the library staff in enduring the Siberian conditions of the Library in the long winter months. A form of steam-heating which made no contribution to human comfort was introduced in 1845, but although the needs of college tutors were reiterated from 1850, nothing effective could be done until in 1861 the Bodleian curators were able to use the Radcliffe Camera as a reading-room which, in a building that could be safely lit and heated, could remain open until 10 p.m. In the first half of the century, the only Bodleian reading-room was Duke Humfrey's Library, and the only provision for book-storage was in the Picture Gallery and two of the first-floor 'schools'.

All this was clearly inadequate for a library which should have been expanding rapidly to meet new needs. Lack of expansion was partly due to the inadequate provision of current English publications as a result of the ineffective operation of the 'copyright deposit' system.[5] The Library had the right, under successive Copyright Acts, to claim all British publications free of charge, but owing to the uncertain scope of the law this right had disappointing results. Publishers held that under the terms of the Copyright Act of 1709 they were required to deposit in the privileged libraries only those publications which they registered at Stationers' Hall, and these were for the most part the smaller, cheaper publications for which registration offered some protection against piracy. Weightier, more expensive publications were, most of them, not then registered or deposited. The average annual intake of material from Stationers' Hall in the years 1801–5, as listed in the Library's records, was about sixty books and sixty 'pamphlets', a category which included novels, poems and children's books.[6] A King's Bench decision in 1812 that all publications, registered or not, should be deposited in the privileged libraries altered the position fundamentally, and this new reading of the law was incorporated in the Copyright Act of 1814. In 1815, when the new Act came into operation, the Bodleian received about 400 books,[7] but still for many years the publishers continued to evade the full requirements of the Act, and the privileged libraries continued to doubt the value of acquiring much of the material which was offered. In a return made to the House of Commons in 1818 of 'Books not deemed by the Curators necessary to be deposited in the Library' Bodley's Librarian listed seventy-two titles of books and three (unnamed) novels as well as music and school-books which had been received, but not incorporated (classified or cata-logued), in the Library in the years 1814–17.[8] But this must have been a very

---

[5] For pre-1800 developments see *The Eighteenth Century*, 727–32, and for details of the 19th-century practice, Craster, 61–4, 172–4. For a general account, R. C. Barrington Partridge, *History of the Legal Deposit of Books* (1938).

[6] Library records, registrum D.

[7] Ibid.

[8] *Returns of the Libraries, Ordered to be Printed by the House of Commons, 6 March 1818.*

inadequate return, for the gaps in the Library's holdings of English novels in this period were great: R. W. Chapman, working on his edition of Jane Austen in the 1920s, discovered that the Bodleian 'contained no edition of Jane Austen's novels [1811–18] of any interest to the bibliographer or of any value to the editor'.[9] The earliest edition he could then find in the Library was one of 1833. But, as publishers were gradually forced to deposit more and better books, the Bodleian curators began to attach greater importance to their privilege. In 1836 they rejected a proposal that the deposit privilege should be commuted for an annual grant of £500, and by mid-century, partly as a result of the Copyright Act of 1842, the annual Bodleian intake of deposited English publications amounted to about 2,500 volumes a year.[10]

In view of the meagre intake of free English publications in the early part of the century, the Library's purchasing policy became all the more important, but the two Librarians who held office up to 1861 did not regard the Library as primarily an institution which had to cater for the needs of those aspiring to graduate in the University, and the more substantial purchases tended to reflect the learned Librarian's personal interests, or, more importantly, those of the more active curators. John Price, who had been appointed Librarian in 1768 and held office until his death in 1813, was a keen botanist and a learned topographer, especially in matters relating to his native Wales, but in 1800 he was 66 and his interests were plainly too restricted. He was succeeded in 1813 by his godson, Bulkeley Bandinel, a Wykehamist fellow of New College, who held office for the next forty-seven years until his retirement at the age of 79 in 1860.[11] Bandinel was an erudite and discriminating bibliophile who for nearly forty years applied himself with great energy and expertise to building up the Bodleian collections. He jealously guarded the treasures he acquired and generally resisted all change which might have led to their use by those with whose qualifications he had no personal acquaintance. For the last fifteen years of his term of office Bandinel, with seriously failing health, was an obstacle to reform of any kind, but up to about 1850 his librarianship was a great period in the growth of Bodleian collections. The Library was then more affluent than it had ever been since Thomas Bodley's own day, and this affluence was devoted, in great part, to the purchase of important collections of classical and oriental learning.

By a statute of 1780 a share in matriculation and other university fees was allocated to the Bodleian, initially as a fund for the purchase of books.[12] Income from this source rose from £450 in 1781 to £750 in 1813 and £2,335 in 1850.[13] Price did not take full advantage of this: in the six years 1800–5 the

[9] *Friends of the Bodleian Fifth Annual Report, 1929–1930,* 8.
[10] Craster, 19.
[11] Ibid. 27–30.
[12] *The Eighteenth Century,* 742.
[13] Library records, purchase catalogues, 1848–57.

average expenditure on books was just over £500 a year; in the next seven years 1806–12 the average annual expenditure was just under £200. The extent of Price's inactivity can be measured by the increase of expenditure in his successor's first year of office, £725 in 1813 compared with £261 in 1812.[14] However, there were advantages in Price's inactivity, for the balances accruing in the book fund during his term of office made it possible for the Library Curators to finance outstanding purchases of special collections, starting with the purchase in 1805 of the D'Orville collection. Jacques Philippe D'Orville, at one time Professor of History, Eloquence and Greek at Amsterdam, died there in 1751 leaving a great collection of classical learning.[15] His main collection of printed books was sold in 1764, but his manuscripts and collated printed texts remained together as a collection and were purchased, almost intact, by the Bodleian for £1,095. The collection then comprised about 570 volumes, chiefly texts of Latin and Greek classics, with thirty-four volumes of correspondence of scholars like Isaac Vossius, Heinsius and Paolo Sarpi. D'Orville's primary object was to collect material for a proposed edition of Theocritus and the Greek Anthology; but his collection contains one unexpected treasure, a manuscript of Euclid written in 888 by Stephanos the clerk. This had belonged to Arethos of Patras, afterwards Bishop of Caesarea, who died c.931. The collection of Edward Daniel Clarke, bought for £1,000 in 1809, contained, remarkably, another manuscript from this source, a volume of twenty-four dialogues of Plato, written by John the Calligrapher in 895 for Arethos of Patras.[16] This had been purchased from the monastery of St John the Evangelist at Patmos in 1801 by Clarke, who travelled widely in countries bordering the eastern Mediterranean collecting Greek, Latin and oriental manuscripts. Clarke, who became Professor of Mineralogy at Cambridge in 1808, and University Librarian there in 1817, had opened negotiations with the Bodleian for the purchase of his manuscripts in 1808; and in 1809 the Library completed the purchase of forty-five volumes of oriental manuscripts and thirty-two Greek and Latin manuscripts, to which Clarke subsequently added another eight. Catalogues of the D'Orville and Clarke collections of Greek and Latin manuscripts published in 1806 and 1812 were compiled by Thomas Gaisford, then a young Student of Christ Church, but this was only one of the Library's many debts to Gaisford. He had been instrumental in persuading the curators to purchase these two collections, and from 1812, when as Regius Professor of Greek he became an ex officio curator of the Library, it was largely due to him that the Library was able to pursue a remarkably successful accessions policy for upwards of forty years, until his death in 1855.

---

[14] Ibid. 1781–1825, Bodl. Bliss B. 417.
[15] *Bodleian Library: summary catalogue of Western manuscripts* iv (1897), 37–150.
[16] Ibid. 297–312.

The first great purchase after Gaisford became a curator was that of the collection of Greek, Latin and Italian manuscripts formed by an Italian Jesuit, Matteo Luigi Canonici, who died in 1807.[17] After his death the collection was divided; but in 1817 the Library was able to buy the major part of the manuscript collection, about 2,045 items, for £5,444, the largest single purchase made by the Library up to that time. Three years later, in 1820, another select group of fifty Greek manuscripts was bought for £500 from the collection of Giovanni Saibante of Verona, a purchase which included a twelfth-century manuscript of Arrian's discourses of Epictetus, the archetype of all existing manuscripts of this work, and a book which ranks among Bodleian treasures with the D'Orville Euclid and the Clarke Plato.

From 1823 until the end of Bandinel's period of office in 1860 the annual expenditure on books was about £1,800 and the range of subjects and sources was very wide. In 1823 over 700 works were brought for £375 at the sale of Professor Te Water's library in Leiden[18] and in the following year £925 was spent when the library of the Dutch scholars Gerard and John Meerman came to be sold by auction at The Hague.[19] Gaisford had drawn the attention of the Curators to this collection and offered to attend the sale in person. At their meeting on 6 May 1824 he was empowered to make such purchases for the Library 'as he shall judge proper'.[20] He bought about 1,500 volumes chiefly of foreign history and law, but also secured fifty-nine manuscripts which included a sixth-century manuscript of St Jerome's translation of the chronicle of Eusebius. One who attended this sale recalled how Gaisford 'attended most assiduously during the sale at the Hague, and managed to get the London booksellers to withdraw their opposition to his acquiring many of [the Greek] MSS. unless at exorbitant prices'.[21] Gentlemanly arrangements of this kind could not, however, be made with one equally assiduous collector. Six years later Gaisford recalled how he had been outbid for some items by Sir Thomas Phillipps; and 'but for his silly interference', he complained, 'I should have placed...the whole of all that was valuable in Meerman's collection in our public library, but he wd. not consent to let me have two or three manuscripts which I much wished— which can never be of use to him—for he is an arrant ignoramus'.[22]

---

[17] Ibid. 313–14.
[18] W. D. Macray, *Annals of the Bodleian Library* (1868, 2nd edn 1890), 312.
[19] Ibid. 314.
[20] Library records, curators' minutes, 1793–1862.
[21] Macray, 314 n.
[22] 'Dean Gaisford and the Meerman collection', *Bodleian Library Record* iv (1952), 7–8; A. N. L. Munby, *The Formation of the Phillipps Library up to 1840* (Phillipps Studies 3 1954), 35–6. The Phillipps papers are in the Bodleian, which also holds a location register of the Phillipps Collection. One Meerman manuscript, a late 14th-cent. Statius (Phillipps MS 1798), was eventually bought by Mrs Chester Beatty. The Phillipps holdings of the Berlin Staatsbibliothek are extensive. For the Bodleian's unsuccessful efforts to acquire the collection, 1851–61 (which culminated in Phillipps's attempt to become Bodley's Librarian), and for the long aftermath, see Craster, 83–7, 195–7, 199.

In the acquisition of the next two important collections the leading part was taken by Alexander Nicoll, Professor of Hebrew, also an ex officio curator, who proposed the purchase of the Finn Magnusen collection of Icelandic manuscripts and of the Oppenheimer Hebrew collection. Nicoll had resigned from his post as Sub-Librarian in 1822 on election to the Regius professorship, but continued, like Gaisford, to be an assiduous Bodleian reader; 'no sooner were his lectures over, than he hastened to the Bodleian Library, where he remained till the hour of closing it'.[23] The Magnusen collection was bought for £350 in 1828; the Oppenheimer purchase involved more expensive and difficult negotiation. At a meeting on 14 November 1826 Nicoll urged that the curators should seize the chance of buying the library which had been formed by David Oppenheimer,[24] Chief Rabbi of Moravia and afterwards of Bohemia, who died in 1736. Since 1782 successive owners of the collection had tried to sell it and in 1826 it was announced that it would be broken up and sold in separate lots by auction unless a purchaser could be found by June 1827.[25] In November 1826 Nicoll reported this to the curators and, after further enquiries about price, it was resolved on 4 June 1827 that he should proceed 'without delay' to Hamburg to complete the purchase 'for a sum not exceeding £2,300'.[26] Legal complexities among the vendors meant that Nicoll had to return empty-handed, but in 1829, after Nicoll's death, the Oppenheimer library was finally acquired for £2,080, a collection of 5,000 volumes of which 780 were manuscripts. Before this purchase the Library possessed about 385 Hebrew manuscripts; the accession of 780 Oppenheimer manuscripts put the Bodleian in the first rank of the world's Hebrew libraries at a time when the British Museum still had no more than 200 Hebrew manuscripts.[27]

While the Library authorities, particularly the professorial curators Gaisford, Nicoll and Pusey, were engaged in the purchase of these very considerable and expensive special collections, the Librarian, Bandinel, continued to collect in those fields of which he himself had special knowledge. His interests were wide-ranging. He built up the Library's collection of Spanish books, expanded the Bible collection, bought a remarkable collection of 43,400 foreign dissertations, chiefly German, in 1827, and greatly increased the Library's holdings of incunabular and other *editiones principes* of classical texts. In the decade 1820–30 Bandinel acquired for the Library 265 incunabula; in the following decade (1830–40) 1,009 were added, of which 470 came with the Douce collection, and then in the next two decades Bandinel

[23] *Sermons by the Late Rev. Alexander Nicoll* (1830), p. xxxviii.
[24] Macray, 319–21.
[25] C. Roth, 'An episode in the history of the Oppenheimer collection', *Bodleian Library Record* v (1954), 104–8.
[26] Library records, curators' minutes, 1793–1862.
[27] Craster, 105.

acquired, mainly by purchase, a further 982. This was indeed a remarkable achievement, and Bandinel's notebooks and correspondence show the very wide range of his bibliographical knowledge and the respect with which he was regarded by collectors and booksellers.[28]

But the Library's major purchases were still, for another decade, in the field of oriental studies.[29] In 1842 the Wilson collection of Sanskrit manuscripts was bought for £500; in 1843 £1,000 was spent on a collection of Arabic and Ethiopic manuscripts collected by James Bruce of Kinnaird; and in 1844 £2,000 was spent on 750 manuscripts, chiefly Persian, gathered during forty years' collecting by Sir William Ouseley. To these were later added in 1858–9, by purchase and gift, over 600 Persian and Indian manuscripts collected by Sir Gore Ouseley. Pusey, now Regius Professor of Hebrew, was no doubt responsible for continued accessions of Hebrew printed books and manuscripts. The Library spent £176 on 483 volumes from the collection of the Semitic philologist H. F. W. Gesenius, whose library was sold by auction at Halle in 1844, and in 1848 a collection of 629 volumes of Hebrew manuscripts, comprising nearly 1,300 separate works, was bought for £1,030 from the library of H. J. Michael, who died in 1846. More came in 1850 with the purchase from Italy of sixty-two Hebrew manuscripts for £100, and with a collection from Berlin of Hebrew books from the library of Isaac Auerbach. Then in 1853 seventy-two manuscripts were bought for £108 from the library of Professor Isaac Reggio of Goritz. These collections were supported by regular purchases of Hebrew printed material for the knowledge of which the Librarian was greatly indebted to the Rabbi Hirsch Edelmann, a frequent reader in the Bodleian, and above all to the assiduous labour and great expertise of the Berlin bookseller Adolf Asher. Finally, in the last decade of the century, the Library built up, mainly by purchase, the second-largest collection (after Cambridge) of Hebrew documents from the Cairo Genizah, amounting to some 10,000 pieces.

While the purchasing policy of the Library in the first half of the nineteenth century concentrated on important collections of Greek and oriental manuscripts, the great donations of the same period added to the Library's resources in quite different fields, particularly in English topography and literature. The first of these was the bequest in 1809 of the topographical collection of Richard Gough.[30] Gough had published the results of his topographical journeyings and research in three great works on English antiquities, *British Topography* (1768), *Sepulchral Monuments of Great Britain* (1786) and an enlarged English translation of Camden's *Britannia* (1789).

---

[28] Bodl. various shelf-marks.
[29] For the oriental collections here referred to see Craster, 105–12.
[30] Macray, 285–9.

These works, particularly the first two, were profusely illustrated and in 1799 Gough tried to get the British Museum to act as a depository for the copperplates used in his work. Even when he offered to add the whole of his topographical collections, the trustees were, he thought, dilatory in finalizing the arrangements, and Gough, impatient at the delay, bequeathed his collections to the Bodleian to be preserved in 'the Antiquaries' Closet erected for keeping Manuscripts printed Books and other Articles relating to British Topography... so that all together they may form one uniform body of British Antiquities'.[31] The Librarian, John Price, who had corresponded helpfully with Gough for over twenty years, seems to have been the author of this ingenious plan, which persuaded Gough to bequeath to the Bodleian a collection ranging far more widely than the term 'British Antiquities' suggested. Besides the collection of maps, engravings and copperplates the preservation of which had caused Gough particular concern, his will specified all his topographical collections with all his books relating to Saxon literature and the Scandinavian North 'for the use of the Saxon Professor', a bequest amounting in all to nearly 4,000 volumes.

After the arrival of this bequest the Antiquaries' Closet became known as Gough's Room, and the concept of a specialized-subject collection, new in the Library's history, led to the building-up of a topographical collection in which all items are still classified as additions to the original Gough collection, a lasting tribute to the importance of Gough's work and a continuing encouragement to like-minded benefactors. In the same way the Library regarded the next great benefaction as the basis for further specialized collecting of English drama. Edmond Malone, editor of Shakespeare, bequeathed his library to his brother Lord Sunderlin, but left the immediate use of all his Shakespearean material to James Boswell the younger, who produced the 'third variorum' edition of Malone's Shakespeare in 1821.[32] On the completion of this work Lord Sunderlin gave Malone's collection to the Bodleian, which thus acquired the library of 'the representative scholar of one of our greatest periods of English studies'.[33] Malone collected anything that threw light on poetry and drama of the Elizabethan age, but the important core of his collection, which contained many great rarities, was the group of twenty-one composite volumes of Elizabethan quartos which he bought at the sale of Narcissus Luttrell's books in 1786.[34] At his death Malone's Shakespearean collection was much richer than that of the British Museum, and that part which came to the Bodleian amounted to over 800 volumes containing more than 3,000 separate items. The Library's collection

---

[31] For Gough's correspondence with the British Museum and the Bodleian see J. Nichols, *Illustrations of the Literary History of the Eighteenth Century* (8 vols 1817–58) v. 552–5.

[32] Macray, 306–8.

[33] D. Nichol Smith, 'Edmund Malone', *Huntington Library Quarterly* iii (1939–40), 28.

[34] J. M. Osborn, 'Reflections on Narcissus Luttrell', *Book Collector* vi (1957), 19.

of sixteenth- and seventeenth-century English literature had been sparse and unorganized: the Malone collection made the Bodleian a centre of Elizabethan studies and encouraged a new pattern of collecting. The effect of this was seen in 1834 when at the Heber sale the Library bought, besides much other valuable material, a collection of between 1,100 and 1,200 plays, chiefly of the seventeenth and eighteenth centuries.

The third great donation of the first half of the nineteenth century was of a quite different scope but superb quality. Francis Douce, one-time Keeper of Manuscripts in the British Museum, died in 1834 bequeathing to the Bodleian a collection of prints, coins and books, numbering about 13,000 volumes, covering his favourite subjects, which his obituary writer defined as 'the History of Art, Manners, Customs, Superstitions, Fiction, Popular Sports and Games of Ancient Times'.[35] To his contemporaries Douce's collection was thought of as a repository of 'old English and French literature', and this element in his collecting still remains an important part of the Library's resources for the study of seventeenth- and eighteenth-century literature. Douce did not go out of his way to collect first editions—though a Shakespearean scholar he had no quarto or folio editions of Shakespeare—but the range of his collecting was unique and from plays and poems he went on to collect ephemeral publications, chapbooks and broadside ballads, which, formerly sparsely represented in the Bodleian, have in modern times become increasingly valued as a rare source for social and literary history. The outstanding individual treasures of the Douce collection, however, were among his early printed books and manuscripts. His bequest included 470 incunabula, by far the Library's largest single accession of such books; and, among the manuscripts, the famous Douce Apocalypse written in France in the thirteenth century, and the Ormesby Psalter completed about 1330 and presented to Norwich Cathedral, arguably the most beautiful example of the East Anglian school of manuscript illumination.

On 4 April 1834 Frederic Madden, a tireless critic of the Bodleian, wrote to Sir Thomas Phillipps: 'I am quite vexed at Douce's disposition of his collections. To leave them to the Bodleian is to throw them down a bottomless pit. They will there be neither catalogued, bound or preserved, but suffered to sleep on with the Gough, Rawlinson and Tanner collections undisturbed above once in a lustre by some prying individual of antiquarian celebrity.'[36] But the comparatively few 'prying individuals' who frequented the Bodleian were not to be so ill served with catalogues as Madden implied. The annual catalogues of Bodleian purchases published from 1780 to 1861 provided an up-to-date record of all individual accessions and some detailed lists of libraries bought *en bloc*. The greater collections could not, of course,

[35] 'Francis Douce, 1757–1834', *Bodleian Quarterly Record* vii (1934), 359–82.
[36] Bodl. MS Phillipps–Robinson b. 128, fo 23ᵛ.

be dealt with so expeditiously, but a consistent attempt was made to make their contents known to scholars. The Gough collection, received in 1809, had its published catalogue by 1814; catalogues of the collections of Icelandic manuscripts and printed dissertations were published in 1832–4; and that of the Malone collection was in hand and published in 1836, the Douce catalogue following in 1840. Nicoll's catalogue of Arabic manuscripts, published in 1835, was followed at intervals up to 1887 by published catalogues of printed books and manuscripts in Hebrew, Chinese and Japanese, while the general catalogue of Western printed books, omitting those special collections already dealt with, was published in four volumes in 1843–51. This was followed from 1853 by catalogues of earlier collections of manuscripts, beginning with the catalogue of Greek manuscripts undertaken by H. O. Coxe[37] at Gaisford's insistence. Catalogues of the great historical collections of Tanner and Rawlinson appeared a little later. These in turn were followed by the *Summary Catalogue of Western Manuscripts*, which, from 1895 to 1905, covered all the manuscript accessions received in the eighteenth and nineteenth centuries.

Meanwhile other cataloguing problems had become more acute. From 1850 the intake of books deposited under the Copyright Act steadily increased. This followed the active lead given by Anthony Panizzi at the British Museum, and after 1882 the Oxford intake increased dramatically when E. W. B. Nicholson, in this respect one of Panizzi's devoted admirers, became Bodley's Librarian. In the previous year (1881) Jowett had instituted a curatorial committee to consider the collection of copyright books, and the committee shared a general approval of a full implementation of the deposit privilege, except for the solitary protest of Professor H. W. Chandler, who warned: 'If we do not take speedy measures to avert the catastrophe, we shall, like Tarpeia, be crushed under the gifts we solicit.'[38] But Nicholson rejoiced in what to others seemed at times a catastrophic growth; by 1888 the annual copyright intake amounted to 30,545 items and by 1891 it was 34,035 items.[39] In that year the Curators recommended that steps should be taken to reduce the number of books received under the Copyright Act, but the other privileged libraries could not agree, and the intake continued to rise until in 1910 the 54,813 items so received amounted to approximately 70 per cent of the Library's total annual intake. Growth on this scale brought many problems. At mid-century the Library's total stock of printed books was about 240,000 volumes. By 1887 the Library had almost doubled in size and by 1914 it had more than doubled again, the book stock being calculated then as about a million printed books.[40] One of the most urgent library

[37] Sub-Librarian 1838–60, Librarian 1860–81.
[38] Craster, 173.
[39] For the following statistics of deposited books see *Library Provision in Oxford* (1931), 151.
[40] F. Madan, 'Statistical survey', *Bodleian Quarterly Record* i (1916), 254–62.

problems of the second half of the century was therefore that of storing and making available this unprecedented influx of current English publications. After 1860 there was to be no more large-scale buying in British or continental sale-rooms—and no more great donations—and, as administrative costs increased, expenditure on books as a proportion of total library expenditure steadily declined. So the second half of the century became a period of anxious grappling with administrative problems, and a continuing decline in the provision of scholarly publications for which the development of honours degree courses had urgently increased the demand.

The members of the 1850 University Commission noted the view that 'the utility of the Library, however great, is not proportionate to the extent and value of the books which it contains', and the first suggestion for Bodleian reform related to the need for longer opening hours or, if that was impracticable, the relaxation of the prohibition on lending.[41] Most of those who gave evidence before the Commission had in mind the needs of senior members, and, like Pusey, probably assumed that the value of a library like the Bodleian to undergraduates was 'very much over-rated'.[42] One witness, however, H. E. Strickland, Deputy Reader in Geology, spoke out for undergraduates on grounds of equity: 'our billiard-rooms, tennis-courts and livery stables are freely open to students, and why should our libraries be closed to them?'[43] His plea for admission and for a special undergraduate reading-room eventually bore fruit: the Bodleian statute was amended in 1856 to allow the admission of undergraduates on tutors' recommendation and the opening of the Radcliffe Camera reading-room, with fifty seats, provided ample space for immediate demand. By 1876 the average number of readers, tutors and undergraduates in the Camera at any one time was about thirty-six, and by 1880 the curators calculated that the total number of students reading there on any one day was between 200 and 275.[44]

The 1850 Commissioners had also had to consider statements of more general tenor and recommendations of more debatable value. The statement that 'of all the great libraries of Europe the Bodleian is the most convenient and generally useful' was based on the testimony of many foreign scholars,[45] but Jowett, then an influential Balliol tutor, put forward a series of detailed recommendations which he thought would make the Library more generally useful in Oxford. His proposal 'that the selection of books in different departments should be placed under the Professors of different branches of knowledge, who might become the Curators of the Library'[46] was not

[41] *RCO* (1850), report, 116.
[42] Craster, 145.
[43] *RCO* (1850), evidence, 101.
[44] Craster, 144.
[45] *RCO* (1850), evidence, 228.
[46] Ibid. 39.

approved by the University, but when, on Gaisford's death in 1855, Jowett succeeded to his Regius professorship and to his position of authority among Bodleian curators, he was able to press for the implementation of other recommendations which he had laid before the Commissioners. His first concern was for the reclassification and rearrangement of the entire Library, and, although he received little support, his opinion never wavered: 'I am aware', he wrote nearly twenty years later, 'that the other Curators and the Librarian disapprove of classificatory arrangement, but that circumstance is immaterial.'[47] Failing in his initial scheme, which would have had disastrous results, Jowett continued to press for the compilation of a classified catalogue, but this, after much expenditure of time and money, proved to be equally impracticable. Jowett was also a firm believer in lending Bodleian books to individual scholars as one way of offsetting the inconvenience of short Library opening hours.[48] The Bodleian statute forbade such lending, but Jowett continued to press the case, at least for limited lending to professors and scholars of similar seniority and weight. Eventually such a scheme won some measure of curatorial support and on a limited scale operated from 1873 to 1887,[49] but it had no general support and it became clear that the most urgent requirement of university teachers was a better supply of current foreign publications and an up-to-date general author catalogue. A new author catalogue compiled in 1860–78 and revised from 1907 was a partial answer, but the need for more scholarly foreign publications was even more difficult to meet.

Since the establishment of the Taylor Institution in 1845 the Bodleian had been relieved of the expense of buying foreign *belles-lettres*, and since 1861 the supply of scientific publications could be left to the Radcliffe Science Library, but, although a greater part of the Library's book grant was now spent on foreign material, this was still quite inadequate. In 1875 the Curators, anxious to improve the Library's service, had wished to apply for an additional £1,000 a year for book purchase, but this was whittled down to £250 for five years,[50] and the 1877 Commission heard many complaints of this aspect of library service. H. A. Pottinger, a friendly witness, reported that 'the foreign department is almost nil at the Bodleian';[51] the Librarian, Coxe, admitted that 'there is a great deal of German and other literature in which we are very deficient indeed',[52] and Stubbs, speaking for the curators, acknowledged that Slavonic is 'altogether conspicuous by its absence'.[53]

[47] Craster, 58.
[48] Ibid. 80–1.
[49] Ibid. 82.
[50] Ibid. 49.
[51] *UOC* (1877), evidence, 264.
[52] Ibid. 244.
[53] Ibid. 248. But this overlooks the purchase of two important collections, the *Hungarica bibliotheca* (400 vols) in 1850, and the *Polonica bibliotheca* (1,200 vols) in 1852.

Again in 1878 the Curators asked for a substantial increase for book purchase, but in the following year Convocation could only agree to a limited
grant of £230 a year for three years.[54] It was not until 1904 that a protest
from the faculty of modern history produced an important series of private
benefactions specifically for the increased purchase of modern historical
literature, and then, in 1907, the refurnishing of the north range of the
Picture Gallery,[55] again by private benefaction, made it possible to provide
a reading-room with, on open access, a substantial range of reference books,
foreign periodicals and transactions of societies and academies. This was the
first step in making that provision for teaching and research which many
members of the University had, for a generation or more, regarded as the
most pressing need in the University's library service.

[54] Craster, 70.   [55] Ibid. 242.

19

The Ashmolean Museum

A. G. MACGREGOR

The role of the Ashmolean envisaged by its founder—that it should be an integrated centre for scientific research—suffered progressive erosion from the early eighteenth century as the unity of Ashmole's foundation gradually broke down.[1] In the Broad Street building the original elements of public display gallery (on the upper floor), lecture-room(s) (on the ground floor) and laboratory (in the basement) still survived in the early 1800s; but the museum element had effectively become isolated from the other functions and had stagnated. The lack of positive impact on the collections by the curators who ushered in the nineteenth century, William Lloyd,[2] Thomas Dunbar[3] and William Philipps,[4] contrasts with indications of more intensive activity from their contemporaries on the lower floors: new apparatus for the readers in experimental philosophy and chemistry was purchased on a number of occasions, while repeated additions were made to the numbers of specimen cabinets in the ground-floor chambers of William Buckland, Professor in Mineralogy from 1813 and in Geology from 1818.[5] Far from benefiting the public displays, however, these developments brought about a further drain on them, for parts of the mineral collection and the important cabinet of fossils amassed by Edward Lhuyd, Keeper of the Ashmolean from 1690 to 1709, were removed at that time from exhibition and were integrated with Buckland's teaching collections.

On taking office as Keeper in 1824, John Shute Duncan[6] was confronted by a scene of considerable neglect. He found that 'the skins of animals

[1] On the beginnings of the Museum see M. Welch, 'The foundation of the Ashmolean Museum' in A. G. MacGregor (ed.), *Tradescant's Rarities: essays on the foundation of the Ashmolean Museum, 1683, with a catalogue of the surviving early collections* (1983), 40–58; A. V. Simcock, *The Ashmolean Museum and Oxford Science, 1683–1983* (1983); A. G. MacGregor and A. J. Turner, 'The Ashmolean Museum' in *The Eighteenth Century*, 639–58; R. F. Ovenell, *The Ashmolean Museum, 1683–1894* (1986). The latter work, exhaustive in scope and meticulous in compilation, appeared after the first draft of this chapter had been submitted for publication; some later rewriting was undertaken to take account of details published for the first time by Ovenell.

[2] William Lloyd, BCL 1784, Keeper 1795–1815.

[3] Thomas Dunbar, BA 1805, MA 1808, Keeper 1815–22.

[4] William Thomas Philipps, BA 1811, MA 1813, BD 1824, Keeper 1822–3.

[5] Ovenell, 186–7.

[6] John Shute Duncan, BA 1791, MA 1794, DCL 1830, Keeper 1823–9.

collected by the Tradescants [whose "closet of rarities" had formed the bulk of the Ashmolean's founding collection] had fallen into total decay, that cabinets for those objects which were liable to injury from time were wholly wanting, and that the apartment dedicated to the exhibition of them had become much dilapidated'.[7]

Duncan's appointment coincided with an upsurge of interest at Oxford in the study of natural history, fuelled by the writings of Paley on 'natural theology' and by the lectures of Kidd on comparative anatomy and Buckland on geology. With the general approval of the University, Duncan set about rearranging the collections into three parts: the first division followed the principles established by Paley, being designed 'to induce a mental habit of associating the view of natural phenomena with the conviction that they are the media of Divine manifestation, and by such association to give proper dignity to every branch of natural science'; the second division exhibited 'relics of antiquity, arranged according to the order of time', while the third featured zoological specimens displayed according to the method of Cuvier, with the name of every exhibit 'conspicuously affixed'.[8]

The extent of Duncan's commitment to the guiding philosophy which he embraced is made clear in the texts of a number of 'tablets' preserved in the Ashmolean library in a folder titled 'Paleyian Museum' (sic) and intended to be hung from the appropriate display cases.[9] That destined for the first cabinet reveals that the exhibits displayed there were chosen to illustrate one of Paley's fundamental tenets, in which the characteristics of 'unorganized objects' (stones, minerals) were contrasted with those of an 'organized object' (a clock displayed under glass in order to show its mechanism), the whole exemplifying 'power directed by Intelligence to good ends in the works of the Divine Creator'. Ten other tablets, several with only the headings described, deal with aspects of human and comparative anatomy, zoology, botany and astronomy, while a number of contemporary printed sheets, also designed to be exhibited, describe the distinguishing characteristics of birds and mammals or outline the classificatory schemes erected by Lacépède and Pennant.[10]

[7] A Catalogue of the Ashmolean Museum (1836), p. vi.

[8] Duncan's draft notes for the new display are preserved in the Ashmolean library: AA AMS 44, 10. His own published works, including Botanical Theology; or, evidences of the existence and attributes of the Deity collected from the appearances of nature (2nd edn 1826), also reveal the influence of Paley. Kidd and Buckland were both contributing authors to the series of Treatises sponsored by the 8th Earl of Bridgwater which collectively formed the most comprehensive exposition of the doctrines of natural theology. These were highly influential in the early decades of the 19th century, so that Duncan's choice of organizing principles should be seen as very much in harmony with the spirit of the age and not as the product of a personal whim.

[9] AA AMS 24.

[10] Appended to the printed sheets is the following note: 'This arrangement is experimental, requiring the confirmation of further observation. Remarks of Naturalists who may visit the Museum will be thankfully received. A book to receive such remarks will be produced when required.'

Throwing himself into his self-appointed task, Duncan financed the re-furbishments (including 'New Cabinets covering entirely each end of the Museum') out of his own pocket, later being reimbursed £320 by the University.[11] A survey of the entire collection by the Keeper—the first that had been undertaken for many decades—revealed losses of many of the older specimens, and the lack of inventories for certain elements of the collections (notably Reinhold Forster's benefactions of material collected on Cook's Pacific voyage of 1772–5). It also showed the addition of numbers of fresh natural history and ethnological specimens from Duncan himself and from his friends. Antiquities formed a much less important feature of the Ashmolean at this time, but in 1829 the Museum received from Sir Richard Colt Hoare a collection of major importance in archaeological and historical terms, in the form of material excavated between 1771 and 1783 by the Revd James Douglas from a series of Anglo-Saxon sites in Kent: with this material, published in his *Nenia Britannica* in 1793, Douglas may be said to have laid the foundations of Anglo-Saxon archaeology in England.

A list of regulations for the running of the Museum, contained in a letter written by Duncan on 26 November 1827, reveals the institution performing its public functions in much the same way as it had in the seventeenth century. The opening hours were 10 a.m. to 4 p.m. Monday to Saturday inclusive, and the admission charge was 6*d*. The collections were to be viewed only in the presence of the Keeper or Under-Keeper; not more than ten persons were to be admitted at any one time, and no one was to spend more than half an hour in viewing the Museum without the consent of the Keeper.[12]

In 1829, after six years in office, J. S. Duncan was succeeded in the keepership by his younger brother, Philip Bury Duncan.[13] No other arrangement could have ensured a greater continuity of purpose than that which marked the transfer of the office from one brother to the other. Philip Duncan too promoted the cause of the natural sciences in Oxford,[14] although his term of office saw the final alienation from the Ashmolean of the geological material which had once formed the principal element of its scientific collections. With the freeing of the ground-floor premises consequent on the departure of the geology professor and his specimens, Philip Duncan put in motion another radical programme of reorganization of the displays. With the internal divisions which had encroached over the years now swept away, the ground floor was for the first time in the Museum's

[11] Ovenell, 190–1.
[12] AA AMS 1, 10, printed in full by Ovenell, 196–7.
[13] Philip Bury Duncan, BA 1794, MA 1798, DCL 1855, Keeper 1829–54.
[14] In a paper entitled 'History and arrangement of the Ashmolean Museum', read to the Ashmolean Society on 12 Feb. 1830, Duncan compared the personal cost of preparing new zoological acquisitions for display (not less than £100 annually) with the salary actually paid to the Keeper (£70 annually).

history given over to exhibits, principally of mammals. Its appearance (including columns newly inserted to support the sagging ceiling) is recorded in the frontispiece of the Museum's first printed catalogue (Plate 26), brought out by Duncan in 1836 on principles laid down by his brother.[15] On the upper floor were displayed birds, reptiles, fish, insects[16] and shells. Philip Duncan's interests also encompassed antiquarian matters[17] and provision was made in the new scheme for the inclusion of antiquities, along with coins and medals and small works of art, in a lesser room on the ground floor. The staircase too was pressed into service, notably for the display of paintings, with which, like his elder brother, Duncan was reluctant to 'dilute' the scientific impact of the galleries.

The Duncans appear to have been exemplary Keepers[18] and indeed model citizens: of the pair of them Archbishop Howley wrote, 'I question whether any two men, with the same means, have ever done the same amount of good,'[19] while a large part of the zoological collections held by the Ashmolean in the 1830s may be attributed to their personal benefactions and the attraction of many other gifts to their influence.[20] More importantly, perhaps, the successive appointment of these two widely respected persons to the keepership re-established the esteem of the Museum in the public eye, and indeed its self-esteem, as exemplified by the founding in 1828 of a new Ashmolean Society 'for the purpose of promoting an interchange of

[15] *A Catalogue of the Ashmolean Museum* (1836). The heavy emphasis in this catalogue on zoological specimens accurately reflects the new direction in which the Duncans moved the Museum, but the section on antiquities, thought to have been delegated to the Under-Keeper William Kirtland, is more perfunctory. For some account of the 19th-century rearrangements of the Ashmolean see D. Sturdy, 'The old Ashmolean', *Ashmolean* no. 1 (1983), 7–9.

[16] The most valuable entomological acquisition during Duncan's keepership was the collection of the Revd F. W. Hope, but it was so vast that it never entered the Ashmolean: instead it found temporary shelter in the 'Taylor buildings' (a term then used to identify the University Galleries as well as the adjoining Taylor Institution) before entering the new University Museum: see Ovenell, 215–16.

[17] His publications included an account of Roman antiquities in England and Wales under the title *Reliquiae Romanae* (1836).

[18] Their full-time presence in Oxford was, however, neither expected nor given. A later Keeper, J. H. Parker, denied that the Duncans had displayed any interest in antiquities and, indeed, much in the Ashmolean as a whole: 'The two Mr. Duncans were gentlemen of property, living at Bath,' he wrote, 'who thought it a great compliment from the University to give them the name of Keeper of the Ashmolean Museum, and they came to Oxford once a year to see that it was "all right", leaving the entire management to their assistants.' This assertion was hotly denied by G. A. Rowell in his *Recent Discoveries in the Ashmolean Museum* (1881), who claimed that the Duncans' contributions to the Museum in terms of new acquisitions and fixtures and fittings qualified them for consideration as second founders of the institution.

[19] *GM* (1864) ii. 125.

[20] R. T. Gunther, *Early Science in Oxford* (14 vols 1923–45) iii. 369, credits the Duncans with almost half of the zoological holdings in the 1830s, but from the comparatively small proportion of specimens attributed to the foundation collection in the 1836 catalogue (120 items out of 2,600, the latter emanating from 140 donors, according to Ovenell, 205) their impact seems to have been even greater.

observations on subjects connected with natural history, experimental philosophy, and other branches of modern research'.[21] Before long, however, the advancement of the natural sciences elsewhere in the University far outstripped the capacity of the Ashmolean to provide adequate and relevant teaching resources, and with the acceptance by Convocation in 1854 of the need for an entirely new museum of natural history, the Ashmolean itself was faced with the need once again to adapt or die.

In that same year the 82-year-old Duncan resigned his keepership, to be succeeded by John Phillips, the University's Deputy Reader in Geology and an obvious candidate for the Ashmolean post, since he had begun his career as curator of the Yorkshire Philosophical Society's museum at York. Phillips also had the task of overseeing the development of the new Natural Science Museum in Parks Road and was appointed its first Keeper, a position he held in plurality with his office at the Ashmolean. Under him the natural history collections (including the geological material previously removed to the Clarendon Building) were transferred to the Natural Science Museum and teaching ceased (in 1855) in the basement laboratory, so extinguishing the role of the Ashmolean as a centre of science.

With little remaining beyond the rump of its seventeenth-century collection of curiosities, the viability of the Ashmolean hung in the balance. As already mentioned, a few antiquities had arrived which were to form the germ of the Museum's later development, but further acquisitions were slow in coming. Amongst modest additions the most notable comprised further collections of Anglo-Saxon material: one such arrived (along with some Romano-British items) in 1855, having been bequeathed eight years earlier by the Revd A. B. Hutchins. Others had been excavated at Brighthampton (given in 1858); at Standlake by J. Y. Akerman and Stephen Stone; and at Fairford by W. M. Wylie (1865).[22] The development of archaeology in general and of the Ashmolean's role in its promotion still lay some time in the future,[23] however, and it is a measure of the scant importance attached to the nascent discipline that in 1858 the Bodleian Library was offered not only the books and manuscripts from the Ashmolean's library (housed in some small chambers on the upper floor) but also the coins and medals, to be added to the Bodleian's own cabinet, and all the antiquities, to join its collection of curiosities. By 1860 the transfer of all but the last element, which the curators of the Bodleian had rejected, had been completed.

---

[21] Ovenell, 189, 203. Ovenell aptly compares the renaissance of spirit embodied in the Ashmolean Society with that of the 17th-century Oxford Philosophical Society, established at the Museum under its first Keeper, Robert Plot.

[22] A summary of these developments, together with descriptions of surviving specimens, is given in A. MacGregor and E. Bolick, *Ashmolean Museum: a summary catalogue of the Anglo-Saxon collections* (1993), 5–10.

[23] Phillips's role in instigating local collections of antiquities was, however, stoutly canvassed by Rowell in his *Recent Discoveries*.

By 1862 a new role for the Ashmolean building was agreed. The upper floor, which had formed the original display gallery, was now to be given up to the examiners as a writing school; a new entrance was opened up on the east side of the building, giving access to the staircase. The internal stairs, meanwhile, were extended down to the basement, which hitherto had been accessible only by an independent entrance, in order to minimize the risk of fire;[24] and the ground floor was designated as 'an Archaeological Museum'. The necessary alterations were completed by the summer of 1864, when the Museum reopened to the public from 10 a.m. to 4 p.m. daily for two weeks, and thereafter from 11 a.m. to 1 p.m. only.[25] A photograph of about this period (Plate 27) reveals extreme crowding of exhibits in the gallery, notwithstanding the earlier losses to the collections. These were already being compensated for by additions of ethnological material, notably in 1863 with specimens from the collections of the explorer W. J. Burchell. Archaeological material also continued to accumulate: in addition to the Anglo-Saxon benefactions already mentioned, Greek, Roman and Egyptian antiquities were acquired from the Christy collection in 1866, and Near Eastern and classical material from the Revd Greville Chester. This latter series of acquisitions began in 1865 and continued until Chester's death in 1892.

It was in the archaeological collections in particular that the salvation of the Ashmolean was to lie.[26] John Phillips was by no means unsympathetic to the archaeological cause; but the curatorship of the University Museum now absorbed so much of his time that he was more than willing to relinquish his responsibilities at the Ashmolean. The moment proved propitious, for there was already waiting in the wings a candidate who not only possessed the appropriate interest and ability to take over the keepership, but was also prepared to underwrite his appointment with an endowment to the University. This was John Henry Parker,[27] already 62 years of age, a successful publisher and an authority on the history of architecture[28] when, in 1868, he

[24] The abatement of this danger had been brought about by the abandonment of the laboratory for teaching and experimental purposes (see above) and its appropriation as a store for some parts of the Arundel marbles and other sculptures.

[25] Ovenell, 218–19.

[26] Just how close the Ashmolean came to losing even this element of its collections is revealed in a letter addressed to the Vice-Chancellor on 26 Jan. 1867 by George Rolleston, the University's Professor of Anatomy and Physiology, and himself an archaeologist, in which he advocates the relocating of the archaeological and anthropological collections to a new gallery to be built adjoining the University Museum: AA AMS 45.

[27] John Henry Parker, MA 1867, CB, Keeper 1870–84.

[28] Parker was a moving spirit behind the Oxford Architectural and Historical Society as he had been in its earlier manifestations, the Oxford Society for the Study of Gothic Architecture (1839–48) and the Oxford Architectural Society (1848–60). As early as 1858 his son James Parker, then librarian of the Oxford Architectural Society, had written to John Phillips on the desirability of reshaping the Ashmolean as a museum of national antiquities: see Ovenell, 216. For the wider context see A. MacGregor, 'Antiquity inventoried: museums and "national antiquities" in the mid-nineteenth century' in V. Brand (ed.), The Victorian Study of the Past (forthcoming).

set out his proposals in two letters to the Dean of Christ Church. Parker proposed himself for the keepership of 'the Historical Museum of the University', undertaking at the same time to make a permanent endowment of £250 per annum, a sum which he recognized as inadequate by itself for the support of the Museum, but which he conjectured would lead to further promises of support from other quarters. Agreement was concluded with the University in 1870, whereon Phillips surrendered the keepership of the Ashmolean to Parker.

While undoubtedly deeply committed to the cause of the Ashmolean, Parker continued his former practice of wintering in Rome, where he excavated, recorded in great detail the surviving antique architecture[29] and bought numerous antiquities for the Ashmolean collections.[30] In time, ill health forced him to spend less time abroad but ensured that his attendances at the Museum were hardly more frequent. None the less, he made an undoubted impact on the Ashmolean. During his period of office a foothold was regained on the upper floor, where plans, photographs, casts and architectural fragments were insinuated while the premises were not required by its new occupants, the public examiners. Having published in 1870 a summary list of donations to the Museum from 1836 to 1868,[31] the Under-Keeper, G. A. Rowell—himself over 70 years old—was now called upon to complete as soon as possible a series of more detailed catalogues of the collections. Subsequent delays and misunderstandings introduced a certain harshness into the relations between the Keeper and his deputy. These were to deteriorate even further following Rowell's resignation in 1879, when his successor discovered in an outside basement of the Museum certain items from the seventeenth-century foundation collection; accusation led to counter-accusation in a wrangle which reached the pages of the local and ultimately the national newspapers.[32]

This public exchange, together with the adverse (and ill-informed) criticism which it brought on the Museum, was regretted by Parker for more than one reason. 'This attack on the Ashmolean', he wrote to the editor of

---

[29] Parker's archive of over 3,000 photographs of Roman monuments, which he was to bequeath to the Ashmolean for the use of the Oxford Architectural and Historical Society, survives today in the care of the Ashmolean library. His work in Rome brought him decorations from the King of Italy and from the Pope.

[30] He was also to make numerous personal benefactions to the Museum: a list entitled 'Things found in Egypt, Rome, etc. given to the Ashmolean by J. H. Parker...' comprises more than 1,100 items: AA AMS 45, item 2, quoted in Ovenell, 249.

[31] *A List of Donations to the Antiquarian and Ethnological Collections in the Ashmolean Museum, 1836 to 1868* (1870).

[32] The relevant press cuttings, mostly in the form of letters from Rowell, Parker, and Rowell's successor as Under-Keeper, E. C. Evans, are preserved in the Ashmolean library: AP 23. Elements of them were reprinted in pamphlet form both by Rowell, in *The Assistant Keepership and the New Catalogue of the Ashmolean Museum* (1879), and *Recent Discoveries in the Ashmolean Museum* (1881), and by Parker, in *The Keeper's Correction of some Misstatements in London Newspapers in November, 1880* (1880) and in *Ashmolean Museum* (1881).

the *Standard*, 'comes at an unfortunate time, just as a friend of mine is proposing to send a valuable collection of articles of virtu to the Ashmolean, as soon as the Public Examiners give up their charge of the upper room, of which they have kept possession for the last dozen years.'[33] The proposed benefaction was linked to a plan, presented in 1878 to the Hebdomadal Council in the form of a memorial signed by 132 senior members of the University, calling for the formal establishment in Oxford of a museum of archaeology and art. Particular emphasis in this institution should, it was suggested, be given to casts of Greek and Roman sculpture and to models of antique architecture; the University's collections of sculpture should be centralized there, and libraries dedicated to classical epigraphy and to numismatics (the latter including casts of antique coins) should form prominent components. It was to this enhanced institution that C. D. E. Fortnum, the benefactor alluded to by Parker, anticipated adding his collection of classical and Renaissance antiquities, although it is evident that he saw it more clearly than most as a development of (rather than a competitor to) the Ashmolean Museum. Fortnum added his support to plans for rationalizing in this centre the University's collections of 'the works of man' (singling out for criticism the omnivorous University Museum, 'which ought to be *confined* to the works of nature'). He also declared that he would make no move with his benefaction until positive action had been taken, for 'to entrust my loved children (my only family) to a baby-farm where they might die for want of proper nursing, clothing, or care, would be the act of an extremely careless and unnatural parent'.[34]

In his efforts to establish the Ashmolean on a firm archaeological footing, Parker also had the support of Greville Chester, who focused attention on the Museum's problems with an eloquent and biting broadsheet entitled *Notes on the Present and Future of the Archaeological Collections of the University of Oxford*.[35] Chester castigated the University for the 'contemptuous and apathetic want of system', through which even the archaeological potential of the Ashmolean was threatened by the dissipation of existing resources amongst five separate institutions, so that no two elements could be studied together. Outside the public areas of the Museum, some of the

---

[33] The 'valuable collection' referred to was that of C. D. E. Fortnum (see p. 609 below).

[34] OUA WP/β/2/4, quoted in full in Ovenell, 243. Later, in a letter addressed to the *Academy* on 10 Dec. 1881, Fortnum elaborated his list of desiderata for the new institution: he saw a need for a comprehensive approach to the study of material culture, in unbroken sequence from the first flint implements, through the classical civilizations and the Renaissance, and up to the present day: Ovenell, 245–6.

[35] Although designed to rally support for the Ashmolean, remarks made by Chester in this pamphlet fuelled the disagreement involving Rowell. Rowell replied to Chester's criticisms (which he took personally) with a pamphlet of his own entitled *Remarks on Mr. Greville Chester's Notes on the Archaeological Collections of Oxford and the Recent Discovery in the Ashmolean Museum* (1891). Chester remained a generous benefactor to the Museum until his death in 1892, when his cabinet of antique gems was bequeathed to the Ashmolean.

Arundel marbles which had come to the University through the intercession of John Evelyn were crammed into the former laboratory in the basement, while others more recently arrived through a gift by the Countess of Pomfret were 'out of sight and out of mind' in the Taylorian basement. The Greek and Etruscan terracottas acquired earlier from Signor Castellani were to be viewed dimly through a glass door in the same institution. The coins languished in the Bodleian Library, while the University Museum, on the principle that 'all is Fish that comes to their net', had started a rival collection of antiquities.

In the absence of any immediate response from the University to these problems, plans were laid to make the best of the resources available at the Ashmolean. During 1882 the Museum was redecorated, and many of the pictures from the foundation collection (some sixty to seventy of them) were retrieved from the Clarendon attics and rehung in the upper room and on the staircase. Little progress had been made with the more radical scheme when, on 31 January 1884 at the age of 77, Parker died. In the ebb and flow of the Ashmolean's fortunes, matters stood in a troubled state. Exceptional measures were required if the Museum was to seize the opportunity to establish a new academic credibility in the fields opening out before it. By good fortune, a candidate with more than enough vigour and tenacity to match the challenge presented himself for consideration as Parker's successor.

Arthur Evans,[36] appointed Keeper on 17 June 1884 at the age of 34, succeeded not only in saving the Ashmolean but in transforming it into a revitalized centre of international repute, fitted to the demands of the century to come. Within a few months of taking office, Evans had prepared for the Visitors a six-part scheme (the outlines of which had already been established by his predecessor) designed to ensure the security of the building and its contents, the reclamation of accommodation 'perverted to other uses' over the years, and the unification and development of the collections in such a manner as 'to secure the greatest possible amount of usefulness to students'.[37]

As an opening gambit, Evans offered for transfer to the new (Pitt Rivers) anthropological museum almost the entire ethnological holdings of the Ashmolean. Some of these were, he pointed out, of the utmost importance, including, for example, the items brought from the Pacific by Forster, and the material collected by the Tradescants and forming part of the Ashmolean's seventeenth-century foundation collection.[38] In return, various hold-

---

[36] Arthur John Evans, BA 1874, Keeper 1884–1908. For Evans see J. Evans, *Time and Chance: the story of Arthur Evans and his forebears* (1943); D. B. Harden, *Sir Arthur Evans, 1851–1941: a memoir* (1983).

[37] A. J. Evans, *The Ashmolean Museum and the Archaeological Collections of the University* (Report of the Keeper of the Ashmolean to the Visitors).

[38] Evans had reread some of the original manuscript inventories of the Museum dated *c.*1685 (AA AMS 8, AMS 18) and had used them to identify items surviving in the collections from this date. The inventory of ethnological material earmarked for transfer (E. C. Evans, 'List of

ings in the University Museum, the Taylorian building, and the Bodleian Library were earmarked by Evans as appropriate for transfer to the Ashmolean. Amongst these was the entire coin cabinet, housed inappropriately and inaccessibly in the Bodleian: Evans pressed strongly his conviction that 'the juxtaposition of the Numismatic Collections with our other antiquities, is of vital importance for the sound study of Archaeology'.[39]

A major priority in Evans's scheme in terms of accommodation was, as in the earlier plans outlined above, the rehabilitation of the upper gallery. The first nineteenth-century Keeper fully to appreciate the historical significance of the Tradescant collection with which the Ashmolean had been founded, Evans presented plans for the full restitution of the portraits and some of the other exhibits that had been retrieved from their 'lurking place' in the attics of the Clarendon Building. Another restoration scheme was presented for the chamber known as 'Wood's study', converted under the regime of the examiners to a lavatory: the Keeper lamented that it 'acts at present as a slow accumulator of sewer gas, but is entirely lost to the services of Archaeology'. A plan to replace the Museum's nine coal fires with a central-heating system was also submitted. A special grant was requested to cover the cost of these exceptional outgoings, but the need for increased annual funding was also spelled out, particularly to develop and to enhance the collections.

Having set out his immediate objectives, Evans sought (even before they had been considered by the Visitors) to rally support for them with a public lecture entitled 'The Ashmolean Museum as a home of archaeology in Oxford'. The dire need for action was restated, tantalizing prospects for substantial benefactions attendant upon such actions were held out and the prevailing shortcomings were outlined with a forthrightness which was, in the speaker's own closing words, 'frank to the verge of indiscretion'.[40] Further canvassing was pursued with a *conversazione* in the Museum at which collections of borrowed material were drafted in to convey an impression of what the Museum might aspire to become. Large numbers of Egyptian, Greek and Roman antiquities were exhibited, along with medieval

---

anthropological objects transferred from the Ashmolean to the Pitt Rivers Museum, 1886', AA AMS 25) includes items then identified as originating in the foundation collection, but most of these were withheld from the subsequent transfer and remain today in the Ashmolean. (For items from the foundation collection which were inadvertently handed over at this time see L. Williamson, 'Ethnological specimens in the Pitt Rivers Museum attributed to the Tradescant collection' in MacGregor (ed.), *Tradescant's Rarities*, 338–45.) Amongst other items which Evans claimed to have discovered at this time was a plaster death-mask of the elder Tradescant: such an item was also mentioned by J. Hamel (*Tradescant der Aeltere 1618 in Russland* (St Petersburg 1847), 305; Hamel, *England and Russia* (1854), 294), but is otherwise unknown.

[39] Evans, *The Ashmolean Museum and the Archaeological Collections*. In due course the coins and medals were returned to the Ashmolean; the Heberden Coin Room emerged as an independent department in 1961: see Christopher White, 'Museums and art galleries' in *The Twentieth Century*, 486.

[40] A. J. Evans, *The Ashmolean Museum as a Home of Archaeology in Oxford* (1884), 32.

European and ethnological material. Amongst those who loaned items for the evening was John (later Sir John) Evans, the Keeper's father, much of whose vast collection of antiquities later came permanently to the Museum through Arthur Evans in 1909 and in 1927.[41]

Although no instant resolution followed of the problems outlined by Evans, the dynamism of the new Keeper soon dispelled the malaise that had settled over the Museum, and new benefactions began to flow in.[42] Fortnum's loan collections of maiolica and bronzes by now almost filled the upper room. First steps had also been taken in the rationalization of the University's holdings: the transfer in 1885–6 to the Pitt Rivers Museum of much of the ethnological material was to some extent compensated for by receipts of antiquities from the University Museum and from the Bodleian Library. In 1888 the evacuation of the Arundel marbles from the basement (where they had been stored rather than displayed) freed this area for the establishment of a lecture-room in which the tenets of the new Ashmolean doctrines could be preached. In the same year, with the aid of a grant from the University, a new library was founded within the Museum where books appropriate to its new disciplinary basis were placed. At the same time, 'Wood's study' was fitted out as an additional library, in which were placed the books and other materials belonging to the Oxford Architectural and Historical Society, including the sixty-eight portfolios containing Parker's photographs. So successful was Evans in expanding the collections that Ashmole's museum, even with its enhanced display facilities, quickly became inadequate to the task which it had been set. At this time an average of over 2,000 accessions a year were being added through Evans's own efforts and by those of others working in the East Mediterranean such as Flinders Petrie, H. M. Kennard, D. G. Hogarth and J. L. Myres.[43] Accordingly, a new plan was prepared envisaging even more radical changes: Evans now proposed that the entire institution should be removed to new, purpose-built premises where the exhibits could be properly appreciated and where there would be room for continuing development.[44]

---

[41] A programme for the *conversazione* is preserved in the Ashmolean library: AMS 16, fo 71.

[42] In mentioning the importance of Evans's galvanizing effect on the Museum, the contributions of others must also be acknowledged. In particular, the Vice-Chancellor of the period, Benjamin Jowett, cast by Joan Evans as a wholly negative influence in the upheavals of the period (*Time and Chance*, 261–87), has been shown in an altogether different light by Geoffrey Faber: *Jowett* (1957), 384–401. Jowett, it seems, had conceived plans of his own for the establishment of an archaeological museum at the Ashmolean and of a museum of Greek antiquities and art. After the appointment of the headstrong Evans, however, Jowett found his function reduced to that of 'a man in a short-term responsible position, with a foot on the brake' (Faber, 398).

[43] For an example of the accessions see M. Vickers, 'Arthur Evans, Sicily and Greek vases in Oxford', *Apollo* cxvii (Apr. 1983), 276–9.

[44] A. J. Evans, *The Scheme for a New Museum of the Arts and Archaeology, in Connexion with Mr. Fortnum's Offer* (1891).

No doubt this proposal too would have run quickly into the sand had not Evans now been able to hold out the prospect of substantial funding for the project and a generous benefaction to secure its future, the source of both being the wealthy Fortnum. Fortnum's extensive collections of antique and Renaissance bronzes, finger-rings and maiolica had almost been secured for the University by Parker, but the offer had been withdrawn when the benefactor (with some justification) felt himself to have been slighted by the university authorities. Now, with much skill and diplomacy, Evans succeeded in mollifying the injured Fortnum and in overcoming all internal opposition to the plan for expanding the Ashmolean's ambit. In his scheme for a new museum, Evans presented the prospective benefits to the University in the form of a simple but persuasive equation:

The University gains	*The University contributes*
1 The Ashmolean Building	1 £10,000 for the New Building
2 £10,000 from Mr. Fortnum	2 £10,000 (approximately) towards
3 The eventual accession of the	the New Museum Fund
remainder of Mr. Fortnum's	
collection	
4 The legacy of Mr. Fortnum's	
Archaeological Library	

When Fortnum wrote again to the Vice-Chancellor his offer was graciously accepted, the University later rewarding him with the honorary degree of DCL.

The new museum premises took the form of an extension to the rear of the University Galleries in Beaumont Street (see Chapter 20).[45] Evans's extension was designed to provide not only display space for the antiquities, which were now to be transferred from the Ashmolean in Broad Street,[46] but also premises for the professor of classical art and archaeology, thus ensuring a closer involvement of the Museum with the teaching faculty. By 1894 the new building work had been completed and on 17 November the transfer of the antiquities was completed 'without loss or breakage'.[47] In the same year Fortnum deposited on loan the residue of his collection not already assigned to the Ashmolean, ownership of the whole magnificent

[45] The architect of the extension was W. H. Moore; for a reappraisal of his work in Oxford, see Pt 2, Ch. 30.

[46] Some material, such as the Castellani collection and those parts of the Arundel marbles previously stored in the Ashmolean's former basement laboratory, were (as mentioned above) already stored in this building.

[47] *Ashmolean Museum: report of the Keeper to the Visitors for the year 1894*, 1. The ground floor of the original Ashmolean building, meanwhile, became the editorial headquarters of the *Oxford English Dictionary*, the basement being occupied by the Bodleian book stacks. In 1924 the upper floor, having been put to various other uses for some years, became home to a historical collection of scientific instruments, from which developed the Museum of the History of Science, which currently occupies the building: see White, 'Museums and galleries', 488–9.

benefaction passing to the Museum by bequest on his death in 1895.[48] The collections of antiquities (under Evans) and of paintings and sculpture (under Alexander Macdonald) coexisted under one roof, while maintaining their separate identities, until 1908.[49] Their unification in that year, at Evans's suggestion, is described in the following chapter.

The transformation from moribund cabinet of curiosities to twentieth-century museum which the Ashmolean had undergone was as vitally necessary as it was timely. The disciplines of archaeology and art history with which it now concerned itself simply had not existed a century earlier and it is difficult to imagine how the Ashmolean could have embraced them without the complete metamorphosis which had been achieved. To have rejected them, on the other hand, would have ensured its continuing slide towards irrelevance and, ultimately, oblivion.

---

[48] See *Ashmolean Museum, Report of the Keeper to the Visitors for the year 1899* for a summary account of the bequest.

[49] On 30 June 1908 Alexander Macdonald resigned his keepership of the University Galleries, the Assistant Keeper, C. F. Bell, being appointed interim Keeper and later Keeper of the Fine Art Department within the combined institution. At the same time, Evans gave notice of his resignation at the end of the year; his successor, D. G. Hogarth, became Keeper of the 'Antiquarium' and of the reconstituted Ashmolean.

20

The University Galleries

J. J. L. WHITELEY

In the early nineteenth century, most of the works of art belonging to the University (excluding those which belonged to the colleges) were exhibited in and around the Bodleian. The Arundel inscriptions, given to the University in 1667, and the busts and statues added by the Countess of Pomfret in 1755 were set out in ground-floor rooms adjoining the Schools Quadrangle.[1] This was not an ideal arrangement, particularly for the Pomfret marbles, which were poorly displayed behind a 'shilling barrier'.[2] The Picture Gallery, one of the oldest public institutions of its kind, was better-organized.[3] For a small fee, visitors could see approximately 200 portraits and a handful of other pictures, arranged in a large, well-lit, panelled gallery which occupied the site of the present Upper Library. But, despite the presence of a few good portraits, acquired chiefly out of interest in the sitters, most were of little value.[4] Connoisseurs, who came to Oxford to see the collections at Christ Church and at Blenheim, did not, as a rule, visit the Bodleian Picture Gallery.[5]

The lack of space for exhibiting the Pomfret marbles prompted the Revd Francis Randolph, Principal of St Alban Hall, to bequeath £1,000 towards the cost of building a new gallery. Randolph does not seem to have taken account of the existing pictures, nor, despite a persistent belief to the contrary, did he mention the Arundel inscriptions, for which he almost certainly did not foresee a place in the new gallery. He did, however, intend that

---

[1] *The New Pocket Companion for Oxford or Guide through the University* (1812), 9–12.

[2] J. W. Burgon, *Some Remarks on Art with Reference to the Studies of the University, a Letter* (1846), 7. I am grateful to Mr Peter Howell for drawing my attention to this book. See also William Westall's water-colour of the Sculpture Gallery in the Ashmolean Print Room, repr. in R. Ackermann, *History of the University of Oxford* (2 vols 1814) ii facing p. 224.

[3] W. D. Macray, *Annals of the Bodleian Library* (2nd edn 1890), 257.

[4] J. Norris, *A Catalogue of the Pictures, Models, Busts etc. in the Bodleian Gallery and Library* (1840); apart from portraits, the largest group of paintings came from the bequest of Dr John King (see A. Wood, *The History and Antiquities of the University of Oxford*, trans. J. Gutch (2 vols in 3 1792–6) ii. 969–70); the pictures, transferred to the University Galleries in 1845, also included twelve pictures donated by the artists.

[5] Neither Passavant nor Waagen appears to have visited the Picture Gallery on their visits to Oxford.

there should be room for future gifts of 'paintings, engravings and other curiosities'.[6]

Randolph's money, received by the University in 1797, was not sufficient to allow work on the gallery to begin, and it put an unexpected difficulty in the way of alternative proposals. Sir Roger Newdigate, who was related by marriage to the Countess of Pomfret and had acted as her agent when she gave the marbles to the University, offered £2,000 to cover the costs of installing them in the main reading-room of the Radcliffe Library and of enclosing the loggia on the ground floor as a space for the inscriptions.[7] His proposals were accepted by the Radcliffe trustees, who promised to provide a salary for the keeper of the statues, and they received the assent of Convocation in March 1806, despite a last-minute attack by the Radcliffe Librarian, Thomas Hornsby, who objected to the apparent misuse of the building under the terms of Radcliffe's will,[8] and despite strong opposition from one of Randolph's trustees, who believed that the University would forfeit Randolph's bequest by accepting an alternative proposal for exhibiting the marbles.[9] Once the money had been handed over, Flaxman proposed a layout for the statues and agreed to repair the damaged pieces.[10] But the Solicitor-General and his predecessor, Sir Samuel Romilly, advised that the University could only reconcile Newdigate's gift and Randolph's bequest by an application to the Court of Chancery and, as a result, despite one or two bolder members of Convocation who were willing to risk a suit in Chancery, Sir Roger's money was returned.[11] His famous candelabra, found in Hadrian's Villa and restored by Piranesi, remained in the Radcliffe Library, but the Pomfret marbles were not moved to new premises for a further thirty years.

Had Randolph's proposal been put in hand without delay, Oxford would have been strongly placed to benefit from the dispersal of works of art in England after the French Revolution. However, by the time the new gallery was begun, forty-three years later, the stakes were less high. This delay was partly caused by the terms of the bequest. Randolph had intended his money as a down-payment on the gallery to gather interest and encourage others.

---

[6] The text of the relevant item in Randolph's will appears in A. J. Butler, *Report for the Committee on the Amalgamation of the Ashmolean Museum and University Galleries* (1893); the notion that Randolph's supposed provision for the Arundel inscriptions was neglected in favour of the Chantrey plasters was wishful thinking by the archaeologists who attempted to demote the Chantrey plasters at the end of the century in favour of the 'Graeco-Roman' collection; the published accounts are, correspondingly, confused: see D. Harden, 'The Ashmolean Museum— Beaumont St', *Museums Journal* lii (Feb. 1953), 265; D. Haynes, *The Arundel Marbles* (1975), 16.

[7] Bodl. G. A. Oxon. b. 19, fo 352.

[8] Bodl. G. A. Oxon. b. 19, fos 354 and 361.

[9] Bodl. G. A. Oxon. b. 19, fo 358, and Don. b. 12, fo 149.

[10] R. Churton, 'Biographical memoirs of Sir Roger Newdigate', lxxvii (1867), 649.

[11] Ibid. 706; see also S. G. Gillam, *The Building Accounts of the Radcliffe Camera* (OHS new series xiii. 1958), pp. xl–iv.

But the hoped-for benefactions did not appear; the best alternative suggestion was disallowed and only an ingenious scheme to amalgamate the Randolph fund with money received in 1835 from the heirs of Sir Robert Taylor to promote the teaching of modern languages permitted work on the new gallery to begin.

On 10 May 1839 a site on Beaumont Street belonging to Worcester College was purchased by means of the joint Randolph and Taylor funds.[12] Three weeks later, Convocation agreed to the insertion of a notice in the press, advertising a competition for two buildings and inviting architects to apply to the University Registrar, Dr Philip Bliss, for details.[13] These were circulated in a document signed by Bliss on 12 June which instructed applicants that the two institutions—an art gallery and a languages library with teaching-rooms—should be internally distinct but should give the appearance from the outside of a single building. The art gallery should consist of a basement, a ground-floor space for sculpture and an upper gallery or galleries, lit from above, for paintings.[14] As an afterthought, Bliss stipulated that the building should be in the 'Grecian' style, no doubt heading off any misconceptions among architects about the uses of the Gothic.[15] No other details of the gallery were supplied, not even the cost of the new building, an omission which puzzled and irritated a number of the competing architects.[16] But Bliss, himself, had no idea how much money would be available. The Taylor Institute was well endowed and did not need the support of the Randolph Gallery but the Gallery was under-funded and could not have been built without a substantial supplement. By making the one institution dependent on the other, Bliss and the trustees perhaps hoped to strengthen their application to the University for a grant to fund the difference. However, at the time of the competition, Bliss could not presume on extra money and could not petition for a subsidy until he had an architect's plan and a builder's estimate to submit to Convocation.

Architects were given four months to send in their designs. This was not enough for several of the competitors, who had not completed their drawings by the closing date on 19 October.[17] By 15 November twenty-eight entries had been received and submitted to a delegacy which included Dr Edward Cardwell, Principal of St Alban Hall, Dr John Antony Cramer, Principal of New Inn Hall, the Revd Lewis Sneyd, Warden of All Souls,

[12] Butler, *Report for the Committee.*
[13] Notice of Convocation, 6 June 1839.
[14] Copies of the document, which was handwritten and reproduced lithographically, are in the Ashmolean: AA W. A. miscellaneous papers.
[15] See H. Colvin, *Unbuilt Oxford* (1987), 122; the clause was added by Bliss to the original draft to the document, which is in the museum archives.
[16] See the letters from the architects to Bliss, AA W. A. letters and papers, 1839.
[17] See ibid.

Henry George Liddell, Student of Christ Church, the Vice-Chancellor, the two proctors and ten other members of the University.[18] In December the delegates submitted a short-list of five entries to Sir Robert Smirke for professional advice.[19] According to Liddell, Anthony Salvin and Charles Robert Cockerell sent in the best designs. Liddell personally preferred Salvin's entry because Cockerell's appeared too expensive.[20] But Smirke's clear preference for the drawings submitted by his pupil, Cockerell, must have carried weight with the delegates, who on 3 February unanimously selected his more costly looking scheme. In Smirke's view, Cockerell was the only competitor who, by designing his building round an open courtyard, had made adequate provision for admitting light. Salvin, too, had devised a courtyard, but it was open to the north, where the light was restricted by the site, and no clear proposal was indicated for lighting the lower galleries.[21] Salvin attributed his failure to the haste in which his drawing had been prepared and to the lack of detail in the instructions, which provided him 'with so little knowledge of the amount Convocation were likely to sanction' he had 'erred on the side of economy'.[22] According to Liddell, however, economy was on Salvin's side; but his failure to indicate a sufficient source of light and Smirke's lack of enthusiasm for his design probably cost him a place among the prize-winners. A majority of the delegates voted for John Plowman to receive the second prize of £50.[23]

Estimates were not available to the delegacy. Smirke had been asked to indicate the likely cost of the proposals, but had refused to do so.[24] This did not affect the award of £100 to Cockerell as the University was not committed to building the winning scheme;[25] but nor did it deter the Vice-Chancellor from immediately asking Convocation to agree to the nomination of a second delegacy to supervise the work of building Cockerell's design and to 'employ in aid of the Randolph Fund such monies, the property of the University, as may be available for that purpose'.[26] This proposal provoked lively opposition, but was accepted after an assurance

---

[18] Proceedings of the delegates, OUA TL/M/1/1 (hereafter cited as Proceedings); twenty-seven entries were listed; a twenty-eighth was received and accepted on 28 Nov.: ibid; the drawings were returned to the architects after the competition; one drawing by Gutch and Trendell is in the Bodleian (Colvin 123); Cockerell's drawings are in the V. & A. Print Room; a lithograph after Salvin's design is reproduced in J. Allibone, *Anthony Salvin* (1988), 59.

[19] Proceedings, 12 Dec. 1839; see also Smirke's correspondence with Bliss, BL Add. MS 54573.

[20] H. L. Thompson, *Henry George Liddell D.D., Dean of Christ Church, Oxford: a memoir* (1899), 50.

[21] Smirke to the Vice-Chancellor, 23 Dec. 1839, Proceedings.

[22] Salvin to Bliss, 10 Feb. 1840, AA W. A. letters and papers, 1840.

[23] Proceedings, 28 Jan. 1839.

[24] Smirke to the Vice-Chancellor, 23 Dec. 1839, Proceedings.

[25] Proceedings, 30 Oct. 1839.

[26] Notice of Convocation, 21 Feb. 1840.

from the Vice-Chancellor that estimates would be submitted to Convocation when they became available.[27]

By 15 December 1840 Bliss had a final set of plans from Cockerell (revised after discussion with the delegates) and an estimate from the builders, George Baker & Son of Lambeth, for £49,373, of which £30,992 was intended for the Galleries and £18,381 for the Taylor Institute.[28] The difference between the available funds and the estimate was supplied by a grant of £10,000 from the accumulated profits of the Clarendon Press.

The designs which Cockerell submitted in 1839 were faithful to the instructions issued to the architects. The exuberant mixture of antique and Italian detail was suitably 'Grecian', and the Taylor Institute, with its 'ornamental' façade on St Giles, was neatly housed in the eastern half, as requested. The upper galleries and the Grand Staircase were top-lit and the two institutions were combined with ingenious symmetry. As a consequence, the Taylor Institute, which was a larger, wider and more complex building than the two-storeyed gallery on the west, dictated the appearance of the gallery façades, which bore little logical relationship to the rooms within.

On receiving the award, Cockerell eliminated all but six of the skylights from his design. The delegates, no doubt recalling Smirke's comments on the need for light and the instructions issued to the architects, invited him to obtain an opinion from William Dyce, Superintendent of the Board of Design, and Charles Eastlake, the future director of the National Gallery and already an acknowledged expert in everything connected with works of art.[29] Dyce and Eastlake, in turn, consulted Dr Gustave Waagen in Berlin, Schnorr von Carolsfeld in Munich, and Baron Friesen in Dresden, and submitted their findings to Cockerell in December 1840.[30] Impressed by recent experiments with side-lighting in German museums, Friesen, Dyce and Eastlake recommended a careful combination of screens and windows for lighting small pictures, with skylights for the larger works of art. Dyce and Eastlake had doubts about the effect of the nine windows in the Great Gallery, inserted simply to balance the Taylor Institute windows on the east, but they approved of the plan to light the long gallery, the present Fortnum Gallery, by windows on the north. Waagen opposed the use of skylights, but

---

[27] William Sewell of Exeter College, who was later deeply involved in the schemes to buy the Lawrence drawings, scathingly criticized the impropriety of these proposals: Bodl. G. A. Oxon. c. 29, fo 656.

[28] D. Watkin, *The Life and Work of C. R. Cockerell* (1974), 200; the contract drawings from the university archives are on deposit in the Print Room of the department of Western art in the Ashmolean; for a detailed discussion of Cockerell's building, see also D. Watkin, 'The making of the Ashmolean', *Country Life* (7 Feb. 1974), 242–5.

[29] Proceedings, 24 Oct. 1840.

[30] A copy of the letter from Dyce and Eastlake with an edited translation of the other letters is in AA W. A. miscellaneous papers; see C. Lloyd, 'Reflexions on the Ashmolean', *Oxford Art Journal* i (1980), 47–9; Watkin, 205–6; and M. Pointon, *William Dyce, 1806–1864* (1979), 64.

favoured high, lateral windows of the kind which Klenze designed for the Hermitage sculptures; Cockerell eventually employed these in the Randolph Gallery.

There is no written evidence that Cockerell or the delegates took account of these recommendations, but the final arrangement of windows and sky-lights suggests they did. The windows in the Great Gallery, to which Dyce and Eastlake objected, were covered over on the inside, making, as Fisher's water-colour shows (Plate 29), a dark south end, which must have been particularly troublesome in winter.[31] All other galleries, as Cockerell in-tended, were lit by windows on the side. The lighting on the ground floor was supplemented by three recesses, a semi-circular apse on the west wall of the west wing, a rectangular space on the west end of the long sculpture gallery, and a nearly circular tribune on the north wall, facing the entrance: all three were roofed with glass. These light-filled projections and the six skylights in the Great Gallery were a source of leaks throughout the nine-teenth century. Cockerell was consulted about the problem as early as 1847,[32] but, despite periodic attempts to exclude the rain,[33] and despite the prediction of Baron Friesen that these would not be a problem in England 'where mechanical skill has overcome so many difficulties',[34] the trouble was never cured.

The balancing of the wings produced a palatial Picture Gallery on the upper floor of the west wing, for which the University had no immediate need. Unlike the Fitzwilliam or the Dulwich Picture Gallery, the Oxford Galleries were not built to house an existing gift of paintings, and the works of art moved from the Picture Gallery in the Bodleian to fill the space were mostly of little interest.[35] Seven full-scale copies of Raphael's tapestry car-toons covered the upper walls,[36] while the space below was filled with portraits and a few indifferent compositions (Plate 29). The Gallery was built, however, as Randolph intended, in the hope that 'the munificence of

[31] Artificial lighting, because of the hazard of fire, was not installed until 1867 when gas was supplied to the art school; it was introduced to the new Sculpture Gallery in 1890 but there was no artificial lighting in the older galleries until the building was wired for electricity in 1895. For Pugin's attack on Cockerell's 'pagan' design, see Pt 2, Ch. 30.

[32] Cockerell to unnamed correspondent, 18 Dec. 1847, AA W. A. letters and papers, 1847; Cockerell was reluctant to insert a raised lantern in place of flat skylights and suggested the problem was caused by condensation. A design for an octagonal skylight by Cockerell in the museum archives (AA W. A. miscellaneous papers) is probably related to the discussions for securing the lights in 1847: minutes of curators, 22 Mar. 1848, AA AMS 41.

[33] Repairs were made in 1848, 1866 and 1889.

[34] AA W. A. miscellaneous papers; the name of the writer is not given; the attribution to Friesen, plausibly based on a reference in the Dyce–Eastlake letter, is due to C. F. Bell.

[35] J. Fisher, *Hand-Book Guide for the University Galleries, Oxford* (1846); only three of the paintings in Fisher's guide, Batoni's *Portrait of Garrick*, Willaerts's *Seapiece* and *Still-Life* by William Claesz Heda, remain on public display.

[36] These were presented to the University by the Duke of Marlborough in 1807 and were exhibited with a doubtful attribution to Henry Cooke.

future benefactors will add to the collection many other more valuable specimens both in Sculpture and Painting'.[37] This hope was vindicated, in part, by an influx of gifts. The widow of the sculptor Sir Francis Chantrey, informed by Cockerell that Oxford was building a gallery for sculpture, offered the University the plaster models from her husband's studio with his collection of sixty casts of ancient busts and statues.[38] The Sculpture Gallery was hastily completed to allow the transfer of the plasters by covered wagon[39] to the Galleries, where they arrived, badly damaged by the journey, in March 1843.[40] By November 1844 the Chantrey models had been repaired[41] and, after some discussion with Cockerell[42] and Chantrey's executors[43] about opening a door to the Taylorian and installing the busts in a lecture-room, the collection was assembled in the lower gallery of the west wing.

The Chantrey gift was not universally welcomed. John William Burgon, author of 'rose-red' *Petra* and a blunt-spoken follower of Newman, who had inherited a love of Greek art from his father, deprecated the gift 'in the strongest terms'.[44] In the eyes of Burgon and the archaeologists who followed him, the Chantrey models were objectionable not because they were casts, but because the originals from which they were taken were less interesting than antique marbles. Burgon's own proposals for the Galleries, set out in a pamphlet addressed to his tutor, Richard Greswell of Worcester College, included a large collection of casts, illustrating the archaic, middle and late periods of Greek art, with a particular emphasis on the sculpture brought to light by recent expeditions: the Parthenon pediments, frieze and metopes; the Phigaleian marbles; the figures from Xanthus; the Venus de Milo; the Aegina pediments; and the Harpy Tomb.[45]

When the Galleries opened, the display of casts fell short of Burgon's ideal. The Phigaleian marbles and the Parthenon frieze were included, but inserted so high in the Chantrey Gallery and stairwell that they were not as

[37] Suppl. to *Herald* 19 June 1841; the text was probably written by Bliss, who was part-owner of the *Herald*.

[38] Lady Chantrey to the Vice-Chancellor, 6 Apr. 1842, AA W. A. letters and papers, 1842; Chantrey's own sculpture gallery, from which the plasters had been removed, is discussed and illustrated in G. Waterfield (ed.), *Palaces of Art: art galleries in Britain, 1790–1990* (Dulwich 1991–2), 81–2. For a full description of the early history of the University Galleries see N. Penny, *Catalogue of European Sculpture in the Ashmolean Museum, 1540 to the present day* (3 vols 1992) iii, pp. xvii–xxxiii. This appeared after the text of this chapter was written, but it should be consulted particularly for the place of sculpture in Cockerell's design and for the development of the sculpture collections.

[39] Proceedings, 4 May 1842.

[40] Jones to unnamed correspondent, 29 Nov. 1844, AA W. A. letters and papers, 1844.

[41] Thomas Jones, Chantrey's assistant, was paid £99 13s 13d for repairing the plasters from 15 July to 26 Oct. 1844: ibid.

[42] Cockerell to Vice-Chancellor, 10 Sept. 1844: ibid.

[43] Turner and Jones to Vice-Chancellor, 4 Sept. 1844: ibid.

[44] Burgon, *Remarks on Art*, 11.

[45] Ibid. 38–42.

visible as he had hoped,[46] and the choice of remaining casts, by Burgon's standards, was somewhat *retardaire*. This is not surprising as all the casts displayed in the Sculpture Gallery derived from existing collections. The Florentine Boar, given by Queen's College, had once belonged to Sir Roger Newdigate; the Nine Muses, cast from the originals in the Sala dei Musei in the Vatican and placed in the tribune opposite the main door, were given by Philip Duncan; the Apollo from the same set was placed in the niche in the stairwell; all the remaining casts came from the collection of Sir Francis Chantrey and reflected his own tastes and professional preoccupations. Most of Chantrey's collection consisted of antique busts. The remainder included the Venus de Milo, two figures from the Parthenon, and a group of casts which more or less corresponded to those which Burgon chose to illustrate the period of decline—the Laocoön (placed dramatically in the niche on the west wall), the Germanicus, the Belvedere torso, the *Diane Chasseresse*, the Medici Venus and others.[47] Burgon discussed his ideas about the uses of the Galleries with Charles Newton of Christ Church,[48] then Assistant Keeper at the British Museum, and probably also with his close friend C. R. Cockerell, whom he had known since his infancy in Greece,[49] and whose views and discoveries were well represented in his imaginary museum. However, despite Burgon's eloquent scholarship and despite his undisguised affection for the contents of the Ashmolean[50] and the Bodleian Picture Gallery,[51] he ridiculed antiquarians who valued artefacts simply because they were old, and would admit nothing into his museum which was not 'Sublime and Beautiful' and admirable for its own sake.[52] This is why, in Burgon's eyes, casts of ancient sculpture and copies of great paintings were preferable to third-rate originals like the Pomfret marbles and the Bodleian portraits.[53] This is also why he did not consider giving a place to the Arundel inscriptions despite his belief that they were 'the greatest treasure we possess'.[54] As he realized, the Oxford Galleries were a museum of art, a type of institution which had developed in the eighteenth and early nineteenth centuries, particularly in Germany, from princely and private collections with the purpose of inspiring artists, educating the eye

[46] Burgon, *Remarks on Art*, postscript.

[47] Fisher, *Hand-Book Guide*, 9; despite the reference to the antique busts in the correspondence and in the museum register, there is no mention of them otherwise and it is doubtful if they were ever sent to Oxford.

[48] Burgon, *Remarks on Art*, 66.

[49] Cockerell had carried the 7-month-old Burgon up to the Parthenon in 1814 and dedicated him to the service of Pallas Athene: E. M. Goulburn, *John William Burgon: a biography* (2 vols 1892) i. 15.

[50] Ibid. 115.

[51] Ibid. 15.

[52] Burgon, *Remarks on Art*, 53.

[53] Ibid. 68.

[54] Ibid. 8.

and awakening a noble sympathy for the 'sublimest efforts of Genius' in the minds of visitors.[55]

The difficulty, as Burgon's contemporaries in Oxford realized, was that the Oxford Galleries, unlike the few other museums of art which existed in England at this date, and unlike most of those on the Continent, were not created to display works of the highest order. Thanks to the Pomfret and Chantrey gifts (followed by a smaller gift of casts of works by Westmacott), the ground floor and basement were filled to capacity with works which could provoke interest but could not inspire veneration. Paintings of quality were also slow to appear. Despite hopes that the Great Gallery would attract important works of art, only three gifts of paintings stand out before the 1900s:[56] a collection of early Italian paintings, given in 1850 by the Hon. William Thomas Fox-Strangways;[57] a group of Flemish, English and Venetian pictures, including a number of important sketches, given by Chambers Hall in 1855;[58] and the Pre-Raphaelite paintings bequeathed by Mrs Thomas Combe in 1894.[59] These were specialized collections consisting mostly of pictures of modest size better suited to a small room than a Great Gallery. Only two accessions in the early years, Bellucci's *Family of Darius*, given by G. C. Percival in 1854,[60] and Van Dyck's *Deposition*, given by Charles Maude in 1869,[61] were pictures of the size and quality which the Gallery required.

Henry Wellesley, one of the three original curators, was less optimistic than Bliss and Randolph about the future of the picture collection. In 1841 he told Dr Cramer that the time was past when Oxford could hope for gifts of major paintings. There was, however, as he pointed out, still scope for collecting drawings by Old Masters.[62] Both statements contained an element of truth, although it has to be said that Wellesley and the other academics who shaped the growth of the collection—Bliss, Cramer, Liddell and Acland—were more familiar with prints and drawings than they were with either antique sculpture or Old Master paintings.[63] A Passavant or an

[55] Ibid. 53; see also Waterfield (ed.), *Palaces of Art*, 153–6.

[56] One should, perhaps, include the bequest of twenty-five pictures, mainly Dutch and including several of interest, from the Revd Thomas Penrose, vicar of Writtle in Essex, together with a library of art books (AA W. A. University Galleries donation-book, Mar. 1851); the prize of his collection, a sea-piece by Turner, is now recognized to be a copy.

[57] See C. Lloyd, 'Fox-Strangways and Fortnum: two collectors of Italian art', *Apollo* cxvii (Apr. 1983), 280–7, with previous literature.

[58] See K. Garlick, 'The Chambers Hall gift', ibid. 296–301.

[59] See J. Whiteley, 'The Combe bequest', ibid. 302–7.

[60] Percival to Chase, 30 Apr. 1854 (extract), AA W. A. letters and papers, 1854.

[61] AA W. A. University Galleries donation-book, 1869.

[62] D. Sutton, 'Studies in the history of collecting of drawings in England: the Arundel collection: the drawings of Raphael in the Ashmolean Museum, Oxford' (Oxford BLitt thesis 2 vols 1943) ii. 66.

[63] For Wellesley's collection of Old Master drawings see F. Lugt, *Les Marques de collections* (Amsterdam 1921), 246–8; for Bliss's prints see *Catalogue of the Select and Important Collection of Engravings Formed by the Late Rev. Philip Bliss D.C.L.*, Leigh, Sotheby, & Wilkinson, 12

Eastlake might have had more success in finding appropriate works for the Great Gallery. As it was, none of the nineteenth-century curators was a professional in the field of post-classical art except, perhaps, for Wellesley, who was a dilettante with a serious interest in Old Master prints and drawings. He alone among the nineteenth-century curators had the contacts in the world of art commerce and collecting which were essential for the pursuit of acquisitions. His friendship with Chambers Hall and Samuel Woodburn resulted in brilliant acquisitions of prints and drawings. But, like his colleagues and successors on the Board of Curators, he had no special taste for Old Master paintings and, notwithstanding the difficulties he anticipated in acquiring major paintings, there is no evidence that either he or the other curators took any steps to overcome them.

Wellesley's preference for prints and drawings was shared by his university colleagues. His scheme, inspired by a visit to Woodburn's final exhibition of the Lawrence collection in 1841, to buy the Raphaels and Michelangelos for the Galleries by subscription for £10,000 would have been impossible without widespread support within the University.[64] Despite a delay of eight months while the University procrastinated and Woodburn became increasingly threatening and bad-tempered,[65] Wellesley's proposal was backed by many academics. There was, apparently, as Bliss explained to Cockerell, 'a hitch with Woodburn',[66] but the nature of this is not clear. The Chancellor of the University, Wellesley's uncle, the Duke of Wellington, whose support was essential, was proving difficult.[67] Dr Cramer, Wellesley's Principal at New Inn Hall, had doubts about the timing of the subscription, perhaps because of the political crisis in the summer of 1841.[68] Whatever the reason, his reluctance was overcome by October when a meeting of the Oxford parties in Bliss's room agreed to set up the promised committee with the support of the Vice-Chancellor.[69] The appeal was launched, officially, in the Radcliffe Library on 13 November when £500 was pledged.[70] By the summer of 1842 the committee had raised more than £2,000 from over 500 subscribers.[71] But London, the court and the aristocracy were less forthcoming, and without the Earl of Eldon's contribution of

June 1858; for Cramer's Old Master drawings see the catalogue of his sale, Sotheby's, 11–14 Feb. 1850 (Lugt 19652).

[64] Sutton, ii. 66–98.

[65] Woodburn bombarded Bliss with letters from May 1841 until June 1842, chiefly about the delays in setting up an Oxford committee, which Woodburn felt was crucial to the success of the appeal in London: BL Add. MS 54513.

[66] Cockerell to Bliss, nd, ibid.

[67] Bliss to Woodburn, 30 Oct. 1841, ibid.

[68] Woodburn to Bliss, 4 June 1841, ibid.

[69] Bliss to Woodburn, 23 Oct. 1841, ibid.

[70] Sutton, ii. 90.

[71] The subscription-book is preserved in AA W. A.

£4,000 and Woodburn's decision to accept a reduction in the price of £3,000 the drawings would not have come to Oxford.[72]

This famous acquisition, exhibited *in toto* in the long gallery, became the basis of many other gifts of prints and drawings. In 1853 the Earl of Ellesmere presented a volume of drawings by or attributed to the Carracci which had previously belonged to Lawrence and Woodburn.[73] The drawings by Rembrandt, Claude, Leonardo, Sodoma, Raphael and others given by Wellesley's friend Chambers Hall in 1855, with a large, choice collection of Old Master prints, were even more important than his gift of paintings.[74] In 1861 Ruskin presented forty-eight drawings by Turner to the Galleries,[75] supplemented in 1878 by the loan of another 249 drawings by Turner from the National Gallery.[76] The transfer of the Douce prints and drawings in 1863 from the Bodleian brought in a huge collection of Italian and Northern prints and several hundred drawings by Old Masters of the Northern Schools, many of great rarity and importance.[77] For lack of funds, prints and drawings were not purchased by the curators until 1887 when a group of eighteen prints was bought by special grant from the Buccleuch sale.[78] The first purchase of drawings, a group of Pre-Raphaelite studies belonging to Mrs Thomas Combe, was made in 1894, at Mallam's auction of her effects. The failure to buy collections of drawings by early German and Italian artists, by Parmigianino and by the Zuccari, offered by Woodburn to Wellesley, was regrettable.[79] But the greatest and the most surprising loss was the sale of Wellesley's own famous collection of drawings, prints and art books, which was dispersed in a series of auctions in the 1850s and 1860s. The gift of these would have transformed the university collection and reunited many of Lawrence's Claude drawings with his Raphaels and Michelangelos.[80]

Largely, it seems, through Bliss's skilful management the new institution moved from the competition stage to a finished building with remarkable speed and, apart from a threatened lawsuit by Wyatt, who owned the yard to

[72] Sutton, ii. 98.

[73] University Galleries donation-book, 1853.

[74] Garlick, 'The Chambers Hall gift', 298–300; like his friend Henry Wellesley, Chambers Hall had a large collection of Claude's drawings.

[75] University Galleries donation-book, 12 Mar. 1861.

[76] Minutes of curators, 17 Oct. 1878.

[77] See C. Lloyd, *Dürer to Cézanne: northern European drawings from the Ashmolean* (Exhibition, New Brunswick NJ 12 Sept. 1982–2 Jan. 1983), v–vii; and *The Douce Legacy: an exhibition to commemorate…Francis Douce 1757–1834* (1984).

[78] Minutes of curators, 5 May 1887.

[79] Sutton, ii. 100.

[80] Wellesley's collection was dispersed in seven sales at Sotheby's between 1858 and 1866; the fifth sale, beginning on 1 Nov. 1866, contained his collection of drawings; see K. Parker, *Catalogue of the Collection of Drawings in the Ashmolean Museum: Italian Schools* (1956), xii–xx.

the north,[81] with surprisingly little friction.[82] The Galleries opened in the autumn of 1845 under the supervision of three curators, the Revd Lewis Sneyd, Dr Edward Cardwell and Wellesley, who succeeded Cramer as Principal of New Inn Hall in 1847. At the first meeting of the curators on 24 January 1845, Joseph Fisher, an engraver of modest talent, was appointed Keeper of the Galleries at a salary of £100 per annum,[83] funded from a grant of £10,000 allocated by the University to cover running-costs.[84] The Keeper was not expected to be a scholar, although, like the janitor at the Bodleian, he was expected to catalogue the works of art and remain in the building during opening hours. The Galleries were open to members of the University in academic dress from 10 a.m. to 4 p.m. every day except Sunday; on days when there was a University Sermon they remained closed until midday. Strangers unaccompanied by a member of the University were admitted on Thursday only, but an appeal to the Keeper secured access at other times.[85]

A new phase in the history of the Galleries began with the appointment of Henry George Liddell as curator in 1858 in succession to Lewis Sneyd. During his studentship at Christ Church from 1833 to 1846, Liddell had become an acknowledged authority in artistic matters.[86] He was appointed to the committee to judge the Taylor competition and, again, to the delegacy which supervised the building work, and he acted as joint secretary to the committee for purchasing the Lawrence drawings. Like his friends Henry Acland and John Ruskin, he was an amateur water-colourist with a keen interest in promoting contemporary art. On the death of Wellesley in 1866, Liddell became senior curator and, with the support of Acland, who succeeded Wellesley on the Board, he brought a new sense of purpose into the care of the collection.[87] The Great Gallery, which had been neglected somewhat since 1846, was redecorated and rehung, with the advice of George Richmond (a friend of Acland) and William Boxall.[88] Although there were no significant gifts of paintings or drawings during Liddell's long curatorship, he supervised the transfer of the Douce collection in 1863 and con-

---

[81] Cockerell to Bliss [June 1841], BL Add. MS 54573; Cockerell to Vice-Chancellor, Proceedings, 28 Oct. 1841.

[82] Cockerell took considerable liberties with the delegacy, but in no important respects did the delegates overturn his wishes or succeed in imposing theirs.

[83] Minutes of curators, 24 Jan. 1845; there is an MS biography of Joseph Fisher by his nephew in the Bodleian (MS Top. Oxon. d. 507, fo 471); I am grateful to David Sturdy for this reference.

[84] Notice of Convocation, 6 Feb. 1845.

[85] Minutes of curators, 29 Oct. 1845.

[86] Thompson, *Liddell*, 51.

[87] Ibid. 208–14.

[88] MS report by Boxall and Richmond inserted in minutes of curators, 1866; the report was written in response to proposals by Liddell, which were accepted entirely by the two artists apart from Liddell's suggestion that the 'indifferent copies' of the Raphael cartoons should be removed; Ruskin, also, was consulted and approved: Boxall to Liddell, 3 Dec. 1866, AA W. A. letters and papers, 1866.

solidated and conserved the existing works. Care of the Douce prints and drawings was paid for by the Bodleian, whose Librarian, Henry Coxe, joined the Board of Curators to keep an eye on the Bodleian loans.[89] To pay for the care of the Italian drawings, Richmond persuaded the third Earl of Eldon, son of the original benefactor, to set up a fund of £1,200.[90] This enabled the curators, with Richmond's help, to purchase books on Italian art, to conserve the drawings and to pay for John Charles Robinson's catalogue of the drawings of Michelangelo and Raphael, published in 1870, which became a landmark in the scholarly study of Old Master drawings.[91]

In the 1840s and 1850s the presence of the Galleries drew attention to the lack of courses for studying art at the University. Richard Greswell, John Burgon, Richard Tyrwhitt and Henry Acland[92] separately urged the University to establish the study of art in the undergraduate curriculum, but with neither adequate resources nor any obvious candidate to teach the subject, their suggestions could not be taken up. Charles Newton, who had known Acland and Ruskin since their undergraduate days at Christ Church, seems to have been a persuasive force behind a number of the schemes to promote the study of art at the University. Although he was a classical archaeologist, his belief that a knowledge of the history and 'figurative language' of art was as important to understanding past cultures as the study of the written word could apply (as he pointed out to an Oxford audience in 1850) to the study of Giotto, Raphael and Michelangelo.[93] The case which Burgon made for classes in the 'language of art'[94] was, to a large extent, based on Newton's theory of integrated culture. Newton also persuaded Thomas Dyke Acland, Henry's brother, that 'Art has a history and language', and that the study of both should be included as a subject in its own right in educating the young.[95] This principle was accepted by the University in 1858, when the practice, history and theory of art were included in the Oxford local examinations after a zealous campaign by Thomas Acland.[96] These examinations were intended for schoolchildren,

[89] Thompson, 208.

[90] Eldon to Richmond, 21 Oct. 1868, AA W. A. letters and papers, 1868; Acland, and perhaps the other two curators, thought that the approach to Eldon was a 'forlorn hope': Richmond to Acland, 22 Oct. 1868, ibid.

[91] J. C. Robinson, *A Critical Account of the Drawings by Michelangelo and Raffaello in the University Galleries, 1870* (1870); Robinson, who could have been a useful ally of the curators, was alienated by Liddell's failure to acknowledge receipt of the catalogue or to thank the author: Robinson to Price, 10 July 1871, AA W. A. letters and papers, 1871.

[92] See R. Greswell, *On Education in the Principles of Art* (1843); Burgon, *Remarks on Art*, 2–3.

[93] C. Newton, *Essays in Art and Archaeology* (1880), 24.

[94] Burgon, 31.

[95] T. D. Acland, *Some Account of the Origins and Objects of the New Oxford Examinations for the Title of Associate in Arts and Certificates for the Year 1858* (1858), 30–7.

[96] Ibid. 73.

but, as Richmond recognized,[97] they were an important first step towards a more comprehensive acceptance of the study of art at the University.

The discussions about the new examinations forced those who advocated the 'study of art' to define what this would mean in practice. The advice which Acland received in 1857 brought to light two opposing points of view. William Dyce and a group of architects argued that if art classes were to become part of a general education, they should concentrate on the history of art and leave instruction in drawing to the very young or to the professionals.[98] But Ruskin, supported by his friends in Oxford, defended the importance of practical tuition and eloquently rejected Dyce's proposals for lessons in the history of art. Ruskin's own proposals, discussed with the Acland brothers in the summer of 1857 and developed in a letter to Frederick Temple,[99] became the basis of the classes which he established in the Galleries in the early 1870s. Because of this, and because Ruskin's friends occupied places of authority in the University, the historical approach to the study of paintings and drawings was not developed as it might have been if Newton had been appointed to the Slade professorship,[100] or as it was at Cambridge where Sidney Colvin, the first Slade Professor, took an 'anti-Ruskin' stand.[101]

Before Ruskin had become a major influence in Oxford, Liddell and his colleagues already associated the idea of the Galleries with the needs of contemporary art. At the launching of the appeal to buy Woodburn's drawings in 1841, Liddell had argued that the presence of the work of Raphael and Michelangelo in Oxford would help raise English art to the level of art in Germany, while Cramer, appealing to a widespread unease about the quality of industrial design, emphasized the effect this would have in improving the work of artisans.[102] These arguments, which were commonplace in 1841, seem implausible in retrospect as reasons for keeping Old Master drawings in the University, but, to those who took them seriously, they pointed to the need for a school of art as a natural complement to the University Galleries.[103]

In 1861 the curators agreed, in principle, to establish a drawing school in the Galleries,[104] but no steps were taken until the end of Michaelmas 1864, when Liddell called a group of colleagues to his rooms in Christ Church to

---

[97] T. D. Acland, 61.

[98] Ibid. 42–5.

[99] Ibid. 54–7.

[100] Newton's name was proposed, along with Holman Hunt's and Ruskin's, by George Butler, the Vice-Chancellor's first choice for the chair; J. Evans, *John Ruskin* (1954), 309.

[101] E. V. Lucas, *The Colvins and their Friends* (1928), 28; Ruskin's friend the Revd Richard Tyrwhitt submitted a proposal to the Senior Censor at Christ Church for a lectureship in the history of art which would supplement Ruskin's professorship. Tyrwhitt's proposals clearly echo those of Newton; Tyrwhitt to T. V. Bayne, 10 Nov. 1874, CA GB vii. c. 1.

[102] Sutton, ii. 102.

[103] Cox, 338.

[104] Minutes of curators, 1861.

discuss the question.[105] This led to a public meeting at the Town Hall on 11 February, at which both townspeople and academics spoke in support of an Oxford school of art.[106] There was a general feeling that the school should be modelled on the South Kensington system, which was already working well in Cambridge, Cheltenham and Gloucester and in most of the bigger industrial cities, but that it should not be confined to the artisans alone. Liddell warned the meeting not to expect too much from the undergraduates and predicted that suitable premises would be hard to find in the University. But Acland, who was more of an enthusiast than Liddell, attacked the University for neglecting the study of art, complained that no educational use had been made of the collections and declared that he 'should strongly object to a school for one class of persons only'.[107] A temporary room was lent, rent-free, in the Taylorian;[108] Alexander Macdonald, a teacher from the South Kensington School, was appointed by a subcommittee to the post of Master;[109] and the school opened on 22 May 1865. All classes of society, as intended, were included, although separated into male and female classes for artisans and male and female classes for the town and University. When the room was reclaimed by the Taylorian in 1866, Liddell offered to install the school in the south end of the Chantrey Gallery, rent-free and fitted up at the expense of the Galleries.[110] Other capital costs were covered by donations. It was hoped that the school would become self-supporting with the help of fees and grants from the government Department of Art and Science, but the finances were never secure.[111] The addition of science classes in 1868, based in the University Museum, helped to steady the budget and increased the service which the school provided to an area which eventually extended over Oxfordshire and Berkshire.[112]

The arrival of John Ruskin, elected to the new Slade professorship in Fine Art in 1869 with the support of Liddell and Acland, brought financial security to the class for townspeople and those with university connections, but almost put an end to the artisan class with which Ruskin had little sympathy. Acland had already tried to involve Ruskin in the affairs of the Galleries by offering him a curatorship in 1867; but Ruskin, who had no illusions about the importance of the post, sent a discouraging reply.[113] In 1869 Acland invited Ruskin to take the chair at the annual public meeting of

[105] Newspaper cutting inserted in Oxford school of art minute-book, Oxford Brookes University archives.
[106] *Jackson's Oxford Journal* 18 Feb. 1865.
[107] Ibid.
[108] Ibid. 25 Mar. 1865; Oxford school of art minute-book, 16 Mar. 1865.
[109] Ibid. 1 May 1865.
[110] Minutes of curators, 21 Feb. 1867.
[111] E. Henry, *Oxford Polytechnic: genesis to maturity, 1865–1980* (1981), 4–7.
[112] C. Batey, *Technical and Art Education in Oxford* (1944), 8.
[113] Atlay, *Acland*, 369.

the art school and present the prizes, but Ruskin, again, declined.[114] The repetitive and mechanical teaching in art schools of the South Kensington type, established in its basic form by William Dyce in the late 1830s, did not appeal to Ruskin, who used his position as Slade Professor to establish a class of his own for undergraduates in the Upper Galleries.[115] Ruskin's class was intended not to train professional artists, but to influence the taste of future patrons and collectors.[116] In 1871, undeterred by the fluctuating enthusiasm of the undergraduates for his class in taste, he turned his attention to providing practical training, prompted, it seems, by Acland and backed, more cautiously, by Liddell.[117] His proposal to fund an alternative to the school of art which would, like the existing school, be based in the Galleries under the supervision of Macdonald was accepted by the curators. The school of art was expelled from the Chantrey wing, and the space was enlarged and refitted for Ruskin's school, which took charge of the more prosperous of Macdonald's students. The school of art was now unable to continue giving classes to the town and University, but the artisan class continued in the evenings, under Macdonald's care, with the help of a pupil teacher. It operated in a room in the basement which was condemned by a Government inspector in 1876 as unsuitable for teaching art.[118]

Macdonald and the managers of the art school saw Ruskin's school not as a successful rival, but as a confirmation of their efforts to secure the teaching of art in the University.[119] The new school continued, much as the old art class had done, in the same place, under the same Master and with the same students, but with an added 'museum' of photographs, prints and drawings and with an endowment, formally ratified by a Deed of Gift in 1875, which ensured the future of the school.[120] But, in securing the teaching of art for the 'Upper and Middle Classes who were desirous of Studying Art for Art's sake',[121] the academics on the Board of Curators sacrificed the interests of the artisans. The class for the latter continued with difficulty, supported mostly by a group of Oxford townspeople until the City took control in 1891.[122] The Slade Professor's class, meanwhile, continued in the Upper Galleries with a painting studio, added by Hubert Herkomer in 1886,[123] so that by the 1890s there were three art schools in the building, all putting

---

[114] Oxford school of art minute-book, 7 and 19 Oct. 1869.
[115] R. Hewison, *Catalogue of the Rudimentary Series in the Arrangements of 1873 with Ruskin's Comments of 1878* (1984), 15–16.
[116] Ibid. 16.
[117] Ibid. 9.
[118] Henry, *Oxford Polytechnic*, 7–8.
[119] *Oxford School of Art and Science Report* (1872), 12.
[120] Hewison, *Catalogue*, 16.
[121] Henry, 5.
[122] Ibid. 7.
[123] Thompson, *Liddell*, 213.

pressure on the exhibition space, especially in the Sculpture Gallery, where casts from the antique were beginning to arrive in quantity.

In 1885 Liddell chaired a committee to consider what works of art belonging to the University might be added to the collection, and to report on the question of space in the Galleries.[124] As a result, the Piranesi candelabra were brought over from the Radcliffe Library in 1894, the Arundel inscriptions were transferred in 1887 and one or two important drawings from the Douce collection, which had remained in the Bodleian, were placed on deposit with the other drawings in the Galleries.[125] On the recommendation of the committee, two small rooms were built in 1889 for the casts, paid for with a grant of £2,000 from the University.[126] In 1895 the school of art and science, which, since 1891, had been funded by the City Technical Instruction Committee, moved from the basement into new premises in St Ebbe's as the City Technical School, where it began its evolution into Oxford Brookes University.[127] The departure of the art school released some needed space, but not enough to provide for the expansion of the collection.

Although Liddell remained chairman of the curators until he retired in November 1891, his influence declined with the appointment of six additional curators in 1884.[128] This expansion of the Board was taken in response to the growing importance of classical archaeology in the University, and to an increase in the archaeological collection at the Galleries. In the early years, the collection of ancient art had expanded less than the collection of paintings, prints and drawings. A group of small bronzes and terracottas, given by Chambers Hall, eleven fragments of antique sculpture, given by John William Burgon, and a slab from Nineveh, given by Henry Layard, were the most important antiquities acquired before 1875, when a group of Etruscan and Roman artefacts was bought from the Castellani collection.[129] This purchase marked the beginning of a tendency to develop a base for archaeology in the Galleries, encouraged by Mark Pattison and confirmed in 1884 when the new Merton and Lincoln professorship in Classical Archaeology was established there. The first professor, William Ramsay, left the chair in 1885, disheartened, it seems, by the lack of support he received in the University for his subject,[130] but his successor, Percy Gardner, who came to Oxford from the British Museum by way of Cambridge and remained in the chair for thirty-seven years, established Oxford as a centre for the study of

---

[124] Minutes of curators, 29 Jan. 1885.

[125] Ibid. 30 Apr. 1885.

[126] Ibid. 24 Oct. 1889.

[127] *Report of the Curators of the University Galleries for the Year 1894* (1894), 2; the move was delayed until July 1895: Minutes of curators, 3 May 1894.

[128] Minutes of curators, 1884.

[129] W. S. W. Vaux, *Catalogue of the Castellani Collection of Antiquities in the University Galleries, Oxford* (1876).

[130] J. Evans, *Time and Chance: the Story of Arthur Evans and his forebears* (1943), 262.

Greek and Roman art according to the principles advocated by Charles Newton and recently introduced by Sidney Colvin at the Fitzwilliam. A departmental library of archaeology, which absorbed the existing art books, was set up with the support of Henry Pelham, a friend of Arthur Evans and one of the most active of the new curators.[131] Gardner, like Colvin, was convinced that a comprehensive museum of casts after the antique was needed for the study of Greek and Roman art. With help from Pelham, who had taken an active part since 1881 in laying the groundwork for a cast collection, Gardner persuaded the University to provide an annual grant for buying casts mostly from collections in Germany and Greece, to illustrate the history of Greek art along the lines which Burgon had proposed in 1846.[132] But, unlike Burgon, Gardner was principally attracted by 'the historic rather than the aesthetic side of the monuments'[133] of which he purchased casts.

The new Board, through numerous subcommittees, was extremely active: entrance fees came and went;[134] the paintings were restored;[135] the galleries were redecorated;[136] the Raphael and Michelangelo drawings were treated and remounted at the British Museum with help from Sidney Colvin.[137] Alexander Macdonald, who was appointed Deputy Keeper in 1886 and Keeper in 1890 on the death of Fisher, took a conscientious interest in the condition of the works of art while continuing in his post as Ruskin Master of Drawing; but, as his time and scholarship were limited, the preparation of a catalogue of paintings, which had been traditionally the responsibility of the keeper, was taken over by two of the curators, Thomas Watson Jackson, fellow and tutor of Worcester, and Henry George Woods, President of Trinity. The new *Provisional Catalogue*, published in 1891, was motivated by the need to revise the uncritical attributions on the labels in the galleries. Although it was a derivative compilation, relying heavily on Waagen and on Crowe and Cavalcaselle, it was also the first attempt to provide a scholarly catalogue of the paintings in the place of Fisher's handbooks, which had been published at intervals since 1846. By contrast with earlier catalogues of prints and drawings, commissioned by the University from Thomas Dodd and J. C. Robinson, the 1891 catalogue was a late arrival. The Oxford amateurs, as always, gave priority to the graphic arts.

---

[131] P. Gardner, *Autobiographica* (1933), 58.

[132] Ibid. 54; before the arrival of Ramsay, the expansion of the cast collection had begun through a subscription, launched in 1881 by Pelham and others. By 1884, when the collection became the responsibility of the University, thirty-two casts had been installed and a further seven were on order. Gardner continued this development of the collection with university funds, but he did not set it in motion. I am grateful to Sir John Boardman for this information.

[133] Ibid. 53.

[134] A charge of 2*d* was introduced on 28 May 1885 and suspended on 20 Nov. 1890; a charge of 6*d* was introduced when the Galleries and the Ashmolean amalgamated in 1908.

[135] Minutes of curators, 6 June 1889.

[136] *Report of the Curators of the University Galleries for the Year 1891* (1891), 1.

[137] Minutes of curators, 2 June 1887.

The influence of the archaeologists brought a change of emphasis. The proposals by Henry Pelham to introduce an entrance charge, restrict access to the galleries at certain times to students only and expel the school of art from the basement,[138] indicate a move away from the idea of the Galleries as a public institution with a commitment to the fine arts towards a narrower, more academic point of view. In Cambridge, where similar developments in archaeology and the study of classical art had put pressure on resources, separate institutions were founded in the 1880s for archaeology and for the display of casts. In Oxford, the University Galleries were used increasingly for both.

The growth of archaeology involved the Galleries in the tenacious campaign waged by Evans round the Ashmolean in Broad Street to find a proper home for Oxford archaeology (see Chapter 19). His search for better premises ended in a scheme, approved by Convocation on 7 June 1892, for amalgamating the two museums.[139] C. D. E. Fortnum, who offered his collection of ancient and Renaissance art to Oxford, together with a contribution of £10,000 for housing it, provided the incentive to build a new Ashmolean in the space adjoining the Galleries in Wyatt's Yard, which the University had recently purchased. From 1894 the Visitors of the Ashmolean and the curators of the Galleries met as a joint body until, on Evans's proposition, they became a single body in 1908.[140] This development was resented by a number of the curators. The study of classical art and archaeology was strengthened by the move, but the prospects for the fine arts were not uniformly improved by the dominance of archaeologists in the administration of the museum. The increased complexity of the institution restricted the space available for expanding the picture galleries and led to the removal of the Chantrey plasters to the basement to make room for Gardner's growing collection of casts. The removal of the plasters provoked a furious protest from Bodley's Librarian, E. W. B. Nicholson, supported, less vigorously, by T. W. Jackson; but they were overruled by the archaeologists, to whom casts of ancient statues were of more interest than a nineteenth-century collection of models by a sculptor whose work, by then, was not as fashionable as it had been in his lifetime.[141]

Given the importance of classical studies at the Universities, it is not surprising that London, Cambridge and Oxford had professorships in Greek and Roman art long before later art became part of the curriculum. Those

---

[138] Ibid. 30 Apr. 1885.

[139] R. F. Ovenell, *The Ashmolean Museum, 1683–1894* (1986), 244–6; I am grateful to Ronald Ovenell for many improvements and corrections which have been incorporated in this chapter.

[140] *Gazette* xxxviii (5 May 1908), 591–6.

[141] E. W. B. Nicholson, *Council, Lady Chantrey and the Bodleian: an appeal to Convocation to reject by a monumental majority the illegal Chantrey casts decree* (1896): for a detailed account of the Chantrey gift and its sorry treatment by the Ashmolean, see N. Penny, 'Chantrey, Westmacott and casts after the antique', *Journal of the History of Collections* iii (1991), 255–64.

who advocated the teaching of art history in Oxford were classicists at heart who were attracted to the idea of studying art in Christian Europe because they were already interested in the link between art and religion in the ancient world. On an analogy with literature, they stressed the role that the study of art should have in a university which aimed at providing a general, culturally based education. However, as the idea of a university education shifted in the later nineteenth century from a broadly based concept towards greater specialization, the argument for studying art lost much of its appeal. The University Galleries, founded as a museum of art, were transformed in the last thirty years of the century into a museum in the modern sense, combining several academic interests.

The division of the new institution into two departments of antiquities and fine art was a sensible arrangement for administering the enlarged collection. The artefacts from the Ashmolean in Broad Street were combined in the department of antiquities with the classical works of art from the Galleries, while the pre-eminent importance of the collection of prints and drawings remained secure in the hands of Charles Bell, the first of a succession of scholars and connoisseurs who occupied the post of Keeper in the new department of fine art after the resignation of Macdonald in 1908.[142]

[142] *Report of the Keeper of the Ashmolean Museum for the Year 1908* (1908), 1, 4–5.

21

The Taylor Institution

GILES BARBER

The foundation, in 1724, of the Regius professorship of Modern History, and of the professor's supporting posts for teaching modern languages, has been described in *The Eighteenth Century*.[1] This initiative petered slowly out as regards the language side, which only moved forward some 120 years later following a delayed benefaction from a remarkable man. Sir Robert Taylor, born at Woodford, Essex, in 1714, was originally a sculptor and a pupil of Sir Henry Cheere. When Taylor's apprenticeship was over his father gave him 'just money enough to travel on a plan of frugal study to Rome'. While the future Sir Robert was in Rome news reached him of his father's death and he decided to return home at once. This he is reputed to have done disguised as a Franciscan friar, since he lacked the passports necessary to cross Europe in time of war. Having thus 'passed unmolested through the enemy's camp', he returned to find that his father had died (in 1743) a bankrupt. Friends came to his aid and he soon made a considerable reputation as a sculptor. Realizing, however, the strength of contemporary competition in this field, he turned to architecture, and by hard work and businesslike methods built up one of the most extensive practices of his day, being surveyor to the Bank of England, the Admiralty, and the Customs, Architect of the King's Works, Master Carpenter, and Deputy Surveyor. He was knighted in 1783 upon his election as Sheriff of London.[2]

Taylor is not known to have had any particular connections with Oxford (where he executed no work) other than the presence there of his only child, Michael Angelo Taylor, who matriculated at Corpus in 1774. Five years later Robert Taylor drew up a will naming Sir Charles Asgill, a City banker, and

[1] *The Eighteenth Century*, 115, 474. The standard history of the Taylorian is Sir Charles Firth, *Modern Languages at Oxford, 1724–1929* (1929), which, although produced as a pamphlet for a debate in Congregation on the allocation of the extension site to the north of the Taylorian, is fully documented and the basic source for this chapter. For the architectural and other aspects of the building see D. Watkin, *The Life and Work of C. R. Cockerell* (1974), N. Penny, *Catalogue of European Sculpture in the Ashmolean Museum* (3 vols 1992) iii pp. xvii–xxv, and G. G. Barber, *Arks for Learning: a short history of Oxford library buildings* (1995).
[2] For information on Sir Robert Taylor see Sir Howard Colvin, *A Biographical Dictionary of English Architects, 1660–1840* (1954), 601–4, and M. Binney, *Sir Robert Taylor* (1984).

John Nightingale as his executors. After certain sums for his wife and others, he left the residue in trust to his son for life and, providing that his son died without issue, subsequently (January 1788) by codicil to the University of Oxford 'for the purpose of applying the interest and produce in purchasing freehold land within, or if possible to be made within, the jurisdiction of the University of Oxford for the erecting of a proper edifice thereon and for establishing a Foundation for the teaching and improving the European languages'.[3] His motives here are not clear. The will uses the language of the building trades where 'improving' means learning, but an interest in things European may have come from his early trip to Rome and can perhaps be deduced from his extensive collection of continental books of ornamentation (now in the Taylor Institution)[4] and from the fact of his son's given name.

As a result of the inefficiency of his solicitors the codicil establishing the bequest to the University was not signed at the time; and when Sir Robert (as he had by then become) fell seriously ill, having caught a chill at the funeral of Sir Charles Asgill in September 1788, it became necessary to sign the document. There are clear contemporary attestations that he wished to sign the codicil, together probably with another raising his lifetime gifts to his son from £45,000 to £50,000. As it turned out he died on 27 September before suitable witnesses could be found. By his will he left his house, fixtures and an annuity to his wife (who died within a few years), and various small legacies to relations, friends, and architectural pupils, while David and John Godfrey of Isleworth (friends of Woodford days) were to act as executors of a trust, the monies from which were to be divided among certain societies for the propagation of the Gospel, some London hospitals, and other charities, particularly those connected with St Martin-in-the-Fields.

The will was proved by the Godfreys, Lady Taylor and her son on 4 January 1789, but one of the legatees having instituted a suit in the Prerogative Court of Canterbury, the judge pronounced against the validity of both draft codicils. The University appealed to the High Court of Delegates, which reversed the decision, and letters of administration were granted to Michael Angelo Taylor on 13 June 1795. From the papers associated with these proceedings it would appear that Sir Robert did not want his estate (amounting finally to some £180,000) to go to people he did not know or, more particularly, to his wife's relatives. He seems to have been certain, early on, that his son would leave no issue and that he would therefore be tempted to leave the estate to his maternal relatives. On leaving Oxford Michael Angelo Taylor had in fact been called to the Bar; and he then sat as a Member of Parliament for various constituencies from 1784 to 1834. Ambitious, he began as a devoted adherent of Pitt; but he then participated in the im-

[3] A copy of Sir Robert's will and other documents relating to the early history of his bequest are in OUA UD/23/1 ff.
[4] D. J. Gilson, *Books from the Library of Sir Robert Taylor* (1973).

peachment of Warren Hastings and became a close friend of the Prince of Wales. Socially a host to the Whig Party for many years, his services here and in the reform of the Court of Chancery, not to mention the paving of the streets of London, were but meanly rewarded by his appointment as Privy Counsellor in 1831. In 1817 he had proposed to the University that their claim on his father's estate should be settled for £50,000 Irish currency, the majority of the estate being in property in Ireland. The University seems to have declined this offer, which, however, reappeared in Taylor's will. Taylor died on 16 July 1834 and his wife, Frances Ann, daughter of the Revd Sir Harry Vane, in January 1835. Michael Angelo bequeathed his estate rather as his father had feared; but the recipient was one of the Vanes, and not a member of his mother's family. As the moneys of father and son had become totally confused over the years, the University accepted a settlement on 18 November 1835 of £65,000.

Ten days later the Hebdomadal Board received the report of a committee on the benefaction which advised adhering closely to the testator's wishes, and proposed the purchase of a site and the erection of a building. The committee had considered the creation of a college or corporate body, but recommended that further expenditure should be for 'teaching and improving the European languages'. It had discussed 'what European languages may be considered, with regard to a knowledge of them, as essential to Diplomatic or Commercial pursuits, and as possessing a Literature sufficient to entitle an able Professor thereof to rank among Literary Persons'. The French, Italian, Spanish, Portuguese, German and Slavonic languages were thought suitable, although French, Italian and German should be put forward first. Sir Robert had foreseen that Convocation ought to have power to alter the field and the committee recommended this, 'the attempt to ingraft a plan for the study of European languages upon our Academical Institution being in itself in the nature of an experiment'.

The trust fund was allowed to accumulate interest for some years and then, supplemented by a sum of about £4,000 originating in a trust bequeathed by Dr Francis Randolph in 1796 for the construction of a building to house the Pomfret statues and other works of art, it was used, together with other University moneys, to finance the building of a combined modern language institution and an art gallery. Land was acquired from Worcester College and each fund charged with the cost of the share of land allotted to it which, in the case of the Taylor Institution, came to £2,093. The architect chosen, C. R. Cockerell, was the distinguished son of Sir Robert Taylor's old pupil Samuel Pepys Cockerell. His design and the construction of the building are described in Chapter 20.

The eastern wing of Cockerell's dual-purpose building, the Taylor Institution, or Taylorian as it is often called, had six lecture-rooms and a library measuring 39 feet by 45 feet with a height of 41 feet. There was also some living accommodation, but the original committee had noted that, while some fireplaces were provided, 'an apparatus for warming by hot water would also be recommended'. The final cost of the Taylor building was £25,647 3s 7d, almost all of which could be met from the accumulated income of the bequest.

The east front of the building was to be decorated with four figures representing the languages of France, Italy, Germany and Spain. Cockerell sketched these as female figures, but the delegates insisted on male ones, 'to represent the literature or national character of the four countries, discarding any peculiarity of national costume that may seem objectionable'. Later they demanded figures representing Corneille, Dante, Schiller and Cervantes. Cockerell won the day, but the figures erected are supported by stands bearing the names of the principal authors of the countries in question, the selection of which casts some light on the interests of the delegates and the focus they saw the Institution as having. From south to north the statues represent the literatures of France (Racine, Molière, Montesquieu), Italy (Dante, Tasso, Guicciardini), Germany (Herder, Goethe, Schiller), Spain (Cervantes, Calderón, Mariana).

Regulations for the Institution were submitted to Convocation on 10 April 1845, but their final adoption was delayed for two years for various reasons: there was opposition to them from the Tractarians, who feared 'Germanism'; there were objections to the powers of the curators to remove the proposed professor of modern European languages; and there were others to 'the entire absence of all provision for the encouragement of the study of the languages and literature' for which teachers were to be supplied. A circular stated:

When it is notorious that the existing Professorships, even when they relate to the most popular branches of modern literature or science, are fast dwindling into sinecures, owing to the diminished interest in such pursuits which seems the natural consequence of the exclusive importance attached to classical studies within this University, it might be expected that any augmentation in the numbers of such professors and teachers should be accompanied, wherever it is practicable, with measures calculated to induce the students to avail themselves more generally of the increased means of instruction henceforward to be afforded them.

The statute of March 1847 established a professor of modern European languages (at a salary of £400 a year), a librarian, and two teachers of languages (at £150 a year each).

Meanwhile in May 1845 the first curators had been appointed. Beside the Vice-Chancellor (Dr B. P. Symons, Warden of Wadham), the proctors, and the Professor of Modern History (Dr J. A. Cramer, Principal of New Inn Hall), they consisted of Dr R. Bullock-Marsham (Warden of Merton), Dr F. C. Plumptre (Master of University), Dr F. Jeune (Master of Pembroke), the Revd Joseph Smith (Trinity) and the Revd H. G. Liddell (Christ Church). It is worth noting that amongst these Dr Cramer was born in Switzerland, that Dr Plumptre was related to the English translator and promoter of Kotzebue and that the future Dean of Christ Church and father of Alice (in Wonderland), like later curators such as Donkin, Lake and Vaughan, was one of the 'Germanizers'; many of the latter were skilled in that language, had visited the country and were associated with the Balliol reform group.[5]

The delays to which Sir Robert Taylor's foundation had been subject were considerable, but the final timing of its establishment was not inopportune. Already the Chancellor's English Essay had been devoted in 1827 to 'The influence of the Crusades on the art and literature of Europe', and in 1832 to 'The study of different languages as it relates to the philosophy of the human mind'. In 1834 the University had received by bequest the art collections and the outstanding library of classical and European literature belonging to Robert Finch.[6] In 1835 George Cornewall Lewis, later Chancellor of the Exchequer but then a recent Student of Christ Church and practising on the Oxford circuit, a man already conversant with French, German, Italian, Spanish, Provençal and Anglo-Saxon, published *An Essay on the Origin and Formation of the Romance Languages* at Oxford. Elsewhere, but at the same period, there also appeared Henry Hallam's last great work, *Introduction to the Literature of Europe during the Fifteenth, Sixteenth, and Seventeenth Centuries* (1837–9). Moreover, the turmoil created by the Oxford Movement was succeeded by a remarkable move towards reform, culminating in the Royal Commission of 1850. Cramer, basically a classicist, was succeeded as Regius Professor of Modern History in 1848 by H. H. Vaughan, more strictly a historian, and by 1853 the curators included among their number Mr Mark Pattison of Lincoln College.

The 1847 Regulations passed, the curators appointed a librarian, one John Macray, a Scot and the author of a volume of translations from the German. Seven months later, in October 1847, Wilhelm Frädersdorff and Jules T. T. Bué were appointed as teachers of German and French respectively. The chair of modern European languages appears to have been offered to the French historian and politician F. P. G. Guizot, who had been French ambassador in London in 1840, but in December 1848 the curators finally appointed F. H. Trithen, a Swiss with a Berlin doctorate. He had formerly been employed in St Petersburg and as a master at Rugby School, but was then on the staff of the British Museum library and Secretary of the Geographical Society. Trithen was in fact a comparative philologist with a sound knowledge of Sanskrit, but as he fell seriously ill in 1850 and gave up his position in 1854, he made little impact. The library opened in early 1849.

[5] The minute-books of the Taylor curators are held in OUA and by the Institution. See also J. S. G. Simmons, 'Slavic studies at Oxford, I: the proposed Slavonic chair at the Taylorian in 1844', *Oxford Slavonic Papers* iii (1952), 125–52.
[6] E. Nitchie, *The Reverend Colonel Finch* (New York 1940).

At this time the curators were still much preoccupied with the routine establishment of the Institution. Porters had to be appointed (and dismissed), book-plates designed, a lecture-room was allocated to the professor of modern history, and plans for a fresco on the ceiling of the main library room (never in fact executed) were discussed, William Dyce and G. F. Watts being approached. In its first decades the Taylor Institution provided lecture-rooms and storage accommodation of the greatest use to the University generally. In 1849 the Hope entomological collection was housed, and in 1854 the Strickland ornithological collection arrived, these needs only being relieved by the opening of the University Museum in 1860. Until then teaching in some scientific subjects such as geography, geology and anatomy was also catered for, and well after that date the lecture-room facilities were made available to professors and others teaching not only languages such as Anglo-Saxon, Greek, Hindustani, and Chinese but also poetry and political economy. Many of these demands for space disappeared only with the building of the Examination Schools in 1883 and the completion of the Indian Institute in 1885.

The elevation of Friedrich Max Müller to the professorship of modern European languages in 1854 gained an outstanding scholar of a very wide range and a most stimulating teacher for the Taylorian. He gave courses on the *Nibelungenlied*, on German civilization and literature to the reign of Charlemagne, on seventeenth-century German literature, on Goethe, Schiller, *Faust* and even on Joinville. His personality, powers of lucid and orderly expression and his rare command of English attracted many. A contemporary reported: 'It was a new star in the Oxford firmament...It was a new light, a new ideal of literature and lecture, that Max imported.' He was, however, equally, if not more, interested in comparative philology and gave courses on that subject itself, on the history of modern language, the origin of the Romance languages, the history of German, the science of language, and the principles of etymology, the latter really a study of the English language. Progressively, however, Max Müller's interests moved further from literature and even from European philology towards mythology and Sanskrit. He was an unsuccessful candidate for the chair in the latter subject offered in 1860, but late in 1865 he became, additionally to his professorial position, a Sub-Librarian of the Bodleian, a cumulation of posts recorded by the curators as being 'not in the best interests of the University and to be avoided in the future'. However, this arrangement did not work out and in 1868 he was appointed to the new chair of comparative philology (which was not attached administratively to the Taylorian). Coincidentally with this, the professorship of modern European languages was abolished, and in 1869 the holder of the new chair became an ex-officio curator of the Taylorian (the other non-administrative curator being the Regius professor of modern history). Müller's meteoric rise in English society and his wide contemporary fame certainly drew the attention of fashionable circles to philological questions, but a number of linguistic scholars soon attacked him for unreliable logic and a romantic rather than scholarly approach to philology.[7]

The teachers of languages operated on a distinctly different, lower and more grammatical level, concentrating on a sound elementary knowledge of their language, a necessary function at a time when the teaching of modern European languages was only just becoming properly established in public schools. Bué held his post for fifty years, publishing a series of 'readers', editions of standard plays and exercises in translation, together with the first French translation of *Alice in Wonderland* (1869). Frädersdorff wrote a number of similar works in German as well as some in Danish, a language in which he regularly conducted classes. In 1862 he resigned to become Professor of Modern Languages at Queen's College, Belfast.

By 1855 the curators found themselves in possession of regular surplus income and so decided to raise the salary of the professor to £500, to raise their expenditure on books for the library, to appoint a teacher in Italian (and two years later one in Spanish), and, mindful perhaps of the strictures made earlier on, to establish scholarships for undergraduates interested in modern languages. The Spanish teacher was Lorenzo Lucena, a Protestant described as an honorary canon of Gibraltar. The teacher of Italian was Count Aurelio Saffi (1819–90), a follower of Mazzini in 1848, who had been one of the triumvirs of the short-lived Roman republic and had come to England as an exile in 1851. He returned to Italy in 1860, resigning his Oxford post in the following year on becoming a deputy in the first Italian Parliament. A thinker rather than a man of action, he devoted much time to educational propaganda and to the collection of Mazzini's writings. His funeral was attended by 20,000 people, the oration being given by Carducci. The University sent a letter of condolence.

The Taylorian scholarships, worth £25 a year, were offered from 1857. They were tenable for two years, and varied in number over the years, ranging from one to four. Papers were set in prose composition, translation and philology and literature. There was also a dictation and an oral examination, the curators (not the teachers of languages) appointing examiners annually. Initially the scholars were expected to sign for the receipt of their scholarships in the curators' account-book, which bears in 1858 and 1859 the signature of A. C. Swinburne, he being, with A. G. Duff, one of the first pair of scholars. Swinburne was a pupil of Count Saffi, to whom he addressed verses duly prefixed to Saffi's tragedy *Marino Faliero* in 1885; subsequently, he wrote a poem on Saffi's death. Other later scholars of note included Henry Sweet, W. P. Ker (later Professor of Poetry), A. A. Macdonell (later Taylor-

---

[7] L. Dowling, 'Victorian Oxford and the science of language', *PMLA* xcvii (1982), 160–78. See also N. C. Chaudhuri, *Scholar Extraordinary: the life of Professor the Rt. Hon. Friedrich Max Müller, P.C.* (1974).

ian teacher in German and subsequently Professor of Sanskrit) and George, first Viscount Cave (later Lord Chancellor and Chancellor of the University).

The presence of a substantial library was clearly integral to the original Taylor delegates' view of the foundation, and the brief given for the architectural competition included major provision for this. Initially, however, the librarian was given little authority or freedom, being indeed reprimanded both for acquiring books without permission and for allowing borrowing. Purchases were made on recommendations made by the teachers and librarian, but only after consideration by the curators. Permission to borrow was highly restricted, and even Max Müller, when Deputy to the Professor, had to apply four times before being granted it. Regular, although limited, borrowing was only allowed from 1856. The original library establishment grant was of £1,000 with an annual budget of £100, but the deposit of the Finch library with its trust fund (both later divided among the Ashmolean, the Bodleian and the Taylorian) was of considerable assistance. A catalogue of the whole library was printed in 1861, and while this contains all the Finch books (some of which are now in the Bodleian) it shows what was available in the Taylorian at that date. The library was remarkably strong in editions of the Greek and Latin classics; it had many modern grammars and dictionaries; and Dante and other Italian authors (especially Foscolo) were well represented in nineteenth-century editions, while there were also earlier ones of Tasso and Guarini in particular. Major French, German and Spanish authors were present in nineteenth-century 'complete works' (and in some late eighteenth-century ones), Goethe and Schiller being the most popular. The best-represented contemporary authors were Lamartine and Guizot. The library budget was increased in 1855, and by 1866 the curators were insuring the building for £12,000, the furniture for £2,000 and the books for £8,000. The abolition of the professorship as a charge to the Taylorian in 1868 allowed for increased library expenditure, and by 1879 the books were valued at £16,000. At this time the second librarian, Dr Heinrich Krebs, who held the office from 1871 until 1921, was able to make interesting purchases of incunabula, of early Luther tracts (duplicates from Heidelberg University) and of some manuscripts. Krebs, who rearranged and recatalogued the whole library, was accurate, scholarly and industrious, having also a considerable reputation as a disciplinarian. He and his family lived sparingly in exiguous quarters in the library, an existence poignantly evoked in the unpublished memoirs of his daughter.[8] In 1895 the bequest of the Martin collection of Spanish and Portuguese books strengthened the early holdings in those fields; but in general acquisitions were made fairly widely, though more on the academic side of current philological and literary production than among strictly contemporary creative authors. By the turn of the

---

[8] Mrs L. Hewitt's autobiography is in Bodl. MS Top. Oxon. d. 440.

century the library possessed some 50,000 volumes. These had by then filled not only the gallery shelves in the main library room: they also required shelving in the curators' room, the room reserved for MAs, and indeed some of the lecture-rooms. Lists of library accessions were printed from 1881 onwards; and, by tacit agreement, the Bodleian has, since the foundation of the Taylorian, left the provision of continental European literature largely to that library.

The 1850 Commission report listed the professorships given to the University by private benefaction since the Reformation, and ended with Sir Robert Taylor's 1847 professorship of modern European languages, commenting, 'The greater part of these foundations are due to the desire of individuals to foster particular branches of study not acknowledged by the University.' Apart from University College London, where chairs of four modern European languages were founded in 1828, the Taylorian was in fact the only British institution of higher learning to provide any instruction in this field during the middle years of the nineteenth century. However, despite the promotion of Taylorian scholarships in 1857 and the addition of teachers of Spanish and Italian (in 1858 and 1861 respectively), the whole of this side of the benefaction was seen as working with the practical aim of acquiring a useful knowledge of any particular language, the first real university recognition of these studies being the acceptance of a French and German option in the pass school, agreed in 1872. Full academic recognition was, however, beginning elsewhere, and during the 1860s chairs of modern languages were established in Belfast, Dublin and Manchester.

The existence of the Taylorian and of its growing library, together with the presence of the Oxford University Press, provided encouraging ground for various learned lexicographical projects. Gúdbrandr Vígfússon came to Oxford in 1866 and, supported by Dean Liddell, published Richard Cleasby's *Icelandic–English Dictionary* in 1874, the first of a number of important Icelandic and Norse publications to appear in the following decade. The 1880s saw work start on Bosworth and Toller's *Anglo-Saxon Dictionary*, on Murray's *New English Dictionary* and, later, on Joseph Wright's *English Dialect Dictionary*, all works of impressive and impeccable scholarship.

Other languages and literatures were not forgotten, and, if the conversion of the Taylor professorship of modern European languages into a chair of comparative philology threatened the study of their literature, the curators' creation of an occasional lecture series could be seen as an attempt to counterbalance this change to some extent. The first of these Taylorian Lectures was delivered by Hippolyte Taine in 1871. At the same time the establishment of the Ilchester Fund in 1869 (set up under the will of the fourth Earl of Ilchester) allowed the occasional appointment from the following year of a lecturer on Slavonic languages, literature and history. This post became a full readership in 1889 and a personal chair in Russian in 1900.

Modern languages were evidently an area of activity in the University, and, as such, the University Commission of 1877 inquired into them. The picture of the regular instruction given, however, was not impressive: the teachers aimed only at a fairly elementary level, and attendance was not striking, the German teacher averaging sixteen in each class, the French twelve, the Italian just over five and the Spanish four. Among the causes of this situation were said to be the poor state of teaching in the public schools and the lack of formal recognition by the University of the subject. R. L. Nettleship suggested, in evidence to the Commission, that the latter difficulty could be removed by the creation of an honours school of 'Modern Literature' comprehending 'English, German, French and other languages'.[9]

The 1880s saw the lexicographical activities referred to above come to fruition. Society meetings and literary lectures increased, and it is clear that general British interest in modern languages was reaching an important level. In 1886 a modern languages tripos was instituted at Cambridge and between 1890 and 1904 Birmingham, Leeds, Liverpool, and Manchester universities, and Nottingham and Sheffield university colleges, all established chairs in the modern languages field. Equally important was the new interest in modern languages shown by the civil service and the army. An account of the long struggle to establish an honour school of modern languages is given in Part 2, Chapter 17. When the proposal at last found favour in 1903 it was argued that the existence of the Taylorian would guarantee the initial expenditure on the new school to be very low.

Although the motives for Sir Robert Taylor's bequest remain obscure, his very practical objectives were assiduously pursued by a perhaps surprisingly well-intentioned university, and promptly carried out once there was the power to do so. The founder's insistence on a building paid off handsomely, providing lecture-rooms for many subjects, a library and a multidisciplinary centre from which both language-teaching and philological and lexicographical research could be carried out. Oxford became the second British university (after University College London) to cater for modern language study; and, although the curricular study of European literature was long delayed, the eventual creation of the honour school was not significantly behind what was happening in other universities. Moreover, the existence of a firm institutional base meant that by 1914 the University had not only one of the largest British departments in the field, but one with a remarkably high academic standard.

[9] *UOC* (1877), evidence, Qs 3671–7.

22

The University Museum and Oxford Science, 1850–1880

ROBERT FOX

The laying of the foundation-stone of the University Museum by the Chancellor, Lord Derby, on 20 June 1855 was a great university occasion. Regrettably, as *The Times* reported, the luncheon in Worcester College, which had preceded the ceremony, had been 'very hurried', and the accommodation for spectators in the Parks was 'rough and poor'.[1] But neither the physical discomfort nor the tedium of the Vice-Chancellor's 'long and ill-composed prayer' and of Lord Derby's speech could efface the memory of that morning's Encaenia, at which Charles Lyell, George Gabriel Stokes, Humphrey Lloyd and other leading men of science had received honorary doctorates, or of a glittering, if over-heated, soirée in the Radcliffe Library which had been attended on the previous evening by over a thousand guests and followed by a Masonic Ball in the Town Hall that went on into the early hours.[2]

Oxford, it seemed, had embraced the natural-sciences ideal and done so with a lavishness and commitment that signalled its determination to end the exclusive stranglehold of classical and religious studies and to foster new subjects more suited to the economic and cultural climate of the age of

I am grateful to R. D. Hutchins, J. B. Morrell, and A. V. Simcock for their comments on an earlier draft, and to Mr Simcock and Stella Brecknell for their help with the manuscripts in their care at the Museum of the History of Science and the University Museum respectively. The starting-points for any study of the Museum and of Oxford science in this period include: H. W. Acland and J. Ruskin, *The Oxford Museum* (1859; 2nd edn 1860; repr. with preface by Acland 1893), and H. M. Vernon and K. D. Vernon, *A History of the Oxford Museum* (1909), esp. 38–104. Other important accounts include: Mallet, iii. 360–7; F. Sherwood Taylor, 'The teaching of science at Oxford in the nineteenth century', *Annals of Science*, viii (1952), 82–112; A. V. Simcock, *The Ashmolean Museum and Oxford Science, 1683–1983* (1984), esp. 14–17.

[1] *The Times* 21 June 1855, 9.

[2] For a distinctly unenthusiastic eye-witness account of the events, including the critical comment on the Vice-Chancellor's prayer, see M. J. Gifford (ed.), *Pages from the Diary of an Oxford Lady* (1932), 55–6. A more detailed and less personal account is in the *Herald* 23 June 1855, 11–14. Copies of the printed *Form of Prayer on Occasion of the Ceremony of Laying the First Stone of the New Museum at Oxford, June XX. M.DCCC.LV* are in Bodl. G. A. Oxon. 4° 13 (6) and MS Acland d. 95, fos 75–8.

reform. In reality, however, the battle for the Museum had been a close-run affair, and the building continued to provide a focus for controversy until, and even after, its opening in 1860. The notion that the University should make such costly provision for the scientific disciplines brought to the surface animosities between, on the one hand, a Hebdomadal Board and, from 1854, a Hebdomadal Council broadly sympathetic to science, and, on the other, reactionary critics who used the more democratic platform of Convocation to impede what they saw as a departure from the true purposes of the University. The Museum, in fact, was a natural focus for the tensions that divided university opinion through the years of liberal agitation and change between the mid-1840s and the 1870s, and its passage from project to realization intersected repeatedly with the broader issues that were firing debate, notably the function and remuneration of university professors and readers, the case for the recruitment of undergraduates from a broader social base and the proper place in Oxford of research, specialization and professional training.

Although the establishment of the new honour school of natural science in 1850 and the Royal Commission's explicit support for the Museum two years later[3] greatly strengthened the case, the proposal for the rehousing of the scientific collections and laboratories had deep roots in unreformed Oxford. The importance of creating a fitting home for the University's collections had been widely recognized in the late 1820s, when subscriptions for the purpose had been gathered. But the campaign had been poorly led and, despite the vogue for science that had briefly propelled the charismatic William Buckland to the forefront of Oxford intellectual life, both as a lecturer and as a practising geologist, it had soon foundered. Two decades later, the position of science within the University was, in important respects, weaker than it had been in Buckland's heyday. Persistently paltry attendances at lectures since the 1830s had demoralized the professoriate in virtually all disciplines (in law, for example, no less than in science), and it had helped to bring Buckland himself to a state of despair, compounded in 1849 by a breakdown of his mental health that had ended his geological career.[4]

Despite the difficulties of the 1830s and 1840s, the cause of science and, more specifically, of the Museum was championed as sternly as ever at the

---

[3] *RCO* (1850), report, 258.

[4] For evidence of the declining numbers attending lectures from the 1830s in chemistry, anatomy, geology, mineralogy and mathematics see C. Daubeny, *Brief Remarks on the Correlation of the Natural Sciences. Drawn up with reference to the scheme for the extension and better management of the studies of the University, now in agitation* (1848), 20–3; the figures given in evidence and published in *RCO* (1850), evidence, 257–9, 267, 284–6; and the list of those attending Daubeny's lectures in R. T. Gunther, *A History of the Daubeny Laboratory, Magdalen College, Oxford* (1904), 65–98. The decline is discussed in G. L'E. Turner, 'Experimental science in early nineteenth-century Oxford', *History of Universities*, viii (1989), 123–31.

mid-century by a circle of campaigners who drew visibility and strength from their elaboration of a determinedly united front. The main inspiration for the circle came from Charles Daubeny, now the senior figure in Oxford science, who held simultaneously the chairs of chemistry, rural economy and botany, aided by the more retiring Reader in Experimental Philosophy, the Revd Robert Walker, and the young, articulate and ambitious Henry Acland, who had been elected to the Dr Lee's readership in Anatomy at Christ Church in 1845 at the early age of 30.[5] The case they put was argued on grounds that broke significantly with Buckland's highly individualistic conception of the role of science in the University. Whereas Buckland had stressed originality and the elucidation, for a committed audience of both senior and junior members, of the scientific and theological implications of his geology, Daubeny and his allies adopted a less exotic trajectory. Their argument, advanced relentlessly, was that a broad foundation in science should be an indispensable element in any liberal education and hence a compulsory part of the undergraduate curriculum.

With appropriately Oxonian twists, the campaign reflected the national mood, which, at the time, made the extension of scientific education a natural plank in any reformist platform.[6] The pace was being made by new foundations, such as the Royal College of Chemistry (1845) and the Government (later Royal) School of Mines (1851) in London and Owens College in Manchester (1851). But the renewal of the laboratory provision for physics at Glasgow after the appointment of William Thomson in 1846 and, about the same time, in chemistry at University College and King's College in London shows how widely a decision to invest in science was regarded as a touchstone of any university's will to engage with the modern world. In Oxford, which had been, with Cambridge, the butt of nearly half a century of public criticism for its arcane curriculum and antiquated modes of government, the pressures were made all the greater by threats, spoken and unspoken, that such an engagement might be forced on the University if reform were not undertaken voluntarily. In liberal Oxford minds, there was also the disturbing sense of having been led by Cambridge, where the natural sciences tripos had been introduced in 1848.

But the main sources of unease on which the scientific reformers played were of a more parochial kind. It was not difficult to convey a sense of

---

[5] Acland's role is stressed, and arguably even exaggerated, in Vernon and Vernon, *History of the Oxford Museum*, esp. chs 2–4. In a similar vein see also Atlay, *Acland*, esp. ch. 8. Daubeny's leading role among the advocates of science at the mid-century is referred to unequivocally in [J. B. Mozley], 'The Oxford Commission', *Quarterly Review* xciii (1853), 178, and explained fully in R. Hutchins, 'Charles Daubeny (1795–1867): the bicentenary of Magdalen's first modern scientist', *Magdalen College Record*, (1995), 81–92; see also the longer version deposited as a typescript in the Magdalen College archives.

[6] On the new educational departures, see D. S. L. Cardwell, *The Organisation of Science in England* (2nd edn 1972), ch. 4.

scandal through the contrast that was repeatedly drawn between the enduring neglect of science, both by undergraduates and by the university authorities, and the importance of Oxford's scientific tradition going back to the
later seventeenth century, when the Ashmolean building in Broad Street had
been erected to house a museum and lecture-room and the first purpose-
built laboratory in Britain. The neglect was most dismally encapsulated in
the unsatisfactory state of the University's scientific collections. While there
was no great cause for concern with regard to the anatomical collection,
which Acland supervised, used and augmented at Christ Church in his
capacity as Dr Lee's Reader, the more general picture was one of dispersal
and disorder. Specimens and other materials were distributed between the
Ashmolean Museum, which housed the zoological collections, and the
Clarendon building, where there were rooms devoted to experimental philosophy (on the first floor at the eastern end of the building) and the
important geological collection which Buckland had installed there in
1832. In both locations, the lack of space and the air of disorder (for which
the geological collection was especially notorious) made it easy to convey
the impression that a rich accumulated asset was being under-exploited.

At the time of its resurgence in the later 1840s, the campaign for science
found only patchy support in the intellectual standing of the holders of the
University's scientific posts. The disenchantment and consequent departure
of William Buckland for the deanery at Westminster in 1845 had deprived
Oxford of its leading scientific light, and the competent but untried deputies
who replaced him—Nevil Story-Maskelyne (Deputy Reader in Mineralogy)
and Hugh Strickland (Deputy Reader in Geology)—were not appointed
until, following his breakdown, Buckland finally retired to the rectory of
Islip in 1850.[7] To a large extent, the vacuum in leadership was filled by
Daubeny. However, even Daubeny's considerable influence was tempered
by his decision to build a laboratory and lecture-room for himself at the
Botanic Garden and, in 1848, to extricate the teaching of chemistry from the
'dark, inconvenient, and confined' home it had occupied since the seventeenth century in the basement of the Ashmolean Museum—a move which
had the effect of satisfying his own worst grievances independently of the
general movement towards improved conditions for science.[8]

Elsewhere, there were few indications of either sustained vigour or real
distinction. Astronomy, for example, suffered from a damaging separation

---

[7] For biographical studies of Strickland and Maskelyne see 'Memoir of the late Hugh Edwin
Strickland', in Sir William Jardine, *Memoirs of the Late Hugh Edwin Strickland, M.A.* (1858),
pp. i–cclxv, and V. Morton, *Oxford Rebels: the life and friends of Nevil Story Maskelyne, 1823–
1911* (Gloucester 1987).

[8] The description is Charles Daubeny's. See his *Oxford Botanic Garden; or, a popular guide to
the Botanic Garden of Oxford* (2nd edn 1853), 13 n. The new laboratory is described in Gunther,
Daubeny Laboratory, 9–19.

between the work of Manuel Johnson, the competent, conscientious and amiable Radcliffe Observer, and the Savilian Professor of Astronomy, William Donkin, who had neither the interest nor the observatory that were required for serious observational astronomy and whose versatile intellect (displayed by his firsts in both Literae Humaniores and mathematics in 1836) was constrained by ill health and a chronically unassuming manner.[9] In physics, Robert Walker was more ambitious and as zealous as anyone for the cause of science; but the lectures that he had given in the Clarendon building since his appointment as Reader in Experimental Philosophy (the first to hold the post independently of other positions in the University) in 1839 were popular and capacious rather than scientifically original.[10] Likewise at the Ashmolean Museum, the eye that Philip Bury Duncan kept on the collections of natural history, paintings and antiquities of which he and before him, his elder brother, John Shute Duncan, had been Keepers since 1823 was vigilant enough, but it was unmistakably ageing: by the time he finally resigned his keepership in favour of John Phillips in 1854, the younger Duncan was 82. Among figures more marginal to science, Baden Powell, as Savilian Professor of Geometry, had done good work in optics and radiant heat. However, his impact on the University had been diminished by consistently poor attendances at his lectures and by his growing preoccupation with the fashioning of a new natural theology in the Broad-Church mould. Two other distant alliances that might have been made were non-existent. The Sedleian Professor of Natural Philosophy, George Leigh Cooke, and the Regius Professor of Medicine and Radcliffe Librarian, John Kidd, were elderly and, in their disciplines, inactive.

Despite the mixed quality and commitment of the scientific community, the call for an improved provision for Oxford science that was voiced in a public memorandum of 12 July 1847 was a forceful one. Although the memorandum was signed by Daubeny, Walker, Philip Duncan and Acland, it drew heavily on views for which Daubeny seems to have been chiefly responsible. It urged the University to erect a building that would provide space not only for the rehousing of the scientific collections in the Clarendon building, the Ashmolean Museum and Christ Church, but also for

---

[9] Roger Hutchins has drawn attention to the harm that was done, from 1839 until the early 1870s, by the decision of the Radcliffe trustees to appoint their own separate observer and to prohibit the use of their observatory by the Savilian Professor of Astronomy. See R. Hutchins, 'John Phillips, "geologist-astronomer", and the origins of the Oxford University Observatory, 1853–1875', *History of Universities*, xiii (1994), 193–249. On the decision and Johnson's work as the Radcliffe Observer see also I. Guest, *Dr. John Radcliffe and his Trust* (1991), 260–72.

[10] On Walker see A. V. Simcock's article in C. S. Nicholls (ed.), *DNB: Missing Persons* (1993), 695–6. Walker's sustained popularity is demonstrated by the certificates of attendance at his lectures, which show that he regularly drew attendances of over thirty, sometimes substantially more, throughout the 1850s. See OUA SP/85, 86 and 88. The numbers were far higher than that of candidates attempting the natural science school.

lecture-rooms, a library and a room for meetings.[11] The vision, fired by the support of visitors to the Oxford meeting of the British Association for the Advancement of Science in the previous month, was an exhilarating one, founded on the ideal of the unity of knowledge and a suspicion of premature specialization which Acland, in particular, was to preach until his death in 1900. But from the moment Buckland failed to give his support to a cause he considered 'utterly hopeless', still less to intercede with his friend Sir Robert Peel, the plan was doomed, and the memorandum was withdrawn.[12]

By the time the proposal for what was now and henceforth referred to as the University Museum resurfaced nearly two years later, the ground had been far better laid. Pamphlets by Daubeny and Walker, both published in 1848, had harped on the related needs to enforce attendance at professorial lectures and to extend the place of science in the curriculum to the point of making some scientific study a normal or even, as Walker maintained, an essential condition for admission to the degree of bachelor of arts.[13] In a similar vein, Acland too had clarified his position in the *Remarks on the Extension of Education in the University of Oxford* that he addressed to the Revd William Jacobson, the Regius Professor of Divinity and a canon of Christ Church, in November 1848.[14] In a choice that echoed Daubeny's triumvirate of 'primary' sciences (on which all the other sciences, described as 'special or subordinate', were claimed to depend),[15] Acland argued for the introduction of natural philosophy, chemistry and general physiology (essentially biology) as compulsory subjects. The aim was not the training of 'professed' scientists, but the disciplining of the mind. For that purpose, as Acland maintained with his characteristically accommodating caution, twenty-four lectures in each subject would be ample, and, at least for pass-men, the examination would be 'slight'. To have aspired to a larger slice of undergraduates' time would have raised the spectre of an intrusive element of specialized training and support for the activity of 'discovery in science' for which Oxford was palpably unready. As Acland believed and as the Royal Commissioners (among them Baden Powell) were to confirm in 1852,[16] if

[11] An MS copy of the memorandum is in the University Museum archives, 'History of the building of the Museum' (hereafter UMA), box 5, folder 1. For a printed version see Devonshire Commn i. 172.

[12] An MS copy of Buckland's letter is in UMA, box 5, folder 1.

[13] Daubeny, *Brief Remarks on the Correlation of the Natural Sciences*, and R. Walker, *A Letter Addressed to the Rev. the Vice-Chancellor, on Improvements in the Present Examination Statute and the Studies of the University* (1848). Walker proposed that all candidates for a BA should pass through a school of moral philosophy and history and either a school of mathematics or a school of physics (embracing all three of Daubeny's 'primary' sciences; see n. 15).

[14] H. Acland, *Remarks on the Extension of Education at the University of Oxford* (1848).

[15] Daubeny argued that his 'primary' sciences—mechanical or natural philosophy, chemistry and physiology—should be part of 'every complete system of Education'. See his *Brief Remarks on the Correlation of the Natural Sciences*, 8–11.

[16] *RCO* (1850), report, 80–1, and evidence, 235–9.

science were to establish itself in the studies of the University, it had to do so as part of the cherished ideal of a 'general education', in which the fashioning of minds and characters was more important than the imparting of information. Acland's overriding goal, in fact, was that scientific studies should be recognized as a branch of instruction comparable in status and style with Literae Humaniores.[17] By comparison, both research and the rather mundane utilitarian ideals that Lord Derby was to espouse (to the surprise of many of his hearers) at the laying of the foundation-stone in 1855 were of secondary importance.[18]

Even among the early champions of science, there were divergences of opinion, in particular on the extent to which attendance at scientific lectures (as opposed to professorial lectures in general) should be enforced and on the point at which science should be incorporated in the *cursus* of examinations. But on the essentials, Daubeny, Walker and Acland maintained a united public front. They were instrumental in calling a meeting of twenty-one members of Convocation in the lodgings of the Warden of New College, the Revd David Williams, at the beginning of May 1849, and in the decision to create an Oxford Museum Committee, with sixty-two members representing a wide range of colleges and disciplinary interests.[19] At this stage, the proposal for a museum was uncontroversial. Pusey and Samuel Wilberforce, as well as several heads of house, were among the non-scientific members of the Committee, and a public meeting of sympathizers in the Sheldonian Theatre on 19 June, under the chairmanship of the Vice-Chancellor, provoked no dissent. The resolution in favour of the erection of the Museum passed easily on the tide of support for the new school of natural science, and promises of donations, including £100 each from Gladstone and Peel, got the raising of funds off to a brisk start.[20] By March 1850 the matter had moved on to the Hebdomadal Board, which resolved that it was 'desirable that a New Museum be built for a collection in illustration of Physical Science and of Natural History, provided the details as to site and expense can be satisfactorily arranged'.[21]

[17] Acland and Daubeny could never have accepted the opinion of an anonymous writer in the *Herald* 14 Jan. 1854, 9, who argued, against Daubeny, that, as a 'means of mental training', science was far inferior not only to classics but also to history, philosophy and mathematics. Nevertheless, they were content to retain the substantial element of classical study in the early stages of the undergraduate curriculum.

[18] One who experienced surprise and disappointment at Lord Derby's argument that science should be supported on the grounds that it was dangerous to allow 'the mob' to advance in science more rapidly than 'us' was Henry Acland's brother Thomas Dyke Acland. See his letter to his father, Sir Thomas Acland, 19 June 1855, in *Memoir and Letters of the Right Honourable Sir Thomas Dyke Acland*, ed. A. H. D. Acland (1902), 173. The report of Lord Derby's speech in *The Times* 21 June 1855, 9, states, less emotively, that he had warned against the 'dangerous separation of feeling between the Universities and the great middle class, which was rapidly increasing in political power'.

[19] An MS record of the meeting on 1 May 1849 is in MS Acland d. 95, fos 71–2.

[20] Records of the early donations are in UMA, box 5, folder 1.

[21] HBM 18 Mar. 1850, 185.

At first, the Board's favourable response, aided by the decision to associate the building of the Museum with a broader plan involving the erection of new examination schools and lecture-rooms as well, suppressed any conservative qualms that might have been felt. But perceptions changed as, after the initial interest, subscriptions struggled to exceed £3,000, despite the efforts of Richard Greswell, the energetic Tractarian, former fellow of Worcester and long-standing friend of science, who led the campaign.[22] Plainly, the scheme, whose cost (including the new examination schools and lecture-rooms) was estimated in February 1851 at 'not less than £40,000', was going to be beyond the resources of individual benefactors, on whom it had at first been decided to rely.[23] In the face of that realization, the scheme would probably have foundered, but suddenly, in the spring of 1851, the availability of £60,000, transferred to the University from the accumulated profits of the University Press, allowed the matter to be reopened. Seeing their chance, the supporters of the museum project immediately secured a recommendation of the Hebdomadal Board that Convocation should allocate £30,000 of the windfall to the combined purposes of the new Museum, the examination schools, and the lecture-rooms, with another £23,100 being earmarked to secure an increase in professorial salaries—a move of special interest to the scientists.[24]

The move smacked of a pre-emptive opportunism, and as such it united the critics and waverers. Pusey, thinly and very briefly disguised as 'a Doctor of Divinity', led the protest with a pamphlet that condemned the proposal as, at best, over-hasty and advanced the characteristically though by no means exclusively Tractarian argument that the fruits of the printing of God's word (the Bible being the main source of the profits of the Press) should be devoted, at least in part, to the support of poor scholars who would go on 'to serve God both in Church and State'.[25] There seems little reason to doubt that Pusey's call, like that of his supporters, was founded on a positive commitment to university extension rather than on any systematic hostility to science. Certainly, for Pusey (as for many of his conservative

[22] In the 1820s Greswell (who took firsts in both Lit. Hum. and mathematics in 1822) had been one of the founders of the scientific discussion group that eventually, in 1828, formed the Ashmolean Society. See J. W. Burgon, *Lives of Twelve Good Men* (2 vols 1888) ii. 115–16, and Greswell's own mention of the sum that had been collected by Mar. 1850, when he abandoned his efforts, in his *Memorial on the (Proposed) Oxford University Lecture-Rooms, Library, Museums, &c. addressed to members of Convocation* (np nd), 20, Bodl. G. A. Oxon. 8° 124(16).

[23] The figure of £40,000 was laid before the Hebdomadal Board on 17 Feb. 1851 by the small committee which the Board appointed on 22 Feb. 1850 to consider the proposal (HBM).

[24] HBM, meetings of 2 Dec. 1850 and 24 and 27 Mar. 1851; see also the draft statute concerning the increases in salaries pasted in the back of this register as document 89. The proposal was guided through the Board by the Principal of St Alban Hall, Edward Cardwell, in the absence of representatives of the scientific interest (membership of the Board being restricted to the Vice-Chancellor, heads of house, and the proctors).

[25] 'A Doctor of Divinity', *On the Proposed Vote of £53,100* (dated 14 June 1851); repr. *Herald* 28 June 1851, 3, with a letter to Edward Cardwell, dated 18 June 1851, identifying Pusey as the author.

contemporaries), science could never fulfil the role of the severer disciplines of classical study, philosophy and mathematics as vehicles for the cultivation of the mind; and in Convocation and elsewhere he made no secret of his conviction that it was capable of fostering irreverence and arrogance when it strayed beyond 'its own limits'.[26] But he appears to have believed quite genuinely that science deserved a place in university studies.[27] In any case, whatever residual qualms he might have felt were tempered by a personal friendship with Acland, a man of unimpeachable piety whose cautious views on the place of science in the undergraduate curriculum were, in fact, close to his own.[28] It was presumably this friendship which led Pusey to lace his pamphlet with a specific plea for the neglected discipline of physiology.

Despite his clear, if qualified, sympathy for the cause of science, Pusey's pamphlet had the effect of rallying opposition, and on 17 June 1851 even an eloquent plea from Daubeny could not prevent Convocation from roundly rejecting the Board's recommendation on the allocation of funds for the Museum and the other buildings by 88 votes to 47.[29] In taking this decision, Convocation was flying in the face of the liberal wind of change that was blowing through Oxford, and displaying its characteristic suspicion of the Board. But within less than a year the report of the Royal Commission, disregarding what it must have seen as Oxonian perversity, had urged the University to proceed with the plan for the Museum as part of a general encouragement for science.[30] Fortified by this support, the Hebdomadal Board's Museum Committee duly went its way as if the rebuff had never occurred. In November 1852 it recommended to the Board that a site not exceeding four acres should be purchased at the southern extremity of the Parks, and in February 1853, Convocation fell in with the Board's wishes by appointing a delegacy to prepare a detailed report on the 'museums, lecture-rooms, and other buildings' that were needed for the scientific subjects.[31] Within three months, however, Convocation had dug its heels in once again. On 24 May 1853, faced with the delegacy's insistence on the desirability of the new Museum if the honour school of natural science were not to become

[26] Despite Pusey's compromising tone towards science, his suggestion that, only a few years before, science had gone beyond these 'limits' and, in an excess of pride, had 'seemed to be lifting itself up against God himself', was interpreted by an unidentified 'Member of Congregation' as an unwarranted attack on 'the Professors and Cultivators of Physical Science'. See the letter to the editor of the *Herald* 28 June 1851, 3.

[27] The point is made strongly in the translation of the Latin text of Pusey's speech in Convocation on 17 June 1851; see *Herald* 21 June 1851, 3.

[28] H. P. Liddon (ed.), *Life of Edward Bouverie Pusey* (4 vols 1893–7) iv. 330–7.

[29] *Herald* 21 June 1851, 3. Daubeny's plea was published as *Brief Remarks on the Statute 'De lectoribus publicis', to be submitted to Convocation on Tuesday, June 17* (1851).

[30] *RCO* (1850), report, 258.

[31] HBM 22 Nov. 1852, 6 Dec. 1852, 17, 24 and 31 Jan. 1853 and 7 Feb. 1853. Convocation gave its approval on 17 Feb. 1853; see OUA Convocation register, 1846–1854, 438, and *Herald* 19 Feb. 1853, 8.

a dead letter, it rejected the report by 35 votes to 31. In taking this stance, it was evidently swayed by a variety of sentiments, ranging from a suspicion of the scientists' ambitions to a concern that the University risked committing itself to a venture which, in view of the other demands that could properly be made, might devour far more than the sum made available by the Press.[32]

The inclusion, in the report, of a provisional estimate of at least £48,000 (excluding fittings, which it was said might cost another £7,500) by the architect and builder Lewis Cubitt gave substance to the concern on financial grounds.[33] And even Greswell, a consistently supportive member of the delegacy and a champion of the new honour school, argued that the report called for further deliberation before it could properly be submitted to Convocation.[34] But a blistering intervention from Daubeny, who had been a driving force on the delegacy, had its desired effect, and soon Convocation swung back to a position of suspicious approval.[35] A rearguard action in favour of a site at the eastern end of Broad Street was silenced, chiefly on the grounds of cost, and in December 1853 the University signed an agreement with Merton College for the purchase of the land in the Parks that had been earmarked more than a year before. The cost was £4,000, raised (with Convocation's backing) by the sale of stock.

By the spring of 1854, with a new delegacy in place, the proposal was assuming an unstoppable momentum. On 30 March Convocation agreed that between £30,000 and £40,000 should be spent on the new Museum,[36] and shortly afterwards, on 8 April, yet another delegacy was appointed to obtain architectural plans and estimates and to advise Convocation on the most suitable design.[37] On this body, the scientific interest had some powerful voices. The established professoriate was represented by Daubeny and Acland; Manuel Johnson was present in his capacity as Radcliffe Observer; and these older hands were joined by two newcomers: Bartholomew Price,

---

[32] Convocation register, 1846–1854, 457, and *Herald* 28 May 1853 (reporting on a Convocation held on 24 May). A four-page leaflet by 'Prometheus', entitled *Considerations Affecting the Museum Report*, and an unsigned reply, *Prometheus vinctus*, reflect the bitterness of the discussion in the days preceding the debate in Convocation, Bodl. G. A. Oxon. c. 69 (109–10). The delegacy's seven-page report was published (apparently about the middle of April, although it bore no date) as *The Report of the Delegates for the Oxford University Museum*, Bodl. G. A. Oxon. 8° 659.

[33] *Report of the Delegates*, 7, and Lewis Cubitt to the members of the museum delegacy, 4 Apr. 1853, in Bodl. MS Acland d. 95, fo 73.

[34] Greswell, *Memorial*, 10–13. Greswell's dissatisfaction centred on what he saw as an inappropriate distribution of space between the disciplines. His own alternative plan, which accompanied the *Memorial*, gave more space to zoology than was envisaged in the report.

[35] Daubeny's attack on what he described as Convocation's 'palpable inconsistency' and 'intentional bad faith' appeared in a note added to his separately paginated 'Address to the members of the University', delivered on 20 May 1853 to mark the University's acceptance of the herbarium, in Daubeny, *Oxford Botanic Garden*, 12–13 n.

[36] *Herald* 1 Apr. 1854, 8. The vote was 18 to 4.

[37] Ibid. 8 Apr. 1854, 8, and 15 Apr. 1854, 8.

recently promoted (following Cooke's death) from a fellowship and mathematical lectureship at Pembroke College to the Sedleian chair of Natural Philosophy, and the quietly influential figure of John Phillips, a former professor at Trinity College, Dublin, who had come from York to succeed Strickland as Deputy Reader in Geology in 1853 and who was soon to become (simultaneously) Duncan's successor as Keeper of the Ashmolean Museum.

Although, on a delegacy of seventeen members, the scientists formed a minority that could easily be outvoted, they were vociferous and of one mind, and the vision of the underlying unity of the sciences which the delegacy endorsed bore their unmistakable thumbprint. The statement of principle was uncompromising: 'To increase the value of the Collections illustrative of Natural History, and to aid the School of Natural Science in the University, it is desirable that a General University Museum be formed with distinct departments under one roof, together with Lecture Rooms and apartments for the use of Professors, and working-rooms for students.'[38] The accompanying guidance for architects wishing to submit plans in the open competition spelled out the vision in more detail, though with the important and quite new gloss that no scheme whose estimated cost exceeded £30,000 (excluding heating and other basic services) would be considered. The building was to be of two storeys. In it, there were to be specialized museums or apparatus rooms for medicine, physiology and anatomy, zoology, geology, mineralogy, chemistry and experimental philosophy. In addition, there were to be seven lecture-rooms (including one capable of seating 500), a library, a detached residence for the Curator (later redesignated as Keeper), accommodation for a porter and two servants, and generous provision for laboratories and dissecting rooms, private work-rooms, store-rooms, workshops, and individual sitting-rooms for the professors and readers, including the Savilian Professors of Astronomy and Geometry and the Sedleian Professor of Natural Philosophy. Most importantly, easy communication was to be ensured by the arrangement of the facilities around the three sides of a common central courtyard roofed in glass, leaving the fourth side for future extension.

It can hardly have escaped the attention of Acland and the other promoters of the scheme that such detailed considerations had the welcome effect of diverting attention from the more fundamental question of whether Oxford should seek to accommodate science on this scale at all. The same was true of the debate about architectural style, which generated contention of an engaging but disarming kind. Here, as in most aspects of the campaign, Acland's reconciling influence was evident. In his capacity as Radcliffe Librarian, he invited members of Convocation and their friends to a convivial viewing of the thirty-two competing designs in the Camera on the

---

[38] *Statement of the Requirements of the Oxford University Museum, Prepared for the Use of Architects by the Delegates who were Appointed in a Convocation held on April 8, 1854 ...* (np nd), 1. Bodl G. A. Oxon. c. 70(254).

afternoon of 6 November 1854, and there can be little doubt that it was his skilful lobbying which guided the delegacy that was appointed to consider the proposals in its narrowing of the choice, first to six and then, after a further viewing, to two.

By the time Convocation met, in the following month, to choose between the two selected designs, Acland had very effectively prepared the ground for the last stage in the process.[39] On the evening of 9 December 1854, members of Convocation and other residents of Oxford were invited to inspect the designs of the two finalists, and on 12 December, after two more days of viewing, the vote was taken.[40] In adopting the 'Rhenish' gothic plan of 'Nisi Dominus aedificaverit domum' (the tag adopted by Benjamin Woodward of the Dublin firm of Deane and Woodward) rather than the Palladian scheme of 'Fiat justitia, ruat coelum' (entered by Edward Middleton Barry, the son of Sir Charles Barry), Convocation was fulfilling Acland's wishes. For him (as for G. E. Street and for the even more influential figure of John Ruskin, Acland's friend since their undergraduate days at Christ Church[41]), the gothic style, unfettered by the constraints of symmetry and unity, offered an incomparable capacity for adaptation and future enlargement. It was also no small consideration in the all-important task of integration with the older traditions of the University that gothic was preeminently in keeping with the collegiate character of Oxford, even if the chosen design was not in the *English* gothic style that one anonymous observer was keen to see adopted.[42]

Both in securing the general principle in favour of building the Museum and in the details of the design, Acland's vigilance had been indispensable. The crucial majority that was obtained on 12 December 1854 in favour of

---

[39] *Report of the Oxford University Museum Delegacy, December 7, 1854* (np nd), Bodl G. A. Oxon. c. 70(253); repr. *Herald* 9 Dec. 1854, 9–10. The report was signed by the Revd Henry Wellesley (Principal of New Inn Hall), John Phillips, Henry Acland and the secretary to the delegacy, the Revd George Butler, a former fellow of Exeter and now a curate at St Giles's Church, who was soon to become Principal of Butler Hall, a short-lived private hall. Although the choice had been guided by professional architectural advice, from Philip Hardwick and his son Philip Charles Hardwick, it must be assumed that even this advice was coloured by Acland's preferences.

[40] A programme for the viewing on 9 Dec. is in UMA, box 5, folder 1.

[41] G. E. Street, *An Urgent Plea for the Revival of the True Principles of Architecture in the Public Buildings of the University of Oxford* (1853). For Ruskin's support for the adoption of the gothic style for the Museum, see his two letters to Acland, the first written on 25 May 1858, the second dated 20 Jan. 1859, which appeared in Acland and Ruskin, *The Oxford Museum*, 44–56 and 60–90 (1st edn); 35–44 and 47–70 (2nd edn); 43–55 and 60–90 (1893 edn). The letters were omitted from the third and fourth editions of the work, published respectively in 1866 and 1867.

[42] *The Old English Style of Architecture, as Applicable to Modern Requirements; or, suggestions for the new museum at Oxford. For private circulation only* (np 1854). See also E. Blau, *Ruskinian Gothic: the architecture of Deane and Woodward* (Princeton NJ 1982), 48–81. Contemporaries also called the style 'Veronese gothic' and 'Lombardo-gothic': M. W. Brooks, *John Ruskin and Victorian Architecture* (New Brunswick 1987), 120. See also *Athenaeum*, 16 Dec. 1854, 1531; Atlay, *Acland*, 207.

choosing one or other of the two final designs (70 to 64) was perilously small, although once that vote had been taken, the majority for 'Nisi Dominus' was much larger: 81 to 38.[43] The emergence of a professional architectural opinion in favour of an Italianate design that would combine the elegance of classical architecture with the picturesqueness of the gothic and provide the foundation for a distinctive national style for public buildings came too late to sway the issue.[44] But real menace had lurked in the flurry of hostile papers in the days preceding the vote, which had resurrected the spectre of financial irresponsibility. The public assurance of the secretary of the museum delegacy, George Butler, that the shortlisted plans could both be realized, at least in their essentials, within the stated budget of £30,000 rang hollow in the face of charges of extravagance in the plans and dark warnings of the additional costs which, as critics maintained, would impoverish the University once the building was open.[45] 'Is there one shilling at hand to endow this gigantic Babylon?', asked one flysheet, signed by a 'Member of Congregation'.[46] What right had the delegates to 'play ducks and drakes' with the University's funds when Oxford already possessed two museums (the Ashmolean and the recently built University Galleries) that were 'as yet unused and unfrequented'?

Such sentiments were fanned by a widespread sense that the grandeur of the scheme was out of all proportion to either the state or the future prospects of science in Oxford, and, more specifically, by memories of Cubitt's estimate of £48,000 or more for a building of the kind that was proposed. The opposition may also have drawn some strength from the remnants of Tractarian unease about the dangers that arose when science strayed from its exclusive concern with the material world into the realms of revelation. However, as Acland later recalled, opposition on this ground was never strong.[47] And it was, in any case, decisively undermined by the decision of Pusey and the Newmanite Charles Marriott, who had attended Acland's lectures as Dr Lee's Reader in Anatomy at Christ Church in the late

---

[43] The majority in the first vote is reported as 70 to 64 in the Convocation register, 1854–71, 31, and in the *Herald* 16 Dec. 1854, 8. However, the figures in the printed flysheet 'To members of Convocation', published by 'A member of Convocation' on the day after the vote, and in *Builder* xii (16 Dec. 1854), 641, are 68 to 64, a result referred to in Atlay, *Acland*, 211.

[44] See the article, signed 'J.F.', in *Builder* xii (18 Nov. 1854), 592.

[45] Butler's assurance appeared in a printed statement dated 11 Dec. 1854; see Bodl. G. A. Oxon. c. 70(246). Butler's optimism, based on 'offers from responsible Contractors', contradicted the view of the two professional judges who had reported on 28 Nov. that none of the final six designs could be completed for the designated sum; see *Report of the Oxford Museum Delegacy*, 3–4.

[46] Flysheet addressed 'To members of Convocation', dated 11 Dec. 1854, Bodl. G. A. Oxon. c. 70(244).

[47] See Acland's preface to Acland and Ruskin, *The Oxford Museum* (1893 edn), p. ix. The point is explored fully in P. B. Nockles, 'An academic counter-revolution: Newman and Tractarian Oxford's idea of a university', *History of Universities* x (1991), 159–64. See also my earlier comments on Greswell's support, pp. 648, 650.

1840s, to rally to the cause of the Museum: simply by voting in favour of the project in Convocation on 12 December 1854, Pusey and Marriott probably won over enough doubters to ensure the passage of the motion.

The influence of non-Tractarian religious opinion is less easily gauged. Evangelicals, for example, might have been expected to take a critical view, inspired by the kind of fundamentalist venom that had led William Cockburn, the Dean of York, to attack even the unimpeachably orthodox Buckland for his allegorical interpretation of the scriptures in the 1830s and 1840s.[48] But the evidence that suspicion of science on these grounds might in any systematic way have fired opposition to the Museum is slight. Walker himself was a noted Evangelical preacher, and it was the Evangelical Provost of Worcester, Richard Lynch Cotton, who did as much as anyone to steer the project through the choppy waters of the mid-1850s. Succeeding the helpful but rather more sceptical Master of University College, Frederick Charles Plumptre, as Vice-Chancellor in 1852, Cotton proved a constructively persuasive ally, especially in his capacity as chairman of Hebdomadal Council, where the scientific professoriate was unrepresented.[49] The figure of £30,000 as the upper limit for the cost of constructing the Museum was, in fact, his estimate of the largest amount that Council might be persuaded to approve. Although the calculation may have reflected Cotton's concern to preserve a substantial part of the windfall from the Clarendon Press for other initiatives somewhat closer to his heart, in particular, for the building of a hall for the education of poor students as clergymen, it was plainly a source of satisfaction to him that the sum he had earmarked was duly delivered.

Even after the victory in Convocation in December 1854, protests continued to be voiced. In the following spring, the proposal for the release of the £29,041 to meet the successful builder's tender, from Lucas Brothers of Lambeth, provoked a round of pamphlets of undiminished virulence.[50] Convocation's approval on 8 May 1855, by 123 votes to 20, was decisive, and within barely six weeks, with the laying of the foundation-stone, what Daubeny represented in a satirical pamphlet as his 'dream' began to become a physical reality.[51] Thereafter, the tone of the opposition gradually changed.

---

[48] J. B. Morrell and A. W. Thackray, *Gentlemen of Science: early years of the British Association for the Advancement of Science* (1981), 240–4.

[49] The contrast between Plumptre and Cotton, who 'took a wider and truer view of man and of truth than his predecessor', was made by Acland in the preface to Acland and Ruskin, *The Oxford Museum* (1893 edn), p. x. However, there is no evidence that Plumptre was anything but wholly supportive; indeed, his role as chairman of the sub-delegacy for the museum building in the late 1850s appears to have been crucial.

[50] See e.g. 'The new museum', a single sheet signed 'A member of Congregation' and dated 3 May 1855, in Bodl. G. A. Oxon. b. 28 (unfoliated) and MS Acland d.95 (88). The author is tentatively, but plausibly, identified as Daubeny in Cordeaux and Merry, 532.

[51] The vote is recorded in Convocation register, 1854–1871, 53. Daubeny's *A Dream of the New Museum* (1855) was probably written at about the time of the laying of the foundation-stone. In his dream, Daubeny was transported to the imaginary University of Icaria, a German mirror image of Oxford, in which the sciences held almost exclusive sway, to the detriment of classical studies.

It now assumed the character of sniping on such matters as the decoration and fittings, and expressions of ill-concealed satisfaction as the work of construction encountered difficulties ranging from the need to replace the original wrought-iron pillars with pillars in the much stronger cast iron that had been recommended by Woodward to the running battles with the self-willed Irish mason James O'Shea. And always the residual animus was reinforced by the inexorably mounting cost. The original tender of £29,041,[52] which had been intended to cover the cost only of the building (without even the provision of basic services), soon receded into inconsequence as the expenditure reached £45,000 by the spring of 1858, almost £57,000 by December 1860, and eventually, by 1867, more than £87,000.[53]

A vote in Convocation on 17 May 1856, which secured an additional £7,500 (including no less than £5,000 for well-seasoned timber for the book- and display-cases), confirmed the critics' most dismal warnings about the voracity of the project,[54] and fears were repeatedly aroused over the next decade as Convocation was called upon time and again to vote on requests for additional sums both for the building and for the materials, equipment and assistance that were required for teaching. Almost invariably the voting was close, and occasionally the opponents of further expenditure had the gratification of a victory calculated to pique the champions of science. However, such votes as those of 14 May 1858 (rejecting the allocation of £500 for the purchase of chemical apparatus) and of 3 June 1858 (against Hebdomadal Council's recommendation that £250 should be expended on the adjustment of the design of the Museum's central tower to allow the construction of a platform for the observation of temperature, humidity and other physical phenomena) were the exception rather than the rule.[55] Still, they served as a reminder of the watchful eye that critics and even some sympathizers kept on the rising cost of supporting science.

A fundamental problem that underlay all these debates was the decision to limit the cost of construction to £30,000. The *Builder* was only one of many voices that predicted, from the start, that the specification could not be met

[52] See the original contract in UMA, box 1, folder 2, which also contains the unsuccessful tenders.

[53] The figure of £87,391 2s 3½d, given in the printed *Statement of Sums Granted by University for Establishing and Maintaining the Museum down to December 1867*, includes not only the cost of construction, fitting out and maintenance and repairs up to that date but also grants of over £6,000 to the various science departments. For a detailed breakdown both of the grants received and of expenditure up to 31 Jan. 1860 see the printed statement in UMA, box 1, folder 3.

[54] Convocation register, 1854–1871, 113–14, and *Herald* 17 May 1856, 8.

[55] Convocation register, 1854–1871, 172 and 174, and *Herald* 22 May 1858, 8, and 5 June 1858, 8. The proposal concerning the adaptation of the tower entailed a partial resurrection of the earliest version of the plan, in which the tower was to have a flat roof; see the illustration in *Builder* xiii (7 July 1855), 319. It was strongly supported by the Radcliffe Observer, Manuel Johnson, and opposed by Greswell, who argued that the tower's conical roof was 'the great beauty of the building'. According to Greswell, the tower of the Bodleian Library, where some observational work had been undertaken, would be a better location and could be fitted out for the purpose for a mere £10. Hebdomadal Council's support for the scheme was expressed on 26 May 1858; see OUA HC/1/2/2, p. 237. Hebdomadal Council minutes, 1854–66.

for this figure: as one contributor put it, if more money were not made available or if the requirements were not modified, the university authorities would have to be content with 'a mere warehouse in which to contain their collections'.[56] It appears remarkable, therefore, that, despite these grave misgivings, the menace of enforced skimping was generally averted, the more so as on occasions even the scientific vote was not unanimous. At one particularly stormy meeting of Convocation on 17 December 1858, for example, the Regius Professor of Medicine, James Adey Ogle, found his complaint about the 'continuous and apparently endless demands' of the advocates for the Museum buttressing the proposal of Henry Wall, the Professor of Logic, for the dismissal of the architect 'for gross ignorance of his business'.[57] This alliance brought together important strands of conservative Oxford opinion. Ogle, though a long-standing advocate of a school of natural science, was uncompromisingly hostile to research, and the view he had expressed in 1841, that 'the prosecution of Truth forms no part of our duties',[58] was clearly behind his scepticism towards the Museum. Wall, for his part, was one of the most notorious opponents of the new academic disciplines. In the event, however, the allocation of an additional £3,995 that Wall was opposing (even though it was for work already completed) was approved, by 41 votes to 17, and precariously the plan moved on to completion.

Such deletions from Woodward's design as did occur, notably in some of the carving on the west front and the plan for an elaborate open arch leading into the recessed main doorway, disturbed Ruskin, as they also disappointed Richard Greswell, who organized a last-minute public appeal for £1,000 to avoid the inevitable paring down.[59] Although the appeal was only partially successful, the casualties were few, and they were compensated for by a surge of interest in other decorative aspects of the building. The success of the appeal for donations to pay for the statues, corbels and miscellaneous carvings that adorned the central court and for the capitals and shafts forming the arcades (which doubled as geological specimens) helped to give the structure an air of at least superficial opulence, while satisfying Ruskin's insistence that decoration was essential to any gothic building. No less importantly, it brought prestige and publicity. It was hard to regard a scheme to which the Queen herself had donated £350 to pay for the statues of Bacon, Galileo, Newton, Leibniz and Oersted as unworthy of support.[60]

[56] 'J. F.', article in *Builder* xii (18 Nov. 1854), 591. Cf. also the doubt expressed ibid. 388.

[57] *Herald*, 18 Dec. 1858, 8.

[58] J. A. Ogle, *A Letter to the Reverend the Warden of Wadham College, on the System of Education Pursued at Oxford; with suggestions for remodelling the examination statutes* (1841), 9. At this conspicuously early date, Ogle advocated the creation of a new honour school of natural science as an alternative for candidates who had passed through classical Moderations.

[59] See the four-page printed appeal circulated by Greswell, in Bodl. G. A. Oxon. c. 75(187) and MS Acland d. 95, fos 81–2. Ruskin's anxiety at what he saw as a menacing parsimony emerges clearly from his two letters to Acland, cited in n. 41.

[60] The success of the appeal to meet the cost of the statues, pillars and other adornments is evident from the annotated list of donations, dated 4 June 1860, in UMA, box 5, folder 2.

As the work progressed, thoughts turned increasingly to the task of transferring the collections and equipment from their various cramped locations. Gradually, under the meticulous supervision of Phillips in his capacity as Keeper of the Museum (a position he held from 1858 until his death in 1874), the preparations for occupation began. The emollient influence that Phillips had exerted on the whole museum project was now more necessary than ever, and once again it paid dividends in restraining the irritation that was only finally defused in the spring of 1860, when the building was structurally complete. Inevitably, there were those who found the wait unbearably frustrating. Benjamin Brodie, for example, had been obliged to work, on a rather makeshift basis, in the recently established Balliol College laboratory since his appointment as Daubeny's successor in the Aldrichian chair of Chemistry in 1855. With no access to the old chemical laboratory in the basement of the Ashmolean Museum, where Maskelyne had taught mineralogical analysis (and lived) since 1850, and with Daubeny comfortably occupying his premises at the Botanic Garden, Brodie displayed his impatience by lecturing in the Museum from October 1858.[61] He did so in the absence of a gas supply and amid many other signs of unreadiness. But it was in these unfinished premises that, in accordance with his father's wishes, the Prince of Wales was instructed by Brodie for two hours a week during the Prince's residence in Oxford in 1859–60.[62]

By the time the work of installation was done, in the early months of 1861, the Museum had already been the setting for one of the most remarkable events in its history: the tempestuous debate on Charles Darwin's theory of evolution by natural selection between the Broad-to-High Bishop of Oxford, Samuel Wilberforce, and Darwin's champion, Thomas Henry Huxley. The occasion was the visit of the British Association for the Advancement of Science, which chose Oxford for its eight-day annual meeting in 1860. It was important for the cause of science in Oxford that the Association's visit (its third since it had been founded in 1831) should pass off smoothly, and the early signs were all favourable. An appropriately calm and congratulatory tone was set by the President for the year, Lord Wrottesley, whose opening address in the Sheldonian Theatre contrasted the marginality of science in Oxford in his own undergraduate days more than forty years before with its present prosperity.[63] And thereafter, the unremarkable proceedings went their way, until the momentous happenings of Saturday 30 June.

In a busy programme, a seemingly innocuous session of the zoological and botanical section, planned for that day, would not normally have drawn

[61] See the printed syllabus of his lectures for Michaelmas term 1858, bound in Bodl. 2626 d. 35.
[62] Sir Sidney Lee, *King Edward VII: a biography* (2 vols 1925–7) i. 77.
[63] The text of Lord Wrottesley's speech is reproduced in *Report of the Thirtieth Meeting of the British Association for the Advancement of Science; held at Oxford in June and July 1860* (1861), pp. lv–lxxv (lv–lix). Also printed, with omissions, in *Oxford Chronicle* 30 June 1860, 4–5, and, in a more abbreviated form, in the *Herald* 7 July 1860, 3–4. John Wrottesley, a former president of the Royal Society, had taken a first in mathematics at Christ Church in 1819.

a large audience. But the announcement of a paper by a well-known speaker, Professor J. W. Draper of New York, 'On the intellectual development of Europe, considered with reference to the views of Mr Darwin and others, that the progression of organisms is determined by law', raised the intriguing prospect of a hostile riposte from Wilberforce. It was enough to attract over 700 people, a mixed bag, mainly of dons, undergraduates and clergy, crammed into the Museum's still unfinished library on the first floor of the west front.[64] After a dull, over-long performance by Draper, Wilberforce's riposte duly came, in the form of a sneering but well-received attack on Darwin's theory and, more specifically, on Huxley.[65] That Huxley was there at all was fortuitous: he had intended to leave Oxford by the Saturday and was only persuaded to stay after a chance meeting with Robert Chambers, the author of the popular evolutionary work *Vestiges of the Natural History of Creation*, published fifteen years before. It was also by chance that another Darwinian, the botanist J. D. Hooker, was there: he had felt distinctly out of sorts in clerical Oxford and, after spending most of his time away from the meeting, had been tempted to leave before Wilberforce's intervention. In the event, the uncompromising position taken by Huxley and Hooker, both of whom replied to Wilberforce in the name of a scientific professionalism that brooked no interference from ill-informed clerics, spawned one of the legendary episodes in the relations between science and religion.

Exactly what happened is far from clear, but the essentials of the traditional account seem true enough. In the course of his address, Wilberforce appears to have challenged Huxley to declare whether he was descended from the ape on his grandmother's or his grandfather's side, whereupon Huxley made the famous reply (in words he recalled two months after the event): 'If...the question is put to me: would I rather have a miserable ape for a grandfather or a man highly endowed by nature and possessed of great means & influence & yet who employs those faculties & that influence for the mere purpose of introducing ridicule into a grave scientific discussion—I unhesitatingly affirm my preference for the ape....'[66] What is less certain is

---

[64] Among the many modern accounts of the event and its context see: J. R. Lucas, 'Wilberforce and Huxley: a legendary encounter', *Historical Journal* xxii (1979), 313–30; S. Gilley and A. Loades, 'Thomas Henry Huxley: the war between science and religion', *Journal of Religion* lxi (1981), 285–307; J. Vernon Jensen, 'Return to the Wilberforce–Huxley debate', *British Journal for the History of Science* xxi (1986), 161–79; and A. Desmond and J. Moore, *Darwin* (1991), 493–9. For contemporary accounts and reminiscences see: *Athenaeum* 14 July 1860, 64–5, and J. D. Hooker to Darwin, 2 July 1860, in *The Correspondence of Charles Darwin, viii: 1860* (1993), 270–2. Also *The Life and Letters of Charles Darwin* ed. F. Darwin (3 vols 1887) ii. 320–3; *Life and Letters of Thomas Henry Huxley* ed. L. Huxley (2 vols 1900) i. 179–89; and Tuckwell, *Reminiscences*, 50–4.

[65] Another contemporary account, which stresses the audience's warm response to Wilberforce's speech and which mentions Huxley only briefly, is in the *Oxford Chronicle* 7 July 1860, 2, and (identically) the *Herald* 7 July 1860, 8.

[66] Huxley to Frederick Dyster, 9 Sept. 1861, quoted in Desmond and Moore, *Darwin*, 497, and Jensen, 'Return to the Wilberforce–Huxley debate', 168.

the effect that the reply had. It seems probable, for example, that Huxley's words were drowned in the hubbub and that his reply was less effective than Hooker's subtle but unyielding response.[67] At all events, there was noise and excitement, sufficient to cause Sir David Brewster's wife to faint and Rear Admiral Robert FitzRoy, the former commander of HMS Beagle (at the time of Darwin's voyage) and now head of the Board of Trade's meteorological department, to be shouted down when he 'solemnly implored the audience to believe God rather than man'.[68]

It is hard to imagine that the champions of science were not concerned by a debate that could too easily be taken to have resurrected the old spectre of the intrinsic hostility of science to religious belief. But whatever fears there may have been were largely allayed by the diversity of the opinions held by the Oxford professors themselves, which were by no means delimited by the modernizing Broad-Church compromise of Baden Powell and his fellow authors of *Essays and Reviews*, to which Wilberforce directed his keenest venom.[69] At one extreme, Brodie's notorious atheism and his refusal to subscribe to the Thirty-nine Articles were an undoubted embarrassment. Maskelyne, too, was a free-thinker, and Daubeny was suspect. But, on the other side, there was ample evidence of piety (ranging from Walker's evangelicalism to Acland's capacious Anglicanism and Johnson's Tractarianism) and even of firm opposition to Darwin's theory, most notably by the Nonconformist Conservator of the Hope Collection and (from 1861) the first Hope Professor of Zoology, John Obadiah Westwood.

The divisions within the ranks of the scientists, which reflected those within the academic community generally, helped Acland in his task of reconciling Oxford's clerical interest to the increasingly intrusive claims of science. Vigilance was still necessary ten years later when Acland and H. P. Liddon had to work hard to placate Pusey, enraged by Lord Salisbury's nomination of Huxley, Darwin and John Tyndall for honorary degrees.[70] But it was never possible for even the most sensitive critic to see the University Museum as a nest of atheists. Certainly, if the boat of science was briefly rocked by the events of June 1860, the waters were calm again by the early months of 1861, when the Museum came fully into use.

The relief that Acland must have felt at the departure of the members of the British Association was soon reinforced by the generally favourable reception that the Museum received on aesthetic grounds. It was plainly

---

[67] The quality and vigour of Hooker's response emerge clearly from the account in the *Athenaeum* and Hooker's letter of 2 July 1860, cited in n. 64.

[68] G. Stoney to F. Darwin, 17 May 1895, Darwin archive, Cambridge University Library, quoted in Desmond and Moore, *Darwin*, 495.

[69] See p. 708.

[70] Lord Salisbury, an amateur scientist and critic of the limitations of an exclusively classical education, made the nominations as part of his inaugural honours list in 1870 on his election as Chancellor of the University. See Atlay, *Acland*, 347–9, and Ward, *Victorian Oxford*, 261–2 and 402 n. 184.

gratifying to read the judgement in *Macmillan's Magazine*, by F. G. Stephens, the art critic and advocate of the Pre-Raphaelite cause, who asserted that 'there is hardly any modern public building which even nearly approaches it in beauty or dignity'.[71] But it was far more important for Acland that the Museum had realized the cherished ideal, inherited from Daubeny, of a single building that would provide for the teaching and study of all the sciences and reflect, in the words of the record of the meeting of May 1849 in New College, a 'Philosophical view of the connexion' between them.[72] In this way, as he saw it, the opportunities for specialization in the different departments could be reconciled with a higher vision of the inextricable bonds that connected the individual branches of scientific knowledge and justified the broadly based common curriculum in science to which Oxford remained wedded until the 1880s.

This vision departed quite deliberately, and in the long run damagingly, from the emerging fashion for separate buildings or even institutions for each science. It was given physical expression in an arrangement, broadly in keeping with the specifications of the competition, that gave the various disciplines immediate access to a common central court roofed in glass. The court, which was bounded by open arcades on the ground-floor and first-floor levels, was devoted to collections, in particular those of geology and mineralogy, palaeontology, zoology and anatomy and physiology, and to cabinets housing the apparatus for experimental philosophy.[73] Around it, on the ground floor, were lecture-rooms, laboratories and other facilities, grouped for each of the sciences: mineralogy and geology and experimental philosophy on the south side, and chemistry and medicine on the west. On the first floor, the galleries also housed collections, and there were further teaching and sitting-rooms, a large general lecture theatre, and space for the Hope Collection and its curator. And occupying the whole length of the west front on this level there were the lofty rooms of the library. Here, the scientific material from the Radcliffe Library, moved from its previous home in the Camera, was housed in what Acland regarded as an appropriately central position in the new building (see Figures 22.1–2).[74]

It was essential to the plan that communication between the departments should be easy. Apart from the curator's house, erected at the south-east corner of the site, the only building that stood completely apart was for

[71] F.G.S. [F. G. Stephens], 'The Oxford University Museum', *Macmillan's Magazine* v (1861–2), 532. Stephens's view was made all the more predictable by Woodward's known sympathies for the Pre-Raphaelite movement.

[72] Bodl. MS Acland d. 95, fos 71–2.

[73] For the layout of the collections see J. Phillips, *Notices of the Rocks and Fossils in the University Museum, Oxford* (1863), esp. the floor plan, p. 4.

[74] The arrangement of the library is described in *Library and Reading-Room, Oxford University Museum* (1861). On the library and its transfer to the Museum, see Guest, *Dr. Radcliffe and his Trust*, 126–206.

astronomy, for which a small free-standing teaching observatory was constructed to the rear of the Museum for the trifling sum of £168 15s. In the
case of the rooms for anatomy, physiology and zoology (around a small
court added to the cooler north side of the building) and the chemistry
laboratory (housed, on the south side, in a charming but impractically lofty
building modelled on the Abbot's Kitchen at Glastonbury), practical considerations enforced some compromise. But the shortness of the corridors
connecting these departments to the main core of the building respected the
essentials of Acland's ideal.

There was just one science that had no place in the scheme, to Acland's
enduring regret.[75] This was botany, the base for which remained in the
Botanic Garden. The separation of the botanical collections, both the herbaria and the living plants, from the new development in the Parks was one
that Daubeny was largely responsible for maintaining. From the time of his
election to the Sherardian professorship of Botany in 1834, Daubeny supervised improvements in the garden and the conservatories which, quite apart
from his understandable preference for concentrating his activities close to
his private chemical lecture-room and laboratory and the accommodation
that he enjoyed as Sherardian Professor, made removal, at least in the short
term, an unrealistic option. Although he was to have a change of heart on the
matter in later life, it was not until 1870, three years after his death, that the
question was reopened.

Now, Phillips and Acland took the lead in seeking to have the glass-
houses, formal plots and laboratories moved to a much larger site adjacent
to the Museum. They founded their case on the arguments of convenience
and the need to foster what Phillips, writing in 1873, called 'that larger &
more comprehensive view of natural phenomena which is sometimes likely
to be forgotten amidst the unceasing toil of special teaching'.[76] This time, the
prospects that botany would be brought fully within the fold of the mu-
seum-based sciences were good. But, after more than five years of debate and
arm-twisting, the proposal was undermined by the vacillation and eventual
opposition of J. D. Hooker (arguing, as an external expert, on aesthetic and
historic grounds) and of Daubeny's successor as Sherardian Professor,
Marmaduke Lawson.[77] With further opposition being voiced outside the

[75] See Acland's statement in his preface to the 1893 edition of Acland and Ruskin, *The
Oxford Museum*, pp. xx–i, where he also laments the failure to accommodate living animals
close to the Museum.

[76] MS Gunther 64, in the Museum of the History of Science, contains a manuscript paper by
Phillips, 'On the suggested removal of the Botanic Garden to a site adjacent to the University
Museum', dated 16 May 1873. The paper, from which the quotation in the text is taken, strongly
supports the proposed move.

[77] The changes in the views advanced by Hooker and Lawson between 1870 and 1875 emerge
clearly from the correspondence and printed pamphlets in OUA, UM/F/4/1; see also the
cuttings and other printed material in Bodl. G. A. Oxon. c. 228 and in MS Gunther 64
(MHS). Acland's determination to win over Hooker is reflected in the ten-page pamphlet *A
Letter to Dr. Hooker from Dr. Acland* (2nd edn 1875).

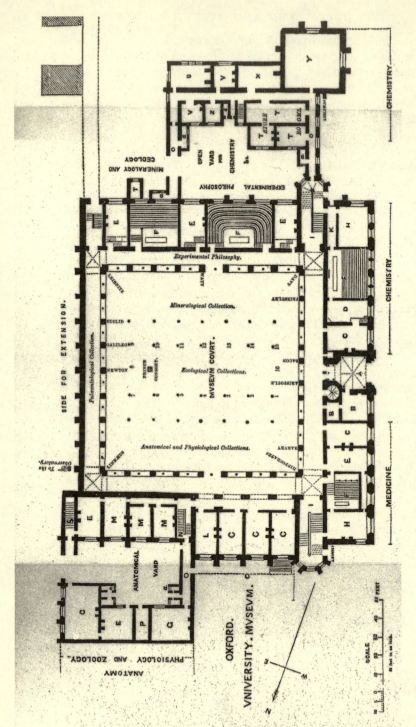

FIGURE 22.1 University Museum ground plan, c.1866. Source: H. W. Acland, *The Oxford Museum: the substance of a lecture* (3rd edn 1866), frontispiece.

A: entrance hall; B. porter; C: sitting-rooms; D. apparatus-room; E: work-rooms; F. lecture-rooms; G. dissecting-room; H: laboratory; I: principal staircase; K: passage; L: sitting-room; M: professors' work-room; N: staircase for anatomical and zoological department; O: covered way; P: macerating-room; S: private stairs to anatomy lecture-room; T: store-rooms; U: praelector's laboratory (mineralogy); V: balance-rooms; X: furnace-room; Y: large laboratory; Z: lavatories

OXFORD UNIVERSITY MUSEUM.

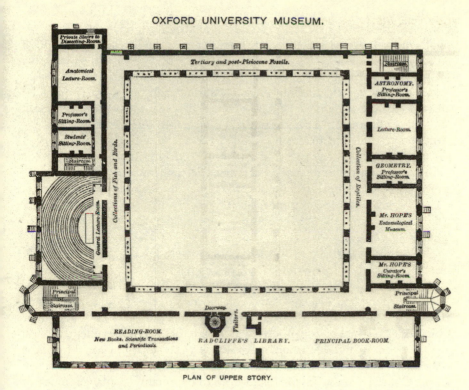

PLAN OF UPPER STORY.

FIGURE 22.2 University Museum upper storey plan, *c.*1866. Source: Acland, *The Oxford Museum* (3rd edn 1866), facing p. 63

University, in sources as diverse as *Nature* and *The Gardeners' Chronicle*, it succumbed in a Convocation deaf to Acland's last-minute plea but receptive to the cheaper alternative of simply repairing the existing facilities, in particular the sadly decayed glass-houses.[78] The conspicuous lack of interest which Lawson took in the garden from 1867 until his departure for a post in India in 1882 and the even more difficult reign of the ailing and retiring Sydney Howard Vines, the Sherardian Professor from 1887 to 1919, ensured that it was well into the twentieth century before at least some of the activities associated with botany were finally removed to the Science Area.

As had always been anticipated, practices in the different sciences soon began to diverge. Brodie responded to the particularly brisk demand for teaching in chemistry not only by lecturing three times a week for two out of

[78] *Gazette* vi (1875–6), 355–7 and 389–90. The decision to spend £2,200 immediately and to earmark £5,580 for future repairs was taken in Convocation on 23 May 1876.

the three terms but also by opening his laboratory in the Museum for six hours every day for practical exercises in analysis; a termly fee of £3 gave pupils the right to work there for three days a week under the supervision of either Brodie himself or his demonstrator.[79] In experimental philosophy, the fee for laboratory tuition (an initial £1, which gave unlimited access thereafter) was lower, reflecting not only a lesser demand but also the outdated character of the equipment and, as age and illness took an increasing toll, Walker's reluctance to change. In physiology, too, there was practical instruction, provided in an energetic and systematic way by the first holder of the new Linacre professorship of Anatomy and Physiology, George Rolleston. And in astronomy, such occasional demands as there were for guidance in observational techniques were met by Donkin, though at an exceedingly modest level commensurate with his fragile health, his mainly mathematical interests and the rudimentary facilities that were available to him.[80]

The flurry of activity in the laboratory-based subjects was more than matched by the busy provision for the disciplines in which instruction rested on a mixture of lectures and the inspection of specimens. The arrangements for the housing and display of the collections in geology and mineralogy, zoology and anatomy in the court and certain of the galleries—though far from perfect—were conspicuously better than those for experimental work, and the opening of the Museum not only allowed existing material from the Ashmolean Museum, the Clarendon building, and other locations (such as Christ Church and the Taylor Institution) to be suitably displayed, much of it for the first time, but also encouraged further bequests and donations that confirmed Oxford's pre-eminence among the provincial centres for the study of natural history.

Throughout the planning of the Museum, Acland and his circle had recognized that the jewel among the collections was the huge accumulation of entomological and other specimens and the accompanying library of natural history and engravings that were donated in 1849 by the Revd Frederick William Hope, a devoted graduate of Christ Church, a pupil of Kidd and one of the leading naturalists of his day.[81] In its original location, in his house in Seymour Street, London, Hope's collection of British and exotic insects had been a magnet for serious students, among them Charles Darwin, since the 1830s. To the benefactor's indignation, the University began by

[79] B. C. Brodie, *Syllabus of a Course of Lectures on Chemistry, to be delivered in the Museum in Michaelmas and Hilary Terms 1864 and 1865* (np nd).

[80] Hutchins, 'John Phillips', 210–14.

[81] On Hope and his collections see A. Z. Smith, *A History of the Hope Entomological Collections in the University of Oxford, with lists of archives and collections* (1986), esp. 1–46, and, for a brief contemporary description, John Obadiah Westwood, 'The Hope collections', a single sheet in Bodl. G. A. Oxon, c. 76 (36). According to Westwood, the collection included about 10,000 books and 200,000 engravings, mainly of natural history and topography.

quibbling unworthily over the terms of the donation, but the transfer was eventually made (to temporary premises in the Taylor Institution, where it was open to visitors on three days each week during term), and Hope proceeded with his plan of providing support to ensure that the collection was properly exploited. In 1857 a grant from Hope allowed his protégé Obadiah Westwood, who knew the collection well from its Seymour Street days, to be appointed curator of the entomological specimens, at a salary of £250 per annum.[82] And four years later Westwood became the first holder of the Hope chair of Zoology, with a salary secured by the income from a further donation of £10,000 in annuities, which Hope made in the face of another display of coolness on the part of the University.

During the 1850s other research materials for natural history had arrived in profusion. Among them, the 80,000 specimens of the Fielding Herbarium and a small but choice botanical library, bequeathed by Henry Borron Fielding of Lancaster in 1852, were especially important.[83] According to Sir William Hooker, the Director of Kew Gardens, Fielding's stood 'at least third in rank' among British herbaria, being surpassed only by those of the British Museum and Kew and by just one collection on the Continent, presumably that of the Muséum d'histoire naturelle in Paris.[84] Other notable additions included materials from the libraries of the French naturalists Jussieu and Brongniart, purchased and donated by Hope,[85] large collections of insects, shells and crustacea, and the Pengelly collection of Devonshire fossils, donated in 1860 by Miss Angela Burdett-Coutts (along with £5,000 consols for the endowment of two studentships, each of about £60 a year, to allow recent graduates to engage in two years of research in geology).[86]

Collections and facilities, however, were one thing; integration with the mainstream of academic life within Oxford quite another. Suspicion of subjects that were pursued primarily by professors and readers was always present among the body of college tutors. Far from impressing traditional opinion, therefore, the perceived opulence of the Museum and the threat

---

[82] On Westwood see Smith, *A History of the Hope Entomological Collections*, 35–46.

[83] Convocation's unanimous decision to accept the bequest and to create a fund of £2,000 for the maintenance of the collection and books and to allocate up to £1,250 for a building to house them in the Botanic Garden is reported in the *Herald*, 19 June 1852, 8 (reporting on the meeting on 15 June 1852). See also the issue for 12 June 1852, 8. For a brief description and history of the herbaria, see H. N. Clokie, *An Account of the Herbaria of the Department of Botany in the University of Oxford* (1964), 43–4 and 103–8.

[84] Daubeny, 'Address to the members of the University', 4.

[85] *Herald*, 24 Apr. 1858, 8.

[86] Papers concerning the donation are in OUA WP/β/2/13. The Burdett–Coutts scholarships quickly established themselves as an important means of access to a successful scientific career. William Boyd Dawkins, Thomas Wyndham (see below, n. 120) and Edwin Ray Lankester were among the holders during the 1860s. For a list of the recipients between 1861 and 1898 see *Calendar* (1899), 52–3.

that expenditure on it posed to other cherished plans, notably for the expansion of the University, served to fan the sense of resentment that many tutors felt towards a professoriate whose specialized intellectual interests and style of teaching (by formal lectures rather than by the catechetical method used in the small classes conducted by college tutors) set them apart from the world of the colleges. The animosity on this score was significantly heightened in the wake of the Royal Commission's report, with its recommendation that professors should be given an enhanced, even dominant, voice in the University.[87] And it gained further strength, from 1853, in the debates of the Tutors' Association, which was reinvigorated in that year in pursuit of such causes as the ending of enforced celibacy and the protection of the intellectual role and status of the tutorial fellows.[88] At best, the science professors were seen, from the collegiate perspective, as indifferent to these causes. At worst, the Museum appeared as a vehicle that would establish a new and uncontrollable source of power founded on subjects outside the mainstream of the curriculum and advance the subordination of college teaching and tutors to professorial authority.

It was symptomatic of such fears that when the scientific professoriate moved, successfully, to secure a determining voice in the electing committee for the professorship of experimental philosophy in 1863 (a position previously filled on the nomination of the Vice-Chancellor alone), the opposition was fierce. What might have been interpreted as a sensible administrative adjustment in keeping with the spirit of reform was seen as the 'revolutionary' tip of an iceberg of centrifugal forces that were threatening college-based Oxford and the ideal of a broadly unified general education. But the tide of change was running strongly enough for the measure to be approved in Convocation. The victory, by 60 votes to 10, was comfortable enough, but the fuss surrounding the proposal served as a reminder that any extension of the autonomy of the scientists would be carefully scrutinized.[89] When chemistry started down a similar road in 1865, as part of the suppression of the Aldrichian chair and its replacement by the new Waynflete professorship, the change was a judiciously less provocative one. Whereas the electoral board for the chair of experimental philosophy was to consist of a majority of three Oxford professors (the Savilian professor of astronomy, the Sedleian professor of natural philosophy, and the professor of chemistry) sitting with the Vice-Chancellor and the Warden of Wadham, the board for the Waynflete chair was composed of two scientific outsiders (the Presidents

[87] *RCO* (1850), report, 92–110 and 257–8.

[88] A. J. Engel, *From Clergyman to Don: the rise of the academic profession in nineteenth-century Oxford* (1983), 43–9.

[89] *Herald*, 30 May 1863, 8. The fear of the emergence of a self-governing clique of science professors is expressed clearly in the printed statements relevant to the debate in Bodl. G. A. Oxon. c. 79(250–2).

of the Royal Society and the College of Physicians) and three non-scientists (the Chancellor, the Visitor and the President of Magdalen). It was by this new mechanism that William Odling was elected in 1872, in contrast with the open vote in Convocation that had led to Brodie's appointment in 1855.[90]

Despite the inevitable drift towards acceptance, the Achilles' heel of the arguments in favour of the Museum and of the disciplines it housed remained the obdurately low numbers of candidates who presented themselves for examination in natural science. Throughout the 1850s and 1860s, high hopes were pinned on the successive changes in the statutes, which at least established a degree structure more favourable to science than it had been during the first half of the century. However, the evolving system of examinations was quickly seen to harbour its own ineradicable snares. The new statutes of 1850, for example, unequivocally brought science (along with certain other 'modern' subjects) to the heart of the undergraduate curriculum by incorporating the controversial innovation, advanced by the Hebdomadal Board but rejected in Convocation in 1839, that candidates for a degree should have attended at least two courses of professorial lectures. The initial stir was considerable, but in reality the requirement was a modest one. Each course normally comprised a mere eight lectures, and the mechanism for certifying attendance was often negligently enforced. Moreover, since there was no restriction on the subject of the lectures that were attended, professors and readers in the sciences were left to compete with one another and with their colleagues in the non-scientific disciplines for fickle undergraduate audiences whose main concern was not learning but the passing of a tiresome administrative hurdle on the way to a degree. It is not surprising that in 1859, after some years of faltering implementation, the obligation to attend professorial lectures was withdrawn altogether. For all its limited effect—and it had fallen far short of Daubeny's vehemently held view that the study of science should be made compulsory[91]—the regulation was valued by most of those in and sympathetic to the science lobby, and its repeal was vigorously opposed. As Walker represented it, the change encapsulated Oxford's retrograde denial of the perfectly proper outside pressure to require a familiarity with physical science of any graduate in

[90] Brodie's election on 13 Nov. 1855 by a majority of 33 votes to the 10 cast for Maskelyne is recorded in the Convocation register, 1854–1871, 82.

[91] Daubeny's argument in favour of obligatory attendance at a course of fifteen science lectures was put forcibly in his pamphlet *Reasons for Voting in Favour of Clauses 2 and 3 in the Examination Statute, to be submitted to Congregation on Tuesday the 16th relative to the attendance on the lectures of professors*, in Bodl. G. A. Oxon. b. 29. In the debate in Congregation, held on 16 June 1857, the Hebdomadal Council's proposal that attendance at a series of lectures in mathematics or physical science should be made compulsory was defeated by 68 votes to 24. Maskelyne and Donkin were among those who deplored the laxity of the control over the attendance at professorial lectures, while favouring the idea that the required lectures need not be in a scientific discipline; see *Herald* 13 June 1857, 8, and 20 June 1857, 8.

the modern world.[92] Only Acland stood conspicuously apart on this issue, looking back on the experiment with compulsory attendance as ill-advised.[93]

A far more promising innovation that was introduced by the statutes of 1850 was the new structure of examinations. The requirement that, after passing the predominantly classical hurdles of Responsions and Moderations, candidates for a degree should be examined not only in Lit. Hum. (in which it remained compulsory to attain either a pass or honours) but also in a second school, of which the new school of natural science was one, opened the possibility for science to compete for at least some serious candidates.[94] In the event, the school of natural science never secured the popularity of either the long-established school of mathematics (formally but somewhat misleadingly designated the Schola Disciplinarum Mathematicarum et Physicarum[95]) or the new school of law and modern history, which until 1870 were the other options open to those who had passed the hurdle in Lit. Hum. As the figures given in Chapter 11 show, the disparity between natural science and the other schools was glaring and persistent. Between 1853, when the first trickle of candidates presented themselves under the new statutes, and 1864, only 114 took honours and 164 took passes in the school of natural science, figures far lower than those for mathematics and law and modern history. Even the publicity and improved facilities that came with the opening of the Museum effected no lasting improvement: a modest increase in enrolments that occurred in 1861 soon evaporated, and by 1863 levels were no higher than they had been in the late 1850s.

The failure of the school of natural science to hold its own under the statutes of 1850, especially in the competition for passmen, reflects a number of damaging impediments. A fundamental and frequently cited difficulty lay in the limited exposure to science that undergraduates had received in their schools. The establishment of the Oxford local delegacy for examinations in 1857 had been one response to this.[96] But despite the committed support of the scientific professoriate (Walker, Brodie, Phillips, Bartholomew Price and Acland were all examiners in 1860, for example[97]), the new delegacy failed to

[92] R. Walker, *Remarks on Certain Parts of the Proposed Form of Statute respecting the Examinations for the Degree of B.A.* (1857), 9–14, and, for Daubeny's earlier espousal of a similarly liberal view, Daubeny, *Correlation of the Natural Sciences*, 18–19.

[93] See his evidence, 19 Dec. 1862, *Public Schools Commission* (1864) iv, evidence, pt. 2, pp. 407–8.

[94] The regulations are reproduced in the successive editions of the *Calendar* and in *RCO*, (1850), report, 64–7.

[95] Designated from 1855 the Schola Scientiarum Mathematicarum et Physicarum.

[96] On this new structure for examinations and its first year of operation see *University of Oxford. Under the statute 'De examinatione candidatorum qui non sunt de corpore universitatis'. First annual report of the delegacy, rendered to Convocation. December 31, 1858* ([1858]), 1–22. Henry Acland's brother Thomas Dyke Acland was a leading figure in the foundation of the delegacy.

[97] For a list of examiners in 1860 see the printed sheet tipped into the Bodleian Library's copy of the third annual report of the delegacy, for 1860, facing p. 6, Bodl. Per. 26269 e. 7 (3).

attract a significant number of candidates in the sciences, and undergraduates coming up with a previous familiarity with, or even an interest in, science remained rare birds. Responding to the Royal Commission on Public Schools (the Clarendon Commission) in 1862, Acland drew modest encouragement from the few signs of improvement he had observed since his appointment as Dr Lee's Reader in 1845.[98] But the place of science in schools remained weak. Indeed, as the delegacy's report for 1863 showed, the number of those wishing to be examined in scientific subjects was diminishing: the need for apparatus and for a specialized knowledge that most schoolmasters did not possess was inexorably fostering a preference for languages, in particular the classical languages, in which crucially there were far more scholarships.[99]

The shortcomings of science teaching in the schools fostered the perception that the school of natural science was difficult. It must be said, however, that its intellectual level was not high. Pusey, in fact, depicted the school as positively easy: it was precisely for this reason, as he observed, that some candidates chose it as their second school under the 1850 statutes.[100] The elementary and straightforwardly descriptive character of the questions, especially in the pass school, would certainly confirm Pusey's view.[101] A paper that was set for the pass school in Easter term 1863 gives the flavour of what was expected in the 1850s and 1860s. The forty-three questions, distributed more or less equally between chemistry, physiology, and mechanical philosophy, were an elementary test of memory requiring brief answers that were entered in designated spaces on the examination paper. A typical question in chemistry asked candidates, first, to 'Write down the names of the elements, distributing them into classes' and then to 'Explain the system of classification which you have adopted'. Another asked: 'What is the composition of atmospheric air? How has its composition been ascertained?' In mechanical philosophy, candidates were asked to 'Enunciate and explain the three Laws of Motion' and to elucidate 'What is meant by the Latent Heat of freezing of water'. The style in physiology was similar, with the emphasis on description rather than analysis. Typical questions in the examination in Easter term 1863 were 'What are the distinctive peculiarities in the Circulatory System in the class Reptilia?' and 'Give the descriptive anatomy of the spinal cord'. The question 'What does the Jaw-bone laid before you enable you to predicate of the structures and habits of the animal to which it belonged?' (a favourite one at about this time) was certainly among the more difficult ones.

---

[98] *Public Schools Commission* iv, evidence, pt. 2, p. 406.

[99] *University of Oxford. Under the statute 'De examinatione candidatorum qui non sunt de corpore universitatis'. Sixth annual report of the delegacy, for the year 1863* (nd), 5–6.

[100] *SCOC* (1867), 191–2.

[101] Sets of examination papers are available in many locations. But of particular interest are those bound, with annotations and notes, in Bodl. 2626 d. 35.

One of the most striking characteristics of the papers, at honours as well as at pass level, was the scarcity of questions that demanded a calculation. This reflected the clear distinction between the syllabus of the school of natural science, in which experimental philosophy was not to be treated mathematically, and that of the school of mathematics, to which 'mathematical reasonings' were said to belong.[102] In marked contrast with papers in the school of mathematics, where relatively sophisticated numerical questions on optics, hydrostatics, mechanics and statics and dynamics were not uncommon, those which appeared in the natural science papers were both rare and elementary. In Michaelmas term 1863, for example, candidates for a pass who opted for the special subject of 'heat' were asked to convert a given temperature from the Centigrade to the Fahrenheit scale and to prove that the same temperature was denoted by $11\frac{3}{7}°$F and $-11\frac{3}{7}°$C. In the following year, only two of the fifteen questions on mechanical philosophy that were set for passmen called for a calculation: both—one on specific gravity, the other on Boyle's law—were exceedingly straightforward. Although the style of the questions for both a pass and for honours changed little during the 1860s, there was a trend towards slightly higher standards. By 1870 questions requiring a simple calculation had become somewhat more common, especially in physics (in the sections on mechanics, heat and light) and in chemistry. But even the honours papers remained primarily tests of memory, with the emphasis on definitions, accounts of experimental procedures and (in chemistry and physiology) the enumeration of the characteristics of a substance or the description of anatomical structures and their operation.

At both the honours and the pass level of the school of natural science, therefore, the intellectual challenge lay less in the intrinsic difficulty of the questions than in the need to acquire sufficient factual knowledge across the wide variety of topics that had to be covered. Such limited specialization as was permitted by the regulations gave only modest relief[103] and did little to diminish the importance of a capacity for the rapid assimilation of large quantities of relatively easy material and the efficient 'spotting' of questions. For a candidate for a pass who had some previous knowledge of science and access to efficient tutoring, the process of cramming could usually be com-

[102] This distinction between the schools of natural science and mathematics was stated explicitly in the *Calendars* between 1854 and 1861, but in reality persisted for far longer.

[103] Under the regulations for honours in the natural science school, both before and after the reforms of 1864, candidates were expected to be familiar with the principles of all three of the main disciplines (mechanical philosophy, chemistry, and physiology) and, within one of these disciplines, to show a special competence in at least one individual science. In the case of mechanical philosophy, for example, such a science might be mechanics, hydrostatics, pneumatics, sound, light, heat, electricity or magnetism. For honours, inorganic chemistry, geology, physical geography, botany, zoology and mineralogy were also cited as possible sciences for specialization. For a pass, candidates were examined in two of the main disciplines and in one of the particular sciences within mechanical philosophy.

pleted within one term after the examination in Lit. Hum., sometimes even more perfunctorily (as a relative of Pusey demonstrated) in as little as three weeks.[104] But potential candidates were often deterred by the fact that tutoring in science was not readily available in most colleges. Further discouragement lay in the strikingly enlightened requirement that candidates in the school of natural science should undertake at least some work in the laboratory. This exposed them both to an added complication and, most notably in chemistry under Brodie, to the need to pay significant supplementary fees.[105]

The revised examination statutes that were finally adopted in 1864, after many months of urging by the Hebdomadal Council and resistance in Convocation, opened the prospect (alluring to the science lobby but anathema to the conservatives) of a move to greater specialization.[106] They did so by allowing candidates who had passed Moderations (in or after their seventh term as undergraduates) and taken at least third-class (or, from 1870, fourth-class) honours in any one of the four schools to proceed to a degree. With the passage through Lit. Hum. no longer obligatory, at least for the more serious honoursmen, natural science was finally placed on an equal footing with the other disciplines, and the scientific professoriate viewed the change with satisfaction. One immediate and predictable consequence was the virtual disappearance of the passmen in the natural science school, but the resulting fall in the numbers reading scientific subjects seems to have been regarded as a small price to pay for the professoriate's new freedom to concentrate on instructing pupils at the more advanced level required for honours.[107] Quite apart from the promise of an enhanced commitment on the part of undergraduates in science, the statutes of 1864 had the merit of bringing Oxford into line with Cambridge, where the necessity for candidates for the natural sciences tripos to be examined first in the mathematical tripos had been abolished in 1860 and, more remotely,

[104] *SCOC* (1867), 191. In fact, it was not uncommon for candidates who had taken a pass or honours in Lit. Hum. to try to complete the work for their second school within two or three weeks. In this way, they could be examined in the same term and avoid waiting for the next round of examinations six months later.

[105] Throughout the 1860s Brodie charged a fee of £3 per term, which gave students access to laboratory instruction in analysis between 10 a.m. and 4 p.m. on alternate days. See Brodie, *Syllabus of a Course of Lectures ... 1864 and 1865*, 6, and the corresponding *Syllabus* for the lectures to be delivered in Michaelmas term 1868 and Hilary term 1869. At about this time, Brodie's demonstrator, H. G. Madan of Queen's (first in natural science, 1861), gave quite separate complementary classes in chemical manipulation.

[106] The vehemence of the debate in Convocation is conveyed in the flysheets that circulated before the vote on 25 Feb. 1864, in Bodl. G. A. Oxon. c. 80 (384–6). On the longer history of the debate see Ward, *Victorian Oxford*, 218–23.

[107] While many classical tutors saw the new statutes as a threat to their subject, some shared the optimism of the scientists at the prospect of having more committed, if fewer, students in their charge. See e.g. the unsigned flysheet 'A true view of the new statute', in Bodl. G. A. Oxon. c. 80 (385).

with London, where broadly based science degrees had been introduced in 1858.[108]

As with the reforms of 1850, however, the anticipated benefits of the statute of 1864 were not fully realized, and the increase in the number of candidates for honours in the school of natural science materialized slowly. Through the 1860s the average number of those obtaining honours remained obdurately at about ten a year, and thereafter its growth, to a peak of about thirty in the late 1870s, was modest. Seen from within Oxford, the pace of expansion was not entirely discouraging: at least, the school of natural science fared somewhat better under the new regulations than the mathematics school.[109] But at no stage did the number of candidates for honours in natural science match the corresponding figures for Lit. Hum. or the highly successful new school of modern history, which, to its advantage, was separated from law in 1872. Moreover, the inevitable comparison with Cambridge had its disturbing as well as its heartening side. For whereas the numbers taking honours in the school of natural science remained virtually the same as those for the Cambridge natural sciences tripos until 1880, there was, from the 1850s, an ineradicable disparity in the numbers reading for honours in mathematics. By the early 1870s an average of over 100 candidates a year were taking honours in the mathematical tripos, compared with a corresponding figure of about twenty for the school of mathematics in Oxford—a figure that was virtually unchanged until the end of the century. Especially after 1868, when new regulations gave Cambridge undergraduates working for the mathematical tripos an exposure to at least certain branches of physics and hence a natural way into the subject, the consequences of the disparity for Oxford's standing in science, relative to that of Cambridge, were serious.

Despite the slowness with which the number of honours candidates in the school of natural science grew and the abrupt reduction in the passmen after the new statutes of 1864 came into effect, the view of the professoriate that the Museum was inadequate for the needs of science began to surface at an early stage. Visitors who enthused about the new building tended to dwell on its appearance and general atmosphere, rather than on detailed practicalities. The observations of the entomologist Hermann Hagen of Königsberg were typical of an outsider's view: he saw the Museum as 'magical' and in the library felt that he was 'carried, in the spirit, into a new world'.[110] But, from the start, the sheer size of the collections, which so impressed Hagen, was a source of anxiety to those who had to manage and work with them. In 1863

---

[108] D. A. Winstanley, *Later Victorian Cambridge* (1947), and Cardwell, *Organisation of Science*, 92–5.
[109] On the numbers of candidates in the various honours schools, see Ch. 11.
[110] H. A. Hagen, 'An entomological trip to Oxford', *Entomologist's Weekly Intelligencer* no. 255 (24 Aug. 1861), 166.

Westwood commented on the shortage of space for the zoological speci-mens: 'you may fancy how wretched the arrangements for zoological pur-poses are when I tell you that Cases covering about 6 square yards are allotted for the general Collection of Mammalia!'[111] But the most humiliat-ing illustration is that of the Strickland collection of birds, which Strickland's widow and father-in-law formally offered to the University in 1860. By 1866, after negotiations that had gone on for twelve years, Phillips had to advise the Vice-Chancellor and Hebdomadal Council that no space for the collection could be found in the University Museum and that the only possible location was the Upper Room of the Ashmolean Building.[112] Embarrassingly, on this occasion the offer was peremptorily withdrawn on the grounds that the Ashmolean was an unworthy setting, and in 1867 the collection was transferred to Cambridge.[113]

Generally, however, Phillips's ingenuity and negotiating skills were better rewarded, though in the face of a relentless and eventually crippling stream of additions for which there was never enough room. In anatomy, for example, the core collection from the Ashmolean was augmented, on the opening of the University Museum, by a substantial transfer, on loan, from the Christ Church Museum. And the Hope Entomological Collection, zealously enlarged under Westwood until his death in 1893 and then by his successor as Hope Professor, Edward Poulton, eventually had to be given additional space: at first, two extra rooms on the south side of the Museum and then, in 1903, when the Radcliffe Library moved out to its new building on Parks Road, space on the first floor of the west front. Further problems arose from serious impracticalities in the design of the building. The heating of the cavernous central court proved to be an unremitting drain on re-sources, and by 1873 the cost of lighting the court was seen as too high to allow its use after dark.[114] The architectural intricacies and high specifica-tions of the structure also harboured a dispiriting menace by making repairs, especially to the roof, ruinously expensive.

Tiresome though these shortcomings were in the eyes of the professors who suffered them, they would not have been sufficient in themselves to sustain any broader swell of indignation, still less to precipitate substantial expenditure on the part of the University. But through the 1850s and 1860s, for all the frustrations, the voice of science in Oxford was becoming un-mistakably louder and less easy to ignore. This was in part a simple question of numbers. The small, discrete caucus of professors and readers of the late

---

[111] Westwood to A. H. Haliday, 21 Jan. 1863, quoted in Smith, *Hope Entomological Collec-tions*, 20.
[112] Phillips to Vice-Chancellor, 1 Nov. 1866, Museum Delegacy minutes, 1858–66, OUA UM/M/1/2, fo 86; C. D. M. Strickland to Vice-Chancellor, 20 Nov. 1866, ibid.
[113] O. Salvin, *A Catalogue of the Collection of Birds Formed by the Late Hugh Edwin Strickland, M.A.* (1882), p. vi.
[114] *Devonshire Commn* 3rd report, p. xxxviii.

1840s, which had the meetings of the Ashmolean Society as its only formalized focus for common activity, had become, twenty years later, a far more visible and well-placed pressure group. Now, science was represented not only by the professors (readers throughout the University having been retitled professors in 1860), but also by a small but significant number of colleagues who had begun to filter into college appointments, either as fellows or, more commonly, as lecturers.[115] Although the main function of tutorial fellows and lecturers was that of preparing the candidates of their various colleges for the school of natural science, at least some of them engaged in research and publication, and all, collectively, contributed to a growing sense of community, the more so as, almost invariably, those who were appointed had themselves passed through the school.

Both in the impetus it gave to research and in the strengthening of new disciplines, what occurred in science between 1850 and 1870 was comparable with developments in the subjects of the other new school—law and modern history—and in mathematics, for which a number of colleges also felt the need to provide teaching, usually in the form of lectureships. But in so far as certain colleges set out to cater for the practical, as well as the purely theoretical, aspects of science, the impact on college life tended to be greater. In the history of college-based teaching, Christ Church has an especially important place. By 1870 advanced college lectures were being given there by two of the ablest early products of the school of natural science: on chemistry by A. G. Vernon Harcourt, Brodie's first pupil and Dr Lee's Reader in Chemistry since 1859, and on physics by A. W. Reinold, the newly appointed first holder of the Dr Lee's readership in the subject.[116] Both men taught in the refurbished laboratory and lecture-room once used by the Dr Lee's Reader in Anatomy, the reassignment of which to chemistry and physics was an important by-product of the centralization of collections and facilities in the Museum. It was at Christ Church that Harcourt performed his outstandingly important and painstaking research in what was to become known as chemical kinetics.[117] Another product of the natural science school, Edward Chapman, had recently been appointed to a new lecturership in natural science at Magdalen, where, with the aid of an assistant, he gave practical instruction and lectures in Daubeny's former laboratory and

[115] For contemporary accounts of the vigour of science teaching in the colleges in 1870 see: Edward Chapman's letter to Henry Acland, Mar. 1870, repr. in A. E. Gunther, *Early Science in Oxford, xv: Robert T. Gunther: a pioneer in the history of science, 1869–1940* (1967), 26–8; J. P. Earwaker, 'Natural science at Oxford', *Nature* iii (1870–1), 170–1; and Robert Clifton's evidence on 12 July 1870, *Devonshire Commn* i, minutes of evidence, Q. 2997.

[116] Vernon Harcourt took a first in natural science in 1858. Reinold took firsts in mathematics in 1866 and in natural science in 1867. He was a fellow of Merton from 1866 until his marriage in 1869.

[117] K. J. Laidler, 'Chemical kinetics and the Oxford college laboratories', *Archive for History of Exact Sciences* xxxviii (1988), 240–6.

in the adjacent college observatory; there, he not only taught chemistry and physiology but also used the excellent $5\frac{1}{2}$-inch equatorially mounted refracting telescope that Daubeny presented to the college in 1855.[118] At Balliol too there was an important college laboratory, installed in 1855 in a basement on staircase XVI of the new Salvin building (at a cost of £165) and supervised until 1860 by a fellow, the very able future Savilian Professor of Geometry and Curator of the Museum, Henry Smith.[119] Elsewhere, Thomas Wyndham at Merton, where a microscope and other rudimentary apparatus was provided for the use of undergraduates, and Richard Abbay at Wadham held college lectureships in science in addition to their fellowships.[120]

But it was not only the size of the scientific community and its facilities that explained its growing prominence. While the college appointments tended to go to Oxford men who had recently emerged from the school of natural science, the University was beginning to take a different path. It did so by introducing to senior positions a new generation of men who, for a variety of reasons, were less marked either by Oxford's gentlemanly traditions or by Acland's ideal of a unified body of sciences thrust together in mutually invigorating proximity. The transition was not sharp. Indeed, two of the most notable early 'outsiders', Phillips and Westwood, broadly concurred with Acland's aims. The same was true, more predictably, of a leading newcomer from within Oxford, George Rolleston, whose opposition to specialization was of a piece with his varied career and interests: it was

[118] The observatory is well described in R. Hutchins, 'Magdalen's astronomy observatory', *Magdalen College Record* (1990), 44–51. Chapman had taken a first in the school of natural science in 1864. He divided his time between his academic duties, mainly at Magdalen but also at Jesus (where he held a lectureship in physical sciences), and his responsibilities as a substantial shareholder in the Great Central Railway, of which he became deputy chairman; see W. D. Macray, *A Register of the Members of St. Mary Magdalen College, Oxford, from the foundation of the college* NS (8 vols 1894–1915) vii. 36–8, and Gunther, *Gunther*, 28–9. Chapman's own account of his work at Magdalen was laid before the Devonshire Commission in the form of a letter of 2 Nov. 1870; see *Devonshire Commn* i appx IX, p. 35. This appendix and appendix VII contain much information on college laboratories, as do Laidler, 'Chemical kinetics and the Oxford college laboratories', 217–39, and the successive editions of *The Student's Handbook to the University and Colleges of Oxford* that were published from 1873.

[119] This laboratory is not to be confused with the new laboratory built by Balliol and shared by Balliol and Trinity Colleges from the late 1870s. See E. J. Bowen, 'The Balliol–Trinity laboratories, Oxford, 1853–1940', *Notes and Records of the Royal Society of London* xxv (1970), 227–36; H. Hartley, *Studies in the History of Chemistry* (1971), 225–8; T. Smith, 'The Balliol–Trinity laboratories', in John Prest (ed.), *Balliol Studies* (1982), 185–224; and Laidler, 'Chemical kinetics and the Oxford college laboratories', 224–8 and 229–33.

[120] One of these fellows, Thomas Wyndham, had taken a first in the school of natural science in 1865 and subsequently held the Burdett–Coutts scholarship in geology; he taught at Merton until his premature death in 1876, also serving in the early 1870s as the first Aldrichian demonstrator in Chemistry, a post created with funds liberated by the suppression of the Aldrichian chair. On the facilities at Merton see *Devonshire Commn* i appx IX, pp. 34–5. Abbay had taken a first in mathematics in 1867 and become a fellow of Wadham in 1869, following a short period as lecturer and demonstrator in physics at King's College, London. He taught at Wadham, travelling extensively, chiefly for astronomical purposes, until 1878, when he began a clerical career in Suffolk.

only after gaining a college fellowship at Pembroke by his performance in Lit. Hum. in 1850 that Rolleston turned to medicine, practised at the Radcliffe Infirmary, and served first as the Dr Lee's Reader in Anatomy at Christ Church (from 1857) and then, from 1860 until his death in 1881, as Linacre Professor of Anatomy and Physiology—a position in which he worked not only across a wide range of physiology and human and comparative anatomy but also in anthropology.[121] A far more deviant tone, however, was set by Maskelyne, with his strong radical temper and very public interest in the applications of science, and the uncompromisingly atheistic Brodie, who came to his chair after working under Liebig at Giessen and then in his own private laboratory in London.[122] Although both Maskelyne and Brodie were Oxford men, they resolutely advanced the cause of research and specialization and the integration of Oxford in the wider community of science, in particular in London, to which they felt an equal allegiance.[123] It is symptomatic of this openness that when the prospect of marriage led Maskelyne to seek an increase in his university salary in 1857, he accepted the post of Keeper of Minerals at the British Museum, holding it simultaneously with the readership in mineralogy, in which he had succeeded Buckland in the previous year (after three years' service as Deputy Reader).[124]

In the 1860s and early 1870s these tendencies were reinforced by further appointments that marginally but unmistakably changed the character of professorial expectations. The most notable new arrival in this respect was Robert Bellamy Clifton, who was elected to the professorship of experimental philosophy in November 1865.[125] The decision to appoint Clifton in

---

[121] M. Pelling, 'The refoundation of the Linacre lectureships in the nineteenth century', in F. Maddison, M. Pelling and C. Webster (eds), *Essays on the Life and Work of Thomas Linacre, c.1460–1524* (1877), 282–3.

[122] Morton, *Maskelyne*, and the obituary notice on Brodie in *Journal of the Chemical Society* xxxix (1881), 182–5.

[123] Maskelyne's interests in utility, and that of certain of his colleagues, are reflected in the public lectures that were given in the spring of 1851. On 17 June 1851, for example, Maskelyne spoke on 'The properties of metals and their adequation to the requirements of machinery and manufactures', as part of a scheme to raise money to assist working men to attend the Great Exhibition. Daubeny and Strickland also gave lectures on practical subjects for members of the University intending to visit the Exhibition; see *Herald* 24 May 1851, 3, and the cuttings in Bodl. G. A. Oxon. b. 27.

[124] Morton, *Maskelyne*, 133. Maskelyne may also have been disenchanted by the neglect of his campaign for the creation of five new professorships in science, medicine and mathematics (including one in 'experimental mechanics and engineering'). His plan for expansion, which would have brought the number of professorships in 'physical and mathematical science' to fourteen, was outlined in a letter of 23 Feb. 1854 to Palmerston: *Corr. on Improvement* (1854), 67–9.

[125] On Clifton see the obituary notice by R. T. Gunther in *Proceedings of the Royal Society* cix A (1921), pp. vi–ix, and the unsigned notices in *Nature* cvii (1921), 18–19, and *Monthly Notices of the Royal Astronomical Society* lxxxii (1921–2), 248. More recent studies include A. J. Croft's sadly uncompleted typescript 'Oxford's Clarendon Laboratory' (1986), ch. 9, and G. J. N. Gooday, 'Precision measurement and the genesis of physics teaching laboratories in Victorian Britain' (University of Kent Ph.D. thesis 1989), ch. 6, currently being revised for publication as a

preference to the only other serious contender, George Griffith of Jesus College, who had assisted and eventually deputized for Walker during the latter's increasingly incapacitating illness, marked a significant rejection of the older, more parochial traditions of Oxford science.[126] It also proclaimed a determination to appoint at the highest possible intellectual level. For although Clifton was in no sense the equal of Hermann Helmholtz, who seems to have been thought of at one stage as a likely candidate, he arrived with a considerable reputation earned at an early age, as well as the backing of a dazzling array of supporters that included William Thomson, J. C. Adams, G. G. Stokes, William Whewell, James Joule, Henry Roscoe, and in Germany Bunsen and Kirchhoff.[127] By comparison, the support that Griffith could muster (expressed in letters from his pupils and from John Phillips, Henry Acland, Henry Smith, Nevil Story-Maskelyne, Robert Main and Charles Daubeny, among others) was of a distinctly local nature; only his work as assistant secretary of the British Association for the Advancement of Science won him significant outside support, including that of Charles Lyell and Francis Galton.[128]

Clifton had every opportunity of making his mark in the University, combining as he did the virtues of both freshness and, for his age, considerable experience. After an undergraduate career at St John's College, Cambridge, where he had been Sixth Wrangler and Second Smith's prizeman, he

book. On the location of copies of Croft's work and the photographs accompanying it see K. D. Watson, *Sources for the History of Science in Oxford* (1994), 9–10 and 26–7.

[126] Griffith, who had taken a first in the school of natural science at Jesus in 1856, had one of the first college appointments in science. Although he was never a fellow of his college, he held the title of lecturer in natural science from 1857 until 1867, when Chapman arrived. While deputizing for Walker in the last few years of the latter's reign, Griffith used the title Deputy Professor of Experimental Philosophy. He also taught for one day a week at Winchester College and eventually, after leaving Jesus, returned to schoolteaching, at Harrow.

[127] The names are given in Gunther's obituary of Clifton, *Proceedings of the Royal Society* cix A (1921), p. vi, but the testimonials do not appear to have survived. On the approach to Helmholtz see N. Kurti, 'Opportunity lost in 1865?', *Nature* cccviii (1984), 313–14, and 'Reflections of an amateur historian of science', in J. Roche (ed.), *Physicists Look Back: studies in the history of physics* (Bristol, 1990), 79–82. It is not clear that Helmholtz was ever formally sounded. As Kurti argues, Max Müller seems to have persuaded the university authorities that Helmholtz would not be interested and that an offer of even a very substantial salary, probably of £700 p.a., would be refused. According to a printed *Statement of the Duties and Emoluments of the Professorship of Experimental Philosophy*, dating from late in 1865 (Bodl. G. A. Oxon. c. 81 (290)), the salary of the professor was to be made up of £30 from Lord Leigh's benefaction, £270 from the University Chest, and the emoluments of a fellowship at Wadham (which could be compounded for a fixed sum of £200 p.a.) and up to £1 for each person attending his lectures—a total of little more than £500 p.a. Even when the salary was subsequently augmented by a fellowship at Merton, it probably left Clifton in an inferior position to that of the Linacre professor of anatomy and physiology, who was offered 'an amount not exceeding £800' per annum, made up of the proceeds from four suspended fellowships at Merton; see the printed announcement of the appointment in OUA WP/γ/26(2), fo 44. However, his salary was substantially higher than the £300 received by Walker.

[128] *Testimonials in Favour of George Griffith, M.A., F.C.S. Candidate for the professorship of experimental philosophy of the University of Oxford* (1865).

had been since 1860 (when he was still only 24) a popular and respected professor of physics at Owens College in Manchester. There, he had forged an alliance with the energetic Professor of Chemistry, Henry Roscoe, and had even published with him on spectroscopy. When he arrived in Oxford, he found a very different world. Several years of faltering activity in Walker's declining years had left physics in a state of indisputable neglect, and it was not hard to argue that facilities which had been adequate for Walker's gentle regime were insufficient for a professor who aspired to secure for Oxford a reputation in teaching and research comparable with that of any European university. With the confidence of a newcomer unaware of, or insensitive to, the contention that had surrounded the struggle for the Museum, Clifton duly assumed the role of a reformer, campaigning for an extension of a provision for science which many observers outside the Museum already regarded as irresponsibly lavish.

Despite his mathematical background and his lack of any exposure to experimental science at Cambridge, Clifton regarded precise measurement as the core of his discipline. For someone with this view, the space and equipment for physics in the Museum were palpably insufficient. Above all, they did not permit him to mount the laboratory exercises which (as he liked to observe) allowed the faculty of observation to be exercised along with that of reasoning. Sums of £150 a year from the University and about £90 a year from Lord Leigh's benefaction, and a quite generous special grant of £1,000 from the University, made in 1869, fell far short of the mark: they allowed some renewal of the apparatus that Walker's modest budget had allowed him to accumulate (with considerable skill) over the years, but they could not remedy the absence of an area designated for the practical teaching which Clifton regarded as an essential complement to his lecture demonstrations.[129]

Clifton's emphasis on the importance of a training in experimental technique, in particular in metrology, placed him firmly among the most progressive teachers of physics in British universities and gave his campaign an air of modernity that appealed at least to his immediate colleagues. By November 1866, within months of his arrival in Oxford, the report of the Museum delegates which Phillips communicated to the Vice-Chancellor stated that the needs of the Professor of Experimental Philosophy for laboratory space and work-rooms and storage space were particularly pressing.[130] A second report, in February 1867, made the point even more

[129] *Royal Commission on Scientific Instruction* i. 186. By 1870 Clifton received £565 p.a., to cover the cost of the demonstrator, a skilled workman to assist in lectures and other general expenses.

[130] See Phillips's letter to the Vice-Chancellor, 1 Nov. 1866, printed on pp. 1–4 of a report prepared by the museum delegacy for members of the Hebdomadal Council. A copy is in the minute-book of the museum delegacy, 1858–66, OUA UM/M/1/2, fo 86.

strongly. According to Phillips, writing on behalf of the professors, even with the help of rooms borrowed from another department, practical instruction in physics could be offered to so few pupils and in such unsatisfactory circumstances that candidates for the highest honours wishing to undertake advanced work in the main branches of the subject were obliged to leave Oxford for the new generation of physical laboratories that were emerging on the Continent, in particular in Germany, and even in England.[131]

The essential requirement, as Clifton insisted in a printed statement accompanying the delegates' second report to Council, was for six rooms that would serve as student laboratories. In addition, Clifton requested outbuildings to house battery rooms, workshops and store-rooms, and a private laboratory in which the professor could pursue his personal research.[132] The case for some improvement had much in its favour. In the existing conditions, which allowed Clifton to admit no more than six pupils in his laboratory class,[133] the strikingly enlightened requirement that candidates for honours who chose physics as their special discipline in the natural science school should undergo not only laboratory training but also a practical examination would have been hard to implement.[134] But even to Clifton's most sympathetic supporters, the scheme he described, which would have entailed a substantial extension, continuing the south front of the Museum in an easterly direction, appeared audacious. The reaction of the retiring Donkin was one of startled admiration. As he confided in a letter to Phillips, Clifton's strategy reminded him of 'the farmer who wanted a new gate, and asked his landlord to build him a new house'.[135] 'However', he added, referring to the extra rooms that Clifton had requested, 'I sincerely hope he will get them.'

At the time Donkin made his comment, in March 1867, Clifton's prospects of securing the funds he was seeking from the University Chest were remote. But within weeks a wholly unexpected windfall from outside the University allowed physics in Oxford to move quite suddenly to the international forefront of laboratory development. The source was the fund held by the Clarendon trustees, which had been started just over 100 years before by Henry Lord Hyde, the great-grandson of the Earl of Clarendon. By his will, Hyde had bequeathed to the University the profits that would arise from the publication of the writings of his great-grandfather in order to start

---

[131] See Phillips's letter to the Vice-Chancellor, 1 Feb. 1867, printed on pp. 1–4 of the second report of the Museum delegacy to members of the Hebdomadal Council, in the minute-book of the Museum delegacy, 1867–75, OUA UM/M/1/3.

[132] Second report of the Museum delegacy, 4–7.

[133] Clifton to Phillips, 8 Mar. 1867, OUA UM/F/4/3.

[134] As early as 1859 there was a practical examination in chemistry and physiology for all candidates for honours. By 1862 this requirement had been extended to mechanical philosophy as well. See the *Calendar* (1862), 140.

[135] Donkin to Phillips, 15 Mar. 1867, OUA UM/F/4/3.

a riding school or, failing that, to pursue other objects which the trustees would regard as 'most for the honour and benefit of the University and most conducive to public utility'.[136] When Hyde's specific proposal for a riding school had been placed before Convocation in December 1864, it had been rejected, and six months later a counter-suggestion that the money should be used for the maintenance of the Parks was, in turn, declined by the trustees, who asked that a new proposal should be made that would perpetuate the name of the trust 'with some visible object'.[137]

The nature and timing of the trustees' invitation could not have been more favourable to Clifton's interests. But, faced with the alternatives of satisfying the long-felt need for new Examination Schools, which offered the great attraction of freeing space for the Bodleian Library, and of constructing a new laboratory of experimental philosophy, the Hebdomadal Council declared a predictable preference for the Schools.[138] It was left for the Clarendon trustees to reverse the decision. On 3 May 1867 Gladstone wrote on their behalf to the Vice-Chancellor, stating clear support for the laboratory, and within six months Clifton's revised and enlarged proposals and T. N. Deane's outline plans for an appropriately gothic building at the north-western corner of the Museum site were endorsed by the trust.[139] On 4 February 1868, in the face of opposition from Charles Neate and J. R. Magrath but without a division, Convocation gave its approval.[140] It was an outcome which, only a year earlier, would have appeared inconceivable. Nevertheless, in Michaelmas term 1870 Clifton and his one young assistant could begin moving into premises which one, admittedly partial contemporary described as 'the most perfect physical laboratory in the world'.[141]

Through this largely fortuitous turn of events, the University found itself endowed with the first purpose-built physics laboratory in Britain, constructed on a scale that matched the grandeur of the Museum. Despite some trimming of the original scheme, it was a model laboratory, planned in the most meticulous detail under Clifton's supervision and containing fittings of the highest quality and apparatus chosen from the best on show at the Universal Exhibition of 1867 in Paris. The arrangement of the rooms ex-

---

[136] From the preamble and correspondence appended to the Vice-Chancellor's printed announcement of the offer from the Clarendon trustees, p. 1, in Convocation register, 1854–71, between pp. 433 and 434.

[137] Ibid.

[138] F. K. Leighton to Gladstone, 5 Apr. 1867, ibid. 2.

[139] Gladstone to the Vice-Chancellor, 3 May 1867, and Sir William Heathcote to the Vice-Chancellor, 22 Nov. 1867, ibid. 2–3.

[140] Convocation register, 1854–71, 434, and Herald 8 Feb. 1868, 8; also Clifton's memorandum urging acceptance of the offer, ibid. 1 Feb. 1868, 8–9.

[141] Earwaker, 'Natural science at Oxford', 171. Earwaker, an undergraduate at Merton, was to take a first in the school of natural science in 1872. After graduation, he pursued his antiquarian interests as Deputy Keeper in the Ashmolean Museum; see R. F. Ovenell, The Ashmolean Museum, 1683–1894 (1986), 232–3.

pressed Clifton's determination to pursue teaching and research that reflected the priority he gave to experiment and, more particularly, to precise measurement. In addition to two lecture theatres (the larger one for experimental demonstrations, the other for theoretical lectures), a library, students' common room and two private laboratories for the professor, the space was divided into a number of small rooms, each devoted to an individual branch of physics.[142] In this way, the often delicate apparatus would remain in position, and it was left for students to move about the building. With rooms for magnetism in the basement, spectrum analysis, heat and radiant heat, acoustics, static electricity and weighing and measuring on the ground floor, optics and current electricity on the first floor, photography above the main lecture theatre and optics again in a long gallery in the roof, the coverage of the main branches of physics was complete.

The Clarendon Laboratory (or Hyde Institute, as it was briefly called) had the great merit, in sympathetic Oxford eyes, of stretching the lead that the University had taken over Cambridge in the provision for science since 1860.[143] The opening of the new museums and lecture-rooms on the Free School Lane site in Cambridge in 1865 came after more than a decade of wrangling that betrayed a noticeably greater scepticism towards science than was apparent in Oxford. And even then it was by no means obvious that the needs of the scientific professoriate had been met. The accommodation was modest by the standards of the University Museum: it housed most of the sciences (zoology, comparative and human anatomy, chemistry, mineralogy and botany) at a cost of under £25,000, less than a third of what had been spent in Oxford by 1867.[144] Moreover, in the Cambridge plan, the physical sciences had fared distinctly worse than they had done in Oxford. The facilities for the teaching of practical chemistry were virtually non-existent until a rehousing in 1872. In physics, the absence of any significant provision was equally glaring and was made all the more so by the statutes of 1868, which admitted heat, electricity and magnetism into the syllabus for honours in the mathematical tripos. Although it was not long before the immediate requirements of the discipline and the newly established Cavendish chair of Experimental Physics were satisfied by the opening of the Cavendish Laboratory, also in Free School Lane, during the academic year 1873/4, the expenditure of £8,450 on the Cavendish was still somewhat less than the

[142] The laboratory is described in *Builder* xxvii (8 May 1869), 366–7 and 369.

[143] For a smug undergraduate view of the superiority of Oxford's facilities for science (though with an acknowledgement of the greater strength of Cambridge mathematics) see *Oxford Undergraduate's Journal* 31 Oct. 1872, 8.

[144] On the provision in Cambridge see R. Willis and J. W. Clark, *The Architectural History of the University of Cambridge, and the Colleges of Cambridge and Eton* (4 vols 1886) iii. 157–90, and A. E. Shipley, *'J.': a memoir of John Willis Clark* (1913), 293–343. A slightly higher figure of 'about £30,000', presumably including the cost of fitting out the building, appears in *Devonshire Commn*, 3rd report, p. xlii.

£10,300 spent on the buildings and fittings (though not the apparatus) of the Clarendon.[145]

In terms of both the facilities and the quality and size of its scientific community, therefore, Oxford entered the 1870s in a strong position. Thomas Henry Huxley commented, in 1871, that 'there was nowhere in the world a more efficient or better school, so far as it went, for teaching the great branches of physical science than was at the present time to be found in the University of Oxford'.[146] Two years later, the Devonshire Commission on Scientific Instruction praised the University's 'great liberality' in providing for the scientific disciplines and its readiness to acknowledge science as 'a great branch of education'.[147] The Commission's praise, though tempered by a warning about the superior conditions that existed elsewhere in Europe, was not misplaced. Moreover, until the late 1870s the momentum was maintained, with Convocation turning its back on its former scepticism and repeatedly endorsing further growth, albeit on a lesser scale than Clifton and certain other professors maintained was desirable.[148]

Both teaching and research were the beneficiaries of the new consensus. The case of astronomy, following Donkin's death in 1869, illustrates this well. When Donkin's successor in the Savilian chair, the Revd Charles Pritchard, arrived in 1870, he came, first and foremost, as a teacher.[149] The priority was a natural one: he was over 60 at the time of his appointment, and his background was that of an amateur astronomer who had spent most of

---

[145] *Devonshire Commn*, 3rd report, p. xxxix gives a figure of £12,000 for the total cost of the Clarendon, which would appear to include the initial expenditure on apparatus. This exceeded the £10,700 which the Clarendon trustees were able to offer.

[146] From an address reported in *Nature* 30 Nov. 1871, 89.

[147] *Devonshire Commn*, 3rd report, p. xli.

[148] The ambitions of the professoriate for further expansion are clearly articulated in the printed replies to the Vice-Chancellor's Letter of Enquiry of 10 May 1873 about the provision for professorial teaching in each of the boards of studies; a copy of this seventy-page document is in the Museum of the History of Science, Oxford (MS Gunther 65). At the time of his reply, dated 21 Feb. 1874, Clifton was still assisted by just one demonstrator. Hence his request for three new professorships of physics and one in experimental mechanics—each with at least one demonstratorship—and his hopes for a future chair and demonstratorship in civil engineering represented a dramatic expansion. Even Clifton himself seems to have felt that his request was extravagant, and he conceded that it might be possible for only one of the chairs to be created immediately. He hoped that the holder of this chair would teach heat and electricity, while he himself would teach acoustics and optics. In the event, no new posts were created, despite the recommendation of the Devonshire Commission that two chairs of physics—one in theoretical physics and one in applied mechanics and engineering—should be established without delay; *Devonshire Commn*, 3rd report, p. xxviii. It was not until 1885 that Trinity College appointed the Revd Frederick John Smith to Oxford's first lectureship in experimental mechanics; see below, pp. 686–7.

[149] On Pritchard see A. Pritchard, *Charles Pritchard D.D., F.R.S., F.R.A.S., F.R.G.S. Late Savilian Professor of Astronomy in the University of Oxford: memoirs of his life* (1897), esp. the section on 'astronomical work' by H. H. Turner, pp. 213–316, and Hutchins, 'John Phillips', 219–37. As Roger Hutchins has observed to me, Pritchard was the last ordained member of the Church of England to be elected to a scientific chair in Oxford.

his life, after leaving Cambridge, as headmaster of a successful private school, Clapham Grammar School. Initially, his strategy was to 'make do' with relatively minor changes to the existing provision. At his own expense, he put the small museum observatory in a fit state for practical teaching and even provided an assistant, who attended for three hours each evening to instruct students. However, with his personal resources alone, he could do little about the equipment. The small altazimuth telescope, astronomical clock and neglected five-foot transit instrument that he inherited from Donkin were gravely inadequate, even for elementary training in observational technique, and Pritchard's own telescope, a 10-inch equatorially mounted reflector, functioned poorly in the museum observatory. By comparison with John Phillips, who had used his 6-inch Cooke equatorial refractor for research in the private observatory next to his house since 1862, Pritchard was poorly equipped. Nevertheless, it seems to have taken Phillips's resolute intervention to persuade Pritchard to go beyond modest, piecemeal improvements and to aspire to major changes in the provision for his subject.[150]

By December 1872 Pritchard had conceived a plan for a 'school of astronomical physics' that would foster research and have only a minor role in undergraduate education.[151] The immediate catalyst for Pritchard's new vision seems to have been the ageing Phillips's concern to ensure the continuation of his own observations, either by the bequest of his Cooke refractor to the University (his initial idea) or by the creation of a completely new observatory with new equipment. In pursuit of the latter objective, Pritchard obtained an estimate for a $12\frac{1}{4}$-inch equatorial refracting telescope by Sir Howard Grubb of Dublin, while Phillips chose a location for a new observatory at the north-eastern extremity of the museum site and commissioned from Charles Barry a plan for an ornate building in the shape of an octagonal tower in the gothic style.[152]

Forced by Phillips, events in the early weeks of 1873 moved with great rapidity. On 4 March Convocation unanimously approved a grant of £2,500 for the purchase and housing of the Grubb instrument and proceeded to commission another design from Barry, with the remarkably liberal rider that the observatory could be placed at any location in the Parks and not necessarily on the Museum's own site.[153] The result was the new university observatory, simpler than Barry's original design but much larger. The main cause of the increase in size, and of an additional allocation of £1,500 for the

[150] Hutchins, 'John Phillips', 223.
[151] See Pritchard's printed appeal to Convocation, dated Dec. 1872, in the minute-book of the Museum delegacy, 1867–75, OUA UM/M/1/3; repr. (with the addition of a short paragraph on the proposed location) in Gazette iv (1873), 43.
[152] Hutchins, 'John Phillips', 226.
[153] Gazette iv (1873), 42–3 and 73, and the unamended cuttings in Convocation register, 1872–91, 36.

building,[154] was yet another windfall. This came in the form of the 13-inch reflecting telescope which the wealthy independent astronomer Warren De la Rue—responding to the unexpected generosity that had been shown to astronomy—offered to the University in June. One of the observatory's two towers was devoted to this fine and very celebrated instrument; the other housed the Grubb refractor.

The new building, with its two telescopes and associated equipment, suddenly placed Oxford among a handful of leading research observatories in the world. It was a condition of De la Rue's gift that his instrument should be put to serious use, and, with his continued help (including, notably, a salary for a second assistant to work under Pritchard), that condition was handsomely fulfilled. The De la Rue reflector was a versatile instrument: lending itself particularly well to celestial photography, it was the foundation for the distinguished research that earned Pritchard the gold medals of the Royal Astronomical Society in 1886 (for his work on visual photometry) and six years later, a few months before his death, of the Royal Society (for his contributions to the study of stellar parallax). The vigour and quality of the research done by and under Pritchard was such that when the project for the creation of a comprehensive photographic star map, the Carte du ciel, was launched in the late 1880s, the decision to engage the Oxford observatory in the international network of contributors was a natural one (although Oxford's participation was only made feasible by De la Rue's readiness to pay for the new photographic refractor which brought the facilities up to scratch).[155] More parochially, the observatory's reputation also helped to restore observational astronomy to the heart of the University's activities, after more than three decades in which such work had been the preserve of Phillips (in his private capacity) and of the successive Radcliffe Observers Manuel Johnson (until his death in 1859) and then Robert Main.

In the wake of the momentous decision on the observatory, it was soon the turn of chemistry. By the time William Odling had succeeded the ailing Brodie in the Waynflete chair in 1872, some extra space had been gained by the removal of experimental philosophy to the Clarendon Laboratory. But there was still accommodation for no more than twenty students. By 1874 the pressure was becoming acute. Forty students were working regularly in this space, though few of them could spend more than three days a week there, and two years later the number of those wishing to undertake laboratory work topped fifty.[156] Odling's account of the overcrowding and the

[154] *Gazette* iv (1873), 323, and Convocation register, 1872–91, 52 and 309–10.

[155] On the Carte du ciel and Oxford's contribution to it, see the editor's introductions, in H. H. Turner (ed.), *Astrographic catalogue 1900. Oxford section Dec. +24° to +32°. From photographs taken and measured at the University Observatory, Oxford* (8 vols Edinburgh 1906–12) i, pp. vii–xlvii, and vii, pp. ix–xxxiii.

[156] W. Odling, 'Statement on the chemical laboratories in the University Museum', *Gazette* vii (1876–7), 126–7.

excessive demands made on the two assistants who conducted the laboratory classes in qualitative and quantitative analysis (John Watts, an organic chemist who had come with him from London, and Walter William Fisher, Thomas Wyndham's successor in the Aldrichian demonstratorship in Chemistry)[157] was a compelling one. While the fittings in the main laboratory remained satisfactory, the additional benches that had been squeezed into other available space provided students with conditions that were 'not only discreditable but seriously disadvantageous to their studies'; moreover, as in physics, students each year had to be turned away. Faced with this evidence, Convocation yet again displayed its liberality, in two decisive votes, one (22 to 2) in favour of seeking architectural advice, the other (62 to 22) in favour of implementing it.[158] A substantial two-storey extension, built between 1877 and 1879 to the south-east of the main museum building, at a cost of just under £6,000 (excluding fittings), and, like the Clarendon, to the designs of T. N. Deane, had the immediate effect of relieving the pressure on the grossly inconvenient Abbot's Kitchen, although even further building in 1902, which helped to create space for as many as 150 students, failed to remove a lingering sense of the inadequacy of both the conditions and the equipment. Even as the building work was in progress, Odling and Fisher predicted that the extension would leave the provision for chemistry no more satisfactory than it had been almost thirty years before.[159]

The investment that was made in astronomy and chemistry demonstrates the strength of the University's commitment to the consolidation of Clifton's achievement in his campaign for the Clarendon. But no amount of investment could conceal weaknesses that were, in due course, to have debilitating consequences for Oxford's reputation, in particular as a centre for research. By no means all the sciences were wanting in this respect. The vigour of the new observatory under Pritchard has already been referred to. Likewise, while the arrival of Joseph Prestwich as Phillips's successor in the chair of geology in 1874 stimulated neither new building nor expansion, there was no slackening of activity.[160] Despite his age (when appointed, he

[157] Fisher, who had taken a first in the school of natural science in 1870, succeeded Wyndham in 1873 and served for forty years.

[158] For a forthright statement of the need for a doubling of the laboratory space and the provision of more assistant teaching staff, see Odling's unpaginated printed pamphlet of 22 Apr. 1874, addressed to the delegates of the Museum: Museum of the History of Science, MS Gunther 65. The votes in Convocation on 30 Jan. and 5 June 1877 are reported in *Gazette* vii (1876–7), 219 and 434, and, in unamended cuttings, in Convocation register, 1872–91, 140 and 150.

[159] W. Odling and W. W. Fisher, 'Memorandum from the Waynflete Professor of Chemistry', in *Statements of the Needs of the University, being replies to a circular letter addressed by the Vice-Chancellor on February 20, 1902, to heads of institutions and departments, to the boards of faculties, and to professors and readers* (1902), 44–7: 45.

[160] *Life and Letters of Sir Joseph Prestwich M.A., D.C.L., F.R.S.*, written and edited by his wife (Edinburgh 1899), esp. Sir Archibald Geikie's 'Summary of the scientific work of Sir Joseph Prestwich, D.C.L., F.R.S.', on pp. 402–21. For a modern assessment see E. A. Vincent, *Geology and Mineralogy at Oxford, 1860–1986* (1994), 5–8.

was already 62), a life's career spent in the City, and a lack of any previous experience as a teacher, Prestwich fitted well in Oxford. Until his retirement in 1888, he lectured and worked zealously on the arrangement of the geological collection, publishing a guide to it that significantly extended Phillips's account, dating from 1863,[161] and a two-volume textbook marked by a striking range and by the scepticism (characteristic of all his work) towards the more extreme forms of uniformitarianism in geology.[162] Away from Oxford, where he pursued the distinguished stratigraphical work on the tertiary and quaternary deposits of southern England and northern France which had engaged his main scientific energies since the 1830s, he was no less active.

In dismal contrast, the pace of research in the two leading physical sciences, physics and chemistry, was very much slower than that set by the rather elderly new professors of astronomy and geology. Here, the root of the difficulty lay with the attitudes of Clifton and Odling, who from the 1870s and on into the less forgiving world of the twentieth century showed little or no interest in research. Clifton's frequently quoted comment that 'the wish to do research betrays a certain restlessness of mind' was typical of the jaundiced attitudes he displayed once the intellectual promise he had displayed in his Manchester days and in the first few years of his reign became submerged in his meticulous and time-consuming attention to the demands of teaching.[163] His influence, which weighed heavily on Oxford physics until his retirement in 1915, was made all the greater by the lack of a powerful rival focus, at least until the appointment of J. S. E. Townsend to the new Wykeham professorship of Physics in 1900 and the opening of the new electrical laboratory in 1910. Robert Edward Baynes, who succeeded Reinold as Dr Lee's Reader in Physics at Christ Church in 1873, after taking firsts in the schools of both mathematics (1871) and natural science (1872), and served for almost fifty years, was an able physicist whose diligence as a teacher earned him, in his prime, a reputation as the best tutor in his subject in Oxford.[164] But he resembled Clifton all too closely in that, through what appears to have been a mixture of excessive modesty and a lack of self-confidence, he published little, apart from two well-informed but unoriginal textbooks on heat and thermodynamics. More effective and visible as a practising scientist was the Revd Frederick John Smith (later Jervis-Smith),

[161] J. Prestwich, *A Short Guide to the Geological Collections in the University Museum Oxford* (1881). Phillips's guide is cited in n. 73. Prestwich included notices both on recent acquisitions and on the Stonesfield fossils and other local collections that Phillips had not treated.

[162] J. Prestwich, *Geology: chemical, physical, and stratigraphical* (2 vols 1886–8). Here and in his inaugural lecture *The Past and Future of Geology* (1875), 34–8, Prestwich endorsed his 'cataclysmic' position, according to which forces of greater intensity than those acting at present, though not of a different kind, might be assumed to have been at work in the distant geological past.

[163] Clifton's comment is cited in B. Bleaney, 'Physics at the University of Oxford', *European Journal of Physics* ix (1988), 285.

[164] See the obituary by H.B.B (H. B. Baker) in *OM* xl (1921–2), 48.

who, as Millard Lecturer in Experimental Mechanics at Trinity College, offered classes in the college's Millard Laboratory to all members of the University from the mid-1880s until his retirement in 1908. But despite his appointment as the University's first lecturer in mechanics in 1888, he remained a somewhat marginal enthusiast, and when a chair of engineering science was finally created in 1908, the appointment went to an outsider, Frewen Jenkin, with qualifications far more impressive than Jervis-Smith's passes in Lit. Hum. and mathematics.[165]

In chemistry, Odling flaunted his attitudes to research less publicly than Clifton. But the contrast between his own indifference and the sustained commitment of his predecessor, Brodie, both to experimental work and to the elaboration of a positivistic, mathematically based 'ideal' chemistry at odds with atomism was unmissable.[166] The contrast was made all the more striking by the disparity between Odling's performance in the chair and the reputation he had had on his arrival in Oxford. By the time of his appointment, when he was in his mid-forties, Odling had been a Fellow of the Royal Society for thirteen years and had held the chair of chemistry at St Bartholomew's Hospital (1863–8) and the Fullerian professorship of Chemistry at the Royal Institution in London (1868–73).[167] In these years, he was respected for his work on the classification of silicates and as a champion of the views of the French chemists Laurent and Gerhardt on the theory of compound radicals. Within a year of taking up the Waynflete chair, he had been elected to the presidency of the Chemical Society after many years' service as the Society's secretary and vice-president, and, by his engagement in the wider world of chemistry, seemed destined to give the discipline in Oxford the vigorous leadership it needed. As events were soon to show, however, his lack of interest in laboratory teaching was as flagrant as his neglect of research and was of a piece with his view that it was no part of the professor's duty to appear for any purpose in the laboratory. His conscientious lectures and the careful eye that he kept on the latest advances in his discipline were some compensation for this self-imposed detachment from the practical aspects of chemistry. But neither his lecturing nor his continued interest in following developments in chemistry could compensate for the fact that for over thirty years he devoted most of his energies to his literary and artistic interests and general university affairs, publishing nothing of consequence between 1876 and his retirement in 1912. In these years, Vernon Harcourt followed a very different trajectory, pursuing research at Christ Church until his retirement in 1902, as did his pupil Harold

---

[165] See A. V. Simcock's article on Jervis-Smith in *DNB: Missing Persons*, 353–4.

[166] On Brodie and his chemical 'calculus' see W. H. Brock (ed.), *The Atomic Debates: Brodie and the rejection of the atomic theory* (Leicester 1967).

[167] See the obituary notice on Odling by J. E. Marsh, *Journal of the Chemical Society: Transactions* cxix (1921), 553–64; also W. A. Tilden's obituary of him in *Nature* cvii (1921), 19–20.

B. Dixon at the new Balliol–Trinity laboratory from 1879 to 1887, following his first in natural science in 1875. But with Chapman (in his twenty-six years at Magdalen) and Fisher (in his forty years as Aldrichian Demonstrator) showing little interest in research, the handicap of Odling's detachment from laboratory work remained a grave one.[168]

In ways that Janet Howarth explores in Part 2, Chapter 20, late nineteenth-century Oxford was to pay a high price for such attitudes and for ideals that had been built into the structure for science in the 1850s, 1860s and 1870s.[169] While areas of real strength persisted after 1880, the scale of Oxford science remained small. It is true that some adjustments to the quickening pace of the wider world of science were made: one of the most significant was the decision, taken within three years of Rolleston's death in 1881, to distribute the responsibilities of the Linacre professorship of Anatomy and Physiology between a Linacre professorship of Human and Comparative Anatomy, a Waynflete professorship of Physiology, and a readership in Anthropology.[170] But expansion comparable with what occurred in many other universities, notably Cambridge, after 1880 was made difficult by the still strong insistence on breadth and gentlemanly status rather than professional training and the formation of specialists.[171] As a result, the Oxford curriculum came to appear irrelevant to many of the careers, notably in medicine and engineering, to which the sons of middle-class families might have aspired. Such families would also have been deterred by the requirement (enshrined in the statutes from 1864 until 1886 and significantly tougher than the requirement in Cambridge) that candidates proceeding to either a pass or an honours degree must have gained at least a pass in a first public examination, Moderations, that was predominantly classical. Since the examination could not be attempted before the seventh (from 1872, the fourth) term after matriculation, the hurdle was not just a trivial irrelevance: it delayed and discouraged candidates eager to press on with their scientific studies.[172]

[168] Such continuing activity as there was is well described in the items cited in nn. 118–20, especially in Hartley, *Studies in the History of Chemistry*, 223–32. Chapman retired from Magdalen in 1894. Fisher served from 1873 to 1913.

[169] See Pt 2, Ch. 20, and J. Howarth, 'Science education in late-Victorian Oxford: a curious case of failure?', *English Historical Review* cii (1987), 334–71.

[170] Pelling, 'Linacre lectureships', 283.

[171] On the increasing number and changing social profile of the candidates for the NST in Cambridge after 1880 see Roy MacLeod and Russell Moseley, 'The "Naturals" and Victorian Cambridge: the anatomy of an elite, 1851–1914', *Oxford Review of Education* vi (1980), 177–95.

[172] However, the delay was diminished by the division of the year at this time into four terms, and even further, for most candidates, by the special provision, introduced in 1872, that those who had matriculated in Michaelmas term could attempt pass Mods as early as their third (Easter) term. Only by taking honours in mathematics could a candidate avoid the strong classical component that was characteristic of Mods even at pass level, although such a candidate would still be required to have passed in both the classical and the mathematical parts of Responsions. Moreover, candidates for honours (in classics as in mathematics) could not attempt

Another damaging legacy from the mid-century, as Howarth has argued, was the school's austere common curriculum, with its continued emphasis on Daubeny's 'primary natural sciences' of physics, chemistry and general physiology (or what increasingly came to be referred to as 'biology'), in all of which, under the regulations of both 1850 and 1864, potential honoursmen had to be examined, in addition to more specialized work in one of the disciplines.[173] Even when, in 1872, the requirement was modified to allow candidates for honours to select only one of the three 'general subjects', a degree of compulsory breadth was preserved by the introduction of a preliminary honour examination in 'mechanics and physics' and chemistry.[174] By comparison, the syllabus of the Cambridge natural sciences tripos came to appear not only more flexible but also more attractive to candidates whose interest lay in such sciences as astronomy, mineralogy, zoology and geology, which in Oxford were all damagingly marginalized by the structure of the syllabus, assuming at best the status of optional supplementary subjects. The point was not lost on Hugh Strickland, whose rather strident claims for the centrality of his discipline, made as early as 1850 in his introductory lecture as Deputy Reader in Geology, seem to have been fired by a sense of exclusion.[175]

Strickland's dissent, like that of the distinctly radical figures of Brodie and Story-Maskelyne, indicates that there were always those in Oxford who were not entirely at one with the principles on which Acland rested his campaign and from which he never departed. But the successes of the science lobby in the 1850s, 1860s and 1870s had the effect of dulling perceptions of the dangers inherent in the course that was being taken. While money in those years never flowed easily, it flowed easily enough to foster the sense that science had finally won acceptance in the University and that Oxford could even be regarded as a pacemaker: it was at once predictable and flattering that when Owens College in Manchester was contemplating the renewal of its premises in 1867, Phillips was asked to supply details of the Museum's facilities.[176] In the light of such marks of success, the decision of Acland and his sympathizers to plead the cause of science primarily on the

---

the examination before their fifth term, or after their eighth. For convenient summaries of the examination regulations and syllabuses see the appropriate editions of *The Student's Handbook to the University and Colleges of Oxford*.

[173] See n. 103; Howarth, 'Science education', 361–2.

[174] Under the modified regulations, which remained in force until the restructuring of the school of natural science into a number of virtually independent subdivisions in 1885, candidates for honours who had passed the preliminary honour examination could elect to be examined in one or more of physics, chemistry and biology. In addition, crystallography and mineralogy, geology and palaeontology, zoology and botany were all offered as optional supplementary (or 'special') subjects for examination.

[175] H. E. Strickland, *On Geology in Relation to the Studies of the University of Oxford* (1852), 6–31.

[176] J. G. Greenwood to Phillips, 27 Apr. 1867, in the minute-book of the Museum delegates: OUA UM/M/1/3.

grounds that it was a proper part of a general education, and only secondarily for its vocational value, appeared eminently sensible. As those who were most sensitive to entrenched Oxonian prejudices perceived very clearly, Acland's strategy had the merit of calming suspicion and of allowing science to be swept along in the same tide of moderate reform that created and sustained the other new honour schools of the mid-century.

The pattern of the development of Oxford science in the third quarter of the century has to be seen, therefore, as sensitively and (albeit only in the short term) successfully adapted to local circumstances. A comparison between the position of science in the 1840s and its position two or three decades later shows how helpful those circumstances had been in invalidating the kind of criticism of the University's failure to encourage science which the Earl of Rosse had voiced in his anniversary address as President of the Royal Society in 1854.[177] It is true that in 1870 Clifton, Brodie and Rolleston still had pupils who had no intention of being examined in the subjects they were studying: in this respect, something of the old tradition of professorial instruction had survived (although the senior members who had swollen the attendances at Buckland's lectures in the 1820s and early 1830s were now conspicuously absent).[178] But by 1870 both lectures and laboratory work responded, first and foremost, to the demands of the syllabus and were seen, at least by a significant proportion of the abler pupils, as relevant to (if not always a qualification for) a career that required some scientific knowledge. As Acland, Clifton and Rolleston all observed in their evidence to the Devonshire Commission in 1870, schoolteaching provided ready openings for a substantial proportion of those emerging from the school, while smaller numbers went on to other science-based careers, including medicine or engineering, for which they had to seek professional training elsewhere.[179]

But, however well the strategy of Acland and his allies was adapted to the conditions that prevailed in Oxford up to the 1870s, the wider world of science was on the brink of growth and other changes with which Oxford failed to keep pace. Within barely a decade of the opening of the Clarendon, the expenditure of just over £10,000, which had appeared generous in 1870, had been eclipsed by the £77,000 that was spent on the erection of a new physics institute at Berlin between 1873 and 1878, and even by the £29,000 that was lavished, with political as well as scientific motives, on the smaller but exquisitely designed laboratory with which August Kundt's chair at Strasbourg was endowed in 1882.[180] By the mid-1880s, the gap between

---

[177] *Proceedings of the Royal Society*, vii (1854–5), 255. While acknowledging that beneficial changes were in train, Rosse stated: 'At present it can scarcely be said that science at Oxford receives any substantial encouragement.'

[178] *Devonshire Commn* i. 174–5.

[179] Ibid., 175, 187, 210.

[180] D. Cahan, 'The institutional revolution in German physics, 1865–1914', *Historical Studies in the Physical Sciences* xv, pt 2 (1985), 15–37.

the laboratory facilities available in Oxford and those that were coming to be expected internationally of a university with a serious commitment to science was widening inexorably. Whereas the chemical institute which the University of Heidelberg built for the recently appointed Robert Bunsen in 1854–5 cost an unremarkable £7,000 or so, the Zurich Polytechnic (the future Eidgenössische Technische Hochschule) spent more than ten times that amount when it built its new chemical laboratory between 1884 and 1886. In Britain, it must be said, the rise in expenditure was slower to appear, but the decision to spend £36,000 on the new physics laboratory at the University of Manchester about the turn of the century is just one pointer to the changing scale of investment within the more ambitious institutions.[181]

It is not, therefore, that activity ceased in the period after 1870, or that changes no longer occurred, or that there was no further expenditure. What happened was rather that Oxford was overtaken by developments elsewhere which quite suddenly made its performance relative to other institutions of higher education appear sluggish. The late nineteenth-century world of what Harold Perkin has analysed as 'professional society' came to make demands, for specialists and practitioners, that the school of natural science and its teachers were not adaptable enough to meet. Research, too, assumed an unprecedented vigour and a centrality in the new styles of late nineteenth-century university life that went unmatched in an Oxford hard hit by the agricultural depression.[182]

As a result, Oxford could be seen, and was widely seen by contemporaries, to have stumbled at the threshold of the modern world. But what critics failed to observe was that the mid-century engagement with modernity, drawing as it did on both a long scientific tradition and a will to reform, had been a resolute and fruitful one. The tragedy for science in Oxford was that the promise of those exhilarating days was only partially realized in the subsequent more difficult period of economic hardship and heightened competition. The momentum of what, by any standards, had been a brisk start in the period discussed in this chapter was arguably maintained after the 1870s, but it was not increased to the degree that had come to be expected of a leading international university at the dawn of the twentieth century.

---

[181] *The Physical Laboratories of the University of Manchester. A record of 25 years' work. Prepared in commemoration of the 25th anniversary of the election of Dr. Arthur Schuster, F.R.S., to a professorship in the Owens College, by his old students and assistants* (Manchester 1906), 129.

[182] H. J. Perkin, *The Rise of Professional Society: England since 1880* (1989). The impact of the agricultural depression on Oxford is controversial. Engel, *From Clergyman to Don*, esp. 202–56, takes the view that it was very great, though he agrees that the interests of science were better protected than most others by the measures introduced in the wake of the 1877 Commission. Dunbabin's stance in Ch. 12 above is more 'revisionist'. The depression hit Cambridge harder than Oxford.

NOTE

The Radcliffe Science Library

H. C. HARLEY

Under the date 13 September 1714 the will of Dr John Radcliffe, physician, instructed his executors to spend £40,000 'for the building a library in Oxford', but did not state that it was to be a science library. Making his benefaction at a period when all knowledge was interwoven, Radcliffe envisaged his library as but a structural extension of the Bodleian. But when the Radcliffe Camera finally opened, in 1749, it was already especially associated with the medical and natural sciences.[1] The allegorical scene depicted in the University Almanack of 1751 ranged four cherubic genii, representing Botany, Chemistry, Anatomy and Physic, behind the skirts of Alma Mater, who is accepting the keys of the library from the Radcliffe trustees. Nevertheless, during the next sixty years the Camera was a repository for oriental manuscripts, coins and sculpture.

In 1811 the Radcliffe Library became a library of reference for scientists. In his inaugural lecture as Professor of Chemistry in 1822, Daubeny described the library as 'exclusively dedicated to works of science and natural history', while P. B. Duncan, Curator of the Ashmolean Museum, paid tribute to the activity of the Radcliffe Librarian, George Williams, in assembling a 'valuable collection of books in every department of science', in aid of the Ashmolean's zoological specimens.[2] Dr Williams, he wrote, was 'always willing to permit students to consult the books in the library'.

In 1861 the scientific books were transferred from the Camera to the University Museum, bringing the science library, with the exception of the botanical works, which remained at the Botanic Garden, under the same roof as the scientific collections, laboratories and work-rooms for the professors. The library occupied the upper storey of the west front, which was rented by the Radcliffe trustees from the University. Over the entrances to the three rooms were inscribed the words 'Radcliffe Library':[3] the name 'Radcliffe Science Library' was not used until many years later.

The need for future extension, as acquisitions mounted, was foreseen by Gladstone, one of the Radcliffe trustees, as early as 1857.[4] The library then contained about 15,000 volumes. By the end of the century there were 50,000 books and runs of 600 periodicals. The offer of £15,000 (later increased to £18,500) by the Drapers' Company enabled the collections to be transferred to a purpose-built library, which opened in 1901 on a site adjoining the Museum.[5]

---

[1] I. G. Philip, 'Libraries and the University Press', in *The Eighteenth Century*, 733.

[2] C. Daubeny, *Inaugural Lecture on the Study of Chemistry* (1823), 38; *A Catalogue of the Ashmolean Museum, Descriptive of the Zoological Specimens, Antiquities, Coins, and Miscellaneous Curiosities* (1836), p. viii.

[3] There were, and are, five inscriptions, two for each of the entrances to what were the main rooms, and one for the small entrance hall or office between them: see Fig. 22.2. Dr Dennis Shaw kindly supplied information about this.

[4] I. Guest, *Dr John Radcliffe and his Trust* (1991), 186.

[5] *Gazette* xxxii (17 June 1902), 632. For this, and the other buildings adjoining the Museum, see Pt 2, Ch. 30.

None of the three librarians who held office in the nineteenth century had any previous experience of librarianship: they were practising physicians, acting as part-time keepers of the Radcliffe Library for a salary of £150 per annum. The august body of electors was headed by the Archbishop of Canterbury assisted by the Lord Chancellor, the Chancellor of the University, the Bishops of London and Winchester, the two principal Secretaries of State, the Lord Chief Justices and the Master of the Rolls. Once appointed the library keepers were responsible to a smaller, more readily convened committee of four elected trustees to whom they submitted reports (oral, manuscript or printed) at the annual audits or special meetings in London.

George Williams, appointed Librarian in 1810, combined the post with the chair of botany. He was the first physician to hold the office, and under him the purchase of books began to be confined to natural science and medicine. An accumulated surplus of £5,000 in the trust fund gave him considerable scope for new purchases, expenditure on which reached £2,000 in 1813 and £1,000 in the following year. Thereafter the annual purchasing grant settled down to £500. Williams laid the foundations for the first general catalogue of the books, which was revised and published by John Kidd, the Regius Professor of Medicine, who succeeded to the keepership on Williams's death in 1834. Kidd's keepership began with high hopes: in addition to the publication of the catalogue, the convenience of the Camera as a place of study was enhanced by the installation of new gas apparatus. But he had the misfortune to be Keeper at a time when, as the evidence of statistics of readers showed, the library was comparatively neglected by members of the University. Committed to heavy expenditure on the trust estate at Wolverton, the Radcliffe trustees reduced Kidd's annual book purchase grant from £500 to £200 in 1841.[6]

On Kidd's death in 1851 the trustees appointed Henry Wentworth Acland, then aged 36, who was Librarian until his resignation in 1900, aged 85.[7] Acland's first achievement was to persuade the trustees of the case for moving the collections to the Museum, presenting a report to them in 1856 supported by a petition signed by forty-six residents, including fourteen heads of houses and Acland's new-found ally in the Museum controversies, E. B. Pusey.[8] Towards the end of Acland's long tenure of office, *Nature* acknowledged that 'the opportunities of scientific study in Oxford are greatly enhanced by the existence within the precincts of the Museum of a first-rate scientific library, such as is not possessed by any other college or university in the kingdom'.[9] Acland was concerned to promote research as well as undergraduate education. 'One advanced student in any department of knowledge' required in his view 'as good a library of reference as 50 students would.'

[6] Guest, 180.
[7] Meeting of trustees, 9 Dec. 1851, Bodl. MS DD Radcl. c. 36.
[8] H. W. Acland, 'Report on the subject of the Radcliffe Library, 8 Nov. 1856', Bodl. MS DD Radcl. c. 36; Radcliffe trustees minutes, 16 July 1857, Bodl. MS DD Radcl. c. 54.
[9] *Nature* 9 July 1896, 225. See also H. W. Acland, 'Report to the Radcliffe Trustees for 1893', Bodl. MS DD Radcl. c. 37. References to the building erected for the Library between the University Museum and South Parks Road, 1898–1900, will be found in Pt 2, Chs 20 and 30. Designed by T. G. Jackson, it resulted from a gift by the Drapers' Companys whose Master in 1896–7 had been Henry Boyd, Principal, Hertford College, 1877–1922, Vice-Chancellor 1890–4.

A NATIONALIZED UNIVERSITY?

23

Reform and Expansion, 1854–1871

CHRISTOPHER HARVIE

AFTER THE ACT OF 1854

In 1859 Thomas Henry Huxley visited Oxford, courted by his friend George Rolleston. He had refused the new Linacre chair of Physiology, which he had helped to create, despite Rolleston's blandishments; and he now wrote of Oxford, 'I see much to admire and like; but I am more and more convinced that it would not suit me as a residence.'[1] Thirty-three years later, only half in jest, he prescribed Oxford for his grandson Lawrence:

Lawrence will go to Oxford & become a real scholar, which is a great thing and a noble. He will combine the new & the old, & show how much better the world would have been if it had stuck to Hellenism. You are dreaming of the schoolboy who does not follow up his work, or becomes a mere poll man. Good enough for parsons, not for men. *Lawrence will go to Oxford.*[2]

The excoriator of the old universities had mellowed; his Liberal Unionist politics were the same as those of most Oxford dons; his residual anti-clericalism had become virtually redundant now that fewer than two-fifths (about 39 per cent in 1882–91) of Oxford's graduates took orders.

In 1854–63 almost two-thirds (63 per cent) had done so, and this secularization was not watched with equanimity by those it dislodged. In 1881, as the work of the second Executive Commission drew to its exhausting close, Canon H. P. Liddon, long the lieutenant of E. B. Pusey, wrote in the *Church Quarterly Review,*

At Oxford before 1854, the Church was still everything & everywhere … henceforth Oxford will belong to the Church of England just as much and just as little as does the House of Commons. It is still a centre of social and intellectual interests; but as a centre of religious force it is no longer what it was, and is unlikely in its future to be what it still is.[3]

Liddon and Pusey had fought hard and resourcefully, but they had been from the start pessimistic, Pusey declaring to Keble in 1854, 'If they [the

[1] Quoted in L. Huxley, *Life of Thomas Henry Huxley* (2 vols 1900) i. 154.
[2] Ibid. ii. 441.
[3] (H. P. Liddon), 'Recent fortunes of the Church in Oxford', *Church Quarterly Review* xii (Apr. 1881), 204, 241. For ordinands as a percentage of all undergraduates, see Table 14.A5.

universities] belong to the Church, no one except members of the Church have a claim to be educated there. A Socinian has no claim. If to the nation, then I do not see how the Church can put any restriction upon it.'[4] Keble tended to accept Gladstone's assurance that a reformed Oxford would 'exercise a far greater sway than heretofore over the mind of England', but Pusey recognized the development foreshadowed in the Introduction to this volume: he knew that he was carrying out a retreat.[5]

Who, then, were the victors? Historians are scarcely unanimous about the motives for university reform. Lewis Campbell, Jowett's biographer, shared, in his *Nationalisation of the Old English Universities* (1901), Pusey's vision of steady secularization. This 'composure', also evident in the final volume of Charles Mallet's *A History of the University of Oxford* (1927), minimized the personal antipathies which had shown their sharp teeth in Mark Pattison's *Memoirs* (1885). It has been subverted by the 'neo-Namierite' approach of W. R. Ward's *Victorian Oxford* (1965), but while this legitimately reassesses some reputations, enhancing those of Charles Savile Roundell and Bartholomew Price at the expense of Jowett and Pattison, the 'condition of England question' still played a greater role in university politics than either interpretation grants it.

This is not to say that Oxford fits snugly into any Marxist analysis. No institutions, surely, came closer to the *'faux frais* of production' Marx and Engels saw the English bourgeoisie ruthlessly discarding; yet instead of stripping Oxford and Cambridge to endow civic and technological universities, the bourgeoisie proved almost pathetically responsive to the 'conservation' programme of such liberal dons as had their ear. This has led the American historian Martin Wiener and others to a neo-Weberian schema, supported to some extent by Correlli Barnett and noisily seconded by various members of the Thatcher Cabinet. In this the dons spirited otherwise rational Victorian capitalists (and, more importantly, their sons) from foundry and shipyard into the Eloi-land of anti-industrialism. Arthur Engel has seen the 'training' function of the colleges systematically 'professionalized' in his *Clergyman into Don* (1983).[6] Others, myself included, have suggested that such processes were less deliberate; that, before institutional pressures closed in, university reformers—desperately unsure of their status—saw visions in which the idea of a university merged with that of a democratic commonwealth to suggest a new integration of university and society.[7]

---

[4] Quoted in I. Ellis, 'Pusey and university reform', in P. Butler (ed.), *Pusey Rediscovered* (1983), 302.

[5] Ibid. 308.

[6] Cf. Simon, *Studies in the History of Education* (1961); M. Wiener, *English Culture and the Decline of the Industrial Spirit* (1981); A. Engel, *From Clergyman to Don* (1983).

[7] C. Harvie, *The Lights of Liberalism: university liberals and the challenge of democracy, 1860–1886* (1976).

These varying interpretations stem, at least in part, from the constant flux of personnel in post-1854 university politics. This affected liberals and conservatives alike. The 1854 Commissioners were different from those of 1850. The protagonists of tests abolition, 1863–71, were different again from the Commissioners of the 1870s, and from the generation which ultimately benefited from their reforms.

This element of change was already visible in 1854. The five (ultimately seven) Executive Commissioners chosen to frame university and college statutes on the basis of Gladstone's 'compromise' (which received the royal assent on 7 August) *were* appreciably older and more conservative than the Commissioners of 1850. As their chairman, Gladstone appointed the 54-year-old Earl of Ellesmere, a graduate of Christ Church and a Peelite landowner. The Tory judge Sir John Taylor Coleridge (Corpus and a fellow of Exeter, 1812–18), Sir John Awdry (Christ Church and a fellow of Oriel, 1820–30), a retired Indian judge, and Charles Longley (Student of Christ Church since 1815), a Low-Church liberal, former headmaster of Harrow, Bishop of Ripon, and after 1856 of Durham, were all in their sixties. The 46-year-old Broad-Church Dean of Wells, G. H. S. Johnson, fellow of Queen's since 1829 and Professor of Moral Philosophy from 1842 to 1845, was the only survivor of the radicals of 1850. By 7 August 1854 these had been supplemented with the 56-year-old Peelite Earl of Harrowby (Christ Church), landowner and, after March 1855, Chancellor of the Duchy of Lancaster, and the 48-year-old Sir George Cornewall Lewis (Student of Christ Church, 1828–39), Whig MP from 1847, classicist and Benthamite political writer. The Secretaries (at £800 per annum, £300 more than the wealthiest Oxford professor) were the 'safe and dull' Samuel Wayte (who was Trinity's representative on the Tutors' Association)[8] and Goldwin Smith, lately a demy of Magdalen and University prizeman. Because he had researched as Stowell law fellow of University College in papers which the colleges withheld from the 1850 Commission, he had been A. P. Stanley's Assistant Secretary in 1850–2.[9]

Christ Church predominated: not a good sign, given its decline in intellectual attainments, which even Gladstone lamented, and—as was subsequently demonstrated—a stubborn imperviousness to reform.[10] But the task of the Commissioners was markedly different from that of their more speculative predecessors. They had to carry out the institutional adaptations required of the colleges by the Act. This was a narrower and less onerous task than that given the Commissioners of 1877; and its routine quality was

[8] Goldwin Smith to Gladstone, 9 June 1854, BL Add. MS 44303, fo 25.
[9] G. Smith, *Reminiscences* (1910), 102.
[10] Emily Wood wrote in May 1859 to her brother, then at the House, that Gladstone 'lamented very much the falling-off of the College of late years. As to book-learning, that, he says, is altogether discarded.' Quoted in J. G. Lockhart, *Charles Lindley, Viscount Halifax* (1935), 64; and see E. G. W. Bill and J. F. A. Mason, *Christ Church and Reform* (1970).

well captured by Anthony Trollope, who visited on them his own nominee, the elusive Dr Proudie of Barchester.[11] Opening fellowships to competition, laicizing a proportion of them, circumscribing the influence of schools (with far-reaching consequences in the cases of St John's and New College), making somewhat tentative precepts from collegiate income to support new university chairs: these were appropriate tasks for a collection of political landlords, church administrators and old official hands.

Given such a reassuring Commission, most colleges were prepared to co-operate, as long as this did not involve too much additional work and disruption. Although they had a year's grace to do so, ten out of eighteen colleges had submitted their statutes within six months.[12] Apart from an excursion to Oxford (in November 1855) the Commission was based in London. Its political centre of gravity was comfortably close to Gladstone's own,[13] and, as Longley wrote, it construed its remit narrowly:

in making ordinances, we were directed to keep in view 'the main designs of the Founder and Donors'—The spirit of this latter portion of the bill then under the general terms in which it was couched seemed to be that of a Conservative Reform ...in short the Commissioners were empowered to do whatever they believed every reasonable founder, were he living to witness the altered state of things, would himself desire to aid in doing...[14]

It increased to a minimum of a third the proportion of lay fellowships in each college, made elections depend on merit, and made provision for up to ten new chairs at £600 each (specifying chemistry, international law, Latin, miner-alogy, modern history, moral and metaphysical philosophy, physical geo-graphy, and physiology).[15] The wholesale financial reform implied by the recommendations of the 1850–2 Commission drove Dean Johnson to anticipate the Cleveland Commission in 1871,[16] but only Exeter and Lincoln seem to have made returns, and nothing more was heard of this.[17]

Almost inevitably the Commission lost momentum in the spring of 1855. While colleges could empower a subcommittee to negotiate on new statutes, college meetings had to ratify these, and the ensuing modifications dragged on. Goldwin Smith warned Gladstone in June: 'you will readily understand that the occasional attendance, even of the ablest men, when they cannot pay attention to the subject between the meetings, sometimes does more harm than good'.[18] The object of his strictures was probably the impatient Corne-

---

[11] See Anthony Trollope, *Barchester Towers* (1857), ch. 5.
[12] 18 Aug. 1854, PRO HO 73.
[13] Gladstone to Longley, 18 Mar. 1854, LPL MS Longley, box 2.
[14] Longley to Gladstone, 29 Feb. 1856, LPL MS Longley, box 2.
[15] *Ordinances and Statutes framed or approved by the Oxford University Commissioners* (1863).
[16] S. W. Wayte to Blackford (with enclosure), 6 Nov. 1854, PRO HO 73.
[17] Wayte to Blackford, 30 Jan. 1855, ibid.
[18] Goldwin Smith to Gladstone, 12 June 1855, BL Add. MS 44303, fo 85.

wall Lewis, who had something of the temperament of his friend Robert Lowe. He was appointed Chancellor of the Exchequer in February 1855 and was replaced by another Liberal lawyer, Edward Turner Boyd Twisleton. A fellow of Balliol, 1830–8, and one of the most energetic of Edwin Chadwick's protégés, Twisleton promptly raised the issue of opening fellowships to Dissenters, something still being pressed in Parliament by James Heywood. Longley reacted with alarm: 'The adoption of the principle involved in Mr Heywood's Resolution would plunge us in the downward path of destructive Revolution instead of our maintaining the line of conservative reform, and the spirit and character of the Oxford Act would to my mind be entirely altered'.[19] Longley's veiled threat of resignation checked further action in this direction. Goldwin Smith squared Twisleton by arguing that Dissenters could become fellows if they conformed with the letter of the law, reporting to Gladstone in March 1857 on the New College statutes:

I wish you particularly to see Clause 40, the effect of which is to enable the College to enforce as a continuing obligation the declaration of conformity made under the Act of Uniformity. This is surely the best kind of safeguard for the religious system of the colleges. Anything in the shape of a test which scrutinizes conscience as opposed to outward conduct, gives you the minimum of security with the maximum of offence. If a Roman Catholic or an infidel will regularly conform to the liturgy of the Church of England for the sake of retaining his fellowship (as some persons suggest) no test will reach him.

These weasel words allowed James Bryce (not just a Dissenter but a Scots 'voluntaryist' opposed root and branch to the notion of an Established Church) to become a scholar of Trinity in 1857 and a fellow of Oriel in 1862 without 'subscribing', and accommodated a growing number of highly nominal Anglicans.[20] When the Commission was dissolved in July 1858 the High-Church *Guardian* professed to be satisfied with its labours:

There cannot be a doubt that they have performed a very considerable work, on the whole well; that, without compromising the main principles of the Act of Parliament, they have dealt tenderly with the Colleges; that their spirit has been conservative and conciliatory; that they have laboured to reform, not to root up, to invigorate, not to revolutionise, the Oxford system.[21]

But Pusey's fears in 1854 that 'the talent of young Oxford is all liberal' were coming home.[22]

The Act was conservative and the Executive Commission timid, yet a revolution had been carried through. Oxford became after 1854 a political

---

[19] Longley to Gladstone, 29 Feb. 1856, LPL MS Longley, box 2.
[20] Goldwin Smith to Gladstone, 27 Mar. 1857, BL Add. MS 44303, fo 121. See H. A. L. Fisher, *James Bryce* (2 vols 1927), i. 37–43, 54–5. Lewis Campbell called Bryce's tenure of the scholarship 'the triumph of liberalism in Oxford'. For declaration see 13 Car. II c. iv. 9.
[21] Quoted in Ward, *Victorian Oxford*, 209.
[22] Quoted in Ellis, 'Pusey and university reform', 311.

system. Before then it had been a close corporation, run by the heads of houses, ecclesiastical beneficiaries elected for life by ever-changing collegiate bodies, only loosely overlooked by the rural clergy in Convocation; not as grotesquely corrupt as Scottish or English town councils before, respectively, 1833 and 1835, but closer in spirit to them than to any educational purpose. Now that Congregation elected all but three of the members of the Hebdomadal Council, Oxford possessed a legislative arm capable of transforming policy, something rare both in the state-run universities of Europe and in the Scottish or later the civic universities, where externally nominated members were prominent in powerful courts and councils.

The implications of such empowerment have been advanced in theoretical terms by Graeme Moodie and Rowland Eustace in their study of British university government:

universities are political in the sense that in making, changing and applying the rules, penalties, and sanctions, they activate or mobilise important, and conflicting, perspectives and attitudes. The consequent disputes must be resolved, in the sense that decisions must be taken on the issues in contention without (if possible) undermining or disrupting the coherence (or even the existence) of the university itself.[23]

And the implication for Oxford was this: that all the parties concerned—secular liberals, Broad-Churchmen, Tractarians, dedicated researchers, or popular tutors—had to find solutions within the system: they had to form parties and manœuvre them, court electors, make alliances and reach consensuses. Some conservatives revealed unexpected talents for this; some liberals collapsed at the challenge. But the result was a *polis*—an accretion of rules and conventions—which propelled its actors to move, however unwillingly, in specific ways.

The settlement of 1858 appeared a secure one: collegiate, classical and clerical. Spectres of a Scots or a German future had been banished, and visions of Oxford, from Newman to Goldwin Smith, located its purposes in catering, in its unique way, to the needs of the English upper classes. In his Inaugural Lecture delivered in 1859, Goldwin Smith, whom Derby had rewarded for his labours on the Commission with the Regius chair of Modern History, supported the bipartisan basis of Gladstone's 1854 settlement, anticipating possible social change, yet also determined to accommodate Oxford's traditional clients: '[The gentry] . . . must know their position, and own their duty to those by whose labour they are fed. They must be resident, they must be well-educated, they must be able and willing to act as the social and moral educators of those below them.'[24] Smith's purposes, didactic rather than scholarly, were in social terms not too far from those of

---

[23] G. Moodie and R. Eustace, 'British universities as political systems', *Political Studies* xix (1979), 296.
[24] G. Smith, *An Inaugural Lecture* (1859), 14.

Pusey, who, in his *Collegiate and Professorial Teaching and Discipline* (1854), had defined 'the problem and special work of a university' as not scholarship or discovery but 'to form minds religiously, morally, intellectually, which shall discharge aright whatever duties God, in His providence, shall appoint to them'.[25] God, naturally, had in mind the duties of squire and rector, as in Pusey's own family of improving Wiltshire landlords. Why, then, did this apparent consensus dissolve so rapidly?

This brings into play some of the interpretations alluded to earlier, in particular Professor Engel's. Since the heads had lost power, which the professors had not gained, the tutors were surely at the centre of affairs. Through their Association, they acted as the voice of Congregation, as its most numerous and best-organized grouping (27 per cent of its 1858 strength, against 8 per cent for the heads and 9 per cent for the professors).[26] Yet subsequent events seemed to shift beyond their control.

The problem was that for college teaching to equal the economic rewards on offer in the Church or at the public schools, it had to pay much better, while it could never provide as alluring an ambience as a fat living with a couple of dutiful and energetic curates. The tutorial constellation was impermanent. Of the twenty members of the Tutors' Association committees in 1851 only three were, for instance, still in Oxford posts in 1865.[27] The Association registered the new political *character* of the University—with Congregation the arena of competition between rival if overlapping groupings—rather than a determined effort to push teaching developments in a particular way.

The importance of the Tutors' Association was its determination to equal the status of the most prestigious comparable outside group, the public school masters, who could (with the management of a school house) command almost double the salary of an Oxford tutor. The Association demarcated the hard-working and ambitious from the 'old corruption' of the heads and the country clergy; it aligned them with government, personified by Gladstone and Lord Derby (Chancellor since 1852). It protected tutors from the threat implied by the professoriate that studies would expand into fields untouched in the public schools, and staked the claims to patronage of men whose considerable ambitions still lay outside the University.

Strong though this position was in the long term—as the products of 'progressive' colleges would gradually colonize the others—the clerical centre found difficulty in capitalizing on it.[28] The Liberal Anglican leaders wavered or fell back, like Jeune and Conington, or left, like Stanley, while the High-Church party showed itself more than competent, and Pusey

---

[25] Pusey, *Collegiate and Professorial Teaching and Discipline*, 215.
[26] Engel, *Clergyman to Don*, 61, 289.
[27] From the list in G. Marshall, *Osborne Gordon: a memoir* (1885), 38.
[28] Ward, *Victorian Oxford*, 210.

established a remarkable, if temporary, ascendancy. But the gulf between religious parties was far too deep for them to maintain any semblance of unity under the hammer-blows that rained on the Church between 1858 and 1865: these claimed as victims both Bishop Wilberforce and Pusey himself. And while this was happening, the acceptance of the 'national education' issue by the University gradually marginalized religious questions.

Although W. R. Ward is, in the strictly legal sense, right to say that 'the chief business of the University was still the management of examinations and the election of its burgesses and Chancellor',[29] in the 1850s it was being pushed towards a specifically educational role in two highly contentious areas which are examined in the next two sections of this chapter: the natural sciences and the organization of national education. The forces pressing for both could not, with any precision, be slotted into the main university parties: the leaders of these parties had therefore to manœuvre in order to accommodate these new factors if they were, in Moodie's and Eustace's terms, to validate the University as an institution.

Pusey faced this problem in 1854 when, after opposing Henry Acland's scheme for a science museum and laboratories, he swung his support behind it to carry it to a narrow victory (70 to 64) in Convocation on 12 December.[30] It was difficult to see how he could have done otherwise, as Acland and his friends were sympathetic to him, and in no way secularist liberals, and Pusey's ideal gentry were supposed to be competent in the natural sciences. Yet the result inevitably created expectations of Oxford as a centre for scientific research—as well as, in 1860, providing the most spectacular collision between science and religion with its *mise-en-scène*.

The Aclands provide the link with the other impulse, the national education question. In 1857, while the University Museum was rising, Henry Acland's elder brother, Sir Thomas, along with Frederick Temple, prevailed on the Hebdomadal Council to undertake the examination of schoolboys from the Devon area.[31] To this the Hebdomadal Council agreed, with very little fuss, doubtless mindful that the University's population had been static since 1820, while that of England had risen by two-thirds. If the University did not co-operate in such initiatives, it would be marginalized: something as apparent to Sir Thomas as to his colleague in 'the Engagement'—that High-Church commitment to social participation—W. E. Gladstone. The upshot was the intrusion into the University of another major political issue at a critical juncture. The Newcastle Commission on elementary education

---

[29] Ward, *Victorian Oxford*, 217–18.
[30] Atlay, *Acland*, 202–4. See also pp. 652–4 above.
[31] A. H. D. Acland, *Memoir and Letters of Sir Thomas Dyke Acland* (1902), 179 ff. His brother remarked on the power of the West Country interest in Convocation (Atlay, *Acland*, 244); might this be linked to the fact that the Great Western main line, with the fastest expresses in England, made Exeter only about three hours distant from Oxford?

started sitting in 1859, the Clarendon Commission on the major public schools in 1860. By the time the Taunton Commission into endowed schools was set up in 1864 with Acland and Temple as members, the 'education interest' had become a major factor in Oxford politics. Taunton's assistant Commissioners—T. H. Green, James Bryce, R. S. Wright—were virtually synonymous with the secularist Left in the University, and Gladstone's London committee in 1865 had a solid phalanx of fourteen senior public school figures, including the heads of Marlborough, Clifton, St Paul's, Merchant Taylors' and Rugby, against which the Tories could manage only the heads of Winchester and Malvern and five very obscure grammar schools.[32]

OXFORD AND THE MARCH OF MIND

As the Executive Commission wound itself up Goldwin Smith contributed 'Oxford University reform' to a volume of *Oxford Essays* brought out by the Oxford publisher James Parker in 1858. He did his best to endorse the conservative settlement he had helped create: 'Good judges thought—and their opinion seems to have been justified by the event—that under a more open and genial constitution, much of the energy of theological agitation would have been absorbed in the practical duties of the place.'[33] Smith thought that religion had been more than adequately secured by the limitation to clergymen of every headship but one (Merton), and of 'almost every professorship for the chance of which a man of ability would remain at Oxford'.[34] Yet he ended pessimistic: 'This combination of heads without defined duties, a houseless and half-alien professoriate, and tutors who must give up their calling when they marry, is such as no human being would have devised if it had not come into our hands through historical accidents of the most capricious kind.'[35] Smith was particularly chagrined at the way the 'empty college' of All Souls had staved off reform. He could also have added St John's, which had refused to accept its new statutes, or Christ Church itself, where the Senior Students were given the same status as fellows in other colleges, but denied any part in its government. The process of settling these issues was to extend into the 1860s, but was now affected by a recrudescence of theological warfare—somewhat different from that of the 1840s, but with even more profound repercussions.

The *casus belli* was provided by the same Broad-Church party which had favoured the settlement of the 1850s. Arthur Stanley (and, at this stage, Smith himself) accepted the Anglican university, seeing the Church as consonant with the nation. F. D. Maurice had opposed the admission of Dis-

---

[32] Gladstone and Gathorne Hardy election flysheets, respectively 6 and 9 May 1865.
[33] Smith, 'Oxford university reform' in *Oxford Essays, Part 4* (1858), 271.
[34] Ibid. 278.
[35] Ibid. 282.

senters in 1834[36] and Smith found Stanley 'an almost fanatical upholder of Church establishments'.[37] Their view, however, was that the formularies of the Church be interpreted as flexibly as possible: a proposition debatable, to say the least, in the Oxford of the 1860s. It was true that most of the educational figures who were to support Gladstone in 1865 had this sort of undogmatic Erastianism. Yet they were only an external arm, admittedly powerful, of a group which within the University felt itself small and perpetually under threat.

Liddon exaggerated when he claimed that the Church had been 'everything and everywhere' in the University before 1854. Yet clergymen were certainly in the vast majority (215 out of 273 in the Congregation of 1855),[38] and although they were always more deeply divided than conscious of any common attitude towards secular political interests, a conservative majority could be constructed through effective leadership. In the High-Church party Pusey had both political expertise and was open to some discussions of an ecumenical sort; by 1858 he was co-operating very effectively with the Evangelical and former liberal leader Jeune of Pembroke, to the chagrin of H. G. Liddell: 'Pusey appears to be dominant on the Council, supporting Jeune where he can and receiving Jeune's support in other cases.'[39] Along this track might have lain the liberal 'worst case': a university federated out of confessional colleges, Church and Dissent. But High-Church–Evangelical co-operation could only be cemented by focusing on a common enemy and minimizing disagreements. In the 1860s Pusey managed, instead, to provide the Broad-Church party with powerful external allies and by 1866 to isolate himself.

The fundamental reason for this clerical débâcle lies in the provocations offered by Broad-Church Oxford. Its attitude to the Bible was eclectic: remote from the blend of mysticism and social mission of F. D. Maurice and his mainly Cambridge followers, closer to the theistic philosophy of history which had been introduced from Germany in the 1820s. In his study of Jowett, Peter Hinchliff argued that it was perhaps closest to the 'moderatism' of the Scots Enlightenment.[40] The Hon. W. H. Fremantle, a Broad-Church clergyman who was a fellow of All Souls in the 1850s, found it thin and unconvincing: 'it was to be noticed that whereas the Tractarian leaders invited young men to a system of ordinances, "Broad Church" was merely a tendency which it was difficult to define, and which, while honouring the existing system of ordinances, was largely occupied in criticism

---

[36] F. D. Maurice, *Subscription No Bondage* (1835). The identity of the author, 'Rusticus', was soon known.

[37] Smith, *Reminiscences*, 84.

[38] List of 8 June 1855, annexed to Hebdomadal Council minutes.

[39] Ellis, 'Pusey and university reform', 320.

[40] P. Hinchliff, *Benjamin Jowett and the Christian Religion* (1987), 18.

which at times was justly called negative'.[41] The Broad Church's power, Ward maintains, lay in the force of the reactions it provoked. Its leading figures, Jowett, Stanley and Liddell, were relatively young men whose teaching ability and assistance during the 1850–4 crisis, rather than their theology, recommended them to the Evangelical-leaning governments of the Palmerston years. Their rewards, however, were limited. Cornewall Lewis, presumably, made Liddell Dean of Christ Church in 1855 and Jowett (sulking since 1854 in Balliol after being defeated for the mastership) got the Regius Chair of Greek. But both posts had inbuilt menaces. Christ Church was still run by its canons; the Greek chair paid only £40 per annum. Stanley, a gentle, conciliatory figure who held the chair of ecclesiastical history, 1856–64, was the nearest the Broad Church had to a leader. But, in contrast to 1850–4, there was no firm Westminster hand on the university tiller. Gladstone, fully in control of the 1854 reform and respected by clerical and liberal alike, was now in opposition. He was, too, in a rather fey mood—in late 1858 he departed for five months to sort out the constitution of the Ionian Islands—which could, in hindsight, be seen as a process of setting his sails for the wind which would carry him into the Liberal Party. But this abstention meant that Oxford politics got out of hand.

Goaded by a clerical majority in Congregation which had impressed itself on Council by 1858, and by such irritants as the foundering of attempts to raise Jowett's stipend on the rocks of Pusey's opposition, the liberals attacked, determined, as Jowett put it to Stanley, 'not to submit to this abominable system of terrorism which prevents the statement of the plainest facts, and makes true theology or theological education impossible'.[42] The chosen weapon was *Essays and Reviews*, one of a series of essay collections which Parkers published in the 1850s. Two of the proposed contributors, Max Müller and Sir Alexander Grant, pulled out; two—the Cambridge theologian Rowland Williams and Bristow Wilson—had more than a whiff of Unitarianism hanging about them; and Jowett and Pattison were already marked men. Yet the reception of the book when it came out in 1860 was very low-key, until, through the Balliol fellow W. L. Newman, Jowett stimulated the Wadham fellow Frederic Harrison to comment on it. The result was a mighty blast against the essayists in the *Westminster Review* of October 1860 entitled 'Neo-Christianity'.[43]

Harrison, an Evangelical turned Comtist and, as Matthew Arnold was to find, tending more to fire and strength than sweetness and light, hit very hard: 'In object, in spirit and in method . . .—this book is incompatible with

[41] *Recollections of Dean Fremantle, chiefly by himself*, ed. W. H. Draper (1921), 35.

[42] Abbott and Campbell, *Jowett* i. 275.

[43] F. Harrison, *Creed of a Layman* (1907), 27–32, *Autobiographic Memoirs* (2 vols 1911) i. 205–6; *Letters of B. Jowett*, ed. E. Abbott and L. Campbell (1899), 14–16; [A. P. Stanley], 'Essays and Reviews', *Ed. Rev.* cxiii (1861), 461–500.

the religious belief of the mass of the Christian public, and the broad principles on which the Protestantism of Englishmen rests.'[44] Harrison argued that the 'scientific' biblical criticism on which the essayists had prided themselves dealt only with partial and selective evidence, ignoring the contribution to world history of the non-Christian religious traditions: 'The old faith consigned them to Hell; the new, it seems, reserves them for annihilation.' *Essays and Reviews*, he argued, showed learning to be diseased, and the University—in its Broad-Church even more than its High-Church form—as the malarial swamp where the contagion bred: 'The pedantic education and the shuffling morality too rife in the Universities, often leads them to adopt the principles of hostile criticism, in the spirit of the rhetorician or the sophist...day after day we see the latest conclusions of philosophy and science travestied into Hebrew phraseology, to defend the pretentions of an official Church.'[45] This brought on the heads of the essayists a chorus of disapproval from the *Saturday Review*, and from Samuel Wilberforce in the *Quarterly*, culminating in an encyclical condemnation signed by the whole bench of bishops, including such *ci-devant* radicals as Hampden, Thirlwall, and Tait. The Church courts arraigned Williams and Wilson on heresy charges; in Oxford Pusey attempted to get Jowett tried before the Chancellor's Court (usually the means of tailors or liverymen dunning defaulting undergraduates). The fact that both prosecutions ended in circumstances of some absurdity—Lord Westbury's famous 'hell dismissed with costs'—was, however, matched by the menacing statistic that 11,000 clergy (equivalent to two-thirds of the parochial clergy) signed a joint High Church–Evangelical declaration affirming 'without reserve or qualification' what they saw Jowett and company as diluting—the truth of eternal damnation.[46]

Harrison's assault drew a tribute from another figure who had recently assaulted Oxford clericalism. T. H. Huxley wrote to the *Westminster's* publisher, John Chapman, 'I take it the author is not a man to care much for praise or blame, but it may interest him to know that he has the entire sympathy and concurrence of a few men of science.'[47] On 30 June, in the half-completed library of the University Museum, had occurred Huxley's famous clash with Bishop Wilberforce. Sheridan Gilley has argued that the impact of this was embellished retrospectively by the Huxley side,[48] but a letter from Robinson Ellis, future Corpus Professor of Latin to James Bryce, the coming man of the younger liberals, makes clear the impressive nature of

[44] Repr. as 'Septem contra fidem' in *The Creed of a Layman*, 98.

[45] Ibid. 115, 120. The original version of the second passage is rather fiercer: *Westminster Review* NS xviii (1860), 309.

[46] Ward, *Victorian Oxford*, 240.

[47] Huxley to John Chapman, 10 Oct. 1860, LSE Harrison MSS, box 5 'c'.

[48] S. Gilley, 'The Huxley–Wilberforce debate: a reconsideration', in Keith Robbins (ed.), *Religion and Humanism*, Studies in Church History xvii (1981), 325–40.

Huxley's impact: 'I thought his speech exceedingly effective. It was the triumph of reason against Rhetoric—not so much that the Bp. of Oxford had confined himself to Rhetoric, as that he is by nature a Rhetorician and cannot get out of that style. The Bp. again replied and was again answered—and altogether got the worst of it. I came away with a strong impression in favour of the Darwin theory.'[49] Henry Fawcett, the blind economist from Trinity Hall, Cambridge, also present, had the same reaction, and defended Darwin in *Macmillan's Magazine* in December.[50]

The significance of the clash was that Wilberforce, far from being an extremist, was a centrist ecclesiastical politician of Broad-to-High views, very close to Gladstone: he had been an influential guarantor of conservative university reform both on the bench of bishops and in his own diocese. By aligning himself so publicly with clerical authoritarianism, not only did he foreshadow the capitulation over *Essays and Reviews* of Hampden, Thirlwall and Tait, but he seemed to promise that the Church would intervene to circumscribe scientific inquiry. That Wilberforce's address was mainly a reasoned critique of Darwin's weaker points, which had impressed Darwin himself, was beside the point; in the circumstances of 1860 Wilberforce was rejecting the Broad-Church compromise and enlisting in the army of reaction.

The year 1860 was in fact crucial for the evolution of the reform movement at the universities. It saw the arena shift from Oxford to London, the participants become laymen rather than clergy, non-residents rather than dons; a political context was established in which links both with Cambridge and with Dissent could be made. At the same time the opponents of reform became both more emphatically political and more deeply entrenched in Oxford.

Much depended on the impact of both controversies on the London literary scene, on which so many non-residents (penurious barristers almost to a man) depended for their bread and butter. The *Saturday Review* had provided an intellectual critique of a Peelite sort throughout the 1850s, and paid well. But the violence of its attack on *Essays and Reviews* drove most of its liberals from it, and ex-*Saturday Reviewers* like Charles Bowen, Frederic Harrison and Mountstuart Grant Duff played central roles first in the committee formed to defend Jowett and then in the bodies pressing for tests abolition.[51]

At the same time Lord Robert Cecil, one of the most dedicated and 'slashing' of the *Saturday Reviewers*, his neurasthenic fears of a general assault on property and status fuelled by the success of European radicalism as much as by critical theology, began to lend himself to a clerical revival of a specifically Conservative type in Oxford.[52] Managed by the layman Mon-

---

[49] R. Ellis to Bryce, 1 July 1860, Bodl. MS Bryce 62 fos 170–3.
[50] L. Stephen, *The Life of Henry Fawcett* (1885), 99–100.
[51] See L. Stephen, *Life of Sir James Fitzjames Stephen* (1895), 184 ff.
[52] See Ward, *Victorian Oxford*, 230.

tagu Burrows (Chichele Professor of History after 1862), who had countered Goldwin Smith on university reform in the *Quarterly* in 1859,[53] and by the Revd George Anthony Denison, this revival shifted university politics on to more party-political lines. These two organized the overwhelmingly Conservative undergraduate body, and, anticipating that more country clergy would be able to vote at burgess elections through the facility of proxy voting (introduced in 1861), worked successfully to destabilize the High-Church–Liberal alliance which had kept Gladstone in his university seat.

On the liberal side, such Broad-Churchmen as Jowett and Stanley shifted from leading to advisory roles. The years 1860 and 1861 had shown that, in national religious politics, they were a red rag to the clerical bull. MPs insisted in debates that the abolition of university tests 'was not in the main a Dissenters' question. Its main effect was to relieve loyal Churchmen who could not hold all her dogmatic teaching.'[54] But in the great rally of the anti-test forces at the Freemasons' Tavern on 10 June 1864 fewer than twenty clergy were present out of an attendance of 120, compared with nine prominent Nonconformists.

The secularism of the liberal movement of the early 1860s was triggered by theological controversy, but the younger dons—Bryce was 23 and T. H. Green 25 in 1861—had far less interest in theology than in abolishing clerical restrictions on freedom of inquiry.[55] When T. H. Green wrote an accomplished undergraduate essay (presumably about 1857) entitled 'The duties of the University to the state', the word 'Church' occurred only once, and the thrust of the argument was secular and democratic:

There is a constant tendency in modern times to substitute 'the Public' for the State, and to exult the transient will of the majority above the eternal principles embodied in law. We try to separate the present from the past, to give to the opinions of the day the force which only belongs to the fundamental ideas that reappear in every generation. It should be the work of the University to raise men above the influence of surrounding opinion. As the constitution is to present Acts of Parliament, so should university learning be to the notions which regulate the manners and professions of the day.'[56]

The members of such undergraduate coteries as the Essay Society or the Old Mortality interested in taking orders were more or less equalled by clergymen slightly older (Thorold Rogers, J. R. Green) trying to escape from the clerical collar; their literary weapons were no longer polemical flysheets circulating in Oxford, but articles in literary and political reviews, which reached a peak in 1864.

Is the importance of this London element exaggerated? Non-residence naturally meant consultation by letter and thus increased the evidence which

---

[53] M. Burrows, *Autobiography* (1908), 208.
[54] Speech of C. H. Buxton MP, 15 Feb. 1864, quoted in Campbell, *Nationalization*, 135.
[55] Bryce to Dicey, 14 Nov. 1913, Bodl. MS Bryce 4 fos 57–62.
[56] Essay-book, nd (presumably 1856–9), BCA T. H. Green MSS, essay-book 2.

survives. Yet the same cadres also organized institutions like the Century Club in 1864 and the *Fortnightly Review* in 1865. The names of such non-residents as C. S. Bowen, Frederic Harrison, C. S. Roundell, James Bryce, A. O. Rutson and G. C. Brodrick continually recur, and indeed were to supply the executive organization of the tests campaign.[57] Their linkages ramified to embrace such sympathetic MPs as William Ewart and J. G. Dodson, editors like G. H. Lewes and later John Morley, publishers like the Macmillan brothers and last, but certainly not least, reformers at the sister university. Political excitement increased with the progress of the American Civil War (1861–5), which found the university liberals almost to a man supporting the North against most of their clerical opponents and practically all of the aristocracy; and the eloquent Cambridge combination of Henry Fawcett and Leslie Stephen (already committed to political radicalism and university reform) seemed to match Goldwin Smith at Oxford, whose disgust with his chosen instrument, when the gentry supported 'the slave power', drove him further and further to the left.

In 1864 this link was given tangible reality by the creation of the Ad Eundem Club, through which Oxford and Cambridge liberals dined together alternately in each other's universities. (The last railway link had been put in place a year earlier.) The Club was largely the work of the most earnest of the Cambridge reformers, Henry Sidgwick, who had good Oxford connections through his brothers, and who made it clear to his Trinity colleague Henry Jackson that its purposes were those of academic reform, not agreeable conversation.[58] The Cambridge connection enabled Oxford to cultivate the Dissenters as a pressure group. At this date there were few in Oxford; and these, like C. P. Scott in Corpus in 1866, felt isolated,[59] although, if the Scots voluntaryists of Balliol are counted in, they were already making their mark on the class lists. But at Cambridge there had been a long tradition of Dissenters matriculating, and success in the tripos (there would be nineteen Dissenting Senior Wranglers between 1860 and 1889) was already making the demand for access to fellowships difficult to resist.[60]

Militant 'old' dissent, notably the Liberation Society, which represented Congregationalists, Independents and Baptists, had strongly supported Heywood's campaigns in the 1850s. By 1862, however, the set-back of 1857, when Cobden and Bright lost their seats, and the failure of various other projects had made its parliamentary committee disconsolate: 'the friends of religious equality have suffered from that reaction in public sentiment which has encouraged the House of Commons to reject almost

---

[57] See F. Harrison, 'The Century Club' in *Realities and Ideals* (1908), 371–6.
[58] Sir George Young to Henry Jackson, 17 June 1907, Trinity College, Cambridge, Add. MS 47.
[59] J. L. Hammond, *C. P. Scott* (1934), 16.
[60] Ward, *Victorian Oxford*, 243.

every measure of reform lately submitted to it'.[61] As a result, the Liberationists were open to university leadership and endorsed contacts made by Heywood with unnamed university men (probably at Cambridge) early in 1862.[62] In 1864 Goldwin Smith, in contact with various Manchester radicals through his tours in support of the North in the Civil War, brought the Oxford liberals and the Liberationists together.[63]

On the eve of the eight-year-long tests campaign, which paved the way for the final instalment of reform in the 1870s, factors were still visible which could have prejudiced the reform movement. At Oxford Goldwin Smith, now far from his Peelite views of the late 1850s, was its chief leader, but his personality, like those of Pattison and H. H. Vaughan, was very unstable. A decade earlier Mrs Jeune, wife of the Master of Pembroke, had noted him as 'a sad, invalidish-looking person, and his bad health gives him a languid and somewhat fretful air'.[64] His hard work was interrupted by bouts of unspecified ill health and, latterly, by the agonizing process of caring for a depressive and suicidal father. He resigned his chair in 1866, only to have his father cut his own throat the following year. Such traumas probably lay behind his seemingly perverse determination to begin a new life in America in 1868, just as his educational and democratic ideas were taking hold in Britain.

By this time a phalanx of younger secular Liberals was there to replace him—and the clerical camp had split apart. The joint High-Church–Evangelical campaign against *Essays and Reviews* had weakened the Gladstonian alliance at Oxford, and when Pusey gave way on Jowett's chair in 1864 Montagu Burrows believed the rationalists could claim a major victory.[65] Gladstone's defeat in the Burgess election of the following year isolated the non-Conservative High-Churchmen, who then went out of control. In 1865 Pusey began to negotiate with the Catholic Church, which had gained some intellectual credibility after Newman's drubbing of Charles Kingsley in 1864. This came to nothing; the ultramontane hierarchy was bitterly suspicious of Oxford, and laid it under ban.[66] Pusey's 'Romanism' and his toleration of the Ritualists—a minority in the High-Church movement but, as Montagu Burrows found, a majority in Oxford[67]—now made him almost as unpopular in the parishes as the Essayists and Reviewers had been. In 1868 another powerful figure left the scene. H. L. Mansel, elevated by Derby to the ecclesiastical history chair in 1867, was now transferred to the

[61] 'Parliamentary action in 1862', Liberation Society, File A/Lib/36, fo 14, London Metropolitan Archives.
[62] Parliamentary committee minutes, 10 Jan 1862, ibid. File A/Lib/13.
[63] Parliamentary committee minutes 4 and 18 Mar. 1864, ibid. File A/Lib/3.
[64] Entry for 2 Feb. 1853 in M. Jeune, *Pages from the Diary of an Oxford Lady* (1932), 21.
[65] Burrows, *Autobiography*, 209.
[66] V. A. McClelland, *English Roman Catholics and Higher Education* (1973), 202–7.
[67] Burrows, 220.

Deanery of St Paul's. In the absence of this shrewd party manager, hostilities between the High-and-Dry Tories and the Ritualists became irreconcilable.[68]

In 1869 the academic Liberals, in a minority of six out of the eighteen elected Council members for most of the 1860s, gained two seats. Equality, which came two years later, was now in prospect. In 1869 the University also gained a new Chancellor, elected by Convocation, and thus inevitably Conservative. The Marquess of Salisbury, after his election, wrote gloomily to his Liberal friend Henry Acland, summing up the forces which had led to his embattled state:

I quite agree with you that a University should be governed, both by its nominal and its real chiefs, without reference to the political struggles of the day.

But the Ethiopian cannot change his skin, nor can I put off my 'Toryism'—my deep distrust of the changes which are succeeding each other so rapidly. Numbers of men support them who are not of the spirit that bred them: but that spirit is essentially a Pagan spirit, discarding the supernatural and worshipping no God but man. It is creeping over Europe rapidly: and I can not put off the conviction that it is dissolving every cement that holds society together.

I have given you enough and too much of my gloomy thoughts. They have been excited by reading in a Liberal paper 'that learning is too high and sacred a thing to be sectarian.' Bah![69]

OXFORD, EDUCATION AND THE STATE

In the 1860s academics and non-residents concentrated their energies on reform, and in particular the abolition of the remaining tests, with remarkable effectiveness. Subsequently, their cohesion was difficult to preserve. They flowed out of that narrow and turbulent channel to diffuse themselves over a wide range of activities—party politics, service on commissions and boards, commitments to university extension or the higher education of women, even to scholarship. Nearly half of the Oxford liberals who turned up at the Freemasons' Tavern meeting in 1864, for example, were college fellows or university teachers; only a quarter were so connected in 1876.[70]

This juncture also coincided with the creation of the crucial myths of—and about—the British educational system. In the later 1860s and early 1870s legislation affected all levels of education and their relation with the state; intellectual leaders such as Mill, Huxley and Arnold spoke authoritatively about educational theory and values: thus the period provides an obvious matrix of British educational ideology, and of equally prehensile critiques.

One influential thesis of the 1980s about British political culture already mentioned saw a 'counter-revolution' of traditional values interdicting the

---

[68] Ward, *Victorian Oxford*, 233.
[69] Salisbury to Acland, 12 Nov. 1869, Acland MSS, Bodleian Library, in J. F. A. Mason, 'The Election of Lord Salisbury as Chancellor...in 1869', *Oxoniensia* xxix (1964–5), 188.
[70] Cf the list appended to Campbell, *Nationalization*, 284–93.

industrial ethos displayed at the Great Exhibition of 1851. In Martin Wiener's theory the 1860s can be identified as a 'wrong turning'; 'nationalized' university and 'reformed' endowed school combined to impose the 'gentleman heresy': a retrospective, 'chivalrous' social ethic which corroded the rational, exploitative, innovating values of the middle class.[71] Within Britain, but not wholly divorced from the above, an influential Scottish critique has alleged that the 'democratic intellect' of a university system quantitatively more extensive than that of England (and hence a major element in British educational pluralism) was undermined by 'Anglicizing' assaults headed by the products of Oxford and Cambridge.[72] Such essentially 'élitist' interpretations assume close collaboration between ideologists and politicians. This is not easy to gainsay, given the 'effortless superiority' of Oxford Greats men in cabinet and Whitehall. But the link between cultural cause and institutional effect requires shared goals which are specific, unity in recruitment and action and enough strategic thinking to overcome the secondary impediments which can arrest institutional reform.[73]

With the tests agitation primarily a political issue, closely linked to the public debate on democracy, strictly educational goals were at a discount. And it was difficult to talk about education—let alone about curriculum—as far as the majority of undergraduates were concerned. In 1864 George Brodrick wrote to this effect in a *Times* leader, blaming the great public schools, which the Clarendon Commission was currently investigating. According to this leader 'about a third at Christ Church and a fifth at Exeter College failed the [college's] matriculation examination', while, of those allowed to come up, 'not less than a fourth' were 'plucked for their "Little-Go"'. Coaches got the weaker survivors through pass finals somehow; but, according to Bartholomew Price, no public schoolboy had ever won a junior mathematical scholarship; and Brodrick commented: 'High-spirited aristocratic youths with great expectations, accustomed to every luxury at home, never braced up to exertion by paternal warnings...that they will have to win their bread for themselves, are not the most promising subjects for any educational experiments.'[74] As far as Brodrick's academic colleagues were concerned, there was confidence neither in the traditional curriculum, nor—as yet—in any alternative, although the alliance with Cambridge and the commitment to university extension opened up the curriculum issue,

---

[71] Cf Wiener, *English Culture and the Decline of the Industrial Spirit*.

[72] G. E. Davie, *The Democratic Intellect: Scotland and her universities in the nineteenth century* (Edinburgh 1961); but see also the critique of this in R. D. Anderson, *Education and Opportunity in Victorian Scotland* (1983).

[73] See E. Ashby and M. Anderson, *Portrait of Haldane at Work on Education* (1974), esp. chs 2 and 3, for the operations of an adept élitist educational reformer.

[74] *Report of the Royal Commission on Public Schools* ii. appx c. 24 (PP 1864 (3288) xx. 276); *The Times* 28 Mar. 1864, 9a. Authorship clear from copy in Merton College MS Brodrick. See also p. 360 above.

notably in a companion volume to the reform essays, F. W. Farrar's *Essays on a Liberal Education*, published by Macmillan in 1867. In this J. R. Seeley, author of the controversially rationalistic apologia for Christianity *Ecce Homo* (1865), attacked the dominance of examinations:

Subjects in which attainments can be accurately tested come to take precedence of subjects in which they cannot. These latter, however important they may be, gradually cease to be taught or valued or learned, while the former come into repute and acquire an artificial value... Both... the taught and the teachers... reject as worthless for educational purposes the greatest questions which can occupy the human mind and attach unbounded importance to some of the least.[75]

Charles Stuart Parker, the only Oxford contributor, implied at the end of his lengthy essay 'On the history of classical education' that, in the light of the reports of the various Commissions, the nature of a liberal education had better change to comply with modern demands:

the question of the 'course' of liberal education has a most important bearing on a larger question, which, if the Universities do not boldly face it, may be settled for them by a Reformed Parliament. If the Universities and the Church mean to remain national, they must do as the legislature has done. They must open their eyes to see the true dimensions of a nation.[76]

Henry Sidgwick was less diffuse: the classics must abdicate in favour of the physical sciences, for the training of the reasoning faculties, and in favour of English literature, for the diffusion of culture.[77]

Sidgwick, however, was hovering on the edge of leaving Cambridge.[78] The coherence of the symposium was, in fact, illusory: it represented a continuing loyalty in Cambridge—and on the part of Macmillan—to a liberal Anglicanism now moribund in Oxford.[79] Macmillan's *Essays on a Liberal Education* were followed a year later by *Essays on Church Policy*, in which the Revd William Berkley, fellow of Trinity, Oxford, and a friend of Bryce's, argued that 'the loss of power from perpetual crossing of purpose' was 'seen to be... deplorable'. Therefore, 'on pragmatic grounds it would seem sounder policy to reform thoroughly Church and University than to abolish both or either, as national institutions, and transfer their work to spontaneously-organised societies'.[80] Sound political sense as this was, by 1868 the 'national' formula of liberal Anglicanism had ceased to grip, even when reformulated in an ecumenical sense by Sidgwick, T. H. Green,

---

[75] J. R. Seeley, 'Liberal education in universities' in F. W. Farrar (ed.), *Essays on Liberal Education* (1867), 157.
[76] Farrar (ed.), *Essays*, 78–9.
[77] Sidgwick, 'The theory of classical education', ibid. 124.
[78] S. Rothblatt, *The Revolution of the Dons* (1968), 218.
[79] C. L. Graves, *Life and Letters of Alexander Macmillan* (1910), 270 ff.
[80] 'The Church and the universities', in W. L. Clay (ed.), *Essays...* (1868), 127.

Frank Newman and James Martineau in the short-lived Free Christian Union of 1866–70.[81]

Newman's desire for a Catholic *rapprochement* with Oxford now became urgent. In 1864 he had asked: 'Can the Oratory, that is I, *when once* set up, without saying a word to anyone, make the Oratory a Hall?' Two years later he had reached the stage of buying land for his project; but it was felled, then and in 1867 finally, by the Hierarchy.[82] Yet in the same year his successor as intellectual magus, John Stuart Mill (who had once regarded Oxford and Cambridge with intense suspicion), showed himself remarkably conciliatory, in his Rectorial Address at St Andrews, delivered on 1 February. Mill invoked the classics as a necessary pendant to the physical sciences, at a time when the tendency was for the more 'masculine' of his devotees to commit themselves to the scientism of T. H. Huxley.[83]

Despite their prestige, Mill, Newman and Huxley were isolated from the politics of education. Mill had never been to a university, Newman defended the idea of one against the narrow seminarism of the Irish Catholics, Huxley's *démarches* in education remained, in comparison with, say, the operations of Lyon Playfair, gauche. It is much more difficult to explain the political marginality of two men who, firmly in the tradition of British higher education, contributed most of its ethos in the 1860s: Matthew Arnold and Mark Pattison.

The Arnold of *Thyrsis* or *The Scholar-Gipsy* contributed as much to the topography of mid-Victorian Oxford as Waterhouse or Butterfield, and the famous lines from *Essays in Criticism* (1865) remind us of its lure for such products of more efficient higher-education systems as Max Müller or James Bryce:

Beautiful city! so venerable, so lovely, so unravaged by the fierce intellectual life of our century, so serene...spreading her gardens to the moonlight, and whispering from her towers the last enchantments of the Middle Age...home of lost causes, and forsaken beliefs, and unpopular names and impossible loyalties. Who will deny that Oxford, by her ineffable charm, keeps ever calling us nearer to the true goal of all of us, to the ideal, to perfection—to beauty, in a word, which is only truth seen from another side?—nearer, perhaps, than all the science of Tübingen.[84]

Born in 1822 and so a coeval of Goldwin Smith, Arnold was, as an inspector of schools, an educational professional, and as Professor of Poetry, 1857–67,

---

[81] J. Drummond and C. B. Upton, *Life and Letters of James Martineau* (1902), 425–37, and Sidgwick letters to and from T. H. Green, 1866–70, Trinity College, Cambridge, Sidgwick MSS, box 94.

[82] Newman to Hope-Scott, 29 Aug. 1864, in *LDN* xxi. 211. See McClelland, *English Roman Catholics and Higher Education*, 196, 214–22.

[83] J. S. Mill, *Inaugural Address Delivered to the University of St Andrews* (1867), quoted in M. Sanderson, *The Universities in the Nineteenth Century* (1975), 127. See also p. 2.

[84] M. Arnold, *Essays in Criticism*, First Series (1865), preface.

enough of a don to know the liberal leaders and sign some of their petitions. That he appreciated them can be seen from the affectionate letter he wrote to Bryce on the latter's election to Parliament in 1880.[85] Besides this, he was well served by the reputation of his father, and well connected: W. E. Forster was a brother-in-law; Huxley was married to a niece. As an unofficial extension of his professional work he produced, in *A French Eton* (1864) and *Schools and Universities on the Continent* (1868), two well-documented studies of the operation of the state in education, which he deployed as propaganda for a system broadly similar to that which came into operation in England after 1902 (and in Scotland and Wales some time earlier).[86] In retrospect, he seems as important to education in the 1860s as Bagehot was to politics. He was—in the sense that neither man was regarded by the actual executants of policy as more than an engaging commentator.

In Bagehot's case this was understandable. The 'Palmerstonian Constitution' which he celebrated scarcely survived publication of *The English Constitution*; but Arnold's prescience was repeatedly endorsed. John Morley, retrospectively fulsome in his *Recollections*, had to admit that 'not many really knew the service of a man who had put his finger on one of our most urgent needs'.[87] In the 1890s the Bryce Commission went to some pains to get a quotation from Arnold into its *Report*,[88] but everything that Arnold had argued for had been just as pressing when he compared the educational organization of England with that of modern Rome in 1865:

the same easy-going and absence of system on all sides, the same powerlessness and indifference of the State, the same independence in single institutions, the same free course for abuses, the same confusion, the same lack of all idea of *co-ordering* things, as the French say—that is, of making them work fitly together to a fit end; the same waste of power, therefore the same extravagance, and the same poverty of result.[89]

Why, during a period of intense discussion of educational problems, was Arnold neglected? There can be no single explanation. Arnold's own character and position were inconvenient. The 'raillery'—the apparent lack of seriousness—which offended some of his Evangelically reared juniors was not simply a mannerism. It was linked to the paradoxes thrown up by the very systems—the French or the Prussian—he expounded as models. 'Abroad' he wrote,

a Minister might have known more about my performances: but then abroad I doubt whether I should ever have survived to perform them. Under the strict bureaucratic

[85] Arnold to Bryce, 6 Apr. 1880, Bodl. MS Bryce 23 fo 25.
[86] I am indebted to Prof. Robert Anderson for information about Arnold's influence on Scots and Welsh educational reform.
[87] J. Morley, *Recollections* (2 vols 1917) i. 127–8.
[88] Fisher, *Bryce* i. 298.
[89] Quoted in G. W. E. Russell, *Matthew Arnold* (1904), 75–6.

system I should have been dismissed ten times over for the freedom with which on various occasions I have expressed myself on matters of religion and politics.[90]

A state system—'a definite plan and course'—facilitated co-ordination of the various levels, but at a cost. Arnold recognized that the continental universities existed to supply state officials—teachers, bureaucrats, clergymen. The recruitment regulations imposed by various ministries (and not simply that formally responsible for the universities) constrained *Lehr- und Lernfreiheit*, and effectively removed the concept of the university as a commonwealth of teachers and scholars.[91] The social integration he praised in German universities ended by provoking an almost melodramatic depression: 'Never surely was there seen a people of so many millions so unattractive.'[92]

Secondly, as Bryce himself admitted twenty-seven years after the Taunton Report, state action was difficult to envisage in the absence of any sort of systematic general-purpose local government, which only came into being after the County Councils Act of 1888.[93] In its absence, academic reformers who wanted to integrate the universities as inspecting and examining bodies for secondary education simply had no *point d'appui*. They could agitate within groups concerned with university extension, women's education, science and art instruction and endowment reform: they had access to the new periodical press, the *Fortnightly* or the *Contemporary*, and could aid the tests abolition cause. But this diffused rather than concentrated the issue of systematic educational reform. Of a hundred articles on education surveyed in representative periodicals between 1865 and 1870, not a single one dealt with the 'co-ordering' role of the state.[94]

Arnold never produced detailed proposals for institutional change. Among Oxford residents Benjamin Jowett disbelieved in such public pressure, regarding the well-directed private letter as far more effective. This had worked in 1852, and in 1867 a memorandum to Lord John Russell probably had some influence in gaining non-collegiate students.[95] But this was his last attempt at reform on any substantial scale. Mark Pattison, on the other hand, in his *Suggestions on Academical Organisation*, produced a remarkably concentrated blueprint for an Oxford which would combine the intimacy of the collegiate system with the intellectual ambitions of the great German universities.

[90] Ibid., 54.

[91] M. Arnold, *Schools and Universities on the Continent* (1866, Ann Arbor 1964), 254 ff.

[92] Arnold to Wyndham Slade, 12 Sept. 1865, in *The Letters of Matthew Arnold*, ed. G. W. E. Russell (1895), 300.

[93] *Report of the Royal Commission on Secondary Education* (PP 1895 xliii C. 7862, 12–13).

[94] *Macmillan's Magazine, Contemporary Review, North British Review, Quarterly*; contents lists in *The Wellesley Index*.

[95] John Prest, 'Jowett on education', suppl. to *Balliol College Record* (1965), 4 ff.

Pattison's forbidding, tragic character, displayed in his *Memoirs* (1885), has made so many novelists' fingers itch that the logic of his proposals has tended to be discounted. Nevertheless, much of the urgency of the *Suggestions* is sharply modern:

the necessity of organised science is likely to force itself upon the convictions of Englishmen, and that at no very distant time. All that we have hitherto accomplished, all of which we have been proud—our colonies, our commerce, our machinery—has been the result of individual enterprise. These splendid results have been due to the energy of will—to character. But civilisation in the West has now reached a point where no further triumphs await mere vigour, undirected by knowledge. Energy will be beaten in the practical field by combined skill. The days when the knight, cased in his armour, lorded it on the field by the prowess of his arm, are gone for ever, and battles are now directed by the evolutions of masses directed by a central intellect. We have lately had some rude reminders—in the *fiasco* of our railway system, in the catastrophe which in a few weeks ruined the edifice of our credit, in the incapacity of our boasted self-government to secure us the most indispensable sanitary regulations—that there is something wrong, somewhere, which is not want of energy of purpose. The conviction must ere long reach us that our knowledge is defective, and that such is the length of art and the shortness of life, that knowledge can only be made available for public purposes by concert and organisation.[96]

Pattison gave the contemporary debate on higher education an Oxford context, taking to logical if ambitious conclusions many of the ideas of his more political juniors. He allowed that the freeing of the fellowships in the 1850s had been a liberating influence, and that the Oxford Greats course could produce remarkable results:

The best papers are no mere schoolboys' themes spun out with hackneyed commonplaces, but full of life and thought, abounding with all the ideas with which modern society, and its best current literature, are charged. . . . I do not believe that there exists at this moment in Europe any public institution for education, where what are called 'the results of modern thought' . . . are so entirely at home.[97]

But he thought that a far greater chance had been missed:

The Commissioners found an enormous abuse existing illegally, and they legalised it. The richest and grandest institution for the cultivation of science remaining in Europe was given into their hands for reform, for restoration to its original national and noble purpose—a purpose which, though forgotten in practice, still remained engrossed in the title-deeds of the colleges. The Commissioners took those title-deeds, erased the purpose, and returned the parchments smilingly to their owners.[98]

As far as the passmen were concerned, he considered that Oxford wasted its substance in attempting to educate the ineducable. In his view the money expended on undergraduate scholarships could instead be used to endow research on a scale greater even than that of Berlin.[99]

[96] M. Pattison, *Suggestions* (1868), 328.   [97] Ibid. 291–2.   [98] Ibid. 90.   [99] Ibid. 231.

Pattison's impressive but flawed book is the intellectual autobiography of the younger men. Yet the conclusions reached were not in themselves new. Defining 'Wissenschaft', Pattison fell back on the *Memoir of Dugald Stewart* by John Veitch:

The first proper and adequate object of philosophical inquiry is...the determination of the various special ends and methods of the sciences, and the analysis of the ground of our certainty regarding real existence as well as formal truth, or the constitution of a rational logic....This general study of human nature affords the exclusive condition and the means of true liberal culture.[100]

The irony is that this endorsement of the Scottish common-sense school came only a couple of years after Mill's demolition of Sir William Hamilton, its last great representative. Pattison's position, *in an English context*, was eccentric.[101] While essentially accepting the Scoto-Germanic conception of the university, he was still deflected by his Oxford loyalties, something which skewed the structure of the book. To plunge, shortly after the introduction, into an eleven-page legal opinion on the alterability of bequests to colleges is less than ingratiating, particularly when Pattison immediately proceeds to deny that his case rests on the grounds cited. But he presented his proposals energetically. He wanted reorganization on the basis of seven faculties: theology, law, medicine, classics, philology and language, historical and moral sciences, mathematical and physical sciences. The faculties would colonize the former colleges, their heads, appointed on merit, being 'senior fellows', researchers of an elevated sort; administration would be by rotation of the professors.[102]

Pattison's 'Germanism' was in fact qualified by an endorsement of Newman's dictum that the socialization of young men at university was superior to even the most elaborate menu of professorial seminars and lectures—an echo, perhaps, of the collegiate loyalties he had shown in his evidence to the 1850 Commissioners.[103] His romanticism, as well as that practicality which was always devising new railway timetables, is shown in its local habitation. Despite the number of references to Berlin and the Scots, this is emphatically an argument about Oxford. Cambridge is scarcely mentioned.

Pattison's *démarche* has subsequently attracted attention as the most fully worked-out unofficial plan for Oxford reform, and the manifesto of the 'endowment of research' party, but was it thus regarded at the time? 'It is the clearest, finest thing that any of us people has put forth,' James Bryce wrote to Henry Sidgwick on reading a pre-publication copy. 'But all the regular

[100] Ibid., 307.
[101] See Davie, *The Democratic Intellect*, 258 ff.; and C. Beveridge and R. Turnbull, *The Eclipse of Scottish Culture* (Edinburgh 1989).
[102] Pattison, *Suggestions*, 175.
[103] Ibid. 248, quoting Newman, *Idea*, 129 (*Discourse* vi, originally vii); and see J. Sparrow, *Pattison and the Idea of a University*, 89 ff.

liberals call out that it is utopian; some that it is self-interested.' And he was sceptical about Pattison's central premiss: 'We may fear that if other things have not produced a learned class in England, endowment will not.'[104]

In fact, the *Suggestions* were not widely noticed, in comparison with F. W. Farrar's *Liberal Education*. This was perhaps attributable to their publication by an Edinburgh firm. Only the *Quarterly* reviewed them at any length, and the writer chosen was the High-Church *matelot* Montagu Burrows, who noisily agreed with Pattison about the superficial radicalism of the Lit. Hum. tutors, quoted Arnold as saying that only a third of German students worked seriously, and (himself a married professor) raised the usual Tory bogy about the quads becoming filled with professors 'and their wives and families'.[105] The 'utopian' accusation stuck, particularly as Pattison had provided no time-scale for such drastic changes, beyond the threat that foreign *savants* might have to take over various of the professorships until Oxford had improved its own products.[106]

Moreover, Pattison then seemed to forget about his own scheme. As John Sparrow remarked, his attitude to scholarship verged on the mystical.[107] Others might suspect that the psychotic was more in evidence: a simultaneous yearning for and rejection of the principle of authority personified by Pattison's former mentor Newman. The *Suggestions* stemmed from a period when these forces seemed more or less in balance, with Pattison adhering to a theism broadly of the Scottish common-sense type.[108] But around 1871, Duncan Nimmo argues, the impossibility of securing space within the Church and the University for this concept led him to a complete, pessimistic scepticism.[109]

This withdrawal—evident in his less than half-hearted support for the 'endowment of research' group and his indifference to the activities of the Selborne Commission—may also have been the result of further philosophical and personal difficulties. That Charles Appleton, the energetic organizer of the group, was an enthusiastic Hegelian cannot have endeared him to Pattison, who believed that the importation of the a priori metaphysic of Hegel was a Tory-sacerdotalist plot.[110] Even more ironically, his estranged wife associated herself openly with Sir Charles Dilke, one of the leading defenders of traditional fellowships.[111] By 1880 he was writing that 'I only

[104] Bryce to Sidgwick, 4 Jan. 1868, Bodl. MS Bryce.
[105] *Quarterly* cxxiv (Apr. 1868), 394 ff.
[106] Pattison, *Suggestions*, 173.
[107] Sparrow, *Pattison*, 125 ff.
[108] Davie, *Democratic Intellect*, 275.
[109] Duncan Nimmo, 'Learning against religion, learning as religion: Mark Pattison and the "Victorian crisis of faith"', in *Religion and Humanism* (1981), 321.
[110] Pattison, *Memoirs*, 91–2.
[111] See his activities when the Universities of Oxford and Cambridge Bill was in committee from late Apr. 1877: *Parl. Deb.* 3S. ccxxxiv.

served to give a decent appearance to the high-handed proceedings of the commission who treated me and our college with supreme contempt, taking at the same time all they could squeeze out of us for their claptrap professors.'[112]

There was also a pervasive anti-statism among the dons. 'No English party of that date foresaw most of the coming changes,' A. V. Dicey reminded Bryce in 1921, in the course of a retrospection, lasting several years, of the values of their youth.[113] 'We all assumed', Bryce had earlier written, 'individualism as obviously and absolutely right.'[114] His memory was unsure here; in the 1860s Mill was as suspect an individualist as Arnold or Ruskin or the Positivists. Goldwin Smith, however, considered himself an individualist *pur sang*, and, as leader of the secular liberals at Oxford, he provided perhaps the most powerful counter-current (as Dicey would have put it) to 'co-ordering' higher education along Arnoldian or Pattisonian lines.

In a passage from his 1859 Inaugural Lecture just quoted Smith saw the universities performing a vocational role in educating the aristocracy and gentry to tread 'the steep path of social duty'.[115] Service on the Newcastle Commission on Elementary Education (1858–61) did not, however, as with Arnold, broaden this into a desire to create an élite to serve a democracy. Instead, it introduced him to the most convinced advocates of voluntaryism, religious and educational. Smith and Edward Miall of the Liberation Society wrote a voluntaryist minority report, only to waive their dissent later.[116] It was the beginning of Smith's conversion to radicalism, which was accelerated by the American Civil War, and led to the violent anti-Toryism and anti-aristocrat animus of his *Plea for the Abolition of Tests* (1864).[117] The 'alliance with Manchester' meant a retreat from the principle of state action. An 'alliance with Birmingham' would have been more *étatiste*, but Joseph Chamberlain did not found his Education League until 1867.[118] At the closest point of their political involvement, the academics were aligned with a personality more hostile to state action than Robert Lowe, closer to Herbert Spencer than to Matthew Arnold.

Hunters after the 'gentleman heresy' have arraigned Arnold for anti-industrialism, while ignoring the motives which inhibited the creation of a co-ordinated educational policy in the 1860s. The apostasy of the academics was only one factor; the Spencerian identification of science with *laissez-faire*; the complacency and tight-fistedness of local business élites; the self-interest of public school headmasters and trustees, which forced the aban-

[112] Quoted in V. H. H. Green, *The Commonwealth of Lincoln College* (1979), 474.
[113] Dicey to Bryce, 22 Apr. 1921, MS Bodl. Bryce 3 fos 260–1.
[114] Bryce to Dicey, 14 Nov. 1913, MS Bodl. Bryce 4 fo 59.
[115] G. Smith, *Inaugural Lecture*, 39. For an earlier passage see p. 702.
[116] Smith, *Reminiscences*, 120.
[117] Smith, *Plea*, 19 ff.
[118] See D. Judd, *Radical Joe* (1977), 44 ff.

donment of the supervisory elements in the Taunton Report in 1869, were cumulatively more important.[119] Against this, Arnold wrote, almost despairingly, in November 1865: 'I have a conviction that there is a real, an almost imminent danger of England losing immeasurably in all ways, declining into a sort of greater Holland, for want of what I must still call ideas, for want of perceiving how the world is going and must go, and preparing herself accordingly.'[120] In November 1871 he commented, anonymously, on the remit of the impending Commission in the *Pall Mall Gazette*. It was 'arithmetic without note or comment in the first instance'; unless the academics achieved some co-ordination, their programme of reform could be indefinitely delayed by party politics. Pattison had made valuable suggestions: 'But now is not the time for the scheme or the testimony of any individual; what we want to hear of is a clear and concerted definition, between competent persons, of available practical heads or bases of reform.'[121] But after the year which saw the tests overthrown, academic opinion would never be as clear and concerted again.

THE TESTS CAMPAIGN

On 24 June 1863 Lord John Russell and John George Dodson MP presented to Parliament a petition signed by 105 Oxford residents, praying for the abolition of the religious tests which governed the Oxford MA. This action signalled the beginning of an eight-year campaign which provided the backbone of mid-Victorian academic liberalism, and which was largely directed by Oxford men. Yet initially they had been stimulated by a petition organized in 1862 by Cambridge residents, praying for college fellowships to be set free. By the time the Oxford petition turned up, the bill to achieve this end, promoted by Edward Pleydell-Bouverie MP, had already been withdrawn because of the lateness of the session.

The rights of Nonconformists, as well as academic discontent at the tardiness of reform, underlay the 'Cambridge Bill'. Nonconformist candidates had performed superlatively in examinations: their nineteen Senior Wranglers in the thirty years after 1860 have already been mentioned.[122] Yet they were debarred from fellowships, and college and University alike forfeited their services. Lord Salisbury was to see in the whole process the insatiability of Nonconformity; the bones of the 1850s settlement gnawed dry, it cried for fresh meat.[123] As Gladstone contemplated the Oxford demand, however, his concern was rather with the dissent within the Church of England surrounding *Essays and Reviews*. The petition of 1863 was an act

[119] T. W. Bamford, *The Rise of the Public Schools* (1967), 183 ff.
[120] Letter of Nov. 1865, in *Letters of Arnold*, 385.
[121] 'University reform', repr. in *Essays, Letters and Reviews by Matthew Arnold*, ed. Fraser Niemen (1960), 180–3.
[122] Liberation Society, *Jubilee Retrospect* (1894), 38. For freeing fellowships see p. 701.
[123] Salisbury to Sir Roundell Palmer, 31 July 1870, LPL MS Selborne 1864, fos 67–70.

of 'gross impolicy...by those who will, at any rate for the time, be chiefly regarded in the outer world as the friends of Mr Jowett'.[124]

Gladstone was, however, far from complacent. 'Alarmed at the weakness of what ought to be the defending force...There are so few *Hoplites*...', he was beginning to move towards his identification with industrial Britain. He could not yet tell whether the prospect opened by abolishing subscription would be one of 'a firmer or a more shifting standing ground'.[125] In a memorandum 'most private' of 6 July, he pondered a project for a settlement which would liberate the professoriate and allow it to instruct undergraduates at Nonconformist-run halls. These would take the MA, but be denied a teaching or governing role in the University. Implicitly, this scheme depended on the Nonconformists and university liberals accepting the MA as the limit of their ambitions. Until this assumption could be tested, it would remain a secret.[126]

A secret it remained. On 12 February 1864 Dodson introduced a bill on the lines of the 1863 petition, and on 4 March Goldwin Smith, by then a fixture on radical platforms, secured Liberation Society support for it.[127] The alliance, however, was soon under strain. At second reading, carried by 211 to 189 on 16 March, Gladstone proposed the 'Cambridge compromise' (the MA as the final concession) and Dodson conceded that this was an option to be discussed in committee. Misreported as acceptance by the *Nonconformist* on 23 March, this provoked strong protests from liberal don and Dissenter alike. Edward Miall, who had probably picked up some notion of Gladstone's mind through the latter's correspondence with the Reverend Newman Hall of the Independents,[128] wrote angrily to Goldwin Smith: 'Private halls would leave us as Gentiles of the Outer Court. Even with money enough we should not care to establish ourselves as an inferior caste.... If [Dodson] prefers acquiescing we must take steps to clear ourselves of participation.'[129] Apprised of this, Dodson charged Goldwin Smith with sounding out Oxford opinion again. Smith convened a meeting on 16 May, after which forty residents signed a memorial rejecting any compromise, although the leading clerical liberals, Jowett and Dean Liddell, announced that they would settle for 'a *negative* test binding the person taking a degree not to impugn the doctrines of the Church of England'.[130] At this meeting preparations must have been made for the rallying together of all influential

---

[124] Gladstone to Dr Henry Wentworth Acland, 18 Mar. 1863, BL Add. MS 44091, fo 55.
[125] Ibid., and see R. T. Shannon, *Gladstone* (1 vol. to date, 1982) i. 474.
[126] BL Add. MS 44752, fo 311.
[127] Parliamentary committee minutes, 4 Mar. 1864, London Metropolitan Archives, Liberation Society, File A/Lib/3.
[128] *Gladstone Diaries* vi. 264, 19 Mar. 1864.
[129] Copy of letter enclosed in Goldwin Smith to J. G. Dodson, 29 Mar. 1864, Bodl. Monk Bretton MSS, 39.
[130] Goldwin Smith to Dodson, 16 May 1864, Ibid.

supporters of both bills (for Bouverie's measure made a belated reappearance on 8 June) at the Freemasons' Tavern in London on 10 June.

Dodson's bill went into committee, by 236 to 226, on 1 June, and Gladstone duly pressed his compromise. The gathering of intellectual *prominenti* who pledged themselves at the Freemasons' Tavern to the bill's integrity on 10 June was remarkable even by Victorian standards. Besides the leading liberals of both universities were representatives from educational administration, the higher journalism, the scientific movement and Nonconformity. Kay-Shuttleworth was there, and Henry Reeve, Huxley and John Bright. It represented the result of academic liberal involvement in national politics—particularly support for the North in the American Civil War—as much as Nonconformist support for the issue of tests abolition itself, and it cemented a relationship which was to endure, with an amicability unusual in Nonconformist–Liberal dealings, until abolition was carried seven years later.[131]

Three weeks later the bill was dead. On 1 July there was a tie at third reading, the Speaker called for a revote, and the bill, unblemished by compromise, was lost 171 to 173. To Charles Roundell, about to take over the London end of the agitation, the exercise had, however, been pure gain. He wrote to Dodson: 'the course of your Bill through the House has raised new hopes, and has elevated the question into the rank of a first-rate Liberal measure...when we recommence the struggle we shall do so with better hopes for we may calculate on the united action of non-University as well as University men.'[132] The manœuvrings of 1864 ensured that the tests abolition campaign would be aimed at 'nationalizing' the universities, not in bestowing some sort of parity of confessional access. They ensured the loyalty, even the deference to academic judgement, of Nonconformity. They also saw the leadership of the campaign slip away from the liberal Churchmen and into the hands of secular radicals—politicians, lawyers and journalists—the sort of men whom Roundell typified. As was mentioned, fewer than 15 per cent of the participants in the Freemasons' Tavern meeting were in Anglican orders.[133] In the small committee which subsequently took over the co-ordinating role, the only minister of religion was the Congregationalist and Liberationist Edward Miall.[134]

Between 1865 and 1867 the two bills were presented annually, got as far as second reading, but perished in the turmoil of the reform crisis. Agitation in the provinces continued, aided by the involvement of many academics in the Taunton inquiry into secondary education. One of them, James Bryce, who helped organize a big rally in the Free Trade Hall, Manchester, on 6 April 1866, began to see that Nonconformists' attitudes were modulating from

---

[131] Campbell, *Nationalization*, 137.
[132] Roundell to Dodson, 8 July 1864, Bodl. Monk Bretton MSS. 39.
[133] List in Campbell, *Nationalization*, 284–93.
[134] Ibid. 136.

aggressiveness into unease about the health of provincial culture.[135] Complacency, lessened by the cotton famine, was jolted by the 1866 slump. However much they resented his style in *Culture and Anarchy*, some leading Dissenters were reluctantly coming to accept Matthew Arnold's conclusions, in *Schools and Universities on the Continent*, that pure voluntaryism was no longer a satisfactory solution to the education issue. The experience of Owen's College, Manchester, showed the necessity of collaborating with the old universities, if a network of civic colleges was to be created. Bryce was to become a professor there in 1868. The influence of Taunton also directly inspired Jowett—at last in the ascendant at Balliol—to produce his own scheme for low-cost university extension through an affiliated hall, an initiative which followed the Hebdomadal Council's informal sanction of four committees on extension after a meeting at Oriel on 16 November 1865.[136]

University extension, like 'middle-class' examinations, was a cause which conservatives felt that they must back, in order to prevent the liberals running away with it. In the reports, which were published in October 1866, they secured endorsement for the idea of a denominational college, the future Keble, and assistance for 'poor students' (generally assumed to be candidates for orders), but the liberals gained publicity for non-collegiate students, residence in lodgings, the reduction of the period of residence, and the affiliation of institutions such as King's College, London, and Owens College, Manchester, to Oxford University.[137] In March 1867 the liberals hammered their point home when the veteran Liverpool radical William Ewart introduced a bill to end the requirement to live within the college walls. Ewart was the uncle of A. O. Rutson, then editing *Essays on Reform*, and the debate on his measure, mercifully free of the religious issue, gave the liberals what they wanted: a Select Committee on university teaching at Oxford and Cambridge, and a declaration from Gladstone in ringing contrast with his previous attitudes:

there never was a period when the deficiency of the universities in the performance of the important work assigned to them was so great and so manifest...there never was a period in the history of the University of Oxford, at all events, when it was able to do so little for the poorer class of students...Go into the great centres of industry and you will hardly find a trace in them of university teaching.[138]

---

[135] James Bryce to E. A. Freeman, 22 May 1865 and 3 Feb. 1866; R. D. Darbishire to James Bryce, 3 and 11 July 1865, Bodl. MS Bryce 9 fos 73–4, 55 fos 66–9, 70–2; Harvie, *Lights of Liberalism*, 86.
[136] Abbott and Campbell, *Jowett* i. 377; Ward, *Victorian Oxford*, 263–4; J. Jones, *Balliol College* (1988), 208.
[137] Goldwin Smith, 'The Oxford reports on university extension', *Macmillan's Magazine* 15 Jan. 1867, 224–7. For Keble College see Pt 2, Ch. 6.
[138] *Parl. Deb.* 5 June 1867, 3S clxxxvii. 1639–40.

The Select Committee of March 1867, which coincided with liberal academia taking the political stage with *Essays on Reform* and *Questions for a Reformed Parliament* and with the climacteric of the Reform Bill's progress through the Commons, was probably the watershed of the campaign, although it came to no conclusions and Ewart's bill proceeded no further. As witnesses, Roundell, Brodie, Jowett and Thomas Fowler were able to demonstrate how the programme of self-reform adumbrated by the Act of 1854 had been checked, and how much a new reforming impulse was required.[139] A move by Liberal MPs on the committee to institute an inquiry into university revenues was negatived (both Gladstone and Roundell Palmer were absent on this occasion), but on 10 April, as the Tests Abolition (Oxford) Bill was going into committee, Henry Fawcett MP moved, successfully, 'an Instruction to the Committee that they have power to extend the provisions of the Bill to the University of Cambridge'.[140] This action, unanticipated by the Oxford liberals, seems to have stemmed directly from his experience on the Select Committee. The blind Cambridge economist, to whom tact was an alien concept, pushed his Oxford colleagues towards a simple joint bill rather than the more comprehensive measure that a conference held at the Ship Hotel on 1 July had delegated Roundell, Goldwin Smith, Fowler and Bryce to prepare. Attacking the Oxford-originated draft as 'an extraordinary jumble of discordant elements' when it appeared in January 1868, he got his way later in the month when, on the casting vote of James Bryce, the Oxford draft was dropped in favour of a joint measure.[141]

1867 was the last occasion on which Gladstone opposed tests abolition. The Ewart Committee—and some prompting from Jowett—had brought Russell (by now an earl) back to the cause of university reform after almost two decades, and the prospect of a series of resolutions from him in the Lords drew Gladstone and Goldwin Smith into consultation.[142] At issue were not only the tests, but the utilization of college revenues, which could be seen as having doubled since Victor Huber had calculated them in 1839.[143] Gladstone may have sensed that the question these revenues raised—that of prize fellowships—placed the academic liberals on awkward ground, opening up divisions between residents who wanted more funds for teaching and/or research, and London politicians such as Fawcett or Brodrick who saw the money as a sort of public endowment of bright young radicals.[144] Roundell

[139] *SCOC* (1867), 1–13, 13–30, 75–7, 123–32, 132–56.

[140] *Parl. Deb.* 10 Apr. 1867, 3S clxxxvi. 1431.

[141] Ward, *Victorian Oxford*, 271; L. Stephen, *Fawcett* (1885), 236; Sir George Young to James Bryce, 15 Feb. 1892, Bodl. MS Bryce 156 fos 51–2.

[142] Hinchcliff, *Jowett*, 101; Goldwin Smith to Gladstone, 27 Nov. and 1 Dec. 1867, BL Add. MS 44303, fos 177–8, 179.

[143] Huber, *English Universities* ii. pt 2, 576, compared with Roundell's evidence to the *SCOC* (1867), 14; see also the Cleveland statistics abstracted in Ward, *Victorian Oxford*, 294, and Ch. 12 above.

[144] G. C. Brodrick, *Memories and Impressions* (1900), 168–73; Stephen, *Fawcett*, 114.

also liaised with Gladstone over the joint bill, which was originally to have been introduced with a further measure confined to Oxford.[145] The imminence of an election meant, however, that only the Tests Abolition (Oxford and Cambridge) Bill was introduced—by J. D. Coleridge. Under its provisions the restrictive Acts were to be repealed, and all lay degrees and appointments in the two universities freed from subscription, but the colleges would be permitted to impose a test for any headship or fellowship which was independent of a university post. Having survived second reading this bill was withdrawn on 22 July 1868. By now, however, the expectation was that a good Liberal majority at the general election, which liberal academia exerted itself to the uttermost to achieve, would make its enactment inevitable.[146]

The 1868 election gave the Liberals a majority of 110, but pressure on legislative time was considerable, and it was not until 1871 that tests abolition became law. By then, however, it was a compulsory measure which applied to all lay posts, whether in the University or in the colleges. It forbade a test for any degrees except those in divinity; and it was accompanied by a pledge to inquire into university and college revenues with a view to further legislation. In 1869 it became plain that the barrier lay in the Lords—they threw the Bill out on 19 July—and in particular in the attitude of the Marquess of Salisbury. Leader of the extreme anti-reform wing of the Conservatives in 1867, Salisbury was elected Chancellor on 12 November 1869. The new Chancellor was a complex figure, intellectually much closer to the modern age than Gladstone (he was a knowledgeable amateur scientist, and had actually defended Bishop Colenso in the *Saturday Review* in 1864), but emotionally repelled by it.[147] Since 'the Ethiopian' could not 'change his skin',[148] an energetic struggle could be expected in the last ditch.

Salisbury's determination increased as Gladstone at last mobilized himself in the reform cause. Following the 1869 failure, Charles Roundell pressed the re-introduction of a 'compulsory' bill on Gladstone,[149] who replied that although a 'permissive' measure would be easier to pass, some sort of enduring settlement ought to be aimed at: 'the Bill, if altered at all in the sense of extension, ought to be altered not in one particular alone but in several. It would not be wise to open the ground of one fresh and stiff battle now with the prospect of its being soon succeeded by another.'[150] The

---

[145] Goldwin Smith to Gladstone, 26 Feb. 1868, BL Add. MS 44303, fos 180–2. Roundell to W. H. Gladstone, 21 Feb. 1868, BL Add. MS 44414, fos 111–12.

[146] Stephen, *Fawcett*, 237; see Harvie, *Lights of Liberalism*, 176–83. For text of Coleridge's bill see PP 1867–8, iii. 589–92.

[147] See Paul Smith (ed.), *Lord Salisbury on Politics* (1972), 15–20; and Michael Pinto-Duschinsky, *The Political Thought of Lord Salisbury* (1967), 71.

[148] Salisbury to H. Acland, 12 Nov. 1869, in Mason, 'The Election of Lord Salisbury', 188; Bodl. Acland MSS. See p. 713 above.

[149] Roundell to Gladstone, 9 Nov. 1869, BL Add. MS 44423, fos 69–70.

[150] Gladstone to Roundell, 10 Nov. 1869, BL Add. MS 44423, fos 75 and 76.

government took up the 'compulsory' bill, with an eye on Nonconformist opinion, increasingly restive over Forster's education proposals. But it was not introduced until 25 April 1870, and its passage depended on the acquiescence of the Lords.

Salisbury stuck fast, insisting on a Lords Select Committee on religious safeguards, and rejecting a proposal by Roundell via his cousin Roundell Palmer to give the Hebdomadal Council some vague police powers to prevent any 'attack upon the Christian faith.'[151] He replied to Palmer, robustly:

I think there are circumstances in which it is better to be openly beaten than to accept a merely nominal compromise. The legislative effect of the two processes is of course exactly the same: but in the one case your friends are indignant with the enemy, in the other case they are indignant with you. The difference has a great effect on their willingness and capacity to fight future battles.[152]

The Lords Committee halted progress on the bill in 1870, but it came first on the cabinet's list of 1871 legislation.[153] It was evident, too, that Salisbury and Gladstone were moving towards some sort of accord on what investigation should accompany it. Salisbury was believed to want 'large organic changes in the relation between the Colleges and the Universities',[154] partly because of his own interest in natural science, but also as a means of establishing a more hierarchical system of authority.

After clearing the Lords the bill received the royal assent on 16 June. The cabinet immediately went on to discuss a commission into university and college income, and Salisbury accepted this proposal on 2 July.[155] The idea had been suggested by Charles Roundell to Gladstone on 4 May 1871:

A Parliamentary Commission, to inquire concerning the revenues present and prospective, of the University and Colleges, and the appropriation thereof, and to Report upon any enlargement of Powers which may be deemed necessary for making the same more conducive to the purposes of learning and education in the University and Colleges ... It is thought that a small and effective Commission of Inquiry would be able to ascertain the required financial facts in the course of a few weeks.[156]

The university liberals wanted a parliamentary, as opposed to a royal, commission, because it would be able to demand information and impose reforms. What Gladstone agreed with Salisbury was a much more sedate affair, reliant on the voluntary collaboration of the universities.

[151] Roundell to Roundell Palmer, 21 July 1870, LPL MS Selborne 1864, fos 62–4.
[152] Salisbury to Roundell Palmer, 31 July 1870, LPL MS Selborne 1864, fos 67–70. The government seem to have rebuffed the 'police powers' proposal.
[153] Gladstone Diaries vii. 390, 2 Nov. 1870.
[154] Roundell Palmer to Salisbury, 22 July 1870, LPC MS Selborne 1864, fos 65–6.
[155] Gladstone Diaries vii. 510, 518, 17 June, and Gladstone's letter, 30 June, with extract from Salisbury's reply, 2 July.
[156] Roundell to Gladstone, 4 May 1871, BL Add. MS 44430, fos 180–1.

This inspired a rather indignant memorial from Cambridge liberals, headed by Fawcett: 'The question of the amount of available funds is only one and by no means the most important element in the matter to be investigated.... when the facts as to the funds were ascertained, the subject would be no further advanced.'[157] Coleridge, forwarding it to Gladstone, partly concurred,[158] but the cabinet on 11 December settled on a royal commission, made up of landowners, college bursars and statisticians, chaired by a duke (Gladstone wanted Somerset but ended up with Cleveland).[159] Roundell tried again to press for statutory powers by sending Gladstone a copy of the draft Oxford Reform Bill which had been aborted in 1868.[160] Almost by return of post he got the offer of the secretaryship of the Cleveland Commission.[161] It was to occupy him for the next three years.

[157] Memorial enclosed in J. D. Coleridge to Gladstone, 11 Dec. 1871, BL Add. MS 44138, fo 128.
[158] Ibid., covering letter, fos 126–7.
[159] *Gladstone Diaries* viii. 75, 11 Dec. 1871. For the help which Cleveland (then the Hon. Harry Vane) had given the United Debating Society in 1824 see p. 45 above.
[160] Roundell to Gladstone, 18 Dec. 1871, BL Add. MS 44432, fos 281–2.
[161] Roundell to Gladstone, 27 Dec. 1871; ibid. fos 320–1.

Nineteenth-Century Oxford, Part 2

INDEX

The longer entries in this index do not follow a single pattern. In some an alphabetical arrangement was judged the most suitable: in others a broadly chronological sequence is followed.

The later titles of a person mentioned are given only when they seem relevant. In succession to hereditary titles the second edition of *GEC's Peerage* has been the guide. Where a person's date of birth is not known it has been calculated approximately from date of, and age at, matriculation.

'Conservative' and 'Liberal' were used with various connotations in nineteenth-century Oxford. They are given an initial capital only where party affiliation is indicated.

Page numbers in bold indicate the principal references to entries.

Abbreviations

Assocn	Association	hon.	honorary
BAAS	British Association for the Advancement of Science	hons	honours
		H. of Commons/	
BNC	Brasenose College	Lords	House of &c.
C.	Cambridge	lab.	laboratory
CCC	Corpus Christi College	Lit. Hum.	*Literae Humaniores*
C.E.	Catholic emancipation	maths	mathematics
cent.	century	Mods	Moderations
Ch.Ch.	Christ Church	movt	movement
Ch. of E.	Church of England	Nat. Sci.	Natural Sciences
coll.	college	O.	Oxford
cr.	created	Parl.	Parliamentary
dept	department	Parlt	Parliament
educn	education	Prof.	Professor
exam.	examination	SCR	Senior Common Room
Exec.	Executive	Sec.	Secretary
Gen. Election	General Election	Soc.	Society
govt	government	Univ.	University
Hebd.	Hebdomadal	V.-C.	Vice-Chancellor

Abbay, Richard (1844–1924) 675
Abbott, Evelyn (1843–1901) 540
Abercrombie, John (1780–1844) 569
Aberdeen, 4th Earl of (1784–1860) 324, 334
Abingdon, Berks. 280, 334
    Abingdon School 170
academic dress *see* Oxford University
accounting and actuarial professions 492
Acland, (Sir) Arthur Herbert Dyke, 13th Bt. (1847–1926) 449, 457
Acland, (Sir) Henry Wentworth, cr. Bt. 1890 (1815–1900):
    All Souls (1840) 168
    anatomy: opposes undergraduate study of 575, 578; Lee's reader in (1845) 572
    art in curriculum 623–5; Art School 625–6

    BM, remodelling of 573
    campaigner on social issues 470
    champions cause of science 643
    in cholera epidemic (1854) xx, 454
    Clinical Medicine, Prof. of (1857) 576
    criticism of (1878) 577
    drawbacks of his influence 689–90
    evidence to Selborne Commission (1877) 576
    'ideal' of 572–3
    'lost medical school' (1878) 491, 576–7, 579
    Medicine, Regius Prof. of (1857) 572; accommodation for 573–4
    national questions 573
    new generation of scientists 675

Index compiled by Eleanor Brock